BIOLOGY OF THE REPTILIA

VOLUME 16, ECOLOGY B
DEFENSE AND LIFE HISTORY

BIOLOGY OF THE REPTILIA

Edited by
CARL GANS
The University of Michigan
Ann Arbor, Michigan

VOLUME 16, ECOLOGY B
DEFENSE AND LIFE HISTORY

Coeditor for this volume
RAYMOND B. HUEY
The University of Washington
Seattle, Washington

ALAN R. LISS, INC., NEW YORK

Address all Inquiries to the Publisher
Alan R. Liss, Inc., 41 East 11th Street, New York, NY 10003

Copyright © 1988 Alan R. Liss, Inc.

Printed in the United States of America

Under the conditions stated below the owner of copyright for this book hereby grants permission to users to make photocopy reproductions of any part or all of its contents for personal or internal organizational use, or for personal or internal use of specific clients. This consent is given on the condition that the copier pay the stated per-copy fee through the Copyright Clearance Center, Incorporated, 27 Congress Street, Salem, MA 01970, as listed in the most current issue of "Permissions to Photocopy" (Publisher's Fee List, distributed by CCC, Inc.), for copying beyond that permitted by sections 107 or 108 of the US Copyright Law. This consent does not extend to other kinds of copying, such as copying for general distribution, for advertising or promotional purposes, for creating new collective works, or for resale.

Library of Congress Cataloging-in-Publication Data
(Revised for vol. 16)

Gans, Carl, 1923–
  Biology of the reptilia.
  Vol. 14–15 published by: New York : Wiley;
  vol. 16– published by: New York : Alan R. Liss.
  Coeditor for v. 16: R.B. Huey.
  Includes biobliographies and indexes.
  B69-06748 (v. 1)
  1. Reptiles—Collected works. I. Title.
QL641.G3   597.9   68-9113
ISBN 0-8451-4402-2

Contents

CONTRIBUTORS vii

PREFACE ix

DEFENSE

1. **ANTIPREDATOR MECHANISMS IN REPTILES** 1
   Harry W. Greene

2. **MIMICRY AND RELATED PHENOMENA** 153
   F. Harvey Pough

3. **CAUDAL AUTOTOMY AS A DEFENSE** 235
   E. N. Arnold

4. **PARENTAL CARE IN REPTILES** 275
   Richard Shine

LIFE HISTORY

5. **METHODS FOR THE STUDY OF REPTILE POPULATIONS** 331
   Arthur E. Dunham, Peter J. Morin, and Henry M. Wilbur

6. **LIFE HISTORY EVOLUTION IN TURTLES** 387
   Henry M. Wilbur and Peter J. Morin

7. **LIFE HISTORY PATTERNS IN SQUAMATE REPTILES**   **441**

Arthur E. Dunham, Donald B. Miles, and David N. Reznick

8. **THE PHYSIOLOGICAL ECOLOGY OF REPTILIAN EGGS AND EMBRYOS**   **523**

Gary C. Packard and Mary J. Packard

AUTHOR INDEX   **607**

SUBJECT INDEX   **635**

Contributors

E. N. ARNOLD, Department of Zoology, British Museum (Natural History), London SW7 5BD, England

ARTHUR E. DUNHAM, Department of Biology, University of Pennsylvania, Philadelphia, Pennsylvania 19104

HARRY W. GREENE, Museum of Vertebrate Zoology and Department of Zoology, University of California, Berkeley, California 94720

DONALD B. MILES, Department of Biology, University of Pennsylvania, Philadelphia, Pennsylvania; present address: Department of Zoological and Biological Sciences, Ohio University, Athens, Ohio 45701

PETER J. MORIN, Department of Zoology, Duke University, Durham, North Carolina 27706; present address: Department of Biological Sciences, Rutgers, The State University, Piscataway, New Jersey 08854

GARY C. PACKARD, Department of Zoology, Colorado State University, Fort Collins, Colorado 80523

MARY J. PACKARD, Department of Zoology, Colorado State University, Fort Collins, Colorado 80523

F. HARVEY POUGH, Laboratory of Functional Ecology, Section of Ecology and Systematics, Cornell University, Ithaca, New York 14853

DAVID N. REZNICK, Department of Biology, University of California, Riverside, California 92521

RICHARD SHINE, Department of Zoology, University of Sydney, Sydney, New South Wales 2006, Australia

HENRY M. WILBUR, Department of Zoology, Duke University, Durham, North Carolina 27706

Preface

The present volume of the Biology of the Reptilia is the second dedicated primarily to topics of ecology and behavior, although volumes 12 and 13 on physiological ecology obviously fit this area. Furthermore, volume 8 included chapters on venoms and envenomation and volumes 14 and 15 provided accounts of reproduction in crocodilians and turtles and in lepidosaurians, respectively. Also, the latter volume included accounts on parthenogenesis, viviparity, and autotomy mechanisms.

The hiatus since the last volume dedicated to Ecology, which appeared in 1976, reflects mainly the untimely demise first of William W. Milstead and then of Donald W. Tinkle. The former had participated in the planning of the ecological components of the series and the latter had coedited the first volume and handled much of the initial contact with prospective authors of future ones.

Consequently, I am delighted to have obtained the assistance of Dr. Raymond B. Huey as a colleague who had the knowledge, skill, and commitment to assume the associate editorship of the next volume on ecology.

This second volume on Ecology contains chapters dealing with two major areas, namely the defensive behavior of reptiles and the parameters of reptilian life histories. Ancillary to these, but clearly associated, are accounts of reptilian parental care and the physiology and ecology of reptilian eggs. The first section begins with a widely ranging account of reptilian defensive behavior and is followed by chapters on mimicry and caudal autotomy, topics separated only because the extensive work permits their authors a much more detailed and informed discussion. The second section starts with a general account of methods for the study of populations. Then follow specific accounts on turtles and squamates, as well as of their eggs. (We regret that logistic and scheduling problems forced omission of the account of crocodilians.) A technique section is included here for two reasons: First, because the series is intended to stimulate much-needed future work rather than merely reporting upon the past. The second is that over the last quarter century, the study of life history phenomena has encountered both a conceptual and a methodological revolution. The methods of the pioneers in the field have been tested repeatedly and sometimes have had to be superceded. The substantial work required to obtain meaningful data on aspects of life history had best benefit from the results of these tests rather than proceed with the use of classical, but now inadequate approaches.

More than anything else, this volume documents the theme of diversity within the Reptilia. Such diversity might be expected in comparisons among turtles and sphenodontids, lizards and crocodilians; however, the degree of interspecific and intraspecific variability within each major reptilian group is important and significant. Analysis within such a framework requires knowledge of the full range of diversity, as well as an unusual breadth of viewpoint. Moreover, it requires parallel information about evolutionary and other biological principles, that lets the information be placed into perspective and thus generates a document that facilitates further study. This volume describes the multiple patterns utilized by these ectothermal amniotes and indicates some of the reasons why this group provides us with an unexcelled indicator of environmental diversity. Also it indicates that this diversity is as yet poorly characterized, so that many major phenomena remain to be discovered. From this viewpoint, we do not yet know enough about reptilian biology to make effective use of Krogh's principle, namely that there is an "optimum" species for the study of any biological phenomenon.

I am very grateful to our contributors for their responsiveness to the comments of multiple reviewers and for their patience while awaiting the completion of the last-arrived manuscripts of the volume. I am again appreciative for George Zug's careful check of Latin names that permits us to refer to species by the currently appropriate terminology. It is my pleasure to acknowledge the assistance of R.B. Huey and of the large numbers of reviewers. Their efforts represent the key to the generation of volumes intended to remain useful to the herpetological, indeed the zoological community. At the risk of omitting some names we would like to mention R. A. Ackerman, A. Ananjeva, S. J. Arnold, A. d'A. Bellairs, J. F. Berry, D. G. Broadley, C. Carey, J. H. Carothers, B. Dial, R. Dmi'el, J. Endler, J. G. Frazier, J. W. Gibbons, A. E. Greer, L. Houck,

PREFACE

F. Jaksić, A. R. Kiester, A. Muth, G. Pasteur, T. Pilorge, T. W. Schoener, R. A. Seigel, I. R. Swingland, J. R. G. Turner, L. Vitt, B. Wilson, as well as the authors of the several chapters. Several colleagues, identified in the captions, furnished pertinent photographs to illustrate the major topics. Ms. Katherine Vernon aided substantially with the correspondence. Finally, we appreciate the support of our institutions toward the ever increasing cost of postage and copying.

CARL GANS

Ann Arbor, Michigan
February 1987

CHAPTER

1

Antipredator Mechanisms in Reptiles

HARRY W. GREENE
Museum of Vertebrate Zoology and Department of Zoology,
University of California, Berkeley, California

CONTENTS

I. INTRODUCTION   3

II. PREDATION ON REPTILES   4
    A. Introduction, 4
    B. Analysis by Region, 5
    C. Analysis by Predator Taxa, 7
    D. Injury Frequencies, 11
    E. Natural and Manipulative Experiments, 12
    F. Some Generalizations, 12

III. INTRASPECIFIC VARIATION IN ANTIPREDATOR MECHANISMS   14
    A. Introduction, 14
    B. Stimulus Control and Context, 15
    C. Genetics and Ontogeny, 16
    D. Intra- and Interindividual Variation, 20
    E. Geographic Variation, 22

IV. SYSTEMATIC VARIATION IN ANTIPREDATOR MECHANISMS   24
    A. Introduction, 24
    B. Testudines, 25
    C. Crocodilia, 27
    D. Rhynchocephalia, 28
    E. Iguanian Lizards, 28
    F. Gekkotan Lizards, 31
    G. Autarchoglossan Lizards, 34
    H. Amphisbaenia, 37
    I. Serpentes, 37
    J. Rattlesnakes, 45

V. EVOLUTION OF ANTIPREDATOR MECHANISMS   48
    A. Function and Biological Roles, 48
    B. Patterns and Processes, 57
    C. Fossils, Anachronisms, and Recent Changes, 60

VI. REPTILES AND ANTIPREDATOR THEORY   61
    A. Reptiles as Study Organisms, 61
    B. Optimality and Limits to Theory, 62
    C. Some Generalizations, 63

INTRODUCTION	3
VII. PROBLEMS AND PROSPECTS	65
ADDENDUM	69
ACKNOWLEDGMENTS	69
REFERENCES	70
APPENDICES	112

A. Some Records of Predation on Reptiles, 112
B. Defensive Behavior in Neonate Reptiles, 122
C. Phenotypic Survey of Antipredator Mechanisms, 124
D. Taxonomic Survey of Antipredator Mechanisms, 134

I. INTRODUCTION

A great German herpetologist, Robert Mertens, published the first comprehensive review of reptilian antipredator mechanisms in 1946, and discussed them in terms of acoustic signals, chemical discharges, and other modes of expression. Although numerous brief descriptions of defensive behavior have appeared subsequently, only a few experimental studies and summaries of a more restricted nature have been published since Mertens' monograph. The present chapter surveys the nature and extent of predation on reptiles, and provides an updated review of their defensive mechanisms. With that perspective and the benefit of some recent advances in evolutionary biology, I then search for generalizations and address certain broader issues.

The study of antipredator mechanisms was a prominent aspect of the post-Darwinian era in evolutionary biology (e.g., Cott, 1940), but, with the notable exception of mimicry (Pough, this volume), defense against predators remains a topic largely without conceptual foundation (Dingle, 1975; Janzen, 1981; Endler, 1986a). A truly comprehensive theory of antipredator mechanisms would enable us to predict structures and responses of an unstudied animal on the basis of other, known aspects of its biology. The extent to which such a general theory is possible and factors that might limit it are addressed in Section VI. The following remarks will orient the reader and provide an interim conceptual framework.

This chapter is restricted to predation in a strict sense, i.e., the killing and consumption of another animal. Parasitism, scavenging, and predation on the eggs of reptiles (see Packard and Packard, this volume; Wilbur and Morin, this volume) are excluded on the grounds that they are not likely to influence the evolution of behavioral and external morphological aspects of organisms. With predation thus defined, defensive mechanisms can be considered in terms of the costs and benefits associated with searching for, pursuing, handling, and processing food. These components incorporate the probabilities of locating and capturing prey, the risk of injury or death to the predator, and the delay or nonperformance of other essential activities while feeding (Schoener, 1971; Griffiths, 1980; Greene, 1982). An antipredator tactic could work by raising any cost component to unacceptably high levels, or by deceptively indicating higher costs and/or lower benefits than a predator would "willingly" accept. Section II reviews predation on reptiles, as background for understanding antipredator mechanisms.

Ethology has traditionally recognized four major issues regarding behavior, viz., development within an individual, sensory and motivational control, evolutionary history, and ecological consequences (Tinbergen, 1963). Parallel questions also are posed with respect to morphological and physiological features of organisms (Gans, 1974; Liem and Wake, 1985), and they highlight important areas that have been largely overlooked in the study of antipredator mechanisms. Factors affecting the individual expression of defensive attributes and intraspecific variation are discussed in Section III. There follows a systematic analysis of variation among species and higher taxa in Section IV and a discussion of the evolution of antipredator mechanisms in Section V. Records of predation on specific taxa in nature, a survey of defensive behavior in neonate reptiles, a descriptive catalogue of antipredator mechanisms, and a taxonomic review are provided in the Appendices.

Case studies are emphasized throughout this chapter and, whenever possible, conceptual discussions are biased toward reptiles as examples. Occasional mention is made of unpublished observations, because they influenced my perspective and in hopes that they will inspire more detailed research. Autotomy (Arnold), mimicry (Pough), and parental care (Shine) are dealt with elsewhere in this volume.

II. PREDATION ON REPTILES

A. Introduction

The kinds and numbers of potential predators involved, the ways in which they interact with prey, and the energetic and reproductive consequences of those interactions are necessary parameters for understanding the ecological and evolutionary significance of antipredator mechanisms. The interaction itself is a "behavioral couple" that can vary irrespective of morphological features of predator and prey (Greene, 1982, 1986a). Energetic consequences of the interaction might reflect the roles of morphological and physiological constraints on predators and/or prey (Pough, 1983; Huey and Bennett, 1986), and might figure heavily in the future fitness of both organisms. Reproductive consequences of an encounter are the ultimate measures of fitness for both predator and prey.

An evaluation of antipredator mechanisms requires knowledge of actual predation on the prey species of interest, as well as of predator taxa that are *not* eating it because the encounter would be too "expensive." The latter information can suggest profitable experiments and appropriate interpretations of the behavior. For example, coatis (*Nasua narica*) and peccaries (*Tayassu tajacu*) were used as experimental predators of coral snake models (Gehlbach, 1972). Although those sympatric mammals are not known to prey upon venomous coral snakes, they do eat small, cryptic vertebrates, and Gehlbach's data demonstrated that coatis and peccaries actually avoid coral snakes (Greene and McDiarmid, 1981: Note 76).

Several sources of information on predation are potentially available, although relatively few data can be applied conclusively to questions about the evolution of antipredator mechanisms. These sources are discussed below, and include autecological studies of hunting techniques and diets, dietary analyses of entire communities of predators, comparative surveys of injury frequencies, and natural and manipulative experiments. Specific records of predation on reptiles in nature are given in Appendix A, and brief summaries for higher taxa are in Section IV.

B. Analysis by Region

Animals and their defensive mechanisms evolve in a community context. Work on marine invertebrates (Vermeij, 1978, 1982), poeciliid fishes (Endler, 1978, 1983), and other organisms (e.g., Moynihan, 1971; Maiorana, 1976) underscores the importance of studying simultaneously predation and antipredator responses in geographic and temporal terms. An especially pertinent example is the suggestion that the large biomass of herbivores and carnivores depresses species richness and overall abundance of reptiles in Africa relative to the neotropics (Janzen, 1976). That complex proposal was based on indirect evidence and crude measures of reptilian densities at African and neotropical sites (see criticisms by Kreulen, 1979, and response by Janzen, 1979). Nevertheless, the hypothesis might explain a major pattern in vertebrate geographical ecology, and thereby illustrates the potential value of comparative studies of predation.

A few surveys examine the diets of several sympatric predators, usually within a narrow taxonomic focus. Among 29 species of raptors in Surinam, at least six feed frequently on reptiles and at least eight feed occasionally on lizards and snakes. Of those, the laughing falcon (*Herpetotheres cachinnans*) specializes on snakes and the gray hawk (*Buteo nitidus*) takes many lizards (Haverschmidt, 1962; Voous, 1969).

In Africa, at least 20 of 89 species of diurnal raptors and 2 of 30 species of owls feed only or in part on reptiles, and their collective diets encompass an impressively large number of species (Brown, 1971; Broadley, 1974). For example, 8 secretary birds (*Sagittarius serpentarius*) contained 61 reptilian prey, including a tortoise, 57 lizards of 6 genera and 11 species, and 1 each of 3 species of snakes. Forty-four reptiles eaten by brown snake eagles (*Circaetus cinerus*) included a *Chamaeleo dilepis*, a *Varanus niloticus*, an *Agama sp.*, and 41 snakes, among which were numerous large, venomous species (*Bitis arietans*, *Dendroaspis polylepis*, *Naja mossambica*; Broadley, 1974).

Reptiles are uncommon in the diets of most of 15 species of medium and large carnivores in southern Africa, but several of those predators might have important impact on them (Pienaar, 1969; Broadley, in litt.). Land tortoises (*Geochelone pardalis*, *Kinixys belliana*) and water turtles (*Pelusios sinuatus*, *P. subrufa*) are eaten by lions (*Panthera leo*) and two species of hyaenas (*Crocuta crocuta*, *Hyaena brunnea*), and the aquatic turtles are eaten commonly by *Crocodylus niloticus* as well. *Python sebae* is eaten by lions and leopards (*Panthera pardus*).

In contrast, the smaller African carnivores are regular predators on reptiles. These include a small cat, *Felis libyca*; all of the canids except wild dogs; all mustelids other than otters; and all viverrids except two insectivorous mongooses (Broadley, in litt.). Most predation is evidently opportunistic (e.g., an amphisbaenian, ten species of lizards, and four species of snakes in the diet of *F. libyca*; a tortoise, an amphisbaenian, eight species of lizards, and nine species of snakes eaten by *Canis mesomelas*), but sometimes predators gorge on particular species or the inhabitants of particular microhabitats. A badger, *Mellivora capensis*, had eaten 22 geckos, *Ptenopus garrulus*, as well as an amphisbaenian, rodents, and scorpions. One mongoose, *Paracynictis selousi*, contained 18 burrowing skinks, *Panaspis wahlbergii*; 3 lacertids, *Nucras taeniolata*; 3 snakes, including 2 *Lycophidion capense* and an *Atractaspis bibroni*; plus a frog, rodents, and crickets.

Comprehensive dietary surveys of entire assemblages of sympatric predators (rather than taxonomic subsets) are available for only four localities, three of them in Mediterranean-type habitats of Spain (Valverde, 1967), Chile (Jaksic et al., 1982), and California (a series of papers by Fitch and colleagues, cited in Jaksic et al., 1982). Among those sites, the overall importance of reptiles as prey is lowest in Chile, intermediate in California, and highest in Spain. The incidence of predation on a species is correlated with its relative abundance in Spain and California, but not in Chile. Behavioral and morphological attributes apparently make some prey species more vulnerable to capture (e.g., a large colubrid snake, *Philodryas chamissonis*, in Chile) and others less so (e.g., a very fast teiid lizard, *Callopistes maculatus*, in Chile; a venomous rattlesnake, *Crotalus viridis*, in California) than their abundances would predict.

In an assemblage of more than 100 sympatric vertebrate predators at Finca La Selva, Costa Rica, a katydid, 2 frogs, 2 lizards, at least 17 snakes, 10 raptors, and 2 mammalian carnivores feed on reptiles. Preliminary data from that locality indicate that most lizards and snakes, particularly smaller species, face the threat of a wide variety of avian, mammalian, and snake predators (van Berkum et al., 1986; Greene, 1987; Greene, Donnelly, Guyer, and Santana, unpubl.).

C. Analysis by Predator Taxa

1. INVERTEBRATES

Although reptiles frequently prey on invertebrates, the reverse is rarely true. Most cases of arthropod predation on terrestrial and aquatic reptiles represent occasional attacks on small individuals by predator species that usually eat other invertebrates, but exceptions exist (see McCormick and Polis, 1982, for a review). Some large centipedes, spiders, and scorpions eat vertebrates, and reptiles are apparently an important part of the diet of a few species. Scorpions are abundant in parts of arid western North America, and blind snakes, *Leptotyphlops humilis*, sometimes form as much as 10% of their diets (McCormick and Polis, 1982). Spiders prey on small snakes (Groves and Groves, 1978; McCormick and Polis, 1982), a mantid ate a gecko (Wright, 1982), a crab caught a hatchling king cobra (Wall, 1926a), a water bug ate a garter snake (Drummond and Wolfe, 1981), and centipedes often eat Galapagos lava lizards (Snell, in litt.). The prevalence of large, predatory invertebrates in the leaf litter of lowland tropical forests might account for the paucity of small reptiles in those habitats (Myers and Rand, 1969), but more information on the geographic incidence of arthropod predation on small litter vertebrates is needed to evaluate that hypothesis.

Marine reptiles are also preyed upon by invertebrates. A large octopus was found eating a medium sized sea turtle, *Eretmochelys imbricata*, and flipper damage to other sea turtles might have been caused by octopi (Buxton and Branch, 1983). Crabs probably are prominent predators on hatchling sea turtles throughout the world (e.g., Stancyk, 1981; Frazier, 1984; Cornelius, 1986).

2. FISHES

Relatively few reptiles are aquatic or marine, and predatory fish are probably rarely important in the evolution of reptiles (see Section V.A). The diet of a chub includes terrestrial iguanid lizards, *Sceloporus spp.* (Neve, 1976); a large catfish had an African viper, *Bitis arietans*, in its stomach (Thorne and Hamman, 1981); a 3-kg African fish contained a 2-m long black mamba (*Dendroaspis polylepis*, Broadley, 1983); and a large Amazonian fish had eaten two blind snakes, *Leptotyphlops macrolepis* (Goulding, 1980). Four *Thamnophis sirtalis* and one *Storeria occipitomaculata* were found in 1724 bass (*Micropterus salmoides*) stomachs in Michigan (Knapik and Hodgson, 1986). An eel (*Anquilla rostrata*) regurgitated two hatchling musk turtles, *Sternotherus odoratus*, that survived the encounter (Pough, in litt.).

Six species of sharks take considerable numbers of sea snakes in the waters off Australia, and also perhaps catch them elsewhere (Heatwole, 1975). On rare occasions marine bony fishes eat *Pelamis platurus*, a surface-feeding sea snake (Pickwell et al., 1983), as well as other marine elapids (Heatwole, 1975). Sharks might pose a significant threat to sea turtles (Stancyk, 1981; Cornelius, 1986) and Galapagos marine iguanas (*Amblyrhynchus cristatus*, Carpenter, 1966). A single dolphin contained nine young sea turtles of two species (Whitham, 1974).

3. AMPHIBIANS

Most amphibians are not predators on reptiles. The few caecilians that have been studied feed mainly on invertebrates (Wall, 1922; Bemis et al., 1983); an *Ameiva undulata* and an *Anolis dollfusianus* in the stomach of a *Dermophis mexicanus* are the only records of predation on vertebrates by those limbless, tropical amphibians (Moll and Smith, 1967). The only records of predation on wild reptiles by salamanders are of *Siren intermedia* on a snake, *Regina alleni* (Godley, 1982); of *Dicamptodon ensatus* on an iguanid lizard, *Sceloporus occidentalis* (Bury, 1972); and of *Ambystoma tigrinum* on a teiid lizard, *Cnemidophorus sexlineatus* (Camper, 1986). *Dicamptodon ensatus* is probably the only salamander in the world that regularly eats terrestrial vertebrates in the field.

Most frogs are insectivorous and too small to prey on vertebrates, but there are some interesting exceptions. *Rana catesbeiana* in North America (Minton, 1949; Clarkson and de Vos, 1986), *Leptodactylus pentadactylus* (Hoogmoed, 1980) in the neotropics, and *Pyxicephalus adspersus* in Africa (Branch, 1976) eat snakes, including highly venomous species in the first and last cases. A *Bufo terrestris* ate a brightly colored colubrid snake, *Cemophora coccinea* (Brown, 1979); a *Rana warschewitchii* regurgitated a small iguanid lizard, *Anolis humilis* (Greene, Donnelly, Guyer, and Santana, unpubl.); and a *R. grylio* ate an *Eumeces laticeps* (Lamb, 1984). Asiatic *B. melanostictus* commonly eats blind snakes (Hahn, 1976). Aquatic turtles occasionally fall prey to frogs (Graham, 1984), as do baby *Alligator mississippiensis* (Neill, 1971).

4. REPTILES

The sole living sphenodontid, *Sphenodon punctatus*, feeds on a variety of prey, including lizards (Gans, 1983a), but the few sympatric geckos and skinks are not a major part of its diet.

Apparently few turtles consume other reptiles in the field, but *Macroclemys temminckii* is an important predator on other turtles (Pritchard and Trebbau, 1984). Captive observations suggest that a few other species also might eat reptiles in nature (e.g., *Terrapene ornata*, Legler, 1960).

Crocodilians feed on a variety of invertebrates and vertebrates, including turtles, lizards, and snakes. *Crocodylus niloticus* even eats highly venomous puff adders, *Bitis arietans* (Cott, 1961). *Alligator mississippiensis* (Neill, 1971) and *C. niloticus* (Pienaar, 1969) frequently eat turtles, and several neotropical species occasionally feed on turtles, lizards, and snakes (Alvarez el Toro, 1974; Medem, 1981). *Crocodylus palustris* sometimes eats sea snakes and marine turtles (Allen, 1974). No crocodilian specializes on reptiles as prey.

Most lizards feed mainly or entirely on arthropods, but some occasionally eat other vertebrates and a few are reptile specialists (for general discussion, see Greene, 1982). Species that feed frequently on other lizards include two large teiids of the genus *Callopistes* (pers. obs.), the iguanid *Gambelia wislizeni* (Tanner and Krogh, 1975; Parker and Pianka, 1976), the pygopodid *Lialis burtonis* (Patchell and Shine, 1986), and several species of Australian varanids (e.g., Pianka, 1986; Losos and Greene, unpubl.).

Snakes are probably important predators on lizards in many regions (e.g., Shine, 1977, for Australia; McKinney and Ballinger, 1966, for Texas; Fitch, 1949, for California; Duellman, 1978, for Ecuador; Henderson, 1984a, for the West Indies). Some species specialize on other snakes (e.g., *Ophiophagus hannah*, M. A. Smith, 1943; *Cylindrophis rufus*, Greene, 1983a; *Micrurus fulvius*, Greene, 1984) or amphisbaenians (Broadley, 1963; Papenfuss, 1982). A few species of snakes occasionally feed on turtles (e.g., *Drymarchon corais*, Ruthven, 1912; *Agkistrodon piscivorus*, Burkett, 1966) and/or crocodilians (e.g., *A. piscivorus*, Allen and Swindell, 1948; *Eunectes murinus*, Wehekind, 1955; an unidentified Eocene henophidian, Greene, 1983a).

5. BIRDS

Birds are often enemies of reptiles throughout the world, and at many sites there exists an array of emphasis ranging from occasional to very frequent predation. Species that eat reptiles regularly, at least at times, include the secretary bird (*Sagittarius serpentarius*) and several other African raptors (Brown, 1971; Sweeney, 1971; Broadley, 1974), roadrunner (*Geococcyx californicus*, Bryant, 1916; Meinzer, 1983), and numerous tropical hawks (Haverschmidt, 1962; Voous, 1969; Greene, Donnelly, Guyer, and Santana, unpubl.). Herons eat many young crocodilians (Alvarez del Toro, 1974; Gorzula, 1985), and pelicans can eat moderately large land turtles (Land, 1931). Several species of marine raptors eat sea snakes (Heatwole, 1975), and a variety of birds eat young sea turtles (Stancyk, 1981). Although many diurnal reptiles are probably safe from nocturnal raptors, by virtue of the use of retreats, some owls regularly take nocturnal gekkonid lizards (Demeter, 1982). In addition to specialists on reptiles, many other birds occasionally or frequently eat them, including shrikes, jays, toucans, puffbirds, cuckoos, and others (for old but still useful reviews of bird predation on snakes, see Wall, 1906a; Guthrie, 1932).

6. MAMMALS

Few mammals regularly take reptiles as prey; examples include some viverrids (Broadley, in litt.), neotropical mustelids (*Galictis sp.*, Jackson, 1979; Rodda and Burghardt, 1985), some foxes (e.g., *Vulpes macrotus*, pers. obs.), badgers (Klauber, 1956; Messick and Hornocker, 1981; Kruuk and Mills, 1983; Broadley, in litt.), and some primates (Gans, 1964, 1965; Lorenz, 1971). Hyaenas in South Africa frequently eat tortoises, "easily cracking their shells" (Pienaar, 1969). Several carnivorous bats eat nocturnal geckos and diurnal agamid and iguanid lizards (Goodwin and Greenhall, 1961; Douglas, 1967; Tuttle, 1967; Valdez and LaVal, 1971; Vaughn, 1976; Advani, 1981). Sea turtles, especially small individuals, are prey to a variety of terrestrial and marine mammals (Stancyk, 1981). Numerous other mammals in several orders prey occasionally on lizards, amphisbaenians, and snakes (e.g., wild pigs, *Sus scrofa*, Valverde, 1967) and even adult crocodilians are sometimes taken by lions (*Panthera leo*, Cott, 1961; Pienaar, 1969) and jaguars (*P. onca*, Alvarez del Toro, 1974). Nesting females of large arboreal lizards, *Iguana iguana*, are seasonally important prey for jaguars in northeastern Costa Rica (Greene, Santana, and Braker, unpubl.). A bear (presumably *Ursus arctos*) perhaps tried to eat a *Testudo graeca* (Reed and Marx, 1959).

D. Injury Frequencies

Scars and missing body parts do not necessarily index the intensity of successful predation (Schoener, 1979; Jaksic and Greene, 1984; Arnold, this volume), but they can provide a minimum estimate of successful escape from predators (Greene, 1973a), assuming no injuries due to social encounters, mishaps, or illness (Vitt et al., 1974; Khan and Tasnim, 1986a). Injuries are thus potential indicators of predator–prey interactions, both in terms of the frequency and nature of the wounds.

Predation is widely assumed to be an all-or-none phenomenon for prey, although unsuccessful predation is clearly essential for the evolution of antipredator mechanisms (Vermeij, 1982). Observations of encounters and scars indicate that reptiles often confront formidable enemies, incur injuries, and escape. I have found adult iguanid lizards (*Callisaurus draconoides*, *Iguana iguana*) with large, healed body scars. A small colubrid snake (*Diadophis punctatus*) that survived more than 5 minutes of mouthing by a captive kit fox (*Vulpes macrotus*) was seemingly healthy 2 weeks later (pers. obs.). Recovery from serious wounds has also been reported for *Sternotherus odoratus* (Ernst, 1986), *Terrapene coahuila* (Brown, 1974), *T. ornata* (Legler, 1960), *Phrynops zuliae* (Pritchard and Trebbau, 1984), *Crocodylus niloticus* (Cott, 1961), *Sauromalus obesus* (Camp, 1916; Berry, 1974), *Eumeces obsoletus* (Fitch, 1955), *Coluber constrictor* (Brunson, 1986), *Pituophis melanoleucus* (Brunson, 1986), *Xenochrophis piscator* (Auffenberg, 1980), and several species of sea snakes (Heatwole, 1975).

The abilities of reptiles to survive serious injuries from a predator has relevance for the efficacy and mechanisms of defense. The responses to danger work because the prey push the costs of predation above an acceptable level, or because they deceive a predator about the magnitude of the costs. Because escape from predators can be accomplished despite actual physical contact, the dynamics of an encounter might influence the behavior of a reptile and a predator in subsequent interactions, but the extent to which this occurs in nature is unknown (see Section III.C).

E. Natural and Manipulative Experiments

Reptiles have existed on some small, isolated islands in the near or total absence of predation for long periods, and numerous cases demonstrate unusual tameness in those animals (e.g., *Anolis agassizi*, Rand et al., 1975). The mechanisms producing such behavior (e.g., selection, habituation) remain unstudied (see Sections III.C, V.C).

Modern introductions provide valuable information on the negative impact of predators on populations of prey that are not capable of defense against them. The arrival of armadillos (*Dasypus novemcinctus*) in peninsular Florida during recent decades occurred contemporaneously with the disappearance of appropriate predators on those generalist hunters, and the result has been a marked reduction in the abundance of leaf litter organisms, including small reptiles (Carr, 1982; see also Redford, 1985; Greene, 1987). Introductions of mongoose and feral cats have had severe effects on the reptilian faunas of several Caribbean islands. In a particularly well documented case, the introduction of dogs and cats on a small island devastated a population of large iguanid lizards, *Cyclura carinata*, in 3 years (Iverson, 1978).

Although widely assumed to be a major source of mortality for many reptiles, the impact of predation on population parameters is poorly known (see Dunham et al., this volume). Experimental exclusion of predators significantly increases the survivorship of particular phenotypes of *Uta stansburiana* (Ferguson and Fox, 1984).

F. Some Generalizations

Reptiles are subject to a wide range of predators, although the risks vary geographically as well as among predator taxa at a locality. Even species that might be expected to be relatively free of enemies are eaten, such as those that are predominantly nocturnal (many geckos), aquatic (crocodilians, many turtles), fossorial (amphisbaenians, scolecophidian snakes), heavily armored (cordylid lizards, tortoises), or highly venomous (*Bitis, Naja*). Studies of experimental populations, of reptiles subject to introduced predators, and of island reptiles underscore the widespread potential importance of predation as a factor in the lives of these animals. Brief speculation regarding the kinds of problems with which reptiles must contend—the sensory and prey-handling characteristics of their predators—is possible from the information presented above, but generalizations are necessarily broad and tentative.

Birds and mammals probably often are the most significant potential factors in the evolution of antipredator mechanisms in reptiles, for several reasons. They are by and large visually hunting predators, although some, especially mammals, are also guided by auditory and chemical cues. Many birds possess particularly acute vision, and thus are particularly likely to circumvent crypsis (Section V.A). Parent birds and mammals often transport immobile, intact prey as food for their offspring, making lack of movement subsequent to capture (i.e., failure to elicit additional prey immobilization tactics) a potentially viable defense option (see Sections V.A, VI.B). Birds and mammals have high metabolic rates and high daily energy needs, such that their consumption rates and impact on a prey population can be high even if the latter constitutes a small part of the overall diet.

Snakes frequently prey on lizards and, to a lesser extent, on other snakes. Although some species appear to have good vision, many rely heavily on chemical cues to locate prey (Burghardt, 1970) and usually begin consuming prey while it is immobilized (e.g., Klauber, 1956; Greene, 1984). At equivalent densities, the impact of snakes and other ectotherms on prey populations will be far less than that of endothermic predators. Probably most terrestrial vertebrate predators are capable of solving at least moderately complex learning problems (see Burghardt, 1977a, for a review of learning in reptiles).

The available evidence suggests that many birds and mammals take species within a broad prey type (e.g., size, higher taxon) and roughly in proportion to their abundances (Jaksic, 1986), although some might avoid preferentially certain dangerous (e.g., *Crotalus viridis*, Fitch 1949) or particularly fleet (e.g., *Callopistes maculatus*, Jaksic et al., 1982) species. Some snakes also might feed indiscriminantly on abundant reptiles, but most species probably specialize on a few prey taxa (e.g., certain African burrowing snakes that eat exclusively amphisbaenians, Broadley, 1963; see also Arnold, 1972; Savitzky, 1983).

Some predators are "hunting habitat specialists" that feed frequently on reptiles as well as on any other appropriately sized, palatable organisms that they encounter. The neotropical crane-hawk (*Geranospiza caerulescens*) systematically searches bromeliads and holes in trees for large insects, frogs, lizards, snakes, and nestling birds (Sutton, 1954; Alvarez del Toro, 1971; Bokermann, 1978). Jamaican cuckoos (*Saurothera vetula*), crows (*Corvus jamaicensis*), and becards (*Platypsaris niger*) hunt for anoles and other prey in bromeliads (Cruz, 1972, 1973, 1975). Nocturnal lyre snakes (*Trimorphodon spp.*) hunt in crevices for resting diurnal iguanid lizards (pers. obs.), and coral snakes (*Micrurus spp.*) search for small reptilian prey in leaf litter (Greene, 1973b, 1984). African honey badgers (*Mellivora capensis*) locate a variety of prey, including many lizards and snakes, by digging at the bases of bushes (Kruuk and Mills, 1983; Broadley, in litt.). Such predators present a constant threat to otherwise hidden, inactive animals (e.g., sleeping iguanids at night, quiescent geckos during the day), implying that selection of retreat site might be an important antipredator mechanism.

In summary, many reptiles, perhaps especially diurnal forms that are active above ground, potentially face a large number of predators with diverse prey detection and handling capabilities. Diurnal species may be vulnerable in the daytime to one set of enemies that perceive them visually and precipitate a chase, and to another set that use chemical cues to locate their retreats at night and simply seize the immobile prey. For example, a diurnal desert lizard, *Cnemidophorus tigris,* may be eaten by kestrels (*Falco sparverius*), roadrunners, and coachwhip snakes (*Masticophis flagellum*) during the day, and dug from its burrows by badgers (*Taxidea taxus*) and long-nosed snakes (*Rhinocheilus lecontei*) at night (Greene, 1986a; pers. obs.). An analogous, reverse dichotomy of predatory problems probably confronts some nocturnal reptiles. A consequence for potential prey of this spectrum of interactions is that *some* defense is probably effective in *some* cases, but almost no defense works *all* the time.

III. INTRASPECIFIC VARIATION IN ANTIPREDATOR MECHANISMS

A. Introduction

Knowledge of variation within an individual during its lifetime can help elucidate developmental mechanisms that shape the phenotype, such as learning and maturation. Variation among individuals and among populations can potentially help explain the nature of genetic and social transmission in the population, and the substrate upon which selection acts. An understanding of those phenomena requires that factors external to the organisms also be understood, including experience, stimulus control, and temperature effects.

B. Stimulus Control and Context

Potential predators might be perceived by visual, thermal, auditory, chemical, and/or tactile cues. Those modalities differ in the distance over which they are effective, and in the extent to which they are relevant to particular predators and prey. Ideally, two kinds of information are of interest: the responses of reptiles to a controlled series of threatening stimuli, and field observations on the reactions of reptiles to potential predators.

Our notions of what constitutes defensive behavior are heavily influenced by reactions to human collectors, and perhaps only for that reason does it appear that reptiles respond defensively primarily to visual and tactile cues. This has led to erroneous conclusions whenever routine or cautious handling was not sufficient to elicit reactions, as in the supposedly docile nature of venomous coral snakes (Gehlbach, 1972; Greene and Pyburn, 1973) and the long-overlooked, noxious secretions of *Lichanura trivirgata* (Ruben, 1976). *Oligodon violaceus* presses a human captor with its tail tip and rarely bites when handled, but strikes vigorously and vibrates the tail when attacked by a mongoose (Wall, 1903; Schmidt, 1927a). In fact, some snakes (Weldon and Burghardt, 1979) and lizards (Prieto and Sorenson, 1975) perceive the proximity of predators by chemical cues, and the significance of that modality is surely widely underestimated (for negative evidence for *Sceloporus jarrovi*, see Simon et al., 1981). Moreover, contextual factors (see below and Section IV.C) might interact with sensory cues to determine whether a response occurs.

Observations and studies on several species demonstrate the role of different stimuli in eliciting antipredator behavior. A *Nephrurus asper* responds to mice, small snakes, and humans with a dramatic threat posture, vocalization, and lunges, but to large snakes by locomotor escape and crouching (Bustard, 1967, 1979). Similarly, *Elgaria multicarinata* actively threatens bird predators but flees from snakes (Fitch, 1935). Close approach and tactile contact prompt higher tongue flick rates than resting levels in three species of *Nerodia*, but tactile cues cause a more dramatic increase (Scudder and Burghardt, 1983). *Thamnophis radix* responds more defensively (head-hiding, etc.) to more severe attacks (tapping the head) and more offensively (e.g., striking) to less severe stimuli (tapping the tail) and at lower temperatures (Arnold and Bennett, 1984; see Fitch, 1965, for similar observations of *T. sirtalis*). A human finger more readily elicits strikes than a cotton swab presented to neonates of three other species of *Thamnophis* (Herzog and Burghardt, 1986). Experimental presentation of carnivores and humans to rattlesnakes (*Crotalus viridis, Sistrurus catenatus*) demonstrated that defensive responses are elicited by generalized visual cues (large moving objects) rather than particular configurational stimuli (Scudder and Chiszar, 1977).

The situation in *Crotalus viridis* is further complicated by environmental and social factors. Solitary prairie rattlesnakes threatened when away from cover emphasized locomotor escape, whereas those near cover usually remained immobile. Grouped rattlesnakes near cover most frequently resorted to escaping and threatening movements, suggesting social facilitation of individual responses to a predator (Duvall et al., 1985). Other examples of the role of context are *Caiman crocodilus*, juveniles of which feign death under water but react aggressively on land (Gorzula, 1978), and *Bungarus caeruleus*, which emphasizes head hiding in daylight but escape and biting at night (Khan and Tasnim, 1986b).

The anatomy and neurophysiology of hearing have been studied extensively in reptiles (e.g., Wever, 1978), but the roles of air- and ground-borne vibrations in eliciting defensive responses remain poorly known. A tropical teiid lizard, *Cnemidophorus lemniscatus*, reacts to alarm cries of small birds by rapid escape to its burrow (Beebe, 1945), and desert geckos, *Ptenopus garrulus*, retreat to their holes if one steps on a nearby dry leaf or twig (Huey, in litt.). Snakes are widely reported to respond to ground-borne vibrations (e.g., Klauber, 1956).

C. Genetics and Ontogeny

The phenotype reflects a complex interaction of genetic heritage, the environment, and factors within the developing organism itself (for general treatments, see Burghardt, 1977a, 1977b, 1978; Alberch et al., 1979). This interaction begins at conception (or cleavage, in the case of uniparental forms), and assumes potentially much larger environmental components after birth or hatching. As a descriptive task, we can inquire whether a particular behavior is present at hatching or birth, whether the behavior varies within and among litters, whether the behavior changes with age, and what factors control those differences and changes.

Failure to exhibit an appropriate response during a first predator encounter could be fatal to a young reptile, and a variety of species typical defensive behavior patterns are elicited in a taxonomically diverse sample of young turtles, lizards, and snakes that lack prior experience with threatening stimuli (Appendix B). Nevertheless, that finding does not imply necessarily the lack of maternal and/or postnatal effects. The widespread survival of reptiles after serious predator encounters (Section II.D), the association of young crocodilians and some lizards with their parents (Shine, this volume), and examples of individual changes in response to humans (see below and Section III.E) all indicate the potential for experiential modification of defensive behavior.

Most descriptions of defensive mechanisms in reptiles either concern adults of unknown background or congenital responses that closely resemble those seen in adults (Appendix B). A few examples illustrate changes with time or lack thereof, but the information provided usually is insufficient to distinguish experience from other factors (e.g., maturation of neuromuscular control mechanisms). Juvenile *Chelodina longicollis* are more likely to expel musk than are adults (Kool, 1981). Recently hatched *Pseudemys scripta* are more likely to remain immobile and less likely to flee than are adults (Moll and Legler, 1971). Large *Geoclemys hamiltoni* are "belligerent," whereas small ones are "shy and gentle" (Minton, 1966). Large *Sceloporus torquatus* are more wary than small ones (Schmidt and Shannon, 1947). Small individuals of *Cnemidophorus lemniscatus* are easily approached and resume foraging within seconds after being frightened, whereas adults flee immediately and subsequently remain immobile for several minutes (Beebe, 1945). Newly hatched *Crotaphytus collaris* run about erratically when chased, whereas those a week or more in age flee directly to a familiar crevice or burrow (Fitch, 1956). Young *Varanus varius* are secretive, but adults are formidable adversaries and far less wary (Bustard, 1968c; Section IV.G). Juveniles of a Kalahari Desert lacertid, *Eremias lugubris*, are brightly colored and use a peculiar, jerky locomotion that resembles sympatric, noxious beetles, whereas adults are cryptic and run rapidly (Huey and Pianka, 1977). A number of lizards (Huey, 1982; Garland, 1985) and snakes (e.g., Pough, 1980) exhibit ontogenetic changes in locomotor performance abilities, and these are likely to be relevant in predator encounters.

Young *Boa constrictor* are quiet, whereas adults hiss loudly (Mertens, 1952a; Donnelly, Santana, and Greene, unpubl.). Adult *Antillophis parvifrons* flatten their necks and elevate the head when threatened; behavior that was not observed in newly hatched young (Sajdak and Henderson, 1982). One-day-old *Epicrates angulifer* strike aggressively, but only exude a mild musk at an age of 13 days (Sheplan and Schwartz, 1974). Juvenile copperheads, *Agkistrodon contortrix*, cannot eject a stream of scent gland liquid until they are 8 days old (Gloyd, 1934). *Pseudaspis cana* do not begin to hiss and strike until 18 hours after birth (Branch, 1973). Neonates of *Ninia sebae* exhibit defensive head displays that resemble those of adults from the same population, but are somewhat wobbly, a difference perhaps attributable to a lack of muscular coordination in the young snakes (Greene, 1975). Young *Masticophis lateralis* typically go under rocks when chased, but adults of that racer will travel 15 m or more to ascend a bush (Sweet, in litt.). Juveniles and adults of six species of Australopapuan elapids resemble each other generally in defensive behavior, but differ interspecifically in the presence of certain component postures during ontogeny (Johnson, 1975). Adult *Pituophis melanoleucus* are less likely than juveniles to hiss, vibrate their tails, and form striking coils (Sweet, 1985). Young *Naja naja* are more aggressive than adults (Wall, 1913a). Newly hatched *Lachesis muta* strike and vibrate their tails, but cease those responses at the age of 1 month (Switak, 1969; Solorzano, Santana, and Greene, unpubl.); that could be attributed to captive habituation, but is also consistent with the phlegmatic behavior of adult wild bushmasters from some populations (Greene and Santana, unpubl.). Young *Vipera russellii* are more alert and more easily provoked into biting than are the adults (Wall, 1907a).

Other potential modifiers of defensive behavior include habituation, learning, and social transmission (see Burghardt, 1977a, for general discussion). A waning of antipredator behavior in response to handling by humans and other aspects of captivity has been seen in *Chelodina longicollis* (Kool, 1981), *Gambelia wislizeni* (Crowley and Pietruszka, 1983), *Heloderma suspectum* (Bogert and del Campo, 1956), *Heterodon platirhinos* (Platt, 1969), *Pituophis melanoleucus* (Sweet, 1985), and some *Crotalus* spp. (Klauber, 1956). Conversely, *Tropidurus albemarlensis* that were initially tame became exceptionally difficult to capture after experience with a noose (Stebbins et al., 1967). *Crocodylus porosus* that have been caught once by humans at night subsequently avoid boats at distances of more than 100 m (Bustard, 1968a).

Most reptiles are not especially social, but the possibility exists that intra- and interspecific responses to predators are more widespread than currently thought. Wild adult *Iguana iguana* typically follow suit when one lizard jumps out of a tree in response to a predator. However, members of a group that were habituated to a human observer over a period of days subsequently failed to exhibit escape behavior in response to that of a nonhabituated, transient iguana at the site (Greene et al., 1978). Parental protection of young crocodilians is well known (Shine, this volume), but recent observations on *Caiman crocodilus* show that distress vocalizations can attract several conspecifics of various sizes and sexes (Gorzula, 1985). The remarkable observation that tropical whiptail lizards, *Cnemidophorus lemniscatus*, flee in response to alarm calls of birds (Beebe, 1945) deserves detailed study.

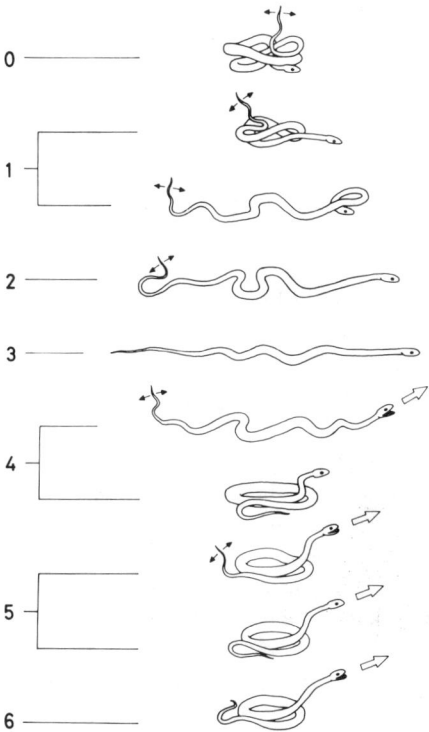

Fig. 1. Antipredator displays in newborn garter snakes, *Thamnophis radix*, arranged in a continuum from defensive (top) to offensive (bottom). Total scores (on the left) were assigned to each display by summing scores for behavioral characteristics of parts of a snake (see Arnold and Bennett, 1984, and text for additional details). (Courtesy of *Animal Behaviour*).

The heritability of antipredator mechanisms in vertebrates is inadequately known (e.g., fishes, Vadasz et al., 1978), and the only estimates for a reptile are based on full-sibling analyses for *Thamnophis radix* (Arnold and Bennett, 1984). The variation among litters in that garter snake is extensive (Fig. 1), some of it context dependent, and encompasses much of the defensive behavioral variation seen among other colubrids. Replicate trials show that there are stable behavioral phenotypes for individual *T. radix*, and heritability estimates ranged from 0.37 for single trials to 0.45 for replicate trials. Selection on defensive responses has not been studied in the field, but the recent work by Arnold, Burghardt, and colleagues suggests that is feasible.

D. Intra- and Interindividual Variation

Apparent intrapopulational variability could be caused by differences in age, stimulus intensity, thermal effects, and/or other undetected contextual variables. Real individual variability might also be dependent on sex. Unfortunately, almost all reports of individual differences in the defensive behavior of reptiles are not controlled with respect to one or more of those variables.

Diadophis punctatus, a small colubrid snake, illustrates the problems of assessing behavioral variability. An initial study within a Kansas population found that 74 of 100 snakes tested with visual and tactile stimuli displayed their tails. Of a second 100 snakes, tested when initially encountered in the field, 96 displayed. The sex ratio in that sample was approximately equal, and the response seemed equally well developed in young and adults (Fitch, 1975). The difference between the two samples suggests that handling subsequent to capture might have reduced the tendency to display in some snakes. Another study in the same area found that ca. 66% of small *D. punctatus* displayed their tails, but only ca. 30% of the larger snakes did so (Smith, 1974; see also Burghardt, 1978). Several factors probably are at work here, and this species is a prime candidate for detailed studies.

Two species of hognose snakes in Kansas are similarly likely to feign death when first observed (71% of 70 *Heterodon nasicus*, 83% of 35 *H. platirhinos*; Platt, 1969). However, in Texas significantly fewer *H. nasicus* feign death (52% of 25) than did sympatric *H. platirhinos* (73% of 51, Kroll, 1977). One species loses this behavior sooner in captivity, judging from the proportions responding when re-examined within 24 hours of capture (9% of 98 *H. nasicus*, 59% of 41 *H. platirhinos*, Platt, 1969). Two individuals of *H. simus* differed in the extent to which various behavioral components were included in their defensive displays (Myers and Arata, 1961).

Four of fifty-six male and three of forty-one female horned lizards, *Phrynosoma cornutum*, squirted blood from their eyes during a total of 118 encounters in which they were handled and toe-clipped by humans. The frequency of that behavior was unaffected by sex of the lizards or by ten environmental variables (Lambert and Ferguson, 1985). Other indications of individual variability include 5 of 65 (7.7%) *P. solare* that squirted blood (Parker, 1971), 12 of 80 (15%) *Diplodactylus williamsi* that ejected caudal gland secretions (Bustard, 1964), 10 of 32 (31.3%) of *Thelotornis kirtlandii* that bit when captured (Sweeney, 1971), and 1 of 26 (3.9%) neonatal *Lampropeltis alterna* that feigned death (Tryon and Guese, 1984). The tendency of *Terrapene carolina* (Nichols, 1939) and of *T.*

ornata (Legler, 1960) to withdraw and close their shells varies individually, but each of 169 *T. coahuila* did so (Brown, 1974; see also Sections IV.B, V.A).

Defensive responses vary with temperature in several species. At high body temperatures, *Agama mutabilis* and *A. savignii* flee rapidly when threatened. At lower temperatures (which reduce sprint speed), the lizards remain stationary, adopt threat postures, and bite readily (Hertz et al., 1982). Several species of iguanids flee from predators at a greater distance at lower body temperatures (*Anolis lineatopus*, Rand, 1964; *Sceloporus cyanogenys*, Greenburg, 1976; *Tropidurus peruvianus*, Huey, 1977; *Uta stansburiana*, Tinkle, 1967). Leopard lizards (*Gambelia wislizeni*) are more aggressive and vocalize more readily at lower temperatures in captivity (Crowley and Pietruszka, 1983) and, presumably for that reason, are more likely to vocalize earlier in the morning in the field (Jorgensen et al., 1963). The defensive behaviors of *Bitis caudalis* (Gans and Mendelsohn, 1972) and *Thamnophis radix* (Arnold and Bennett, 1984) vary with body temperature, and flight distance of *Regina septemvittata* varies inversely with body temperature (Layne and Ford, 1984). However, there is no relationship between incidence of death feigning and temperature in *Masticophis flagellum* (Gehlbach, 1970) or *Natrix natrix* (Heusser and Schlumpf, 1962).

Gravid female *Lacerta vivipara* allow a human to approach more closely and flee for shorter distances than do nongravid conspecifics under field conditions, presumably reflecting increased reliance on crypsis in the face of reduced ability to flee during pregnancy (Bauwens and Thoen, 1981). Gravid females of *Leiolopisma entrecasteauxi* run slower, bask more often, and are more likely to be caught by snakes than are males (Shine, 1980a). Males of three species of *Nerodia* (Scudder and Burghardt, 1983) and of *Telescopus dhara* (Zinner, 1985) are more aggressive toward simulated predators than are females. Old males of *Acanthodactylus schreiberi* are perhaps less able to flee than younger individuals (Zinner, 1967). Camouflage, age, and sex affect flight distance in certain iguanids (Heatwole, 1968; Johnson, 1970). Fatigue alters defensive behavior in some snakes (Gans and Mendelsohn, 1972; Pough, 1978; Arnold and Bennett, 1984) and agamid lizards (Anderson, 1963; Heatwole, 1970). The physiological bases for such differences remain unstudied.

The complexities of individual variation are further illustrated by two recent studies. Evasion distances (from a human) by the adder, *Vipera berus*, are short during cool spring and fall conditions, but longer during the summer. There are no differences among males, females, and subadults, and all flee at significantly shorter distances when rodents are scarce and adders are undernourished (Andren, 1982). Male

Galapagos lava lizards, *Tropidurus albemarlensis,* are faster and allow closer approach then do females; lizards held in captivity a short time are faster than those held for longer periods; and gravid females are slower than nongravid females. Males from sparsely vegetated areas are faster than those from heavily vegetated areas, and both sexes are more wary in sparsely vegetated areas (Snell et al., in litt.). [Note added in proof: Hailey and Davies (1986) reported detailed experimental studies on variable defensive behavior in *Natrix maura.*]

Antipredator responses that are currently rare within populations deserve further study. Examples include ball forming in *Chionactis occipitalis* (Mitchell, 1978), and death feigning in *Masticophis flagellum* (Gehlbach, 1970) and *Storeria occipitomaculata* (Jordan, 1970). Rare behavior might represent lack of observations (not likely for the above examples, all of which are of common, widespread North American snakes), chance occurrences that have no consequences for individuals, or the behavioral variation upon which selection can act (see also Section III.C).

E. Geographic Variation

Individual variation can be translated into geographic variation as a result of selection across an environmental gradient (Endler, 1977, 1986b), or because of geographic variation in some other variable (e.g., experience) that is correlated with the expression of an antipredator mechanism. The only examination to date of the latter possibility found no relationship between presence or absence of regenerated tails (presumably an indication of predator encounters, see Section II.D) and wariness in *Cnemidophorus tigris* (Schall and Pianka, 1980). However, the fact that defensive behavior can be modifiable and that reptiles show evidence of surviving encounters (Section II.D) suggest that this topic deserves further study.

Most reports of geographic variation in defensive behavior are anecdotal and potentially confounded by the unknown roles of temperature, sex, stimulus strength, experience, and other factors discussed in the previous sections. Individuals of *Kinosternon subrubrum* from peninsular Florida are much more prone to bite in defense than are those from farther north (Carr, 1940). At three localities in Baja California, *Callisaurus draconoides* either allows close approach and runs only a short distance, runs far along arroyo bottoms, or runs up steep slopes (Tevis, 1944; Asplund, 1967). Throughout most of its range in western North America this species displays the brightly marked underside of the tail, but does not do so in the southern half of Baja California (Tevis, 1944).

Sauromalus obesus and *Sceloporus orcutti* are much more wary in Baja California than farther north, and the differences are correlated with conspicuous dark coloration, occurrence on pale granite, and increased abundance of raptors at the southern localities (Welsh, in litt.). *Urosaurus ornatus* is a very shy lizard at some places in the Guadeloupe Mountains of New Mexico, but quite tame in nearby parts of the same range in Texas (Mosauer, 1932). *Eremias barbouri* escapes into rocks at one locality in China and into bushes at another (Schmidt, 1927a). Geographic variation is weakly indicated for presence or absence of a tail display in *Sphaerodactylus glaucus* (Harris and Kluge, 1984) and *Phrynocephalus arabicus* (Arnold, 1984a).

Each of 19 *Ninia sebae* from southern Mexico exhibited a head display (Greene, 1975), but only 1 of ca. 15 (6.7%) from Belize did so (Henderson, 1977). *Coluber constrictor* frequently ascends trees to escape in Georgia and North Carolina, but almost never does so in Florida (Carr, 1940). *Masticophis flagellum piceus* in southern California typically defends itself by rapid escape and vigorous striking if cornered; animals from farther north in the state, *M. f. ruddocki,* form a stiff, irregular coil with the head concealed when restrained (Sweet, in litt.). Boomslangs (*Dispholidus typus*) in a treeless, mountain region of southern Africa are more aggressive than elsewhere (Broadley, 1983). Adults of *Lachesis muta* are usually mild mannered on the Atlantic versant of Costa Rica (Solorzano, Santana, and Greene, unpubl.), but very aggressive on the Osa Peninsula of that country (Bolaños et al., 1978). *Pituophis melanoleucus* and *Crotalus viridis* show concordant geographic variation in the tendency to vibrate their tails, hiss, and form striking coils (Sweet, 1985).

Cnemidophorus tigris, a fast moving teiid lizard found in much of the western United States, exhibits considerable geographic variation in defensive responses (Schall and Pianka, 1980). Escape behavior diversity varies positively with incidence of regenerated tails among 12 sites, suggesting a possible relation to predation intensity. This species relies on high speed, but variation among the frequencies of 12 possible responses to approach by an observer at one site varies from 0.3% (for "run from shrub into open") to 38% (for "run from one shrub to another").

Diadophis punctatus in the western United States, peninsular Florida, and northern Mexico has bright orange or red posterior ventral surfaces and a spectacular defensive tail display. In most of the eastern United States the same species has a yellow venter and lacks the tail display. The two types intergrade in Illinois and northern Florida, where snakes with yellow venters have tail displays (Myers, 1965; Greene, 1973a).

Although further studies on stimulus control and ontogeny are needed (see above), this appears to be a case of true geographic variation.

Intraspecific geographic variation in morphological defense mechanisms (other than color pattern) is evidently uncommon. Among cobras, all *Hemachatus haemachatus, Naja mossambica,* and *N. nigricollis* eject venom in streams, but "spitting" only occurs in some populations of *N. naja* in Asia (Bogert, 1943). Short-horned lizards, *Phrynosoma douglassi*, are more spinose in southern parts of the species range, where predators are more common (Pianka and Parker, 1975).

IV. SYSTEMATIC VARIATION IN ANTIPREDATOR MECHANISMS

A. Introduction

This section summarizes the taxonomic occurrence of antipredator mechanisms in reptiles, and seeks to identify patterns of evolution in those attributes. The latter involves a search for taxon-typical patterns and their assessment in terms of phylogenetic relationships. Given a sufficiently large sample of taxa and a phylogeny for the group in question, inferences can be made about the origins and changes that have occurred in those traits.

The term adaptation is used herein to describe a feature that promotes a performance advantage (relative to the next most ancestral condition) that was associated with the origin of that feature. This usage is tantamount to saying that a feature and a performance advantage are derived at the same level of descent within a clade, and in the absence of additional data (e.g., Arnold, 1983; Arnold and Bennett, 1984; Endler, 1986b), does not imply a particular process such as natural selection in the origin of an adaptation (see Greene, 1986b). Evidence for performance advantages is given in Section V.A, and some general trends are discussed in Sections V.B and VI.C.

The separate consideration of taxa in this section is according to their assignment to monophyletic lineages, except as noted, and the extent to which they can be conveniently and accurately characterized in terms of antipredator mechanisms. Figure 2 summarizes current views on the phylogenetic relationships of major tetrapod taxa. A feature is judged to be derived if it is absent in two successive outgroups, or, in the absence of precise information on relationships, rare in most other closely related taxa (Wiley, 1981; Maddison et al., 1984). Unless otherwise noted, sources for this section are listed by specific taxa in Appendices A, B, and D. Detailed descriptions of antipredator mechanisms are given in Appendix C.

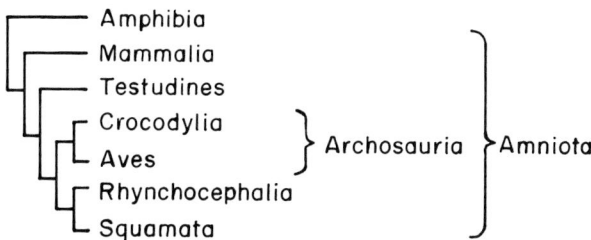

Fig. 2. Phylogenetic relationships of major groups of tetrapods as treated in this chapter (based on Gauthier et al., 1988).

Fig. 3. Gaping threat display in a Mexican kinosternid turtle, *Claudius angustatus*. (Photograph by H. B. Shaffer).

B. Testudines

Few predators seem to specialize on turtles, with the possible exception of some birds and crocodilians, alligator snapping turtles (*Macroclemys temminckii*), and humans. Turtles of various species, particularly as juveniles, are sometimes eaten by a variety of fishes, frogs, snakes, birds, and mammals (Section II, Appendix A; Auffenberg and Iverson, 1979).

Antipredator behavior in turtles emphasizes crypsis, flight into water or a burrow, withdrawal into the shell, cloacal discharge, postural threats, and biting (Fig. 3). Other defense mechanisms are less common, and include chemical deterrents (e.g., *Pelomedusa subrufa*, Pienaar et al., 1978; *Sternotherus odoratus*, Eisner et al., 1977) aposematic coloration (perhaps juveniles of *Chelus fimbriatus*, Pritchard and Trebbau, 1984, and *Platysternon megacephalum*, Campbell and Evans, 1972), death feigning

(*Kinixys belliana,* Schmidt, 1919), and sound production (kinosternids, Gans and Maderson, 1973; *P. megacephalum,* Campbell and Evans, 1972). *Malacochersus tornieri* has an unusually flat and flexible shell for a testudinid, and escapes predators by rapid movements into rock crevices (Proctor, 1922; Ireland and Gans, 1972).

The defensive behaviors of only a few turtles have been described in detail. *Chelydra serpentina* (Chelydridae) is a large, aquatic species of eastern and southern North America. This common snapping turtle is cryptic and moves away if a threat is perceived at a distance, especially if the turtle is in water. If approached closely on land, a snapping turtle elevates the posterior part of its body, hisses loudly, and gapes. The turtle pivots, sometimes using the tail for additional support, such that the shell and gaping mouth continue to orient toward a moving aggressor. If the threat is nearby, a snapping turtle strikes violently and hangs on firmly if the attacker is seized. If handled, a snapping turtle emits an offensive glandular secretion, struggles with its limbs, and continues to attempt to bite (Mertens, 1946; Ernst and Barbour, 1972; Dodd and Brodie, 1975).

Bell's hinge-backed tortoise, *Kinixys belliana* (Testudinidae), occurs in savanna and swampy areas throughout much of Africa. This turtle responds to an approaching person by walking away, and if halted withdraws the limbs into the shell and sometimes feigns death. If picked up, it scratches, withdraws the head into the shell, snaps the beak and hisses, and sometimes discharges small quantities of a strong smelling fluid from the cloaca. If further harrassed, it expels air from the lungs, draws the forelimbs in over the head, and shuts down the hinged, posterior portion of the carapace (Schmidt, 1919).

Terrapene ornata (Emydidae) is a terrestrial inhabitant of relatively open areas in the south-central United States. If an ornate box turtle sees an approaching predator at a distance it instantly freezes with limbs and head extended. If the threat draws near, the turtle either moves away with surprising speed, or withdraws and retracts the plastral elements to form a tightly closed box around its head and extremeties. Some individuals struggle violently, bite, expel a pungent secretion from integumentary glands, and urinate copiously if handled. Others simply remain closed up in their shells until danger has passed (Norris and Zweifel, 1950; Legler, 1960).

The shell is a defining characteristic of turtles, and most authors have concluded without explicit arguments that it was a structural adaptation against predators in a semiaquatic ancestor (e.g., Carr, 1952; Pritchard, 1979). Böker's (1935) hypothesis, that the shell functions as a plow in pushing through dense brush, was soon labeled "sheer nonsense"

(Schmidt, 1939). A consideration of the phylogeny and ecology of living turtles supports the traditional view and suggests an interaction between feeding and defense in the origin of the shell. Although diversity in the feeding behavior of turtles is substantial, most species in most higher taxa evidently search actively for relatively immobile food such as plant parts (e.g., South American pelomedusids that eat submerged palm fruit) or mollusks and other slow-moving animals (see Ernst and Barbour, 1972; Pritchard, 1979, 1984; Pritchard and Trebbau, 1984; Bury, 1986). The domed shell configuration typical of fully terrestrial turtles is an independently derived feature of testudinids and some emydids (*Terrapene*), as are the fast active (trionychids, some chelids) and stationary ambush (*Macroclemys, Chelus*) modes of hunting (for discussions of turtle phylogeny, see Bickham and Carr, 1983; Gaffney, 1984, 1985). These considerations imply that primitive turtles were relatively slow-moving animals; their feeding tactics of sustained searching and/or long handling time were correlated with protection by the shell. The turtle shell was evidently a key innovation that facilitated a potentially dangerous feeding mode, and specialized defense mechanisms also typify several other reptilian lineages with those foraging characteristics (Sections V.B, VI.C).

Shell-closing mechanisms have evolved at least seven times in turtles, and provide particularly interesting examples of the interactions of feeding, locomotion, and defense. For example, phylogenetic analyses of functional and ecological attributes suggest that anterior plastral kinesis evolved independently in two lineages of kinosternid turtles, in each case apparently associated with opening the shell to permit large head size, durophagous feeding, and defensive gaping (e.g., *Claudius angustatus*; Dodd, 1978; Fig. 3). In *Kinosternon*, the primitive condition has been converted to a shell-closing mechanism, and there is also posterior plastral kinesis. The morphoclines within kinosternids are correlated with shifts away from durophagous feeding, increased emphasis on locomotion and protection of body parts rather than aggressive defense, and life in arid regions (Bramble 1974; Bramble and Hutchinson, 1981; Bramble et al., 1984).

C. Crocodilia

Adult crocodilians generally are not subject to predation, except by humans (Neill, 1971), although lions (*Panthera leo*), jaguars (*P. onca*), and sharks eat large *Crocodylus* spp. (Section II, Appendix A). These reptiles generally respond to intruders by flight into water or aggressive attacks with their jaws and tails, but there are few detailed descriptions of antipredator behavior by crocodilians. Other responses to predators include death feigning, hissing, vocalization, cloacal discharge, exuding secretions from throat glands, gaping, and writhing.

In Venezuela, individuals of *Caiman crocodilus* typically swim away from a potential predator. They often dive, and subadults bury in the bottom mud. Hatchlings feign death when handled under water, but struggle, vocalize, and bite when handled on land. Nearby caimans sometimes respond to the distress calls of juveniles by attacking a potential predator (Gorzula, 1978, 1985). Juvenile crocodilians are subject to heavy predation, and perhaps this has played a major role in the evolution of parental care in these animals (Shine, this volume).

Some features of crocodilians used in defense (e.g., stout tails and strong jaws) are undoubtedly coopted for that role, because those attributes function primarily and primitively in locomotion and feeding. However, the distribution and development of bony scutes varies among living crocodilians, and the possibility that these structures are adaptations for resisting injury from predators should be investigated (cf. Seidel, 1979; Ross and Mayer, 1983).

D. Rhynchocephalia

The sole living member of this group, *Sphenodon punctatus*, is largely free of native predators, but might be subject to diurnal predation by hawks (Saint Girons et al., 1981). These animals are colored cryptically and freeze or take refuge in burrows when approached. Responses to handling and/or intraspecific aggression include erection of a dorsal crest, inflating the body, gaping, biting, and hissing (Carpenter and Ferguson, 1977; Gans, 1983a; Gans et al., 1984). Tail autotomy is present, but regenerated tails might reflect the incidence of aggressive social interactions rather than attempted predation.

E. Iguanian Lizards

This taxon includes the Agamidae, Chamaeleonidae, and Iguanidae. The first two are more closely related to each other than either is to the third (Estes, 1983). Iguanians are generally diurnal, terrestrial or aboreal, small, and insectivorous. They are eaten by a variety of reptilian, avian, and mammalian predators (Section II, Appendix A). As a group they tend to have somewhat stocky bodies, with the notable exception of the laterally flattened chamaeleonids. Evolutionary limb loss is unknown in the Iguania.

Most iguanians are probably cryptic, and initially respond to a threat by immobility and locomotor escape. Flight is often to an adjacent

SYSTEMATIC VARIATION IN ANTIPREDATOR MECHANISMS

Fig. 4. Threat display in an Asian agamid lizard, *Phrynocephalus mystaceus*. (Photograph by E. Haubt, courtesy of the Senckenberg Museum).

microenvironment where pursuit by a predator would be difficult, such as up a tree or into a burrow. In a few instances it involves a radical shift in habitat, such as into air or water. Morphological specializations for locomotor escape are infrequent, but include features associated with running on sand (e.g., fringes in *Uma*, Pough, 1970; Carothers, 1986), running on water (e.g., fringes in *Hydrosaurus*, Luke, 1986), gliding (*Draco*, Colbert, 1967), and blocking burrows or crevices with the tail (e.g., *Ctenosaura clarki*, Duellman and Duellman, 1959).

Some iguanians have exaggerated threat displays, which may be accompanied by morphological adjuncts (e.g., the frill and its erection mechanism in *Amphibolurus barbatus*, Throckmorten et al., 1985, and the black throats of *Gambelia* and some species of *Agama*, Hertz et al., 1982; see below and Fig. 4). Most species will bite if handled, and in some this can be a formidable defense (e.g., *Gambelia wislizeni*, Crowley and Pietruszka, 1983; *Cyclura carinata*, Iverson, 1979). Less common defensive mechanisms include rigid immobility (*Brookesia sp.*, Böhme, 1974), tail display (*Cophosaurus texanus*, Dial, 1986; *Phrynocephalus helioscopus*, Obst, 1959), lashing with the tail (*Iguana iguana*, Greene et al., 1978; *Uracentron azureum*, Greene, 1977; *Hydrosaurus pustulosus*, pers. obs.), vocalization (*Gambelia wislizeni*, Crowley and Pietruszka, 1983; *Liolaemus chiliensis*, Carothers, 1987; *Otocryptis wiegmanni*, Matuschka, 1978), and group responses (*Agama stellio*, Zinner, 1967; *Iguana iguana*, Greene et al., 1978).

Fourteen species of the iguanid genus *Phrynosoma* are characterized by flattened, spinose bodies and the presence of sharp, sturdy spines ("horns") on the head. There is ample evidence of the efficacy of those structures in thwarting predation, both direct in the reactions of predators (e.g., Tollestrup, 1981; Section V.A) and indirect in the fact that *P. douglassi* has highly reduced horns in parts of its range where predation evidently is lower than elsewhere (Pianka and Parker, 1975). Some species of *Phrynosoma* squirt a stream of blood from the eyes, hitting objects up to 2 m away (Section III.D). This response involves derived aspects of the cephalic circulation, themselves modified from a vascular mechanism of head temperature regulation, and contraction of the protrusor oculi muscles (Burleson, 1942; Heath, 1966). Observations on captive predators suggest that blood squirting by horned lizards is specifically effective against canids (Cowles, 1977). The Australian agamid *Moloch moloch* is convergent in some respects with *Phrynosoma*, including a flattened, spinose body and stationary foraging for considerable periods of time at ant nests and trails (Pianka and Pianka, 1970; Greene, 1982; Sections V.A, V.B).

Detailed descriptions of antipredator mechanisms in iguanians are few, but three case studies illustrate some of the diversity in this group:

Corytophanes cristatus (Iguanidae) is a slow-moving, cryptic, arboreal neotropical forest lizard. Individuals remain stationary unless disturbed, then move away with a hopping gait and frequent changes of direction. When ceasing voluntary locomotion, this helmeted iguana maintains whatever position it happens to be in. If threatened by a snake, the lizard orients perpendicularly to the attacker, elevates its trunk, depresses a throat fan, and lowers the head, thus elevating a dorsal crest. The overall effect is to increase the apparent lateral aspect of the animal approximately four-fold. If the threatening stimulus changes position, the lizard shifts its position to maintain a lateral presentation, and occasionally bobs its head. Sometimes a lunge is made at the threat, the lizard bites fiercely if grasped, and jaw strength is enhanced by elongate adductor muscles (Davis, 1953; Schwenk, 1980; pers. obs.).

Iguana iguana (Iguanidae) is a large, cryptic, herbivorous neotropical forest lizard. Juveniles are highly social, and tend to move during periods in which the wind is moving the vegetation around them. They respond to the approach of a predator by mass flight on the ground, into low vegetation, or across the surface of the water. Juveniles thrash and sometimes defecate when handled. Adults leap off their perches in the canopy and either disappear into the vegetation below or take refuge in an adjacent stream or lake. Prolonged submergence is facilitated by high tolerance for anaerobic metabolism. If cornered or seized, adults thrash and scratch with their claws, lash with their tails, and sometimes bite (Moberly, 1969; Burghardt et al., 1977; Greene et al., 1978; Meritt, 1981).

Phrynocephalus mystaceus (Agamidae) is a small, cryptic, Asiatic desert lizard. This animal sometimes burrows rapidly in sand with its feet if threatened. If the source of danger is nearby, the lizard jumps, rises high on its legs, and faces the attacker. The tail is elevated and curled repeatedly, both vertically in its entirety and laterally at its curled tip. The mouth is opened widely, unfolding the fringed flaps at the angles of the jaws. At this time the body is inflated and the buccal tissues are engorged with blood, such that the mouth appears bright red. The tongue is not protruded. If seized, the lizard bites fiercely and hangs on to the predator (Nikolskii, 1915; Mertens, 1952b; Polynova, 1982; Fig. 4).

Interfamilial trends among iguanians are few. Chamaeleonids depend heavily on crypsis and aggressive defenses, rather than on flight. Iguanids tend to have lateral displays, whereas agamids more frequently have frontal displays that emphasize enlarged teeth, flaps, fringes, and other cephalic structures. The reasons for this difference are unknown, but it parallels differences in social displays (Davis, 1953; Carpenter and Ferguson, 1977). In any case, agamids perhaps are derived from within the Iguanidae (Estes et al., 1988; Fig. 5), so their frontal displays might represent modifications of a more primitive lateral posture.

F. Gekkotan Lizards

All recent considerations of squamate relationships agree that gekkonids and pygopodids are sister taxa (together the Gekkota), and in turn the sister taxon of other noniguanian squamates (Fig. 5). The Gekkota is of particular interest, in that it clearly involves the evolution of limblessness (Shine, 1986) in a group that is distinctive in defense relative to other lizards.

The Gekkonidae is a large cosmopolitan group, currently divided into four subfamilies (Kluge, 1967). Gekkonines and diplodactylines are usually nocturnal, have specialized scansorial pads on their feet, and rely on crypsis and rapid locomotion for initial escape from predators. These geckos are eaten by diurnal predators, such as snakes, that catch them in retreats, and by snakes, owls, and bats at night (Section II, Appendix A). Most species probably adopt elevated threat postures when cornered, and vocalize and bite if seized (e.g., *Teratoscincus scincus*, Mebs, 1966; *Nephrurus asper*, Bustard, 1967). Tail autotomy is almost ubiquitous. Less frequent antipredator mechanisms that are

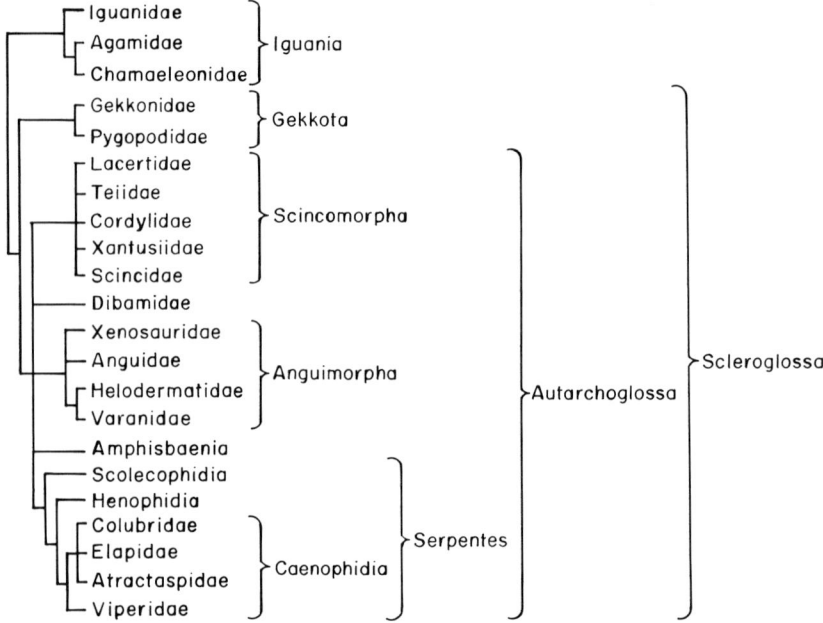

Fig. 5. Phylogenetic relationships among higher taxa of squamate reptiles (based on Dessauer et al., 1987; Estes et al., 1988).

derived within the family include epidermal sound production (all species of *Teratoscincus,* Gans and Maderson, 1973), gliding with the aid of skin flaps (all species of *Ptychozoon,* Marcellini and Keefer, 1976), skin loss (e.g., *Aristelliger hechti,* pers. obs.), and glandular secretions from the tail (some *Diplodactylus,* Rosenberg and Russell, 1980; Fig. 6).

Eublepharines are nocturnal, terrestrial geckos that vocalize, flee, and in some cases tail display from an elevated posture when threatened by predators. Sphaerodactylines are diurnal geckos that apparently rely only on crypsis and flight, although little is known of their responses to potential predators. One species has a defensive tail display (*Sphaerodactylus glaucus,* Harris and Kluge, 1984), and one has large eyespots that possibly frighten predators (*S. semasiops,* Thomas, 1975).

Exaggerated postures and vocalizations have been reported as antipredator mechanisms in eublepharine, diplodactyline, and gekkonine gekkonids (e.g., Mebs, 1966, 1973; Johnson and Brodie, 1974; Frankenberg, 1975; Bustard, 1977). The Eublepharinae include terrestrial, slow-moving species that are not known to use vocalizations during social behavior (Marcellini, 1977, 1978). It is the sister taxon of other geckos, and the latter as a group are probably primitively

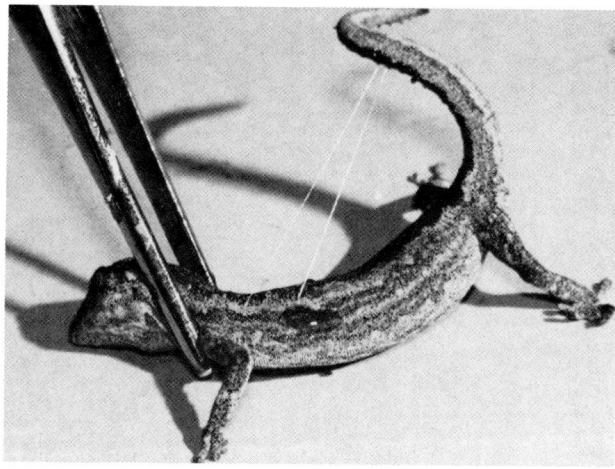

Fig. 6. Defensive ejection of caudal secretions by a gecko, *Diplodactylus spinigerus* has been elicited by artificial disturbance. Note two strands of dried, viscous secretion extending from the caudal rupture zones to the anterior part of the trunk and the gob of secretion just anterior to the second strand. (Photograph by H. I. Rosenberg, courtesy of the *Canadian Journal of Zoology*).

nocturnal, specialized for climbing, and use complex intraspecific vocalizations. Milton and Jenssen (1979) concluded that vocalizations in certain *Anolis* function in defense (as they do in a few other iguanids, e.g., *Gambelia wislizeni*, *Liolaemus chiliensis*, see above), and they speculated that such sounds could represent precursors of intraspecific vocal communications. Phylogenetic relationships among gekkonids imply that the evolutionary sequence hypothesized by Milton and Jenssen actually occurred in that family: Vocalizations arose as a defensive adaptation in ancestral geckos and were later coopted and adaptively modified (for increasing complexity; see Marcellini, 1978; Werner et al., 1978) within the noneublepharine geckos for intraspecific communicative functions.

Pygopodids are limbless or nearly limbless, elongate relatives of geckos. Their predators include bats and snakes (Appendix A). Three species in two genera exhibit threat displays and false strikes that might mimic venomous elapid snakes (Bustard, 1968b; but see Kluge, 1974:161), and also use saltation as an antipredator mechanism (Bauer, 1986). A captive *Lialis burtonis* writhed and defecated when restrained, but did not bite (pers. obs.). Interestingly, pygopodids are not known to gape in response to predators, a behavioral pattern that is widespread in geckos. [Note added in proof: Kluge (1987) analyzed phylogenetic relationships among higher taxa in the Gekkota, reviewed literature on defensive vocalizations in that group (including pygopodids), and tentatively concluded that response is primitive for tetrapods.]

G. Autarchoglossan Lizards

1. GENERAL

The Autarchoglossa are a diverse group of ten families, the precise relationships of which to each other and to amphisbaenians and snakes are uncertain (Estes, 1983; Estes et al., 1988; Fig. 5). This uncertainty restricts the extent to which generalizations are possible, a problem made even more serious by the extreme heterogeneity of body form and life styles among the species in these families.

2. XANTUSIIDAE

These secretive lizards are eaten by snakes, other lizards, and perhaps other predators (Appendix A). They struggle, defecate, autotomize their tails, and bite fiercely when handled.

3. SCINCIDAE

Most skinks probably are usually solitary, territorial during the breeding season, and feed by intensive searching (Stamps, 1977; Regal, 1978). They are eaten occasionally by a variety of vertebrates, but few predators specialize on skinks (Section II, Appendix A; exceptions include certain snakes, see below).

A defensive response that is nearly ubiquitous for skinks and possibly primitive for the family is strong, effective writhing when grasped. Skinks generally have elongate bodies and shiny scales that are underlain by osteoderms, and axial bending makes them even more difficult for predators to manipulate. Some owls (Janzen and Pond, 1976) and snakes (Vinson, 1975) have difficulty holding these lizards, and lizards and snakes that feed predominantly on skinks have specializations for holding them (Greene, 1978; Savitzky, 1981; Patchell and Shine, 1986). The hypothesis that smooth overlapping scales and enhanced axial bending are defensive adaptations is confounded by the fact that they also are functionally associated with lateral undulatory locomotion, which serves a variety of biological roles (Gans, 1975). Most skinks typically flee into cover when chased, and squirm effectively, bite, and defecate when handled. Several large Australasian species have threat displays that include gaping, tongue extrusion, hissing, and lunging at a predator (e.g., *Tiliqua scincoides*, Carpenter and Murphy, 1978).

4. LACERTIDAE AND TEIIDAE

Species in these families are heterogeneous in terms of size, morphology, and ecology, and the monophyly of the Teiidae is arguable (e.g., Harris, 1985). Among one of the undoubtedly monophyletic lineages, the "macroteiids," at least some species have unusual abilities for sustained locomotion (van Berkum et al., 1986; Garland, 1987). A number of macroteiids are eaten by fast moving predators (Section II, Appendix A), and search widely and intensively for hidden prey (Stamps, 1977; Regal, 1978). Teiids and lacertids typically employ crypsis and rapid locomotion to escape, sometimes into burrows. *Holaspis guentheri* glides out of trees as a means of site change (Schiøtz and Volsøe, 1959), and might use that behavior to escape predators. Most species probably struggle when handled; large ones use postural threats and bite violently (e.g., *Callopistes flavipunctatus*, *Lacerta lepida*, pers. obs.), and a *C. flavipunctatus* feigned death when dug from its burrow (pers. obs.).

5. CORDYLIDAE

Cordylids are eaten by snakes, birds, and mammals (Appendix A). They often flee to rock crevices or into burrows, and lash with their tails and bite when handled. *Cordylus cataphractus* grasps its tail when threatened, forming an immobile circle (Rose, 1962). *Gerrhosaurus major* runs, takes refuge in a burrow, feigns death, scratches, lashes the tail, inflates its body, and bites (Schmidt, 1919).

6. DIBAMIDAE

The two genera in this family are limbless, secretive, and of uncertain relationships (Greer, 1985; Estes et al., 1988). *Anelytropsis papillosus* of Mexico burrows when uncovered, and bites and defecates when handled (Greer, 1985).

7. ANGUIDAE

Alligator lizards and their allies are occasionally eaten by various vertebrates (Appendix A), and glass lizards (*Ophisaurus spp.*) are often taken by coral snakes in the southeastern United States (Greene, 1984).

Anguids typically have elongated bodies and shiny scales underlain by osteoderms. They are usually secretive, and take cover when disturbed. Typical responses to handling include violent axial bending, defecation, open mouth threats, biting, and hissing. Species of *Elgaria* sometimes seize their own tail and encircle a branch, use their tails as "shields," and vocalize (Fitch, 1935).

8. XENOSAURIDAE

The Xenosauridae includes two genera of poorly known lizards and is possibly polyphyletic (Hu et al., 1984). *Xenosaurus grandis* of Mexico and Central America hides in crevices and will inflate, gape, lunge, and bite when cornered and handled (Alvarez del Toro, 1982). *Shinisaurus crodilurus* is aquatic, dives into water to escape, and bites readily when handled (Fan, 1931).

9. HELODERMATIDAE

The two living species of helodermatids are relatively large, slow moving, venomous lizards. They are evidently rarely eaten by predators. The black and yellow color pattern of *Heloderma horridum* is primitively cryptic, whereas the black and pink coloration of *H. suspectum* is derived and probably aposematic. If approached by a potential predator, beaded lizards and Gila monsters attempt to escape, sometimes into a burrow or up a nearby tree. If threatened closely, they hiss, inflate the body, elevate the foreparts and gape, then lunge laterally at the intruder. They struggle, discharge their cloacal contents, and bite hard if handled. Use of the jaws in defense is surely facilitated by toxic secretions, but whether venom injection in helodermatids is primarily an adaptation for feeding or for defense against predators is uncertain (Bogert and del Campo, 1956; Pregill et al., 1986; Lowe et al., 1986).

10. VARANIDAE

Monitor lizards (Varanidae, Varaninae) are eaten by a variety of other vertebrates. They are generally shy, fast animals that run to shelter at the first hint of danger. When approached closely, a varanid typically elevates its foreparts, arches the neck, and inflates the throat while hissing and slowly flicking the tongue. If a potential predator approaches closely, the lizard lashes accurately with its tail and lunges. Some monitors defecate, struggle violently, extrude the hemipenes, and bite when handled; at least three species feign death (e.g., *Varanus exanthematicus*, Schmidt, 1919). *Lanthanotus borneensis*, the only living lanthanotine varanid (Pregill et al., 1986), squirms, defecates, struggles violently, and sometimes bites when handled (Proud, 1978).

H. Amphisbaenia

All amphisbaenians are fossorial (Gans, 1969), but at least some do move above ground in the daytime (e.g., Beebe, 1945; Busack, 1978). They are eaten by burrowing snakes, armadillos, and at least occasionally by diurnal birds and mammals (Section II, Appendix A; Greegor, 1980).

The few species of amphisbaenians that have been studied resemble autarchoglossans in that they bite, defecate, and writhe with exaggerated body movements when grasped by a predator. Some species are capable of rapid disappearance by burrowing when uncovered (e.g., *Blanus cinereus*, pers. obs.). Species of *Blanus* and *Trogonophis* sometimes freeze in "pretzel" postures (e.g., Stemmler, 1970; Malkmus, 1982a), and *Agamodon anguliceps* sometimes lies with its bright pink venter exposed (Gans, 1969). At least two species of *Amphisbaena* have defensive tail displays, and these might direct attacks to the expendable tail as well as serve as tactile cues for retaliatory biting (Greene, 1973a). The success of the former is demonstrated by the incidence of scars and incomplete tails in those animals (Gans, 1962; Greene, 1973a; Papenfuss, 1982), and the efficacy of the latter becomes obvious in handling them (Gans, pers. comm.; pers. obs.).

The defensive behavior of *Amphisbaena fuliginosa* has been described in some detail (Beebe, 1946; Greene, 1973a). This moderately large, brightly patterned, neotropical species burrows rapidly when uncovered, and waves its elevated, curled tail if restrained. At times the display stops and the tail makes burrowing movements. Intensity of the tail movements increases when the animal is grasped firmly, but if lifted free from the substrate it swings the head back and forth with mouth gaping, and bites readily.

I. Serpentes

1. GENERAL

Living snakes typically are divided into three infraorders of uncertain relationships (e.g., Dessauer et al., 1987). Three families comprise the Scolecophidia ("blind snakes"), together the sister taxon of other living snakes. A second group, the Henophidia ("primitive snakes"), includes taxa with various primitive and derived features, and might not be monophyletic (Aniliidae, Uropeltidae, Boidae, Tropidophiidae, and perhaps others). A third group, the Caenophidia ("advanced snakes") is evidently monophyletic and includes most of the living snakes (Colubridae, Atractaspidae, Elapidae, Viperidae). Although sometimes linked to particular families of autarchoglossans (e.g., dibamids or varanids), a conservative view is that snakes are part of a largely unresolved clade (Scleroglossa) that is the sister taxon of Gekkota (Estes et al., 1988; Fig. 5).

Paired, postcloacal scent glands are ubiquitous among snakes and are apparently a derived characteristic of that group (Underwood, 1957; see Whiting, 1969, for survey and terminology). Cloacal discharge, widespread in autarchoglossans (see above), was primitively present in snakes and the scent gland products can be far more offensive in terms of odor than fecal material (e.g., *Tropidophis greenwayi*, pers. obs.; *Lichanura trivirgata*, Ruben, 1976). Active searching is probably also primitive for snakes, since it occurs widely in autarchoglossan lizards (Pregill et al., 1986; Losos and Greene, unpubl.), amphisbaenians (Riley et al., 1986), scolecophidians (Watkins et al., 1967), aniliids (pers. obs. on captive *Cylindrophis rufus*), and many advanced snakes (e.g., Savitzky, 1980). Offensive scent gland secretions probably enhance the effects of cloacal discharge during predatory encounters, and their presence in snakes might be adaptively associated with a wide foraging mode (see Section V.B).

Snakes have the most elaborate antipredator mechanisms yet described among reptiles, and numerous species have been characterized briefly. Among 129 species in 77 genera and 5 families, tail displays and horizontal head displays were associated disproportionately with terrestrial habits and vertical head displays were correlated with arboreality (Greene, 1979). That scheme undoubtedly conceals interesting variability, and the imperfect correlation with habitats deserves further study. In addition to those three behavioral categories, others seen in snakes include rigid postures (e.g., *Trachyboa boulengeri*, Lehmann, 1970), death feigning (e.g., *Heterodon platirhinos*, see below), killing the predator by constriction (e.g., *Charina bottae*, Peabody et al., 1975), and rolling into a ball (e.g., *Calabaria reinhardtii*, Bustard, 1969). Nevertheless, most snake taxa are characterized by defensive behavior as species, genera, or tribes (e.g., spreading hoods in *Naja* and other cobras, tail displays by *Micrurus*, see below) rather than at the family or higher level (Greene, 1979; Myers, 1986; but see below).

Morphological adjuncts are widespread among snakes with defensive displays, and include putative aposematic coloration (*Diadophis punctatus*, Greene, 1973a; micrurine elapids, Greene and McDiarmid, 1981), tracheal rings that facilitate throat inflation (e.g., *Dasypeltis scabra*, Gans and Richmond, 1957; *Spilotes pullatus*, Brongersma, 1957; Rossman and Williams, 1966), a glottal keel that enhances hissing in *Pituophis* (Martin and Huey, 1971; Saif, 1975), elongate anterior ribs that form a hood when abducted (*Naja* and other cobra genera), reinforced caudal vertebral structures in some erycine boas that elevate the tail (Greene, 1973a; Section V.C), modification of the fangs for "spitting" in *Hemachatus* and some *Naja* (Bogert, 1943), nuchodorsal glands in some natricine colubrids (Smith, 1938), the rattle (*Crotalus, Sistrurus*, Klauber, 1956; see below), and perhaps vertebral protrusion in *Mehelya* and *Bungarus* (Savitzky, 1985). Conversely, snakes have fewer known locomotor specializations associated primarily with defense than do lizards. Flying snakes (*Chrysopelea* spp.) have keeled ventral scales that facilitate gliding (Heyer and Pongsapipatana, 1970; Mertens, 1970), and sidewinding and saltation might utilize neuromuscular specializations that serve a defensive role (e.g., Gans and Mendelssohn, 1972).

2. SCOLECOPHIDIA

Three families of blind snakes are all characterized by slender bodies, short tails, smooth scales, and reduced eyes. All are fossorial, but occasionally emerge and even climb trees (e.g., Vanzolini, 1970). They are eaten by scorpions, fishes, frogs, lizards, snakes, birds, and mammals (Section II, Appendix A).

Leptotyphlopids thrash when handled, sometimes displaying a brightly colored tail tip (e.g., *Leptotyphlops goudotii*, Greene, 1973a); one species feigns death (*L. scutifrons*, Visser, 1966), and another "takes to water" when pursued (*L. longicauda*, Pienaar et al., 1978). Typhlopids thrash, discharge the cloaca, and press a captor with the tail spine. A few specimens of *Rhinotyphlops schlegelii* squeaked when handled (Sweeney, 1971).

3. HENOPHIDIA

This infraorder includes several families that retain primitive features relative to caenophidians, but their relationships to each other and to the latter group are unclear (Dessauer et al., 1987). Henophidians are conveniently discussed in terms of two superfamilies, although the monophyly of those groups also is questionable.

Anilioids (Aniliidae, Loxocemidae, Uropeltidae) are burrowing snakes with several lizard-like attributes. Some species respond to predators by thrashing, cloacal discharge, head hiding, and tail display (e.g., *Cylindrophis rufus,* Greene, 1973a). Snakes and perhaps birds eat uropeltids (Gans, 1976; Appendix A), but nothing else is known of predation. Although most species are probably cryptic, some aniliids and uropeltids have bright, contrasting colors that are perhaps aposematic, mimetic, or deflective (e.g., *Anilius scytale,* Greene, 1973a; *Uropeltis blythi,* Gans, 1973). Uropeltids also respond to predators by coiling around twigs and other objects, and have reinforced tails that attract dirt and form protective caudal plugs (Gans, 1973, 1976; Gans and Baic, 1977).

Booids (Boidae, Tropidophiidae, and perhaps others) are more diverse ecological and morphological than anilioids (Greene, 1983a), and are eaten by crabs, lizards, snakes, birds, and mammals (Section II, Appendix A). Tropidophiids generally respond to threats like anilioids, and some exude blood from the eyes and nostrils (e.g., *Tropidophis sp.,* Hecht et al., 1955). Many boids hiss, strike, and bite fiercely (e.g., *Boa constrictor,* Greene, 1983b).

4. CAENOPHIDIA

This infraorder includes more than half of the living snakes, but familial limits and relationships among them are uncertain despite much attention (e.g., McDowell, 1986; Dessauer et al., 1987; Fig. 5).

One species with a particularly complex repertoire illustrates much of the range of antipredator mechanisms in the largest caenophidian family, Colubridae. *Heterodon platirhinos* is a moderately large, nonvenomous or slightly venomous snake found in the eastern United States. The dorsal pattern typically consists of dark dorsal blotches on a lighter ground color, but in some areas many individuals are melanistic. When first disturbed, an eastern hognose snake assumes an exaggerated S-coil, hisses loudly, and makes false strikes if approached closely. The tail is tightly coiled and in some instances elevated. That suite of behavior is repeated if the snake is grasped, but after repeated harrassment an *H. platirhinos* begins to writhe violently with its mouth open limply and to defecate. If placed on the ground the snake continues to writhe for a short time, then assumes an inverted, limp posture, usually with the mouth open and tongue hanging out. If turned onto its ventral surface, the hognose snake immediately inverts the entire body. If the threatening stimulus is removed, the snake slowly rights itself and crawls away (Edgren, 1955; Platt, 1969; Kroll, 1977; Sexton, 1979). Controlled observations on two litters demonstrated that the complete repertoire occurs in neonates, that false strikes habituate more rapidly than does death feigning, and that stable variation among individuals in a litter is substantial (Burghardt, Greene, and Klinghammer, unpubl.; see also Section V.A, Appendix B).

Another widespread colubrid, *Coluber constrictor*, illustrates the responses of a slender, fast-moving species. A startled racer reacts by violent, undulatory movement that quickly changes to rapid, graceful locomotion for 30 m or more. It readily climbs or enters water in the course of escape. If startled at very close range, a racer sometimes coils with its head hidden and writhes, smearing scent gland secretions over its body. Alternatively, the snake assumes an S-coil, vibrates the tail, and strikes repeatedly. If seized, the racer continues to bite and discharge the cloacal contents, and twists its entire body so strongly that sometimes the tail is broken off (Fitch, 1963; Section III.E).

Atractaspidae includes a single genus of African burrowing snakes with powerful venom and long, movable fangs. The only record of predation was by a mammal (Section II, Appendix A). Species of *Atractaspis* respond to threats by rapid locomotion, thrashing, tail display, cloacal discharge, and biting. The head is held in a peculiar, ventrally flexed position when these snakes are disturbed; that is probably a prestrike posture, because biting prey is accomplished by a posteriorly directed, ventral and/or lateral movement (pers.obs. on *A. bibroni* and *A. microlepidotus*). Greene (1979) interpreted the similar defensive behavior of *Atractaspis* and certain elapids (see below) as convergence, but their response to predators might be homologous if the two families are indeed closely related (Cadle, 1982; McDowell, 1986; Fig. 5).

The large family Elapidae includes dangerously poisonous snakes with predominantly neurotoxic venoms and short, relatively immobile fangs. Terrestrial and arboreal elapids are eaten by lizards, other snakes, birds, and mammals (Section II, Appendix A). Most are nervous snakes that respond to predators with rapid, often erratic locomotion. Many elapids bite readily, and one or more major clades within the family consist of species that elevate and flatten the foreparts as a threat (Fig. 7). This behavior and its structural correlates occur to varying degrees in "cobras" (two species of *Aspidelaps*, two species of *Boulengerina*, *Hemachatus haemachatus*, six species of *Naja*, and *Ophiophagus hannah*) and some mambas (*Dendroaspis sp.*, Armitage, 1956). Three species of African cobras (*H. haemachatus*, *N. mossambica*, *N. nigricollis*) and some populations of Asiatic *N. naja* eject streams of venom that are aimed accurately at the face of an enemy (Bogert, 1943). The relationships among cobras are not well understood, so it is not yet possible to evaluate the origins of hoods and spitting, but the phylogenesis of these antipredator mechanisms invites detailed study.

Fig. 7. Defensive head and neck display in a neonatal king cobra, *Ophiophagus hannah* (Elapidae). (Photograph by Sam Dunton, courtesy of the New York Zoological Society ©).

The approximately 50 species of New World elapids are characterized as a group by a suite of antipredator attributes (Appendix D), illustrated by the Sonoran coral snake. *Micruroides euryxanthus* is a small, crepuscular and nocturnal coral snake found in the southwestern United States and Mexico. Its bright red, black, and white or yellow ringed pattern might be both cryptic and aposematic. A Sonoran coral snake crawls rapidly away if touched lightly. When restrained or touched firmly, it writhes rapidly and violently, with the head tucked laterally and the tail elevated into a coiled loop or spiral (Fig. 8). As the snake writhes and displays its tail, loops of the body move erratically in vertical and horizontal planes. The cloacal contents are expelled with a series of sharp, popping sounds that are audible to a human ear from a distance of at least 1 m. If released immediately, a Sonoran coral snake crawls rapidly away or freezes for a moment, often with its head tucked under a loop of the body and its tail elevated and coiled. It continues to writhe and bites repeatedly when restrained, and even a small adult is capable of envenomating a large mammal with serious consequences.

Fig. 8. Defensive tail display by a Sonoran coral snake, Micruroides euryxanthus, from near Portal, Cochise County, Arizona (specimen now Museum of Vertebrate Zoology 200000).

Eventually a Sonoran coral snake may disgorge a recently swallowed prey snake, sometimes weighing ca. 50% of the weight of the Micruroides (Woodin, 1953; Bogert, 1960; Russell, 1967; Vitt and Hulse, 1973; Greene, 1973a; Greene and McDiarmid, 1981; pers. obs.; Pough, this volume).

Venomous sea snakes probably represent two or more independent marine radiations from terrestrial, Australasian elapid ancestors (McDowell, 1986). Some species are evidently inoffensive (e.g., Laticauda spp.), while others bite fiercely (e.g., Aipysurus). Pelamis platurus has noxious flesh as well as a venomous bite, and the bright tail display is aposematic (Rubinoff and Kropach, 1970; Caldwell and Rubinoff, 1983).

Fig. 9. Gaping threat display by a Middle American eyelash viper, *Bothrops schlegeli*. (Photographed in Guatemala by J. A. Campbell; specimen now University of Kansas Museum of Natural History 187441).

Most species of Viperidae assume an S-coil and strike when threatened, and many vibrate the tail and hiss (e.g., *Agkistrodon contortrix*, Fitch, 1960; *Azemiops feae*, Kardong, 1986); those behavior patterns are found in all three viperid subfamilies as well as several other families and are probably retained primitive traits (see Henophidia, above, and Fig. 5). Terrestrial *Bothrops asper* occasionally gape at threatening humans (pers. obs.), and aquatic *Agkistrodon piscivorus* routinely do that (Allen and Swindell, 1948). Arboreal species in the predominantly terrestrial subfamilies Crotalinae (*B. schlegeli*) and Viperinae (*Atheris squamifer*) also gape defensively (Kratzer, 1969; Fig. 9), implying the independent evolution of that display several times. Species of *Cerastes* and *Echis* do not hiss (a loss perhaps functionally related to problems of water loss in desert environments, Mendelssohn, 1963, 1965), but instead produce a loud, "hissing" sound by rubbing obliquely keeled scales on adjacent body coils against each other (Gans and Baic, 1974; Fig. 10). Similar behavior and sound production in snakes of the colubrid genus *Dasypeltis* are mimetical convergence (Gans and Richmond, 1957; Pough, this volume). Whether the sound producing mechanisms of *Cerastes* and *Echis* result from a single evolutionary event is not resolved (cf. Marx and Rabb, 1965), but the shifting, exaggerated threat displays and loud hissing of other African Viperinae perhaps represent the antecedent defensive response (e.g., *Causus resimus*, Fig. 11).

Fig. 10. Defensive coil for epidermal sound production by a Middle Eastern carpet viper, *Echis coloratus*. (Photographed at the Atlanta Zoo).

J. Rattlesnakes

Approximately 31 species of New World pit vipers in the genera *Crotalus* and *Sistrurus* form a monophyletic group characterized by the presence of a rattle. That complex, epidermally derived caudal structure is associated with specialized shaker muscle (Martin and Bagby, 1972), and rattlesnakes are prominent creatures in a variety of North American ecosystems.

A particularly widespread, well studied species illustrates the range of rattlesnake defensive mechanisms. *Crotalus viridis* is a moderately large, diurnal or nocturnal species that occurs in much of the western half of the United States and southern Canada. These snakes vary geographically in color and are probably cryptic. When approached from a distance by a potential predator, a western rattlesnake is either already immobile or freezes. If approached closely it usually crawls rapidly away from a threat. If cornered or restrained, the rattlesnake assumes a prestrike posture, with its head elevated and foreparts drawn into an S-shaped coil. By that stage, the snake is typically rattling vigorously and continuously. If the predator remains in close proximity or touches the rattlesnake, it may strike and bite, hide its head under a body coil, or first hide its head and then suddenly strike from under a coil. If the predator is a kingsnake (*Lampropeltis getulus*), the rattler forms long, low "body bridges," which are sometimes jerked slightly up and down. *C. viridis* struggles violently if restrained, attempts to bite, continues to rattle, and discharges the cloacal contents in a fine spray (Bogert, 1941;

Fig. 11. Defensive coil by an African night adder, *Causus resimus*. (Photographed at the Fort Worth Zoological Garden).

Klauber, 1956; Carpenter and Gillingham, 1975; Weldon and Burghardt, 1979; Kardong, 1980; Duvall et al., 1985; Sweet, 1985).

The rattle is fundamentally a defensive signaling device today, and it is never regularly used in any other context. Hay (1887) and some subsequent authors favored an original role in warning large, trampling ungulates of a rattler's presence. Others suggested that the rattling sound originally diverted attention away from the snake's head and toward its tail (Garman, 1889; Williams, 1966). As Klauber (1956) noted, the first scenario entailed inconsistencies if, as he thought likely, the most primitive living rattlesnakes are small species restricted to high, forested areas on the Mexican Plateau (Klauber's reasons for choosing a particular phylogeny were only vaguely supported in print). Such forms probably would not be susceptible to trampling by ungulates. Klauber (1956) also pointed out that no evidence supports the second scenario either; he marshalled extensive evidence that the rattle is a warning device in all extant species that possess it, and by my reading, preferred no particular hypothesis beyond that.

Schuett et al. (1984) inferred from variation in size and construction among species that the rattle did not arise in a single step. They concluded therefore that at some stage an incipient rattle was small and inaudible, and could not have served as a warning device. Instead,

Schuett et al. (1984) proposed that a proto-rattle served as a caudal lure during hunting, because caudal luring is widespread among viperids and could be more advantageous in two ways with a keratinized caudal appendage. They supposed that a proto-rattle would have increased the optical attractiveness of a lure to potential prey, and that it would have protected a rattler from injuries delivered by the prey.

It is refreshing to have alternative hypotheses regarding the origin of the rattle, but the Schuett et al. (1984) hypothesis is not strongly supported by evidence at this time. Whether or not the rattle arose gradually or suddenly is not known, although the occurrence of occasional anomalous individuals demonstrates that it can be lost abruptly (Klauber, 1956; Smith et al., 1985). Nevertheless, although rattles vary interspecifically in relative size and shape (Klauber, 1956), all are so similar in structural details that this feature surely has arisen only once. Most *Crotalus* and *Sistrurus* make noise with their rattles that is audible to a human ear from a distance of more than a meter (e.g., small *C. lepidus, C. mitchelli,* and *C. pricei* in rock slides, pers. obs.). Granting there might have been transitional stages not evident in living taxa and prior to the origin of rattlesnakes, but assuming the rattles of *Crotalus* and *Sistrurus* are homologous as rattles, their ancestor had a rattle that functioned in a defensive context.

Caudal luring probably is primitive for Viperidae or a more inclusive taxon, because it occurs in numerous crotalines, at least two viperines, one elapid, and at least one boid. However, although the effectiveness of the tail as a lure can be enhanced structurally (e.g., swollen and pink in *Bothrops bilineatus,* Greene and Campbell, 1972), no convincing case has been made for damage to that appendage by prey. Schuett et al. (1984) cited data on tail injuries and mortality in *Thamnophis* (Willis et al., 1982), but those scars probably resulted from bites of predators rather than from small prey items. Finally, caudal luring occurs in a feeding context and involves relatively slow, sinuous movements (e.g., Greene and Campbell, 1972; Schuett et al., 1984, for *Sistrurus catenatus*). Tail vibration by viperids and many colubrids occurs in a defensive context, is typically rapid, and produces obvious noise on some substrates (e.g., *Agkistrodon halys,* Maslin, 1950; *Bothrops sp.,* Darwin, 1859; an adult *Lachesis muta* produces a distinct buzzing noise on dry leaves that can be perceived by the human ear from a distance of several meters, Greene and Santana, unpubl.).

Defensive tail vibration and caudal luring might both be ritualized versions of intention movements to escape, or of conflicting tendencies to attack and escape (cf. Parker, 1965; Greene, 1973a; Radcliffe et al., 1980); whether one evolved from the other is not known. However, defensive tail vibration clearly was the behavioral precursor of rattling and the rattle almost certainly evolved solely in a defensive context. Beyond that, the origin of the rattle remains an important problem, the solution to which has bearing on the adaptive radiation of a major group of snakes. Progress will require a convincing phylogeny of rattlesnakes and their closest relatives, and a survey of variation in the natural history of these animals.

Rattlesnakes vary considerably in their responses to danger (Klauber, 1956) and in venom composition (e.g., Minton and Weinstein, 1984). Some species are remarkably phlegmatic (e.g., *Crotalus ruber*), some have particularly dramatic threat displays (e.g., *C. durissus*), and some have especially toxic venom (e.g., some *C. scutulatus, C. tigris*). The rattle has been lost independently in *C. catalinensis* and an island population of *C. ruber*, although individuals of at least the former still make "rattling" movements of the tail (Radcliffe and Maslin, 1975; pers. obs.). The possible ecological significance of such differences and of other variation remains to be investigated, but rattlesnakes are clearly of great potential interest for studying diversification subsequent to major antipredator innovation.

V. EVOLUTION OF ANTIPREDATOR MECHANISMS

A. Function and Biological Roles

1. CRYPSIS

Cryptic animals resemble a random sample of the relevant aspects of their environment (Endler, 1978). A rigorous demonstration of crypsis requires comparisons with a specified hypothesis of resemblance, and consideration of other potential influences. The latter include biological roles in social interactions, mechanical protection, thermoregulation, asposematism, mimicry, and even hunting (e.g., Norris, 1967; Ficken et al., 1971; Pough et al., 1978; Burtt, 1979; Pough, this volume). Egg-eating snakes (*Dasypeltis,* Gans, 1961, 1970), gopher snakes (*Pituophis melanoleucus,* Sweet, 1985), and several vipers (e.g., *Crotalus spp.,* Klauber, 1956; *Cerastes* and *Echis,* Gans, 1961) illustrate multiple functions, in that their color patterns are concurrently cryptic, mimetic, and/or aposematic.

Field reports often emphasize the resemblance, sometimes remarkable, of reptiles to the substrates upon which they are found (e.g., Gans, 1976, for uropeltids). Numerous reports mention parallel geographic variation in substrate and lizard color, the most impressive of which are those concerned with dramatic differences from nearby habitats (e.g., *Holbrookia maculata* at White Sands, New Mexico, Ruthven, 1907; *Uta stansburiana* at Pisgah Lava Flow, California, Norris, 1967; the *Amphibolurus decresii* species group in Australia, Gibbons and Lillywhite, 1981). Several field studies have documented selection among morphs within a population (e.g., *Nerodia sipedon,* Camin and Ehrlich, 1958; Beatson, 1976; King, 1986; *Thamnophis sirtalis*, Sattler and Guttman, 1976), but only a single study to date has quantified in detail the extent to which variation in color patterns tracks environmental color variation (Sweet, unpubl.). Individuals of *Pituophis melanoleucus* are substantially less cryptic when displaced from their original capture site to another along a subspecific intergrade transect. Furthermore, a broad range of phenotypes is present among hatchlings at any point on the cline, suggesting that there is a selective gradient that maintains geographic variation in the adults.

A few experimental studies have examined the relationship between color and predation. Models of the black morph of *Vipera berus* are subject to more disturbance by predators than are those of the normal, striped morph in the field, and the continued presence of black vipers in the population is attributed to a thermal advantage associated with melanism (Andren and Nilson, 1981). *Phrynocephalus arabicus* that had cryptic coloration disrupted by small paint marks suffered increased mortality (Arnold, 1984a), but survivorship did not differ significantly between paint-marked and normal *Sceloporus undulatus* (Jones and Ferguson, 1980). A study of *S. jarrovi* demonstrated no significant differences in mortality between paint-marked and unmarked lizards, even when juveniles and adult males were examined separately (Simon and Bissinger, 1983).

Several kinds of indirect evidence support the hypothesis that cryptic coloration in reptiles is important in avoiding predation. Bright, contrasting colors are often used in social signaling by lizards (Carpenter and Ferguson, 1977), but these are almost always on hidden body surfaces that are either protruded (e.g., the dewlaps of *Anolis* and *Sitana,* the patagia of *Draco*) or exposed by rapid body movements (e.g., the bright ventral patches emphasized by the "pushups" of many small iguanids).

Another source of evidence for adaptive coloration is found in the correlations among pattern types and escape responses in snakes. Unicolored and striped species tend to live in grassy habitats and respond to threat by rapid crawling. Blotched and ringed snakes more often rely on immobility or other responses that emphasize defenses other than flight (Jackson et al., 1976). Other discussions of alternative cryptic color patterns in snakes include Klauber (1939), Brattstrom (1955a), Van Devender (1973), Pough (1976), Bechtel (1978), Dunson (1979), Jackson and Pounds (1980), Kardong (1980), Vitt (1980), and Gregory et al. (1983).

Cryptic coloration is often accompanied by behavior that facilitates the effect. Crocodilians and some turtles possess elevated nostrils and eyes, and typically rest in the water with only those sensory structures protruding (e.g., Neill, 1971; Alvarez del Toro, 1974). Iguanids (e.g., *Urosaurus graciosus*, pers. obs.) and agamids (e.g., *Draco maculatus*, Schmidt, 1927a) often remain immobile and crouch against the substrate when a predator is perceived nearby. Slender, arboreal snakes sway like a branch in the wind (e.g., *Ahaetulla sp.*, Gans, 1974; *Opheodrys aestivus*, Goldsmith, 1984; *Oxybelis aenus*, Fleishman, 1985), and some small lizards conduct many of their movements during periods when wind is causing their surroundings to move (Jackson, 1974; Greene et al., 1978).

2. LOCOMOTOR ESCAPE

The advantage of movement away from a predator is obvious, but that option is limited for most reptiles by their restricted aerobic capacities (e.g., Bennett, 1980; Christian and Tracy, 1981; Pough, 1983). Exceptions include certain teiids and varanids, which have unusual endurance at high speeds compared to other reptiles. Most species seemingly seek inaccessible retreats (vegetation, burrows, rock crevices, etc.) as soon as possible, and some lizards and snakes apparently know the location of those refuges (e.g., *Ameiva ameiva*, Beebe, 1945; *Tropidurus torquatus*, Rand and Rand, 1966; *Uromastyx hardwicki*, Minton, 1966). Many arboreal lizards move to the opposite side of a tree from the pursuer (e.g., *Sceloporus magister*, Parker and Pianka, 1973). Lizards that take refuge in crevices of rocks and trees sometimes watch potential predators from concealment (e.g., *Varanus tristis*, Pianka, 1971a), and some venomous snakes turn once they reach shelter and prepare to strike (e.g., *Agkistrodon piscivorus*, *Bothrops asper*, pers. obs.).

A common gambit is to escape into a radically different microenvironment that is inaccessible to most predators in the original site. An adult *Iguana iguana* evaded several coatis (*Nasua narica*) by diving into a lake in Panama (Greene et al., 1978), a response typical of many aquatic turtles, crocodilians, snakes, and other large lizards when approached by humans. That behavior is also seen as an occasional tactic in a variety of small and medium-sized lizards (e.g., *Hoplodactylus pacificus*, Whitaker, 1968; *Cnemidophorus sexlineatus*, Dillon and Baldauf, 1945; *Crotaphytus* collaris, McAllister, 1983; *Eumeces septentrionalis*, Black, 1976; *Lacerta lepida*; Malkmus, 1982b), and a regular escape method in several species of semiaquatic *Anolis* (e.g., Campbell, 1973) and skinks (e.g., *Leiolopisma suteri*, Whitaker, 1968). A specialization among several distantly related lineages is to run across the surface of water, a behavior that is facilitated by fringe-toed hind feet, and emerge on the opposite bank (e.g., *Basiliscus, Hydrosaurus*; Rand and Marx, 1967; Laerm, 1973; Luke, 1986). Small lizards that jump into water are susceptible to predation by fish at some sites (Campbell, 1973) and perhaps that risk favored the evolution of fringe-toed water runners in tropical areas.

Two other widespread specialized locomotor modes are running on fine sand, which is often facilitated by toe fringes (Carothers, 1986; Luke, 1986), and climbing relatively smooth, vertical surfaces. The latter task is associated with highly derived and convergent digital scansors in anoline iguanids, geckos, and a few species of skinks (Russell, 1979a; Williams and Peterson, 1982).

An even rarer escape behavior involves leaping into the air from an elevated perch, then gliding or parachuting to another location (e.g., *Draco spp.*, Colbert, 1967; *Anolis carolinensis*, Oliver, 1951; *Ptychozoon lionotum*, Marcellini and Keefer, 1976; *Chrysopelia paradisi*, Mertens, 1970; *Philothamnus spp.*, Sweeney, 1971). Gliding and parachuting are significantly more common in southeast Asia than in other rainforest areas, where there are fewer vines than in African and neotropical forests (Emmons and Gentry, 1983). Experiments in which the lateral cutaneous flaps of *P. lionotum* were tied against the body demonstrated that those structures improve gliding performance (Marcellini and Keefer, 1976). Although relatively uncommon among extant lineages, adaptive modifications for gliding have been a recurrent theme in the evolution of reptiles (Colbert, 1967, 1970).

Field observations suggest that forming a ball of coils might have surprising locomotor consequences in predator encounters for *Lichanura trivirgata*: twice when these small boas were discovered under rocks, they rolled out of reach into nearby crevices (B. M. McGurty, pers. comm.). Humans might be the only predators that can reach rose boas in rock shelters, but ringtails (*Bassariscus astutus*) occur in the same habitat and eat snakes (W. P. Taylor, 1954). In any case, that behavior represents a rare use of a gravity powered "wheel" by a vertebrate (cf. LaBarbera, 1983).

Escape from a predator that has grasped them might be facilitated in a few species of gekkonids and scincids by the extreme fragility of their skin (e.g., *Aristelliger hechti*, pers. obs.; *Gehyra mutilata*, Bustard, 1970; *Pachydactylus namaquensis*, Huey, in litt.; *Phelsuma sp.*, J. B. Losos, pers.

comm.; *Teratoscincus scincus*, Minton, 1966; a few species of *Ctenotus* and *Lerista*, Greer, 1986).

3. BLUFFS AND THREATS

Bluffs and threats are signals that differ in terms of consequences if they are ignored, in that the latter imply potential injury to an attacker and the former are deceptive in that regard. That distinction can be difficult to make in practice or actually variable for an individual because of relative characteristics of the participants (e.g., size). Such signals are present sporadically among several groups of reptiles (e.g., some turtles, some iguanids), and predominate in certain others (e.g., agamids, anguimorphans, geckos, many snakes). Bluffs and threats typically include increases in apparent size, intention movements to bite, explosive noises, and sudden exposure of bright colors or, rarely, fake eyes (e.g., *Sphaerodactylus semasiops*, Thomas, 1975).

Some observational and experimental evidence demonstrates that bluffs and threats work. A *Varanus niloticus* kept at bay a full grown, hungry lioness (*Panthera leo*, Schaller, 1972), and an *Iguana iguana* repulsed several coatis (*Nasua narica*) with its tail (Chapman, 1938). A *Calotes cristatellus* repelled a snake (*Chrysopelea paradisi*, Lim, 1959) and a *C. versicolor* successfully evaded a crow (Minton, 1966). A "*Natrix sp.*" (perhaps = *Rhabdophis tigrinus*, a dangerously poisonous colubrid) repeatedly rebuffed an attacking house sparrow with a head display before eventually gaining the safety of a bush (Sen Gupta, 1969). A 35-kg malamute that effectively defended me against a larger dog was later rebuffed by the vigorous hissing and strikes of a 20-gm *Pituophis melanoleucus*. An adult *P. melanoleucus* held two adult raccoons (*Procyon lotor*) at bay for an hour and then crawled away unharmed (Carr, 1940). The defensive display of *Phrynosoma platyrhinos* (lateral presentation of the tilted, flattened body accompanied by hissing and lunges) is almost certainly a bluff, because leopard lizards (*Gambelia wislizeni*) will approach and avoid horned lizards of a weight they could easily subdue (based on confrontations with nonspinose lizards, Tollestrup, 1981).

Many defensive displays of reptiles probably are bluffs, in the sense that the consequences for a predator of actually attacking would be trivial. In each of the cases described above, the predator probably could have easily overcome the potential prey had it chosen to "attack anyway." This poses the question, why do those displays work? Perhaps predators simply cannot afford to make mistakes unless they are really hungry, because real danger is sufficiently common, stimulus generalization is so widespread (Werner, 1983, 1986; see also Pough, this volume), and size alone is sometimes not an accurate indicator of fighting ability. An *Elgaria multicarinata* immobilized an attacking adult *Masticophis lateralis* by biting it on the head, and another held off an adult *Coluber constrictor* by gaping at it (Sweet, in litt.). Naive mammalian predators and nonraptorial birds that eat small litter vertebrates avoid coral snake models (Gehlbach, 1972; Smith, 1975, 1977; Greene and McDiarmid, 1981: Note 76), herons avoid yellow-bellied sea snakes (Caldwell and Rubinoff, 1983), and predatory fishes avoid yellow-bellied sea snakes (Rubinoff and Kropach, 1970), all situations in which attack might be fatal in nature. Likewise, numerous field observations demonstrate that a variety of vertebrates respond with avoidance to the sound of a rattlesnake (Klauber, 1956).

On the other hand, bluffs sometimes fail because the handling abilities of predators are not always strictly size dependent. A shrike (*Lanius ludovicianus*) readily attacked and flew off with a *Phrynosoma platyrhinos* that was displaying vigorously (pers. obs.). In this case the bird is capable of reducing a relatively large prey lizard to ingestable chunks, whereas a predatory leopard lizard (*Gambelia wislizeni*) of equivalent size (ca. 50 gm) must swallow it intact and is limited by gape. Coatis (*Nasua narica*) are rebuffed by models of venomous coral snakes (Gehlbach, 1972), but other carnivores of smaller or similar size (*Grison sp.*) readily attack living *Micrurus* (Jackson, 1979).

4. DIVERSION OF ATTACK

Many defensive responses apparently work by diverting attack, either completely or to an expendable portion of the animal. Absolute diversion is not common, but might include the tail displays of certain iguanids (*Cophosaurus texanus, Callisaurus draconoides,* Dial, 1986) and agamids (*Phrynocephalus sp.;* see Arnold, 1984a, 1984b, and this volume). *Cophosaurus texanus* has a ventrally striped tail, which is sometimes elevated and waved at an approaching predator before the lizard flees. Individuals are significantly more likely to display if they perceive a predator at a long distance, and to flee without displaying if surprised at a short distance. The former behavior might signal a predator that there is no chance of capture, thereby decreasing the likelihood of an actual chase (Dial, 1986).

Many tail displays in snakes and amphisbaenians probably divert attacks to an especially sturdy or disposable portion of the body, a role that is facilitated by the tendencies of many avian and mammalian predators to attack the head of a prey (Kaufmann and Kaufmann, 1965; Ewer, 1968; Lorenz, 1971; Curio, 1976; Jackson, 1979). Among certain snakes and amphisbaenians, high incidence of tail scars is associated with vertebral structures that strengthen the tail (Greene, 1973a; Section V.C; but see Nussbaum and Hoyer, 1974, for a feeding role of that modification in *Charina bottae*). Field observations indicated that a jackal (*Canis sp.*) attacked an *Eryx johnii*, but abandoned the sand boa with a bleeding tail but otherwise uninjured (Minton, 1966). Lizards that form a ring by seizing a body part in their jaws (e.g., some *Elgaria*, Fitch, 1935; *Cordylus cataphractus*, Rose, 1962) are probably abandoned unharmed because a predator cannot locate the head or because the resultant "object" is too large to swallow (*Lacerta saxicola*, Darevsky, 1967).

Some snakes occasionally miscarry young (uropeltids, Gans, in litt.; *Sistrurus catenatus*, pers. obs.) or regurgitate recent meals (e.g., *Heterodon*, Platt, 1969; *Python sebae*, Pienaar et al., 1978) when disturbed, and the latter is especially likely in New World venomous coral snakes (*Micruroides*, *Micrurus*) that have eaten relatively heavy meals (cf. Greene, 1984; pers. obs.; Section IV.I). Such behavior might be an incidental effect of fright and of the difficulties of struggling or locomoting while containing a developing young or a large prey item, but it might also be advantageous in diverting a predator. A potential predator could be repulsed by the sudden appearance of a large, smelly mass or could consume it. In either case, the predator would be distracted and the snake could escape. This hypothesis could be tested easily with captive predators and appropriate snakes.

5. REMOVAL OF CUES

Predatory behavior is typically controlled by particular sign stimuli, and some kinds of defensive behavior might succeed because they remove or obscure those cues from the potential prey's appearance (Platt, 1969; Alcock, 1975). Two classes of stimuli that are particularly widespread in eliciting killing behavior by vertebrate predators are movement and presence of a "head" (Curio, 1976). Tactics that likely involve removal of one or both of those cues include concealing the head under coils in snakes (Fig. 8); extended, rigid postures in lizards (e.g., *Echinosaura horrida*, Leviton and Anderson, 1966) and snakes (e.g., *Trachyboa boulengeri*, Lehmann, 1970); and death feigning by some lizards (e.g., *Varanus exanthematicus*, Schmidt, 1919; Pienaar et al., 1978) and snakes (see below). The efficacy of those responses might depend in part upon the ability of a prey to withstand some manipulation by a predator, which seems likely in reptiles (see Section II.D).

The possible biological role of death feigning is intriguing and controversial. McDonald (1974) documented bradycardia in death feigning *Heterodon platirhinos,* and noted that most snakes that death feign feed heavily on toads and have enlarged adrenal glands (e.g., *Hemachatus, Heterodon*). He proposed that the suite of activities involved in death feigning represents a "parasympathetic syndrome," facilitated by typically high levels of circulating catecholamines. McDonald (1974) and other authors recognized no obvious, specific advantage to death feigning, and he suggested that it might be a nonadaptive consequence of toad-eating. That nonadaptive hypothesis has yet to be directly refuted, but additional considerations are relevant. Removal of cues that elicit prey-killing behavior might provide an animal with subsequent opportunities for escape (Alcock, 1975), an event that seems especially likely in the case of predators that carry intact, immobile prey to a nest or den (e.g., raptors, some canids). Furthermore, the response (including slight bradycardia, McDonald, 1974) occurs repeatedly if a threat is rapidly presented and removed from a *Heterodon platirhinos* (Burghardt, Klinghammer, and Greene, unpubl.), and *Hemachatus haemachatus* remains alert and ready to bite during death feigning (Broadley, 1983). These observations perhaps imply an evoked behavioral response rather than neurohormonal phenomena.

6. NOVELTY, STARTLE EFFECTS, AND ASPECT DIVERSITY

Numerous behavioral responses among reptiles are so bizarre relative to normal behavior that they might delay or prevent attacks by virtue of their novel or startling qualities. Possible examples include erratic movements and noises, sudden appearance of bright colors or eye spots, and behavior or appearance that is novel to the predator relative to other members of the prey population (Gans and Richmond, 1957; Humphries and Driver, 1967, 1970). Color pattern polymorphism is relatively rare in reptiles (reviewed by Neill, 1963, for snakes), but might represent a response to predation via aspect diversity (see Rand, 1967a; Harvey and Greenwood, 1978). Examples include *Hoplodactylus pacificus* (Whitaker, 1968), *Anolis cuvieri* (Rand and Andrews, 1975), *Gambelia wislizeni* (Montanucci, 1978), *Sonora aemula* (Nickerson and Heringhi, 1966), *S. michoacanensis* (Echternacht, 1973), *S. semiannulata* (Gehlbach, 1972), *Lampropeltis getulus* (Zweifel, 1981, 1982), and *Scaphiodontophis* (Henderson, 1984b).

An example of interspecific behavioral diversity as a response to predation is found in whiptail lizards of the western United States. One to five species of *Cnemidophorus* occur at various sites, and the diversity of total behavioral response is positively correlated with tail break frequencies among assemblages (Schall and Pianka, 1980).

7. OFFENSIVE DEFENSE

Many reptiles are capable of delivering one or more "noxious consequences" to an attacking predator. Features and displays that emphasize unpalatability or danger (e.g., Figs. 3, 4, 9) are likely to be defensive adaptations, because they have no other apparent role, and because the behavior of the predators in rejecting prey sometimes supports that conclusion. Examples include distasteful or toxic flesh (*Pelamis platurus*, Rubinoff and Kropach, 1970; perhaps some *Eumeces*, but see Cooper and Vitt, 1985) and odoriferous glandular secretions (e.g., *Diplodactylus sp.*, Bustard, 1978; Fig. 6; kinosternid and pelomedusid turtles, Eisner et al., 1977, 1978; but see Kool, 1981, for contradictory evidence). Offensive mechanisms involving the digestive system (biting, cloacal discharge) have obviously been coopted for defense against predators, and in some cases adaptively elaborated for that role (e.g., the modified fangs of spitting cobras).

The recognition of "active combat" as an antipredator mechanism can be difficult. Casual observations suggest that aggression by some snakes (e.g., *Coluber constrictor*, Fitch, 1963; *Dendroaspis polylepis*, Broadley, 1983) and crocodilians (e.g., *Crocodylus niloticus*, Jackson, 1962) might be mediated by social and hormonal factors, and thus represent misdirected territoriality rather than a real defensive response. Another problem is that threatening and bluffing movements such as tail lashing, lunging, and even biting can merge into actual active combat (see Part 3, this Section). Examples of overt aggression (usually as biting) include snapping turtles (*Chelydra serpentina*, Section IV.B), most large lizards (e.g., *Lacerta lepida, Callopistes flavipunctatus*, several *Varanus*, Section IV.G), some amphisbaenians (e.g., *Amphisbaena alba, Trogonophis wiegmanni*, Section IV.H), and many snakes (e.g., *Ophiophagus hannah*, Howe, 1931; Section IV.I). A further problem is that aggressive defense tactics easily can be misinterpreted as real attacks, as when venomous snakes suddenly change directions, seek shade, or turn to face a threat (e.g., *Dendroaspis polylepis*, Broadley, 1983; *Bothrops asper*, pers. obs.; *Echis carinatus*, Minton, 1966).

8. MORPHOLOGICAL ADJUNCTS

Morphological features that facilitate defense include cryptic and aposematic color patterns, structures that enhance locomotion or sound production, structures that improve the utility of other adaptations as defensive weapons (see above), and structures that are evidently adaptive only in defensive roles. The latter include such things as the turtle shell (which of course has other properties, e.g., hydrodynamic and thermoregulatory), certain glands, body and tail spines, and the rattle.

Shell closure mechanisms have evolved repeatedly in turtles, and are believed to be antipredator adaptations (Bramble et al., 1984; Iverson, 1984; Section IV.B). Field observations on *Terrapene coahuila* at a marsh in Mexico support that hypothesis, because they indicate that secondarily aquatic box turtle is better able to avoid predation than other sympatric turtles that lack plastral kinesis. A coyote (*Canis latrans*) caught and began to open a slider turtle, *Pseudemys scripta*. Along the nearby shoreline were remains of nine other sliders and two soft-shelled turtles (*Trionyx sp.*), and signs indicated that coyotes had eaten both species (which, like most turtles, lack plastral hinges). Box turtles were common in the marsh, and one was found with fresh scratches on its closed shell and coyote tracks nearby. It was alive and unharmed, and no carcasses of that species were found around the marsh (Minckley, 1966).

Experimental work has confirmed the locomotor advantage conferred by fringed toes of lizards on water (Laerm, 1973) and sand (Carothers, 1986), and of cutaneous flaps and other specializations for gliding in a lizard (*Ptychozoon lionotum*, Marcellini and Keever, 1976) and a snake (*Chrysopelea ornata*, Heyer and Pongsapipitana, 1970). Whether these locomotor adaptations actually reduce predation is not yet documented.

B. Patterns and Processes

1. PRIMITIVE REPTILES AND OTHER AMNIOTES

Crypsis, locomotor escape, struggling, defecating, biting, and perhaps hissing are probably primitive for amniotes, judging from their near ubiquity among the living lineages of reptiles (Section IV), their presence in a number of mammals (Ewer, 1968), and the presence of all except hissing in at least some living amphibians (Duellman and Trueb, 1985; cf. Fig. 2). The prevalence of crypsis, inaccessability, and brief flight in living reptiles thus reflects retention of effective primitive features, and probably also the potentially high energetic costs of more direct responses (Pough, 1983). Among the latter, threatened or actual biting perhaps is the most frequently observed. There have been no thorough reviews of defense in mammals (see Ewer, 1968; Curio, 1976; Eisenberg, 1983; Wemmer and Wilson, 1983) or birds (see Curio, 1975, 1976; Brunton, 1986), but the antipredator mechanisms postulated as primitive for reptiles are evidently also widespread in those classes. Future attempts to evaluate the phylogenesis and ecological significance of defense in birds and mammals should include consideration of their reptilian relatives (see Section IV.C).

2. MAJOR TRENDS WITHIN REPTILIA

Defense against predators in ancestral turtles included the shell and retained, primitive tetrapod mechanisms. Subsequent evolution involved the occasional gain of new features associated with defense (e.g., plastral kinesis, odoriferous glands, spines, bright colors) and perhaps the repeated gains and losses of biting. Crocodilians and *Sphenodon* evidently retain primitive amniote responses to predation with little in the way of subsequent antipredator specializations, although large size no doubt affords freedom from most predators in the former.

The greatest diversity of antipredator mechanisms is in squamates, perhaps in part because this is by far the largest clade of living reptiles and because they occupy a greater number of microhabitats than do other lineages. The first major split in extant squamate taxa was between iguanians and scleroglossans (gekkotans plus autarchoglossans, amphisbaenians, and snakes, Estes et al., 1988; Fig. 5), and clear-cut differences in many behavioral and ecological attributes parallel that dichotomy. Scleroglossans are frequently secretive and/or nocturnal, solitary and nonterritorial (Stamps, 1977), and cover substantial distances in foraging. Although usually cryptic, they often rely on struggling, defecation, powerful jaws, and/or ritualized displays when discovered by a predator, rather than further rapid flight. Iguanians are diurnal, territorial, sedentary predators that usually rely on crypsis and brief bursts of locomotion to avoid predators. Exceptions exist for both generalizations, including iguanians with impressive stationary threat displays and some teiids and lacertids that surely rely mainly on crypsis and speed. Less frequent themes among scleroglossans include epidermal sound protection (e.g., *Echis, Teratoscincus*), limbless lateral undulation (e.g., *Elgaria multicarinata*, pers. obs.; all snakes), bizarre behavior (e.g., *Cordylus cataphractus*), and venomous bites (found only in *Heloderma* and many snakes). Tail autotomy is widespread in some scleroglossan families, but is absent in xenosaurids, helodermatids, varanids, and most snakes (Arnold, this volume).

Snakes and amphisbaenians retain the antipredator responses of a primitive scleroglossan squamate, but thrashing and cloacal discharge are enhanced by specialized, postcloacal scent glands in the former. Several major subsequent radiations of snakes have evolved innovative antipredator mechanisms, such as hoods in certain colubrids and elapids, aposematic coloration and displays in New World venomous coral snakes, and the rattle in one lineage of viperids. Several amphisbaenians (perhaps most) include erratic movements and novel postures, not seen elsewhere among scleroglossans, in their defensive repertoires.

3. ADAPTATION AND CONVERGENCE

Two classes of innovations are evident in the evolutionary diversification of reptilian defense against predators. Small changes that solve restricted problems have been widespread among squamates, often in the form of individual, intraspecific, or intrageneric variation. Perhaps because the number of options is limited, convergence is common. Examples include behavioral displays in snakes (Greene, 1979; Myers, 1986), and several pairs of iguanids and agamids, respectively: fringe-toed water runners (*Basiliscus, Hydrosaurus*), fringe-toed sand runners (*Uma, Phrynocephalus*), and spinose bodies (*Phrynosoma, Moloch*). Such innovations are minor in the sense that they apparently have not led to major radiations (typically a dozen species or less), and usually involve either postural changes or minor morphological modifications (e.g., spines and other elaborated epidermal structures).

A few defense-related changes apparently served as key innovations, by solving a problem in a way difficult for some predators to overcome, and facilitated major radiations. Possible examples include the shell of turtles (ca. 230 living species), shiny scales and body elongation in skinks (ca. 31% of 3400 lizards), scent glands in snakes (ca. 42% of 6000 living reptiles), and the rattle (ca. 16% of 190 living vipers). The total number of species encompassed by these relatively few evolutionary events is potentially very large, suggesting that antipredator problems have played a significant role in the diversification and persistence of reptiles.

Although the relevant data on foraging styles are incomplete, major antipredator innovations among reptiles apparently are often associated with a shift to active searching and/or with relatively long handling times under exposed conditions. Recent studies on fishes, birds, and mammals confirm an intuitively appealing proposition, that preoccupation with feeding activities decreases the ability of an animal to watch for predators (Milinski, 1984; Lawrence, 1985; Lima, 1985; Carey and Moore, 1986). Slow, careful foraging behavior, particularly in an open environment, probably makes an animal especially vulnerable to attack by a mobile predator. Interestingly, a desert gekkonid, *Ptenopus garrulus*, suffered increased mortality when it switched from its usual sit-and-wait to widely foraging tactics (Huey and Pianka, 1981). The problem of increased vulnerability while feeding is evidently surmounted in many birds and some mammals by social vigilance and group defense, but most reptiles are solitary (Wilson, 1975). *Iguana iguana* provides an instructive exception: Juveniles feed on young leaves and flowers in sustained bouts (pers. obs.), are virtually incapable of active defense, and are among the few highly social squamates (Burghardt et al., 1977; Greene et al., 1978). An implication of these considerations is that the repeated coupling of preoccupied foraging styles, antipredator innovations, and life history traits (Dunham et al., this volume) has been a major theme in reptilian evolution (see Section VI.C).

C. Fossils, Anachronisms, and Recent Changes

The evolutionary study of antipredator mechanisms in modern reptiles will utlimately profit from information on extinct taxa. Indirect evidence from fossil lineages can suggest new and surprising tactics, as in the bony tail club of some ancient turtles (Gaffney, 1985) and the putative defensive adaptations of extinct archosaurian reptiles (Bakker, 1986). This information might be important to the evaluation of constraints and optimal design, because it delimits the bounds of possible defensive responses (Section VI.B). Fossil members of extant clades can provide further evidence of the homology of defensive features and minimal estimates of their times of origin, as in the heavily reinforced caudal vertebrae of Eocene and Recent erycine boas (Hoffstetter and Rage, 1972; Greene, 1973a).

The analysis of putative defensive adaptations in living taxa is confounded by the possibility that they arose in concert with conditions no longer present (Gans, 1976; cf. Janzen and Martin, 1982), especially in places where there have been recent changes in the relative and absolute abundances of predators. Conversely, burgeoning human populations might affect antipredator mechanisms, via the experience of individual reptiles and/or selection on heritable variation in populations. A few examples will illustrate these problems.

Jaksic et al. (1982) compared predation on reptiles in Spain, Chile, and California, and discussed the role of predators in shaping the evolution of reptilian phenotypes (see Section II.B). They could not evaluate, however, the former role of grizzly bears (*Ursus arctos*) as predators, even though that large omnivore was common throughout much of California until the end of the last century (Storer and Tevis, 1955). The jaguar (*Panthera onca*), a generalist predator on many vertebrates (including tortoises, crocodilians, and iguanas; Schaller and Vasconcelos, 1978; Greene, Baker, and Santana, unpubl.), occurred in the southern United States until recently (Brown, 1983). Even when predators remain present, their abundances probably are far lower than carrying capacities in the recent past. For example, more than 50,000 bobcats (*Lynx rufus*) were killed in the western United States in one year recently (Schueler, 1980), and for several hundred years the trade in skins of spotted cats has drastically reduced their populations throughout the neotropics (Myers, 1973).

Recent effects of humans on antipredator mechanisms would have potential for elucidating causes of rapid change, but few cases have been suggested and none have been studied as yet. Some lay people believe that rattlesnakes in the vicinity of humans are at a disadvantage if they rattle, and that this has favored a reduced tendency for that behavior in such places (Cope, 1871; Klauber, 1956). No evidence supports that hypothesis, but experimental and comparative field research might be feasible on a wide-ranging, common species the distribution of which encompasses areas of high and low human densities, different attitudes toward snakes, etc. (e.g., *Crotalus viridis* in the western United States). Such studies should elucidate the roles of selection and individual modification as mechanisms underlying the behavioral shifts (see Section III).

VI. REPTILES AND ANTIPREDATOR THEORY

A. Reptiles as Study Organisms

Reptiles are becoming widely recognized as convenient organisms for studies of functional morphology (Gans, 1974) and behavioral ecology (Huey et al., 1983), and there are several reasons why the study of their antipredator mechanisms might contribute to those and other broad areas in evolutionary biology. First, searching for food and avoiding being eaten probably are the two most likely tasks facing a reptile on a daily basis, and the systems utilized in those two roles are often mechanically and functionally identical or interrelated. Second, because reptiles have a rich fossil record, they can serve as case studies for as yet unsolved macroevolutionary questions, especially in the context of evolutionary morphology (e.g., Vrba, 1984). For example, why are certain innovations correlated with at least modest radiations in some lineages whereas similar changes are exhibited only by single species in other clades (e.g., there are 14 species of *Phrynosoma* versus 1 species of *Moloch*)? Finally, Reptilia encompasses a sufficiently large and diverse group of organisms that its members can contribute to general theory as well as to the understanding of the limits of generality.

B. Optimality and Limits to Theory

Optimization is an approach to research in which design principles are used to evaluate and predict the functional significance of features of organisms (for general discussions, see Oster and Wilson, 1978; Lauder, 1981; Townsend and Calow, 1981). It proceeds by specifying the task (e.g., rebuff a particular type of predator under certain conditions) and a currency by which to measure performance (e.g., time, energy, mortality rate, clutch size), designing a solution to the task (using engineering or economic criteria, demographic models, etc.) such that benefits are maximized relative to costs, evaluating the role of possible constraints on the system, and then comparing the results with reality. Optimization can provide a design hypothesis against which organisms are evaluated, it can lead to general theories for examining the diversity of life, and it can clarify factors that need to be investigated (Greene, 1986b; for reptilian examples, see Gans, 1974). A disadvantage is that optimization inherently involves a number of assumptions, often unrecognized by the investigator, some of which might be inappropriate and misleading (Gans, 1966, 1983b; Levins and Lewontin, 1985).

At this point only a few, very general predictions seem possible. Most birds and mammals possess aerobic exercise abilities far in excess of those of reptiles (Bennett, 1980; Pough, 1983). For that reason, reptiles generally are expected to be cryptic and to rely on brief movements into inaccessible microhabitats for escape, rather than on long distance flight or sustained combat. Defenses against predators that encounter active prey should emphasize crypticity and brief flight if possible, whereas an encounter when the prey is inactive necessarily involves actual contact. Death-feigning will not work for species taken primarily by reptilian predators, because the immobile prey would simply be eaten sooner (cf. Gehlbach, 1970; McDonald, 1974:162; Greene, 1984). Antipredator mechanisms that capitalize on visual, auditory, and chemical perception by a predator might be especially effective in particular cases, but as yet no attempt has been made to predict which of these would obtain.

Theories in biology are rarely both precise and general, and this might be especially true for defensive mechanisms. Thus far only a few generalizations are possible: We can make reasonably good predictions about the antipredator strategy of an unstudied snake, based on a knowledge of its size, coloration, and preferred microhabitat (Jackson et al., 1976; Greene, 1979), but very few about those of a bird, a spider, or even a lizard based on studies of snakes. That situation is in contrast to allometry (e.g., Calder, 1984) and some aspects of life history theory (e.g., Dunham et al., this volume), for which fairly precise predictions have held true across a wide variety of animals and plants.

Perhaps a general theory of antipredator mechanisms for animals (let alone for animals plus plants!) is not possible, because the component phenomena are so complex. What "works" as a defensive response depends on predictable characteristics of the predator, the prey, the context for the interaction between them, and the particular aspect of feeding (e.g., pursuit, search, etc.) that is being manipulated by each animal. Those components and perhaps stochastic factors offer the potential of tremendous complexity, in turn multiplied by the number of possible interactions, so that the number of possible combinations is very high (see also Endler, 1986a). Because antipredator mechanisms are so often idiosyncratic, their explanation is more likely to be informed by functional biology and natural history than by theories based on considerations of optimality (see Gans, 1974, 1986; Greene, 1986a). As with some other problems in evolutionary biology (Colwell, 1984), we may have to settle for sets of restricted theories of antipredator mechanisms.

C. Some Generalizations

A few general principles concerning antipredator mechanisms seem likely, given the above caveats:

1. There is extensive evidence for a set of design rules with respect to crypsis, aposematic coloration, and mimicry. They follow from certain principles of psychophysics, and apply across a wide range of taxa, including reptiles (e.g., Cott, 1940; Wickler, 1968; Endler, 1978; Hailman, 1979; Owen, 1982; Pough, this volume). Examples include widespread, particular patterns of counter-shading and disruptive coloration, and the use of only a few hues and patterns in warning displays. It is noteworthy that most considerations of aposematic coloration are biased toward invertebrates, and sometimes start from assumptions that probably do not apply widely to reptiles (e.g., kin selection, see Harvey and Greenwood, 1978; Harvey and Paxton, 1981; Guilford, 1985; Endler, 1986b; Engen et al., 1986; Pough, this volume).

2. Although many descriptions emphasize a single defensive component, without mentioning the stimuli eliciting a reaction, animals typically react to the threat of predation with a hierarchy of responses that follows from consideration of relative risks, energetic demands, and intrinsic constraints (e.g., Rand and Rand, 1976; Pough, 1983). Numerous cases suggest that a reptile attempts to avoid detection whenever

possible, to flee if located and rapid escape is possible, and to engage a predator directly only as a last alternative. Examples of that hierarchy of responses include *Corytophanes cristatus* (Davis, 1953), *Thamnophis radix* (Arnold and Bennett, 1984), and *Micruroides euryxanthus* (see Section IV.I). This generality holds across a wide variety of other taxa (Ewer, 1968; Robinson, 1969, 1970; Edmunds, 1974; Alcock, 1984).

There are exceptions to the above pattern. Some large or particularly noxious forms immediately threaten a potential predator rather than flee (e.g., some *Lachesis muta*, pers. obs.), recourse to threat versus flight sometimes is dependent on type of predator (Section III.B), and some aposematic organisms apparently never behave cryptically. However, in some contexts even animals as dangerous as *Crotalus viridis* (Section IV.J), *Ophiophagus hannah* (Oliver, 1956), and *Heloderma horridum* (Pregill et al., 1986) exhibit the general hierarchy described above.

3. Features used in defense by plants and animals are usually adaptations for another biological role, and either coopted outright or modified in minor ways (Janzen, 1981). This appears to be true for reptiles, and the structures coopted are usually those used primarily for feeding and locomotion. Indeed, it can be difficult to distinguish primary from secondary roles, as in the cranial modifications of *Corytophanes* (Section IV.E). Many defensive displays of reptiles are plausibly interpreted as ritualized locomotor "intention movements" to attack, or of conflicting tendencies to attack and flee (cf. Daanje, 1950; Greene, 1973a; Chiszar, 1978), although those possibilities have not been rigorously examined.

4. There is a clear tendency among ectotherms for wide-searching and preoccupied foragers to rely on sudden (or omnipresent), highly effective, and often active defenses (Section V.B). That pattern is reasonably consistent for several lineages of reptiles, including several higher taxa (e.g., turtles, snakes), and anurans (Taigen et al., 1982). Certain solitary mammals also fit the pattern (e.g., tenrecs, porcupines, armadillos, skunks; Ewer, 1968; Eisenberg, 1983), suggesting that the coupling of preoccupied foraging and specialized defense might have been a significant factor in the evolution of tetrapods and deserves detailed consideration.

5. Predictable functional relationship, more taxonomically restricted than the pattern described above (4), exist among lizards and snakes. Lizards that forage widely across diverse microhabitats and use speed to escape have longer tails than species that are sedentary predators, habitat specialists, and use crypsis as a predominant antipredator tactic (Huey and Pianka, 1981; Vitt, 1983; Arnold, 1984a). Lizards with high exercise abilities typically rely on speed, whereas those with low aerobic

scope and work capacity exhibit more complex, static defense repertoires (Bennett, 1980). Snakes that depend on rapid locomotion for escape are often unicolored or striped, whereas those with static defenses are usually banded or blotched (Jackson et al., 1976).

6. Earlier considerations suggested that defensive mechanisms should be minor innovations that are closely tuned to local, contemporary problems, and that convergence should be widespread (Alcock, 1975; Greene, 1979; Janzen, 1981). Similar, independently evolved displays are indeed widespread among snakes (Gans and Baic, 1974; Greene, 1979; Myers, 1986; see above), but the broader conclusion that antipredator mechanisms have not played a significant role in reptilian evolution (Pough, 1983) is strongly contradicted by the survey in this chapter. Furthermore, as with the courtship of salamanders (S. J. Arnold, 1977) and the constricting behavior of some snakes (Greene and Burghardt, 1978), certain defensive adaptations have persisted for very long periods. Why some attributes of organisms should be tightly correlated with contemporary local conditions and others remain stable throughout ancient adaptive radiations is an intriguing question for evolutionary biology.

VII. PROBLEMS AND PROSPECTS

Brief descriptions have continued to accumulate during the four decades since Mertens' (1946) monograph appeared, but much remains to be learned about antipredator responses in reptiles. The following kinds of studies are needed to understand more fully the topic.

1. Thorough accounts of antipredator mechanisms, either in the field or under naturalistic captive conditions, will continue to be of value. A good description must recreate details with sufficient precision and accuracy to be useful to future workers (see Drummond, 1981, 1985). It should be quantitative to the extent possible, and the conditions under which the observations were made should be mentioned in detail. To resolve future uncertainties about identification, published reports should include collecting data and the location of representative museum specimens or photographs (Wickler, 1960, documented unresolved, conflicting conclusions because of the lack of voucher specimens).

The following guidelines are offered in the interest of standardization, to be modified as necessitated by specific circumstances (see also Scudder and Burghardt, 1983; Arnold and Bennett, 1984; Duvall et al., 1985; Herzog and Burghardt, 1986). Describe the behavior of a reptile in the field when first perceived visually by the observer, when lightly touched (if feasible), when handled lightly, and then when handled firmly. Take its body temperature, then note sex and reproductive condition, if appropriate. Record the reaction of the animal if given the opportunity to escape, then repeat the handling regime. Laboratory conditions will permit more sophisticated descriptions and analyses, including the use of video and film recordings (e.g., Inglehart and Chiszar, 1977). Unusual features (e.g., prominent vertebrate eyes, a particular odor) might be necessary components of the threatening stimuli for some reptiles.

Not one species of reptile has been studied thoroughly in terms of antipredator responses, but certain kinds are especially worthy of particular types of research. Common, easily maintained animals are best suited for studies of variation, genetics, and ontogeny, as exemplified by recent work on *Cnemidophorus tigris* (Schall and Pianka, 1980), *Nerodia sipedon* (Scudder and Burghardt, 1983), species of *Thamnophis* (Arnold and Bennett, 1984; Herzog and Burghardt, 1986), and *Crotalus viridis* (Duvall et al., 1985). Paradoxically, the most spectacular and complex defensive repertoires are often found in tropical species (cf. Robinson, 1970; Greene, 1987), for which rarity and other factors frequently make detailed studies difficult. Careful descriptive accounts, even of rare animals and isolated events, will continue to be of interest because they enlarge the scope of theoretical concern (Gans, 1978; Greene, 1986a). Even though many of the records in the appendices are "anecdotes," buried in faunal and systematic works, they are particularly valuable when the investigator has made an effort to record the full repertoire of defensive responses in as many sympatric species as possible (e.g., Schmidt, 1919; Beebe, 1944a, 1944b, 1945, 1946; Whitaker, 1968; Arnold, 1984a).

Although additional descriptive studies of antipredator mechanisms in snakes will be of interest, they are now known better in this regard than any other group of reptiles. Turtles and crocodilians remain especially poorly understood, and otherwise fine books on their biology typically either ignore the topic or scatter comments on defense among sections on habitat, reproduction, and feeding! Because turtles and crocodilians are cladistically outside *Sphenodon* and the squamates, studies of the former groups are particularly important for conclusive analyses of other tetrapods. A detailed study of even one diverse turtle fauna could quickly make the present review of those animals outdated.

2. The study of evolution in an ecological context requires natural historical (Greene, 1986a, 1986b) and quantitative genetic (Arnold, 1983)

PROBLEMS AND PROSPECTS

approaches. Observations of natural and staged encounters between predators and prey are a necessary first step in interpreting the function and biological role of putative defensive behavior. Predator–prey interactions are rarely observed in the field, but that can perhaps be facilitated by special techniques (e.g., remote cinematography, Greene et al., 1978). Staged encounters have been infrequent (e.g., Gehlbach, 1972; Gans, 1976; Jackson, 1979) and are inevitably subject to problems of interpretations, but might be facilitated by the participation of zoos.

Interpretation of descriptive and experimental approaches to the study of biological roles should assess potential predators as thoroughly as possible, and consider the possibility that the responses are currently anachronistic. Recent advances in the study of subfossil assemblages might prove helpful in the latter regard (cf. Steadman, 1986; Pregill, 1986).

3. Morphological defense mechanisms remain poorly studied in reptiles, but excellent examples include epidermal sound production (Gans and Richmond, 1957; Gans and Baic, 1974) and hissing (Martin and Huey, 1971; Saiff, 1975) in some snakes, the shell of turtles (Bramble and Hutchison, 1981; Iverson, 1984), and frill erection in *Amphibolurus barbatus* (Throckmorton et al., 1985). Such structural features are both challenging and interesting for evolutionary biology because they often reflect the overlapping functional demands of multiple biological roles (cf. Gans, 1974).

4. Experimental studies of the energetic costs and benefits of alternative tactics are needed to translate the significance of antipredator mechanisms into overall energy budgets and differential reproduction. Recent technical advances in physiological ecology hold much promise for that area (e.g., Bennett, 1980, 1986; Feder and Arnold, 1982; Pough and Andrews, 1985).

5. The relationship between injuries and antipredator mechanisms warrants additional attention. For example, increased frequencies of serious wounds might occur in taxa the defensive tactics of which include actual contact (e.g., species of *Phrynosoma*) or those for which there is a substantial experiential component to the response (Sections II.D, III.C).

6. Elucidation of the physiological and behavioral phenomena underlying adaptive modification of organisms continues to be a major challenge. Standardized descriptive studies of naive young and of subsequent stability of modification of behavior are necessary for understanding the proximal processes that affect different phenotypes. This is another area in which zoos, by virtue of their emphasis on

captive breeding, could make significant contributions. Carefully structured breeding studies are required to understand better the genetic bases for variation in defensive mechanisms (see Arnold, 1983; Arnold and Bennett, 1984). Studies of intra- and interspecific variation in antipredator behavior also will help, ideally to encompass (1–5, above); recent studies of *Pituophis melanoleucus* (Sweet, 1985, and in litt.) and species of *Thamnophis* (Arnold and Bennett, 1984; Herzog and Burghardt, 1986) are exemplary in that regard.

The influence of age, sex, and context on defensive responses in reptiles (Section III) implies underlying mechanisms of motivation and arousal, topics that have received scarcely any attention (e.g., Gehlbach, 1970; Hennig and Dunlap, 1978). Conversely, physiological responses to stress (e.g., defecation, labored breathing) might be misinterpreted as antipredator mechanisms (Noble, 1921; Section V.A), as might increased aggressivity as a nonadaptive correlate of highly reactive feeding behavior (e.g., perhaps among species of *Pseudemys*, Pritchard, 1979:122; among species of *Thamnophis*, Herzog and Burghardt, 1986). However, either might have served as precursors to real adaptive responses (Daanje, 1950; see Section IV.J).

7. This chapter has emphasized behavioral and morphological innovations as antipredator adaptations, but there are additional characteristics that should receive attention: (a) Juvenile *Anolis aeneus* compete for open microhabitats in order to avoid predation by *A. richardi* in shady areas, which are preferred by adult *A. aeneus* (Stamps, 1983). Such ontogenetic shifts might be a widespread response by reptiles vulnerable to size-restricted predators. (b) The potential for predation on inactive reptiles suggests that choice and/or alteration of retreat sites might be subject to selection (see Sections II.F, V.A). (c) Reptiles might escape by evolving smaller or larger size relative to particular predators (e.g., perhaps some *Sauromalus sp.*, Case, 1982; *Varanus varius*, Bustard, 1970; for general treatments see Paine, 1977; Power, 1987). (d) High risks from predation can be met with compensatory life history tactics (Dunham et al., this volume), and in many species that might be the only response other than crypsis and avoidance behavior.

8. The study of organisms in an evolutionary historical context is dependent on an understanding of their phylogenetic relationships. An investigator must keep abreast of and evaluate evidence for the relationships of the taxa under study, and choose a method for analysis (e.g., outgroup comparison, Maddison et al., 1984), such that the direction of evolution for the trait of interest can be inferred. A major opportunity lies in combining ontogenetic and phylogenetic approaches (e.g., Fink, 1982; Lauder, 1986).

Taken as a whole, these suggestions emphasize that systematics, descriptive natural history, and experimental studies all will be necessary for a thorough understanding of antipredator mechanisms. Our efforts are more likely to succeed if they avoid false dichotomies (e.g., history *versus* adaptation), and stress instead the integration of genetics, development, and multiple biological roles in shaping the lives of reptiles.

ADDENDUM

Several important references came to my attention after this chapter was submitted for publication. Armstrong and Murphy (1979) described defensive behavior in 17 species of Mexican rattlesnakes, and a natural encounter between an ocelot (*Felis pardalis*) and an adult *Crotalus durissus*. Lowe et al. (1986) summarized the defensive behavior of Arizona rattlesnakes and adduced cogent arguments for the biological role of venom in the defensive repertoire of helodermatids. Kluge (1987) analyzed phylogenetic relationships among higher taxa in the Gekkota, reviewed literature on defensive vocalizations in that group (including pygopodids), and tentatively concluded that response is primitive for tetrapods. Hailey and Davies (1986) reported detailed experimental studies on variable defensive behavior in *Natrix maura*.

ACKNOWLEDGMENTS

My studies on reptilian behavior have been supported by the American Museum of Natural History (Theodore Roosevelt Memorial Fund); Field Museum of Natural History (Karl P. Schmidt Fund); Committee on Research, Center for Latin American Studies, and Museum of Vertebrate Zoology (Annie M. Alexander Fund), University of California, Berkeley; Smithsonian Tropical Research Institute (Noble Fund); Organization for Tropical Studies; World Wildlife Fund (U.S.); American Philosophical Society; and National Science Foundation (BNS 76-19903, BSR 83-00346). Many constructive criticisms of the manuscript were received from N. B. Ananjeva, S. J. Arnold, D. G. Broadley, G. M. Burghardt, J. H. Carothers, J. A. Endler, A. Lockhardt, J. B. Losos, F. H. Pough, S. S. Sweet, and P. J. Weldon. I am grateful to N. B. Ananjeva and I. S. Darevsky for help with the Russian literature; D. G. Broadley for generously allowing me to quote his important manuscript on African carnivores; K. de Queiroz for advice on systematic matters; J. B. Iverson for aiding me with the turtle literature; Layla for saving me from the doberman; and especially C. Gans, R. B. Huey, and C. Luke for reading and talking about it all over and over. This is an appropriate place to pay special tribute to my mentors and teachers, especially P. Anderson, G. M. Burghardt, C. C. Carpenter, H. S. Fitch, C. Gans, W. F. Pyburn, A. S. Rand, J. C. Streett, and G. B. Wolcott.

REFERENCES

Adolph, S. C. and Roughgarden, J. (1983). Foraging by passerine birds and *Anolis* lizards on St. Eustatius (Neth. Antilles): Implications for interclass competition, and predation. Oecologia 56, 313–317.
Advani, R. (1981). Seasonal fluctuations in the feeding ecology of the Indian false vampire, *Megaderma lyra lyra* (Chiroptera: Megadermatidae) in Rajasthan. Z. Säugetierkunde 46, 90–93.
Alberch, P., Gould, S. J., Oster, G. F. and Wake, D. B. (1979). Size and shape in ontogeny and phylogeny. Paleobiology 5, 296–317.
Alcock, J. (1975). *Animal Behavior: An Evolutionary Approach*. Sinauer Assoc., Sunderland, MA.
Alcock, J. (1984). *Animal Behavior: An Evolutionary Approach* (3rd ed.). Sinauer Assoc., Sunderland, MA.
Allen, E. R. and Swindell, D. (1948). Cottonmouth moccasin of Florida. Herpetologica 4 (first suppl.), 1–16.
Allen, G. R. (1974). The marine crocodile, *Crocodylus porosus*, from Ponape, Eastern Caroline Islands, with notes on food habits of crocodiles from the Palau Archipelago. Copeia 1974, 553.
Alvarez del Toro, M. (1971). *Los Aves de Chiapas*. Inst. Hist. Nat. Est., Dept. Zool., Tuxtla Gutierrez, Chiapas, Mexico.
Alvarez del Toro, M. (1974). *Los Crocodylia de Mexico (Estudio Comparativo)*. Inst. Mex. Recur. Nat. Renov., Mexico, D.F.
Alvarez del Toro, M. (1982). *Los Reptiles de Chiapas*. Inst Hist. Nat. Est., Dept. Zool., Tuxtla Gutierrez, Chiapas, Mexico.
Amaral, A. do A. (1929). Notes on *Spilotes pullatus*. Bull. Antivenin Inst. Am. 3, 98–99.
Amaral, A. do A. (1932). Contribução a biologia dos ophidios do Brasil. Mem. Inst. Butantan 7, 91–94.
Amores, F. (1980). Feeding habits of the stone marten, *Martes foina* (Erxleben, 1777), in south western Spain. Säugetierkundl. Mitt. 28, 316–322.
Anderson, J. (1898). *Zoology of Egypt. I. Reptilia and Batrachia*. B. Quaritch, London.
Anderson, J. D. (1956). A blind snake preyed upon by a scorpion. Herpetologica 12, 327.
Anderson, S. C. (1963). Amphibians and reptiles from Iran. Proc. Cal. Acad. Sci. 31, 417–498.
Andren, C. (1982). Effect of prey density on reproduction, foraging and other activities in the adder, *Vipera berus*. Amphibia–Reptilia 3, 81–96.
Andren, C. and Nilson, G. (1981). Reproductive success and risk of predation in normal and melanistic colour morphs of the adder, *Vipera berus*. Biol. J. Linn. Soc. (London) 15, 235–246.
Angel, F. (1933). *Les Serpents de l'Afrique Occidentale Française*. Larose, Paris.

REFERENCES

Armitage, W. W. (1965). Observations on differences in morphology and behavior of *Dendroaspis angusticeps* and *D. polylepis*. J. Herpetol. Assoc. Africa 1, 12–16.
Armstrong, B. L., and Murphy, J. B. (1979). The natural history of Mexican rattlesnakes. Spec. Publ. Univ. Kansas Mus. Nat. Hist. 5, 1–88.
Arnold, E. N. (1977). Little-known geckoes (Reptilia: Gekkonidae) from Arabia with descriptions of two new species from the Sultanate of Oman. J. Oman Stud. Spec. Rep. 1, 81–110.
Arnold, E. N. (1980). The reptiles and amphibians of Dhofar, southern Arabia. J. Oman Stud. Spec. Rep. 2, 273–332.
Arnold, E. N. (1984a). Ecology of lowland lizards in the eastern United Arab Emirates. J. Zool. (London) 204, 329–354.
Arnold, E. N. (1984b). Evolutionary aspects of tail shedding in lizards and their relatives. J. Nat. Hist. 18, 127–169.
Arnold, E. N., and Gallagher, M. D. (1977). Reptiles and amphibians from the mountains of Oman with special reference to the Jebel Akhdar region. J. Oman Stud. Spec. Rep. 1, 59–80.
Arnold, S. J. (1972). Species densities of predators and prey. Am. Nat. 106, 220–236.
Arnold, S. J. (1977). The evolution of courtship behavior in New World salamanders with some comments on Old World salamanders. In *The Reproductive Biology of Amphibians* (D. H. Taylor and S. I. Guttman, eds.). Plenum Press, New York, pp. 141–183.
Arnold, S. J. (1983). Morphology, performance and fitness. Am. Zool. 23, 347–361.
Arnold, S. J. and Bennett, A. F. (1984). Behavioural variation in natural populations. III. Antipredator displays in the garter snake *Thamnophis radix*. An. Behav. 32, 1108–1118.
Asplund, K. K. (1967). Ecology of lizards in the relictual cape flora, Baja California. Am. Midl. Nat. 77, 462–475.
Auffenberg, W. (1980). Autoecological notes on *Xenochrophis piscator* (Reptilia: Serpentes) from Keoladeo Ghana Sanctuary. Int. J. Environ. Sci. 6, 77–82.
Auffenberg, W. (1981). *The Komodo Monitor*. Univ. Florida Press, Gainesville.
Auffenberg, W. (1983). The burrows of *Varanus bengalensis:* Characteristics and use. Rec. Zool. Surv. India 80, 375–385.
Auffenberg, W., and J. B. Iverson. (1979). Demography of terrestrial turtles. In *Turtles: Perspectives and Research*. (M. Harless and H. Morlock, eds.). Wiley, New York, pp. 541–569.
Bakker, R. T. (1986). *Dinosaur Heresies*. William Morrow and Co., New York.
Balgooyen, T. G. (1976). Behavior and ecology of the American kestrel (*Falco sparverius* L.) in the Sierra Nevada of California. Univ. Cal. Publ. Zool. 103, 1–83.
Banta, B. H. (1960). Notes on the feeding of the western collared lizard, *Crotaphytus collaris baileyi* Stejneger. Wasmann J. Bio. 18, 309–311.
Barber, H. S. (1906). (Untitled abstract concerning attack on ringneck snake by beetle larva.) Proc. Biol. Soc. Washington 19, xv.
Barbour, R. W. (1956). A study of the cottonmouth, *Ancistrodon piscivorus leucostoma* Troost, in Kentucky. Trans. Kentucky Acad. Sci. 17, 33–41.
Barbour, T. (1921). Aquatic skinks and arboreal monitors. Copeia 97, 42–44.
Barbour, T. and Loveridge, A. (1928). A comparative study of the herpetological fauna of the Uluguru and Usambara Mountains, Tanganyika Territory, with descriptions of new species. Mem. Mus. Comp. Zool. 50, 87–265.
Barbour, T. and Ramsden, C. T. (1919). The herpetology of Cuba. Mem. Mus. Comp. Zool. 47, 69–213.

Bauer, A. M. (1986). Saltation in the pygopodid lizard, *Delma tincta*. J. Herpetol. 20, 462–463.
Bauwens, D. and Thoen, C. (1981). Escape tactics and vulnerability to predation associated with reproduction in the lizard *Lacerta vivipara*. J. An. Ecol. 50, 733–743.
Beasom, S. L. and Pattee, O. H. (1975). An encounter between a turkey and a bullsnake. Wilson Bull. 85, 281–282.
Beatson, R. R. (1976). Environmental and genetical correlates of disruptive coloration in the water snake, *Natrix s. sipedon*. Evolution 30, 241–252.
Beavers, R. A. (1976). Food habits of the western diamondback rattlesnake, *Crotalus atrox*, in Texas (Viperidae). Southwest. Nat. 20, 503–515.
Bechtel, H. B. (1978). Color and pattern in snakes (Reptilia, Serpentes). J. Herpetol. 12, 521–532.
Beebe, W. (1944a). Field notes on the lizards of Kartabo, British Guiana, and Caripito, Venezuela. Part 1. Gekkonidae. Zoologica (N. Y.) 29, 145–160.
Beebe, W. (1944b). Field notes on the lizards of Kartabo, British Guiana, and Caripito, Venezuela. Part 2. Iguanidae. Zoologica (N. Y.) 29, 195–216.
Beebe, W. (1946). Field notes on the snakes of Kartabo, British Guiana, and Caripito, Venezuela. Zoologica (N. Y.) 31, 11–52.
Bellairs, A. d'A. and Bryant, S. V. (1985). Autotomy and regeneration in reptiles. In *Biology of the Reptilia*. C. Gans and F. Billet (eds.). Wiley, New York. Volume 15, 301–410.
Bellemin, J. M. and Stewart, G. R. (1977). Diagnostic characters and color convergence of the garter snakes *Thamnophis elegans terrestris* and *Thamnophis couchii atratus* along the central California coast. Bull. S. Cal. Acad. Sci. 76, 73–84.
Belt, T. (1874). *The Naturalist in Nicaragua*. J. Murray, London.
Bemis, W. E., Schwenk, K. and Wake, M. H. (1983). Morphology and function of the feeding apparatus in *Dermophis mexicanus* (Amphibia: Gymnophiona). Zool. J. Linn. Soc. (London) 77, 73–96.
Bennett, A. F. (1980). The metabolic foundations of vertebrate behavior. Bioscience 30, 444–469.
Bennett, A. F. (1986). Measuring behavioral energetics. In *Predator–Prey Relationships: Perspectives and Approaches From the Study of Lower Vertebrates*. (M. Feder and G. V. Lauder, eds.) Univ. Chicago Press, Chicago, pp. 69–81.
Berry, K. H. (1974). The ecology and social behavior of the chuckwalla, *Sauromalus obesus obesus* Baird. Univ. Cal. Publ. Zool. 101, 1–60.
Bickham, J. W. and Carr, J. L. (1983). Taxonomy and phylogeny of the higher categories of cryptodiran turtles based on a cladistic analysis of chromosomal data. Copeia 1983, 918–932.
Binder, M. H. and Henderson, R. W. (1982). Tail waving as a diversionary tactic in *Anolis carolinensis*. Herpetol. Rev. 13, 10.
Biswas, S. (1983). Food habits of the banded krait. Hamadryad 8, 16–17.
Biswas, S. and Acharjyo, L. N. (1977). Notes on ecology and biology of some reptiles occurring in and around Nandankanan Biological Park, Orissa. Rec. Zool. Surv. India 73, 95–109.
Black, J. H. (1976). Escape behavior of the southern plains skink. Herpetol. Rev. 7, 111.
Bogert, C. M. (1941). Sensory cues used by rattlesnakes in their recognition of opidian enemies. Ann. New York Acad. Sci. 41, 329–343.
Bogert, C. M. (1943). Dentitional phenomena in cobras and other elapids with notes on adaptive modifications of fangs. Bull. Am. Mus. Nat. Hist. 81, 285–360.
Bogert, C. M. (1960). The influence of sound on the behavior of amphibians and reptiles.

REFERENCES

In *Animal Sounds and Communication*. (W. E. Lanyan and W. N. Tavolga, eds.). Am. Inst. Biol. Sci. Publ. 7, 137–320.

Bogert, C. M. and Martin del Campo, R. (1956). The Gila monster and its allies. The relationships, habits, and behavior of lizards of the family Helodermatidae. Bull. Am. Mus. Nat. Hist. 109, 1–238.

Böhme, W. (1974). Ein seltenes Zwergchamaeleon aus Madagaskar. Salamandra 10, 80–82.

Böker, H. (1935). *Einführung in die vergleichende biologische Anatomie der Wirbeltiere*. Gustav Fischer Verlag, Jena.

Bokermann, W. C. A. (1978). Observações sobre habitos alimentares do gavião *Geranospiza caerulescens* (Viellot, 1817) (Aves, Accipitridae). Rev. Brasil. Biol. 38, 715–720.

Bolaños, R., Muñoz, G. and Cerdas, L. (1978). Toxicidad, neutralizacion e immunoelectroforesis de los venenos de *Lachesis muta* de Costa Rica y Colombia. Toxicon 16, 295–300.

Boulenger, G. A. (1888). An account of the Reptilia obtained in Burma, north of Tenasserim, by M. L. Fea, of the Genoa Civic Museum. Ann. Mus. Civ. Stor. Genova 6, 563–604.

Boulenger, G. A. (1912). *A Vertebrate Fauna of the Malay Peninsula from the Isthmus of Kra to Singapore, Including the Adjacent Islands. Reptilia and Batrachia*. Taylor and Francis, London.

Bourquin, O. and Channing, A. (1980). Herpetofauna of the Natal Drakensburg: An annotated checklist. Lammergeyer 30, 1–20.

Bouskila, A. (1983). The burrows of the dabb-lizard, *Uromastyx aegyptius*. Israel J. Zool. 32, 151–152.

Brain, C. K. (1961). Observations on the birth of young *Chamaeleo jacksoni*. J. Herpetol. Assoc. Rhodesia 17–18, 11–12.

Bramble, D. M. (1974). Emydid shell kinesis: Biomechanics and evolution. Copeia 1974, 707–727.

Bramble, D. M. and Hutchinson, J. H. (1981). A reevaluation of platral kinesis in African turtles of the genus *Pelusios*. Herpetologica 37, 205–212.

Bramble, D. M., Hutchinson, J. H. and Legler, J. M. (1984). Kinosternid shell kinesis: Structure, function and evolution. Copeia 1984, 456–475.

Branch, W. R. (1973). Birth in the mole snake *Pseudaspis cana*. J. Herpetol. Assoc. Rhodesia 10, 24–29.

Branch, W. R. (1976). Two exceptional food records for the African bullfrog *Pyxicephalus adspersus* (Amphibia, Anura, Ranidae). J. Herpetol. 10, 266–268.

Branch, W. R. (1981). Cape lizards. II. The leguans (Varanidae). The Naturalist 25, 15–19.

Brattstrom, B. H. (1955a). The coral snake "mimic" problem and protective coloration. Evolution 9, 217–219.

Brattstrom, B. H. (1955b). Notes on the herpetology of the Revillagigeo Islands, Mexico. Am. Midl. Nat. 54, 219–229.

Broadley, D. G. (1959). The herpetology of Southern Rhodesia, Part 1. Snakes. Bull. Mus. Comp. Zool. 120, 1–100.

Broadley, D. G. (1963). Two rare fossorial reptiles in southeastern Rhodesia—predator and prey. J. Herpetol. Assoc. Rhodesia 20, 7–8.

Broadley, D. G. (1974). Predation by birds on reptiles and amphibians in south-eastern Africa. Honeyguide 78, 11–19.

Broadley, D. G. (1983). *FitzSimons' Snakes of Southern Africa*. Delta Books, Johannesburg.

Broadley, D. G. and Cock, E. V. (1975). *Snakes of Rhodesia*. Longman Rhodesia, Salisbury.

Broadley, D. G. and Gans, C. (1978a). Southern forms of *Chirindia* (Amphisbaenia, Reptilia). Ann. Carnegie Mus. 47, 29–51.

Broadley, D. G. and Gans, C. (1978b). Distribution, variation, and systematic status of *Zygaspis violacea* (Peters) (Amphisbaenia: Reptilia) endemic to southeastern Africa. Ann. Carnegie Mus. 47, 319–334.

Broadley, D. G. and Stevens, R. A. (1971). A review of *Chamaetorntus aulicus* Gunther, with the description of a new subspecies from Malawi (Serpentes: Colubridae). Arnoldia 5 (11), 1–11.

Bröer, W. and Engelhardt, M. (1981). Haltung und Zucht einer selten importierten Schlange: *Elaphe helena* (Daudin 1803) (Reptilia: Serpentes: Colubridae). Salamandra 17, 63–70.

Brongersma, L. D. (1957). Notes upon the trachea, the lungs, and the pulmonary artery of snakes. I–II. Proc. Kon. Ned. Akad. Wetensch. 60, 299–313.

Brown, D. E. (1983). On the status of the jaguar in the Southwest. Southwest Nat. 28, 459–460.

Brown, E. E. (1979). Some snake food records from the Carolinas. Brimleyana 1, 113–124.

Brown, L. (1971). *African Birds of Prey*. Houghton-Mifflin Co., Boston.

Brown, W. S. (1974). Ecology of the aquatic box turtle, *Terrapene coahuila* (Chelonia, Emydidae) in northern Mexico. Bull. Florida State Mus. 19, 1–67.

Brunner, A. (1968). Über die Black Forest Cobra, *Pseudohaje goldii*. Salamandra 4, 56–59.

Brunson, K. (1986). Some unusual injuries to snakes. Kansas Herpetol. Soc. Newsletter 65, 13–14.

Bryant, H. C. (1916). Habits and food of the roadrunner in California. Univ. Cal. Publ. Zool. 17, 21–58.

Buden, D. W. (1975). Prey remains of barn owls in the southern Bahama Islands. Wilson Bull. 86, 336–343.

Burghardt, G. M. (1970). Chemical perception in reptiles. In *Communication by Chemical Signals*. (J. W. Johnston, Jr., D. G. Mouton, and A. Turk, eds.). Appleton-Century-Crofts, New York, pp. 241–308.

Burghardt, G. M. (1977a). Learning processes in reptiles. In *Biology of the Reptilia*, Vol. 7. *Ecology and Behavior*. (C. Gans and D. W. Tinkle, eds.). Academic Press, New York, pp. 555–681.

Burghardt, G. M. (1977b). Ontogeny of communication. In *How Animals Communicate*. (T. A. Sebeok, ed.). Indiana Univ. Press, Bloomington, pp. 71–97.

Burghardt, G. M. (1978). Behavioral ontogeny in reptiles: Whence, whither, and why? In *The Development of Behavior: Comparative and Evolutionary Aspects*. (G. M. Burghardt and M. Bekoff, eds.). Garland STPM Press, New York, pp. 149–174.

Burghardt, G. M., Greene, H. W. and Rand, A. S. (1977). Social behavior, in hatchling green iguanas: Life at a reptile rookery. Science 195, 689–691.

Burkett, R. D. (1966). Natural history of the cottonmouth moccasin, *Agkistrodon piscivorus* (Reptilia). Univ. Kansas Publ. Mus. Natl. Hist. 17, 435–491.

Burkholder, G. L. and Tanner, W. W. (1974). Life history and ecology of the Great Basin sagebrush swift, *Sceloporus graciosus graciosus* Baird and Girard, 1852. Brigham Young Univ. Sci. Bull. 19, 1–44.

Burleson, G. L. (1942). The source of blood ejected from the eye of horned toads. Copeia 1942, 246–248.

Burrage, B. R. (1973). Comparative ecology and behavior of *Chamaeleo pumilis pumilis* (Gmelin) and *C. namaquensis* A. Smith (Sauria: Chamaeleonidae). Ann. S. Afr. Mus. 61, 1–158.

Burt, C. E. (1949). Baby garter snake victim of garden spider. Herpetologica 5, 127.

REFERENCES

Burt, C. E. and Hoyle, W. L. (1934). Additional reports of the reptiles of the prairie region of the United States. Trans. Kansas Acad. Sci. 37, 193–216.
Burtt, E. H., Jr. (ed.) (1979). *The Behavioral Significance of Color*. Garland STPM Press, New York.
Bury, R. B. (1972). Small mammals and other prey in the diet of the Pacific giant salamander (*Dicamptodon ensatus*). Am. Midl. Nat. 87, 524–526.
Bury, R. B. (1979). Review of the ecology and conservation of the bog turtle, *Clemmys muhlenbergii*. U.S. Department of the Interior Fish and Wildlife Service Special Scientific Report—Wildlife No. 219, Washington, D.C.
Busack, S. D. (1978). Diurnal surface activity in the amphisbaenian, *Blanus cinereus* (Vandelli) 1797 (Reptilia, Lacertilia, Amphisbaenidae). J. Herpetol. 12, 428.
Bustard, H. R. (1955). Observations on the birth of two species of lizard in the vivarium. Br. J. Herpetol. 2, 6–9.
Bustard, H. R. (1964). Defensive behavior shown by Australian geckos, genus *Diplodactylus*. Herpetologica 20, 198–200.
Bustard, H. R. (1965). Observations on Australian geckos. Herpetologica 21, 294–302.
Bustard, H. R. (1967). Defensive display behavior of the Australian gecko *Nephrurus asper*. Herpetologica 23, 126–129.
Bustard, H. R. (1968a). Rapid learning in wild crocodiles (*Crocodylus porosus*). Herpetologica 24, 173–175.
Bustard, H. R. (1968b). *Pygopus nigriceps* (Fischer): A lizard mimicking a venomous snake. Br. J. Herpetol. 4, 22–24.
Bustard, H. R. (1968c). The reptiles of Merridindi State Forest, Pilliga West, northern New South Wales, Australia. Herpetologica 24, 131–140.
Bustard, H. R. (1969). Defensive behavior and locomotion of the Pacific boa, *Candoia aspera*, with a brief review of head concealment in snakes. Herpetologica 25, 164–170.
Bustard, H. R. (1979). Defensive mechanisms and predation in gekkonid lizards. Br. J. Herpetol. 6, 9–11.
Butler, W. H. (1970). A record of an invertebrate preying on a vertebrate. W. Austr. Nat. 11, 146.
Buxton, C. D. and Branch, W. R. (1983). Octopus predation on the hawksbill turtle, *Eretmochelys imbricata* (Cryptodira: Cheloniidae). J. Assoc. Africa 29, 15–16.
Buys, P. J. and Buys, P. J. C. (1983). *Slange van Suidwes-Afrika*. Gamsberg Uitgewers, Windhoek.
Cadle, J. E. (1982). Problems and approaches in the interpretation of the evolutionary history of venomous snakes. Mem. Inst. Butantan 46, 255–274.
Calder, W. A., III. (1984). *Size, Function, and Life History*. Harvard Univ. Press, Cambridge, MA.
Caldwell, G. S. and Rubinoff, R. W. (1983). Avoidance of venomous sea snakes by naive herons and egrets. Auk 100, 195–198.
Camin, J. H. and Ehrlich, P. R. (1958). Natural selection in water snakes (*Natrix sipedon* L.) on islands in Lake Erie. Evolution 12, 504–511.
Camp, C. C. (1916). Notes on the local distribution and habits of the amphibians and reptiles of southeastern California in the vicinity of the Turtle Mountains. Univ. Cal. Publ. Zool. 12, 503–544.
Campbell, B. (1934). Report on a collection of reptiles and amphibians made in Arizona during the summer of 1933. Occ. Pap. Mus. Zool. Univ. Michigan 289, 1–10.
Campbell, H. W. (1973). Ecological observations on *Anolis lionotus* and *Anolis poecilopus* (Reptilia, Sauria) in Panama. Am. Mus. Novitates 2516, 1–29.

Campbell, H. W. and Evans, W. E. (1967). Sound production in two species of tortoises. Herpetologica 23, 204–209.

Campbell, H. W. and Evans, W. E. (1972). Observations on the vocal behavior of chelonians. Herpetologica 28, 277–280.

Campbell, J. A. and Armstrong, B. L. (1979). Geographic variation in the Mexican pygmy rattlesnake, *Sistrurus ravus*, with the description of a new species. Herpetologica 35, 304–317.

Campbell, J. A. and Quinn, H. R. (1975). Reproduction in a pair of Asiatic cobras, *Naja naja* (Serpentes, Elapidae). J. Herpetol. 9, 229–233.

Campden-Main, S. M. (1970). *A Field Guide to the Snakes of South Vietnam.* U.S. Natl. Mus., Washington, D.C.

Camper, J. D. (1986). Life history notes: *Ambystoma trigrinum tigrinum* (feeding). Herpetol. Rev. 17, 19.

Cansdale, G. S. (1961). *West African Snakes.* Longmans, London.

Carey, W. M. (1975). The rock iguana, *Cyclura pinguis*, on Anegada, British Virgin Islands, with notes on *Cyclura ricordi* and *Cyclura cornuta* on Hispaniola. Bull. Florida St. Mus. Biol. Sci. 19, 189–233.

Carothers, J. H. (1981). Dominance and competition in an herbivorous lizard. Behav. Ecol. Sociobiol. 8, 261–266.

Carothers, J. H. (1986). An experimental confirmation of morphological adaptation: Toe fringes in the sand-dwelling lizard *Uma scoparia*. Evolution 40, 871–874.

Carothers, J. H. (1987). Aspects of the ecology of lizards of the genus *Liolaemus* in the central Chilean cordillera. Doctoral diss., Univ. California, Berkeley.

Carpenter, C. C. (1966). The marine iguana of the Galapagos Islands, its behavior and ecology. Proc. Cal. Acad. Sci. (4th Ser.) 34, 329–376.

Carpenter, C. C. and Ferguson, G. W. (1977). Variation and evolution of stereotyped behavior in reptiles. In *Biology of the Reptilia, Vol. 7. Ecology and Behavior A.* (C. Gans and D. W. Tinkle, eds.). Academic Press, New York, pp. 335–554.

Carpenter, C. C. and Gillingham, J. C. (1975). Postural responses to kingsnakes by crotaline snakes. Herpetologica 31, 293–302.

Carpenter, C. C. and Murphy, J. B. (1978). Tongue display by the common bluetongue (*Tiliqua scincoides*) Reptilia, Lacertilia, Scincidae). J. Herpetol. 12, 428–429.

Carr, A. (1982). Armadillo dilemma. Animal Kingdom 85(5), 40–43.

Carr, A. F. (1934). Notes on the habits of the short-tailed snake, *Stilosoma extenuatum* Brown. Copeia 1934, 138–139.

Carr, A. F. (1940). A contribution to the herpetology of Florida. Univ. Florida Publ., Biol. Sci. Ser. 3, 1–118.

Carr, A. F. (1952). *Handbook of Turtles.* Comstock Publ. Assoc., Ithaca, New York.

Case, T. J. (1982). Ecology and evolution of the insular gigantic chuckawallas, *Sauromalus hispidus* and *Sauromalus varius*. In *Iguanas of the World: Their Behavior, Ecology, and Conservation.* (G. M. Burghardt and A. S. Rand, eds.). Noyes Publ., Park Ridge, NJ, pp. 184–212.

Chapman, F. (1938). *Life in an Air Castle.* D. Appleton-Century Co., New York.

Cheke, A. S. (1984). Lizards of the Seychelles. In *Biogeography and Ecology of the Seychelles Islands.* (D. R. Stoddart, ed.). Dr. W. Junk Publ., The Hague, Boston, Lancaster, pp. 332–360.

Chenowith, W. L. (1948). Birth and behavior of young copperheads. Herpetologica 4, 162.

Chiszar, D. (1978). Lateral displays in the lower vertebrates: Forms, functions, and origins. In *Contrasts in Behavior.* (E. S. Reese and F. J. Lighter, eds.). Wiley, New York, pp. 105–135.

REFERENCES

Christian, K. A. and Tracy, C. R. (1981). The effect of the thermal environment on the ability of hatchling Galapagos land iguanas to avoid predation during dispersal. Oecologica 49, 218–223.
Cissé, M. (1972). L'alimentation des varanides au Sénégal. Bull. I. F. A. N. Ser. A, 34, 503–515.
Clark, R. F. (1949). Snakes of the hill parishes of Louisiana. J. Tennessee Acad. Sci. 24, 244–261.
Clark, R. J. and Clark, E. D. (1973). Report on a collection of amphibians and reptiles from Turkey. Occ. Pap. Cal. Acad. Sci. 104, 1–62.
Clark, R. J., Clark, E. and Anderson, S. C. (1966). Report on two small collections of reptiles from Iran. Occ. Pap. Cal. Acad. Sci. 55, 1–9.
Clark, R. J., Clark, E. D., Anderson, S. C. and Leviton, A. E. (1969). Report on a collection of amphibians and reptiles from Afghanistan. Proc. Cal. Acad. Sci. 36, 279–316.
Clarkson, R. W. and de Vos, J. C., Jr. (1986). The bullfrog, *Rana catesbeiana* Shaw, in the Lower Colorado River, Arizona–California. J. Herpetol. 20, 42–49.
Cochran, D. M. (1930). The herpetological collections made by Dr. Hugh M. Smith in Siam from 1923–1929. Proc. U. S. Natl. Mus. 77, 1–39.
Colbert, E. H. (1967). Adaptations for gliding in the lizard *Draco*. Am. Mus. Novitates 2283, 1–20.
Colbert, E. H. (1970). The Triassic gliding reptile *Icarosaurus*. Bull. Am. Mus. Nat. Hist. 143, 85–142.
Colwell, R. K. (1984). What's new? Community ecology discovers biology. In *A New Ecology: Novel Approaches to Interactive Systems*. (P. W. Price, C. N. Slobodchikoss, and W. S. Gaud, eds.). Wiley, New York, pp. 387–396.
Compton, L. V. (1933). A garter snake attempting to eat an alligator lizard. Copeia 1933, 225.
Conant, R. (1938a). A note on eggs and young of *Leioheterodon madagascariensis* (Duméril & Bibron). Zoologica 23, 389–392.
Conant, R. (1938b). The reptiles of Ohio. Am. Midl. Nat. 20, 1–200.
Conant, R. (1942a). Notes on the young of three recently described snakes, with comments upon their relationships. Bull. Chicago Acad. Sci. 6, 193–200.
Conant, R. (1942b). Amphibians and reptiles from Dutch Mountain (Pennsylvania) and vicinity. Am. Midl. Nat. 27, 154–170.
Cooper, W. E. and Vitt, L. J. (1985). Blue tails and autotomy: Enhancement of predator avoidance in juvenile skinks. Z. Tierpsychol. 70, 265–276.
Cope, E. D. (1871). The method of creation of organic forms. Proc. Am. Phil. Soc. 12, 89–123.
Coppinger, R. P. (1970). The effect of experience and novelty on avian feeding behavior with reference to the evolution of warning coloration in butterflies. II. Reactions of naive birds to novel insects. Am. Nat. 104, 323–335.
Corkill, N. L. (1932). The snakes of Iraq. J. Bombay Nat. Hist. Soc. 35, 552–572.
Cornelius, S. E. (1986). *The Sea Turtles of Santa Rosa National Park*. Fund. Parq. Nac. Costa Rica, San Jose.
Cott, H. B. (1961). Scientific results of an inquiry into the ecology and economic status of the Nile crocodile (*Crocodylus niloticus*) in Uganda and Northern Rhodesia. Trans. Zool. Soc. London 29, 211–357.
Cott, H. G. (1940). *Adaptive Coloration in Animals*. Methuen and Co., London.
Cowles, R. B. (1930). The life history of *Varanus niloticus* (Linnaeus) as observed in Natal South Africa. J. Ent. Zool. 22, 3–31.

Cowles, R. B. (1938). Unusual defense posture assumed by a rattlesnake. Copeia 1938, 13–16.
Cowles, R. B. (1977). *Desert Journal*. Univ. California Press, Berkeley.
Crother, B. (1986). Life history notes: *Alsophis cantherigerus* (diet). Herpetol. Rev. 17, 47.
Crowley, S. R. and Pietruszka, R. D. (1983). Aggressiveness and vocalization in the leopard lizards (*Gambelia wislizenii*): The influence of temperature. An. Behav. 31, 1055–1060.
Cruz, A. (1972). Food and feeding behavior of the Jamaican crow, *Corvus jamaicensis*. Auk 89, 445–446.
Cruz, A. (1973). Food and foraging ecology of the Jamaican becard. Auk 90, 905–906.
Cruz, A. (1975). Ecology and behavior of the Jamaican lizard cuckoo. Stud. Fauna Curacao Carib. Is. 46, 109–111.
Cruz, A. (1976). Food and foraging ecology of the American kestrel in Jamaica. Condor 78, 409–412.
Cunningham, J. D. (1956). Food habits of the San Diego alligator lizard. Herpetologica 12, 225–230.
Cunningham, J. D. (1959). Reproduction and food of some California snakes. Herpetologica 15, 17–19.
Curio, E. (1976). *The Ethology of Predation*. Springer-Verlag, New York.
Curran, E. J. (1932). Tuchtoo versus dhaman. J. Bombay Hist. Soc. 35, 901–902.
Cutter, W. L. (1959). An instance of blood-squirting by *Phrynosoma solare*. Copeia 1959, 176.
Daanje, A. (1950). On locomotor movements in birds and the intention movements derived from them. Behaviour 3, 49–98.
Darevsky, I. S. (1966). Ecology of rock viper (*Viper xanthina raddei* Boettger) in the natural surroundings of Armenia. Mem. Inst. Butantan Simp. Internac. 33, 81–83.
Darevsky, I. S. (1967). *Rock Lizards of the Caucasus*. Smithsonian Inst., Washington, D. C.
Darlington, P. J. (1927). Autohemorrhage in *Tropidophis semicinctus*. Bull. Antivenom Inst. Am. 1, 59.
Darwin, C. (1859). *On the Origin of Species by Means of Natural Selection*. J. Murray, London.
Davis, D. D. (1948). Flash display of aposematic colors in *Farancia* and other snakes. Copeia 1948, 208–211.
Davis, D. D. (1953). Behavior of the lizard *Corythophanes cristatus*. Fieldiana: Zool. 35, 1–8.
Dawbin, W. H. (1962). The tuatara in its natural habitat. Endeavour 21(81), 16–24.
Demeter, A. (1982). Prey of the spotted eagle-owl *Bubo africanus* in the Awash National Park, Ethiopia. Bonn. Zool. Beitr. 33, 283–292.
de Silva, A. (1980). *Cercaspis carinatus*. A relict snake of Sri Lanka. Loris 16, 105–107.
de Silva, A. (1983). *Haplocercus ceylonensis* Gunther, a relict snake of Sri Lanka. Loris 16, 105–107.
Dessauer, H. D., Cadle, J. E. and Lawson, R. (1987). Patterns of snake evolution suggested by their proteins. Fieldiana: Zool., n.s. (34), 1–34.
DeWitte, G. F. (1962). Genera des serpents du Congo et du Ruanda-Urundi. Ann. Mus. Roy. Afr. Cen., Ser. B, 104, 1–203.
Dial, B. E. (1965). Distributional notes on reptiles and amphibians from northeastern Texas. Southwestern Nat. 10, 143–144.
Dial, B. E. (1978). Aspects of the behavioral ecology of two Chihuahuan desert geckos (Reptilia, Lacertilia, Gekkonidae). J. Herpetol. 12, 209–216.
Dial, B. E. (1986). Tail display in two species of iguanid lizards: A test of the "predator signal" hypothesis. Am. Nat. 127, 103–111.
Diller, L. V. and Wallace, R. L. (1986). Aspects of the life history and ecology of the desert

REFERENCES

night snake, *Hypsiglena torquata deserticola:* Colubridae, in southwestern Idaho. Southwestern Nat. 31, 55–64.
Dillon, L. S. and Baldauf, R. J. (1945). Unusual behavior of *Cnemidophorus sexlineatus.* Copeia 1945, 174.
Dingle, H. (1975). (Review of) *Defence in Animals,* by M. Edmunds. Science 188, 1105–1106.
Dodd, C. K., Jr. (1978). A note on the defensive posturing of turtles from Belize, Central America. Herpetol. Rev. 9, 11–12.
Dodd, C. K., Jr. and Brodie, E. D., Jr. (1975). Notes on the defensive behavior of the snapping turtle, *Chelydra serpentina.* Herpetologica 31, 286–288.
Donoso-Barros, R. (1969). Consideraciones sobre un reflejo postural de *Tachymenis peruviana chilensis.* Bol. Soc. Biol. Concepcion 41, 157–160.
Douglas, A. M. (1967). The natural history of the ghost bat, *Macroderma gigas* (Microchiroptera, Megadermatidae), in Western Australia. W. Austr. Nat. 10, 125–137.
Drummond, H. (1981). The nature and description of behavior patterns. In *Perspectives in Ethology.* (P. G. Bateson and P. H. Klopfer, eds.). Plenum Press, New York, Volume 4, 1–33.
Drummond, H. (1985). Towards a standard ethogram: Do ethologists really want one? Z. Tierpsychol. 68, 338–339.
Drummond, H. and Wolfe, G. W. (1981). An observation of a diving beetle larva (Insecta: Coleoptera: Dytiscidae) attacking and killing a garter snake, *Thamnophis elegans* (Reptilia: Serpentes: Colubridae). Coleopterists Bull. 35, 121–124.
Dryden, G. L. (1965). The food and feeding habits of *Varanus indicus* on Guam. Micronesica 2, 73–76.
Duellman, W. E. (1978). The biology of an equatorial herpetofauna in Amazonian Ecuador. Misc. Publ. Mus. Univ. Kansas Mus. Nat. Hist. 65, 1–352.
Duellman, W. E. and Duellman, A. S. (1959). Variation, distribution, and ecology of the iguanid lizard *Enyaliosaurus clarki* of Michoacan, Mexico. Occ. Pap. Mus. Zool. Univ. Michigan 598, 1–10.
Duellman, W. E. and Trueb, L. (1985). *Biology of Amphibians.* McGraw-Hill Book Co., New York.
Dundee, H. A. (1950). Additional records of *Hypsiglena* from Oklahoma, with notes on the behavior and the eggs. Herpetologica 6, 28–30.
Dunn, E. R. (1927). Results of the Douglas Burden expedition to the island of Komodo. II. Snakes from the East Indies. Am. Mus. Novitates 287, 1–7.
Dunn, E. R. (1937). New or unnamed snakes from Costa Rica. Copeia 1937, 213–215.
Dunson, W. A. (1979). Occurrence of partially striped forms of the mangrove snake *Nerodia fasciata compressicauda* Kennicott and comments on the status of *N. f. taeniata* Cope. Florida Sci. 42, 102–112.
Durham, F. E. (1956). Amphibians of the North Rim, Grand Canyon, Arizona. Herpetologica 12, 220–224.
Duvall, D., King, M. B. and Gutzwiller, K. J. (1985). Behavioral ecology and ethology of the prairie rattlesnake. Natl. Geogr. Res. 1, 80–111.
Easterla, D. A. (1975). Giant desert centipede preys upon snake. Southwestern Nat. 20, 411.
Echternacht, A. C. (1973). The color pattern of *Sonora michoacanensis* (Duges) (Serpentes, Colubridae) and its bearing on the origin of the species. Bull. Mus. Comp. Zool. 410, 1–18.
Edgren, R. A. (1955). The natural history of the hog-nosed snakes, genus *Heterodon:* A review. Herpetologica 11, 105–117.

Edgren, R. A. and Edgren, M. K. (1955). Experiments on bluffing and death-feigning in the hognose snake *Heterodon platyrhinos*. Copeia 1955, 2–4.
Edmunds, M. (1974). *Defense in Animals*. Longman Group, Ltd., Essex.
Eisenberg, J. F. (1983). *The Mammalian Radiations: an Analysis of Trends in Evolution, Adaptation, and Behavior*. Univ. Chicago Press, Chicago.
Eisner, T., Conner, W. E., Hicks, K., Dodge, K. R., Rosenberg, H. I., Jones, T. H., Cohen, M. and Meinwald, J. (1977). Stink of stinkpot turtle identified: W-phenylalkanoic acids. Science 196, 1347–1349.
Eisner, T., Jones, T. H. and Meinwald, J. (1978). Chemical composition of the odorous secretion of the Australian turtle, *Chelodina longicollis*. Copeia 1978, 714–715.
Elzen, P. van den. (1980). Zur Abwehrreaktion von *Blanus strauchi aporus* Werner, 1898 (Reptilia: Sauria: Amphisbaenidae). Salamandra 16, 52–56.
Emmons, L. H. and Gentry, A. H. (1983). Tropical forest structure and the distribution of gliding and prehensile-tailed vertebrates. Am. Nat. 121, 513–524.
Endler, J. A. (1977). *Geographic Variation, Speciation, and Clines*. Princeton Univ. Press, Princeton, NJ.
Endler, J. A. (1978). A predator's view of animal color patterns. In *Evolutionary Biology*. (M. K. Hecht, W. C. Steere and B. Wallace, eds.). Plenum, New York, Volume 11, 319–364.
Endler, J. A. (1983). Natural selection on color patterns in poeciliid fishes. Envir. Biol. Fishes 9, 173–190.
Endler, J. A. (1986a). Defense against predators. In *Predator–Prey Relationships: Perspectives and Approaches From the Study of Lower Vertebrates*. (M.E. Feder and G. V. Lauder, eds.). Univ. Chicago Press, Chicago, pp. 109–134.
Endler, J. A. (1986b). *Natural Selection in the Wild*. Princeton Univ. Press, Princeton.
Engen, S., Jarvi, T. and Wiklund, C. (1986). The evolution of aposematic coloration by individual selection: A life-span survival model. Oikos 46, 397–403.
Ernst, C. H. (1986). Ecology of the turtle, *Sternotherus odoratus*, in southeastern Pennsylvania. J. Herpetol. 20, 341–352.
Ernst, C. H. and Barbour, R. W. (1972). *The Turtles of the United States*. Univ. Kentucky Press, Lexington.
Estes, R. (1983). The fossil record and early distribution of lizards. In *Advances in Herpetology and Evolutionary Biology: Essays in Honor of Ernest E. Williams*. (A. G. J. Rhodin and K. Miyata, eds.). Mus. Comp. Zool., Cambridge, MA, pp. 365–398.
Estes, R., de Queiroz, K. and Gauthier, J. (1988). Phylogenetic relationships within squamate reptiles. In *Phylogenetic Relationships of the Lizard Families*. (R. Estes and G. K. Pregill, eds.). Stanford University Press, Palo Alto, CA, in press.
Ewer, R. F. (1968). *Ethology of Mammals*. Logos Press, Ltd., London.
Fan, T. H. (1931). Preliminary report of the reptiles from Yaoshan, Kwangsi, China. Bull. Dept. Biol. Coll. Sci. Sun Yatsen Univ., 11, 1–154.
Feder, M. E. and Arnold, S. J. (1982). Anaerobic metabolism and behavior during predatory encounters between snakes (*Thamnophis elegans*) and salamanders (*Plethodon jordani*). Oecologia 53, 93–97.
Ferguson, G. W. and Fox, S. F. (1984). Annual variation of survival advantage of large juvenile side-blotched lizards, *Uta stansburiana*: Its causes and evolutionary significance. Evolution 38, 342–349.
Ficken, R. W., Matthiae, P. E. and Horwich, R. (1971). Eye marks in vertebrates: Aids to vision. Science 173, 936–939.

REFERENCES

Fink, W. S. (1982). The conceptual relationship between ontogeny and phylogeny. Paleobiology 8, 254-264.
Fitch, H. S. (1935). Natural history of the alligator lizards. Trans. Acad. Sci. St. Louis 29, 1-38.
Fitch, H. S. (1949). Study of snake populations in central California. Am. Midl. Natl. 41, 1-150.
Fitch, H. S. (1954). Life history and ecology of the five-lined skink, *Eumeces fasciatus*. Univ. Kansas Publ. Mus. Nat. Hist. 8, 1-156.
Fitch, H. S. (1955). Habits and adaptations of the Great Plains skink (*Eumeces obsoletus*). Ecol. Monogr. 25, 59-83.
Fitch, H. S. (1956). An ecological study of the collard lizard (*Crotaphytus collaris*). Univ. Kansas Publ. Mus. Nat. Hist. 8, 213-274.
Fitch, H. S. (1958). Natural history of the six-lined racerunner (*Cnemidophorus sexlineatus*). Univ. Kansas Publ. Mus. Nat. Hist. 11, 11-62.
Fitch, H. S. (1960). Autecology of the copperhead. Univ. Kansas Publ. Mus. Nat. Hist. 13, 85-288.
Fitch, H. S. (1963). Natural history of the racer *Coluber constrictor*. Univ. Kansas Publ. Mus. Nat. Hist. 15, 351-468.
Fitch, H. S. (1965). An ecological study of the garter snake, *Thamnophis sirtalis*. Univ. Kansas Publ. Mus. Nat. Hist. 15, 493-564.
Fitch, H. S. (1975). A demographic study of the ringneck snake (*Diadophis punctatus*) in Kansas. Misc. Publ. Univ. Kansas Mus. Nat. Hist. 62, 1-53.
Fitzpatrick, J. W. and Woolfenden, G. E. (1978). Red-tailed hawk predation on juvenile gopher tortoise. Florida Field Nat. 6, 49.
FitzSimons, V. F. M. (1962). *The Snakes of Southern Africa*. Macdonald and Co., London.
Fleay, D. (1961). Beware—This small snake is dangerous. Vict. Nat. 77, 284-287.
Fleishman, L. J. (1985). Cryptic movement in the vine snake *Oxybelis aeneus*. Copeia 1985, 242-245.
Flower, S. S. (1899). Notes on a second collection of reptiles made in the Malay Peninsula and Siam, from November 1896 to September 1898, with a list of species recorded from those countries. Proc. Zool. Soc. London 1899, 600-697.
Fox, S. F. (1978). Natural selection on behavioral phenotypes of the lizard *Uta stansburiana*. Ecology 59, 834-847.
Frank, W. (1969). *Cylindrophis rufus*—eine nur selten gehaltene ostasiatische Schlange aus der Überfamilie Booidea. Salamandra 5, 105-112.
Frankenberg, E. (1975). Distress calls of gekkonid lizards from Israel and Sinai. Israel J. Zool. 24, 43-53.
Frazier, J. (1984). Misidentification of sea turtles in the East Pacific: *Caretta caretta* and *Lepidochelys olivacea*. J. Herpetol. 19, 1-11.
Funk, R. S. (1964). On the food of *Crotalus m. molosus*. Herpetologica 20, 134.
Gaffney, E. S. (1984). Historical analysis of theories of chelonian relationships. Syst. Zool. 33, 283-301.
Gaffney, E. S. (1985). The cervical and caudal vertebrae of the cryptodiran turtle, *Meiolania platyceps*, from the Pleistocene of Lord Howe Island, Australia. Am. Mus. Novitates 2805, 1-29.
Gallardo, J. M. (1972). Observaciones biologicas sobre una falsa yarara, *Tomodon ocellatus* Dumeril, Bibron et Dumeril. Neotropica 18, 57-63.
Gans, C. (1961). Mimicry in procyptically colored snakes of the genus *Dasypeltis*. Evolution 15, 72-91.

Gans, C. (1962). Notes on amphisbaenids (Amphisbaenia: Reptilia). 5. A redefinition and a bibliography of *Amphisbaena alba* Linné. Am. Mus. Novitates 2105, 1–31.
Gans, C. (1965). Empathic learning and the mimicry of African snakes. Evolution 18, 705.
Gans, C. (1966). Some limitations of and approaches to problems in functional anatomy. Folia Biotheor. 6, 41–50.
Gans, C. (1969). Amphisbaenians—reptiles specialized for a burrowing existence. Endeavour 28, 146–151.
Gans, C. (1970). Beobachtungen an afrikanischen Eierschlangen. Nat. Mus. 100, 460–471.
Gans, C. (1973). Uropeltid snakes—survivors in a changing world. Endeavour 32, 60–65.
Gans, C. (1974). Biomechanics: An Approach to Vertebrate Biology. J. P. Lippincott, Philadelphia.
Gans, C. (1975). Tetrapod limblessness: Evolution and functional corollaries. Am. Zool. 15, 455–467.
Gans, C. (1976). Aspects of the biology of uropeltid snakes. In *Morphology and Biology of Reptiles*. (A. d'A. Bellairs and C. B. Cox, eds.). Linnean Soc. Symp. Ser., 3, pp. 191–204.
Gans, C. (1978). All animals are interesting! Am. Zool. 18, 3–9.
Gans, C. (1983a). Is *Sphenodon punctatus* a maladapted relict? In *Advances in Herpetology and Evolutionary Biology: Essays in Honor of Ernest E. Williams*. (A. G. J. Rhodin and K. Miyata, eds.). Mus. Comp. Zool., Cambridge, MA, pp. 613–620.
Gans, C. (1983b). On the fallacy of perfection. In *Perspectives of Modern Auditory Research: Papers in Honor of E. G. Wever*. (R. Fay and G. Gourevitch, eds.). Amphora Press, Groton, CT, pp. 101–114.
Gans, C. (1986). Functional morphology of predator–prey relationships. In *Predator–Prey Relationships: Perspectives and Approaches From the Study of Lower Vertebrates*. (M. E. Feder and G. V. Lauder, eds.). Univ. Chicago Press, Chicago, pp. 6–23.
Gans, C. and Baic, D. (1974). Convergent surface structures in the sound producing scales of some snakes (Reptilia: Serpentes). In *Recherches Biologiques Contemporaines, Ouvrage Dedié à Manfred Gabe (1916–1973)*. (L. Arvey, ed.). Vagner, Nancy, pp. 265–272.
Gans, C. and Baic, D. (1977). Regional specialization of reptilian scale surfaces: Relation of texture and biologic role. Science 195, 1348–1350.
Gans, C., Gillingham, J. C. and Clark, D. L. (1984). Courtship, mating and male combat in tuatara, *Sphenodon punctatus*. J. Herpetol. 18, 194–197.
Gans, C. and Latifi, M. (1973). Another case of presumptive mimicry in snakes. Copeia 1973, 801–802.
Gans, C., Laurent, R. F. and Pandit, H. (1965). Notes on a herpetological collection from the Somali Republic. Ann. Zool. R. G. Mus. Afr. Cen. 134, 1–93.
Gans, C. and Maderson, P. F. A. (1973). Sound producing mechanisms in Recent reptiles: Review and comment. Am. Zool. 13, 1195–1203.
Gans, C. and Mendelssohn, H. (1972). Sidewinding and jumping progression of vipers. In *Proc. 2nd Int. Symp., Toxins of Animal and Plant Origin*. (A. de Vries and E. Kochva, eds.). Gordon and Breach Sci. Publ., London, pp. 17–38.
Gans, C. and Richmond, N. D. (1957). Warning behavior in snakes of the genus *Dasypeltis*. Copeia 1957, 269–274.
Garland, T., Jr. (1985). Ontogenetic and individual variation in size, shape and speed in the Australian agamid lizard *Amphibolurus nuchalis*. J. Zool. (London) 207, 425–439.
Garland, T., Jr. (1987). Locomotory performance and activity metabolism in *Cnemidophorus tigris* in relation to natural behaviors. In *The Biology of Whiptail Lizards (Genus*

REFERENCES

Cnemidophorus). (J.W. Wright, ed.). Spec. Publ. Nat. Hist. Mus. Los Angeles Co., in press.
Garman, S. (1889). On the evolution of the rattlesnake. Proc. Boston Soc. Nat. Hist. 24, 170–182.
Garrick, L. D. and Lang, J. W. (1977). Social signals and behavior of adult alligators and crocodiles. Am. Zool. 17, 225–239.
Gates, G. O. (1957). A study of the herpetofauna in the vicinity of Wickenburg, Maricopa County, Arizona. Trans. Kansas Acad. Sci. 60, 403–418.
Gauthier, J., Estes, R. and de Queiroz, K. (in press). A phylogenetic analysis of Lepidosauromorpha. In *Phylogenetic Relationships of the Lizard Families*. (R. Estes and G. K. Pregill, eds.). Stanford Univ. Press, Palo Alto, CA.
Gaymer, R. (1968). The Indian Ocean giant tortoise *Testudo gigantica* on Aldabra. J. Zool. (London) 154, 341–363.
Gehlbach, F. R. (1970). Death-feigning and erratic behavior in leptotyphlopid, colubrid, and elapid snakes. Herpetologica 26, 24–34.
Gehlbach, F. R. (1972). Coral snake mimicry reconsidered: The strategy of self-mimicry. Forma et Functio 5, 311–320.
Gharpurey, K. G. (1931). An unusually large Shaw's rat snake (*Zamenis fasciolatus*). J. Bombay Nat. Hist. Soc. 34, 1084.
Gibbons, J. R. H. and Lillywhite, H. B. (1981). Ecological segregation, color matching, and speciation in lizards of the *Amphibolurus decresii* species complex (Lacertilia: Agamidae). Ecology 62, 1573–1584.
Glass, B. P. (1946). A collection of reptiles from Hunan and Anhwei provinces, China. Copeia 1946, 249–252.
Gloyd, H. K. (1934). Studies on the breeding habits and young of the copperhead, *Agkistrodon mokasen* Beauvois. Pap. Michigan Acad. Sci. Art. Let. 19, 587–604.
Goddard, P. (1984). Morphology, growth, food habits and population characteristics of the smooth snake *Coronella austriaca* in southern Britain. J. Zool. (London) 204, 241–257.
Godley, J. S. (1982). Predation and defensive behavior of the striped swamp snake (*Regina alleni*). Fla. Field. Nat. 10, 31–36.
Golder, F. (1972). Beitrag zur Fortpflanzungsbiologie einiger Nattern (Colubridae). Salamandra 8, 1–20.
Golder, F. (1983). Beitrag zur Kenntnis der Fortpflanzung von *Oxybelis fulgidus* (Daudin, 1803) (Serpentes: Colubridae). Salamandra 19, 55–60.
Goldsmith, S. K. (1984). Aspects of the natural history of the rough green snake, *Opheodrys aestivus* (Colubridae). Southwestern Nat. 29, 445–452.
Gonzales, D. (1979). Bissverletzungen durch *Malpolon monspessulanus* (Reptilia: Serpentes: Colubridae). Salamandra 15, 266–268.
Goodwin, G. C. and Greenhall, A. M. (1961). A review of the bats of Trinidad and Tobago: Descriptions, rabies infection, and ecology. Bull. Am. Mus. Nat. Hist. 122, 187–302.
Gorman, G. C., Huey, R. B. and Williams, E. E. (1969). Cytotaxonomic studies on some unusual iguanid lizards assigned to the genera *Chamaeleolis, Polychrus, Polychroides,* and *Phenacosaurus*, with behavioral notes. Breviora 316, 1–17.
Gorzula, S. J. (1978). An ecological study of *Caiman crocodilus crocodilus* inhabiting savanna lagoons in the Venezuelan Guayana. Oecologia 35, 21–34.
Gorzula, S. J. (1985). Are caimans always in distress? Biotropica 17, 343–344.
Gosner, K. J. (1942). Lip curling of the red-bellied snake. Copeia 42, 181–183.
Goulding, M. (1980). *The Fishes and the Forest*. Univ. California Press, Berkeley.
Gove, D. (1979). The evolution of tongue-flicking in reptiles. Z. Tierpsychol. 41, 58–76.

Gove, D. and Burghardt, G. M. (1983). Context-correlated parameters of snake and lizard tongue-flicking. An. Behav. 31, 718–723.

Gracie, A. E. and Murphy, R. W. (1986). Life history notes: *Gambelia wislizenii* (food). Herpetol. Rev. 17, 47.

Graf, W., Jewett, S. G., Jr., and Gordon, K. L. (1939). Records of amphibians and reptiles from Oregon. Copeia 1939, 101–104.

Graham, T. E. (1984). Life history notes: *Pseudemys rubriventris* (predation). Herpetol. Rev. 15, 19–20.

Grant, C. (1946). Notes on *Tretanorhinus* of Cuba and the Isle of Pines. J. Agricul. Univ. Puerto Rico 30, 102–117.

Greegor, D. H., Jr. (1980). Diet of the little hairy armadillo, *Chaetophractus vellerosus*, of northwestern Argentina. J. Mamm. 61, 331–334.

Greenberg, N. (1977). An ethogram of the blue spiny lizard, *Sceloporus cyanogenys* (Reptilia, Lacertilia, Iguanidae). J. Herpetol. 11, 177–195.

Greene, H. W. (1973a). Defensive tail display by snakes and amphisbaenians. J. Herpetol. 7, 143–161.

Greene, H. W. (1973b). *The Food Habits and Feeding Behavior of New World Coral Snakes*. M. A. Thesis, Univ. Texas at Arlington.

Greene, H. W. (1975). Ecological observations on the red coffee snake, *Ninia sebae*, in southern Veracruz, Mexico. Am. Midl. Nat. 93, 478–484.

Greene, H. W. (1977). Lizards of the genus *Uracentron* (Iguanidae) in east-central Colombia. Herpetologica 33, 256–260.

Greene, H. W. (1979). Behavioral convergence in the defensive displays of snakes. Experientia 35, 747–748.

Greene, H. W. (1982). Dietary and phenotypic diversity in lizards: Why are some organisms specialized? In *Environmental Adaptation and Evolution: A Theoretical and Empirical Approach*. (D. Mossakowski and G. Roth, eds.). G. Fischer Verlag, Stuttgart, pp. 107–128.

Greene, H. W. (1983a). Dietary correlates of the origin and radiation of snakes. Am. Zool. 23, 431–441.

Greene, H. W. (1983b). *Boa constrictor* (Boa, Bequer, Boa Constrictor). In *Costa Rican Natural History*. (D. H. Janzen, ed.). Univ. Chicago Press, Chicago, pp. 380–382.

Greene, H. W. (1984). Feeding behavior and diet of the eastern coral snake, *Micrurus fulvius*. In *Vertebrate Ecology and Systematics—A Tribute to Henry S. Fitch*. (R. A. Seigel, L. E. Hunt, J. L. Knight, L. Malaret and N. Zischlag, eds.). Univ. Kansas Mus. Nat. Hist. Spec. Publ. 10, 147–162.

Greene, H. W. (1986a). Natural history and evolutionary biology. In *Predator–Prey Relationships: Perspectives and Approaches From the Study of Lower Vertebrates*. (M. E. Feder and G. V. Lauder, eds.). Univ. Chicago Press, Chicago, pp. 99–108.

Greene, H. W. (1986b). Diet and arboreality in the emerald monitor, *Varanus prasinus*, with comments on the study of adaptation. Fieldiana, Zool. (New Ser.) 31, 1–12.

Greene, H. W. (1987). Species richness in tropical predators. In *Diversity and Conservation of Tropical Rainforests*. (F. Alameda and C. M. Pringel, eds.). Mem. Cal. Acad. Sci., in press.

Greene, H. W. and Burghardt, G. M. (1978). Behavior and phylogeny: Constriction in ancient and modern snakes. Science 200, 74–77.

Greene, H. W., Burghardt, G. M., Dugan, B. A. and Rand, A. S. (1978). Predation and the defensive behavior of green iguanas (Reptilia, Lacertilia, Iguanidae). J. Herpetol. 12, 169–176.

REFERENCES

Greene, H. W. and Campbell, J. A. (1972). Notes on the use of caudal lures by arboreal green pit vipers. Herpetologica 28, 32–34.

Greene, H. W. and McDiarmid, R. W. (1981). Coral snake mimicry: Does it occur? Science 213, 1207–1212.

Greene, H. W. and Oliver, G. V., Jr. (1965). Notes on the natural history of the western massasauga. Herpetologica 21, 225–228.

Greene, H. W. and Pyburn, W. F. (1973). Comments on aposematism and mimicry among coral snakes. Biologist 55, 144–148.

Greer, A. E. (1985). The relationships of the lizard genera *Anelytropsis* and *Dibamus*. J. Herpetol. 19, 116–156.

Greer, A. E. (1986). Diagnosis of the *Lerista bipes* species-group (Lacertilia: Scincidae), with a description of a new species and an updated diagnosis of the genus. Rec. W. Austr. Mus. 13, 121–127.

Greer, A. E. and Parker, F. (1968). A new species of *Tribolonotus* (Lacertilia: Scincidae) from Bougainville and Buka, Solomon Islands, with comments on the biology of the genus. Breviora 291, 1–23.

Gregory, P. T., Gregory, L. A. and Macartney, J. M. (1983). Color-pattern variation in *Thamnophis melanogaster*. Copeia 1983, 530–534.

Griffiths, D. (1980). Foraging costs and relative prey size. Am. Nat. 116, 743–752.

Grinnell, J. and Grinnell, H. (1907). Reptiles of Los Angeles County, California. Bull. Throop Polytech. Inst. (Sci. Ser.) 35, 1–64.

Grinnell, J. and Storer, T. I. (1934). *Animal Life in the Yosemite*. Univ. California Press, Berkeley.

Groves, J. D. and Groves, F. (1978). Spider predation on amphibians and reptiles. Bull. Maryland Herpetol. Soc. 14, 44–46.

Gudger, E. W. (1925). Spiders as fisherman and hunters. Nat. Hist. 25, 261–275.

Gudynas, E. (1981). Some notes from Uruguay on the behavior, ecology, and conservation of the macroteiid lizard, *Tupinambis teguixin*. Bull. Chicago Herpetol. Soc. 16, 29–39.

Guidry, E. V. (1953). Herpetological notes from southeastern Texas. Herpetologica 9, 49–56.

Guilford, T. (1984). Is kin selection involved in the evolution of warning coloration? Oikos 45, 31–36.

Guthrie, J. E. (1932). Snakes versus birds; birds versus snakes. Wilson Bull. 44, 88–113.

Haacke, W. D. and Bruton, M. N. (1978). On two little known snakes from the tropical subtraction zone of south-eastern Africa. Ann. Transvaal Mus. 31, 43–50.

Hadley, N. F. and Williams, S. C. (1968). Surface activities of some North American scorpions in relation to feeding. Ecology 49, 726–734.

Hahn, D. E. (1960). Collecting notes on central Korean reptiles and amphibians. J. Ohio Herpetol. Soc. 2, 16–24.

Hahn, D. E. (1976). Worm snakes in the diet of a toad, *Bufo melanostictus*. Herpetol. Rev. 7, 167.

Hailey, A. and Davies, P. M. C. (1986). Effects of size, sex, temperature and condition on activity metabolism and defence behaviour of the viperine snake, *Natrix maura*. J. Zool. (London) 208, 541–558.

Hailman, J. P. (1979). *Optical Signals*. Indiana Univ. Press, Bloomington.

Hairston, N. G. (1957). Observations on the behavior of *Draco volans* in the Philippines. Copeia 1957, 262–265.

Hamilton, W. J., Jr. (1951). The food and feeding behavior of the garter snake in New York State. Am. Midl. Nat. 46, 385–390.

Hamilton, W. J., Jr. and Pollack, J. A. (1956). The food of some colubrid snakes from Fort Benning, Georgia. Ecology 37, 519–526.
Hanley, G. H. (1943). Terrarium notes of California reptiles. Copeia 1943, 145–147.
Harris, D. M. (1985). Infralingual plicae: Support for Boulenger's Teiidae (Sauria). Copeia 1985, 560–565.
Harris, D. M. and Kluge, A. G. (1984). The *Sphaerodactylus* (Sauria: Gekkonidae) of Middle America. Occ. Pap. Mus. Zool. Univ. Michigan 706, 1–59.
Harvey, P. H. and Greenwood, P. J. (1978). Anti-predator defence strategies: Some evolutionary problems. In *Behavioural Ecology: An Evolutionary Approach*. (J. R. Krebs and N. B. Davies, eds.). Sinauer Assoc., Sunderland, MA, pp. 129–151.
Harvey, P. H. and Paxton, R. J. (1981). The evolution of aposematic coloration. Oikos 37, 391–396.
Haverschmidt, F. (1962). Notes on the feeding habits and food of some hawks of Surinam. Condor 64, 154–158.
Hay, O. P. (1887). The massasauga and its habits. Am. Nat. 21, 211–218.
Hay, O. P. (1892). On the breeding habits, eggs, and young of certain snakes. Proc. U. S. Natl. Mus. 15, 385–397.
Hayes, F. E. (1985). Life history notes: *Hypsiglena torquata deserticola* (behavior). Herpetol. Rev. 16, 79–80.
Hayes, F. E. and Baker, W. S. (1986). Life history notes: *Thamnophis couchi hammondi* (behavior). Herpetol. Rev. 17, 22–23.
Heath, J. E. (1966). Venous shunts in the cephalic sinuses of horned lizards. Physiol. Zool. 39, 30–35.
Heatwole, H. (1968). Relationship of escape behavior and camouflage in anoline lizards. Copeia 1968, 109–113.
Heatwole, H. (1975). Predation on sea snakes. In *The Biology of Sea Snakes*. (W. Dunson, ed.). Univ. Park Press, Baltimore, pp. 233–249.
Heatwole, H. and Finnie, E. P. (1980). Seal predation on a sea snake. Herpetofauna 8, 24.
Hecht, M. K., Walters, V. and Ramm, G. (1955). Observations on the natural history of the Bahaman pigmy boa, *Tropidophis pardalis*, with notes on autohemorrage, Copeia 1955, 249–251.
Henderson, R. W. (1974). Aspects of the ecology of the neotropical vine snake, *Oxybelis aeneus* (Wagler). Herpetologica 30, 19–24.
Henderson, R. W. (1976). Notes on the reptiles in the Belize City, Belize area. J. Herpetol. 10, 143–146.
Henderson, R. W. (1977). The head-neck display of *Ninia s. sebae* (Reptilia, Colubridae) in northern Belize. J. Herpetol. 11, 106–108.
Henderson, R. W. (1984a). The diets of Hispaniolan colubrid snakes. 1. Introduction and prey genera. Oecologia 62, 234–239.
Henderson, R. W. (1984b). *Scaphiodontophis* (Serpentes: Colubridae): Natural history and test of a mimicry related hypothesis. Spec. Publ. Mus. Nat. Hist. 10, 185–194.
Henderson, R. W. and Binder, M. (1980). The ecology and behavior of vine snakes (*Ahaetulla, Oxybelis, Thelotornis, Uromacer*): A review. Contr. Biol. Geol. Milwaukee Publ. Mus. 37, 1–38.
Hennig, C. W. and Dunlap, W. P. (1978). Tonic immobility in *Anolis carolinensis*: Effects of time and conditions of captivity. Behav. Biol. 23, 75–86.
Hertz, P. E., Huey, R. B. and Nevo, E. (1982). Fight versus flight: Body temperature influences defensive responses of lizards. Ann. Behav. 30, 676–679.
Herzog, H. A. and Burghardt, G. M. (1986). Development of antipredator responses in

REFERENCES

snakes. I. Defensive and open-field behaviors of newborns and adults of three species of garter snakes (*Thamnophis melanogaster, T. sirtalis, T. butleri*). J. Comp. Psychol. 100, 372–379.

Herzog, H. A. and Drummond, H. (1984). Tail autotomy inhibits tonic immobility in geckos. Copeia 1984, 763–764.

Heyer, W. R. and Pongsapipatana, S. (1970). Gliding speeds of *Ptychozoon lionatum* (Reptilia: Gekkonidae) and *Chrysopelea ornata* (Reptilia: Colubridae). Herpetologica 26, 317–319.

Hillis, D. M. (1977a). An incident of death-feigning in *Sonora semiannulata blanchardi*. Bull. Maryland Herpetol. Soc. 13, 116–117.

Hillis, D. M. (1977b). A note on predation of *Eumeces fasciatus* by a fish. Bull. Maryland Herpetol. Soc. 13, 117.

Hoffstetter, R. and Rage, J. C. (1972). Les erycines fossiles de France (Serpentes, Boidae). Comprehension et histoire de la sus-famille. Ann. Paleont., Vertébres 58, 81–124.

Hoogmoed, M. S. (1980). Revision of the genus *Atractus* in Surinam, with the resurrection of two species (Colubridae, Reptilia). Notes on the herpetofauna of Surinam VII. Zool. Verh. Rijksmus. Nat. Hist. 175, 1–47.

Horn, H. G. and Petters, G. (1982). Beitraege zur Biologie des Rauhnackenwarans *Varanus* (*Dendrovaranus*) *rudicollis* Gray (Reptilia: Sauria: Varanidae). Salamandra 18, 29–40.

Horn, H. G. (1977). Notizen zur Systematik, Fundortangaben und Haltung von *Varanus* (*Varanus*) *karlschmidti* (Reptilia, Sauria, Varanidae). Salamandra 13, 78–88.

Horn, H. G. (1980). Bisher unbekannte Details zur Kenntnis von *Varanus varius* auf Grund von feldherpetologischen und terraristischen Beobachtungen (Reptilia: Sauria: Varanidae). Salamandra 16, 1–18.

Horn, H. G. and Schurer, U. (1978). Bemerkungen zu *Varanus* (*Odatria*) *glebopalma* Mitchell 1955 (Reptilia: Sauria: Varanidae). Salamandra 14, 105–116.

Hotz, H. (1969). Gefangenschaftsbeobachtungen an einigen südwestasiatischen Geckos. Aquar. Terrar. Z. 22. 279–282.

Howe, P. A. W. (1931). Encounter with a hamadryad (*Naia bungarus*). J. Bombay Nat. Hist. Soc. 35, 225–226.

Hu, Q., Jiang, Y. and Zhao, E. (1984). A study of the taxonomic status of *Shinisaurus crocodilurus*. Acta Herpetol. Sin. 3, 1–7.

Huey, R. B. (1974). Winter thermal ecology of the iguanid lizard *Tropidurus peruvianus*. Copeia 1974, 149–155.

Huey, R. B. (1982). Phylogenetic and ontogenetic determinants of sprint performance in some diurnal Kalahari lizards. Koedoe 25, 43–48.

Huey, R. B. and Bennett, A. F. (1986). A comparative approach to field and laboratory studies in evolutionary biology. In *Predator–Prey Relationships: Perspectives and Approaches From the Study of Lower Vertebrates*. (M. E. Feder and G. V. Lauder, eds.). Univ. Chicago Press, Chicago, pp. 82–98.

Huey, R. B. and Pianka, E. R. (1977). Natural selection for juvenile lizards mimicking noxious beetles. Science 195, 201–203.

Huey, R. B. and Pianka, E. R. (1981). Ecological consequences of foraging mode. Ecology 62, 991–999.

Huey, R. B., Pianka, E. R. and Schoener, T. W. (1983). *Lizard Ecology: Studies of a Model Organism*. Harvard Univ. Press, Cambridge, MA.

Hulme, J. H. (1951). The "playing possum" habits of the ringhals cobra. Herpetologica 7, 132.

Hulse, A. (1981). Ecology and reproduction of the parthenogenetic lizard *Cnemidophorus uniparens* (Teiidae). Ann. Carnegie Mus. 50, 353–369.
Humphries, D. A. and Driver, P. M. (1967). Erratic display as a device against predators. Science 156, 1767–1768.
Humphries, D. A. and Driver, P. M. (1970). Protean defense by prey animals. Oecologia 5, 285–302.
Inglehart, F. and Chiszar, D. (1977). Covariation among elements of rattlesnake posture: Potential interspecific signals. Bull. Psychol. Soc. 9, 294–296.
Ionides, C. J. P. and Pitman, C. R. S. (1965). Notes on three east African venomous snake populations. Occ. Pap. Dept. Game and Fisheries, Zambia 3, 87–95.
Ireland, L. C. and Gans, C. (1972). The adaptive significance of the flexible shell of the tortoise *Malacochersus tornieri*. Anim. Behav. 20, 778–781.
Iverson, J. B. (1978). The impact of feral cats and dogs on populations of the West Indian rock iguana, *Cyclura carinata*. Biol. Conserv. 14, 63–73.
Iverson, J. B. (1979). Behavior and ecology of the rock iguana, *Cyclura carinata*. Biol. Conserv. 14, 63–73.
Iverson, J. B. (1984). Proportional skeletal mass in turtles. Florida Sci. 47, 1–11.
Iverson, J. B. (1986). Notes on the natural history of the Oaxaca mud turtle, *Kinosternon oaxacae*. J. Herpetol. 20, 119–123.
Jackson, D. R. and Franz, R. (1981). Ecology of the eastern coral snake (*Micrurus fulvius*) in northern peninsular Florida. Herpetologica 37, 213–228.
Jackson, J. F. (1971). Intraspecific predation in *Coluber constrictor*. J. Herpetol. 5, 196.
Jackson, J. F. (1974). Utilization of periods of high sensory complexity for site change in two lizards. Copeia 1974, 785–787.
Jackson, J. F. (1979). Effects of some ophidian tail displays on the predatory behavior of grison (*Galictis sp.*). Copeia 1979, 169–172.
Jackson, J. F., Ingram, W. F., III. and Campbell, H. W. (1976). The dorsal pigmentation pattern of snakes as an antipredator strategy: A multivariate approach. Am. Nat. 110, 1029–1053.
Jackson, J. F. and Pounds, J. A. (1980). On differential head–body pigmentation in snakes. J. Herpetol. 14, 307–311.
Jackson, P. B. N. (1962). Why do Nile crocodiles attack boats? Copeia 1962, 204–206.
Jaksic, F. M. (1986). Predator–prey interactions in terrestrial and intertidal ecosystems: Are the differences real? Rev. Chilena Hist. Nat. 59, 9–17.
Jaksic, F. M. and Greene, H. W. (1984). Empirical evidence of noncorrelation between tail loss frequency and predation intensity of lizards. Oikos 42, 407–411.
Jaksic, F. M., Greene, H. W., Schwenk, K. and Seib, R. L. (1982). Predation upon reptiles in Mediterranean habitats of Chile, Spain and California: A comparative analysis. Oecologia 53, 152–159.
Jaksic, F. M. and Schwenk, K. (1983). Natural history observations on *Liolaemus magellanicus*, the southernmost lizard in the world. Herpetologica 39, 457–461.
Janzen, D. H. (1976). The depression of reptile biomass by large herbivores. Am. Nat. 110, 371–400.
Janzen, D. H. (1979). Reply to Kreulen's note. Am. Nat. 114, 166.
Janzen, D. H. (1981). Evolutionary physiology of personal defence. In *Physiological Ecology: An Evolutionary Approach to Resource Use*. (C. R. Townsend and P. Calow, eds.). Sinauer Associates, Inc., Sunderland, MA, pp. 145–164.
Janzen, D. H. and Martin, P. S. (1982). Neotropical anachronisms: Fruits the gomphotheres ate. Science 215, 19–27.
Janzen, D. H. and Pond, C. M. (1976). Food and feeding behavior of a captive Costa Rican

REFERENCES

least pygmy owl *Glaucidium minutissimum rarum* Griscom (Aves: Strigidae). Brenesia 9, 71–80.

Jennings, M. R. (1984). Predation on Sonoran spotted whiptails, *Cnemidophorus sonorae* (Teiidae), by the great-tailed grackle, *Quiscalus mexicanus* (Icteridae). Southwestern Nat. 29, 280–282.

Johnson, C. R. (1970). Escape behavior and camouflage in two subspecies of *Sceloporus occidentalis*. Am. Midl. Nat. 84, 280–282.

Johnson, C. R. (1975). Defensive display behaviour in some Australian and Papuan-New Guinean pygopodid lizards, boid, colubrid and elapid snakes. Zool. J. Linn. Soc. (London) 56, 265–282.

Johnson, J. A. and Brodie, E. D., Jr. (1974). Defensive behavior of the western banded gecko *Coleonyx variegatus*. An. Behav. 22, 684–687.

Jones, S. M. and Ferguson, G. W. (1980). The effect of paint marking on mortality in a Texas population of *Sceloporus undulatus*. Copeia 1980, 850–854.

Jordon, R. (1970). Death-feigning in a captive red-bellied snake, *Storeria occipitomaculata* (Storer). Herpetologica 26, 466–468.

Jorgensen, C., Orton, A. M. and Tanner, W. W. (1963). Voice of the leopard lizard *Crotaphytus wislizeni* Baird and Girard. Proc. Utah Acad. Sci. Art. Lett. 40, 115–116.

Kalmbach, E. R. (1944). *The Armadillo: Its Relation to Agriculture and Game*. Game, Fish and Oyster Comm., Austin, Texas, pp. 1–57.

Kalmus, H. (1984). Zu Haltung und Nachzucht von *Dasypeltis scabra* (Linnaeus, 1758) (Serpentes: Colubridae). Salamandra 20, 11–20.

Kamel, S. and Gatten, R. E., Jr. (1983). Aerobic and anaerobic activity metabolism of limbless and fossorial reptiles. Physiol. Zool. 56, 419–429.

Kardong, K. V. (1980). Gopher snakes and rattlesnakes: Presumptive Batesian mimicry. Northwest Sci. 54, 1–4.

Kardong, K. V. (1986). Observations on live *Azemiops feae*, Fea's viper. Herpetol. Rev. 17, 81–82.

Kästle, W. (1966). Beobachtungen an ceylonesischen Taubagamen (*Cophotis ceylanica*). Salamandra 2, 78–87.

Kaufmann, J. H. and Kaufmann, A. (1965). Observations of the behavior of tayras and grisons. Z. Säugetierkunde 30, 146–155.

Keenlyne, K. D. and Beer, J. R. (1973). Food habits of *Sistrurus catenatus catenatus*. J. Herpetol. 7, 381–382.

Kennedy, J. P. (1961). Eggs of the eastern hognose snake, *Heterodon platyrhinos*. Texas J. Sci. 13, 416–422.

Kennedy, J. P. (1964). Natural history notes on some snakes of eastern Texas. Texas J. Sci. 16, 210–215.

Kennedy, J. P. (1965a). Observations on the distribution and ecology of Barker's anole, *Anolis barkeri* Schmidt (Iguanidae). Zoologica (N.Y.) 50, 41–44.

Kennedy, J. P. (1965b). Notes on the habitat and behavior of a snake, *Oxybelis aeneus* Wagler, in Veracruz. Southwestern Nat. 10, 136–139.

Kennedy, J. P. (1968). Observations on the ecology and behavior of *Cnemidophorus guttatus* and *Cnemidophorus deppei* (Sauria, Teiidae) in southern Veracruz. J. Herpetol. 2, 87–96.

Kenneweg, F. H. (1956). Meine Beobachtungen an der Netzwühle, *Blanus cinereus* Vand.. Aquar. Terrar. Z. 9, 77–78.

Khan, M. S. and Tasnim, R. (1986a). A note on tail injury in *Eryx johnii*. The Snake 18, 57–58.

Khan, M. S. and Tasnim, R. (1986b). Balling and caudal luring in young *Bungarus caeruleus*. The Snake 18, 42–46.

King, R. B. (1986). Population ecology of the Lake Erie water snake, *Nerodia sipedon insularum*. Copeia 1986, 757–772.

Kirk, V. M. (1969). An observation of a predator-escape technique practiced by a worm snake *Potamophis striatulus* (L.). Turtox News 47, 44.

Klages, H. G. (1982). Pflege and Nachzucht der australischen Bodenagame *Amphibolurus nuchalis* (Reptilia: Sauria: Agamidae). Salamandra 18, 65–70.

Klauber, L. M. (1928). The *Trimorphodon* (lyre snake) of California, with notes on the species of adjacent areas. Trans. San Diego Soc. Nat. Hist. 5, 183–194.

Klauber, L. M. (1931). A statistical survey of the snakes of the southern border of California. Bull. Zool. Soc. San Diego 8, 1–93.

Klauber, L. M. (1939). Studies of reptile life in the arid Southwest. Bull. Zool. Soc. San Diego 14, 1–100.

Klauber, L. M. (1940). Two new subspecies of *Phyllorhynchus*, the leaf-nosed snake, with notes on the genus. Trans. San Diego Soc. Nat. Hist. 9, 195–214.

Klauber, L. M. (1941). The long-nosed snakes of the genus *Rhinocheilus*. Trans. San Diego Soc. Nat. Hist. 9, 289–332.

Klauber, L. M. (1949). The subspecies of the ridge-nosed rattlesnake, *Crotalus willardi*. Trans. San Diego Soc. Nat. Hist. 11, 121–140.

Klauber, L. M. (1956). *Rattlesnakes, their Habits, Life Histories, and Influence on Mankind*. Univ. California Press, Berkeley.

Klimstra, W. D. (1959). Food habits of the cottonmouth in southern Illinois. Nat. Hist. Misc. 168, 1–8.

Kluge, A. G. (1967). Higher taxonomic categories of gekkonid lizards and their evolution. Bull. Am. Mus. Nat. Hist. 135, 1–59.

Kluge, A. G. (1974). A taxonomic revision of the lizard family Pygopodidae. Misc. Publ. Mus. Zool. Univ. Michigan 147, 1–221.

Kluge, A. G. (1987). Cladistic relationships in the Gekkonoidea (Squamata, Sauria). Misc. Publ. Mus. Zool. Univ. Michigan 173, 1–54.

Knapik, P. G. and Hodgson, J. R. (1986). Life history notes: *Storeria occipitomaculata* (predation). Herpetol. Rev. 17, 22.

Knight, J. L. and Collins, J. T. (1977). The amphibians and reptiles of Ceyenne County, Kansas. Rept. St. Biol. Surv. Kansas 15, 1–18.

Kofron, C. P. (1978). Foods and habitats of aquatic snakes (Reptilia, Serptentes) in a Louisiana swamp. J. Herpetol. 12, 543–554.

Kool, K. (1981). Is the musk of the long-necked turtle, *Chelodina longicollis*, a deterrent to predators? Austr. J. Herpetol. 1, 45–53.

Kratzer, H. (1965). Über die Tanganyika-Wasserkobra (*Boulengerina annulata stormsi*). Salamandra 1, 61–67.

Kratzer, H. (1969). Über eine ungewöhnliche Warnreaktion bei *Atheris squamiger* Hallowell. Aqua Terra 6, 82–84.

Kreulen, D. A. (1979). Factors affecting reptile biomass in African grasslands. Am. Nat. 114, 157–165.

Kreyenberg, M. (1907). Briefe aus China. V. Die Reptilien und Amphibien unseres Schutzgebietes. Wochenschr. Aquarienkunde, Braunschweig 4, 209–210, 224–225.

Kroll, J. C. (1977). Self-wounding while death feigning by western hognose snakes (*Heterodon nasicus*). Copeia 1977, 372–373.

Kruuk, H. and Mills, M. G. L. (1983). Notes on food and foraging of the honey badger *Mellivora capensis* in the Kalahari Gemsbok National Park. Koedoe 26, 153–157.

REFERENCES

LaBarbera, M. (1983). Why the wheels won't go. Am. Nat. 121, 395–408.

Laerm, J. (1973). Aquatic bipedalism in the basilisk lizard: The analysis of an adaptive strategy. Am. Midl. Nat. 89, 314–333.

Lamar, W. W. and Medem, F. (1984). Notes on the chelid turtle, *Phrynops rufipes* in Colombia (Reptilia: Testudines: Chelidae). Salamandra 18, 305–321.

Lamoral, B. H. (1971). Unusual prey of some African scorpions. Bull. Br. Arachnol. Soc. 2, 13.

Lamb, T. (1984). The influence of sex and breeding condition on microhabitat selection and diet in the pig frog *Rana grylio*. Am. Midl. Nat. 111, 311–318.

Lambert, S. and Ferguson, G. M. (1985). Blood ejection frequency by *Phrynosoma cornutum* (Iguanidae). Southwestern Nat. 30, 616–617.

Lamborn, W. A. (1913). Notes on the habits of certain reptiles in the Lagos district. Proc. Zool. Soc. London 1913, 218–224.

Land, D. S. (1931). Pelicans and turtles. J. Bombay Nat. Hist. Soc. 34, 1081.

Lardie, R. L. (1961). Ejection of a secretion from the vent of *Rhinocheilus lecontei*. Bull. Philadelphia Herp. Soc., 9, 18.

Lauder, G. V. (1981). Form and function: Structural analysis in evolutionary morphology. Paleobiology 7, 430–442.

Lauder, G. V. (1986). Homology, analogy, and the evolution of behavior. In *Evolution of Animal Behavior*. (M. H. Nitecki and J. A. Kitchell, eds.). Oxford Univ. Press, New York, pp. 9–40.

Laughlin, H. (1959). Stomach contents of some aquatic snakes from Lake McAlester, Pittsburgh County, Oklahoma. Texas J. Sci. 11, 83–85.

Lawrence, E. S. (1985). Vigilance during "easy" and "difficult" foraging tasks. An. Behav. 33, 1373–1375.

Lawrence, R. F. (1953). *The Biology of the Cryptic Fauna of Forests*. Cape Town.

Layne, J. R., Jr. and Ford, N. B. (1984). Flight distance of the queen snake, *Regina septemvittata*. J. Herpetol. 18, 496–498.

Lee, H. T. (1964). Letter to the editor. Texas Game and Fish Mag. 22(3), 32.

Legler, J. M. (1960). Natural history of the ornate box turtle, *Terrapene ornata ornata* Agassiz. Univ. Kansas Publ., Mus. Nat. Hist. 11, 527–669.

Lehmann, H. D. (1966). Daten zur Fortpflanzung von *Chelydra serpentina* in Gefangenschaft. Salamandra 2, 1–5.

Lehmann, H. D. (1970). Beobachtungen bei der Haltung und Aufzucht von *Trachyboa boulengeri* (Serpentes, Boidae). Salamandra 6, 32–42.

Lehmann, H. D. (1971). Notizen über Nahrungsaufnahme und Abwehrverhalten von *Calabaria reinhardtii* (Serpentes, Boidae). Salamandra 7, 55–60.

Lema, T. de (1983). Bipedalia em *Tupinambis tequixin* (Linnaeus, 1758), (Sauria, Teiidae). Iheringia. Ser. Zool., Porto Alegre 62, 89–119.

Levins, R. and Lewontin, R. C. (1985). *The Dialectical Biologist*. Harvard Univ. Press, Cambridge, MA.

Leviton, A. E. and Anderson, S. C. (1966). Further comments on the behavior of the Panamanian microteiid *Echinosaura horrida*. Herpetologica 22, 160.

Liem, K. F. and Wake, D. B. (1985). Morphology: Current approaches and concepts. In *Functional Vertebrate Morphology*. (M. Hildebrand, D. M. Bramble, K. F. Liem and D. B. Wake, eds.). Harvard Univ. Press, Cambridge, MA, pp. 366–377.

Lim, B. L. (1958). The harlequin monitor lizard. Malayan Nat. J. 13, 70–72.

Lim, B. L. (1959). Paradise tree snake versus green crested lizard. Malayan Nat. J. 14, 33–34.

Lima, S. L. (1985). Maximizing feeding efficiency and minimizing time exposed to predators: A trade-off in the black-capped chickadee. Oecologia 66, 60–67.

Lindberg, K. (1932). Snakes on the Barsi Light Railway (Deccan). J. Bombay Nat. Hist. Soc. 35, 690–697.
Liner, E. A. (1977). Letistimulation in *Storeria dekayi limnetes* Anderson. Trans. Kansas Acad. Sci. 80, 81–82.
Longman, H. A. (1913). Herpetological notes. Mem. Queensland Mus. 2, 39–45.
Longman, H. A. (1915). Reptiles from Queensland and the Northern Territory. Mem. Queensland Mus. 3, 30–34.
Longman, H. A. (1918). Notes on some Queensland and Papuan reptiles. Mem. Queensland Mus. 6, 37–44.
Longman, H. A. (1937). Herpetological notes. Mem. Queensland Mus. 11, 165–168.
Longstaff, G. G. and Poulton, E. B. (1907). A few notes on South African chamaeleons, etc. Linn. J. Zool. 30, 45–48.
Lönnberg, E. (1902). On a collection of snakes from northwestern Argentina and Bolivia containing new species. Ann. Mag. Nat. Hist. Ser. 7, 10, 457–462.
Lorenz, R. (1971). Goeldi's monkey *Callimico goeldii* Thomas 1904 preying on snakes. Folia Primatol. 15, 133–142.
Louw, G. N. and Holm, E. (1972). Physiological, morphological and behavioural adaptations of the ultrapsammophilous, Namib Desert lizard *Aporosaura anchietae* (Bocage). Madoqua, (Ser. II) 1, 67–85.
Loveridge, A. (1918). Notes on snakes in East Africa. J. E. African and Uganda Nat. Hist. Soc. 4, 315–338.
Loveridge, A. (1928). Notes on snakes and snake-bites in East Africa. Bull. Antivenin Inst. Am. 1, 106–117; 2, 32–41.
Loveridge, A. (1938). On a collection of reptiles and amphibians from Liberia. Proc. New Engl. Zool. Club 17, 49–74.
Loveridge, A. (1941). Revision of the African lizards of the family Amphisbaenidae. Bull. Mus. Com. Zool. 87, 353–451.
Loveridge, A. (1951). On reptiles and amphibians from Tanganyika territory, collected by C. J. P. Ionides. Bull. Mus. Comp. Zool. 106, 176–204.
Lowe, C. H., Schwalbe, C. R., and Johnson, T. B. (1986). *The Venomous Reptiles of Arizona*. Arizona Game and Fish Dept., Phoenix.
Luke, C. (1986). Convergent evolution of lizard toe fringes. Biol. J. Linn. Soc. London 16, 1–16.
Lynch, W. (1978). Death-feigning in the eastern yellow-bellied racer. Blue Jay 36, 92–93.
Maddison, W. P., Donoghue, M. J. and Maddison, D. R. (1984). Outgroup analysis and parsimony. Syst. Zool. 33, 83–103.
Maehr, D. S. and Brady, J. R. (1986). Food habits of bobcats in Florida. J. Mammol. 67, 133–138.
Mahendra, B. C. (1931). The coloration of the tail of the common blue tail skink (*Lygosoma punctatum*). J. Bombay Nat. Hist. Soc. 35, 463–465.
Maiorana, V. C. (1976). Predation, submergent behavior, and tropical diversity. Evol. Theory 1, 157–177.
Malkmus, R. (1982a). Einige Bemerkungen zur Abwehrreaktion bei *Blanus cinereus* sowie zur Verbreitung dieser Art in Portugal (Reptilia: Sauria: Amphisbaenidae). Salamandra 18, 71–77.
Malkmus, R. (1982b). Ungewöhnliche Fluchtreaktion einer *Lacerta lepida* (Reptilia: Sauria: Lacertidae). Salamandra 18, 357–358.
Malkmus, R. (1983). Nachtrag zur Verbreitung der Amphibien und Reptilien Portugals. Salamandra 19, 71–83.

REFERENCES

Malnate, E. (1939). A study of the yellow-lipped snake, *Rhadinaea flavilata* (Cope). Zoologica (N.Y.) 24, 359–366.

Malnate, E. V. (1944). Notes on South Carolinian reptiles. Am. Midl. Nat. 32, 728–731.

Mandaville, J. (1967). The hooded *Malpolon, M. moilensis* (Reuss) and notes on other snakes of north-eastern Arabia. J. Bombay Nat. Hist. Soc. 64, 115–118.

Marcellini, D. (1977). Acoustic and visual display behavior of gekkonid lizards. Am. Zool. 17, 251–260.

Marcellini, D., and Keefer, T. E. (1976). Analysis of the gliding behavior of *Ptychozoon lionatum* (Reptilia: Gekkonidae). Herpetologica 32, 362–366.

Marcellini, D. L. (1978). The acoustic behavior of lizards. In *Behavior and Neurology of Lizards*. (N. Greenberg and P. D. MacLean, eds.). Nat. Inst. Mental Health, Rockville, MD, pp. 287–300.

March, D. H. (1928). Field notes on the neotropical rattlesnake (*Crotalus terrificus*). Bull. Antivenin Inst. Am. 2, 55–61.

Marchisin, A. (1978). Observations on an audiovisual "warning" signal in pigmy rattlesnake, *Sistrurus miliarius* (Reptilia, Serpentes, Crotalidae). Herpetol. Rev. 9, 92–93.

Marr, J. C. (1944). Notes on amphibians and reptiles from the central United States. Am. Midl. Nat. 32, 478–490.

Martin, J. H. and Bagby, R. M. (1972). Temperature-frequency relationship of the rattlesnake rattle. Copeia 1972, 482–485.

Martin, P. S. (1955). Herpetological records from the Gomez Farias region of southwestern Tamaulipas, Mexico. Copeia 1955, 173–180.

Martin, W. F. and Huey, R. B. (1971). The function of the epiglottis in sound production (hissing) of *Pituophis melanoleucus*. Copeia 1971, 752–754.

Marx, H. and Rabb, G. B. (1965). Relationships and zoogeography of the viperine snakes (Family Viperidae). Fieldiana: Zool. 44, 161–206.

Maslin, T. P. (1950). Snakes of the Kiukiang–Lushan area, Kiangsi, China. Proc. California Acad, Sci. 26, 419–466.

Matuschka, F.-R. (1978). Beobachtungen bei der Haltung von *Otocryptis wiegmanni* (Reptilia: Sauria: Agamidae). Salamandra 14, 207–211.

McAllister, C. T. (1983). Aquatic behavior of collared lizards, *Crotaphytus c. collaris*, from Arkansas. Herpetol. Rev. 14, 11.

McCormick, S. and Polis, G. A. (1982). Arthropods that prey on vertebrates. Biol. Rev. 57, 29–58.

McCoy, C. J. (1967). Natural history notes on *Crotaphytus wislizeni* (Reptilia: Iguanidae) in Colorado. Am. Midl. Nat. 77, 138–146.

McCoy, C. J. and Gehlbach, F. R. (1967). Cloacal hemorrhage and the defense display of the colubrid snake *Rhinocheilus lecontei*. Texas J. Sci. 19, 349–352.

McCrystal, H. K. and Green, R. J. (1986). Life history notes: *Agkistrodon contortrix pictigaster* (feeding). Herpetol. Rev. 17, 61.

McDonald, H. S. (1974). Bradycardia during death-feigning of *Heterodon platyrhinos* Latreille (Serpentes). J. Herpetol. 8, 157–164.

McDowell, S. B. (1986). The architecture of the corner of the mouth of colubroid snakes. J. Herpetol. 20, 353–407.

McGowan, N. (1963). Something in scales. Texas Game and Fish Mag. 21(4), 20–22, 27.

McIlhenny, E. H. (1935). *The Alligator's Life History*. Christopher Publ. House, Boston.

McKinney, C. O. and Ballinger, R. E. (1966). Snake predators of lizards in western Texas. Southwestern Nat. 11, 410–412.

Meade, G. P. (1940). Observations on Louisiana captive snakes. Copeia 1940, 165–167.

Meade, G. P. (1946). The natural history of the mud snake. Sci. Monthly 63, 21–29.
Mebs, D. (1966). Studien zum aposematischen Verhalten von *Teratoscincus scincus*. Salamandra 2, 16–20.
Mebs, D. (1973). Drohreaktionen beim Blattschwanzgecko, *Phyllurus platurus*. Salamandra 9, 71–74.
Mebs, D. (1974). Haltungserfahrungen mit *Tiliqua casuarinae* (Sauria, Scincidae). Salamandra 10, 104–114.
Medem, F. (1962). La distribucion geographica y ecologia de los Crocodylia y Testudinata en el departmento del Choco. Rev. Acad. Colombiana Cien. Exactas, Fis. Natur. 11, 79–303.
Medem, F. (1981). *Los Crocodylia de Sur America. Volumen 1. Los Crocodylia de Colombia*. Min. Ed. Nac., Bogota.
Meinzer, W. P. (1983). Trailing the roadrunner. Texas Parks Wildlife 41(4), 22–25.
Mendelssohn, H. (1963). On the biology of the venomous snakes of Israel. Part I. Israel J. Zool. 12, 143–170.
Mendelssohn, H. (1965). On the biology of the venomous snakes of Israel. II. Israel J. Zool. 14, 185–212.
Meritt, D. A. (1981). The green iguana, *Iguana iguana:* Behavioral observations and natural history. Bull. Chicago Herpetol. Soc. 16, 59–64.
Mertens, R. (1929). Über eine kleine herpetologische Sammlung aus Java. Senckenbergiana 11, 22–33.
Mertens, R. (1930). Die Amphibien und Reptilien der Inseln Bali, Lombok, Sumbawa und Flores (Beiträge zur Fauna der Kleinen Sunda-Inseln. I.). Abh. Senckenberg. Naturforsch. Ges. 42, 115–344.
Mertens, R. (1931). Eine eigentümliche Schreckstellung mancher Schlangen. Bl. Aquar. Terrarienkunde 42, 8–9.
Mertens, R. (1946). Die Warn- und Droh-Reaktionen der Reptilien. Abh. Senckenberg. Naturforsch. Ges. 471, 1–108.
Mertens, R. (1952a). Die Amphibien und Reptilien von El Salvador, auf Grund der Reisen von R. Mertens und A. Zilch. Abh. Senckenberg. Naturforsch. Ges. 487, 1–120.
Mertens, R. (1952b). Der "Bärtige Krötenkopf" und seine Warnstellung. Natur Volk 82, 15–19.
Mertens, R. (1955). Die Amphibien und Reptilien Südwestafrikas. Abh. Senckenberg. Naturforsch. Ges. 490, 1–172.
Mertens, R. (1960). *The World of Amphibians and Reptiles*. McGraw-Hill Book Co., New York.
Mertens, R. (1969). Die Amphibien und Reptilien West-Pakistan. Stuttgart. Beitr. Naturkunde 197, 1–96.
Mertens, R. (1970). Zur Frage der "Fluganpassungen" von *Chrysopelea* (Serpentes, Colubridae). Salamandra 6, 11–14.
Mertens, R. (1971). Beobachtungen an Schlanknattern der Gattung *Leptophis*. Salamandra 7, 117–122.
Messick, J. P. and Hornocker, M. G. (1981). Ecology of the badger in southwestern Idaho. Wildlife Monogr. 76.
Mienis, H. K. (1979). Predation on *Testudo graeca* by the little owl in Israel (Reptilia: Testudines: Testudinidae). Salamandra 15, 107–108.
Mienis, H. K. (1980). A case of predation on *Natrix tessellata* by the Smyrna kingfisher (Reptilia: Serpentes: Colubridae). Salamandra 16, 135.
Mienis, H. K. (1982). A case of predation on *Typhlops vermicularis* by a Blackbird in Israel (Reptilia: Serpentes: Typhlopidae). Salamandra 18, 116–117.

REFERENCES

Milinski, M. (1984). A predator's costs of overcoming the confusion-effect of swarming prey. Anim. Behav. 32, 1157–1162.
Miller, A. H. and Stebbins, R. C. (1964). *The Lives of Desert Animals in the Joshua Tree National Monument*. Univ. Calif. Press, Berkeley.
Milstead, W. W. (1961). Notes on teiid lizards in southern Brazil. Copeia 1961, 493–495.
Milstead, W. W. and Tinkle, D. W. (1969). Interrelationships of feeding habits in a population of lizards in southwestern Texas. Midl. Nat. 81, 491–499.
Milton, T. H. and Jenssen, T. A. (1979). Description and significance of vocalizations by *Anolis grahami* (Sauria: Iguanidae). Copeia 1979: 481–489.
Minckley, W. L. (1966). Coyote predation on aquatic turtles. J. Mammal. 47, 137.
Minton, J. E. (1949). Coral snake preyed upon by bullfrog. Copeia 1949, 288.
Minton, S. A. (1966). A contribution to the herpetology of West Pakistan. Bull. Am. Mus. Nat. Hist. 134, 27–184.
Minton, S. A., and Mebs, D. (1978). Vier Bissfälle durch Colubriden (Reptilia: Serpentes: Colubridae). Salamandra 14, 41–43.
Minton, S. A. and Minton, J. E. (1948). Notes on a herpetological collection from the Middle Mississippi Valley. Am. Midl. Nat. 40, 378–390.
Minton, S. A. and Minton de Cervantes, B. (1977). Observations on the snakes of Queretaro, Mexico. Bull. Chicago. Herpetol. Soc. 12, 69–74.
Minton, S. A. and Weinstein, S. A. (1984). Protease activity and lethal toxicity of venoms from some little known rattlesnakes. Toxicon 22, 828–830.
Mitchell, J. C. (1978). Balling behavior in *Chionactis occipitalis* (Reptilia, Serpentes, Colubridae). J. Herpetol. 12, 435–436.
Mitchell, J. C. (1984). Observations on the ecology and reproduction of the leopard lizard, *Gambelia wislizenii* (Iguanidae) in southeastern Arizona. Southwestern Nat. 29, 509–511.
Mitchell, J. C. (1985). Life history: *Hypsiglena torquata ochrorhyncha* (behavior). Herpetol. Rev. 16, 54–56.
Moberly, W. R. (1968). The metabolic responses of the common iguana, *Iguana iguana*, to walking and diving. Comp. Biochem. Physiol. 27, 21–32.
Mole, R. R. (1924). The Trinidad snakes. Proc. Zool. Soc. London 1924, 235–278.
Mole, R. R. and Urich, F. W. (1894). Biological notes upon some of the Ophidia of Trinidad, B. W. I, with a preliminary list of the species recorded from the island. Proc. Zool. Soc. London 1894, 499–518.
Moll, E. and Smith, H. M. (1967). Lizards in the diet of an American caecilian. Nat. Hist. Misc. 187, 1–2.
Moll, E. O. and Legler, J. M. (1971). The life history of a neotropical slider turtle, *Pseudemys scripta* (Schoepff), in Panama. Bull. Los Angeles Co. Mus. Nat. Hist. Sci. 11, 1–102.
Montanucci, R. R. (1965). Observations on the San Joaquin leopard lizard, *Crotaphytus wislizenii silus* Stejneger. Herpetologica 21, 270–283.
Montanucci, R. R. (1968). Notes on the distribution and ecology of some lizards in the San Joaquin valley, California. Herpetologica 24, 316–320.
Montanucci, R. R. (1971). Ecological and distributional data on *Crotaphytus reticulatus* (Sauria: Iguanidae). Herpetologica 27, 183–197.
Montanucci, R. R. (1978). Dorsal pattern polymorphism and adaptation in *Gambelia wislizenii* (Reptilia, Lacertilia, Iguanidae). J. Herpetol. 12, 73–81.
Mosauer, W. W. (1932). The amphibians and reptiles of the Guadelupe Mountains of New Mexico and Texas. Occ. Pap. Mus. Zool. Univ. Michigan 246, 1–18.

Mosauer, W. W. (1934). The reptiles and amphibians of Tunisia. Publ. Univ. California Los Angeles Biol. Sci. 1, 49–64.
Mosse, A. H. E. (1931). On the food of the vampire bat (*Lyroderma lyra*). J. Bombay Nat. Hist. Soc. 34, 1052–1053.
Moynihan, M. (1971). Successes and failures of tropical mammals and birds. Am. Nat. 105, 371–383.
Müller, P. (1971). Herpetologische Reiseeindrücke aus Brasilien. Salamandra 7, 9–30.
Murphy, J. B., Lamoreaux, W. E. and Carpenter, C. C. (1978). Threatening behavior in the angle-headed dragon, *Goniocephalus dilophus* (Reptilia, Lacertilia, Agamidae). J. Herpetol. 12, 455–460.
Myers, C. W. (1965). Biology of the ringneck snake, *Diadophis punctatus*, in Florida. Bull. Florida St. Mus. 10, 43–90.
Myers, C. W. (1967). The pine woods snake, *Rhadinaea flavilata* (Cope). Bull. Florida St. Mus. 2, 47–97.
Myers, C. W. (1969). Snakes of the genus *Coniophanes* in Panama. Am. Mus. Novitates 2372, 1–28.
Myers, C. W. (1971). Central American lizards related to *Anolis pentaprion*: Two new species from the Cordillera de Talamanca. Am. Mus. Novitates 2471, 1–40.
Myers, C. W. (1986). An enigmatic new snake from the Peruvian Andes, with notes on the Xenodontini (Colubridae: Xenodontinae). Am. Mus. Novitates 2853, 1–12.
Myers, C. W. and Arata, A. A. (1961). Remarks on "defensive" behavior in the hognose snake *Heterodon simus* (Linnaeus). Quart. J. Florida Acad. Sci. 24, 108–110.
Myers, C. W. and Rand, A. S. (1969). Checklist of the amphibians and reptiles of Barro Colorado Island, Panama, with comments on faunal change and sampling. Smithsonian Contr. Zool. 10, 1–11.
Myers, N. (1973). The spotted cats and the fur trade. In *The World's Cats, Vol. I: Ecology and Conservation.* (R. L. Eaton, ed.). World Wildlife Safari, Winston, Oregon, pp. 276–326.
Neill, W. T. (1948b). Spiders preying upon reptiles and amphibians. Herpetologica 4, 150.
Neill, W. T. (1948c). Use of scent glands by prenatal *Sternotherus minor*. Herpetologica 4, 148.
Neill, W. T. (1948d). Odor of young box turtles. Copeia 1948, 130.
Neill, W. T. (1960). The caudal lure of various juvenile snakes. J. Florida Acad. Sci. 23, 173–200.
Neill, W. T. (1963). Polychromatism in snakes. Quart. J. Florida Acad. Sci. 26, 194–216.
Neill, W. T. (1964). Taxonomy, natural history, and zoogeography of the rainbow snake, *Farancia erythrogramma* (Palisot de Beauvois). Am. Midl. Nat. 71, 257–295.
Neill, W. T. (1971). *The Last of the Ruling Reptiles.* Colombia Univ. Press, New York.
Netting, M. G. (1936). Notes on a collection of reptiles from Barro Colorado Island, Panama Canal Zone. Ann. Carnegie Mus. 25, 113–120.
Neve, L. C. (1976). Predation on iguanid lizards by the roundtail chub, *Gila robusta grahami*, at Fossil creek, Arizona. Herpetol. Rev. 7, 113.
Nichols, J. T. (1939). Disposition in the box turtle. Copeia 1939, 107.
Nickerson, M. A. and Heringhi, H. L. (1966). Three noteworthy colubrids from southern Sonora, Mexico. Great Basin Nat. 26, 136–140.
Nickerson, M. A. and Mays, C. E. (1970). A preliminary herpetofaunal analysis of the Graham (Pinaleno) Mountain Region, Graham Co., Arizona with ecological comments. Trans. Kansas Acad. Sci. 72, 492–505.
Nikolskii, A. M. (1915). *Fauna of Russia and Adjacent Countries. Reptiles, Vol. I: Chelonia and Sauria.* Israel Program for Sci. Trans., Jerusalem.

REFERENCES

Noble, G. K. (1921). Snakes that inflate. Nat. Hist. 21, 166–171.
Norris. K. S. (1967). Color adaptation in desert reptiles and its thermal relationships. In *Lizard Ecology: A Symposium*. (W. W. Milstead, ed.). Univ. Missouri Press, Columbia, pp. 162–229.
Norris, K. S. and Zweifel, R. G. (1950). Observations on the habits of the ornate box turtle, *Terrapene ornata* (Agassiz). Nat. Hist. Misc. 58, 1–4.
Nussbaum, R. A. and Diller, L. V. (1976). The life history of the side-blotched lizard, *Uta stansburiana* Baird and Girard, in north-central Oregon. Northwest. Sci. 50, 243–260.
Nussbaum, R. A. and Hoyer, R. F. (1974). Geographic variation and the validity of subspecies in the rubber boa, *Charina bottae* (Blainville). Northwest. Sci. 48, 219–229.
Obst, F. J. (1959). Kroetenkoepfe. Aquar. Terrar. Z. 12, 187–188.
Oliver, J. A. (1948). The relationships and zoogeography of the genus *Thalerophis* Oliver. Bull. Am. Mus. Nat. Hist. 92, 157–280.
Oliver, J. A. (1951). "Gliding" in amphibians and reptiles, with a remark on an arboreal adaptation in the lizard, *Anolis carolinensis carolinensis* Voigt. Am. Nat. 85, 171–176.
Oliver, J. A. (1956). Reproduction in the king cobra, *Ophiophagus hannah* Cantor. Zoologica (N.Y.) 41, 145–152.
Orejas-Miranda, B. (1966). The snake genus *Lystrophis* in Uruguay. Copeia 1966, 193–205.
Oster, G. F. and Wilson, E. O. (1978). *Caste and Ecology in Social Insects*. Princeton Univ. Press, Princeton.
Owen, C. E. and Owen, D. (1959). Lizard killed by a beetle. Br. J. Herpetol. 2, 167.
Owen, D. (1982). *Camouflage and Mimicry*. Univ. Chicago Press, Chicago.
Paine, R. T. (1977). Controlled manipulations in the marine intertidal zone and their contributions to ecological theory. In *The Changing Scenes in Natural Sciences, 1776–1976*. (C. Goulden, ed.). Spec. Publ. Acad. Nat. Sci. Philadelphia, 12, pp. 245–270.
Papenfuss, T. J. (1982). The ecology and systematics of the amphisbaenian genus *Bipes*. Occ. Pap. California Acad. Sci. 136, 1–42.
Parker, F. (1983). The prehensile-tailed skink (*Corucia zebrata*) on Bougainville Island, Papua New Guinea. In *Advances in Herpetology and Evolutionary Biology: Essays in Honor of Ernest E. Williams*. (A. G. J. Rhodin, and K. Miyata, eds.). Mus. Comp. Zool., Cambridge, MA, pp. 435–440.
Parker, H. W. (1949). The snakes of Somaliland and the Sokotra Islands. Zool. Verh. Rijksmus. Nat. Hist. 6, 1–115.
Parker, H. W. (1965). *Natural History of Snakes*. Br. Mus. (Nat. Hist.), London.
Parker, W. S. (1971). Ecological observations on the regal horned lizard (*Phrynosoma solare*) in Arizona. Herpetologica 27, 333–338.
Parker, W. S. (1972). Aspects of the ecology of a Sonoran desert population of the western banded gecko, *Coleonyx variegatus* (Sauria, Eublepharinae). Am. Midl. Nat. 88, 209–224.
Parker, W. S. and Pianka, E. R. (1973). Notes on the ecology of the iguanid lizard, *Sceloporus magister*. Herpetologica 29, 143–152.
Parker, W. S. and Pianka, E. R. (1974). Further ecological observations on the western banded gecko, *Coleonyx variegatus*. Copeia 1974, 528–531.
Parker, W. S. and Pianka, E. R. (1976). Ecological observations on the leopard lizard (*Crotaphytus wislizeni*) in different parts of its range. Herpetologica 32, 95–114.
Patchell, F. C. and Shine, R. (1986). Hinged teeth for hard-bodied prey: A case of convergent evolution between snakes and legless lizards. J. Zool. (London) 208, 269–275.
Paulson, D. R. (1967). Searching for sea serpents. Sea Frontiers 13, 244–250.

Peabody, R. B., Johnson, J. A. and Brodie, E. D., Jr. (1975). Intraspecific escape from ingestion of the rubber boa, *Charina bottae*. J. Herpetol. 9, 237.

Perez-Rivera, R. A. (1985). Nota sobre el habitat, los habitos alimentarios y los depredadores del lagarto *Anolis cuvieri* (Lacertilia: Iguanidae) de Puerto Rico. Carib. J. Sci. 21, 101–103.

Petzold, H. G. (1968). Zur Fortspflanzungsbiologie asiatischer Kobras (*Naja naja*). Zool. Gart. 36, 133–146.

Petzold, H. G. (1969). Zur Haltung und Fortpflanzungsbiologie einiger kubanischer Schlangen im Tierpark Berlin. Salamandra 5, 124–140.

Pianka, E. R. (1968). Notes on the biology of *Varanus eremius*. West. Austr. Nat. 11, 39–44.

Pianka, E. R. (1970a). Notes on the biology of *Varanus gouldi flavirufus*. W. Austr. Nat. 11, 141–144.

Pianka, E. R. (1970b). Comparative autecology of the lizard *Cnemidophorus tigris* in different parts of its geographic range. Ecology 51, 703–720.

Pianka, E. R. (1971a). Comparative ecology of two lizards. Copeia 1971, 129–138.

Pianka, E. R. (1971b). Ecology of the agamid lizard *Amphibolurus isolepis* in Western Australia. Copeia 1971, 527–536.

Pianka, E. R. (1971c). Notes on the biology of *Varanus tristis*. W. Austr. Nat. 11, 180–183.

Pianka, E. R. (1982). Observations on the ecology of *Varanus* in the Great Victorian Desert. West. Austr. Nat. 15, 37–44.

Pianka, E. R. and Parker, W. S. (1975). Ecology of horned lizards: A review with special reference to *Phrynosoma platyrhinos*. Copeia 1975, 141–162.

Pianka, E. R. and Pianka, H. D. (1970). The ecology of *Moloch horridus* (Lacertilia: Agamidae) in western Australia. Copeia 1970, 90–103.

Pickwell, G. V., Bezy, R. L. and Fitch, J. E. (1983). Northern occurrences of the sea snake, *Pelamis platurus*, in the eastern Pacific, with a record of predation in the species. Cal. Fish and Game 69, 172–177.

Pienaar, U. de V. (1969). Predator–prey relationships amongst the larger mammals of the Kruger National Park. Koedoe 12, 108–176.

Pienaar, U. de V., Haakce, W. D. and Jacobsen, N. H. G. (1978). *The Reptiles of the Kruger National Park*. Natl. Parks Board S. Africa, Pretoria. Revised 1983.

Pitman, C. R. S. (1965). Hood-spreading by the mambas of the African genus *Dendroaspis* Schlegel. J. E. Africa Nat. Hist. Soc. 25, 110–115.

Platt, D. R. (1969). Natural history of the hognose snakes *Heterodon platyrhinos* and *Heterodon nasicus*. Univ. Kansas Publ. Mus. Nat. Hist. 18, 253–420.

Polis, G. A. (1979). Prey and feeding phenology of the desert sand scorpion *Paruroctonus mesaensis* (Scorpionida: Vaejovidae). J. Zool. (London) 188, 333–346.

Polynova, G. V. (1982). Demonstration behavior of *Phrynocephalus mystaceus*. Zool. Zhr. 61, 734–741 (in Russian).

Pope, C. H. (1929). Notes on reptiles from Fukien and other Chinese provinces. Bull. Am. Mus. Nat. Hist. 58, 335–487.

Pope, C. H. (1935). *The Reptiles of China*. Nat. Hist. Cent. Asia 10, Am. Mus. Nat. Hist., New York.

Pope, C. H. (1958). Fatal bite of a captive African rear-fanged snake (*Dispholidus*). Copeia 1958, 280–282.

Pough, F. H. (1970). The ecology of burrowing in the sand lizard, *Uma notata*. Copeia 1970, 145–157.

Pough, F. H. (1976). Multiple cryptic effects of crossbanded and ringed patterns of snakes. Copeia 1976, 834–836.

REFERENCES

Pough, F. H. (1980). Blood oxygen transport and delivery in reptiles. Am. Zool. 20, 173-185.
Pough, F. H. (1983). Amphibians and reptiles as low-energy systems. In *Behavioral Energetics*. (W. P. Aspey and S. I. Lustick, eds.). Ohio St. Univ. Press, Columbus, pp. 141-188.
Pough, F. H. and Andrews, R. M. (1985). Use of anaerobic metabolism by free-ranging lizards. Physiol. Zool. 58, 205-213.
Pough, F. H., Kwiencinski, G. and Bemis, W. (1978). Melanin deposits associated with the venom of snakes. J. Morphol. 155, 63-72.
Power, M. (1987). Predator avoidance by grazing fishes in temperate and tropical streams: Importance of stream depth and prey size. In *Predation: Direct and Indirect Impacts on Aquatic Communities*. (W. C. Kerfoot and A. Sikh, eds.). Univ. Presses of New England, Hanover, NH, pp. 333-351.
Prakash, I. (1959). Foods of the Indian false vampire. J. Mammal. 40, 545-547.
Pregill, G. K. (1986). Body size of insular lizards: A pattern of Holocene dwarfism. Evolution 40, 997-1008.
Pregill, G. K., Gauthier, J. A. and Greene, H. W. (1986). The evolution of helodermatid squamates, with description of a new taxon and an overview of Varanoidea. Trans. San Diego Soc. Nat. Hist. 21, 167-202.
Prestrude, A. M. and Crawford, F. T. (1970). Tonic immobility in the lizard, *Iguana iguana*. An. Behav. 18, 391-395.
Prestt, I. (1971). An ecological study of the viper *Vipera berus* in southern Britain. J. Zool. (London) 164, 373-418.
Prieto, A. A. and Sorenson, M. W. (1975). Predator-prey relationships of the Arizona chuckwalla (*Sauromalus obesus tumidus*). Bull. New Jersey Acad. Sci. 20, 12-13.
Pritchard, P. C. H. (1979). *Encyclopedia of Turtles*. T. F. H. Publications, Neptune, NJ.
Pritchard, P. C. H. (1984). Piscivory in turtles, and evolution of the long-necked Chelidae. In *The Structure, Development and Evolution of Reptiles: A Festschrift in Honour of Professor A. d'A. Bellairs on the Occasion of His Retirement*. (M. W. J. Ferguson, ed.). Academic Press, London, pp. 87-110.
Pritchard, P. C. H. and Trebbau, P. (1984). *The Turtles of Venezuela*. Soc. Study of Amph. Rept., Oxford, Ohio.
Procter, J. B. (1922). A study of the remarkable tortoise, *Testudo loveridgii* Blgr., and the morphogeny of the chelonian carapace. Proc. Zool. Soc. London 1922, 483-526.
Proud, K. R. S. (1978). Some notes on a captive earless monitor lizard, *Lanthanotus borneensis*. Sarawak Mus. J. 26, 235-242.
Radcliffe, C. W., Chiszar, D. and Smith, H. M. (1980). Prey-induced caudal movements in *Boa constrictor* with comments on the evolution of caudal luring. Bull. Maryland Herpetol. Soc. 16, 19-22.
Radcliffe, C. W. and Maslin, T. P. (1975). A new subspecies of red rattlesnake, *Crotalus ruber*, from San Lorenzo Sur Island, Baja California Norte, Mexico. Copeia 1975, 490-493.
Rajendran, M. V. (1985). *Studies in Uropeltid Snakes*. Madurai Kamaraj Univ., Madurai.
Rand, A. S. (1964). Inverse relationship between temperature and shyness in the lizard *Anolis lineatopus*. Ecology 45, 863-864.
Rand, A. S. (1967). Predator-prey interactions and the evolution of aspect diversity. Atas Simp. Biota Amazonica 5, 73-83.
Rand, A. S. and Andrews, R. (1975). Adult color dimorphism and juvenile pattern in *Anolis cuvieri*. J. Herpetol. 9, 257-260.

Rand, A. S., Gorman, G. C. and Rand, W. M. (1975). Natural history, behavior, and ecology of *Anolis agassizi*. Smithsonian Contr. Zool. 176, 27–38.

Rand, A. S. and Marx, H. (1967). Running speed of the lizard *Basiliscus basiliscus* on water. Copeia 1967, 230–233.

Rand, A. S. and Ortleb, E. P. (1969). Defensive display in the colubrid snake *Pseustes poecilonotus shropshirei*. Herpetologica 25, 46–48.

Rand, A. S. and Rand, P. J. (1966). Aspects of the ecology of the iguanid lizard *Tropidurus torquatus* at Belem, Para. Smithsonian Misc. Coll. 151, 1–16.

Rand, W. M. and Rand, A. S. (1976). Agonistic behavior in nesting iguanas: A stochastic analysis of dispute settlement dominated by the minimization of energy cost. Z. Tierpsychol. 40, 279–299.

Raun, G. G. (1962). Observations on behavior of newborn hognose snakes, *Heterodon p. platyrhinos*. Texas J. Sci. 14, 3–6.

Redford, K. (1985). Food habits of armadillos (Xenarthra: Dasypodidae). In *The Evolution and Ecology of Armadillos, Sloths, and Vermilinguas*. (G. G. Montgomery, ed.). Smithsonian Inst. Press, Washington, D. C., pp. 429–437.

Reed, C. A. (1956). Temporary bipedal locomotion in the lizard *Agama caucasica* in Iraq. Herpetologica 12, 128.

Reed, C. A. and Marx, H. (1959). A herpetological collection from northeastern Iraq. Trans. Kansas Acad. Sci. 62, 91–122.

Regal, P. J. (1978). Behavioral differences between reptiles and mammals: An analysis of activity and mental capabilities. In *Behavior and Neurobiology of Lizards*. (N. Greenberg and P. D. MacLean, eds.). Dept. Health, Education and Welfare, Washington, D. C., pp. 183–202.

Reid, W. H. and Fulbright, H. J. (1981). Impaled prey of the loggerhead shrike in the northern Chihuahuan desert. Southwestern Nat. 26, 204–205.

Reynolds, H. C. (1945). Some aspects of the life history and ecology of the opossum in central Missouri. J. Mammal. 26, 361–379.

Ridley, H. N. (1899). The habits of Malay reptiles. J. Straits Branch Roy. Asiat. Soc., 32, 185–210.

Rieppel, O. (1970). Nachwuchs bei *Dryophis nasutus* (Lacepede) 1789. Aqua Terra 7, 85–88.

Rieppel, O. (1971). Zum Verhalten von *Trogonophis wiegmanni elegans* (Gervais, 1835). Aqua Terra 4, 44–48.

Riley, J., Winch, J. M., Stimson, A. F. and Pope, R. D. (1986). The association of *Amphisbaena alba* (Reptilia: Amphisbaenia) with the leaf-cutting ant *Atta cephalotes* in Trinidad. J. Nat. Hist. 20, 459–470.

Robinson, M. H. (1969). Defenses against virtually hunting predators. In *Evolutionary Biology*. (T. Dobzhansky, M. K. Hecht, and W. C. Steere, eds.). Appleton-Century-Crofts, New York, Volume 3, pp. 225–259.

Robinson, M. H. (1970). Insect anti-predator adaptations and the behavior of predatory primates. Act IV Congr. Latin. Zool. 2, 811–836.

Rodda, G. H. and Burghardt, G. M. (1985). Life history notes: *Iguana iguana* (terrestriality). Herpetol. Rev. 16, 112.

Rose, W. (1962). *The Reptiles and Amphibians of Southern Africa*. Maskew Miller, Ltd., Cape Town.

Rosenberg, H. I. and Russell, A. P. (1980). Structural and functional aspects of tail squirting: A unique defense mechanism of *Diplodactylus* (Reptilia: Gekkonidae). Can. J. Zool. 58, 865–881.

Rosenberg, H. I., Russell, A. P. and Kapoor, M. (1984). Preliminary characterization of the

REFERENCES

defensive secretion of *Diplodactylus* (Reptilia: Gekkonidae). Copeia 1984, 1025–1028.

Rosler, H. (1984). First observation of bipedal locomotion in a gecko, *Homopholis* (*Blaesodactylus*) *sakalava* (Reptilia: Sauria: Gekkonidae). J. Herpetol. Assoc. Africa 3, 13–14.

Ross, F. D. and Mayer, G. C. (1983). On the dorsal armor of the Crocodylia. In *Advances in Herpetology and Evolutionary Biology: Essays in Honor of Ernest E. Williams*. (A. G. J. Rhodin and K. Miyata, eds.). Mus. Comp. Zool., Cambridge, MA, pp. 305–311.

Rossman, D. A. and Williams, K. L. (1966). Defensive behavior of the South American colubrid snakes *Pseustes sulphureus* (Wagler) and *Spilotes pullatus* (Linnaeus). Proc. Louisiana Acad. Sci. 29, 152–156.

Rowe-Rowe, D. T. (1978). The small carnivores of Natal. Lammergeyer 25, 1–48.

Roze, J. A. (1958). Los reptiles del Auyantepui, Venezuela, basandose en las colecciones de las expediciones de Phelps-Tate, del American Museum of Natural History, 1937–1938, ye de la Universidad Central de Venezuela, 1956. Acta Biol. Venezuelica 2, 243–270.

Roze, J. A. (1964). Pilgrim of the river. Nat. Hist. 73, 34–41.

Rubinoff, I. and Kropach, C. (1970). Differential reactions of Atlantic and Pacific predators to sea snakes. Nature 228, 1288–1290.

Ruben, J. A. (1976). Aerobic and anaerobic metabolism during activity in snakes. J. Comp. Physiol. 109, 147–157.

Russell, A. P. (1979a). Parallelism and integrated design in the foot structure of gekkonine and deplodactyline geckos. Copeia 1979, 1–21.

Russell, A. P. (1979b). The origin of parachuting locomotion in gekkonid lizards. Zool. J. Linn. Soc. 65, 233–249.

Russell, F. E. (1967). Bites by the Sonoran coral snake *Micruroides euryxanthus*. Toxicon 5, 39–42.

Ruthven, A. G. (1907). A collection of reptiles and amphibians from southern New Mexico and Arizona. Bull. Am. Mus. Nat. Hist. 23, 483–603.

Ruthven, A. G. (1912). The amphibians and reptiles collected by the University of Michigan–Walker Expedition in southern Vera Cruz, Mexico. Zool. Jahrb. (Syst.) 32, 295–332.

Saiff, E. (1975). Preglottal structures in the family Colubridae. Copeia 1975, 589–592.

Saint Girons, H., Bell, B. D. and Newman, D. G. (1980). Observations on the activity and thermoregulation of the tuatara, *Sphenodon punctatus* (Reptilia: Rhynchocephalia), on Stephens Island. New Zealand J. Zool. 7, 551–556.

Sajdak, R. A. and Henderson, R. W. (1982). Notes on the eggs and young of *Antillophis parvifrons stygius* (Reptilia, Serpentes, Colubridae). Florida Sci. 45, 200–204.

Salt, G. W. (1943). The lungs and inflation mechanisms of *Sauromalus obesus*. Copeia 1943, 193.

Sanchez-Herrera, O., Smith, H. M. and Chiszar, D. (1981). Another suggested case of ophidian deceptive mimicry. Trans. Kansas Acad. Sci. 84, 121–127.

Sattler, P. W. and Guttman, S. I. (1976). An electrophoretic analysis of *Thamnophis sirtalis* from western Ohio. Copeia 1976, 352–356.

Savitzky, A. H. (1980). The role of venom delivery strategies in snake evolution. Evolution 34, 1194–1204.

Savitzky, A. H. (1981). Hinged teeth in snakes: An adaptation for swallowing hard-bodied prey. Science 212, 346–349.

Savitsky, A. H. (1983). Coadapted character complexes among snakes: Fossoriality, piscivory, and durophagy. Am. Zool. 23, 397–409.
Savitzky, A. H. (1985). Vertebral protrusion in snakes: Evidence for a novel defense mechanism. Am. Phil. Soc. Grantee's Rept. 1984, 42–43.
Schall, J. J. and Pianka, E. R. (1980). Evolution of escape behavior. Am. Nat. 115, 551–566.
Schaller, G. B. (1972). *The Serengeti Lion.* Univ. Chicago Press, Chicago.
Schaller, G. B. and Crawshaw, P. G., Jr. (1982). Fishing behavior of Paraguayan caiman (*Caiman crocodilus*). Copeia 1982, 66–72.
Schaller, G. B. and Vasconcelos, J. M. C. (1978). Jaguar predation on capybara. Z. Säugetierkunde 43, 296–301.
Schiøtz, A. and Volsøe, H. (1959). The gliding flight of *Holaspis guentheri* Gray, a west-African lacertid. Copeia 1959, 259–260.
Schleich, H.-H. (1979). Feldherpetologische Beobachtungen in Persien, nebst morphologischen Daten zu den Agamen *Agama agilis, A. caucasica,* and *A. erythrogaster* (Reptilia: Sauria: Agamidae). Salamandra 15, 237–253.
Schleich, H.-H. (1982). Ein Fall von Cheloniophagie bei der griechischen Eidechsennatter, *Malpolon monspessulanus insignitus* (Geoffroy) (Reptilia: Serpentes: Colubridae). Salamandra 18, 354–355.
Schmidt, A. A. (1970). Zur Fortpflanzung der Kreuzbrustschildkröte (*Staurotypus slavinii*) in Gefangenschaft. Salamandra 6, 3–10.
Schmidt, K. P. (1919). Contributions to the herpetology of the Belgian Congo based on the collection of the American Museum Congo Expedition, 1909–1915. Part I. Turtles, crocodiles, lizards, and chameleons. Bull. Am. Mus. Nat. Hist. 39, 385–612.
Schmidt, K. P. (1923). Contributions to the herpetology of the Belgian Congo based on collections of the American Museum Congo Expedition, 1909–1915. Part II. Snakes. Bull. Am. Mus. Nat. Hist. 49, 1–148.
Schmidt, K. P. (1926). Amphibians and reptiles from the James Simpson-Roosevelt Asiatic Expedition. Field Mus. Nat. Hist. Publ., Zool. Ser., 22, 167–173.
Schmidt, K. P. (1927a). Notes on Chinese reptiles. Bull. Am. Mus. Nat. Hist. 54, 467–551.
Schmidt, K. P. (1927b). The reptiles of Hainan. Bull. Am. Mus. Nat. Hist. 54, 395–465.
Schmidt, K. P. (1928). Reptiles collected in Salvador for the California Institute of Technology. Field Mus. Nat. Hist. Publ., Zool. Ser., 22, 193–201.
Schmidt, K. P. (1939). Review of Böker (1935). Copeia 1939, 116–117.
Schmidt, K. P. (1957). Anent the "dangerous" bushmaster. Copeia 1957, 233.
Schmidt, K. P. and Inger, R. F. (1957). *Living Reptiles of the World.* Doubleday Co., Garden City, New York.
Schmidt, K. P. and Shannon, F. A. (1947). Notes on amphibians and reptiles of Michoacan, Mexico. Fieldiana 31, 63–85.
Schoener, T. W. (1971). Theory of feeding strategies. Ann. Rev. Ecol. Syst. 2, 369–404.
Schoener, T. W. (1979). Inferring the properties of predation and other injury-producing agents from injury frequencies. Ecology 60, 1110–1115.
Schueler, D. G. (1980). *Incident at Eagle Ranch.* Sierra Club Books, San Francisco.
Schurer, U. and H. G. Horn. (1976). Freiland- und Gefangenschaftsbeobachtungen am australischen Wasserwaran, *Varanus mertensi.* Salamandra 12, 176–188.
Schuett, G. W., Clark, D. L. and Kraus, F. (1984). Feeding mimicry in the rattlesnake *Sistrurus catenatus* with comments on the evolution of the rattle. An. Behav. 32, 625–626.
Schwartz, A. (1978). Some aspects of the herpetogeography of the West Indies. In *Zoogeography in the Caribbean.* (F. B. Gill, ed.). Spec. Publ. Acad. Nat. Sci. Philadelphia, Vol. 13, pp. 31–51.

REFERENCES

Schwartz, A. and Garrido, O. H. (1981). A review of the Cuban members of the genus *Arrhyton* (Reptilia, Serpentes, Colubridae). Ann. Carnegie Mus. 50, 207–230.

Schweitzer, H. (1956). Die Levante-Otter von Nordwest-Afrika—*Vipera lebetina mauritanica* (Guichenot). Aquar. Terrar. Z. 9, 190–192.

Schwenk, K. (1980). Functional morphology of cranial crests in lizards. Am. Zool. 20, 783.

Scudder, K. M. and Chiszar, D. (1977). Effects of six visual stimulus conditions on defensive and exploratory behavior in two species of rattlesnakes. Psychol. Rec. 3, 519–526.

Scudder, R. M. and Burghardt, G. M. (1983). A comparative study of defensive behavior in three sympatric species of water snakes (*Nerodia*). Z. Tierpsychol. 63,17–26.

Seib, R. L. (1980). Human envenomation from the bite of an aglyphous false coral snake, *Pliocercus elapoides* (Serpentes: Colubridae). Toxicon 18, 399–401.

Seidel, M. R. (1979). The osteoderms of the American alligator and their functional significance. Herpetologica 35, 375–380.

Seigel, R. A. (1986). Ecology and conservation of an endangered rattlesnake, *Sistrurus catenatus*, in Missouri, USA. Biol. Conserv. 35, 333–346.

Sen Gupta, S. N. (1969). Indian house sparrow attacks grass snake. Auk 86, 339.

Sexton, O. J. (1979). Remarks on defensive behavior of hognose snakes, *Heterodon*. Herpetol. Rev. 10, 86–87.

Sexton, O. J. and Heatwole, H. (1965). Life history notes on some Panamanian snakes. Caribbean J. Sci. 5, 39–43.

Sheplan, B. R. and Schwartz, A. (1974). Hispaniolan boas of the genus *Epicrates* (Serpentes, Boidae) and their Antillean relationships. Ann. Carnegie Mus. 45, 57–143.

Shine, R. (1977). Habitats, diet and sympatry in snakes: A study from Australia. Can. J. Zool. 55, 1118–1128.

Shine, R. (1980a). "Costs" of reproduction in reptiles. Oecologia 46, 92–100.

Shine, R. (1980b). Reproduction, feeding and growth in the Australian burrowing snake *Vermicella annulata*. J. Herpetol. 14, 71–77.

Shine, R. (1984). Ecology of small fossorial Australian snakes of the genera *Neelaps* and *Simoselaps* (Serpenter, Elapidae). Univ. Kansas, Spec. Publ. Mus. Nat. Hist. 10, 173–183.

Shine, R. (1986). Evolutionary advantages of limblessness: Evidence from pygopodid lizards. Copeia 1986, 525–529.

Shreve, B. (1957). Reptiles and amphibians from Selva Lacandona. In *Biological Investigations in the Selva Lacandona, Chiapas, Mexico*. (R. A. Paynter Jr., ed.). Bull. Mus. Comp. Zool. 116, 242–248.

Sight, W. P. (1949). Annotated list of reptiles taken in western Bengal. Herpetologica 5, 81–83.

Simon, C. A. and Bissinger, B. (1983). Paint marking lizards: Does the color affect survivorship? J. Herpetol. 17, 184–186.

Simon, C. A., Gravelle, K., Bissinger, B. E., Eiss, I. and Ruibal, R. (1981). The role of chemoreception in the iguanid lizard *Sceloporus jarrovi*. An. Behav. 29, 46–54.

Slevin, J. R. (1928). Description of a new species of lizard from Malpelo Island. Proc. Cal. Acad. Sci. 16, 681–684.

Slevin, J. R. (1939). Notes on a collection of reptiles and amphibians from Guatemala. I. Proc. Cal. Acad. Sci. 23, 392–414.

Smedley, N. (1931). Notes on some Malaysian snakes. Bull. Raffles Mus. 5, 49–54.

Smith, A. K. (1974). Incidence of tail coiling in a population of ringneck snakes (*Diadophis punctatus*). Trans. Kansas Acad. Sci. 77, 237–238.

Smith, D. D. (1983). *Anolis carolinensis* (green anole) predation. Herpetol. Rev. 14, 46.
Smith, D. D., Laposha, N. A., Powell, R. and Parmerlee, J. S. (1985). Life history notes: *Crotalus molossus* (anomaly). Herpetol. Rev. 16, 78–79.
Smith, H. M. (1943). Summary of the collection of snakes and crocodilians made in Mexico under the Walter Rathbone Bacon traveling scholarship. Bull. U.S. Nat. Mus. 93, 393–504.
Smith, H. M. (1946). *Handbook of Lizards*. Comstock Publ. Assoc., Ithaca, New York.
Smith, H. M. (1949). Miscellaneous notes on Mexican lizards. J. Wash. Acad. Sci. 39, 34–43.
Smith, M. A. (1938). The nucho-dorsal glands of snakes. Proc. Zool. Soc. London, Ser, B 100, 575–583.
Smith, M. A. (1943). *The Fauna of British India, Ceylon and Burma, Including the Whole of the Indo-chinese Sub-region. Reptilia and Amphibia. Vol. III. Serpentes*. Taylor and Francis, London.
Smith, N. G. (1969). Avian predation of coral snakes. Copeia 1969, 402–404.
Smith, S. M. (1975). Innate recognition of coral snake pattern by a possible avian predator. Science 187, 757–760.
Smith, S. M. (1977). Coral snake pattern recognition and stimulus generalization by native great kiskadees (Aves. Tyrannidae). Nature 265, 535–536.
Soderberg, P. (1966). *On Twelve Asiatic Elapid Snakes With Specific Reference to Their Occurrence in Thailand*. Privately publ., Bangkok.
Soderberg, P. S. (1971). Striking behaviour of the common green whip snake (*Ahaetulla nasutus*). J. Bombay Nat. Hist. Soc. 68, 839.
Spawls, S. (1985). Life history notes: *Dispholidus typus* (behavior). Herpetol. Rev. 16, 111.
Stamps, J. A. (1977). Social behavior and spacing patterns in lizards. In *Biology of the Reptilia, Vol. 7, Ecology and Behavior*. (C. Gans and D. W. Tinkle, eds.). Academic Press, New York, pp. 265–334.
Stamps, J. A. (1983). The relationship between ontogenetic habitat shifts, competition and predator avoidance in a juvenile lizard (*Anolis aeneus*). Behav. Ecol. Sociobiol. 12, 19–33.
Stancyk, S. E. (1981). Non-human predators of sea turtles and their control. In *Biology and Conservation of Sea Turtles*. (K. A. Bjordal, ed.). Smithsonian Inst. Press, Washington, D. C., pp. 139–152.
Steadman, D. W. (1986). Holocene vertebrate fossils from Isla Floreana, Galapagos. Smithsonian Contr. Zool. 413, 1–103.
Stebbins, R. C. (1954). *Amphibians and Reptiles of Western North America*. McGraw-Hill Book Co., New York.
Stebbins, R. C., Lowenstein, J. M. and Cohen, N. W. (1967). A field study of the lava lizard (*Tropidurus albemarlensis*) in the Galapagos Islands. Ecology 48, 839–851.
Stemmler-Gyger, O. (1965). Zur Biologie der Rassen von *Echis carinatus* (Schneider) 1801. Salamandra 1, 29–46.
Stemmler, O. (1970). Beobachtungen an marokkanischen Schachbrettschleichen, *Trognophis wiegmanni* Kaup 1830 (Amphisbaenia, Trogonophidae). Aquar. Terrar. 17, 343–347.
Stemmler, O. (1971). Auffällige Schwanzhaltung bei zwei Riesenschlangen (*Python sebae* and *Epicrates cenchria*). Salamandra 7, 137–142.
Stille, W. T. (1947). The aquatic habits of *Cnemidophorus sexlineatus*. Copeia 1947, 143.
Storer, T. I. and Tevis, L. P. Jr. (1955). *California Grizzly*. Univ. Nebraska Press, Lincoln.
Strasser, F. D. (1931). An encounter between a collared lizard and a rattlesnake. Bull. Antivenin Inst. Am., 5, 41.

REFERENCES

Stuart, L. C. (1935). A contribution to the knowledge of a portion of the savannah region of Central Peten, Guatemala. Misc. Publ. Mus. Zool. Univ. Michigan 29, 1–56.

Stull, O. G. (1928). A revision of the genus *Tropidophis*. Occ. Pap. Mus. Zool. Univ. Michigan 195, 1–49.

Stumpel, A. H. P. (1981). Water snake (*Xenochrophis piscator*) imitates cobra (Reptilia: Serpentes: Colubridae). Salamandra 17, 203–204.

Sutton, G. M. (1954). Blackish crane-hawk. Wilson Bull. 66, 237–242.

Sweeney, R. C. H. (1971). *Snakes of Nyasaland* (Second ed., revised). A. Asher and Co., Amsterdam.

Sweet, S. S. (1985). Geographic variation, convergent crypsis and mimicry in gopher snakes (*Pituophis melanoleucus*) and western rattlesnakes (*Crotalus viridis*). J. Herpetol. 19, 55–67.

Switak, K. H. (1969). First captive hatching of bushmasters *Lachesis muta*. Int. Zoo. Yrbk. 9, 56–57.

Taigen, T. L., Emerson, S. B. and Pough, F. H. (1982). Ecological correlates of anuran exercise physiology. Oecologia 52, 49–56.

Tanner, W. W. and Krogh, J. E. (1975). Ecology of the zebra-tailed lizard *Callisaurus draconoides* at the Nevada test site. Herpetologica 31, 302–316.

Tanner, W. W. and Robison, W. G., Jr. (1960). New and unusual serpents from Chihuahua, Mexico. Herpetologica 16, 67–70.

Taylor, E. H. (1922). *The Lizards of the Philippine Islands*. Bureau of Printing, Manila.

Taylor, E. H. (1931). Notes on two specimens of the rare snake *Ficimia cana* and the description of a new species of *Ficimia* from Texas. Copeia 1931, 4–7.

Taylor, E. H. (1951). A brief review of the snakes of Costa Rica. Univ. Kansas Sci. Bull. 34, 3–188.

Taylor, E. H. (1965). The serpents of Thailand and adjacent waters. Univ. Kansas Sci. Bull. 45, 609–1096.

Taylor, E. H. and Smith, H. M. (1942). The snake genera *Conopsis* and *Toluca*. Univ. Kansas Sci. Bull. 28, 325–363.

Taylor, W. P. (1954). Food habits and notes on life history of the ring-tailed cat in Texas. J. Mammal. 35, 55–63.

Telford, S. R. (1952). A herpetological survey in the vicinity of Lake Shipp, Polk County, Florida. J. Florida Acad. Sci. 15, 175–185.

Test, F. H., Sexton, O. J. and Heatwole, H. (1966). Reptiles of Rancho Grande and vicinity, Estado Aragua, Venezuela. Misc. Publ. Mus. Zool. Univ. Michigan 128, 1–63.

Tevis, L., Jr. (1944). Herpetological notes from Lower California. Copeia 1944, 6–18.

Thomas, R. (1975). The *argus* group of West Indian *Sphaerodactylus* (Sauria: Gekkonidae). Herpetologica 31, 177–195.

Thomas, R. and Schwartz, A. (1965). Hispaniolan snakes of the genus *Dromicus*. Rev. Biol. Trop. 13, 59–83.

Thomas, R. A. and Hendricks, F. S. (1967). Letistimulation in *Virginia striatula* (Linnaeus). Southwestern Nat. 21, 123–124.

Thorne, S. C. and Hamman, K. C. D. (1981). Predation by the sharptooth catfish *Clarias gariepinus* (Siluriformes: Clariidae) on the common puff-adder *Bitis arietans* (Squamata: Viperidae). J. Herpetol. Assoc. Africa 25, 14–15.

Throckmorton, G. S., Bavay, J. E., Chaffey, W., Merrotsy, B., Noske, S. and Noske, R. (1985). The mechanisms of frill erection in the bearded dragon *Amphibolurus barbatus* with comments on the jacky lizard *A. muricatus* (Agamidae). J. Morphol. 183, 285–292.

Tinbergen, N. (1963). On the aims and methods of ethology. Z. Tierpsychol. 20, 410–429.

Tinkle, D. W. (1967). The life and demography of the side-blotched lizard, *Uta stansburiana*. Misc. Publ. Mus. Zool. Univ. Michigan 132, 1–182.

Tinkle, D. W. (1976). Comparative data on the population ecology of the desert spiny lizard, *Sceloporus magister*. Herpetologica 32, 1–6.

Tollestrup, K. (1981). The social behavior and displays of two species of horned lizards, *Phrynosoma platyrhinos* and *Phrynosoma coronatum*. Herpetologica 37, 130–141.

Tonge, S. and Morgan, D. (1984). Notes on the herpetofauna of southern Malawi. Br. Herpetol. Soc. Bull. 9, 35–42.

Townsend, C. R. and Calow, P. (1981). *Physiological Ecology: An Evolutionary Approach to Resource Use*. Sinauer Assoc., Inc., Sunderland, MA.

Trowbridge, A. H. (1937). Ecological observations on amphibians and reptiles collected in southeastern Oklahoma during the summer of 1934. Am. Midl. Nat. 18, 285–303.

Tryon, B. (1975). How to incubate reptile eggs: A proven technique. Bull. New York Herpetol. Soc. 11, 33–37.

Tryon, B. W. and Guese, R. K. (1984). Death-feigning in the gray-banded kingsnake, *Lampropeltis alterna*. Herpetol. Rev. 15, 108–109.

Tyron, B. W. and Whitehead, J. (1986). Life history notes: *Naja melanoleuca* (caudal use). Herpetol. Rev. 17, 61.

Tschambers, B. (1949). Birth of the Australian blue-tongued lizard, *Tiliqua scincoides*. Herpetologica 5, 141–142.

Tuttle, M. D. (1967). Predation by *Chrotopterus auritus* on geckos. J. Mammal. 48, 319.

Tweedie, M. F. W. (1953). *The Snakes of Malaya*. Govt. Printing Off., Singapore.

Underwood, G. (1947). Reptiles of Cocanada. J. Bombay Nat. Hist. Soc. 46, 613–628.

Underwood, G. (1957). *Lanthanotus* and the anguinomorphan lizards: A critical review. Copeia 1957, 20–30.

Uzzell, T. M., Jr. (1965). Teiid lizards of the genus *Echinosaura*. Copeia 1965, 82–89.

Uzzell, T. M., Jr. (1966). Teiid lizards of the genus *Neusticurus* (Reptilia, Sauria). Bull. Am. Mus. Nat. Hist. 132, 277–328.

Vadasz, C., Kiss, B. and Csanyi, V. (1978). Defensive behaviour and its inheritance in the anabantoid fish, *Macropodus opercularis* and *Macropodus opercularis concolor*. Behav. Proc. 3, 107–124.

Valdez, R. and LaVal, R. K. (1971). Records of bats from Honduras and Nicaragua. J. Mammal. 52, 247–250.

Valverde, J. A. (1967). *Estructura de una Communidad Mediterranea de Vertebrados Terrestres*. Conseja superior de Investigascions Cientificas, Madrid.

van Berkum, F., Huey, R. B. and Adams, B. A. (1986). Physiological consequences of thermoregulation in a tropical lizard (*Ameiva festiva*). Physiol. Zool. 59, 464–472.

Van Denburgh, F. (1922). *The Reptiles of Western North America. Vol. 1. Lizards*. Occas. Pap. Cal. Acad. Sci. 10:1–611.

Vanderhaege, M. (1971). Reproduction en captivite de *Dracaena guianensis* Daudin 1802. Aquarama 5, 28.

Van Devender, T. R. (1973). Behavior and disruptive coloration in the New Mexico gartersnake *Thamnophis sirtalis ornata*. Southwestern Nat. 18, 247–248.

Van Devender, T. R. (1977). Observations on the Argentine iguanid lizard *Leiosaurus bellii* Duméril and Bibron (Reptilia, Lacertilia, Iguanidae). J. Herpetol. 11, 238–241.

Van Mater, J. (1971). The natural history of two generations of *Chamaeleo jacksoni* in captivity. Herpetology 5, 1–23.

Vanzolini, P. E. (1970). Climbing habits of Leptotyphlopidae (Serpentes) and Wall's theory of the evolution of the ophidian eye. Pap. Avul. Zool. 23, 13–16.

REFERENCES

Vanzolini, P. E., Ramos-Costa, A. M. M. and Vitt, L. J. (1980). *Repteis das Caatingas*. Acad. Cien. Brasileira, Rio de Janero.
Vaughn, T. A. (1976). Nocturnal behavior of the African false vampire bat (*Cardioderma cor*). J. Mammal. 57, 227–248.
Venning, F. E. W. (1910a). A collection of Ophidia from the Chin Hills. J. Bombay Nat. Hist. Soc. 20, 331–344.
Venning, F. E. W. (1910b). Further notes on snakes from the Chin Hills. J. Bombay Nat. Hist. Soc. 20, 770–775.
Vermeij, G. J. (1978). *Biogeography and Adaptation: Patterns of Marine Life*. Harvard Univ. Press, Cambridge, MA.
Vermeij, G. J. (1982). Unsuccessful predation and evolution. Am. Nat. 120, 701–720.
Vetter, R. S. and Brodie, E. D., Jr. (1977). Background color selection and antipredator behavior of the flying gecko, *Ptychozoon kuhli*. Herpetologica 33, 464–467.
Villa, J. (1969). Notes on *Conophis nevermanni*, an addition to the Nicaraguan herpetofauna. J. Herpetol. 3, 169–171.
Vinson, J. M. (1975). Notes on the reptiles of Round Island. Mauritius Inst. Bull. 8, 49–67.
Visser, J. (1966). Colour change in *Leptotyphlops scutifrons* (Peters) and notes on its defensive behaviour. Zool. Afr. 2, 123–125.
Vitt, L. J. (1980). Ecological observations on sympatric *Philodryas* (Colubridae) in northeastern Brazil. Pap. Avul. Zool. 34, 87–98.
Vitt, L. J. (1983). Tail loss in lizards: The significance of foraging and predator escape modes. Herpetologica 39, 151–162.
Vitt, L. J., Congdon, J. D., Hulse, A. C. and Platz, J. E. (1974). Territorial aggressive encounters and tail breaks in the lizard *Sceloporus magister*. Copeia 1974, 990–993.
Vitt, L. J. and Hulse, A. C. (1973). Observations on feeding habits and tail display of the Sonoran coral snake, *Micruroides euryxanthus*. Herpetologica 29, 302–304.
Vitt, L. J. and Lacher, T. E., Jr. (1981). Behavior, habitat, diet, and reproduction of the iguanid lizard *Polychrus acutirostris* in the caatinga of northeastern Brazil. Herpetologica 37, 53–63.
Voous, K. (1969). Predation potential in birds of prey from Surinam. Ardea 57, 117–148.
Vrba, E. S. (1984). Evolutionary pattern and process in the sister-group Alcelaphini-Aepycerotini (Mammalia: Bovidae). In *Living Fossils*. (N. Eldredge and S. M. Stanley, eds.). Springer-Verlag, New York, pp. 62–79.
Wall, F. (1903). A prodromus of the snakes hitherto recorded from China, Japan, and the Loo Choo Islands; with some notes. Proc. Zool. Soc. London 1903, pp. 84–102.
Wall, F. (1906a). The snake and its natural foes. J. Bombay Nat. Hist. Soc. 17, 375–395.
Wall, F. (1906b). A popular treatise on the common Indian Snakes. Part III. J. Bombay Nat. Hist. Soc. 17, 259–273.
Wall, F. (1906c). A popular treatise on the common Indian snakes. Part I. J. Bombay Nat. Hist. Soc. 16, 533–554.
Wall, F. (1906d). A popular treatise on the common Indian snakes. Part II. J. Bombay Nat. Hist. Soc. 17, 1–8.
Wall, F. (1907a). A popular treatise on the common Indian snakes. Part V. J. Bombay Nat. Hist. Soc. 18, 1–17.
Wall, F. (1907b). Notes on snakes collected in Fyzabad. J. Bombay Nat. Hist. Soc. 18, 101–129.
Wall, F. (1907c). A popular treatise on the common Indian snakes. Part IV. J. Bombay Nat. Hist. Soc. 17, 857–870.

Wall, F. (1907d). A popular treatise on the common Indian snakes. Part VI. J. Bombay Nat. Hist. Soc. 18, 227–243.
Wall, F. (1908a). Notes on a collection of snakes from the Khasi Hills, Assam. J. Bombay Nat. Hist. Soc. 18, 312–337.
Wall, F. (1908b). A popular treatise on the common Indian snakes. Part VII. J. Bombay Nat. Hist. Soc. 18, 525–554.
Wall, F. (1908c). A popular treatise on the common Indian snakes. Part VIII. J. Bombay Nat. Hist. Soc. 18, 711–735.
Wall, F. (1909a). Notes on snakes from the neighborhood of Darjeeling. J. Bombay Nat. Hist. Soc. 19, 337–357.
Wall, F. (1909b). A popular treatise on the common Indian snakes. Part IX. J. Bombay Nat. Hist. Soc. 19, 87–106.
Wall, F. (1909c). Notes on snakes collected in upper Assam. J. Bombay Nat. Hist. Soc. 19, 608–623.
Wall, F. (1909d). A popular treatise on the common Indian snakes. Part XI. J. Bombay Nat. Hist. Soc. 19, 555–563.
Wall, F. (1909e). A popular treatise on the common Indian snakes. Part X. J. Bombay Nat. Hist. Soc. 19, 287–298.
Wall, F. (1910a). A popular treatise on the common Indian snakes. Part XII. J. Bombay Nat. Hist. Soc. 19, 775–792.
Wall, F. (1910b). Notes on snakes collected in upper Assam. J. Bombay Nat. Hist. Soc. 19, 825–845.
Wall, F. (1910c). A popular treatise on the common Indian snakes. Part XIII. J. Bombay Nat. Hist. Soc. 20, 65–79.
Wall, F. (1911a). A popular treatise on the common Indian snakes. Part XV. J. Bombay Nat. Hist. Soc. 20, 933–953.
Wall, F. (1911b). A popular treatise on the common Indian snakes. Part XIV. J. Bombay Nat. Hist. Soc. 20, 603–633.
Wall, F. (1911c). Reptiles collected in Chitral. J. Bombay Nat. Hist. Soc. 21, 132–145.
Wall, F. (1911d). A popular treatise on the common Indian snakes. Part XVI. J. Bombay Nat. Hist. Soc. 21, 1–9.
Wall, F. (1912a). A popular treatise on the common Indian snakes. Part XVII. J. Bombay Nat. Hist. Soc. 21, 447–475.
Wall, F. (1912b). A popular treatise on the common Indian snakes. Part XVIII. J. Bombay Nat. Hist. Soc. 21, 1009–1021.
Wall, F. (1913a). A popular treatise on the common Indian snakes. Part XX. J. Bombay Nat. Hist. Soc. 22, 242–259 and 550–568.
Wall, F. (1913b). A popular treatise on the common Indian snakes. Part XXII. J. Bombay Nat. Hist. Soc. 23, 34–43.
Wall, F. (1913c). A popular treatise on the common Indian snakes. Part XIX. J. Bombay Nat. Hist. Soc. 22, 22–28.
Wall, F. (1913d). A popular treatise on the common Indian snakes. Part XXI. J. Bombay Nat. Hist. Soc. 22, 749–760.
Wall, F. (1914). A popular treatise on the common Indian snakes. Part XXIII. J. Bombay Nat. Hist. Soc. 23, 206–215.
Wall, F. (1918a). A popular treatise on the common Indian snakes. Part XXIV. J. Bombay Nat. Hist. Soc. 25, 375–382.
Wall, F. (1918b). A popular treatise on the common Indian snakes. Part XXV. J. Bombay Nat. Hist. Soc. 25, 628–635.

REFERENCES

Wall, F. (1918c). A popular treatise on the common Indian snakes. Part XXVI. J. Bombay Nat. Hist. Soc. 26, 89–92.

Wall, F. (1919a). Notes on a collection of snakes made in the Nilgiri Hills and the adjacent Wynaad. J. Bombay Nat. Hist. Soc. 26, 552–584.

Wall, F. (1919b). A popular treatise on the common Indian snakes. Part XXVIII. J. Bombay Nat. Hist. Soc. 26, 803–810.

Wall, F. (1921). *Ophidia Taprobanica or the Snakes of Ceylon*. H. R. Cottle, Government Printer, Colombo, Ceylon.

Wall, F. (1922). Notes on some lizards, frogs and human beings in the Nilgiri Hills. J. Bombay Nat. Hist. Soc. 28, 493–499.

Wall, F. (1924). The hamadryad or king cobra, *Naia hannah*. J. Bombay Nat. Hist. Soc. 30, 189–195.

Wall, F. (1925). Notes on snakes collected in Burma in 1924. J. Bombay Nat. Hist. Soc. 30, 805–821.

Wall, F. (1926a). Snakes collected in Burma in 1925. J. Bombay Nat. Hist. Soc. 31, 558–566.

Wall, F. (1926b). The reticulate python. *Python reticulatus* (Schneider). J. Bombay Nat. Hist. Soc. 31, 84–90.

Warren, E. (1923). Notes on a lizard-eating S. African spider. Ann. Natal Mus. London 5, 95–100.

Watkins, J. F. II, Gehlbach, F. R. and Kroll, J. C. (1967). Ability of the blind snake, *Leptotyphlops dulcis*, to follow pheromone trails of army ants, *Neivamyrmex nigrescens* and *N. opacithorax*. Southwestern Nat. 12, 455–462.

Webb, G. J. W., Manolis, S. C. and Buckworth, R. (1982). *Crocodylus johnstoni* in the McKinlay River Area, N. T. I. Variation in the diet, and a new method of assessing the relative importance of prey. Aust. J. Zool. 30, 877–899.

Webb, R. G. (1970). *Reptiles of Oklahoma*. Univ. Oklahoma Press, Norman.

Webster, T. P. (1969). Ecological observations on *Anolis occultus* Williams and Rivero (Sauria, Iguanidae). Breviora 312, 1–5.

Weldon, P. J. and Burghardt, G. M. (1979). The ophiophage defensive response in crotaline snakes: Extension to new taxa. J. Chem. Ecol. 5, 141–151.

Wellman, J. (1963). A revision of snakes of the genus *Conophis* (Family Colubridae, from Middle America). Univ. Kansas Publ. Mus. Nat. Hist. 15, 251–295.

Wemmer, C. and Wilson, D. E. (1983). Structure and function of hair crests and capes of African Carnivora. In *Advances in the Study of Mammalian Behavior*. (J. F. Eisenberg and D. G. Kleiman, eds.). Amer. Soc. Mamm. Spec. Publ. 7.

Werler, J. E. (1970). Notes on young and eggs of captive reptiles. Int. Zoo Yrbk. 10, 105–116.

Werner, Y. (1983). Behavioural triangulation of the head in three boigine snakes: Possible cases of mimicry. Israel J. Zool. 32, 205–228.

Werner, Y. (1985). Defensive behaviour in a boigine snake: First record of throat inflation in *Psammophis*. Israel J. Zool. 33, 69–71.

Werner, Y. (1986). Evolutionary implications of occasional (non-mimetic) behavioural triangulation of the head in snakes (*Coluber rhodorhachis* and *Malpolon monspessulanus*). The Snake 18, 37–41.

Werner, Y. L., Frankenberg, E. and Adar, O. (1978). Further observations on the distinctive vocal repertoire of *Ptyodactylus hasselquistii* cf. *hasselquistii* (Reptilia: Gekkonidae). Israel J. Zool. 27, 176–188.

Werth, R. J. (1973). Implications of aquatic behavior in the collared lizard, *Crotaphytus collaris collaris*. HISS News-Journal 1, 192.

Wever, E. G. (1978). *The Reptile Ear: Its Structure and Function.* Princeton Univ. Press, Princeton, NJ.
Whitaker, A. H. (1968). The lizards of the Poor Knights Islands, New Zealand. New Zeal. J. Sci. 11, 623–651.
White, S. R. (1948). Observations on the mountain devil. West. Aust. Nat. 1, 78–81.
Whitham, R. (1974). Neonate sea turtles from the stomach of a pelagic fish. Copeia 1974, 548.
Whiting, A. M. (1969). Squamate cloacal glands: Morphology, histology, and histochemistry. Doctoral dissertation, Pennsylvania State Univ.
Wickler, W. (1960). Belegexemplare zu Ethogrammen. Z. Tierpsychol. 17, 141–142.
Wickler, W. (1968). *Mimicry in Plants and Animals.* McGraw-Hill Book Co., New York.
Wiley, E. O. (1981). *Phylogenetics, the Theory and Practice of Phylogenetic Systematics.* John Wiley and Sons, New York.
Williams, E. E. and Peterson, J. A. (1982). Convergence and alternative designs in the digital adhesive pads of scincid lizards. Science 215, 1509–1511.
Williams, E. E., Rivero, J. A. and Thomas, R. (1965). A new anole from Puerto Rico. Breviora 231, 1–18.
Williams, G. C. (1966). *Adaptation and Natural Selection, A Critique of Some Current Evolutionary Thought.* Princeton Univ. Press, Princeton, NJ.
Williamson, M. A. (1986). *Trail of the Snake: From Big Bend to Baja.* Sunstone Press, Santa Fe, NM.
Willis, L., Threlkeld, S. T. and Carpenter, C. C. (1982). Tail loss patterns in *Thamnophis* (Reptilia: Colubridae) and the probable fate of injured individuals. Copeia 1982, 98–101.
Wilson, E. O. (1975). *Sociobiology: The New Synthesis.* Harvard Univ. Press, Cambridge.
Wilson, L. D. (1967). Generic reallocation and review of *Coluber fasciolatus* Shaw (Serpentes: Colubridae). Herpetologica 23, 260–275.
Wilson, V. J. (1965). The snakes of the eastern province of Zambia, Puku 3, 149–170.
Wolda, H. (1975). The ecosystem on Malpelo Island. Smithsonian Contr. Zool. 176, 21–26.
Woodin, W. H. (1953). Notes on some reptiles from the Huachuca area of southeastern Arizona. Bull. Chicago Acad. Sci. 9, 285–296.
Wright, A. H., and A. A. Wright. (1957). *Handbook of Snakes of the United States and Canada.* Comstock Publ. Assoc., Ithaca, NY.
Wright, P. (1982). Observations of predator/prey relationships between praying mantids and geckos. N. Terr. Nat. 1(5), 10–11.
Wunderle, J. M. (1981). Avian predation upon *Anolis* lizards on Grenada, West Indies. Herpetologica 37, 104–108.
Zingg, A. (1968). Zur Fortpflanzung von *Dispholidus typus* (Reptilia, Colubridae). Salamandra 4, 37–43.
Zinner, H. (1967). Herpetological collection trips to the Lebanon 1965 and 1966. Israel J. Zool. 16, 49–58.
Zinner, H. (1985). On behavioral and sexual dimorphism of *Telesocopus dhara* Forscal 1776 (Reptilia: Serpentes, Colubridae). J. Herpetol. Assoc. Africa 31, 5–6.
Zug, G. R. (1974). Crocodile galloping: An unique gait for reptiles. Copeia 1974, 550–552.
Zweifel, R. G. (1981). Genetics of color patterns polymorphism in the California kingsnake. J. Heredity 72, 238–244.
Zweifel, R. G. (1982). Color pattern morphs of the kingsnake (*Lampropeltis getulus*) in southern California: Distribution and evolutionary status. Bull. S. Cal. Acad. Sci. 80, 70–81.

REFERENCES

ADDITIONAL REFERENCES

Brunton, D. H. (1986). Fatal antipredator behavior of a killdeer. Wilson Bull. 98, 605–607.

Carey, H. V. and Moore, P. (1986). Foraging and predation risk in yellow-bellied marmots. Amer. Midl. Nat. 116, 267–275.

Cokendolpher, J. (1977). Comments on a lizard-eating *Arqiope* (Araneidae: Araneae). J. Arachnol. 5, 184.

Douglass, J. F. and Weingarner, C. E. (1977). Predation of eggs and young of the gopher tortoise, *Gopherus polyphemus* (Reptilia, Testudines, Testudinidae) in southern Florida. J. Herp. 11, 236–238.

Heusser, H. and Schlumpf, H. U. (1962). Totsellen bei der Barren-Ringelnatter—*Natrix natrix helvetica*. Aquar. Terr. Z. 15, 214–218.

Ramsey, L. W. (1946). Captive specimens of *Tropidoclonion lineatum*. Herpetologica 3, 112.

Sanchez-Herrera, O., Smith, H. M. and Chiszar, D. (1981). Another suggested case of ophidian deceptive mimicry. Trans. Kansas Acad. Sci. 84, 121–127.

Smith, N. G. (1969). Avian predation on coral snakes. Copeia 1969, 402–404.

Wehekind, L. (1955). Notes on the foods of the Trinidad snakes. Brit. J. Herp. 2, 9–13.

Wetmore, A. (1965). The birds of the Republic of Panama. Part I. Smithsonian Misc. Coll. 150, 1–483.

APPENDICES

A. Some Records of Predation on Reptiles

The following abbreviations are used for predator taxa below: I, invertebrates; Fi, fishes; Ca, caecilians; Sa, salamanders; Fr, frogs; T, turtles; Cr, crocodilians; L, lizards; Sn, snakes; Bi, birds; Ba, bats; M, other mammals. References to predation by humans and by captive animals are not included.

TESTUDINES

Chelidae

Phrynops rufipes (M, Lamar and Medem, 1984).

Cheloniidae

Caretta caretta (Fi, Witham, 1974); *Chelonia mydas* (I, Fi, Bi, Sn, Brattstrom, 1955b; Witham, 1974; Pritchard and Trebbau, 1984; Frazier, 1985); *Eretmochelys imbricata* (I, L, Sn, Auffenberg, 1981a; Buxton and Branch, 1983; Crother, 1986).

Chelydridae

Chelydra serpentina (Fr, Sn, Ruthven, 1912; Guidry, 1953; Klimstra, 1959; Ernst and Barbour, 1972; Graham, 1984).

Emydidae

Chrysemys picta (Fr, Graham, 1984); *Graptemys sp.* (Fr, Graham, 1984); *G. geographica* (Fr, Graham, 1984); *Malaclemys terrapin* (Bi, Pritchard and Trebbau, 1984); *Mauremys caspica* (M, Amores, 1980); *Pseudemys concinna* (Sn, Laughlin, 1959; Brown, 1979); *P. rubriventris* (Fr, Graham, 1984); *P. scripta* (I, Cr, Fr, Sn, Bi, M, Shreve, 1957; Laughlin, 1959; Burkett, 1966; Minckley, 1966; Klimstra, 1969; Moll and Legler, 1971; Graham, 1984). *Rhinoclemmys punctularia* (Cr, Medem, 1962); *Terrapene carolina* (Fr, Sn, Klimstra, 1969; Graham, 1984); *T. ornata* (Fr. T, Sn, Bi, M, Legler, 1960; Graham, 1984).

Kinosternidae

Kinosternon flavescens (Sn, Platt, 1969); *K. scorpioides* (Bi, Pritchard and Trebbau, 1984); *K. subrubrum* (Sn, Barbour, 1956; Hamilton and Pollack,

1956; Brown, 1979); *Sternotherus odoratus* (Sn, Hamilton and Pollack, 1955).

Pelomedusidae

Pelomedusa subrufa (Bi, Broadley, 1974); *Pelusios subniger* (Cr, Cott, 1961); *P. sinuatus* (Cr, Bi, Cott, 1961; Broadley, 1974); *Podocnemis expansa* (Fi, Cr, Bi, Pritchard and Trebbau, 1984; Roze, 1964); *P. vogli* (Cr, Sn, M, Pritchard and Trebbau, 1984).

Testudinidae

Geochelone sp. (M, L. Emmons, pers. comm.); *G. pardalis* (Bi, M, Broadley, 1974, in litt.); *Gopherus agassizii* (Bi, M, Berry, in litt.); *G. polyphemus* (Bi, Sn, M, Douglass and Weingarner, 1977; Fitzpatrick and Woolfenden, 1978); *Kinixys belliana* (Bi, M, Schmidt, 1919; Broadley, 1974); *Psammobates sp.* (M, Broadley, in litt.); *P. oculifer* (Bi, Broadley,1974); *Testudo graeca* (Bi, M, Reed and Marx, 1959; Mienis, 1979); *T. marginata* (Sn, Schleich, 1982).

Trionychidae:

Trionyx sp. (M, Minckley, 1966); *T. spiniferus* (Fr, Clarkson and de Vos, 1986).

CROCODILIA

Alligatoridae

Alligator mississippiensis (Sn, Bi, M, McIlhenny, 1935; Allen and Swindell, 1948; Neill, 1971); *Caiman crocodilus* (Fi, Sn, Bi, M, Wehekind, 1955; Alvarez del Toro, 1974; Gorzula, 1978).

Crocodylidae

Crocodylus acutus (Fi, Bi, M, Alvarez del Toro, 1974); *C. moreletii* (Fi, T, Sn, Bi, M, Alvarez del Toro, 1974). *C. niloticus* (Fi, Cr, L, Bi, M, Cott, 1961; Broadley, 1974).

RHYNCHOCEPHALIA

Sphenodontidae

Sphenodon punctatus (Bi, Saint Girons et al., 1980).

AMPHISBAENIA

Amphisbaenidae

Amphisbaena fuliginosa (Sn, Greene, 1973b); *Ancylocranium ionidesi* (Sn, Loveridge, 1951); *Blanus cinereus* (Bi, M, Amores, 1980; Valverde, 1967); *Chirindia swynnertoni* (Sn, Bi, Broadley, 1974; Broadley and Gans, 1978a); *Dalophia pistillum* (Sn, Bi, M, Broadley, 1963, 1974, in litt.); *Monopeltis sp.* (M, Broadley, in litt.); *M. capensis* (Bi, Broadley, 1974); *M. leonardi* (M, Broadley, in litt.); *M. sphenorhynchus* (Sn, Broadley, 1963); *Zygaspis quadrifrons* (Sn, M, Broadley, 1963; in litt.); *Z. violacea* (Sn, Broadley and Gans, 1978b); unidentified (Sn, Greene, 1973b, 1983a).

Bipedidae

Bipes biporus (Sn, Papenfuss, 1982); *B. canaliculatus* (Sn, Papenfuss, 1982).

Rhineuridae

Rhineura floridana (Sn, Bi, M, Carr, 1940, 1982; Jackson and Franz, 1981; Greene, 1984).

SAURIA

Agamidae

Agama sp. (Bi, Broadley, 1974); *A. aculeata* (M, Broadley, in litt.); *A. agama* (L, Cissé, 1972); *A. agilis* (Sn, Bi, M, Minton, 1966); *A. atricollis* (M, Broadley, in litt.); *A. cyanogaster* (Bi, Broadley, 1974); *A. hispida* (Bi, Broadley, 1974; Bourquin and Channing, 1980); *A. kirkii* (Bi, M, Broadley, 1974, in litt.); *Amphibolurus barbatus* (L, Pianka, 1971b); *A. nuchalis* (L, Sn, Pianka, 1968, 1970a); *A. isolepis* (L, Pianka, 1968); *Calotes sp.* (Sn, Wall, 1909a); *C. jerdoni* (Sn, Wall, 1908a); *C. versicolor* (Bi, L, Sn, Minton, 1966); *Japalura variegata* (Sn, Wall, 1909a); *Moloch horridus* (Bi, Pianka and Pianka, 1970); *Phrynocephalus arabicus* (Bi, Arnold, 1984a); *Lophognathus longirostris* (Ba, Douglas, 1967). *Uromastyx hardwickii* (Bi, M, Minton, 1966); *U. microlepis* (L, Bi, Arnold, 1979, 1984a).

Anguidae

Abronia lythrochila (Bi, pers. obs.); *Anguis fragilis* (Sn, Prestt, 1971; Goddard, 1984); *Elgaria kingii* (Sn, Klauber, 1949); *E. multicarinata* (L, Sn, Cunningham, 1959; pers. obs.); *Gerrhonotus liocephalus* (M, W. P. Taylor, 1954); *Ophisaurus sp.* (Sn, Hamilton and Pollack, 1956; Brown, 1979; Jackson and Franz, 1981; Greene, 1984); *O. attenuatus* (Sn, Fitch, 1960; Brown, 1979; Greene, 1984); *O. gracilis* (Sn, Venning, 1910); *O. ventralis* (Sn, Jackson and Franz, 1981).

Chamaeleontidae

Bradypodion dracomontanum (L, Bourquin and Channing, 1980); *Chamaeleo chamaeleon* (Sn, Arnold, 1980); *C. dilepis* (I, Sn, Bi, Burrage, 1973; Tonge and Morgan, 1984); *C. namaquensis* (Bi, M, Burrage, 1973); *C. pumilis* (Bi, Burrage, 1973).

Cordylidae

Gerrhosaurus sp. (Bi, Broadley, 1974); *G. major* (Bi, Broadley, 1974); *G. multilineatus* (M. Broadley, in litt.); *G. nigrolineatus* (Sn, M, Loveridge, 1951; Broadley, in litt.); *G. validus* (Bi, Broadley, 1974); *Pseudocordylus sp.* (M, Broadley, in litt.); *P. melanotus* (Sn, Bourquin and Channing, 1980).

Gekkonidae

Afroedura africana (Sn, Boulenger, 1888); *A. transvaalica* (M, Broadley, in litt.); *Ailuronyx seychellensis* (M, Cheke, 1984); *Chondrodactylus angulifer* (M, Broadley, in litt.); *Coleonyx variegatus* (I, L, SN, pers. obs.; Hadley and Williams, 1968; Parker, 1972); *Colophus wahlbergi* (M, Broadley, in litt.); *Gekko gecko* (L, Auffenberg, 1981b); *G. subpalmata* (Sn, Wall, 1903); *Gehyra australis* (Ba, Douglas, 1967); *Hemidactylus sp.* (L, Sn, Parker, 1949; Arnold and Gallagher, 1977; Auffenberg, 1981a); *H. brookii* (Bi, Minton, 1966); *H. flaviviridis* (Ba, Advani, 1981; Mosse, 1931; Prakash, 1959); *H. frenatus* (L, Dryden, 1965); *H. mabouia* (Ba, M, Vaughn, 1976; Broadley, in litt.); *H. platycephalus* (M, Broadley, in litt.); *Homopholis wahlbergii* (M, Broadley, in litt.); *Lygodactylus capensis* (I, Bi, Warren, 1923; Broadley, 1974); *L. chobiensis* (Bi, M, Broadley, 1974, in litt.); *Oedura reticulata* (I, Butler, 1970); *Pachydactylus sp.* (I, Lawrence, 1953); *P. bibronii* (M, Broadley, in litt.); *P. capensis* (I, M, Lamoral, 1971; Broadley, in litt.); *P. punctatus* (M, Broadley, in litt.); *Palmatogecko rangei* (I, Lamoral, 1971); *Phelsuma abbotti* (Bi, Cheke, 1984); *P. longinsulae* (Bi, Cheke, 1984); *Ptenopus garrulus* (M, Kruuk and Mills, 1983; Broadley, in litt.);

Ptyodactylus hasselquisti (Sn, Arnold and Gallagher, 1977); *Rhoptropus sp.* (M, Broadley, in litt.); *Stenodactylus doriae* (Sn, Arnold, 1980); *Thecadactylus rapicaudus* (Ba, Goodwin and Greenhall, 1961; Tuttle, 1967).

Helodermatidae

Heloderma suspectum (Sn, Funk, 1964).

Iguanidae

Amblyrhynchus cristatus (Bi, Carpenter, 1966); *Anolis sp.* (I, Bi, Gudger, 1925; Cruz, 1972, 1973, 1975, 1976; Wunderle, 1981; Adolph and Roughgarden, 1983); *A. agassizi* (I, Wolda, 1975); *A. carolinensis* (Sn, Bi, M, Burkett, 1966; Kalmbach, 1944; Kennedy, 1964; Brown, 1979; Smith, 1983); *A. cuvieri* (Bi, M, Perez-Rivera, 1985); *A. lemurinus* (Ba, Valdez and LaVal, 1971). *A. limifrons* (Sn, Sexton and Heatwole, 1965); *A. poecilopus* (Fi, L, Sn, Campbell, 1973); *A. pulchellus* (L, Perez-Rivera, 1985); *A. sagrei* (I, Sn, M, Henderson, 1976); *A. scriptus* (Bi, Iverson, 1979); *Basiliscus basiliscus* (Sn, Sexton and Heatwole, 1965); *Callisaurus draconoides* (L, Sn, Camp, 1916; Gates, 1957; Nickerson and Mays, 1970; Tanner and Krogh, 1975; Parker and Pianka, 1976); *Cophosaurus texanus* (Bi, Reid and Fulbright, 1981); *Crotaphytus collaris* (I, Sn, Bi, M, Fitch, 1956; Messick and Hornocker, 1981); *C. reticulatus* (Bi, Montanucci, 1971); *Dipsosaurus dorsalis* (Bi, Camp, 1916); *Gambelia silus* (Sn, Bi, Montanucci, 1965); *Holbrookia sp.* (Sn, M, McKinney and Ballinger, 1966; W. P. Taylor, 1954); *H. maculata* (Sn, Bi, Marr, 1944; Platt, 1969); *Iguana iguana* (Cr, L, Sn, Bi, M, Beebe, 1944b; Greene et al., 1978; Rodda and Burghardt, 1985); *Leiocephalus psammodromus* (Bi, Buden, 1974; Iverson, 1979); *Phrynosoma sp.* (Sn, McKinney and Ballinger, 1966; Parker and Pianka, 1976); *P. cornutum* (Bi, Sn, Beavers, 1976; Meinzer, 1983); *P. coronatum* (Bi, Bryant, 1916); *P. modestum* (Bi, Reid and Fulbright, 1981); *P. platyrhinos* (Sn, Bi, Bryant, 1916; Gates, 1957; Pianka and Parker, 1975); *Polychrus marmoratus* (Bi, Beebe, 1944b); *Sauromalus obesus* (Bi, M, Camp, 1916; VanDenburgh, 1922; Miller and Stebbins, 1964; Berry, 1974; Prieto and Sorenson, 1975); *Sceloporus sp.* (L, Sn, M, Schmidt, 1928; McKinney and Ballinger, 1966; W. P. Taylor, 1954; Parker and Pianka, 1976); *S. clarki* (Fi, Sn, Neve, 1976; pers. obs.); *S. graciosus* (L, Sn, Bi, Cunningham, 1956, 1959; Burkholder and Tanner, 1974; Balgooyen, 1976); *S. horridus* (Sn, Schmidt and Shannon, 1947); *S. jarrovi* (Sn, Bi, Klauber, 1949; Simon and Bissinger, 1983); *S. magister* (L, Tinkle, 1976); *S. occidentalis* (Sa, L, Bi, Sn, Bryant, 1916; Cunningham, 1956, 1959; Bury, 1972; Balgooyen, 1976); *S. orcutti* (Sn, Bi, Cunningham, 1959; Welsh, in litt.); *S. poinsetti* (Sn, Marr, 1944); *S. undulatus* (Sn, Bi, Marr, 1944; Hamilton and Pollack, 1956; Platt,

APPENDICES

1969; Knight and Collins, 1977; Brown, 1979; Reid and Fulbright, 1981; Greene, 1984); *S. variabilis* (L, Kennedy, 1968); *Uma scoparia* (L, Gracie and Murphy, 1986); *Urosaurus ornatus* (Fi, Sn, Gates, 1957; Neve, 1976); *Uta stansburiana* (I, L, Sn, Bi, M, Bryant, 1916; Cunningham, 1956, 1959; Montanucci, 1968; Milstead and Tinkle, 1969; Platt, 1969; Nussbaum and Diller, 1976; Parker and Pianka, 1976; Messick and Hornocker, 1981; Reid and Fulbright, 1981; Diller and Wallace, 1986).

Lacertidae

Acanthodactylus erythrurus (L, Sn, Bi, Valverde, 1967); *A. schmidti* (L, Arnold, 1984a); *Eremias sp.* (M, Broadley, in litt.); *E. lineocellata* (Bi, Broadley, 1974); *E. lugubris* (Bi, Broadley, 1974); *E. multiocellata* (Sn, Schmidt, 1926); *E. namaquensis* (Bi, M, Broadley, 1974, in litt.); *Ichnotropis capensis* (Bi, M, Broadley, 1974, in litt.); *I. squamulosus* (Bi, Broadley, 1974); *Lacerta lepida* (M, Amores, 1980); *L. vivipara* (I, Sn, Bi, Owen and Owen, 1959; Prestt, 1971; Bauens and Thoen, 1981; Goddard, 1984); *Latastia boscai* (Sn, Parker, 1949); *Meroles suborbitalis* (M, Broadley, in litt.); *Nucras intertexta* (Bi, M, Broadley, 1974, in litt.); *N. lalandii* (M, Bourquin and Channing, 1980); *N. taeniolata* (M, Broadley, in litt.); *N. tessellata* (Bi, Broadley, 1974); *Podarcis agilis* (Bi, Prestt, 1971); *Psammodromus algirus* (M, Amores, 1980); *Tachydromus sp.* (Sn, Maslin, 1950).

Pygopodidae

Aprasia sp. (Sn, Shine, 1984); *A. repens* (Sn, Shine, 1984); *Delma sp.* (Ba, Douglas, 1967); *Lialis burtonis* (Ba, Douglas, 1967).

Scincidae

Ablepharus lineoocellatus (I, Bustard, 1968); *Acontias sp.* (M, Broadley, in litt.); *A. percivali* (M, Broadley, in litt.); *Chalcides bedriagai* (M, Amores, 1980); *C. chalcides* (M, Amores, 1980); *C. ocellatus* (L, pers. obs.); *Ctenotus sp.* (Sn, Shine, 1984); *Ctenotus pantherinus ocellifer* (L, Pianka, 1971); *Emoia cyanura* (L, Dryden, 1965); *Eumeces sp.* (L, Sn, M, Maslin, 1950; W. P. Taylor, 1954; Montanucci, 1971; Brown, 1979; Jackson and Franz, 1981; Greene, 1984; Henderson, 1984b); *E. egregius* (Sn, Hamilton and Pollack, 1956); *E. fasciatus* (L, Sn, M, Fitch, 1954; Hamilton and Pollack, 1956; Burkett, 1966; Greene, 1984); *E. inexpectatus* (Sn, Burkett, 1966; Jackson and Franz, 1981; Greene, 1984); *E. laticeps* (I, Fr, Cokendolpher, 1977; Lamb, 1984); *E. obsoletus* (L, Sn, Bi, Fitch, 1955a; Montanucci, 1971); *E. septentrionalis* (I., Sn, Burt and Hoyle, 1934; Platt, 1969); *E. skiltonianus* (L, Sn, Cunningham, 1956; pers. obs.); *E. tetragrammus* (Sn, Beavers, 1976;

Greene, 1984); *Lerista sp.* (Sn, Greene, 1984); *L. elegans* (Sn, Shine, 1984); *L. lineata* (Sn, Shine, 1984); *L. praepedita* (Sn, Shine, 1984); *L. picturata* (Sn, Shine, 1984); *Lygosoma afer* (M, Broadley, in litt.); *L. himalayana* (Sn, Wall, 1911a); *L. indica* (Sn, Wall, 1908a, 1909a); *L. sundevalli* (M, Broadley, in litt.); *Mabuya sp.* (L, Cissé, 1972); *M. hildae* (Bi, Broadley, 1974); *M. homalacephala* (M, Broadley, in litt.); *M. multifasciatus* (Sn, Wall, 1910a); *M. occidentalis* (M, Kruuk and Mills, 1983); *M. sechellensis* (L, Bi, M, Cheke, 1984); *M. striata* (I, Bi, M, Broadley, 1974; Rowe-Rowe, 1978; McCormick and Polis, 1982); *M. varia* (Bi, M, Broadley, 1974, in litt.); *M. variegata* (Bi, Broadley, 1974); *M. wrighti* (L, Bi, M, Cheke, 1984); *Menetia sp.* (Sn, Shine, 1984); *Morethia sp.* (Sn, Shine, 1984); *Neoseps reynoldsi* (Sn, Jackson and Franz, 1981; Greene, 1984); *Panaspis wahlbergi* (Bi, M, Broadley, 1974, in litt.); *Scelotes braueri* (M, Cheke, 1984); *S. gardineri* (M, Cheke, 1984); *Scincella lateralis* (I, Sn, M, Malnate, 1939; Kalmback, 1944; Neill, 1948a; Hamilton and Pollack, 1955, 1956; Myers, 1965, 1967; Burkett, 1966; Jackson and Franz, 1981; Greene, 1984); *Scincus mitranus* (L, Arnold, 1984a); *Sphenomorphus cherriei* (Sn, Henderson, 1984b); *S. florensis* (L, Auffenberg, 1981a); *S. undulatus* (Sn, Dunn, 1927); *Typhlacontias gracilis* (M, Broadley, in litt.); *Typhlosaurus cregoi* (M, Broadley, in litt.); *T. lineatus* (M, Broadley, in litt.).

Teiidae

Ameiva ameiva (Bi, Beebe, 1945; Voous, 1969); *Cnemidophorus sp.* (Sn, M, W. P. Taylor, 1954; Wellman, 1963; McKinney and Ballinger, 1966; Beavers, 1976); *C. gularis* (L, Sn, Montanucci, 1971; Greene, 1984); *C. hyperthyrus* (Bi, H, Welsh, in litt.); *C. lemniscatus* (Sn, Bi, Sexton and Heatwole, 1965; Voous, 1969); *C. sexlineatus* (Sa, Sn, Bi, M, Fitch, 1958; Hamilton and Pollack, 1955, 1956; Platt, 1969; Camper, 1986); *C. sonorae* (Bi, Jennings, 1984); *C. tigris* (L, Sn, Bi, Bryant, 1916; Cunningham, 1959; Pianka, 1970; Parker and Pianka, 1976; Messick and Hornocker, 1981; Mitchell, 1984); *C. uniparens* (L, Bi, Hulse, 1981); *Dicrodon guttulatum* (L, pers. obs.); *Dracaena paraguayensis* (Cr, Schaller and Crawshaw, 1982; *Gymnophthalmus sp.* (Sn, Bi, Henderson, 1984; Voous, 1969); *G. speciosus* (Sn, Schmidt, 1928).

Varanidae

Varanus sp. (Cr, Sn, Wall, 1907b; Webb et al., 1982); *V. exanthematicus* (L, Bi, M, Cissé, 1972; Broadley, 1974, in litt.); *V. niloticus* (Cr, Bi, M, Cott, 1961; Broadley, 1974, in litt.; Bourquin and Channing, 1980).

APPENDICES

SERPENTES

Acrochoridae

Acrochordus arafurae (Cr, Webb et al., 1982).

Atractaspidae

Atractaspis bibroni (M, Broadley, in litt.).

Boidae

Boa constrictor (Sn, Beebe, 1946); *Eunectes notaeus* (Cr, Schaller and Crawshaw, 1982); *Python molurus* (M, Wall, 1912a); *P. sebae* (Cr, Bi, M, Cott, 1961; Broadley, 1974, in litt.).

Colubridae

Amblyodipsas ventrimaculata (M, Broadley, in litt.); *Amphiesma stolata* (Sn, Bi, Wall, 1906a, 1910a, 1911b); *Aparallactus sp.* (M, Broadley, in litt.); *A. capensis* (M, Broadley, in litt.); *A. lunulatus* (Bi, Broadley, 1974); *Arizona elegans* (Sn, M, Greene, 1984, unpubl.); *Aspidura trachyprocta* (Sn, Wall, 1906a, 1921); *Atractus torquatus* (Sn, Hoogmoed, 1980); *A. trilineatus* (Sn, Beebe, 1946); *A. zidocki* (Fr, Hoogmoed, 1980); *Boiga gokool* (Sn, Wall, 1906a); *B. trigonata* (Sn, Wall, 1906a); *Calamaria sp.* (Sn, Wall, 1906a); *Carphophis amoenus* (Sn, Hamilton and Pollack, 1956; Brown, 1979); *Cemophora coccinea* (Fr, Brown, 1979); *Coluber constrictor* (Sn, Hamilton and Pollack, 1956; Fitch, 1963; Platt, 1969; Jackson, 1971; Brown, 1979; Jackson and Franz, 1981; Greene, 1984); *C. rhodorhachis* (Bi, Wall, 1911a); *Chrysopelea ornata* (Sn, Wall, 1906a); *Conopsis nasus* (Sn, Minton and Minton-Cervantes, 1977); *Crotaphopeltis hotamboeia* (Sn, Bi, M, Loveridge, 1951; Broadley, 1974, in litt.); *Dasypeltis scabra* (Cr, Cott, 1961); *Dendrelaphis pictus* (L, Auffenberg, 1981a); *Diadophis punctatus* (I, Fi, Fr, Sn, M, Barber, 1906; Graf et al., 1939; Reynolds, 1945; W. P. Taylor, 1954; Hamilton and Pollack, 1955, 1956; Myers, 1965; Fitch, 1975; Groves and Groves, 1978; Brown, 1979; Jackson and Franz, 1981; Greene, 1984); *Dispholidus typus* (Bi, M, Broadley, 1974, in litt.); *Duberria lutrix* (Bi, Broadley, 1974); *Elaphe guttata* (Sn, Jackson and Franz, 1981; Greene, 1984); *E. obsoleta* (Sn, Kennedy, 1964; Greene, 1984); *E. subradiata* (L, Sn, Auffenberg, 1981a; Dunn, 1927); *Farancia abacura* (Sn, Telford, 1952; Greene, 1984); *Ficimia olivacea* (Sn, Greene, 1984); *Haplocercus ceylonensis* (Sn, de Silva, 1983); *Heterodon nasicus* (Bi, M, Platt, 1969); *H. platirhinos* (Fr, T, Sn, Bi, Hamilton and Pollack, 1955, 1956; Platt, 1969); *Hypsiglena torquata* (Bi, Diller and Wallace, 1986); *Lampropeltis alterna* (M, Tryon and

Guese, 1984); *L. calligaster* (Sn, Brown, 1979; Greene, 1984); *Lamprophis fuliginosus* (Cr, Bi, M, Cott, 1961; Broadley, 1974, in litt.); *Liophis* cf. *reginae* (Bi, Voous, 1969); *Lycodon aulicus* (Sn, Wall, 1906a, 1909b, Dunn, 1927); *L. fasciatus* (Sn, Wall, 1911c); *Lycodonomorphus rufulus* (I, Fi, Cr, L, Bi, M, Sweeney, 1971); *Lycophidion capense* (M, Broadley, in litt.); *Macropisthodon rhodomelas* (Sn, Wall, 1906a); *Malpolon monspessulana* (M, Amores, 1980); *Masticophis flagellum* (Sn, Bi, Bryant, 1916; Carr, 1940; Guidry, 1953; Hamilton and Pollack, 1956; Gates, 1957); *Meizodon semiornatus* (Bi, Broadley, 1974); *Mehelya capensis* (Sn, Sweeney, 1971); *Natriciteres olivacea* (Cr, Cott, 1961); *Natrix maura* (M, Amores, 1980); *N. natrix* (M, Amores, 1980); *N. tesselata* (Bi, Mienis, 1980); *Nerodia sp.* (Sn, Hamilton and Pollack, 1955; Klimstra, 1959; Burkett, 1966); *N. erythrogaster* (Sn, Trowbridge, 1937; Hamilton and Pollack, 1956; Burkett, 1966); *N. fasciata* (Sn, Clark, 1949; Kofron, 1978; Brown, 1979); *N. sipedon* (Sn, Hamilton and Pollack, 1956); *Opheodrys aestivus* (Sn, M, Taylor, 1954; Hamilton and Pollack, 1956; Kennedy, 1964; Brown, 1979; Jackson and Franz, 1981; Greene, 1984); *O. vernalis* (I, Neill, 1948); *Philodryas chamissonis* (M, Jaksic et al., 1982); *P. viridissimus* (Bi, Voous, 1969); *Philothamnus sp.* (Bi, Sweeney, 1971); *P. heterolepidotus* (Bi, Broadley, 1974); *P. hoplogaster* (Cr, Cott, 1961); *P. semivariegatus* (M, Broadley, in litt.); *Pituophis melanoleucus* (Bi, M, Beasom and Pattee, 1975; Messick and Hornocker, 1981); *Prosymna bivittata* (M, Broadley, in litt.); *P. sundevalli* (M, Broadley, in litt.); *Psammophis sp.* (Bi, Wall, 1906a); *P. angolensis* (M, Broadley, in litt.); *P. condanarus* (Sn, Wall, 1906a); *P. crucifer* (Fi, Wall, 1906a); *P. jallae* (Bi, Broadley, 1974); *P. phillipsii* (M, Broadley, in litt.); *P. semivariegatum* (M, Broadley, in litt.); *P. sibilans* (Bi, Broadley, 1974); *P. subtaeniatus* (Bi, Broadley, 1974); *Psammophylax tritaeniatus* (Bi, Broadley, 1974); *Pseudaspis cana* (M, Kruuk and Mills, 1983; Broadley, in litt.); *Ptyas korros* (Sn, Wall, 1910a); *P. mucosus* (Sn, Wall, 1906d, 1919a; Biswas, 1983); *Regina alleni* (I, Sa, Sn, Bi, M, Godley, 1982); *R. rigida* (Sn, Kofron, 1978); *Rhamphiophis oxyrhynchus* (Sn, Loveridge, 1951); *Rhinocheilus lecontei* (I, Sn, Cunningham, 1959; Easterla, 1975); *Salvadora grahamiae* (L, Sn, Montanucci, 1971; Greene, 1984); *Seminatrix pygaea* (Sn, Jackson and Franz, 1981; Greene, 1984); *Sibon sartorii* (Sn, Greene, 1984); *Sonora semiannulata* (Sn, Greene, 1984); *Stilosoma extenuatum* (Sn, Jackson and Franz, 1981; Greene, 1984); *Storeria dekayi* (I, Sn, Barbour, 1956; Greene, 1984; Hamilton, 1951; Hamilton and Pollack, 1956; Jackson and Franz, 1981; Neill, 1948b; Seigel, 1986); *S. occipitomaculata* (Fi, Sn, Jackson and Franz, 1981; Knapik and Hodgson, 1986; *Tantilla sp.* (Sn, M, W. P. Taylor, 1954; Greene, 1984); *T. coronata* (Sn, Hamilton and Pollack, 1956; Brown, 1979; Jackson and Franz, 1981; Greene, 1984); *T. gracilis* (Sn, M, Greene, 1984; Kalmbach, 1944); *T. longifrontale* (Sn, Beebe, 1946); *T.*

nigriceps (I, McCormick and Polis, 1982); *T. planiceps* (Sn, Bi, Greene, 1984; E. Ely, pers. comm.); *T. relicta* (Sn, Greene, 1984; Jackson and Franz, 1981); *T. rubra* (Sn, Greene, 1984); *Telescopus semiannulatus* (Bi, Broadley, 1974); *Thamnophis sp.* (Sn, M, W. P. Taylor, 1954; Klimstra, 1959; Greene, 1984); *T. elegans* (I, Bi, Balgooyen, 1976; Drummond and Wolfe, 1981; *T. marcianus* (Sn, Greene, 1984); *T. proximus* (Sn, Kofron, 1978; Greene, 1984); *T. radix* (Sn, Platt, 1969); *T. sirtalis* (I, Fi, Bi, Sn, M, Gudger, 1925; Burt, 1949; Fitch, 1965; Keenlyne and Beer, 1973; Balgooyen, 1976; Knapik and Hodgson, 1986; Seigel, 1986); *Thelotornis capensis* (Bi, M, Broadley, 1974, in litt.); *Tretanorhinus variabilis* (I, Grant, 1946); *Tropidoclonion lineatum* (Sn, Greene, 1984); *Virginia striatula* (Sn, Greene, 1984); *V. valeriae* (Sn, Greene, 1984); *Xenocalamus bicolor* (M, Broadley, in litt.); *X. mechowii* (M, Broadley, in litt.); *X. sabiensis* (Bi, Broadley, 1974); *Xenochrophis piscator* (Sn, Wall, 1906a; Biswas, 1983); *Xylophis perroteti* (Sn, Wall, 1919a).

Elapidae

Aspidelaps scutatus (M, Broadley, in litt.); *Bungarus fasciatus* (Sn, Wall, 1906a); *Dendroaspis polylepis* (Bi, M, Broadley, 1974, in litt.); *Micrurus sp.* (Sn, Bi, Beebe, 1946; Voous, 1969); *M. fulvius* (Sn, Bi, Carr, 1940; Greene and McDiarmid, 1981; Jackson and Franz, 1981; Greene, 1984); *Naja sp.* (Bi, Broadley, 1974); *N. haje* (Bi, Broadley, 1974); *N. melanoleuca* (Cr. Cott, 1961); *N. mossambica* (Bi, M, Broadley, 1974, in litt.); *N. naja* (L, Sn, Bi, M, Wall, 1906a; Wall, 1913a; Auffenberg, 1981a); *N. nigricollis* (Bi, Sweeney, 1971); *Ophiophagus hannah* (I, Sn, Wall, 1906a, 1926a); *Pelamis platurus* (Fi, Bi, M, Wetmore, 1965; Paulson, 1967; Heatwole and Finnie, 1980; Pickwell et al., 1983).

Leptotyphlopidae

Leptotyphlops sp. (Bi, M, Broadley, 1974, in litt.); *L. dulcis* (Sn, M, Kalmbach, 1944; W. P. Taylor, 1954; Greene, 1984); *L. humilis* (I, Sn, Anderson, 1956; Greene, 1973b; Vitt and Hulse, 1973; Polis, 1979; McCormick and Polis, 1982); *L. longicaudus* (M, Broadley, in litt.); *L. scutifrons* (M, Broadley, in litt.).

Typhlopidae

Rhamphotyphlops braminus (Fr, L, Sn, Wall, 1907b, 1918a; Dryden, 1965; Hahn, 1976); *Typhlops sp.* (Sn, Bi, M, Broadley, 1974, in litt.; Greene, 1983); *T. beddomii* (Sn, Wall, 1919a); *T. fletcheri* (Sn, Wall, 1919a); *T. schlegeli* (Sn, Bi, M, Loveridge, 1951; Broadley, 1974, in litt.); *T. vermicularis* (Bi, Mienis, 1982).

Uropeltidae

Rhinophis sp. (Sn, Wall, 1906a); *R. oxyrhynchus* (Sn, Greene, 1983a); *R. sanguineus* (Sn, Wall, 1919a).

Viperidae

Agkistrodon sp. (M, W. P. Taylor, 1954); *A. contortrix* (Sn, Bi, M, Fitch, 1960; Kennedy, 1964; Greene, 1984); *A. piscivorus* (Fi, T, Cr, Sn, Bi, Carr, 1940; Allen and Swindell, 1948; Clark, 1949; Klauber, 1956; Klimstra, 1959; Lee, 1964; Burkett, 1966); *Bitis arietans* (Fi, Cr, Bi, M, Cott, 1961; Broadley, 1974, in litt.; Thorne and Hamman, 1981); *B. caudalis* (M, Broadley, in litt.); *B. peringueyi* (L, Burrage, 1973); *Bothrops atrox* (Sn, Beebe, 1946); *Causus defilippi* (Sn, Loveridge, 1951); *C. rhombeatus* (Bi, M, Broadley, 1974, in litt.); *Crotalus sp.* (see Klauber, 1956, for review; Sn, Burkett, 1966); *Echis carinatus* (Sn, Wall, 1906a, 1908b); *Lachesis muta* (Sn, M, Greene and Santana, unpubl.); *Sistrurus miliaris* (M, Maehr and Brady, 1986); *Trimeresurus albolabris* (L, Auffenberg, 1981a); *T. gramineus* (Sn, Cochran, 1930); *Vipera berus* (Bi, Prestt, 1971); *V. russellii* (L, Auffenberg, 1981a).

B. Defensive Behavior in Neonate Reptiles

Numbers following each taxon refer to phenotypic categories that are described in Appendix C. An asterisk indicates that an author stated only that newborn or newly hatched animals exhibited defensive behavior similar or identical to that seen in adults.

TESTUDINES

Chelydridae

Chelydra serpentina (44, 48, Carr, 1952).

Kinosternidae

Sternotherus minor (15, Neill, 1948c); *S. odoratus* (48, Carr, 1952); *Staurotypus salvinii* (46, Schmidt, 1970).

SAURIA

Chamaeleonidae

Chamaeleo jacksonii (*, Van Mater, 1971); *C. pumilis* (40, 48, Bustard, 1955).

APPENDICES

Gekkonidae

Gonatodes annularis (7a, 33, Beebe, 1944a).

Iguanidae

Iguana iguana (7a, 7c, 73, 60, Burghardt et al., 1977; Greene et al., 1978).

Scincidae

Tiliqua scincoides (46, Tschambers, 1949).

Teiidae

Dracaena guianensis (44, 46, Werler, 1970; Vanderhaege, 1971); *Tupinambis tequixin* (7a, 31, 48, Beebe, 1945).

Varanidae

Varanus niloticus (12, 48, Cowles, 1930).

SERPENTES

Boidae

Eryx johni (33, Greene, 1973a).

Colubridae

Ahaetulla nasuta (30, Rieppel, 1970); *Chrysopelea ornata* (43, 48, Golder, 1972); *Coluber constrictor* (43, 48, Golder, 1972); *Conophis vittatus* (46, Werler, 1970); *Dasypeltis scabra* (*, Kalmus, 1984); *Dispholidus typus* (25, Zing, 1969); *Elaphe guttata* (43, 48, Golder, 1974); *E. longissima* (43, 48, Golder, 1972); *E. obsoleta* (43, 48, Golder, 1972); *Gyalopion canum* (10, 37, Williamson, 1986); *Heterodon platirhinos* (3, 12, 28, 40, 43, Hay, 1892; Kennedy, 1961; Raun, 1962); *Lampropeltis alterna* (3, 14, 20, Tryon and Guese, 1984); *Lycodon aulicus* (48, Wall, 1907c); *Natrix maura* (27, 43, 48, Golder, 1972); *Ninia sebae* (27, 41, Greene, 1975); *Oxybelis fulgidus* (48, Golder, 1983); *Pituophis melanoleucus* (12, 34, 46, 48, pers. obs.); *Psammodynastes pulverulentus* (43, 48, Wall, 1910b); *Ptyas mucosus* (44, 48, Wall, 1906c); *Thamnophis radix* (3, 19, 20. 27, 33, 39, 43, 44, 45, Arnold and Bennett, 1984); *T. sirtalis* (43, 48, Golder, 1972); *Tomodon ocellatus* (*, Gallardo, 1972); *Trimorphodon biscutatus* (46, Werler, 1970); *Xenocrophis piscator* (44, 48, Wall, 1907c).

Elapidae

Naja melanoleuca (28, 41, Tryon, 1975); *N. naja* (12, 28, 44, Wall, 1913a; Campbell and Quinn, 1975); *Ophiophagus hannah* (28, 41, 48, Oliver, 1956; see Fig. 7).

Viperidae

Agkistrodon contortrix (34, 43, 48, Chenowith, 1948); *Echis carinatus* (9, 43, 48, Stemmler-Gyger, 1965); *Lachesis muta* (30, 34, 43, 48, Switak, 1969; Solorzano, Santana, and Greene, unpubl.).

C. Phenotypic Survey of Antipredator Mechanisms

Several phenotypic categories used here subsume more than one response, but are lumped because they sometimes cannot be distinguished on the basis of published descriptions. Homology of antipredator mechanisms is not implied among taxa for these categories (e.g., tail displays in lizards and snakes), although it certainly exists in some cases (see Sections IV, V). The categories are listed to some extent in order of the parts of the animal involved, but a strictly topographic, kinematic, or functional classification is neither possible nor advisable at this time. This is because similar components are often expressed in different combinations in different taxa, and because every attempt should be made initially to avoid functional descriptions (see Drummond, 1981). The reader is encouraged to consult the original literature for details of the diverse components. Examples with references are cited for each category, containing an illustration whenever possible. The summaries of taxonomic distribution are based on Appendix D.

1. CONCEALING COLORATION

This category includes crypsis, masquerading, countershading, obliterative marks, and perhaps other phenomena. Concealing coloration is undoubtedly widespread in reptiles, but Appendix D includes only references in which the authors emphasized the topic (see also Section V.A). Particularly obvious or well studied examples include *Chelus fimbriatus* (Pritchard and Trebbau, 1984), *Uta stansburiana* (Norris, 1967), *Uroplatus fimbriatus* (Cott, 1940), and *Pituophis melanoleucus* (Sweet, 1985).

2. IMMOBILITY

The animal remains still ("freezing") but not rigid or unresponsive, either in a retreat or exposed and alert. Immobility is a very widespread initial response among reptiles (e.g., aquatic turtles, cryptic desert lizards, and arboreal snakes; pers. obs.), and probably is confused with items 3 and 4 in some published accounts.

3. CATALEPSY, LETISTIMULATION, DEATH FEIGNING, TONIC IMMOBILITY

The animal assumes a state of external unresponsiveness to stimulation. This can include retention of a rigid posture (e.g., *Echinosaura horrida*, Leviton and Anderson, 1966) or limp condition (e.g., *Heterodon platirhinos*, Section IV.I). Tonic immobility is apparently rare as a naturally exhibited behavior (but see Herzog and Drummond, 1984), although it can be induced in many species during handling (Prestrude and Crawford, 1970; Greene et al., 1978).

4. CROUCHING

A reptile flattens as much of its body against the substrate as possible (e.g., *Phrynosoma douglassi*, pers. obs.; *Phrynocephalus helioscopus*, Obst, 1959).

5. INOFFENSIVE

No response to real or simulated predation occurs other than crypsis and flight. Probably not common, but occurrence unknown. Included in Appendix D when mentioned by authors, in order to indicate variation in the presence of defensive behavior.

6. WIND MOVEMENTS

Parts or all of the body are moved during wind-induced movements of the adjacent microhabitat. Known only in a few small lizards, (*Sceloporus woodi*, Jackson, 1974; juvenile *Iguana iguana*, Greene et al., 1978) and slender, arboreal snakes (e.g., *Oxybelis aeneus*, Fleishman, 1985; *Ahaetulla sp.*, Gans, 1974).

7. LOCOMOTOR ESCAPE

This includes any attempt to move beyond the immediate capture range of the predator, including over the surface of the land (7a), into the substrate (7b), including rock crevices, cracks in bark, etc.), into or over water (7c), through the air (7d), and into vegetation (7e). It might be facilitated in amphibious forms by stirring up the substrate (e.g., *Shinisaurus crocodilurus*, Fan, 1931). Locomotor escape is widespread among all higher taxa of reptiles, and may or may not lead to inaccessability (see 8).

8. INACCESSABILITY

Presence in, or locomotion to a site that cannot be reached by a predator. Examples of this widespread response include the pancake tortoise, *Malachochersus tornieri*, that scuttles into rock crevices (Ireland and Gans, 1972); and an arboreal, spiny-tailed iguana, *Ctenosaura clarki*, that takes refuge in hollow tree limbs (Duellman and Duellman, 1959).

9. EPIDERMAL SOUND PRODUCTION

Sound is produced by movements of adjacent body parts against each other. Found in a few lizards (e.g., *Teratoscincus scincus*) and snakes (e.g., *Echis carinatus*), but rare or absent in other groups of reptiles (see Gans and Maderson, 1973, for a review; Section IV.I).

10. CLOACAL SOUND PRODUCTION

Sound is produced by contraction of and expulsion of gas and/or liquid from the cloaca. Rare in reptiles (e.g., *Micruroides euryxanthus*, see Bogert, 1960, and Section IV.I), and perhaps only an epiphenomenon (see also 14).

11. VOCALIZATION

Sound is produced from the mouth and/or throat (excluding hissing, see 12). Found only rarely in most groups of reptiles (e.g., *Gambelia wislizeni, Liolaemus chiliensis*, some *Anolis*; Section IV.E) but widespread in gekkonid lizards (see Gans and Maderson, 1973; Frankenberg, 1975; Section IV.F).

12. HISS

Sound is produced by expulsion of air from the mouth. Found in a variety of reptiles, usually either those that are large or especially pugnacious (e.g., *Pituophis melanoleucus*, Martin and Huey, 1971; see Gans and Maderson, 1973, for a review). Usually not accompanied by morphological specialization (cf. Saiff, 1975).

APPENDICES

13. NOXIOUS FLESH

Tissue is distasteful and/or toxic. Not definitely known to occur in any reptiles, although suspected in certain skinks (*Eumeces*, but see Cooper and Vitt, 1985) and a sea snake (*Pelamis platurus*, Rubinoff and Kropach, 1970).

14. CLOACAL DISCHARGE

The contents of the cloaca are expelled, including feces, uric acid, urine, glandular products, and/or gas (see also 10). A widespread response in turtles (e.g., *Chelodina longicollis*, Kool, 1981), some lizards (e.g., *Elgaria multicarinata*, Fitch, 1935), and many snakes (e.g., *Diadophis punctatus*, Greene, 1973a; Section IV.I). In some vipers the result is a fine stream or spray, sometimes ejected a considerable distance (e.g., *Trimeresurus monticola*, Wall, 1908a; *Crotalus sp.*, Klauber, 1956; *Agkistrodon contortrix*, Fitch, 1960).

15. EXTERNAL GLANDULAR DISCHARGES

The contents of the glands are discharged outside the body. Found sporadically in several families of turtles (e.g., *Sternotherus odoratus* and *Chelodina longicollis*, Eisner et al., 1977, 1978), a genus of gekkonid lizard (*Diplodactylus*, Rosenberg and Russell, 1980; Rosenberg et al., 1984; Fig. 6), and a few genera of snakes (e.g., *Macropisthodon*, Smith, 1938).

16. SKIN LOSS

Pieces of skin are lost during contact with a predator, perhaps facilitating locomotor escape (see 7). Known to occur in some gekkonids (e.g., *Aristelliger hechti*, pers. obs.; Bellairs and Bryant, 1985; Section IV.F) and scincids (Greer, 1986).

17. SEIZE PART OF OWN BODY

An appendage or piece of the body is grasped in the mouth, forming a loop. Known in only a few lizards (e.g., *Cordylus cataphractus*, Rose, 1962; *Lacerta saxicola*, Darevsky, 1967; *Varanus exanthematicus*, Schmidt, 1919).

18. ELEVATE BODY LOOPS

Single or multiple segments of the body are elevated and held immobile. Occurs regularly in an elapid snake, *Vermicella annulata* (Longman, 1918; Shine, 1980b).

19. FORM BALL

Coils of the body are arranged into an irregular or approximately circular mass. Known in several species of snakes (e.g., *Charina bottae*, VanDenburg, 1922; see Bustard, 1969, and Greene, 1973a, for reviews).

20. HIDE HEAD

The head is hidden under one or more parts of the body, as in 18, but the body is not necessarily in a spherical mass (see Bustard, 1969, and Greene, 1973a, for reviews). Known in a few species of lizards and many species of snakes (e.g., *Calabaria reinhardtii*, Bustard, 1969; various uropeltids, Gans, 1973).

21. RETRACT APPENDAGES

Limbs, head, and/or tail are withdrawn against the body. Probably ubiquitous in turtles, which the retract the extremeties into a shell.

22. INVERT BODY

Rare in reptiles (e.g., *Agamodon anguliceps*, Gans, 1969), although occurs in concert with other behavior patterns (e.g., with 3 in *Heterodon*).

23. LATERAL FACE-OFF

The long axis of the body is positioned approximately perpendicular to an approaching predator. This posture is widespread, particularly in iguanid (e.g., *Phrynosoma platyrhinos*, Tollestrup, 1981), anguid (e.g., *Gerrhonotus liocephalus*, pers. obs.), and gekkonid (e.g., *Teratoscincus scincus*, Mebs, 1966) lizards.

24. FRONTAL DISPLAY

The body and head are aligned facing a predator (see also 46). This posture occurs occasionally in turtles (e.g., *Claudius angustatus*, Dodd, 1978; Fig. 3), and is widespread in agamid lizards (e.g., *Phrynocephalus mystaceus*, Section IV.E; Fig. 4) and snakes (e.g., *Bothrops schlegeli*, Kratzer, 1969; Fig. 9).

25. LATERAL NECK EXPANSION

The anterior part of the body is flattened laterally and/or inflated (these cannot be distinguished in some descriptions). Known for lizards of the genus *Varanus* (e.g., *V. komodoensis*, Auffenberg, 1981b) and several snakes (e.g., *Spilotes pullatus*, Rossman and Williams, 1966; *Pseustes poecilonotus*, Greene, 1979).

26. LATERAL BODY EXPANSION

The body is flattened laterally in a few lizards (e.g., *Corytophanes cristatus*, Davis, 1953).

27. DORSOVENTRAL BODY COMPRESSION

The body is flattened dorsoventrally, presumably by abducting the ribs, as seen in certain lizards (e.g., *Lanthanotus borneensis*, Proud, 1978) and many snakes (e.g., *Micrurus fulvius*, Greene, 1973a).

28. DORSOVENTRAL NECK COMPRESSION

Only the anterior part of the body is flattened dorsoventrally, by abduction of ribs in that region, forming a "hood." Found only in some snakes (e.g., *Ophiophagus hannah*, Fig. 7; *Erythrolamprus sp.*, Greene, 1979; Myers, 1986).

29. HEAD ENLARGEMENT

The head is made to appear larger, e.g., by spreading laterally the quadratomandibular joints. Widespread in some colubrid snakes (e.g., *Dasypeltis scabra*, Gans and Richmond, 1957; *Pseustes poecilonotus*, Greene, 1979; three species of *Telescopus*, Werner, 1983), and found in some lizards (e.g., *Corytophanes cristatus*, Davis, 1953). Perhaps often mimetic (Gans and Richmond, 1957; Werner, 1983; Pough, this volume).

30. TONGUE EXTENSION

The tongue is protruded and moved or held stationary, as in some lizards (e.g., *Tiliqua scincoides*, Carpenter and Murphy, 1978) and snakes (e.g., many *Crotalus*, Klauber, 1956; *Heterodon*, Platt, 1969). Exploratory tongue flicks in *Thamnophis sirtalis* have shorter durations than do defensive tongue flicks (Gove and Burghardt, 1983), a pattern that is probably widespread in snakes (Klauber, 1956; Gove, 1979).

31. SCRATCH WITH CLAWS

A potential effect of any struggling, but probably especially significant for large turtles, crocodilians, and varanid lizards (e.g., *Varanus niloticus*, Cowles, 1930).

32. TAIL LASH

The tail is moved back and forth, and sometimes aimed accurately at a predator. Exhibited by many crocodilians (Neill, 1971), by large iguanids (e.g., *Iguana iguana*, Greene et al., 1978) and varanids (e.g., *Varanus griseus*, Nikolskii, 1915), and by small agamid and iguanid lizards with spiny tails (e.g., *Uracentron azureum*, Greene, 1977). In some instances this might be kinematically indistinguishable from diversionary tail display (item 33).

33. TAIL DISPLAY

Refers to all behavior in which the tail is elevated or otherwise made more prominent but not used as a weapon (item 32); see Greene, 1973a, for a review in amphisbaenians and snakes). Known in some amphisbaenians, a few lizards, and many snakes (e.g., *Micruroides euryxanthus*, Fig. 8). There is great variation in the display; the tail can be elevated and held stationary (e.g., *Amphisbaena alba*, Greene, 1973a), curled over the back and wagged (e.g., *Cophosaurus texanus*, Dial, 1986; *Phrynocephalus helioscopus*, Obst, 1959) or inverted in a tight spiral (*Diadophis punctatus*, Greene, 1973a).

34. TAIL VIBRATION

The tail is moved rapidly back and forth, and often produces a noise when it occurs against a dry substrate (see Section IV.I, IV.J). Restricted to and widespread among snakes (e.g., *Pituophis melanoleucus*, Kardong, 1980). In one species of large viper, *Lachesis muta*, sound production is evidently enhanced by the peculiar shape and arrangement of the terminal scales on the tail (pers. obs.).

35. RATTLING

Restricted to members of the pit viper genera *Crotalus* and *Sistrurus*, and facilitated by a keratinized rattle and specialized shaker musculature (Klauber, 1956; Martin and Bagby, 1972; Section IV.J).

36. PRESS WITH TAIL SPINE

The sharp tip of the tail is pressed against a predator. Occurs only in a few advanced snakes (e.g., *Farancia abacura*, Davis, 1948), but perhaps widespread in scolecophidians (Section IV.I).

37. BODY THRASH

Probably most reptiles struggle when grasped by a potential predator, using axial bending and/or limb movements. Examples include *Elgaria multicarinata* (Fitch, 1935) and *Masticophis flagellum* (Wright and Wright, 1957).

38. BODY BRIDGE

A portion of the body is raised in the direction of a predator. This posture is characteristic of pit vipers approached by ophiophagous snakes (e.g., *Agkistrodon contortrix,* Carpenter and Gillingham, 1975; Weldon and Burghardt, 1979).

39. COIL BODY

A spiral, circular, or pretzel-shaped (*Blanus*) coil is formed by the body; in some cases it is rapidly formed, uncoiled, and reformed (e.g., *Prosymna*).

40. INFLATE BODY

A very widespread response in reptiles (e.g., Noble, 1921), particularly obvious in some lizards (e.g., *Sauromalus obesus,* Prieto and Sorenson, 1975) and snakes (e.g., *Crotalus adamanteus,* Klauber, 1956).

41. ELEVATE HEAD AND NECK

A widespread behavior among snakes (e.g., *Ophiophagus hannah,* Fig. 7), in which the head and anterior part of the body are lifted from the substrate.

42. ELEVATE BODY

Part or all of the body is lifted free of the substrate. Occurs in some turtles (e.g., *Chelydra serpentina,* Dodd and Brodie, 1975; *Claudius angustatus,* Dodd, 1978), some lizards (e.g., *Teratoscincus scincus,* Mebs, 1966), and some snakes.

43. S-COIL

The head and neck are retracted in a striking posture (e.g., *Heterodon platirhinos,* Section IV.I). Widespread in snakes and also found in some lizards (e.g., *Varanus gouldii*).

44. STRIKE, LUNGE, OR CHARGE

Implies that a real strike occurred (see 43), such that contact is likely, although in many instances that is not recorded in the description.

45. FALSE STRIKES

The head is moved rapidly forward, as if to bite, but contact is not made with the predator or, if so, the mouth remains closed on impact (e.g., *Heterodon platirhinos*, Section IV.I). Found in several snakes.

46. GAPE

The mouth is opened and pointed at a predator (see also 24). Widespread in reptiles (e.g., *Claudius angustatus*, Dodd, 1978; Fig. 3; *Tiliqua scincoides*, Carpenter and Murphy, 1978; *Bothrops schlegeli*, Kratzer, 1969; Fig. 9).

47. FLAIR LIPS

The jaws or adjacent flaps of skin are moved laterally, exposing the teeth. Apparently exhibited only by a few small snakes (e.g., *Storeria occipitomaculata*, Gosner, 1942) and some agamid lizards (e.g., *Agama savignii*, Hertz et al., 1982; *Phrynocephalus mystaceus*, Section IV.E; Fig. 4).

48. BITE

The jaws are brought to bear on a potential predator, but not necessarily aimed at a particular body part (see 49). Widespread in reptiles of all living higher taxa (e.g., *Chelydra serpentina*, Dodd and Brodie, 1975), and enhanced by venom in helodermatid lizards and numerous advanced snakes (Sections IV.G, IV.I, IV.J).

49. BITE GLOTTIS

Recorded only for *Virginia striatula*, in which this small snake repeatedly hung limply while being ingested by a kingsnake (*Lampropeltis getulus*), then suddenly turned and bit the predator's glottis (Kirk, 1969).

50. "SPIT" VENOM

Venom is ejected through anterior openings in maxillary fangs, a response seen regularly only in certain cobras of the genera *Hemachatus* and *Naja* (Bogert, 1943). An individual *N. nigricollis* "spit" 57 times in 20 minutes, after which the venom glands seemed exhausted (Sweeney, 1971).

51. CONSTRICT

Portions of the potential prey's body are used to restrain and/or suffocate a predator. This is typically a prey-handling tactic (Greene and

APPENDICES

Burghardt, 1978), but it is used in a defensive context by a few snakes (e.g., *Conopsis nasus*, Minton and Minton-Cervantes, 1977).

52. DISGORGE MEAL

Food is regurgitated by a potential prey. This might be simply a side effect of fear, but it is much easier to elicit in certain taxa (e.g., *Micrurus fulvius*, pers. obs.) than others.

53. EVERT HEMIPENES

Perhaps an epiphenomenon of fright, but a conspicuous component of defensive display in *Micrurus frontalis* (Greene, 1973a).

54. CLOACAL AUTOHEMORRAGE

A few species of snakes expel blood from the cloaca when harrassed (e.g., *Rhinocheilus lecontei*, Lardie, 1961).

55. CEPHALIC AUTOHEMORRAGE

A few snakes expel blood from the head region, including perhaps the mouth, nares, and borders of the orbits (e.g., *Tropidophis*, Hecht et al., 1955).

56. SQUIRTING BLOOD

Some species of horned lizards (*Phrynosoma*) expel a stream of blood from the eyes (Stebbins, 1954; Heath, 1966; Section IV.E).

57. APOSEMATIC COLORATION

Color patterns that signal a noxious or dangerous quality to a potential predator. Demonstrably present in venomous coral snakes (Greene and McDiarmid, 1981; Pough, this volume), and perhaps occurring in some other snakes (e.g., *Diadophis punctatus*, Greene, 1973a) and a few turtles (e.g., juvenile *Platysternon megacephalum*, Campbell and Evans, 1972).

58. MORPHOLOGICAL ADJUNCTS

Structural features that enhance or make possible a defensive response; a poorly studied but probably widespread phenomenon in reptiles. Examples include the shell of turtles (Section IV.B), oral flaps in *Phrynocephalus mystaceus* (Section IV.E), spines in *Phrynosoma* (Pianka and Parker, 1975), flash colors in *Farancia abacura* (Davis, 1948), the glottal keel in *Pituophis melanoleucus* (Martin and Huey, 1971; Saiff, 1975), and tracheal rings that promote neck inflation in snakes (e.g., *Dasypeltis scabra*, Gans and Richmond, 1957; *Pseustes* and *Spilotes*, Rossman and Williams, 1966).

59. PHYSIOLOGICAL ADJUNCTS

A poorly investigated but possibly widespread phenomenon (e.g., unusual capacity for submergence in *Iguana iguana*, Moberly, 1969; and for locomotion in *Cnemidophorus tigris*, Garland, 1987).

60. SOCIAL RESPONSES

Two or more individuals react in concert to the presence of a predator. Widespread in iguanine lizards (e.g., *Ctenosaura hemilopha*, Carothers, 1980; *Iguana iguana*, Burghardt, et al., 1977; Greene et al., 1978) and perhaps in turtles (Ernst and Barbour, 1972), but rare in other reptiles (e.g., *Agama stellio*, Zinner, 1967). The iguanine lizards are unquestionably responding in a socially coordinated fashion, but that has not been rigorously distinguished from simultaneous, independent responses to threat in the case of turtles. This category includes interspecific warning signals (*Crocodylus niloticus*, Pienaar et al., 1978; *Cnemidophorus lemniscatus*, Beebe, 1945).

D. Taxonomic Survey of Antipredator Mechanisms

Numbers following each taxon refer to phenotypic categories described in Appendix C.

TESTUDINES

Chelidae

Chelodina longicollis (15, Eisner et al., 1978; Kool, 1981); *Chelus fimbriatus* (1, 42, 45, 48, 58, Neill, 1971; Pritchard and Trebbau, 1984); *Phrynops gibbus* (14, Pritchard and Trebbau, 1984); *P. zuliae* (14, 48, Pritchard and Trebbau, 1984); *Platemys platycephala* (1, Pritchard and Trebbau, 1984).

Chelydridae

Chelydra serpentina (1, 7, 15, 21, 24, 31, 37, 42, 44, 46, 48, Dodd and Brodie, 1975; Lehmann, 1966; Mertens, 1946); *Platysternon megacephalum*

APPENDICES

(11, 23, 42, 48, 58, Schmidt, 1927a; Pope, 1935; Campbell and Evans, 1972).

Emydidae

Chinemys reevesii (7c, Schmidt, 1927b); *Clemmys muhlenbergi* (1, 7b, 7c, Bury, 1979); *Hardella thurgi* (5, Minton, 1966); *Kachuga smithi* (5, 7c, Minton, 1966); *K. tecta* (48, Minton, 1966); *Melanochelys trijuga* (14, Pritchard, 1979); *Pseudemys scripta* (1, 7c, Moll and Legler, 1971); *Rhinoclemmys punctularia* (7c, Pritchard and Trebbau, 1984); *Terrapene carolina* (15, Neill, 1948d); *T. coahuila* (1, 2, 7a, 7b, 7c, 8, 21, Brown, 1974); *T. ornata* (1, 7a, 15, 37, 48, 58, Legler, 1960; Norris and Zweifel, 1950).

Kinosternidae

Claudius angustatus (46, Pritchard and Trebbau, 1984); *Kinosternon oaxacae* (5, 21, 46, Iverson, 1986); *Staurotypus salvinii* (46, 48, Schmidt, 1970); *Sternotherus odoratus* (15, Eisner et al. 1977).

Pelomedusidae

Peltocephalus tracaxus (1, 48, Pritchard and Trebbau, 1984); *Podocnemis expansa* (7c, Pritchard and Trebbau, 1984).

Testudinidae

Gopherus agassizii (5, 7b, 8, 11, 14, Camp, 1916; Campbell and Evans, 1967); *Geochelone elegans* (5, Minton, 1966); *Kinixys belliana* (7a, 7c, 12, 14, 21, 31, 48, Schmidt, 1919); *Malacochersus tornieri* (7b, 8, 58, Ireland and Gans, 1972); *Geochelone gigantea* (12, 21, Gaymer, 1968); *Testudo graeca* (21, Reed and Marx, 1959); *T. horsfieldii* (5, 21, Minton, 1966).

Trionychidae

Chitra indica (5, Minton, 1966); *Lissemys punctata* (15, 21, Minton, 1966); *Pelochelys bibroni* (45, Pritchard, 1979); *Trionyx gangeticus* (48, Minton, 1966).

CROCODILIA

Alligatoridae

Alligator mississippiensis (7, 12, 24, 32, 37, 44, 46, 48, McIlhenny, 1935; Neill, 1971); *Caiman crocodilus* (3, 7b, 7c, 11, 15, 20, Gorzula, 1978).

Crocodylidae

Crocodylus sp. (3, 7, 14, 15, 32, 48, Schmidt, 1919); *C. niloticus* (60, Pienaar et al., 1978); *C. palustris* (11, 12, Minton, 1966); *C. porosus* (7a, Zug, 1974).

RHYNCHOCEPHALIA

Sphenodontidae

Sphenodon punctatus (1, 11, 40, 46, 48, Dawbin, 1962; Carpenter and Ferguson, 1977).

AMPHISBAENIA

Amphisbaenidae

Amphisbaena alba (7a, 7b, 33, 37, 46, 48, Beebe, 1945; Gans, 1969; Greene, 1973a); *A. fuliginosa* (7a, 7b, 33, 37, 46, 48, Greene, 1973a); *Blanus cinereus* (7, 37, 39, Kenneweg, 1956; Malkmus, 1982a); *B. strauchi* (7b, 14, 19, 20, 39, Clark and Clark, 1973; Elzen, 1980).

Rhineuridae

Rhineura floridana (7b, Carr, 1940).

Trogonophidae

Agamodon anguliceps (1, 22, Gans, 1969); *Trogonophis wiegmanni* (19, 37, 39, 48, Stemmler, 1970; Rieppel, 1971; pers. obs.).

SAURIA

Agamidae

Agama aculeata 4, 7a, 33, Pienaar et al., 1978); *A. agama* (7a, Schmidt, 1919); *A. agilis* (4, 7a, 7e, Minton, 1966; Clark et al., 1969); *A. atricollis* (1, 7a, 46, Schmidt, 1919; Pienaar et al., 1978); *A. blanfordi* (44, 48, Anderson, 1963); *A. caucasica* (7, 8, Clark et al., 1966; Clark et al., 1969; Mertens, 1960; Reed, 1956; Reed and Marx, 1959); *A. erythrogastra* (7a, 7b, 8, Clark et al., 1966; Schleich, 1979); *A. flavimaculata* (48, Arnold, 1984a); *A. himalayana* (7b, Wall, 1911a); *A. mutabilis* (7, 32, 42, 44, 46, 48, 58, Hertz et al., 1982); *A. nupta* (7b, Minton, 1966); *A. ruderata* (1, 2, 7a, 48, Clark et al., 1969; Clark and Clark, 1973; Reed and Marx, 1959); *A. savignii* (7a, 32, 42, 44, 46, 48, 58, Hertz et al., 1982); *A. sinaita* (Hertz et

APPENDICES

al., 1982); *A. stellio* (7a, 8, 60, Zinner, 1967; Clark and Clark, 1973; Hertz et al., 1982); *A. tuberculata* (7b, Minton, 1966); *Amphibolurus barbatus* (24, 29, 46, 58, Longman, 1913; Throckmorton et al., 1985); *A. nuchalis* (32, 48, Klages, 1982); *Calotes cristatellus* (46, 48, Lim, 1959); *C. versicolor* (7b, 7e, 48, Clark et al., 1969; Minton, 1966); *Chlamydosaurus kingii* (24, 29, 46, 58, Longman, 1913); *Cophotis ceylanica* (1, Kästle, 1966); *Draco maculatus* (1, Schmidt, 1927a); *D. volans* (7d, Hairston, 1957); *Gonocephalus dilophus* (7, 12, 23, 24, 25, 26, 30, 32, 42, 44, 46, 48, 58, Murphy et al., 1978); *Hydrosaurus pustulosus* (37, Taylor, 1922; pers. obs.); *Leiolepis belliana* (7a, 7b, Schmidt, 1927a); *Moloch horridus* (1, 2, 7a, 37, 58, Pianka and Pianka, 1970; White, 1948); *Otocryptis wiegmanni* (11, Matuschka, 1978); *Phrynocephalus arabicus* (1, 2, 5, 7b, 7e, 48, Arnold, 1984a); *P. frontalis* (7b, 33, Schmidt, 1927b); *P. helioscopus* (1, 2, 7a, 7b, 22, 27, 33, Clark et al., 1966; Clark and Clark, 1973; Obst, 1959); *P. luteoguttatus* (7a, 7b, Minton, 1966; Clark et al., 1969); *P. maculatus* (4, 7a, 7e, 33, 48, Minton, 1966; Arnold, 1984a); *P. mystaceus* (1, 2, 4, 7, 24, 27, 29, 33, 42, 44, 46, 47, 48, 58, Mertens, 1952b, 1960; Nikolskii, 1915); *P. ornatus* (1, 2, 7a, 7b, 33, Clark et al., 1969); *P. scutellatus* (1, 2, 7a, Clark et al., 1969); *Uromastyx hardwicki* (7b, 32, 60, Minton, 1966); *U. loricatus* (7b, 32 Anderson, 1963); *U. princeps* (7b, Gans et al., 1965).

Anguidae

Abronia deppei (12, 14, 23, 37, 46, 48, pers. obs.); *A. taeniata* (48, Martin, 1955); *Anguis fragilis* (7e, Clark and Clark, 1973); *Elgaria coerulea* (1, 11, 42, 48, Fitch, 1935); *E. kingi* (7a, 14, 48, pers. obs.); *E. multicarinata* (2, 7a, 7c, 14, 17, 37, 42, 38, Compton, 1933; Fitch, 1935); *E. panamintina* (14, 48, pers. obs.); *Gerrhonotus liocephalus* (7, 12, 14, 23, 37, 40, 46, 48, McGowan, 1963; pers. obs.); *Diploglossus millepunctatus* (7c, Slevin, 1928); *Ophisaurus apodus* (7b, 8, Clark and Clark, 1973; *O. ventralis* (7a, 48, 59, Carr, 1940; Malnate, 1944; Kamel and Gatten, 1983).

Chameleonidae

Brookesia sp. (3, Böhme, 1974; Mertens, 1960); *Chamaeleo chamaeleon* (Arnold, 1984a); *C. jacksoni* (6, Van Mater, 1971); *C. dilepis* (1, 3, 12, 40, 46, 48, Longstaff and Poulton, 1907; Brain, 1961); *C. gracilis* (12, 25, 40, 46, 48, Schmidt, 1919); *C. johnstoni* (1, Schmidt, 1919); *C. laterispinis* (3, Böhme, 1982); *C. namaquensis* (2, 7a, 12, 26, 40, 42, 44, 46, 48, Burrage, 1973); *C. oweni* (7e, 12, 31, 32, 40, 44, 48, Schmidt, 1919); *C. pumilis* (73, 48, Burrage, 1973); *C. zeylanicus* (12, 46, 48, Wall, 1922; Biswas and Acharjyo, 1977); *Brookesia spectrum* (1, 2, 3, 40, Schmidt, 1919).

Cordylidae

Cordylus cataphractus (17, Rose, 1962); *C. warreni* (7b, 8, Pienaar et al., 1978); *Gerrhosaurus flavigularis* (7a, 48, Pienaar et al., 1978); *G. major* (3, 7a, 7b, 31, 33, 40, 48, Schmidt, 1919); *G. vallidus* (7b, 8, Pienaar et al., 1978); *Platysaurus intermedius* (7b, 8, Pienaar et al., 1978).

Dibamidae

Anelytropsis papillosus (7b, 14, 48, Greer, 1985).

Gekkonidae

Agamura femoralis (4, 33, Minton, 1966); *A. persica* (4, 7a, Minton, 1966); *Alsophylax* cf. *pipiens* (7b, 8, Clark et al., 1969); *Aristelliger hechti* (16, pers. obs.); *Bunopus tuberculatus* (48, Arnold, 1984a); *Coleonyx brevis* (7a, 33, Dial, 1978); *C. reticulatus* (7a, Dial, 1978); *C. variegatus* (7a, 33, Johnson and Brodie, 1974; Parker and Pianka, 1974); *Cyrtodactylus scaber* (7a, 7e, 11, Minton, 1966; Arnold, 1984a); *C. serpeninsula* (7b, 7e, 11, 26, 33, 42, 48, Vinson, 1975); *Diplodactylus ciliarus* (15, 58, Bustard, 1964; Rosenberg and Russell, 1980); *D. elderi* (15, 58, Bustard, 1964; Rosenberg and Russell, 1980); *D. michaelsoni* (15, 58, Rosenberg and Russell, 1980); *D. spinigerus* (15, 32, 37, 58, Bustard, 1964; Rosenberg and Russell, 1980); *D. strophurus* (15, 58, Rosenberg and Russell, 1980); *D. taenicauda* (15, 58, Rosenberg and Russell, 1980); *D. vittatus* (40, 42, 46, 48, Bustard, 1965); *D. williamsi* (15, 42, 46, 58, Bustard, 1964; Rosenberg and Russell, 1980; Rosenberg et al., 1984); *Eublepharis macularius* (11, 14, 23, 33, 42, 48, Anderson, 1963; Minton, 1966; Marcellini, 1977); *Geckolepis sp.* (16, Mertens, 1960); *Gehyra mutilata* (16, Bustard, 1970); *Gekko gecko* (48, Curran, 1932); *Gonatodes annularis* (7a, 7b, Beebe, 1944a); *Hemidactylus brookii* (11, 37, 48, Schmidt, 1919); *H. mabouia* (7b, Schmidt, 1919); *H. triedrus* (11, 33, 42, Minton, 1966); *Homopholis sakalava* (7a, 46, Rosler, 1984); *Hoplodactylus duvaucelii* (7e, 11, 12, 48, Whitaker, 1968); *H. pacificus* (7c, 7e, 37, 48, Whitaker, 1968); *Nephrurus asper* (11, 42, 44, 46, 48, Longman, 1918; Bustard, 1967); *Pachydactylus bibronii* (7b, Pienaar et al., 1978); *Phyllodactylus asaccus* (7b, Anderson, 1963); *P. lanei* (3, Herzog and Drummond, 1984); *Phyllurus platurus* (1, 11, 24, 33, 42, 44, 46, 48, Mebs, 1973); *Ptychozoon kuhli* (1, 2, 3, 7d, 7e, 11, 23, 33, 42, 44, 46, 48, 58, Vetter and Brodie, 1977); *P. lionotum* (7d, 58, Heyer and Pongsapipatana, 1970; Marcellini and Keefer, 1976; Russell, 1979b); *Sphaerodactylus glaucus* (33, Harris and Kluge, 1984); *S. molei* (7a, Beebe, 1944a); *Stenodactylus arabicus* (1, 7a, 7e, 33, Arnold, 1984a); *S. doriae* (1, 7a, 7e, 48, Arnold, 1984a); *S. leptocosymbotes* (1, 7a, 7e, 33, Arnold, 1984a); *S. khobarensis* (1, 7e, Arnold, 1984a); *S. orientalis* (11, 14, Minton, 1966); *S. slevini* (1, 33, Arnold, 1984a); *Teratolepis fasciatus* (7a, 33, Minton, 1966; Hotz, 1969);

APPENDICES

Teratoscincus przewalskii (2, 7a, 9, 23, 33, 42, 58, pers. obs.); *T. scincus* (7a, 9, 11, 16, 23, 25, 33, 42, 44, 46, 48, 58, Arnold, 1977, 1984a; Mebs, 1966; Minton, 1966); *Thecadactylus rapicauda* (7a, 7e, 33, 48, Beebe, 1944a; pers. obs.).

Helodermatidae

Heloderma horridum (7a, 7e, 12, 14, 23, 24, 31, 40, 42, 44, 46, 48, 58, Bogert and del Campo, 1956; Alvarez del Toro, 1982; Pregill et al., 1986); *H. suspectum* (7a, 7e, 12, 14, 23, 24, 31, 40, 42, 44, 46, 48, 58, Bogert and del Campo, 1956; Pregill et al., 1986).

Iguanidae

Amblyrhynchus cristatus (7, 8, 48, Carpenter, 1966); *Anolis sp.* (7e, Belt, 1874); *A. barkeri* (7c, Kennedy, 1965a); *A. biporcatus* (11, Myers, 1971); *A. carolinensis* (7e, 33, Oliver, 1951; Henderson and Binder, 1982); *A. chocorum* (11, Myers, 1971); *A. chlorocyanus* (11, Milton and Jenssen, 1979); *A. coelestinus* (11, Milton and Jenssen, 1979); *A. cybotes* (11, Milton and Jenssen, 1979; *A. fuscoauratus* (7e, Beebe, 1944b; *A. garmani* (11, Milton and Jenssen, 1979; *A. grahami* (11, Milton and Jenssen, 1979); *A. hendersoni* (11, Milton and Jenssen, 1979); *A. lionotus* (7c, Campbell, 1973); *A. nitens* (1, 2, 7, Beebe, 1944b); *A. occultus* (11, Webster, 1969; Williams et al., 1965); *A. opalinus* (11, Milton and Jenssen, 1979); *A. poecilopus* (7, 8, Campbell, 1973); *A. roquet* (11, Myers, 1971); *A. valencienni* (11, Milton and Jenssen, 1979); *A. vociferans* (11, Myers, 1971); *Basiliscus basiliscus* (7c, Rand and Marx, 1967); *B. plumifrons* (7c, Laerm, 1973); *B. vittatus* (7a, 7c, Laerm, 1973; Schmidt and Shannon, 1947); *Callisaurus draconoides* (2, 7a, 7b, 8, 33, Asplund, 1967; Gates, 1957; Tanner and Krogh, 1975; Tevis, 1944); *Conolophus pallidus* (7a, 60, Christian and Tracy, 1981); *Cophosaurus texanus* (7a, 33, Mosauer, 1932; Dial, 1986); *Corytophanes cristatus* (1, 2, 12, 23, 26, 40, 41, 42, 44, 46, 48, 58, Davis, 1953); *Crotaphytus collaris* (7a, 7b, 7c, 46, 48, Camp, 1916; Strasser, 1931; Burt and Hoyle, 1934; Fitch, 1956; Marr, 1944; Werth, 1973; McAllister, 1983); *C. reticulatus* (12, 23, 25, 26, 42, 46, 48, Montanucci, 1971); *Ctenosaura pectinata* (1, 7a, 7c, 8, Schmidt and Shannon, 1947); *Cyclura carinata* (7a, 8, 32, 40, 48, Iverson, 1979; pers. obs.); *C. cornuta* (7c, Carey, 1975); *C. nubila* (7a, 7c, 8, 12, Carey, 1975); *C. pinguis* (7a, 8, Carey, 1975); *Dipsosaurus dorsalis* (7a, 7b, Camp, 1916); *Gambelia silus* (12, 32, 46, 48, Montanucci, 1965); *G. wislizeni* (2, 7a, 7b, Camp, 1916; Tevis, 1944; McCoy, 1967); *Holbrookia propinqua* (7a, Dial, 1986); *Iguana iguana* (1, 2, 3, 6, 7a, 7c, 7d, 7e, 14, 26, 31, 32, 42, 46, 48, 60, Beebe, 1944b; Schmidt and Shannon, 1947; Burghardt et al., 1977;

Greene et al., 1978; Meritt, 1981); *Liolaemus chiliensis* (11, 46, 48, Carothers, 1987, in press); *Leiosaurus bellii* (1, 48, Van Devender, 1977); *Liolaemus magellanicus* (7a, 8, Jaksic and Schwenk, 1983); *Petrosaurus mearnsi* (7a, Tevis, 1944); *Phrynosoma coronatum* (7a, 8, 56, Klauber, 1939; Tevis, 1944); *P. douglassi* (1, 4, 7, Durham, 1956; pers. obs.); *P. platyrhinos* (7a, 7e, Camp, 1916; Tollestrup, 1981); *P. solare* (3, 22, 56, Cutter, 1959; Parker, 1971); *Polychrus acutirostris* (1, 7e, Vanzolini et al., 1980; Vitt and Lacher, 1981); *P. femoralis* (2, 3, Gorman et al., 1969); *P. gutturosus* (1, 7e, 26, 46, 48, pers. obs.); *P. marmoratus* (1, 2, 7a, 7e, 25, 48, Beebe, 1944b); *P. peruvianus* (3, 46, 48, Gorman et al., 1969); *Sauromalus obesus* (3, 5, 7a, 8, 32, 40, Camp, 1916; Salt, 1943; Berry, 1974; Prieto and Sorenson, 1975; Welsh, in litt.); *Sceloporus graciosus* (3, 7b, Burkholder and Tanner, 1974); *S. grammicus* (7a, Schmidt and Shannon, 1947); *S. horridus* (7a, Schmidt and Shannon, 1947); *S. magister* (7a, 7b, 7e, 8, Gates, 1957; Parker and Pianka, 1973); *S. occidentalis* (1, 2, 4, 7a, 7b, 7e, 8, 48, pers. obs.); *S. poinsetti* (2, 7a, 7b, 8, 48, Mosauer, 1932; pers. obs.); *S. pyrocephalus* (7a, 8, Schmidt and Shannon, 1947); *S. undulatus* (7e, 6, Minton and Minton, 1948); *S. woodi* (6, 7a, 7e, Carr, 1940; Jackson, 1974); *Tropidurus torquatus* (7a, 8, Rand and Rand, 1966); *Uma notata* (1, 7a, 7b, Camp, 1916); *Uracentron azureum* (7, 32, 48, Greene, 1977); *Uranoscodon superciliosa* (1, 2, 5, Beebe, 1944b); *Urosaurus graciosus* (7e, Camp, 1916); *U. nigricaudus* (7a, Tevis, 1944); *U. ornatus* (1, 7b, Mosauer, 1932); *Uta gadovii* (73, Schmidt and Shannon, 1947); *U. stansburiana* (7e, Tevis, 1944).

Lacertidae

Acanthodactylus cantoris (7a, 8, Clark et al., 1969); *A. pardalis* (7b, Zinner, 1967); *A. schmidti* (1, 7b, 7e, 48, Arnold, 1984a); *A. schreiberi* (7a, Zinner, 1967); *Aporosaura anchietae* (7b, 42, 44, 46, 48, Louw and Holm, 1972); *Bedriagaia tropidopholis* (7a, 7d, 32, 48, Schmidt, 1919); *Eremias barbouri* (7b, 7e, Schmidt, 1927b); *E. velox* (7a, 7e, 8, Clark et al., 1969; Clark and Clark, 1973); *Holaspis guentheri* (7b, 7d, 7e, Schmidt, 1919; Loveridge, 1951; Schiøtz and Volsøe, 1959); *Ichnotropis squamulosa* (7a, Pienaar et al., 1978); *Lacerta agilis* (7a, 8, Clark and Clark, 1973); *L. brandtii* (7a, 8, Clark et al., 1966); *L. cappadocica* (7b, 8, Clark and Clark, 1973); *L. echinnata* (7e, Schmidt, 1919); *L. lepida* (7a, 7c, 8, 37, 46, 48, Malkmus, 1982b; pers. obs.); *L. princeps* (1, 7a, Clark and Clark, 1973); *L. schreiberi* (46, Malkmus, 1983); *L. trilineata* (7a, 8, Clark and Clark, 1973); *L. viridis* (7a, Clark and Clark, 1973); *Mesalina adramitana* (7a, 7e, Arnold,

APPENDICES

1984a); *M. guttulata* (7a, 7b, 8, Anderson, 1963; Clark et al., 1969); *Ommateremias aria* (7a, Clark et al., 1969); *Ophisops elegans* (7a, 7e, Clark and Clark, 1973); *Podarcis taurica* (7a, 8, Clark and Clark, 1973); *Rhabderemias pleski* (7a, Clark et al., 1966; Clark and Clark, 1973).

Scincidae

Ablepharus pannonicus (7, Minton, 1966); *Acontias plumbicolor* (37, Pienaar, et al., 1978); *Chalcides ocellatus* (7a, 8, Clark and Clark, 1973); *Corucia zebrata* (12, 26, 30, 46, 48, Parker, 1983); *Ctenotus sp.* (16 Greer, 1986); *Eumeces fasciatus* (1, 7a, 7c, 7e, Fitch, 1954); *E. gilberti* (7b, 48, Montanucci, 1968; pers. obs.); *E. inexpectatus* (7a, 7c, Carr, 1940); *E. multivirgatus* (7c, 7e, Mosauer, 1932); *E. obsoletus* (7a, 14, 37, 48, Trowbridge, 1937; Smith, 1946; Fitch, 1955); *E. schneideri* (7a, 37, 48, Minton, 1966; Clark and Clark, 1973); *E. septentrionalis* (7c, Black, 1976); *Feylinia currori* (3, 37, Schmidt, 1919); *Leiolopisma moco* (7b, Whitaker, 1968); *L. oliveri* (7b, 12, 37, 48, Whitaker, 1968); *L. suteri* (7c, Whitaker, 1968); *Lerista connivens* (16, Greer, 1986); *L. nichollsi* (16, Greer, 1986); *L. onsloviana* (16, Greer, 1986); *L. uniduo* (16, Greer, 1986); *Lygosoma fernandi* (7b, 37, 48, Schmidt, 1919); *Mabuya acutilabris* (7b, Schmidt, 1919); *M. aurata* (7a, 7b, 8, Anderson, 1963; Clark and Clark, 1973); *M. dissimilis* (7a, 7c, 7e, 8, Minton, 1966; Clark et al., 1969); *M. homolacephala* (7b, Pienaar et al., 1978); *M. mabouya* (1, Beebe, 1945); *M. maculilabris* (7a, 7d, Schmidt, 1919); *M. multifasciata* (48, Schmidt, 1927a); *M. perroteti* (7a, 7c, Schmidt, 1919); *M. brevicollis* (7a, 7e, Schmidt, 1919); *M. vittata* (7e, Clark and Clark, 1973); *Ophiomorus tridactylus* (7b, Clark et al., 1969); *Scelotes bidigittata* (7a, Pienaar et al., 1978); *Scincella lateralis* (7a, 7c, Carr, 1940); *Scincus mitranus* (1, 5, 7b, Arnold, 1984a); *S. scincus* (7a, 7b, Anderson, 1963; Arnold, 1984a); *Sphenomorphus assatum* (7a, Smith, 1949); *Tiliqua casaurinae* (48, Mebs, 1974); *T. gigas* (7a, 12, 23, 46, 48, pers. obs.); *T. scincoides* (12, 30, 40, 46, 48, 58, Carpenter and Murphy, 1978); *Tribolonotus blanchardi* (7, Greer and Parker, 1968); *T. pseudoponceleti* (4, Greer and Parker, 1968); *Tropidophorus brookei* (7c, Barbour, 1921).

Teiidae

Ameiva ameiva (7a, 7b, Beebe, 1945); *A. undulata* (7a, Schmidt and Shannon, 1947); *Buchia cophias* (7a, Beebe, 1945); *Callopistes flavipunctatus* (3, 7a, 8, 14, 37, 46, pers. obs.); *C. maculatus* (7a, 8, 48, pers. obs.); *Cnemidophorus deppei* (7b, Kennedy, 1968; Schmidt and Shannon, 1947);

C. gularis (Schall and Pianka, 1980); *C. guttatus* (7b, Kennedy, 1968); *C. hyperythrus* (7a, 8, Tevis, 1947); *C. lemniscatus* (7a, 60, Beebe, 1945); *C. sexlineatus* (1, 4, 7b, 7c, 46, Dillon and Baldauf, 1945; Minton and Minton, 1948; Stille, 1947; Fitch, 1958); *C. tesselatus* (7a, 7b, 7e, Schall and Pianka, 1980); *C. tigris* (7b, Schall and Pianka, 1980; Welsh, in litt.); *C. velox* (7a, Durham, 1956); *Dracaena guianensis* (44, 46, Werler, 1970); *Echinosaura horrida* (7c, 3, Leviton and Anderson, 1966; Uzzell, 1965); *Kentropyx calcaratus* (5, Beebe, 1945); *Leposoma percarinatum* (7a, Beebe, 1945); *Neusticurus ecpleopus* (7c, Uzzell, 1966); *N. rudis* (7c, Roze, 1958); *Tupinambis teguixin* (7a, 7c, 7e, 12, 32, 46, 48, Milstead, 1961; Gudynas, 1981; Lema, 1983).

Varanidae

Lanthanotus borneensis (12, 14, 27, 46, 48, Proud, 1978); *Varanus acanthurus* (20, 32, 58, Auffenberg, 1983); *V. bengalensis* (7a, 7c, 7e, 12, 32, 48, Minton, 1966; Clark et al., 1969; Auffenberg, 1983); *V. exanthematicus* (3, 7a, 12, 32, 37, 40, 48, Schmidt, 1919); *V. giganteus* (3, 46, 48, Pianka, 1982); *V. glebopalma* (7a, 8, Horn and Schuerer, 1978); *V. gouldii* (2, 7a, Bustard, 1968c); *V. griseus* (12, 25, 26, 32, 40, 44, 48, Mosauer, 1934; Anderson, 1963; Minton, 1966); *V. karlschmidti* (25, 26, 32, 42, Horn, 1977); *V. komodoensis* (12, 32, 44, 48, Auffenberg, 1981b); *V. mertensi* (7c, 7e, 12, 25, 30, 32, 42, 44, 48, Schurer and Horn, 1976); *V. niloticus* (3, 7a, 7c, 7d, 7e, 8, 12, 14, 28, 31, 32, 48, Cowles, 1930; Pienaar et al., 1978; Branch, 1981a); *V. rudicollis* (3, 7a, 12, 25, 30, 32, Lim, 1958: Horn and Petters, 1982); *V. salvator* (12, 25, 32, 48, Schmidt, 1927a; Biswas and Acharjyo, 1977); *V. tristis* (7e, Pianka, 1971a); *V. varius* (7a, 7e, 12, 25, 27, 31, 32, 41, 46, Bustard, 1968c; Horn, 1980).

Xantusiidae

Lepidophyma flavimaculatum (1, 7a, 7b, 14, 37, 48, pers. obs.); *L. pajapanensis* (1, 7a, 7b, 14, 37, 48, pers. obs.); *L. tuxtlae* (1, 7a, 7b, 7e, 14, 37, 48, pers. obs.); *Xantusia vigilis* (1, 7a, 7b, 14, 37, 48, pers. obs.).

Xenosauridae

Shinisaurus crocodilurus (7c, 48, Fan, 1931); *Xenosaurus grandis* (7b, 8, 12, 23, 40, 42, 44, 46, 48, Alvarez del Toro, 1982; pers. obs.).

SERPENTES

Acrochordidae

Acrochordus arafurae (48, Boulenger, 1912; Flower, 1899).

APPENDICES

Aniliidae

Anilius scytale (7b, 14, 20, 27, 33, Greene, 1973a); *Cylindrophis celebensis* (14, 33, Greene, 1973a); *C. maculatus* (14, 33, Greene, 1973a); *C. opisthorhodus* (14, 33, Greene, 1973a); *C. rufus* (14, 20, 27, 33, Frank, 1969; Greene, 1973a).

Atractaspidae

Atractaspis aterrima (48, Schmidt, 1923); *A. bibroni* (14, 37, 48, Broadley, 1959, 1983; Broadley and Cock, 1975; Loveridge, 1918; Mertens, 1955; Pienaar et al., 1978); *A. irregularis* (48, Loveridge, 1938); *A. microlepidota* (33, 37, 48, pers. obs.).

Boidae

Aspidites melanocephalus (12, 25, 43, 48, Johnson, 1975; Longman, 1937); *Boa constrictor* (12, 43, 48, Greene, 1983b; Mertens, 1952a); *Calabaria reinhardtii* (19, 20, 33, 43, 45, Angel, 1933; Bustard, 1969; Cansdale, 1961; Greene, 1973a; Lehmann, 1971); *Candoia aspera* (43, 48, Bustard, 1969; Johnson, 1975); *C. carinata* (12, 43, Johnson, 1975); *Charina bottae* (14, 19, 33, 51, 58, Greene, 1973a; Peabody et al., 1975); *Chondropython viridis* (43, 48, Johnson, 1975; Mertens, 1946); *Corallus annulatus* (1, 43, 48, pers. obs.); *C. caninus* (48, pers. obs.); *C. enydris* (43, 48, Mole, 1924; pers. obs.); *Epicrates angulifer* (14, 43, 48, Sheplan and Schwartz, 1974); *E. cenchria* (33, 43, 48, Stemmler, 1971); *E. chrysogaster* (7b, 14, 37, pers. obs.); *Eryx johni* (5, 7b, 19, 20, 33, Wall, 1911d; Underwood, 1947; Greene, 1973a); *E. somalicus* (5, Gans et al., 1965); *E. tataricus* (5, 33, Minton, 1966; Greene, 1973a); *Gonyophis conicus* (20, 27, 37, 43, 44, 48, 51, Wall, 1911d; Mahendra, 1931a; Minton, 1966; Greene, 1973a); *Liasis albertisii* (43, 48, Johnson, 1975); *L. amethystinus* (43, 48, Johnson, 1975); *L. boa* (7a, Johnson, 1975); *L. boeleni* (43, 48, Johnson, 1975); *L. childreni* (43, 48, Johnson, 1975); *L. mackloti* (7a, Johnson, 1975); *L. papuanus* (7a, Johnson, 1975); *Lichanura trivirgata* (7, 14, 19, Grinnell and Grinnell, 1907; Ruben, 1976; Wright and Wright, 1957); *Python molurus* (5, 12, 44, 48, Wall, 1912b, 1926a; Schmidt, 1927a; Minton, 1966); *P. regius* (19, 20, Cansdale, 1961); *P. reticulatus* (5, 7c, 20, Wall, 1926b); *P. sebae* (5, 12, 33, 43, 44, 48, 52, Sweeney, 1971; FitzSimons, 1962; Stemmler, 1971; Broadley, 1983); *P. spilotes* (43, 48, Johnson, 1975).

Bolyeriidae

Bolyeria multocarinata (12, Vinson, 1975); *Casarea dussumieri* (5, 7e, Vinson, 1975).

Colubridae

Ahaetulla mycterizans (1, 24, 30, 40, 43, 44, 46, 48, 50, Wall, 1906a); *A. nasuta* (12, 25, 30, 34, 41, 44, 46, 48, Wall, 1905; Soderberg, 1971); *A. prasina* (25, 30, 40, 43, 44, 48, Boulenger, 1912; Mertens, 1930; Henderson and Binder, 1980); *Alsophis cantherigerus* (28, 32, Barbour and Ramsden, 1919); *Amblycephalus moellendorffi* (34, Wall, 1903); *Amblyodipsas polylepis* (5, 20, 37, Pienaar et al., 1978; Broadley, 1983); *Amphiesma platyceps* (7a, 28, 41, Wall, 1908a, 1909c); *A. sanguinea* (48, Taylor, 1954); *A. stolata* (5, 7a, 7e, 27, 28, 41, 58, Wall, 1909, 1911b; Schmidt, 1927a); *Amphlorhinus multimaculatus* (39, 43, 48, FitzSimons, 1962; Broadley, 1983); *Antillophis parvifrons* (7e, 28, Sadjak and Henderson, 1982; Schwartz and Thomas, 1966; Schwartz, 1978); *Aparallactus capensis* (37, 48, FitzSimons, 1962; Pienaar et al., 1978; Broadley, 1983); *Aplopeltura boa* (3, Taylor, 1965); *Argyrogena fasciolatus* (27, 28, 41, 43, 44, 48, Wall, 1907b, 1913b; Gharpurey, 1931; Minton, 1966; Wilson, 1967); *Arrhyton landoi* (7b, Schwartz and Garrido, 1981); *Atractus poeppigi* (27, 33, Greene, 1973a); *Boiga cyanea* (46, 48, 58, Campden-Main, 1970); *B. cynodon* (25, Lim, 1958); *B. dendrophila* (25, 29, 34, 43, 46, 48, Boulenger, 1912, Greene, 1979); *B. gokool* (34, 41, 43, 44, Wall, 1910a); *B. irregularis* (25, 29, 41, 43, 48, Longman, 1915, 1937; Johnson, 1975); *B. multomaculata* (29, 34, 43, 44, 48, Schmidt, 1927a); *B. trigonata* (20, 40, 42, 43, 45, 48, Wall, 1908b; Minton, 1966; Gans and Latifi, 1973); *Blythia reticulata* (5, Wall, 1908a); *Calamaria leucocephala* (43, 46, 48, Flower, 1899); *C. septentrionalis* (3, 4, 36, 48, Fan, 1931; Maslin, 1950; Schmidt, 1927b); *Cemophora coccinea* (20, 33, Greene, 1973a); *Cerberus rynchops* (5, 7c, 12, 14, 27, 30, 43, 44, 48, Wall, 1918b; Mertens, 1930); *Cercaspis carinatus* (19, 20, 48, de Silva, 1980); *Chilomeniscus cinctus* (33, 34, Greene, 1973a; Sweet, pers. comm.); *Chilorhinophis gerardi* (33, 58, Broadley, 1983); *Chionactis occipitalis* (5, 12, 43, 44, 48, Camp, 1916; Wright and Wright, 1957; Greene, 1973a; pers.obs.); *Chironius carinatus* (25, 32, 34, 37, 40, 43, 48, Mole, 1924; Test et al., 1966; pers. obs.); *Chrysopelea ornata* (7d, 43, 44, 48, 58, Wall, 1907d; Golder, 1972); *C. paradisi* (7d, 58, Mertens, 1970); *Clelia clelia* (14, 20, 33, Greene, 1973a); *Coluber constrictor* (3, 7a, 7c, 7e, 14, 37, 46, 48, Carr, 1940; Minton and Minton, 1948; Telford, 1952; Golder, 1972; Lynch, 1978; pers. obs.); *C. jugularis* (7a, 8, Clark and Clark, 1973); *C. karelini* (7e, Clark et al., 1969); *C. najadum* (7a, 8, Clark and Clark, 1973); *C. nummifer* (29, Werner, 1986); *C. rhodorhachis* (7a, 7b, 29, 43, Wall, 1911a; Minton, 1966; Werner, 1986); *C. ventrimaculatus* (7a, 48, Wall, 1913b; Corkhill, 1932; Minton, 1966); *Coniophanes imperialis* (33, Greene, 1973a); *C. fissidens* (48, Myers, 1969); *C. frangivirgatus* (48, Minton and Mebs, 1978); *Conophis vittatus* (46, Werler, 1970); *Crisantophis nevermanni* (43, 45, 48,

APPENDICES

Villa, 1969); *Crotaphopeltis hotamboeia* (12, 27, 29, 39, 40, 43, 44, 48, Loveridge, 1928; Broadley, 1959; 1983; FitzSimons, 1962; Sweeney, 1971); *Dasypeltis scabra* (9, 12, 25, 28, 29, 39, 40, 43, 45, 46, 58, Anderson, 1898; FitzSimons, 1962; Gans and Richmond, 1957; Gans et al., 1965; Sweeney, 1971; Pienaar et al., 1978; Broadley, 1983; Kalmus, 1984; Mertens, 1955); *Dendrelaphis caudolineatus* (14, Boulenger, 1912); *D. punctulatus* (25, 40, 43, 46, 48, Longman, 1913; Johnson, 1975); *Dendrelaphis pictus* (25, 29, 43, 46, 48, 58, Mertens, 1930); *Dendrophidion percarinatus* (14, 29, 34, 37, 43, Test et al., 1966); *Diadophis punctatus* (3, 7b, 8, 14, 33, 37, 48, Conant, 1942b; Fitch, 1975; Gates, 1957; Gehlbach, 1970; Greene, 1973a; Grinnell and Storer, 1924; Klauber, 1931; Minton and Minton, 1948; Pickwell, 1947; Wright and Wright, 1957); *Dinodon rufozonatus* (5, 48, Wall, 1903; Maslin, 1950; Pope, 1935); *Dipsadoboa aulicus* (41, 44, 43, 48, Broadley and Stevens, 1971; Pienaar et al., 1978; Broadley, 1983); *Dispholidus typus* (1, 2, 3, 5, 7a, 7e, 12, 28, 30, 40, 43, 46, 48, Broadley, 1959; 1983; FitzSimons, 1962; Mertens, 1955; Pope, 1958; Zingg, 1968; Sweeney, 1971; Pienaar et al., 1978; Buys and Buys, 1983; Spawls, 1985); *Drymarchon corais* (14, 33, 37, 43, 48, Mole, 1924; Mole and Urich, 1894; Neill, 1960); *Drymobius margaritiferus* (7a, Schmidt and Shannon, 1947); *Duberria lutrix* (5, 37, 39, FitzSimons, 1962; Sweeney, 1971; Broadley, 1983); *D. variegata* (5, 14, Broadley, 1983); *Eirenis lineomaculata* (29, Werner, 1983); *Elaphe carinata* (5, 43, 46, 48, Maslin, 1950; Pope, 1929); *E. dione* (48, Hahn, 1960); *E. guttata* (34, Golder, 1974; Schenck, 1880); *E. helenae* (25, 42, 43, 44, 48, Wall, 1913c, 1919a; Bröer and Engelhardt, 1981); *E. hohenackeri* (43, 48, Clark and Clark, 1973); *E. longissima* (43, 48, Golder, 1972); *E. mandarina* (34, 43, 48, Golder, 1974); *E. obsoleta* (34, Golder, 1972; Schenck, 1880); *E. radiata* (25, 41, 43, 44, 46, 48, 58, Wall, 1910a, 1914; Campden-Main, 1970); *E. rufodorsata* (34, 43, 48, Hahn, 1960); *E. subradiata* (25, Mertens, 1930); *E. taeniura* (7a, 7c, 12, 19, 20, 43, 45, 46, Maslin, 1950); *E. triaspis* (43, 48, pers. obs.); *E. vulpina* (34, Schenck, 1880); *Elapomorphus bilineatus* (33, Greene, 1973a); *Enhydris chinensis* (27, 48, Schmidt, 1927a); *E. enhydris* (5, 7c, Wall, 1912b; Biswas and Acharjyo, 1977); *E. pakistanica* (48, Minton, 1966); *E. plumbea* (1, 48, Boulenger, 1912; Schmidt, 1927a); *E. schistosus* (7a, 7e, 5, 27, 41, 48, Boulenger, 1912; Wall, 1912b, 1919b); *E. sieboldi* (27, 41, 44, 46, 48, Wall, 1907b); *Erythrolamprus aesculapii* (33, 48, Greene, 1973a; Myers, 1986); *E. bizona* (7a, 14, 27, 33, 37, 41, 48, Smith, 1969, Myers, 1986; pers. obs.); *E. mimus* (7a, 14, 27, 33, 37, 41, 48, Myers, 1986; pers. obs.); *Farancia abacura* (19, 20, 33, 36, 33, 45, 58, Davis, 1948; Meade, 1946; Greene, 1973a); *F. erytrogramma* (33, Neill, 1964); *Gomesophis brasiliensis* (19, Amaral, 1932); *Gyalopion canum* (8, 14, 37, Tanner and Robinson, 1960; Taylor, 1931; Woodin, 1953); *Haplocercus ceylonensis* (2, de Silva, 1983); *Helicops* *angulatus* (40, 43, 48, Mole, 1924); *H. carinicaudus* (34, Mueller, 1971); *Hemirhagerrhis notataenia* (5, 48, Sweeney, 1971; Broadley, 1983); *Heterodon nasicus* (3, 7a, 12, 14, 20, 28, 29, 30, 32, 33, 37, 40, 41, Platt, 1969); *H. platirhinos* (3, 7a, 12, 14, 20, 22, 28, 29, 30, 32, 33, 37, 40, 41, 43, 45, 46, 52, Platt, 1969); *H. simus* (12, 14, 20, 22, 28, 30, 37, 46, Myers and Arata, 1961); *Homoroselaps lacteus* (37, FitzSimons, 1962; Broadley, 1983); *Hydrodynastes gigas* (27, 48, Minton and Mebs, 1978; Mueller, 1971); *Hypsiglena torquata* (5, 12, 14, 20, 33, 37, 39, 43, Dundee, 1950; Webb, 1970; Hayes, 1985; Mitchell, 1985); *Lampropeltis alterna* (3, 14, 20, Tryon and Guese, 1984); *L. getulus* (2, 7a, 14, 34, 37, 43, 48, Malnate, 1944; pers. obs.); *L. triangulum* (33, 37, 48, Greene, 1973a, pers. obs.); *Lamprophis aurora* (5, Broadley, 1983); *L. fiskii* (12, 39, Broadley, 1983); *L. fuliginosus* (14, 43, 44, 48, Barbour and Loveridge, 1928; FitzSimons, 1962; Sweeney, 1971; Broadley, 1983); *L. inornatus* (5, Broadley, 1983); *Leptophis ahaetulla* (29, 43, 46, 48, Beebe, 1946; Mertens, 1971; Minton and Mebs, 1978; Mole, 1924; Mole and Urich, 1894); *L. depressirostris* (29, 43, 46, 48, Mertens, 1971); *L. diplotropis* (5, 29, 43, 46, 48, Oliver, 1948; Mertens, 1971); *L. mexicanus* (1, 7e, 43, 46, 48, Stuart, 1935; Slevin, 1939; Mertens, 1971); *L. nebulosus* (43, 46, 48, pers. obs.); *L. occidentalis* (25, 29, 30, 46, Oliver, 1948); *Lioheterodon madagascariensis* (28, Conant, 1938a); *Liophis sp.* (28, Myers, 1986); *L. anomalus* (33, Mertens, 1931); *L. epinephalus* (14, 20, 27, 28, 40, 48, 58, Dunn, 1937; Taylor, 1951; Myers, 1986; pers. obs); *L. melanotus* (28, Mole, 1924); *L. miliaris* (34, Mueller, 1971); *L. reginae* (28, Mole, 1924; Mole and Urich, 1894); *L. williamsi* (5, 14, 28, Myers, 1986); *L. zweifeli* (14, 28, Test et al., 1966; Myers, 1986); *Lycodon aulicus* (19, 20, 34, 43, 44, 46, 48, Wall, 1907b, 1909c, 1909b; Mertens, 1930); *L. fasciatus* (14, 44, 48, Wall, 1908a, 1911c); *L. striatus* (5, 20, 26, 27, 34, 37, 48, Wall, 1909b, Minton, 1966); *L. subcinctus* (34, 48, Mertens, 1930); *Lycodonomorphus laevissimus* (5, Broadley, 1983); *L. rufulus* (5, 7c, Sweeney, 1971; Pienaar et al., 1978; Broadley, 1983); *Lycophidion capense* (12, 29, 37, 44, 48, Sweeney, 1971); *Lystrophis dorbignyi* (20, 27, 33, Orejas-Miranda, 1966; Greene, 1973a); *Lytorhynchus diadema* (12, 33, 39, Greene, 1973a); *L. maynardi* (7a, 7b, 34, 43, 45, Minton, 1966); *L. paradoxus* (20, 33, 39, Minton, 1966; Greene, 1973a); *L. ridgewayi* (20, 39, Minton, 1966); *Macropisthodon plumbicolor* (5, 27, Wall, 1906b); *M. rhodomelas* (15, 28, Ridley, 1899; Taylor, 1965; Tweedie, 1953); *Malpolon moilensis* (28, Arnold, 1980; Mandaville, 1967; Mosauer, 1934); *M. monspessulana* (7a, 12, 28, 29, 41, 42, 48, Anderson, 1898; Reed and Marx, 1959; Clark and Clark, 1973; Gonzales, 1979; Werner, 1986); *Masticophis flagellum* (3, 7a, 7b, 7e, 34, 37, 46, 48, Carr, 1940; Gates, 1957; Wright and Wright, 1957; Gehlbach, 1970); *M. lateralis* (7a, Fitch, 1949); *Mastigodryas bifossatus* (34, Mueller, 1971); *M. boddaerti* (34, 48, Mole, 1924); *M.

APPENDICES

melanolomus (34, 48, Mertens, 1952a); *M. pleei* (34, 48, Mertens, 1952a); *Mehelya capensis* (5, 14, Broadley, 1959, 1983; Sweeney, 1971; Pienaar, et al., 1978); *Natriciteres olivacea* (12, 25, 29, 37, 44, 48, Barbour and Loveridge, 1928; FitzSimons, 1962; Sweeney, 1971; Broadley, 1983); *Natrix maura* (27, Golder, 1972); *N. natrix* (3, Owen, 1982); *N. percarinata* (7c, 48, Maslin, 1950); *N. sanguinea* (48, E. H. Taylor, 1954); *N. stolata* (5, 7a, Schmidt, 1927a); *Nerodia erythrogaster* (14, 27, 43, 48, Conant, 1938b); *N. sipedon* (1, 7, Pough, 1976); *N. taxispilota* (48, Telford, 1952); *Ninia atrata* (27, 41, Greene, 1975); *N. diademata* (20, 27, 33, Greene, 1975); *N. sebae* (1, 14, 27, 29, 37, 41, Greene, 1975; Henderson, 1977); *Oligodon arnensis* (5, 7a, 27, 29, 40, 43, 44, 48, Wall, 1907b, 1913d; Minton, 1966); *O. bitorquatus* (12, 33, 42, 43, 45, 58, Mertens, 1931); *O. cyclurus* (33, 48, Taylor, 1965; Greene, 1973a); *O. quadrilineatus* (33, Greene, 1973a); *O. subgriseus* (5, 48, Wall, 1909e); *O. taeniatus* (33, Greene, 1973a); *O. taeniolatus* (29, 33, Minton, 1966; Greene, 1973a); *O. violaceus* (5, 33, 34, 36, 44, 48, Wall, 1903; Schmidt, 1927a); *Opisthotropis balteatus* (5, 14, 33, Schmidt, 1927a; Fan, 1931); *Opheodrys vernalis* (21, Conant, 1942b); *Oxybelis aeneus* (1, 6, 14, 30, 34, 46, 48, Mertens, 1952a; Kennedy, 1965b; Henderson, 1974; Henderson and Binder, 1980); *O. argenteus* (30, Henderson and Binder, 1980); *O. fulgidus* (30, 48, Henderson and Binder, 1980; Golder, 1983); *Philothamnus angolensis* (25, 44, 48, Broadley, 1983); *P. hoplogaster* (5, 7d, 7e, Sweeney, 1971; Pienaar et al., 1978; Broadley, 1983); *P. irregularis* (25, 37, 43, 48, 58, Broadley, 1959; Sweeney, 1971; FitzSimons, 1962; Wilson, 1965); *P. ornatus* (25, 44, Broadley, 1983); *P. semivariegatus* 1, 7d, 12, 25, 30, 44, 48, 58, Mertens, 1955; Broadley, 1959, 1983; Sweeney, 1971; FitzSimons, 1962; Wilson, 1965; Pienaar et al., 1978); *Phyllorhynchus decurtatus* (12, 25, 43, Klauber, 1940; Wright and Wright, 1957); *Pituophis melanoleucus* (5, 12, 29, 34, 43, 48, 58, Carr, 1940; Durham, 1956; Sanchez-Herrera et al., 1981; Kardong, 1980); *Plagiopholis styani* (36, Maslin, 1950); *Pliocercus elapoides* (33, 46, Greene, 1973a; Seib, 1980); *Prosymna bivittata* (37, 39, Pienaar et al., 1978; Broadley, 1983); *P. janii* (37, 39, 40, 41, 46, Broadley, 1983; Haacke and Bruton, 1978); *P. sundevalli* (29, 37, Broadley, 1959; FitzSimons, 1962); *Psammodynastes pulverulentus* (1, 5, 7a, 41, 43, 44, 48, Wall, 1908a, 1910b, Boulenger, 1912; Schmidt, 1927a; Mertens, 1930); *Psammophis aegyptius* (25, Werner, 1985); *P. condanarus* (37, 48, Wall, 1911b); *P. leightoni* (2, 7a, 7c, Pienaar et al., 1978; Broadley, 1983); *P. leithi* (2, 7, 48, Minton, 1966); *P. phillipsii* (7a, 48, Broadley, 1983); *P. schokari* (7a, 48, Minton, 1966); *P. sibilans* (1, 7a, 48, Broadley, 1959, 1983; Sweeney, 1971; FitzSimons, 1962; Pienaar et al., 1978); *P. subtaeniatus* (1, 7e, 48, FitzSimons, 1962; Pienaar et al., 1978); *Psammophylax rhombeatus* (5, 7e, 27, 37, Sweeney, 1971; Pienaar et al., 1978; FitzSimons, 1962; Broadley, 1983); *P. variabilis* (1, 7e, 27, 37, 48, Broadley, 1983); *Pseudaspis cana* (12, 39, 41, 43, 44, 46, 48, Broadley, 1959, 1983; FitzSimons, 1962; Sweeney, 1971; Branch, 1973; Buys and Buys, 1983); *Pseudoxenodon macrops* (28, 41, 44, Wall, 1909a); *P. nothus* (28, 37, 43, Maslin, 1950); *Pseustes poecilonotus* (12, 25, 29, 34, 43, 45, 46, 48, 58, Greene, 1979; Mole, 1924; Netting, 1936; Rand and Ortleb, 1969); *P. sulphureus* (25, 29, 34, 58, Mole, 1924; Rossman and Williams, 1966); *Ptyas korros* (5, 7a, 37, 48, Wall, 1908a; Schmidt, 1927a); *P. mucosus* (7a, 7b, 7c, 11, 12, 25, 27, 43, 45, 48, 58, Wall, 1906b, 1909c, 1911a; Boulenger, 1912; Flower, 1899; Gharpurey, 1931); *Regina alleni* (7a, 7c, Carr, 1940; 14, 19, 20, 27, 48, Godley, 1982); *Rhabdophis subminiatus* (5, 27, 41, 58, Wall, 1909a; Taylor, 1965); *R. tigrina* (5, 15, 27, 28, 41, 45, 48, Hahn, 1960; Kreyenberg, 1907; Maslin, 1950; Minton and Mebs, 1978; Schmidt, 1927a); *Rhabdops bicolor* (2, 5, 19, 20, Wall, 1908a); *Rhadinaea flavilata* (14, Myers, 1967); *Rhamphiophis oxyrhynchus* (5, 12, 25, 43, 44, 48, Sweeney, 1971; FitzSimons, 1962; Pienaar et al., 1978; Broadley, 1983); *Rhinocheilus lecontei* (14, 20, 33, 34, 37, 43, 48, 54, McCoy and Gehlbach, 1967; Hanley, 1943; Klauber, 1941; Lardie, 1961; Greene, 1973a); *Salvadora grahamiae* (7e, 34, 43, 48, Mosauer, 1932; Conant, 1942a); *Scaphiodontophis annulatus* (5, 33, 37, Henderson, 1984b); *S. venustissimus* (5, 33, 37, Henderson, 1984b); *Sibon nebulata* (28, 36, 43, Mole, 1924); *Sibynophis collaris* (5, 7, 14, Wall, 1908a); *Sinonatrix aequifasciata* (14, Fan, 1931); *S. chrysarges* (48, Boulenger, 1912); *Sonora semiannulata* (3, 7b, 22, 30, 37, Camp, 1916; Hillis, 1977); *Spalerosophis diadema* (7a, 12, 37, Wall, 1911d, 1914); *Spilotes pullatus* (25, 30, 37, 43, 48, Amaral, 1929; Mole, 1924; Mole and Urich, 1894; Rossman and William, 1966; Vanzolini et al., 1980; pers. obs.); *Stilosoma extenuatum* (34, 43, 48, Carr, 1934); *Storeria dekayi* (3, Liner, 1977); *S. occipitomaculata* (3, 47, Dial, 1965; Gosner, 1942; Jordon, 1970; Wright and Wright, 1957); *Tachymenis peruvianus* (19, 20, 33, Donoso-Barros, 1969); *Tantilla brevicauda* (33, Mertens, 1952a); *Telescopus dhara* (29, 30, 43, 44, Werner, 1983); *T. fallax* (5, 29, 43, Werner, 1983); *T. hoogstraali* (5, 29, 43, 44, Werner, 1983); *T. semiannulatus* (12, 40, 43, 44, 48, Sweeney, 1971; FitzSimons, 1962; Pienaar et al., 1978; Broadley, 1983); *Thamnophis couchi* (7a, 7c, 14, 20, 27, 38, 48, Tevis, 1944; Hayes and Baker, 1986); *T. cyrtopsis* (7a, 7c, Gates, 1957); *T. elegans* (37, Drummond and Wolfe, 1981); *T. eques* (33, Greene, 1973a); *T. sirtalis* (1, 7e, 27, 30, 37, 43, 45, 48, 58, Fitch, 1965; Golder, 1972; Gove and Burghardt, 1983; Van Devender, 1973); *Thelotornis capensis* and *T. kirtlandi* (1, 25, 40, 43, 48, 58, (Loveridge, 1928; Broadley, 1959, 1983; FitzSimons, 1962); *Toluca lineata* (28, Smith, 1943; Taylor and Smith, 1942); *T. megalodon* (28, Taylor and Smith, 1942); *Tomodon ocellatus* (29, 33, 43, 48, Gallardo, 1972); *Trachischium fuscum* (5, Wall, 1909a); *T. guentheri* (5, Wall, 1909a); *T. monticola* (5, Wall, 1908a); *Tretanorhinus variabilis* (5, 19, 51, Barbour and

Ramsden, 1919; Grant, 1946; Petzold, 1969); *Trimorphodon biscutatus* (34, 43, 48, Klauber, 1928; Campbell, 1934; Wright and Wright, 1957); *T. tau* (41, 43, 44, pers. obs.); *Tropidoclonion lineatum* (27, 29, 43, Ramsey, 1946); *Umbrivaga mertensi* (28, Myers, 1986); *Uromacer catesbyi* (44, 46, Henderson and Binder, 1980); *U. oyxrhynchus* (44, 46, Henderson and Binder, 1980); *U. wetmorei* (44, 46, Henderson and Binder, 1980); *Virginia striatula* (3, 48, 49, Kirk, 1969; Thomas and Hendricks, 1976); *Waglerophis merremii* (28, 41, 45, Vanzolini et al., 1980); *Xenochropis cerasogaster* (5, 7, 7c, 30, 40, 41, 48, Wall, 1907b; Minton, 1966); *X. piscator* (7a, 7b, 12, 27, 28, 40, 41, 44, 46, 48, Wall, 1907b, 1907c; Boulenger, 1912; Schmidt, 1927a; Stumpel, 1981); *Xenodon neuwiedi* (28, Mueller, 1971); *X. rabdocephalus* (28, Myers, 1986; pers. obs.); *Zaocys dhumnades* (7a, 7c, 12, 14, 40, 43, 48, Wall, 1903; Maslin, 1950).

Elapidae

Acanthophis antarcticus (40, 41, 43, 48, Johnson, 1975); *Aspidelaps lubricus* (12, 28, 41, FitzSimons, 1962; Mertens, 1955; Pienaar et al., 1978; Broadley, 1983); *A. scutatus* (3, 12, 22, 28, 41, 43, 48, FitzSimons, 1962; Mertens, 1955; Broadley, 1983); *Austrelaps superbus* (27, 41, 43, 48, Johnson, 1975); *Boulengerina annulata* (7c, 28, 41, 46, Ionides and Pitman, 1965; Kratzer, 1965); *Bungarus candidus* (20, 27, 37, 40, 44, 48, Wall, 1908; Soderberg, 1966); *B. caeruleus* (5, 20, 27, 33, 37, 39, 40, 48, Wall, 1908c; Minton, 1966; Khan and Tasnim, 1986b); *B. fasciatus* (5, 7e, 12, 19, 20, 27, 37, Wall, 1910a, 1911c; Soderberg, 1966); *B. lividus* (48, Wall, 1910a) *B. multicinctus* (20, 27, 33, 37, 48, Schmidt, 1927a; Pope, 1935; Glass, 1946); *Cacophis harriettae* (20, 37, 41, Johnson, 1975; Longman, 1918); *Calliophis gracilis* (5, 33, 37, Soderberg, 1966); *C. macclellandii* (5, 7a, 14, 27, 48, Wall, 1908a, 1910a, 1918b, 1926a; Venning, 1910; Schmidt, 1927a; Soderberg, 1966); *C. maculiceps* (7a, 30, 33, 37, 48, Soderberg, 1966); *C. melanurus* (20, 33, Lindberg, 1932; Greene, 1973a); *Cryptophis nigrescens* (20, 27, 34, 37, 48, Johnson, 1975); *Demansia olivacea* (28, 37, 41, 43, 48, Johnson, 1975); *D. psammophis* (28, 37, 41, 43, 48, Johnson, 1975); *Dendroaspis angusticeps* (5, 7a, 7e, 12, 28, 28, 48, Ionides and Pitman, 1965; Loveridge, 1928; Pitman, 1965; Sweeney, 1971; Broadley, 1983); *D. jamesoni* (25, 28, Pitman, 1965); *D. polylepis* (7a, 7b, 12, 25, 28, 41, 43, 44, 46, 48, Armitage, 1965; Broadley, 1959, 1983; FitzSimons, 1962; Pitman, 1965; Sweeney, 1971; Pienaar et al., 1978; Buys and Buys, 1983); *D. viridis* (28, Pitman, 1965); *Echiopsis curta* (27, 37, 41, Johnson, 1975); *Elapsoidea guentheri* (33, DeWitte, 1962); *E. sundevalli* (5, 7a, 12, 33, 40, 48, FitzSimons, 1962; Sweeney, 1971; Greene, 1973a; Broadley, 1983); *Enhydrina schistosa* (5, 48, Minton, 1966; *Hemachatus haemachatus* (3, 7, 28, 41, 43, 48, 50, 58,

FitzSimons, 1962; Hulme, 1951; Buys and Buys, 1983; Broadley, 1983); Hemiaspis daemelii (20, 28, 37, 45, Johnson, 1975); *H. signata* (27, 34, 41, Johnson, 1975); *Hydrophis cyanocinctus* (48, Minton, 1966); *H. spiralis* (40, 48, Minton, 1966); *Leptomicrurus sp.* (33, Schmidt and Inger, 1957); *Maticora bivirgata* (33, 37, 43, 48, Soderberg, 1966; Greene, 1973a); *M. intestinalis* (7a, 33, 37, 48, Mertens, 1929; Soderberg, 1966; Greene, 1973a); *Micruroides euryxanthus* (7a, 10, 14, 20, 33, 37, Vitt and Hulse, 1973; Woodin, 1953; Bogert, 1960; Greene, 1973a); *Micrurus browni* (33, Greene, 1973a); *M. clarki* (33, Greene, 1973a); *M. diastema* (33, Greene, 1973a); *M. dissoleucus* (33, Greene, 1973a); *M. distans* (33, Greene, 1973a); *M. filiformis* (33, Greene, 1973a); *M. frontalis* (33, Greene, 1973a); *M. fulvius* (31, 33, 48, Carr, 1940; Gehlbach, 1970, 1972; Greene, 1973a; Greene and Pyburn, 1975); *M. ibiboboca* (33, Vanzolini et al., 1980); *M. isozonus* (33, Greene, 1973a); *M. lemniscatus* (48, Mole, 1924; Greene, 1973a); *M. limbatus* (33, 37, 48, Greene, 1973a); *M. mipartitus* (33, Greene, 1973a); *M. nigrocinctus* (33, Greene, 1973a); *M. psyches* (33, Greene, 1973a); *M. spixi* (Greene, 1973a); *M. surinamensis* (Greene, 1973a); *Naja haje* (3, 7a, 12, 28, 41, 48, Anderson, 1898, Broadley, 1959, 1983; FitzSimons, 1962; Sweeney, 1971; Pienaar et al., 1978; Buys and Buys, 1983); *N. melanoleuca* (28, 36, 41, Broadley, 1959, 1983; FitzSimons, 1962; Sweeney, 1971; Tryon and Whitehead, 1986); *N. mossambica* (3, 7a, 7c, 28, 41, 46, 48, 50, Broadley, 1959, 1983; Pienaar et al., 1978); *N. naja* (5, 7a, 12, 28, 41, 44, 46, 48, 50, 58, Wall, 1911a, 1913a; Boulenger, 1912; Dunn, 1927; Minton, 1966; Petzold, 1968; Soderberg, 1966); *N. nigricollis* (3, 28, 41, 48, 50, Loveridge, 1928; FitzSimons, 1962; Mertens, 1955; Sweeney, 1971; Broadley, 1983); *N. nivea* (7, 28, 41, 43, 48, FitzSimons, 1962; Mertens, 1955; Buys and Buys, 1983; Broadley, 1983); *Notechis scutatus* (27, 41, 43, 48, Johnson, 1975); *Ophiophagus hannah* (7a, 7c, 12, 28, 41, 44, 48, Wall, 1908a, 1910a, 1919a, 1924; Oliver, 1956; Soderberg, 1966); *Oxyuranus scutellatus* (30, 34, 40, 41, 48, Johnson, 1975); *Pelamis platurus* (33, 48, 58, Minton, 1966; Rubinoff and Kropach, 1970; Greene, 1973a; Caldwell and Rubinoff, 1983); *Pseudechis australis* (7a, 28, 41, 43, 48, Johnson, 1975); *P. colletti* (28, 30, 43, 48, Johnson, 1975); *P. guttatus* (12, 28, Bustard, 1968c); *P. porphyriacus* (12, 27, 33, 37, 41, 43, 48, Johnson, 1975; Greene, 1973a); *Pseudohaje goldii* (5, 28, 41, Brunner, 1968); *Pseudonaja textilis* (28, 41, 43, 48, Johnson, 1975); *Simoselaps warro* (7b, 19, 27, 37, Johnson, 1975); *Suta dwyeri* (20, 27, 34, 37, 48, Johnson, 1975); *S. suta* (20, 27, 37, 41, 43, 48, Johnson, 1975); *Tropidechis carinatus* (12, 27, 29, 43, 48, Fleay, 1961; Johnson, 1975); *Vermicella annulata* (7b, 18, 20, 33, Johnson, 1975; Longman, 1918, 1937; Mertens, 1946; Thompson, 1934; Shine, 1980b); *Walterinnesia aegyptii* (12, 44, Corkill, 1932; Reed and Marx, 1959).

APPENDICES

Leptotyphlopidae

Leptotyphlops cairi (37, Anderson, 1898); *L. dulcis* (3, 14, 37, Gehlbach, 1970; Watkins et al., 1972); *L. goudotii* (Greene, 1973a); *L. longicauda* (7c, 37, Sweeney, 1971; Pienaar et al., 1978); *L. macrorhynchus* (37, Clark and Clark, 1973; Corkhill, 1932); *L. scutifrons* (3, 37, Visser, 1966).

Tropidophiidae

Exiliboa placata (14, 20, pers. obs.); *Trachyboa boulengeri* (3, 14, 19, 20, Lehmann, 1970; pers. obs.); *Tropidophis canus* (2, 7b, 14, 19, 20, pers. obs.); *T. caymanensis* (19, 20, 54, Thomas, 1963); *T. greenwayi* (2, 7b, 14, 19, 20, 33, 58, pers. obs.); *T. jamaicensis* (19, Barbour, 1910); *T. melanurus* (14, 19, 20, 55, Barbour and Ramsden, 1919; Petzold, 1969; Stull, 1928); *T. pardalis* (5, 19, 20, 33, 55, Hecht et al., 1955; Petzold, 1969); *T. semicinctus* (14, 19, 55, Barbour and Ramsden, 1919; Darlington, 1927).

Typhlopidae

Rhamphotyphlops braminus (7b, 36, 37, Wall, 1909c, 1918a); *Typhlops acutus* (7b, Wall, 1918a); *T. diardi* (7, 33, 37, Wall, 1909c, 1910, 1918a; Smedley, 1931); *T. platycephalus* (36, Schmidt, 1928); *Rhinotyphlops schlegelii* (11, 14, 36, 37, 46, Broadley, 1959; Sweeney, 1971; Pienaar et al., 1978).

Uropeltidae

Plecturus perroteti (5, Wall, 1919a); *Rhinophis travancoricus* (7b, 36, Rajendran, 1985); *Uropeltis myhendrae* (7b, 37, Rajendran, 1985); *U. ocellatus* (5, Wall, 1918b, 1919a).

Viperidae

Agkistrodon bilineatus (34, 43, 48, pers. obs.); *A. blomhoffi* (27, 34, Wall, 1903); *A. contortrix* (7a, 34, 37, 38, 40, 43, 48, Carpenter and Gillingham, 1975; Chenowith, 1948; Fitch, 1960; Mead, 1940; Trowbridge, 1937; McCrystal and Green, 1986); *A. halys* (27, 34, 43, Hahn, 1960; Maslin, 1950); *A. piscivorus* (34, 37, 38, 40, 43, 46, 48, Carpenter and Gillingham, 1975; Mead, 1940; Minton and Minton, 1948); *Atheris squamiger* (46, Kratzer, 1969); *Azemiops feae* (7, 27, 29, 34, 44, Kardong, 1986); *Bitis arietans* (1, 2, 12, 40, 43, 48, Broadley, 1959, 1983; FitzSimons, 1962; Ionides and Pitman, 1965; Sweeney, 1971; Pienaar et al., 1978); *B. atropos* (12, 43, 44, 48, FitzSimons, 1962; Broadley, 1983); *B. caudalis* (1, 2, 12, 40, 43, 44, 48,

Broadley, 1959, 1983; FitzSimons, 1962; Mertens, 1955; Pienaar et al., 1978); *B. cornuta* (7, 12, 37, FitzSimons, 1962; Broadley, 1983); *B. gabonica* (1, 5, 12, 43, 48, FitzSimons, 1962; Ionides and Pitman, 1965; Sweeney, 1971; Broadley, 1983); *B. nasicornis* (48, Ionides and Pitman, 1965); *B. peringueyi* (12, 43, 48, Mertens, 1955); *B. xeropaga* (12, 43, 45, 48, Haacke, 1975; Broadley, 1983); *Bothrops asper* (1, 7a, 34, 37, 43, 44, 46, 48, pers. obs.); *B. schlegeli* (1, 7e, 43, 46, 48, Kratzer, 1969; pers. obs.); *Causus defilippii* (12, 37, 48, Broadley, 1959, 1983; Sweeney, 1971); *C. resimus* (12, 43, 48, pers. obs.); *C. rhombeatus* (5, 7a, 12, 28, 39, 40, 41, 43, 48, Broadley, 1959, 1983; FitzSimons, 1962; Loveridge, 1918, 1928; Pitman, 1961); *Cerastes cerastes* (9, 12, 40, 43, 48, Anderson, 1898; Mendelssohn, 1963; pers. obs.); *C. vipera* (9, Mosauer, 1934); *Crotalus sp.* (see Klauber, 1956, and Armstrong and Murphy, 1979, for extensive summaries); *C. adamanteus* (5, Carr, 1940); *C. atrox* (38, Bogert, 1941; Inglehart and Chiszar, 1977); *C. cerastes* (38, Bogert, 1941; Cowles, 1938); *C. durissus* (34, 43, March, 1928); *C. enyo* (38, Bogert, 1941); *C. horridus* (38, Meade, 1940); *C. lepidus* (1, Vinson, 1975); *C. mitchelli* (38, Bogert, 1941); *C. ruber* (38, Bogert, 1941); *C. scutulatus* (38, Bogert, 1941); *C. triseriatus* (7a, Schmidt and Shannon, 1947); *C. viridis* (1, 7a, 14, 20, 24, 30, 35, 37, 38, 40, 41, 43, 48, 58, Bogert, 1941; Carpenter and Gillingham, 1975; Cowles, 1938; Durham 1956; Duvall et al., 1985); *C. willardi* (1, 7a, 48, Wright and Wright, 1957; pers. obs.); *Echis carinatus* (1, 7a, 7c, 9, 40, 43, 44, 48, 58, Anderson, 1898; Wall, 1908b; Gans and Latifi, 1973; Sight, 1949; Anderson, 1963; Stemmler-Gyger, 1965; Minton, 1966); *E. coloratus* (7a, 9, 43, 44, 48, Mendelssohn, 1965); *Eristicophis macmahoni* (12, 41, 43, 44, Minton, 1966); *Hypnale himalayanus* (5, 7a, 27, 34, 44, 48, Wall, 1910, 1911a); *Lachesis muta* (1, 5, 34, 43, 48, Schmidt, 1957; Solorzano, Santana, and Greene, unpubl.); *Pseudocerastes persica* (5, 12, Mendelssohn, 1965; Minton, 1966); *Sistrurus catenatus* (35, 43, 44, Greene and Oliver, 1965); *S. miliaris* (35, 37, 38, 40, 41, 48, Carr, 1940; Carpenter and Gillingham, 1975; Inglehart and Chiszar, 1977; Marchisin, 1978); *S. ravus* (27, 35, 39, 44, Campbell and Armstrong, 1979); *Trimeresurus gramineus* (12, 33, 34, 43, 44, 48, Wall, 1906c, 1926a; Schmidt, 1927a; Greene and Campbell, 1972); *T. monticola* (14, 44, 48, Wall, 1908a, 1909a); *T. mucrosquamatus* (5, Maslin, 1950); *T. puniceus* (43, 48, Taylor, 1965); *T. wagleri* (46, Ridley, 1899); *Vipera lebetina* (27, 28, 37, 48, Clark and Clark, 1973; Schweitzer, 1956); *V. russellii* (7e, 12, 44, 48, Wall, 1907a); *V. palestinae* (7a, 7e, 12, 27, 28, 41, 43, 48, Mendelssohn, 1963); *V. raddei* (7a, 12, 42, 43, 48, Darevsky, 1966).

Xenopeltidae

Xenopeltis unicolor (14, 19, 27, 33, 34, 48, Flower, 1899; Wall 1909e).

CHAPTER 2

Mimicry and Related Phenomena

F. HARVEY POUGH
Laboratory of Functional Ecology, Section of Ecology and Systematics,
Cornell University, Ithaca, New York

CONTENTS

I. THE STUDY OF MIMICRY   **155**
    A. Historical Development of the Theory of Mimicry, 155
    B. Mimicry and Behavior, 158
    C. The Distribution of Mimicry Among Taxa of Animals, 162

II. MIMICRY OF VENOMOUS SNAKES   **164**
    A. Theoretical Aspects, 164
    B. Tests of the Predictions, 170

III. MIMICRY OF INVERTEBRATES BY REPTILES   **205**

IV. INTRASPECIFIC MIMICRY   **208**

V. POSSIBLE MIMICRY OF UNPROFITABLE PREY BY LIZARDS   **210**

VI. THE USE OF LURES TO ATTRACT PREY   **212**

VII. SUMMARY   **215**
    ACKNOWLEDGMENTS   **217**
    REFERENCES   **217**
    APPENDIX   **230**

I. THE STUDY OF MIMICRY

A. Historical Development of the Theory of Mimicry

In 1862 H. W. Bates introduced the term "mimetic analogies" to describe the "resemblances in external appearance, shape, and colors between members of distinct families." In particular, he proposed that edible species of Amazonian butterflies were protected from attack by predators by virtue of their resemblance to inedible species that insectivorous animals had learned by experience to avoid. This sort of resemblance is now known as Batesian mimicry.

Although Bates was the first to formulate a coherent explanation for mimicry, the existence of resemblances among unrelated animals had long been recognized. Eighteenth century names of day-flying moths like *Apiformis* and *Ichneumoniformis* called attention to the similarity in appearance of the newly described taxon to an unrelated noxious insect (Remington, 1963). Studies of mimicry have concentrated largely upon insects since the early work by Bates and by A. R. Wallace (1865); but examples of mimicry have been noted among vertebrates, and reptiles were among the first of these to be described. In 1860 E. D. Cope called attention to the similarity of several African colubrid snakes to the venomous *Atractaspis* and of some New World colubrids to coral snakes. In 1867 Wallace pointed out that species of coral snakes (*Micrurus*) from different parts of Latin America differed in pattern, and that in a number of localities some colubrid snakes bore the pattern of the local coral snake. Mimetic resemblances of egg-eating snakes (*Dasypeltis*) to night adders (*Causus*) and of a water snake, *Nerodia fasciata*, to the water moccasin (*Agkistrodon piscivorus*) were proposed by Weale (1871) and Goode (1873), respectively.

The second major step in the understanding of mimicry was F. Müller's (1879) solution to a paradox that had baffled Bates—the mutual resemblance of two unpalatable species of butterfly. Bates had recorded this phenomenon, but had been unable to accommodate it within his hypothesis of a defenseless species gaining protection via a resemblance to a noxious species. Müller proposed that two noxious species could mutually benefit from a shared pattern because predators would consume fewer of each species in the process of learning to reject all animals with that pattern. Mimetic phenomena of this sort are called Müllerian mimicry.

Bates had observed (1862:511) that "the process by which a mimetic analogy is brought about in nature is a problem that involves that of the origin of all species and all adaptations." That succinct characterization explains the controversy that surrounded the phenomenon of mimicry during the late nineteenth and twentieth centuries. Proponents and opponents of evolutionary theory and adherents of different views of evolutionary mechanisms chose mimicry as a battleground, a phenomenon that continues today—see Turner (1983a, b). Three major lines of argument sought to discredit the view that mimetic resemblances were functional or the result of natural selection (Remington, 1963):

1. The putative selective agents (birds, in most instances) were said not to eat butterflies, or eat them too rarely to have any effect upon butterfly populations and evolution.
2. Alternatively, if the predators do eat butterflies, they eat as many noxious ones as palatable species.
3. The similarities attributed to mimicry are in fact the result of some other factor; either (a) chance, (b) common ancestry, or (c) a common response to some unknown condition of the physical environment—that is, *genius loci*.

Publication of a review of insect mimicry in 1933 by G. D. H. Carpenter and E. B. Ford refuted these objections to mimicry as it was observed in insects. Carpenter and Ford documented the occurrence of predation by birds on butterflies and thereby established the existence of the necessary selective agents and selective pressures. The use of evidence from beak marks on butterfly wings as an indication of actual or attempted predation by birds was a critical link in the chain of evidence. (Predators often release unpalatable insects after tasting them (Boyden, 1976; Wirklund and Järvi, 1982); thus beak marks on the wings of butterflies provide evidence of rejection by predators as well as of the inefficiency of predators. For a review of early studies of beak marks and more recent data see Pough and Brower, 1977, and L. Brower, 1984.)

In the second half of the twentieth century, studies of mimicry among insects have shifted their focus from the question of whether mimicry occurs to investigations of the mechanisms by which it operates. The importance of different relative frequencies of models and mimics or of different degrees of noxiousness of the model have been investigated experimentally and mathematically with a gratifying degree of agreement among the conclusions drawn from different approaches. (See J. Brower, 1958a, b, c, 1960, 1963; Huheey, 1961, 1964, 1976, 1980a; L. Brower et al., 1963, 1964, 1967a, 1971; Holling, 1963, 1965; O'Donald and Pilecki, 1970; Pough et al., 1973; Estabrook and Jespersen, 1974; Pilecki and O'Donald, 1971; Bobisud and Potratz, 1976; Arnold, 1978; Turner et al., 1984 for examples and additional references.) Fulfilling

Bates' prediction, the study of mimicry has made important general contributions to evolutionary biology. Of particular significance have been questions about the origin and evolution of aposematic colors (Boyden, 1976; Turner, 1977; Gittleman et al., 1980; Harvey and Paxton, 1981a, b; Järvi et al., 1981a, b; Harvey et al., 1982; Wirklund and Järvi, 1982). The experimental demonstration of a selective advantage for artificially created mimetic color patterns exposed to natural predators under field conditions has provided data to test the predictions of theoretical studies (L. Brower et al., 1964, 1967b; Cook et al., 1969; Waldbauer and Sternburg, 1976; Sternburg et al., 1977; Jeffords et al., 1979, 1980). Further light has been shed on evolutionary mechanisms by experiments showing that very small changes in color and pattern, of the magnitude that could be produced by a mutation at a single locus, can confer measurable protection from predators (L. Brower et al., 1963, 1971).

These experiments were pivotal in establishing the validity of mimicry theory because some critics of mimicry maintained that only a very close resemblance of a mimic to its model would confer protection on the mimic (Punnet, 1915; Goldschmidt, 1945). Experimental studies have demonstrated that even poor mimics can receive protection. Predators appear to generalize the salient features of noxious prey and consequently a very slight resemblance between model and mimic can provide a measurable degree of protection. For example, birds that had learned that two species of orange butterflies were distasteful subsequently rejected a blue and yellow butterfly that was the same size and shape as the unpalatable orange butterflies, but accepted brown butterflies of a different size and shape (L. Brower et al., 1963). In a second experiment, birds trained to avoid an unpalatable butterfly also avoided three other species of butterflies with varying degrees of resemblance to the model (L. Brower et al., 1971). Generalization of unpleasant experiences can extend to quite dissimilar prey items. Chickens trained to reject quinine-treated meal, which was presented on a glass slide with a pattern of yellow and black stripes, subsequently refused to peck a cinnabar moth caterpillar with a similar striped pattern (Morgan, 1900). Birds trained to avoid cinnabar caterpillars also avoided wasps that had the same yellow and black pattern but an entirely different shape (Windecker, 1939). This generalization of the characteristics of noxious prey by predators has led to an hypothesis for the evolution of Batesian mimicry by a two-step process, the first step providing an inaccurate resemblance that is subsequently refined by selection (Nicholson, 1927; Sheppard, 1962; Ford, 1964).

An important advance in the study of mimicry is the concept of a "palatability spectrum" (L. Brower et al., 1967a). Like many butterflies, the monarch (*Danaus plexippus*) derives its noxious characteristics from its larval foodplant. Monarch caterpillars feed upon a number of species of milkweeds that contain different mixtures and concentrations of cardenolides. As a consequence of their varied larval diets, adult monarchs vary in their cardenolide concentrations. Some individuals are entirely palatable, others have more than a lethal dose of toxin and are extremely emetic to a predator. Butterflies at both extremes of palatability as well as at intermediate points may occur in a population (L. Brower et al., 1972, 1978; Brower and Moffitt, 1974). Predators feeding on a population of monarchs can experience widely different stimuli depending upon the cardenolide content of a particular butterfly. In its original form the concept of a palatability spectrum embraced variation in the degree of palatability within a single species, but it can logically be extended to apply to a Müllerian mimicry complex or to a Müllerian complex with Batesian mimics (L. Brower et al., 1963; Pough et al., 1973; Huheey, 1976; but see Turner et al., 1984).

The study of mimicry among reptiles has not shared the progress made recently by studies of insect mimicry. Investigations of reptilian mimicry have been largely descriptive rather than experimental. With a few notable exceptions, the topic has remained mired in speculative arguments about potential predators and their hypothetical effects on models and mimics, as did the discussions that characterized the study of insect mimicry at the turn of the century.

B. Mimicry and Behavior

Mimicry is only one mode of defense or offense potentially available to an organism (cf. Greene, this volume), and the distinction between mimicry and other mechanisms is necessarily blurred. Mimicry grades into other forms of protective or exploitative resemblances and into resemblances that function during intraspecific social behavior. The tendency of scientists to classify natural phenomena in two-dimensional arrays is severely challenged by the multi-dimensional complexity of mimicry. Even the distinction between matching an inanimate background and imitating a living organism has been a point of repeated controversy. Pasteur (1982:Fig. 1) presented an amusing graphic representation of the scope of the definitions of mimicry employed by various authors during the last 150 years.

Classifications of mimicry systems have proven to be short-lived and have often stimulated as much criticism as clarification. The year 1976 saw the inception of two such controversies: J. E. Huheey published the seventh of his "Studies in Warning Colors and Mimicry," drawing responses from Benson (1977) and Sheppard and Turner (1977), to which Huheey subsequently replied (1980b). Also in 1976, R.I. Vane-Wright published "A Unified Classification of Mimetic Resemblances" (slightly amended in Vane-Wright, 1980), which elicited responses by Huheey (1980b), Cloudsley-Thompson (1981), Edmunds (1981), Endler (1981), Robinson (1981), and Rothschild (1981) and a rebuttal of these criticisms by Vane-Wright (1981). These examples illustrate the enthusiasm with which competing views of mimicry are expressed and debated.

Rothschild (1981) suggested that an elastic definition of mimicry would best accommodate new examples and new concepts in a series of categories that grade into each other, and Pasteur (1982) emphasized that too rigid a system of classification can blind us to examples of mimicry that are not readily accommodated by that particular system. Perhaps this is a time to consider examples of mimicry in all their perplexing charm and not a time to construct pigeonholes. For the purposes of this review, I will avoid proposing, even by implication, a system of classification of mimicry. Instead I will draw upon distinctions, definitions, and terminology from three recent reviews: Wickler (1968), Vane-Wright (1976), and Pasteur (1982). (Citations in the following paragraphs identify the sources of terminology, not necessarily the originator of an idea.)

Mimicry systems of the sorts considered in this chapter are tripartite (Wickler, 1968). They include three protagonists—a model, a mimic, and a dupe (Pasteur, 1972, 1982). A *model* is a "living or material agent" with perceptible characteristics such as color, odor, or sound. A *mimic* is a living organism that plagiarizes the characteristics of the model, and a *dupe* is the organism that is deceived by the mimic.

A major dichotomy in systems of protective resemblance can be based on the response of the dupe to the model (Vane-Wright, 1976, 1980; Pasteur, 1982). Some models are of no interest to the dupe (background objects like leaves or the substrate, and inedible objects like twigs or bird droppings), whereas other models are of interest (potential prey, predators, or mates, for example). Imitation of an object that is not of interest to the dupe can be called *camouflage*. The central feature of camouflage is failure of the model to elicit any reaction—attraction or avoidance—from the dupe.

Imitation of models that are of interest to the dupes can be designated *homotypy* ("assimilation of another type"). The model in these systems is normally a living organism, and it is to the advantage of the mimic to elicit the same reaction from the dupe as does the model. This review will be limited to consideration of examples of homotypy.

Two major sorts of homotypy can be distinguished: In *concrete homotypy* the model is a definite (actual) species or group of similar species, whereas in *abstract homotypy* the model is an abstraction of a general category of organism that cannot be identified at the species level (Pasteur, 1982). Abstract homotypy appears to be particularly well represented among vertebrates, especially by mimics of venomous snakes.

Another dichotomy within homotypic resemblances can be based on the relationship between the model and the dupe: The model may be either attractive or forbidding. This distinction underlies most systems of classification of mimicry (Wickler, 1968; Vane-Wright, 1976; Pasteur, 1982), but can be difficult to determine in practice because the response of a dupe to a model may not be stable. The proper allocation of a particular relationship may vary in time or in space as population numbers or densities change. Even at one place and time, the role of model and mimic may be different for different species of dupes, or even for different age classes of a single species of dupe. For example, in the absence of alternative prey, hungry predators attack moderately unpalatable prey that they had previously learned to reject (Holling, 1965; Sexton et al., 1966; Alcock, 1970b); tolerance of aposematically colored prey may increase during the ontogeny of an individual (Rothschild, 1981); some species of predators are more tolerant of unpalatable prey than others (Alcock, 1971; Brower, 1984); and some species of predators have behaviors that allow them to separate toxin-containing portions of prey from edible parts (Calvert et al., 1979; Fink and Brower, 1981; Brower, 1984).

An additional division of homotypic resemblances can be based on the taxonomic relationships of the model, mimic, and dupe (Vane-Wright, 1976). If all three protagonists belong to different species, the system is *disjunct*. Batesian and Müllerian mimicry are examples of disjunct relationships among the protagonists. When two protagonists belong to one species and the third to a different species, the system is *bipolar*. Mimicry of female hymenopterans by orchid flowers is bipolar; a dupe (the male hymenopteran) tries to copulate with the mimic (an orchid flower) that resembles the model (a female hymenopteran), and in the process carries pollinia from one flower to another. In *conjunct* mimicry, all three protagonists are conspecific. For example, male scorpion flies (*Hylobittacus apicalis*) can obtain mates only by offering insect prey to a female as a nuptial gift. Males obtain these nuptial gifts in one of three ways: by catching them, by stealing them by force from other males, or by mimicking female behavior so that they are offered a nuptial gift by another male (Thornhill, 1979).

Homotypic resemblances do not operate in an ecological or behavioral vacuum. Protective mimicry is normally part of a primary defense that operates before a predator initiates an attack (Edmunds, 1974:1), or of a secondary defense that operates after the prey has responded to the presence of a predator (Edmunds, 1974:136), or both. For example, egg-eating snakes (*Dasypeltis*) have a cryptic pattern of dark dorsal blotches that is similar to the patterns of several species of sympatric vipers (see Section II.B.2.b). Camouflage is the initial primary defense for both egg-eating snakes and for vipers. If a predator discovers an egg-eating snake, the predator may mistake it for a viper because of its similarity to the viperid pattern. Thus, homotypy is a second line of primary defense for the egg-eating snake. If both primary defensive mechanisms fail, the egg-eating snake engages in an active display that incorporates body movements and sound production in imitation of a similar display by vipers. This secondary defense enhances the original visual homotypic resemblance of *Dasypeltis* to a viper by adding movement to the visual stimulus and by adding sound as an additional stimulus. This progression of synergistic defense mechanisms may be a general rule among reptiles, as it is among other vertebrates (Edmunds, 1974). Homotypic resemblances among reptiles are often associated with *protean defense* (a sudden, erratic change in appearance or movement (Humphries and Driver, 1970)), *deimatic behavior* (a frightening display, posture, or noise (Maldonado, 1970)), and *thanatosis* (feigning death (Edmunds, 1974)).

Two categories of resemblances have posed particularly knotty problems for students of mimicry: Müllerian mimicry and homotypic resemblances that are the result of phylogenetic relationship. In Müllerian mimicry two or more noxious species resemble each other, and both species benefit from the resemblances because fewer individuals of each species are lost in the process of educating predators to avoid animals with the shared pattern. Various authors (Poulton, 1890; Wickler, 1968; Wiens, 1978; Pasteur, 1982) have maintained that this situation involves no deceit because avoidance of equally noxious models and mimics is the correct response for the dupe. Because no deceit occurs, they argue that it should not be called mimicry. However, two or more species of animals are unlikely to be equally noxious for all their potential predators, and Batesian and Müllerian mimicry may form a continuum (Huheey, 1976) or a step function (Turner et al., 1984). This distinction has implications for the direction in which selection may act on the stronger and weaker members of a Müllerian mimicry situation (Benson, 1977; Sheppard and Turner, 1977; Turner, 1977, 1984; Huheey, 1980a).

A different problem is posed by homotypic resemblances that reflect phylogenetic relationships rather than being the product of evolutionary convergence resulting from selection by predators. These situations may involve deceit of predators, but selection for homotypy cannot necessarily be inferred. For example, Gingerich (1975) has suggested that the inoffensive, termite-eating aardwolf (*Proteles cristatus*) is a Batesian mimic of one or both species of *Hyaena* (*H. brunnea* and *H. hyaena*), both of which are formidable predators. This proposal has been strongly criticized (Goodhart, 1975) and endorsed (Greene, 1977). One point of controversy has been the significance of the phylogenetic relationship of hyaenas and aardwolves: Both are hyaenids and their similarity in color and pattern may be a shared–ancestral character. (Of course, no information is available about changes through time in the similarity in appearance of the two genera.) If mimicry is viewed as an evolutionary process by which two species become more similar through time as a result of selection by predators, a homotypy that embodies a shared ancestral character does not qualify for inclusion unless it can be shown that selection by predators has increased the resemblance of the mimic to the model. On the other hand, if mimicry is viewed in an ecological context as an antipredator strategy, the important question becomes whether a predator is deceived. A resemblance based on a phylogenetic relationship could qualify as mimicry by that criterion. The question of how to interpret mimicry that derives from ancestral characters is particularly relevant to snakes because many instances of mimicry of vipers probably have their origins in a shared ancestral pattern of blotches (Section II.B.2.b).

C. The Distribution of Mimicry Among Taxa of Animals

Homotypy and camouflage can occur in any sensory modality to which a dupe is capable of responding, and may involve different characteristics within one modality. For example, visual homotypy may include similarities of reflected or emitted light, pattern and form, body outline, or movement. Similarly, a mimic may duplicate the thermal or electrical emissions of a model and its odors or sounds. All of these potential mimicries, except duplication of electrical properties, are known to occur (Pasteur, 1982).

Examples of visual mimicry dominate the literature, probably because humans are primarily visually oriented. Humans as dupes are particularly sensitive to visual homotypies, and visual mimicry is over-represented in our sample (Pasteur, 1982). Furthermore, the diurnality and visual sensitivity of humans make us especially likely to recognize mimetic resemblances that result from selection by other animals that are diurnal and visually oriented. Thus, birds and lizards appear to be the selective agents in most of the well-known cases of mimicry. Like humans, these animals attend to details of color, pattern, and movement, and form search images. Humans are not sensitive to visual properties of objects at wavelengths in the ultraviolet or infrared portions of the spectrum, but other vertebrates may be. Some mimetic resemblances among insects are as good in the ultraviolet as in the visible part of the spectrum (Silberglied, 1979).

Most animals probably rely on smell and hearing more than on vision, and these species seem likely to exert selective pressures that would favor the evolution of olfactory or auditory mimicries that humans would not perceive (Pasteur, 1982). Various species of predators and even individuals of a species may respond to different characteristics of a model or mimic (Alcock, 1971; Terhune, 1977; Vasconcello-Neto and Lewinsohn, 1984). Antipredator mechanisms are equally diverse; some deter certain types of predators but may increase the risk of attack by other predators (Pearson, 1985). Mimetic relationships combine the effects of all these different types of selection.

To illustrate his system of classification of mimicry, Vane-Wright (1976) listed 56 examples of mimicry, most of which were drawn from previous summaries (Wickler, 1968; Edmunds, 1974). (I have omitted from this list the "egg mimics" on the anal fin of the cichlid fish *Haplochromis* because these are probably not examples of mimicry (Otte, 1974:398–399; Hailman, 1977:309) and all of the mimetic activities described for humans.) Vane-Wright's list was not intended to be exhaustive, and it would probably be impossible to compile a truly complete list of examples of mimicry because so much of the literature on the subject consists of anecdotes without experimental data (Pasteur, 1982). Nevertheless, these 56 examples provide a representative sample of known examples to assess the incidence of mimicry among different groups of organisms. Precisely half the examples refer to mimicry by insects, and two more concern spiders. Relatively few examples of mimicry are known among vertebrates; only 14 were cited by Vane-Wright (see Edmunds, 1974; Pasteur, 1982; and Pough, in press, for a few additional examples). The paucity of mimetic relationships among vertebrates is almost certainly an artifact of a mismatch between the sensory modalities to which humans attend and those in which mimicry of vertebrates is most likely to occur. Carefully designed and controlled experiments are necessary to investigate the possible existence of mimicry in sensory modalities to which we are not attuned.

In addition to the mismatch of sensory modalities of humans and other vertebrates, some kinds of protective mimicry among vertebrates may differ qualitatively from the mimicry of insects that has dominated thinking about homotypy (Pough, in press). These differences may reflect the potentially disastrous consequences for a dupe of mistaking a model for a mimic. The advantage gained by a mimic depends in part on the properties of its model. A mildly noxious model protects good mimics, whereas a very noxious model extends protection even to poor mimics (Brower and Brower, 1965; Duncan and Sheppard, 1965; Goodale and Sneddon, 1977).

Vertebrates as a group may be more noxious models than are insects, partly because vertebrates are larger than insects in absolute terms and relative to the size of their predators. A model that combines an effective defense with large body size may pose a substantial risk for a dupe that mistakenly attacks it. If that is true, homotypy among vertebrates may in general be less precise than the insect homotypy that has shaped much of our thinking, and vertebrate mimicry would be correspondingly harder to recognize. In the terminology of Pasteur (1982), abstract (rather than concrete) homotypies may be the rule among vertebrates. Of all vertebrates, the venomous snakes seem to be the animals most likely to translate risk to a dupe into widespread abstract mimicry.

II. MIMICRY OF VENOMOUS SNAKES

A. Theoretical Aspects

1. PROPERTIES OF REPTILIAN MIMICRY

Venomous snakes provided the earliest examples of mimicry among vertebrates (Cope, 1860; Wallace, 1867, 1870; Weale, 1871; Goode, 1873; Lönnberg, 1902) and have continued to attract attention from biologists. The dramatic defensive displays and conspicuous colors of some snakes emphasize the risk they represent to a predator. Indeed, some snakes (particularly vipers) are so dangerous that certain assumptions, terms, and mathematical models that have been developed for mimetic relationships among insects may be only marginally applicable to the mimicry of venomous snakes.

2. VENOMOUS SNAKES AS MODELS

Venom is probably an ancestral character for caenophidian snakes (colubrids, elapids, hydrophiids, and vipers), and venom is widespread among living colubirds (Savitzky, 1980). At our present state of knowledge, even the distinction between venomous snakes and harmless ones is uncertain. The widespread development of toxic oral secretions by a variety of colubrid snakes and the possibility that these secretions are specialized for particular functions make allocations of snakes to categories of risk very speculative (Gans, 1978). For example, the colubrid genus *Pliocercus* lacks fangs and is considered harmless, but recently an adult human was hospitalized by the effects of a bite from *P. elapoides* (Seib, 1980). For small foliage-gleaning birds any snake, venomous or not, may be a potential predator and a dangerous model for a mimicry system.

The most specialized venomous snakes are the approximately 500 species in the families Elapidae, Hydrophiidae, and Viperidae. Most of these snakes produce toxins that are potentially lethal to vertebrate predators (see Gans, 1978, for a list of these species). These families of snakes include the species most often cited as models that are mimicked by a variety of colubrid snakes and by a wide variety of other animals, including vertebrates and invertebrates.

The unusual features of mimicry of venomous snakes are the result of three features of these animals: their venom, their size, and the unpredictability of their success in biting a predator.

a. Venom

Considerations of the potential lethality of a bite from a venomous snake have focused primarily on the toxicity of snake venom (Brattstrom, 1955; Hecht and Marien, 1956; Mertens, 1957; Gans, 1961; Wickler, 1968). Many factors interact in determining the severity of a bite from a venomous snake: Venomous snakes can bite without delivering venom or can vary the quantity of venom they inject (Kochva, 1978). Venom displays individual, ontogenetic, seasonal, and geographic variation in toxicity (Gans, 1978). The properties of snake venoms also vary phylogenetically (Mebs, 1978). Neurotoxic symptoms are prominent features of bites from elapids and hydrophiids, and include systemic effects such as depression, paralysis of the hind limbs, and respiratory failure. The venom of viperids produces local discoloration and hemorrhage, followed by symptoms of cardiovascular shock and generalized internal hemorrhage. However, classifying snake venoms as neurotoxic or hemorrhagic is an oversimplification. Elapid venoms may produce cardiovascular failure and hemorrhage, and viperid venoms can lead to paralysis and respiratory arrest. The quantity of venom injected, the species of animal being tested, and the route of envenomation are important variables (Mebs, 1978).

The delayed effects of envenomation have usually been ignored in considerations of mimicry of venomous snakes, but these effects seem likely to pose a substantial risk for mammals and birds that prey on snakes. A snake need not deliver a fatal dose of venom to expose an animal to the debilitating effects of envenomation. Tissue necrosis and bacterial infections of damaged tissues are secondary consequences of sublethal doses of venom, even for animals as large as humans (Russell, 1980). Indeed, these secondary effects can be clinically significant results of untreated snakebites, and the loss of digits or limbs was a common aftermath of snakebite before the introduction of massive antivenin therapy (Russell, 1980).

Tissue destruction, infection, or the potential loss of a limb may be as important as the chance of rapid death in determining the risk of preying on venomous snakes. When the short-term and long-term effects of snakebite are considered, the potential risk for a predator of attacking a venomous snake appears to be substantially greater than the risk associated with eating an unpalatable insect, or even of being stung by most wasps. Only among some marine invertebrates that possess lethally toxic venoms (some coelenterates, gastropods, and cephalopods (Halstead, 1965)), do we find potential models that may be as formidable to their predators as are venomous snakes.

b. Size

Snakes are not only larger than insects, but snakes increase in size ontogenetically without changing their appearance, unlike the holometabolous insects that have formed the basis for most considerations of mimicry. A large individual of a particular species of venomous snake may represent a very much greater threat to a predator than a small individual of the same species.

c. Uncertainty

Venomous snakes probably must bite a predator to deliver a noxious stimulus. (Some venoms are not toxic when ingested. The possibility that the flesh of some snakes is unpalatable to predators is discussed in Section II.B.2.a.) If a snake does not succeed in biting a predator, the experience of the predator with a model is probably not different from its experience with a mimic. (Stinging insects represent a parallel situation in this respect.)

The probability that a predator will be bitten depends on at least two interrelated factors: How good is the snake at delivering venom, and how good is the predator at killing snakes without being bitten? Nature presents a range of specializations on both sides. Front-fanged snakes, especially vipers, are probably capable of killing most predators if they succeed in biting. Elapids, which have short fangs at the front of the mouth, and colubrid snakes, with fangs at the rear of the mouth, may or may not administer a lethal dose of venom. Some snakes, like the nearly toothless colubrids of the genus *Dasypeltis* and the blunt-toothed sibynophine colubrids, are probably incapable of deterring a predator by biting it (Gans, 1974; Savitzky, 1983).

The specializations of predators interact with the specializations of snakes in determining the probability that a snake will succeed in biting and the consequences of a bite. Many snakes, both venomous and nonvenomous, are immune to snake venom (Kochva et al., 1983). Some predators, especially snake-eating birds like the neotropical laughing falcon (*Herpetotheres cachinanns*) and the African secretary bird (*Sagittarius serpentarius*), probably can prey upon even the most dangerous snakes with little risk to themselves. Less specialized birds and most mammals seem likely to face some risk of being bitten if they attack a venomous snake. Risk to a predator may vary intraspecifically as a result of ontogenetic change in its body size and its experience in capturing prey. Chance will play a role, too. If the snake is partly concealed, is its head where the predator assumes it is? Which direction will the snake strike when it is first seized? If the snake has an erratic display (Tweedie, 1953; Gehlbach, 1970; Greene, 1973, this volume), will it bite the predator as it thrashes about?

As a consequence of these variations in venom delivery capability of snakes and in predatory capacity of predators, one cannot assign a constant degree of noxiousness to a particular venomous snake that is serving as a model. The outcome of an encounter between a venomous snake and a predator might be death or injury for the snake, death or illness for the predator, or possibly the deaths of both or neither of the participants. This situation is different from that known in insects for which models and mimics (species or individuals) can usually be ranked in order of noxiousness. The closest analogy to this situation among insects is the palatability spectrum (L. Brower et al., 1967a). However, in a palatability spectrum the variation in noxiousness results from differences in the quantity and quality of toxic chemicals present in individual models, and each individual has a definable noxious quality.

3. SPECIAL FEATURES OF THE MIMICRY OF VENOMOUS SNAKES

The differences in the properties of snakes and insects as models give rise to special features of the selection exerted on predators by venomous snakes, and the selection exerted by those predators on mimics of the snakes. Conventionally, mimicry has been assumed to act through the ability of predators to learn to avoid noxious prey after one or more experiences. The initial learning process is reinforced by subsequent experiences once the initial conditioned avoidance is forgotten. In that situation a mimic benefits from being treated like its model by the predator. A recurrent theme in discussions of mimicry of venomous snakes has been the paradox of the deadly model—that is, the inability of a dead predator to profit from its experience with the model or to avoid a mimic as a result of that experience. To some extent this problem has been overcome by postulating that empathic learning teaches predators that observe a fatal snakebite to avoid the snake in the future (Gans, 1964; Jouventin et al., 1977). This mechanism appears plausible for social animals but is less appropriate for solitary predators. The demonstration of innate avoidance of venomous snakes by predators (Smith, 1975, 1977; Caldwell and Rubinoff, 1983) supplies a mechanism that creates a selective advantage for mimics of venomous snakes in the face of even solitary predators. This situation differs from the sort of response by predators involved in insect mimicry in that the effect produced by experience with the model is not learning in ecological time, but instead genetically fixed alteration of the behavior of a species of predator in evolutionary time.

4. PREDICTIONS

Both the magnitude of the potential noxious experience and the mechanism of avoidance of models and mimics have special features in the case of mimicry of venomous snakes that are not present in mimicry of insects. These features should be reflected in various aspects of the mimicry of venomous snakes. Several testable predictions can be formulated on the basis of that assumption.

a. Ratio of Models to Mimics

For insects the degree of protection received by a mimic varies inversely with the frequency of the mimic in relation to the model. A variety of factors interact to determine the precise degree of protection a mimic experiences including the noxiousness of the model and the length of time a predator remembers its experience with the model (J. Brower, 1960; Holling, 1963, 1965; Huheey, 1964; Emlen, 1968; Alcock, 1970a, b; L. Brower et al., 1970; O'Donald and Pilecki, 1970; Pough et al., 1973). The common assertion that models must outnumber mimics is incorrect, but the degree of protection a mimic experiences is sensitive to the frequency with which a predator encounters models and mimics, particularly if the model is not very noxious or if the memory of the predator is short.

Mimicry of venomous snakes may be less sensitive to variation in the ratio of mimics to models than is mimicry of insects. If a single noxious experience with a venomous snake can kill a predator, a frequency of models that exposes a predator to one such experience in its normal reproductive lifespan would be effective in creating a selective advantage for those individuals in the predator species with an innate tendency to avoid the model. Mimics of venomous snakes could be considerably more conspicuous or abundant than their models with little loss of protection from predators.

b. Abstract Mimicry

A second consequence of the extreme noxiousness of venomous snakes as models should be broad generalization of the features of the model by the predator and the avoidance of snakes with even minor similarities to the model. Thus, venomous snakes probably serve as abstract models. Because even a very slight similarity to a venomous snake would be selectively advantageous, mimetic resemblances could evolve readily and functional mimicry may be widespread among snakes. Much of this mimicry is likely to be relatively imprecise provided that, once an inaccurate resemblance to a venomous snake is achieved, the very noxious quality of the model limits the selective advantage of modifications that would perfect the mimicry. If predators generalize the characteristics of venomous snakes broadly, one can predict that areas with coral snakes will have higher proportions of nonvenomous snakes with banded patterns incorporating red, yellow (or white), and black than are found in areas without coral snakes because mimics with only superficial similarities to coral snakes should often be avoided by predators.

c. Dual Mimics

In mimicry of insects, predators learn specific characteristics of one or more models, and mimics are often remarkably precise duplicates of one or another of those models. Dual mimics that combine features of two or more models do not occur as part of normal mimetic assemblages. When such hybrid mimics do occur, they are a result of perturbation of the geographic ranges of different mimetic patterns, and the hybrid mimics appear to be less protected than either of the normal forms. However, a mimic that combined the features of two or more species of venomous snakes would not be expected to lose protection, and might even benefit by having more of the abstract features of venomous models because, even within a species of predator, individuals respond to different characteristics of a mimic (Terhune, 1977). The occurrence among snakes of mimics combining the features of two or more models would be evidence that mimicry of venomous snakes is different from the single-model mimicry of most insects.

B. Tests of the Predictions

1. MIMICRY OF REPTILES BY INSECTS

Examples of mimicry of reptiles by insects are particularly useful in testing the hypothesis that mimicry of venomous snakes can be effective without being precise because most examples of mimicry of insects by other insects are concrete. That is, the models are identifiable species or groups of species and the mimicry involves extraordinarily exact duplications of the pattern, color, and even body form of the models. (For examples of this precision, see the color plates in Bates (1862), L. Brower et al. (1963), Turner (1975), and Papageorgis (1975)). If mimicry of reptiles by insects is less precise than this, the reason is probably to be sought in the characteristics of the models, not of the predators.

The larvae, and in some cases the pupae, of butterflies and moths in the families Sphingidae, Notodontidae, Oxytenidae, Noctuidae, Geometridae, and Papiliionidae have markings and behaviors that are reminiscent of snakes (Figs. 1, 2). These caterpillars occur in both the Old and New World and represent many independent origins of the phenomenon, probably facilitated by the general similarity of the body forms of snakes and caterpillars. In Santa Rosa National Park in northwestern Costa Rica, caterpillars of some 50 species, belonging to five families, have eyespots and may be mimics of snakes (D. H. Janzen, pers. comm.). In general the mimicry consists of a display in which the anterior portion of the caterpillar's body is inflated, often revealing eyespots, and waved from side to side. Bates (1862:509) described the display of such a caterpillar in South America:

> The most extraordinary instance of imitation I ever met with was that of a very large Caterpillar, which stretched itself from amidst the foliage of a tree which I was one day examining, and startled me by its resemblance to a small Snake. The first three segments

MIMICRY OF VENOMOUS SNAKES

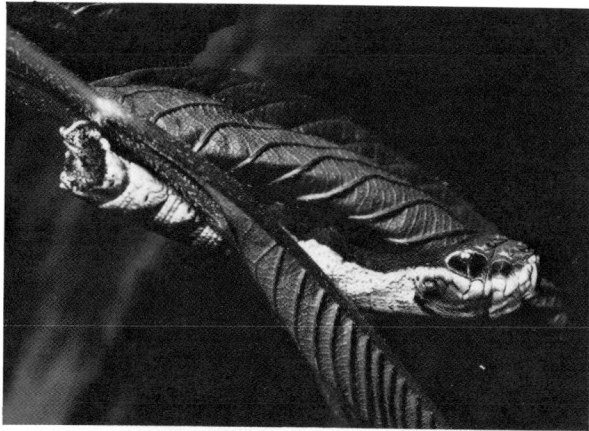

Fig. 1. Abstract mimicry of snakes by a caterpillar. The larva of the neotropical sphingid moth *Hemeroplanes triptolemus* normally rests upside down beneath a twig. When it is disturbed, the caterpillar inflates the anterior part of its body and reveals a pair of eyespots on its ventral surface. The resemblance to a snake is clear, but abstract. That is, the caterpillar does not look like any particular species of snake or even more like a viper than a nonvenomous snake. Foliage-gleaning birds are likely to treat any snake as a potential predator, and may provide selective pressure favoring this abstract mimicry. (Photographs by Daniel H. Janzen.)

behind the head were dilatable at the will of the insect, and had on each side a large black pupillated spot, which resembled the eye of the reptile: it was a poisonous or viperine species mimicked, and not an innocuous or colubrine Snake; this was proved by the imitation of keeled scales on the crown which were produced by the recumbent feet, as the Caterpillar threw itself backwards.

Fig. 2. Abstract mimicry of snakes by the chrysalis of the nymphalid butterfly *Dynastor darius*. (Photograph by Daniel H. Janzen.)

Other descriptions and photographs can be found in Morrell (1954, 1969), L. Brower (1968, 1971), Edmunds (1974, pl. 7b), Aiello and Silberglied (1978), and Janzen (1980).

The similarity of snake-mimicking caterpillars to snakes is not precise, and it may have a simple genetic basis. Turner (1984) has suggested that the combination of four mutations (Moricaud, Zebra, quail, and Multilunar) can convert the larva of the domestic silk moth (*Bombyx*) into a "snake mimic."

Snake-mimicking caterpillars are found in areas without arboreal vipers or without any vipers, and such caterpillars appear no more nor less viper-like than species that live in sympatry with arboreal vipers. The Malayan hawk moth (*Panacra mydon*) has been suggested as a mimic of the juvenile pattern of *Trimeresurus wagleri*, largely because the caterpillar has a dark stripe on its head that resembles the dark line that runs horizontally through the eye of the juvenile viper (Morrell, 1969). However, eyestripes of this sort are usual markings of vipers; among 48 species of vipers, 92% had an eyestripe and similar marks are common among arboreal colubrids (Pough et al., 1978). Because of the ubiquity of eyestripes in potential models, more evidence is required to support the suggestion that the caterpillar of *P. mydon* is specifically mimicking *T. wagleri*.

MIMICRY OF VENOMOUS SNAKES

Third and fourth instar larvae of the neotropical sphingid moth *Hemeroplanes triptolemus* are said to mimic the vine snake *Oxybelis*, whereas the last instar is described as a "formidable mimic" of the pit viper *Bothrops schlegelii* (Haber, 1983). The pupa of the nymphalid butterfly *Dynastor darius* has a snake-like appearance (Aiello and Silberglied, 1978). The yellow-and-black banded caterpillar of the neotropical sphingid *Pseudosphinx tetrio* may be sufficiently like a coral snake to be considered a mimic, but the caterpillars are probably distasteful and are perhaps better regarded as being aposematic in their own right (Janzen, 1980, 1983).

Any caterpillar that looks enough like a snake to startle a foraging bird is likely to benefit—if not from the bird's previous experience with snakes, then perhaps from a tendency for a bird to flee from a startling or potentially dangerous stimulus (Coppinger, 1969, 1970). The eyespots displayed by many insects as part of a deimatic display may be analogous to snake mimicry in certain functional respects. Realistic eyespots (with eccentric pupils and an apparent reflective highlight) elicited more escape responses by small birds than a pattern of simple concentric circles, and the concentric circles were more effective than a single circle (Blest, 1957a). The eyespots on the wings of some moths are very realistic; like the eyespots in Blest's experiments, they contain eccentric pupils and a light mark resembling reflection of light from the moist surface of the cornea (Blest, 1957b). Nonetheless, they are an abstract representation of the eyes of vertebrates, not mimics of the eyes of a particular predator of the birds they frighten (Pasteur, 1982); and four or more false eyes are displayed simultaneously by many animals (Wickler, 1968).

Eyelike markings occur among a wide variety of vertebrates including fishes, birds, snakes, lizards, frogs, and turtles (Cott, 1940; Wickler, 1968; Edmunds, 1974; Owen, 1980), and many such animals have more than one pair of eyespots. Some of these markings may deter predators, but eyelike patterns may be only a particularly conspicuous way of combining contrasting colors (Hailman, 1977).

Other insects may be still less precise mimics of reptiles. The head of the neotropical fulgorid bug *Laternaria* bears a large hollow structure of vaguely reptilian appearance (Poulton, 1924; Hogue, 1984). Other examples of proposed mimicry of reptiles by insects are probably illusory. A mimetic resemblance between markings on the hind wings of the tropical butterflies *Caligo* and *Eryphanis* and the heads of hylid frogs and anoline lizards respectively (Stradling, 1976) seems problematic. Such mimicry might protect the butterflies from predation by some birds, but other species of birds would be equally likely to prey on treefrogs or anoles. The proposal that *Eryphanis* is left unmolested by territorial

Anolis that mistake it for a larger individual of their own species (Stradling, 1976) seems improbable in light of the complexities of the species-specific displays of most anoles. The marks on the wings of the butterflies may be primarily deflection marks that induce predators to misdirect their attacks or to misjudge the direction in which the insect will flee (Smith, 1978).

Detailed information about geographic variation in snake-mimicking insects and their potential snake models is necessary to test the hypothesis, but in the light of the ability of insect mimics of insect models to achieve extraordinarily precise resemblances, differences in the quality of the models may well explain the imprecision of mimicry of snakes by insects.

2. WARNING AND DEFENSIVE MIMICRY AMONG SNAKES

a. The Coral-Snake Mimicry Complex

The problem. The very conspicuous similarities of the colors and patterns of coral snakes and of a number of nonvenomous or mildly venomous snakes was noted by Cope (1860) before a coherent theory of mimicry had been formulated. In the earliest synthesis of mimicry theory, Wallace (1867), an ardent supporter of Bates' (1862) suggestion of mimicry as a defensive mechanism, cited coral snakes and their mimics as the preeminent examples of mimicry among vertebrates. Wallace immediately perceived the inadequacy of the bare fact of a similarity in appearance to substantiate a claim of mimicry. In particular, he appears to have been the first to appreciate the significance of parallel geographic variation among models and mimics. In 1867 he gave four examples of similarity of color and pattern of coral snakes and their colubrid mimics within limited geographic areas; and, in his 1870 revision of that essay, he added two more examples. Unfortunately Wallace's interests in mimicry were centered on butterflies, and he did not continue his investigation of coral snakes. Indeed, after its promising start the study of coral-snake mimicry was largely overlooked until the middle of the twentieth century. The chronological development of hypotheses in this period has been summarized (Dunn, 1954; Hecht and Marien, 1956; Mertens, 1957; Grobman, 1978) and will not be repeated here. Instead I will consider the major questions that have been raised about coral snakes and their presumed mimics.

The hypothesis that underlies what has become known as "the coral-snake mimicry problem" states that nonvenomous and mildly venomous colubrid snakes with bicolor or tricolor banded patterns mimic the patterns of highly venomous coral snakes of the genera *Micrurus* and *Micruroides*. In the absence of direct evidence of mimicry, the proposal that the similarity in color and pattern is protective has been received with a skepticism that does credit to the abstract ideal of scientific objectivity, although not all publications on the subject have embodied that objectivity. Discussion of the occurrence and mechanics of mimicry of coral snakes has focused on several aspects of the biology of the snakes and of their potential predators. The possible functions of regularly banded color patterns in snakes have formed another area of speculation.

Are the patterns of coral snakes cryptic or aposematic? The patterns of coral snakes vary among species and vary geographically within species. (See Roze (1967), Savage and Vial (1974), Amaral (1978), and Duellman (1978) for illustrations.) A coral-snake pattern is any pattern of "alternating black and red (or yellow or white) dorsally" (Savage and Vial, 1974:334). A complex terminology has been used to classify patterns as "bicolor," "tricolor," "tricolor triad," and "tricolor quartet" (Dunn, 1954; Hecht and Marien, 1956).

The earliest papers on coral-snake mimicry were apparently written by people who had no experience with coral snakes in the field. In a museum collection, a coral-snake pattern is so conspicuous that an aposematic function was implicitly assumed and was not a subject for comment (Cope, 1860; Wallace, 1867, 1870). The first suggestion that coral-snake patterns are cryptic rather than (or in addition to) being aposematic came from Gadow (1911:2), who may have carried out the earliest experimental investigation of the function of the coral-snake pattern:

> . . . In their natural surroundings . . . they are . . . conspicuous at a close distance, the red catching the eye at once, but at a distance, say beyond five yards, they seem to vanish, at least parts of them according to the pattern. It may not appeal to the closet zoologist, but it is nevertheless a most instructive experiment to have some flexible tubes painted with the various patterns and colours of these snakes and to study the effect of those toys when thrown at random into an herbaceous border, upon the grass, into shrubs in bright sunshine or on a dull day. In most cases the effacive effect is surprising, whilst a similar toy painted monochrome, draws attention at once.

The strongest proponent of a cryptic function for the coral-snake pattern was Brattstrom (1955) who pointed out that most snake patterns appear to be cryptic and suggested that coral snakes and their mimics are the coincidental result of convergent evolution of similar cryptic patterns. He suggested two cryptic effects of a ringed pattern: (1) The alternating bands of strongly contrasting color may have the effect of disrupting the impression of an elongate object, thereby making a motionless snake hard to perceive. (2) When a banded snake moves, an observer's eye may become fixed on one portion of the background scene, and the regular appearance of bands may give the impression that the snake is motionless. (This illusion is readily perceived with striped snakes.)

A view of coral-snake patterns as primarily aposematic was advanced by Hecht and Marien (1956) who stressed the importance of the absence of countershading and the continuation of the colored dorsal bands onto the ventral surface. A snake with a pattern of this sort is recognizable even when it is overturned in a struggle with a predator, whereas there is no apparent reason why a cryptic pattern should be continued onto the ventral surface, and the dorsal patterns of most snakes terminate near the border between lateral scales and ventral scutes. Additional functions that have been suggested for coral-snake patterns include the hypothesis that a ringed pattern is especially conspicuous and functions to induce nesting birds to attack a snake, thereby guiding the snake to the vicinity of the birds' nest (Goodman, 1974; Goodman and Goodman, 1976a; but see Smith and Mostrom, 1985) and the proposal that the colorful patterns of coral snakes and their mimics have no function in either crypsis or warning, but have evolved in the absence of any selective pressure (Grobman, 1978).

Much controversy about the function of coral-snake patterns has stemmed from a tendency to seek a single function for the pattern, but coral-snake patterns are probably aposematic in some circumstances and cryptic in others. Evidence for an aposematic function is provided by experiments that have demonstrated innate avoidance of coral-snake patterns by birds and possibly by mammals as well (Gehlbach, 1972; Smith, 1975, 1977). Additional evidence suggesting an aposematic function for a coral-snake pattern comes from the Central American colubrid snake *Liophis epinephalus*, which is normally solid colored. However, its defensive display reveals a red pattern on the skin (Fig. 3). Because the coral-snake pattern of this species is revealed only as a part of a defensive display it clearly serves a warning function (H. W. Greene, pers. comm.).

Cryptic effects of coral-snake patterns include a visual illusion,

Fig. 3. Defensive display of *Liophis epinephalus*. The neotropical colubrid snake *L. epinephalus* normally appears to be a solid black. Bands of red and black pigment between the scales are revealed when the lungs are inflated during the defensive display, giving *L. epinephalus* the appearance of a coral snake. (Photograph by R. W. Van Devender.)

apparent when banded or blotched snakes move, that depends upon the rate of passage of light–dark transitions across a viewer's visual field. If this rate exceeds the flicker-fusion frequency of the viewer, the eye cannot resolve individual bands and perceives the snake as a solid-colored object that is a blend of the band colors (Jackson et al., 1976; Pough, 1976). This illusion is well illustrated by water snakes: Juvenile water snakes (*Nerodia sipedon*) are prominently banded, whereas the adults are unicolored. The escape behavior of juveniles, in contrast to that of adults, consists of crawling very rapidly for a few seconds and then stopping abruptly. While the snake crawls, the light and dark bands on its body pass an observer's field of view at a speed above the flicker-fusion frequency of most predators and the snake appears to be a unicolored light grey (Fig. 4). The instantaneous transition from motion to immobility removes the elongate, solid-colored stimulus a predator had perceived and substitutes one in which the sharply contrasting bands conceal the elongate form. A similar blending of colors of individual bands occurs in coral snakes during their erratic displays (Gehlbach, 1970 and pers. comm.).

In addition to the change in the visual stimulus that a banded snake can present to a predator by suddenly becoming immobile, the banded pattern could conceivably be employed to produce a flickering stimulus that might be unpleasant to a predator, or to create an illusion that the bands are flowing in a direction opposite to that in which the snake is

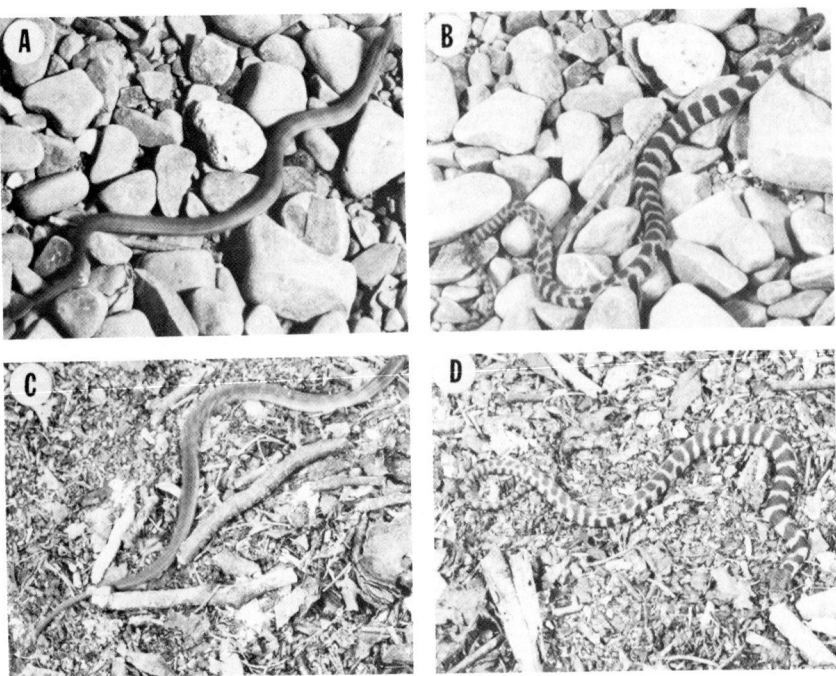

Fig. 4. Cryptic effects of a banded pattern. An optical illusion produced by flicker fusion changes the appearance of a banded snake when it moves rapidly. A juvenile *Nerodia sipedon* appears to be a solid grey color when it is crawling (A, C.) and reverts to its usual banded pattern when it stops moving (B, D). All photographs were exposed at 1/30 of a second and show the snake as it would appear to a predator with a flicker fusion frequency about twice that of a human. The optical illusion is greater when the snake is crawling on gravel because forward progress is more rapid, but a motionless snake is more cryptic on a background of plant material than on gravel. (From Pough, 1976. Copyright by the American Society of Ichthyologists and Herpetologists and reproduced with permission.)

moving (Jackson et al., 1976). These phenomena depend upon the visual properties of particular species of predators as well as the details of the patterns of the snakes (high or low contrast, bicolored or tricolored, sharp borders to the bands or irregular ones) and on the viewing conditions (bright or dim, full solar spectrum or light filtered through vegetation). These variations in the physical and biological systems probably contribute to the high degree of variation in banded patterns of snakes and to multiple functions that probably include both aposematism and crypsis.

Can predators of coral snakes perceive the colors? Much debate has focused on the twin questions of what predators might kill snakes and whether certain potential predators are capable of perceiving and responding to the bicolor or tricolor patterns of coral snakes. These questions involve complex interactions between the visual sensitivities of the predators and the behaviors of the predators and snakes. Simple answers are not likely to be available. The assertion that coral snakes are nocturnal or fossorial and therefore rarely if ever exposed to diurnal predators originated with Gadow (1911) and has been frequently repeated. Several lines of evidence suggest that the nocturnal and fossorial habits of coral snakes have been exaggerated, at least insofar as they affect the possibility of encounters among coral snakes and diurnal predators. Coral snakes and their mimics have been found in the open during the day. In Costa Rica individuals of *Micrurus nigrocinctus* have been observed in Santa Rosa and Corcovado National Parks moving slowly across the forest floor during the day, poking their heads into holes and doubling back on their paths (D. H. Janzen and W. Hallwachs, pers. comm.). This behavior suggests that the snakes were foraging for food, not escaping from predators or moving from one retreat site to another. Coral snakes and their mimics are eaten by diurnal birds and discovered by diurnal mammalian predators (see Greene and McDiarmid, 1981). Innate avoidance of the coral-snake pattern by two species of diurnal birds has been demonstrated (Smith, 1975, 1977), a phenomenon that is hard to explain unless those species of birds encounter coral snakes during their daily foraging. The protean defensive display of coral snakes appears to be directed against predators that can see the snake clearly. In Costa Rica the yellow, black, and red colubrid snake *Scolecophis atrocinctus* has been reported to thrash violently from side to side in its defensive display, even propelling itself into the air (D. H. Janzen, pers. comm.). This display is like that of the sympatric venomous coral snake *Micrurus nigrocinctus*. The possibility that foraging birds or mammals overturn ground litter and expose hidden snakes (Gehlbach, 1972) appears to have been underemphasized. A preponderance of evidence suggests that coral snakes and their mimics are encountered by predators during the day with sufficient regularity to have produced stereotyped reactions to that situation among both the snakes and the predators.

The assertion that most mammals lack color vision because histological examination of their retinae revealed few cone cells (Walls, 1942) directed the search for potential selective agents toward birds (Hecht and Marien, 1956). Recent behavioral and biochemical evidence suggests that most mammals are capable of distinguishing colors and of responding to different colors (Muntz, 1974), although the qualitative aspects of color vision are unknown (Jacobs, 1982). Color vision of this sort has been demonstrated in both diurnal mammals (dogs, squirrels, ungulates) and nocturnal species (cats, opossums, tree shrews), and color vision must be assumed to be widespread among mammals. This realization greatly broadens the scope of the potential selective agents for an aposematic function of color patterns of coral snakes and a mimetic function of similar patterns in colubrid snakes. The proclivity of many mammals for searching through the ground litter appears to make them particularly likely to encounter small snakes. Few mammals are specialized for killing venomous snakes, consequently mammals may be the animals most likely to evolve innate avoidance responses to venomous snakes and thus to favor the evolution of mimics of those snakes.

The relative frequency of models and mimics. The idea that models must outnumber their mimics if the mimics are to benefit can be traced directly to Bates (1862) and Wallace (1865, 1867). It persists in the mimicry literature despite the existence of both experimental and mathematical demonstrations that mimics can receive protection even when they outnumber models by 9:1 (J. Brower, 1960; Holling, 1965; Emlen, 1968). In practice, the protection received by a mimic depends upon the interaction of many factors: A very noxious model protects a higher ratio of mimics to models, and protects less precise mimics, than does a less noxious model (Brower and Brower, 1965; Duncan and Sheppard, 1965; Goodale and Sneddon, 1977). The availability of alternate prey enhances the protection received by a mimic, and poor mimics receive less protection if a predator can compare them with the model than they do if they are encountered separately (Sexton, 1960). These and other conditions that affect the precision and selective advantage of mimicry are discussed by Edmunds (1974:81–135).

Various reports have listed the proportions of coral snakes, rear-fanged snakes, and aglyphous snakes in collections from different regions (Dunn, 1954; Mertens, 1966). In Panama 62% of 1175 snakes with the coral-snake pattern were *Micrurus*, whereas in the state of São Paulo, Brazil, only 17% of 1227 snakes with that pattern were *Micrurus*. When the sample area was expanded to all of southern Brazil, the proportion of *Micrurus* rose to 29% of 1691 snakes with the coral-snake pattern.

These data may not be directly applicable to a consideration of coral-snake mimicry because the different foraging modes of various species of predators will expose them to different portions of the snake fauna in a habitat. For example, hawks will see only those snakes that move by daylight on top of the ground. Birds scratching on the forest floor will see those snakes plus some partly concealed beneath small pieces of ground litter. Mammals may dig deeper and move larger pieces of litter than birds and are more likely to be active before dawn or at dusk. Only mammals and perhaps owls are likely to sample snakes at night. Each of these kinds of predators is likely to encounter a different frequency of models and mimics, and their samples are all likely to be different from a sample gathered by human collectors. These considerations make it difficult to know what significance to attach to the frequencies of coral snakes and their mimics that have been reported. Nevertheless, two useful points do emerge from these data: The coral-snake pattern is well represented in the Americas and the proportions of the total number of snakes with that pattern that are comprised by *Micrurus*, rear-fanged, and aglyphous species are extremely variable.

The number of independent origins of a coral-snake pattern in different lineages of snakes would probably be the best measure of the selective forces favoring that pattern. In the absence of detailed phylogenetic information about snake faunas, this analysis is not feasible. As an alternative, the number of species of snakes in a region with the coral-snake pattern is an index of the occurrence of the pattern that may be less subject to the sampling errors inherent in different foraging methods of predators than is the number of individuals. Table I shows the frequencies of the coral-snake pattern among aniliid, boid, and colubrid snakes of several regions. (For the census method and lists of snakes considered to have coral-snake patterns see the Appendix.) The coral-snake pattern is clearly more common in the neotropics than in other parts of the world. The average frequency of coral-snake patterns in Central and northern South America is 18%, four times the average for Europe, Asia, and Africa. Furthermore, an average of 80% of the neotropical species of snakes with coral-snake patterns include red, whereas the average incidence of red is only 20% for the rest of the world. Conspicuously banded elapids in Asia and Australia (*Calliophis, Bungarus, Vermicella, Simoselaps, Pseudonaja*) might form the basis for a mimicry complex like that of the neotropics (Hecht and Marien, 1956), but this does not seem to have happened. Coral snake patterns in these regions are largely confined to elapids.

The high proportion of snakes with coral-snake patterns in the neotropics compared to the lower frequency of that pattern in most of the rest of the world suggests that many species of snakes mimic coral snakes, as was predicted by a consideration of the consequences of mimicking a deadly model. The great variation in the proportions of coral snakes, rear-fanged snakes, and aglyphous snakes among the coral-snake pattern group suggests that, as expected, the advantage for

TABLE I
The Frequency of Coral-Snake Patterns Among Aniliid, Boid, and Colubrid Snakes[a]

Region	Coral-snake patterns			Total number of species classified	Reference
	Number of species	Percentage of total species	Percentage with red		
The Americas					
Temperate					
Canada and United States	12–14	10–12	86	120	Stebbins, 1966; Conant, 1975
Argentina	1–2	4–12	100	24	Abalos et al., 1964
Tropical					
Guatemala	7–9	20–26	78	35	Duellman, 1963
Venezuela	15–21	14–20	86	107	Roze, 1966
Ecuador	7–13	15–28	62	46	Duellman, 1978
Brazil	15–22	10–14	95	155	Amaral, 1978; Freiberg, 1982
Europe and Asia					
Temperate					
Europe and Soviet Union	1–3	2–5	67	63	Bannikov et al., 1971; Steward, 1971
Iraq	0–1	0–4	0	27	Khalaf, 1959
Indian Subcontinent	25–31	7–9	26	346	Smith, 1943; Minton, 1966
Japan	1–3	4–12	67	25	Nakamura and Ueno, 1963
Taiwan	1–2	3–6	0	31	Kuntz, 1963
Tropical					
Thailand	7–10	6–8	10	121	Taylor, 1965
South Vietnam	1–3	1–4	33	71	Campden-Main, 1970
Malaya	5–11	5–10	18	105	Tweedie, 1953
Philippines	3–5	3–5	20	89	Taylor, 1922
Africa					
West Africa	1–4	1–3	0	117	Villiers, 1975
Uganda	1	1	0	118	Pitman, 1974
Southern Africa	1–3	1–2	0	116	FitzSimons, 1970; Broadley and Cock, 1975
Australia					
Temperate	4–6	6–10	0	64	Cogger, 1979
Tropical	4–7	6–10	14	67	Cogger, 1979

[a] The incidence of such patterns among Australian elapids is included for comparison.

a mimic of a coral snake is relatively insensitive to the proportion of models and mimics in a region.

The paradox of the deadly model and the palatability of coral snakes. The assumption that a bite from a coral snake is lethal has led several investigators to doubt that coral snakes could serve as models because a predator that dies from the bite of a coral snake has not learned to avoid a mimic of a coral snake. As an alternative, it has been suggested that rear-fanged species of snakes with coral-snake patterns are the models, and that the nonvenomous and front-fanged species are, respectively, Batesian and Müllerian mimics (Hecht and Marien, 1956; Mertens, 1957; Emsley, 1966). The name "Mertensian mimicry" has been applied to this hypothesis (Wickler, 1968). Uncertainties about the probability of envenomation of a predator by a snake and the toxicity of different venoms preclude complete evaluation of this hypothesis, but under some circumstances a bite from a coral snake probably can elicit conditioned avoidance by a predator (Greene and McDiarmid, 1981). Colubrid snakes may be weak Müllerian mimics of venomous coral snakes, but they are unlikely to be the species on which the mimicry complex is based.

Nonetheless, additional mechanisms of conditioning predators to avoid coral snakes may operate. Unpalatability of a prey species is a common basis for discrimination by predators, and coral snakes might be unpalatable. W. Hallwachs and D. H. Janzen (pers. comm.) report that in Costa Rica scavengers (mostly birds) that quickly consume road-killed snakes of other species leave dead coral snakes undisturbed. Although the phenomenon has not been widely investigated, other vertebrates may use unpalatability as a predator-avoidance mechanism. Nurse sharks (*Ginglymostoma cirratum*) rejected the flesh of yellow-bellied sea snakes (*Pelamis platurus*) even when it was concealed inside a piece of squid (Rubinoff and Kropach, 1970). Various species of birds and their eggs may be unpalatable to vertebrate and invertebrate predators and scavengers (see Cott, 1969, for a review).

Evidence for an aposematic function of coral snake patterns and for mimicry of coral snakes: Parallel geographic variation of coral snakes and colubrids. Because of the improbability of observing rare events like encounters between predators and models or mimics in nature, the evaluation of alleged examples of mimicry is based on indirect evidence. Concordant geographic change in color or pattern of presumed models and mimics has been particularly useful. Among butterflies of the genus *Heliconius*, for example, local variation in patterns of Müllerian mimicry complexes may reflect Pleistocene fragmentation of the Amazonian forest (Brown et al., 1974). In the presence of a model the butterfly *Limenitis* is mimetic, but in areas in which the model does not occur, it is cryptically colored (Platt and Brower, 1968).

Geographic variation and correspondence in the patterns of coral snakes and their mimics were appreciated by Wallace, who cited four examples in his 1867 review and added two more in his 1870 revision. Conversely, the occurrence of snakes with patterns similar to those of coral snakes in areas lacking models has been used to argue against mimicry (Gadow, 1911; Brattstrom, 1955; Grobman, 1978). These lines of reasoning have been complicated by differences in the perception of particular species as mimics or nonmimics by different authors. (Compare Grobman (1978) and Greene and McDiarmid (1981) for an example of these sorts of differences in perception.) Similar differences in the perception of mimics probably occur among predators of the snakes. Some of the predators appear to have dichromatic color vision, whereas others (including humans) have trichromatic color perception (Muntz, 1974; Jacobs, 1982). Banded patterns are probably differentially visible in different lighting conditions. Even the determination of sympatry of a model and mimic is not simple. A mimic and model need not occur syntopically, provided a predator includes the ranges of both the model and mimic in its foraging area. If migratory birds are predators and avoidance of coral snakes is innate, models that occur in the tropical regions in which the birds overwinter could protect mimics in North America where the birds spend the summer.

The colubrid snake *Lampropeltis triangulum* shows a clinal change from a cryptic pattern of dark blotches in the northeastern United States to a coral snake pattern of red, yellow, and black bands in the southeastern United States where it is sympatric with *Micrurus fulvius* (Conant, 1943). Several subspecies of *L. triangulum* in central and western North America have patterns generally like those of coral snakes in the absence of sympatric models. These patterns, too, become less mimetic as one moves away from the region of sympatry with coral snakes (see color plates in Williams, 1978). *L. zonata*, which was probably derived from *L. triangulum* (Zweifel, 1952), also has a coral-snake pattern. In some parts of the range of the species, the red areas of the pattern are largely obscured by black; this may be an example of an originally mimetic pattern changing to a cryptic one (Hecht and Marien, 1956).

Several species of coral-snake mimics show both close similarity to their models and concordant geographic variation. The patterns of milksnakes (*Lampropeltis triangulum*) in Latin America vary in parallel with the patterns of coral snakes. In Mexico two subspecies of *L. triangulum* resemble local species of *Micrurus* in band width and color (Zweifel, 1960): In Guerrero *L. t. blanchardi* occurs with *M. browni* and both have red rings that are heavily spotted with black. In contrast, in Nayarit, Sinaloa, and southern Sonora, where *L. t. nelsoni* occurs with *M. distans distans*, the coral snake and milksnake both have broad immaculate red rings. A second coral snake in this region, *Micruroides euryxanthus australis*, has wider red rings in its area of overlap with *Micrurus distans* than it does in more northern parts of its range. In Oaxaca *L. t. oligozona* and *Micrurus ephippifer* have an encroachment of black into red rings. On the Yucatán Peninsula the crossbanded pattern of *L. triangulum* breaks down in some localities where *Micrurus diastema* exhibits the same effect, and in Honduras the pattern changes to one of black and orange rings like that of *Micrurus nigrocinctus* (Greene and McDiarmid, 1981). In Costa Rica and northwestern Panama juveniles of *L. t. gaigae* and *Micrurus alleni* have a tricolor pattern that darkens with age. The milksnakes become bicolored red and black and eventually the red also is obscured leaving a black snake. In the coral snakes the process terminates with a bicolored pattern of black and yellow (Savage and Vial, 1974). (Experiments are needed before the hypothesis that the black color is significant in thermoregulation (Williams, 1978) can be accorded credence.)

The parallels in color patterns of coral snakes and some sympatric colubrids extend even to very local variations (Greene and McDiarmid, 1981). For example, a form of *Micrurus limbatus* from the eastern shore of Lago Catemaco, Veracruz, Mexico, is orange with a black nape band and a few large dorsal spots. A *Pliocercus* from that locality and one of its offspring had the same pattern, and a second offspring was banded with black and orange like the normal pattern of *M. limbatus* from the surrounding region. *M. bernadi* from Necaxa, Puebla, Mexico, is red with dorsal black cross bars or spots; three of four *Pliocercus* from that locality had the same pattern. Similar local variation in *Pliocercus* and *Erythrolamprus* with local variations in *Micrurus* has been reported from Guatemala, Honduras, Ecuador, and Peru (Fig. 5).

Some coral-snake mimics combine features of two or more models. Most striking is the situation in southern Mexico and northern Guatemala where *Pliocercus elapoides* combines elements of the patterns of two local coral snakes (Fig. 6). Another example of a mimetic pattern that combines features of two models is *Oxyrhopus trigeminus*; some individuals from Peru have bicolor patterns on some parts of the body and tricolor patterns on other parts. Both bicolor and tricolor coral snakes occur in sympatry with the *Oxyrhopus* (Hecht and Marien, 1956). The same authors noted examples of polymorphisms in the mimetic patterns

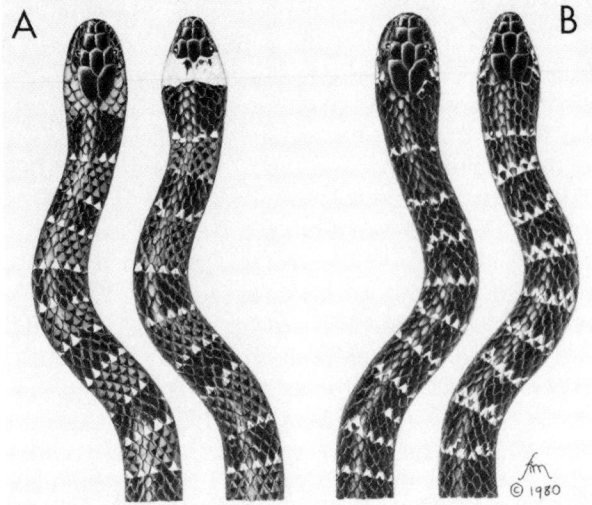

Fig. 5. Mimicry of different models. In Peru the colubrid snake *Erythrolamprus guentheri* shows geographic variation in mimicry of coral snakes. The coral snake is on the left in each pair. (A) *Micrurus langsdorfii*, which occurs in the Amazonian region of southeastern Ecuador and adjacent Peru, has a tricolored pattern with red and black bands about four dorsal scales in width separated by light yellow or white bands about one scale wide. This pattern is mimicked by *E. guentheri*. (B) *Micrurus margaretiferus*, which has a very limited geographic range in the lower reaches of the Rio Cenepa and Rio Santiago in northern Peru, has speckled white bands on a black background. A black and white form of *E. guentheri* in the Rio Cenepa area mimics this bicolored coral snake. (From Greene and McDiarmid, 1981. Illustration copyright by the artist Frances J. Irish, and used by permission.)

of *Atractus elaps* and *A. latifrons* that parallel variation in *Micrurus* and might involve some individuals with patterns that combine features of two models. In Argentina, the colubrid snake *Lystrophis dorbignyi* has a dorsal pattern of dark blotches and a subcaudal pattern of alternating red and black bands. The defensive behavior of this species includes a tail display that exposes the red and black markings and resembles the caudal display of the sympatric coral snake *Micrurus frontalis*. In addition, *L. dorbignyi* flattens its body and may spread the posterior tips of the quadrate bones, giving the head a triangular shape and enhancing its resemblance to the sympatric viper *Bothrops alternatus* (A. A. Yanosky, pers. comm.). Such dual mimics are to be expected if the proposed differences between mimicry of venomous snakes and conventional mimicry are correct.

Concordant variation in the patterns of venomous and nonvenomous snakes permits the inference that coral-snake patterns are aposematic

MIMICRY OF VENOMOUS SNAKES

Fig. 6. Simultaneous mimicry of two models. In southern Mexico and Guatemala the colubrid snake *Pliocercus elapoides* (in the center of the illustration) combines elements of the patterns of two venomous coral snakes. *Micrurus diastema* (on the left) has broad bands of red and very narrow secondary black rings bordering the yellow rings. *Micrurus elegans* (on the right) has narrow red rings and broad secondary black rings. In this region *P. elapoides* has relatively broad red rings in addition to well-developed secondary black rings. (From Greene and McDiarmid, 1981. Illustration copyright by the artist Frances J. Irish, and used by permission.)

and that the colubrid snakes are mimics of the coral snakes. A mechanism by which such mimicry can be selectively advantageous is provided by recent experimental studies of predatory behavior of birds and mammals.

Responses of predators to coral-snake patterns. Two important experimental studies have investigated the responses of probable avian and mammalian predators of coral snakes to artificial models painted in banded patterns that resemble coral snakes and in a variety of control patterns. Zoo-reared coatimundis (*Nasua narica*) and javelinas (*Tayassu pecari*) in open enclosures and a group of free-ranging coatis were presented with two rubber replicas of snakes (Gehlbach, 1972). One rubber snake was painted to resemble a species of *Micrurus* (not *Micruroides*, which is the coral snake that occurs in the area of origin of the coatis and javelinas). An olive-green rubber snake was used as a control. The snakes could be manipulated by threads to simulate serpentine crawling or the tail display of *Micrurus*.

Juvenile coatis, both zoo-reared and wild, were startled by the replica of the coral snake giving a tail display. The coati closest to the snake vocalized and ran away and one or more of the other juveniles also ran. Neither the individual that had been startled by the snake nor the others approached the model subsequently. When the olive-green rubber snake was moved in simulation of serpentine locomotion, it was attacked eight times and avoided once. In serpentine locomotion the coral-snake replica was attacked only once and avoided five times. Adult coatis, both wild and zoo-reared, paid little attention to either rubber snake, a response reminiscent of an encounter between coatis and a *Micrurus nigrocinctus* in the wild (Kaufmann, 1962). Adult zoo-reared javelinas were frightened by the tail display of the coral-snake replica and avoided it after one individual had examined it and run away. Data presented in Table I of Gehlbach (1972) suggest that a tail display induced fright more often than serpentine locomotion, and that the coral-snake pattern induced fright more often than the control pattern (Greene and McDiarmid, 1981).

In two carefully controlled experiments, Smith (1975, 1977) presented wooden dowels painted in a variety of colors and patterns to hand-reared birds, thus ensuring that the birds, unlike the mammals in Gehlbach's experiments, had no contact with anything resembling the experimental stimuli before they were tested. The species of birds Smith used, motmots (*Eumomota superciliosa*) and great kiskadees (*Pitangus sulphuratus*), are neotropical ground-foraging predators that capture a variety of small reptiles including snakes.

Motmots attacked dowels painted in solid colors (red, yellow, green, blue), in a neutral banded pattern (green with crosswise blue bands), or in a pattern of yellow with lengthwise red stripes. They fled to the opposite corner of their cage and uttered alarm notes when they were presented with a dowel painted yellow with red bands. In a subsequent experiment, kiskadees also attacked solid-colored models (white, green, red, yellow, and black), neutral patterns (white with green bands), and a pattern of yellow with red stripes. They fled, giving high intensity alarm cries, from a dowel painted to resemble a coral snake (black-yellow-red-yellow-black). A yellow dowel with red bands also caused the birds to flee, but to give lower intensity alarm calls. The response of the birds to a dowel painted with red, yellow, and black stripes was particularly revealing: Only four of the six birds attacked it, and they did so only with great hesitation and adopting a defensive posture as they attacked. The birds gave a total of only seven pecks to the red, yellow,

Fig. 7. The coral-snake pattern of some individuals of the colubrid *Scaphiodontophis annulatus* appears only on the anterior part of the body. Attacks by predators may be directed at the long and apparently fragile tail of snakes with such patterns. (Photograph by Alan H. Savitzky.)

and black striped model compared to 59 pecks on the white and green banded model and 44 pecks on the red and yellow striped model.

Smith also used models that were painted for only one-third of their length—the remaining two-thirds was bare wood. She found that the birds attacked the painted ends of dowels that had patterns they did not fear, and the unpainted ends of dowels with patterns they treated as being like coral snakes. Some Latin American snakes, particularly *Scaphiodontophis*, have a coral-snake pattern that is sometimes limited to the head and anterior part of the body; the rest of the body is solid colored (Fig. 7). If predators respond to these snakes as Smith's birds responded to her models, that pattern should reduce the intensity of predation and deflect attacks to the tail of the snake. *Scaphiodontophis* has an extremely long tail that is readily broken when it is seized (Henderson, 1984; Arnold, this volume).

Smith's carefully designed experiments show that birds are capable of making very precise discriminations among a variety of solid, striped, and banded patterns but that in practice they generalize their response broadly. The types of alarm calls the kiskadees gave when they were presented with the models indicate that they made a distinction between the red, yellow, and black banded dowel and the red and yellow banded one, but they did not attack either. Similarly, their responses suggest that they perceived that the red, yellow, and black striped model was less like a coral snake than the banded combination of the same colors. Despite their ability to make that distinction, the birds showed only a slight inclination to attack the striped dowel. The implications of these responses for the establishment and function of coral-snake mimicry are critical. The birds generalized sufficiently to provide a selective advantage for even a poor mimic of the coral-snake pattern—the red, yellow, and black striped dowel, for example. Predation on coral-snake mimics by birds that behaved like Smith's experimental animals would not produce very precise mimicry of the coral-snake pattern because the birds failed to attack even a poor mimic, the red and yellow banded dowel. This is exactly the sort of response predicted from a consideration of the consequences of having a deadly model, and some coral-snake mimics fall into the categories of Smith's dowels. The species of *Elapomorphus*, *Apostolepis*, and *Scaphiodontophis* with the coral-snake pattern limited to the anterior portion of the body are one such group (Henderson, 1984). In some populations, *Elapomorphus bilineatus* has red, yellow, and black stripes and might derive protection from that pattern in a manner analogous to the red, yellow, and black striped dowel in Smith's experiments.

Predators that respond like motmots and kiskadees would produce a situation in which mimics with even a small resemblance to coral snakes would benefit from reduced predation. This sort of response by predators is probably the reason for the high incidence of snakes with coral-snake patterns in the neotropics. Snakes like *Anilius*, *Dipsas*, and *Liophis* are poor mimics; they do not really look very much like coral snakes, but they look as much like coral snakes as some of the painted dowels that frightened Smith's birds. Apparently broad generalization by predators makes even that degree of resemblance advantageous. The very precise resemblances to the patterns of coral snakes and the parallel geographic variation with coral snakes seen among species of *Lampropeltis* and *Pliocercus* are a different situation. Apparently in this case some predators are making fine distinctions that have refined an initial imprecise resemblance of the colubrids to coral snakes. This situation may be the only example among snakes of the second stage of the two-step evolution of Batesian mimicry that may be the norm for insects.

The clear demonstration of innate avoidance of the coral-snake pattern by two potential avian predators of coral snakes offers a mechanism for the evolution of aposematic color and mimicry that avoids the difficulties of requiring a predator to experience the lethal consequences of the noxious qualities of a venomous snake (Greene and Pyburn, 1973). Empathic learning appears to be another plausible method of learning to avoid coral snakes. More than a century after

Cope first called attention to the situation, the two thorniest issues of the "coral-snake mimicry problem" appear to be resolved.

b. Mimicry of Vipers by Egg-Eating Snakes

On comparing the two snakes I was much struck by their general resemblance, although, of course, the *Dasypeltis* has a very dissimilar head; but the curious way it has of blowing itself out, and distending its neck, and darting at intruders heightened the resemblances. I cannot help thinking that these habits must be serviceable to so harmless a snake (Weale, 1871).

Distinctive or conspicuous colors and patterns are not essential components of the aposematic displays of snakes. Most vipers, for example, are cryptically colored. Terrestrial vipers have cryptic patterns that match the substrate color and incorporate obliterative shading or disruptive colors. African vipers of the genera *Causus*, *Echis*, *Bitis*, and *Cerastes* fit this general description (Gans, 1961). They may be unicolored or have dorsal saddles and lateral bars. The predominant hue of a snake matches the color of the substrate on which it is found. Many of these African vipers have a prominent V-shaped mark on the head or neck. Crypsis appears to be the primary function of these patterns; aposematism is secondary and associated with distinctive behavior after a snake is discovered by a predator.

Interspecific differences in the components of these displays have been described and intraspecific variation probably occurs as well, but the general aspects can be characterized (Gans, 1961):

Night adders. *Causus rhombeatus* and *C. defilippii* inflate and flatten their bodies, coil and strike, sometimes leaping from the ground.

Horned viper. *Bitis caudalis* rests in a C-shaped coil and strikes repeatedly to the accompaniment of loud hissing.

Saw-scaled viper. *Echis carinatus* also forms a C-shaped coil, but in this species a hissing noise is produced by rubbing together specialized scales that are distributed in a band occupying the lower several rows of lateral scales.

Two species of the nearly toothless egg-eating snakes, *Dasypeltis scabra* and *D. palmarum*, appear to mimic both the patterns and behaviors of these vipers. Gans (1961) reviewed this subject and summarized the parallels in geographic variation of the vipers and their mimics. The ranges of the species of *Dasypeltis* are not mutually coextensive with any of the vipers and consequently the most widespread egg-eating snake, *D. scabra*, mimics different vipers in different parts of Africa. Through most of sub-Saharan Africa, *D. scabra* closely resembles local populations of the night adders *Causus rhombeatus* and *C. defilippii*. These adders have dark brown saddles and lateral bars outlined with cream on a light brown background and a V-shaped mark on the neck. In western Africa the lateral body markings of *C. rhombeatus* are fused with the dorsal blotches, whereas in central Africa the lateral blotches alternate with the dorsal marks. This geographic pattern variation is paralleled by *D. scabra*. In regions where a unicolor phase of *C. rhombeatus* occurs, *D. scabra* is also unicolored. *Causus defilippii* has a pattern very like that of *C. rhombeatus*. *Causus* is a stouter snake than *Dasypeltis* and shows an ontogenetic change in pattern. As the adders grow their patterns become less distinct and large adults may be unicolored. The patterns of egg-eating snakes resemble those of adders with body girth, but not length, equal to those of the egg-eating snakes.

In the horn of Africa, Angola, Egypt, and Arabia, *Dasypeltis scabra* resembles *Echis carinatus*. In eastern Africa both egg-eating snakes and saw-scaled vipers have patterns of elongate saddles and dark heads without markings. This is the only part of its range in which *D. scabra* has a dark, unpatterned head. Night adders and egg-eating snakes from western Africa have square or hexagonal blotches and a V-shaped marking on the head. This pattern is shared with *Causus rhombeatus* as well.

In parts of southwestern Africa *Bitis caudalis* appears to be a model for *Dasypeltis scabra*. The patterns of the horned vipers and egg-eating snakes change in concert from square saddles in the west to hexagonal blotches in the east. In addition Sternfeld (1908, 1910) has suggested that a north-to-south reduction in the length of the tail of egg-eating snakes is mimicry of the short tail of *Bitis caudalis*.

In Angola *Bitis heraldica* has a distinctive dorsal pattern formed by a light middorsal band that encloses diamond-shaped markings that are bordered by dark lines. This middorsal pattern contrasts sharply with the dark coloring adjacent to it on the back and sides of the body. *Dasypeltis palmarum* appears to mimic the distinctive middorsal pattern of the body of that viper. Mimicry of only a portion of the pattern, one that may be perceived as separate from the rest of the pattern of the snake, may make the difference between the slim body of *Dasypeltis* and the thick body of the viper less apparent to potential predators.

The mimicry of vipers by egg-eating snakes extends to their aposematic displays. Like *Echis*, *Dasypeltis* throws its body into a series of concentric C-shaped coils that are moved in opposite directions so that each coil rubs against adjacent ones (Fig. 8). Modified lateral scales produce a hissing sound (Gans and Richmond, 1957; Gans, 1974). Examination of the surface configuration with electron microscopy shows that the sound-producing structures on the scales of the vipers and egg-eating snakes are quite different. In *Echis carinatus, E. coloratus,* and *Cerastes cerastes* the scales have central keels that terminate in one or two longitudinal series of rounded knobs, whereas in *Dasypeltis* the keels of the modified lateral scales are covered by longitudinal ridges (Gans and Baic, 1974).

As an egg-eating snake rubs its body coils together, it appears as a swirling object, and its body proportions are difficult to judge (Weale, 1871). The snake inflates its tracheal air sac, lung, and posterior air sac, increasing its girth and causing the dark markings to become more conspicuous and its body form more viper-like (Gans and Richmond, 1957). Inflation is facilitated by the structure of the tracheal air sac, a ventral expansion of the trachea that originates immediately behind the hyoid. The cartilaginous tracheal bars are not joined ventrally; hence they straighten as the tracheal air sac is inflated and press against the flattened esophagus and subvertebral muscles. The inflated tracheal air sac, lung, and posterior air sac may act as resonating chambers and amplify the hissing sound produced by the modified scales.

During this display some egg-eating snakes spread the posterior tips of the quadrates, giving the head a triangular shape and a more viper-like appearance. The head is the only part of the body of the snake that is motionless and thus readily visible to a predator through most of the defensive display. During the culminating phase of the display, the egg-eating snake gapes its jaws widely and strikes repeatedly but without actually biting (Gans and Richmond, 1957; Gans, 1961).

The combination of a cryptic color and pattern shared by the egg-eating snakes and vipers with an aposematic display mimicked by the egg-eating snakes is a noteworthy example of the multiple uses of colors and patterns by animals. The clearly cryptic function of a blotched pattern in snakes has led some authors to deny the hypothesis of mimicry by egg-eating snakes (Werner, 1909; Mertens, 1955). Convergence on a similar cryptic pattern by vipers and egg-eating snakes would be a plausible hypothesis were it not for the mimicry of the vipers' display. Five of six species of egg-eating snakes have populations with blotched patterns, but Gans (1961) considered that only in *D. scabra* and *D. palmarum* was the resemblance close enough to the vipers to be considered mimetic. The remaining species of *Dasypeltis* do have modified lateral scales and engage in a defensive display similar to that described for *D. scabra*. If predators generalize the features of vipers as broadly as they appear to do those of coral snakes, all species of *Dasypeltis* might benefit to some extent from their resemblance to vipers.

The similarity of the patterns of the several species of vipers that are models for *Dasypeltis* suggests that this group may be an assemblage of Müllerian mimics (Gans, 1961). Evaluation of that hypothesis is complicated by the ubiquity of snake patterns that consist of irregular dorsal markings. Patterns of this sort often characterize relatively slow-moving species of snakes that are exposed to predators in daylight and are capable of defending themselves effectively (Brattstrom, 1955; Jackson et al., 1976). Blotched patterns are found in many species of boids as well as among colubrids, and blotched patterns may be an ancestral characteristic of caenophidian snakes. Nonetheless, predators that avoid vipers, whether innately or as a result of experience, might mistake another blotched snake for a viper. Thus, a shared ancestral pattern of blotches could function like mimicry in an antipredator display. Parallel geographic variation of the patterns of presumed models and mimics (as seen among vipers and egg-eating snakes) suggests that predators may have exerted selective pressure on the resemblance. If that is the case, the resemblance would be mimetic in an evolutionary as well as in an ecological sense. However, a parallel response by model and mimic to some other feature of the physical or biological environment cannot be dismissed. (See Sweet, 1985, for an example of convergent selection for camouflage among snakes.) Additional similarities of colubrids and vipers, especially stout bodies, large heads, and the ability to spread the ventral tips of the quadrate bones, may represent convergent adaptations for swallowing large prey (Marx et al., 1982; Pough and Groves, 1983), or they might be mimetic (Werner, 1985).

The viperid models of egg-eating snakes pose at least as much risk to predators as do coral snakes. Empathic learning has been suggested as the primary mechanism by which predators learn to avoid vipers, although Gans (1961) noted that innate responses were also possible. Baboons (*Papio cephalus*), mandrills (*Mandrillus sphinx*), and warthogs (*Phocochoerus aethiopicus*) are among the potential predators of African snakes. These mammals forage in groups and might learn avoidance from seeing another individual bitten by a venomous snake. Foraging baboons overturn ground litter and uproot plants, and they do eat snakes; older individuals may be more cautious than young ones about

---

Fig. 8. *(facing page)* The egg-eating snake, *Dasypeltis scabra*. (Top) In its defensive display the egg-eating snake throws its body into C-shaped loops that originate at the neck and pass posteriorly along the body in the sequence a–d. Adjacent portions of the body move past each other in opposite directions, as indicated by the arrows. (Bottom) Several rows of lateral scales are inclined at an angle to the long axis of the body of the snake and have serrated keels. The tips of the keels on adjacent loops click together, and the sound is summated to a sustained hiss. (From Gans, 1974; Copyright by The University of Michigan and reproduced by permission.)

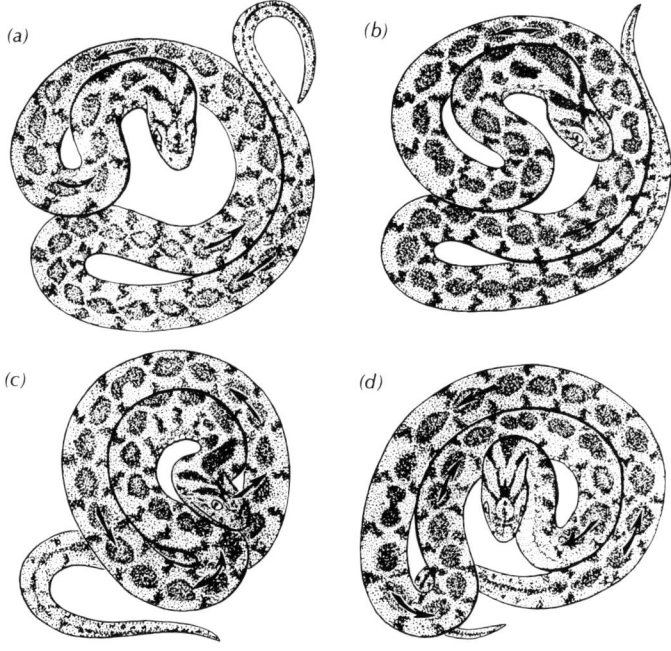

attacking snakes (Gans, 1964). In captivity mandrills fed slices of banana dyed different colors learned to avoid the color made unpalatable by quinine (Jouventin et al., 1977). Empathic learning was more effective than direct experience in this situation. Animals that watched another individual sample the palatable and unpalatable colors made fewer mistakes when tested subsequently than the animals that had done the sampling. Discrimination achieved by observation was retained for at least 2 weeks without intervening reinforcement.

These experiments demonstrate that empathic learning by predators is a feasible basis for selection of mimetic color patterns and behaviors among egg-eating snakes. The possibility that some avian or mammalian predators of snakes have evolved innate avoidance of vipers akin to that shown for coral snakes remains to be investigated. Experiments utilizing naive predators and a variety of models could determine whether innate avoidance of vipers exists, and if so, what features of the appearance or behavior of a viper elicit that avoidance. With this information it would be possible to evaluate the numerous suggestions of mimicry of vipers by other snakes.

c. Mimicry of Vipers by *Boiga*

The distinctive pattern and defensive display of the saw-scaled viper *Echis carinatus* seem most reasonably interpreted as a compromise between the cryptic and aposematic functions of a pattern of dorsal blotches. The light lines that cross the dorsum are outlined by black scales. This contrast renders the total pattern of a saw-scaled viper more conspicuous than that of vipers with unicolored dark blotches on a lighter background. Inflation of the body in the defensive display emphasizes the contrast of the crossbands.

In southeastern Iran, the rear-fanged *Boiga trigonata melanocephala*, a larger snake than *Echis*, has a dorsal pattern and a defensive display that resemble those of the saw-scaled viper (Gans and Latifi, 1973). In the region of sympatry with *Echis* the anterior and midbody of *Boiga* are crossed by light lines with black margins; the posterior part of the body lacks these brightly contrasting marks. As a result of the distribution of the two sorts of pattern on *Boiga*, the portion of the body that bears an *Echis*-like pattern has the same length–diameter ratio as *Echis* despite the difference in the size and relative girth of the two species. The defensive display of *Boiga* in Iran consists of using the contrastingly marked portions of the body to form a C-shaped loop that resembles the loop formed by *Echis*. Unlike the viper, *Boiga* from Iran are said to hide the head beneath a coil of the body, but in other parts of the range of the genus *Boiga* may strike during the display (Kroon, 1975).

These similarities of pattern and behavior suggest that *Boiga* is a mimic of *Echis* (Gans and Latifi, 1973). Both species have extensive geographic ranges and the situation in Iran may be a local manifestation of a more general relationship between *Boiga* and *Echis* (Gans and Latifi, 1973). Furthermore, the eight species of *Boiga* that have overlapping ranges with *Echis* and have patterns like that of *B. t. melanocephala* may also mimic *Echis* or form a Müllerian mimicry complex that includes *Echis* (Kroon, 1975). In Africa, *B. pulverulenta*, *Rhamphiophis multimaculatus*, *Telescopus variegatus*, and *Pseudaspis cana* may mimic vipers (Gans, 1961).

d. Additional Examples of Mimicry of Vipers

Many vipers and colubrids have a pattern of dark blotches on a light background (Fig. 9). This similarity has startled observers sufficiently to inspire repeated suggestions of mimicry of vipers by colubrids, but other interpretations are also plausible. A blotched pattern is widespread among caenophidian snakes, and is characteristic of slow-moving terrestrial species (Jackson et al., 1976), so that convergence on a common cryptic pattern cannot be dismissed as an explanation for the similarities of some vipers and colubrids. Furthermore, blotched patterns are common among henophidians, and may be an ancestral character for caenophidians.

Most suggestions of mimicry of vipers by colubrid snakes are anecdotal, and few have considered these alternative hypotheses. For example, the assertion that *Coluber ravergieri* mimics *Vipera palaestinae* in Israel (Arbel, 1979) is apparently based on the coincidence of a pattern of dorsal blotches in both species; the photographs that accompany the description do not show any noticeable similarity between them, and geographic variation is not considered. The Great Basin gopher snake (*Pituophis melanoleucus deserticola*) has been proposed as a mimic of the northern Pacific rattlesnake (*Crotalus viridis oreganus*) because both species have dark dorsal blotches and coil the body and vibrate the tail when they are disturbed (Kardong, 1980). However, a quantitative comparison of geographic variation in color and pattern of *Pituophis melanoleucus* and *Crotalus viridis* in coastal and inland areas of central southern California suggested that camouflage is the primary factor involved, and that mimicry is of no more than secondary importance (Sweet, 1985). Coastal populations of rattlesnakes and gopher snakes occur in different plant associations, do not resemble each other, and are cryptic in different habitats: Coastal *Crotalus viridis helleri* are matched to their background in chaparral and woodland areas, whereas *Pituophis melanoleucus annectans* from the coast are cryptic in brushy grasslands. Inland populations of *P. m. catenifer* and *C. v. oreganus* from the Carrizo

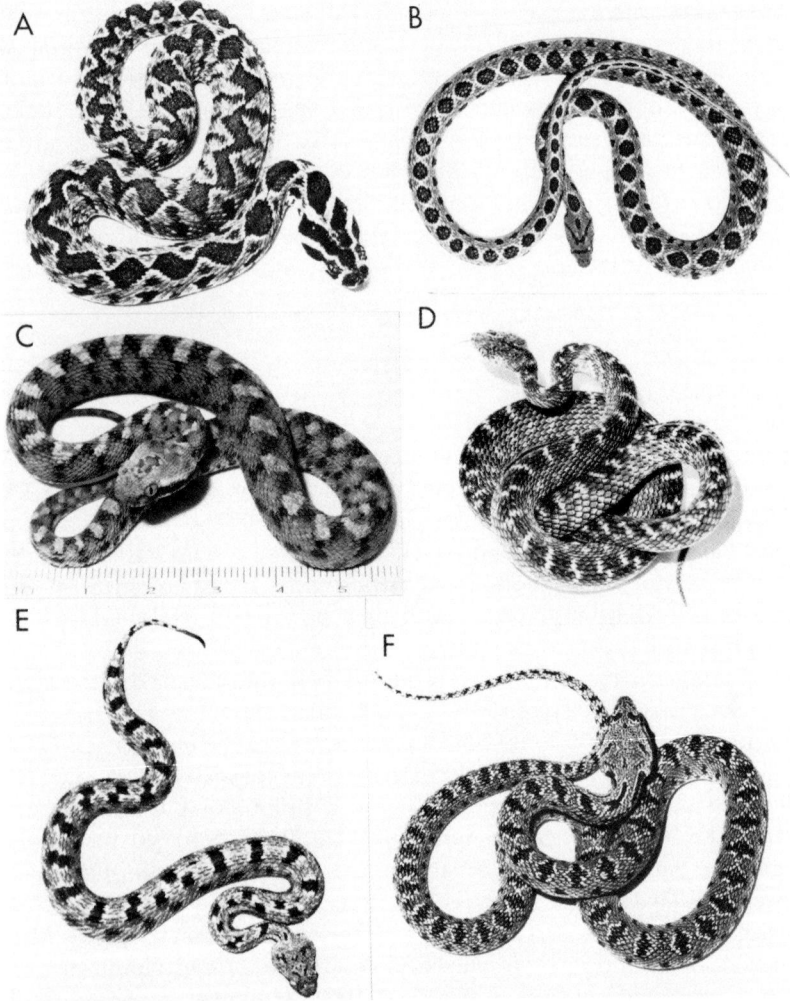

Fig. 9. Viperid snakes and their presumed colubrid mimics. In the mesic Mediterranean region of Israel the dark dorsal blotches of *Vipera palaestinae* (A) may be mimicked by *Coluber nummifer* (B). In the desert of southern Israel the vipers *Echis coloratus* (C) and *Pseudocerastes persica fieldi* (E) have alternating light and dark dorsal bands that find counterparts in the dorsal patterns of the colubrids *Telescopus dhara* (D) and *Spalerosophis diadema cliffordi* (F). These very general resemblances may be enhanced by defensive behaviors including hissing, striking and triangulation of the head that increase the resemblance of the colubrid snakes to vipers. (Photographs by Yehudah L. Werner.)

Plain, where habitat diversity is less than on the coast, show more overlap of habitat utilization and are more similar to each other in color than are coastal populations. The inland populations of both species of snakes are cryptic in open grasslands. The populations of rattlesnakes and gopher snakes from the Carrizo Plain are also more aggressive than are the coastal snakes. Nearly all the individuals of both species from the inland habitat hissed or rattled the tail when they were disturbed, whereas fewer than 20% of the gopher snakes and only 50% of the rattlesnakes from the coast gave these responses. Crypsis and mimicry are not incompatible mechanisms of predator avoidance for these snakes, but mimicry cannot be inferred from the information currently at hand; convergent evolution of camouflage is a more likely explanation of the similarity of the two species in open grassland habitats (Sweet, 1985).

Colubrid snakes can produce a triangular outline of the head when it is seen in dorsal view by spreading the ventral tips of the quadrate bones laterally (Fig. 10). This behavior may increase the resemblance of a colubrid to a viper, and a snake may enhance the effect by tilting its head so that the triangular shape is more readily apparent to a predator (Rand and Ortleb, 1969; Greene, 1975; Werner, 1986), and by keeping the head motionless while the body moves (Gans and Richmond, 1957). Head triangulation may be combined with coiling, hissing, and striking (Gans and Richmond, 1957; Gans, 1961; Sapwell, 1968; Rand and Ortleb, 1969; Kardong, 1980; Werner and Frankenberg, 1982; Werner, 1983, 1985; Sweet, 1985). The neotropical colubrid *Xenodon* has been reported to resemble a terrestrial species of the pit viper *Bothrops* (Lönnberg, 1902; Neill, 1965; Fig. 11). *Waglerophis merremii, Tomodon ocellatus*, and *Lystrophis dorbignyi* also may mimic species of *Bothrops* (Astort, 1983).

Vocalizations by nestling birds sound to some observers like the hiss of a snake and have been described as auditory mimicry that deters predators of the birds (Leroy, 1979), but this hypothesis has not been tested experimentally. In western North America burrowing owls (*Athene cunicularia*) and rattlesnakes (*Crotalus*) both live in tunnels dug by rodents. The defensive hiss of the owl is sonagraphically similar to the rattling of the snake (Martin, 1973), but similar hisses are produced by two other small North American owls that do not inhabit burrows, and the young of several owl species use hisses to solicit food from adults (Thomsen, 1971). Thus, the vocalizations might be an ancestral character of burrowing owls (Rowe, 1984). Wild-caught ground squirrels (*Spermophilus beecheyi*) showed interpopulation differences in their responses to the rattling of a snake and the hiss of owl (Rowe, 1984; Rowe et al., 1986): Squirrels from a population sympatric with rattlesnakes

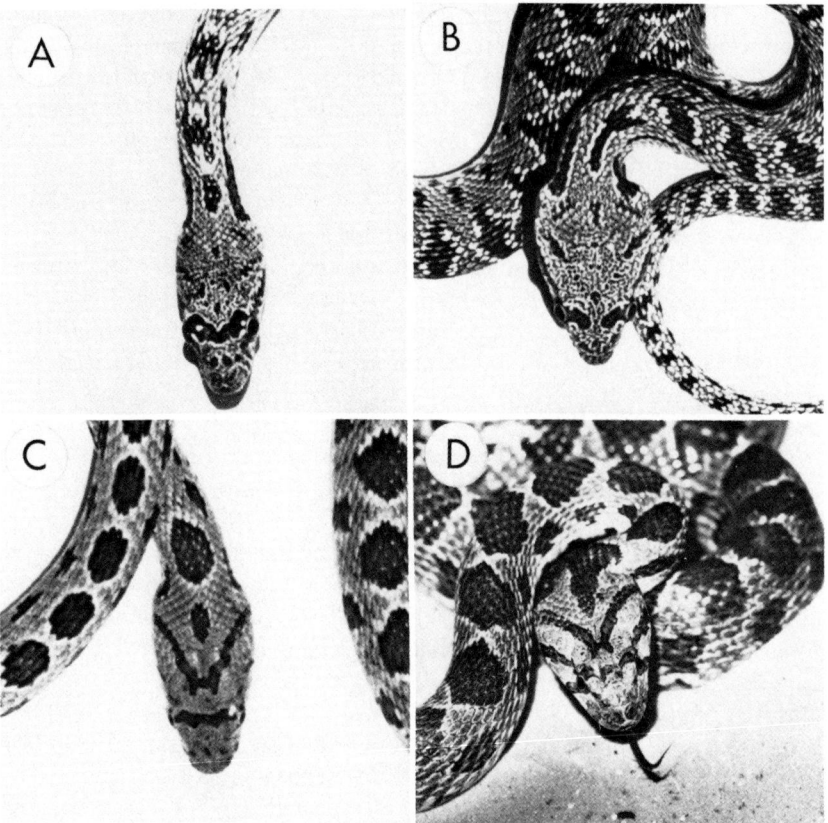

Fig. 10. Head triangulation by colubrid snakes. By spreading the posterior ends of the quadrate bones laterally, the colubrids *Spalerosophis diadema cliffordi* (A and B) and *Coluber nummifer* (C and D) impart a triangular shape to the head that makes it appear more viper-like. (Photographs by Yehudah L. Werner.)

treated both sounds with greater caution than squirrels from a population that has probably not been exposed to rattlesnakes for some 3000 years, raising the possibility that the hiss of the owl may have a mimetic function.

Several lizard species have been reported to mimic vipers. In Pakistan the gecko *Teratolepis fasciata* has a dorsal pattern of light bands on a darker background. The bands on the head are bent into shallow Vs and the bands continue on the broad tail. The defensive display of the gecko consists of curling and flattening the body and raising the tail so its dorsal surface is presented to a predator. In this position the gecko is said to resemble the sympatric saw-scaled viper, *Echis carinatus*

Fig. 11. Mimicry of the pit viper *Bothrops asper* (A) by the colubrid *Xenodon rhabdocephalus* (B). At La Selva, Costa Rica, the similarity of *Xenodon* to *Bothrops* includes a dorsal pattern of blotches and a dark postorbital stripe that is displayed when the neck is spread into a hood. (Photographs by H. W. Greene.)

(Anderson, 1964). Further disturbance causes the lizard to hiss and strike with its head at an assailant. Legless lizards (*Anguis fragilis*) are polymorphic; juveniles and some adult females are golden brown with a dark dorsal stripe, whereas some females and all adult males are a uniform grey dorsally (M. Smith, 1969). Retention of the dark stripe by some females has been interpreted as mimicry of the adder, *Vipera berus* (R. H. Smith, 1974).

Individually most of these accounts leave much to be desired, but in sum they suggest that mimicry of vipers may be a worldwide phenomenon. If other predators share human perceptions of snake patterns, mimics may derive benefit from quite imprecise resemblances to their models. J. R. G. Turner (pers. comm.) described a color variant of the smooth snake, *Coronella austriaca*, in England that was "grey with a black V-mark on the head and a series of zig-zag black dots down the back, the whole having a sufficient resemblance to the viper, although the V was the wrong way round and the dots not joined up into a zig-zag, to have us looking at the first one we caught for ten minutes before we dared touch it with bare hands." Hesitation of that sort by a predator may provide an opportunity for a snake to escape. Further investigations, especially controlled experiments with potential predators, are necessary to define the role of mimicry of vipers in the defensive repertoires of reptiles.

e. Mimicry of Other Venomous Snakes

Colubrid, elapid, and hydrophiid snakes, although they may be less formidable models than vipers, have been implicated in a number of suggested examples of mimicry. As is the case with mimicry of vipers, the evidence is anecdotal and alternative hypotheses have not been tested. A resemblance has been noted between the boa *Candoia aspera* and the elapid *Acanthophis antarcticus* (Bustard, 1969). *Candoia* from Lae, New Guinea, have the dorsal and lateral blotches joined to form bands and are said to be particularly like *Acanthophis* (McDowell, 1979:59). The terrestrial neotropical turtle *Rhinoclemmys pulcherrima* has a pattern of alternating red, black, and yellow bands on the ventral surfaces of the marginal scutes of the carapace. (A color photograph is presented in Janzen, 1980.) These bands bear a strong resemblance to the pattern of a coral snake when the turtle is viewed from beneath, as it would be seen by a predator that overturned it. In addition, the dorsal aspect of the gular scutes of the plastron bears the same colors, and this pattern is revealed in dorsal view when the turtle retracts its head into its shell.

In Malaya the inoffensive pipe snake, *Cylindrophis rufus* (Aniliidae), is said to mimic the colors and defensive display of the elapid snake *Maticora intestinalis* (Tweedie, 1953). In this region, the elapid has a dorsal pattern consisting of three narrow yellow stripes bordered with black and separated by the brown ground color. The ventral surface is boldly patterned with black bands on a white background, and the underside of the tail is bright red with black bars. The defensive behavior of the snake consists of a display that reveals this pattern:

> When molested this snake makes no attempt to escape, but will often raise its tail, displaying the bright red under surface, and will

writhe and tumble about, turning the conspicuously barred belly uppermost. This behavior is doubtless aposematic, and both it and the coloration are mimicked by the harmless pipe snake, *Cylindrophis rufus* (Tweedie, 1953:95–96).

A color photograph of the ventral pattern of a *Maticora* appears in Fogden and Fogden (1974:114). Tweedie (1953:13) also proposed that the elapid snake *Calliophis gracilis*, which has a ventral pattern like that of *M. intestinalis*, is another mimic. Two of the three species of kraits in Malaya (*Bungarus fasciatus* and *B. candidus*) are banded with black and yellow or white. Tweedie (1953) suggested that several colubrid snakes with banded patterns are mimics of the banded kraits, particularly the mangrove snake (*Boiga dendrophila*) and the banded juveniles of some species including the banded wolf snake, *Lycodon subcinctus*. The third species of krait in Malaya, *B. flaviceps*, is a solid blue-black with a red head and tail. The same pattern is seen in *Maticora bivirgata*.

A number of species of the venomous sea snakes (Hydrophiidae) have alternating black and white bands, and sympatric species of eels share this pattern. These coincidences of pattern have been interpreted as Müllerian mimicry among sea snakes and Batesian mimicry of the sea snakes by the eels (Sternfeld, 1913; Pernetta, 1977), but no feeding trials have been conducted with these banded species. Another sea snake, the pelagic yellow-bellied sea snake, *Pelamis platurus*, has the widest geographic distribution of any species of snake (Minton, 1975). It has been recorded from southern Siberia to New Zealand, Tasmania, and the Cape of Good Hope, and it is the only species of sea snake in the western Indian Ocean and on the west coast of the Americas. *Pelamis* has a bright yellow venter and a black dorsum. The pattern varies from solid blocks of the two colors to spots of yellow and black. *Pelamis* are frequently found where converging surface currents create a drift line of floating debris, and aggregations of snakes may number in the thousands. Despite their local abundance, no *Pelamis* were found in the stomachs of 457 fishes, 214 porpoises, or 1000 sharks examined (Kropach, 1975).

No species of sea snake occurs on the Atlantic side of the Americas, and fishes from the Caribbean have presumably had no experience with sea snakes, at least since the Pliocene when the Isthmus of Panama took its present form. Closely related species of fishes from the Atlantic and Pacific coasts of Panama responded differently to *Pelamis* in experimental feeding trials (Rubinoff and Kropach, 1970). Atlantic fishes attacked *Pelamis* in 38 of 383 trials, and in three of those attacks the fish was fatally bitten by the snake. Only one attack on *Pelamis* was recorded in

316 trials with Pacific fishes, and that fish immediately regurgitated the snake.

Avoidance of *Pelamis* by predatory fishes from the Pacific coast of Panama appears to provide an opportunity for mimicry of the sea snakes by eels, and ophichtid and muraenid eels from Panama (*Murichthys tigris* and *Priodonophis equatorialis*) have some resemblance to *Pelamis* in pattern and color. However, if this resemblance is mimetic, fishes do not appear to have been the predators responsible for its evolution because Pacific fishes readily attacked the eels. In contrast, potential avian predators did respond to *Pelamis* and eels in a manner that would favor mimicry. Naive, hand-reared herons (*Butorides striatus*) and egrets (*Casmerodius albus* and *Egretta thula*) fled from live and dead *Pelamis* with signs of distress (Caldwell and Rubinoff, 1983). The birds largely ignored an arboreal snake (*Imantodes cenchoa*), immediately ate a speckled snake eel (*Murophis punctatus*), and ignored a synbranchid eel (*Synbranchus marmoratus*) that was too large for them to eat. They alternately approached and retreated from a spotted snake eel (*Myrichthys tigris*), which has a pattern of creamy yellow with dark brown or black spots reminiscent of the pattern of some *Pelamis*. Both species of egrets occur on the Pacific coast of Panama where they may frequently encounter *Pelamis* as they forage on tidal mudflats. The herons tested were from the Atlantic side of the isthmus, but are sufficiently mobile to move between regions with and without sea snakes. However, herons normally feed on land or in shallow water and would not be expected to encounter sea snakes frequently. The high toxicity of sea-snake venom may have favored innate avoidance by even an occasional predator (Caldwell and Rubinoff, 1983).

Many snakes spread the neck as part of their defensive display. The dorsoventral neck flattening of the neotropical colubrid *Ninia sebae* may enhance its resemblance to sympatric coral snakes, or may be part of a more generalized threat display (Greene, 1975; Henderson, 1977). Some authors have suggested that neck displays by colubrid snakes mimic the neck spreading of cobras (Flower, 1899; Wall, 1913; Gharpurey, 1962; Deoras, 1965; Werner and Frankenberg, 1982). The descriptions on which these assertions are based do not always distinguish between a cobra-like dorsoventral flattening of the neck and a lateral display. Lateral flattening of the neck is a widespread defensive behavior among colubrids (Mertens, 1946; Greene 1979, this volume). A cobra-like display is not limited to species of colubrids that occur in sympatry with cobras as this extract illustrates: "When [the neotropical colubrid *Liophis reginae* is] angered, the head is raised and the neck flattened and widely expanded, becoming a cobra in miniature" (Beebe, 1946). Coincidences of this sort are as likely to represent shared ancestral characters as they are to be the result of selection by predators for mimicry of venomous snakes.

Even colubrids may serve as models. The innocuous neotropical colubrid *Rhadinaea fulvivittis aemula* takes its subspecific epithet from the suggestion that it mimics the more aggressive colubrid *Coniophanes piceivittis* (Myers, 1974).

Alternative explanations have been suggested for other allegedly mimetic resemblances of reptiles to venomous snakes. For example, the pygopodid lizard *Delma fraseri* has a dark head and a light brown body. Hall (1905) proposed that this pattern mimicked the juvenile color and pattern of the unbanded form of the elapid *Pseudonaja textilis*. The pygopodid lizards *Pygopus nigriceps* and *P. lepidopodus* also have dark heads. When threatened they raise the head off the ground and flatten the neck laterally. This behavior has been likened to the defensive display of small elapid snakes like *Unechis flagellum* and *U. gouldii* (Bustard, 1968). Juvenile oak skinks (*Tiliqua casuarinae*) have black bands on the head and neck. Like the pygopodids, oak skinks raise their heads when molested, a behavior described as mimicry of juvenile brown snakes (*Pseudonaja textilis*) (Rankin, 1973). However, another interpretation is plausible: Nearly 60% of the species of pygopodids have heads that are colored differently from the body, as do 30% of Australian snakes. These dichromatisms of the head and body are most common among elongate reptiles, and may conceal the location of the head and induce predators to seize the body instead (Jackson and Pounds, 1980). Mimicry and crypsis are not mutually exclusive explanations of the high incidence of dichromatism among Australian snakes and pygopodids. The Australian snake fauna is unique in being composed largely of elapids, many of which are probably dangerously toxic to predators. A much lower incidence of venomous snakes in other parts of the world has apparently produced widespread abstract mimicry. What are the consequences for mimicry of having a snake fauna that is composed nearly entirely of venomous species? Experiments with Australian snakes and predators of snakes might reveal hitherto unrecognized aspects of mimicry.

III. MIMICRY OF INVERTEBRATES BY REPTILES

Three examples of apparent mimicry of invertebrates by reptiles have been described. The geckos *Chondrodactylus angulifer* and *Coleonyx variegatus* raise their tails over their backs and wave them from side to side when they detect the presence of a predator; this behavior has been regarded as mimicry of scorpions (FitzSimons and Brain, 1958; Parker and Pianka, 1974). Experiments with *Coleonyx variegatus* using the snake *Hypsiglena torquata* as a predator, however, suggest that tail-waving directs the attack of a predator to a relatively unimportant part of the lizard's body that may be autotomized if it is seized, giving the lizard time to escape (Congdon et al., 1974; Arnold, this volume).

Many uropeltid snakes have bright colors on the sides of the trunk or near the tail that contrast with their normally dark, unpatterned dorsal surfaces. These bright markings may represent Batesian mimicry of large centipedes that are themselves probably aposematically colored (Gans, 1976; 1987). Ground-foraging birds such as jungle fowl, spur fowl, and pea fowl seem likely to have been important selective agents in the evolution of such a mimetic resemblance. Several aspects of the defensive behavior of the uropeltid snakes support that inference: Fowl were often slow to attack uropeltids. When they did attack a snake, most pecks were directed at its tail. The snake was seized and flipped through the air repeatedly before being swallowed, whereas worms were swallowed after only a few flips. The usual defensive behavior of uropeltids consists of coiling the body around a projection such as a root or stem, extending the tail horizontally from the coiled body, and burrowing into the soil with the head. This behavior seems likely to frustrate attempts to flip the snake into the open and the tail may deflect attack from the head. Under these circumstances a snake burrows rapidly and may be able to conceal itself before a predator can do serious harm.

The contrasting colors of uropeltids may function in one or more of several ways. As mimicry of the presumably aposematic colors of centipedes, which are capable of inflicting at least a painful bite upon a predator, the colors may deter attack upon the harmless snakes. If a predator does attack, markings on the tail may act as flash colors, causing the attacker to hesitate, or they may aid in deflecting attack from the head. These potential functions are mutually compatible (Gans, 1976).

Juveniles of the lacertid lizard *Heliobolus lugubris* in the Kalahari Desert of southern Africa appear to mimic abundant, conspicuous oogpister beetles (*Anthia* spp.) that are protected by a noxious fluid they spray at attackers (Huey and Pianka, 1977). The body color, posture, and locomotion of the juvenile lizards differ from those of the adults and instead resemble the beetles. Adult *H. lugubris* from the Kalahari are red-tan and blend with the sand on which they occur, whereas the bodies of the juveniles, like those of the beetles, are black with white markings (Fig. 12). The juvenile lizards attain the adult color and pattern at snout–vent lengths of 40–50 mm; these correspond to the maximum body size of the oogpisters. Adult *H. lugubris* move with the lateral

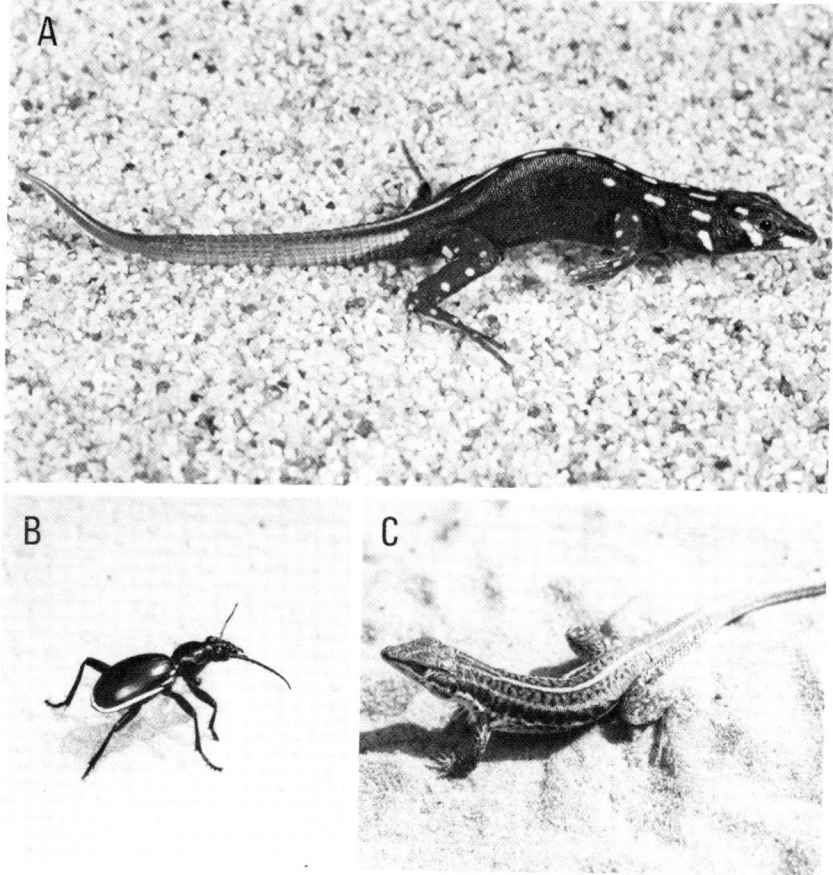

Fig. 12. Mimicry of a beetle by a lizard from the Kalahari Desert. (A) Juveniles of the lacertid lizard *Heliobolus lugubris* are black with broken light lateral and dorsal stripes. Most of the tail is buff or red-yellow, closely matching the color of the substrate. Juvenile *H. lugubris* walk stiffly and jerkily, with the back arched and the tail pressed against the ground. (B) Sympatric oogpister beetles (*Anthia* spp.) are black with lateral white stripes on the elytral borders and sometimes on the thorax and head. Oogpister beetles squirt a pungent acidic fluid when they are attacked. (C) Adult *H. lugubris* are a pale red-tan color that blends with the sand, and they move with lateral undulations. (From Huey and Pianka, 1977. Copyright by the American Association for the Advancement of Science, reproduced by permission.)

undulations of the body that are characteristic of elongate lizards. In contrast, the juveniles move stiffly and jerkily, holding the body arched and the tail pressed to the sand. They resemble the beetles closely enough to deceive human observers.

The frequency of broken tails among samples of juveniles of three species of lacertids in the Kalahari was used as an index of the intensity of predation on the lizards. Juvenile *Heliobolus lugubris* had the lowest frequency of broken tails (10.5%) and differed significantly from juveniles of *Pedioplanes lineoocellatus* (22.3%) and *P. namaquensis* (34.8%). Juveniles of the latter two species resemble their adults in color, pattern, and behavior. The low frequency of broken tails among the beetle-mimicking juvenile *H. lugubris* was interpreted as evidence that the mimicry does deter some potential predators of the lizards (Huey and Pianka, 1977). However, recent reconsiderations of tail-break frequencies among lizards cast doubt on their usefulness as indicators of the intensity of predation (Schoener, 1979; Schoener and Schoener, 1980; Jaksić and Greene, 1984; Arnold, this volume).

IV. INTRASPECIFIC MIMICRY

Deceptive actions or appearances may be directed toward conspecific individuals, and some examples of intraspecific deception may represent conjunct mimicry. For example, the apparent resemblance of certain markings on the faces and ears of mammals to horns or teeth has generated an unverified hypothesis that these patterns (called "weapon automimicry") fool conspecifics into thinking their possessor a formidable opponent (Guthrie and Petocz, 1970).

A better substantiated example of the same phenomenon was reported among lizards by Rand (1967). Male *Anolis lineatopus* behaved as if they were predicting the outcome of agonistic encounters partly on the basis of the size of their opponent. The larger individual was the victor in 85% of the disputes observed, and encounters between individuals of different sizes were less likely to lead to actual physical contact than were encounters between individuals of nearly the same size. A male *Anolis* has many behavioral and structural mechanisms for increasing its apparent size during agonistic encounters (see illustrations in Crews, 1978): A lizard orients itself laterally to its opponent, arches its back and flattens its sides, thereby increasing the apparent depth of its body. The gular region of the throat is engorged, making the head appear larger, and a dark spot appears behind the eye. Tissue along the neck and back can be raised into a crest to enhance that effect, and some species of *Anolis* and other lizards have a permanently erect crest on the back or tail. By the reasoning applied to "weapon automimicry" among mammals, these structures of lizards would be considered "automimicry." However, the employment of threatening displays and devices to make an individual appear larger and fiercer is nearly universal among vertebrates, and occurs during both interspecific and intraspecific interactions (Edmunds, 1974). Extending the term "mimicry" to include these behaviors robs the word of much of its usefulness without illuminating the phenomena so designated. Colors, patterns, structures, and behaviors of this nature can be included in a general category of "intraspecific deception" (Otte, 1975).

A different manifestation of intraspecific deception fits more comfortably into the framework of concrete homotypy: mimicry of females of a species by males of the same species. This form of sexual mimicry is one of many alternative mating strategies for males, a topic that is currently of much interest to students of social behavior (Austad and Howard, 1984). Mimicry of females may be a facultative response to transient conditions, or (apparently rarely among vertebrates) it may be genetically fixed in some individuals of a population (Dominey, 1984). Reptiles appear to provide examples of both situations.

Some male green iguanas (*Iguana iguana*) employ female mimicry as a mating strategy when they are small (Dugan, 1982). During the breeding season large adult male iguanas maintain territories from which they display to females. The adult males exclude medium-size males from these territories, but small males that have not developed secondary sex characters are apparently not recognized from a distance as males and are not excluded. These small males adopt female behaviors (or at least they refrain from engaging in conspicuously male behaviors), thereby escaping the notice of territorial males. Fifteen forced copulation attempts by these small males were observed. The small male ran to a female, leaped on her back, and tried to secure a grip on the female with his mouth. In all 15 attempts the female tried to escape from the male. On five occasions the territorial male chased the small male away, and in three of the remaining ten attempts small males apparently copulated successfully. Of course, successful copulation does not necessarily ensure fertilization. Nonetheless, the long period before full body size is attained by iguanas (approximately 7 years in the Panama population), the low turnover of territorial males (a minimum tenure of 2½ years), and the apparent lack of prospects for copulation by medium-size males may combine to make even a small chance of successful breeding by small males an important factor in their lifetime reproductive success. Female mimicry may be a normal alternative mating strategy for young males of long-lived species of reptiles in which dominant adult males monopolize access to females. The distinctive characteristics of the social systems of some of the large herbivorous species of iguanine lizards (Stamps, 1983) appear particularly conducive to female mimicry. However, similar behaviors have been reported for small, short-lived species of lizards. Young male *Anolis lineatopus* and *A. garmani*, which are the same size as adult females of the species, may occupy sites within the territory of an adult male (Rand, 1967; Trivers, 1976). These males occasionally succeed in mating with resident females.

Red-sided garter snakes (*Thamnophis sirtalis parietalis*) apparently exhibit a genetically fixed form of alternative mating strategy in which certain males possess a physiological feminization that may enhance mating success in some situations (Mason and Crews, 1985). Red-sided garter snakes mate on emergence from their winter den. As females emerge they are courted by multiple males, usually 10 to 20 but sometimes as many as 100 males simultaneously forming a mating ball entwined about the female. Male garter snakes apparently use the vomeronasal system to detect a pheromone produced by females (Kubie et al., 1978). Certain individual males of the red-sided garter snake are female mimics. The mimics were structurally normal males and did not differ in length or mass from randomly sampled males. However, pheromone samples obtained from the skin surface of female snakes and female mimics elicited courtship by males, but samples from the skin of males did not elicit this response. The mimics maintained their attraction to male garter snakes after 40 weeks in captivity. In simultaneous courtship choice tests, a majority of males preferred a female snake to a female mimic, but some males courted the female mimic in every test. Competitive mating trials showed that female mimics were more successful than normal males in copulating with females; the female mimic mated in 69% of the trials, the male in 21%. The female mimics in this system may derive their advantage from confusing other males during the formation of a courtship ball, causing them to ignore a female and court the mimic while the mimic courts the real female. Garter snakes appear to be the first example of female mimicry in which the mimics actually seduce normal males away from females.

V. POSSIBLE MIMICRY OF UNPROFITABLE PREY BY LIZARDS

Aposematism is only one possible function of conspicuous colors or behaviors of vertebrates. Tail displays during encounters with predators have been interpreted as warning signals directed to conspecifics, or as signals informing the predator that it has been observed by its potential prey (Harvey and Greenwood, 1978). Some lizards that live in open habitats and escape from predators by running have conspicuous dark bars on the ventral side of the tail. These markings are revealed by a display in which the lizard arches its tail over its body and undulates the tail slowly from side to side (Greene, this volume).

Two species of iguanid lizards that occur in xeric habitats in North America, *Cophosaurus texanus* and *Holbrookia propinqua*, allow a distinction between the hypotheses that these signals are directed to conspecifics or to predators (Dial, 1986). *C. texanus* has a pattern of dark bars on the ventral surface of the tail, whereas *H. propinqua* lacks markings on the tail. These two species differ in their modes of escape from predators: *C. texanus* runs rapidly from predators, relying on speed to evade capture, whereas *H. propinqua* runs only a short distance and then remains motionless, trusting to crypsis to avoid detection. The species differ also in population structure: *C. texanus* occurs at low population densities, whereas *H. propinqua* occurs at high densities. Thus, the use of tail displays to warn conspecifics of the presence of a predator would be expected for *H. propinqua*, whereas a tail display directed toward a predator is more likely to be seen in *C. texanus*.

C. texanus employed tail displays in 19 of 35 encounters with a human observer, and in 6 of those encounters the lizards displayed a second time after fleeing, whereas none of 31 *Holbrookia* tested used a tail display. No conspecifics were in sight during tail displays by *C. texanus*, whereas a conspecific was nearby in every trial with *H. propinqua*. Thus, the tail display of *C. texanus* is probably directed toward predators, and no warning of conspecifics can be demonstrated for *H. propinqua*.

A tail display might inform a predator that its presence had been detected and that the prey was prepared to flee, thereby reducing the chance that the predator would attack. A similar function has been proposed for the alarm calls of birds and mammals (Maynard Smith, 1965; Charnov and Krebs, 1975). An additional hypothesis suggests that predators might learn to associate a tail display with lizards that are difficult to capture and are probably not worth chasing ("unprofitable prey"); this function has been proposed for the bright colors of some birds (Baker and Parker, 1979; Baker and Hounsome, 1983).

If the tail displays of lizards like *C. texanus* that flee swiftly do identify them to predators as unprofitable prey, a less agile species of lizard might be able to dupe a predator by mimicking the tail display of a fleet-footed species. This hypothesis could be tested in parts of the southwestern United States and Mexico where several species of sand lizards occur sympatrically: *Callisaurus draconoides* and *Cophosaurus texanus* are lizards that can run fast and have conspicuous bars on the ventral surface of their tails, the four species of *Uma* in the United States and Mexico have dark bars on their tails but do not run as rapidly as *Callisaurus* or *Cophosaurus*, and *Holbrookia maculata* and *H. propinqua* lack dark markings and run only a short distance when a predator approaches. Experiments with natural predators like roadrunners (*Geococcyx californianus*) that pursue lizards on the ground during the day could test the predictions that predators are more likely to chase and capture slow species than fast ones, and that they are less likely to chase and capture lizards that exhibit a tail display than those that do not display. If those predictions are supported by experimental evidence, the ability of naive predators to learn to ignore lizards that exhibit a tail display could be tested, as could the ability of a *Uma* to deter a predator by giving a tail display like that of *Callisaurus* or *Cophosaurus*.

VI. THE USE OF LURES TO ATTRACT PREY

Portions of the bodies of certain reptiles bear a presumed resemblance to a larval insect and may be moved in a manner that has been interpreted as an attempt to attract prey within reach of the reptile. This behavior has been called "feeding mimicry" (Schuett et al., 1984). In all instances of which I am aware, the homotypy is abstract. That is, the model is a general category of objects (larval insects), but not a particular species of insect.

The tongue of the alligator snapping turtle, *Macroclemys temminckii*, bears a bifurcate wormlike appendage on its dorsal surface that is used to attract fishes (Fig. 13). The lure can be made to wiggle by contractions of the muscular base on which it rests, and the moving lure attracts fish to the turtle (Allen and Neill, 1950; Carr, 1952:58–59; Drummond and Gordon, 1979). Twelve of nineteen prey captures occurred when a fish swam into the mouth of a turtle and bit the lure, and the remaining seven captures were of fish that swam into the mouth of the turtle without biting the lure (Drummond and Gordon, 1979). In contrast, three attacks on fish that were swimming near the head of the turtle were unsuccessful.

Use of the tail to attract prey has been inferred for a number of species of snakes, but actual success in luring and capturing prey has not often been documented. Putative caudal lures are particularly common among vipers (Fig. 14), but have been suggested also for boids and elapids (Neill, 1960; Greene and Campbell, 1972; Heatwole and Davison, 1976; Murphy et al., 1978; Carpenter et al., 1978).

In many instances, the tip of the tail is bright yellow and contrasts with the cryptic color of the remainder of the body. The bright color and the use of the tail as a lure are generally confined to juvenile snakes, but there are exceptions to that generalization. An adult *Bothrops bilineatus* captured an *Anolis* lizard that was attracted within striking distance by

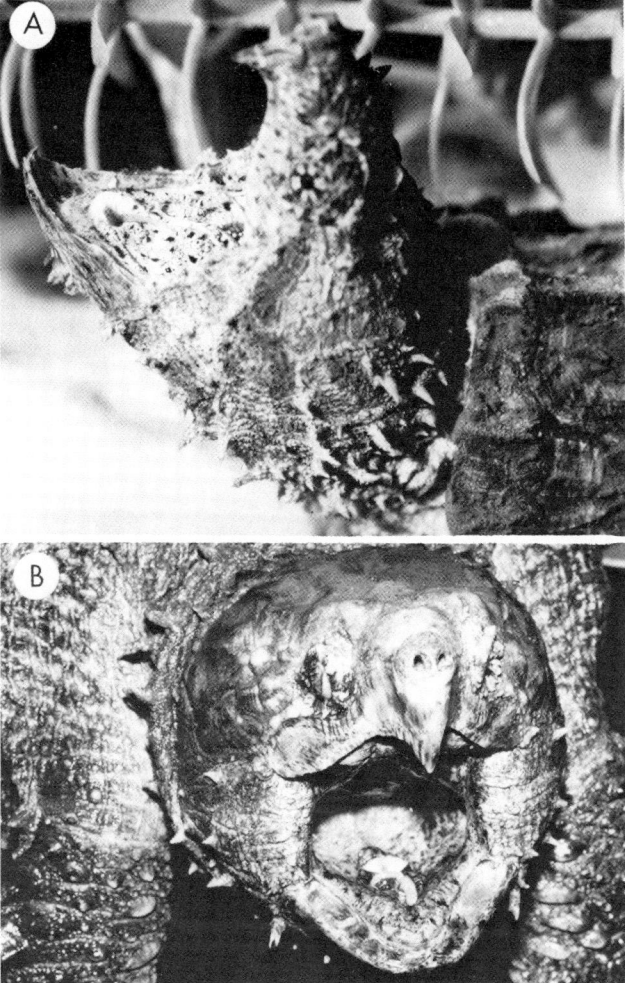

Fig. 13. Luring behavior of the alligator snapping turtle, *Macroclemys temminckii*. (A) In its luring posture the turtle rests with its mouth open. (B) The bifurcate reddish lure is set against a cream-colored patch on the grey and black tongue and resembles the larva of a midge (Tendipedidae). (Photograph (A) by R. W. Van Devender, (B) by F. H. Pough.)

the twitching of the snake's tail (Greene and Campbell, 1972), and an adult *Cerastes vipera* captured a lizard, *Acanthodactylus* (Heatwole and Davison, 1976). Captive adult *Acanthophis antarcticus* waved their tails, apparently in response to the presence of mice on the wire screen tops of their cages (Carpenter et al., 1978). The function of the tail as a lure in

Fig. 14. Luring behavior of a juvenile cantil. The tip of the tail of the neotropical crotalid *Agkistrodon bilineatus howardgloydi* is held in the air and moved to attract potential prey. (Photograph copyright by David L. Hardy and used with permission.)

this instance is inferential; the mice were not in the cages with the snakes and there is no indication that these or other prey were attracted to the tail movements of the snakes. Alternative explanations of tail movements by snakes include various defensive behaviors and an analogy to the tail twitching of stalking felines (Hecht et al., 1955; Greene and Campbell, 1972; Greene, 1973, this volume).

Photographs of juvenile *Agkistrodon bilineatus* waving their tails appear in Neill (1960: Fig. 1). Lizards and toads in the cage with the snakes appear to be orienting toward the tails in some of the photographs. A white mouse and a frog were captured by juvenile *Vipera russellii* when they moved toward the snakes' bright yellow tail tips (Henderson, 1970). A young *Calloselasma rhodostoma* successfully lured and captured a frog (Schuett, 1984). Frogs (*Rana clamitans* and *R. sylvatica*) approached and snapped at the undulating tails of juvenile *Sistrurus catenatus* (Schuett et al., 1984). Only after a frog had seized its tail did the snake strike, even though other frogs were within striking range before that. These experiments led the authors to suggest that the rattle of rattlesnakes had its origin as a structure that enhanced the effectiveness of a caudal lure (see Greene, this volume).

The legend that snakes charm birds has been explicitly invoked to describe the defensive display of an African vine snake, *Thelotornis*, and the coral-snake pattern of the California mountain kingsnake,

Lampropeltis zonata (Goodman, 1974; Goodman and Goodman, 1976a, b). These hypotheses suggest that the snakes exploit the responses of birds to potential predators. The ringed pattern of *Lampropeltis*, it is said, makes the snakes conspicuous and thereby facilitates their discovery by nesting birds. (The term "thelgosematic" was coined to describe this unlikely function of a pattern.) The birds, in the process of defending their nest, are said inadvertently to guide the snake to it by a process of "hot and cold": The intensity of the defense by the birds supposedly increases as the snake approaches the nest and decreases when the snake moves away, thereby providing directional cues to the predator. However, an experimental test of this hypothesis showed that nesting birds mobbed a cryptic model snake as often as a brightly banded model (Smith and Mostrom, 1985).

The defensive display of *Thelotornis* includes inflation of the anterior part of the body. This behavior, it has been suggested, converts the snake to a mimic of a fledgling bird with the result that adult birds are presented with conflicting stimuli. On one hand, they perceive the snake as a predator and simultaneously, it is suggested, the resemblance to a fledgling confuses adult birds with possibly fatal effect (Goodman and Goodman, 1976b). The slow tongue movements of *Thelotornis*, which are shared by the neotropical vine snake *Oxybelis*, have been suggested as creating an additional alluring effect. Alternative interpretations suggest a combination of cryptic and chemosensory functions for the slow tongue movements (Beebe, 1946; Keiser, 1975).

VII. SUMMARY

The study of mimicry has been marked by controversy from its inception, and divergent views continue to be strongly expressed. Reptilian mimicry has remained a scientific backwater for most of the twentieth century, largely because of a lack of systematic experimental studies in appropriate biological contexts. Few of the approaches developed for the study of insect mimicry have penetrated herpetology. The objections advanced to a mimetic function for patterns and colors of reptiles (Grobman, 1978) are similar to arguments raised against mimicry among insects half a century ago. Hypotheses about the functions of reptilian colors and behaviors (Goodman, 1974; Goodman and Goodman 1976a, b) are as speculative as those suggested for insects at the turn of the century.

Fortunately, an increasing frequency of exceptions to this bleak generalization gives promise of better days to come. The significance of parallel geographic variation of models and mimics has been appreciated and exploited (Gans, 1961; Greene and McDiarmid, 1981), and those studies provide the only well-documented examples of snake mimicry. Experimental approaches, using artificial models and mimics, played a pivotal role in the development and testing of hypotheses about insect mimicry. Initial attempts to use experiments to test reptilian mimicry have been equally influential (Gehlbach, 1972; Smith, 1975, 1977, 1980; Caldwell and Rubinoff, 1983). Largely as a result of the studies just cited, one can conclude that mimicry of venomous snakes is a real phenomenon. No alternative explanation as readily accounts for both parallel geographic variation among venomous and nonvenomous species and for innate avoidance of aposematic patterns by predators.

Mimicry among reptiles differs in certain respects from mimicry among insects, partly because reptiles are potentially more noxious models than insects. The high risk associated with mistaking a model for a mimic appears to have led predators of reptiles to generalize the characteristics of models broadly. As a consequence of this broad generalization, even a slight resemblance to a model may be advantageous for a mimic. Because an encounter with a model is potentially lethal for a predator, selection may act in evolutionary time to produce innate avoidance of models and mimics, rather than acting by educating predators in ecological time. Abstract mimicry, in which the model is a general category of objects rather than a particular species or group of species, is widespread among reptiles and, probably, among vertebrates generally.

Venomous snakes may be the vertebrates most likely to induce broad generalization by predators. Experimental studies have shown that predators do generalize the characteristics of coral snakes, and this result is consistent with the high incidence in the neotropics of colubrid snakes with patterns like those of venomous coral snakes. However, coral snakes and some of their mimics show very precise parallel geographic variation, indicating that some predators do attend closely to the details of the mimics.

Mimicry of vipers may be widespread, but interpretation of resemblances between vipers and colubrids is complicated by the possibility that a viper-like pattern of dark dorsal blotches may be ancestral for both groups of snakes. One must distinguish between mimicry as an evolutionary process in which selection by predators increases a resemblance between model and mimic, and mimicry as an ecological process of predator avoidance. These two interpretations may be impossible to separate without information about changes in the patterns of models and mimics through time.

Mimicry of invertebrates by vertebrates is far less common than the reciprocal situation, possibly because vertebrates in general are more dangerous to predators than invertebrates and therefore are more effective models. A few reptiles mimic noxious arthropods, but most cases of mimicry of invertebrates by reptiles involve the use of lures to attract prey. Intraspecific mimicry as an alternative male-mating strategy is probably more widespread among reptiles than is currently recognized. Nonetheless, two well-documented examples already appear to illustrate both transient and genetically fixed female mimicry, the latter being an unusual situation among vertebrates.

Color and pattern are the features of an organism traditionally considered in studies of mimicry, but that perspective reflects primarily the limitations of human sensory systems. Auditory and, particularly, olfactory mimicry are probably widespread among vertebrates, and experimental investigations of these possibilities are particularly important. The difficulty of working with sensory modalities to which we ourselves are not attuned is obvious, but elegant studies of olfactory communication by salamanders show what must be done (Jaeger and Gergits, 1979; Jaeger, 1981; Dawley, 1984).

ACKNOWLEDGMENTS

The lengthy process of preparing this review has been greatly aided by the efforts and suggestions of Ray Huey and Carl Gans. In addition, Lincoln P. Brower, Alan de Queiroz, Harry W. Greene, Alan H. Savitzky, Susan M. Smith, and John R. G. Turner reviewed a preliminary draft of the manuscript and made many helpful suggestions, as did two anonymous reviewers. Discussions of mimicry with Ben Dial, Paul Feeny, Douglas Futuyma, Carl Gans, Winnifred Hallwachs, James Huheey, Daniel Janzen, James Mallet, Roy McDiarmid, Janis Roze, Ellen Smith, and Yehudah Werner have challenged and sometimes changed my views, helped to clarify my ideas, and provided much additional information. George R. Zug kindly provided the currently accepted taxonomy of the reptilian taxa cited, and Linda Maloney translated German literature. I am very grateful to Carl Gans, Harry Greene, David Hardy, Ray Huey, Frances Irish, Daniel Janzen, Alan Savitzky, Wayne Van Devender, and Yehudah Werner for allowing me to reproduce their photographs and drawings in this chapter.

REFERENCES

Abalos, J. W., Baez, E. C. and Nader, R. (1964). Serpientes de Santiago del Estero. Acta Zool. Lilloana 20, 211–283.

Aiello, A. and Silberglied, R. E. (1978). Life history of *Dynastor darius* (Lepidoptera: Nymphalidae, Brassolinae) in Panama. Psyche 85, 331–345.

Alcock, J. (1970a). Punishment levels and the response of black-capped chickadees (*Parus atricapillus*) to three kinds of artificial seeds. Anim. Behav. 18, 592–599.

Alcock, J. (1970b). Punishment levels and the response of white-throated sparrows (*Zonotrichia albicollis*) to three kinds of artificial models and mimics. Anim. Behav. 18, 733–739.

Alcock, J. (1971). Interspecific differences in avian feeding behavior and the evolution of Batesian mimicry. Behaviour 40, 1–9.

Allen, E. R. and Neill, W. T. (1950). The alligator snapping turtle, *Macrochelys temminckii*. Ross Allen's Reptile Institute Spec. Publ. 4, 1–15.

Amaral, A. do. (1978). *Serpentes do Brasil*. Ed. da Universidade de São Paulo.

Anderson, J. A. (1964). A report on the gecko *Teratolepis fasciata* (Blyth, 1853). J. Bombay Nat. Hist. Soc. 61, 161–171.

Arbel, A. (1979). The coin-marked snake—a case of animal mimicry. Israel—Land and Nature 4, 112–114.

Arnold, S. J. (1978). The evolution of a special class of modifiable behaviors in relation to environmental pattern. Am. Nat. 112, 415–427.

Astort, E. (1983). Fauna Argentina: las falsas yacaraes. Centro Editor Am. Latina, No. 64.

Austad, S. N. and Howard, R. D. (eds). (1984). Alternative reproductive tactics. Am. Zool., 24, 307–418.

Baker, R. R. and Hounsome, M. V. (1983). Bird coloration: Unprofitable prey model supported by ringing data. Anim. Behav. 31, 614–615.

Baker, R. R. and Parker, G. A. (1979). The evolution of bird coloration. Phil. Trans. R. Soc. B, 287, 63–130.

Bannikov, A. G., Darevsky, I. S. and Rustamov, A. K. (1971). *Zemnovodny i presmuikaiushchiesya SSSR*. Izdatelstvo "Muisl," Moscow.

Bates, H. W. (1862). Contributions to an insect fauna of the Amazon Valley, Lepidoptera: Heliconidae. Trans. Linn. Soc. Lond. 23, 495–566.

Beebe, W. (1946). Field notes on snakes of Kartabo, British Guiana, and Caripito, Venezuela. Zoologica 31, 11–52.

Benson, W. W. (1977). On the supposed spectrum between Batesian and Müllerian mimicry. Evolution 31, 454–455.

Blest, A. D. (1957a). The function of eyespot patterns in the Lepidoptera. Behaviour 11, 209–256.

Blest, A. D. (1957b). The evolution of protective displays in the Saturnioidea and Sphingidae (Lepidoptera). Behaviour 11, 257–309.

Bobisud, L. E. and Potratz, C. J. (1976). One-trial learning versus multi-trial learning for a predator encountering a model-mimic system. Am. Nat. 110, 121–128.

Boyden, T. C. (1976). Butterfly palatability and mimicry: Experiments with *Ameiva* lizards. Evolution 30, 73–81.

Brattstrom, B. H. (1955). The coral snake "mimic" problem and protective coloration. Evolution 9, 217–219.

Broadley, D. G. and Cock, E. V. (1975). *Snakes of Rhodesia*. Longman Rhodesia, Salisbury.

Brower, J. V. Z. (1958a). Experimental studies of mimicry in some North American butterflies. I. *Danaus plexippus* and *Limenitis archippus archippus*. Evolution 12, 32–47.

Brower, J. V. Z. (1958b). Experimental studies of mimicry in some North American butterflies. II. *Battus philenor* and *Papilio troilus*, *P. polyxenes*, and *P. glaucus*. Evolution 12, 123–136.

Brower, J. V. Z. (1958c). Experimental studies of mimicry in some North American butterflies. III. *Danaus gilippus berenice* and *Limenitis archippus floridensis*. Evolution 12, 273–285.

REFERENCES

Brower, J. V. Z. (1960). Experimental studies of mimicry. IV. The reactions of starlings to different proportions of models and mimics. Am. Nat. 44, 271–282.

Brower, J. V. Z. (1963). Experimental studies and evidence on the evolution of mimicry in butterflies. In *Mimicry* (L.P. Brower, ed.). *Proc. XVI Internat. Congr. Zool.* 4, pp. 156–161.

Brower, J. V. Z. and Brower, L. P. (1965). Experimental studies of mimicry. 8. Further investigations of honeybees (*Apis mellifera*) and their dronefly mimics (*Eristalis* sp.). Am. Nat. 49, 173–188.

Brower, L. P. (1968). Motion picture, *Patterns for Survival: Study of Mimicry and Protective Coloration in Tropical Insects*. Amherst College, Amherst, MA.

Brower, L. P. (1971). Prey coloration and predator behavior. In *Topics in the Study of Life: The BIO Source Book. Section 6*. Harper and Row, New York, pp. 360–370.

Brower, L. P. (1984). Chemical defense in butterflies. In *The Biology of Butterflies*. (R. I. Vane-Wright and P. R. Ackery, eds.). Symp. Roy. Entomol. Soc. London. 11, 109–134.

Brower, L. P., Alcock, J. and Brower, J. V. Z. (1971). Avian feeding behaviour and the selective advantage of incipient mimicry. In *Ecological Genetics and Evolution*. (R. Creed, ed.). Blackwell Sci. Publ., Oxford, pp. 261–274.

Brower, L. P., Brower, J. V. Z. and Collins, C. T. (1963). Experimental studies of mimicry. 7. Relative palatability and Mullerian mimicry among neotropical butterflies of the subfamily Heliconiinae. Zoologica 48, 65–84.

Brower, L. P., Brower, J. V. Z. and Corvino, J. M. (1967a). Plant poisons in a terrestrial food chain. Proc. Natl. Acad. Sci. USA 57, 893–898.

Brower, L. P., Brower, J. V. Z., Stiles, F. G., Croze, H. J. and Hower, A. S. (1964). Mimicry: Differential advantage of color patterns in the natural environment. Science, 144, 183–185.

Brower, L. P., Cook, L. M. and Croze, H. J. (1967b). Predator responses to artificial Batesian mimics released in a neotropical environment. Evolution 21, 11–23.

Brower, L. P., Gibson, D. O., Moffitt, C. M. and Panchen, A. L. (1978). Cardenolide content of *Danaus chrysippus* butterflies from three areas of East Africa. Biol. J. Linn. Soc. Lond. 10, 251–273.

Brower, L. P., McEvoy, P. B., Williamson, K. L. and Flannery, M. A. (1972). Variation in cardiac glycoside content of monarch butterflies from natural populations in eastern North America. Science, 177, 426–429.

Brower, L. P. and Moffitt, C. M. (1974). Palatability dynamics of cardenolides in the monarch butterfly. Nature, 249, 280–283.

Brower, L. P., Pough, F. H. and Meck, H. R. (1970). Theoretical investigations of automimicry. I. Single trial learning. Proc. Natl. Acad. Sci. USA 66, 1059–1066.

Brown, K. S., Jr., Sheppard, P. M. and Turner, J. R. G. (1974). Quaternary refugia in tropical America: Evidence from race formation in *Heliconius* butterflies. Proc. Roy. Soc. Lond. B 187, 369–378.

Bustard, H. R. (1968). *Pygopus nigriceps* (Fischer): A lizard mimicking a venomous snake. Br. J. Herpetol. 4, 22–24.

Bustard, H. R. (1969). Defensive behavior and locomotion of the Pacific boa, *Candoiaaspera*, with a brief review of head concealment in snakes. Herpetologica 25, 164–170.

Caldwell, G. S. and Rubinoff, R. W. (1983). Avoidance of venomous sea snakes by naive herons and egrets. Auk 100, 195–198.

Calvert, W. H., Hedrick, L. E. and Brower, L. P. (1979). Mortality of the monarch butterfly (*Danaus plexippus*) due to avian predation at five overwintering sites in Mexico. Science, 204, 847–851.

Campden-Main, S. M. (1970). *A Field Guide to the Snakes of South Vietnam*. Division of Reptiles and Amphibians, United States National Museum, Washington, DC.
Carpenter, C. C., Murphy, J. B. and Carpenter, G. C. (1978). Tail luring in the death adder, *Acanthophis antarcticus* (Reptilia, Serpentes, Elapidae). J. Herpetol. 12, 574–577.
Carpenter, G. D. H. and Ford, E. B. (1933). *Mimicry*. Metheun & Co. Ltd., London.
Carr, A. F. (1952). *Handbook of Turtles*. Cornell Univ. Press, Ithaca, NY.
Charnov, E. L. and Krebs, J. R. (1975). The evolution of alarm calls: Altruism or manipulation? Am. Nat. 109, 107–112.
Cloudsley-Thompson, J. L. (1981). Comments on the nature of deception. Biol. J. Linn. Soc. (Lond.) 16, 11–14.
Cogger, H. G. (1979). *Reptiles and Amphibians of Australia*. Revised ed. A. H. & A. W. Reed, Sydney.
Conant, R. (1943). The milk snakes of the Atlantic coastal plain. Proc. New Engl. Zool. Club 22, 3–24.
Conant, R. (1975). *A Field Guide to Reptiles and Amphibians of Eastern and Central North America*. 2nd ed. Houghton Mifflin, Boston.
Congdon, J. D., Vitt, L. J. and King, W. W. (1974). Geckos: Adaptive significance and energetics of tail autotomy. Science 184, 1379–1380.
Cook, L. M., Brower, L. P. and Alcock, J. (1969). An attempt to verify mimetic advantage in a neotropical environment. Evolution 23, 339–345.
Cope, E. D. (1860). Catalogue of the Colubridae in the Museum of the Academy of Natural Sciences of Philadelphia, with notes and descriptions of new species. Proc. Acad. Nat. Sci. Philadelphia 12, 241–266.
Coppinger, R. P. (1969). The effect of experience and novelty on avian feeding behaviour with reference to the evolution of warning coloration in butterflies. Part I: Reactions of wild caught adult blue jays to novel insects. Behaviour 35, 45–60.
Coppinger, R. P. (1970). The effect of experience and novelty on avian feeding behaviour with reference to the evolution of warning coloration in butterflies. Part II: Reactions of naive birds to novel insects. Am. Nat. 104, 323–335.
Cott, H. B. (1940). *Adaptive Coloration in Animals*. Oxford Univ. Press, New York.
Cott, H. B. (1969). The palatability of birds, mainly based upon the observations of a tasting panel in Zambia. Ostrich, suppl. 8, 357–384.
Crews, D. (1978). Integration of internal and external stimuli in the regulation of lizard reproduction. In *Behavior and Neurobiology of Lizards*. (N. Greenberg and P. D. MacLean, eds). NIHM, Rockville, Maryland, pp. 149–171.
Dawley, E. M. (1984). Recognition of individual, sex, and species odours by salamanders of the *Plethodon glutinosus–P. jordani* complex. Anim. Behav. 32, 353–361.
Deoras, P. J. (1965). *Snakes of India*. National Book Trust, New Delhi.
Dial, B. E. (1986). Tail display in two species of iguanid lizards: A test of the "predator signal" hypothesis. Am. Nat. 127, 103–111.
Dominey, W. J. (1984). Alternative mating tactics and evolutionarily stable strategies. Am. Zool. 24, 385–396.
Drummond, H. and Gordon, E. R. (1979). Luring in the neonate alligator snapping turtle (*Macroclemys temminckii*): Description and experimental analysis. Z. Tierpsychol. 50, 136–152.
Duellman, W. E. (1963). Amphibians and reptiles of the rainforests of southern El Petén, Guatemala. Univ. Kansas Publ. Mus. Nat. Hist. 15, 205–249.
Duellman, W. E. (1978). The biology of an equatorial herpetofauna in Amazonian Ecuador. Univ. Kansas Mus. Nat. Hist. Misc. Publ. 65, 1–352.

REFERENCES

Dugan, B. (1982). The mating behavior of the green iguana, *Iguana iguana*. In *Iguanas of the World*. (G. M. Burghardt and A. S. Rand, eds). Noyes Publications, Park Ridge, NJ, pp. 320–341.
Duncan, C. J. and Sheppard, P. M. (1965). Sensory discrimination and its role in the evolution of Batesian mimicry. Behaviour 24, 269–282.
Dunn, E. R. (1954). The coral snake "mimic" problem in Panama. Evolution 8, 97–102.
Edmunds, M. (1974). *Defence in Animals*. Longman, Harlow, Essex, England.
Edmunds, M. (1981). On defining "mimicry." Biol. J. Linn. Soc. (Lond.) 16, 9–10.
Emlen, J. M. (1968). Batesian mimicry: A preliminary theoretical invetigation of quantitative aspects. Am. Nat. 102, 235–241.
Emsley, M. G. (1966). The mimetic significance of *Erythrolamprus aesculapii ocellatus* Peters from Tobago. Evolution 20, 663–664.
Endler, J. A. (1981). An overview of the relationships between mimicry and crypsis. Biol. J. Linn. Soc. (Lond.) 16, 25–31.
Estabrook, G. F. and Jespersen, D. C. (1974). Strategy for a predator encountering a model-mimic system. Am. Nat. 108, 443–457.
Fink, L. S. and Brower, L. P. (1981). Birds can overcome the cardenolide defense of monarch butterflies in Mexico. Nature, 291, 67–70.
FitzSimons, V. F. M. (1970). *A Field Guide to the Snakes of Southern Africa*. Collins, London.
FitzSimons, V. F. M. and Brain, C. K. (1958). A short account of the reptiles of the Kalahari Gemsbok National Park. Koedoe 1, 99–104.
Flower, S. S. (1899). Notes on a second collection of reptiles made in the Malay Peninsula and Siam, from November 1896 to September 1898, with a list of species recorded from those countries. Proc. Zool. Soc. Lond., 600–696.
Fogden, M. and Fogden, P. (1974). *Animals and Their Colors*. Crown, New York.
Ford, E. B. (1964). *Ecological Genetics*. Chapman and Hall Ltd., London.
Freiberg, M. (1982). *Snakes of South America*. T. F. H. Publs., Neptune City, NJ.
Gadow, H. (1911). Isotely and coralsnakes. Zool. Jahrb. Abt. Syst. 31, 1–24.
Gans, C. (1961). Mimicry in procryptically colored snakes of the genus *Dasypeltis*. Evolution 15, 72–91.
Gans, C. (1964). Empathic learning and the mimicry of African snakes. Evolution 18, 705.
Gans, C. (1974). *Biomechanics, An Approach to Vertebrate Biology*. J. B. Lippincott, Philadelphia; Univ. Michigan Press, Ann Arbor.
Gans, C. (1976). Aspects of the biology of uropeltid snakes. In *Morphology and Biology of Reptiles*. (A. d'A. Bellairs and C. B. Cox, eds.). Linnean Soc. Symp. Ser. 3,191–204.
Gans, C. (1978). Reptilian venoms: Some evolutionary considerations. In *Biology of the Reptilia*. (C. Gans and K. A. Gans, eds.). Academic Press, London, Volume 8, pp. 1–42.
Gans, C. (1987). Automimicry and Batesian mimicry in uropeltid snakes: Pigment, proportions, pattern, and behavior. J. Bombay Nat. Hist. Soc., 83 (Suppl.), 153–158.
Gans, C. and Baic, D. (1974). Convergent surface structures in the sound producing scales of some snakes (Reptilia: Serpentes). In *Recherches Biologie Contemporaine*. (L. Arvie, ed.), pp. 265–272.
Gans, C. and Latifi, M. (1973). Another case of presumptive mimicry in snakes. Copeia 1973, 801–802.
Gans, C. and Richmond, N. D. (1957). Warning behavior in snakes of the genus *Dasypeltis*. Copeia 1957, 269–274.
Gehlbach, F. R. (1970). Death-feigning and erratic behavior in leptotyphlopid, colubrid, and elapid snakes. Herpetologica 26, 24–34.

Gehlbach, F. R. (1972). Coral snake mimicry reconsidered: The strategy of self-mimicry. Forma et Functio 5, 311–320.

Gharpurey, K. G. (1962). *The Snakes of India and Pakistan*. 5th ed. Popular Book Depot, Bombay.

Gingerich, P. D. (1975). Is the aardwolf a mimic of the hyaena? Nature 253, 191–192.

Gittleman, J. L., Harvey, P. M. and Greenwood, P. J. (1980). The evolution of conspicuous coloration: Some experiments in bad taste. Anim. Behav. 28, 897–899.

Goldschmidt, R. B. (1945). Mimetic polymorphism, a controversial chapter of Darwinism. Quart. Rev. Biol. 20, 147–164, 205–230.

Goodale, M. A. and Sneddon, I. (1977). The effect of distastefulness of the model on the predation of artificial Batesian mimics. Anim. Behav. 25, 660–665.

Goode, G. B. (1873). Mimicry in snakes. Am. Nat. 7, 747–748.

Goodhart, C. G. (1975). Does the aardwolf mimic a hyaena? Zool. J. Linn. Soc. 57, 349–356.

Goodman, J. D. (1974). Birds and snakes—A neglected study. Indiana Audubon Quarterly 52, 56–57.

Goodman, J. D. and Goodman, J. M. (1976a). Contrasting color and pattern as enticement display in snakes. Herpetologica 32, 145–148.

Goodman, J. D. and Goodman, J. M. (1976b). Possible mimetic behavior of the twig snake, *Thelotornis kirtlandi kirtlandi* (Hallowell). Herpetologica 32, 148–150.

Greene, H. W. (1973). Defensive tail displays by snakes and amphisbaenians. J. Herpetol. 7, 143–161.

Greene, H. W. (1975). Ecological observations on the red coffee snake, *Ninia sebae*, in southern Veracruz, Mexico. Am. Midl. Nat. 93, 478–484.

Greene, H. W. (1977). The aardwolf as a hyaena mimic: An open question. Anim. Behav. 25, 245.

Greene, H. W. (1979). Behavioral convergence in the defensive displays of snakes. Experientia 35, 747–748.

Greene, H. W. and Campbell, J. A. (1972). Notes on the use of caudal lures by arboreal green pit vipers. Herpetologica 28, 32–34.

Greene, H. W. and McDiarmid, R. W. (1981). Coral snake mimicry: Does it occur? Science 213, 1207–1212.

Greene, H. W. and Pyburn, W. F. (1973). Comments on aposematism and mimicry among coral snakes. Biologist 55, 144–148.

Grobman, A. B. (1978). An alternative solution to the coral snake mimic problem (Reptilia, Serpentes, Elapidae). J. Herpetol. 12, 1–11.

Guthrie, R. D. and Petocz, R. G. (1970). Weapon automimicry among mammals. Am. Nat. 104, 585–588.

Haber, W. A. (1983). Checklist of Sphingidae. In *Costa Rican Natural History*. (D. H. Janzen, ed.). Univ. Chicago Press, Chicago, pp. 645–650.

Hailman, J. P. (1977). *Optical Signals: Animal Communication and Light*. Indiana Univ. Press, Bloomington.

Hall, T. S. (1905). A lizard mimicking a poisonous snake. Vict. Nat. 22, 74.

Halstead, B. W. (1965). *Poisonous and Venomous Marine Animals of the World*. Vol. 1, Invertebrates. U.S. Gov. Printing Office, Washington, DC.

Harvey, P. M., Bull, J. J., Pemberton, M. and Paxton, R. J. (1982). The evolution of aposematic coloration in distasteful prey: A family model. Am. Nat. 119, 710–719.

Harvey, P. M. and Greenwood, P. J. (1978). Anti-predator defence strategies: Some evolutionary problems. In *Behavioural Ecology: An Evolutionary Approach*. (J. R. Krebs and N. B. Davies, eds.). Blackwell, Oxford, pp. 129–151.

REFERENCES

Harvey, P. M. and Paxton, P. J. (1981a). The evolution of aposematic coloration. Oikos 37, 391–393.
Harvey, P. M. and Paxton, P. J. (1981b). On aposematic coloration: A rejoinder. *Oikos* 37, 395–396.
Heatwole, H. and Davison, E. (1976). A review of caudal luring in snakes with notes on its occurrence in the Saharan sand viper, *Cerastes vipera.* Herpetologica 32, 332–336.
Hecht, M. K. and Marien, D. (1956). The coral snake mimic problem: A reinterpretation. J. Morphol. 98, 335–356.
Hecht, M. K., Walters, V. and Ramm, G. (1955). Observations on the natural history of the Bahaman pygmy boa, with notes on auto hemorrhage. Copeia 1955, 249–251.
Henderson, R. W. (1970). Caudal luring in a juvenile Russell's viper. Herpetologica 26, 276–277.
Henderson, R. W. (1977). The head-neck display of *Ninia s. sebae* (Reptilia, Serpentes, Colubridae) in northern Belize. J. Herpetol. 11, 106–108.
Henderson, R. W. (1984). *Scaphiodontophis* (Serpentes: Colubridae): Natural history and test of a mimicry-related hypothesis. In *Vertebrate Ecology and Systematics, A Tribute to Henry S. Fitch.* (R. A. Seigel, L. E. Hunt, J. L. Knight, L. Malaret, and N. L. Zuschlag, eds.). Univ. Kansas Mus. Nat. Hist., Spec. Publ. 10, 185–194.
Hogue, C. L. (1984). Observations on the plant hosts and possible mimicry models of "lantern bugs" (*Fulgora* spp.) (Homoptera: Fulgoridae). Rev. Biol. Trop. 32, 145–150.
Holling, C. S. (1963). Mimicry and predator behavior. In *Mimicry.* (L. P. Brower, ed.). Proc. XVI Internat. Congr. Zool. 4, 166–177.
Holling, C. S. (1965). The functional response of predators to prey density and its role in mimicry and population regulation. Mem. Entomol. Soc. Canada 45, 1–60.
Huey, R. B. and Pianka, E. R. (1977). Natural selection for juvenile lizards mimicking noxious beetles. Science 195, 201–203.
Huheey, J. E. (1961). Studies in warning coloration and mimicry. III. Evolution of Mullerian mimicry. Evolution 15, 567–568.
Huheey, J. E. (1964). Studies of warning coloration and mimicry. IV. A mathematical model of model-mimic frequencies. Ecology 45, 185–188.
Huheey, J. E. (1976). Studies in warning coloration and mimicry. VII. Evolutionary consequences of a Batesian–Müllerian spectrum: a model for Müllerian mimicry. Evolution 30, 86–93.
Huheey, J. E. (1980a). Studies in warning coloration and mimicry. VIII. Further evidence for a frequency dependent model of predation. J. Herpetol. 14, 223–230.
Huheey, J. E. (1980b). Batesian and Müllerian mimicry: Semantic and substantive differences of opinion. Evolution 34, 1212–1215.
Humphries, D. A. and Driver, P. M. (1970). Protean defence by prey animals. Oecologia (Berl.) 5, 285–302.
Jackson, J. F., Ingram, W., III, and Campbell, H. W. (1976). The dorsal pigmentation pattern of snakes as an antipredator strategy: A multivariate approach. Am. Nat. 110, 1029–1053.
Jackson, J. F. and Pounds, J. A. (1980). Of differential head-body pigmentation in snakes. J. Herpetol. 14, 307–311.
Jacobs, G. H. (1982). *Comparative Color Vision.* Academic Press, New York.
Jaeger, R. G. (1981). Dear enemy recognition and the costs of aggression between salamanders. Am. Nat. 117, 962–974.
Jaeger, R. G. and Gergits, W. F. (1979). Intra- and interspecific communication in salamanders through chemical signals on the substrate. Anim. Behav. 27, 150–156.

Jaksić, R. M. and Greene, H. W. (1984). Empirical evidence of non-correlation between tail loss frequency and predation intensity on lizards. Oikos 42, 407–411.
Janzen, D. H. (1980). Two potential coral snake mimics in a tropical deciduous forest. Biotropica 12, 77–78.
Janzen, D. H. (1983). *Pseudosphinx tetrio*. In *Costa Rican Natural History*. (D. H. Janzen, ed.). Univ. Chicago Press, Chicago, pp. 764–765.
Järvi, T., Sillen-Tullberg, B. and Wirklund, C. (1981a). The cost of being aposematic. An experimental study of predation on larvae of *Papilio machon* by the great tit *Parus major*. Oikos 36, 267–272.
Järvi, T., Sillen-Tullberg, B. and Wirklund, C. (1981b). Individual versus kin selection for aposematic coloration: A reply to Harvey and Paxton. Oikos 37, 393–395.
Jeffords, M. R., Sternburg, J. G. and Waldbauer, G. P. (1979). Batesian mimicry: Field demonstration of the survival value of the pipevine swallowtail and monarch color patterns. Evolution 33, 275–286.
Jeffords, M. R., Waldbauer, G. P. and Sternburg, J. G. (1980). Determination of the time of day at which diurnal moths painted to resemble butterflies are attacked by birds. Evolution 34, 1205–1211.
Jouventin, P., Pasteur, G. and Cambefort, J. P. (1977). Observational learning of baboons and avoidance of mimics: exploratory tests. Evolution 31, 214–218.
Kardong, K. V. (1980). Gopher snakes and rattlesnakes: Presumptive Batesian mimicry. Northwest Sci. 54, 1–4.
Kaufmann, J. H. (1962). Ecology and social behavior of the coati (*Nasua narica*) on Barro Colorado Island, Panama. Univ. Calif. Publ. Zool. 60, 95–222.
Keiser, E. D., Jr. (1975). Observations on tongue extension of vine snakes (genus *Oxybelis*) with suggested behavioral hypotheses. Herpetologica 31, 131–133.
Khalaf, K. T. (1959). *Reptiles of Iraq*. Ar-Rabitta Press, Baghdad.
Kochva, E. (1978). Oral glands of the Reptilia. In *Biology of the Reptilia*. (C. Gans and K. A. Gans, eds.). Academic Press, London, Volume 8, pp. 43–161.
Kochva, E., Nakar, O. and Ovadia, M. (1983). Venom toxins: Plausible evolution from digestive enzymes. Am. Zool. 23, 427–430.
Kroon, C. (1975). A possible Müllerian mimetic complex among snakes. Copeia 1975, 425–428.
Kropach, C. (1975). The yellow-bellied sea snake, *Pelamis*, in the eastern Pacific. In *The Biology of Sea Snakes*. (W. A. Denson, ed.). Univ. Park Press, Baltimore, pp. 185–213.
Kubie, J. L., Vagvolgyi, A. and Halpern, M. (1978). Roles of the vomeronasal and olfactory systems in courtship behavior of male garter snakes. J. Comp. Physiol. Psychol. 92, 627–641.
Kuntz, R. E. (1963). *Snakes of Taiwan*. U.S. Medical Research Unit No. 2.
Leroy, Y. (1979). *L'Universa Sonore Animal*. Bordas, Paris.
Lönnberg, E. (1902). On a collection of snakes from north-western Argentina and Bolivia containing new species. Ann. Mag. Nat. Hist. 10, (seventh series), 457–462.
Maldonado, H. (1970). The deimatic reaction in the praying mantis *Stagmatoptera biocellata*. Z. vergl. Physiol. 68, 60–71.
Martin, D. J. (1973). A spectrographic analysis of burrowing owl vocalizations. Auk 90, 564–578.
Marx, H., Rabb, G. B. and Arnold, S. J. (1982). *Pythonodipsas* and *Spalerosophis*, colubrid snake genera convergent to the vipers. Copeia 1982, 553–561.
Mason, R. T. and Crews, D. (1985). Female mimicry in garter snakes. Nature 316, 59–60.
Maynard Smith, J. (1965). The evolution of alarm calls. Am. Nat. 99, 59–63.

REFERENCES

McDowell, S. B. (1979). A catalogue of the snakes of New Guinea and the Solomons, with special reference to those in the Bernice P. Bishop Museum. Part III. Boinae and Acrochordoidea (Reptilia, Serpentes). J. Herpetol. 13, 1–92.

Mebs, D. (1978). Pharmacology of reptilian venoms. In *Biology of the Reptilia*. (C. Gans and K. A. Gans, eds). Academic Press, London, Volume 8, 437–560.

Mertens, R. (1946). Die Warn- und Droh-Reaktionen der Reptilien. Abh. Senckenb. Naturforsch. Ges. 471, 1–108.

Mertens, R. (1955). Die Amphibien und Reptilien Südwestafrikas. Aus den Ergebnissen einer im Jahre 1952 ausgeführten Reise. Abh. Senckenb. Naturforsch. Ges. 490, 1–172.

Mertens, R. (1957). Gibt es eine Mimikry bei Korallenschlangen? Nat. Volk 87, 56–66.

Mertens, R. (1966). Das Problem der Mimikry bei Korallenschlangen. Zool. Jahrb. Syst. 84, 541–576.

Minton, S. A., Jr. (1966). A contribution to the herpetology of West Pakistan. Bull. Am. Mus. Nat. Hist. 134, 27–184.

Minton, S. A. (1975). Geographic distribution of sea snakes. In *The Biology of Sea Snakes*. (W. A. Dunson, ed.). Univ. Park Press, Baltimore, pp. 21–31.

Morgan, C. L. (1900). *Animal Behaviour*. Edward Arnold, London.

Morrell, R. (1954). Eyes that are no eyes. Malay. Nat. J. 9, 94–97.

Morrell, R. (1969). Play snake for safety. Animals 12, 154–155.

Müller, F. (1879). *Ituna* and *Thyridia*; a remarkable case of mimicry in butterflies. Proc. Entomol. Soc. Lond. 1879, xx–xxix.

Muntz, W. R. A. (1974). Comparative aspects in behavioural studies of vertebrate vision. In *The Eye*. (H. Davson, ed.). Academic Press, London, Volume 6, pp. 155–226.

Murphy, J. B., Carpenter, C. C. and Gillingham, J. C. (1978). Caudal luring in the green tree python, *Chondropython viridis* (Reptilia, Serpentes, Boidae). J. Herpetol. 12, 117–119.

Myers, C. W. (1974). The systematics of *Rhadinaea* (Colubridae), a genus of New World snakes. Bull. Am. Mus. Nat. Hist. 153, 1–262.

Nakamura, K. and Uéno, S.-I. (1963). *Japanese Reptiles and Amphibians in Colour*. Hoikusha, Osaka.

Neill, W. T. (1960). The caudal lure of various juvenile snakes. Quart. J. Fla. Acad. Sci. 23, 173–200.

Neill, W. T. (1965). New and noteworthy amphibians and reptiles from British Honduras. Bull. Florida State Museum 9, 77–130.

Nicholson, A. J. (1927). A new theory of mimicry in insects. Aust. Zool. 5, 10–104.

O'Donald, P. and Pilecki, C. (1970). Polymorphic mimicry and natural selection. Evolution 24, 395–401.

Otte, D. (1974). Effects and functions in the evolution of signalling systems. Ann. Rev. Ecol. Syst. 5, 385–417.

Otte, D. (1975). On the role of intraspecific deception. Am. Nat. 109, 239–242.

Owen, D. (1980). *Camouflage and Mimicry*. Univ. Chicago Press, Chicago.

Papageorgis, C. (1975). Mimicry in neotropical butterflies. Am. Sci. 63, 522–532.

Parker, W. S. and Pianka, E. R. (1974). Further ecological observations on the western banded gecko, *Coleonyx variegatus*. Copeia 1974, 528–531.

Pasteur, G. (1972). *Le Mimétisme*. Presses Universitaires de France, Paris.

Pasteur, G. (1982). A classificatory review of mimicry systems. Ann. Rev. Ecol. Syst. 13, 169–199.

Pearson, D. L. (1985). The function of multiple anti-predator mechanisms in adult tiger beetles (Coleoptera: Cicindelidae). Ecol. Entomol. 10, 65–72.

Pernetta, J. C. (1977). Observations on the habits and morphology of the sea snake *Laticauda colubrina* (Schneider) in Fiji. Can. J. Zool. 55, 1612–1619.

Pilecki, C. and O'Donald, P. (1971). The effects of predation on artificial mimetic polymorphisms with perfect and imperfect mimics at varying frequencies. Evolution 25, 365–370.

Pitman, C. R. S. (1974). *A Guide to the Snakes of Uganda*. Revised ed. Wheldon and Wesley, Ltd., Codicote.

Platt, A. P. and Brower, L. P. (1968). Mimetic versus disruptive coloration in intergrading populations of *Limenitis arthemis* and *Astyanax* butterflies. Evolution 22, 699–718.

Pough, F. H. (1976). Multiple cryptic effects of crossbanded and ringed patterns of snakes. Copeia 1976, 834–836.

Pough, F. H. (In press). Mimicry of vertebrates: Are the rules different? Am. Nat.

Pough, F. H. and Brower, L. P. (1977). Predation by birds on great southern white butterflies as a function of palatability, sex, and habitat. Am. Midl. Nat. 98, 50–58.

Pough, F. H., Brower, L. P., Meck, H. R. and Kessell, S. R. (1973). Theoretical investigations of automimicry: Multiple trial learning and the palatability spectrum. Proc. Natl. Acad. Sci. USA 70, 2261–2265.

Pough, F. H. and Groves, J. D. (1983). Specializations of the body form and food habits of snakes. Am. Zool. 23, 443–454.

Pough, F. H., Kwiecinski, G. and Bemis, W. (1978). Melanin deposits associated with the venom glands of snakes. J. Morphol. 155, 63–72.

Poulton, E. B. (1890). *The Colors of Animlas*. Appleton, New York.

Poulton, E. B. (1924). The terrifying appearance of *Laternaria* (Fulgoridae) founded on the most prominent features of the alligator. Proc. Entomol. Soc. Lond., xlii–xlix.

Punnet, R. C. (1915). *Mimicry in Butterflies*. University Press, Cambridge.

Rand, A. S. (1967). Ecology and social organization in the iguanid lizard *Anolis lineatopus*. Proc. U.S. Natl. Mus. 122, No. 3595, 1–79.

Rand, A. S. and Ortleb, E. P. (1969). Defensive display of the colubrid snake *Pseustes poecilonotus shropshirei*. Herpetologica 25, 46–48.

Rankin, P. R. (1973). Lizard mimicking a snake—juvenile *Tiliqua casuarinae* (Duméril and Bibron). Herpetofauna 5(4), 13–14.

Remington, C. L. (1963). Historical backgrounds of mimicry. In *Mimicry*. (L. P. Brower, ed.). Proc. XVI Internat. Congr. Zool. 4, 145–149.

Rettenmeyer, C. W. (1970). Insect mimicry. Ann. Rev. Entomol. 15, 43–76.

Robinson, M. H. (1981). A stick is a stick and not worth eating: On the definition of mimicry. Biol. J. Linn. Soc. (Lond.) 16, 15–20.

Rothschild, M. (1981). The mimicrats must move with the times. Biol. J. Linn. Soc. (Lond.) 16, 21–23.

Rowe, M. P. (1984). *California Ground Squirrels and Their Burrow Coinhabitants: Communicatory Coevolution Between Predators and Prey*. Ph.D. Thesis, University of California, Davis.

Rowe, M. P., Goss, R. G. and Owings, D. H. (1986). Rattlesnake rattles and burrowing owl hisses: A case of acoustic Batesian mimicry. Ethology 72, 53–71.

Roze, J. A. (1966). *La Taxonomia y Zoogeographia de las Ofidios en Venezuela*. Univ. Central de Venezuela, Caracas.

Roze, J. A. (1967). A check list of the New World venomous coral snakes (Elapidae), with descriptions of new forms. *Am. Mus. Novitates* 2287, 1–60.

Rubinoff, I. and Kropach, C. (1970). Differential reactions of Atlantic and Pacific predators to sea snakes. Nature 228, 1288–1290.

REFERENCES

Russell, F. E. (1980). *Snake Venom Poisoning.* J. B. Lippincott Co., Philadelphia.
Sapwell, J. (1968). An unusual defensive display by a West African snake, *Crotaphopeltis hotamboeia hotamboeia* (Laurenti). Herpetologica 25, 314–315.
Savage, J. M. and Vial, J. L. (1974). The venomous coral snakes (genus *Micrurus*) of Costa Rica. Rev. Biol. Trop. 21, 295–349.
Savitzky, A. H. (1980). The role of venom delivery strategies in snake evolution. Evolution 34, 1194–1204.
Savitzky, A. H. (1983). Coadapted character complexes among snakes: Fossoriality, piscivory, and durophagy. Am. Zool. 23, 397–409.
Schoener, T. W. (1979). Inferring the properties of predation and other injury-producing agents from injury frequencies. Ecology 60, 1110–1115.
Schoener, T. W. and Schoener, A. (1980). Ecological and demographic correlations of injury rates in some Bahamian *Anolis* lizards. Copeia 1980, 839–850.
Schuett, G. W. (1984). *Calloselasma rhodostoma* (Malayan pit viper): Feeding mimicry. Herpetol. Rev. 15, 112.
Schuett, G. W., Clark, D. L. and Kraus, F. (1984). Feeding mimicry in the rattlesnake *Sistrurus catenatus* with comments on the evolution of the rattle. Anim. Behav. 32, 625–626.
Seib, R. L. (1980). Human envenomation from the bite of an aglyphous false coral snake, *Pliocercus elapoides* (Serpentes: Colubridae). Toxicon 18, 399–401.
Sexton, O. J. (1960). Experimental studies of artificial Batesian mimics. Behaviour 15, 244–252.
Sexton, O. J., Hoger, C. and Ortleb, E. (1966). *Anolis carolinensis*: Effects of feeding on reactions to aposematic prey. Science 153, 1140.
Sheppard, P. M. (1962). Some aspects of the geography, genetics, and taxonomy of a butterfly. Publ. Syst. Assoc. 4, 135–152.
Sheppard, P. M. and Turner, J. R. G. (1977). The existence of Müllerian mimicry. Evolution 31, 452–453.
Silberglied, R. (1979). Communication in the ultraviolet. Ann. Rev. Ecol. Syst. 10, 373–398.
Smith, M. A. (1943) *Fauna of British India. Amphibia and Reptilia, Vol. 3, Serpentes.* Taylor and Francis, London, reprinted 1961 by Manager of Publication, Delhi.
Smith, M. A. (1969). *The British Reptiles and Amphibians.* 4th ed. Collins, London.
Smith, R. H. (1974). Is the slow worm a Batesian mimic? Nature 247, 571–572.
Smith, S. M. (1975). Innate recognition of coral snake pattern by a possible avian predator. Science 187, 759–760.
Smith, S. M. (1977). Coral-snake pattern recognition and stimulus generalisation by naive great kiskadees (Aves: Tyrannidae). Nature 265, 535–536.
Smith, S. M. (1978). Predatory behaviour of young great kiskadees (*Pitangus sulphuratus*). Anim. Behav. 26, 988–995.
Smith, S. M. (1980). Responses of naive temperate birds to warning colors. Am. Midl. Nat. 103, 346–352.
Smith, S. M. and Mostrom, A. M. (1985). "Coral snake" rings: Are they helpful in foraging? Copeia 1985, 384–387.
Stamps, J. A. (1983). Sexual selection, sexual dimorphism, and territoriality. In *Lizard Ecology, Studies of a Model Organism.* (R. B. Huey, E. R. Pianka, and T. W. Schoener, eds.). Harvard Univ. Press, Cambridge, MA.
Stebbins, R. C. (1966). *A Field Guide to Western Reptiles and Amphibians.* Houghton Mifflin, Boston.
Sternburg, J. G., Waldbauer, G. P. and Jeffords, M. R. (1977). Batesian mimicry: Selective advantage of color pattern. Science 195, 681–683.

Sternfeld, R. (1908). Mimicry bei afrikanischen Schlangen. *Sitzber. Ges. Naturf. Freunde Berlin* 1, 89–91.
Sternfeld, R. (1910). Zur Schlangenfauna Deutsch-Südwestafricas. *Mitt. Zool. Mus. Berlin* 5, 51–60.
Sternfeld, R. (1913). Die Erscheinungen der Mimicry bei den Schlangen. *Sitzber. Ges. Naturf. Freunde Berlin* 2, 98–117, plates 10–13.
Steward, J. W. (1971). *The Snakes of Europe*. David and Charles, Newton Abbot.
Stradling, D. J. (1976). The nature of the mimetic patterns of the brassolid genera, *Caligo* and *Eryphanis*. *Ecol. Entomol.* 1, 135–138.
Sweet, S. S. (1985). Geographic variation, convergent crypsis and mimicry in gopher snakes (*Pituophis melanoleucus*) and western rattlesnakes (*Crotalus viridis*). *J. Herpetol.* 19, 55–67.
Taylor, E. H. (1922). *The Snakes of the Philippine Islands*. Publ. No. 16, Bureau of Printing, Department of Agriculture and Natural Resources, Manila.
Taylor, E. H. (1965). The serpents of Thailand and adjacent waters. *Univ. Kansas Sci. Bull.* 45, 609–1096.
Terhune, E. C. (1977). Components of a visual stimulus used by scrub jays to discriminate a Batesian model. *Am. Nat.* 111, 435–451.
Thomsen, L. (1971). Behavior and ecology of burrowing owls on the Oakland Municipal Airport. *Condor* 73, 177–192.
Thornhill, R. (1979). Adaptive female-mimicking behavior in a scorpionfly. *Science* 205, 412–414.
Trivers, R. L. (1976). Sexual selection and resource-accruing abilities in *Anolis garmanii*. *Evolution* 30, 253–269.
Turner, J. R. G. (1975). A tale of two butterflies. *Nat. Hist.* 84(2), 28–37.
Turner, J. R. G. (1977). Butterfly mimicry: The genetical evolution of an adaptation. *Evol. Biol.* 10, 163–206.
Turner, J. R. G. (1983a). The hypothesis that explains mimetic resemblance explains evolution; the gradualist-saltationist schism. In *Dimensions of Darwinism*. (M. Greene, ed.). Cambridge Univ. Press, Cambridge, pp. 129–169.
Turner, J. R. G. (1983b). Mimetic butterflies and punctuated equilibria: Some old light on a new paradigm. *Biol. J. Linn. Soc.* 20, 277–300.
Turner, J. R. G. (1984). Mimicry: The palatability spectrum and its consequences. In *The Biology of Butterflies*. (R. I. Vane-Wright and P. R. Ackery, eds.). Symp. Roy. Entomol. Soc. 11, 141–161.
Turner, J. R. G., Kearney, E. P. and Exton, L. S. (1984). Mimicry and the Monte Carlo predator: The palatability spectrum and the origins of mimicry. *Biol. J. Linn. Soc.* (Lond.) 23, 247–268.
Tweedie, M. W. F. (1953). *The Snakes of Malaya*. Government Printing Office, Singapore.
Vane-Wright, R. I. (1976). A unified classification of mimetic resemblances. *Biol. J. Linn. Soc.* (Lond.) 8, 25–56.
Vane-Wright, R. I. (1980). On the definition of mimicry. *Biol. J. Linn. Soc.* (Lond.) 13, 1–6.
Vane-Wright, R. I. (1981). Only connect. *Biol. J. Linn. Soc.* (Lond.) 16, 33–40.
Vasconcellos-Neto, J. and Lewinsohn, T. M. (1984). Discrimination and release of unpalatable butterflies by *Nephila clavipes*, a neotropical orb-weaving spider. *Ecol. Entomol.* 9, 337–344.
Villiers, A. (1975). *Les Serpents de l'Ouest Africain*. Initiations et Etudes Africaines, No. 2, 3rd ed. I.F.A.N., Dakar.
Waldbauer, G. P. and Sternburg, J. G. (1976). Saturniid moths as mimics: An alternative

REFERENCES

interpretation of attempts to demonstrate mimetic advantage in nature. Evolution 29, 650–658.

Wall, F. (1913). *The Poisonous Terrestrial Snakes of our British Indian Dominions (Including Ceylon) and How to Recognize Them*. Bombay Nat. Hist. Soc., Bombay.

Wallace, A. R. (1865). On the phenomena of variation and geographical distribution as illustrated by the Papilionidae of the Malayan region. Trans. Linn. Soc. Lond. 25, 1–71.

Wallace, A. R. (1867). Mimicry and other protective resemblances among animals. The West Minster and Foreign Quarterly Review, New Series 32, 1–43.

Wallace, A. R. (1870). *Contributions to the Theory of Natural Selection*. Macmillan and Co., London.

Walls, G. L. (1942). *The Vertebrate Eye, and Its Adaptive Radiation*. Cranbrook Inst. Sci., Bloomfield Hills, MI.

Weale, J. P. M. (1871). Protective resemblances. Nature (April 27, 1871), 507–508.

Werner, F. (1909). Review of *Mimikry bei afrikanischen Schlangen* (Sternfeld 1908). Zool. Zentralblatt, Leipzig 16, 514–515.

Werner, Y. L. (1983). Behavioural triangulation of the head in three boigine snakes: A possible case of mimicry. Israel J. Zool. 32, 205–228.

Werner, Y. L. (1985). Similarities of the colubrid snakes *Spalerosophis* and *Pythonodipsas* to vipers: An additional hypothesis. Copeia 1985, 266–268.

Werner, Y. L. (1986). Evolutionary implications of occasional (non-mimetic) behavioural triangulation of the head in snakes (*Coluber rhodorhachis* and *Malpolon monspessulanus*). Snake 18, 37–41.

Werner, Y. L. and Frankenberg, E. (1982). Head triangulation in two colubrine snakes: Probably behavioural reinforcement of Batesian mimicry. Israel J. Zool. 31, 137–150.

Wickler, W. (1968). *Mimicry in Plants and Animals*. Weidenfeld and Nicolson, London.

Wiens, D. (1978). Mimicry in plants. In *Evolutionary Biology*. (M. K. Hecht, W. C. Steere, and B. Wallace, eds.). Plenum Press, New York. Volume 10, pp. 365–403.

Williams, K. L. (1978). Systematics and natural history of the American milk snake, *Lampropeltis triangulum*. Milwaukee Public Mus. Publ. Biol. Geol. 2, 1–258.

Windecker, W. (1939). *Euchelia (Hypocrita) jacobaeae* L. und das Schutztrachtenproblem. Z. Morphol. Okol. Tiere 35, 84–138.

Wirklund, C. and Järvi, T. (1982). Survival of distasteful insects after being attacked by naive birds: A reappraisal of the theory of aposematic coloration evolving through individual selection. Evolution 36, 998–1002.

Zweifel, R. G. (1952). Pattern variation and evolution of the mountain kingsnake, *Lampropeltis zonata*. Copeia 1952, 152–168.

Zweifel, R. G. (1960). Results of the Puritan-American Museum of Natural History expedition to western Mexico. 9. Herpetology of the Tres Marias Islands. Bull. Am. Mus. Nat. Hist. 119, 77–128.

APPENDIX

Coral-Snake Patterns from Different Geographical Regions

The frequencies of coral-snake patterns summarized in Table I are based on descriptions of regional snake faunas that provided sufficient detail to assign species to categories of "coral-snake pattern" and "not-coral-snake pattern." For this survey, the coral-snake category included any pattern of "alternating black and red (or yellow or white) dorsally" (Savage and Vial, 1974:334). Some patterns could not be assigned unequivocally to either category and are listed as "questionable." Coral-snake patterns were further classified as containing or not containing red. (Species lacking red are indicated by an asterisk in the list below.) Allocation to a category depended upon the description in each source; consequently the same species may have different allocations in different places. Presumably these inconsistencies reflect geographic variation within a species. In some instances, only juveniles have a coral snake pattern. Frequencies listed in Table I for Costa Rica and Panama are those reported by Savage and Vial (1974) and Dunn (1954), respectively, and are not included here. This list includes elapids whereas frequencies in Table I were calculated by omitting elapids.

UNITED STATES (STEBBINS, 1966; CONANT, 1975)

Coral-snake patterns:

Cemophora coccinea, Chionactis occipitalis, C. palorostris, Lampropeltis getulus, L. mexicana, L. pyromelana, L. triangulum, L. zonata, Micruroides euryxanthus, Micrurus fulvius, Rhinocheilus lecontei, Sonora semiannulata, Stilosoma extenuatum.* Questionable: *Chilomeniscus cinctus,* Leptodeira septentrionalis.**

GUATEMALA (DUELLMAN, 1963)

Coral-snake patterns:

(Recorded from Guatemala) *Lampropeltis triangulum, Micrurus diastema, Ninia sebae, Pliocercus euryzonus.* (Expected but not recorded) *Micrurus elegans, Oxyrhopus petola, Pliocercus elapoides, Scaphiodontophis annulatus, Tropidodipsas sartori.* Questionable: (Recorded from Guatemala) *Sibon dimidiata,* S. nebulata.**

VENEZUELA (ROZE, 1966)

Coral-snake patterns:

Anilius scytale, Atractus badius, A. elaps, A. erythromelas, Dipsas pavonina, D. variegata, Erythrolamprus aesculapii, E. bauperthuisii,*

APPENDIX

E. bizona, E. pseudocorallus, Hydrodynastes bicinctus, Hydrops triangularis, Lampropeltis triangulum, Micrurus carinicauda, M. dissoleucus, M. hemprichii, M. isozonus, M. lemniscatus, M. mipartitus,* M. psyches, M. spixii, M. surinamensis, Oxyrhopus petola,* O. venezuelanus. Questionable: *Attractus major, Clelia clelia, Dipsas copei, D. latifrontalis, Micrurus collaris, Pseudoboa coronata, P. neuwiedii.**

ECUADOR (DUELLMAN, 1978)

Coral-snake patterns:

Anilius scytale, Atractus elaps, Dipsas pavonina,* Erythrolamprus aesculapii, Oxyrhopus formosus,* O. petola, O. melanogenys, Micrurus langsdorfii, M. lemniscatus, M. spixii, M. surinamensis. Questionable: *Dipsas catesbyi, Drepanoides anomalus, Imantodes cenchoa,* Micrurus narducci,* Pseudoboa coronata, Tripanurgos compressus,* Xenopholis scalaris.**

BRAZIL (AMARAL, 1978; FREIBERG, 1982)

Coral-snake patterns:

Anilius scytale, Atractus baduus, A. guentheri, Erythrolamprus aesculapii, Hydrops triangularis, Liophis poecilogyrus, Liophis brazili, Lystrophus semicinctus, Micrurus albicinctus,* M. corallinus, M. decoratus, M. filiformis, M. fischeri, M. frontalis, M. ibiboboca, M. lemniscatus, M. spixii, M. surinamensis, Oxyrhopus petola, O. rhombiferus, O. trigemina, Simophis rhinostoma. Questionable: *Apostolepis assimilis, A. cearensis, A. coronata, Drymoluber brazili,* Elapomorphus lepidus, E. mertensi, Waglerophis merremii.*

ARGENTINA (ABALOS ET AL., 1964)

Coral-snake patterns:

Lystrophis semicinctus, Micrurus lemniscatus. Questonable: *Elapomorphus tricolor, Oxyrhopus rhombifer.*

EUROPE AND RUSSIA (BANNIKOV ET AL., 1971; STEWARD, 1971)

Coral-snake pattern:

Rhabdophis tigrina. Questionable: *Elaphe schrencki,* Rhynchocalamus melanocephalus.*

IRAQ (KHALAF, 1959)

Questionable:

Coluber ventromaculatus.*

WEST PAKISTAN (MINTON, 1966)

Coral-snake patterns:

Bungarus caeruleus,* Lycodon striatus,* Lytorhynchus maynardi.* Questionable: *Lycodon travancoricus** (juvenile), *Naja naja** (juvenile).

INDIA (SMITH, 1943)

Coral-snake patterns:

Azemiops feae,* Bungarus bungaroides,* B. fasciatus,* B. caeruleus,* B. ceylonicus,* B. multicinctus,* B. candidus,* B. magnimaculatus,* B. walli,* Calliophis macclellandi, C. bibroni, C. kelloggi, Cantoria violacea,* Cercaspis carinatus,* Chrysopelea ornata,* Cylindrophus rufus,* Dinodon septentrionalis,* D. gammei,* D. flavozonatus,* Dryocalamus nympha,* D. davisoni,* D. gracilis,* Enhydris smithi,* Elaphe porphyracea,* Lycodon subcinctus,* L. travancoricus,* L. laoensis,* L. kundui,* L. fasciatus,* L. paucifasciatus,* Naja naja,* Oligodon juglandifer, O. albocinctus, O. cinereus, O. arnensis, Plectrurus aureus.* Questionable: *Boiga ochracea, Coluber argyrogena,* Lycodon aulicus,* Oligodon cyclurus, Plectrurus guentheri, Uropeltis nitidus.**

JAPAN (NAKAMURA AND UÉNO, 1963)

Coral-snake patterns:

Calliophis japonicus, C. macclellandi, Dinodon semicarinatus. Questionable: *Dinodon orientalis,* D. rufozonatus.*

TAIWAN (KUNTZ, 1963)

Coral-snake patterns:

Bungarus multicinctus,* Calliophis macclellandi, Dinodon septentrionalis,* Questionable: *Dinodon rufozonatus.**

THAILAND (TAYLOR, 1965)

Coral-snake patterns:

Boiga dendrophila,* Bungarus candidus,* Bungarus fasciatus,* Calliophis macclellandi, Dinodon septentrionalis,* Dryocalamus davisoni,* Elaphe porphyracea, Homalopsis buccata* (juvenile), *Lycodon laoensis,* L. fasciatus.** Questionable: *Calamaria parimentata,* Cylindrophus rufus,* Lycodon subcinctus** (juvenile).

APPENDIX

SOUTH VIETNAM (CAMPDEN-MAIN, 1970)

Coral-snake patterns:

Boiga dendrophila,* *Bungarus candidus.** Questionable: *Lycodon laoensis,** *Rhabdophis subminiata.*

MALAYA (TWEEDIE, 1953)

Coral-snake patterns:

Bungarus fasciatus,* *B. candidus,** *Cantoria violacea,** *Elaphe porphyracea,** *Lycodon subcinctus,** *L. effrenis,** *L. laoensis.** Questionable: *Bitia hydroides,** *Boiga dendrophila,** *Cylindrophis rufus,** *Macropisthodon flaviceps,** *Maticora intestinalis, Oligodon signatus, Pareas margaretophorus.*

PHILIPPINES (TAYLOR, 1922)

Coral-snake patterns:

Boiga dendrophila,* *Calamaria lumbricoidea* (juvenile), *Calliophis calligaster,** *Lycodon subcinctus.** Questionable: *Maticora intestinalis,** *Oligodon maculatus,** *Naja naja,** *Stegonotus dumerilii.**

AUSTRALIA (COGGER, 1979)

Coral-snake patterns:

Pseudechis colletti* (juvenile), *Pseudonaja textilis,** *Simoselaps australis, S. bertholdi,** *Vermicella annulata,** *V. multifasciata.** Questionable: *Hoplocephalus bungaroides,** *H. stephensi,** *Pseudonaja guttata,** *P. modesta.**

WEST AFRICA (VILLIERS, 1975)

Coral-snake patterns:

Dromophis praeornatus,* *Elapsoidea semiannulata** (juvenile). Questionable: *Crotaphopeltis hotamboeia,** *Grayia smythii,** *Meizodon coronatus.**

UGANDA (PITMAN, 1974)

Coral-snake pattern:

Telescopus semiannulatus.* Questionable: *Elapsoidea laticincta,** *E. loveridgei.**

SOUTHERN AFRICA (FITZSIMONS, 1970; BROADLEY AND COCK, 1975)

Coral-snake patterns:

Aspidelaps lubricus, Elaps lacteus,* *Elapsoidea guentheri** (juvenile), *E. sundevalli,** *Naja haje,** *Telescopus semiannulatus.** Questionable: *Aparallactus guentheri,** *Prosymna janii.**

CHAPTER

3

Caudal Autotomy as a Defense

E. N. ARNOLD

Department of Zoology, British Museum (Natural History),
London, United Kingdom

CONTENTS

I. INTRODUCTION 237

II. THE EFFECTIVENESS OF CAUDAL AUTOTOMY 238
  A. The Strategy, 238
  B. Evidence From Predator Stomachs and Encounters in Captivity, 238
  C. The Meaning of Broken Tails in Wild Populations, 239

III. CAUDAL AUTOTOMY AND THE DETERMINANTS OF ITS VARIATION 244
  A. Mechanisms of Caudal Autotomy and Regeneration, 244
  B. How Autotomy Mechanisms May Change, 244
  C. Evolutionary History of Autotomy Mechanisms in the Squamata, 245
  D. Factors Determining Ease of Autotomy: Costs, Benefits, and History, 246
  E. Benefits of Autotomy, 247
  F. Costs of Autotomy, 248
  G. Alternative Defensive Uses of Tails, 251
  H. Modifications That Increase the Effectiveness of Autotomy, 253

IV. VARIATIONS IN THE AUTOTOMY PROCESS AND THEIR CAUSES 255
  A. Total Loss of Intravertebral Autotomy, 255
  B. Re-evolution of Autotomy, 258
  C. Restriction of Autotomy to the Caudal Base, 259
  D. Ontogenetic Loss of Autotomy, 260
  E. Short-term Changes Within the Individual, 261
  F. Interspecific Variation in the Readiness With Which the Tail Is Shed, 262
  G. Brightly Colored Tails, 263
  H. Regeneration of the Tail, 265

V. FURTHER RESEARCH 267

ACKNOWLEDGMENTS 267

REFERENCES 267

I. INTRODUCTION

Caudal autotomy, the ability to shed the tail, occurs in many lepidosaurians (Bellairs and Bryant, 1985), some salamanders (Wake and Dresner, 1967) and a few rodents (Matthews, 1969–1971). Tail shedding usually takes place if an animal is attacked by a predator and often appears to facilitate escape. Despite its apparent survival value, caudal autotomy is not universal; the ease with which breakage occurs also varies. There are differences among taxa, among ontogenetic stages of the same species, and even within the same individual over short periods of time. Recent selective pressures may influence these differences, but historical factors may also be important; absence of autotomy may be due to loss in the distant past rather than through lack of present survival value. As with all selective pressures, both costs and benefits need to be considered. In recent years information about caudal autotomy has increased substantially and it is now easier to assess the factors controlling its variation.

Autotomy is a deceptive phenomenon; it is often thought of as a simple adaptation that enables a potential prey animal to escape from predators. However, autotomy is actually highly complex as are other defensive phenomena, such as mimicry (Pough, this volume). Ramifications extend to many aspects of the animal and even to the proclivities and perceptive capacities of its predators. As such, caudal autotomy gives insight into the complexity of natural selection, the interconnections of parts and activities of animals to each other, and of animals to the situations in which they live. The interactions of which caudal autotomy is a nexus resemble Darwin's famous evolutionary analogy of the tangled bank (Darwin, 1859), in which many things are interlinked so that proximate effects may have very distant and interwoven causes.

Historically, autotomy has provided support for natural selection as the mechanism of evolution rather than Lamarckian inheritance of characters acquired by successful use. Detached parts of animals, like moving lizard tails, may act to the benefit of their recent owners by actively distracting predators. That tails should act in this way after disconnection is understandable in terms of natural selection, for lizards having such tails will tend to survive and pass on this trait to their offspring. However, such separated organs could not be perfected by Lamarckian systems of inheritance as their success could not be transmitted to the gonads of their owners (Poulton, 1895; Gould, 1983).

Many aspects of caudal autonomy have been recently reviewed elsewhere, including its detailed systematic distribution, histological mechanisms, and evolutionary history (Arnold, 1984; Bellairs and Bryant, 1985). These three topics are only considered briefly here; but new work, especially on behavioral and ecological aspects of autotomy, has been incorporated.

II. THE EFFECTIVENESS OF CAUDAL AUTOTOMY

A. The Strategy

Caudal autotomy seems able to benefit lizards and some other reptiles in two quite distinct ways: It lets them break away from a predator that has seized them by the tail and it allows the tail to be used as a distraction, engaging the attention of the predator while the lizard escapes. In distraction the tail is sometimes "offered" to a predator while still attached to the lizard thus diverting attack from the unexpendable head and body. Bright or contrasting markings and movements of the tail (Section III.H) may enhance this process by making the tail more conspicuous. Autotomy usually occurs once a predator has grasped the tail, either after such a display or while a lizard is feeding; the writhing tail may then act to distract the attacker from further pursuit of the rest of the potential prey.

Shed tails usually move vigorously for some time and seem to attract the attention of the predators (Section III.H). Indeed the rate of caudal movement often increases if the tail is touched and may well increase further if the tail is bitten. Eating the shed tail may in fact be a more beneficial course for the predator than pursuing the lizard itself. Although the tail may sometimes be a poorer potential meal than the rest of the lizard, it has the advantage of being already secured, whereas the rest of the lizard may well evade capture (the tail is like the proverbial bird in the hand worth two in the bush). Furthermore, if the predator temporarily abandoned the moving tail to chase the lizard, the tail might attract another animal and be eaten by it. Movement may also increase the time that may be spent subduing and swallowing the tail, thus allowing the lizard more time to escape (Section III.H). The two strategies, distraction and breaking away, are of course not necessarily complete alternatives; some species use one or the other according to circumstance (see, for instance, Bustard, 1968, on *Gehyra variegata*).

B. Evidence From Predator Stomachs and Encounters in Captivity

The frequent efficacy of autotomy in allowing escape is well known to anyone who has tried to catch lizards. It is also supported by the recovery of substantial numbers of detached tails, but not their owners, from the stomachs and crops of predators (Cott, 1957). For instance, tails have been reported from the stomachs of other lizards (Milstead, 1957; Dixon and Medica, 1966; Cunningham, 1956), and of snakes (Brooks, 1967; Mount, 1963; Carpenter, 1958; McKinney and Ballinger, 1966; Fitch, 1940; Greene, 1984).

Direct evidence of the importance of the tail in escape strategies comes from observation in captivity of controlled encounters among lizards and their enemies. Of 30 geckos *Coleonyx variegatus* with complete tails that were exposed to the spotted night snake (*Hypsiglena ochrorhyncha*), 19 were captured while 11 escaped by losing parts of the tail; but all tailless geckos were captured (Congdon et al., 1974). Similarly, tailed geckos (*Phyllodactylus marmoratus*) were more successful in escaping from the shrew-like marsupial *Antechinus swainsoni* than were tailless ones. Of 35 tailed individuals contacted, 54% escaped by caudal autotomy, whereas all 15 tailless animals were captured (Daniels, 1983; other experiments reported by Daniels et al., 1986). Exposure of skinks (*Scincella lateralis*) to the snake *Lampropeltis triangulum*, resulted in capture of only 8 out of 19 tailed individuals grasped by the predator, whereas all 12 tailless ones were captured (Fig. 1; Dial and Fitzpatrick, 1984). Caudal autotomy also significantly enhances escape of hatchling *Eumeces* spp. from *Lampropeltis triangulum elapsoides* (Cooper and Vitt, 1985; Vitt and Cooper, 1986). The survival value of autotomy to plethodontid salamanders exposed to chickens has also been demonstrated (Labanick, 1984). Although autotomy is clearly advantageous in many circumstances, its benefits vary. Thus the slender tail of *Anolis carolinensis*, which does not move much after autotomy, is not very effective in distracting cats from pursuing the rest of the lizard (Dial and Fitzpatrick, 1983).

C. The Meaning of Broken Tails in Wild Populations

The frequency of broken and regenerated tails in populations has been interpreted as an indication of the effectiveness of autotomy (Haldane and Huxley, 1927). Each lizard with a damaged tail might be an individual saved from death by predation. Alternatively, the incidence of broken tails has been regarded as an indicator of predation intensity; the more damaged tails in a population the greater the intensity of predation (Rand, 1954; Tinkle, 1972, 1973, 1976; Parker and Pianka, 1973, 1975, 1976; Pianka, 1967; Pianka and Pianka, 1976; Schall

Fig. 1. Attack of king snake, *Lampropeltis triangulum*, on the small skink, *Scincella lateralis*. (A) (bottom) The snake has grabbed the tail and the lizard autotomized it. (B) (top) Some seconds later. The snakes remains preoccupied with the undulating tail, whereas the lizard is escaping. (A, Copyright Benjamin E. Dial and the American Association for the Advancement of Science, 1983, from Dial and Fitzpatrick, 1983; B. Copyright B. E. Dial.)

and Pianka, 1980). Frequency of damage has also been postulated as an index of age difference among populations (Bustard and Hughes, 1966). In fact a number of independent factors may possibly affect the perceived frequency of damaged tails in a sample. At a trivial level, collecting bias is possible. This is likely to apply especially when museum material is used to compare damage rates among taxa, for there is often a tendency to reject damaged specimens during assembly of specimens for taxonomic and morphological work. Again, samples collected from one locality may not be typical of the taxon as a whole (Schall and Pianka, 1980). Although in many species, regenerated tails are conspicuously different from the originals and consequently easy to recognize, this is not always the case (for instance in *Teratoscincus scincus*, see Werner, 1967); it is sometimes possible to underestimate the number of regenerates as they may closely resemble original tails. However, as the vertebrae in regenerated tails are replaced by a cartilaginous tube, such tails can always be identified by radiography.

Tails, or portions thereof, may be lost in conspecific fights. In *Agama agama*, such damage occurs when males strike each other with their tails (Harris, 1964). Similarly, territorial fighting has been blamed for high frequency of caudal breakage in males of the iguanid *Sceloporus magister* (Vitt et al., 1974) and of the xantusiid *Xantusia vigilis* (Zweifel and Lowe, 1966), although this is disputed in the latter case (Vitt et al., 1977). In some groups, such as lacertid lizards, tail loss rarely seems to result from intraspecific conflicts, even in captivity. The importance of this factor in increasing natural incidence of broken tails can only be assessed properly by field observation of the species concerned.

The probability that an individual lizard will have lost its tail necessarily increases with time, although the increase is often not uniform, and young animals are frequently more prone to caudal autotomy than are adults (see, for instance, data in Cooke, 1979; Blair, 1960). All other things being equal, long-lived species will tend to have higher aggregate levels of caudal breakage than will short-lived ones (Brown and Ruby, 1977; Schoener, 1979; Schoener and Schoener, 1980). This complication can be countered by comparing samples of known age, either recognized by relative size or by previous individual marking.

The frequency of autotomized tails in a population will increase only if tail shedding significantly improves the chances that a lizard will escape. If predation efficiency is high and animals are often caught, broken tails may remain rare in samples even though predation levels are high (Schoener, 1979). On the other hand, incidence of broken tails will be higher in species and populations that show frequent encounters with predators and subsequent escape after autotomy. Moreover, tail-break frequencies can be minimal estimates of escape, because predators striking at tails, sometimes miss their prey entirely (Vitt and Cooper, 1986). Finally taxa appear to differ in the ease with which autotomy takes place (Section IV.F).

In principle, it is possible to assess all of these factors; however, the necessary substantial ecological knowledge of the species concerned is rarely available. In particular, predator pressure is hard to estimate without extensive collateral studies of other animals in the communities in which the lizards live. Also, the readiness with which autotomy takes place is difficult to measure realistically (Section IV.F). Because of these problems, it is difficult to unravel the contributions of intraspecific conflict, age, predation efficiency and intensity, and ease of autotomy to the incidence of broken tails. This means that the use of caudal damage as an indirect source of information about any of these factors generally requires additional information. Schoener (1979) and Schoener and Schoener (1980) derive and explore a method of estimating predation parameters from tail break and demographic data in *Anolis*.

Comparison of geographically close populations of the same species is likely to be most useful, for this controls for potential differences in behavioral traits and inherent longevity; in such comparisons, predation level is the most probable cause of substantial differences in frequency of breakage. The same assumptions can be made, but with less confidence, if widely separated populations of the same species, or closely related species, are compared. For instance, the low level of caudal breakage found in juvenile *Heliobolus lugubris*, compared with that of the young of related forms in the same area has been attributed to reduced predator pressure arising from mimicry of noxious beetles (Huey and Pianka, 1977; Pough, this volume). This is not unreasonable, because samples are alike in age and are quite similar in many aspects of behavior and environment.

In several cases for which predation intensity could be quantified, tail break frequency shows some correlation with this. In *Cnemidophorus tigris*, frequency of regenerated tails increases from north to south and correlates with an increase in the number and variety of predators (Pianka, 1970), a trend also found in juvenile *Uta stansburiana* (Parker and Pianka, 1975). Yearly variation in frequencies of broken tails among hatchling *Uta stansburiana* from southern Nevada correlates with the density of one of its important predators, *Gambelia wislizeni* (Turner et al., 1982). In *Sceloporus jarrovi* in southeast Arizona, a higher frequency of autotomy at low altitudes correlates with higher numbers of potential predators and increased mortality (Ballinger, 1979). In three taxa of *Sceloporus*, the one with the highest tail break frequency has the lowest survivorship (Vinegar, 1975). In an analogous experimental case, caudal injury frequency in tadpoles of the toad *Scaphiopus holbrooki* correlates with predation intensity (Morin, 1985). On the other hand, incidence of autotomy in Bahamian *Anolis* (Schoener, 1979) and in lizards from a site in California, at which diets of predators are known (Jaksić and Greene, 1984), shows no correlation with predation level and appears to reflect predator inefficiency.

It might be thought that tail-break incidence does at least give an indication of the relative success with which autotomy enables lizards of different species to evade predators. This would be correct, if each lizard with a broken tail had survived a predator attack, and if survival had been linked with autotomy in each case. However, in some species autotomy may not involve great costs; such forms may shed the tail at a time at which the risks of capture by a pursuing predator are still relatively low. In such cases, a shed tail is unlikely to represent a lizard saved from certain death by autotomy, whereas this may be more nearly so in species in which lost tails involve a great cost and are given up less willingly. Moreover, as already noted, tail-break incidence gives no evidence of the frequency of predator strikes at tails during which the predator missed the prey entirely (Vitt and Cooper, 1986).

Autotomy levels do often show a broad correlation with particular ecological circumstances. Thus, among geckos occurring in Israel, broken tails are commoner in climbing species than among ground dwelling ones (Werner, 1968), and this is also true among Chilean iguanids (*Liolaemus*: Jaksić and Fuentes, 1980). Similar correlations exist among European lizards of the genera *Lacerta* and *Podarcis*, in communities of lizards in eastern Arabia and in species of *Agama* in Africa (Arnold, 1984). The causes of this correlation are uncertain, largely because many of the relevant ecological data are lacking. Nevertheless, at present, there are no indications that climbing species are more prone to intraspecific combat, to longer life, or to higher rates of predation. On the other hand, subjective impressions suggest that climbing species relinquish their tails more easily than do ground dwellers (Section IV.F). If this impression is valid, it could indicate that tail loss might be less costly in these forms, perhaps because the tail is less important in the locomotion of climbers. Here, the body is not counterbalanced by the tail, as is possible and necessary in cursorial forms (Section III.F). Also, because the feet are firmly attached to the substrate during climbing, lateral oscillation of the hindquarters is less of a problem.

In summary, tail-break frequencies are often unreliable indices of predation rates, especially in interspecific comparisons that fail to control for age and other factors. However, approaches that incorporate demographic data may yield useful estimates of predation rates (Schoener, 1979).

III. CAUDAL AUTOTOMY AND THE DETERMINANTS OF ITS VARIATION

A. Mechanisms of Caudal Autotomy and Regeneration

The term, caudal autotomy, is used here to describe a fracture of the tail that occurs in a regular and predictable way at a distinct region of weakness. Its mechanisms are described in detail by Bellairs and Bryant (1985) and will consequently only be dealt with briefly here. Among modern reptiles, caudal autotomy is unknown in the Testudines and Crocodilia but is widespread in the Lepidosauria, including *Sphenodon;* it is absent in the great majority of snakes. It also occured in some extinct groups (Bellairs and Bryant, 1985).

There are two distinct autotomy mechanisms. The first and more widespread is intravertebral autotomy, in which breakage takes place at preformed areas of weakness—the autotomy or fracture planes—that cross each vertebra transversely. In the soft tissues surrounding the vertebra, the autotomy plane follows the myoseptum that separates adjacent segments of axial musculature and the segments of fat that often lie between these and the vertebra itself. In some cases, there may be clear regions of weakness in the skin corresponding to the autotomy planes (Woodland, 1920; Quattrini, 1954). In the second kind of tail breakage, namely intervertebral autotomy, fracture takes place between vertebrae. Species with intervertebral autotomy do not show any obvious caudal modifications relative to nonautotomizing species. It is difficult to distinguish the two conditions, as the degree of caudal fragility is variable. In most cases of autotomy the tail is regenerated after breakage.

B. How Autotomy Mechanisms May Change

Intravertebral autotomy is probably the ancestral condition in squamate reptiles. Consequently loss or a substantial reduction in the ability to shed all or part of the tail is a derived feature (Section III.C). Loss or reduction can take place in a number of ways, the most obvious involving whole or partial fusion of the anterior and posterior sections of each vertebra across the fracture plane, so that its inherent weakness is lessened. This may occur in all the post-pygal vertebrae or only the more distal ones. Whenever such fusion occurs, it proceeds from the tip of the tail forwards and from the top of the neural arch downwards in each vertebra (Etheridge, 1967). Vertebral fusion is easy to detect in skeletal material and often in radiographs as well, so it is widely used as an indicator of restricted autotomy. However, ease of autotomy may be reduced by stronger attachment of the muscle segments to the myosepta and loss of planes of weakness in the skin, if originally present. These modifications usually accompany vertebral fusion but sometimes occur in forms in which intravertebral autotomy planes remain, for instance in the geckos of *Pristurus carteri* group (Arnold, 1984). Neurological factors also seem to be able to change autotomy thresholds (Section IV.E). Whereas all these mechanisms seem to be capable of reducing the facility with which autotomy takes place, they may not be unidirectional in their action and reversal may be possible, although this would not necessarily apply to fusion of the autotomy planes in the vertebrae once it is established throughout ontogeny.

Of the various mechanisms for changing the facility with which autotomy occurs, all seem able to act on evolutionary and ontogenetic time scales. They then produce differences among taxa and among different ontogenetic stages of the same taxon, but neurological factors are likely to be effective only on shorter time scales.

C. Evolutionary History of Autotomy Mechanisms in the Squamata

The evolutionary history of autotomy mechanisms in the Squamata has been discussed elsewhere (Arnold, 1984); hence it is only summarized here. Intravertebral autotomy with capacity to regenerate appears to be the ancestral condition in the group. This is supported by its presence in *Sphenodon*, the primitive living sister taxon of the Squamata, by its generally wide occurrence, and by its early appearance in ontogeny. Phylogenies of particular groups, such as the macroteiids (Presch, 1974) and the gecko genus *Pristurus* (Arnold, 1984), also indicate that intravertebral autotomy is ancestral. Absence of intravertebral autotomy in some members of many holophyletic families indicates that the ability to shed the tail in this way has been lost a number of times. In many instances, this loss may have been relatively recent, for instance, it may only be lacking in a few members of a genus or even of a species (e.g., *Amphisbaena angustifrons*, Gans and Diefenbach, 1972). On the other hand, its absence from whole superfamilial groupings, such as the Platynota (Helodermatidae, Lanthanotidae, and Varanidae) or the Agamidae plus Chamaeleonidae, indicate that its loss may be very long standing.

Intervertebral autotomy seems to represent a re-evolution of tail shedding ability, developed in stocks where intravertebral autotomy was previously lost. Within the Agamidae, comparison of the distribution of intervertebral autotomy with a hypothetical phylogeny of the group (Moody, 1980) suggests that it may have arisen as many as eight times; multiple origins are also likely among the colubrid snakes that possess it. Not all intervertebral autotomizers among the Agamidae are able to regenerate shed portions of the tail (Section IV.B), although regenerative ability appears to have developed or been reactivated up to five times in the family.

D. Factors Determining Ease of Autotomy: Costs, Benefits, and History

If natural selection acted without constraint on totally plastic phenotypes, variations in the ease with which caudal autotomy takes place, or whether it takes place at all, would represent adaptations to different situations that maximized their fitness. This would apply to differences among taxa and among ontogenetic stages, and to short term changes within the same individual. Autotomy would be retained wherever it increased the chances that a lizard or other reptile would approach its full reproductive potential; it would be lost whenever it reduced such chances. In autotomizing forms the facility with which the tail is shed should be determined by similar considerations.

The value of caudal autotomy depends essentially on the balance of its costs and benefits; only if the latter exceed the former is autotomy selectively advantageous. However, the presence or absence of autotomy is frequently explained mainly in terms of variations in cost. Thus, loss or reduction of the ability to autotomize is often attributed to the tail being of especial survival value in other ways (cf. Woodland, 1920; Boring et al., 1948). Variation in benefits must also be taken into account. In some situations, the advantages of autotomy are so great that they justify the sacrifice of even a very valuable tail; conversely, in other situations, the benefits are so low that even the shedding of a tail with little positive function is unjustified.

Furthermore, phenotypes may not be totally plastic, so variations in the autotomy mechanism need not represent precise adaptation to different situations. In rapidly altering environments, the phenotype may not change swiftly enough to become fully adapted to current conditions. Also, some kinds of phenotypic change may be less likely than others. The mechanism of intravertebral autotomy appears to have been lost independently many times, yet there is no evidence that it has ever been redeveloped in its original form. Functionally analogous intervertebral autotomy appears to have evolved in some of the stocks that previously lost the intravertebral mechanism (Section III.C). Lineages might well differ in the facility with which the ability to autotomize and regenerate the tail is lost and regained. If this is so, absence of autotomy may sometimes result from the phylogenetic history of a taxon rather than from disadvantage of autotomy in the present environment. Therefore, species without autotomy should not always show the predicted excess of likely costs over likely benefits. Consequently, loss of autotomy should be less precisely correlated with excess cost, than should the presence of autotomy with excess benefit. As the environments in which animals and their descendants live probably change substantially through time, the longer since a stock has lost autotomy, the less precise the expected correlation. Because of this, better correlations should be expected at low taxonomic levels than at higher ones; this is the observed condition (Section IV.A).

E. Benefits of Autotomy

The frequent effectiveness of autotomy has already been described (Section II), but its benefits are likely to vary in different situations. (1) Benefits will be slight if predation is very rare. (2) Simply breaking away from a predator is only beneficial if the lizard can elude further pursuit by speed and agility or otherwise reach a secure refuge. Distraction techniques probably demand less speed; however, the lizard must leave the vicinity of the predator before the shed tail has been consumed, and must deny it the choice between the shed and the rest of the prey. The problem may be aggravated, as tail loss itself may reduce the speed of a lizard (Section III.F). Consequently, autotomy has only slight benefits to very slow-moving lizards. (3) Autotomy will be of limited importance for lizards that have other means of deterring predators. For instance, a large species might more effectively defend itself with teeth and claws than with autotomy. (4) Conversely, autotomy may be more beneficial to small species, and use of the tail to divert attention from the head and body will be more important for delicately constructed forms with limited ability to fight back, than for more robust ones. (5) The effectiveness of the tail as a distraction device depends on its being an acceptable item of diet, or apparently so. Therefore, tails and tail fragments that are very small, or spiny, or that do not move much are likely to have little effect. As will be seen (Section IV.A), the actual taxonomic distribution of autotomy shows some correlation with these factors.

F. Costs of Autotomy

In most lizards, tails have survival value in areas other than the evasion of predators by autotomy. Indeed these uses are so widespread that the simple classification of tails into "actively" and "passively" functional types (Vitt et al., 1977) appears inappropriate. (In this scheme, actively functional tails include those with obvious functions apart from autotomy for predator escape, such as swimming, climbing, defense and balance; passively functional tails include those without an obvious function, other than autotomy.) Nevertheless, the aggregate selective value of the tail differs substantially among taxa, and probably among ontogenetic stages; the cost of losing the tail must show a similar variation. Apart from the transient loss of alternative function, this cost also includes the price of replacing the original tail by regeneration.

In many cursorial lizards, the tail is raised during running and acts as a counterpoise to the head and body. The weight is concentrated over the hind limbs, which are often the main source of forward propulsion. This role is particularly important in bipedal forms; thus the iguanid *Basiliscus* is unable to run bipedally after losing only the distal third of the tail (Snyder, 1949). The tail is also important as a counterpoise in quadrupedal species, such as the lacertid, *Podarcis sicula*, and loss of the tail results in more weight being transferred to the front legs (Arnold, 1984). The tail may function as an inertial damper in reducing lateral swing of the hind quarters. In most cursorial lizards the legs move in more or less horizontal arcs and the rump tends consequently to oscillate from side to side; the presence of a large tail with substantial inertia limits this by inducing bending within the limbs (Arnold, 1984).

In a number of cases, experiment has shown that maximum speed is reduced after caudal amputation. Thus, amputation reduces the velocity of the teiid *Cnemidophorus sexlineatus* by 36% over distances of 3 m (Ballinger et al., 1979); similar results are obtained for the iguanids *Dipsosaurus dorsalis* (Pond, 1981), *Cophosaurus texanus* and *Uma notata* (Punzo, 1982) and for the lacertid *Podarcis sicula* (Arnold, 1984). Such changes make lizards more vulnerable to predators. Tailed *Scincella lateralis* are more adept at evading capture by snakes than are tailless ones; 11 out of 30 intact *S. lateralis* escaped without being contacted by the predator, compared with none of 12 that lacked tails (Dial and Fitzpatrick, 1984). However, tail loss does not always reduce speed; *Phyllodactylus marmoratus*, in which the robust tail perhaps plays no part in locomotion, runs faster after the tail is removed, at least for distances of 10–30 cm (Daniels, 1983). In the iguanid *Sceloporus merriami*, maximal sprint speed on a 2-m track is unaltered by the loss of even two-thirds of the length of the tail (R. B. Huey and A. E. Dunham, personal communication).

The tail contributes directly to locomotion in many long-bodied squamates that have very small legs or no legs at all. In many of these species, the tail makes up a large proportion of their total length, and its loss may significantly reduce the ability to move.

In climbing forms, the tail may be important in balancing. *Polychrus marmoratus* can stand erect on a branch whenever reaching upwards to grasp a twig because the long tail hanging downwards promotes stability (Cott, 1926). The tail is also important in balancing *Anolis carolinensis*, and its loss reduces ability to perch in unstable situations (Ballinger, 1973). *Urosaurus graciosus* also use their tail in balancing (Vitt and Ohmart, 1975).

Lizards that climb in flimsy vegetation or travel across its surface often distribute their weight over as large an area as possible via a long, often slender tail. Among lacertids this occurs in such forms as *Lacerta viridis*, *Psammodromus algirus*, and especially among the East Asian grass runners, *Takydromus*.

Tails may be coiled spirally around twigs or stems to maintain position in vegetation. This is best known and particularly developed in the chameleons but occurs in other forms such as the iguanids *Polychrus* (Cott, 1926; Vitt and Lacher, 1981), *Phenacosaurus* (Schmidt and Inger, 1957) and *Chamaeleolis*, the geckos *Naultinus*, *Heteropholis*, and *Aeluroscalabotes*, and even such unspecialized climbers as *Lacerta viridis* and *Podarcis muralis*. The gecko *Lygodactylus* has an adhesive pad on the caudal tip, similar in structure to those on the digits, and uses it as a fifth point of attachment, for instance during jumps (cf. Vitt and Ballinger, 1982).

Many kinds of lizards use the tail in swimming, and in the more regularly aquatic forms, it is laterally compressed. Such forms, include the iguanids *Anolis barkeri* (Robinson, 1962), *Amblyrhynchus cristatus* and *Basiliscus*, the agamids *Lophosaurus* and *Physignathus*, the teiids *Crocodilurus* and *Dracaena*, the xenosaurid *Shinosaurus crocodilurus*, some *Varanus* species and the skink *Sphenomorphus quoyii*. In the latter species, loss of the tail severely restricts swimming ability (Daniels, 1985b), as it does in *Amblyrhynchus* (Bartholomew et al., 1976).

In at least some arboreal lizards that can glide, such as the gecko *Ptychozoon* (Cantor, 1847; Tweedie, 1950; Marcellini and Keeper, 1976) and the lacertid *Holaspis guentheri* (Schiøtz and Volsøe, 1959), the tail promotes aerodynamic stability and contributes to lift. Loss of the tail in these autotomous forms may well reduce gliding ability.

The tail is sometimes used in intraspecific signalling (Carpenter and

Ferguson, 1977), for example in geckos of the genus *Pristurus* (Arnold and Gallagher, 1977; Arnold, 1980), and tail loss sometimes decreases social status in encounters with conspecifics. This has been demonstrated experimentally in juvenile *Uta stansburiana*, in which such decreases may impose a social handicap on successful home range acquisition, thereby increasing the risk of death (Fox and Rostker, 1982). A similar loss of social status has been reported for tailless *Anolis carolinensis* (Hennig, 1979).

Lizards frequently have substantial caudal fat deposits, especially forms such as *Heloderma* with very plump tails. In the gecko *Phyllodactylus marmoratus*, 32.6% of the tail may be lipid, compared with 18.3% of the body (Daniels, 1984). In the skink *Scincella lateralis*, 12–15% of the tail is fat, and this represents 47–75% of the total fat reserves of the lizard. In female *Coleonyx brevis* 60% of fat reserves are in the tail (Dial and Fitzpatrick, 1981). In *Eumeces skiltonianus* and *E. gilberti*, about 47% of the undamaged tail is fat (Vitt et al., 1977). These reserves are apparently mobilized whenever feeding does not occur, such as during hibernation in *Lacerta vivipara* (Avery, 1970) and *Eumeces fasciatus* (Fitch, 1954). Viability can be reduced if lizards are deprived of caudal fat by autotomy. Juvenile *Lacerta vivipara* survived less well in hibernation after the tail had been lost and only partly regenerated (Bauwens, 1981). *Scincella lateralis* may survive about 35 days if starved but only 24 days after the tail has been lost (Clark, 1971). In *Phyllodactylus marmoratus*, animals with original tails survived 90.4 days, those with regenerates 142.4 days and tailless animals only 49.2 days (Daniels, 1984). Tail loss negatively affects growth in *Uta stansburiana* (Ballinger and Tinkle, 1979), but not in juvenile *Eumeces* (Vitt and Cooper, 1986).

Tail loss may also affect reproductive capacity (Vitt and Cooper, 1986). In *Coleonyx brevis*, energy reserves account for 53% of reproductive energy in females with tails but only 29% in ones that have autotomized. The latter females produce eggs that are significantly lower in mass (17%) and energy content (19%) (Dial and Fitzpatrick, 1981). In the skink, *Morethia boulengeri* tail loss results in reduced egg mass, whereas in *Hemiergis peronii*, tail loss reduces clutch size (Smyth, 1974).

If a substantial part of the tail is shed, the tail cannot be used as an effective antipredator device until regeneration takes place. This applies whether such use involves further autotomy or some other strategy (Section III.G). A significant proportion of the short-lived iguanid *Uta stansburiana* regenerate the tail more than once, indicating that predatory attacks are probably quite frequent (Tinkle, 1967). This suggests that such lizards may stand an appreciable risk of meeting a predator before the autotomized tail has been fully replaced.

Fragile tails may sometimes be lost inadvertently. Also, they can be damaged whenever used as weapons in intraspecific combats, for instance in *Agama agama* (Harris, 1964), or they may possibly be broken off by the jaws of a rival, although it is uncertain how common this is (Section II.C). Similar loss may also occur by accident, and some predators may even take advantage of caudal fragility to crop tails of lizards that are otherwise too large to eat. For instance, *Varanus caudolineatus* appears to harvest the tails of *Gehyra* that are too large to be subdued in their entirety (Pianka, 1969). In captivity at least, the lacertid *Podarcis lilfordi* often pulls the tails off similarly sized lizards including conspecifics. Finally, autotomy exposes bone and soft tissue to infection and attack of invertebrate predators.

Regenerating a new tail must divert energy and material from other bodily functions or, alternatively, involve increased food intake. For instance, up to 50% of total growth energy may be allocated to caudal regeneration in the skink, *Eumeces gilberti* (Vitt et al., 1977). Energy contained in a regenerated tail of the gecko *Coleonyx variegatus* has been calculated to be equivalent to 47% of the energy in one egg of this species; this figure underestimates the actual cost of regeneration because it ignores losses of metabolic energy (Vitt et al., 1977). In plethodontid salamanders, autotomized tails are regenerated at some expense to future reproduction (Maiorana, 1977).

G. Alternative Defensive Uses of Tails

Loss of the tail may also prevent it being used for defensive purposes other than autotomy. These are discussed elsewhere (Greene, this volume) and will be only summarized here. In some lizards, the tail is used as a weapon in intraspecific combat. Thus, males of *Agama agama* strike each other about the head with their tails (Harris, 1964), and this sort of behavior may also be directed at potential predators, as occurs in the iguanids *Iguana* (Schmidt and Inger, 1957) and *Ctenosaura*, in a number of *Varanus* species (cf. FitzSimons, 1943; Auffenberg, 1981), and in some forms with thick, spiny, club shaped tails such as several species of the agamid genus *Uromastyx*. Some geckos of the genus *Diplodactylus* can expel a very viscous exudate from subcutaneous glands in the tail that probably deters predators (Zietz, 1914; Bustard, 1964, 1970; Rosenberg and Russell, 1980).

The agamid *Uromastyx thomasi* has a disk-shaped tail with a spiny upper surface. Whenever it enters burrows, the tail is turned downwards so that any predator following the lizard will be presented with an effective blockage that prevents further progress (Arnold, 1980). This also occurs in *U. princeps* (Laurent and Gans, 1965), and *Agama (Xenagama) battilifera* and *A. (X.) taylori* probably use their rather similar tails in this way. The gecko *Diplodactylus conspicillatus*, which inhabits the abandoned holes of trap-door spiders, also plugs entrances with its expanded tail (Bustard, 1970).

The tail may also give defense through mimicry (Pough, this volume). The boid *Charina bottae* uses its tail to distract and deter female mice while eating their young (Nussbaum et al., 1983). In some lizards the tail is very similar to the head in shape and coloring and may mimic it. Such similarity occurs, for example, in the skink *Tiliqua (Trachydosaurus) rugosus* and in at least some amphisbaenians. In some *Amphisbaena*, the tail is also moved conspicuously whenever the animal is disturbed; this may direct the attention of a predator away from the more vulnerable head to the expendable tail (Greene, 1973). Another area of defense in which the tail may be involved is crypsis. The flattened, fringed, leaf-shaped tails of such geckos as *Phyllurus* and *Uroplatus* improve the match of these lizards with the surfaces on which they usually occur.

It has been suggested that various lizards that habitually raise the tail in the presence of a predator are scorpion mimics, for example *Chondrodactylus* (FitzSimons and Brain, 1958), *Coleonyx variegatus* (Parker and Pianka, 1974), and *Phrynocephalus*. However, in at least the latter two taxa, caudal tail movement is not scorpion-like (Section III.H; also Pough, this volume).

Members of the gecko genus *Teratoscincus* have the dorsal caudal scales modified, so that they produce a hissing noise as lateral waves of movement pass down the tail (Mertens, 1946; Mebs, 1966). This behavior occurs in the presence of predators and might deter them (although this is not documented), perhaps being similar to the noise produced by the vipers of the genus *Echis*, which are sympatric with *Teratoscincus*. The vipers generate the noise by rubbing their lateral scales together during threat displays.

The brilliant tails of the juveniles of some North American species of *Eumeces* have been thought to indicate that their owners were unpalatable (Clark, 1971), but experiments with predators suggest they are not actually distasteful (Cooper and Vitt, 1985). Bright caudal markings may be "flash coloring": In lizards in which the underside of the tail is conspicuously marked, exposure and the sudden concealment of this pattern by a running animal may fix the attention of a predator on the spot at which the bright coloring was last seen, even though the otherwise cryptically colored prey has moved on (Arnold, 1984) or become hidden in litter as a refuge. Finally, movement of conspicuous tails might warn a predator that it has been seen and that pursuit will be expensive (Arnold, 1980). This strategy has been demonstrated in *Cophosaurus texanus* (Dial, 1986).

H. Modifications That Increase the Effectiveness of Autotomy

As observed earlier (Section I), caudal autotomy in reptiles is often a much more elaborate phenomenon than mere possession of a breakable tail; refinements increase the effectiveness of autotomy, either by enhancing its efficiency or by reducing its costs.

There is evidence that ease of shedding may be adjusted so tails are shed or retained in accordance with the balance between the degree of danger and the value of the tail (Section IV.E). Also, the amount of tail shed seems to be related to the kind of escape strategy employed (Section IV.C). In the breaking-away strategy, the minimal amount of the tail necessary to escape is shed, whereas in the distraction strategy, most of the organ is lost.

Tail size appears to alter the effectiveness of autotomy. Thus, the relatively and absolutely smaller tails of juvenile *Phyllodactylus marmoratus* are less efficient than those of adults at attracting the attention of the marsupial predator, *Antechinus swainsonii* (Daniels et al., 1986). High risk of predation may favor the evolution of relatively long tails (Vitt and Congdon, 1978) as this would increase the chances that a pursuing predator would grasp the appendage rather than the lizard. In the Kalahari desert, species of widely foraging lacertid lizards appear to be at greater risk from predators and have longer tails than do sit-and-wait species (Huey and Pianka, 1981). A similar correlation occurs in lizards from northeast Brazil (Vitt, 1983), and members of the amphisbaenian genus *Bipes* have longer tails wherever they coexist with coral snakes, *Micrurus*, which are one of their main predators (Papenfuss, 1982).

Tails of lizards with intravertebral autotomy have a high energy content, containing large amounts of fat, which could be interpreted as increasing their attractiveness to predators familiar with lizards. However, the caudal fat of the lizard may simply be part of its energy resources that cannot be stored anywhere else (Dial and Fitzpatrick, 1983); perhaps, it is also a necessary component of the intravertebral autotomy mechanism. This last hypothesis receives some support because squamates with intervertebral autotomy or no autotomy lack well developed fat deposits in the tail.

Many lizards have bright coloring on the tail, especially when young (Section IV.G; Greene, this volume). In many cases this may attract the attention of predators so that attack is diverted away from the head and body (Section IV.A). The bright blue tails of hatchling *Eumeces fasciatus* and *E. laticeps* appear to function in this way (Cooper and Vitt, 1985; Vitt and Cooper, 1986). In trials with the snake *Lampropeltis triangulum elapsoides*, a total of 9 out of 18 young skinks were bitten on the tail and escaped by autotomy, but in animals in which caudal color was obliterated, nearly all attacks were directed at the body and only 1 out of 15 individuals evaded the predator.

The tail is often moved conspicuously in the presence of a predator and may be directed towards it. Thus, *Coleonyx* may turn so that its tail is towards an attacking snake (Dial, 1978), holding the tail upwards and waving it back and forth (Congdon et al., 1974; Dial, 1978). The tail is also held upwards in *Chondrodactylus* and *Palmatogecko* (Haacke, 1976a,b). In young *Stenodactylus leptocosymbotes* and *S. slevini*, sinusoidal waves pass slowly along the extended tail (Arnold, 1984), and *Phyllodactylus marmoratus* may undulate the tail laterally (Daniels, 1984). Such displays are frequent and readily elicited in geckos, such as those just mentioned, that use the distraction strategy and shed the whole tail (Section IV.C). Other species also exhibit this behavior, particularly if flight is impossible. For instance, many lacertids wave the distal part of the tail in the presence of predators; *Lacerta oxycephala* does this vigorously if cornered by a snake (Arnold, 1984). As they dive into the litter to avoid snakes, hatchling blue-tailed skinks (*Eumeces*) wave their tails and thus distract predators away from more vulnerable parts of the skink's body (Cooper and Vitt, 1985; Vitt and Cooper, 1986).

In many lizards, the tail continues to move after autotomy, in some cases for 5 minutes or more (Vitt et al., 1977). The vigor and duration of activity differs among species. Thus autotomized tails thrash rapidly in *Hemidactylus turcicus* and *Scincella lateralis*, whereas caudal movements are much more restrained in *Anolis carolinensis* (Hennig, 1979; Dial and Fitzpatrick, 1983). Movement attracts the attention of predators to the detached tail and increases handling time, thus enhancing the opportunity for the lizard to escape. Thrashing tails of *Scincella lateralis* are far more effective than exhausted tails of this species, or than active or exhausted tails of *Anolis carolinensis*, in enabling lizards to escape from a feral cat (Dial and Fitzpatrick, 1983). Snakes (*Lampropeltis triangulum*) also take longer to ingest thrashing than exhausted tails of *Scincella* and are more likely to give them prolonged attention; the snakes appear to treat them as they would a live lizard. Tails of *Scincella* have high anaerobic capacities and appear to be physiologically adapted for extended postautotomy movement; autotomized tails accumulate higher levels of lactate than do autotomized tails of *Anolis carolinensis* (Dial and Fitzpatrick, 1983).

Shed tails are not always eaten by the predators that caused them to become detached. In such circumstances, the individuals that autotomized may return and eat their tail, enabling them to recoup some of its contained material and energy. This behavior is known in *Scincella lateralis* (Clark, 1971) and has been demonstrated in captive *Eumeces* and *Xantusia* (Vitt et al., 1977). Experiments suggest that postautotomy movements propels tails of *Scincella* through leaf litter, so that they move out of sight, facilitating their retrieval and eating by the owner (Clark, 1971).

By modifying its behavior until the tail is at least partly regenerated, a lizard could avoid some of the likely functional costs of autotomy. For instance, by stopping close to cover, it could reduce the risk of being attacked by a predator at a time at which caudal autotomy could not be used successfully and locomotory ability is impaired. *Anolis carolinensis* may compensate for tail loss in this manner (Hennig, 1979). The skink, *Sphenomorphus quoyii* usually escapes by diving into water and swimming away using its tail; after autotomy it changes its escape strategy, either by fleeing onto land or by hiding on the bottom of water courses (Daniels, 1985b). *Phyllodactylus marmoratus* appears to have some automatic behavioral compensation for tail loss (Daniels, 1983). After the tail is lost, the fleeing lizard almost doubles its speed. On the other hand, not all behavioral changes are likely to decrease predator contact. In captivity, autotomy of the tail by female *Coleonyx brevis* is followed by a substantial increase in the rate of food ingestion; apparently they compensate for the lost energy reserves of the tail. In natural conditions, this would increase foraging time and exposure of the lizard to predators during a period when primary defense mechanisms are impaired (Dial and Fitzpatrick, 1981).

The cost of tail replacement can be avoided by not regenerating it, or spread by doing so only slowly. However, this is likely only if tail shedding does not involve substantial net long-term costs.

IV. VARIATIONS IN THE AUTOTOMY PROCESS AND THEIR CAUSES

A. Total Loss of Intravertebral Autotomy

If the loss of intravertebral autotomy frequently resulted from environmental selective pressures similar to those still acting on the taxa concerned, its distribution should correlate with particular modes of life in which the likely costs of autotomy exceed its likely benefits. Appraisal of likely costs is difficult, even in an informal qualitative way, as none of the numerous possible components has been fully assessed for any species. Variations in likely benefits are perhaps easier to discern, as fewer factors are liable to be significant, and these are easier to estimate. On the whole, the magnitude of benefits may be more important than that of costs in determining whether autotomy is lost, as the former vary more. Costs tend to be substantial. In most cases, regeneration of the tail requires considerable metabolic input, and during this time some significant caudal functions are lost. On the other hand, costs are rarely extremely high. Presumably, most lizards survive the transient effects of tail loss, which may be of quite short duration, as regrowth is often swift and functional losses may be substantially reduced by the time that the tail is partially regrown. Furthermore, behavioral considerations during this period, such as stopping closer to cover or changing escape strategy, may sometimes reduce the risks of subsequent predation (Section III.H). In contrast, benefits of autotomy range from great (i.e., the lizard escapes) to nonexistent. The latter involves species too slow to escape from predators. Most lizards that do not autotomize fall into three groups, in each of which the potential benefits of autotomy appear to be low.

The first group is made up of large forms and includes the iguanids *Amblyrhynchus, Conolophus, Ctenosaura, Cyclura,* and *Iguana,* and the teiid *Tupinambis.* In some *Conolophus,* and *Ctenosaura, Iguana iguana,* and *Tupinambis,* the ability to autotomize is lost during ontogeny. Adults of these forms are often capable of active defense against predators by biting, clawing, and tail lashing. Several of the species occur on small islands, on which predation levels are likely to be low, at least for adults. Both these factors would be expected to reduce the benefits of tail shedding.

The second group comprises slow-moving forms with unpalatable tails, including the iguanids *Hoplocercus, Leiosaurus, Phrynosoma,* and *Uracentron,* the gecko *Nephrurus laevis,* and the skinks *Egernia depressa, Tiliqua (Trachydosaurus) rugosa,* and *Tiliqua scincoides.* In the latter two species, the ability to autotomize is lost only during ontogeny. Most of these species move slowly and the tail is either very small compared with the body (for instance in *Phrynosoma* and *Nephrurus*) or spiny (*Hoplocercus, Uracentron, Egernia depressa*). Inability to flee very effectively and tails that are unlikely to capture the attention of a predator for long again restrict the possible benefits of caudal autotomy.

The third group is made up of forms that climb in vegetation, such as the iguanids *Anisolepis, Anolis etheridgei, Anolis latifrons* series, *Apty-*

cholaemus, Basiliscus, Chamaeleolis, Chamaelinorops, Corythophanes, Enyalius, Enyalioides, Laemanctus, Phenacosaurus, Polychroides, Polychrus, and *Urostrophus,* and the skink *Corucia zebrata.* This assemblage includes a range of lizards that appear to spend all, or a substantial part, of their time among small branches, twigs and leaves or other complex vegetation. Rapid escape from predators, such as birds and snakes, is often difficult in such an environment; surfaces are discontinuous and refuges rare. Many of these lizards are sluggish, at least at times, and frequently adopt slow gaits. Some are capable of hopping from branch to branch (for instance *Corythophanes,* Davis, 1953; *Laemanctus,* McCoy, 1968; *Polychrus,* Cott, 1926; Böker, 1935), but even this mode of progression is not especially fast. Antipredator mechanisms may involve aggressive displays or postures that increase apparent body size (Davis, 1953), rather than immediate resort to flight.

Caudal autotomy is likely to have reduced value in enabling such lizards to break away from predators or distract them. The tails of such lizards do not show much postautotomy movement (Vitt, 1983) and are often very slender rather than stout. Hence, they are unlikely to deflect the attention of an attacker. Experiments with *Anolis carolinensis,* which approaches this group in many caudal features, show that its tail is ineffective in deflecting predator attacks (Dial and Fitzpatrick, 1983). This line of explanation is less convincing for the basiliscines (*Basiliscus, Corythophanes,* and *Laemanctus*); many of their species are known to descend from vegetation and are capable of bursts of fast locomotion on horizontal surfaces (Duellman, 1963; McCoy, 1968; Davis, 1953). Although they could theoretically benefit from autotomy, these lizards run bipedally and, at least for *Basiliscus,* the tail is essentially for maintaining running posture (Section III.F).

Loss of autotomy also occurs in some other forms, namely *Gambelia,* some *Ophisaurus,* many Agamidae, Chamaeleonidae, Helodermatidae, Lanthanotidae, and Varanidae. The bipedal ground dweller *Gambelia* may have lost autotomy for the same reasons as the basiliscines, but it is not obvious why loss should have occurred in some species of *Ophisaurus.* Many Agamidae, Chamaeleonidae, and Varanidae are ecologically similar to species from other families that lack autotomy mechanisms. Thus many varanids are large and capable of actively deterring some predators, whereas chameleons and some agamids generally live in vegetation, are slow moving, and rely on their tails for support whenever moving among twigs; however, numerous forms are ecologically analogous to members of other families that retain intravertebral autotomy. For instance, some of the small Australian species of *Varanus* are ecologically similar to some autotomizing skinks, teiids, and lacertids.

In the same way, the agamid, *Leiolepis* is quite like the iguanid, *Dipsosaurus*, and the small ground dwelling agamids, *Phrynocephalus* and *Tympanocryptis*, superficially resemble such iguanids as *Holbrookia*. This lack of correlation tends to support the view (Section III.C) that absence of intravertebral autotomy in the Platynota, Agamidae, and Chamaeleonidae is due to loss early in the history of these groups rather than to its being universally disadvantageous to present species.

It might be asked why intravertebral autotomy has not been lost more widely, given the apparent facility with which this trait disappears. This may simply be because the great majority of species retaining it do not have the sort of life mode favoring loss. For example, among fully autotomous geckos, pygopodids, lacertids, teiids, xantusiids, cordylids, and agamids, few species are large, very slow, or possess unappetizing tails; also, the great majority of these forms do not inhabit the sort of vegetation in which many nonautotomous iguanids occur.

B. Re-evolution of Autotomy

Tail breakage by intervertebral fracture occurs in some agamids and snakes and is the only kind of autotomy occurring in these groups. Breakage in agamids was thought to take place across the centra of the more distal vertebrae, which are narrow in many species, and not between them (Siebenrock, 1895). This impression is incorrect and probably arose because the last vertebra remaining after autotomy undergoes some ablation before healing or regeneration, so its posterior section is absent (Arnold, 1984). Intervertebral autotomy appears to represent a re-evolution of tail-shedding ability, involves relatively slight modification of caudal structure and has apparently arisen a number of times (Section III.C). Even so, in the Agamidae it is by no means universal and is almost entirely confined to two ecomorphological types of lizard. The first are climbing forms, nearly all of which live on rock surfaces and include *Agama (Agama)*, *Agama (Pseudotrapelus)*, *Agama (Stellio)*, and *Psammophilus*. The second includes terrestrial species and some that climb in vegetation. They have relatively long hind legs and very long tails that become extremely slender distally. A number of these forms are known or suspected to be bipedal (Russell and Rewcastle, 1979) and autotomy is usually restricted to the distal parts of the tail. They include some *Amphibolurus* species, (*A. caudicinctus, A. cristatus, A. isolepis, A. maculatus,* and *A. pictus*), *Diporiphora bilineata, Gonocephalus subcristatus, Lophognathus temporalis, Otocryptis wiegmanni, Physignathus lesueurii,* and *Sitana ponticeriana*. Neither of these groups appears to be holophyletic.

Thus, although appparently quite easily evolved, intervertebral autotomy has not developed in a variety of fast, ground-dwelling agamids that, by analogy with intravertebrally autotomizing iguanids (Section IV.A) might be expected to have it. One possible reason for this is that the evolution of autotomy and regenerative ability in agamids may be independent events. Forms like *Diporiphora, Otocryptis, Psammophilus,* and *Sitana* can only autotomize and do not regenerate, whereas most of the other agamids listed above do both. If intervertebral autotomy usually evolves before the ability to regenerate, it will only become established in situations in which permanent loss of much of the tail does not carry heavy penalties, or in which loss can usefully be limited to a small portion of it. Such situations may be rather rare.

Circumstantial evidence suggests that the tail is often less important to rock-dwelling species than to those in other habitats (Section IV.F), so tail loss may be survivable by the former even without regeneration. In long-tailed, frequently bipedal agamids in which autotomy is usually restricted to the distal part of the organ, such modest loss may have only a minimal effect on the balancing function of the tail. This suggests that analogous bipedal forms, such as the basiliscine iguanids, should also have distal autotomy, but they do not. Perhaps this reflects the way in which the ability to shed the tail has been lost in groups such as iguanids that were originally intravertebral autotomizers. Both in ontogeny and phylogeny, the fracture planes in the vertebrae fuse from the caudal tip forwards (Etheridge, 1967). Consequently, if selection favors retaining the greater part of the tail for balancing purposes in bipedal forms, the whole organ must become nonautotomous.

Among snakes, intervertebral autotomy is reported in *Pliocercus, Rhadinea decorata, Scaphiodontophis,* and *Sibynophis*. It is uncertain what factors may have caused its development in these few forms, all of which are characterized by very long tails. The rarity of the condition suggests that it has arisen only in rather special circumstances, but what these were is still a matter for conjecture. In *Scaphiodontophis*, the tail may be used to flush prey out of litter but also shows high incidence of damage (Henderson, 1984).

C. Restriction of Autotomy to the Caudal Base

Restriction of autotomy planes to the vertebrae of the caudal base occurs quite widely in geckos (Arnold, 1984), including the eublepharine *Hoplodactylus,* the diplodactylines *Carphodactylus, Diplodactylus stenodactylus, D. strophurus, D. vittatus, Heteropholis, Naultinus, Nephrurus laevis, Oedura castelnaui, O. marmoratus, Phyllurus,* and *Gymnodactylus,* and the gekkonines *Colopus, Kaokogecko, Geckonia, Pachydactylus mariquensis, Palmatogecko, Paroedura, Stenodactylus affinis, S. doriae, S. grandiceps, S. leptocosymbotes, S. petrii, S. slevini, S. sthenodactylus, S. yemenicus, Tetratolepis fasciata,* and *Uroplatus.* In others, autotomy planes may occur more widely but autotomy is still most usually basal, for example among the eublepharines *Aeluroscalabotes, Eublepharis,* and *Hemitheconyx,* and the gekkonines *Chondrodactylus, Crossobamon eversmanni, Phyllodactylus marmoratus* (Daniels, 1985a), *Pristurus carteri, P. collaris, P. ornithocephalus,* and *Ptenopus.* Basal restriction of autotomy planes also occurs in some species of *Anolis,* but in some cases autotomy can still occur more distally (Cox, 1969). Because of this, discussion will be limited to geckos.

In most lizards, the tail is autotomous throughout its length distal to the pygal vertebrae, and breakage often takes place just in front of the place at which the tail is seized, or contacted, by a predator. This "economy of autotomy" minimizes costs for a lizard breaking away from the grip of a pursuer. Nevertheless, some species always shed the whole tail, although it often contains substantial amounts of stored fat (for example in *Phyllodactylus marmoratus;* Daniels, 1983). However, breaking away from a predator is only likely to be successful if the lizard has the speed to evade further pursuit or if a refuge is close.

Relatively slow species, particularly ones living in habitats with few secure shelters, probably rely on a different strategy in which the tail is used to deflect the attention of predators from the more vulnerable head and body. However, sacrifice of the smallest portion of the tail possible may not be sufficient to retain the attention of a predator and restriction of autotomy to the caudal base could be a means of ensuring that a large enough "bait" is provided to deflect an attacker. The distribution of basal autotomy tends to support such an interpretation. Many of the geckos listed above are indeed relatively slow, slower than relatives with functioning autotomy planes throughout the tail (Arnold, 1984). Thus, basally autotomizing *Pristurus* and *Stenodactylus* are slower than other members of these genera. Further, many basal autotomizers occupy open arid country, in which refuges are likely to be sparse; most other basal autotomizers climb in bushy vegetation in which the same may be true.

D. Ontogenetic Loss of Autotomy

Juveniles of many species of lizards possess well developed autotomy mechanisms and reduce, or more often, obliterate them by maturity. Examples are *Iguana iguana, Cyclura* spp., *Ctenosaura acanthura, Sauro-*

malus, Basiliscus, Enyalioides, most members of the *Anolis latifrons* series, *Trachydosaurus, Tiliqua rugosus, Tiliqua scincoides,* and some *Tupinambis teguixin.*

Presumably the change results from a shift in the balance of costs and benefits, either the former rising or the latter falling with increase in body size, or both. The benefits of autotomy are probably greater in young animals, because of their more obvious vulnerability compared with adults (Section IV.G). Not surprisingly, ontogenetic loss of autotomy is commonest in quite large species.

E. Short-term Changes Within the Individual

The strength of individual fracture planes determines the maximum force necessary to produce physical breakage of a particular part of the tail; but much smaller stimuli may initiate autotomy, and the threshold for this often varies considerably within individual lizards.

Such variation has undergone little formal investigation but a number of observations indicate that it exists. (1) Conscious animals typically shed their tails more readily than unconscious ones (see for example Slotopolsky, 1922). (2) Ease of autotomy may vary with temperature, for example in *Uta stansburiana* (Brattstrom, 1965), *Podarcis sicula* (Quattrini, 1952), *Stenodactylus* (Werner, 1964), *Gehyra variegata* (Bustard, 1968), and *Phyllodactylus marmoratus* (Daniels, 1984). In most cases, autotomy occurs most easily at high temperatures, but in *Gehyra* it takes place readily at high or at low temperatures. (3) Captive lizards, including many lacertids, that become tame will tolerate a degree of handling of the tail that would produce immediate autotomy in wild animals. (4) In some species, such as the lacertids *Podarcis sicula* and *Lacerta vivipara*, the tail is shed quite readily if grasped as the lizard runs away. However, if the tail is pulled or twisted while the lizard is held by the body, the tail can be detached only with difficulty. (5) Ease of autotomy may change with physiological state; thus, starved *Phyllodactylus marmoratus* shed the tail less readily than well fed ones (Daniels, 1984). (6) *Scincella* (Dial and Fitzpatrick, 1983), *Coleonyx* (Congdon et al., 1974), and *Eumeces* (Vitt and Cooper, 1986) do not autotomize their tails immediately upon being grasped by a predator. This may allow the lizard the opportunity to escape with an intact tail if the predator's grasp is poor.

These examples suggest that tail shedding threshold is modified in the individual by neurological means in response to external circumstances. If the mechanism is optimally adjusted by natural selection, autotomy should only occur easily in situations for which likely benefits exceed likely costs. The likely costs of losing a given portion of tail are probably quite constant in the short term (although they may vary seasonally, for instance if large amounts of fat are stored in the tail at certain times of the year). Likely benefits on the other hand change very rapidly. The benefits of autotomizing the tail are probably low until a predator is at close quarters. They will rise further if the predator actually makes contact with the tail and would be expected to be higher still if the predator is of a kind that is efficient at capturing lizards.

At least some of the known individual variation in autotomy threshold appears to be adaptive, and Brattstrom (1965) and Bustard (1968) provide functional hypotheses for temperature-correlated change in *Uta* and *Gehyra*, respectively. In the case of a lizard held by the body, tail shedding is probably of little advantage as it will not aid escape. In this situation, a high autotomy threshold would make retention of the tail more probable; if the lizard subsequently breaks free, it could still utilize caudal autotomy in any further pursuit.

F. Interspecific Variation in the Readiness With Which the Tail Is Shed

Not only should the complete loss of autotomy mechanisms be determined by the balance of costs and benefits but so should relative readiness with which the tail is shed by different autotomizing species. Tails should be relinquished most easily in those species with the lowest costs of loss, in terms of future reproduction. If the loss of the tail is comparatively inexpensive, the lizard can "afford" not to take high risks and autotomy can be brought into operation even in circumstances in which the chances of capture are not especially high. Conversely, if loss of the tail is likely to be very costly, autotomy should be delayed until the risk of capture without autotomy approaches certainty. For example, if loss of the tail only slightly reduces future reproduction on average, autotomy should be initiated whenever the risks of being caught and killed by the pursuing predator are also low. However, if the chances of failing to reproduce after tail loss are high, autotomy should be delayed until the probability of being killed by the predator rises to this level. Animals with low-cost tails should therefore autotomize earlier in response to a particular kind of attack and at lower levels of tactile stimulation.

That such interspecific differences in autotomy threshold exist is apparent to anyone who has tried to catch diverse species of lizards. Some species shed the tail if it is only lightly touched during pursuit, whereas others only break it if the organ is grasped very firmly. Among European lacertids, tails appear to break most readily in rock climbing species, such as *Lacerta oxycephala*, and, in Arabian geckos, fragility seems to be greater in climbing forms than in ground dwellers. Such assessments are, of course, subjective as we lack satisfactory comparative measurements of tail fragility. This is largely because of the difficulty of delivering calibrated stimuli to lizards under natural conditions. Moreover, habituation and restraint may alter autotomy thresholds of captive animals, perhaps differentially among species. In addition, applied stimuli should mimic the kinds of contacts made by predators; the attachment of weights to the tail (Quattrini, 1952; Brattstrom, 1965; Daniels, 1984), though easy to apply and measure, are unlike anything that lizards usually encounter.

G. Brightly Colored Tails

Many lizards have their tails colored in a way that contrasts with that of the rest of the body. This can enhance the effectiveness of caudal autotomy (Section III.H), although a number of alternative functions are possible (Cooper and Vitt, 1985). Markings, such as bold transverse bars, may be disruptive, breaking up the outline of the tail. Caudal coloring might be used in intraspecific signalling or contribute to other antipredator devices (Section III.F, III.G). None of the available explanations of conspicuous caudal markings necessarily rules out the others. Conspicuous tail markings occur in some nonautotomous species, for instance some *Varanus* and *Phrynocephalus*, although not as commonly as in autotomous ones. In many cases, the main function is probably not to direct attention to the tail. However, this explanation cannot be completely excluded, as diversion of attack from more vital areas to the tail may be advantageous although the tail cannot be shed. This usage is suggested for snakes with bright, nonautotomic tails (Greene, 1973).

Regularities in the occurrence of bright caudal coloring have been surveyed in lizard faunas of Arabia and in those of Europe west of the U.S.S.R. (Arnold, 1984); the following remarks are largely based on these surveys. In nearly all cases in which conspicuously colored tails occur, the caudal coloring is substantially exposed in the living lizard. It typically occurs on the dorsal caudal surface and is most intense here; although a few species have bright coloring on the underside of the tail so colored. In species that practice economy of autotomy, caudal coloring is more intense distally; it presumably directs attention away from the more vulnerable body and towards the caudal tip, so that the amount of tail lost will be minimal. In forms that shed the whole tail, coloring tends to be more uniformly distributed.

Permanently exposed bright caudal coloring carries the risk of attracting the attention of predators that would not have otherwise detected the lizard. At first sight, a better strategy would be to have conspicuous coloring concealed, for instance beneath the tail, and only exposed once a predator is at close quarters. This, however, would require the approach of the predator to be detected sufficiently early to allow time for the caudal coloring to be deployed. Most lizards, particularly active foragers, may not be able to afford the high degree of vigilance involved, especially at times during which their attention is largely devoted to hunting. The risk inherent in permanently exposed bright coloring, namely that of sometimes attracting a predator that otherwise might have ignored the lizard, may be offset by the advantage that the attention of the predator will be constantly directed toward the tail.

Conspicuous caudal coloring is better developed in young than in adults, and often disappears entirely before maturity. This may reflect the greater vulnerability of juveniles to predation. Being small, they can be tackled by a greater range of predators. Frequently, they are built more delicately than equivalent-sized adult lizards and are likely to be slower. Newly hatched or dispersing juveniles are unfamiliar with their immediate surroundings and cannot flee to refuges or otherwise evade capture with the speed and facility provided by detailed knowledge of a home range. The loss of the color at maturity may partly relate to the disastrous effect of loss of tail lipids on reproduction of females (Vitt and Cooper, 1986).

Conspicuous caudal marking is typically associated with open situations lacking much vegetation and the shadows it throws. Lizards living in open, uniform habitats are quite easily seen; this may increase the need for diverting attention from head to the tail. In Arabia, ground dwelling forms from open sand and gravel substrates have contrastingly colored tails, as do species climbing on continuous open surfaces, such as rock faces. In contrast, bright tails are absent in species inhabiting litter, dense vegetation and rocky surfaces with good plant cover. Most European lizard habitats are relatively enclosed and bright caudal color here is uncommon and largely confined to rock-dwelling forms. In Arabia and Europe, most species with conspicuous tails are active, widely-ranging foragers. These place limited reliance on crypsis and may be more vulnerable to predators than are sit-and-wait species. Whether bright caudal coloring and activity are really correlated is difficult to confirm in these areas, as autotomizing passive foragers are uncommon. In the New World, conspicuous caudal coloring is more frequent in actively hunting groups, such as teiids and skinks, than among sit-and-wait iguanids; however, the above association with type of habitat is unsupported (Vitt and Cooper, 1986).

Nocturnal species (predominantly geckos) with conspicuous tails nearly always have the tail patterned with light and dark areas, often forming transverse bands. In contrast, most diurnal forms have bright colors of which blue and blue-green are by far the most common. This difference correlates with the usual visual capacity of nocturnal and diurnal predators. Night operating hunters have poor color vision and probably the objects most conspicuous to them are ones in which light and dark areas are juxtaposed; on the other hand, many diurnal hunters such as birds can distinguish colors.

The predominance of blue and blue-green coloring in diurnal lizards may be adaptive because these colors are conspicuous from a short distance but much less arresting from far away compared to reds and yellows. This may have the advantage of making the tail stand out at close quarters without attracting more distant predators.

H. Regeneration of the Tail

Most lizards that autotomize the tail regenerate the shed portion. In many cases, the greater part is replaced quite rapidly. For instance, *Lacerta dugesii* takes only 12 weeks to regenerate 90% of the length of the portion originally lost (Bryant and Bellairs, 1976), and the tail of *Coleonyx brevis* may regenerate in 4–5 weeks (Dial, 1978). In contrast, a number of forms reproduce the tail very slowly, if at all. This is the case in snakes and some agamids; autotomizing amphisbaenians do not regenerate (Gans, 1978). Rate and extent of caudal regeneration differs not only among taxa but also among ontogenetic stages and sexes of the same species and even in the same individual in different situations.

Except, perhaps, in some forms that have completely lost the ability to regenerate, rate and extent of caudal replacement should be determined by the balance between present costs and benefits. Benefits of regeneration include the restitution of the tail as an antipredator device and all the other things listed as costs of autotomy in Section III.F. Costs of regeneration, on the other hand, involve the energetic and material expense of regenerating the tail and that of maintaining it subsequently. As we have seen, these costs may possibly be met by increased food intake or diversion of energy from other functions, such as somatic growth or reproductive effort (Section III.F). The optimal balance between these factors varies with circumstances and, in many cases, there is considerable compromise between them. Thus, young *Uta stansburiana* may curtail general growth while the tail regenerates (Ballinger and Tinkle, 1979). In contrast, juveniles of *Coleonyx variegatus*, *Eumeces skiltonianus* and *E. gilberti* devote a smaller proportion of their disposable energy to regeneration than do adults. In female *Coleonyx brevis*, the rate of regeneration is generally less than in males, apparently because of the need to use energy during vitellogenesis; regeneration of the tail is slow until vitellogenesis has been completed (Dial and Fitzpatrick, 1983).

The rate of regeneration might correlate with the life history of species. Long-lived, slowly maturing forms with short annual breeding seasons are thought to give precedence to reproduction and to regenerate slowly, whereas short-lived species that have several breeding episodes each year will reproduce the tail rapidly (Vitt et al., 1977). *Elgaria multicarinata* conforms to the first type, and *Coleonyx* approaches the second (Vitt et al., 1977; Dial and Fitzpatrick, 1981). More data are needed to test this supposed regularity. *Mabuya heathi*, which has a very short annual breeding season, regenerates the tail very quickly (Vitt, 1981).

Slow regeneration rates appear to be most frequent in elongate, usually legless lepidosaurians that burrow or live cryptically close to the earth-vegetation interface or under objects. Thus, *Anguis fragilis* typically produces a regenerate less than 5 mm long in 14 weeks (Bryant and Bellairs, 1976) and the skink *Ophiomorus streeti* may regenerate even more slowly (Rathor, 1971). Similarly, a captive *Anniella pulchra* developed a regenerate of only 4.1 mm in 11 months (Miller, 1944). Detailed information on regeneration rates is not available for other lizards with this general mode of life history. Only small regenerates are found in museum material of many such species, suggesting that caudal replacement is very incomplete, or at least extremely slow. This appears to be true of the anguids, *Ophisaurus* and *Ophiodes* and such skinks as *Acontias*, *Melanoseps*, and *Ophiomorus* species, in addition to *O. streeti*, *Parachalcides*, *Scelotes*, and *Sphenops*. As previously noted, caudal regeneration is lacking in all of the autotomizing amphisbaenians and in the few colubrid snakes that are known to shed portions of the tail.

Benefits of regeneration may not be high in these squamates for few of the potential advantages of possessing a tail seem likely to be important to them. The tail may contribute to locomotion, but in limbless forms moving among herbage or loose soil, additional length beyond a critical level may not increase velocity. Also, a long tail may be less important as an antipredator device in these largely cryptic forms. Nevertheless, in at least some of them, it seems to allow breaking way from predators and may do so more than once, in spite of poor regenerative capacity. In *Anguis*, for instance, although many animals have damaged tails, these are rarely broken close to the vent. Often most of the organ is retained, suggesting that losses are often small and that the tail may be able to function in a number of predator encounters, even without intervening regrowth. Costs of regeneration may be considerable. Possibly they are important in dictating very restricted replacement in slowly-growing forms such as *Anguis*.

V. FURTHER RESEARCH

Although work on caudal autotomy has blossomed in the last few years, many areas remain that merit investigation. Indeed, research in the topic tends to generate as many questions as answers. Not infrequently, the information needed involves much wider aspects of the animal than autotomy itself. For instance, broad studies of predation intensity and efficiency are necessary for the interpretation of tail break frequencies in natural populations. Again, very little is known about the relative survivorship of lizards in nature that have autotomized the tail relative to those that retain them. Experimental determination of speed in a wide range of fleeing lizards is required to determine whether forms that shed most of the tail are indeed slower than those that practice economy of autotomy.

Another area of interest is the facility with which autotomy takes place. Do delicately built species or ones that mainly use the tail for autotomy relinquish it more easily than others? Do individual lizards really alter their autotomy threshold over short periods so that it is optimally adapted to current circumstances? These questions involve formidable technical problems of delivering natural but calibrated stimuli to lizards (of known behavioral history) and to their tails. Predator response is also poorly known. For instance, experiments are needed to determine whether blue tails are really less likely to attract predators from a distance than are red and yellow ones.

ACKNOWLEDGMENTS

I am most grateful to C. Gans, R. B. Huey, and H. Greene for reading drafts of this chapter and making helpful comments, and to A. d'A. Bellairs for useful discussion.

REFERENCES

Arnold, E. N. (1980). The reptiles and amphibians of Dhofar, Southern Arabia. J. Oman Stud., Spec. Rep. 2, 273–332.

Arnold, E. N. (1984). Evolutionary aspects of tail shedding in lizards and their relatives. J. Nat. Hist. 18, 127–169.

Arnold, E. N. and Gallagher, M. D. (1977). Reptiles and amphibians from the mountains of northern Oman with special reference to the Jebel Akhdar region. J. Oman Stud., Spec. Rep. 1, 58–80.

Avery, R. A. (1970). Utilization of caudal fat by hibernating common lizards, *Lacerta vivipara*. Comp. Biochem. Physiol. 37, 119–121.

Auffenberg, W. (1981). *The Behavioral Ecology of the Komodo Monitor.* University of Florida, Gainesville.

Ballinger, R. E. (1973). Experimental evidence of the tail as a balancing organ in the lizard, *Anolis carolinensis*. Herpetologica 29, 65–66.

Ballinger, R. E. (1979). Intraspecific variation in demography and life history of the lizard *Sceloporus jarrovi* along an altitudinal gradient in southeastern Arizona. Ecology 60, 901–909.

Ballinger, R. E., Nietfeldt, J. W. and Krupa, J. J. (1979). An experimental analysis of the role of the tail in attaining high running speed in *Cnemidophorus sexlineatus* (Reptilia: Squamata: Lacertilia). Herpetologica 35, 114–116.

Ballinger, R. E. and Tinkle, D. W. (1979). On the cost of tail regeneration to body growth in lizards. J. Herpetol. 13, 374–375.

Bartholomew, G. A., Bennett, A. F. and Dawson, W. R. (1976). Swimming, diving and lactate production of the marine iguana, *Amblyrhynchus cristatus*. Copeia 1976, 709–720.

Bauwens, D. (1981). Survivorship during hibernation in the European common lizard, *Lacerta vivipara*. Copeia 1981, 741–744.

Bellairs, A. d'A. and Bryant, S. V. (1985). Autotomy and regeneration in reptiles. In *Biology of the Reptilia*, Volume 15, Development B (C. Gans and F. Billett, eds.). John Wiley & Sons, New York, pp. 301–410.

Blair, W. F. (1960). *The Rusty Lizard. A Population Study.* University of Texas Press, Austin.

Böker, H. (1935). *Einführung in die vergleichende biologische Anatomie der Wirbeltiere. 1. Aufgaben und Methoden: Die morphologische Typologie: Biologische Anatomie der Fortbewegung.* G. Fischer, Jena.

Boring, A. M., Chang, L.-F. and Chang, W.-H. (1948). Autotomy and regeneration in the tails of lizards. Peking Nat. Hist. Bull. 17, 85–108.

Brattstrom, B. H. (1965). Body temperatures of reptiles. Am. Midl. Nat. 73, 376–422.

Brooks, G. R., Jr. (1967). Population ecology of the ground skink, *Lygosoma laterale* (Say). Ecol. Monogr. 37, 71–87.

Brown, C. K. and Ruby, D. E. (1977). Sex-associated variation in the frequencies of tail autotomy in *Sceloporus jarrovi* (Sauria: Iguanidae) at different elevations. Herpetologica 33, 380–387.

Bryant, S. V. and Bellairs, A. d'A. (1976). Tail regeneration in the lizards *Anguis fragilis* and *Lacerta dugesii*. J. Linn. Soc. (Zool.) Lond. 46, 297–305.

Bustard, H. R. (1964). Defensive behavior shown by Australian geckos, genus *Diplodactylus*. Herpetologica 20, 198–200.

Bustard, H. R. (1968). Temperature dependent tail autotomy mechanism in gekkonid lizards. Herpetologica 24, 127–130.

Bustard, H. R. (1970). *Australian Lizards.* Collins, Sydney and London.

Bustard, H. R. and Hughes, R. D. (1966). Gekkonid lizards: Average ages derived from tail loss data. Science 153, 1670–1671.

Cantor, T. (1847). Catalogue of reptiles inhabiting the Malayan peninsula and islands,

REFERENCES

collected and observed by Theodore Cantor, Esq., M. D. J. Asiat. Soc. Bengal 16, 607–656.
Carpenter, C. C. (1958). Reproduction, young, eggs and food of Oklahoma snakes. Herpetologica 14, 113–115.
Carpenter, C. C. and Ferguson, G. W. (1977). Variation and evolution of stereotyped behavior in reptiles. In *Biology of the Reptilia*, Volume 7, Ecology and Behavior A (C. Gans and D. W. Tinkle, eds.). Academic Press, London, pp. 335–554.
Clark, D. R. (1971). The strategy of tail-autotomy in the ground skink, *Lygosoma laterale*. J. Exp. Zool. 176, 295–302.
Congdon, J. D., Vitt, L. J. and King, W. W. (1974). Geckos: Adaptive significance and energetics of tail autotomy. Science 184, 1379–1380.
Cooke, L. M. (1979). Variation in the Madeiran wall lizard *Lacerta dugesii*. J. Zool. 187, 327–340.
Cooper, W. E. and Vitt, L. J. (1985). Blue tails and autotomy: Enhancement of predation avoidance in juvenile skinks. Z. Tierpsychol. 70, 265–276.
Cott, H. B., 1926. Observations on the life habits of some batrachians and reptiles from the lower Amazon: And a note on some mammals from Marajó Island. Proc. Zool. Soc. Lond. 1926, 1159–1178.
Cott, H. B. (1957). *Adaptive Colouration in Animals*. Methuen, London.
Cox, P. G. (1969). Some aspects of tail regeneration in the lizard, *Anolis carolinensis*. 1. A description based on histology and autoradiography. J. Exp. Zool. 171, 127–150.
Cunningham, J. D. (1956). Food habits of the San Diego alligator lizard. Herpetologica 12, 225–230.
Daniels, C. B. (1983). Running: An escape strategy enhanced by autotomy. Herpetologica 39, 162–165.
Daniels, C. B. (1984). The importance of caudal lipid in the gecko *Phyllodactylus marmoratus*. Herpetologica 40, 337–344.
Daniels, C. B. (1985a). Economy of autotomy as a lipid conserving mechanism: An hypothesis rejected for the gecko *Phyllodactylus marmoratus*. Copeia 1985, 468–472.
Daniels, C. B. (1985b). The effect of tail autotomy on the exercise capacity of the water skink, *Sphenomorphus quoyii*. Copeia 1985, 1074–1077.
Daniels, C. B., Flaherty, S. P. and Simbotwe, M. P. (1986). Tail size and effectiveness of autotomy in a lizard. J. Herpetol. 20, 93–96.
Darwin, C. R. (1859). *The Origin of Species by Means of Natural Selection*. J. Murray, London.
Davis, D. D. (1953). Behavior of the lizard *Corythophanes cristatus*. Fieldiana: Zool. 35, 1–8.
Dial, B. E. (1978). Aspects of the behavioral ecology of two Chihuahuan desert geckos (Reptilia, Lacertilia, Gekkonidae). J. Herpetol. 12, 209–216.
Dial, B. E. (1986). Tail display in two species of iguanid lizards: A test of the "predator signal" hypothesis. Am. Nat. 127 103–111.
Dial, B. E. and Fitzpatrick, L. C. (1981). The energetic costs of tail autotomy to reproduction in the lizard *Coleonyx brevis* (Sauria: Gekkonidae). Oecologia, Beil. 51, 310–317.
Dial, B. E. and Fitzpatrick, L. C. (1983). Lizard tail autotomy: Function and energetics of postautotomy tail movement in *Scincella lateralis*. Science 219, 391–393.
Dial, B. E. and Fitzpatrick, L. C. (1984). Predator escape success in tailed versus tailless *Scincella lateralis* (Sauria: Scincidae). Anim. Behav. 32, 301–302.
Dixon, J. R. and Medica, P. A. (1966). Summer food of four species of lizards from the vicinity of White Sands, New Mexico. Los Angeles Co. Mus. Contr. Sci. 121, 1–6.
Duellman, W. E. (1963). Amphibians and reptiles of the rainforests of southern El Petén, Guatemala. Univ. Kans. Publs. Mus. Nat. Hist. 15, 205–249.

Etheridge, R. (1967). Lizard caudal vertebrae. Copeia 1967, 699–721.
Fitch, H. S. (1940). A field study of the growth and behavior of the fence lizard. Univ. Calif. Publs. Zool. 44, 151–172.
Fitch, H. S. (1954). Life history and ecology of the five-lined skink, *Eumeces fasciatus*. Univ. Kans. Publs. Mus. Nat. Hist. 8, 1–156.
FitzSimons, V. F. (1943). *The Lizards of South Africa*. Transvaal Museum, Pretoria.
FitzSimons, V. F. and Brain, C. K. (1958). A short account of the reptiles of the Kalahari Gemsbok National Park. Koedoe 1, 99–102.
Fox, S. F. and Rostker, M. A. (1982). Social cost of tail loss in *Uta stansburiana*. Science 218, 692–693.
Gans, C. (1978). The characteristics and affinities of the Amphisbaenia. Trans. Zoo. Soc. London 34, 347–416.
Gans, C. and Diefenbach, C. O. (1972). Description and geographical variation of the South American *Amphisbaena angustifrons:* The southernmost amphisbaenian in the world. Am. Mus. Novitates 2494, 1–20.
Gould, S. J. (1983). A life and death tail. Nat. Hist. 1983 (6), 12–16.
Greene, H. W. (1973). Defensive tail display by snakes and amphisbaenians. J. Herpetol. 7, 143–161.
Greene, H. W. (1984). Feeding behavior and diet of the eastern coral snake, *Micrurus fulvius*. Spec. Publ. Mus. Nat. Hist. Univ. Kansas 10, 147–163.
Haacke, W. (1976a). The burrowing geckos of southern Africa, 2 (Reptilia: Gekkonidae). Ann. Transv. Mus. 30, 13–28.
Haacke, W. (1976b). The burrowing geckos of southern Africa, 4 (Reptilia: Gekkonidae). Ann. Transv. Mus. 30, 53–70.
Haldane, J. B. S. and Huxley, J. S. (1927). *Animal Biology*. Oxford University Press, Oxford.
Harris, V. A. (1964). *The Life of the Rainbow Lizard*. Hutchinson, London.
Henderson, R. W. (1984). *Scaphiodontophis* (Serpentes, Colubridae): Natural history and test of a mimicry-related hypothesis. Spec. Publ. Mus. Nat. Hist. Univ. Kansas 10, 185–194.
Hennig, C. W. (1979). A functional investigation of tail autotomy in lizards. Diss. Abstr. Int. B 39(11), 5634.
Huey, R. B. and Pianka, E. R. (1977). Natural selection for juvenile lizards mimicking noxious beetles. Science 195, 201–203.
Huey, R. B. and Pianka, E. R. (1981). Ecological consequences of foraging mode. Ecology 62, 991–999.
Jaksić, F. M. and Fuentes, E. R. (1980). Correlates of tail loss in 12 species of *Liolaemus* lizards. J. Herpetol. 14, 137–141.
Jaksić, F. M. and Greene, H. W. (1984). Empirical evidence of non-correlation between tail loss frequency and predation intensity on lizards. Oikos 42: 407–411.
Labanick, G. M. (1984). Anti-predator effectiveness of autotomized tails of the salamander *Desmognathus ochrophaeus*. Herpetologica 40, 110–118.
Laurent, R. F. and Gans, C. (1965). Lizards. In Notes on a herpetological collection from the Somali Republic. Ann. Mus. Roy. Afr. Centr. 134, 25–46.
Maiorana, V. C. (1977). Tail autotomy, functional conflicts and their resolution in a salamander. Nature 265, 533–535.
Marcellini, D. L. and Keeper, T. E. (1976). Analysis of the gliding behavior of *Ptychozoon lionatum* (Reptilia: Gekkonidae). Herpetologica 32, 362–366.
Matthews, L. H. (1969–1971). *The Life of Mammals*. 2 Vols. Weidenfeld and Nicolson, London.
McCoy, C. J. (1968). A review of the genus *Laemanctus* (Reptilia, Iguanidae). Copeia 1968, 665–678.

REFERENCES

McKinney, C. O. and Ballinger, R. E. (1966). Snake predators of lizards in western Texas. *Southwest. Nat.* 11, 410–412.

Mebs, D. (1966). Studien zum aposematischen Verhalten von *Teratoscincus scincus*. *Salamandra* 2, 16–20.

Mertens, R. (1946). Die Warn- und Droh-Reaktionen der Reptilien. *Abhandl. Senck. Naturf. Ges.* 47, 1–108.

Miller, C. M. (1944). Ecological relations and adaptations of the limbless lizards of the genus *Anniella*. *Ecol. Monogr.* 14, 271–289.

Milstead, W. W. (1957). Some aspects of competition in natural populations of whiptail lizards (genus *Cnemidophorus*). *Texas J. Sci.* 9, 410–447.

Moody, S. M. (1980). *Phylogenetic and Historical Biogeographical Relationships of the Genera of the Family Agamidae (Reptilia: Lacertilia)*. Ph. D. Thesis, The University of Michigan.

Morin, P. J. (1985). Predation intensity, prey survival and injury frequency in an amphibian predator-prey interaction. *Copeia* 1985, 638–644.

Mount, R. H. (1963). The natural history of the red-tailed skink, *Eumeces egregius* Baird. *Am. Midl. Nat.* 70, 356–385.

Nussbaum, R. A., Brodie, E. D., Jr. and Storm, R. M. (1983). *Amphibians and Reptiles of the Pacific Northwest*. University Press of Idaho, Moscow, Idaho.

Papenfuss, T. J. (1982). The ecology and systematics of the amphisbaenian genus *Bipes*. *Occ. Pap. Calif. Acad. Sci.* 136, 1–42.

Parker, W. S. and Pianka, E. R. (1973). Notes on the ecology of the iguanid lizard, *Sceloporus magister*. *Herpetologica* 29, 143–152.

Parker, W. S. and Pianka, E. R. (1974). Further ecological observations on the western banded gecko, *Coleonyx variegatus*. *Copeia* 1974, 528–530.

Parker, W. S. and Pianka, E. R. (1975). Comparative ecology of populations of the lizard *Uta stansburiana*. *Copeia* 1975, 615–632.

Parker, W. S. and Pianka, E. R. (1976). Ecological observations on the leopard lizard (*Crotaphytus wislizeni*) in different parts of its range. *Herpetologica* 32, 95–114.

Pianka, E. R. (1967). Lizard species diversity. *Ecology* 48, 333–351.

Pianka, E. R. (1969). Notes on the biology of *Varanus caudolineatus* and *Varanus gilleni*. *W. Aust. Nat.* 11, 76–82.

Pianka, E. R. (1970). Comparative autecology of the lizard *Cnemidophorus tigris* in different parts of its geographical range. *Ecology* 51, 703–720.

Pianka, E. R. and Pianka, H. D. (1976). Comparative ecology of twelve species of nocturnal lizards (Gekkonidae) in the western Australian desert. *Copeia* 1976, 125–142.

Pond, C. M. (1981). Storage. In *Physiological Ecology—An Evolutionary Approach to Resource Use*. (C. R. Townsend and P. Calow, eds.). Blackwell Scientific Publications, Oxford, pp. 190–219.

Poulton, E. B. (1895). Theories of evolution. *Proc. Boston Soc. Nat. Hist.* 26, 371–393.

Presch, W. (1974). Evolutionary relationships and biogeography of the macroteiid lizards (family Teiidae, subfamily Teiinae). *Bull. S. Calif. Acad. Sci.* 73, 23–32.

Punzo, F. (1982). Tail autotomy and running speed in the lizards *Cophosaurus texanus* and *Uma notata*. *J. Herpetol.* 16, 329–331.

Quattrini, D. (1952). Richerche anatomiche e sperimentali sulla autotomia della coda delle lucertole. I. Dinamica dell'autotomia e conseguenza nel tegumento (Osservazioni nella *Lacerta sicula sicula* Rat.). *Arch. Zool. Ital.* 37, 131–170.

Quattrini, D. (1954). Piano di autotomia e rigenerazione della coda nei Sauri. *Arch. Ital. Anat. Embriol.* 59, 225–282.

Rand, A. S. (1954). Variation and predator pressure in an island and a mainland population of lizards. *Copeia* 1954, 260–262.

Rathor, M. S. (1971). The autotomy and regeneration of the tail of an Indian sand lizard, *Ophiomorus streeti* Anderson and Leviton. Zool. Pol. 21, 110–125.
Robinson, D. C. (1962). Notes on the lizard *Anolis barkeri* Schmidt. Copeia 1962, 640–642.
Rosenberg, H. I. and Russell, A. P. (1980). Structural and functional aspects of tail squirting: A unique defense mechanism of *Diplodactylus* (Reptilia: Gekkonidae). Can. J. Zool. 58, 865–881.
Russell, A. P. and Rewcastle, S. C. (1979). Digital reduction in *Sitana* (Reptilia: Agamidae) and the dual role of the fifth metatarsal in lizards. Can. J. Zool. 57, 1129–1135.
Schall, J. J. and Pianka, E. R. (1980). Evolution of escape behavior diversity. Am. Nat. 115, 551–566.
Schiøtz, A. and Volsøe, H. (1959). The gliding flight of *Holaspis guentheri* Gray, a West African lacertid. Copeia 1959, 259–260.
Schmidt, K. P. and Inger, R. F. (1957). *Living Reptiles of the World*. Hamish Hamilton, London.
Schoener, T. W. (1979). Inferring the properties of predation and other injury-producing agents from injury frequencies. Ecology 60, 1110–1115.
Schoener, T. W. and Schoener, A. (1980). Ecological and demographic correlates of injury rates in some Bahamian *Anolis* lizards. Copeia 1980, 839–850.
Siebenrock, F. (1895). Das Skelet der Agamidae. Sber. k. Akad. Wiss. Wien Math.-nat. Cl. 104, 1089–1196.
Slotopolsky, B. (1922). Beiträge zur Kenntnis der Verstümmelungs- and Regenerations-vorgänge am Lacertilierschwanze. Zool. Jahrb. Anat. 43, 219–322.
Smyth, M. (1974). Changes in the fat stores of the skinks *Morethia boulengeri* and *Hemiergis peronii* (Lacertilia). Aust. J. Zool. 22, 135–145.
Snyder, R. C. (1949). Bipedal locomotion of the lizard *Basiliscus basiliscus*. Copeia 1949, 129–137.
Tinkle, D. W. (1967). The life and demography of the side-blotched lizard, *Uta stansburiana*. Misc. Publs. Mus. Zool. Univ. Michigan 132, 1–182.
Tinkle, D. W. (1972). The dynamics of a Utah population of *Sceloporus undulatus*. Herpetologica 28, 351–359.
Tinkle, D. W. (1973). A population analysis of the sagebrush lizard, *Sceloporus graciosus* in southern Utah. Copeia 1973, 284–296.
Tinkle, D. W. (1976). Comparative data on the population ecology of the desert spiny lizard, *Sceloporus magister*. Herpetologica 32, 1–6.
Tweedie, M. W. F. (1950). The flying gecko, *Ptychozoon kuhli* Stejn. Proc. Zool. Soc. Lond. 120, 13.
Turner, F. B., Medica, P. A., Jennrich, R. I. and Maza, B. G. (1982). Frequencies of broken tails among *Uta stansburiana* in southern Nevada and a test of the predation hypothesis. Copeia 1982, 835–840.
Vinegar, M. B. (1975). Comparative aggression in *Sceloporus virgatus*, *S. undulatus consobrinus*, and *S. u. tristichus* (Sauria: Iguanidae). Anim. Behav. 23, 279–286.
Vitt, L. J. (1981). Tail autotomy and regeneration in the tropical skink, *Mabuya heathi*. J. Herpetol. 15, 454–457.
Vitt, L. J. (1983). Tail loss in lizards: The significance of foraging and predator escape modes. Herpetologica 39, 151–162.
Vitt, L. J. and Ballinger, R. E. (1982). The adaptive significance of a complex caudal adaptation in the tropical gekkonid lizard, *Lygodactylus klugei*. Can. J. Zool. 60, 2582–2587.
Vitt, L. J. and Congdon, J. D. (1978). Body shape, reproductive effort, and relative clutch mass in lizards: Resolution of a paradox. Am. Nat. 112, 595–608.

REFERENCES

Vitt, L. J., Congdon, J. D. and Dickson, N. A. (1977). Adaptive strategies and energetics of tail autotomy in lizards. Ecology 58, 326–337.
Vitt, L. J., Congdon, J. D., Hulse, A. C. and Platz, J. E. (1974). Territorial aggressive encounters and tail breaks in the lizard *Sceloporus magister*. Copeia 1974, 990–993.
Vitt, L. J. and Cooper, W. E., Jr. (1986). Tail loss, tail color and predator escape in *Eumeces* (Lacertilia: Scincidae): Age-specific differences in costs and benefits. Can. J. Zool. 64, 583–592.
Vitt, L. J. and Lacher, T. E., Jr. (1981). Behavior, habitat, diet, and reproduction of the iguanid lizard *Polychrus acutirostris* in the Caatinga of northeastern Brazil. Herpetologica 37, 53–63.
Vitt, L. J. and Ohmart, R. D. (1975). Ecology, reproduction, and reproductive effort of the iguanid lizard *Urosaurus graciosus* on the lower Colorado River. Herpetologica 31, 56–65.
Wake, D. B. and Dresner, I. G. (1967). Functional morphology and evolution of tail autotomy in salamanders. J. Morphol. 122, 265–306.
Werner, Y. L. (1964). Frequencies of regenerated tails, and structure of caudal vertebrae in Israeli desert geckos (Reptilia: Gekkonidae). Israel J. Zool. 13, 134–136.
Werner, Y. L. (1967). Regeneration of specialized scales in tails of *Teratoscincus* (Reptilia: Gekkonidae). Senck. Biol. 48, 117–124.
Werner, Y. L. (1968). Regeneration frequencies in geckos of two ecological types (Reptilia: Gekkonidae). Vie et Milieu (C) 19, 199–222.
Woodland, W. N. F. (1920). Some observations on caudal autotomy and regeneration in the gecko (*Hemidactylus flaviviridis*, Rüppell), with notes on the tails of *Sphenodon* and *Pygopus*. Quart. J. Microsc. Sci. 65, 63–100.
Zietz, F. R. (1914). Lacertilia from central Australia. Trans. Roy. Soc. S. Aust. 38, 440–444.
Zweifel, R. G. and Lowe, C. H. (1966). The ecology of a population of *Xantusia vigilis*, the desert night lizard. Am. Mus. Novitates 2247, 1–57.

CHAPTER

4

Parental Care in Reptiles

RICHARD SHINE
Department of Zoology, University of Sydney, Sydney,
New South Wales, Australia

CONTENTS

I. INTRODUCTION AND TERMINOLOGY — 277

II. THE OCCURRENCE OF PARENTAL CARE — 278
  A. Taxa Reported to Show Parental Care, 278
  B. Taxonomic Biases, 293
  C. Number of Independent Evolutionary Origins, 294
  D. Male, Female, and Biparental Care, 297

III. HYPOTHESES ON THE EVOLUTION OF PARENTAL CARE — 298
  A. Cost-Benefit Models, 298
  B. Intermediate Stages in the Evolution of Parental Care, 305
  C. Factors Increasing the Benefits of Parental Care, 306
  D. Factors Reducing the Costs of Parental Care, 308
  E. Which Sex Should Show Parental Care?, 312
  F. Why Is Parental Care Rare in Reptiles?, 313

IV. SUMMARY — 314

ACKNOWLEDGMENTS — 316

REFERENCES — 316

"Parental feeling is not a strong character in reptiles, and for that reason it is all the more interesting when it does occur." (Smith, 1937)

I. INTRODUCTION AND TERMINOLOGY

Prolonged care of eggs or offspring is a common feature of vertebrate reproduction. Parental care takes diverse forms, and presumably has evolved independently many times (e.g., Gross and Shine, 1981). Although parental care is exhibited by only a minority of reptilian species, these include a diverse array of lizards, snakes and crocodilians. The present chapter (a) reviews the occurrence and nature of reptilian parental care and (b) poses and tests hypotheses on the selective forces responsible for the evolution of such behavior. The only previous comprehensive reviews of reptilian parental care are those of Noble and Mason (1933) on squamates and of Cott (1971) on crocodilians.

I define "parental care" as any form of postovipositional parental behavior; that is, any action of the parent after oviposition or parturition, that increases the chances of survival of the offspring. This definition differs from the concept of "parental investment" (Trivers, 1972), which (a) includes investment prior to oviposition, and (b) is restricted to behavior that decreases the probable survivorship or future fecundity of the parent. This latter condition is difficult to verify empirically and hard to apply to certain cases. For example, if the "costs" of a female guarding her eggs are independent of the number of eggs guarded, the addition of more eggs would not increase the mother's "parental investment"; however, her behavior towards those additional eggs clearly would qualify as "parental care."

Parental care may be divided conveniently into two major categories: care of the eggs and care of the young. Care of the eggs is widespread but uncommon in reptiles, and generally consists of the parent remaining with the eggs for some time after oviposition (Figs. 1,2). This behavior usually is termed "egg-brooding" or "egg-guarding." However, although protection against predators is probably the major advantage conferred by the parent's presence (see below), actual defense against predators has been witnessed only rarely. Hence, the terms "nest-guarding" and "egg-guarding" should be applied only to species in which active nest defense has been observed. Cases in which the parent remains with the eggs, but without documentation of nest defense, may be termed "nest attendance" or "egg attendance" (Tryon, 1979). Finally, the term "egg-brooding" may be restricted to species in which the female facilitates incubation by raising nest temperatures above ambient (Campbell and Quinn, 1975). I prefer this terminology to the proposal (Groves, 1982) that the term "egg-brooding" should be reserved for species that actively manipulate their eggs.

Fig. 1. *Ophiophagus hannah*. King cobra within a nest containing a clutch of eggs. As far as is known, these snakes do not raise the temperature of the clutch. (Photo courtesy of the New York Zoological Society ©).

II. THE OCCURRENCE OF PARENTAL CARE

A. Taxa Reported to Show Parental Care

1. TESTUDINES

Parental care is rare or absent in turtles; apparently the only record is that of Hodsdon and Pearson (1943), who described maternal behavior in the Bahamian emydid *Pseudemys malonei*. According to these authors (and see Oliver, 1955), the female turtles returned to their nest sites immediately before hatching and dug away hard-packed soil above the nest-chambers so that the hatchlings could emerge successfully. Freshwater turtles have attracted considerable ecological study since the time of Hodsdon and Pearson's observations, and if maternal behavior of the type described above is a general phenomenon, it is surprising that it has not been noted by other workers.

2. CROCODILIANS

In contrast to the turtles, parental care is common (possibly ubiquitous) among crocodilians (Table I). Descriptions of crocodilian nest defense may be found in the works of Pliny and Aristotle (and see

Fig. 2. Uncovered nests. (A) *Ophisaurus apodus*. Female coiled around clutch. (B) *Elgaria multicarinata*. Multiclutch nest with several females. (Photo courtesy of B. Langerwerf.)

TABLE I
Crocodilian Taxa Reported to Show Parental Care

Species	Form of parental care					Authority
	Attends nest	Defends nest	Opens nest	Carries young	Defends young	
Alligator mississippiensis	♀	♀	♀	♀	♀	Clarke, 1888; Devenish, 1893; Reese, 1907; McIlhenny, 1934; Joanen, 1970; Joanen and McNease, 1970, 1980; Kushlan, 1973; Fogarty, 1974; Herzog, 1975; Ogden, 1976; Metzen, 1977; Goodwin and Marion, 1978; Kushlan and Kushlan, 1980; Dietz and Hines, 1980; Kushlan and Simon, 1981
Caiman crocodilus	♀	♀, ♂	♀, ♂	♂(?)	♀, ♂	Alvarez del Toro, 1969, 1974; Staton and Dixon, 1977; Gorzula, 1978; Staton, 1978
C. yacare	♀	–	♀	–	♀	Crawshaw and Schaller, 1980
Crocodylus acutus	♀	♀	♀	♀	♀	Descourtilz, 1809; Brehm, 1885; Ogden and Singletary 1973; Ogden, 1978; Dugan et al., 1981
C. cataphractus	♀	–	♀	–	–	Waitkuwait, 1982
C. intermedius	♀	–	–	–	–	Medem, 1958
C. johnsoni	♀	♀(?)	♀	♀	–	Worrell, 1952; Compton, 1981
C. morelettii	♀	–	♀	♀	♀, ♂	Hunt, 1974, 1975
C. niloticus	♀	♀	♀, ♂	♀, ♂	♀, ♂	Pliny (trs. Holland, 1601); Aristotle (trs. Creswell, 1862); Vansleb, 1678; Pitman, 1930, 1941; Chadwick, 1931; Cott, 1961, 1971; Modha, 1967; Pooley, 1969, 1974, 1976, 1977; Hadley, 1969; Pooley and Gans, 1976
C. novaeguineae	♀	♀	♀	♀, ♂	♂	Neill, 1946; J. W. Lang, pers. comm.
C. palustris	♀	♀	♀	–	♀, ♂	Waytialingham, 1880; Deraniyagala, 1939; Dharmakumarsinji, 1947; David, 1970; Whitaker and Whitaker, 1977, 1978

THE OCCURRENCE OF PARENTAL CARE

TABLE I (Continued)

Species	Form of parental care					Authority
	Attends nest	Defends nest	Opens nest	Carries young	Defends young	
C. porosus	♀	♀	♀	♀	♀, ♂	Boake, 1870; Shelford, 1916; Deraniyagala, 1939; Loveridge, 1946; Robinson, 1948; Neill, 1971; Webb, 1977; Biswas, 1977; Webb et al., 1977; Bustard and Choudhury, 1980; Bustard and Kar, 1981; Magnusson, 1980; Jelden, 1981; Bustard and Maharana, 1982; Choudhury and Bustard, 1979; Acharjyo and Mishra, 1981
Gavialis gangeticus	♀	♀	♀	♀	♀	Whitaker and Whitaker, 1977b; Singh and Bustard, 1977; Bustard, 1980; Basu and Bustard, 1981; Bustard and Singh, 1981
Melanosuchus niger	No(?)	♀	(?)	–	♀	Hartwig, 1873; Medem 1971
Osteolaemus tetraspis	♀	♀	♀	♀, ♂	–	Schmidt, 1919; Cansdale, 1955; Tryon, 1980
Palaeosuchus palpebrosus	♀	♀	–	–	–	Medem, 1958
P. trigonatus	–	–	Yes	–	–	Magnusson et al., 1985

Table indicates sex of parent reported to care for young. A dash indicates that parental care is not reported.

discussion by Böhme, 1977), and more recent scholars have documented parental behavior in virtually every crocodilian species studied in detail.

Although the frequency of nest attendance and active nest defense varies interspecifically, and even intraspecifically (references in Table I), the broad outlines of parental care are similar in all crocodilians for which data are available. The pattern is quite different from that described in any squamate reptile. The female parent remains in the vicinity of the nest after laying, or returns to it at intervals. Potential predators on the eggs may or may not be attacked; species that are not egg predators are ignored (e.g., Modha, 1967; Cott, 1971; Dietz and Jackson, 1979). The female opens the nest at the time of hatching, and carries full-term eggs and newly-hatched young to the water (Pooley, 1977). The young remain in a group for days or weeks and are actively defended by the adults. If attacked, even older juveniles will give "distress calls" that will initiate aggressive behavior from adult crocodilians toward the attacker (e.g., Hunt, 1974, 1975). Parental behaviors, such as nest-guarding and nest-opening, are probably universal among present-day crocodilians (Greer, 1971; Kushlan and Simon, 1981).

3. SQUAMATES

Postovipositional parental behavior by squamate reptiles can take many forms, of which the simplest is concealment of eggs immediately after oviposition. Oviparous squamates generally lay eggs in places with appropriate conditions of temperature and humidity (Muth, 1980) and away from the attention of egg predators (see Packard and Packard, this volume). Several species of lizards manipulate their eggs after oviposition, presumably to place them into suitable microhabitats. This behavior has been reported in lacertids (Hilzheimer, 1910), iguanids (Gordon, 1960; Smith et al., 1972; Tokarz and Jones, 1979; Jones and Guillette, 1982), scincids (Noble and Mason, 1933), agamids (Asana, 1941), and gekkonids (Nettman and Rykena, 1979; *Phyllurus platurus*, Shine, pers. obs.). Presumably such behavior is widespread among reptiles.

More complex, or at least longer-term, parental care is shown by many species. Among the squamates, at least 103 species have been reported to have one or both parents remain with the eggs after oviposition (Table II). These species include a taxonomically diverse array of lizards and snakes. Unfortunately, some of the cases listed in Table II are poorly documented; at least 15 of the 103 examples depend upon single observations of adults found near eggs. Undoubtedly, some of the cases do not indicate parental care, but may be coincidental or reflect incipient oophagy or discovery of a female with a recently oviposited clutch. The force of this objection is diminished by the consistency with which the adult is reported to be coiled around the eggs rather than merely close to them, but nonetheless these reports should be regarded with caution. I once found a small snake (*Unechis gouldi*) only a few centimeters from four eggs under a piece of tin; the obvious inference would have been parental care, except that the snake species is viviparous, and the eggs were those of an agamid lizard.

Records of parental care for the Varanidae are particularly difficult to evaluate. No well-documented case is available, but at least three anecdotal reports are suggestive. For example, Cogger (1967:60) notes that "on several occasions when adult goannas have been disturbed at

TABLE II
Squamate Taxa in Which the Female Parent Has Been Reported to Remain With the Eggs After Oviposition

Family	Species	Authority
Lizards		
Anguidae	*Diploglossus delasagra*	Barbour and Ramsden, 1919; Greer, 1967
	D. bilobatus	Taylor, 1956; Fitch, 1970
	Gerrhonotus liocephalus	Greene and Dial, 1966; Tinkle and Gibbons, 1977
	Elgaria multicarinatus	Langerwerf, 1981
	Ophisaurus apodus	Langerwerf, 1981
	O. attenuatus	Fitch, 1970
	O. gracilis	Daniel, 1983
	O. harti	Smith, 1935
	O. ventralis	Noble and Mason, 1933; Vinegar, 1968; Mount, 1975
Iguanidae	*Amblyrhynchus cristatus*	Carpenter, 1966; Eibl-Eibesfeldt, 1966; Trillmich, 1979
	Brachylophus fasciatus	Cogger, 1974; Gibbons and Watkins, 1982
	B. vitiensis	Gibbons and Watkins, 1982
	Conolophus pallidus	Christian and Tracy, 1982
	C. subcristatus	Werner, 1982
	Cyclura carinata	Iverson, 1979
	C. stejnegeri (= *C. cornuta*)	Wiewandt, 1977, 1979
	C. cyclura	Carey, 1975
	C. nubila	Shaw, 1954
	Iguana iguana	Rand, 1968; Alvarez del Toro, 1972; Rand and Rand, 1976; Wiewandt, 1982
Scincidae	*Emoia cyanura* (?)	Fitch, 1970
	Eumeces anthracinus	Smith, 1946; Dowling, 1950; Collins, 1974
	E. brevilineatus	Werler, 1951
	E. callicephalus	Campbell and Simmons, 1961
	E. chinensis	Wang, 1966
	E. egregius	Mount, 1963
	E. elegans	Mell, 1929; Hikida, 1981

(Continued)

TABLE II (Continued)

Family	Species	Authority
Lizards (Continued)		
Scincidae	E. fasciatus	Ruthven, 1911; Dunn, 1920; Blanchard, 1922; Smith, 1882; Brimley, 1904; Ditmars, 1904; Brady, 1927; Burt, 1928; Corrington, 1929; Klots, 1930; Cagle, 1940; Fitch, 1954; Strecker, 1908; Allard, 1909; Hurter, 1911; McCauley, 1939, 1945; Bishop, 1926; Evans and Roecker, 1951; Minton, 1972; Cooper et al., 1983
	E. inexpectatus	Duellman and Schwartz, 1958
	E. laticeps	Smith, 1946; Martof, 1956; Vitt and Cooper, 1985
	E. latiscutatus	Hikida, 1981
	E. multivirgatus	Gehlbach, 1965; Van Devender and Van Devender, 1975
	E. obsoletus	Smith, 1946; Evans, 1959; Fitch, 1955, 1970; Hall, 1971
	E. okadae	Hikida, 1975; Hasegawa, 1984
	E. oshimensis	Toyama, 1975
	E. quadrilineatus	Mell, 1929
	E. "pekinensis" (= xanthi)	Mell, 1929
	E. septentrionalis	Breckenridge, 1943; Smith, 1946
	E. skiltonianus	Tanner, 1943, 1957; Smith, 1946
	E. stimsoni (?)	Taylor, 1935
	E. tetragrammus	Behler and King, 1979
	E. xanthi	Schmidt, 1927; Taylor, 1935
	Neoseps reynoldsi	Telford, 1959
Teiidae	Tupinambis teguixin	Krieg, 1925
Varanidae	Varanus mitchelli (?)	G. Gow, pers. comm.
	V. salvator (?)	Biswas and Kar, 1981
	V. varius (?)	Cogger, 1967

THE OCCURRENCE OF PARENTAL CARE

TABLE II (Continued)

Family	Species	Authority
Snakes		
Boidae	*Aspidites melanocephalus*	Boos, 1979; Barker, 1981; Charles et al., 1985
	Chondropython viridis	Kratzer, 1962; Mackay, 1973; Walsh, 1979; Switak, 1975
	Liasis albertisii	Ross, 1978
	L. amethystinus	Pope, 1961; Boos, 1979; Charles et al., 1985
	L. boa	Barker, 1981
	L. childreni	Ross, 1973; Dunn, 1979a; Barker, 1981
	L. fuscus	Kinghorn, 1956; Ross, 1978; Boos, 1979; Shine, pers. obs.
	L. mackloti	Ross and Larman, 1977; Barker, 1981
	Morelia bredli	Gow, 1981
	M. spilotes	Cogger and Holmes, 1960; Boos, 1979; Harlow and Grigg, 1983; Charles et al., 1983
	Python curtus	Noble, 1935; Pope, 1961; Vinegar et al., 1970
	P. molurus	Lamarre-Picquot, 1835, 1842; Valenciennes, 1841; Forbes, 1881; Abercromby, 1913; Wall, 1921; Stemmler-Morath, 1956; Pope, 1961; Hutchinson et al., 1966; Yadav, 1967; Vinegar et al., 1970; Wagner, 1973, 1976; Van Mierop and Barnard, 1976, 1978. Acharjyo and Misra, 1976; Coborn, 1975; Foekema, 1975
	P. regius	Logan, 1973; Pitman, 1938; Walsh, 1979; Boos, 1979; Schivre, 1972; Van Mierop and Bessette, 1981

(Continued)

TABLE II (Continued)

Family	Species	Authority
Snakes (Continued)		
Boidae	*P. reticulatus*	Wray, 1862; Wall, 1926; Lederer, 1944; Pope, 1961; Taylor, 1965; Vinegar et al., 1970; Honegger, 1970; La Panouse and Pellier, 1973; Hediger, 1968; Müller, 1970
	P. sebae	Sclater, 1862; FitzSimons, 1930; Benedict, 1932; Pitman, 1938; Broadley, 1959; Dowling, 1960; Pope, 1961; Schutte, 1970; Vinegar et al., 1970; Dunn, 1979b; Schmidt, 1973
	P. timoriensis	Murphy et al., 1981; Barker, 1981
Colubridae	*Amphiesma mairii*	J. Bredl, pers. comm.
	A. stolata	Wall, 1921; Mell, 1929
	Cemophora coccinea	Ditmars, 1942
	Elaphe climacophora	Fukada, 1965
	E. guttata	D. Kent, pers. comm.
	E. obsoleta	Oliver, 1955; Medsger, 1919
	E. quadrivirgata	Fukada, 1965
	Farancia abacura	Meade, 1940; Goldstein, 1941; Riemer, 1957; Ashton and Ashton, 1981
	F. erytrogramma (?)	Ashton and Ashton, 1981
	Heterodon platyrhinos (?)	Hahn, 1909
	Lampropeltis triangulum	Babcock, 1929; Ditmars, 1942; Minton and Minton, 1973; G. Marsec, pers. comm.
	Lycodon aulicus	Smith, 1943
	L. striatus (?)	Wall, 1921
	Natrix natrix	Gallwey, 1932; Smith, 1973
	Opheodrys vernalis (?)	Blanchard, 1933
	Opisthotropis latouchi (?)	Pope, 1935
	Pituophis melanoleucus (?)	Carl, 1944

TABLE II (Continued)

Family	Species	Authority
Snakes (Continued)		
Colubridae	*Psammophylax rhombeatus*	FitzSimons, 1962; Le Roux, 1964; Bourquin, 1970; Visser, 1971; Broadley, 1977
	P. tritaeniatus (?)	Sweeney, 1961: but see Broadley, 1977
	P. variabilis	Broadley, 1977
	Ptyas korros	Mell, 1929
	P. mucosus	Wall, 1907, 1921; Mell, 1929; Pope, 1935
	Rhabdophis subminiatus	Mell, 1929
	Xenochrophis piscator	Mell, 1929; Abercromby, 1913
Elapidae	*Bungarus caeruleus*	Smith, 1943; Wall, 1921
	B. candidus	Mell, 1929
	B. ceylonicus	Green, 1905; Wall, 1921
	B. fasciatus	Mell, 1929; Pope, 1935; Smith, 1943
	Calliophis maculiceps (?)	Frith, 1977
	Demansia papuensis (?)	Parker, 1982
	Laticauda colubrina	Smedley, 1931; Neill, 1964; Taylor, 1965; but see Dunson, 1975
	Micrurus corallinus	Mole, 1924
	M. fulvius	Campbell, 1973
	Naja naja	Wall, 1921; Mell, 1929; Smith, 1937; Kopstein, 1938; Smith, 1943; Tweedie, 1957; Petzold, 1968; Campbell and Quinn, 1975
	N. melanoleuca	Tryon, 1979
	Ophiophagus hannah	W. Smith, 1935; H. Smith, 1936; Mustill, 1936; M. Smith, 1943; Oliver, 1956; Leakey, 1969; Shaw and Shebbeare, 1931
	Pseudechis butleri (?)	Fitzgerald and Mengden, 1987
	Pseudonaja textilis (?)	Fleay, 1943; R. Wells, pers. comm.; J. Edwards, pers. comm.

(Continued)

TABLE II (Continued)

Family	Species	Authority
Snakes (Continued)		
Leptotyphlopidae	*Leptotyphlops dulcis*	Hibbard, 1964
Typhlopidae	*Rhinotyphlops caecus*	Bogert, 1940; but see Erasmus and Branch, 1983
	Rhamphotyphlops braminus (?)	Mell, 1929
Viperidae	*Causus rhombeatus* (?)	Sweeney, 1961; Broadley, 1983
	Calloselasma rhodostoma	Smith, 1915, 1943; Tweedie, 1957; Leakey, 1969
	Lachesis muta	Mole, 1924
	Trimeresurus monticola	Leigh, 1910; Pope, 1935

A question mark indicates that the data are anecdotal and possibly unreliable.

termite mounds, newborn young have been found emerging. This suggests that the female may remain near the nest until the young are ready to hatch, at which time she makes a new tunnel to release the young." In each case, the species involved was *Varanus varius* (H. Cogger, pers. comm.). On two separate occasions, a captive female *Varanus mitchelli* was found with the tail coiled around the eggs (G. Gow, pers. comm.). Parental care is suggested by the behavior of a female *Varanus salvator* that remained at the nest site for several days after oviposition (Biswas and Kar, 1981). A less reliable account of possible parental care in varanids, probably a case of misinterpreted egg predation, has been reported by Berney (1936).

Parental care in squamates may be divided into four major categories, the first three of which deal with care of the eggs rather than the offspring: (1) female buries eggs and defends nest site briefly against conspecific females; (2) female coils around eggs, defends them against predators and warms them by shivering thermogenesis; (3) female remains with eggs after oviposition and may defend them against predation or pathogens; (4) female aids newly born or newly hatched young.

1. Nest-site defense against conspecific females is widespread in iguanine lizards (Table II) but has not been reported in any other squamate group. In some cases, the nest site is defended even prior to

TABLE III
Shivering Thermogenesis in Brooding Female Pythons: Disagreements in the Literature

Species	Shivering thermogenesis	
	Occurs	Does not occur
Aspidites melanocephalus	Boos, 1979; Charles et al., 1983	Murphy et al., 1981
Liasis amethystinus	Boos, 1979	Charles et al., 1983
L. mackloti	Charles et al., 1985	Ross and Larman, 1977
Morelia spilotes	Harlow and Grigg, 1983	Charles et al., 1985
Python curtus	Vinegar et al., 1970	Noble, 1935
P. regius	Pitman, 1974; Logan, 1973	Van Mierop and Bessette, 1981
P. reticulatus	Hediger, 1968; Müller, 1970	Honegger, 1970; La Panouse and Pellier, 1973; Pitman, 1974; Vinegar et al., 1970
P. sebae	Benedict, 1932; Noble, 1935	Vinegar et al., 1970; Pitman, 1974

oviposition (Wiewandt, 1982). The intensity of nest site defense varies considerably among species, and even among geographic areas within a species. Some of this variability may be attributed to the physical condition of the females: only animals in good condition can engage in vigorous nest defense (Wiewandt, 1982; references in Table II).

2. Egg brooding (shivering thermogenesis) has been recorded only in pythons (Table II; Fig. 3). The female coils tightly around the clutch, so that the eggs are completely hidden. In at least some species, rhythmic muscular contractions of the mother's body produce sufficient heat to maintain a relatively high and constant temperature in the egg mass. This phenomenon has been described in *Aspidites melanocephalus*, *Chondropython viridis*, *Liasis amethystinus*, *L. mackloti*, *Morelia spilotes*, *Python curtus*, *P. reticulatus*, and *P. sebae* (references in Table II), and may be universal within the pythons.

Certainly the pythons known to show shivering thermogenesis cover a broad taxonomic range, including small as well as large species, and exclusively tropical as well as temperate-zone taxa. Although several authors (especially Vinegar et al., 1970) have stressed that only some python species utilize shivering thermogenesis, the evidence for interspecific differences in such behavior is weak. Commonly, studies of the same species by different workers are contradictory with respect to whether or not shivering thermogenesis is exhibited (Table III). These

Fig. 3. *Python sebae*. Python coiled around a clutch of eggs and contracting its muscles at a regular rate, thus raising the temperature of body and clutch. (Photo courtesy of the New York Zoological Society ©).

disagreements are due to several factors, including (a) the type of evidence used (e.g. temperature measurement versus presence of muscular twitching), (b) the temperature-dependence of shivering thermogenesis (if the room is warm, no shivering is observed), (c) the difficulties in interpreting slight temperature differences between the egg mass and ambient, because of the great thermal inertia of these large reptiles (e.g., Cogger and Holmes, 1960), and (d) the low sample sizes (often only one or two animals). Some python species may not utilize metabolic heat production during brooding but convincing data are currently unavailable.

The maintenance of high temperatures during incubation undoubtedly quickens embryonic development (e.g., Joshi, 1967) and also may increase embryonic survivorship. Python embryos develop normally only at high temperatures (approximately 30°C), and are much more stenothermic in this regard than embryos of most other squamates (Joshi, 1967; Vinegar, 1973; Harlow and Grigg, 1984). One hypothesis is that maternal brooding is an adaptation to this embryonic thermal sensitivity (Vinegar, 1973). However, distinguishing cause and effect is difficult in such a correlation. Equally plausibly, the embryonic sensitivity may have evolved because of maternal brooding rather than vice versa. If the eggs are always kept warm by the brooding female, selection to maintain embryonic tolerance of low temperature would be weak or absent. An additional hypothesis is that maternal thermogenesis allows pythons to reproduce successfully under colder climatic conditions than would otherwise be possible (Harlow and Grigg, 1984).

The apparent restriction of shivering thermogenesis to pythons might be a function of their massively developed lateral musculature. Presumably, most reptiles would lack the physiological ability for sustained muscular contraction and hence, significant metabolic heat production. The substantial increase in metabolic rate of brooding female pythons (Hutchinson et al., 1966; Van Mierop and Barnard, 1976, 1978; Harlow and Grigg, 1984) means that maternal care in these snakes confers a massive energetic cost. Curiously, this group has not followed the boines in evolving viviparity, a strategy allowing egg temperatures to be raised by maternal behavioral (rather than physiological) thermoregulation. One reason may be that an egg-retaining female python could not subdue prey by constriction, because of the risk of damaging the eggs. An egg-brooding female would not face this restriction.

3. The most widespread form of squamate parental care consists of the female remaining with the eggs after oviposition. Her presence presumably serves some function, which has rarely been demonstrated. Functions documented in some species include defense against predators, and regulation of egg temperature or moisture levels (discussed further in Section III.A). Many of the reported cases of egg-attending (Table II) are likely to be invalid inferences, because they are based on single observations of adults with eggs. Nonetheless, the consistency with which this behavior has been reported in particular species clearly indicates that egg-attendance is widespread in squamates (Table II).

4. Parental care of offspring rather than of eggs is remarkably rare in reptiles, perhaps because the mother and neonates are rarely in close proximity. One exception involves egg-attending (or guarding or brooding) species in which the female often is present at hatching. In at least one such species (*Eumeces obsoletus*), a female was observed to help the young hatch, and later "groom" the offspring (Evans, 1959). Even more remarkable is the observation (unfortunately uncorroborated) of newly-hatched *Python molurus* returning to their empty eggshells at night, with the mother then coiling around them and heating them by shivering thermogenesis (Döflein, 1932; cited in La Panouse and Pellier, 1973). An aborigine from Mudginberri Station (Alligator Rivers region, tropical Australia) suggested that female water pythons (*Liasis fuscus*) "took the babies down to the water and taught them how to swim" (R. Lambeck, pers. comm.).

If the scarcity of posthatching parental care in squamates is due to the lack of physical association between mother and young in most oviparous forms, this problem is overcome in viviparous squamates, which comprise approximately one-fifth of all species of lizards and snakes (Shine, 1985). Observations of viviparous females at parturition confirm that mothers in some squamate species may stimulate the young to emerge from their membranous sacs by pushing with the snout, or may actually tear open the membranes themselves. This occurs in xantusiid lizards (Cowles, 1944; Miller, 1954), scincid lizards (Niekisch, 1975; Rebouças-Spieker and Vanzolini, 1978; Shine, pers. obs. for *Sphenomorphus quoyii*), and boid snakes (Groves, 1981).

However, mothers apparently do not open the fetal membranes at birth in viviparous iguanid, diploglossid, or lacertid lizards (Rebouças-Spieker and Vanzolini, 1978). In some colubrid and boid snakes, the mother ingests dead young and birth debris after the living young have emerged from their membranes (Neill and Allen, 1962; Rieppel, 1970; Groves, 1981; Holmstrom and Behler, 1981). A similar phenomenon occurs in oviparous reptiles, the mothers of which ingest spoiled eggs (e.g., crocodilians: Kushlan and Simon, 1981; squamates: Groves, 1982). Such behavior has been interpreted as parental care, because (a) it may prevent fungal infection spreading to other eggs, and (b) it may prevent odors attracting predators (Groves, 1982). Alternatively, rotting eggs may have a different odor than healthy eggs, and the females may mistake them for food items (R. B. Huey, pers. comm.).

One further form of squamate parental care, which has received great publicity, is the alleged ability of female snakes to swallow their young for protection when danger threatens. The first published reference to this behavior comes from the Egyptians at about 2500 B.C. (Speck, 1923), whereas the first reference in the English language is in Spenser's "The Faerie Queene" (1590). The story has been applied to many species, especially to viviparous forms, and often to species that have been observed in detail by other workers who have failed to report the same phenomenon (e.g., *Bothrops neuwiedi*: Schupp, 1913; Melgarejo, 1977). The extensive literature on the subject has been summarized and evaluated multiple times (Noble, 1921; Ortenburger, 1930; Schmidt, 1929; Angel, 1950; Rose, 1962; Klauber, 1972). The consensus is that no satisfactory evidence of the phenomenon has ever been produced. The stories seem unlikely to be true because (a) the behavior has never been reported in captivity or from field observations of scientists; (b) undigested young have never been discovered in stomachs of snakes dissected for dietary studies; (c) offspring are probably unable to survive for significant periods inside the stomach of the mother (e.g., Klauber, 1972). Nevertheless, the occurrence of mouth-brooding and transport of

THE OCCURRENCE OF PARENTAL CARE

young in cichlid fishes and crocodilians, as well as the recent discovery of gastric brooding in an Australian frog (Corben et al., 1974), suggest that gastric protection of young in snakes is not impossible. Nonetheless, reliable data are totally lacking.

Other popular tales concerning reptilian parental care include the mother snake nourishing the young inside her stomach (Rivers, 1874; Stanley, 1897; Burroughs, 1908), the mother rattlesnake crooning (by rattling mildly) to her newborn young (Crites, 1952), and the mother rattlesnake caring for her young until they are well-grown, and then finding suitable home sites for them (Meek, 1946). Charming as these stories are, their validity seems doubtful.

Although the present review is concerned only with living reptiles, parental care also may have been shown in a variety of groups that are now extinct (e.g., Coombs, 1982; Horner, 1984).

B. Taxonomic Biases

1. GENERAL

The incidence of reptilian parental care is not distributed randomly among different taxonomic groups. This taxonomic bias is evident at the levels of order, suborder, family, and genus.

2. COMPARISONS AMONG ORDERS

The three orders of living reptiles are only distantly related to each other, having been evolving as separate lineages for almost 300 million years (e.g., Romer, 1966). This long divergence has resulted in great differences among the living orders in morphology and, as shown by the present review, in the frequency and form of parental care. Parental behavior appears universal in crocodilians (and in their relatives, the birds) but seems to be lacking in testudines. Parental care is seen in many squamate taxa, but has been described in only about 2% of all oviparous squamate species (7% of oviparous genera). Of course, many species have yet to be examined in this regard.

3. COMPARISONS BETWEEN SUBORDERS

Among the squamate suborders, parental care is unknown in amphisbaenians (possibly because of a paucity of field data), rare in lizards (recorded in 41 of approximately 3000 oviparous species, or 1.3%), and more common in snakes (47 of 1700 species, or 2.8%). If each species is treated as an independent data point (see Ridley, 1983, for a critique of this assumption), the proportion of oviparous species recorded to show parental care is significantly lower in lizards than in snakes (2 × 2 table, 1 d.f., $\chi^2 = 18.5$, $p < 0.001$). However, this may simply reflect a greater tendency for herpetologists to keep and observe snakes rather than lizards.

4. COMPARISONS AMONG FAMILIES

Among the squamates, the percentage of oviparous species reported to show clutch attendance ranges from zero in many families (Agamidae, Chamaeleonidae, Cordylidae, Dibamidae, Gekkonidae, Helodermatidae, Lacertidae, and Pygopodidae) up to virtually 100% in the oviparous Boidae. The variation in percentages among families is too great to be attributed to chance alone (combining families to ensure adequate sample sizes; 7 × 2 table, 6 d.f., $\chi^2 = 103.2$, $p < 0.001$).

5. COMPARISONS AMONG GENERA

The 103 squamate species showing parental care are distributed among 13 genera of lizards and 33 of snakes. If parental care was randomly distributed with respect to taxonomy, the proportion of genera containing more than one nest-attending species should be low. In reality, many instances of squamate parental care are found in congeneric species; for example, half of all the examples in lizards (20 of 41 cases) belong to the single scincid genus *Eumeces*. Parental care is probably ubiquitous in this genus, as well as in others such as *Ophisaurus* and *Python*. Such data are clearly sufficient to reject the null hypothesis of taxonomically random occurrence of parental care. Instead, parental care, although rare overall, is very common within certain taxonomic groups.

A strong taxonomic bias is evident not only in the frequency of parental care, but also in its form. Simple clutch attendance is usually the only form of parental care, but different behaviors are exhibited by iguanine lizards (eggs buried, and nests defended against conspecifics), boid snakes (eggs warmed by shivering thermogenesis), and crocodilians (complex biparental behavior before and after hatching).

C. Number of Independent Evolutionary Origins

The tendency for parental care to be widespread within a single phylogenetic lineage suggests by parsimony that in such cases it has evolved only once, early in the group's history, and has been retained during subsequent speciation (Ridley, 1983). The extreme case of the alternative hypothesis is that all species showing parental care have independently evolved this behavior. Although the strong taxonomic bias in parental care argues against this latter hypothesis, it is difficult to dismiss in specific cases, particularly should only a few distantly-related species show the trait. This could result from either (a) lack of data on other related species, which show parental care although it has not been recorded, (b) an evolutionary loss of parental behavior in these related forms, or (c) separate evolutionary origins of parental care in each species showing this trait.

A typical example of such ambiguity occurs in the colubrid snake genus *Elaphe*, two species of which show maternal care for several days after laying (*E. climacophora, E. quadrivirgata*), whereas a close relative (*E. conspicillata*) does not (Fukada, 1956). Nest attendance also occurs in a distantly related North American congener (Table II).

In the following analysis, I have adopted a conservative approach by considering any cases of parental care in the same subfamily as representing a single evolutionary origin, except in the cases of the speciose snake subfamilies Colubrinae and Elapinae. In these groups, available phylogenetic reconstructions suggest multiple origins of parental care, based on low probability of relatedness among the species involved.

1. COLUBRINAE

Omitting the doubtful record for *Opheodrys* (Table II), all of the North American colubrids reported to show parental care (*Elaphe, Cemophora, Lampropeltis,* and *Pituophis*) probably are derived from a single adaptive radiation from Old World *Elaphe* (Underwood, 1967). Hence, parental care may parsimoniously be regarded as having a single evolutionary origin in these snakes. However, the other colubrine taxa showing parental care (*Farancia, Lycodon, Ptyas*) are only distantly related to each other and to *Elaphe* (Underwood, 1967), suggesting that egg-attending has evolved independently several times in colubrids.

2. NATRICINAE

The natricine snakes (family Colubridae) pose a similar problem. Parental care has been reported in five genera (six species), which appear to be relatively closely related (Malnate, 1960; Underwood, 1967). Hence, these cases will be treated as a single evolutionary origin of parental care. This decision may be overly conservative because parental care has been reported from only one or two species within each genus; if it were a primitive character for the entire natricine radiation, one might expect to see more occurrences of the trait. The high probability that parental behavior has been overlooked in many taxa represents a problem with enumerating the number of independent evolutionary origins (as in Ridley, 1983) by application of a specific method. Hence it seems most parsimonious to count this as a single example of the evolution of parental care.

This analysis suggests that parental care has evolved independently remarkably few times in extant reptiles; the number may be as low as 21

TABLE IV
The Incidence of Parental Care in Reptiles at the Level of Family, Subfamily, Genus and Species With Estimates of the Probable Number of Independent Evolutionary Origins of Parental Care

Family	Subfamily	Number of taxa in which parental care recorded		Probable number of evolutionary origins
		Genera	Species	
Squamata				
Anguidae	Anguinae	1	5	⎫
	Diploglossinae	1	2	⎬ 1
	Gerrhonotinae	1	2	⎭
Iguanidae	Iguaninae	4	10	1
Scincidae	Lygosominae	1	1	doubtful record
	Scincinae	2	21	1
Teiidae	Teiinae	1	1	1
Varanidae	Varaninae	1	3	1
Boidae	Pythoninae	5	16	1
Colubridae	Boiginae	1	3	1
	Colubrinae	8	13	4
	Natricinae	5	6	>1
	Xenodontinae	1	1	doubtful record
Elapidae	Elapinae	6	11	>4
	Laticaudinae	1	1	1
Leptotyphlopidae	Leptotyphlopinae	1	1	1
Typhlopidae	Typhlopinae	1	2	1
Viperidae	Crotalinae	4	4	1
Testudines				
Emydidae	Emydinae	1	1	doubtful record
Crocodylia				
Crocodylidae	Alligatorinae	4	6	⎫
	Crocodylinae	2	10	⎬ 1
Gavialidae	Gavialinae	1	1	⎭

(Table IV). Of these origins, only 5 have occurred among the lizards compared to 15 among the snakes. The ratio of evolutionary origins to the number of present-day oviparous taxa in the suborder thus is much higher (5 in 3000 versus 15 in 1700) in the latter group.

3. ELAPINAE

The six elapine genera recorded to show parental care are only distantly related to each other (e.g., Underwood, 1967; Mao et al., 1983), and hence are likely to represent independent evolutionary origins of the trait. The records for Australasian species are questionable and may be omitted, but this still leaves four probable origins within the elapines.

D. Male, Female, and Biparental Care

Parental care in reptiles is performed almost always by the female (Table II), sometimes in conjunction with the male (Table I). Even in crocodilians, the only group in which male parental care has been reported commonly, the male plays a much less significant role than does the female in nest-guarding or transport of young. However, males may be important in subsequent defense of hatchlings from predators (references in Table I).

Records of male parental care in squamate reptiles are often anecdotal or poorly documented. Egg-attendance by a male *Diploglossus delasagra* was reported by Barbour and Ramsden (1919), but they did not note how the parent's gender was determined. Egg-attendance has also been reported for a female of this species (Taylor, 1956), and for several related forms (Table II); Barbour and Ramsden's (1919) animal may have been incorrectly sexed.

Biparental care has been reported in four species of snakes: the Asian elapids *Bungarus ceylonicus, Ophiophagus hannah* and *Naja naja*, and the north American colubrid *Elaphe obsoleta*. The record for *Bungarus* (Green, 1905) is suspect; two adults of unspecified sex were observed curled up in a hollow with eggs and hatchlings. Other records of parental care in this genus involve only the female remaining with the eggs (Table II). The record for *Ophiophagus* rests upon Wall's statement that "during the incubation period there is no doubt at any rate in some instances, that the male is in close attendance on his mate" (1924:193). This statement is repeated by Tweedie (1957), but detailed studies in captivity (Oliver, 1956), and collection of adults from 15 nests in the wild (Leakey, 1969) provide strong evidence that only the female remains with the eggs.

The record of biparental care in *Naja naja* is based upon a captive pair; the female usually stayed with the eggs but "the male, which was always near the mound, (took) the place of the female during the three hours that she left the eggs to drink and feed. Both reptiles were particularly vicious during the incubation period" (Jennison, 1931; repeated by Smith, 1937; Tweedie, 1957). Deraniyagala (1955) reported that both male and female of a captive pair of *Naja naja* attended the nest, but that only the female resumed this behavior after disturbance. A recent detailed study of reproduction in captive *Naja naja* did not report any assistance by the male to the egg-attending female (Campbell and Quinn, 1975). A statement by Jennison (1931) that the female *Naja* comes obediently to the whistle of the keeper, also seems inconsistent with observations of captive snakes. Hence, I am skeptical of the reliability of the reported biparental care.

The remaining case of parental care is in *Elaphe obsoleta* at Jacob's Creek, Pennsylvania (Medsger, 1919). The eggs were buried in an old sawdust pile, and the two "parent" snakes remained on, in, or near the pile for at least 3 weeks. At one point, "Mr. Medsger secured a fork, and at a depth of twelve inches dug up 44 eggs of the pilot snake. The male snake was coiled around the eggs" (Medsger, 1919:28). Mr. Medsger's talk on this subject was illustrated by photographs, so there seems no reason to doubt his observations. However, his means of sexing the adult snakes may have been in error. The reported clutch size is very high; usual clutches for this species are 7–12 eggs (Fitch, 1970), and communal oviposition has been recorded (Lynch, 1966). Hence, the clutch was probably a communal one, and the two snakes observed by Medsger may both have been females. Further observations on reproduction of this relatively common snake would be of interest.

III. HYPOTHESES ON THE EVOLUTION OF PARENTAL CARE

A. Cost-Benefit Models

1. GENERAL

The selective forces responsible for the evolution of reptilian parental care may be investigated by an analysis of the possible "costs" and "benefits" of such behavior. Thus, the fitness (lifetime reproductive success) of a hypothetical reptile showing parental care is compared to that of an otherwise identical animal not showing care, and the ecological conditions or species characteristics conferring a higher fitness to the former individual are considered.

As described in theoretical models for the evolution of viviparity (Shine, 1985), the primary "costs" of parental care are likely to be decrements in the food intake, survivorship, or subsequent fecundity of the parent. Remaining with the eggs may increase vulnerability of the parent to predators, depending on the site chosen and on whether the eggs have an odor detectable to predators. Remaining with the eggs certainly is likely to reduce the feeding opportunities of the parents. This in turn may prevent the accumulation of energy required for production of a second clutch. In males, restriction to the nest site and guarding of young may reduce opportunities for further copulation.

The "benefit" of parental care presumably is to increase offspring fitness, either by increasing survivorship of embryos and hatchlings or by accelerating embryogenesis so that hatching occurs at a favorable time. The increase in offspring survivorship could result from parental protection against many potential sources of mortality (e.g., predation, dessication, flooding, and fungal attack). These factors are considered in more detail below.

2. BENEFITS OF PARENTAL CARE

Table V summarizes published hypotheses and available evidence on the functions (benefits) of reptilian parental care. Several of these presumed benefits may be valid, and indeed any single case of parental care may well have evolved for a variety of reasons. The common observations that females are particularly aggressive during the defense of nests (Table V) suggests that deterring predators is a major function of parental care. This phenomenon is particularly striking in cases in which the individual reptile, or the species to which it belongs, is generally nonaggressive (e.g., *Bungarus, Laticauda, Naja naja, Python regius*; Table V). However, many nest-attending females are not aggressive: females of several pythons and crocodilians, as well as those of *Ophisaurus apodus, O. ventralis, Naja melanoleuca,* and *Ophiophagus hannah*, have all been reported to be relatively quiescent (in some cases, almost comatose) while attending eggs (Barker, 1981; Cott, 1971; Langerwerf, 1981; Noble and Mason, 1933; Tryon, 1979; Oliver, 1956). Nonetheless, it cannot be claimed unambiguously that any of these changes in maternal behavior (e.g., increased or decreased levels of aggression) are *adaptations* to parental care. The behavior of the parents could alternatively be interpreted as a direct response to a changed thermal environment, endocrine modifications associated with oviposition, the physiological stress of oviposition, or some other factor. This does not mean that the behavior of the parent fails to protect the eggs, but merely that it may be a direct consequence of the physiology of the parent rather than an adaptation per se.

Although the studies cited in Table V show that females may actively defend their eggs against potential predators, the only work to compare predation rates on defended versus undefended clutches is that of Metzen (1977), who studied 110 nests of *Alligator* in the Okefenokee swamp. Most nests (96) were not defended by females, and almost all of these nests (92, or 96%) were destroyed by predators, especially bears. However, in 14 actively-defended nests, predation was rare (four nests destroyed, or 29%).

An alternative threat to eggs may come from their being dug up by other nesting females. This has been reported to occur in sea turtles (Carr, 1967) and presumably is the selective force favoring nest-site defense in iguanine lizards (Table V). Suitable nesting areas are rare in some habitats occupied by these lizards, so that disturbance of an earlier clutch by an ovipositing female is frequent. In these species, nests are defended only until the end of the egg-laying season. A similar situation

TABLE V
"Benefits" of Parental Care: Hypotheses and Evidence

Benefit	Species	Evidence	Authority
1. Deter potential egg predators	*Elgaria multicarinatus*	♀ Aggressive to humans	Langerwerf, 1981
	Eumeces egregius	♀ Aggressive to potential predators	Mount, 1963
	E. fasciatus	♀ Aggressive to potential predators	Noble and Mason, 1933
	E. laticeps	♀ Aggressive to potential predators	Noble and Mason, 1933
	Tupinambis teguixin	♀ Aggressive to humans	Kreig, 1925
	Brachylophus fasciatus	♀ Aggressive to humans	Gibbons and Watkins, 1982
	Liasis albertisii	♀ Aggressive to humans	Ross and Larman, 1977
	Morelia spilotes	♀ Aggressive to humans	Charles et al., 1983
	Python regius	♀♂ Aggressive to humans	Van Mierop and Bessette, 1981
	Natrix natrix	♀ Aggressive to humans	Gallwey, 1932
	Bungarus candidus	♀ Aggressive to humans	Mell, 1929
	Laticauda colubrina	♀ Aggressive to humans	Smedley, 1931
	Naja naja	♀ Aggressive to humans	Jennison, 1931; Campbell and Quinn, 1975
	Alligator mississippiensis	♀ Aggressive to potential predators, humans	McIlhenny, 1934; Dietz and Jackson, 1979
		Presence reduces egg predation	Metzen, 1977
	Crocodylus acutus	♀ Aggressive to potential predators	Dugan et al., 1981
	C. niloticus	♀ Aggressive to potential predators	Modha, 1967; Cott, 1971
	C. palustris	♀ Aggressive to potential predators, humans	Dharmakumarsinhji, 1947; Anon, 1982
	C. porosus	♀ Aggressive to potential predators, humans	Cott, 1971; Biswas, 1977; Acharjyo and Mishra, 1981; Bustard and Choudhury, 1980; Bustard and Kar, 1981; Bustard and Maharana, 1982
	Gavialis gangeticus	♀ Aggressive to humans	Bustard and Singh, 1981
	All iguanine species listed in Table II	Attacks conspecifics if they attempt to excavate nest	References in Table II
2. Prevent disturbance to nest by other ovipositing females	*Alligator mississippiensis*	♀ Stops turtles digging into nest	Dietz and Jackson, 1979

3. Provide additional heat to speed embryonic development	Probably all pythons *Eumeces fasciatus*	♀ Produces heat by "shivering" ♀ Basks, returns to eggs	References in Tables II, V Noble and Mason, 1933, but see Fitch, 1954
	Python regius *Morelia spilotes*	♀ Basks, returns to eggs ♀ Basks, returns to eggs	Van Mierop and Bessette, 1981 Harlow and Grigg, 1984; Charles et al., 1985
4. Regulate egg temperatures	*Elaphe obsoleta*	Parents bask, return to eggs	Medsger, 1919
	Ophisaurus ventralis	♀ Adjusts depth to which eggs are buried	Vinegar, 1968
	Eumeces fasciatus	♀ Adjusts depth to which eggs are buried	Fitch, 1954
	Crocodylus porosus	♀ Lies on nest on sunny day	Deraniyagala, 1939
5. Prevent eggs drowning	*Eumeces fasciatus* *Opisthoropis latouchi*	♀ Moves eggs from flooded burrows Nest site is vulnerable to flooding	Fitch, 1954 Fitch, 1970
6. Provide moisture for eggs	*Eumeces fasciatus* *Crocodylus palustris* *C. niloticus* *C. porosus*	♀ Urinates on nest ♀ Urinates on nest Guarded nest is damp Guarded nest is damp	Fitch, 1954 Whitaker and Whitaker, 1977b Pooley, 1976 Webb et al., 1977
7. Eat or remove spoilt eggs, to deter fungal attack or discovery by predators	*Eumeces fasciatus* *Gerrhonotus liocephalus* *Ophisaurus attenuatus*	♀ Eats spoilt eggs ♀ Eats eggs ♀ Eats eggs	McCauley, 1945; Groves, 1982 Tinkle and Gibbons, 1977 Fitch, 1970
8. Open nest to enable hatchlings to emerge	*Pseudemys malonei* *Varanus varius* Probably all crocodilians	♀ Opens nest at hatching time ♀ In vicinity of nest at hatching time ♀ Opens nest	Hodsdon and Pearson, 1943 Cogger, 1967 References in Table I
9. Keep eggs covered and hidden	*Iguana iguana*	♀ Returns to nest daily, makes repairs	Alvarez del Toro, 1972
10. Deter predators of hatchlings	*Ophiophagus hannah* Many crocodilians	♀ Recovers exposed eggs Adults respond to alarm call	Oliver, 1956 References in Table II
11. Turn eggs to prevent growth of mould	*Eumeces fasciatus*	♀ Turns eggs; unattended eggs rot	Fitch, 1954

occurs in *Alligator*. Turtles attempting to nest on their nest mounds may disturb their eggs and nest-attending female *Alligator* attack them under such circumstances (Dietz and Jackson, 1979).

The only other major function of reptilian parental care is likely to be its effect on the thermal environment of the eggs (Packard and Packard, this volume). Egg temperatures may be modified by (a) the parent adjusting the depth at which the eggs are laid beneath the soil surface (Fitch, 1954; Vinegar, 1968); (b) the parent basking and then returning to the eggs (Medsger, 1919; Noble and Mason, 1933, but see Fitch, 1954; also Harlow and Grigg, 1984, for *Morelia*); or (c) the parent producing heat metabolically to warm the eggs. The last of these alternatives is employed commonly by boid snakes; shivering thermogenesis has been reported in at least nine species (see above).

Apart from benefits accruing from defense against predators or disturbance, and from thermoregulation, other functions of parental care have only been hypothesized rather than demonstrated (Table V). Most seem intuitively reasonable, but are likely to be important only in a restricted number of cases. Other hypotheses seem invalid; for example, Coborn's (1975) explanations for "shivering" in brooding pythons are that this behavior (1) promotes circulation of air around the eggs, (2) increases maternal circulation, and (3) is a maternal reaction to the presence of eggs between the coils. Undoubtedly, the posthatching parental care of crocodilians protects offspring from predatory attacks (e.g., Hunt, 1974, 1975). The parent–offspring bond in crocodilians also may enable the parents to "teach" specific behavior patterns to their offspring, but no data are available to test this hypothesis.

3. COSTS OF PARENTAL CARE

By staying with the eggs after oviposition, the adult reptile may forego opportunities for feeding. This in turn may reduce energy intake to the point that production of a subsequent clutch of eggs is delayed. Alternatively, a lower growth rate may depress subsequent fecundity. In either case, the reproductive success of the animal is reduced. A more direct "cost" of parental care may be a decrement in survivorship, due to increased exposure to predators or other hazards. This might be likely if parental care occurs in a habitat different from that normally occupied by adults, or if predators can detect eggs more easily than they detect adults. The high metabolic expenditure of brooding pythons, which raise metabolic rate to warm the eggs, is another clear "cost" of parental care.

A reduced food intake, often a total cessation of feeding, has been documented in several egg-attending species both in the field and in captivity (Table VI). Observations of captive specimens indicate that

TABLE VI
"Costs" of Parental Care: Hypotheses and Evidence

Cost	Species	Evidence	Authority
1. Reduction of food intake	*Eumeces egregius*	♀ Remains with eggs constantly	Mount, 1963
	E. fasciatus	♀ Remains with eggs constantly	Fitch, 1954
	E. obsoletus	♀ Remains with eggs constantly	Fitch, 1955
	E. okadae	♀ Remains with eggs constantly	Hasegawa, 1984
	E. septentrionalis	♀ Remains with eggs constantly	Breckenridge, 1943
	Ophisaurus attenuatus	Empty stomachs in egg-attending ♀	Fitch, 1970
	Ophiophagus hannah	Empty stomachs in nest-attending ♀	Leakey, 1969
	Morelia spilotes	Captive ♀ refuse food	Shine, 1980
	Python molurus	Captive ♀ refuse food	Taylor, 1965; Van Mierop and Barnard, 1978
	P. reticulatus	Captive ♀ refuse food	La Panouse and Pellier, 1973
	P. regius	Captive ♀ refuse food	Boos, 1979; Ross, 1978; Van Mierop and Bessette, 1981
	P. sebae	Captive ♀ refuse food	FitzSimons, 1930
	Aspidites melanocephalus	Captive ♀ refuse food	Charles et al., 1985
	Liasis amethystinus	Captive ♀ refuse food	Charles et al., 1985
	Crocodylus niloticus	Empty stomachs in nest-attending ♀	Pitman, 1930; Pooley, 1977; Cott, 1971
	C. porosus	Empty stomachs in nest-attending ♀	Deraniyagala, 1939; Choudhury and Bustard, 1979; Bustard and Maharana, 1982
2. Reduction of subsequent fecundity	*Python reticulatus*	♀ Breeds less often than annually	Fitch, 1970
	Morelia spilotes	♀ Breeds less often than annually	Harlow and Grigg, 1984
	Eumeces obsoletus	♀ Breeds less often than annually	Fitch, 1970
	Alligator mississippiensis	♀ Breeds less often than annually	Neill, 1971

inanition during this period is due to a specific disinclination to feed rather than a lack of encounters with suitable prey. Apart from the cases cited in Table VI, many other reports of nest attendance refer to the constant presence of the female with the eggs. Presumably, food intake is reduced in most or all of these species. Egg-attending females often are reported as appearing emaciated by the time that parental care terminates (e.g., Mell, 1929). Interspecific differences may occur in fidelity to the nest; females of some species regularly leave the eggs and forage, whereas those of other species never do so (Mell, 1929). However, specific data on this point are lacking. Females remaining with eggs potentially could obtain considerable quantities of food by consuming potential egg-predators attracted to the nest (Tinkle and Gibbons, 1977). Again, data are lacking.

A reduced food intake probably is common, but not universal, in egg-attending females (e.g., Ross, 1978; Boos, 1979). The same situation occurs with other reproductive modes in reptiles; for example, food intake is reduced during gestation in many, but not all, viviparous species (Shine, 1980).

Without direct experimental manipulation (such as removal of clutches), longer-term costs of parental care are difficult to assess. The hypothesized delay in subsequent reproduction is supported by long intervals (greater than 1 year) among successive clutches in at least four egg-attending species of reptiles (Table VI). Indeed, a strong correlation has been demonstrated both for reptiles and amphibians, among low frequencies of reproduction and "accessory costs", such as parental care, viviparity, and long breeding migrations (Bull and Shine, 1979). Low reproductive frequencies are common in taxa that do have such "costs." However, this correlation may not reflect the fact that parental care confers a high cost per se, but rather that the cost is relatively independent of fecundity. For example, the reduction in food intake of a brooding female python probably is independent of the number of eggs she is brooding. Under these circumstances, calculations suggest that infrequent reproduction, in each case with the production of a large clutch, will be the optimal life-history strategy (Bull and Shine, 1979). A recent study of *Eumeces okadae* (Hasegawa, 1984) confirmed that postovipositional weight loss of egg-attending females was not correlated with their fecundity.

Although the egg-attending species with low frequencies of reproduction (Table VI) provide circumstantial evidence in support of "costs" of parental care, the opposite extreme also occurs; many egg-attending species, especially those from tropical areas, have been reported or suggested to produce more than a single clutch per year. These include *Gerrhonotus liocephalus, Elgaria multicarinatus, Tupinambis teguixin, Rhab-*

dophis subminiatus, Xenochrophis piscator, Cemophora coccinea, Lycodon aulicus, Pituophis melanoleucus, Ptyas korros, and *P. mucosus* (data and references in Fitch, 1970). However, these records may be based on females that have lost or abandoned their first clutch (Fitch, 1970).

4. CONCLUSION

Overall, the available data are consistent with hypothesized "benefits" and "costs" of parental care, but are generally circumstantial in nature. The only direct demonstration of the effectiveness of parental care in increasing egg survivorship comes from a study of *Alligator* (Metzen, 1977). Good quantitative estimates of costs of parental care are lacking. These inadequacies in the available data are regrettable, because studies to measure the relevant variables are entirely feasible. Experimental manipulations could provide measurements both of the benefits of parental care (what is the survivorship of attended and unattended eggs?) and its associated costs (what are the differences in food intake, growth rate, and in the time of subsequent reproduction, between those females that are attending eggs and females of which the clutches of eggs have been removed?). Sample manipulations might involve (a) removal of part or all of the clutch of an egg-attending female, and (b) removal of the female from the clutch. Studies on parental care in salamanders (e.g., Tilley, 1973; Huheey and Brandon, 1975; Forester, 1979a, b), frogs (e.g., Taigen et al., 1984), and insects (e.g., Tallamy and Denno, 1982) have progressed much further in this respect, than have those on reptiles.

B. Intermediate Stages in the Evolution of Parental Care

The vast majority of reptilian species do not show any form of parental care, but a small minority have been reported to remain with the eggs after oviposition (Tables I, II). In most cases, the parent is believed to remain with the clutch for the entire duration of incubation, and only to leave after the eggs have hatched. This situation raises the question of intermediate stages in the evolution of parental care. Presumably, a species without egg-attending behavior does not give rise by a single mutation to individuals that remain with eggs throughout development. Instead, the two more likely scenarios are as follows.

1. The female remains with the eggs for only a short time after oviposition and then leaves. This could occur if the female was "exhausted" by oviposition. Given the chance association between parent and eggs, selection could then favor "parental" behavior (e.g., defense against predators) and ultimately prolonged nest-attendance (Noble, 1931). The feasibility of short-term egg attendance as an intermediate stage towards prolonged parental care is supported by records of short-

term egg attendance in several squamate species (e.g., Gallwey, 1932; Fukada, 1959). Unfortunately, many cases of this phenomenon have been reported in captive animals, even in species known to attend eggs throughout incubation in the wild state (e.g., FitzSimons, 1930; Boos, 1979). This suggests that nest desertion in captivity may be an artifact arising from human disturbance. Variation in the duration of nest defense in iguanine lizards may reflect maternal condition; emaciated females defend nests only briefly, then leave to feed (Wiewandt, 1982).

2. The female leaves the eggs after oviposition, but returns to them regularly because they are located under a favored refuge. This intermittent proximity of parent and eggs provides the opportunity for selection to favor "parental" behavior, and perhaps leads eventually to more persistent nest attendance. We do not know how commonly this phenomenon occurs in nature, although Mell (1929) suggests that there is a continuum among species from intermittent to constant egg attenders.

Both pathways may well have been involved in the evolution of parental care, as is suggested by the apparent occurrence of both putative "intermediate stages" in modern reptiles. However, such strategies in modern reptiles may be secondary modifications of prolonged nest attendance, and not intermediates in the evolution of this trait.

C. Factors Increasing the Benefits of Parental Care

1. PREDICTION

If the primary benefit of parental care is an increase in egg survivorship, then parental care should evolve most readily in situations in which it has a large effect on survival of the eggs. This may occur in species or environments in which the attending parents are unusually successful at reducing mortality rates of eggs, either because of the abilities of the parents, or the high susceptibility of the unprotected eggs.

2. EXPOSED VERSUS HIDDEN NEST SITES

Eggs that are laid under superficial cover on the surface of the ground, rather than being deeply buried, may be particularly vulnerable to predation. Hence, parental care might evolve more readily in species that do not bury their eggs (Noble and Mason, 1933). This hypothesis has been used to explain the presence of parental care in *Tupinambis teguixin*, and its absence in the synonymous *T. nigropunctatus*, which oviposits inside termite mounds (Noble and Mason, 1933; but see Goeldi, 1902 and Riley et al., 1985, who report that *T. teguixin* oviposits in termitaria). However, the argument can be generalized to predict that parental care should be more common in snakes, which typically do not bury their eggs (probably because of the lack of limbs with which to excavate a nest-hole) than in lizards, which typically dig nest-holes. For the same reason, parental care should be more common in limbless (nonburrowing) lizards than in species with fully-developed limbs.

Data presented earlier support the prediction that parental care is more common in snakes than in lizards (3% of oviparous species versus 1%) and has evolved more often in the former group (15 origins in 11 families versus 5 origins in 15 families). Limblessness has evolved many times among lizards, but is shown by only a small proportion of taxa (Gans, 1975). Hence, the parental care of the limbless *Ophisaurus* offers further, although weak, support for the hypothesis that limblessness favors the evolution of parental care.

3. ABILITY OF PARENTS TO DEFEND EGGS

If a major benefit of parental care is the repulsion of potential egg-predators, then parental care should evolve most often in species in which the parent is capable of deterring predators. This is most likely to be true of large and of venomous species. No such trend is evident among the lizards, except for *Tupinambis* and the tentative records for *Varanus*.

However, in snakes there is a strong bias for such parental care in large and venomous species. The only major taxon in which parental care is common (probably universal) is the Pythoninae, and this group contains the largest oviparous snakes of the world. Parental care also occurs in 4 of the 8 oviparous genera of the Viperidae (50%) and 7 of the 17 oviparous genera of the Elapidae (41%). In contrast, the much larger (>200 genera) Colubridae, which consists primarily of nonvenomous (or less venomous) species, shows parental care less commonly (15 genera, or 7.5%). Several of the colubrids reported to show parental care are unusually large (e.g., *Elaphe, Farancia, Ptyas*), or belong to the minority of venomous forms within the family (e.g., *Psammophylax, Rhabdophis*). The prevalence of parental care in crocodilians—most of which are large and formidable—also is consistent with the prediction that this behavior should be shown most frequently by groups in which parents are well able to defend their eggs. Interestingly, many taxa of marine invertebrates show the opposite trend; parental care is most common in the smaller species of marine invertebrates (Strathmann and Strathmann, 1982). Nonetheless, extended parental care may also be common in highly venomous forms (e.g., *Hapalochlaena, Chironex*; Sutherland, 1983).

4. LIMITED AVAILABILITY OF NEST SITES

If nest sites are scarce relative to the number of nesting females, older nests may be excavated and destroyed by new arrivals. This situation has been described in sea turtles (e.g., Carr, 1967) and island populations of iguanine lizards (Rand and Rand, 1976; Wiewandt, 1982). Active defense of nest sites by postovipositional females is common in iguanines (references in Table II). Intraspecific variations in intensity of iguanine nest defense are correlated with the degree to which suitable nest sites are available, and the ease of digging burrows (Wiewandt, 1982). The selective advantage of parental care in this situation is increased by the relatively synchronous nesting of the population; thus even brief nest defense is effective.

Although these arguments are consistent with the behavior seen in iguanines, they are unlikely to be of general importance because scarcity of suitable nesting sites may be a rare phenomenon. The only parallels to iguanine nest defense may be in alligators, in which the nest-guarding female prevents ovipositing turtles from digging into the nest mound (Dietz and Jackson, 1979), and tuataras, in which resting females defend nesting sites against other females (M. Thompson, pers. comm.).

D. Factors Reducing the Costs of Parental Care

1. PREDICTION

If the major "costs" of parental care are a reduction in food intake, probable survivorship, or subsequent fecundity of the reproducing female, then parental care would be expected to evolve most often in species and environments in which such costs were minor or insignificant.

2. SELECTION FOR "RISKY" LIFE-HISTORY STRATEGIES

Life-history theory predicts that small, short-lived species are more likely to pursue "risky" reproductive strategies than are large, long-lived ones (Williams, 1966). Although parental care was suggested to be "risky," a test on fishes revealed no clear trend for more parental care in smaller species, possibly because the smaller species were not capable of deterring egg-predators (Williams, 1966). Similarly, a compilation of data on 49 species of lizards showed a trend reverse to that predicted; parental care was more common in late-maturing species (5 of 14, or 36%) than in those that matured early (2 of 35, or 6%) (Tinkle, 1969). This contradiction has been explained by suggesting that parental care is not as "risky" as it appears; "lizards that practice it usually remain with their eggs in a well-hidden site in which they may be less exposed to dangers than a female that does not tend her eggs" (Tinkle, 1969:505). Indeed, following a general discussion of the evolution of lizard life histories, Tinkle (1969) predicted that parental care will generally be found in long-lived iteroparous species, especially those with a short, annual breeding season.

To the degree that large body size is correlated with late attainment of maturity (Williams, 1966; Dunham, Miles, and Reznick, this volume), the trend for parental care in large reptiles (see previous section) is consistent with Tinkle's (1969) prediction. However, it is consistent also with the hypothesis that parental care by small species is ineffective against predators, or the alternative hypothesis that in small species, parents themselves are too vulnerable to predation to permit the evolution of parental care. Certainly, the data on reptiles (Table II) are inconsistent with the prediction that parental care will be most common in small, short-lived species (Williams, 1966).

3. FREQUENCY OF REPRODUCTION

Egg-attending reduces food intake of the reproducing female (Table VI), and thus may delay the time at which a subsequent clutch can be produced. Hence, parental care is likely to evolve in species that produce only a single clutch of eggs per year. The costs of remaining with the eggs may be independent of the number of eggs guarded, whereas the benefits increase with the number of eggs. Hence, parental care might be more likely to evolve in species that produce large but infrequent clutches rather than in those that produce small and frequent clutches. Both hypotheses predict that parental care should be most common in species that produce clutches only once a year or less often. Data on lizards support the prediction (Tinkle, 1969), although there are some puzzling cases of multiple-clutching, egg-attending species (see previous section on "costs"). The correlation between parental care and extremely low frequencies of reproduction (Bull and Shine, 1979) also is consistent with this prediction, but is open to the other interpretations discussed earlier.

Because the annual production of multiple clutches is common only in the tropics (Dunham, Miles, and Reznick, this volume), parental care should typify temperate rather than tropical species (Tinkle, 1969). The available data are biased by the concentration of scientific study in the temperate zone, but even so, the prediction is refuted; parental care is widespread in tropical reptiles (Tables I, II). The reptilian subfamilies in which parental care is most common (Iguaninae, Pythoninae, Alligatorinae, Crocodylinae) are all primarily tropical groups. Overall, the predicted bias toward temperate-zone species is conspicuously lacking.

4. SUITABILITY OF HABITAT FOR CLUTCH ATTENDANCE

Parental care might be unlikely to evolve whenever eggs are laid in a habitat different from that usually occupied by the adult. In such a situation, the parent may be unusually susceptible to predation or physiological stress. This hypothesis suggests that parental care should be rare in aquatic or arboreal species. It is an obvious explanation for the lack of testudinian parental care, but is unconvincing because (a) many turtles are terrestrial; and (b) many other aquatic reptiles show parental care (e.g., crocodilians, laticaudid sea snakes).

5. HARSH AND UNPREDICTABLE ENVIRONMENT

Prolonged attendance on the clutch might be most likely to be favored in environments in which resources for the adult, at about the time of egg deposition, become increasingly scarce or unpredictable so that searching for such resources becomes a high-risk endeavor (Tinkle and Gibbons, 1977). Under these circumstances, parental care might strongly benefit egg survivorship while conferring only a minor cost on the opportunities of the adult for future reproduction. This hypothesis predicts that parental care will most often be found in environments in which resources for adults are limited at the time of egg deposition (Tinkle and Gibbons, 1977). The prediction is difficult to test, but seems inconsistent with the strong taxonomic bias in the distribution of reptilian parental care. If specific environmental variables are important, one might expect to see parental care restricted to particular habitat types rather than to all species within a given taxon (e.g., *Eumeces*). However, available data are insufficient to convincingly refute the prediction.

6. BRIEF INCUBATION PERIODS

Parental care might be associated with brief incubation periods for three reasons:

(1) The "costs" of remaining with the eggs depend upon the incubation period: if the eggs hatch soon after oviposition, the female is burdened only briefly by egg attendance.

(2) Natural selection may favor prolonged oviducal retention of eggs in species with parental care, because the costs of this retention may be no higher than the costs of parental care (Shine and Bull, 1979). In

contrast, species without parental care are less likely to evolve egg retention; in this case, the physical burdening of the gravid female imposes too high a cost on survivorship and subsequent fecundity.

(3) Parental care and prolonged uterine retention of eggs are both examples of increased maternal investment, and may be favored by the same selective forces. Hence, they are likely to occur in the same species and the same environments.

A recent review of incubation periods showed "at least an indication that egg-guarding species may have slightly shorter development times than those that do not guard eggs" (Tinkle and Gibbons, 1977:27). More detailed analysis of the data from Tinkle and Gibbons (1977:Table 13) confirms that the mean incubation period of egg-attending species (57.5 days; n = 39; s.d. = 23.2) is lower than that of nonattending species (74.4 days; n = 124, s.d. = 44.0), but the variances are so high that the difference fails to reach statistical significance (median test, 1 d.f., $\chi^2 = 0.6$, n.s.). One confounding variable in this test, however, is the trend for parental care in larger species (see earlier); large species tend to have larger eggs, which in turn have longer incubation periods.

An alternative test involves the examination of the embryonic stage of development at oviposition in egg-attending and non-egg-attending species. "Visible embryonic development at oviposition" has been reported more commonly in species with parental care (Shine and Bull, 1979). However, a more recent study, which used objective criteria to stage embryonic development, found that relatively prolonged retention of eggs is the rule rather than the exception in oviparous squamates (Shine, 1983a). No evidence exists to show that uterine retention is more prolonged among egg-attending species (Shine, 1983a).

A recent analysis of parental care in salamanders (Nussbaum, 1985) argues that parental care should evolve in species with long incubation periods; that is, it predicts the reverse of the above-discussed prediction. Nussbaum notes that salamanders with parental care tend to have large eggs, and that such eggs take a long time to develop. From these data, he argues that parental care has evolved to reduce the otherwise high rate of mortality of these slowly-developing embryos. An alternative interpretation of the same data is that natural selection has favored an increase in egg size in species with parental care, because the offspring may thereby be kept for longer in a low-risk situation (protected eggs) rather than as unprotected free-living juveniles (Shine, 1978; the "safe harbor" hypothesis). The association of parental care with large offspring is less clear in reptiles than in many other animal taxa, possibly because of the concentration of most reptilian embryonic mortality to a short postovipositional period (Shine, 1978).

E. Which Sex Should Show Parental Care?

One consistent feature of reptilian parental care (Section II.D) is that involvement by the male is nonexistent (squamates) or relatively minor (crocodilians). In contrast, male parental care is common in amphibians, fishes, and birds (Ridley, 1978). The evolutionary basis for sex differences in the tendency to show parental care has been the subject of several recent discussions (e.g., Trivers, 1972; Ridley, 1978; Perrone and Zaret, 1979; Blumer, 1979; Gross and Shine, 1981; Nussbaum, 1985). Two hypotheses for the selection of parental care have received wide attention:

1. Selection against male parental care, because internal fertilization results in a delay between insemination and oviposition, making the paternity of any given clutch uncertain (unlike the situation in most external fertilization). This low reliability of paternity may select against male parental care in species with internal fertilization (Trivers, 1972), including reptiles (Tinkle and Gibbons, 1977; Perrone and Zaret, 1979).

2. The unlikelihood of selection for male parental care in species with internal fertilization, because the time delay between insemination and oviposition means that a male and his offspring may never be in close proximity (Williams, 1966; Gross and Shine, 1981).

Both of these hypotheses correctly predict that reptilian parental care should be performed by females rather than males. Although the reptilian data therefore do not permit a test between the two hypotheses, the latter (parent–offspring proximity) model seems more accurately to predict the distribution of parental care in teleosts and amphibians (Gross and Shine, 1981). The paternity hypothesis also has been criticized on the grounds of faulty logic (Werren et al., 1980).

An alternative approach is to consider the effects of reproductive activities on the parents. If the female is "exhausted" by oviposition, she may be likely to stay with the eggs until she recovers, protoadapting the species for female parental care (Noble, 1931). However, exactly the opposite prediction is made by Maynard Smith (1977); because the female is exhausted, she has a greater need than the male to recommence feeding as soon as possible. Thus, Maynard Smith predicts that this situation should favor the evolution of male parental care. The reptilian pattern is consistent with the prediction of Noble rather than with that of Maynard Smith, but does not provide strong support for the former hypothesis, because the predominance of maternal care is consistent with several alternative theories.

HYPOTHESES ON THE EVOLUTION OF PARENTAL CARE

A related question is why biparental care is virtually unknown in squamates, and probably rare even in crocodilians (Tables I, II). This result is consistent with a general trend for biparental care to be less common in ectotherms than in endothermic vertebrates (Case, 1978; Gross and Shine, 1981). Biparental care may be most likely to evolve when the form of care is such that two parents are much more effective than one; for example, feeding or guarding mobile young, rather than merely guarding eggs (Maynard Smith, 1977; Perrone and Zaret, 1979). This hypothesis predicts that biparental care in reptiles should be restricted to crocodilians (the only group to guard offspring after hatching), and that the contribution of the male should commence only after the eggs hatch. This prediction is strongly supported by data in Table I.

F. Why Is Parental Care Rare in Reptiles?

An analysis of parental care at the familial level reveals major differences among reptiles, teleost fishes, and amphibians in the frequency and form of parental care they exhibit (Table VII). The proportion of families containing care-giving species is highest among amphibians, in terms of parental care by either sex, or overall. Reptiles differ strongly from the other two groups in their low frequency of male parental care (Table VII). This probably reflects the lack of externally-fertilizing reptilian species (see earlier discussion). Although the overall proportion of families showing parental care is similar in fishes and reptiles, this direct comparison is misleading. Most fish species produce pelagic eggs, so that parental care is impossible. The proportion of species showing parental care would be much higher in demersal-spawning teleosts than in reptiles. This difference may be attributable to (a) the high incidence of external fertilization in teleosts, protoadapting for male parental care (Gross and Shine, 1981), and (b) the brief incubation period of teleost eggs, requiring only a short duration of parental care.

Although parental care is proportionally less common among reptiles than among other ectothermic vertebrates, an alternative form of increased parental investment—viviparity—is strikingly more common in reptiles (Table VII). This may reflect two reptilian features: internal fertilization and behavioral thermoregulation. The former protoadapts the species to viviparity (Gross and Shine, 1981), whereas the latter enables rates of embryonic development to be accelerated greatly by uterine retention of eggs (Shine, 1983b). Because parental care of eggs may serve as a protoadaptation to viviparity, the incidence of reptilian parental care may be lowered by a trend for viviparity to evolve in care-giving species (Shine and Bull, 1979; Shine, 1985).

TABLE VII
The Distribution of Parental Care and Viviparity Among Families of Teleost Fishes, Amphibians, and Reptiles

	Teleosts	Amphibians	Reptiles
Number of families for which data available	182	35	43
Number with male parental care (and proportion with male parental care)	63 (.35)	16 (.46)	1 (.02)
Number with female parental care (and proportion)	28 (.15)	17 (.49)	13 (.30)
Number with parental care by either parent (and proportion)	68 (.37)	23 (.66)	13 (.43)
Number with viviparity (and proportion)	11 (.06)	6 (.17)	18 (.42)
Number with parental care and/or viviparity (and proportion)	77 (.42)	25 (.71)	24 (.56)

Data for teleosts and amphibians from Gross and Shine (1981), and references therein.

IV. SUMMARY

1. Parental care in reptiles occurs in at least four different forms: egg-attending (female remains with clutch), egg-guarding (female defends clutch against potential predators), egg-brooding (female keeps clutch temperature above ambient), and the complex parental behavior of crocodilians (including guarding of eggs and young, nest opening, and mouth transport of eggs and young). Parental care in squamates is typically directed towards the eggs rather than the young.

2. Parental care has been reported in over 100 species of reptiles, but many records are inadequate. Parental care is rare or lacking in testudinians, probably universal in crocodilians, and has been reported in approximately 2% of oviparous squamate species.

3. Both the frequency and the form of parental care show a strong taxonomic bias, which may be detected at the level of order, suborder, family, and genus. Despite the overall scarcity of care-giving species

SUMMARY

among reptiles, this behavior is abundant (universal?) among a few taxonomic groups (Crocodilia, Iguaninae, Pythoninae, Crotalinae, and the scincine genus *Eumeces*).

4. The strong taxonomic bias in parental care suggests that it has evolved only rarely (once within each such group). A phylogenetic analysis suggests that the number of independent evolutionary origins of reptilian parental care among extant species may be as low as 21 (5 in lizards, 15 in snakes, 1 in crocodilians).

5. All well-documented cases of squamate parental care involve only the female parent. Among crocodilians, nest-guarding is undertaken by the female, but the male may contribute also to subsequent protection of the young. These biases to female parental care of eggs, and biparental care of young, are consistent with patterns observed in teleost fishes and amphibians.

6. Parental care imposes both "benefits" (to egg survivorship) and "costs" (to parental survivorship and subsequent reproduction). Major "benefits" of parental care probably come from deterring either potential egg-predators or conspecific females that otherwise would disturb the nest. In pythons, maternal care also helps to keep the eggs at high and constant temperature throughout incubation. The main "cost" of parental care probably is a reduction in food intake of the reproducing female.

7. This paper attempts to test several hypotheses on the evolution of reptilian parental care. The available data are consistent with predictions that parental care is likely to be shown by: (a) Species utilizing exposed rather than hidden nest sites (i.e., snakes rather than lizards); (b) species in which adults are large (e.g., crocodilians, pythons) and/or venomous (e.g., vipers), and hence able to deter potential predators; (c) species that compete intraspecifically for limited nest sites (iguanine lizards); (d) females rather than males because of the low probability that a male will be in close proximity with his offspring; and (e) both parents in species that guard mobile young (crocodilians), because two parents are more effective deterrents than one.

8. The proportion of species with parental care is lower among reptiles than among amphibians or freshwater teleost fishes. This difference reflects the absence of male parental care in squamates, which in turn may be due to internal fertilization. However, the high incidence of viviparity in this group means that increased parental investment (of which parental care is a special case) is a common phenomenon in the Reptilia.

ACKNOWLEDGMENTS

I dedicate this chapter to my father, Patrick Shine, who died while the work was in progress. Without his support of my unconventional career aspirations, I would never have had the opportunity to become a professional scientist. I also thank Terri, James, and Benjamin Shine for insights into parental care, and for their encouragement. Translations were kindly performed by Ruth Holmes, Maria S. Holmes, and A. J. Underwood. Robert Lambeck and Geoffrey Ross helped with bibliographic work, and Terri Shine and Sylvia Warren typed the paper. I am grateful also to the workers who allowed me to cite their unpublished observations of reptilian parental care. Comments on the manuscript were provided by R. Lambeck, D. Slip, and R. Huey.

REFERENCES

Abercromby, A. F. (1913). Some notes on the breeding habits of some Ceylon snakes and reptiles. Spolia Zeylanica 9, 144–147.
Acharjyo, L. N. and Misra, R. (1976). Aspects of reproduction and growth of the Indian python, *Python molurus molurus*, in captivity. Br. J. Herpetol. 5, 562–565.
Acharjyo, L. N. and Mishra, C. G. (1981). Egg-laying and nest-guarding behaviour of estuarine crocodile (*Crocodylus porosus* Schneider) in captivity. J. Bombay Nat. Hist. Soc. 78, 387–390.
Allard, H. A. (1909). Notes on some salamanders and lizards of north Georgia. Science 30, 122–124.
Alvarez del Toro, M. (1969). Breeding the spectacled caiman *Caiman crocodylus* at Tuxtla Gutiérrez Zoo. Int. Zoo Ybk. 9, 35–36.
Alvarez del Toro, M. (1972). *Los Reptiles de Chiapas*. Gobierno del Estado Chiapas, Tuxtla Gutiérrez, Mexico.
Alvarez del Toro, M. (1974). *Los Crocodylia de Mexico*. Inst. Mexicanos de Recursos Naturales Renovables, A.C. Mexico D.F.
Angel, F. (1950). *Vie et Moeurs des Serpents*. Payot, Paris.
Anon (1982). Attack by a nest-guarding female mugger (*Crocodylus palustris*). Hamadryad 7, 3.
Asana, J. J. (1941). Further observations on the egg-laying habits of the lizard *Calotes versicolor* (Boulenger). J. Bombay Nat. Hist. Soc. 42, 937–940.
Ashton, R. E., Jr. and Ashton, P. S. (1981). *Handbook of Reptiles and Amphibians of Florida. Part I. The Snakes*. Windward Publ., Inc., Miami.
Babcock, H. L. (1929). *The Snakes of New England*. Nat. Hist. Guides, No. 1, Boston Soc. Nat. Hist.
Barbour, T. and Ramsden, C. T. (1919). The herpetology of Cuba. Mem. Mus. Comp. Zool. 47, 69–213.
Barker, D. G. (1981). Maintenance and reproduction of pythons at the Dallas Zoo. Proc. Fifth Annual Symposium on Reptile Reproduction and Propagation, Oklahoma City Zoo, June 11–14, 1981.

REFERENCES

Basu, D. and Bustard, H. R. (1981). Maternal behaviour in the gharial (*Gavialis gangeticus* (Gmelin). J. Bombay Nat. Hist. Soc. 78, 390-391.

Behler, J. L. and King, F. W. (1979). *The Audubon Society Field Guide to North American Reptiles and Amphibians*. A.A. Knopf, New York.

Benedict, F. G. (1932). The physiology of large reptiles with special reference to the heat production of snakes, tortoises, lizards and alligators. Carnegie Instit., Wash., Publ. 425, 1-539.

Berney, F. L. (1936). Gould's monitor (*Varanus gouldi*). Queensland Naturalist 1936.

Bishop, C. (1926). Records of some amphibians and reptiles from Kentucky. Copeia 1926, 118-120.

Biswas, S. (1977). Nesting behaviour of estuarine crocodile, *C. porosus* Schneider. J. Bombay Nat. Hist. Soc. 74, 361.

Biswas, S. and Kar, S. (1981). Some observations on nesting habits and biology of *Varanus salvator* of Bhitarkanika Sanctuary, Orissa, India. J. Bombay Soc. Nat. Hist. 78, 303-308.

Blanchard, F. N. (1922). The amphibians and reptiles of western Tennessee. Occas. Pap. Mus. Zool., Univ. Mich. (117), 1-18.

Blanchard, F. N. (1933). Eggs and young of the smooth green snake, *Liopeltis vernalis* (Harlan). Pap. Mich. Acad. Sci. Arts Lett. 17, 493-508.

Blumer, L. S. (1979). Male parental care in the bony fishes. Quart. Rev. Biol. 54, 149-161.

Boake, B. (1870). The nest of the crocodile. Zoologist 2, 2000-2004.

Bogert, C. M. (1940). Herpetological results of the Vernay Angola Expedition with notes on African reptiles in other collections. Bull. Am. Mus. Nat. Hist. 77, 1-107.

Böhme, W. (1977). Discoverer priority of mouth transport in crocodiles. Salamandra 13, 185-186.

Boos, H. E. A. (1979). Some breeding records of Australian pythons. Int. Zoo Ybk. 19, 87-89.

Bourquin, O. (1970). A note on the growth of spotted skaapsteker embryos (*Psammophylax rhombeatus*). J. Herpetol. Assoc. Afr. 6, 8-9.

Brady, M. (1927). Notes on the reptiles and amphibians of the Dismal Swamp. Copeia 162, 26-29.

Breckenridge, W. J. (1943). The life history of the black-banded skink *Eumeces septentrionalis septentrionalis* (Baird). Am. Midl. Nat. 29, 591-606.

Brehm, A. E. (1885) *Merveilles de la Nature. Les Reptiles et les Batraciens*. E. Sauvage, Paris.

Brimley, C. S. (1904). Further notes on the reproduction of reptiles. J. Elisha Mitchell Soc. 20, 139-140.

Broadley, D. G. (1959). The herpetology of southern Rhodesia. Part 1. Snakes. Bull. Mus. Comp. Zool. 120, 1-100.

Broadley, D. G. (1977). A revision of the African snakes of the genus *Psammophylax* Fitzinger (Colubridae). Occas. Pap. Natl. Mus. Rhodesia B 6, 1-43.

Broadley, D. G. (1983). *FitzSimons' Snakes of Southern Africa*. Delta Books, Johannesburg.

Bull, J. J. and Shine, R. (1979). Iteroparous animals that skip opportunities for reproduction. Am. Nat. 114, 296-316.

Burroughs, J. (1908). *Leaf and Tendril*. Boston and New York.

Burt, C. E. (1928). The lizards of Kansas. Trans. Acad. Sci. St. Louis 26, 1-81.

Bustard, H. R. (1980). Maternal care in the gharial (*Gavialis gangeticus* (Gmelin)). Br. J. Herpetol. 6, 63-64.

Bustard, H. R. and Choudhury, B. C. (1980). Parental care in the saltwater crocodile *Crocodylus porosus* and management implications. J. Bombay Nat. Hist. Soc. 77, 64-69.

Bustard, H. R. and Kar, S. K. (1981). Nest defence against man by the saltwater crocodile (*Crocodylus porosus*). Br. J. Herpetol. 6, 143.
Bustard, H. R. and Maharana, S. (1982). The behaviour of the nest-guarding saltwater crocodile (*Crocodylus porosus* Schneider)—a preliminary quantitative study. J. Bombay Nat. Hist. Soc. 79, 87–92.
Bustard, H. R. and Singh, L. A. K. (1981). Gharial attacks on man. J. Bombay Nat. Hist. Soc. 78, 610–611.
Cagle, F. R. (1940). Eggs and natural nests of *Eumeces fasciatus*. Am. Midl. Nat. 23, 227–233.
Campbell, H. and Simmons, R. S. (1961). Notes on the eggs and young of *Eumeces callicephalus* Bocourt. Herpetologica 17, 212–213.
Campbell, J. A. (1973). A captive hatching of *Micrurus fulvius tenere* (Serpentes, Elapidae). J. Herpetol. 7, 312–315.
Campbell, J. A. and Quinn, H. R. (1975). Reproduction in a pair of Asiatic cobras, *Naja naja* (Serpentes, Elapidae). J. Herpetol. 9, 229–233.
Cansdale, G. (1955). *Reptiles of West Africa*. Penguin Books, Middlesex.
Carey, W. M. (1975). The rock iguana, *Cyclura pinguis*, on Anegada, British Virgin Islands, with notes on *Cyclura ricordi* and *Cyclura cornuta* on Hispaniola. Bull. Florida State Mus., Biol. Sci. 19, 189–233.
Carl, G. C. (1944). *The Reptiles of British Columbia*. British Columbia Provincial Museum, Vancouver, Handbook No. 3.
Carpenter, C. C. (1966). The marine iguana of the Galápagos Islands, its behavior and ecology. Proc. Calif. Acad. Sci. 34, 329–376.
Carr, A. F. (1967). *So Excellent a Fishe*. Natural History Press, Garden City, NY.
Case, T. J. (1978). Endothermy and parental care in the terrestrial vertebrates. Am. Nat. 112, 861–874.
Chadwick, W. S. (1931). *Hunters and the Hunted: Some Glimpses of Man and Beast in the African Bush*. H. F. & G. Whitley, London.
Charles, N., Field, R. and Shine, R. (1985). Notes on the reproductive biology of Australian pythons, genera *Aspidites*, *Liasis* and *Morelia*. Herpetol. Rev. 16, 45–48.
Choudhury, B. C. and Bustard, H. R. (1979). Predation on natural nests of the saltwater crocodile *Crocodylus porosus* on North Andaman island, India, with notes on the crocodile population. J. Bombay Nat. Hist. Soc. 76, 311–323.
Christian, K. A. and Tracy, C. R. (1982). Reproductive behavior of Galapagos land iguanas, *Conolophus pallidus*. In *Iguanas of the World*. (G. M. Burghardt and A. S. Rand, eds.). Noyes Publ., Park Ridge, NJ, pp. 366–379.
Clarke, S. F. (1888). The nest and eggs of the alligator, *A. lucius* Cuv. Zool. Anz. 11, 568–570.
Coborn, J. (1975). Report on the reproduction of captive Indian pythons (*Python molurus bivittatus*). Br. J. Herpetol. 5, 471–472.
Cogger, H. G. (1967). *Australian Reptiles in Colour*. A. H. and A. W. Reed, Sydney.
Cogger, H. G. (1974). Voyage of the banded iguana. Austr. Nat. Hist. 18, 144–149.
Cogger, H. G. and Holmes, A. (1960). Thermoregulatory behaviour in a specimen of *Morelia spilotes variegata* Gray (Serpentes: Boidae). Proc. Linnaean Soc. N.S.W. 85, 328–333.
Collins, J. T. (1974). Observations on reproduction in the southern coal skink (*Eumeces anthracinus pluvialis* Cope). Trans. Kans. Acad. Sci. 77, 126–127.
Compton, A. W. (1981). Courtship and nesting behaviour of the freshwater crocodile, *Crocodylus johnstoni*, under controlled conditions. Austr. Wildl. Res. 8, 443–450.
Coombs, W. P., Jr. (1982). Juvenile specimens of the ornithischian dinosaur *Psittacosaurus mongoliensis*. Palaeontology (Lond.) 25, 89–108.

REFERENCES

Cooper, W. E., Vitt, L. J., Vangilder, L. D. and Gibbons, J. W. (1983). Natural nest sites and brooding behavior of *Eumeces fasciatus*. Herpetol. Rev. 14, 65-66.
Corben, C. J., Ingram, G. J. and Tyler, M. J. (1974). Gastric brooding care in an Australian frog. Science 186, 946-947.
Corrington, J. D. (1929). Herpetology of the Columbia, South Carolina Region. Copeia 1929, 58-83.
Cott, H. B. (1961). Scientific results of an inquiry into the ecology and economic status of the Nile crocodile (*Crocodylus niloticus*) in Uganda and Northern Rhodesia. Trans. Zool. Soc. Lond. 29, 211-358.
Cott, H. B. (1971). Parental care in the Crocodilia, with special reference to *Crocodylus niloticus*. IUCN Publ. New Series, Suppl. Paper 32, 166-180.
Cowles, R. B. (1944). Parturition in the yucca night lizard. Copeia 1944, 98-100.
Crawshaw, P. G. Jr. and Schaller, G. B. (1980). Nesting of Paraguayan caiman (*Caiman yacare*) in Brazil. Pap. Avulsos Zool., S. Paulo 33, 283-292.
Creswell, R. (1862). *Aristotle's History of Animals*. Bohn: London.
Crites, A. S. (1952). *A Hunter's Tale of the Great Outdoors*. W. Ritche Press, Los Angeles.
Daniel, J.C. (1983). *The Book of Indian Reptiles*. Bombay Nat. Hist. Soc., Bombay.
David, R. (1970). Breeding of the mugger crocodile (*Crocodylus palustris*) and water monitor (*Varanus salvator*) at Ahmedabad Zoo. Int. Zoo Yrbk. 10, 116-117.
Deraniyagala, P. E. P. (1939). *The Tetrapod Reptiles of Ceylon. Vol. I. Testudinates and Crocodilians*. Colombo Museum, Ceylon.
Deraniyagala, P. E. P. (1955). *A Coloured Atlas of Some Vertebrates From Ceylon. Vol. 3. Serpentoid Reptilia*. Government Press, Ceylon.
Descourtilz, M. E. (1809). *Voyages d'un Naturaliste, et Ses Observations*. Dufart père, Paris, Lib. 3, 71-92.
Devenish, S. (1893). A few notes on alligator shooting in Trinidad. J. Trinidad Field-Nat. Club 1, 142-147.
Dharmakumarsinji, K. S. (1947). Mating and the parental instinct of the marsh crocodile (*C. palustris* Lesson). J. Bombay Nat. Hist. Soc. 47, 174-176.
Dietz, D. C. and Hines, T. C. (1980). Alligator nesting in north-central Florida. Copeia 1980, 249-258.
Dietz, D. C. and Jackson, D. R. (1979). Use of American alligator nests by nesting turtles. J. Herpetol. 3, 510-512.
Ditmars, R. L. (1904). Observations on lacertilians. Eighth Ann. Rept. N.Y. Zool. Soc., pp. 146-160.
Ditmars, R. L. (1942). *The Reptiles of North America*. Doubleday Doran, New York.
Dowling, H. G. (1950). A new southeastern record for the coal skink. Copeia 1950, 235.
Dowling, H. G. (1960). Thermistors, air conditioners and insecticides. Anim. Kingdom 63, 202-207.
Duellman, W. E. and Schwartz, A. (1958). Amphibians and reptiles of southern Florida. Bull. Fla. State. Mus. 3, 181-324.
Dugan, B. A., Rand, A. S., Burghardt, G. M. and Bock, B. C. (1981). Interactions between nesting crocodiles and iguanas. J. Herpetol. 15, 409-414.
Dunn, E. R. (1920). Some reptiles and amphibians from Virginia, North Carolina, Tennessee and Alabama. Proc. Biol. Soc. Wash. 33, 129-138.
Dunn, R. W. (1979a). Breeding children's pythons *Liasis childreni* at Melbourne Zoo. Int. Zoo Yearbk. 19, 89-90.
Dunn, R. W. (1979b). Breeding African pythons *Python sebae* at Melbourne Zoo. Int. Zoo Yearbk. 19, 91-92.

Dunson, W. A. (1975). Adaptations of sea snakes. In *The Biology of Sea Snakes*. (W. A. Dunson, ed.). University Park Press, Baltimore, pp. 3–20.

Eibl-Eibesfeldt, I. (1966). Das verteidigen der eiablageplatze bei der Hood-Meerechse (*Amblyrynchus cristatus venustissimus*). Z. Tierpsychol. 23, 127–213.

Erasmus, H. and W. R. Branch. (1983). Egg retention in the South African blind snake *Typhlops bibronii*. J. Herpetol. 17, 97–99.

Evans, H. E. and Roecker, R. M. (1951). Notes on the herpetology of Ontario, Canada. Herpetologica 7, 69–71.

Evans, L. T. (1959). A motion picture study of maternal behavior of the lizard, *Eumeces obsoletus* Baird and Girard. Copeia 1959, 103–110.

Fitch, H. S. (1954). Life history and ecology of the five-lined skink, *Eumeces fasciatus*. Univ. Kansas Publ. Mus. Nat. Hist. 8, 1–156.

Fitch, H. S. (1955). Habits and adaptations of the great plains skink (*Eumeces obsoletus*). Ecol. Monogr. 25, 59–83.

Fitch, H. S. (1970). Reproductive cycles in lizards and snakes. Univ. Kansas Mus. Nat. Hist., Misc. Publ. 52, 1–247.

Fitzgerald, M. and Mengden, G. A. (1987). Oviparity and captive breeding in an Australian snake, *Pseudechis butleri*. *Amphibia-Reptilia*, in press.

FitzSimons, F. W. (1930). *Pythons and Their Ways*. G. G. Harrap & Co., London.

FitzSimons, V. F. M. (1962). *Snakes of Southern Africa*. MacDonald, London.

Fleay, D. (1943). The brown snake—dangerous fellow. Vict. Nat. 59, 147–152.

Foekema, G. M. M. (1975). Ontwikkeling en voortplanting von *Python molurus bivittatus* in een huiskamerterrarium. Lacerta 33, 123–139.

Fogarty, M. J. (1974). The ecology of the Everglades alligator. In *Environments of South Florida: Present and Past*. (P. J. Gleason, ed.). Mem. Miami Geol. Survey 2, 367–374.

Forbes, M. (1881). Observations on the incubation of the Indian python (*Python molurus*), with special regard to the alleged increase of temperature during that process. Proc. Zool. Soc. Lond., 960–967.

Forester, D. C. (1979a). The adaptiveness of parental care in *Desmognathus ochrophaeus* (Urodela: Plethodontidae). Copeia 1979, 332–341.

Forester, D. C. (1979b). Homing to the nest by female mountain dusky salamanders (*Desmognathus ochrophaeus*) with comments on the sensory modalities essential to clutch recognition. Herpetologica 35, 330–335.

Frith, C. B. (1977). A survey of the snakes of Phuket Island and the adjacent mainland areas of peninsular Thailand. Nat. Hist. Bull. Siam. Soc. 26, 263–316.

Fukada, H. (1956). Biological studies on the snakes. III. Observations on hatching of *Elaphe climacophora* (Boie), *E. conspicillata* (Boie), and *Natrix v. vibakari* (Boie). Bull. Kyoto Gakugei Univ., Ser. B, Maths. Nat. Sci. 9, 1–29.

Fukada, H. (1965). Breeding habits of some Japanese reptiles (critical review). Bull. Kyoto Gakugei Univ., Ser. B, Maths. Nat. Sci. 27, 65–82.

Gallwey, E. (1932). Eggs of grass snake. The Naturalist, Lond. 910, 320.

Gans, C. (1975). Tetrapod limblessness: Evolution and functional corollaries. Am. Zool. 15, 455–467.

Gehlbach, F. R. (1965). Herpetology of the Zuni Mountains region, northwestern New Mexico. Proc. U.S. Natl. Mus. 116, 243–322.

Gibbons, J. R. H. and Watkins, I. F. (1982). Behavior, ecology and conservation of south Pacific banded iguanas including a newly discovered species. In *Iguanas of the World*. (G. M. Burghardt and A. S. Rand, eds.). Noyes Publ., Park Ridge, NJ, pp. 418–441.

Goeidi, E. (1902). Lacertilios. Lagartos do Brazil. Bolm. Mus. Para. Hist. Nat. Ethnogr. 3, 499–560.

REFERENCES

Goldstein, R. C. (1941). Notes on the mud snakes in Florida. Copeia 1941, 49-50.

Goodwin, T. M. and Marion, W. R. (1978). Aspects of the nesting ecology of American alligators (*Alligator mississippiensis*) in north-central Florida. Herpetologica 34, 43-47.

Gordon, R. E. (1960). The influence of moisture on variation in the eggs and hatchlings of *Anolis c. carolinensis* Voigt. Nat. Hist. Misc. 173, 1-6.

Gorzula, S. J. (1978). An ecological study of *Caiman crocodilus crocodilus* inhabiting savanna lagoons in the Venezualan guayana. Oecologia 35, 21-34.

Gow, G. F. (1981). A new species of *Python* from central Australia. Austr. J. Herpetol. 1, 29-34.

Green, E. E. (1905). On the nesting of the snake *Bungarus ceylonicus*. Spolia Zeylanica 3, 158-159.

Greene, H. W. and Dial, B. E. (1966). Brooding behavior by female Texas alligator lizards. Herpetologica 22, 303.

Greer, A. E. (1967). Notes on the mode of reproduction in anguid lizards. Herpetologica 23, 94-99.

Greer, A. E. (1971). Crocodilian nesting habits and evolution. Fauna 2, 20-28.

Gross, M. R. and Shine, R. (1981). Parental care and mode of fertilization in ectothermic vertebrates. Evolution 35, 775-793.

Groves, J. D. (1981). Observations and comments on the post-parturient behavior of some tropical boas of the genus *Epicrates*. Br. J. Herpetol. 6, 89-91.

Groves, J. D. (1982). Egg-eating behavior of brooding five-lined skinks, *Eumeces fasciatus*. Copeia 1982, 969-971.

Hadley, D. (1969). Breeding of crocodile in Livingstone Game Park. Puku 5, 226-228.

Hahn, W. L. (1909). Notes on the mammals and cold-blooded vertebrates of the Indiana University Farm, Mitchell, Indiana. Proc. U.S. Natl. Mus. 35, 545-581.

Hall, R. J. (1971). Ecology of a population of the Great Plains skink (*Eumeces obsoletus*). Univ. Kansas Sci. Bull. 49, 357-388.

Harlow, P. and Grigg, G. C. (1984). Shivering thermogenesis in a brooding diamond python, *Python spilotes spilotes*. Copeia 1984, 959-965.

Hartwig, G. (1873). *The Tropical World: Aspects of Man and Nature in Equatorial Regions of the Globe*. Longmans Green, London.

Hasegawa, M. (1984). Biennial reproduction in the lizard *Eumeces okadae* on Miyake-Jima, Japan. Herpetologica 40, 194-199.

Hediger, H. (1968). Der Akademiestreit über die brütende Pythons. Neue Zürcher Zeitung, 11-6-1968, nr. 351.

Herzog, H. A. (1975). An observation of nest opening by an American alligator, *Alligator mississippiensis*. Herpetologica 31, 446-447.

Hibbard, C. W. (1964). A brooding colony of the blind snake, *Leptotyphlops dulcis dissecta* Cope. Copeia 1964, 222.

Hikida, T. (1975). An observation of the brooding habit in *Eumeces okadae* (in Japanese). Niigata Herpetol. J. 1, 6-7.

Hikida, T. (1981). Reproduction of the Japanese skink (*Eumeces latiscutatus*) in Kyoto. Zool. Mag. 90, 85-92.

Hilzheimer, M. (1910). Die Brutpflege der Reptilien. Aus der Natur, Leipzig 6, 361-367.

Hodsdon, L. A. and Pearson, J. F. W. (1943). Notes on the discovery and biology of two Bahaman fresh-water turtles of the genus *Pseudemys*. Proc. Fla. Acad. Sci. 6, 17-23.

Holland, P. (1601). *The Historie of the World, Commonly Called the Naturall Historie of C. Plinius Secundus*. A. Islip, London.

Holmstrom, W. F., Jr., and Behler, J. L. (1981). Post-parturient behavior of the anaconda, *Eunectes murinus*. Zool. Garten (NF) 51, 353–356.

Honegger, R. E. (1970). Beitrag zur Fortpflanzungsbiologie von *Boa constrictor* und *Python reticulatus* (Reptilia, Boidae). Salamandra 6, 73–79.

Horner, J. R. (1984). The nesting behavior of dinosaurs. Sci. Am. 250, 130–137.

Huheey, J. E. and Brandon, R. A. (1975). Another function of maternal brooding behavior in salamanders of the genus *Desmognathus*. J. Herpetol. 9, 257.

Hunt, R. H. (1974). Hatching and rearing of Morelet's crocodile, *C. moreleti*. In Conf. Am. Ass. Zool. Parks and Aquaria. Arlington, TX, April 1974.

Hunt, R. H. (1975). Maternal behavior in the Morelet's crocodile, *Crocodylus moreleti*. Copeia 1975, 763–764.

Hurter, J. (1911). *Herpetology of Missouri*. Missouri Acad. Sci., St. Louis.

Hutchinson, V. H., Dowling, H. G. and Vinegar, A. (1966). Thermoregulation in a brooding female Indian python, *Python molurus bivittatus*. Science 151, 694–696.

Iverson, J. B. (1979). Behavior and ecology of the rock iguana *Cyclura carinata*. Bull. Florida State Mus., Biol. Sci. 24, 175–358.

Jelden, D. C. (1981). Preliminary studies on the breeding biology of *Crocodylus porosus* and *Crocodylus n. novaeguinae* on the Middle Sepik (Papua New Guinea). Amphibia-Reptilia 3/4, 353–358.

Jennison, G. (1931). Cobras bred at Belle Vue Zoological Gardens, Manchester. Proc. Zool. Soc. Lond. 2, 1413.

Joanen, T. (1970). Nesting ecology of alligators in Louisiana. Proc. Southeast Assoc. Game and Fish Comm., 23rd Ann. Conf. 1969, pp. 141–151.

Joanen, T. and McNease, L. (1970). A telemetric study of nesting female alligators on Rockefeller Refuge, Louisiana. Proc. Southeast Assoc. Game and Fish Comm. 24th Ann. Conf. 1970, pp. 175–193.

Joanen, T. and McNease, L. (1980). Reproductive biology of the American alligator in southwest Louisiana. SSAR Contrib. Herpetol. 1, 153–159.

Jones, R. E. and Guillette, L. J., Jr. (1982). Hormonal control of oviposition and parturition in lizards. Herpetologica 38, 80–93.

Joshi, P. N. (1967). Reproduction of *Python sebae*. Br. J. Herpetol. 3, 310–311.

Kinghorn, J. R. (1956). *The Snakes of Australia*. Second edition. Angus and Robertson, Sydney.

Klauber, L. M. (1972). *Rattlesnakes. Their Habits, Life Histories, and Influence on Mankind*. Second edition. University of California Press, Berkeley.

Klots, A. B. (1930). Notes on Amphibia and Lacertilia collected at Weymouth, N.J. Copeia 1930, 107–111.

Kopstein, F. (1938). Ein Beitrag zur Eierkunde und zur Fortpflanzung der malaiischen Reptilien. Bull. Raffles Mus. 14, 81–167.

Kratzer, H. (1962). Ueberraschende Nachzucht von *Chondropython viridis*. Aquar. Terrar. Z. 4, 177–179.

Kreig, H. (1925). Biologische Reisestudien in Südamerika. IV. Beobachtungen über die "Iguana" (*Tupinambis teguixin* L.). Z. Wiss. Biol. Abt. A3, 441–451.

Kushlan, J. A. (1973). Observation on maternal behavior in the American alligator *Alligator mississippiensis*. Herpetologica 29, 256–257.

Kushlan, J. A. and Kushlan, M. S. (1980). Function of nest attendance in the American alligator (Reptilia: Crocodilia: Crocodylidae). Herpetologica 36, 27–32.

Kushlan, J. A. and Simon, J. C. (1981). Egg manipulation by the American alligator. J. Herpetol. 15, 451–454.

Lamarre-Picquot, P. (1835). L'Institut 3, 70 (not seen).

REFERENCES

Lamarre-Picquot, P. (1842). Troisième mémoire sur l'incubation et autres phénomènes obsérvés chez les ophidiens. C. R. Hebd. Séances Acad. Sci., Paris 14, 164.

Langerwerf, B. (1981). The southern alligator lizard *Gerrhonotus multicarinatus* Blainville 1935: Its care and breeding in captivity. Br. Herpetol. Soc. Bull. 4, 21–25.

La Panouse, R. de, and Pellier, C. (1973). Ponte d'un python réticulé (*Python reticulatus*) élévé en terrarium, et incubation des ouefs. Bull. Mus. Nat, Hist. Natur. Paris (3rd series) 105, 37–48.

Leakey, J. H. E. (1969). Observations made on king cobras in Thailand during May 1966. J. Natl. Res Council Thailand 5, 1–10.

Lederer, G. (1944). Nahrungserwerb, Entwicklung, Paarung und Brutfürsoge von *Python reticulatus* (Schneider). Zool. Jahrb. (Anat.) 68, 363–398.

Lederer, G. (1956). Fortpflanzungsbiologie und Entwicklung von *Python molurus molurus* (Linné) und *Python molurus bivittatus* (Kuhl). Aquar. Terrar. Z. 9, 243–248.

Leigh, C. (1910). An oviparous Indian pit viper. Field, London, 115, 3.

Le Roux, S. F. (1964). A note on the spotted skaapsteker (*Psammophylax rhombeatus* Linnaeus). E. Afr. Wildlife 18, 113–115.

Logan, T. (1973). Observations on the ball python (*Python regius*) in captivity at Houston Zoological Gardens. J. Herpetol. Assoc. East Africa 10, 5–8.

Loveridge, A. (1946). *Reptiles of the Pacific World*. MacMillan, New York.

Lynch, J. D. (1966). Communal egg laying in the pilot blacksnake, *Elaphe obsoleta obsoleta*. Herpetologica 22, 305.

Mackay, R. D. (1973). The green python. Wildlife in Australia 10, 108.

Magnusson, W. E. (1980). Hatching and creche formation by *Crocodylus porosus*. Copeia 1980, 359–362.

Magnusson, W. E., Lima, A. P. and Sampaio, R. M. (1985). Sources of heat for nests of *Paleosuchus trigonatus* and a review of crocodilian nest temperatures. J. Herpetol. 19, 199–207.

Malnate, E. V. (1960). Systematic division and evolution of the colubrid snake genus *Natrix*, with comments on the subfamily Natricinae. Proc. Acad. Nat. Sci. Philadelphia 112, 41–71.

Mao, S-H., Chen, B-Y., Yin, F-Y. and Guo, Y-W. (1938). Immunotaxonomic relationships of sea snakes to terrestrial elapids. Comp. Biochem. Physiol. 74A, 869–872.

Martof, B. (1956). A contribution to the biology of the skink, *Eumeces laticeps*. Herpetologica 12, 111–114.

Maynard Smith, J. (1977). Parental investment: A prospective analysis. Anim. Behav. 25, 1–9.

McCauley, R. H., Jr. (1939). Differences in the young of *Eumeces fasciatus* and *Eumeces laticeps*. Copeia 1939, 93–95.

McCauley, R. H., Jr. (1945). *The Reptiles of Maryland and the District of Columbia*. Hagerstown, MD.

McIlhenny, E. A. (1934). Notes on incubation and growth of alligators. Copeia 1934, 80–88.

Meade, G. P. (1940). Maternal care of eggs by *Farancia*. Copeia 1940, 15–20.

Medem, F. J. (1958). The crocodilian genus *Paleosuchus*. Fieldiana Zool. 39, 227–247.

Medem, F. (1971). The reproduction of the dwarf caiman *Paleosuchus palpebrosus*. IUCN Publ., New Series Suppl. Pap. 32.

Medsger, O. P. (1919). Egg-laying habits of the pilot snake (*Callopeltis obsoletus*). Copeia 1919, 28–29.

Meek, G. (1946). *Creatures of Mystery*. J. W. Burke Co., Macon, GA.

Melgarejo, A. R. (1977). Observaciones sobre nacimiento en el laboratorio de *Bothrops neuwiedi pubescens* (Cope, 1870) (Ophidia, Crotalinae). Revista Biol. Urug. 1, 35–41.

Mell, R. (1929). *Beitrage zur Fauna sinica. IV. Grundzüge einer Ökologie der chinesischen Reptilien und einer herpetologischen Tiergeographie Chinas.* Walter de Gruyter & Co., Berlin.

Metzen, W. D. (1977). Nesting ecology of alligators on the Okefenokee National Wildlife Refuge. Proc. Ann. Southeast. Assn. Game and Fish Comm. 31, 29–32.

Miller, M. R. (1954). Further observations on reproduction in the lizard *Xantusia vigilis*. Copeia 1954, 38–40.

Minton, S. A., Jr. (1972). Amphibians and reptiles of Indiana. Indiana Acad. Sci., Monogr. 3, 1–346.

Minton, S. A., Jr., and Minton, M. R. (1973). *Giant Reptiles.* Charles Scribner's Sons, New York.

Modha, M. L. (1967). The ecology of the Nile crocodile (*Crocodylus niloticus* Laurenti) on Central Island, Lake Rudolf. E. Afr. Wildlife J. 5, 74–95.

Mole, R. R. (1924). The Trinidad snakes. Proc. Zool. Soc. Lond. 1924, 235–278.

Mount, R. H. (1963). The natural history of the red-tailed skink, *Eumeces egregius* Baird. Am. Midl. Nat. 70, 356–385.

Mount, R. H. (1975). *The Reptiles and Amphibians of Alabama.* Auburn Univ. Agr. Exp. Station, Auburn, AL.

Müller, P. (1970). Einige Beobachtungen zur Fortpflanzungsbiologie bei Riesenschlangen im Zoologischen Garten Leipzig. Aquar. Terr. Z. 17, 162–164.

Murphy, J. B., Lamoreaux, W. E. and Barker, D. G. (1981). Miscellaneous notes on the reproductive biology of reptiles. 4. Eight species of the family Boidae, genera *Acrantophis, Aspidites, Candoia, Liasis* and *Python*. Trans. Kansas Acad. Sci. 84, 39–49.

Mustill, F. J. (1936). A hamadryad's nest and eggs. J. Bombay Nat. Hist. Soc. 39, 186–187.

Muth, A. (1980). Physiological ecology of desert iguanas (*Dipsosaurus dorsalis*) eggs: Temperature and water relations. Ecology 61, 1335–1343.

Neill, W. T. (1946). Notes on *Crocodylus novae-guineae*. Copeia 1946, 17–20.

Neill, W. T. (1964). Viviparity in snakes: Some ecological and zoogeographical considerations. Am. Nat. 98, 35–55.

Neill, W. T. (1971). *The Last of the Ruling Reptiles: Alligators, Crocodiles and Their Kin.* Columbia University Press, New York.

Neill, W. T. and Allen, E. R. (1962). Parturient anacondas, *Eunectes gigas* Latreille, eating own abortive eggs and foetal membranes. Quart. J. Florida Acad. Sci. 25, 73–75.

Nettman, H. K. and Rykena, S. (1979). Moorish geckos (*Tarentola mauritanica*) that bury their eggs in the sand (Reptilia, Sauria, Gekkonidae). Salamandra 15, 53–57.

Niekisch, M. (1975). Pflege und Nachzucht von *Egernia cunninghami* (Sauria, Scincidae). Salamandra 11, 130–135.

Noble, G. K. (1921). Do snakes swallow their young for protection? Copeia 1921, 54–57.

Noble, G. K. (1931). *The Biology of the Amphibia.* McGraw-Hill, New York.

Noble, G. K. (1935). The brooding habit of the blood python and of other snakes. Copeia 1935, 1–3.

Noble, G. K. and Mason, E. R. (1933). Experiments on the brooding habits of the lizards *Eumeces* and *Ophisaurus*. Am. Mus. Novitates 619, 1–29.

Nussbaum, R. A. (1985). The evolution of parental care in salamanders. Misc. Publ. Mus. Zool., Univ. Mich. 169, 1–50.

Ogden, J. C. (1976). Crocodilian ecology in southern Florida. In *Research in the Parks:*

REFERENCES

Transactions of the National Park Centennial Symposium, 1971. U.S. Dept. Interior, National Park Services Symposium series, No. 1.

Ogden, J. C. (1978). Status and nesting biology of the American crocodile, *Crocodylus acutus* (Reptilia, Crocodylidae) in Florida. J. Herpetol. 12, 183–196.

Ogden, J. C. and Singletary, C. (1973). Night of the crocodile. Audubon 75, 32–37.

Oliver, J. A. (1955). *The Natural History of North American Amphibians and Reptiles*. D. Van Nostrand Co., Princeton, NJ.

Oliver, J. A. (1956). Reproduction in the king cobra, *Ophiophagus hannah* Cantor. Zoologica 41, 145–152.

Ortenburger, A. I. (1930). Some common snake stories. School Sci. Math. 30, 420–428.

Parker, F. (1982). *The Snakes of Western Province*. Wildlife in Papua New Guinea No. 82/1. Division of Wildlife, Dept. of Lands and Environment, Konedobu.

Perrone, M., Jr., and Zaret, T. M. (1979). Parental care patterns of fishes. Am. Nat. 113, 351–361.

Petzold, H. (1968). Zur Fortpflanzungbiologie asiatischer Kobras (*Naja naja*). Zool. Garten (NF) 36, 133–146.

Pitman, C. R. S. (1930). Ann. Rept. Game Dept., Entebbe. (Not seen).

Pitman, C. R. S. (1938). *A Guide to the Snakes of Uganda*. Uganda Society, Kampala.

Pitman, C. R. S. (1941). About crocodiles. Uganda J. 8, 84–114.

Pitman, C. R. S. (1974). *A Guide to the Snakes of Uganda*. Revised edition. Wheldon and Wesley, Ltd., Codicote.

Pooley, A. C. (1969). Preliminary studies on the breeding of the Nile crocodile, *Crocodylus niloticus*, in Zululand. Lammergeyer 3, 22–44.

Pooley, A. C. (1974). Parental care in the Nile crocodile: A preliminary report on behaviour of a captive female. Lammergeyer 21, 43–45.

Pooley, A. C. (1976). Mother's Day in the crocodile pool. Animal Kingdom 79, 7–13.

Pooley, A. C. (1977). Nest opening responses of the Nile crocodile *Crocodylus niloticus*. J. Zool. Lond. 182, 17–26.

Pooley, A. C. and Gans, C. (1976). The Nile crocodile. Sci. Am. 234, 114–124.

Pope, C. H. (1935). *The Reptiles of China. Turtles, Crocodilians, Snakes, Lizards*. Natural History of Central Asia, Volume 10. American Museum of Natural History, New York.

Pope, C. H. (1961). *The Giant Snakes*. Alfred Knopf, New York.

Rand, A. S. (1968). A nesting aggregation of iguanas. Copeia 1968, 552–561.

Rand, W. M. and Rand, A. S. (1976). Agonistic behavior in nesting iguanas: A stochastic analysis of dispute settlement dominated by the minimization of energy cost. Z. Tierpsychol. 40, 279–299.

Rebouças-Spieker, R. and Vanzolini, P. E. (1978). Parturition in *Mabuya macrorhyncha* Hoge, 1946 (Sauria, Scincidae), with a note on the distribution of maternal behavior in lizards. Pap. Avulsos Zool., S. Paulo 32, 95–99.

Reese, A. M. (1907). The breeding habits of the Florida alligator. Smithson. Misc. Coll. 48, 381–387.

Ridley, M. (1978). Paternal care. Anim. Behav. 26, 904–932.

Ridley, M. (1983). *The Explanation of Organic Diversity*. Clarendon Press, Oxford.

Riemer, W. J. (1957). The snake *Farancia abacura*: An attended nest. Herpetologica 13, 31–32.

Rieppel, O. (1970). Nachwuchs bei *Dryophis nasutus* (Lacépède) 1789. Aqua. Terra 7, 85–88.

Riley, J., Stimson, A. F. and Winch, J. M. (1985). A review of Squamata ovipositing in ant and termite nests. Herpetol. Rev. 16, 38–43.

Rivers, G. M. (1874). The rattlesnake—its poison and antidote. Soc. Med. Rec. 4, 505–517.
Robinson, St. J. (1948). The crocodile at the nest. North Qld. Natur. 16, 3–4.
Romer, A. S. (1966). *Vertebrate Paleontology*. Univ. Chicago Press, Chicago.
Rose, W. (1962). *The Reptiles and Amphibians of Southern Africa*. Maskew Miller, Cape Town.
Ross, R. (1973). Successful mating and hatching of children's python, *Liasis childreni*. HISS News J. 1, 181–182.
Ross, R. (1978). *The Python Breeding Manual*. Institute for Herpetological Research, Stanford, CA.
Ross, R. and Larman, R. (1977). Captive breeding in two species of python *Liasis albertisii* and *L. mackloti*. Int. Zoo Yrbk. 17, 133–136.
Ruthven, A. G. (1911). A biological survey of the sand-dune region on the south shore of Saginaw Bay, Michigan. Mich. Geol. Biol. Survey Publ. 4, Biol. Ser. 2, 1–347.
Schivre, M. (1972). Observations sur la reproduction de *Python regius* (Shaw). Aquarama 6, 67.
Schmidt, C. H. M. (1973). Verslag van een geslaagde kweek met de afrikaanse python (*Python sebae*). Lacerta 31, 91–101.
Schmidt, K. P. (1919). Contributions to the herpetology of the Belgian Congo based on the collection of the American Museum Congo Expedition, 1909–1915. Part 1. Turtles, crocodiles, lizards, and chamaeleons. Bull. Am. Mus. Nat. Hist. 39, 385–624.
Schmidt, K. P. (1927). Notes on Chinese reptiles. Bull. Am. Mus. Nat. Hist. 54, 467–551.
Schmidt, K. P. (1929). The truth about snake stories. Sci. Am. 141, 134–136.
Schupp, A. (1913). As cobras do Rio Grande do Sul. Petropolis. *Typ. Voces de Petropolis, Biblioteca Universal* 10, 1–116.
Schutte, G. W. (1970). Reptile incubation (*Python sebae*). Lammergeyer 11, 85.
Sclater, P. L. (1862). Notes on the incubation of *Python sebae*, as observed in the Society's gardens. Proc. Zool. Soc London 1862, 365–368.
Shaw, C. E. (1954). Captive-bred Cuban iguanas *Cyclura macleayi macleayi*. Herpetologica 19, 73–78.
Shaw, G. E. and Shebbeare, E. O. (1931). The snakes of northern Bengal and Sikkim. J. Darjeeling Nat. Hist. Soc. 5, 3–8.
Shelford, R. W. C. (1916). *A Naturalist in Borneo*. Fisher Unwin, London.
Shine, R. (1978). Propagule size and parental care: The "safe harbor" hypothesis. J. Theor. Biol. 75, 417–424.
Shine, R. (1980). "Costs" of reproduction in reptiles. Oecologia, 46, 92–100.
Shine, R. (1983a). Reptilian reproductive modes: The oviparity–viviparity continuum. Herpetologica 39, 1–8.
Shine, R. (1983b). Reptilian viviparity in cold climates: Testing the assumptions of an evolutionary hypothesis. Oecologia 57, 397–405.
Shine, R. (1985). The evolution of reptilian viviparity: An ecological analysis. In *Biology of the Reptilia*. Vol. 15. *Developmental Biology*. (C. Gans and F. Billett, eds.). John Wiley, New York, pp. 605–694.
Shine, R. and Bull, J. J. (1979). The evolution of live-bearing in lizards and snakes. Am. Nat. 113, 905–923.
Singh, L. A. K. and Bustard, H. R. (1977). Studies on the Indian gharial (*Gavialis gangeticus*) (Gmelin) (Reptilia, Crocodilia). V. Preliminary observations on maternal behaviour. Indian Forester 103, 671–678.
Smedley, M. A. (1931). Oviparity in a sea-snake, *Laticauda colubrina* (Schneid.). Bull. Raffles Mus. 5, 54–58.

REFERENCES

Smith, H. C. (1936). A hamadryad's (*Naia bungarus*) nest and eggs. J. Bombay Nat. Hist. Soc. 39, 186.
Smith, H. M. (1946). *Handbook of Lizards*. Comstock Publ. Co., Ithaca, NY.
Smith, H. M., Sinelnik, G., Fawcett, J. D. and Jones, R. E. (1972). A unique reproductive cycle in *Anolis* and its relatives. Bull. Philadelphia Herpetol. Soc. 20, 28–30.
Smith, M. A. (1915). Notes on some snakes from Siam. J. Bombay Nat. Hist. Soc. 23, 784–789.
Smith, M. A. (1937). Breeding habits of the Indian cobra. J. Siam. Soc., Nat. Hist. Supp. 11, 62–63.
Smith, M. A. (1943). *The Fauna of British India. Volume III. Serpentes.* Taylor & Francis, London.
Smith, M. A. (1973). *The British Amphibians and Reptiles*. Collins, London.
Smith, W. H. (1882). Report on the reptiles and amphibians of Ohio. Rept. Geol. Surv. Ohio 4, 633–734.
Smith, W. J. L. (1935). Mating of the hamadryad or king cobra (*Naia bungarus* Schleg.). J. Bombay Nat. Hist. Soc. 38, 200–201.
Speck, F. G. (1923). Snake folk-lore: The snake who swallows her young. J. Am. Folk-Lore 36, 298–300.
Stanley, C. (1897). *The Life and Adventures of the American Cow-boy*. Providence, RI.
Staton, M. A. (1978). "Distress calls" of crocodilians—whom do they benefit? Am. Nat. 112, 327–332.
Staton, M. A. and Dixon, J. R. (1977). Breeding biology of the spectacled caiman, *Caiman crocodilus crocodilus*, in the Venezualan Llanos. U.S. Fish Wildl. Service, Wild. Res. Report 5, 1–21.
Stemmler-Morath, C. (1956). Beitrag zur Gefangenschafts—und Fortpflanzungsbiologie von *Python molurus* L. Zool. Garten NF 21, 347–364.
Strathmann, R. R. and Strathmann, M. F. (1982). The relationship between adult size and brooding in marine invertebrates. Am. Nat. 119, 91–101.
Strecker, J. K. (1908). Notes on the breeding habits of *Phrynosoma cornutum* and other Texas lizards. Proc. Biol. Soc. Wash. 21, 165–170.
Sutherland, S. K. (1983). *Australian Animal Toxins*. Oxford University Press, Oxford.
Sweeney, R. C. H. (1961). *Snakes of Nyasaland*. Government Printer, Zomba.
Switak, K. H. (1975). Der grüne Baumpython aus dem Land der Menschenfresser. Aquar. Mag. 9, 366–372.
Taigen, T. L., Pough, F. H. and Stewart, M. M. (1984). Water balance of terrestrial anuran (*Eleutherodactylus coqui*) eggs: Importance of parental care. Ecology 65, 248–255.
Tallamy, D. W. and Denno, R. F. (1982). Life-history trade-offs in *Gargaphia solani* (Hemiptera; Tingidae): The cost of reproduction. Ecology 63, 616–620.
Tanner, W. W. (1943). Notes on the life history of *Eumeces skiltonianus skiltonianus*. Great Basin Natur. 4, 81–88.
Tanner, W. W. (1957). A taxonomic and ecological study of the western skink (*Eumeces skiltonianus*). Great Basin Natur. 17, 59–94.
Taylor, E. H. (1935). A taxonomic study of the cosmopolitan scincid lizards of the genus *Eumeces* with an account of the distribution and relationships of its species. Univ. Kansas Sci. Bull. 23, 1–643.
Taylor, E. H. (1956). A review of the lizards of Costa Rica. Univ. Kansas Sci. Bull. 38, 1–322.
Taylor, E. H. (1965). The serpents of Thailand and adjacent waters. Univ. Kansas Sci. Bull. 45, 609–1096.

Telford, S. R. Jr. (1959). A study of the sand skink, *Neoseps reynoldsi* Stejneger. Copeia 1959, 110-119.

Tilley, S. G. (1972). Aspects of parental care and embryonic development in *Desmognathus ochrophaeus*. Copeia 1972, 532-540.

Tinkle, D. W. (1969). The concept of reproductive effort and its relation to the evolution of life histories of lizards. Am. Nat. 103, 501-516.

Tinkle, D. W. and Gibbons, J. W. (1977). The distribution and evolution of viviparity in reptiles. Misc. Pub. Museum Zool., Univ. Mich. 154, 1-54.

Tokarz, R. R. and Jones, R. E. (1979). A study of egg-related maternal behavior in *Anolis carolinensis* (Reptilia, Lacertilia, Iguanidae). J. Herpetol. 13, 283-288.

Toyama, M. (1975). On the embryos obtained from eggs of *Eumeces oshimensis*. Jap. J. Herpetol. 6, 39-42.

Trillmich, K. (1979). Feeding behaviour and social behaviour of the marine iguanas. Noticias de Galapagos 29, 19-20.

Trivers, R. L. (1972). Parental investment and sexual selection. In *Sexual Selection and the Descent of Man*. (B. Campbell, ed.). Aldine Press, Chicago, pp. 136-179.

Tryon, B. W. (1979). Reproduction in captive forest cobras, *Naja melanoleuca* (Serpentes: Elapidae). J. Herpetol. 13, 499-504.

Tryon, B. W. (1980). Observations on reproduction in the West African dwarf crocodile with a description of parental behaviour. SSAR Contrib. Herpetol. 1, 167-185.

Tweedie, M. W. F. (1957). *The Snakes of Malaysia*. R. D. Gillespie, Govt. Printer, Singapore.

Underwood, G. (1967). *A Contribution to the Classification of Snakes*. Trustees of the British Museum (Natural History), London.

Valenciennes, A. (1841). Observations faites pendant l'incubation d'une femelle du python a deux raies (*Python bivittatus*, Kuhl.) pendant les mois de mai et de juin 1841. C. R. Hebd. Séanc. Acad. Sci., Paris 13, 126-133.

Van Devender, T. R. and Van Devender, W. (1975). Ecological notes on two Mexican skinks (genus *Eumeces*). Southwest. Nat. 20, 279-282.

Van Mierop, L. H. S. and Barnard, S. M. (1976). Thermoregulation in a brooding female *Python molurus bivittatus* (Serpentes, Boidae). Copeia 1976, 398-401.

Van Mierop, L. H. S. and Barnard, S. M. (1978). Further observations on thermoregulation in the brooding female *Python molurus bivittatus* (Serpentes, Boidae). Copeia 1978, 615-621.

Van Mierop, L. H. S. and Bessette, E. L. (1981). Reproduction of the ball python, *Python regius* in captivity. Herpetol. Rev. 12, 20-22.

Vansleb, F. (1678). *The Present State of Egypt*. John Starkey, London.

Vinegar, A. (1968). Brooding of the eastern glass lizard, *Ophisaurus ventralis*. Bull. S. Calif. Acad. Sci. 67, 65-68.

Vinegar, A. (1973). The effects of temperature on the growth and development of embryos of the Indian python, *Python molurus* (Reptilia: Serpentes: Boidae). Copeia 1973, 171-173.

Vinegar, A., Hutchinson, V. H. and Dowling, H. G. (1970). Metabolism, energetics, and thermoregulation during brooding of snakes of the genus *Python* (Reptilia, Boidae). Zoologica 55, 19-48.

Visser, J. (1971). Unusually large skaapsteker eggs from the Cape Peninsula. J. Herpetol. Assoc. Afr. 7, 9.

Vitt, L. J. and Cooper, W. E., Jr. (1985). The relationship between reproduction and lipid cycling in the skink *Eumeces laticeps* with comments on brooding ecology. Herpetologica 41, 419-432.

Wagner, E. P. (1973). Breeding *Python molurus bivittatus*. HISS News J. 1, 112.

REFERENCES

Wagner, E. (1976). Breeding of the Burmese python *Python molurus bivittatus* at Seattle Zoo. Int. Zoo Yearbk. 16, 83–85.

Waitkuwait, W. E. (1982). Investigations into the breeding biology of the slender-snouted crocodile *Crocodylus cataphractus*. IUCN Crocodile Specialist Group, Zimbabwe Meeting, August 1982 (verbal presentation).

Wall, F. (1907). Hatching of dhaman (*Zamenis mucosus*) eggs, and observations on the egg tooth. J. Bombay Nat. Hist. Soc. 17, 1033–1035.

Wall, F. (1921). *Ophidia Taprobanica, or the Snakes of Ceylon*. H. R. Cottle, Govt. Printer, Colombo.

Wall, F. (1924). The hamadryad or king cobra, *Naia hannah* (Cantor). J. Bombay Nat. Hist. Soc. 30, 189–195.

Wall, F. (1926). The reticulate python *Python reticulatus* (Schneider). J. Bombay Nat. Hist. Soc. 31, 84–90.

Walsh, T. (1979). Further notes on the husbandry, breeding and behaviour of *Chondropython viridis*. Proc. Third Annual Symp. Reptile Repro. and Propagation, Aug. 20–21, 1979. Knoxville Zoo, Knoxville, TN, pp. 102–110.

Wang, B. (1966). Studies on the ecology of four species of lizards in Hangchow. II. Breeding. Acta Zool. Sinica 19, 170–186.

Waytialingham, S. (1880). Notes on the breeding of *C. palustris*. Proc. Zool. Soc. Lond. 1880, 186–187.

Webb, G. J. W. (1977). The natural history of *Crocodylus porosus*. In *Australian Animals and Their Environment*. (H. Messel and S. Butler, eds.). Shakespeare Head Press, Sydney, pp. 237–312.

Webb, G. J. W., Messel, H. and Magnusson, W. (1977). The nesting of *Crocodylus porosus* in Arnhem Land, northern Australia. Copeia 1972, 238–249.

Werler, J. E. (1951). Miscellaneous notes on the eggs and young of Texan and Mexican reptiles. Zoologica 36, 37–48.

Werner, D. I. (1982). Social organization and ecology of land iguanas on Isla Fernandina, Galapagos. In *Iguanas of the World*. (G. M. Burghardt and A. S. Rand, eds.). Noyes Publ., Park Ridge, NJ, pp. 342–365.

Werren, J. H., Gross, M. R. and Shine, R. (1980). Paternity and the evolution of male parental care. J. Theor. Biol. 82, 619–631.

Whitaker, R. and Whitaker, Z. (1977). Notes on vocalization and protective behaviour in the mugger. J. Bombay Nat. Hist. Soc. 75, 227–228.

Whitaker, Z. and Whitaker, R. (1978). Notes on captive breeding in mugger (*Crocodylus palustris*). J. Bombay Nat. Hist. Soc. 75, 228–231.

Wiewandt, T. (1977). Ecology, Behavior, and Management of the Mona Island Ground Iguana *Cyclura stejnegeri*. Ph.D. dissertation, Cornell Univ., Ithaca, NY.

Wiewandt, T. A. (1979). La gran Iguana de Mona. Nat. Hist. 88, 56–65.

Wiewandt, T. A. (1982). Evolution of nesting patterns in iguanine lizards. In *Iguanas of the World*. (G. M. Burghardt and A. S. Rand, eds.). Noyes Publ., Park Ridge, NJ, pp. 119–141.

Williams, G. C. (1966). *Adaptation and Natural Selection*. Princeton Univ. Press, Princeton, NJ.

Worrell, E. (1952). The Australian crocodiles. Proc. Roy. Soc. New South Wales 1951–52, 18–23.

Wray, G. O. (1982). Extract of letter communicated to the secretary of the Zoological Society. Proc. Zool. Soc. Lond. 1862, 108.

Yadav, R. N. (1967). A note on the breeding of Indian pythons, *Python molurus*, at Jaipur Zoo. Int. Zoo Yearbk. 7, 182–183.

CHAPTER 5

Methods for the Study of Reptile Populations

ARTHUR E. DUNHAM, PETER J. MORIN,
AND HENRY M. WILBUR

Department of Biology, University of Pennsylvania, Philadelphia, Pennsylvania, (A.E.D.); Department of Zoology, Duke University, Durham, North Carolina (P.J.M., H.M.W.)

The present address for Peter J. Morin is Department of Biological Sciences, Rutgers, The State University, Piscataway, New Jersey.

CONTENTS

I. **INTRODUCTION**   333
   A. The Importance of Life Table Data, 333
   B. The Components of a Life Table, 335

II. **METHODS OF DATA ACQUISITION**   336
   A. Capture Techniques, 336
   B. Marking Methods, 340

III. **MARK–RECAPTURE ESTIMATES OF POPULATION PARAMETERS**   343
   A. Estimation of Population Size, 343
   B. Estimation of Survival, 347
   C. Estimation of Fecundity, 353

IV. **SUMMARY AND CONCLUSIONS**   368

   ACKNOWLEDGMENTS   369

   REFERENCES   369

I. INTRODUCTION

A. The Importance of Life Table Data

Data on age-specific rates of birth, death, immigration, and emigration are essential for testing theory in many areas of central importance to ecology. Predictions concerning the dynamics of natural populations require the quantitative study of birth and death processes that determine age-specific survival, fecundity, and migration rates. Environmentally induced variation in population dynamics must be mediated through variation in these rates. Similarly, processes, such as competition and predation, influence the dynamics of interacting populations and, hence, community structure, by their effects on birth, death, and migration rates. Understanding mechanisms whereby environmental variation (either temporal or geographic) influences the distribution or abundance of organisms requires detailed understanding of the mechanisms that couple environmental variation to variation in age-specific birth, death, and migration rates. Obviously, detailed data on these rates and the magnitude and nature of variation in them are necessary to test hypotheses involving such mechanisms. Testing theories or elucidating mechanisms of population regulation require data on variation in these rates as a function of population density.

Rigorous tests of life history theory require data on age-specific birth, death, and migration rates, the magnitude of variation in them in natural populations, and the extent to which variation in them is density dependent. All sources of natural selection operating on age-structured populations act solely on heritable variation in these rates. Thus, these rates are primary components of Darwinian fitness and may themselves be determined by the life history phenotypes characteristic of a particular population. In addition, data on variation in life history characters, such as age-specific clutch size and frequency, age and size at first reproduction, size of offspring, and life expectancy, and the patterns of covariation among them are essential to testing and refining theories of life history evolution (see Wilbur and Morin, this volume; and Dunham et al., this volume).

In addition, an understanding of the factors that influence the birth, death, and migration rates and of the mechanisms whereby these factors exert their effects is essential to the formulation of management policies for any population.

Although detailed data on the nature and magnitude of variation in life history characters and demography both within and among populations are essential, these data will only be produced by detailed, long-term studies (Tinkle, 1979).

The dynamics of a population can be predicted if the age distribution, and the age-specific schedules of fecundity and mortality are available. The relationship among these data in a population with discrete age classes are summarized by the following equations:

$$f(0,t) = \sum_x g(x) \times f(x,t-1) \qquad (1)$$

$$f(x+1,t) = a(x) \times f(x,t-1) \qquad (2)$$

where $a(x)$ = the proportion of females in the xth age interval at the tth point in time ($x = 0,1,2,...; t = 0,1,2,...$) that will be alive and in age class $(x+1)$ at time $(t+1)$; $g(x)$ = the number of daughters born during the time interval $(t,t+1)$ per female in the xth age group at time t that will be alive and in the 0th age group at time $(t+1)$, and $f(x,t)$ = the number of females in xth age class at time t.

Survivorship (l_x) is the probability of living from birth (age 0) to age x. That is:

$$l_x = \prod_{y=0}^{x-1} a(y) \qquad (3)$$

Similarly, age-specific fecundity is often denoted m_x and is estimated as the average number of daughters born to females in the age interval whose midpoint is x (Mertz, 1970; Wilbur, 1975a).

These relationships can be used iteratively to project (predict) population size and age structure at any future time, provided the age-specific survival $(a(x))$ and fecundity $(g(x)$ or $m_x)$ schedules are constant. Mertz (1970), Goodman (1968), and Keyfitz (1968) provide excellent treatments of population projection methods. Caughley (1977) provides a clear exposition of methods involved in life table calculations. Details of the calculation of population parameters, such as rate of population growth, stable age distribution, and age-specific reproductive value, are given in Mertz (1970), Goodman (1968), Caughley (1977), and Wilbur (1975a). A stage-specific model of a sea turtle population that has been analyzed using conventional age-based models (Frazer, 1983, 1984; Richardson, 1982) is provided by Crouse and Crowder (1987).

This paper reviews methods for estimating age structure, age-specific survival rates, and age-specific fecundity rates of reptilian populations. Estimates of age structure require unbiased samples, which may require several capture techniques and stratified mark–recapture analysis. The age of individuals must be measured directly or estimated from a model relating growth in body size to age. Age-specific survival rates are usually obtained from mark–recapture procedures or indirectly from estimates of age structure. Estimation of age-specific fecundity requires careful study of ages at first and last reproduction and reproductive

INTRODUCTION

cycles. Requisite data include data on clutch or brood size and frequency as functions of age or body size. The techniques used to obtain these data vary among groups of reptiles, and we review those methods separately for each group.

Methods for studying populations of crocodilians are very specialized due to the size of the animals and the danger involved in working with them. Therefore, we have chosen to restrict our review to methods that have proven useful in the study of reptiles other than crocodilians. The most intensively studied species is the *Alligator mississippiensis* and a very useful bibliography of studies on that species is provided by Brisban et al. (1986). Demographic studies of crocodilians are reviewed by Turner (1977) and many of the important studies of crocodilian reproduction are summarized by Ferguson (1984).

B. The Components of a Life Table

Vertical life tables infer survival from proportionate representation of individuals in the successive age classes in an age distribution. Because the data can be gathered in a single sample, these are the most readily constructed type of life table for most reptilian populations. However, they are subject to a number of stringent assumptions and are, therefore, the least likely to be accurate. Vertical life tables infer age-specific survivorship by assuming a stable age distribution and the absence of pronounced environmental fluctuations, which may have influenced the age distribution. Furthermore, the population must be stationary (not growing), and the number of individuals in a particular age class must be less than the number in the next youngest class. Due to sampling bias, this frequently does not occur in younger age classes, and these must be excluded from the analysis. In addition, the number of individuals in the 0th age class (newborn) must be estimated independently. This can often be obtained, under the assumption of a stationary population, by multiplying the adult female population size by the mean fecundity for the year preceding the year for which the size of the 1-year-old class is estimated.

Horizontal life tables result from the direct and longitudinal observation of survival of marked individuals in single cohorts of even aged animals. This method is preferable because it requires no assumptions about age distribution and allows measurement of temporal variation in age-specific survival within a given population. However, horizontal life tables are impractical for the description of populations of many long-lived species, such as many turtles, tortoises, crocodilians, and some squamates. Longevity and the small sample sizes of old individuals complicate data collection and analysis. If sampling bias is unimportant, "hybrid" life tables, which combine vertical and horizontal approaches, may represent the most accurate method of estimating age-specific survival schedules for long-lived reptiles. To construct hybrid life tables, several cohorts are followed for varying periods of time, usually several years. Estimates of survival from age x to age x + 1 are then available for each cohort that was followed over that age interval during the study.

Methods of life table construction for turtles have been discussed in further detail by Wilbur (1975a). Survival rates in turtle populations are reviewed by Wilbur and Morin (this volume). Examples of horizontal life table construction in lizard populations are found in the studies of Ballinger (1973, 1979), Dunham (1981), Ruby and Dunham (1984), Tinkle (1967, 1972, 1973, 1976), Tinkle and Ballinger (1972), Tinkle and Dunham (1986), Turner et al. (1969, 1970), Van Devender (1982), and other studies reviewed by Turner (1977). Examples of horizontal life table construction for snake populations are found in the studies of Brown and Parker (1984), Parker and Brown (1980), Plummer (1985), and Feaver (1977).

II. METHODS OF DATA ACQUISITION

The importance of proper deposition in a museum research collection of any animal sacrificed cannot be stressed too strongly. Due to high rates of extinction, these collections will be the only source of research material for many populations. In addition, these collections provide a valuable source of data for measurement of temporal change in populations that remain extant and are subsequently restudied.

A. Capture Techniques

Demographic analyses require the capture and recapture of individuals. Capture techniques range in sophistication from simple hand capture to the use of various types of cleverly designed traps; capture methods are sometimes highly species-specific. Methods of capture, handling, and marking obviously should not alter age-specific mortality or fecundity rates or introduce significant capture heterogeneity among cohorts or age classes. Capture techniques that alter the habitat may alter these rates indirectly and should not be used. Lack of suitable recapture techniques make demographic study extremely difficult for fossorial and subterranean species and for those (e.g., *Xantusia*) living under exfoliating rock or in fallen vegetation. The effectiveness and

METHODS OF DATA ACQUISITION

biases of each technique are often species- and habitat-specific. Biased sex ratios or the disproportionate representation of particular size or age classes resulting from particular capture techniques are factors that must be recognized and offset or measured. Combining two or more capture strategies may negate the biases inherent in any single technique. A summary of general capture techniques used in the study of reptiles is presented below.

1. TURTLES

Hand capture generally results in over-representation of juveniles (*Pseudemys scripta*, Cagle, 1950; Moll and Legler, 1971; *Chrysemys picta*, Ream and Ream, 1966; *Chelydra serpentina*, Froese and Burghardt, 1975). However, hand capture may be a relatively unbiased method of capturing *Chrysemys picta* in some populations (Bayless, 1975). Capturing sleeping *Graptemys* at night by using a boat and spotlight may be productive (Chaney and Smith, 1950; Cagle, 1953), but samples consist mainly of juveniles and adult males.

"Muddling" is a type of hand capture in which turtles are found by probing with the hands and feet through aquatic vegetation and debris. Muddling may be particularly useful in the capture of *Clemmys guttata* (Ernst, 1975) as well as *Sternotherus odoratus*, *Chrysemys picta* (but see Gibbons, 1968a), *Pseudemys scripta* and *Chelydra serpentina* in shallow water, and *Pseudemys scripta* and *Chelydra serpentina* in deeper water (Cagle, 1942, 1944a).

Spotting and hand capture of aquatic turtles in relatively clear water may be facilitated by using a diving mask (Carr and Marchand, 1942). However, this technique produces a preponderance of males in *Pseudemys scripta* (Moll and Legler, 1971) or of larger individuals in *Graptemys pulchra* (Shealy, 1976).

Dipnetting may favor the capture of juvenile *Chrysemys picta* and *Pseudemys scripta* (Ream and Ream, 1966; Moll and Legler, 1971) and adult *Emydoidea blandingii* (Gibbons, 1968c). However, dipnetting from a boat may be the most successful means of capturing *Chrysemys picta* in some populations (Wilbur, 1975a). Similarly, hunting with a dipnet while disguised by a floating blind may result in a relatively unbiased sample of *Chrysemys picta* (Bider and Hoek, 1971) and dipnetting while drifting almost submerged downriver yielded a diversity of size classes for *Graptemys pulchra* (Shealy, 1976).

Seines and trammel nets are occasionally used to capture turtles, but may yield samples biased toward male and juvenile *Pseudemys scripta* (Moll and Legler, 1971). Other somewhat limited means of capture include trot, set, and float lines (Lagler, 1943, 1945; Dobie, 1971; Vogt, 1980), poleing and sounding (Carpenter, 1955; Mahmoud, 1969; Dobie, 1971), gaffing (Lagler, 1943; Hammer, 1969), spearing (Lagler, 1943, 1945), shooting (Lagler, 1943, 1945; Cagle, 1950), and electrical shocking (Gunning and Lewis, 1957; Dobie, 1971). The use of these techniques is limited to a rather restrictive set of circumstances, and is inappropriate when captured individuals are to be marked and released in hope of future recapturing.

Alternative capture techniques involve the use of various traps. Trapping techniques take advantage of the turtle's movement or attraction to bait, to other turtles, or to basking habits. Baited hoop nets and box traps are commonly used but can only be used in shallow water, unless a flotation device assures that trapped animals have access to air. Baited traps have been used with variable success even in studies of different populations of the same species (Arndt and Potter, 1973; Chaney and Smith, 1950; Moll, 1976; Shealy, 1976; Timkin, 1968). Yields are affected by type of bait, type of netting, and the nature of the first turtle to enter the trap (Cagle and Chaney, 1950). Trapping results are also influenced by water temperature, availability of food, water turbidity, phase of the annual cycle, trap location, bait, type of trap, and length of trapping period (Cagle, 1950; Gibbons, 1968b; Ream and Ream, 1966; White and Murphy, 1973). Baited traps may yield sex- or age-biased samples (Ream and Ream, 1966; Wade and Gifford, 1965). Trapping bias in favor of males may be due to attraction by females already in the trap (Ream and Ream, 1966). Baited traps often work poorly in the capture of the adults of many herbivorous species (Carr, 1952). In some studies, baited traps may yield apparently unbiased samples (e.g., Moll and Legler, 1971).

Unbaited swim-in traps (e.g., Gibbons, 1968b, c, 1969) take advantage of the aquatic movements of turtles. Drift fences are placed at angles to the shore and funnel moving animals into the trap.

Basking traps take advantage of the basking habit of many pond and river turtles. These traps vary greatly in the details of their construction, but all employ similar operating principles. Basking turtles are frightened from basking sites by the collector and become trapped in a restraining device which has been previously placed beneath the basking site. Many designs offer the entrapped turtles free access to food, air, and water and thus require less rigorous maintenance than baited traps. Capture bias in these traps is discussed by Moll and Legler (1971) and especially by Ream and Ream (1966).

Terrestrial drift fences combined with pitfall traps are useful for the monitoring of immigration, emigration, nesting, and hatchling recruit-

METHODS OF DATA ACQUISITION

ment of aquatic turtles (Gibbons and Semlitsch, 1981). Terrestrial trapping indicated that *Kinosternon subrubrum* was much more abundant than other trapping methods had suggested (Gibbons, 1970c).

Terrestrial turtles are usually captured by hand, although trapping may be useful for *Terrapene ornata* (Legler, 1960). Trained dogs can be very useful for location and capture of some terrestrial species (Carr, 1952; Loveridge and Williams, 1957; Schwartz et al., 1984). Marine turtles are almost always captured by hand on nesting beaches, but researchers often make opportunistic use of the commercial turtle fisheries (Carr, 1967).

2. LIZARDS AND SNAKES

Most lizards and snakes are spotted visually or heard while moving through vegetation. Nocturnal species (e.g., many geckos and crocodilians) are sometimes spotted using eyeshine (Pianka and Huey, 1978). Diurnal lizards sleeping at night are sometimes easy to spot using artificial light (e.g., Harris, 1964; Ruibal and Philibosian, 1974; T. W. Schoener, pers. comm.; Webster, 1969; Van Devender, 1982) and hand caught. For demograpic studies, most lizards are either captured by hand (e.g., Bustard, 1971; Heulin, 1985; Ruby and Dunham, 1984; Tinkle, 1967; Turner et al., 1970; Van Devender, 1982) or noosed (Dunham, 1980, 1981, 1982; Harris, 1982; Smith, 1981; and Tinkle and Dunham, 1983, 1986), or by a mixture of the two methods (e.g., Ballinger 1973, 1979; Ruibal and Philibosian, 1974). Traps attached to tree trunks may be used to capture arboreal species (e.g., *Sceloporus olivaceus*, Blair, 1960). Pitfall traps are occasionally used in lizard population studies (e.g., Spoecker, 1967). Fixed drift fences are sometimes used in capturing widely foraging, mobile species (e.g., *Cnemidophorus*, Milstead, 1959), and portable ones may also work well (J. W. Wright, pers. comm.). *Varanus komodoensis* may be captured in a variety of funnel-based traps baited with carrion (Auffenberg, 1981). Modified insect nets are effective in capturing wary lizards (Stebbins et al., 1967). In a surprising number of studies the method of capture is not specified. The fraction of the population marked as well as the efficiency of capturing individuals may be increased when fenced populations are studied (e.g., Turner et al., 1969). However, confining individuals within a circumscribed area may introduce errors into demographic estimates because of edge effects, crowding, and altered mortality rates.

In most comprehensive studies of snake populations, animals are captured by hand or in pitfall traps as they enter or leave fenced hibernacula or other areas (e.g., Brown and Parker, 1984; Feaver, 1977; Gregory, 1977;

Parker and Brown, 1980). For other species, hand capture of individuals in unfenced populations works well (e.g., Spellerburg and Phelps, 1977). A number of ingenious funnel traps (both with and without drift fences) have been used to capture snakes and lizards (e.g., Auffenberg, 1981; Banta, 1957; Clark, 1966; Fitch, 1951). Frequently drift fences used in combination with pitfall traps are superior to other methods capturing both lizards and snakes (Campbell and Cristman, 1982; Gibbons and Semlitsch, 1981; Vogt and Hine, 1982).

B. Marking Methods

No marking technique is universally accepted for any group of reptiles. Methods appropriate for each group vary greatly and several recent reviews have appeared (Ferner, 1979; Plummer, 1979; Spellerberg and Prestt, 1978; Swingland, 1978). We briefly review these methods.

1. TURTLES

The testudinian shell offers an ideal substrate for marking individuals. The unambiguous identification of individuals can be accomplished by systematically scoring the shell, or by using the shell as an attachment site for identifying tags. Perhaps the most elegant and widely used marking technique is the one described by Cagle (1939). Each marginal or plastral scute is given a code number. Turtles are then marked according to their assigned code by notching the appropriate scutes with a fine toothed hack saw blade, rasp, or knife. Marks are permanent in older turtles and some turtles have been captured 17 years after being marked with this technique, with the marks clearly visible (Wilbur, 1975a). Young turtles may regenerate notched bone, and notches must be recut during the years of rapid growth. The identification of juveniles may be assisted by assigning them an auxiliary toe clip. This system and those derived from it (e.g., Stubbs et al., 1984; Bury and Luckenbach, 1977) allow large numbers of individuals to be uniquely marked; this marking does not appear to affect the survival of the turtles. Other variations on this technique involve drilling holes in the marginal scutes for the insertion of color coded plastic tags (Pough, 1970), and the use of a leather punch to punch holes in the margin of the leathery carapace of *Trionyx ferox* (Breckenridge, 1955). Metal tags have also been used on Aldabra tortoises (Bourn, 1976; Swingland and Lessells, 1979).

Marine turtles have traditionally been marked with a numbered, metal cow-ear tag that is affixed to the trailing edge of the forelimb (Harrisson, 1956). This technique appears to be fairly reliable, although

METHODS OF DATA ACQUISITION

tag loss is occasionally high (e.g., Simon and Parkes, 1976). This method also has the advantage of allowing instructions for reporting turtle recovery to be inscribed on the tag. Such reports have been used to gather data on migration patterns of marine turtles (e.g., Carr, 1967; Bell and Richardson, 1978). This technique superseded the use of monel metal plates wired to the posterior portion of the carapace (Carr and Giovanolli, 1957).

Painting identifying marks with fingernail polish or lacquer on the carapace is useful for short-term behavioral or nesting studies, but is of limited usefulness for demographic studies because many species regularly undergo ecdysis of the outer layer of the plastral and carapacial shields (e.g., Cagle, 1946; Sexton, 1965). Painting is a fairly reliable method for marking terrestrial species and has been used with some success for *Terrapene carolina* (e.g., Ewing, 1933; Nichols, 1939; Stickel, 1950), *Terrapene ornata* (e.g., Blair, 1976), *Geochelone gigantea* (Gaymer, 1968; Grubb, 1971), and *Gopherus agassizii* (Woodbury and Hardy, 1948). Marking techniques are reviewed by Woodbury (1953) and other examples of marking techniques are in Pearse (1923), Miller (1955), Kaplan (1958), Hammer (1969), and Clark (1971).

Marking techniques that also assist in the observation of movements of released turtles, or which aid in the recapture of marked animals are also sometimes of use in demographic studies. Thread trailers have been used with *Terrapene carolina* (Breder, 1927; Stickel, 1950), *Terrapene ornata* (Legler, 1960), and *Rhinoclemmys annulata* (Mittermeir, 1971) among others. Sonic tags have been used for relocation of *Pseudemys scripta* (Moll and Legler, 1971), and small radio transmitters (Schubauer, 1981) have been used for relocation of *Caretta caretta* (Stoneburner et al., 1982), *Chelydra serpentina* (Obbard and Brooks, 1981), *Terrapene carolina* (Lemaku, 1970; Kiester et al., 1982; Munger, 1984), *Gopherus agassizii* (Turner et al., 1984), and others. The use of radiotelemetry is reviewed by Legler (1979). Radioactive tags, such as radio-tantalum pins allow relocation with gamma scintillation detectors of terrestrially active or hibernating animals (e.g., Bennett et al., 1970; Ward et al., 1976).

2. LIZARDS

In demographic studies, lizards are almost always assigned unique identifying numbers and permanently marked using a system of clipping off the distal phalanx of one or more toes. The most commonly used system is that described by Tinkle (1967). Toe clips are permanent and apparently cause little trauma. The system has worked well in a number of studies including Ballinger (1973, 1979), Barbault (1976), Blair

(1960), Brooks (1967), Bustard (1971), Dunham (1981), Fitch (1956), Heulin (1985), Ruby and Dunham (1984), Ruibal and Philibosian (1974), Schoener and Schoener (1982), Smith (1981), Tinkle (1967), Tinkle and Ballinger (1972), Tinkle and Dunham (1986), Turner et al. (1970), Van Devender (1982), and Vinegar (1975a). Numbered, two-piece plastic cattle ear tags inserted through a hole punched in the lateral body fold may be used to mark *Varanus komodoensis* (Auffenberg, 1981). Branding has occasionally been used to mark lizards (Burrage 1973, 1974).

In addition to making permanent marks, investigators frequently apply unique paint marks to individuals. These marks are generally color-coded dots or symbols applied to the dorsum or over the hind limb insertions that allow visual identification of individuals without the necessity of capturing them. They are very useful in studies of home range dynamics and other behavioral studies. Examples of the use of this technique include Blair (1960), Dunham (1981), Ruby and Dunham (1984), Smith (1981), Tinkle (1967), Schoener and Schoener (1980a, 1982), Tinkle and Ballinger (1972), Tinkle and Dunham (1986), and numerous others. However, colors are sometimes difficult to distinguish in poor light and abrasion can change one symbol into another.

Two studies suggest that paint marking does not increase the mortality rate of marked individuals (Jones and Ferguson, 1980; Simon and Bissinger, 1983). However, these studies were conducted on wait-ambush sceloporines (*Sceloporus*), and the assumption that paint marking does not affect mortality rates should be tested on widely foraging species (e.g., *Cnemidophorus*) before it is used in demographic studies of these species. Toe clipping does not influence sprint speed in *Sceloporus* (R. B. Huey and A. E. Dunham, unpubl.).

3. SNAKES

Snakes are, perhaps, the group that has been subjected to the widest range of marking techniques (see review in Spellerberg and Prestt, 1978). Marking methods include tattooing (Woodbury, 1948), branding with heat (Clark, 1971; Weary, 1969) and cold (Lewke and Stroud, 1974), clipping ventral scales (see below), metal jaw tags (Hirth, 1966), inserting plastic plugs through the caudal scales and musculature (Pough, 1970), and small colored, plastic beads sewn through the dermis (Hudnall, 1982). Rattlesnakes have been marked with colored plastic disks sewn through the second rattle with nylon fishing line (Pendlebury, 1972) and by painting the rattles with a long-lasting, waterproof paint (Brown et al., 1984). Both methods allow visual identification and behavioral observation without disturbing the animal.

Photographs of ventral patterns can be used to identify recaptured individuals (Calstrom and Edelstam, 1946). This technique seems promising but has not been used in reptile demographic studies.

The most widely used method for marking snakes involves clipping out a portion of the enlarged ventral or subcaudal scutes in a coded pattern that allows each individual in the population to be given a unique number (Blanchard and Finster, 1933). Most recent investigators of the demography of natural populations of snakes favor clipping the ventral scutes according to the system described by Prestt (1971) and Brown and Parker (1976). This system has been successfully used to study the population dynamics of colubrids (e.g., Brown and Parker, 1984; Feaver, 1977; Parker and Brown, 1974a, 1980; Plummer, 1985; Spellerberg and Phelps, 1977) and viperids (e.g., Parker and Brown, 1974b; Prestt, 1971).

II. MARK–RECAPTURE ESTIMATES OF POPULATION PARAMETERS

A. Estimation of Population Size

1. OVERVIEW

This section briefly reviews mark–recapture techniques that have been employed in studies of reptilian populations, and the limitations imposed on the use of these techniques by the biology of different groups of reptiles. Detailed accounts of mark–recapture estimation theory are available in Caughley (1977), Chapman (1951), Cormack (1968), Feinberg (1977), Manly and Seber (1973), Schumacher and Eschmeyer (1943), and Seber (1973). Methods that have been employed to estimate the size of reptile populations include the Lincoln-Petersen index (Seber, 1973), both with and without Bailey's (1952) small sample correction, the methods of Hayne (1949), Fienberg (1977), Fitch (1963b), Marten (1970), Schnabel (1938), Tanaka (1951), Bailey's triple catch method, (Bailey, 1951, 1952), the Jolly-Seber technique (Jolly, 1965), and the method of Schumacher and Eschmeyer (1943).

There are two types of bias in recapture estimates of population density (Seber, 1973). Bias may arise from consistent differences in catchability among individuals or classes of individuals (capture heterogeneity) and from contagion (in which the probability of capture of an animal varies as a function of capture history), and the resultant error introduced into the estimation of the size of a cohort, age class, or population may be large. Investigators should test for significant capture heterogeneity and contagion before using these methods. Methods of testing for violations of the assumptions of various estimation procedures are given by Caughley (1977), Feinberg (1977), Heckel and Roughgarden (1979), Marten (1970), Seber (1973), and Wilbur and Landwehr (1975). A complete census is preferable to population estimation and should be used whenever possible.

The Lincoln-Petersen index has been the most widely used method of estimating population size in reptiles. The underlying assumptions of this method include (a) negligible migration, mortality, and recruitment over the period of estimation, (b) equal catchability of individuals on first and subsequent capture occasions, (c) random capture, and (d) that marks will be permanently recognizable and do not affect probability of recapture. In practice few of these assumptions are justified, and investigators should always test whether the population under study meets the assumptions of the particular estimation procedure being used. Equal likelihood of capture and recapture is a fundamental assumption, and the validity of any recapture estimate is seriously compromised when this assumption is violated. Criteria for testing the assumption of equal catchability, as well as procedures to follow when that assumption is not valid, are outlined by Wilbur and Landwehr (1974), Marten (1970), and Heckel and Roughgarden (1979).

Bailey's triple-catch and the Jolly-Seber methods include estimates of survival rates. To obtain age-specific survival rates, these methods must be applied to the data for each age class, a process that usually results in small samples and therefore large standard errors of estimates.

2. TURTLES

Studies using the Lincoln-Petersen index to estimate the size of turtle populations include those by Williams (1961), Mahmoud (1969), Gibbons (1968b), Bider and Hoek (1971), Moll and Legler (1971), Brown (1974), Ernst (1971a, 1974, 1976), Froese and Burghardt (1975), and Shealy (1976). In one study (Froese and Burghardt, 1975), migration during the recapture period may have biased estimates of population size. Moreover, mark–recapture techniques may be of limited value in estimating population size in some river turtles (Tinkle, 1958; Shealy, 1976). Low recapture rates for *Graptemys* may result from an increase in wariness of marked turtles (Tinkle, 1958). In such situations, a basking turtle census may yield a more accurate census than one derived from mark–recapture statistics (Tinkle, 1958). Other possible sources of error in population estimates associated with Lincoln-Petersen estimates are evaluated by Gibbons (1968b) and include behavioral change following marking, migration, and the nonrandom redistribution of marked animals. Studies of *Terrapene coahuila* (Brown, 1974) and *Chrysemys picta* (Wilbur and Landwehr, 1974) suggest that the assumption of equal catchability may not hold for most turtle populations.

Other studies of turtles have employed the Haynes method (Tinkle, 1958; Mahmoud, 1969; Brown, 1974; Major, 1975), the Schnabel method (Wade and Gifford, 1965; Brown, 1974; Major, 1975), Fitch's method (Brown, 1974), Bailey's triple-catch method (Wilbur, 1975a) and the Jolly-Seber method (Wilbur, 1975a). Useful information on the comparative accuracy of population estimates obtained using closed population techniques is contained in Brown (1974) and Major (1975).

Aerial surveys of nesting sea turtles can yield crude estimates of population size (Hoffman and Fritts, 1982; LeBuff and Hagen, 1978; Pritchard 1982).

3. SQUAMATES

The most widely used method of estimating the size of any cohort, age class, or population in lizard population studies has been simply to count the number of individuals in each cohort or age class directly. Generally, one attempts to register all of the individuals in the population at each census. This involves repeated searches of the study area until all (or some very high fraction) of the individuals captured or seen are registered. If every individual can be assigned to a cohort or age class, then the age structure, age-dependent mortality (see below), and total population size can be determined. This approach has been very successful in studies of populations of conspicuous, diurnal, or easily captured lizards. Studies of lizard populations using this method include Ballinger (1973, 1979), Barbault (1976), Blair (1960), Brooks (1967), Dunham (1980, 1981, 1982), Fitch (1956), Ferguson et al. (1980), Heulin, 1985; Ruby and Dunham (1984), Schoener and Schoener (1980a, 1982), Smith (1981), Tinkle (1967, 1972, 1973, 1976), Tinkle and Ballinger (1972), Tinkle and Dunham (1983, 1986), Turner et al. (1970), Van Devender (1982), and Vinegar (1975a, 1975b).

Some impressive studies of snake demography have also relied on direct counts to estimate the size of individual cohorts or age classes. Species that use hibernacula are especially suitable because the entire population can be fenced and captured. Such studies include those of Brown and Parker (1984), Gregory (1977), Parker and Brown (1980), Feaver (1977), Prestt (1971), Plummer (1985), Spellerberg and Phelps (1977).

Direct counts only work well when all cohorts or age classes can be completely enumerated. When this is not the case, mark–recapture methods must be used. One of the most promising methods of estimating population size, especially when it is unnecessary to mark individuals uniquely, is given by Heckel and Roughgarden (1977). This method is very powerful and utilizes the hierarchical multiway contingency table analysis developed by Fienberg (1975). This method allows the possibility of correlations between censuses (capture heterogeneity) and has been used to estimate the densities of *Anolis* populations by Heckel and Roughgarden (1977) and Schoener and Schoener (1982, 1983). The regression method of Tanaka (1951) is also useful in cases where unequal catchability is a problem and has been used effectively by Schoener and Schoener (1982) to estimate size of *Anolis* populations.

The effectiveness of a particular census effort can be estimated by examining the proportion of animals that are recorded in a particular census given that they are known to be at risk. In this method, a chain of three (or more) censuses is used and the fraction of animals that are recorded in both the first and third census that are also recorded in the second census is used as an index of the effectiveness of the second census. Studies that have used this method include Dunham (1980, 1981), Tinkle and Dunham (1983, 1986), and Smith (1981).

A number of studies have compared certain population estimation procedures and direct counts and have generally found close agreement between direct counts and estimated numbers of animals, at least when the fraction of animals registered is high (Lincoln-Petersen and small-sample Lincoln-Petersen methods: Andrews et al., 1983; Dunham, 1981; Ruibal and Philibosian, 1974; Tinkle and Dunham, 1983, 1986; the Jolly-Seber method: Andrews et al., 1983; Smith, 1981; and the Schumacher-Eschmeyer method: Turner et al., 1970). A number of other studies have used mark–recapture procedures to estimate population size (the Schumacher-Eschmeyer method: Plummer, 1985; Carpenter, 1952; the Jolly-Seber method: Auffenberg, 1981; Brown and Parker, 1984).

Virtually all demographic studies of reptiles use indirect methods to estimate the initial size of a given cohort (i.e., the number of newborn during a particular time interval). This estimate is usually calculated using data on age or size structure at the time of oviposition or parturition and age- or size-specific fecundity of females. Examples of this approach include Ballinger (1973, 1979), Barbault (1976), Blair (1960), Brooks (1967), Brown and Parker (1984), Dunham (1980, 1981, 1982), Feaver (1977), Fitch (1956), Gregory (1977), Parker and Brown (1980), Prestt (1971), Plummer (1985), Ruby and Dunham (1984), Schoener and

Schoener (1980a), Smith (1981), Spellerberg and Phelps (1977), Tinkle (1967, 1972, 1973, 1976), Tinkle and Ballinger (1972), Tinkle and Dunham (1983, 1986), Turner et al. (1970), Van Devender (1982), Vinegar (1975a,b), and many others.

B. Estimation of Survival

1. ESTIMATION OF AGE STRUCTURE

a. Turtles

Criteria used to assign turtles to appropriate age classes are generally derived from the relationship between age, growth marks on the plastral or carapacial shields, and plastron or carapace length. The correlation between growth marks and the age is the subject of an extensive literature, and reviews include: Risely (1933), Cagle (1946, 1950), Sexton (1959), Legler (1960), Gibbons (1967, 1976), Moll and Legler (1971), and Schwartz et al. (1984). The mechanism of annulus formation has been described by Legler (1971). True annuli are thought to be a product of cessation in growth of the shields during unfavorable periods (e.g., hibernation, flooding, drought, or whenever feeding activity is reduced). To the extent that these occur on an annual cycle, the growth marks are annual and, therefore, accurate indicators of age.

This method of aging turtles is not without complications. "False annuli," which are relatively indistinct, may occur as a result of unfavorable growth conditions during the course of a normal growing season. The length of time that true annuli can be distinguished depends on several aspects of the biology of the species and of the habitat occupied by the population. Species that undergo regular ecdysis may retain annuli for only 3–5 years (e.g., Cagle, 1946; Sexton, 1959; Wilbur, 1975b). At the other extreme, some species such as *Geochelone gigantea* (Grubb, 1971) may retain complete sets of annuli for more than 20 years.

Annuli also occur in some of the long bones or dermal bones of turtles and may be correlated with age in some species (Mattox, 1935). This technique is described and evaluated in detail by Peabody (1961), Hammer (1969), and Zug et al. (1986). It is obviously inappropriate when animals must be kept alive. Bone annuli may be more reliable indicators of the age of *Chelydra serpentina* than are epidermal annuli (Hammer, 1969). Periosteal rings are laid down annually in *Testudo hermanni* (Castanet and Cheylan, 1979). However, bone annuli are apparently unreliable indicators of age for *Terrapene ornata* (Legler, 1960) and *Macroclemys temmincki* (Dobie, 1971). Tetracycline can be used to label bones *in vivo* for later use in aging recaptured turtles (Frazier, 1985).

Numerous studies have employed plastral or carapacial annuli as a means of generating age–length relationships. Examples of these studies additional to those already mentioned include Bourn and Coe (1978), Cagle (1950), Gibbons (1967, 1968a, b, c), Tinkle (1961), Graham (1970, 1971), Christiansen and Dunham (1972), Dobie (1971), Ernst et al. (1973), Ernst (1975), Gibson and Hamilton (1984), Hulse (1976), and Moll (1976). Studies where annuli were useless or of limited value due to rapid obliteration or irregular growth include Miller (1932, 1955), Wade and Gifford (1965), Brown (1974), and Shealy (1976).

The growth models described by Sexton (1959) and Wilbur (1975a) illustrate the usefulness of annuli for generating age–length relationships even when the annuli are retained for only a limited period of time. Turtles with complete sets of annuli are used to compute the mean and standard error of plastron length for the first few growth seasons using Sergeev's formula (Sergeev, 1937), $A/P = A_t/P_t$ where A and P are the current lengths of the measured annulus and plastron, A_t the annulus length at time t, and P_t the plastron length to be calculated at time t. Because the ratio of annulus length to plastron length varies considerably among individuals, individual growth histories must be calculated for each turtle (Wilbur, 1975b). These growth histories are then used to calculate the mean and standard error of the plastron length for each age class. Having back-calculated the plastral lengths for turtles with complete growth records to age zero, one can assign turtles with the first few annuli obliterated to an appropriate age class by matching their growth history to the relationship developed from absolutely aged turtles. However, this analysis becomes uncertain for turtles of an age much beyond sexual maturity, because growth and annuli production slows or ceases at that time. Moreover, such growth models are specific for particular populations, due to the strong environmental component of variation in growth rate (Gibbons, 1967, 1970a; Hulse, 1976; Sexton, 1959).

Species lacking annuli such as *Trionyx* and other trionychids must be aged using an age–length relationship based on age-specific growth rates inferred from mark–recapture data (Breckenridge, 1955).

Until very recently, no reliable criteria had been developed to allow the aging of marine turtles (Rebel, 1974; Bjorndal, 1980). The use of skeletal growth marks (Zug et al., 1986) as aging criteria may enhance demographic analysis of their populations. Only long-term studies of known individuals will establish the longevity and life expectancy of most turtles (Gibbons and Semlitsch, 1982).

b. Squamates

In most mark–recapture studies of lizards and snakes, animals are aged according to size at initial capture and their subsequent growth history (e.g., Ballinger, 1973, 1979; Barbault, 1976; Blair, 1960; Brooks, 1967; Brown and Parker, 1984; Dunham, 1980, 1981; Feaver, 1977; Ferguson et al., 1980; Fitch, 1956, 1958, 1960, 1963a, b, 1965, 1975; Gregory, 1977; Heulin, 1985; Parker and Brown, 1980; Prestt, 1971; Plummer, 1985; Ruby and Dunham, 1984; Schoener and Schoener, 1980a; Smith, 1981; Spellerberg and Phelps, 1977; Tinkle, 1960, 1967, 1972, 1973, 1976; Tinkle and Ballinger, 1972; Tinkle and Dunham, 1983, 1986; Turner et al., 1970; Van Devender, 1982; Vinegar, 1975a, b). This method involves establishing growth models based on animals of known age (e.g., Dunham, 1978; Schoener and Schoener, 1978; Andrews, 1982) or frequency distributions of size (snout–vent length (SVL) or mass) of known-age animals as a function of age, and comparing the size of animals the age of which is not absolutely known to these growth trajectories or frequency distributions to obtain an estimate of age. Because there is considerable variation among conspecific populations with regard to individual growth (e.g., Andrews, 1976, 1982; Ballinger, 1977, 1983; Ferguson et al., 1980; Tinkle, 1967; Tinkle and Ballinger, 1972; Tinkle and Dunham, 1983, 1986; Ruby and Dunham, 1984; Ballinger, 1983) , such estimates are valid only when the growth trajectories or size–age distributions are derived from the population under study. Moreover, because individual growth rates often vary significantly within single populations in response to proximal environmental variation in resources (e.g., Andrews, 1976, 1982; Schoener and Schoener, 1978; Dunham, 1978), it may be better to establish unique relationships for each cohort or to base estimates of age-dependent population parameters on animals of known (not estimated) age.

Skeletochronological techniques have also been applied to squamate populations (Castanet et al., 1977). This method generally involves removing, preserving, sectioning, and staining an appropriate skeletal element (usually a long bone or phalanx). Periosteal bands may then be examined and counted under a light microscope (Castanet, 1974, 1978; Castanet and Cheylan, 1979; Francillon, 1979; Buffrenil, 1980; Pilorge and Castanet, 1981; Castanet and Roche, 1981; Nouira et al., 1982; Zug and Rand, 1987).

Use of this technique requires three critical assumptions: (a) Regular, cyclical growth occurs in at least some skeletal element. This implies the existence of periods of active growth interspersed with periods of little or no growth. This cyclic growth leaves visible, permanent markers in the bone. (b) These markers cycle with a known period and these periods represent specific times in the life of an individual (e.g., winter hibernation, food shortage, or drought). (c) If a block of bone markers is lost through remodeling, the number of lost markers can be estimated from those markers that remain. Annual cycles of slow and rapid growth have been confirmed in a few lizards: *Cophosaurus texanus* (Nouira et al., 1982), *Lacerta lepida* and *L. viridis* (Castanet, 1978), *L. vivipara* (Heulin, 1985; Pilorge and Castanet, 1981), and *Iguana iguana* (Zug and Rand, 1987). Not all lizards produce periosteal growth markings, possibly because growth is continuous and variations in rate are insufficient for periosteal rings to be produced. Examples include the gecko *Tarentola mauritanica* and the sand skink *Chalcides ocellatus* (Castanet, 1978).

The reliability of age estimates produced by this technique has been studied using known-aged *Iguana iguana* from Panama (Zug and Rand, 1987). This study demonstrated annual cycles of periosteal growth in the phalanges. The number of periosteal rings matched closely the known ages of the animals based on mark–recapture data. There was, however, significant variation between two observers in age determination and in the ages assigned to individuals when the same material was re-examined by one observer after 6–9 months. The lack of close matches for all specimens by all observers led Zug and Rand (1987) to recommend caution in interpreting skeletochronological ages as real ages. Also, the number of growth rings in the surangular bone of *Crotalus atrox* is an unreliable indicator of age (Tinkle, 1962). In short, although the technique is certainly promising, it still requires careful validation using animals of known age before being applied in demographic studies.

In summary, reliable morphological criteria have not been developed to allow the aging of most lizard and snake species. Until such criteria are available, demographic analysis of squamate populations should rely on mark–recapture data to establish age structure.

2. CALCULATING SURVIVORSHIP

Survivorship, l_x, is defined as the proportion of newborn animals in any given cohort that are alive at age x. Hence, l_x is simply calculated as the number of individuals in age class x divided by the number of individuals in age class zero. If a high proportion of the individuals in the population is marked, l_x should be calculated from age distributions derived from actual marked animals, not from estimates of the number of animals in each age class. Survival estimates based on relative frequency of adjacent age classes in the population are valid only if the population is stationary and at stable age distribution. These assumptions should be tested (Wilbur, 1975a) before such estimates are used. In general, squamate populations do not meet these criteria (e.g., Ballinger, 1973, 1979; Barbault, 1976; Dunham, 1981, 1982; Tinkle, 1967, 1972, 1973, 1976; Tinkle and Dunham, 1986; Turner et al., 1970; Van Devender, 1982), and only cohort (horizontal) life table estimates should be used for such populations.

The number of individuals in age class zero can also be estimated using regression analysis, as was done for *Chrysemys picta* (Wilbur, 1975a; Tinkle et al., 1981). The logarithm of the number of individuals in each age class is regressed on age. Under-represented age classes (usually younger age classes) are excluded from the regression model. The number of individuals in "missing" age classes are then estimated by extrapolation from the regression equation. This analysis assumes a stationary population with a stable age distribution. The assumption of a stable age distribution can be supported if there is a high correlation between the number of individuals in different age classes and age, if the slopes of regressions for different years do not differ, and if an exponential survivorship curve adequately fits the data (Wilbur, 1975a). Otherwise, l_x may still be calculated using a_x from the ratio of adjacent age classes providing the age classes are declining in size.

If age-specific mortality rates do not vary with age (exponentially decreasing survivorship curves), $\ln(l_x)$ will be a rectilinear function of age (x) and survivorship may be estimated as

$$l_x = a \times e^{bt} \tag{4}$$

where the parameters (a and b) are estimated by linear regression of $\ln(l_x)$ on age (Schoener and Schoener, 1982).

When mortality rates do not vary with age, this method may be used and the life expectancy of an animal in the initial cohort may be calculated exactly as

$$F_1 = a \times e^{bt} \, dt = -a/b \tag{5}$$

An empirical check on F_1 may be calculated as

$$F_2 = (l_x - l_{x+1})(x + 1/2) \tag{6}$$

where n is the smallest unattained age (Schoener and Schoener, 1982). F_2 is slightly biased, but Schoener and Schoener (1982) noted no systematic discrepencies between these estimates in their analysis of survival in several *Anolis* populations.

If age-specific mortality rates are not constant (vary as a function of age), life expectancy [E(x)] must be calculated from age-specific survivorship (l_x) (Wilbur, 1975a) as

$$E(x) = T(x)/L(x) \tag{7}$$

where

$$L(x) = \int_x^{x+1} l_x \, dx \tag{8}$$

and

$$T(x) = \sum_{y=x}^{\infty} L(y) \tag{9}$$

If the age intervals are reasonably small L(x) may be approximated as

$$L(x) = [l_x + l_{x+1}]/2.0 \tag{10}$$

Injury frequency is often used as an indicator of the intensity of predation in natural populations (Rand, 1954; Pianka, 1967; Tinkle, 1967). In studies of lizard populations, the frequency of broken and regenerated tails is used to estimate and compare intensity of predation among populations. This method makes a number of assumptions about demography (Schoener, 1979; Arnold, this volume). In particular, age-specific mortality rates must be equivalent in all populations being compared. A valuable theoretical analysis (Schoener, 1979) suggests that, under a wide range of reasonable assumptions, injury rates in age-structured populations are unrelated or only weakly related to predation intensity. In such populations, injury rates reflect the number of predation attempts that are unsuccessful and, therefore, estimate predator efficiency rather than intensity of predation (Schoener, 1979; Schoener and Schoener, 1980b). Injuries, such as broken tails, lost toes, and various types of scars, may also result from intraspecific fights in aggressively territorial species (Blair, 1960; Pianka, 1967; Tinkle, 1967; Zweifel and Lowe, 1966). Methods for adjusting injury frequencies to reflect differences in age-specific mortality are given in Schoener (1979) and Schoener and Schoener (1980b).

Collection of turtle shells, with their records of growth and age preserved as annuli provides a convenient way of generating age at death statistics (Deevey, 1947). Because shells are most frequently found on land, they do not represent a complete mortality record for pond turtles, but rather represent the risk of terrestrial mortality. Juvenile mortality is often under-represented using this technique, since the shells of juveniles may be largely destroyed by predators or scavengers or simply overlooked. Examples of the information that may be obtained from age at death statistics are given in Wilbur (1975a) and Ruckdeschel and Zug (1982). To our knowledge, no one has used shell damage in living turtles as an index of mortality risk.

C. Estimation of Fecundity

1. OVERVIEW

Age-specific fecundity, m_x, is the per capita number of female offspring produced per breeding season by a female of age x. The value for m_x becomes non-zero at the age of first reproduction and returns to zero if an age of reproductive senescence is reached. The calculation of m_x requires knowledge of age-specific clutch (brood) size, including the number of clutches produced per year (clutch frequency), over the reproductive life span. Knowledge of any interactions between clutch size and clutch frequency is also useful in scaling m_x.

Several techniques are used to estimate clutch size and frequency in turtles and squamate reptiles. Under the assumption of an average sex ratio of 1:1, m_x is taken to be one-half the age-specific fertile egg production for a clutch produced by a female of age x. The assumption of equal sex ratio in some turtle populations is indirectly supported by the work of Gibbons (1969, 1970b). However, the mechanism of sex determination in most turtles is complex (Raynard and Pieau, 1985; Packard and Packard, this volume), and sex ratio is influenced by incubation temperature in many species of turtles, crocodilians, and some lizards (e.g., Bull, 1980; Bull and Vogt, 1979, 1981; Bull et al., 1982; Morreale et al., 1982; Pieau, 1971, 1972, 1973, 1975; Yntema, 1976). Therefore, it is important to know whether the population under study has environmental sex determination and whether the sex ratio is 1:1. Reproductive ecology of turtles is reviewed by Wilbur and Morin (this volume) and life history patterns of squamates are reviewed by Dunham et al. (this volume). Aspects of the reproductive biology of squamates and *Sphenodon* are reviewed by Saint Girons (1985) and Moffat (1984).

2. AGE AT FIRST AND LAST REPRODUCTION

There are two complementary approaches for establishing sexual maturity in reptiles. The first relies upon the recognition of secondary sexual characters or behaviors appearing after sexual maturity. The second relies upon dissection and direct observation of mature gonads or gametes. The first approach is subject to more sources of error but does not require the sacrifice of animals. The second approach, while more accurate, involves either disturbing the population under study by the permanent removal of individuals or alternatively risking inaccuracies from making inferences about one population from the study of other nearby populations. Errors resulting from extrapolation may be considerable, because even geographically close populations may differ in population parameters (Gibbons, 1967; Gibbons and Tinkle, 1969; Ballinger, 1979; Ruby and Dunham, 1984).

Turtles and Squamates

Depending on the species, maturity may be reached as a function of size (e.g., Hildebrand, 1932; Cagle, 1948, 1954; Legler, 1960; Gibbons, 1968b; Gibbons et al., 1981; Moll, 1977, 1979) or as a function of age (e.g., Risley, 1938; Tinkle, 1961). External criteria for the determination of sexual maturity are much more easily defined for males than for females. Agassiz (1857) recognized that adult male turtles display a relatively enlarged preanal region, and often display some degree of concavity of the plastron. The enlarged preanal region appears to be a widespread character of mature males in most families (e.g., Risley, 1938, *Sternotherus odoratus*; Mosiman and Bider, 1960, *Chelydra serpentina*; Cagle, 1948, *Pseudemys scripta*; Gaymer, 1968, *Geochelone gigantea*; Breckenridge, 1955, *Trionyx ferox*; Pritchard, 1971, *Dermochelys coriacea*; Pritchard and Marquez, 1973, *Lepidochelys kempii*; Rhodin and Mittermeier, 1976, *Chelodina siebenrocki*). Moreover, the age or size at which the preanal region begins to enlarge is often correlated with the age or size at which sperm production begins (Cagle, 1948; Webb, 1956; Risley, 1938). Other secondary sexual characters (e.g., elongation of foreclaws in some emydid turtles, Cagle, 1948; Gibbons, 1968a, b; the striking color changes of *Callagur borneoensis*, Moll, 1977) may be useful for determination of maturity, but their usefulness must be established for each population studied. Courtship and mating behavior may be indicative of maturity for both males and females.

Females generally lack obvious secondary sexual characters that appear with the onset of sexual maturity. Consequently, many workers determine mature females only by size and the lack of male sexual secondary characters (Cagle, 1942, 1946). This technique may result in highly biased estimates of sex ratio when the threshold size is improperly chosen (Gibbons, 1970b). Oviductal eggs, which indicate maturity, can be detected by palping females at the hind limb insertions (e.g., Cagle, 1944b, Gibbons, 1969; Wilbur, 1975a). The presence and number of oviductal eggs may also be detected by X-radiography (Gibbons and Greene, 1979). Females observed nesting may also be assumed to be mature.

In squamates, a number of external criteria allow unambiguous determination of the sex of individuals. The base of the tail is frequently enlarged to accomodate the hemipenes in males. In individuals of all ages, the cloaca may be carefully examined (using a blunt probe) for the existence of hemipenial openings. In addition, many species possess external scale characters that allow determination of sex even in hatchling animals. For example, males of many species of iguanid lizards possess enlarged postanal scales ("propellar" scales) at hatching that they retain throughout life. Femoral pores are frequently larger in males than in females, although this difference may appear only at sexual maturity.

Secondary sexual characteristics that allow unambiguous determination of the age or size of attainment of sexual maturity are uncommon in squamate reptiles, especially snakes. However, gravidity is readily established by palpation (e.g., Tinkle, 1967; Dunham, 1981; Brown and Parker, 1984; Feaver, 1977). In many lizards color changes may signal sexual maturity and breeding condition of both males and females (e.g., Clark, 1965; Ferguson, 1976; Fitch, 1956; Harris, 1964; Medica et al., 1973; Montanucci, 1965; Vitt and Cooper, 1985).

Internal anatomical criteria for maturity are often less ambiguous than external criteria, but dissection requires an artificial change in mortality rates. The presence of motile sperm in the testes, epididymides, or vasa deferentia is generally taken to indicate male sexual maturity (e.g., Risley, 1938; Cagle, 1948; Mosimann and Bider, 1960). Once males reach maturity, sperm is present in the epididymides in varying quantities throughout the year (Dobie, 1971; White and Murphy, 1973). A number of standard histological stains, such as Wright's stain, Toluidine Blue O, and Heidenhain's Iron Hematoxylin, have occasionally been used to study sperm smears (e.g., Webb, 1961; Dobie, 1971). Attainment of a particular testicular size or convoluted condition of the vas deferens is sometimes used to determine sexual maturity (e.g., Brown and Parker, 1984; Dunham, 1981; Feaver, 1977; Gibbons, 1972; Gregory, 1977; Parker and Brown, 1980; Plummer, 1985; Ruby and Dunham, 1984; Swingland and Coe, 1978; Tinkle, 1960, 1961, 1967, 1972, 1973, 1976; Tinkle and Ballinger, 1972; Tinkle and Dunham, 1983, 1986).

Internal maturity criteria for females include the presence of enlarged ovarian follicles undergoing vitellogenesis, oviductal eggs, or corpora lutea (e.g., Ballinger, 1973, 1979; Barbault, 1976; Blair, 1960; Brown and Parker, 1984; Christiansen and Moll, 1973; Dunham, 1981; Feaver, 1977;

Fitch, 1956, 1958, 1960, 1963a, b, 1965, 1975; Gregory, 1977; Moll and Legler, 1971; Moll, 1973; Parker and Brown, 1980; Prestt, 1971; Plummer, 1985; Ruby and Dunham, 1984; Smith, 1981; Spellerberg and Phelps, 1977; Swingland and Coe, 1978; Tinkle, 1960, 1967, 1972, 1973, 1976; Tinkle and Ballinger, 1972; Tinkle and Dunham, 1983, 1986; Turner et al., 1970; Van Devender, 1982; Vinegar, 1975a, b). Other maturational changes in the female reproductive tract include enlargement and color changes of the oviducts (e.g., Webb, 1961; Timken, 1968; Mosimann and Bider, 1960).

Reproductive senescence has not yet become clearly established for turtles or squamates (Gibbons, 1976; but see Swingland and Coe, 1978). The absence of enlarged follicles in a mature-sized individual may indicate senescence or merely skipping reproduction in a particular year as with biennially reproducing species (e.g., most viperids, Dunham et al., this volume). Evidence of reproductive senescence has been found in some turtles (*Emydoidea blandingii*, Gibbons, 1968c; *Deirochelys reticularia*, Gibbons, 1969; and *Pseudemys scripta*, Cagle, 1944c; but see Moll and Legler, 1971). No indication of senescence has been observed for other testudines (*Terrapene ornata*, Legler, 1960; *Graptemys pulchra*, Shealy, 1976; or *Chrysemys picta*, Wilbur, 1975a). Convincing evidence of reproductive senescence is nonexistent in squamates.

3. GONADAL CYCLES

The study of the gonadal cycles can yield valuable demographic information on the timing of reproduction, the occurrence of senescence, the regularity of breeding cycles, and the number of clutches produced per season (Licht et al., 1970; Moll, 1979). This information and similar data are often difficult to obtain using other methods.

Seasonal fluctuation in gonad size is usually expressed as a change in linear measurement or mass. Mass probably represents a superior index of size change, since it is not subject to the inaccuracies inherent in the comparison of lengths and widths of irregularly-shaped organs. Gonads should be weighed or measured prior to preservation, which results in some shrinkage (Legler, 1960; Vitt et al., 1985).

In demographic studies, the data of relevance concerning testicular cycles are those allowing estimation of age at which sexual maturity is attained, length of the reproductive lifespan (if reproductive senescence occurs), and seasonal periodicity of reproductive activities. These traits vary greatly within and among species of squamates (reviews in Dunham and Miles, 1985; Dunham et al., this volume) and general patterns will not be described here.

a. The Testicular Cycle

Testicular cycles can indicate the attainment of sexual maturity and senescence. In addition, the onset of spermatogenesis indicates the end of the breeding season in some species of turtles in which spermatogenesis follows a postnuptual pattern (Lofts, 1969).

Standard histological techniques are employed in the study of testicular cycles. Due to the relatively large size of maturing ovarian follicles, ovarian cycles can be monitored simply by measuring and counting ovarian follicles. Testes and epididymides are usually fixed in Bouin's fluid or other formaldehyde-based fixative. The tissue is then embedded in paraffin, sectioned between 4 μ and 10 μ, and stained for cytological examination (e.g., Asplund and Lowe, 1964; Atland, 1951; Ernst, 1971b; Christiansen and Dunham, 1972; Christiansen and Moll, 1973; Krohmer and Aldridge, 1985a; Mayhew and Wright, 1970; Moll, 1973; Moll and Legler, 1971; Lofts and Boswell, 1961; Lofts and Tsui, 1977; Risley, 1938; White and Murphy, 1973).

An excellent discussion of chelonian testicular cycles is found in Moll (1979), which we summarize below. The male reproductive cycle of turtles consists of three phases: (1) reproduction, (2) postnuptual gonadal recrudescence, and (3) hibernation or gonadal quiescence in nonhibernating species (Lofts and Tsui, 1977). Testicular size displays a clear pattern of fluctuation in most studies. During reproduction, testis size is usually at or near the cyclic minimum. As gonadal recrudescence commences, testis size gradually increases until it reaches a maximum coinciding with the peak of spermatogenic activity. As hibernation begins or approaches, testis size decreases as sperm are emptied into the epididymides. Testes remain small until a new cycle of spermatogenic activity is initiated. Epididymal size and sperm content are generally maximal just prior to the period of mating, with a rapid decrease in size associated with the expenditure of sperm in mating. Epididymal size remains small throughout the period of spermatogenesis and does not increase until sperm are evacuated from the testes prior to or during hibernation.

Pronounced spermatogenic changes occur in the testes during the spermatogenic cycle. During reproduction, spermatic tubules are regressed and inactive, with the lumina much reduced or occluded by Sertoli cells. During spermatogenic recrudescence, the tubules increase in diameter and a proliferation of primary and secondary spermatocytes, spermatids, and sperm occurs. Sertoli cells become less numerous. During hibernation, the spermatogenic tubules decrease in size as sperm is evacuated into the epididymides; only spermatogonia and newly proliferating Sertoli cells are now obvious within the tubules.

Studies of testudinean testicular cycles supporting the general pattern outlined above include Risley (1938), Atland (1951), Legler (1960), Lofts and Boswell (1961), Gibbons (1968a), Moll and Legler (1971), Christiansen and Dunham (1972), Christiansen and Moll (1973), Moll (1973), Mahmoud and Klicka (1972), White and Murphy (1973), Brown (1974), Shealy (1976), and Lofts and Tsui (1977). The only clear exception to this pattern has been reported in *Chrysemys picta* (Ernst, 1971b). Testicular size remained relatively large during hibernation, only becoming smaller following emergence from hibernation in the spring. Studies describing testicular cycles of squamates and methods for studying them include Asplund and Lowe (1964), Krohmer and Aldridge (1985a), and Mayhew and Wright (1970).

b. The Ovarian Cycle

The study of ovarian cycles allows estimation of age at which sexual maturity is attained, length of the reproductive lifespan, periodicity of reproductive activities, and age-specific clutch (brood) size and frequency. Commonly studied variables include seasonal variation in ovarian weight or size, the sequence of vitellogenesis (by the size and number of ovarian follicles and oviductal eggs), and the occurrence and significance of follicular atresia and corpora lutea. These traits vary greatly within and among species of squamates and will not be reviewed here. Patterns of variation and covariation among these traits in squamates are reviewed elsewhere (Dunham and Miles, 1985; and Dunham et al., this volume). Studies in which ovarian cycles of squamates have been described and which contain methods for studying them include Aldridge (1979), Krohmer and Aldridge (1985b), Goldberg (1970, 1971, 1975, 1976), Goldberg and Bezy (1974), Goldberg and Lowe (1966), and many others.

Ovarian cycles of turtles are reviewed by Moll (1979). Fluctuations in ovarian size and weight follow a clearly defined pattern with respect to the sequence of follicular development. Ovarian size gradually increases concurrently with follicular enlargement. During quiescent periods of follicular development, as in hibernation in *Chrysemys picta* (Moll, 1973), the increase in ovarian size also ceases. Examples of studies concerned with seasonal change in ovarian size include Atland (1951), Legler (1960), Ernst (1971b), Moll (1973), Bourn (1977), and Swingland and Coe (1978). However, no seasonal variation in ovarian size was detected in *Macroclemys temminckii* (Dobie, 1971).

The relative length of the ovarian cycle tends to be compressed in boreal populations (e.g., Powell, 1967) and is either extended or continuous for some tropical species (e.g., Moll and Legler, 1971). Ovarian cycles of *Terrapene coahuila* in Mexico are intermediate in length compared to those of boreal and tropical cycles (Brown, 1974). Ovarian cycles of tropical species in general are poorly known, and are in need of further study.

Enlargement of follicles destined for the second or third clutches of a season can occur concurrently with the enlargement and ovulation of the first clutch (e.g., Shealy, 1976). The presence of multiple size classes of ovarian follicles may indicate the production of more than one clutch per season (e.g., Moll and Legler, 1971; Moll, 1973; Christiansen and Moll, 1973; Wilbur, 1975a; Swingland and Coe, 1978), or it may simply be a foreshadowing of the follicles to be ovulated as single clutches in future seasons (e.g., Dobie, 1971; Ernst, 1971b). The fate of enlarged follicles at the end of the nesting season is frequently unclear. Such enlarged follicles may be oviposited during the next breeding season or resorbed (Powell, 1967). Studies of follicular atresia in turtles include Atland (1951), Legler (1960), Webb (1961), Tinkle (1961), Milstead and Tinkle (1967), Powell (1967), Dobie (1971), Moll and Legler (1971), Christiansen and Dunham (1972), Christiansen and Moll (1973), Brown (1974), Shealy (1976), Bourn (1977), and Swingland and Coe (1978).

Ovulation of mature follicles results in the production of corpora lutea, which are often of use in the indirect determination of clutch size and the number of clutches produced per season. Corpora lutea are short-lived in turtles, and often disappear completely within several weeks of ovulation. Corpora lutea are not known to be retained from one year to the next. The occurrence of corpora lutea in turtles has been discussed by Atland (1951), Legler (1960), Tinkle (1961), Powell (1967), Ernst (1971b), Moll and Legler (1971), Christiansen and Dunham (1972), Mahmoud and Klicka (1972), Moll (1973), White and Murphy (1973), Brown (1974), Shealy (1976), Bourn (1977), Cyrus et al. (1978), and Congdon and Tinkle (1982).

Following ovulation, eggs remain in the oviducts for varying lengths of time. Under periods of stress, such as captivity, eggs may be retained for inordinately long periods (Cagle and Tihen, 1948; Cagle, 1950). This phenomenon casts considerable doubt on the general validity of clutch size estimates based on the observation of captive turtles. Observations made on dissected turtles and turtles observed nesting in the field are often sufficient for delimitation of the nesting season (e.g., Cagle, 1950). Accounts of the ovarian cycles of turtles include Risley (1938), Atland (1951), Legler (1960), Tinkle (1961), Powell (1967), Ernst (1971b), Moll and Legler (1971), Mahmoud and Klicka (1972), Christiansen and Dunham (1972), Christiansen and Moll (1973), Moll (1973), White and Murphy (1973), Brown (1974), Shealy (1976), Bourn (1977), and Congdon and Tinkle (1982). Ovulation can be induced with oxytocin (Ewert and Legler, 1978).

4. CLUTCH SIZE

Clutch size of female reptiles may be considered conveniently on three levels. Primary clutch size is the number of enlarged, yolked preovarian follicles that are likely to be ovulated in a single bout of nesting. Secondary clutch size represents the number of enlarged follicles that are actually ovulated. Tertiary clutch size represents the number of fertile eggs in the nest. In some instances any one of these may be an accurate estimate of the other two, but often the distinction between these classifications is nontrivial. Tertiary clutch size is the valid parameter to employ in the estimation of m_x, and the substitution of primary or secondary clutch size must be independently justified.

Primary clutch size is often estimated by a count of enlarged ovarian follicles that would presumably be ovulated at the next nesting opportunity. Several different estimates of clutch size (counts of enlarged and preovulatory follicles, corpora lutea, oviductal eggs, and eggs within the nest) are not significantly different in *Chrysemys picta* (Moll, 1973). Similarly, several clutch size estimates (counts of follicles, corpora lutea, and oviductal eggs) were similar for *Kinosternon flavescens* (Christiansen and Dunham, 1972). In contrast, follicle counts and other measures sometimes yield disparate estimates of clutch size (Webb, 1961; Bourn, 1977; Shealy, 1976). However, clutch size estimates based on mean ovarian follicle counts can frequently be corrected by subtracting the mean number of atretic follicles from the initial estimates (White and Murphy, 1973). Clearly, the presence of a significant level of follicular atresia, the retention of follicles over more than one reproductive season, or the division of enlarged follicles into multiple clutches may result in erroneous estimates of clutch size based on counts of enlarged follicles (Swingland and Coe, 1978, 1979). Examples of other studies that have employed follicle counts in the estimation of clutch size include Cagle (1952), Barton and Price (1955), Tinkle (1958), Legler (1963, 1966), Gibbons (1969), and Legler and Webb (1970).

Secondary clutch size is normally estimated by counting the number of eggs in nests, in the oviduct, or the corpora lutea. In turtles, estimation of secondary clutch size by counts of eggs in nests or by X-radiography (Gibbons and Greene, 1979) is probably ideal; but, unless

MARK–RECAPTURE ESTIMATES OF POPULATION PARAMETERS 361

the investigator is studying a species that nests conspicuously, nesting females will not be captured with their clutches, and valuable data on the relationships among female size, age, and clutch size will go unrecorded. Counts of corpora lutea and oviductal eggs are probably sound estimates of secondary clutch size, as their validity as clutch size estimates rests only on the assumption that all eggs ovulated at a given time are deposited in the nest (but see Congdon and Tinkle, 1982). Fresh sets of corpora lutea may be readily distinguished from older sets (e.g., Legler, 1960; Moll and Legler, 1971; Moll, 1973) and there is generally a good correlation between counts of corpora lutea and oviductal eggs (Legler, 1960). However, corpora lutea fade rapidly in many species (Powell, 1967), which limits their usefulness. Moreover, counts of corpora lutea or oviductal eggs are restricted to females found dead in the population under study, or to females obtained from nearby populations. These and related pitfalls in using counts of corpora lutea or oviductal eggs (in the absence of X-ray techniques) are discussed by Gibbons (1967), Gibbons and Tinkle (1969), and Ruby and Dunham (1984). Another complicating factor arises if females divide their complement of eggs between more than one nest per nesting excursion (e.g., *Trionyx muticus*, Fitch and Plummer, 1975). Notable exceptions to the problems of obtaining clutch size–female size data from nesting females are the many studies of large, conspicuously nesting chelonid and dermochelid turtles (e.g., Caldwell et al., 1959a; Bustard, 1972). Turtle studies using corpora lutea or oviductal egg counts as estimates of clutch size include Barton and Price (1955), Bourn (1977), Cagle (1944c), Christiansen and Dunham (1972), Dobie (1971), Gibbons (1969), Legler (1960), Moll (1973), Moll and Legler (1971), Powell (1967), Tinkle (1961), Wilbur (1975a), Webb (1961, 1962), and White and Murphy (1973).

Examples of turtle studies employing counts of eggs in nests for the estimation of secondary clutch size include Arndt (1977), Baldwin and Lofton (1959), Bourn (1977), Cagle (1950), Ernst (1970), Fitch and Plummer (1975), Moll (1973), Moll and Legler (1971), Taylor (1935), Whillans and Crossman (1977), and Wilbur (1975a).

In demographic studies of squamates, estimates of secondary clutch size, derived from counts of corpora lutea or oviductal eggs, are almost always the method used to infer age specific fecundity. Examples of lizard studies that have used this method include Ballinger (1973, 1974, 1979), Ballinger and Congdon (1981), Ballinger and Hipp (1985), Ballinger et al. (1981, 1972), Barbault (1976), Blair (1960), Burrage (1973, 1974), Dunham (1980, 1981, 1982), Fitch (1954, 1956, 1958), Goldberg and Robinson (1979), Mayhew (1965, 1966a, 1966b, 1971), Medica and Turner (1976), Ruby and Dunham (1984), Smith (1981), Tinkle (1967,

1972, 1973, 1976), Tinkle and Ballinger (1972), Tinkle and Dunham (1983, 1986), Turner et al. (1969, 1970), Van Devender (1982), Vinegar (1975a, b), Vitt (1973, 1982a, b, 1983a, b), Vitt and Goldberg (1983), Vitt and Lacher (1981), and Vitt et al. (1978). Examples of studies using this method to obtain data for inferring age-specific clutch size in snakes include Brown and Parker (1984), Clark (1970), Feaver (1977), Fitch (1960, 1963a, b, 1965, 1975), Gannon and Secoy (1984), Gibbons (1972), Gregory (1977), Parker and Brown (1974a, 1980), Plummer (1984), Semlitsch et al. (1981), Semlitsch and Moran (1984), and Tinkle (1960, 1962).

Tertiary clutch size (the number of fertile eggs deposited by a female) may be identical to or very near the secondary clutch size for many species; however, there are virtually no data on the frequency of infertile eggs in the clutches of oviparous squamates. Many turtle species produce infertile eggs: examples of this phenomenon are known for *Dermochelys coriacea* (e.g., Deraniyagala, 1939; Carr and Ogren, 1959; Pritchard, 1969, 1971; Anders and Schoelkopf, 1981) and *Caretta caretta* (e.g., LeBuff and Beatty, 1971). Often clutch size can be easily corrected for the occurrence of infertile eggs, because infertile eggs are frequently smaller than fertile eggs and may be yolkless. Estimates of infertility based on the number of hatchlings or embryos found per nest may confound fertility with early embryonic death in demographic calculations. Estimates of fertility based on artificial incubation of eggs may be of questionable value because rotation of the developing egg may result in increased embryonic mortality (Pritchard, 1969; Bustard, 1972). However, artificial incubation may impose no additional mortality on embryos of *Chelonia mydas* (Carr and Hirth, 1962).

5. AGE, BODY SIZE AND CLUTCH SIZE RELATIONSHIPS

It is important to recognize and elucidate any characters of reproductive females such as age, weight, or body size that are correlated with clutch size or frequency. An increase in clutch size or frequency with body size could imply that older females produce more eggs per time and the m_x schedules should reflect such effects.

Studies of turtles that have demonstrated or suggested a correlation between female size and clutch size include Cagle (1944c, 1950), Gibbons (1970d), Moll and Legler (1971), and Congdon and Gibbons (1983) for *Pseudemys scripta*; Brown (1974) for *Terrapene coahuila*; Tinkle (1961) and Gibbons (1970a) for *Sternotherus odoratus*; Cahn (1937) for *Graptemys geographica* and *Trionyx muticus*; Yntema (1970) for *Chelydra serpentina*; Dobie (1971) for *Macroclemys temminckii*; Carr (1967), Bustard (1972),

Simon (1975), and Simon and Parks (1976) for *Chelonia mydas*, and Iverson (1977) and Gibbons (1982) for various species of North American turtles. Species for which no correlation between clutch size and body size has been observed include *Chrysemys picta* (Cagle, 1954), *Terrapene nelsoni* (Milstead and Tinkle, 1967), and *Caretta caretta* (Caldwell et al., 1959b). Gibbons and Tinkle (1969) found no correlation between clutch size and body size within three separate populations of *Chrysemys picta*, but observed a correlation of mean clutch size with mean body size among populations. Such correlations are discussed in detail by Wilbur and Morin (this volume).

In most demographic studies of squamate populations, age-specific fecundity relationships are generated from regression models relating clutch size to some measure of body size (usually snout–vent length or mass). The data for these models are generally derived from destructive sampling of females taken from near the study population. Occasionally more than one size-related variable may be included in the model used to predict clutch size. For example, Smith (1977) used a polynomial model relating clutch size to both snout–vent length and mass in his study of *Sceloporus virgatus* and *Urosaurus ornatus*. In a surprising number of cases in the literature on squamate demography, there is significant serial autocorrelation of the residuals about the regression line relating clutch size to body size. In such cases, the model may seriously over- or underestimate size-specific (and, hence, age-specific) clutch size. This may seriously bias estimates of egg or juvenile mortality. In many cases the regression models differ significantly among different clutches produced within a given year as well as among years in which resource availability differs (e.g., Dunham, 1980, 1981). These sources of variation must be considered in developing models that predict clutch size as a function of size or age.

Once an appropriate predictive relationship between body size and clutch size has been developed, the total egg production in any given clutch can then be estimated from the size frequency distribution of mature females in the population at the time of parturition or oviposition. This provides an indirect estimate of the size of the newborn cohort that is used in estimation of the l_x schedule. Finally, if a size–age relationship is available, age-specific fecundity (m_x) is estimated as one-half the expected clutch size of females of age x for a sexually reproducing species, assuming a 1:1 sex ratio in eggs (but see Section III.C), or as the expected clutch size of a female of age x in parthenogenetic species. Studies of squamate demography using this approach include Ballinger (1973, 1974, 1979), Ballinger et al. (1972, 1981), Blair (1960), Brown and Parker (1984), Dunham (1981), Feaver

(1977), Gregory (1977), Parker and Brown (1974a, 1980), Plummer (1984), Ruby and Dunham (1984), Smith (1981), Tinkle (1967, 1972, 1973, 1976), Tinkle and Ballinger (1972), Tinkle and Dunham (1986), Turner et al. (1969, 1970), Van Devender (1982), Vinegar (1975a, b), and Zweifel and Lowe (1966).

Relative clutch mass (RCM), and index of a female's reproductive investment, has attracted considerable attention in studies of reptilian life histories (Tinkle and Hadley, 1975; Vitt and Congdon, 1978; Seigel and Fitch, 1984). Nonetheless, as an estimate of reproductive investment, RCM suffers from serious methodological and analytical problems, which are described below, as well as certain technical problems (see Cuellar, 1984; Vitt et al., 1985).

RCM is typically computed as the ratio of the mass of the clutch (litter) to the mass of a near-term gravid female plus that of her clutch. This method of calculating RCM is inappropriate because clutch mass is included in both numerator and denominator (Shine, 1980; Atchley et al., 1976). Unfortunately, most published RCM estimates are based on this method.

Moreover, even if RCM is computed with only the mass of the female in the denominator, RCM is a ratio, and may be prone to statistical problems associated with ratios (Sokal and Rohlf, 1981; Atchley et al., 1976). Perhaps the most serious problem results because clutch mass and female mass do not scale isometrically (Seigel and Fitch, 1984). Therefore, any comparison of RCMs between reptiles of different body sizes will be necessarily confounded by the difference in body size. Hence an observed difference in RCM (or the lack thereof) might merely reflect the influence of size rather than of biology.

Several alternatives are possible. When comparing two populations that overlap in body size, analysis of covariance (e.g., Seigel and Fitch, 1984) is an appropriate technique for testing for differences in size-specific clutch mass. Regressions of appropriately transformed (logarithmic transformations are usually appropriate) clutch mass on nongravid female mass or SVL may be compared for significant differences in intercept. The population with the higher intercept will have the higher reproductive investment (if the slopes of these regressions are homogeneous). Alternatively, one can either analyze the residuals about the pooled regression or standardize female size to a common value. All of these techniques may be inappropriate if the groups being compared differ greatly in size.

In any case, the continued calculation of RCM as a ratio is inadvisable. Much more useful would be regression equations of (appropriately transformed) clutch mass versus (nongravid) female mass along with summary statistics of average clutch and female masses. However, because virtually all available estimates of RCM involve ratios, comparative analyses of RCM (e.g., Dunham et al., this volume) should be interpreted with caution due to potential confounding effects of body size.

6. MULTIPLE CLUTCHES

The number of clutches deposited in a nesting season by a female of given size or age is a crucial but difficult parameter to estimate for many species.

a. Turtles

Species for which multiple clutches are known or suspected are reviewed in Moll and Legler (1971) and Moll (1973). Ideally, the existence of multiple clutches could be established by observing the actual number of times females nest each season. This approach has been used successfully in marine turtles (Pritchard 1969, 1971 for *Dermochelys coriacea*; Caldwell, 1962; LeBuff and Beatty, 1971; Bustard, 1972; Limpus, 1973; LeBuff, 1974 for *Caretta caretta*; Carr and Giovanolli, 1957; Harrisson, 1956; Hendrickson, 1958; Carr and Ogren, 1960; Carr and Hirth, 1962; Carr, 1967; Carr and Carr, 1970a, b; Limpus, 1971; Bustard, 1972; Simon and Parkes, 1976 for *Chelonia mydas*; and Carr, 1963; Pritchard, 1969; Bustard, 1972; Pritchard and Marquez, 1973 for *Lepidochelys* sp.). The success of these efforts has doubtless been due not only to diligent observation, but also to the large size and conspicuous nesting habits of marine turtles. Equivalent information can be obtained with drift fences that catch pond turtles as they search for nesting sites (Congdon et al., 1983; Tinkle et al., 1981).

Multiple nesting can also be demonstrated indirectly (e.g., Moll and Legler, 1971; Christiansen and Dunham, 1972; Moll, 1973; Swingland and Coe, 1978). Because corpora lutea regress rapidly following ovulation and are not retained from year to year, the presence of sets of different ages implies multiple clutches. However, the rapid regression of corpora lutea often leaves only two sets discernible at any time, and the regressed corpora lutea of earlier clutches will be unnoticed (Congdon and Tinkle, 1982). Examples of studies utilizing corpora lutea in determination of clutch numbers include Tinkle (1958) for *Sternotherus*, Legler (1960) for *Terrapene ornata*, Moll and Legler (1971) for *Pseudemys scripta*, and Moll (1973) for *Chrysemys picta*.

The presence of a set of enlarged preovulatory ovarian follicles, plus a set or sets of corpora lutea is also evidence of multiple clutches.

However, this approach requires that the enlarged follicles are present at a time in the nesting season when ovulation is still probable and they are not ultimately reabsorbed. In *Pseudemys scripta* enlarged preovulatory follicles are not retained from one season to the next nor are they reabsorbed (Moll and Legler, 1971). Clutch number could therefore be estimated by counting distinct sets of corpora lutea, and dividing the remaining number of enlarged follicles by the maximum clutch size (Moll and Legler, 1971; see also Shealy, 1976). Other examples of studies estimating clutch number from ovarian follicles and corpora lutea include Tinkle (1958) for *Sternotherus* and Brown (1974) for *Terrapene coahuila*. A similar technique involves the simultaneous presence of oviductal eggs and enlarged follicles for the determination of multiple clutch numbers (e.g., Brown, 1974).

Follicle size-class analysis may yield some insight as to whether multiple clutches occur. Whether size classes represent discrete clutches within or among years will affect the accuracy of this form of inference. Examples of studies that have employed follicle size class analysis in the inference of the number of clutches produced per season include Cagle (1944c) and Gibbons (1970d) for *Pseudemys scripta*, Einem (1956) for *Kinosternon bauri*, Gibbons (1970a) for *Sternotherus odoratus*, and Moll (1973) for *Chrysemys picta*.

Other forms of inference may occasionally be of use in the determination of the production of multiple clutches. Repeated palpation of marked females may yield evidence of multiple nesting (Gibbons, 1969). Marked females returning to the pond on more than one occasion in the nesting season with swollen cloacae and dirt on their shells suggests multiple nesting (Wilbur, 1975a). Richmond suggested that a multimodal distribution of nesting dates and an extended nesting season may be circumstantial evidence for the occurrence of multiple clutches (Richmond, 1945). Sudden decreases in body mass are sometimes used as evidence of clutch deposition (Turner et al., 1984).

The relationship between female size or age and the number of clutches produced each season remains uncertain for most turtles. The number of clutches produced is not correlated with the size of the female in *Chelonia mydas* (Hendrickson, 1958), but is in many other species (e.g., Moll and Legler, 1971; Shealy, 1976).

Some investigators have observed an inverse correlation between clutch size and the sequence in which the clutches are deposited during the nesting season. An understanding of this relationship, should it exist generally, would facilitate the construction of accurate m_x schedules. Studies suggesting this relationship include Mast (1911) and LeBuff and Beatty (1971) for *Caretta caretta*, Carr and Hirth (1962) for *Chelonia mydas*, Hildebrand (1963) for *Lepidochelys kempii*, Legler (1960) for *Terrapene ornata*, Grant (1936) for *Pseudemys scripta*, Fitch and Plummer (1975) for *Trionyx muticus*, and Brown (1974) for *Terrapene coahuila*.

No clear evidence for multiple clutches has been observed in some species (e.g., *Sternotherus odoratus*, Tinkle, 1961; *Terrapene nelsoni*, Milstead and Tinkle, 1967; *Chelydra osceola*, Iverson, 1977; *Gopherus polyphemus*, Iverson, 1980). However, multiple clutches are probably more common than usually realized, but they are difficult to detect (cf., Moll and Legler, 1971).

The timing and regularity of female reproductive cycles is poorly known for most turtle species, with the exception of marine turtles. Some turtles may reproduce on an annual cycle. Others may reproduce regularly but follow a 2–3-year cycle. It is also becoming increasingly well known that a year of poor feeding or a heavy parasite load could cause females to reproduce irregularly.

Reproductive periodicity has been the subject of intense study in marine turtles. The only marine turtles with regular annual reproduction are *Lepidochelys kempii* (Carr, 1967; Pritchard and Marquez, 1973) and *Lepidochelys olivacea* (Pritchard, 1969). Other species of marine turtles tend to follow a 2–4-year internesting cycle. A 3-year cycle has been proposed for *Eretmochelys imbricata* (Carr et al., 1966). *Chelonia mydas* may follow a 2–4-year cycle depending on the population and the individual turtle (Harrisson, 1956; Carr and Hirth, 1962; Carr, 1967; Carr and Carr, 1970a; Carr and Goodman, 1970). Similarly, *Caretta caretta* may nest on a 1–3-year internesting cycle (Caldwell, 1962; Bustard, 1972; Limpus, 1973; LeBuff, 1974).

Until recently, reproduction in freshwater turtles was thought to be annual for mature females. However, the regular reproduction by only a portion of the mature females could seriously bias life table analyses, as this would lead to overestimates of survival in the zero-age class. Irregular reproduction is now documented for several species (Coe et al., 1979; Congdon and Tinkle, 1982; Congdon et al., 1983; Frazer, 1984; Gibbons, 1983; Gibbons et al., 1983; Tinkle et al., 1981; Swingland, 1977; Swingland and Coe, 1978). Obviously the fraction of females that do not reproduce at any given time must be accounted for in constructing fecundity schedules.

b. Squamates

In squamates, accurate estimates of the number of clutches produced per season require frequent capture and palpation of marked individuals (as in Turner et al., 1970; Dunham, 1981). Few studies meet this strict criterion. Lacking such data, brood frequency is frequently estimated by dividing the time required for the production of one clutch by the length of the active season. This procedure generates erroneous estimates if the time required to produce a single clutch varies significantly among clutches (Turner et al., 1970) or if the reproductive season is much shorter than the active season. Unfortunately, literature estimates of clutch (brood) frequency within a given year lack standardization and reliability.

In squamates, variation in fertility cycles is marked and frequently correlated with family level taxonomy (see reviews in Dunham and Miles 1985; Dunham et al., this volume). For example, viperid snakes usually exhibit a biennial reproductive periodicity and, in studies of the demography of such species, the proportion of the mature female population that reproduce in a given year must be estimated (e.g., Tinkle, 1962). This proportion can generally be obtained from dissection of samples taken from near the population of interest. The problem is identical to that of determining clutch frequency for individuals within a given year and the methods are the same. In addition there is often significant latitudinal variation in reproductive periodicity that is unrelated to family level taxonomy (e.g., see review in Licht and Gorman, 1970).

The method developed by Gibbons and Greene (1979) of radiographing female turtles at each capture deserves greater attention by ecologists studying squamate populations. Their method directly reveals clutch size for each clutch as well as clutch frequency. Pilot studies (Dunham and Miles, unpubl.) show the technique is feasible for small iguanid lizards. Development of this methodology should be given priority.

IV. SUMMARY AND CONCLUSIONS

Life tables are important to population biology because they permit the analysis of reproductive and life history adaptations as well as the prediction of population dynamics. Adequate tests of life history theory and theories of population regulation are impossible without life table data. Life tables are also important to applied ecology because they allow derivation of sound management programs for commercially important species (e.g., large marine turtles) and for rare and endangered species. Unfortunately, adequate life tables are currently available for only one population of turtle (*Chrysemys picta*; see Wilbur and Morin, this volume), fewer than a dozen snakes, and fewer than 30 lizard populations, most of which are iguanids (see Dunham et al., this volume). Data on the nature and magnitude of variation in life history characters and demography both within and among populations of reptiles are essential, but these data will only be produced by detailed, long-term studies (Tinkle, 1979). Comprehensive understanding of reptilian population biology must await the collection of key life history data (complete age structures and age-specific survival and fecundity schedules) from a much larger and more diverse sample of reptiles.

In this chapter we have described useful methods for the study of demography and life history variation in reptile populations. Although we strongly advocate long-term, intensive studies, many of the methods described are suitable for use in short-term studies.

ACKNOWLEDGMENTS

We thank Steve Beaupre, Carl Gans, Ray Huey, Karen Overall, Tom Schoener, Ian Swingland, George Zug, and an anonymous reviewer for many valuable comments and suggestions for improving the manuscript.

REFERENCES

Agassiz, L. (1857). *Contributions to the Natural History of the United States*. Little, Brown, Boston. Volume 2, pp. 451–641 27 (34) plates.

Aldridge, R. D. (1979). Female reproductive cycles of the snakes *Arizona elegans* and *Crotalus viridis*. Herpetologica 35, 256–261.

Allen, E. R. (1938). Notes on the feeding and egg-laying habits of the *Pseudemys*. Proc. Fla. Acad. Sci. 3, 105–108.

Anders, G. J. R. and Schoelkopf, R. C. (1981). Reproductive data on a female leatherback turtle, *Dermochelys coriacea*, stranded in New Jersey. Copeia 1982, 181–183.

Andrews, R. M. (1976). Growth rate in island and mainland anoline lizards. Copeia 1976, 477–482.

Andrews, R. M. (1982). Patterns of growth in reptiles. In *Biology of the Reptilia*. (C. Gans and F. H. Pough, eds.). Academic Press, London. Volume 13, pp. 273–320.

Andrews, R. M., Rand, A. S. and Guerrero, S. (1983). Seasonal and spatial variation in the annual cycle of a tropical lizard. In *Advances in Herpetology and Evolutionary Biology. Essays in Honor of Ernest E. Williams*. (A. G. J. Rhodin and K. Miyata, eds.). Museum of Comparative Zoology, Harvard University, pp. 441–454.

Arndt, R. G. (1977). Notes on the natural history of the bog turtle, *Clemmys muhlenbergi* (Schoepff), in Delaware. Chesapeake Sci. 18, 67–76.

Arndt, R. G. and Potter, W. A. (1973). A population of the map turtle, *Graptemys geographica*, in the Delaware river, Pennsylvania, J. Herpetol. 7, 375–377.

Altland, P. D. (1951). Observations on the structure of reproductive organs of the box turtle. J. Morphol. 89, 599–616.

Asplund, K. K. and Lowe, C. H. (1964). Reproductive cycles of the iguanid lizards *Urosaurus ornatus* and *Uta stansburiana* in southeastern Arizona. J. Morphol. 115, 27–34.

Atchley, W. R., Gaskins, C. T. and Anderson, D. (1976). Statistical properties of ratios. I. Empirical results. Syst. Zool. 25, 137–148.

Auffenberg, W. (1981). *The Behavioral Ecology of the Komodo Monitor.* University of Florida Presses, Gainesville.

Auffenberg, W. and Weaver, W. G. (1969). *Gopherus berlandieri* in southeastern Texas. Bull. Fla. State Mus. 13, 141–203.

Bailey, N. J. T. (1951). On estimating the size of mobile populations from recapture data. Biometrika 38, 293–306.

Bailey, N. J. T. (1952). Improvements in the interpretation of recapture data. J. Anim. Ecol. 21, 120–127.

Baldwin, W. P., Jr., and Lofton, J. P., Jr. (1959). III. The loggerhead turtles of Cape Romain, South Carolina. Bull. Fla. State Mus. Biol. Sci. 4, 319–348.

Ballinger, R. E. (1973). Comparative demography of two viviparous iguanid lizards (*Sceloporus jarrovi* and *Sceloporus poinsetti*). Ecology 54, 269–283.

Ballinger, R. E. (1974). Reproduction of the Texas horned lizard, *Phrynosoma cornutum*. Herpetologica 30, 321–327.

Ballinger, R. E. (1979). Intraspecific variation in demography and life history of the lizard, *Sceloporus jarrovi*, along an altitudinal gradient in southeastern Arizona. Ecology 60, 901–909.

Ballinger, R. E. (1983). Life history variations. In *Lizard Ecology. Studies of a Model Organism* (R. B. Huey, E. R. Pianka, and T. W. Schoener, eds.). Harvard University Press. Cambridge, MA, pp. 241–260.

Ballinger, R. E. and Congdon, J. D. (1981). Population ecology and life-history strategy of a montane lizard (*Sceloporus scalaris*) in southeastern Arizona. J. Nat. Hist. 24, 347–363.

Ballinger, R. E., Droge, D. L. and Jones, S. M. (1981). Reproduction in a Nebraska sandhills population of the northern prairie lizard *Sceloporus undulatus garmani*. Am. Midl. Nat. 106, 157–164.

Ballinger, R. E. and Hipp, T. G. (1985). Reproduction in the collared lizard *Crotaphytus collaris* in west central Texas. Copeia 1985, 976–980.

Ballinger, R. E., Tyler, E. D. and Tinkle, D. W. (1972). Reproductive ecology of a west Texas population of the greater earless lizard, *Cophosaurus texanus*. Am. Midl. Nat. 88, 419–428.

Banta, B. H. (1957). A simple trap for collecting desert reptiles. Herpetologica 13, 174–176.

Barbault, R. (1976). Population dynamics and reproductive patterns of three African skinks. Copeia 1976, 483–490.

Barton, A. J. and Price, J. W., Jr. (1955). Our knowledge of the bog-turtles, surveyed and augmented. Copeia 1955, 159–165.

Bayless, L. E. (1975). Population parameters for *Chrysemys picta* in a New York pond. Am. Midl. Nat. 93, 168–176.

Bell, R. and Richardson, J. I. (1970). An analysis of tag recoveries from loggerhead sea turtles (*Caretta caretta*) nesting on Little Cumberland Island, Georgia. Fla. Marine Res. Publ. 33, 20–24.

Bennett, D. H., Gibbons, J. W. and Franson, J. C. (1970). Terrestrial activity in aquatic turtles. Ecology 51, 738–740.

Bider, J. R. and Hoek, W. (1971). An efficient and apparently unbiased sampling technique for population studies of painted turtles. Herpetologica 27, 481–484.

Bjorndal, K. A. (1980). Demography of the breeding population of the green turtle, *Chelonia mydas*, at Tortuguero, Costa Rica. Copeia 1980, 525–530.

Blair, W. F. (1960). *The Rusty Lizard. A Population Study.* University of Texas Press, Austin.

REFERENCES

Blair, W. F. (1976). Some aspects of the biology of the ornate box turtle *Terrapene ornata*. Southwest. Nat. 21, 89–104.

Blanchard, F. N. and Finster, E. B. (1933). A method of marking living snakes for future recognition, with a discussion of some problems and results. Ecology 14, 334–347.

Bourn, D. (1976). The giant tortoise population of Aldabra (Cryptodira: Testudinidae). Part 1. Preliminary results. Zool. Afr. 11, 275–284.

Bourn, D. (1977). Reproductive study of the giant tortoises on Aldabra. J. Zool., Lond. 182, 27–38.

Bourn, D. and Coe, M. J. (1978). The size, structure, and distribution of the giant tortoise population of Aldabra. Phil. Trans. Roy. Soc., Lond. B. 282, 139–175.

Breckenridge, W. J. (1955). Observation on the life history of the soft-shelled turtle *Trionyx ferox*, with special reference to growth. Copeia 1955, 5–9.

Breder, R. B. (1927). Turtle trailing: A new technique for studying the life habits of certain Testudinata. Zoologica 9, 232–241.

Brisban, I. L., Ross, C. A., Downes, M. C., Staton, M. A. and Gammon, B. R. (1986). *A Bibliography of the American Alligator*. Savannah River National Environmental Research Park. SRO-NERP 13, 1–310.

Brooks, G. R., Jr. (1967). Population ecology of the ground skink, *Lygosoma laterale* (Say). Ecol. Monogr. 37, 72–87.

Brown, W. S. (1974). Ecology of the aquatic box turtle, *Terrapene coahuila* (Chelonia, Emydidae) in northern Mexico. Bull. Fla. St. Mus. Biol. Sci. 19, 1–67.

Brown, W. S., Gannon, V. P. J. and Secoy, D. M. (1984). Paint-marking the rattle of rattlesnakes. Herpetol. Rev. 15, 75–76.

Brown, W. S. and Parker, W. S. (1976). A ventral scale clipping system for permanently marking snakes (Reptilia, Serpentes). J. Herpetol. 10, 247–249.

Brown, W. S. and Parker, W. S. (1984). Growth, reproduction and demography of the racer, *Coluber constrictor mormon*, in northern Utah. In *Vertebrate Ecology and Systematics: A Tribute to Henry S. Fitch* (R. A. Seigel, L. E. Hunt, J. L. Knight, L. Malaret, and N. L. Zuschlag, eds.). Mus. Nat. Hist. Univ. Kansas Spec. Publs. Volume 10, pp. 13–40.

Buffrenil, V. de. (1980). Mise en évidence de l'incidence des conditions de milieu sur la croissance de *Crocodylus siamensis* (Schneider, 1801) et valeur des marques de croissance squelettiques pour l'évaluation de l'âge individuel. Arch. Zool. Exp. Gén. 12, 63–76.

Bull, J. J. (1980). Sex determination in reptiles. Quart. Rev. Biol. 55, 3–21.

Bull, J. J. and Vogt, R. C. (1979). Temperature-dependent sex determination in turtles. Science 206, 1186–1188.

Bull, J. J. and Vogt, R. C. (1981). Temperature-sensitive periods of sex determination in emydid turtles. J. Exp. Zool. 212, 435–444.

Bull, J. J., Vogt, R. C. and Bulmer, M. C. (1982). Heritability of sex ratio in turtles with environmental sex determination. Evolution 36, 333–341.

Burrage, B. R. (1973). Comparative ecology and behaviour of *Chamaeleo pumilus pumilus* (Gmelin) and *C. namaquensis* Smith (Sauria: Chamaeleonidae). Ann. S. Afr. Mus. 61, 1–158.

Burrage, B. R. (1974). Population structure in *Agama atra* and *Cordylus cordylus cordylus* in the vicinity of de Kelders, Cape Province. Ann. S. Afr. Mus. 66, 1–23.

Bury, R. B. and Luckenbach, R. A. (1977). Censusing desert tortoise populations using a quadrat and grid location system. In *Desert Tortoise Council Proceedings of Second Symposium 1977* (M. Trotter and C. G. Jackson, eds.), pp. 169–178.

Bustard, H. R. (1971). A population study of the eyed gecko, *Oedura ocellata* Boulenger, in northern New South Wales, Australia. Copeia 1971, 658–669.
Bustard, H. R. (1972). *Sea Turtles.* Taplinger, New York.
Bustard, H. R. (1979). Population dynamics of sea turtles. In *Turtles: Perspectives and Research* (M. Harless and H. Morlock, eds.). Wiley, New York, pp. 523–540.
Cagle, F. R. (1939). A system for marking turtles for future identification. Copeia 1939, 170–173.
Cagle, F. R. (1942). Turtle populations in southern Illinois. Copeia 1942, 155–162.
Cagle, F. R. (1944a). Home range, homing behavior, and migration in turtles. Misc. Publ. Mus. Zool. Univ. Mich. 61, 1–34.
Cagle, F. R. (1944b). A technique for obtaining turtle eggs for study. Copeia 1944, 60.
Cagle, F. R. (1944c). Sexual maturity in the turtle *Pseudemys scripta elegans*. Copeia 1944, 149–152.
Cagle, F. R. (1946). The growth of the slider turtle *Pseudemys scripta elegans*. Am. Midl. Nat. 36, 685–729.
Cagle, F. R. (1948). Sexual maturity in the male turtle *Pseudemys scripta troostii*. Copeia 1948, 108–111.
Cagle, F. R. (1950). The life history of the slider turtle *Pseudemys scripta troostii* (Holbrook). Ecol. Monogr. 20, 31–54.
Cagle, F. R. (1952). A Louisiana terrapin population (*Malaclemmys*). Copeia 1952, 74–76.
Cagle, F. R. (1953). The status of the turtle *Graptemys oculifera* (Baur.) Zoologica 38, 137–144.
Cagle, F. R. (1954). Observations on the life cycle of painted turtles (genus *Chrysemys*). Am. Midl. Nat. 52, 225–235.
Cagle, F. R. and Chaney, A. H. (1950). Turtle populations in Louisiana. Am. Midl. Nat. 43, 383–388.
Cagle, F. R. and Tihen, J. (1948). Retention of eggs by the turtle *Deirochelys reticularia*. Copeia 1948, 66.
Cahn, A. R. (1937). The turtles of Illinois. Illinois Biol. Monogr. 16, 1–218.
Caldwell, D. K. (1962). Comments on the nesting behavior of the Atlantic loggerhead sea turtles based primarily on tagging returns. Quart. J. Fla. Acad. Sci. 25, 287–302.
Caldwell, D. K., Berry, F. H., Carr, A. F. and Rogotzkie, R. A. (1959a). The Atlantic loggerhead sea turtle, *Caretta caretta caretta* (L.), in America. II. Multiple and group nesting by the Atlantic loggerhead turtle. Bull. Fla. St. Mus. Biol. Sci. 4, 309–318.
Caldwell, D. K., Carr, A. F. and Ogren, L. H. (1959b). The Atlantic loggerhead sea turtle, *Caretta caretta caretta* (L.), in America. I. Nesting and migration of the Atlantic loggerhead turtle. Bull. Fla. St. Mus. Biol. Sci. 4, 295–308.
Calstrom, D. and Edelstam, C. (1946). Methods of marking reptiles for identification after recapture. Nature 158, 748–749.
Campbell, H. W. and Cristman, S. P. (1982). Field techniques for herpetological community analysis. In *Herpetological Communities* (N. J. Scott, Jr. ed.). Wildlife Research Report No. 13. U. S. Fish and Wildlife Service. Washington, DC, pp. 193–200.
Carpenter, C. C. (1952). Comparative ecology of the common garter snake (*Thamnophis s. sirtalis*), the ribbon snake (*Thamnophis s. sauritus*), and Butler's garter snake in mixed populations. Ecol. Monogr. 22, 235–258.
Carpenter, C. C. (1955). Sounding turtles: A field locating technique. Herpetologica 11, 120.
Carr, A. and Giovannoli, L. (1957). The ecology and migrations of sea turtles. 2. Results of field work in Costa Rica, 1955. Am. Mus. Novitates 1835, 1–32.

REFERENCES

Carr, A. and Goodman, D. (1970). Ecologic implications of size and growth in *Chelonia*. Copeia 1970, 783–786.

Carr, A. and Hirth, H. (1962). The ecology and migrations of sea turtles. 5. Comparative features of isolated green turtle colonies. Am. Mus. Novitates 2091, 1–42.

Carr, A., Hirth, H. and Ogren, L. (1966). The ecology and migrations of sea turtles. 6. The hawks bill turtle in the Caribbean Sea. Am. Mus. Novitates 2248, 1–29.

Carr, A. F. (1952). *Handbook of Turtles*. Comstock, Ithaca.

Carr, A. F. (1963). Panspecific reproductive convergence in *Lepidochelys kempii*. Ergeb. Biol. 26, 298–303.

Carr, A. F. (1967). *So Excellent a Fishe*. Natural History Press, N. Y.

Carr, A. F. and Carr, M. H. (1970a). Modulated reproductive periodicity in *Chelonia*. Ecology 51, 335–337.

Carr, A. F. and Carr, M. H. (1970b). Recruitment and remigration in a green turtle nesting colony. Biol. Conserv. 2, 282–284.

Carr, A. F. and Ogren, L. (1959). The ecology and migrations of sea turtles. 3. *Dermochelys* in Costa Rica. Am. Mus. Novitates 1958, 1–29.

Carr, A. F. and Ogren, L. (1960). The ecology and migrations of sea turtles. 4. The green turtle in the Caribbean Sea. Bull. Am. Mus. Nat. Hist. 121, 1–48.

Carr, A. F., Jr., and Marchand, L. J. (1942). A new turtle from the Chipola River, Florida. Proc. New Engl. Zool. Club. 20, 95–100, pl. 14–15.

Castanet, J. (1974). Étude histologique des marques squelettiques des croissance chez *Vipera aspis* (L.) (Ophidia, Viperidae). Zool. Scripta 3, 137–151.

Castanet, J. (1978). Les marques de croissance osseuse comme indicateurs de l'âge chez les lézards. Acta Zool. 59, 35–48.

Castanet, J. and Cheylan, M. (1979). Les marques de croissance des os et des écailles comme indicateur de l'âge chez *Testudo hermanni* et *Testudo graeca* (Reptilia, Chelonia, Testudinidae). Can. J. Zool. 57, 1649–1665.

Castanet, J., Meunier, F. J. and de Ricqles, A. (1977). L'enregistrement de la croissance cyclique par le tissu osseux chez les vertébrés poikilothermes: Données comparatives et essai de synthèse. Bull. Biol. France Belg. 111, 183–202.

Castanet, J. and Roche, E. (1981). Determination de l'âge chez le lézard des murailes, *Lacerta muralis* (Laurenti, 1768) au moyen squelettochronologie. Rev. Suisse Zool. 88, 215–226.

Caughley, G. (1977). *The Analysis of Vertebrate Populations*. John Wiley, New York.

Chaney, A. and Smith, C. L. (1950). Methods for collecting map turtles. Copeia 1950, 323–324.

Chapman, D. G. (1951). Some applications of the hypergeometric distribution with applications to zoological sample censuses. Univ. Calif. Pub. Stat. 1, 131–160.

Christiansen, J. L. and Dunham, A. E. (1972). Reproduction of the yellow mud turtle (*Kinosternon flavescens flavescens*) in New Mexico. Herpetologica 28, 130–137.

Christiansen, J. L. and Moll, E. O. (1973). Latitudinal reproductive variation within a single subspecies of the painted turtle *Chrysemys picta belli*. Herpetologica 29, 152–163.

Clark, D. R., Jr. (1966). A funnel trap for small snakes. Trans. Kans. Acad. Sci. 69, 91–95.

Clark, D. R., Jr. (1970). Ecological study of the worm snake *Carphophis vermis* (Kennicott). Univ. Kansas Publ. Mus Nat. Hist. 19, 85–194.

Clark, D. R., Jr. (1971). Branding as a marking technique for amphibians and reptiles. Copeia 1971, 148–151.

Clark, R. F. (1965). An ethological study of the iguanid lizard genera *Callisaurus, Cophosaurus* and *Holbrookia*. Emporia State Res. Studies 13, 1–66.

Coe, M. J., Bourn, D. and Swingland, I. R. (1979). The biomass, production and carrying capacity of giant tortoises on Aldabra. Phil. Trans. Roy. Soc. London B. 286, 163–176.

Congdon, J. D. and Gibbons, J. W. (1983). Relationships of reproductive characteristics to body size in *Pseudemys scripta*. Herpetologica 39, 147–151.

Congdon, J. D. and Tinkle, D. W. (1982). Reproductive energetics of the painted turtle (*Chrysemys picta*). Herpetologica 38, 228–237.

Congdon, J. D., Tinkle, D. W., Breitenbach, G. L. and Van Loben Sels, R. C. (1983). Nesting behavior and hatching success in the turtle *Emydoidea blandingi*. Herpetologica 39, 417–429.

Cormack, R. M. (1968). The statistics of capture–recapture methods. Oceanogr. Mar. Biol. Ann. Rev. 6, 455–506.

Crouse, D. T. and Crowder, L. B. (1987). A stage-based population model for loggerhead sea turtles and implications for conservation. Ecology, in press.

Cuellar, O. (1984). Reproduction in a parthenogenetic lizard: With a discussion of optimal clutch size and a critique of the clutch weight/body weight ratio. Am. Midl. Nat. 111, 242–258.

Cyrus, R. V., Mahmoud, I. Y. and Klicka, J. (1978). Fine structure of the corpus luteum in the snapping turtle. *Chelydra serpentina*. Copeia 1978, 622–627.

Deevey, E. S., Jr. (1947). Life tables for natural populations of animals. Quart. Rev. Biol. 22, 283–314.

Deraniyagala, P. E. P. (1939). *The Tetrapod Reptiles of Ceylon. Vol. I. Testudinates and Crocodilians*. Dulau, London.

Dobie, J. L. (1971). Reproduction and growth in the alligator snapping turtle, *Macroclemmys temmincki* (Troost). Copeia 1971, 645–658.

Dunham, A. E. (1978). Food availability as a proximate factor influencing individual growth rates in the iguanid lizard *Sceloporus merriami*. Ecology 59, 770–778.

Dunham, A. E. (1980). An experimental study of interspecific competition between the iguanid lizards *Sceloporus merriami* and *Urosaurus ornatus*. Ecol. Monogr. 50, 309–330.

Dunham, A. E. (1981). Populations in a fluctuating environment: The comparative population ecology of *Sceloporus merriami* and *Urosaurus ornatus*. Misc. Publ. Univ. Mich. Mus. Zool. 158, 1–62.

Dunham, A. E. (1982). Demographic and life history variation among populations of the iguanid lizard *Urosaurus ornatus*: Implications for the study of life-history phenomena in lizards. Herpetologica 38, 208–221.

Dunham, A. E. and Miles, D. B. (1985). Patterns of covariation in life history traits of squamate reptiles: The effects of size and phylogeny reconsidered. Am. Nat. 126, 231–257.

Einem, G. E. (1956). Certain aspects of the natural history of the mud turtle, *Kinosternon bauri*. Copeia 1956, 186–188.

Ernst, C. H. (1970). Reproduction in *Clemmys guttata*. Herpetologica 26, 228–232.

Ernst, C. H. (1971a). Sexual cycles and maturity of the turtle *Chrysemys picta*. Biol. Bull. 140, 191–200.

Ernst, C. H. (1971b). Population dynamics and activity cycles of *Chrysemys picta* in southeastern Pennsylvania. J. Herpetol. 5, 151–160.

Ernst, C. H. (1974). Effects of hurricane Agnes on a painted turtle population. J. Herpetol. 8, 237–240.

REFERENCES

Ernst, C. H. (1975). Growth of the spotted turtle, *Clemmys guttata*. J. Herpetol. 9, 313–318.
Ernst, C. H. (1976). Ecology of the spotted turtle, *Clemmys guttata* (Reptilia, Testudinea, Testudinidae), in southeastern Pennsylvania. J. Herpetol. 10, 25–33.
Ernst, C. H., Barbour, R. W., Ernst, E. M. and Butler, J. R. (1973). Growth of the mud turtle *Kinosternon subrubrum* in Florida. Herpetologica 29, 247–250.
Ewert, M. A. and Legler, J. M. (1978). Hormonal induction of oviposition in turtles. Herpetologica 34, 314–318.
Ewing, H. E. (1933). Reproduction in the eastern box turtle, *Terrapene carolina carolina* (Linne). Copeia 1933, 95–96.
Feaver, P. E. (1977). The demography of a Michigan population of *Natrix sipedon* with discussions of ophidian growth and reproduction. Ph. D. Thesis. Univ. Michigan, Ann Arbor.
Ferguson, G. W. (1976). Color change and reproductive cycling in female collared lizards (*Crotaphytus collaris*). Copeia 1976, 491–494.
Ferguson, G. W., Bohlen, C. H. and Woolley, H. P. (1980). *Sceloporus undulatus*: Comparative life history and regulation of a Kansas population. Ecology 61, 312–322.
Ferguson, M. W. J. (1984). Reproductive biology and embryology of the crocodilians. In *Biology of the Reptilia* (C. Gans, F. Billett, and P. F. A. Maderson, eds). John Wiley and Sons. Volume 14, pp. 329–492.
Ferner, J. W. (1979). A review of marking techniques for amphibians and reptiles. SSAR Herpetol. Circ. 9, 1–41.
Fienberg, S. E. (1975). The multiple recapture census for closed populations and incomplete 2^k contingency tables. Biometrika 59, 591–603.
Fitch, H. S. (1951). A simplified type of funnel trap for reptiles. Herpetologica 7, 77–80.
Fitch, H. S. (1949). Study of snake populations in central California. Am. Midl. Nat. 41, 513–579.
Fitch, H. S. (1954). Life history and ecology of the five-lined skink, *Eumeces fasciatus*. Univ. Kansas Publ. Mus. Nat. Hist. 8, 1–156.
Fitch, H. S. (1956). An ecological study of the collared lizard (*Crotaphytus collaris*). Univ. Kansas Publ. Mus. Nat. Hist. 8, 213–274.
Fitch, H. S. (1958). Natural history of the six-lined racerunner (*Cnemidophorus sexlineatus*). Univ. Kansas Publ. Mus. Nat. Hist. 11, 11–62.
Fitch, H. S. (1960). Autecology of the copperhead. Univ. Kansas Publ. Mus. Nat. Hist. 13, 85–288.
Fitch, H. S. (1963a). Natural history of the black rat snake (*Elaphe o. obsoleta*) in Kansas. Copeia 1963, 649–658.
Fitch, H. S. (1963b). Natural history of the racer *Coluber constrictor*. Univ. Kansas Publ. Mus. Nat. Hist. 15, 351–468.
Fitch, H. S. (1965). An ecological study of the garter snake *Thamnophis sirtalis*. Univ. Kansas Publ. Mus. Nat. Hist. 15, 493–564.
Fitch, H. S. (1975). A demographic study of the ringneck snake *Diadophis punctatus* in Kansas. Univ. Kansas Publ. Mus. Nat. Hist. 62, 1–53.
Fitch, H. S. and Plummer, M. V. (1975). A preliminary ecological study of the soft shelled turtle, *Trionyx muticus*, in the Kansas River. Israel J. Zool. 24, 28–42.
Francillion, H. (1979). Etude expérimentale des marques de croissance sur les humérus et les femurs des tritons crétés *Triton cristatus cristatus* (Laurenti) en relation avec la détermination de l'âge individuel. Acta Zool. 60, 223–232.
Frazer, N. B. (1983). Demography and life history evolution of the Atlantic loggerhead sea turtle, *Caretta caretta*. Ph. D. Dissertation. Univ. of Georgia, Athens.

Frazer, N. B. (1984). A model for assessing mean age-specific fecundity in sea turtle populations. Herpetologica 40, 281–291.

Frazier, J. (1985). Tetracycline as an in vivo label in bones of green turtles, *Chelonia mydas* (L.). Herpetologica 41, 228–234.

Froese, A. D. and Burghardt, G. M. (1975). A dense natural population of the common snapping turtle (*Chelydra s. serpentina*). Herpetologica 31, 204–208.

Gannon, V. P. J. and Secoy, D. M. (1984). Growth and reproductive rates of a northern population of the prairie rattlesnake, *Crotalus v. viridis*. J. Herpetol. 18, 13–19.

Gaymer, R. (1968). The Indian Ocean giant tortoise *Testudo gigantea* on Aldabra. J. Zool. (Lond.) 154, 341–363.

Gibbons, J. W. (1967). Variation in growth rates in three populations of the painted turtle, *Chrysemys picta*. Herpetologica 23, 296–303.

Gibbons, J. W. (1968a). Reproductive potential, activity, and cycles in the painted turtle, *Chrysemys picta*. Ecology 49, 399–409.

Gibbons, J. W. (1968b). Population structure and survivorship in the painted turtle, *Chrysemys picta*. Copeia 1968, 260–268.

Gibbons, J. W. (1968c). Observations on the ecology and population dynamics of the Blanding's turtle, *Emydoidea blandingii*. Can. J. Zool. 46, 288–290.

Gibbons, J. W. (1969). Ecology and population dynamics of the chicken turtle, *Deirochelys reticularia*. Copeia 1969, 699–676.

Gibbons, J. W. (1970a). Reproductive characteristics of a Florida population of musk turtles (*Sternotherus odoratus*). Herpetologica 26, 268–270.

Gibbons, J. W. (1970b). Sex ratio in turtles. Res. Pop. Ecol. 12, 252–254.

Gibbons, J. W. (1970c). Terrestrial activity and the population dynamics of aquatic turtles. Am. Midl. Nat. 83, 404–414.

Gibbons, J. W. (1970d). Reproductive dynamics of a turtle (*Pseudemys scripta*) population in a reservoir receiving heated effluent from a nuclear reactor. Can. J. Zool. 48, 881–885.

Gibbons, J. W. (1972). Reproduction, growth, and sexual dimorphism in the canebreak rattlesnake. Copeia 1972, 222–226.

Gibbons, J. W. (1976). Aging phenomena in reptiles. In *Experimental Aging Research* (M. F. Elias, B. E. Eleftheriou and P. K. Elias, eds.). E. A. R. Inc., Bar Harbor, ME, pp. 454–475.

Gibbons, J. W. (1982). Reproductive patterns in freshwater turtles. Herpetologica 38, 222–227.

Gibbons, J. W. (1983). Reproductive characteristics and ecology of the mud turtle *Kinosternon subrubrum* (Lacepede). Herpetologica 39, 254–271.

Gibbons, J. W. and Greene, J. L. (1979). X-ray photography, a technique to determine reproductive patterns of freshwater turtles. Herpetologica 35, 286–89.

Gibbons, J. W., Greene, J. L. and Congdon, J. D. (1983). Drought-related responses of aquatic turtle populations. J. Herpetol. 17, 242–246.

Gibbons, J. W. and Semlitsch, R. D. (1981). Terrestrial drift fences with pitfall traps: An effective technique for quantitative sampling of animal populations. Brimleyana 7, 1–16.

Gibbons, J. W. and Semlitsch, R. D. (1982). Survivorship and longevity of a long-lived vertebrate species: How long do turtles live? J. Anim. Ecol. 51, 523–527.

Gibbons, J. W., Semlitsch, R. D., Greene, J. L. and Schubauer, J. P. (1981). Variation in age and size at maturity of the slider turtle (*Pseudemys scripta*). Am. Midl. Nat. 117, 841–845.

REFERENCES

Gibbons, J. W. and Tinkle, D. W. (1969). Reproductive variation between turtle populations in a single geographic area. Ecology 50, 340–341.

Gibson, C. W. D. and Hamilton, J. (1984). Population processes in a large herbivorous reptile: The giant tortoise of Aldabra atoll. Oecologia (Berl.) 61, 230–240.

Goldberg, S. R. (1970). Seasonal ovarian histology of the ovoviviparous iguanid lizard *Sceloporus jarrovi* Cope. J. Morphol. 132, 255–276.

Goldberg, S. R. (1971). Reproductive cycle of the ovoviviparous iguanid lizard *Sceloporus jarrovi* Cope. Herpetologica 27, 123–131.

Goldberg, S. R. (1975). Reproduction in the sagebrush lizard, *Sceloporus graciosus*. Am. Midl. Nat. 93, 177–187.

Goldberg, S. R. (1976). Reproduction in a mountain population of the coastal whiptail lizard, *Cnemidophorus tigris multiscutatus*. Copeia 1976, 260–266.

Goldberg, S. R. and Bezy, R. L. (1974). Reproduction in the island night lizard, *Xantusia riversiana*. Herpetologica 30, 350–360.

Goldberg, S. R. and Lowe, C. H. (1966). The reproductive cycle of the western whiptail lizard (*Cnemidophorus tigris*) in southern Arizona. J. Morphol. 118, 543–548.

Goldberg, S. R. and Robinson, M. D. (1979). Reproduction in two Namib desert lacertid lizards (*Aporosaura anchietae* and *Meroles cunierostris*). Herpetologica 35, 169–175.

Goodman, L. A. (1968). An elementary approach to the population projection matrix, to the population reproductive value, and to related topics in the mathematical theory of population growth. Demography 5, 382–409.

Graham, T. E. (1970). Growth rate of the spotted turtle, *Clemmys gutata*, in southern Rhode Island. J. Herpetol. 4, 87–88.

Graham, T. E. (1971). Growth rate of the red-bellied turtle, *Chrysemys rubriventris*, at Plymouth, Massachusetts. Copeia 1971, 353–356.

Grant, C. (1936). Breeding biology of *Pseudemys elegans* in California and notes on other captive reptiles. Copeia 1936, 112–113.

Gregory, P. T. (1977). Life-history parameters of the red-sided garter snake (*Thamnophis sirtalis parietalis*) in an extreme environment, the Interlake region of Manitoba. Natl. Mus. Canada Publ. Zool. 13, 1–44.

Grubb, P. (1971). The growth, ecology and population structure of giant tortoises on Aldabra. Phil. Trans. Roy. Soc. London B. 260, 327–372.

Gunning, G. E. and Lewis, W. M. (1957). An electrical shocker for the collection of amphibians and reptiles in the aquatic environment. Copeia 1957, 52.

Hammer, D. A. (1969). Parameters of a marsh snapping turtle population, Lacreek Refuge, South Dakota. J. Wildl. Mgmt. 33, 995–1005.

Harless, M. and Morlock, H. (1979). *Turtles: Perspectives and Research.* Wiley, New York.

Harris, D. M. (1982). The phenology, growth and survival of the green iguana, *Iguana iguana*, in northern Colombia. In *Iguanas of the World. Their Behavior, Ecology and Conservation* (G. M. Burghardt and A. S. Rand, eds.). Noyes Publications, Park Ridge, NJ, pp. 150–161.

Harris, V. A. (1964). *Life of the Rainbow Lizard.* Hutchinson and Co. London.

Harrisson, J. (1956). Tagging green turtles, 1951–1956. Nature 178, 1479.

Hayne, D. W. (1949). Two methods for estimating population from trapping records. J. Mammal. 30, 399–411.

Heckel, D. G. and Roughgarden, J. (1979). A technique for determining the size of lizard populations. Ecology 60, 966–975.

Hendrickson, J. R. (1958). The green turtle *Chelonia mydas* (Linn.) in Malaya and Sarawak. Proc. Zool. Soc. Lond. 130, 455–535.

Heulin, B. (1985). Demographie d'une population de *Lacerta vivipara* de basse altitude. Acta Oecol., Oecol. Gener. 6, 261–280.

Hildebrand, S. F. (1932). Growth of diamond-back terrapins: Size attained, sex ratio, and longevity. Zoologica 9, 551–563.

Hildebrand, H. H. (1963). Hallzago del area de Anidacion de la tortuga marina "lora," *Lepidochelys kempi* (Garman), en la costa occidental del Golfo de Mexico. Ciencia 22, 105–112.

Hudnall, J. A. (1982). New methods for measuring and tagging snakes. Herpetol. Rev. 13, 97–98.

Hirth, H. F. (1966). Weight changes and mortality of three species of snakes during hibernation. Herpetologica 22, 8–12.

Hoffman, W. and Fritts, J. H. (1982). Sea turtles along the boundary of the Gulf Stream current off eastern Florida. Herpetologica 38, 405–409.

Hulse, A. C. (1976). Growth and morphometrics of *Kinosternon sonoriense* (Reptilia, Testudines, Kinosternidae). J. Herpetol. 106, 341–348.

Iverson, J. B. (1977). Reproduction in freshwater and terrestrial turtles of north Florida. Herpetologica 33, 205–212.

Iverson, J. B. (1980). The reproductive biology of *Gopherus polyphemus* (Chelonia: Testunidae). Am. Midl. Nat. 103, 353–359.

Jolly, G. M. (1965). Explicit estimates from capture-recapture data with both death and immigration—stochastic model. Biometrika 52, 225–248.

Jones, S. M. and Ferguson, G. W. (1980). The effect of paint marking on mortality in a Texas population of *Sceloporus undulatus*. Copeia 1980, 850–854.

Kaplan, H. M. (1958). Marking and banding frogs and turtles. Herpetologica. 14, 131–132.

Keyfitz, N. (1968). *Introduction to the Mathematics of Populations*. Addison-Wesley, New York.

Kiester, A. R., Schwartz, C. W. and Schwartz, E. R. (1982). Promotion of gene flow by transients in an otherwise sedentary population of box turtles (*Terrapene carolina triunguis*). Evolution 36, 617–619.

Krohmer, R. W. and Aldridge, R. D. (1985a). Male reproductive cycle of the lined snake (*Tropidoclonion lineatum*). Herpetologica 41, 33–38.

Krohmer, R. W. and Aldridge, R. D. (1985b). Female reproductive cycle of the lined snake (*Tropidoclonion lineatum*). Herpetologica 41, 39–44.

Lagler, K. F. (1943). Methods of collecting freshwater turtles. Copeia 1943, 21–25.

Lagler, K. F. (1945). Economic relations and utilization of turtles. Invest. Ind. Lakes Streams 3, 139–165.

LeBuff, C. R., Jr. (1974). Unusual nesting relocation in the loggerhead turtle, *Caretta caretta*. Herpetologica 30, 29–31.

LeBuff, C. R., Jr., and Beatty, R. W. (1971). Some aspects of nesting of the loggerhead turtle, *Caretta caretta* (Linne) on the coast of Florida. Herpetologica 27, 153–156.

LeBuff, C. R., Jr., and Hagan, P. D. (1978). The role of aerial surveys in estimating nesting populations of the loggerhead turtle. Fla. Marine Res. Publ. 33, 31–33.

Legler, J. M. (1960). Natural history of the ornate box turtle, *Terrapene ornata ornata* Agassiz. Univ. Kansas Publ. Mus. Nat. Hist. 11, 527–669.

Legler, J. M. (1963). Tortoises (*Geochelone carbonaria*) in Panama: Distribution and variation. Am. Midl. Nat. 70, 490–503.

Legler, J. M. (1966). Notes on the natural history of a rare Central American turtle, *Kinosternon angustifrons* Legler. Herpetologica 22, 118–122.

Legler, J. M. and Webb, R. G. (1970). A new slider turtle (*Pseudemys scripta*) from Sonora, Mexico. Herpetologica 26, 157–168.

REFERENCES

Legler, W. K. (1979). Telemetry. In *Turtles: Perspectives and Research*. (M. Harless and H. Morlock, eds.). Wiley, New York, pp. 61–72.

Lemaku, P. J. (1970). Movements of the box turtle *Terrapene c. carolina* (Linnaeus) in unfamiliar territory. Copeia 1970, 781–783.

Lewke, R. E. and Stroud, R. K. (1974). Freeze branding as a method of marking snakes. Copeia 1974, 997–1000.

Licht, P., Breitenbach, G. L. and Congdon, J. D. (1970). Seasonal cycles in testicular activity, gonadotropin, and thyroxine in the painted turtle, *Chrysemys picta*, under natural conditions. Gen. Comp. Endocrinol. 59, 130–139.

Licht, P. and Gorman, G. C. (1970). Reproductive and fat cycles in Caribbean *Anolis* lizards. Univ. Calif. Publ. Zool. 95.

Limpus, C. J. (1971). The flatback turtle, *Chelonia depressa* Garman, in southeast Queensland, Australia. Herpetologica 27, 431–446.

Limpus, C. J. (1973). Loggerhead turtles, (*Caretta caretta*) in Australia: Food sources while nesting. Herpetologica 29, 42–45.

Lofts, B. (1969). Seasonal cycles in reptilian testes. Gen. Comp. Endocrinol., Suppl. 2, 146–155.

Lofts, B. and Boswell, C. (1961). Seasonal changes in the distribution of testis lipids of the Caspian terrapin, *Clemmys caspica*. Proc. Zool. Soc. Lond. 136, 581–592.

Lofts, B. and Tsui, H. W. (1977). Histological and histochemical changes in the gonads and epididymides of the male soft shelled turtle *Trionyx sinensis*. J. Zool. (Lond.) 181, 57–68.

Loveridge, A. and Williams, E. E. (1957). Revision of the African tortoises and turtles of the suborder Cryptodira. Bull. Mus. Comp. Zool. 115, 163–557.

Mahmoud, I. Y. (1969). Comparative ecology of the kinosternid turtles of Oklahoma. Southwest. Nat. 14, 31–66.

Mahmoud, I. Y. and Klicka, J. (1972). Seasonal gonadal changes in kinosternid turtles. J. Herpetol. 6, 183–189.

Major, P. D. (1975). Density of snapping turtles, *Chelydra serpentina*, in western West Virginia. Herpetologica 31, 332–335.

Manly, B. J. F. and Seber, G. A. F. (1973). Animal life tables from capture recapture data. Biometrics 29, 487–500.

Marten, G. G. (1975). A regression method for mark–recapture estimates with unequal catchability. Ecology 51, 291–295.

Mast, S. O. (1911). Behavior of the loggerhead turtle in depositing its eggs. Pap. Tortugas Lab. Carnegie Inst. Wash. 3, 63–67.

Mattox, N. T. (1935). Annular rings in the long bones of turtles and their correlation with size. Trans. Illinois St. Acad. Sci. 28, 255–256.

Mayhew, W. W. (1965). Reproduction in the sand-dwelling lizard, *Uma inornata*. Herpetologica 21, 39–55.

Mayhew, W. W. (1966a). Reproduction in the arenicolous lizard, *Uma notata*. Ecology 47, 9–18.

Mayhew, W. W. (1966b). Reproduction in the psammophilous lizard, *Uma scoparia*. Copeia 1966, 114–122.

Mayhew, W. W (1971). Reproduction in the desert lizard *Dipsosaurus dorsalis*. Herpetologica 27, 57–77.

Mayhew, W. W. and Wright, S. J. (1970). Seasonal changes in testicular histology of three species of the lizard genus *Uma*. J. Morphol. 130, 163–186.

Medica, P. A. and Turner, F. B. (1976). Reproduction by *Uta stansburiana* in southern Nevada. J. Herpetol. 10, 123–128.

Medica, P. A., Turner, F. B. and Smith, D. D. (1973). Hormonal induction of color change in female leopard lizards *Crotaphytus wislizeni*. Copeia 1973, 658–661.
Mertz, D. B. (1970). Notes on methods used in life history studies. In *Readings in Ecology and Ecological Genetics* (J. H. Connell, D. B. Mertz, and W. W. Murdoch, eds.). Harper and Row, New York, pp. 4–17.
Miller, L. (1932). Notes on the desert tortoise (*Testudo agassizi*). Trans. San Diego Soc. Nat. Hist. 7, 187–208.
Miller, L. (1955). Further observations on the tortoise, *Gopherus agassizi* of California. Copeia 1955, 113–118.
Milstead, W. W. (1959). Drift-fence trapping of lizards on the Black Gap Wildlife Management Area of southwestern Texas. Tex. J. Sci. 11, 150–157.
Milstead, W. W. and Tinkle, D. W. (1967). *Terrapene* of western Mexico, with comments on the species groups within the genus. Copeia 1967, 180–187.
Mittermeier, R. A. (1971). Notes on the behavior and ecology of *Rhinoclemys annulata* Gray. Herpetologica 27, 485–488.
Moffat, L. A. (1984). Embryonic development and aspects of reproductive biology in the tuatara, *Sphenodon punctatus*. In *Biology of the Reptilia* (C. Gans, F. Billet, and P. F. A. Maderson, eds.). Wiley, New York. Volume 14, pp. 493–522.
Moll, E. O. (1973). Latitudinal and intersubspecific variation in reproduction of the painted turtle, *Chrysemys picta*. Herpetologica 29, 307–318.
Moll, E. O. (1976). Environmental influence on growth rate in the Ouachita map turtle, *Graptemys pseudogeographica ouachitensis*. Herpetologica 32, 439–443.
Moll, E. O. (1977). Reproduction and color change in *Callagur borneoensis* (Testudines—Emydidae). Am. Soc. Ichthyol. Herpetol. Abstr.
Moll, E. O. (1979). Reproductive cycles and adaptations. In *Turtles: Perspectives and Research* (M. Harless and H. Morlock, eds.). Wiley, New York, pp. 305–331.
Moll, E. O. and Legler, J. M. (1971). The life history of a neotropical slider turtle, *Pseudemys scripta* (Schoepff), in Panama. Bull. Los Angeles Co. Mus. Nat. Hist. Sci. 11, 1–102.
Montanucci, R. R. (1965). Observations on the San Joaquin leopard lizard *Crotaphytus wislizeni silus*. Herpetologica 21, 270–283.
Morreale, S. J., Ruiz, G. J., Spotila J. R., and Standora, E. A. (1982). Temperature-dependent sex determination: Current practices threaten conservation of sea turtles. Science 216, 1245–1247.
Mosimann, J. E. and Bider, J. R. (1960). Variation, sexual dimorphism, and maturity in a Quebec population of the common snapping turtle, *Chelydra serpentina*. Can. J. Zool. 38, 19–38.
Munger, J. C. (1984). Home ranges of horned lizards (*Phrynosoma*): Circumscribed and exclusive? Oecologia (Berlin) 62, 351–360.
Nichols, J. T. (1939). Data on size, growth, and age in the box turtle, *Terrapene carolina*. Copeia 1939, 14–20.
Nouria, S., Maury, M. E., Castanet, J., and Barbault R. (1982). Détermination squelettochronologique de l'âge dans une population de *Cophosaurus texanus* (Sauria, Iguanidae). Amphibia-Reptilia 3, 213–219.
Obbard, M. E. and Brooks, R. J. (1981). A radio-telemetry and mark–recapture study of activity in the common snapping turtle, *Chelydra serpentina*. Copeia 1981, 630–637.
Parker, W. S. and Brown, W. S. (1974a). Notes on the ecology of regal ringneck snakes (*Diadophis punctatus regalis*) in northern Utah. J. Herpetol. 8, 262–263.
Parker, W. S. and Brown, W. S. (1974b). Mortality and weight changes of Great Basin rattlesnakes (*Crotalus viridis*) at a hibernaculum in northern Utah. Herpetologica 30, 234–239.

REFERENCES

Parker, W. S. and Brown, W. S. (1980). Comparative ecology of two colubrid snakes, *Masticophis t. taeniatus* and *Pituophis melanoleucus deserticola*, in northern Utah. Milwaukee Pub. Mus. Publ. Biol. Geol. 7, 1–104.

Peabody, F. E. (1961). Annual growth zones in living and fossil vertebrates. J. Morphol. 108, 11–62.

Pearse, A. S. (1923). The abundance and migration of turtles. Ecology 4, 24–28.

Pendlebury, G. B. (1972). Tagging and remote identification of rattlesnakes. Herpetologica 28, 349–350.

Pianka, E. R. (1967). On lizard species diversity: North American flatland deserts. Ecology 48, 333–351.

Pianka, E. R. and Huey, R. B. (1978). Comparative ecology, resource utilization, and niche segregation among gekkonid lizards in the southern Kalahari. Copeia 1978, 691–701.

Pieau, C. (1971). Sur la proportion sexuelle les embryons de deux chéloniens (*Testudo graeca* L. et *Emys orbicularis* L.) issus d'oeufs incubés artificiellement. C. R. Acad. Sci. (Paris) 272, Serie D., 3071.

Pieau, C. (1972). Effects de la témperature sur le développement des glands génitales chez les embryons de deux chéloniens *Emys orbicularis* L. et *Testudo graeca* L. C. R. Acad. Sci. (Paris) 274, 719–722.

Pieau, C. (1973). Nouvelles données expérimentales concernant les effets de la température sur la différenciation sexuelle chez les embryons de Chéloniens. C. R. Acad. Sci. (Paris) 277, 2789–2792.

Pieau, C. (1975). Effects des variations thermiques sur la differenciation du sexe chez les vertébrés. Bull. Soc. Zool. France 100, 67–76.

Pilorge, T. and Castanet, J. (1981). Détermination l'âge dans une population naturelle du lézard vivipare (*Lacerta vivipara* Jacquin 1787). Acta Oecologica 2, 3–16.

Plummer, M. V. (1979). Collecting and marking. In *Turtles: Perspectives and Research*. (M. Harless and H. Morlock, eds.). Wiley, New York, pp. 45–60.

Plummer, M. V. (1984). Female reproduction in an Arkansas population of rough green snakes (*Opheodrys aestivus*). In *Vertebrate Ecology and Systematics, a Tribute to Henry S. Fitch*. (R. A. Seigel, L. E. Hunt, J. L. Knight, L. Malaret, and N. L. Zuschlag, eds.). Mus. Nat. Hist. Univ. Kansas Spec. Publs. 10.

Plummer, M. V. (1985). Demography of green snakes (*Opheodrys aestivus*). Herpetologica 41, 373–381.

Pough, F. H. (1970). A quick method for permanently marking snakes and turtles. Herpetologica 26, 428–430.

Powell, C. B. (1967). Female sexual cycles of *Chrysemys picta* and *Clemmys insculpta* in Nova Scotia. Can. Field. Nat 81, 134–140.

Prestt, I. (1971). An ecological study of the viper *Vipera berus* in southern Britain. J. Zool. (Lond.) 164, 373–418.

Pritchard, P. C. H. (1969). Sea turtles of the Guianas. Bull. Fla. St. Mus. 13, 85–140.

Pritchard, P. C. H. (1971). The leatherback or leathery turtle. Int. Un. Conserv. Nat., Nat. Res. Monogr. 1, 1–39.

Pritchard, P. C. H. (1982). Nesting in the leather-back turtle, *Dermochelys coriacea*, Pacific Mexico, with a new estimate of the world population status. Copeia 1982, 741–747.

Pritchard, P. C. H. and Marquez, M. R. (1973). Kemp's Ridley or Atlantic Ridley: *Lepidochelys kempi*. Int. Un. Conserv. Nat. Nat. Res. Monogr. 2, 1–30.

Rand, A. S. (1954). Variation and predator pressure in an island and mainland population of lizards. Copeia 1954, 260–262.

Raynaud, A. and Pieau, C. (1985). Embryonic development of the genital system. In *Biology of the Reptilia*. Volume 15. (C. Gans and F. Billett, eds.). Wiley, New York, pp. 149–300.

Ream, C. and Ream, R. (1966). The influence of sampling methods on the estimation of population structure in painted turtles. Am. Midl. Nat. 75, 325–338.

Rebel, T. P. (1974). *Sea Turtles and the Turtle Industry of the West Indies, Florida, and the Gulf of Mexico*. Univ. Miami Press, Coral Gables.

Rhodin, A. G. J. and Mittermeier, R. A. (1976). *Chelodina parkeri*, a new species of chelid turtle from New Guinea, with a discussion of *Chelodina siebenrocki* Werner, 1901. Bull. Mus. Comp. Zool. Harv. 147, 465–488.

Richardson, J. I. (1982). A population model for adult loggerhead sea turtles (*Caretta caretta*) nesting in Georgia. Ph.D. Dissertation, Univ. Georgia, Athens.

Richmond, N. D. (1945). Nesting habits of the mud turtle. Copeia 1945, 217–219.

Risley, P. L. (1933). Observations on the natural history of the common musk turtle, *Sternotherus odoratus* (Latreille). Pap. Mich. Acad. Sci. 17, 685–711.

Risley, P. L. (1938). Seasonal changes in the testes of the musk turtle, *Sternotherus odoratus* L. J. Morphol. 63, 301–317.

Ruby, D. E. and Dunham, A. E. (1984). A population analysis of the ovoviviparous lizard *Sceloporus jarrovi* in the Pinaleño Mountains of southeastern Arizona. Herpetologica 40, 425–436.

Ruckdeschel, C. and Zug, G. R. (1982). Mortality of sea turtles *Caretta caretta* in coastal waters of Georgia. Biol. Conserv. 22, 5–9.

Ruibal, R. and Philibosian, R. (1974). The population ecology of the lizard *Anolis acutus*. Ecology 55, 525–537.

Saint Girons, H. (1985). Comparative data on lepidosaurian reproduction and some time tables. In *Biology of the Reptilia*. Volume 15. (C. Gans and F. Billett, eds.). Wiley, New York, pp. 35–58.

Schnabel, Z. E. (1938). The estimation of the total fish population of a lake. Am. Math. Monogr. 45, 348–352.

Schoener, T. W. (1979). Inferring the properties of predation and other injury-producing agents from injury frequencies. Ecology 60, 1110–1115.

Schoener, T. W. and Schoener, A. (1978). Estimating and interpreting body size growth in some *Anolis* lizards. Copeia 1978, 390–405.

Schoener, T. W. and Schoener, A. (1980a). Densities, sex ratios, and population structure in four species of Bahamian *Anolis* lizards. J. Anim. Ecol. 49, 19–53.

Schoener, T. W. and Schoener, A. (1980b). Ecological and demographic correlates of injury rates in some Bahamian *Anolis* lizards. Copeia 1980, 839–850.

Schoener, T. W. and Schoener, A. (1982). The ecological correlates of survival in some Bahamanian Anolis lizards. Oikos 39, 1–16.

Schoener, T. W. and Schoener, A. (1983). The time to extinction of a colonizing propagule of lizards increases with island area. Nature 302, 332–334.

Schubauer, J. P. (1981). A reliable radio-telemetry tracking system suitable for studies of chelonians. J. Herpetol. 15, 117–120.

Schumacher, F. X. and Eschmeyer, R. W. (1943). The estimate of fish populations in lakes or ponds. J. Tenn. Acad. Sci. 18, 228–249.

Schwartz, E. R., Schwartz, C. W. and Kiester, A. R. (1984). The three-toed box turtle in central Missouri. Part II. A nineteen year study of home range, movements and population. Missouri Department of Conservation Terrestrial Series No. 12.

Seber, G. A. F. (1973). *The Estimation of Animal Abundance*. Griffin, London.

Seigel, R. A. and Fitch, H. S. (1984). Ecological patterns of relative clutch mass in snakes. Oecologia (Berl.) 61, 293–301.

REFERENCES

Semlitsch, R. D., Brown, K. L., and Caldwell, J. P. (1981). Habitat utilization, seasonal activity, and population size structure of the southeastern crowned snake *Tantilla coronata*. Herpetologica 37, 40–46.

Semlitsch, R. D. and Moran, G. B. (1984). Ecology of the red-bellied snake (*Storeria occipitomaculata*) using mesic habitats in South Carolina. Am. Midl. Nat. 111, 33–40.

Sergeev, A. (1937). Some materials to the problem of the reptilian post-embryonic growth. Zool. J. Moscow 16, 723–735 (in Russian).

Sexton, O. J. (1959). A method of estimating the age of painted turtles for use in demographic studies. Ecology 40, 716–718.

Sexton, O. J. (1965). The annual cycle of growth and shedding in the midland painted turtle, *Chrysemys picta marginata*. Copeia 1965, 314–318.

Shealy, R. M. (1976). The natural history of the Alabama map turtle, *Graptemys pulchra* (Baur), in Alabama. Bull. Fla. St. Mus. 21, 47–111.

Shine, R. (1980). "Costs" of reproduction in reptiles. Oecologia 46, 92–100.

Simon, C. A. and Bissinger, B. E. (1983). Paint marking of lizards: Does the color affect survivorship? J. Herpetol. 17, 184–186.

Simon, M. (1975). The green sea turtle (*Chelonia mydas*): Collection, incubation, and hatching of eggs from natural rookeries. J. Zool. (Lond.) 176, 39–48.

Simon, M. H. and Parkes, A. S. (1976). The green sea turtle (*Chelonia mydas*): Nesting on Ascension Island, 1973–1974. J. Zool. (Lond.) 179, 153–163.

Smith, D. C. 1977. Interspecific Competition and the Demography of Two Lizards. Ph. D. Dissertation, University of Michigan, Ann Arbor.

Smith, D. C. (1981). Competitive interactions of the striped plateau lizard (*Sceloporus virgatus*) and the tree lizard (*Urosaurus ornatus*). Ecology 62, 679–687.

Sokal, R. R. and Rohlf, F. J. (1981). *Biometry*. Second edition. Freeman, San Francisco.

Spellerberg, I. F. and Phelps, T. E. (1977). Biology, general ecology and behavior of the snake, *Coronella austriaca* Laurenti. Biol. J. Linn. Soc. (Lond.) 9, 133–164.

Spellerberg, I. F. and Prestt, I. (1978). Marking snakes. In *Animal Marking*. (B. Stonehouse, ed.). Univ. Park Press, Baltimore.

Spoecker, P. D. (1967). Movement and seasonal activity cycles of the lizard *Uta stansburiana stejnegeri*. Am. Midl. Nat. 77, 484–494.

Stebbins, R. C., Lowenstein, J. M. and Cohen, N. W. (1967). A field study of the lava lizard (*Tropidurus albemarlensis*) in the Galapagos Islands. Ecology 48, 839–851.

Stickel, L. F. (1950). Populations and home range relationships of the box turtle, *Terrapene c. carolina* (Linnaeus). Ecol. Monogr. 20, 351–378.

Stoneburner, D. L., Richardson, J. I. and Williamson, G. K. (1982). Observation on the movement of hatchling sea turtles. Copeia 1982, 963–965.

Stubbs, D., Hailey, A., Pulford, E. and Tyler, W. (1984). Population ecology of European tortoises: Review of field techniques. Amphibia-Reptilia 5, 75–68.

Swingland, I. R. (1977). Reproductive effort and life history strategy of the Aldabra giant tortoise. Nature 269, 402–404.

Swingland, I. R. (1978). Marking reptiles. In *Animal Marking* (B. Stonehouse, ed.). Univ. Park Press, Baltimore, pp. 119–132.

Swingland, I. R. and Coe, M. J. (1978). The natural regulation of giant tortoise populations on Aldabra atoll: Reproduction. J. Zool. 186, 285–309.

Swingland, I. R. and Coe, M. J. (1979). The natural regulation of giant tortoise populations on Aldabra atoll: Recruitment. Phil. Trans. Roy. Soc. Lond. B. 286, 177–188.

Swingland, I. R. and Lessells, C. M. (1979). The natural regulation of giant tortoise populations on Aldabra atoll: Movement, polymorphism, reproductive success and mortality. J. Anim. Ecol. 48, 639–654.

Tanaka, R. (1951). Estimates of vole and mouse populations on Mount Ishizuchi and on the uplands of southern Shikoku. J. Mammal. 32, 450–458.

Taylor, E. H. (1935). Arkansas amphibians and reptiles in the Kansas University Museum. Kan. Univ. Sci. Bull. 22, 207–218.

Timken, R. L. (1968). *Graptemys pseudogeographica* in the upper Mississippi River of the north central United States. J. Herpetol. 1, 76–82.

Tinkle, D. W. (1958). The systematics and ecology of the *Sternotherus carinatus* complex. Tulane Stud. Zool. 6, 1–56.

Tinkle, D. W. (1960). Ecology, maturation and reproduction of *Thamnophis sauritus proximus*. Ecology 38, 69–77.

Tinkle, D. W. (1961). The systematics and ecology of the *Sternothaerus carinatus* complex. Tulane Stud. Zool. 6, 1–56.

Tinkle, D. W. (1961). Geographic variation in reproduction, size, sex ratio, and maturity of *Sternotherus odoratus* (Testudinata: Chelydridae). Ecology 42, 68–76.

Tinkle, D. W. (1962). Reproductive potential and cycles in female *Crotalus atrox* from northwestern Texas. Copeia 1962, 306–313.

Tinkle, D. W. (1967). The life and demography of the side-blotched lizard, *Uta stansburiana*. Misc. Publ. Univ. Mich. Mus. Zool. 132, 1–182.

Tinkle, D. W. (1972). The dynamics of a Utah population of *Sceloporus undulatus*. Herpetologica 28, 351–359.

Tinkle, D. W. (1973). A population analysis of the sagebrush lizard, *Sceloporus graciosus* in southern Utah. Copeia 1973, 284–296.

Tinkle, D. W. (1976). Comparative data on the population ecology of the spiny lizard, *Sceloporus magister*. Herpetologica 32, 1–6.

Tinkle, D. W. (1979). Long-term field studies. Bioscience 29, 717.

Tinkle, D. W. and Ballinger, R. E. (1972). *Sceloporus undulatus*: A study of the interspecific comparative demography of a lizard. Ecology 53, 570–584.

Tinkle, D. W., Congdon, J. D. and Rosen, P. C. (1981). Nesting frequency and success: Implications for the demography of painted turtles. Ecology 62, 1426–1432.

Tinkle, D. W. and Dunham, A. E. (1983). Demography of the tree lizard, *Urosaurus ornatus*, in central Arizona. Copeia 1983, 585–598.

Tinkle, D. W. and Dunham, A. E. (1986). Comparative life histories of two syntopic sceloporine lizards. Copeia 1986, 1–18.

Tinkle, D. W. and Hadley, N. F. (1975). Lizard reproductive effort: Caloric estimates and comments on its evolution. Ecology 56, 427–434.

Turner, F. B. (1977). The dynamics of populations of squamates, crocodilians and rhynchocephalians. In *Biology of the Reptilia*. Volume 7. (C. Gans and D. W. Tinckle, eds.). Academic Press, New York, pp. 157–264.

Turner, F. B., Hoddenbach, G. A., Medica, P. A. and Lannom, J. R. (1970). The demography of the lizard, *Uta stansburiana* Baird and Girard, in southern Nevada. J. Anim. Ecol. 39, 505–519.

Turner, F. B., Medica, P. A., Lannom, J. R. and Hoddenbach, G. A. (1969). A demographic analysis of fenced populations of the whiptail lizard, *Cnemidophorus tigris*, in southern Nevada. Southwest. Nat. 14, 189–201.

Turner, F. B., Medica, P. A. and Lyons, C. L. (1984). Reproduction and survival of the desert tortoise (*Scaptochelys agassizii*) in Ivanpah Valley, California. Copeia 1984, 811–820.

Van Devender, R. W. (1982). Comparative demography of the lizard *Basiliscus basiliscus*. Herpetologica 38, 189–208.

REFERENCES

Vinegar, M. B. (1972). Function of breeding coloration in the lizard *Sceloporus virgatus*. Copeia 1972, 660–664.

Vinegar, M. B. (1975a). Demography of the striped plateau lizard, *Sceloporus virgatus*. Ecology 56, 172–182.

Vinegar, M. B. (1975b). Life history phenomena in two populations of the lizard *Sceloporus undulatus* in southwestern New Mexico. Am. Midl. Nat. 93, 388–402.

Vitt, L. J. (1973). Reproductive biology of the anguid lizard, *Gerrhonotus coeruleus principis*. Herpetologica 29, 176–184.

Vitt, L. J. (1982a). Reproductive tactics of *Ameiva ameiva* (Lacertilia, Teiidae) in a seasonally fluctuating tropical habitat. Can. J. Zool. 60, 3113–3120.

Vitt, L. J. (1982b). Sexual dimorphism and reproduction in the microteid lizard, *Gymnophthalmus multiscutatus*. J. Herpetol. 16, 325–329.

Vitt, L. J. (1983a). Reproductive ecology of two tropical iguanid lizards, *Tropidurus torquatus* and *Platynotus semitaeniatus*. Copeia 1983, 131–141.

Vitt, L. J. (1983b). Reproduction and sexual dimorphism in the tropical teiid lizard *Cnemidophorus ocellifer*. Copeia 1983, 359–366.

Vitt, L. J. and Cooper, W. E., Jr. (1985). The evolution of sexual dimorphism in the skink *Eumeces laticeps*, an example of sexual selection. Can. J. Zool. 63, 995–1002.

Vitt, L. J. and Goldberg, S. R. (1983). Reproductive ecology of two tropical iguanid lizards, *Tropidurus torquatus* and *Platynotus semitaeniatus*. Copeia 1983, 131–141.

Vitt, L. J., Howland, J. M. and Dunham, A. E. (1985). The effect of formalin fixation on the weight of lizard eggs. J. Herpetol. 19, 298–299.

Vitt, L. J. and Lacher, T. E. (1981). Behavior, habitat, diet and reproduction of the iguanid lizard *Polychrus acutirostris* in the Caatinga of northeastern Brazil. Herpetologica 37, 53–63.

Vitt, L. J., Van Loben Sels, R. C. and Ohmart, R. D. (1978). Lizard reproduction: Annual variation and environmental correlates in the iguanid lizard *Urosaurus graciosus*. Herpetologica 34, 241–253.

Vogt, R. C. (1980). New methods for trapping aquatic turtles. Copeia 1980, 368–371.

Vogt, R. C. and Hine, R. L. (1982). Evaluation of techniques for assessment of amphibian and reptile populations in Wisconsin. In *Herpetological Communities. Wildlife Research Report No. 13*. (N. J. Scott, Jr., ed.). U. S. Fish and Wildlife Service. Washington, DC.

Wade, E. S. and Gifford, C. E. (1965). A preliminary study of the turtle population of a northern Indiana lake. Proc. Ind. Acad. Sci. 74, 371–374.

Ward, F. P., Hohmann, C. J., Ulrich, J. F. and Hill, S. E. (1976). Seasonal microhabitat selection of spotted turtles (*Clemmys guttata*) in Maryland elucidated by radioisotope tracking. Herpetologica 32, 60–64.

Weary, G. G. (1969). An improved method of marking snakes. Copeia 1969, 854–855.

Webb, R. G. (1956). Size of sexual maturity in the male softshell turtle, *Trionyx ferox emoryi*. Copeia 1956, 121–122.

Webb, R. G. (1961). Observations on the life histories of turtles (genus *Pseudemys* and *Graptemys*) in Lake Texoma, Oklahoma. Am. Midl. Nat. 65, 193–214.

Webb, R. G. (1962). North American recent soft-shelled turtles (family Trionychidae). Univ. Kans. Publs. Mus. Nat. Hist. 13, 429–611.

Webster, T. P. (1969). Ecological observations on *Anolis occultus* Williams and Rivero (Sauria, Iguanidae). Breviora Mus. Comp. Zool., Harvard 312, 1–5.

Whillans, T. H. and Crossman, E. J. (1977). Morphological parameters and spring activities in a central Ontario population of the midland painted turtle, *Chrysemys picta marginata* (Agassiz). Can. Field. Nat. 91, 47–57.

White, J. B. and Murphy, G. G. (1973). The reproductive cycle and sexual dimorphism of the common snapping turtle, *Chelydra serpentina serpentina*. Herpetologica 29, 240–246.

Wilbur, H. M. (1975a). The evolutionary and mathematical demography of the turtle *Chrysemys picta*. Ecology 56, 64–77.

Wilbur, H. M. (1975b). A growth model for the turtle *Chrysemys picta*. Copeia 1975, 337–343.

Wilbur, H. M. and Landwehr, J. M. (1974). The estimation of population size with equal and unequal risks of capture. Ecology 55, 1339–1348.

Williams, E. C. (1961). A study of the box turtle, *Terrapene carolina carolina* (L.), population in Allee Memorial Woods. Proc. Ind. Acad. Sci. 71, 399–406.

Woodbury, A. M. (1948). Marking reptiles with an electric tatooing outfit. Copeia 1948, 127–128.

Woodbury, A. M. (1953). Methods of field study in reptiles. Herpetologica 9, 87–92.

Woodbury, A. M. and Hardy, R. (1948). Studies of the desert tortoise, *Gopherus agassizii*. Ecol. Monogr. 18, 145–200.

Yntema, C. L. (1970). Observations on females and eggs of the common snapping turtle, *Chelydra serpentina*. Am. Midl. Nat. 84, 69–76.

Yntema, C. L. (1976). Effects of incubation temperatures on sexual differentiation in the turtle, *Chelydra serpentina*. J. Morphol. 150, 453–462.

Zug, G. R. and Rand, A. S. (1987). Estimation of age in nesting female *Iguana iguana*: Testing skeletochronology in a tropical lizard. Amphibia-Reptilia, in press.

Zug, G. R., Wynn, A. H. and Ruckdeschel, C. (1986). Age determination of loggerhead sea turtles, *Caretta caretta*, by incremental growth marks in the skeleton. Smithsonian Contrib. Zool. No. 427, 1–34.

Zweifel, R. G. and Lowe, C. H. (1966). The ecology of a population of *Xantusia vigilis*, the desert night lizard. Am. Mus. Novitates 2247, 1–57.

CHAPTER 6

Life History Evolution in Turtles

HENRY M. WILBUR AND PETER J. MORIN
Department of Zoology, Duke University, Durham,
North Carolina

The present address for Peter J. Morin is Department of Biological Sciences, Rutgers, The State University, Piscataway, New Jersey.

CONTENTS

I. INTRODUCTION   **389**

II. METHODS   **390**
    A. General, 390
    B. The Ecological and Reproductive Characters, 394

III. RESULTS   **396**
    A. The Diversity of Turtle Life Histories, 396
    B. Multivariate Analysis of Clutch Parameters and Ecological Groups, 406
    C. Taxonomic Constraints on Life History Patterns, 412
    D. Geographic Variation Within Species, 414

IV. SUMMARY   **420**
    ACKNOWLEDGMENTS   **421**
    REFERENCES   **421**
    APPENDIX   **436**

I. INTRODUCTION

Among tetrapods, turtles are the paragon of delayed reproduction, longevity, and repeated cycles of reproduction (iteroparity). Since at least the Triassic, the order has been committed to a unique body plan, involving a hard shell—a defensive tactic that dominates their life history in interesting ways. The construction of a shell demands resources, and its protective value increases as its owner grows; the delayed maturity of turtles may be the result of selection by predators favoring juveniles that commit resources to growth rather than reproduction. The costs of delayed maturity are offset by a potentially long reproductive life (Gibbons, 1976; Gibbons and Semlitsch, 1982; Wilbur, 1975a).

This chapter reviews the diversity of life histories among turtles and attempts to relate this to the ecology and taxonomy of the group. Turtles are conservative in some regards: For example, all are oviparous, and all lay eggs on land. Nevertheless, they have resolved conflicts between egg size and egg number, and between growth and reproduction, in a variety of ways.

Turtles have a nearly worldwide distribution; there are marine, freshwater, and terrestrial forms. About 236 extant species are distributed among 12 families (four are monospecific) and 73 genera (38 are monospecific) (Pritchard, 1979). We take a comparative approach using published data on nearly half the species of the world to search for interspecific evolutionary patterns that may have an adaptive basis.

Such comparative studies of different species permit inferences about evolutionary processes (Hendrickson, 1980); but such inferences only represent hypotheses subject to test by additional empirical work. A few studies of geographic variation in life history traits are reviewed, as are variation within populations and within known individuals that have been followed for more than one breeding season. Such documentation of phenotypic variation at several levels provides only weak tests of evolutionary hypotheses. However, we know of no direct genetic studies of life history variation in turtles. Reciprocal transplant studies with turtles are feasible and could provide strong evidence for the genetic basis of geographic variation in life history characteristics. The ease of marking and following individuals for much of their life and of identifying and observing their offspring, makes feasible a formal quantitative genetic analysis (Falconer, 1981). We know nothing of the genetic correlations among life history traits within populations, but need such information to generate robust tests of theories on the effects of constraints on adaptive change. The ecological techiques that could be

Fig. 1. *Geochelone gigantea*. Detail of nocturnal egg-laying on Malabar island, Aldabra atoll during July, 1976. The turtle urinated into the cavity prior to laying. (In order to take the picture, the photographer scraped away the rear wall of the nest.) (Courtesy of Dr. I. Swingland.)

used in conjunction with the methods of quantitative genetics are reviewed by Dunham, Morin, and Wilbur (this volume). Our analyses suggest several hypotheses that can be tested by additional field studies.

II. METHODS

A. General

The literature on turtles was searched for life history facts. These data were then examined statistically to discover patterns in reproductive characters that might correlate with taxonomic or ecological groupings. Pritchard's (1979) taxonomic arrangement of the extant turtles of the world was used as a convenient reference; although we made some nomenclatural changes in the family Testudinidae following Auffenberg (1974) and Bramble (1982). Our literature search was not exhaustive, but we were able to collect reproductive data on about two-thirds of the genera and about 44% of the living species (Table I and Appendix). The species was used as the unit of observation for most of the analyses. Hypothesis testing demands that observations be statistically independent estimates of the veracity of the hypothesis being tested. In

METHODS

TABLE I
Life History Characteristics of Turtles

Species	Habitat	Food	Latitude	Egg size (cc)	Clutch size	Number nests	Carapace length (cm)
Cheloniidae							
Caretta caretta	M	C	H	37.4	126	3	927
Chelonia depressa	M	H	L	73.6	50	4	927
C. mydas	M	H	L	56.8	110	3	1000
Eretmochelys imbricata	M	O	L	28.7	161	3	831
Lepidochelys kempi	M	C	L	30.8	110	3	646
L. olivacea	M	C	L	32.3	116	2	686
Chelydridae							
Chelydra serpentina	F	C	H	10.1	37	1	242
C. osceola	F	C	H				
Macroclemys temminckii	F	C	H	26.8	24.3	1	270
Dermatemydidae							
Dermatemys mawii	F	?	L	35.5	15	?	470
Dermochelyidae							
Dermochelys coriacea	M	C	L	73.6	85.5	?	1594
Emydidae							
Batagur baska	F	?	L	?	27	3	463
Callagur borneoensis	F	?	L	59.9	12	2	440
Chrysemys picta	F	O	H	4.6	6.8	2	130
Mauremys caspica	F	C	H	14.5	7	?	238
Clemmys guttata	F	H	H	4.8	3.6	?	132
C. insculpta	F	C	H	14.2	8.2	1	154
C. marmorata	F	O	H	9.1	7	?	148
C. muhlenbergii	F	O	H	3.9	4.5	?	88
Deirochelys reticularia	F	O	H	8.8	6	3	186
Emydoidea blandingii	F	C	H	12.2	8	?	159
Emys orbicularis	F	C	H	7.5	10	?	103
Rhinoclemmys funerea	F	O	L	43.6	3.2	2.5	?00
R. punctularia	F	H	L	49.4	1.5	?	194
Graptemys barbouri	F	C	H	17.9	8.5	3	209
G. geographica	F	C	H	7.4	13.0	2	202
G. oculifera	F	C	H	9.1	3.0	1.5	176
G. ouachitensis	F	?	H				
G. pseudogeographica	F	C	H	8.7	9.5	?	198
G. pulchra	F	C	H	13.7	6.9	4	250
Kachuga dhongoka	F	C	L	?	35	?	406
K. smithii	F	O	H	12.2	7	?	182
Malaclemys terrapin	F	C	H	11.2	8.5	?	194
Pseudemys concinna	F	O	H	13.4	18	?	328
P. decussata	F	H	L	14.7	7	?	192
P. floridana	F	H	H	12.6	19	2	250
P. rubiventris	F	O	H	5.9	11	?	230
P. scripta	F	O	H	9.4	16.5	?	196
P. terrapen	F	O	L	15.8	3.5	?	?
Terrapene carolina	T	H	H	6.6	5.5	1.5	132

(Continued)

TABLE I (Continued)

Species	Habitat	Food	Latitude	Egg size (cc)	Clutch size	Number nests	Carapace length (cm)
Emydidae (Continued)							
T. coahuila	F	O	L	5.0	2.3	3	101
T. nelsoni	T	O	L	17.9	2.7	1	128
T. ornata	T	O	H	8.9	4.7	1	110
Kinosternidae							
Claudius angustatus	F	C	H	?	5.0	?	122
Sternotherus carinatus	F	C	H	4.5	3.6	2	105
S. depressus	F	C	H	?	5.5	2	112
S. minor	F	C	H	?	7	2	112
S. odoratus	F	C	H	3.4	3	1	102
Kinosternon angustipons	F	O	L	10.1	2.5	2	113
K. baurii	F	C	H	4.0	2	2	75
K. dunni	F	C	L	14.6	2	?	150
K. flavescens	F	O	H	4.4	5	?	100
K. hirtipes	F	O	H	4.2	5.5	?	115
K. leucostomum	F	O	L	7.3	1.2	2	106
K. scorpioides	F	?	L	6.7	2.3	?	150
K. spurrelli	F	C	L	7.4	3.0	2	102
K. subrubrum	F	C	H	3.8	5	?	90
Platysternidae							
Platysternon megacephalum	F	C	H	?	2	?	127
Testudinidae							
Geochelone chilensis	T	H	H	26.4	3	2	222
G. denticulata	T	O	L	36.7	3	?	330
G. elegans	T	O	H	26.4	5.5	2.5	217
G. elephantopus	T	H	L	90.5	9.5	1	717
G. gigantea	T	H	L	?	3.8	2.5	750
G. pardalis	T	H	L	28.4	12	6	296
G. radiata	T	H	L	27.6	4.3	?	342
G. sulcata	T	L	H	38.7	17.0	?	517
Gopherus agassizii	T	H	H	34.7	5	?	236
G. polyphemus	T	H	H	37.8	5.5	?	233
Homopus areolatus	T	H	H	7.7	3	?	95
H. boulengeri	T	H	H	9.9	1	?	92
Kinixys belliana	T	O	H	26.9	2.7	?	164
K. erosa	T	O	L	27.1	5	?	204
K. homeana	T	O	L	22.4	4	?	159
Malacochersus tornieri	T	H	L	20.2	1	?	177
Psammobates geometricus	T	H	H	?	13.5	?	125
P. oculifera	T	H	H	19.9	?	?	133
P. tentorius	T	H	H	7.6	2.5	?	121
Testudo graeca	T	O	H	11.5	2	?	192
T. horsfieldii	T	H	H	16.8	?	?	197
T. kleinmanni	T	H	L	7.8	?	?	137

METHODS

TABLE I (Continued)

Species	Habitat	Food	Latitude	Egg size (cc)	Clutch size	Number nests	Carapace length (cm)
Trionychidae							
Cyclanorbis senegalensis	F	C	L	24.4	6	?	225
Cycloderma frenatum	F	C	L	20.6	18	?	560
Lissemys punctata	F	C	L	15.8	3.2	?	370
Trionyx ferox	F	C	H	8.2	19.5	?	266
T. gangeticus	F	O	L	17.2	?	?	425
T. muticus	F	O	H	6.4	17.1	2	121
T. sinensis	F	C	L	4.2	22.5	3	210
T. spiniferus	F	C	H	11.9	18.1	?	281
T. triunguis	F	O	L	20.3	28	?	700
Chelidae							
Chelodina expansa	F	C	L	?	15.4	?	199
C. longicollis	F	C	L	6.0	15.0	1	318
C. novaeguinee	F	C	L	?	10.5	?	219
C. siebenrocki	F	C	L	15.2	10.5	?	181
Chelus fimbriatus	F	C	L	?	16.0	?	275
Elseya dentata	F	C	L	?	12.0	?	350
Emydura macquarrii	F	C	L	8.9	15.3	?	156
Pelomedysidae							
Pelomedusa subrufa	F	C	L	5.9	31.0	1	196
Pelusios subniger	F	?	L	17.7	7.0	?	245
Podocnemis expansa	F	H	L	?	83	1	890
P. unifilis	F	C	L	22.8	20.7	?	515

See text for how character values were determined. Habitat: M, marine; F, Freshwater; T, terrestrial; Food: C, carnivorous; H, herbivorous; O, omnivorous; Latitude: L, low, tropical; H, high, temperate; Egg, egg volume in cubic centiameters (usually estimated from egg length and width); Clutch, number of eggs per nest; Number, number of nests per season; Carapace, linear length of carapace in centimeters. See Appendix for the references from which the values were taken.

evolutionary studies in which the comparative method rather than an experiment is used to test hypotheses, this problem is difficult. A conservative approach would be to use the genus as the unit of observation, but this would greatly misrepresent the diversity found in such genera as *Pseudemys* and *Terrapene*. The other extreme would be to include data for every well-studied population. Our choice of species as the unit of analysis reflects practical problems of incomplete data for most populations on the one hand and the high level of monotypy at all taxonomic levels in this ancient group on the other.

For the multivariate analyses only a single value for each character was used to represent a species. The choice of particular values for some reproductive characters was sometimes arbitrary as we attempted to choose the "most representative" data; usually we choose all values from the same population and from the population that had the largest sample sizes. Dunham, Morin, and Wilbur (this volume) discuss methodological difficulties in measuring life history traits. Geographic variation within species was studied separately.

B. The Ecological and Reproductive Characters

Latitude. Each species was classified as tropical or temperate based on the location of the primary study used in the analysis. Elevation was not used, which may obscure differences between tropical and temperate populations.

Habitat. Each species was classified as freshwater, marine, or terrestrial. Species living in brackish water (e.g., *Batagur* and *Malaclemys*: Emydidae) were classified as freshwater species.

Food. Adult feeding habits were divided into herbivory, omnivory, and carnivory. This classification may be inaccurate because most freshwater turtles that were classified as heribivores will not ignore carrion or easily captured prey. Terrestrial herbivores (e.g. *Terrapene ornata*: Emydidae; Legler, 1960b) may consume insects and large amounts of mammal feces.

Body size. Minimum, maximum, and mean body sizes of adults were taken from the literature as straight linear lengths of the carapace. Records of lengths along the curve of the carapace were not used. Minimum size of reproductively active adults was used as a measure of size at sexual maturity. Few papers report mean adult carapace length; therefore, regressions of mean length on minimum length, maximum length, and both minimum and maximum lengths were used to estimate mean length for the many species with partial data. Carapace length is a good index of body mass (e.g., $r = 0.86$ between the logarithm of mass and carapace length for 558 individuals of *Kinosternon subrubrum*, Gibbons, 1983).

Age at maturity. Only explicit reports of age at maturity were used.

Clutch size. Either published means or the midpoint of ranges of "typical" clutch sizes were used. Most values represent either the number of eggs in nests or counts of oviducal eggs.

Egg size. Volumes of eggs were computed from the radii of spherical eggs ($V = 1.333 \pi r^3$) or from the lengths (2a) and widths (2b) of nonspherical eggs, which we assumed were prolate spheroids ($V = 1.333 \pi ab^2$). These estimates are useful for a comparative study even though they may not closely reflect the true volume of eggs of different shapes.

METHODS

Clutch number. The number of clutches of eggs each female lays in a year in which she is reproductively active is poorly known for most species. Only explicit estimates based on recapture data or examination of size classes of ovarian follicles and corpora lutea are used.

Female cycle. The number of years between bouts of reproduction was used to measure the length of the female ovarian cycle. As field studies accumulate, more and more species have been found to have irregular schedules of reproductive activity (Bull and Shine, 1979; Congdon et al., 1983b). This may not hold for males.

Egg volume, clutch size, and female carapace length were obtained for 84 species and subjected to the most intensive analysis. Total clutch volume, the product of mean egg volume and the number of eggs in the clutch, is an index of the maternal investment of energy and nutrients in a single nest. This clutch volume was used as a separate dependent variable because a given total clutch volume could be composed of a few large eggs or many small ones.

For several reasons, we transformed the three dependent variables, clutch size, egg volume, and clutch volume, by their natural logarithms. They are lognormally distributed within a species, so that logarithmic transformations made variances homogeneous within groups, an assumption of the analysis of variance. This transformation also simplifies the study of the components of clutch volume because clutch volume equals mean egg volume multiplied by the number of eggs in the clutch. On a logarithmic coordinate system clutch size and egg size are additive and linearly related to female carapace length, which allows the use of the General Linear Model for analysis of the differences among taxonomic and ecological groups. Body size was measured as carapace length because body mass is known for relatively few species. Finally, the use of log–log plots allows direct comparison of the allometry of reproductive characters in turtles with similar relationships in other vertebrate groups (Calder, 1984; Dunham, Miles, and Reznick, this volume; Peters, 1983).

Absolute differences between groups of species in egg size or clutch size may be accounted for entirely by the relationship between these reproductive characteristics and body size (e.g. Congdon and Gibbons, 1985). If this is the case, the interesting comparison may involve growth rate and body size rather than egg size or clutch size per se (Gibbons et al., 1982). The analysis of covariance is a statistical technique that allows one first to adjust for differences in body size between groups and then to compare their egg or clutch sizes. Most of our tests are based on analyses of covariance following a stepwise procedure. First the logarithm of each dependent variable (egg size, egg number, or clutch volume) is regressed separately on the logarithm of carapace length in each group of species. The residual mean squares in the groups are tested for homogeneity with an F test to see if the two groups have the same scatter about their own regression lines. If the residual mean squares are homogeneous, then the regression slopes are compared by Student's t tests to see if the form of the relationship is the same in the groups being compared. If the slopes of the regressions are parallel, then the elevations of the lines are tested by analyses of covariance to determine if differences among groups are due to differences in mean female size or some other, more interesting, attribute of the groups. Statistical analyses used procedures of the Statistical Analysis System (SAS Institute, 1982) maintained at the Triangle Universities Computation Center.

III. RESULTS

A. The Diversity of Turtle Life Histories

The natural histories of turtles have been reviewed previously by Bustard (1979), Auffenberg and Iverson (1979), Bury (1979) in Harless and Morlock (1979), and several regional accounts (e.g., Ernst and Barbour, 1972; Pritchard and Trebbau, 1984). In this paper we summarize data from throughout the order and apply a statistical approach to seek broad reproductive patterns.

1. EGG SIZE

Because egg volume correlates positively with yolk content, egg size can be used as an index of the amount of nutrients and energy invested in each offspring. Egg sizes vary among species from 20 mm in diameter in *Trionyx sinensis* to 60 mm in *Dermochelys coriacea* and *Geochelone elephantopus*, a 27-fold difference in volume. Species with large clutches of small eggs tend to produce spherical eggs. Species with small clutch sizes tend to produce elongate eggs, presumably due to limitations on the size of a flexible egg that can be extruded through the pelvic aperture (Congdon et al., 1983b; Ewert, 1979).

Within a population, large eggs produce larger hatchlings (Congdon and Tinkle, 1982; Congdon et al., 1983a; Cox and Marion, 1978; Ewert, 1979; Iverson, 1979b). Larger hatchlings have a greater survival rate and larger absolute growth rate during their first year than smaller hatchlings in the same population. Swingland and Coe (1979), for example,

RESULTS

assume that the positive correlation between egg size and survival rate during the first year of life in Aldabra subpopulations of *Geochelone gigantea* reflects a causal link. In many populations predation is probably high on hatchling turtles, and rapid growth to a large size many be required before the armored shell is an effective defense against vertebrate predators (Wilbur, 1975b, Greene, this volume).

Differences in egg size among species may influence susceptibility of hatchlings to predation. For example, *Chelonia depressa* has eggs 50% heavier than *C. mydas*. Silver gulls *(Larus novaehollandiae)* and ghost crabs *(Ocypoda ceratophthalma)* are important predators of hatchling *C. mydas*, but they have very low success preying on the larger hatchlings of *C. depressa* (Bustard, 1979).

Energy stored in the yolk is used both to fuel development and to fuel the early period of hatchling independence (Congdon and Tinkle, 1982; Congdon and Gibbons, 1985). Only 39% of the lipid in the yolk of freshwater turtles is used to fuel embryogenesis (Congdon et al., 1983c), with much of the remainder presumably used to escape the nest and reach a suitable juvenile feeding site.

Hatchlings of many species delay emergence from the nest beyond the time required for embryogenesis. Such species tend to have eggs high in lipids used to fuel hatchlings (Congdon et al., 1983c). Gibbons and Nelson (1978) observed firsthand and found literature reports of delayed emergence in 19 species from 5 families; including most temperate zone turtles. They found no evidence that delayed emergence occurs simply because the soil covering the nest hardens or soil temperature drops, but they agreed with the earlier arguments of Carr and Ogren (1959) and Wilbur (1975a) that delayed emergence is an adaptation that allows hatchlings to use the sanctuary of the nest during a season when opportunities for growth in the juvenile habitat are poor. In more northern zones, the advantage of remaining in the nest overwinter can be offset by the risk of freezing. Winter-kill of *Chrysemys picta* varies between 0 and 80% with a 5-year mean of 18.6% (Breitenbach et al., 1984). Hatchlings of the more northerly distributed, but geographically overlapping, *Emydoidea blandingii* do not overwinter in the nest (Congdon et al., 1983b), perhaps as an adaptation to life in zones with deep frost penetration. On the other hand, incubation is accelerated in species that nest in the uncertain environment of sandbars (Ewert, 1979).

2. GROWTH AND MATURITY

Most hatchling turtles are carnivores (there may be exceptions within the family Testudinidae), but adults range from carnivores specializing on molluscs (several species of *Graptemys*), sponges *(Eretmochelys)*, siponophores *(Dermochelys)*, vertebrates *(Macrochelys)* to strict herbivores *(Chelonia mydas* and most *Geochelone)*. Many species shift from carnivory to herbivory during growth, often with a pronounced slowing of growth at the time of the dietary shift from food high in protein to an herbivorous diet (Bury, 1979; Clark and Gibbons, 1969). Juvenile growth rates are not well-known even though many species of turtles carry at least a partial record of their recent growth history by externally visible rings on their shells (Dunham, Morin, and Wilbur, this volume).

Turtles vary greatly in the length of their juvenile period. For example, *Sternotherus odoratus* (Kinosternidae) may reproduce for the first time as early as age two (Tinkle, 1961), but *Geochelone gigantea* may delay as late as perhaps age 25 in some populations (Grubb, 1971b; Bourn, 1977). Growth patterns on long bones suggests that *Testudo hermanni* and *T. graeca* mature in 12–13 years (Castanet and Cheylan, 1979). Estimates based on von Bertalanfy growth curves indicate that *Caretta caretta* reproduce for the first time at age 12–30 and *Chelonia mydas* at 18–27 (Frazier and Ehrhart, 1985). The prevailing notion is that most species mature at a species-specific size rather than a specific age (Moll, 1979), but there is little rigorous analysis of this problem as comparative studies must control for habitat and annual differences in growth rates. Both age and nutritional state probably determine when an individual reproduces for the first time (Gibbons et al., 1981; Parmenter, 1980). Gibbons et al. (1981) suggest that male *Pseudemys scripta* mature at a fixed size, but females mature at a fixed age. Their argument is based on comparisons of ages and sizes at maturity of turtles in thermally altered habitats compared to nearby reference habitats. Large-bodied populations on coastal islands also have large clutch sizes (Gibbons et al., 1979b, 1981). Growth slows greatly at maturity; adults of some species do not appear to grow at all (e.g., *Chelonia mydas*; Bjorndal, 1980). If the size of the pelvic canal determines the maximum egg size that a female can lay, size at maturity could be set by the minimum size a female must be to lay an egg with a sufficient energy store to provide fuel for embryogenesis and the nestling period (Congdon and Tinkle, 1982). This idea is supported by geographic comprisons in egg size (Mitchell, 1985a).

The evolution of adult body size entails physiological, behavioral, and ecological characteristics involving such adaptations as feeding habits, survival rates, fecundity schedules, and sexual selection. Early maturity is advantageous, *ceteris paribus*, and a delay in maturity in turtles probably indicates strong selection for growth towards an optimal size, which is obtained at the cost of additional risk of mortality by prolonging the period before reproduction (Wilbur, 1975b).

RESULTS

As in many large vertebrates, turtles have evolved races of giants on isolated islands, such as *Geochelone* on the Galapagos (Fritts, 1984) and on islands in the Indian Ocean (Arnold, 1979). These very large species could permit extrapolation to the reproductive biology of even larger extinct reptiles.

3. SEXUAL DIMORPHISM

Berry and Shine (1980) retrieved from the literature reports of adult body sizes and breeding behavior for 75 species of 7 families. Most terrestrial species (most testudinids and a few emydids) are sexually dimorphic and large males engage in combat for access to females. If male combat is an important selective force, then males may evolve larger sizes than females because larger males win more contests and therefore father more offspring. Terrestrial habitats may permit visually oriented behavior and control of the outcome of contests (Berry and Shine, 1980). If males are able to control copulation with females despite interference by other males, then males will exceed females in body size to enable them to inseminate females forcibly. Females of semiaquatic and "bottom-walking" aquatic species (chelydrids, kinosternids, a few emydids, and one chelid) cannot easily evade advances by a male not of their choice. In these groups males generally mature at a larger size than females. In truly aquatic species (most emydids, most chelids, cheloniids, and trionychids) male combat or forcible insemination are rare, rather males engage in elaborate precoital displays. Females appear to be able to exercise choice by evading the advances of courting males. Males are smaller than females, perhaps because small size allows greater maneuverability in pursuit of females.

The optimal size at maturity may differ between sexes because of complex interactions among the demands of sexual selection, viability selection, and fertility selection. Wilbur (1975b) suggested that males of the aquatic *Chrysemys picta* mature as soon as they have achieved a size at which they have a low risk of predation, whereas females continue to grow for several more years (apparently to increase fecundity). Work on eastern populations of *Chrysemys* supports this interpretation (Mitchell, 1985a,b). The minimum necessary egg size imposes constraints on female size not felt by males (Iverson, 1985). Males move more than females, thus they devote less energy to growth and attain smaller sizes at maturity (Parker, 1984).

4. FEMALE REPRODUCTIVE CYCLE

The fraction of females in a population that breeds in a given year has only recently been studied rigorously. Apparently, females often do not have regular cycles (Bull and Shine, 1979), but rather become reproductive only when they have sufficient energy stores (Congdon and Tinkle, 1982; Congdon et al., 1983b; Gibbons, 1982). A major drought affected the reproductive cycles of *Pseudemys scripta*, *P. floridana*, *Sternotherus odoratus*, and *Deirochelys reticularia*, but not those of *Kinosternon subrubrum* (Gibbons et al., 1983). In southeastern Michigan, only 40–50% of mature female *Chrysemys picta* nest each year (Tinkle et al., 1981; Congdon and Tinkle, 1982). About 4% nest twice in a year. Only 23–48% of mature *Emydoidea blandingii* females nest in a given year (Congdon et al., 1983b). *Chelonia mydas* lays three to five or perhaps more clutches in a year, but females may breed only once every 2–4 years (Bustard, 1979). Only 3% of female *Caretta caretta* on Little Cumberland Island, Georgia nest each year (Richardson and Hillestad, 1978). Populations of *Gopherus polyphemus* may go 7 years without successful recruitment (Auffenberg and Iverson, 1979). The Aldabra population of *Geochelone gigantea* has three isolated subpopulations that differ in the fraction of females that breed each year as well as in clutch size, egg mass, and size at maturity (Swingland, 1977) The determination of the distribution of intervals between reproductive activity is a critical fact that must be determined before models of life history evolution can be rigorously tested (Dunham, Morin, and Wilbur, this volume).

5. CLUTCH SIZE AND NUMBER OF CLUTCHES

Clutch size is the number of eggs laid in a nest. Clutch sizes in turtles range from one egg in several testudinids (e.g., *Chersina angulata*, *Homopus boulengeri*, and *Malacochersus tornieri*; Loveridge and Williams, 1957) to about 150 in *Chelonia mydas* in Surinam (Pritchard, 1969) and Yemen (Frazier, 1971). The maximum number of eggs a female can carry is limited by the space available in her body cavity and the sizes of individual eggs. Larger species produce larger hatchlings than do smaller species (Andrews, 1982). Larger turtles may lay larger eggs as well as more eggs (Auffenberg and Iverson, 1979; Congdon and Tinkle, 1982; Congdon et al., 1983a; Cox and Marion, 1978; Iverson, 1977; Landers et al., 1982). The correlation between clutch size and body size is strong when observations are from different species (see below). The correlation is usually weakened when observations are of different populations of the same species (Congdon and Gibbons, 1985). Within a population the correlation is usually weak; whenever sequential observations are made on individuals, correlations often become weaker and are obvious only if sample sizes are large (Bjorndal, 1980; Gibbons, 1982; Gibbons et al., 1979a, 1982; Iverson, 1977; Tinkle et al., 1981).

RESULTS

The maximum clutch volume of a female must certainly be strongly correlated with the volume of her body cavity. Departures from a perfect correlation provide weak evidence that females are unable to reproduce to their full potential each time they form a clutch. Long-lived iteroparous organisms may be adjusting individual clutch sizes to maximize lifetime reproductive success rather than short-term gains (Congdon and Tinkle, 1982). Females with a recent experience of low food availability or high maintenance costs may facultatively reduce clutch size by reducing the number of ova that develop or by resorbing partially yolk-filled ova. Food availability may act to determine recruitment in just this way in the *Geochelone gigantea* on Aldabra (Swingland, 1977; Swingland and Coe, 1978; Swingland and Coe, 1979).

No turtles are known to have any parental care after the nest is completed (Shine, this volume). Many species lay more than one clutch per year; some tropical testudinids may be continuous breeders. The terrestrial *Geochelone pardalis* may lay as many as five clutches in a year (Auffenberg and Iverson, 1979). Individual sea turtles, *Chelonia mydas*, lay as many as 11 clutches in a season (Hendrickson, 1958). The sequential development of several clutches may liberate female fecundity from the apparent constraint imposed by the limited volume of the body cavity. We argue below that this mechanism may operate in marine turtles, some of which migrate several thousand kilometers between feeding grounds and nesting beaches (Carr and Hirth 1962).

For some species the clutch complement must exceed a minimum number of eggs. For example, hatchling sea turtles must work together to dig out of the nest and then they rapidly move across the beach as a group and swim out to sea past the surf and offshore predators (Carr and Ogren, 1960; Bustard, 1972; Kraemer and Bennett, 1981).

6. NESTING

The eggs of all turtles are laid on land. Usually the female excavates an elaborate nest in the soil and then conceals it from predators (Packard and Packard, this volume). Some kinosternids may make no nest at all, just laying their small clutch in a rotting stump or in other organic debris. Viviparity has not evolved in turtles, as it has in many freshwater and marine snakes (Shine, 1985); consequently many sea turtles, but not all (Frazier, 1971), must migrate thousands of kilometers from feeding grounds to nesting beaches, perhaps to have higher temperatures for incubation of eggs.

A few species have mass migrations to nesting areas, and many females lay eggs on a single night (*Podocnemis expansa* on sandbars, Alho and Padua, 1982; Roze, 1964). The *arribada* of *Lepidochelys kempii* on the coastal beaches of Tamaulipas, Mexico (Pritchard, 1967) is an extreme example of breeding synchrony with estimates of 40,000 turtles nesting on a mile (1.6 km) of beach. Such synchrony may have the effect that predators are swamped.

7. SEX DETERMINATION

Perhaps the most interesting aspect of the nesting biology of turtles is that the female's choice of a nest site can determine the sex of her offspring. The study of sex determination is relevant to the central issues of the evolutionary advantages of sex itself and the prevalence of 1:1 sex ratios in most species (Bull, 1983). Turtles offer tremendous advantages for the study of sex ratios and sex determination because they are so well suited for ecological studies that require detailed knowledge of individuals.

Not surprizingly, sex determination in turtles is currently being studied vigorously (Bull et al., 1982a; Bulmer and Bull, 1982; Charnov and Bull, 1977; Packard and Packard, this volume; Raynaud and Pieau, 1985). Only a few species have a mechanism of genetic control of sex determination via morphologically distinct sex chromosomes. Only one member of the large family Emydidae, *Siebenrockiella crassicollis*, is known to possess sex chromosomes (Carr and Bickham, 1981); scanty knowledge of the evolutionary history and current selective regime of this species hinders speculation on this apparent exception. Both species of *Staurotypus* have sex chromosomes; but the third species of staurotypid, *Claudius angustatus*, does not (Bickham and Carr, 1983). Most species appear to have environmentally determined sex controlled by the temperature at which eggs are incubated (Bull, 1980, 1985; Bull and Vogt, 1979, 1981; Bull et al., 1982b; Gutzke and Paukstis 1983, 1984; McCoy et al., 1983; Morreale et al., 1982; Mrosovsky, 1982; Pieau, 1972, 1982; Raynaud and Pieau, 1985; Schwarzkopf and Brooks, 1985; Standora and Spotila, 1985; Yntema, 1976, 1979, 1981; Yntema and Mrosovsky, 1980, 1982). In general, higher temperatures produce female hatchlings and lower temperatures produce male hatchlings. Only in a narrow range of intermediate temperatures are both sexes produced. Sex ratios of hatchlings may change seasonally in response to prevailing temperatures (Mrosovsky et al., 1984a, b). In *Chelydra*, eggs near the top of the nests at warmer temperatures produced females while eggs in the cooler, bottom part of the nest produced males (Wilhoft et al., 1983). Natural nests of *Graptemys* tend to be all female if they are located in open, sunny areas and all male if in shaded microhabitats (Vogt and Bull, 1984). The phenomenon of envi-

RESULTS

ronmentally controlled sex determination is becoming well-documented, but the adaptive basis for it remains elusive. A quantitative genetic approach to temperature sensitivity and female choice of nest site is needed to test evolutionary hypotheses. It is critical to understand sex determination before the conservation tactic of moving nests to protect them from predators can be evaluated (e.g., Morreale et al., 1982).

8. NEST SUCCESS

The majority of studies of natural populations suggest that mortality of eggs and nestlings is high in turtles. Causes of death in the nest may be attributed to both abiotic and biotic factors. River turtles that nest on sandbars subject to inundation often suffer high egg mortality from high water (e.g., *Podocnemis expansa*, Roze, 1964; *Trionyx muticus*, Plummer, 1976). Unusually heavy rainfall and high tides may also result in increased nest mortality in some cheloniids (e.g., *Caretta caretta*, Ragotzkie, 1959).

Colonially nesting turtles may suffer high egg mortality as females disturb previous nests as they excavate for their own eggs (Bustard and Tognetti, 1969; Henrickson, 1958).

Procyon lotor (Mammalia: Procyonidae) is a ubiquitous North American predator that is known to prey on the nests of many species, including *Pseudemys scripta* (Cagle, 1950), *Pseudemys floridana* (Carr, 1952); *Chrysemys picta* (Wilbur, 1975a); *Emydoidea blandingii* (Congdon et al., 1983c) *Sternotherus odoratus* (Cahn, 1937; Mahmoud, 1969); *Kinosternon subrubrum*, *Kinosternon flavescens*, and *Sternotherus carinatus* (Mahmoud, 1969); *Gopherus berlandieri* (Auffenberg and Weaver, 1969); *Trionyx muticus* (Cahn, 1937; Fitch and Plummer, 1975); *Trionyx ferox* (Goldsmith, 1944); *Chelydra serpentina* (Hammer, 1969); *Malaclemys terrapin* (Seigel, 1980); and *Caretta caretta* (Baldwin and Lofton, 1959; Phillips, 1972). *Mephitis mephitis* (Mammalia; Mustelidae) appears not to endanger the nests of marine turtles, but it does prey on most of the other species exploited by *Procyon*. *Geochelone elephantopus* have a 65% emergence success as burros destroyed 32.1% and 11.7% of nests in two areas (deNiera and Roe, 1984). *Dasypus novemcinctus* (Mammalia: Dasypodidae) and *Ameiva ameiva* (Sauria: Teiidae) have been implicated as important nest predators of neotropical turtles (Moll and Legler, 1971). Birds of many species, such as *Corvus* and *Corogyps*, often eat turtle eggs (e.g., Roze, 1964; Mondolfi, 1955; Baldwin and Lofton, 1959; Phillips, 1972). *Canis latrans* (Mammalia: Canidae) may also contribute to nest destruction (Fitch and Plummer, 1975; Pritchard and Marquez, 1973). *Ocypoda sp. (Crustacea: Oxypodidae)* often cause heavy mortality among marine turtles (Pritchard and

Marquez, 1973; Hendrickson, 1958; Frazier, 1971; Baldwin and Lofton, 1959; Phillips, 1972; Honegger, 1967). Old World predators that contribute to nest destruction include *Varanus* sp. (Sauria: Varanidae) (Raven, 1946; Bustard, 1972; Hendrickson, 1958) and *Sus* (Mammalia: Suidae) (Raven, 1946; Bustard, 1972). Island nest sites reduce predation on freshwater turtles (Drummond, 1983). Reviews of predation on turtle nests include Moll and Legler (1971), Loveridge and Williams (1957), Pritchard (1971a), Lagler (1945), and Minton (1966).

Most reports of nest predation say that if the nest is found by a predator, all eggs are killed. Moreover, many nests are found by predators. As examples, 65 of 73 (89%) nests of *Gopherus polyphemus* were destroyed by mammalian predators in southwestern Georgia (Landers et al., 1980); and, greater than 90% of nests of *Testudo hermanni* were destroyed (Swingland and Stubbs, 1985). Egg success of *Chelonia mydas* at Tortuguero, Costa Rica was low because 39.7% of 350 natural nests were destroyed by predators (Fowler, 1979). Including all sources of mortality only 35.26% of eggs that are laid emerge as hatchlings. *Caretta caretta* nesting in South Carolina may suffer 10–97% destruction in different years depending on the local population density of raccoons (*Procyon lotor*) (Talbert et al., 1980). Predators destroyed 21% of 43 nests of *Chrysemys picta*; 14% in the first night after they were laid (Tinkle et al., 1981). Similar levels of predation on *Emydoidea blandingii* nests occur in the same area (63% predation on 73 nests with 74% of the destruction occurring within 5 days of nest construction) (Congdon et al., 1983b). Other reports of nest predation include 50–97% losses for *Pseudemys scripta* (Moll and Legler, 1971), 95% for *Pseudemys floridana* (Allen, 1938), 42% for *Clemmys guttata* (Ernst, 1970), 90% for *Graptemys pulchra* (Shealy, 1976), 95% for *Podocnemis expansa* (Roze, 1964), 90% for *Lepidochelys olivacea* (Pritchard, 1969), 48% for *Trionyx muticus* (Fitch and Plummer, 1975), 63% for *Chelydra serpentina* (Hammer, 1969), and 56% (Baldwin and Lofton, 1959) and 90% (Phillips, 1972) for *Caretta caretta*. The impact of humans on turtle nesting has been discussed in numerous papers (e.g. Harrisson, 1952; Carr, 1967; Pritchard, 1966; Roze, 1964). Wilbur (1977) has shown that multiple nesting within a season could be an adaptation to reduce the variance (Gillespie, 1974) in nest success among years due to losses of entire nests.

9. MORTALITY RATES OF ADULTS

Very little is known about juvenile mortality despite its critical position in any population model (Frazer, 1983; Thompson, 1980; Wilbur, 1975a). The often high egg mortality and long juvenile period of

RESULTS

turtles are balanced by high adult survival rates, which can result in adults potentially breeding for many years. Only long-term field studies on marked individuals can provide accurate estimates of adult survival rates that account for differences due to years, ages, and sexes. Stickel (1978) has followed a population of individually marked *Terrapene carolina* for 30 years and found no evidence that mortality rate increased with age. Nearly 20% of her population was older than 20 years at each of four censuses over the last 30 years. Gibbons (1968b) reported that survival rate decreases at maturity in *Chrysemys picta*, but Wilbur (1975a) suggests that survival rates are probably constant once adult sizes are reached. Blair's (1976) data for the long-lived *Terrapene ornata* suggest an annual survival of adults of 77.9% (we used the 1952 cohort for our computations). Once a female has attained sexual maturity (8 years), the life expectancy is only 4 years; only 10% of females are expected to live longer than 9 years after maturity. *Chrysemys picta* has a life expectancy of about 5 years after reaching maturity (Wilbur, 1975a); the average female *Chelonia mydas* lives perhaps 16 years as an adult (Carr and Carr, 1970b). Ten percent of a population of *Kinosternon subrubrum* live more than 16 years (Gibbons, 1983). Annual survival rates of 98% may occur in adult desert tortoises (*Gopherus agassizii*) (Turner and Berry, 1984). In female *Caretta caretta*, the annual survival rate is 81% and the probability of a female's returning in the future is associated with the number of clutches she laid (Richardson, 1982). Females that laid two or fewer clutches had a 77% chance of returning, but females that laid three or more clutches had a probability of 94% of returning.

The literature contains many claims of very old turtles. Records of longevity of captive turtles are useful indicators of the physiological capacity to remain reproductively active in advanced ages, but they provide little insight to life expectancies in natural populations. Well-documented records that some individuals of *Terrapene carolina*, a small terrestrial emydid, live beyond 100 years have been reviewed by Graham and Hutchison (1969). Captive *Testudo graeca* and *Geochelone gigantea* have also lived more than a century (Pritchard, 1967). Nevertheless, these estimates of maximum longevity may differ considerably from those of life expectancy in nature. If constant annual mortality rates are a reasonable assumption for turtles, then very old turtles should be rare. For example, given an annual survival rate of 90%, only one in a hundred turtles would live for another 44 years.

10. SUMMARY OF LIFE HISTORY DIVERSITY

In summary, all turtles can probably be characterized by a juvenile period of at least 2 years, no viviparity or postnesting parental care, high mortality rates of eggs and hatchlings, and low mortality rates of adults. Life history theory (Bell, 1976) predicts that such a mortality schedule of high juvenile mortality and low adult mortality should favor iteroparity. As a group, turtles indeed have the greatest development of iteroparity and the lowest intrinsic rates of increase of any large order of tetrapods. Data are abundant on the easily obtained characters of body size, clutch size, and egg size, the traits we discuss in detail above. Nevertheless, data on juvenile growth and survival (Hirth and Schaffer, 1974) and on the reproductive histories of individuals are badly needed. Gibbons and his colleagues in South Carolina and Congdon in Michigan are making valuable progress using drift fences to obtain complete records of movements of females and juveniles into and out of ponds (Gibbons and Semlitsch, 1981). They also use radiographs to determine clutch sizes of females each time they leave a pond for nesting (Gibbons and Greene, 1979). There is also a tremendous level of activity, much of it productive, in the study of sea turtles (e.g., Bjorndal, 1982; Crouse, 1985; Frazer, 1983; Mrosovsky, 1983; Owens, 1980; Pritchard and Trebbau, 1984; Richardson, 1982; Thompson, 1980).

The collection of life histories *sensu stricto* of individuals will eventually allow direct tests of evolutionary theory, only when coupled with a genetic analysis of correlated life history traits. Perhaps the most exciting area in which turtle biologists can contribute to evolutionary theory is in the ecology and behavior of females in determining the sex of their offspring.

B. Multivariate Analysis of Clutch Parameters and Ecological Groups

1. GENERAL

Reproductive data are here used in multivariate statistical analyses to uncover patterns that might help explain the diversity of turtle life histories in terms of taxonomic constraints and ecological pressures. The central technique is regression analysis in which egg volume and clutch size are used as dependent variables and female body size is considered as an independent variable, or covariate. The relationship among these variables in a logarithmic coordinate system is compared among different groups of species. The focus is on differences in size-specific reproductive characters rather than differences in body size itself.

The first analysis examines the multivariate distribution of egg volume and clutch size. The analysis uses carapace length as a covariate and habitat, food, and latitude as main effects in a multivariate analysis of covariance. That is, we ask whether egg volumes and clutch sizes,

RESULTS

adjusted for differences in carapace length, differ between ecological groups defined by the combinations of the habitats (freshwater, marine, and terrestrial), food habits (herbivore, carnivore, and omnivore) and latitude (tropical and temperate). Complete data are available for 80 species. The only significant main effect is habitat ($P \ll 0.001$). We conclude that the effects of adult diet and latitude are unimportant after the two dependent variables have been adjusted for female size and habitat. A univariate analysis of covariance of total clutch volume also shows that only female size ($P < 0.001$) and habitat ($P < 0.0001$) are significant in explaining variation among species.

The differences among species in different habitats have been studied in a stepwise fashion. First separate regressions of each dependent variable on female size have been computed for each group (Table II). Then each pair of habitats is compared with respect to each dependent variable. Separate tests are made for each pair of the three habitat groups for differences in both clutch size and egg size for a total of six simultaneous tests. A single test should use a probability level of 0.0085 to maintain an overall confidence of 95% against a Type I error (rejecting the null hypothesis when it is in fact true) in the analysis.

2. COMPARISONS AMONG FRESHWATER AND MARINE SPECIES

Marine turtles have absolutely larger eggs and larger clutch sizes than do freshwater turtles, but the differences are only what would be expected given the differences in body sizes between the two groups. The regressions of egg volume on carapace length (Table II) are the same in the two groups (homogeneous residual mean squares, homogeneous slopes, no differences in elevation). The much larger eggs of marine turtles are only as large as would be predicted for freshwater turtles of the same body size. The regressions of clutch size on carapace length (Table II) have homogeneous residual mean squares and slopes, but the elevation for marine turtles is close to being significantly higher than that for freshwater species ($P = 0.0098$). Additional data might show convincingly that sea turtles have larger clutches than predicted from the extrapolation of the relationship between clutch size and body size in freshwater turtles.

The statistical comparison may not be entirely fair because no data are available for an estimate of the expected annual fecundity of each species. This estimate would require information for each species about both the average number of clutches and the probability of nesting at all in a given year. Sea turtles may nest several times in a short period (Section III.A.5), making their annual egg production even greater than

TABLE II
Analysis of Covariance of Dependent Variables ($\log_e$ Transformed) Adjusted for $\log_e$ (Carapace Length)

	Freshwater	Marine	Terrestrial
Carapace length (mm)	232.5	942.2	240.7
Egg volume (ml)			
Unadjusted mean	13.4	46.3	24.3
Mean adjusted for size	11.99	10.96	22.49
Sample size	53	8	20
Residual mean square	0.262	0.075	0.121
r^2	0.46	0.57	0.76
Slope + SE	0.932 + 0.141	1.067 + 0.376	1.090 + 0.146
Intercept + SE	−2.557 + 0.742	−3.490 + 2.564	−2.743 + 0.779
Clutch size			
Unadjusted mean	11.9	110.6	5.3
Mean adjusted for size	9.41	28.97	4.45
Sample size	53	8	20
Residual mean square	0.459	0.130	0.321
r^2	0.37	0.09	0.40
Slope + SE	1.019 + 0.187	−0.379 + 0.495	0.819 + 0.238
Intercept + SE	−3.315 + 0.982	7.239 + 0.495	−2.980 + 1.270
Total volume of clutch (ml)			
Unadjusted mean	142.1	4675.1	160.6
Mean adjusted for size	107.5	315.1	99.4
Sample size	53	8	20
Residual mean square	0.439	0.021	0.375
r^2	0.70	0.66	0.75
Slope + SE	1.952 + 0.181	0.686 + 0.201	1.908 + 0.258
Intercept + SE	−5.872 + 0.952	3.749 + 1.372	−5.723 + 1.372

Means are reported on an arithmetic scale.

would be predicted for freshwater species of the same size. Sea turtles also tend to have a tremendous reproductive output only once every 2–4 years, presumably because females in some populations must migrate long distances from feeding grounds to nesting beaches and store energy for several years prior to this great expenditure. For example, *Chelonia mydas* makes a 4000-km trip during its migration between its feeding grounds in the western Caribbean and its nesting beach at Tortuguero, Costa Rica (Carr and Carr, 1970b). This trip is made without food; thereafter, females may deposit 5 or more clutches of about 110 eggs each over about a 10-week period, losing about a fifth of their body mass during the nesting season. No female has been known to make

RESULTS

this trip 2 years in a row; most nest once every 2–4 years (mean = 3.26 yr, N = 447). Clutch sizes in marine turtles are remarkably constant geographically within a species, but egg weight varies considerably (Bustard, 1979; Bustard and Greenham, 1968, 1969; Hendrickson, 1958).

The regression of total clutch volume on female size is different in the two groups. Even on the logarithmic scale, the residual mean squares are significantly different ($P < 0.008$) precluding further testing for differences in slope or elevations. Clutch volume is much more variable for a species of a given size in freshwater turtles than in marine species.

3. COMPARISONS BETWEEN FRESHWATER AND TERRESTRIAL SPECIES

Freshwater and terrestrial species invest similar amounts of resources in a nest (Tables I and II), but they package the investment differently. Terrestrial species lay a few large eggs, freshwater species lay many small ones. The regressions of egg volume on carapace length have homogeneous residual variances and slopes in freshwater and terrestrial groups, but the adjusted means differ significantly ($P < 0.001$). Terrestrial species have larger eggs with respect to female body size than do freshwater species. For example, a 200-mm terrestrial species would be predicted to produce eggs with a volume of 21 ml, but an aquatic species of the same size would be predicted to have an egg volume of only 11 ml. The regressions of clutch size on carapace length also have homogeneous residual mean squares and slopes, but adjusted means are significantly different in the two groups ($P < 0.001$). Terrestrial species have fewer eggs per clutch than freshwater species of the same body size. For example the hypothetical 200-mm terrestrial species would have a clutch of four eggs, but the aquatic species of the same size would have a clutch of eight eggs. The product of clutch and egg size, total clutch volume, is the same (equal residual mean squares, slopes and elevations) in the two groups.

The difference between freshwater and terrestrial turtles have been examined more closely by comparing only the data for the families Emydidae and Testudinidae. Emydidae is the largest family of extant turtles with 30 genera and about 88 species distributed on all continents except Australia. The group inhabits bogs, ponds, rivers, and lakes. Two species, *Batagur baska* and *Malaclemys terrapin* live in the tidal marshes. Two genera (*Terrapene* and *Rhinoclemmys*) have species that have become terrestrial; some species have strong terrestrial tendencies (e.g., *Clemmys insculpta*). The terrestrial family Testudinidae is a large group of 10 genera and about 39 extant species, including the giant

TABLE III
Analyses of Covariance of Dependent Variables ($\log_e$ Transformed) Adjusted for $\log_e$ (Carapace Length)

	Testudinidae	Emydidae
Carapace length (mm)	257.1	203.7
Egg volume (ml)		
Unadjusted mean	26.2	14.6
Mean adjusted for size	19.47	12.09
Sample size	17	28
Residual mean square	0.103	0.295
r^2	0.76	0.37
Slope + SE	1.037 + 0.149	1.126 + 0.288
Intercept	−2.436 + 0.806	−3.402 + 1.492
Clutch size		
Unadjusted mean	5.4	9.3
Mean adjusted for size	3.72	7.86
Sample size	17	28
Residual mean square	0.296	0.303
r^2	0.52	0.25
Slope + SE	1.018 + 0.253	0.866 + 0.292
Intercept + SE	−4.137 + 1.365	−2.573 + 1.512
Total volume of the clutch (ml)		
Unadjusted mean	181.5	109.2
Mean adjusted for size	68.32	88.54
Sample size	17	28
Residual mean square	0.403	0.260
r^2	0.77	0.68
Slope + SE	2.055 + 0.234	1.992 + 0.270
Intercept + SE	−6.572 + 1.592	−5.979 + 1.400

Means are reported on an arithmetic scale.

tortoises of the Galapagos Archipelago and the islands in the Indian Ocean. All land tortoises are primarily herbivorous, although some species eat large amounts of carrion and dung. Testudinids are thought to have evolved from emydids with intermediate forms similar to extant *Terrapene* (Auffenberg and Iverson, 1979).

The regressions of egg volume, clutch size, and clutch volume on carapace length have homogeneous residual mean squares and regression slopes (Table III). Testudinids have significantly larger eggs (mean of 24 ml versus 11 ml) and fewer eggs per clutch (four versus six) than emydids, but the total clutch volumes adjusted for body-size differences

RESULTS

are the same in the two groups. These results, as expected, are the same as those from the comparisons of all freshwater species with all terrestrial species.

The production of large numbers of offspring is advantageous, *ceteris paribus*, because it increases the chances that a female will successfully contribute to the next generation. Quantity of offspring may be tempered by quality; therefore the question becomes why the eggs of terrestrial species are larger than those of freshwater species of the same adult size. We here offer a set of hypotheses for testing with direct comparisons of feeding behavior and growth rates in hatchlings and juveniles of freshwater and terrestrial species.

Hatchlings of freshwater species are apparently carnivorous regardless of their feeding habits after attaining maturity. This carnivory is possible because of the speed and maneuverability of aquatic turtles and the high density of suitable prey (of appropriate size) in the productive ponds, marshes, and lake margins where most freshwater turtles live (Parmenter, 1980; Clark and Gibbons, 1969). Herbivory may also be limited to individuals above a certain body size strictly by physiological limitations imposed by metabolic demand and feeding mode as argued for lizards by Pough (1973). Large turtles may be unable to meet total energy demands by carnivory in most habitats. An apparent counterexample is *Pseudemys rubiventris* the juveniles of which are herbivorous until they become large enough to capture crayfish; growth rate increases when they are able to exploit this food source, which is high in protein (Graham, 1971). We know of no strictly carnivorous terrestrial species. Most terrestrial turtles are herbivorous, although carrion and dung are common adult foods, and some juveniles eat easily captured insects. Herbivorous diets may preclude rapid growth. Terrestrial species may also be limited by climatological factors in the time available for activity. It would be interesting to test the prediction that juvenile terrestrial turtles are less efficient carnivores than juvenile aquatic turtles.

The risk of predation in turtles declines with increase in size. We argue elsewhere (Wilbur, 1975b; Dunham, Morin, and Wilbur, this volume) that maturity may be set by the size at which this risk of predation is balanced by the advantage of switching energy from growth to reproduction. Large eggs produce large hatchlings and therefore shorten the time required to reach a size where the risk of predation declines sharply. There is always a conflict between offspring size and number (Wilbur, 1977); the balance is tipped towards size in terrestrial turtles and towards number in freshwater ones.

4. COMPARISONS AMONG MARINE AND TERRESTRIAL SPECIES

The differences among marine and terrestrial species parallel those of the freshwater–terrestrial comparison. Marine species have smaller eggs than terrestrial species after egg volume has been adjusted for the body size of the female ($P < 0.001$). Marine species also have significantly larger clutch size ($P < 0.001$). The regressions of total clutch volume on female carapace length could not be compared because residual mean squares about the log–log regression lines were significantly different ($P < 0.01$). Terrestrial species are more variable within a size class than marine species.

If marine and freshwater species are considered to have the same scaling of clutch parameters, then the hypotheses outlined above would also apply to comparisons among marine and terrestrial groups of turtles. Marine turtles are playing a sweepstakes with predators (Carr, 1967). This game, which may involve predator satiation mechanisms, favors large numbers of small eggs; perhaps the principal predators on the beaches and offshore are so large that small increments in hatchling size would not confer additional protection. Synchronous breeding will also enhance predator satiation. Because much mortality occurs at the level of whole nests, multiple nesting would be advantageous by reducing the variance in fitness (Gillespie, 1974). Nevertheless these advantages of multiple nesting must be balanced by the increased costs of constructing several nests (Frazer and Richardson, 1986) and by the positive effects of cooperation among hatchlings in escaping the nest (Carr, 1967) and moving en mass to the surf as a "selfish herd" (*sensu*, Hamilton, 1971) to reduce the individual's risk of predation.

C. Taxonomic Constraints on Life History Patterns

Turtle families tend to be ecological groups. Pelomedusidae, Chelidae, Dermatemyidae, Platysternidae, Chelydridae, Kinosternidae, and Trionychidae, each exploit freshwater habitats. Emydidae is a predominately aquatic family, but it has secondary trends towards terrestriality in the genera *Terrapene, Clemmys,* and *Rhinoclemmys*. Dermochelyidae and Cheloniidae are strictly marine. The family Testudinidae is terrestrial. Habitat also implies some limit to adult diet (Table IV). Hendrickson (1980) gives a detailed discussion of adaptive radiation in sea turtles.

Three large, well-studied freshwater families were compared to examine taxonomic constraints during the adaptive radiation within a single habitat. Kinosternidae, the mud and musk turtles, comprises 4

RESULTS

TABLE IV
Association Between Adult Food and Habitat

	Herbivore	Omnivore	Carnivore
Freshwater	6 (7.59)[a]	17 (0.00)	40 (4.57)
Marine	2 (0.00)	1 (0.41)	4 (0.21)
Terrestrial	19 (0.12)	8 (0.08)	0 (12.24)

$\chi^2 = 25.23$; $P < 0.001$.
[a]Entries are numbers of species and contributions of cells to chi-square.

genera and about 20 species. All are small carnivores that tend to forage on the bottom of lakes and ponds in the New World. Trionychidae, the softshelled turtles, consists of 6 genera and about 23 species of moderate to large-sized carnivores, which occur in rivers and lakes in North America, Africa, and Asia. Emydidae, the largest family of turtles, includes many active swimmers and has representatives throughout the world except Australia.

These three families have been compared with respect to the regressions of the logarithms of egg volume, clutch size, and total clutch volume on the logarithm of female carapace length (Table V). Among the three families, residual mean squares and regression slopes are homogeneous within all three sets of regressions. Egg volume and clutch size had similar elevations; i.e., these two variables have the same relationship to body size in all three families. This result supports the notion that the aquatic mode of life, not taxonomic constraints, determines the allometric relationship between clutch parameters and body sizes. In other words, the interesting differences between ecological groups discussed above may be due to differences in environmental factors rather than in taxonomic history.

Total clutch volume, however, has different regression elevations ($P < 0.005$) in the groups. Emydids and trionychids have nearly the same clutch volume when adjusted for carapace length. Kinosternids, however, have significantly smaller clutch volume per body size as a group than do emydids or trionychids. Kinosternids have the weakest correlation between clutch volume and body size, but they clearly fall below the line for emydids and trionychids. The adaptive value, if any, may be related to their high degree of terrestriality. The statistical difference may be only an artifact caused by differences in shape not manifested in the use of carapace length as a measure of body size. Trionychids tend to be larger and dorso-ventrally flattened compared to emydids and kinosternids.

TABLE V
Analyses of Covariance of Dependent Variables (log$_e$ Transformed) Adjusted for log$_e$ (Carapace Length)

	Emydidae	Kinosternidae	Trionychidae
Carapace length (mm)	203.7	111.0	350.9
Egg volume (ml)			
Unadjusted mean	14.6	6.4	14.3
Mean adjusted for size	11.14	9.38	6.97
Sample size	28	11	8
Residual mean square	0.295	0.135	0.265
r^2	0.37	0.43	0.43
Slope + SE	1.126 + 0.298	1.515 + 0.580	0.738 + 0.347
Intercept + SE	−3.402 + 1.492	−5.343 + 2.718	−1.724 + 1.982
Clutch size			
Unadjusted mean	9.3	3.8	16.9
Mean adjusted for size	6.99	4.77	9.16
Sample size	28	11	8
Residual mean square	0.303	0.235	0.641
r^2	0.25	0.03	0.01
Slope + SE	0.866 + 0.292	−0.408 + 0.765	0.123 + 0.539
Intercept + SE	−2.577 + 1.512	2.976 + 3.584	1.927 + 3.085
Total volume of the clutch (ml)			
Unadjusted mean	109.2	18.1	214.4
Mean adjusted for size	71.95	33.90	70.86
Sample size	28	11	8
Residual mean square	0.260	0.164	0.419
r^2	0.68	0.25	0.39
Slope + SE	1.992 + 0.270	1.107 + 0.639	0.861 + 0.436
Intercept + SE	−5.979 + 1.400	2.367 + 2.995	0.203 + 2.495

Means are reported on an arithmetic scale.

D. Geographic Variation Within Species

1. GENERAL

One way to illuminate the origin of differences among species is by the use of the comparative method to study geographic variation within a widely distributed species. A few species of turtles have been studied in enough populations to make some comparisons among geographic areas and among populations in different habitats in the same geographic region. Although our multivariate analysis did not disclose differences among tropical and temperate species (Section III.B.; contra Moll and Legler, 1971), several studies have demonstrated geographic

RESULTS

TABLE VI
Geographic Variation in Reproductive Traits of *Sternotherus odoratus*

Locality	Female carapace length (mm)	Clutch size	Number of clutches	Age at maturity (yr)	Reference
"Northern"	80 (min)	4.6	1	3–7	Tinkle, 1961
Michigan	122 (max)	3–5	1	9–11	Risley, 1933
Illinois	82–119	3–5	–	–	Cahn, 1937
"Southern"	61 (min.)	2.2	–	2–3	Tinkle, 1961
Virginia	66–77	3.2	1–2	4	Mitchell, 1985a
Alabama	70	–	3?	–	McPherson and Marion, 1983
Florida	65–92	2.4	2+	–	Gibbons, 1970a

variation among populations within a species. Geographic differences are generally attributed to correlations of climate and latitude, but the comparative biologist must remain vigilant to the possibility of spurious correlation. Several studies of populations within a local area, reviewed in a next section, have demonstrated the potentially strong effects of local conditions on the life history of a species.

2. GEOGRAPHICALLY DISTANT POPULATIONS

Tinkle (1961) examined museum specimens of *Sternotherus odoratus* to compare reproductive traits in northern and southern populations in the United States. His broad conclusions have been supported by more recent work (Table VI). Females in southern populations mature earlier, at a smaller size, and have more clutches per year than females in northern populations. Females in northern populations have a larger clutch size, as expected from their larger body size.

Kinosternon subrubrum is a highly terrestrial member of the aquatic family Kinosternidae, which is thought to be closely allied with the chelydrids. Body size shows little geographic variation, but females are about 3% larger than males (Gibbons, 1983; Iverson, 1979a). Together with the fact that local populations have a balanced sex ratio, this suggests that both sexes mature at the same age. Clutch size is typically two or three eggs with extremes of one to eight. In contrast to *Sternotherus odoratus* (above), clutch size in *K. subrubrum* decreases with an increase in climatic temperature without a concordant change in body size. Within a population, the clutch size decreases in successive clutches; perhaps the geographic trend merely reflects the inclusion of more second clutches from the southern populations (Gibbons 1983).

Chrysemys picta, including its four recognized subspecies, has been studied throughout its range. Variation in body size, clutch size, clutch number, and age at maturity correspond well with taxonomic divisions (Moll, 1973; Christiansen and Moll, 1973; Table VII). In the North, turtles mature at a larger size and later age and produce fewer, but larger, clutches each year than southern populations (MacCulloch and Secoy, 1983; Moll, 1977). Small size in the south might result from competition with species of the closely related genus *Pseudemys*, primarily *P. scripta* (Moll, 1973). Total annual egg production varies from perhaps as few as 9 eggs per year in Minnesota (Legler, 1954), but the mean clutch size is 19.8 in Saskatchewan, Canada (MacCulloch and Secoy, 1983), to as high as 36 eggs in New Mexico (Christiansen and Moll, 1973). The careful studies of Tinkle et al. (1981) demonstrate that in Michigan fewer than half of all mature females reproduce in a given years. *Chrysemys picta* have lower densities than northern populations (Cagle, 1954). Mammalian nest predators would be expected to have a density-dependent effect on nesting success.

We predict that the life table of a southern population will be found to differ in several ways from the life table of the Michigan population described by Wilbur (1975a) and adjusted by Tinkle et al. (1981). Southern populations will probably turnover at faster rates (individuals have a shorter life expectancy) because of earlier maturity, larger annual egg production, and probably higher juvenile and adult mortality rates. Southern populations are less likely to suffer mortality from hatchlings freezing in the nest during the winter. Earlier maturity would increase the intrinsic rate of increase, but small size might result in lower adult survival. Geographic variation in the proportion of adults that reproduce each year could have a profound effect on reproductive rates.

Hirth (1980) reviewed the reproductive biology of sea turtles and provides tables of life history characteristics for many populations. *Chelonia mydas*, the economically important green sea turtle, has been studied throughout its range. The population nesting at Tortuguero, Costa Rica, has been the subject of long-term studies by Carr and his coworkers. Adults have a very high fidelity to a certain beach, but the pattern of gene flow among populations is unknown because of a lack of data on these sites at which hatchlings first nest after they mature.

On Ascension Island, females nest only every 3–4 years and must travel nearly 5000 km and fast 6–8 weeks during the migration between the feeding grounds off Brazil and the nesting beaches (Carr and Hirth,

RESULTS

TABLE VII
Geographic Variation in Reproductive Characters in *Chrysemys picta*

Locality	Female size (mm)	Plastron or carapace	Female age (yrs)	Clutch size	Clutch number	Authority
Saskatchewan	140	P		19.8	1	MacCulloch and Secoy (1983)
British Columbia				7–13		Thacker (1924)
British Columbia				12–13		Carl (1944)
Nova Scotia				8.5	1–2	Powell (1967)
Ontario	120	C		7.2		Williams and Crossman (1977)
Minnesota	123	P		8.8	1	Legler (1954)
Minnesota				11.9		Gemmell (1970)
Wisconsin	136	P	7	10	1–2	Christiansen and Moll (1973)
Wisconsin	130	C		7		Cunningham (1922)
Wisconsin				7		Mahmoud (1968)
Wisconsin	136	P	7–8	10.7	1–2	Moll (1973)
Iowa				6–13		Stromsten (1923)
Iowa				8.8		Blanchard (1923)
Michigan				4.7		Cagle (1954)
Michigan	115	P	7	6.1–6.6	1–2	Gibbons (1968a)
Michigan				5.2		Gibbons and Tinkle (1969)
Michigan	113	P		6.4		ibid.
Michigan	122	P		8.2		ibid.
Michigan	119		7	6.8		Wilbur (1975a)
Michigan	139.9	C		7.55	0–2	Tinkle et al. (1981)
New York	165	C		11		Wilcox (1933)
Connecticut				5.9		Finneran (1948)
Pennsylvania	100	P	6	4.7		Ernst (1971b)
Illinois	122	P		6.3		Cagle (1954)
Illinois	130	P	4–6	8.7	1–3	Moll (1973)
Illinois	106	P		6–7		Cahn (1973)
Illinois	125	P		6		ibid.
Illinois	142	P		6–7		ibid.
Virginia	105	P	6	4.2	1–2	Mitchell (1985a)
Tennessee	106			4.3		Cagle (1954)
Tennessee	108		4–5	4.8	1–5	Moll (1973)
Louisiana	100		4	4.1	1–5	ibid.
New Mexico	132	P	5–6	9	2–3	Christiansen and Moll (1973)

1962; Simon and Parkes, 1976). Females are larger than at Tortuguero (Carr and Goodman, 1970), the clutch size is slightly larger, and females lay fewer clutches per nesting season. Presumably the long migration causes selection for larger body sizes and also results in a longer reproductive cycle. Many adults are injured by the surf and rocks at the beaches, and evidence of shark injury is common. Both observations suggest that adults may have a lower survival than do those of Caribbean populations, at least lower than values before humans became important predators of sea turtles throughout the Caribbean and Gulf of Mexico.

On three islands of Sarawak, adult turtles have been protected by Moslem custom for centuries and egg predation has been regulated by local chiefs and sultans since at least the early 1800s. These populations of *Chelonia* can be compared to Caribbean populations with a long history of predation by humans. In Sarawak, breeding and nesting occur year-round, and females lay up to 11 times in 1 year, although the average number of nests per female is between 6 and 7 (Hendrickson, 1958). Clutch sizes are significantly lower than at Tortuguero, but because each female lays more often, annual egg production is higher. Adults feed throughout the South China Sea, and presumably are able to expend more energy on reproduction than females in other populations. The high density of females, perhaps due to the absence of predation by humans, results in severe crowding at the beaches. Hendrickson estimates that each point of the beach is dug up by nesting females about three times each year. This interference results in the destruction of about 50% of all eggs laid. Bustard and Tognetti (1969) have modeled the effects of nest destruction on population dynamics.

In Queensland, populations of *Chelonia mydas* have had little human disturbance of either nesting females or eggs, although the lizard *Varanus varius* may be an important nest predator. Females travel to beaches only once in every 4 years, and they may lay three to six clutches (Bustard, 1972; Limpus, 1971).

The largest *Chelonia* with the largest clutch sizes nest on the beaches of Surinam (Pritchard, 1969). Here clutches average about 140 eggs and may exceed 226 eggs, the largest clutch known for an amniote vertebrate. The location of the feeding grounds is uncertain, but a single recapture of a marked turtle suggests that it may be the coast of Brazil.

A comparison of the life tables for these various populations would be interesting. In Sarawak, moslems have been preying heavily on eggs, but not on adults, for several hundred years. In Costa Rica, humans have preyed on both eggs and nesting females since pre-Columbian time. Turnover times should be shorter in the Costa Rican populations because of lower life expectancies, but density-dependent mortality and growth should be lower than in the South China Sea, where egg mortality, and perhaps natural adult mortality, is very high. These different selective regimes could well have resulted in genetic differences in the life histories of isolated *Chelonia* populations.

3. VARIATION AMONG LOCAL POPULATIONS

The interpretation of geographic gradients should be made in light of comparative studies of local populations in different habitats. A few gradients have been compared, but they seldom include measurements of movement, and hence gene flow, between the study areas. Without genetic evidence, such as provided by Schribner et al. (1984), the comparison of local populations may be interpreted as either phenotypic plasticity or genetic adaptation to local conditions.

Three populations of *Chrysemys picta* in Michigan inhabiting a lake, a marsh, and a river have significantly different clutch sizes, which may reflect differences in body size and diet (Gibbons, 1967 and Gibbons and Tinkle, 1969). Turtles in the river are more carnivorous and larger than the turtles in the marsh, which are primarily herbivorous.

The studies of Gibbons and his associates (Gibbons, 1970c; Gibbons et al., 1981), which compare populations of *Pseudemys scripta* in ponds thermally altered by nuclear reactor effluents with populations in nearly natural ponds, are particularly illuminating as to the plasticity of turtle life histories. A heated pond is a more favorable habitat for growth. Juveniles have a significantly higher growth rate, males mature at an earlier age and females mature at a larger size in the heated pond. Differences in female size at maturity result in different clutch sizes, although both the reference and the experimental populations lie on the same regression line of clutch size on body size.

Thornhill (1982) also compared populations of *Pseudemys scripta* in a heated and natural ponds. The heated pond had larger females with larger clutches. Females in the heated pond began reproduction earlier in the year and produced slightly more clutches in a season.

A very complete comparison among local populations is the study of Swingland and his colleagues of *Geochelone gigantea* on Aldabra. In one population, on Grande Terre, some tortoises migrate during the rainy season from inland to the coast where food is relatively more abundant. The benefit of migration is a potentially higher reproductive output, but the cost is higher mortality risk from overheating. The costs and benefits are density-dependent (Swingland and Lessels, 1979). Three of the islands of the Aldabra Atoll have isolated populations that differ in population density (Coe et al., 1979). These densities result in different ages at sexual maturity, clutch sizes, number of clutches per year, proportion of females that are reproductively active each year, and annual reproductive success (Swingland and Coe, 1978, 1979). Recruitment is sensitive to population differences as well as to differences in food availability. This metapopulation provides an excellent opportunity to study genetic differentiation in a long-lived vertebrate.

IV. SUMMARY

Turtles are an ancient order in which life history evolution has been constrained by the morphological limits imposed by a rigid shell and the need to deposit eggs in a safe terrestrial site. The shell of a turtle only becomes an effective defense against predation, after the turtle has reached a threshold size. The order has remained committed to a life history of terrestrial nesting, high egg mortality, and iteroparity despite adaptive radiations in freshwater, terrestrial, and marine habitats.

Size at maturity may be a balance between the advantages of early reproduction and the advantage of large size, which reduces the risk of predation and may increase fecundity. If females benefit from the delay in maturity and consequent increase in fecundity, they may postpone maturity longer and reach a larger size than adult males. This is the commonest form of sexual dimorphism in turtles. In other species, male–male aggression or possibly forcible insemination may result in sexual selection for large size in adult males and the dimorphism will be reversed. In some species, maturity occurs at the same age and nearly the same size in both sexes. These species are generally small and early maturing; perhaps selection has favored rapid reproduction in both sexes due to high levels of predation or environmental uncertainty.

Analysis of life history data from two-thirds of the genera and about 40% of the extant species reveals no correlations between latitude or diet and egg size or clutch size between species when adjusted for differences in body size. Adult habitat has highly significant effects on egg volume, the number of eggs per clutch, and total clutch volume after these variables have been adjusted for female body size. Females of freshwater and terrestrial species deposit the same volume of eggs on a size-specific basis, but they package the clutch differently. A typical terrestrial species lays about half the number of eggs in each clutch, but each egg is about twice as large as that of a freshwater species of the same size. Terrestrial turtles appear to have sacrificed clutch size to increase individual egg size. Large hatchlings are suggested to have faster growth rates and to mature at an earlier age than small hatchlings, an advantage in the low productivity terrestrial environment. Aquatic species are usually carnivorous as juveniles and have fast growth rates.

Most marine species must migrate long distances between feeding areas and nesting beaches, a journey that may be dangerous and requires large stores of energy. Females typically migrate only once every 2–4 years; but on each trip they make several nests, each with many eggs. The eggs are no larger than would be predicted from the regression of egg volume on body size in freshwater species.

Comparisons among populations within a species demonstrate that reproductive characteristics vary in adaptive ways at both the local scale or different habitats and in broad geographic patterns. Taxonomic constraints are not sufficient to prevent convergence in reproductive characters of species in similar habitats. There remains a need for both detailed population studies and experimental studies of the genetic basis of such differences between populations and between species.

ACKNOWLEDGMENTS

We thank the late Professor Donald W. Tinkle who taught us how to apply the comparative method to problems in life history evolution and first asked us to attempt this synthesis. J. Whitfield Gibbons and Justin Congdon read an early draft of the manuscript and provided current information on their studies of turtle populations. Computer time and other support was from the Department of Zoology, Duke University.

REFERENCES

Alho, C. J. R. and Pádua, L. F. M. (1982). Reproductive parameters and nesting behavior of the Amazon turtle *Podocnemis expansa* (Testudinata: Pelomedusidae) in Brazil. Can. J. Zool. 60, 97–103.

Allen, E. R. (1938). Notes on the feeding and egg-laying habits of the *Pseudemys*. Proc. Fla. Acad. Sci. 3, 105–108.

Andrews, R. M. (1982). Patterns of growth in reptiles. In *Biology of the Reptilia*. (C. Gans and F. H. Pough, eds.). Academic Press, London. Volume 13, 273–305.

Arata, A. A. (1958). Notes on the eggs and young of *Gopherus polyphemus* (Daudin). Quart. J. Fla. Acad. Sci. 21, 274–280.

Archer, W. H. (1967). The geometric tortoise (*Psammobates* sp.). Afr. Wildlife 21, 321–329.

Arndt, R. G. (1977). Notes on the natural history of the bog turtle, *Clemmys muhlenbergi* (Schoepff), in Delaware. Chesapeake Sci. 18, 67–76.

Arnold, E. N. (1979). Indian Ocean giant tortoises: Their systematics and island adaptations. Phil. Trans. Roy. Soc. B. 286, 127–145.

Ash, R. P. (1951). A preliminary report on the size, egg number, incubation period, and hatching in the common snapping turtle *Chelydra serpentina*. Va. J. Sci. 2, 312.

Auffenberg, W. (1969). Land of the Chaco tortoise *Geochelone chilensis*. Int. Turtle Tortoise Soc. J. 3, 16–19, 36–37.

Auffenberg, W. (1974). Checklist of fossil land tortoises (Testudinidae). Bull. Fla. St. Univ. Bio. Sci. 18, 125–251.

Auffenberg, W. and Iverson, J. B. (1979). Demography of terrestrial turtles. In *Turtles: Perspectives and Research*. (M. Harless and H. Morlock, eds.). Wiley, New York, pp. 541–569.

Auffenberg, W. and Weaver, W. G. (1969). *Gopherus berlandieri* in southeastern Texas. Bull. Fla. St. Mus. 13, 141–203.

Bacon, P. R. (1969). Studies on the leatherback turtle, *Dermochelys coriacea* (L) in Trinidad, West Indies. Biol. Conserv. 2, 213–218.

Balasingham, E. (1967). The ecology and conservation of the leathery turtle, *Dermochelys coriacea* (Linn.) in Malaya. Micronesia 3, 37–43.

Baldwin, W. P., Jr. and Lofton, J. P. Jr. (1959). III. The loggerhead turtles of Cape Romain, South Carolina. Bull. Fla. State Mus. Biol. Sci. 4, 319–348.

Barbour, T. and Carr, A. F., Jr. (1940). Antillean terrapins. Mem. Mus. Comp. Zool. Harvard 54, 381–415.

Barton, A. J. and Price, J. W., Jr. (1955). Our knowledge of the bog-turtles, *Clemmys muhlenbergi*, surveyed and augmented. Copeia 1955, 159–165.

Bell, G. (1976). On breeding more than once. Am. Nat. 110, 57–77.

Beltz, R. E. (1954). Miscellaneous observations on captive testudininae. Herpetologica 10, 45–47.

Berry, J. F. and Shine, R. (1980). Sexual size dimorphism and sexual selection in turtles (Order Testudines). Oecologia 44, 185–191.

Bickham, J. W. and Carr, J. L. (1983). Taxonomy and phylogeny of the higher categories of cryptodiran turtles based on a cladistic analysis of chromosomal data. Copeia 1983, 918–932.

Bjorndal, K. A. (1980). Demography of the breeding population of the green turtle, *Chelonia mydas*, at Tortuguero, Costa Rica. Copeia 1980, 525–530.

Bjorndal, K. A. (ed.). (1982). *Biology and Conservation of Sea Turtles*. Smithsonian Institution Press, Washington, DC.

Blackwell, K. (1968). Some observations on the hatching and growth of the African tortoise, *Kinixys homeana*. Br. J. Herpetol. 4, 40–41.

Blair, W. F. (1976). Some aspects of the biology of the ornate box turtle, *Terrapene ornata*. Southwest. Nat. 21, 89–104.

Blanchard, F. N. (1923). The amphibians and reptiles of Dickinson County, Iowa. Stud. Nat. Hist. Iowa Univ. 10, 19–26.

Bourn, D. (1977). Reproductive study of giant tortoises on Aldabra. J. Zool., Lond. 182, 27–38.

Bramble, D. M. (1982). *Scaptochelys*: Generic revision and evolution of gopher tortoises. Copeia 1982, 852–867.

Breckenridge, W. J. (1955). Observation on the life history of the soft-shelled turtle *Trionyx ferox*, with especial reference to growth. Copeia 1955, 5–9.

Breckenridge, W. J. (1960). A spring soft-shelled turtle nest study. Herpetologica 16, 284–285.

REFERENCES

Breitenbach, G. L., Congdon, J. D. and van Loben Sels, R. C. (1984). Winter temperatures of *Chrysemys picta* nests in Michigan: Effects on hatchling survival. Herpetologica 40, 76–81.

Brown, W. S. (1974). Ecology of the aquatic box turtle, *Terrapene coahuila* (Chelonia, Emydidae) in Northern Mexico. Bull. Fla. St. Mus. Biol. Sci. 19, 1–67.

Bull, J. J. (1980). Sex determination in reptiles. Quart. Rev. Biol. 55, 3–21.

Bull, J. J. (1983). *Evolution of Sex Determining Mechanisms*. Benjamin/Cummings, Menlo Park, CA.

Bull, J. J. (1985). Sex ratio and nest temperature in turtles: Comparing field and laboratory data. Ecology 66, 1115–1122.

Bull, J. J. and Shine, R. (1979). Iteroparous animals that skip opportunities for reproduction. Am. Nat. 114, 296–316.

Bull, J. J. and Vogt, R. C. (1979). Temperature-dependent sex determination in turtles. Science 206, 1186–1188.

Bull, J. J. and Vogt, R. C. (1981). Temperature-sensitive periods of sex determination in emydid turtles. J. Exp. Zool. 212, 435–444.

Bull, J. J., Vogt, R. C. and Bulmer, M. G. (1982a). Heritability of sex ratio in turtles with environmental sex determination. Evolution 36, 333–341.

Bull, J. J., Vogt, R. C. and McCoy, C. J. (1982b). Sex determining temperatures in turtles: A geographic comparison. Evolution 36, 326–332.

Bulmer, M. G. and Bull, J. J. (1982). Models of polygenic sex determination and sex ratio evolution. Evolution 36, 13–26.

Burns, T. A. and Williams, K. L. (1972). Notes on the reproductive habits of *Malaclemys terrapin pileata*. J. Herpetol. 6, 237–238.

Bury, R. B. (1979). Population ecology of freshwater turtles. In *Turtles: Perspectives and Research*. (M. Harless and H. Morlock eds.). Wiley, New York, pp. 571–602.

Bustard, H. R. (1972). *Sea Turtles*. Taplinger, New York.

Bustard, H. R. (1979). Population dynamics of sea turtles in *Turtles: Perspectives and Research*. (M. Harless and H. Morlock eds.). Wiley, New York, pp. 523–540.

Bustard, H. R. and Greenham, P. (1968). Physical and chemical factors affecting hatching in the green sea turtle, *Chelonia mydas* (L.). Ecology 49, 269–276.

Bustard, H. R. and Greenham, P. (1969). Nesting behavior of the green sea turtle on a Great Barrier Reef island. Herpetologica 25, 93–102.

Bustard, H. R. and Limpus, C. (1969). Observations on the flatback turtle, *Chelonia depressa* Garman. Herpetologica 25, 29–34.

Bustard, H. R. and Tognetti, K. P. (1969). Green sea turtles: A discrete simulation of density-dependent population regulation. Science 163, 939–941.

Cagle, F. R. (1937). Egg laying habits of the slider turtle (*Pseudemys troostii*), the painted turtle (*Crysemys picta*), and the musk turtle (*Sternotherus odoratus*). J. Tenn. Acad. Sci. 12, 87–95.

Cagle, F. R. (1944). Sexual maturity in the female of the turtle, *Pseudemys scripta elegans*. Copeia 1944, 149–152.

Cagle, F. R. (1946). The growth of the slider turtle, *Pseudemys scripta elegans*. Am. Midl. Nat. 36, 685–729.

Cagle, F. R. (1948a). The growth of turtles in Lake Glendale, Illinois. Copeia 1948, 197–203.

Cagle, F. R. (1948b). Sexual maturity in the male turtle, *Pseudemys scripta troostii*. Copeia 1948, 108–111.

Cagle, F. R. (1950). The life history of the slider turtle, *Pseudemys scripta troostii* (Holbrook). Ecol. Monogr. 20, 31–54.

Cagle, F. R. (1952). The status of the turtles *Graptemys pulchra* Baur and *Graptemys barbouri* Carr and Marchand, with notes on their natural history. Copeia 1952, 223–234.

Cagle, F. R. (1953). The status of the turtle *Graptemys oculifera* (Baur). Zoologica 38, 137–144.

Cagle, F. R. (1954). Observations on the life cycle of painted turtles (genus *Chrysemys*). Am. Midl. Nat. 52, 225–235.

Cahn, A. R. (1937). The turtles of Illinois. Ill. Biol. Monogr. 16, 1–218.

Calder, W. A. III. (1984). *Size, Function and Life History.* Harvard, Cambridge, MA.

Caldwell, D. K. (1958). On the status of the Atlantic leatherback turtle, *Dermochelys coriacea coriacea*, as a visitant to Florida nesting beaches, with natural history notes. Quart. J. Fla. Acad. Sci. 21, 285–291.

Caldwell, D. W. (1959). The loggerhead turtles of Cape Romain, South Carolina. Bull. Fla. St. Mus. 4, 319–348.

Caldwell, D. K. (1962a). Comments on the nesting behavior of Atlantic loggerhead sea turtles, based primarily on tagging returns. Quart. J. Fla. Acad. Sci. 25, 287–302.

Caldwell, D. K. (1962b). Carapace length–body weight relationship and size and sex ratio of the northeastern Pacific green sea turtle, *Chelonia mydas carrinegra*. Los Angeles Co. Mus. Contr. Sci. 62, 1–10.

Caldwell, D. K., Carr, A. F. and Hellier, T. R. (1955). A nest of the Atlantic leatherback turtle, *Dermochelys coriacea coriacea* (Linnaeus), on the Atlantic coast of Florida, with a summary of North American nesting records. Quart. J. Fla. Acad. Sci. 18, 279–284.

Caldwell, D. K., Berry, F. H., Carr, A. F. and Ragotzkie, R. A. (1959). The Atlantic loggerhead sea turtle, *Caretta caretta caretta* (L.), in America. II. Multiple and group nesting by the Atlantic loggerhead turtle. Bull. Fla. St. Mus. 4, 309–318.

Carl, C. (1944). The reptiles of British Columbia. Brit. Columbia Prov. Mus. Handbook 3, 5–60.

Carr, A. (1952). *Handbook of Turtles.* Comstock, Ithaca, NY.

Carr, A. (1963). Panpacific reproductive convergence in *Lepidochelys kempi*. Ergeb. Biol. 26, 298–303.

Carr, A. (1967). *So Excellent a Fishe.* Natural History Press, New York.

Carr, A. and Carr, M. H. (1970a). Modulated reproductive periodicity in *Chelonia*. Ecology 51, 335–337.

Carr, A. and Carr, M. H. (1970b). Recruitment and remigration in a green turtle nesting colony. Biol. Conserv. 2, 282–284.

Carr, A. and Hirth, H. (1962). The ecology and migrations of sea turtles. 5. Comparative features of isolated green turtle colonies. Am. Mus. Novitates No. 2091.

Carr, A., Hirth, H. and Ogren, L. (1966). The ecology and migrations of sea turtles. 6. The hawksbill turtle in the Caribbean Sea. Am. Mus. Novitates No. 2248.

Carr, A. and Ogren, L. (1960). The ecology and migration of sea turtles. 4. The green turtle in the Caribbean Sea. Bull. Am. Mus. Nat. Hist. 121, 1–48.

Carr, A. F., Carr, M. H. and Meylan, A. B. (1978). The ecology and migrations of sea turtles. 7. The West Caribbean green turtle colony. Bull. Am. Mus. Nat. Hist. 162, 1–46.

Carr, A. F. and Goodman, D. (1970). Ecologic implications of size and growth in *Chelonia*. Copeia 1970, 783–786.

Carr, A. F. and Ogren, L. (1959). The ecology and migration of sea turtles. 3. *Dermochelys* in Costa Rica. Am. Mus. Novitates No. 1958.

REFERENCES

Carr, J. L. and Bickham, J. W. (1981). Sex chromosomes of the Asian black pond turtle, *Siebenrockiella crassicollis* (Testudines: Emydidae). Cytogenet. Cell Genet. 31, 178–183.

Castanet, J. and Cheylan, M. (1979). Les marques de croissance des os et des écailles comme indicateur de l'âge chez *Testudo hermanni* et *Testudo graeca* (Reptilia, Chelonia, Testudinidae). Can. J. Zool. 57, 1649–1665.

Charnov, E. L. and Bull, J. J. (1977). When is sex environmentally determined? Nature 266, 828–830.

Christiansen, J. L. and Dunham, A. E. (1972). Reproduction of the yellow mud turtle (*Kinosternon flavescens flavescens*) in New Mexico. Herpetologica 27, 130–137.

Christiansen, J. L. and Moll, E. O. (1973). Latitudinal reproductive variation within a single subspecies of painted turtle, *Chrysemys picta belli*. Herpetologica 29, 152–163.

Clark, D. B. and Gibbons, J. W. (1969). Dietary shift in the turtle *Pseudemys scripta* (Schoepff) from youth to maturity. Copeia 1969, 704–706.

Cloudsley-Thompson, J. L. (1970). On the biology of the desert tortoise *Testudo sulcata* in Sudan. J. Zool. 160, 17–33.

Coe, M. J., Bourn, D. and Swingland, I. R. (1979). The biomass, production and carrying capacity of giant tortoises on Aldabra. Phil. Trans. Roy. Soc. B. 286, 163–176.

Cogger, A. G. (1975). *Reptiles and Amphibians of Australia*. Reed, London.

Cogger, A. G. and Lindner, D. A. (1969). Marine turtles in Northern Australia. Aust. Zool. 15, 150–159.

Congdon, J. D. and Gibbons, J. W. (1983). Relationships of reproductive characteristics to body size in *Pseudemys scripta*. Herpetologica 39, 147–151.

Congdon, J. D. and Gibbons, J. W. (1985). Egg components and reproductive characteristics of turtles: relationships to body size. Herpetologica 41, 194–205.

Congdon, J. D., Gibbons, J. W. and Greene, J. L. (1983a). Parental investment in the chicken turtle (*Deirochelys reticularia*). Ecology 64, 419–525.

Congdon, J. D. and Tinkle, D. W. (1982). Reproductive energetics of the painted turtle (*Chrysemys picta*). Herpetologica 38, 228–237.

Congdon, J. D., Tinkle, D. W., Breitenbach, G. L. and Van Loben Sels, R. C. (1983b). Nesting behavior and hatching success in the turtle *Emydoidea blandingi*. Herpetologica 39, 417–429.

Congdon, J. D., Tinkle, D. W. and Rosen, P. C. (1983c). Egg component and utilization during development in aquatic turtles. Copeia 1983, 264–268.

Cox, W. A. and Marion, K. R. (1978). Observations on the female reproductive cycle and associated phenomena in spring-dwelling populations of *Sternotherus minor* in north Florida (Reptilia: Testudines). Herpetologica 32, 20–33.

Crouse, D. T. (1985). The biology and conservation of sea turtles in North Carolina. PhD Dissertation (Zoology). University of Wisconsin–Madison.

Cunningham, B. (1922). Some phases in the development of *Chrysemys cinerea*. J. Elisha Mitchell Sci. Soc. 38, 51–73.

De Koningh, H. L. (1968). An oriental big-head. Int. Turtle Tortoise Soc. J. 2, 14–17.

DeNeira, L. E. F. and Roc, J. H. (1984). Emergence success of tortoise nests and the effect of feral burros on nest success on Vulcan Alcedo, Galapagos. Copeia 1984, 702–707.

Deraniyagala, P. E. P. (1939). *The Tetrapod Reptiles of Ceylon*. Vol. I. Testudinates and Crocodilians. Dulau, London.

DeSola, C. R. and Abrams, F. (1933). Testudinata from south-eastern Georgia, including the Okefinokee Swamp. Copeia 1933, 10–12.

Dobie, J. L. (1971). Reproduction and growth in the alligator snapping turtle, *Macroclemmys temmincki* (Troost). Copeia 1971, 645–658.

Drummond, H. (1983). Adaptiveness of island nest-sites of green iguanas and slider turtles. Copeia 1983, 529–530.

Duellman, W. and Schwartz, A. (1958). Amphibians and reptiles of southern Florida. Bull. Fla. St. Mus. 3, 181–324.

Dunson, W. A. (1967). Relationship between length and weight in the spiny softshell turtle. Copeia 1967, 483–485.

Edgren, R. A. (1956). Egg size in the musk turtle, *Sternotherus odoratus* Latreille. Chicago Acad. Sci. Nat. Hist. Misc. 152, 1–3.

Edgren, R. A. (1960). Ovulation time in the musk turtle, *Sternotherus odoratus*. Copeia 1960, 60–61.

Eglir, A. (1963). Nesting of a parrot-beaked tortoise. Herpetologica 19, 66–68.

Ehrengart, W. (1971). Zür Pflege und zucht der Griechischen Landschildkröte (*Testudo h. hermanni*). Salamandra 7, 71–80.

Einem, G. E. (1956). Certain aspects of the natural history of the mud turtle, *Kinosternon bauri*. Copeia 1956, 186–188.

Ernst, C. H. (1970). Reproduction in *Clemmys guttata*. Herpetologica 26. 228–232.

Ernst, C. H. (1971a). Sexual cycles and maturity of the turtle *Chrysemys picta*. Biol. Bull. Mar. Biol. Lab., Woods Hole 140, 191–200.

Ernst, C. H. (1971b). Population dynamics and activity cycles of *Chrysemys picta* in southeastern Pennsylvania. J. Herpetol. 5, 151–160.

Ernst, C. H. (1971c). Growth of the painted turtle, *Chrysemys picta*, in southeastern Pennsylvania. Herpetologica 27, 135–144.

Ernst, C. H. (1971d). Observation on the egg and hatching of the American turtle, *Chrysemys picta*. Br. J. Herpetol. 4, 224–227.

Ernst, C. H. (1975). Growth of the spotted turtle, *Clemmys guttata*. J. Herpetol. 9, 313–318.

Ernst, C. H. (1976). Ecology of the spotted turtle, *Clemmys guttata* (Reptilia, Testudinea, Testudinidae), in southeastern Pennsylvania. J. Herpetol. 10, 25–33.

Ernst, C. H. and Barbour, R. W. (1972). *Turtles of the United States*. Univ. Kentucky Press, Lexington.

Ewert, M. A. (1976). Nests, nesting and aerial basking of *Macroclemys* under natural conditions, and comparison with *Chelydra* (Testudines: Chelydridae). Herpetologica 32, 150–156.

Ewert, M. A. (1979). The embryo and its egg: Development and natural history. In *Turtles: Perspectives and Research*. (M. Harless and H. Morlock, eds.). Wiley, New York, pp. 333–413.

Ewing, H. E. (1935). Further notes on the reproduction of the eastern box turtle, *Terrapene carolina* (Linné). Copeia 1935, 102.

Ewing, H. E. (1943). Continued fertility in female box turtles following mating. Copeia 1943, 112–114.

Falconer, D. S. (1981). *Introduction to Quantitative Genetics*. Second Edition. Longman, New York.

Finneran, L. C. (1948). Reptiles at Branford, Connecticut. Herpetologica 4, 123–126.

Fitch, H. S. and Plummer, M. V. (1975). A preliminary ecological study of the soft shelled turtle, *Trionyx muticus*, in the Kansas River. Israel J. Zool. 24, 28–42.

Foote, R. W. (1978). Nesting of *Podocnemis unifilis* (Testudines: Pelomedusidae) in the Columbian Amazon. Herpetologica 34, 333–339.

REFERENCES

Fowler, L. E. (1979). Hatching success and nest predation in the green sea turtle, *Chelonia mydas*, at Tortuguero, Costa Rica. Ecology 60, 946–955.

Frazer, N. B. (1983). Demography and life history evolution of the Atlantic Loggerhead sea turtle, *Caretta caretta*. PhD. Dissertation (Zoology), Univ. Georgia.

Frazer, N. B. and Ehrhart, L. M. (1985). Preliminary growth models for green, *Chelonia mydas*, and loggerhead, *Caretta caretta*, turtles in the wild. Copeia 1985, 73–79.

Frazer, N. B. and Richardson, J. I. (1986). The relationship of clutch size and frequency to body size in loggerhead turtles, *Caretta caretta*. J. Herpetol. 20, 81–84.

Frazier, J. (1971). Observations on sea turtles at Aldabra Atoll. Phil. Trans. Roy. Soc. B. 260, 373–410.

Fritts, T. H. (1984). Evolutionary divergence of giant tortoises in Galapagos. Biol. J. Linnean Soc. 21:165–176.

Gaymer, R. (1968). The Indian Ocean giant tortoise *Testudo gigantea* on Aldabra. J. Zool., Lond. 154, 341–363.

Gemmell, D. J. (1970). Some observations on the nesting of the western painted turtle, *Chrysemys picta belli*, in northern Minnesota. Can. Fld. Nat. 84, 308–309.

Gibbons, J. W. (1967). Variation in growth rates in three populations of the painted turtle, *Chrysemys picta*. Herpetologica 23, 269–303.

Gibbons, J. W. (1968a). Reproductive potential, activity, and cycles in the painted turtle, *Chrysemys picta*. Ecology 49, 399–409.

Gibbons, J. W. (1968b). Population structure and survivorship in the painted turtle. *Chrysemys picta*. Copeia 1968, 260–268.

Gibbons, J. W. (1968c). Observations on the ecology and population dynamics of the Blanding's turtle, *Emydoidea blandingi*. Can. J. Zool. 46, 288–290.

Gibbons, J. W. (1969). Ecology and population dynamics of the chicken turtle, *Deirochelys reticularia*. Copeia 1969, 669–676.

Gibbons, J. W. (1970a). Reproductive characteristics of a Florida population of musk turtles (*Sternothaerus odoratus*). Herpetologica 26, 268–270.

Gibbons, J. W. (1970b). Terrestrial activity and the population dynamics of aquatic turtles. Am. Midl. Nat. 83, 404–414.

Gibbons, J. W. (1970c). Reproductive dynamics of a turtle (*Pseudemys scripta*) population in a reservoir receiving heated effluent from a nuclear reactor. Can. J. Zool. 48, 881–885.

Gibbons, J. W. (1976). Aging phenomena in reptiles. In *Experimental Aging Research*. (M. F. Elias, B. E. Eleftheriou and P. K. Elias, eds.). E. A. R. Inc, Bar Harbor, ME, pp. 454–475.

Gibbons, J. W. (1982). Reproductive patterns in freshwater turtles. Herpetologica 38, 222–227.

Gibbons, J. W. (1983). Reproductive characteristics and ecology of the mud turtle *Kinosternon subrubrum* (Lacepede). Herpetologica 39, 254–271.

Gibbons, J. W. and Coker, J. W. (1977). Ecological and life history aspects of the cooter, *Chrysemys floridana* (Le Conte). Herpetologica 33, 29–33.

Gibbons, J. W. and Greene, J. L. (1979). X-ray photography: A technique to determine reproductive patterns of freshwater turtles. Herpetologica 38, 86–89.

Gibbons, J. W., Greene, J. L. and Congdon, J. D. (1983). Drought-related responses of aquatic turtle populations. J. Herpetol. 17, 242–246.

Gibbons, J. W., Greene, J. L. and Patterson, K. K. (1982). Variation in reproductive characteristics of aquatic turtles. Copeia 1982, 776–784.

Gibbons, J. W., Greene, J. L. and Schubauer, J. P. (1979a). Variability in clutch size in aquatic chelonians. Br. J. Herpetol. 6, 13–14.
Gibbons, J. W., Keeton, G. H., Schubauer, J. P., Greene, J. L., Bennett, D. H., McAuliffe, J. R. and Sharitz, R. R. (1979b). Unusual population size structure in freshwater turtles on barrier islands. Ga. J. Sci. 37, 155–159.
Gibbons, J. W. and Nelson, D. H. (1978). The evolutionary significance of delayed emergence from the nest by hatchling turtles. Evolution 32, 297–303.
Gibbons, J. W. and Semlitsch, R. D. (1981). Terrestrial drift fences with pitfall traps: An effective technique for quantitative sampling of animal populations. Brimleyana 7, 1–16.
Gibbons, J. W. and Semlitsch, R. D. (1982). Survivorship and longevity of a long-lived vertebrate species: How long do turtles live? J. Anim. Ecol. 51, 523–527.
Gibbons, J. W., Semlitsch, R. D., Greene, J. L. and Schubauer, J. P. (1981). Variation in age and size at maturity of the slider turtle (*Pseudemys scripta*). Am. Nat. 117, 841–845.
Gibbons, J. W. and Tinkle, D. W. (1969). Reproductive variation between turtle populations in a single geographic area. Ecology 50, 340–341.
Gillespie, J. H. (1974). Natural selection for within-generation variance in offspring number. Genetics 76, 601–606.
Goff, C. C. and Goff, D. S. (1932). Egg laying and incubation of *Pseudemys floridana*. Copeia 1932, 92–94.
Goff, C. C. and Goff, D. S. (1935). On the incubation of a clutch of eggs of *Amyda ferox* (Schneider). Copeia 1935, 156.
Goldsmith, W. M. (1944). Notes on the egg laying habits of soft shelled turtles. Proc. Iowa Acad. Sci. 51, 447–449.
Goode, J. (1967). *Freshwater Tortoises of Australia and New Guinea (in the family Chelidae)*. Lansdowne, Melbourne.
Goode, J. and Russell, J. (1968). Incubation of eggs of three species of chelid tortoises, and notes on their embryological development. Aust. J. Zool. 16, 749–761.
Graham, T. E. (1969). Pursuit of the Plymouth turtle. J. Int. Turtle Tortoise Soc. 3, 10–13.
Graham, T. E. (1971). Growth rate of the red-bellied turtle, *Chrysemys rubriventris*, at Plymouth, Massachusetts. Copeia 1971, 353–356.
Graham, T. E. and Hutchison, V. H. (1969). Centenarian box turtles. J. Int. Turt. Tort. Soc. 3, 25–29.
Grubb, P. (1971a). Comparative notes on the behavior of *Geochelone sulcata*. Herpetologica 27, 328–333.
Grubb, P. (1971b). The growth, ecology and population structure of giant tortoises on Aldabra. Phil. Trans. Roy. Soc. B. 260, 327–372.
Gutzke, W. H. N. and Paukstis, G. L. (1983). Influence of hydric environment on sexual differentiation of turtles. J. Exp. Zool. 226, 467–469.
Gutzke, W. H. N. and Paukstis, G. L. (1984). A low threshold temperature for sexual differentiation in the painted turtle, *Chrysemys picta*. Copeia 1984, 546–547.
Hamilton, W. D. (1971). Geometry for the selfish herd. J. Theoret. Biol. 31, 295–311.
Hamilton, W. J., Jr. (1940). Observations of reproductive behavior of the snapping turtle. Copeia 1940, 124–216.
Hamilton, W. J., Jr. (1947). Egg laying of *Trionyx ferox*. Copeia 1947, 209.
Hammer, D. A. (1969). Parameters of a marsh snapping turtle population Lacreek Refuge, South Dakota. J. Wildl. Mgmt. 33, 995–1005.
Harding, J. H. (1977). Record egg clutches for *Clemmys insculpta*. Herpetol. Rev. 8, 34.
Harless, M. and Morlock, H. (1979). *Turtles: Perspectives and Research*. Wiley, New York.

REFERENCES

Harrisson, J. (1952). Breeding of the edible turtle. Nature 169, 198.
Hausmann, P. (1968a). *Claudius angustatus.* J. Int. Turtle Tortoise Soc. 2, 14–15.
Hausmann, P. (1968b). Mata mata. J. Int. Turtle Tortoise Soc. 2, 18–19, 36.
Henderson, R. W. (1972). Notes on the reproductive habits of *Malaclemys terrapin pileata*. J. Herpetol. 6, 237–238.
Hendrickson, J. D. (1966). The Galapagos tortoise, *Geochelone* Fitzinger 1835 (*Testudo* Linnaeus 1758 in part). In *The Galapagos*. (R. I. Bowman, ed.). Univ. Calif. Press, Berkeley, pp. 252–257.
Hendrickson, J. R. (1958). The green turtle, *Chelonia mydas* (Linn.) in Malaya and Sarawak. Proc. Zool. Soc. Lond. 130, 455–535.
Hendrickson, J. R. (1962). The programme for conservation of the giant leathery turtle. 1961. Malay. Nat. J. 16, 64–69.
Hendrickson, J. R. (1980). Ecological strategies of sea turtles. Am. Zool. 20, 597–608.
Hirth, H. F. (1980). Some aspects of the nesting behavior and reproductive biology of sea turtles. Am. Zool. 20, 507–523.
Hirth, H. F. and Schaffer, W. M. (1974). Survival rate of the green turtle, *Chelonia mydas*, necessary to maintain stable populations. Copeia 1974, 544–546.
Holman, J. A. (1963). Observations on dermatemyid and staurotypine turtles from Vera Cruz, Mexico. Herpetologica 19, 277–279.
Honegger, R. E. (1967). The green turtle (*Chelonia mydas japonica*) Thunberg in the Seychelles Islands. Br. J. Herpetol. 4, 8–11.
Iverson, J. B. (1976). The genus *Kinosternon* in Belize (Testudines: Kinosternidae). Herpetologica 32, 258–262.
Iverson, J. B. (1977). Reproduction in freshwater and terrestrial turtles of North Florida. Herpetologica 33, 205–212.
Iverson, J. B. (1978). Reproductive cycle of female loggerhead musk turtles (*Sternotherus minor minor*) in Florida. Herpetologica 34, 33–39.
Iverson, J. B. (1979a). Reproduction and growth of the mud turtle, *Kinosternon subrubrum* (Reptilia, Testudines, Kinosternidae), in Arkansas. J. Herpetol. 13, 105–112.
Iverson, J. B. (1979b). The female reproductive cycle in North Florida *Kinosternon baurii* (Testudines: Kinosternidae). Brimleyana 1, 37–46.
Iverson, J. B. (1980). The reproductive biology of *Gopherus polyphemus* (Chelonia: Testudinidae). Am. Midl. Nat. 103, 353–359.
Iverson, J. B. (1985). Geographic variation in sexual dimorphism in the mud turtle *Kinosternon hirtipes*. Copeia 1985, 388–393.
Jackson, C. G., Jr., Trotter, J. G., Trotter, T. H. and Trotter, M. W. (1976). Accelerated growth rate and early maturity in *Gopherus agassizii* (Reptilia: Testudinae). Herpetologica 32, 139–145.
Jacques, J. (1966). Some observations on the Cape terrapin. Afr. Wild Life 20, 137–150.
Jayaker, S. D. and Spurway, H. (1964). Bi-modality of laying-hatching times in *Testudo elegans* Schoepff (Chelonia). Nature 204, 603.
Jayaker, S. D. and Spurway, H. (1966). Contributions to the biology of the Indian starred tortoise *Testudo elegans* Schoepff I. J. Bombay Nat. Hist. Soc. 63, 83–114.
Kaufmann, R. (1975). Studies on the loggerhead sea turtle *Caretta caretta caretta* (Linné) in Columbia, South America. Herpetologica 31, 323–326.
Khan, M. K. B. M. (1964). A note on *Batagur baska* (The river terrapin or tuntong). Malay. Nat. J. 18, 184–186.
Kirsche, W. (1967). Zür Haltung, Zucht und Ethologie der griechischen Landschildkröte (*Testudo hermanni hermanni*). Salamandra 3, 36–66.

Kraemer, J. E. and Bennett, S. H. (1981). Utilization of posthatching yolk in loggerhead sea turtles, *Caretta caretta*. Copeia 1981, 406–411.
Lagler, K. F. (1945). Economic relations and utilization of turtles. Invest. Indiana Lakes Streams 3, 139–165.
Lambert, M. R. K. (1969). Tortoise drain in Morocco. Oryx 10, 161–166.
Lambert, M. R. K. (1982). Studies on the growth, structure and abundance of the Mediterranean spur-thighed tortoise, *Testudo gracea*, in field populations. J. Zool., Lond. 196, 165–190.
Landers, J. L., Garner, J. A. and McRae, W. A. (1980). Reproduction of gopher tortoises (*Gopherus polyphemus*) in southwestern Georgia. Herpetologica 36, 353–361.
Landers, J. L., McRae, W. A. and Garner, J. A. (1982). Growth and maturity of the gopher tortoise in southwestern Georgia. Bull. Fla. St. Mus. 27, 81–110.
Lardie, R. L. (1973). Notes on eggs and young of *Trionyx ferox* (Schneider). J. Herpetol. 7, 377–378.
Lardie, R. L. (1975a). Observations on reproduction in *Kinosternon*. J. Herpetol. 9, 260–264.
Lardie, R. L. (1975b). Courtship and mating behavior in the yellow mud turtle, *Kinosternon flavescens flavescens*. J. Herpetol. 9, 223–227.
LeBuff, C. R., Jr. and Beatty, R. W. (1971). Some aspects of nesting of the loggerhead turtle, *Caretta caretta* (Linné), on the Gulf Coast of Florida. Herpetologica 27, 153–156.
Legler, J. M. (1954). Nesting habits of the western painted turtle, *Chrysemys picta belli* (Gray). Herpetologica 10, 137–144.
Legler, J. M. (1960a). Natural history of the ornate box turtle, *Terrapene ornata ornata* Agassiz. Univ. Kans. Publs. Mus. Nat. Hist. 11, 527–669.
Legler, J. M. (1960b). Remarks on the natural history of the Big Bend slider, *Pseudemys scripta gaigeae* Hartweg. Herpetologica 16, 139–140.
Legler, J. M. (1963). Tortoises (*Geochelone carbonaria*) in Panama: Distribution and variation. Am. Midl. Nat. 70, 490–503.
Legler, J. M. (1966). Notes on the natural history of a rare Central American turtle, *Kinosternon angustipons* Legler. Herpetologica 22, 118–122.
Limpus, C. L. (1971). The flatback turtle, *Chelonia depressa* Garman, in southeast Queensland, Australia, Herpetologica 27, 431–446.
Limpus, C. L. (1973). Loggerhead turtles (*Caretta caretta*) in Australia: Food sources while nesting. Herpetologica 29, 42–45.
Lofts, B. and Boswell, C. (1961). Seasonal changes in the distribution of the testis lipids of the Caspian terrapin *Clemmys caspica*. Proc. Zool. Soc. Lond. 136, 581–592.
Lofts, B. and Tsui, H. W. (1977). Histological and histochemical changes in the gonads and epididymides of the male soft shelled turtle, *Trionyx sinensis*. J. Zool., Lond. 181, 57–68.
Loveridge, A. and Williams, E. E. (1957). Revision of the African tortoises and turtles of the suborder Cryptodira. Bull. Mus. Comp. Zool. Harvard 115, 163–557.
MacCulloch, R. D. and Secoy, D. M. (1983). Demography, growth, and food of western painted turtles, *Chrysemys picta belli* (Gray), from southern Saskathchewan. Can. J. Zool. 61, 1499–1509.
Mahmoud, I. Y. (1967). Courtship behavior and sexual maturity in four species of kinosternid turtles. Copeia 1967, 314–319.
Mahmoud, I. Y. (1968). Nesting behavior in the western painted turtle, *Chrysemys picta belli*. Herpetologica 24, 158–162.
Mahmoud, I. Y. (1969). Comparative ecology of the kinosternid turtles of Oklahoma. Southwest. Nat. 14, 31–66.

REFERENCES

McCoy, C. J., Vogt, R. C. and Censky, E. J. (1983). Temperature-controlled sex determination in the sea turtle *Lepidochelys olivacea*. J. Herpetol. 17, 404–406.

McPherson, R. J. and Marion, K. R. (1983). Reproductive variation between two populations of *Sternotherus odoratus* in the same geographic area. J. Herpetol. 17, 181–184.

Medem, F. (1961). Contribuciónes al conocimiento sobre la morfología ecología y distribución geográfica de la tortuga *Kinosternon dunni* K. P. Schmidt. Novedades Columbianas 1, 446–476.

Medem, F. (1962). La distribución geográfica y ecología de los crocodylia y testudinada en el departmento del Chaco. Rev. Acad. Colomb. Cienc. Exact. Fis. Nat. 11, 229–303.

Miller, L. (1955). Further observations on the desert tortoise, *Gopherus agassizi* of California. Copeia 1955, 113–118.

Milstead, W. W. and Tinkle, D. W. (1967). *Terrapene* of western Mexico, with comments on the species groups in the genus. Copeia 1967, 180–187.

Minton, S. A. Jr. (1966). A contribution to the herpetology of West Pakistan. Bull. Am. Mus. Nat. Hist. 134, 113–118.

Mitchell, J. C. (1985a). Female reproductive cycle and life history attributes in a Virginia population of painted turtles, *Chrysemys picta*. J. Herpetol. 19, 218–226.

Mitchell, J. C. (1985b). Variation in the male reproductive cycle in a population of painted turtles, *Chrysemys picta*, from Virginia. Herpetologica 41, 45–51.

Mitsukuri, K. (1905). The cultivation of marine and fresh-water animals in Japan. Bull. Bur. Comm. Fish., Washington, DC 24, 257–289.

Moll, E. O. (1973). Latitudinal and interspecific variation in reproduction of the painted turtle, *Chrysemys picta*. Herpetologica 29, 307–318.

Moll, E. O. (1977). Reproduction and color change in *Callagur borneoensis* (Testudines-Emydidae). Am. Soc. Ichthyol. Herpetol. Herpetol. Abstr.

Moll, E. O. (1979). Reproductive cycles and adaptations. In *Turtles: Perspectives and Research*. (M. Harless and H. Morlock, eds.). Wiley, New York, pp. 305–331.

Moll, E. O. and Legler, J. M. (1971). The life history of a neotropical slider turtle, *Pseudemys scripta* (Schoepff), in Panama. Bull. Los Angeles Co. Mus. Nat. Hist. Sci. 11, 1–102.

Mondolfi, E. (1955). Anotáciones sobre la biología de trés quelonios de los Llanos de Venezuela. Mem. Soc. Cient. Nat. La Salle Caracas 15, 177–183.

Morreale, S. J., Ruiz, G. J., Spotila, J. R. and Standora, E. A. (1982). Temperature-dependent sex determination: Current practices threaten conservation of sea turtles. Science 216, 1245–1247.

Mosimann, J. E. and Bider, J. R. (1960). Variation, sexual dimorphism, and maturity in a Quebec population of the common snapping turtle, *Chelydra serpentina*. Can. J. Zool. 38, 19–38.

Mrosovsky, N. (1982). Sex ratio bias in hatchling sea turtles from artificially incubated eggs. Biol. Conserv. 23, 309–314.

Mrosovksy, N. (1983). *Conserving Sea Turtles*. British Herpetological Society, London.

Mrosovsky, N., Dutton, P. H. and Whitmore, C. P. (1984a). Sex ratios of two species of sea turtle nesting in Suriname. Can. J. Zool. 62, 2227–2239.

Mrosovsky, N., Hopkins-Murphy, S. R. and Richardson, J. I. (1984b). Sex ratio changes of sea turtles: Seasonal changes. Science 225, 739–741.

Muller, J. F. (1921). Notes on the habits of the soft-shell turtle *Amyda mutica*. Am. Midl. Nat. 7, 180–184.

Nichols, J. T. (1947). Notes on the mud turtle. Herpetologica 3, 147–148.

Nichols, U. G. (1953). Habits of the desert tortoise, *Gopherus agassizi*. Herpetologica 9, 65–69.

Nichols, U. G. (1957). The desert tortoise in captivity. Herpetologica 13, 141–144.

Owens, D. W. (ed.). (1980). Behavioral and reproductive biology of sea turtles. Am. Zool. 20, 485–617.
Pallas, D. C. (1960). Observations on a nesting of the wood turtle, *Clemmys insculpta*. Copeia 1960, 155–156.
Parker, W. S. (1984). Immigration and dispersal of slider turtles *Pseudemys scripta* in Mississippi farm ponds. Am. Midl. Nat. 112, 280–293.
Parmenter, R. R. (1980). Effects of food availability and water temperture on the feeding ecology of pond sliders (*Chrysemys s. scripta*). Copeia 1980, 503–514.
Peters, R. H. (1983). *The Ecological Implications of Body Size*. Cambridge University Press, Cambridge.
Petzold, H. (1968). Zur Kenntnis der kubanischen Antillen-Schmuckschildkröte (*Psudemys terrapen rugosa*). Salamandra 4, 73–90.
Phillips, E. J. (1972). 100 to 1. Int. Turtle Tortoise Soc. J. 6, 23–37.
Pieau, C. (1972). Effets de la température sur le développement des glands génitales chez les embryons de deux cheloniens *Emys orbicularis* L. et *Testudo graeca* L. C. R. Hebd. Senc. Acad. Sci., Paris. 274, 719–722.
Pieau, C. (1982). Modalities of the action of temperature on sexual differentiation in field-developing embryos of the European pond turtle *Emys obicularia* (Emydidae). J. Exp. Zool. 220, 353–360.
Plummer, M. V. (1976). Some aspects of nesting success in the turtle, *Trionyx muticus*. Herpetologica 32, 353–359.
Pough, F. H. (1973). Lizard energetics and diet. Ecology 54, 837–844.
Powell, C. B. (1967). Female sexual cycles of *Chrysemys picta* and *Clemmys insculpta* in Nova Scotia. Can. Fld. Nat. 81, 134–140.
Pritchard, P. C. H. (1966). Sea turtles of shell beach, British Guiana. Copeia 1966, 123–125.
Pritchard, P. C. H. (1967). *Living Turtles of the World*. T. H. F. Publications, Neptune City, NJ.
Pritchard, P. C. H. (1969). Sea turtles of the Guianas. Bull. Fla. St. Mus. 13, 85–140.
Pritchard, P. C. H. (1971a). The leatherback or leathery turtle. Int. Un. Conserv. Nat. Nat. Res. Monogr. 1, 1–39.
Pritchard, P. C. H. (1971b). Galapagos sea turtles—preliminary findings. J. Herpetol. 5, 1–9.
Pritchard, P. C. H. (1979). *Encyclopedia of Turtles*. T. F. H. Publications, Neptune City, NJ.
Pritchard, P. C. H. and Márquez, M. R. (1973). Kemp's ridley or Atlantic ridley: *Lepidochelys kempi*. Int. Un. Conserv. Nat. Nat. Res. Monogr. 2, 1–30.
Pritchard, P. C. H. and Trebbau, P. (1984). *The Turtles of Venezuela*. Society for the Study of Amphibians and Reptiles.
Ragotzkie, R. A. (1959). Mortality of loggerhead turtle eggs from excessive rainfall. Ecology 40, 303–305.
Raven, H. C. (1946). Predators eating turtle eggs in the East Indies. Copeia 1946, 48.
Raynaud, A. and Pieau, C. (1985). Embryonic development of the genital system. In *Biology of the Reptilia*. (C. Gans and F. Billett, eds.). Wiley, New York, Vol. 15, 149–300.
Rhodin, A. G. J. and Mittermeier, R. A. (1976). *Chelodina parkeri*, a new species of chelid turtle from New Guinea, with a discussion of *Chelodina siebenrocki* Werner, 1901. Bull. Mus. Comp. Zool. Harvard 147, 465–488.
Richardson, J. I. (1982). A population model for adult female loggerhead sea turtles (*Caretta caretta*) nesting in Georgia. PhD Dissertation (Zoology), Univ. Georgia.

REFERENCES

Richardson, J. I. and Hillestad, H. O. (1978). Ecology of a loggerhead sea turtle population in Georgia. Proc. Rare and Endangered Wildlife Symp. Georgia Game and Fish Tech. Bull. WL4, 1–22.

Richmond, N. D. (1945). Nesting habits of the mud turtle. Gopeia 1945, 217–219.

Ricklefs, R. E. and Burger, J. (1977). Composition of eggs of the diamondback terrapin. Am. Midl. Nat. 97, 232–235.

Risley, P. L. (1933). Observations on the natural history of the common musk turtle, *Sternotherus odoratus* (Latreille). Pap. Mich. Acad. Sci. 17, 685–711.

Roze, J. A. (1964). Pilgrim of the river. Life cycle of the Orinoco river turtle has many unusual features. Nat. Hist. 73, 34–41.

SAS Institute (1982). *SAS User's Guide: Statistics*. SAS Institute, Cary, NC.

Schmidt, K.P. (1919). Contributions to the herpetology of the Belgian Congo based on the collection of the American Congo Expedition, 1909–1915. Bull. Amer. Mus. Nat. Hist. 39, 385–624.

Schribner, K. T., Smith, M. H. and Gibbons, J. W. (1984). Genetic differentiation among local populations of the yellow-bellied slider (*Pseudemys scripta*). Herpetologica 40, 382–387.

Schwartz, E. R., Schwartz, C. W. and Kiester, A. R. (1984). The three-toed box turtle in central Missouri. Part II. A nineteen-year study of home range, movements and population. Missouri Dep. Conserv. Terrestrial Ser. No. 12, pp. 1–29.

Schwarzkopf, L. and Brooks, R. J. (1985). Sex determination in northern painted turtles: Effect of incubation at constant and fluctuating temperatures. Can. J. Zool. 63, 2543–2547.

Schweizer, H. (1965). Ei-Zeitigung, Aufzucht und Entwicklung einer Strahlenschildkröte (*Testudo radiata* Shaw). Salamandra 1, 67–73.

Seigel, R. A. (1980). Predation by raccoons on diamondback terrapins, *Malaclemys terrapin tequesta*. J. Herpetol. 14, 87–89.

Sexton, O. J. (1960). Notas sobre la reproducción de una tortuga Venezolana, la *Kinosternon scorpioides*. Mem. Soc. Cienct. Nat. la Salle 20, 189–197.

Shaw, C. E. (1963). Notes on the eggs, incubation and young of some African reptiles. Br. J. Herpetol. 3, 63–70.

Shaw, C. E. (1966). Breeding the Galapagos tortoise—success story. Oryx 9, 119–126.

Shealy, R. M. (1976). The natural history of the Alabama map turtle, *Graptemys pulchra* (Baur), in Alabama. Bull. Fla. St. Mus. 21, 47–111.

Shine, R. (1985). The evolution of viviparity in reptiles: An ecological analysis. In *Biology of the Reptilia*. (C. Gans and F. Billett, eds.). Wiley, New York. Vol 15, 605–694.

Simon, M. H. and Parkes, A. S. (1976). The green sea turtle (*Cheldonia mydas*): Nesting on Ascension Island, (1973)–(1974). Zool., Lond. 179, 153–163.

Simon, M. H., Ulrich, G. F. and Parkes, A. S. (1975). The green sea turtle (*Chelonia mydas*): Mating, nesting, and hatching on a farm. J. Zool., Lond. 177, 411–423.

Skorepa, A. C. and Ozment, J. E. (1968). Habitat, habits and variations of *Kinosternon subrubrum* in southern Illinois. Trans. Ill. St. Acad. Sci. 61, 247–251.

Snedigar, R. and Rokosky, E. J. (1950). Courtship and egg laying of captive *Testudo denticulata*. Copeia 1950, 46–48.

Snow, J. E. (1980). Second clutch laying by painted turtles. Copeia 1980, 534–536.

Spoczynska, J. O. I. (1969). The fascinating kachugas. J. Int. Turtle Tortoise Soc. 3, 8–11.

Standora, E. A. and Spotila, J. R. (1985). Temperature dependent sex determination in sea turtles. Copeia 1985, 711–722.

Stickel, L. F. (1978). Changes in a box turtle population during three decades. Copeia 1978, 221–225.

Storer, T. I. (1930). Notes on the range and life history of the Pacific freshwater turtle, *Clemmys marmorata*. Univ. Calif. Publs. Zool. 32, 429–441.

Stromsten, F. A. (1923). Nest digging and egg laying habits of Bell's turtle, *Chrysemys marginata belli* (Gray). Stud. Nat. Hist. Iowa Univ. 10, 67–76.

Stuart, G. R. (1954). Observations on reproduction in the tortoise *Gopherus agassizi* in captivity. Copeia 1954, 61–62.

Swingland, I. R. (1977). Reproductive effort and life history strategy of the Aldabra giant tortoise. Nature 269, 402–404.

Swingland, I. R. and Coe, M. J. (1978). The natural regulation of giant tortoise populations on Aldabra Atoll: Reproduction. J. Zool., Lond. 186, 285–309.

Swingland, I. R. and Coe, M. J. (1979). The natural regulation of giant tortoise populations on Aldabra Atoll: Recruitment. Phil. Trans. Roy. Soc. B 286, 177–188.

Swingland, I. R. and Lessells, C. M. (1979). The natural regulation of giant tortoise populations on Aldabra Atoll: Movement, polymorphism, reproductive success and mortality. J. Anim. Ecol. 48, 639–654.

Swingland, I. R. and Stubbs, D. (1985). The ecology of a Mediterranean tortoise (*Testudo hermanni*): Reproduction. J. Zool., Lond. A. 205, 595–610.

Talbert, O. R. Jr., Stancyk, S. E., Dean, J. M. and Will, J. M. (1980). Nesting activity of the loggerhead turtle (*Caretta caretta*) in South Carolina I. A rookery in transition. Copeia 1980, 709–718.

Tardent, P. (1972). Haltung und Zucht der Sternschildkröte *Testudo elegans*. Salamandra 8, 165–175.

Thacker, J. L. 1924. Notes on Bell's painted turtle (*Chrysemys marginata belli*) in British Columbia. Can. Field. Nat. 38, 164–167.

Thompson, N. B. (1980). Population dynamics of the Atlantic green sea turtle, *Chelonia mydas* (Linnaeus) 1758. PhD Dissertation (Zoology), Univ. Rhode Island.

Thornhill, G. M. (1982). Comparative reproduction of the turtle, *Chrysemys scripta elegans*, in heated and natural lakes. J. Herpetol. 16, 347–353.

Timkin, R. L. (1968). *Graptemys pseudogeographica* in the upper Missouri River of the North Central United States. J. Herpetol. 1, 76–82.

Tinkle, D. W. (1958). The systematics and ecology of the *Sternothaerus carinatus* complex. Tuland Stud. Zool. 6, 1–56.

Tinkle, D. W. (1961). Geographic variation in reproduction, size, sex ratio, and maturity of *Sternotherus odoratus* (Testudinata: Chelydridae). Ecology 42, 68–76.

Tinkle, D. W., Congdon, J. D. and Rosen, P. C. (1981). Nesting frequency and success: Implications for the demography of painted turtles. Ecology 62, 1426–1432.

Turner, F. B. and Berry, K. H. (1984). Population ecology of the desert tortoise at Goffs, California. Rep. Southern California Edison Co.

Turner, F. B., Hayden, P., Burge, B. L. and Roberson, J. B. (1986). Egg production by the desert tortoise (*Gopherus agassizii*) in California. Herpetologica 42, 93–104.

Turner, F. B., Medica, P. A. and Lyons, C. L. (1984). Reproduction and survival of the desert tortoise (*Scaptochelys agassizii*) in Ivanpah Valley, California. Copeia 1984, 811–820.

Vanzolini, P. E. (1967). Notes on the nesting behavior of *Podocnemis expansa* in the Amazon Valley (Testudines, Pelomedusidae). Pap. Avulsos Zool., S. Paulo 20, 191–215.

Vestjens, W. J. M. (1969). Nesting, egg-laying and hatching of the snake-necked tortoise at Canberra, A. C. T. Aust. Zool. 15, 141–149.

Vogt, R. C. (1980). Natural history of the map turtles *Graptemys pseudogeographica* and *G. ouachitensis* in Wisconsin. Tulane Stud. Zool. Bot. 22, 17–48.

REFERENCES

Vogt, R. C. and Bull, J. J. (1984). Ecology of hatchling sex ratio in map turtles. Ecology 65, 582–587.

Wahlquist, H. and Folkerts, G. W. (1973). Eggs and hatchlings of Barbour's map turtle, *Graptemys barbouri* Carr and Marchand. Herpetologica 29, 236–237.

Webb, R. G. (1956). Size at sexual maturity in the male softshell turtle, *Trionyx ferox emoryi*. Copeia 1956, 121–122.

Webb, R. G. (1961). Observations on the life histories of turtles (genus *Pseudemys* and *Graptemys*) in Lake Texoma, Oklahoma. Am. Midl. Nat. 65, 193–214.

Webb, R. G. (1962). North American recent soft-shelled turtles (family Trionychidae). Univ. Kans. Publs. Mus. Nat. Hist. 13, 429–611.

White, J. B. and Murphy, G. G. (1973). The reproductive cycle and sexual dimorphism of the common snapping turtle, *Chelydra serpentina serpentina*. Herpetologica 29, 240–246.

Wilbur, H. M. (1975a). The evolutionary and mathematical demography of the turtle *Chrysemys picta*. Ecology 56, 64–77.

Wilbur, H. M. (1975b). A growth model for the turtle *Chrysemys picta*. Copeia 1975, 337–343.

Wilbur, H. M. (1977). Propagule size, number, and dispersion pattern in *Ambystoma* and *Ascelpias*. Am. Nat. 111, 43–68.

Wilcox, L. R. (1933). Incubation of painted turtle eggs. Copeia 1933, 41.

Williams, T. H. and Crossman, E. J. (1977). Morphological parameters and spring activities in a central Ontario population of midland painted turtle, *Chrysemys picta marginata* (Agassiz). Can. Field Nat. 91, 47–57.

Wilhoft, D. C., Hotaling, E. and Franks, P. (1983). Effects of temperature on sex determination in embryos of the snapping turtle, *Chelydra serpentina*. J. Herpetol. 17, 38–42.

Woodbury, A. M. and Hardy, R. (1948). Studies of the desert tortoise, *Gopherus agassizii*. Ecol. Monogr. 18, 145–200.

Yntema, C. L. (1970). Observations on females and eggs of the common snapping turtle, *Chelydra serpentina*. Am. Midl. Nat. 84, 69–76.

Yntema, C. L. (1976). Effects of incubation temperatures on sexual differentiation in the turtle, *Chelydra serpentina*. J. Morphol. 150, 453–462.

Yntema, C. L. (1979). Temperature levels and periods of sex determination during incubation of eggs of *Chelydra serpentina*. J. Morphol. 159, 17–28.

Yntema, C. L. (1981). Characteristics of gonads and oviducts in hatchlings and young of *Chelydra serpentina* resulting from three incubation temperatures. J. Morphol. 167, 297–304.

Yntema, C. L. and Mrosovsky, N. (1980). Sexual differentiation in hatchling loggerheads (*Caretta caretta*) incubated at different controlled temperatures. Herpetologica 36, 33–36.

Yntema, C. L. and Mrosovsky, N. (1982). Critical periods and pivotal temperatures for sexual differentiation in loggerhead sea turtles. Can. J. Zool. 60, 1012–1016.

Zovickian, W. H. (1973). Reproduction of the radiated turtle. J. Int. Turtle Tortoise Soc. 7, 26–29, 35.

APPENDIX
References to Life History Data of Turtles

Species	Reference
Cheloniidae	
Caretta caretta	Caldwell, 1959, 1962a; Caldwell et al., 1959; Carr, 1967; Frazer and Ehrhart, 1985; Frazer and Richardson, 1986; Kaufmann, 1975; LeBuff and Beatty, 1971; Limpus, 1973; Richardson, 1982
Chelonia depressa	Bustard and Limpus, 1969; Limpus, 1971
C. mydas	Bustard, 1972; Bustard and Greenham, 1969; Bustard and Tognetti, 1969; Caldwell, 1962b; Carr, 1967; Carr and Carr, 1970a; Carr et al., 1978; Carr and Goodman, 1970; Carr and Hirth, 1962; Frazier, 1971; Frazer and Ehrhart, 1985; Hendrickson, 1958; Hirth, 1980; Pritchard, 1969, 1971b; Simon and Parkes, 1976; Simon et al., 1975
Eretmochelys imbricata	Carr et al., 1966; Deraniyagala, 1939; Pritchard, 1969; Talbert et al., 1980
Lepidochelys kempii	Pritchard and Márquez, 1973; Carr, 1963
L. olivacea	Cogger and Lindner, 1969; Pritchard, 1969
Chelydridae	
Chelydra serpentina	Ash, 1951; Cahn, 1937; Hamilton, 1940; Hammer, 1969; Mosimann and Bider, 1960; White and Murphy, 1973; Yntema, 1970, 1976
C. osceola	Iverson, 1977
Macroclemys temminckii	Dobie, 1971; Ewert, 1976
Dermatemydidae	
Dermatemys mawii	Holman, 1963
Dermochelyidae	
Dermochelys coriacea	Bacon, 1969; Balasingam, 1967; Caldwell, 1958; Caldwell et al., 1955; Carr and Ogren, 1959; Deraniyagala, 1939; Hendrickson, 1962; Pritchard, 1971a
Emydidae	
Batagur baska	Kahn, 1964; Moll, pers. comm.
Callagur borneoensis	Moll, 1977
Chrysemys picta	Cahn, 1937; Cagle, 1954; Christiansen and Moll, 1973; Ernst, 1971a, b, c, d; Gemmell, 1970; Gibbons, 1967, 1968a; Gibbons and Tinkle, 1969; MacCulloch and Secoy, 1983; Mitchell, 1985a, b; Moll, 1973; Powell, 1967; Snow, 1980; Wilbur, 1975a, b

APPENDIX

References to Life History Data of Turtles (Continued)

Species	Reference
Emydidae (Continued)	
Mauremys caspica	Lofts and Boswell, 1961
Clemmys guttata	Cahn 1937; Ernst, 1970, 1975, 1976
C. insculpta	Harding, 1977; Pallas, 1960; Powell, 1967
C. marmorata	Ernst and Barbour, 1972; Storer, 1930
C. muhlenbergii	Arndt, 1977; Barton and Price, 1955
Deirochelys reticularia	Congdon et al., 1983a; Duellman and Schwartz, 1958; Gibbons, 1969, Ernst and Barbour, 1972; Iverson, 1977
Emydoidea blandingii	Cahn, 1937; Gibbons, 1968c; Wilbur, unpubl.
Emys orbicularis	Loveridge and Williams, 1957; Pieau, 1972
Rhinoclemmys funerea	Moll and Legler, 1971
R. punctularia	Medem, 1962
Graptemys barbouri	Cagle, 1952; Wahlquist and Folkerts, 1973
G. geographica	Cahn, 1937; Ernst and Barbour, 1972
G. oculifera	Cagle, 1953
G. ouachitensis	Vogt, 1980
G. pseudogeographica	Cahn, 1937; Timkin, 1968; Vogt, 1980; Webb, 1961
G. pulchra	Cagle, 1952; Shealy, 1976
Kachuga dhongoka	Spoczynska, 1969
K. smithii	Minton, 1966
Malaclemys terrapin	Burns and Williams, 1972; Carr, 1952; Henderson, 1972; Ricklefs and Burger, 1977; Seigel, 1980
Pseudemys concinna	Cahn, 1937; Ernst and Barbour, 1972
P. decussata	Barbour and Carr, 1940
P. floridana	Gibbons, 1970b; Gibbons and Coker, 1977; Goff and Goff, 1932; Iverson, 1977
P. rubriventris	Graham, 1969, 1971
P. scripta	Cagle, 1937, 1944, 1946, 1948a, b, 1950; Congdon and Gibbons 1983; Gibbons, 1970c; Moll and Legler, 1971; Parker, 1984; Webb, 1961
P. terrapen	Petzold, 1968
Terrapene carolina	Cahn, 1937; Ewing, 1935, 1943; Iverson, 1977; Schwartz et al., 1984
T. coahuila	Brown, 1974
T. nelsoni	Iverson, 1977; Milstead and Tinkle, 1967
T. ornata	Blair, 1976; Legler, 1960a
Kinosternidae	
Claudius angustatus	Hausmann, 1968a
Sternotherus carinatus	Mahmoud, 1967; Tinkle, 1958
S. depressus	Tinkle, 1958

(Continued)

References to Life History Data of Turtles (Continued)

Species	Reference
Kinosternidae (Continued)	
S. minor	Cox and Marion, 1978; Iverson, 1978, 1979a; Tinkle, 1958
S. odoratus	Edgren, 1956, 1960; Gibbons, 1970a; Iverson, 1977; Mahmoud, 1967; Risley, 1933; Tinkle, 1961
Kinosternon angustipons	Legler, 1966
K. baurii	Einem, 1956; Iverson, 1977, 1979b; Lardie, 1975a
K. dunni	Medem, 1961
K. flavescens	Cahn, 1937; Christiansen and Dunham, 1972; Lardie, 1975a, b; Skorepa and Ozment, 1968
K. hirtipes	Ernst and Barbour, 1972; Iverson, 1985
K. leucostomum	Moll and Legler, 1971
K. scorpioides	Iverson, 1976; Sexton, 1960
K. spurrelli	Medem, 1962
K. subrubrum	Gibbons, 1983; Iverson, 1977; Lardie, 1975a, b; Mahmoud, 1967; Nichols, 1947; Richmond, 1945; Skorepa and Ozment, 1968
Platysternidae	
Platysternon megacephalum	De Koningh, 1968
Testudinidae	
Geochelone carbonaria	Legler, 1963
G. chilensis	Auffenberg, 1969
G. denticulata	Beltz, 1954; Snedigar and Rokosky, 1950
G. elegans	Deraniyagala, 1939; Tardent, 1972; Jayaker and Spurway, 1964, 1966
G. elephantopus	DeNeira and Roe, 1984, Hendrickson, 1966; Shaw, 1966
G. gigantea	Bourn, 1977; Gaymer, 1968; Grubb, 1971b; Honegger, 1967
G. pardalis	Loveridge and Williams, 1957
G. radiata	Schweizer, 1965; Zovickian, 1973
G. sulcata	Cloudsley-Thompson, 1970; Grubb, 1971a
Gopherus agassizii	Jackson et al., 1976; Miller, 1955; Nichols, 1953, 1957; Stuart, 1954; Turner and Berry, 1984; Turner et al., 1986; Turner et al., 1984; Woodbury and Hardy, 1948
G. polyphemus	Arata, 1958; Carr, 1952; Desola and Abrams, 1933; Iverson, 1980, Landers et al., 1982
Homopus areolatus	Eglir, 1963; Loveridge and Williams, 1957
H. boulengeri	Loveridge and Williams, 1957
Kinixys belliana	Loveridge and Williams, 1957

APPENDIX

References to Life History Data of Turtles (Continued)

Species	Reference
Testudinidae (Continued)	
K. erosa	Loveridge and Williams, 1957; Schmidt, 1919
K. homeana	Blackwell, 1968
Malacochersus tornieri	Loveridge and Williams, 1957; Shaw, 1963
Psammobates geometricus	Loveridge and Williams, 1957
P. oculifera	Loveridge and Williams, 1957
P. tentorius	Archer, 1967; Loveridge and Williams, 1957
Testudo graeca	Castanet and Cheylan, 1979; Lambert, 1969, 1982; Loveridge and Williams, 1957
T. hermanni	Castanet and Cheylan, 1979; Ehrengart, 1971; Kirsche, 1967; Swingland and Stubbs, 1985
T. horsfieldii	Minton, 1966
T. kleinmanni	Loveridge and Williams, 1957
Trionychidae	
Cyclanorbis senegalensis	Loveridge and Williams, 1957
Cycloderma frenatum	Loveridge and Williams, 1957
Lissemys punctata	Deraniyagala, 1939
Trionyx ferox	Breckenridge, 1955; Goff and Goff, 1935; Hamilton, 1947; Iverson, 1977; Lardie, 1973; Webb, 1956, 1962
T. gangeticus	Minton, 1966
T. muticus	Cahn, 1937; Fitch and Plummer, 1975; Muller, 1921; Plummer, 1976; Webb, 1962
T. sinensis	Mitsukuri, 1905; Lofts and Tsui, 1977
T. spiniferus	Breckenridge, 1960; Cahn, 1937; Dunson, 1967; Webb, 1962
T. triunguis	Loveridge and Williams, 1957
Chelidae	
Chelodina expansa	Goode and Russell, 1968
C. longicollis	Vestjens, 1969
C. novaeguineae	Goode, 1967
C. siebenrocki	Rhodin and Mittermeier, 1976
Chelus fimbriatus	Hausmann, 1968b; Mondolfi, 1955
Elseya dentata	Cogger, 1975
Emydura macquarrii	Goode and Russell, 1968
Pelomedusidae	
Pelomedusa subrufa	Jacques, 1966
Pelusios subniger	Schmidt, 1919
Podocnemis expansa	Alho and Padua, 1982; Roze, 1964; Vanzolini, 1967
P. unifilis	Foote, 1978; Mondolfi, 1955

CHAPTER 7

Life History Patterns in Squamate Reptiles

ARTHUR E. DUNHAM, DONALD B. MILES, AND DAVID N. REZNICK

Department of Biology, University of Pennsylvania, Philadelphia, Pennsylvania (A.E.D., D.B.M.); Department of Biology, University of California, Riverside, California (D.N.R.)

The present address for Donald B. Miles is Department of Zoological and Biomedical Sciences, Ohio University, Athens, Ohio.

CONTENTS

I. INTRODUCTION — 443

II. DATA AND ANALYSES — 447
  A. The Data, 447
  B. Statistical Analyses, 450

III. RESULTS — 454
  A. Life History Variation in Squamate Reptiles, 454
  B. Life History Patterns in Lizards, 456
  C. Life History Patterns in Snakes, 477
  D. Family Effects and Phylogenetic Constraints, 485

IV. CONCLUSIONS — 494
  A. General Patterns of Variation in Life History Traits, 494
  B. Evaluation of the Patterns, 497
  C. Future Directions, 497

ACKNOWLEDGMENTS — 500
REFERENCES — 500
APPENDIX — 512

I. INTRODUCTION

Lizards and snakes exhibit a great diversity of life histories. Although this diversity is well known, there have been few credible attempts to summarize or explain the patterns of life history variation within this group. The general processes by which such diversity may be generated have been delineated, but current theory has largely failed to explain the range of life history variation seen in any group of organisms. One reason for this failure is that constraints that are the unique evolutionary heritage of any species or clade have not been incorporated into theory. These constraints include those imposed by physiological and developmental processes (Stearns, 1980), by morphology and scaling, and by underlying genetic correlations (Lande, 1983). An approach to understanding these constraints and patterns of covariation involves the comparative study of patterns of life history variation across a spectrum of taxonomic organization. Comparative studies sample a wide range of variation in any given trait and allow detection both of correlations among life history traits, and associations between life history variation and environmental variation that are inaccessible within a single species. Such associations suggest causal relationships and become the source of hypotheses to account for the evolution of life history variation.

The classic comparative studies of Tinkle (1969) and Tinkle et al. (1970) demonstrated remarkable variability in life histories among lizards and provided a vital stimulus to the study of life history evolution in reptiles. These studies indicated that lizards maturing at a larger size tend to be larger throughout life, to be older at maturity, and to produce larger clutches. Comparisons of lizards grouped according to mode of reproduction (oviparous versus viviparous), age at first reproduction ("early" versus "late"), frequency of reproduction (single versus multiple broods per season), and distribution (temperate versus tropical) indicated that species with delayed maturity tend to be larger at maturity and throughout life, to produce a single, large brood per season, and to be either oviparous or viviparous. These species were more likely to be found in a temperate environment. Females from early-maturing species tend to be oviparous, to be smaller at maturity and throughout life, and to produce multiple broods per season, but to have fewer young per brood.

Tinkle et al. (1970) characterized the overall association between life history traits through a Prim network analysis, a technique that determines whether populations cluster in discrete groups characterized by unique combinations of life history traits. The analysis revealed four distinct clusters, each describing a major "life history strategy." The largest cluster consisted of early-maturing, multiple-brooded species with small clutch sizes. Species characterized by delayed reproduction and a single large clutch per season comprised a second cluster. A third cluster consisted of viviparous species, which exhibited delayed reproduction and one large brood per season. The final cluster involved populations that matured early and had large, multiple broods per season.

Given such patterns of variation and covariation in life history traits, a key question is: "Why do they occur?" Tinkle et al. (1970) focused their discussion on potential compensation for delayed maturity. Earlier theoretical work (Cole, 1954; Lewontin, 1965) demonstrated that delayed maturity could result in a substantial decrement in individual fitness. Tinkle et al. (1970) argued that if delayed maturity were to evolve, this decrement must be balanced by a corresponding gain in fitness elsewhere. Their hypotheses included three mechanisms: (a) increased clutch size due to the allometric relationship of clutch size and body size, (b) increased adult survival, partly as a result of increased body size, and (c) increased survival from birth to sexual maturity, possibly as a result of increased parental investment (viviparity or larger eggs).

Answering such questions and testing such hypotheses demands a larger and more reliable data set than that available to Tinkle et al. (1970). Those authors recognized that the patterns they detected were drawn from data that were insufficient both in the number of species represented and in the variables measured for each species. They argued that the minimum data set for comparative evolutionary study of patterns of life history variation and covariation in lizards must include better estimates of: (1) age at first reproduction, (2) number of clutches per season, (3) absolute egg size and egg size relative to female size (relative clutch mass), (4) age-specific survival and fecundity, and (5) survival from birth to age at first reproduction.

Additional explanations for how and why life histories evolve have been developed since 1970. Current life history theory has proposed several mechanisms that could select for the observed patterns of variation and covariation in life histories. Such mechanisms include differences in the mean or variance of age-specific survival and reproduction (e.g., Gadgil and Bossert, 1970; Schaffer, 1974; Pianka and Parker, 1975; Law, 1979; Michod, 1979; Charlesworth, 1980), in resource availability and in environmental predictability (Pianka, 1970; Wilbur et al., 1974; Boyce, 1984). Besides providing additional hypotheses for the evolution of patterns such as those observed in lizards, these theories

INTRODUCTION

reinforce the importance of estimating the additional variables suggested by Tinkle et al. (1970). Only by estimating variation in age-specific reproduction and survival can such hypotheses be evaluated.

The variation in life history traits observed among a group of populations may arise from both genetic and nongenetic sources. Nongenetic life history differences between populations result from plastic phenotypic responses to local environmental conditions that alter individual time and energy budgets. Life history differences between populations may also be due to the genetic changes that have accumulated since those populations diverged from a common ancestor. These genetic differences include those due to evolutionary adaptation to local environmental conditions and those due to architectural or design constraints. Ballinger (1983) suggested a nested analysis of variance model of partitioning life history variation into components arising from each of these sources, but was unable completely to carry out this partitioning in the species (*Urosaurus ornatus*) he studied.

Recent empirical workers have also suggested some ecological causes for observed life history patterns. Vitt and Congdon (1978) proposed that foraging mode ("sit-and-wait" versus "active" foragers), body shape, and reproductive allocation are coevolved traits in lizards. They argued that relative clutch mass is a function of body shape, foraging mode, and predator escape tactics. Widely foraging lizards rely on speed to avoid predation, are typically streamlined in form, and have clutches that comprise a relatively low proportion of total body mass. In contrast, sit-and-wait species rely on crypsis to avoid predation and have a short, stocky body form and high relative clutch mass. This idea was developed further by Huey and Pianka (1981), Vitt (1981), Anderson and Karasov (1981), Bauwens and Thoen (1981), Vitt and Price (1982), Andrews (1984), Seigel and Fitch (1984), Bennett et al. (1984), Huey et al. (1984), Nagy et al. (1984), Dunham and Miles (1985), and Huey and Bennett (1986). These authors have demonstrated that a reptile's foraging mode is highly correlated with a number of ecological factors and phenotypic traits. For example, sit-and-wait predators tend to have relatively low metabolic expenditures per unit time, consume a relatively lower mass of food, feed on mobile prey, have limited physiological endurance, are primarily visual predators, and are vulnerable to actively foraging predators. On the other hand, actively foraging species tend to have higher metabolic expenditures per unit time, consume a greater mass of food per unit time, feed on sedentary, clumped or large prey, have high physiological endurance, may be visual or olfactory predators, and be preyed upon primarily by ambush predators. In some special cases, preferred habitat (e.g., arboreality) has also been suggested as a constraint on life history pattern (e.g., Andrews and Rand, 1974, 1983; Vitt, 1981; Ballinger, 1983). The evolution of reproductive mode has been considered in detail (e.g., Shine, 1985).

We surveyed the literature on life history variation in squamate reptiles. The present report includes at least partial life history data on 185 populations of lizards from 149 species. Complete data on the five variables used by Tinkle et al. (1970) are available on 122 populations from 92 species of lizards. Also included are estimates of some of the additional life history variables suggested by Tinkle et al. (1970) for several lizard populations. An important addition is a parallel data set for 58 populations/species of snakes. Finally, for two lizard species (*Sceloporus undulatus* and *Urosaurus ornatus*), we have relatively complete data from multiple populations; these data provide a basis for considering trends in intraspecific variation. We use this enlarged data set to answer the following questions:

(1) Are the trends recognized by Tinkle et al. (1970) evident in the enlarged data set? We also examine the effect on the reported trends of the inclusion of species with invariant clutch sizes; such species were excluded from the analyses of Tinkle et al. (1970).

(2) Do snakes and lizards have similar patterns of life history variation? We analyze the patterns of life history variation and covariation in snakes and contrast those patterns with those occurring in lizards.

(3) Are observed patterns a consequence of allometric relationships with body size or of biased taxonomic representation? Because body size and other life history variables are tightly correlated, Stearns (1983, 1984) recently argued that the observed patterns of covariation in life history traits within any taxonomic group may be a by-product of evolutionary changes in body size rather than the products of direct selection on life history phenotypes per se (but see Dunham and Miles, 1985). We summarize the evidence for and against this argument. Clutton-Brock and Harvey (1984) recently demonstrated that uneven representation of taxa potentially distorts conclusions derived from comparative studies. Consequently, because iguanids are more heavily represented than any other family of lizards in our data set and in that analyzed by Tinkle et al. (1970), observed patterns of variation may reflect differences between iguanids and other lizards rather than general trends within lizards as a whole. Taxonomic affinity is important for a second reason: If a significant amount of variation in life histories is accounted for by the order, family, or genus to which a species belongs, then the common biology (evolutionary history) of the group may canalize and constrain life history evolution to an unknown extent (Felsenstein, 1985; Cheverud et al., 1985; Huey and Bennett, 1986).

DATA AND ANALYSES

(4) What are the causes of the observed patterns of life history variation? We adopt a linear models approach to evaluate the role of foraging mode, preferred habitat, and taxonomic affinity in molding life history patterns in squamate reptiles. This analysis provides an initial test of the hypothesis that habitat specialization may impose constraints on the particular reproductive characteristics of squamate reptiles (e.g., Vitt, 1981).

II. DATA AND ANALYSES

A. The Data

Our data set includes the same seven variables considered by Tinkle et al. (1970): (1) female snout–vent length (SVL) at first reproduction, (2) age at first reproduction, (3) mean adult female SVL, (4) mean clutch size, (5) mode of reproduction, (6) frequency of broods per year, and (7) distribution. We summarize the literature on 185 lizard and 73 snake species/populations. We include studies that provided data on at least four of the seven variables listed above. Studies in which the data were a composite taken from several populations are eliminated. Whenever full data sets are available on multiple populations of a given species, each population was entered as an independent data set. These data are presented in the Appendix. Methods for obtaining such data are detailed in Dunham et al. (this volume). Our conventions for assigning values to these variables are as follows.

1. SVL AT FIRST REPRODUCTION

The snout–vent length in millimeters when vitellogenesis for the first clutch is evident in oviparous species and the snout–vent length when development of embryos comprising the first litter is evident in viviparous species.

2. AGE AT FIRST REPRODUCTION OF FEMALES

Age (months) when vitellogenesis for the first clutch is evident in oviparous species and that corresponding to snout–vent length when development of embryos comprising the first clutch is evident in viviparous species. Following Tinkle et al. (1970), species maturing and reproducing in their first reproductive season after hatching are classified as "early maturing" species; those species maturing in subsequent reproductive seasons are classified as "delayed maturing" species.

3. MEAN ADULT FEMALE SVL

Mean adult female SVL (FSVL) is the average SVL in millimeters of females with a SVL greater than that of the smallest sexually mature female in the population.

4. MEAN CLUTCH SIZE

The mean clutch or brood size is the mean number of offspring per clutch (brood) for all reproductive females.

5. MODE OF REPRODUCTION

Species are classified as either oviparous or viviparous (Blackburn, 1982; Blackburn et al., 1984; Shine, 1985). Following Bellairs (1970), we do not attempt to distinguish between ovoviviparous and viviparous species.

6. CLUTCH FREQUENCY (NUMBER OF BROODS PER YEAR)

Accurate estimates of the number of clutches produced per season require frequent capture and palpation of marked individuals (as in Turner et al., 1970; Dunham, 1981). Few studies meet this criterion. Lacking such data, brood frequency is frequently estimated by dividing the time required for the production of one clutch by the length of the active season. This procedure generates erroneous estimates if the time required to produce a single clutch varies significantly among clutches (Turner et al., 1970) or if the reproductive season is much shorter than the active season. We classify brood frequency as a binary variable (i.e., single versus multiple broods per year) because of the lack of standardization and reliability in the literature estimates of brood frequency.

7. DISTRIBUTION

Species are classified as either tropical or temperate in their distribution based on the locality at which a particular study was conducted.

For as many species as possible, we include data on the following additional variables:

8. RELATIVE CLUTCH MASS (RCM)

Relative clutch mass as normally computed, equals the proportion of the total mass of a near-term female that consists of the clutch or brood of young. As noted by Vitt and Price (1982) and Cuellar (1984), various methods are used to estimate RCM and authors do not always clearly state what method they use. Sources of variation include whether fresh or preserved material is used (Vitt et al., 1985), whether the ratio is based on wet or dry mass, and whether the denominator represents total mass or (preferably) just somatic mass (Cuellar, 1984). Unfortunately, most estimates of RCM are confounded by body mass (Seigel and Fitch, 1984; Dunham and Miles, 1985; see Dunham et al., this volume). Because of these problems with the measurement and analysis of RCM, our analysis of this variable should be considered tentative (see Dunham et al., this volume).

9. FORAGING MODE

Species are classified as either "sit-and-wait" (SW) or "actively foraging" (AF) based on literature descriptions. A more formal means of classification was used by Huey and Pianka (1981), based on timed observations of several individuals of each species. Such data are clearly preferable, but rarely available.

10. PREFERRED HABITAT TYPE

We classify species into six categories (terrestrial, saxicolous, psammophilous, arboreal, fossorial, and aquatic), which describe the predominant microhabitat (substrate) occupied by a given population.

11. OTHER SOURCES OF INACCURACY IN DATA

In addition to sampling error, we recognize two potential sources of inaccuracy in these data. Because many, if not most, data come from relatively short-term studies, inaccuracies may exist in estimates of life history traits due to exogenous variation. Annual variation in life history characteristics has been found in most lizard and snake populations that have been studied over extended periods of time (e.g., Tinkle, 1967; Ballinger, 1977; Martin, 1977; Dunham, 1981; Pilorge, 1981; Andren and Nilson, 1983; Seigel et al., 1986). We have no way of assessing the effects of such variation on the reported mean values of life history variables. We can only assume that this does not represent a source of bias, meaning that a particular group is not affected by such variation in a fashion that is systematically different from any other group to which it is being compared. In comparative studies such variation, which is generally included in the error or residual variation, is likely to be small relative to the magnitude of differences among species.

Another source of inaccuracy may result from the inclusion of species with genetically invariant clutch size. Within the Iguanidae, all species of *Anolis* have a single egg per clutch but relatively high clutch frequencies. Within the Gekkonidae, all members of two subfamilies (Eublepharinae, Diplodactylinae) lay two eggs per clutch, whereas all members of two other subfamilies (Sphaerodactylinae, Gekkoninae) lay a single egg per clutch. The over- or underrepresentation of such groups biases estimates of mean clutch size and brood frequency within these families. Furthermore, clutch size conceivably constrains the values of other life history traits and hence may bias the means for those variables also. For this reason Tinkle et al. (1970) excluded species with invariant clutch size from their analyses. We follow their convention for most analyses, but also repeat selected analyses including these species to determine whether species with fixed clutch sizes fit the same patterns of covariation seen in species with variable clutch sizes or whether they represent a separate constellation of life history patterns.

B. Statistical Analyses

We performed a series of statistical tests to answer the following questions:

(1) Are there significant correlations among the life history variables (SVL at maturity, mean SVL of adult females, and clutch size)? Age at maturity (age at first reproduction) was also included in this analysis and was represented as the actual age when the first clutch was produced and not as a binary variable.

(2) Are the categorical variables (distribution, mode of reproduction, and brood frequency) associated with significant differences in the mean values of the life history variables? Such differences may suggest causal relationships. A separate t-test was performed for every combination of life history and categorical variables.

(3) Are there any associations among the categorical variables? This question was answered with chi-square tests of association, or Fisher's Exact Probability tests, where demanded by small sample sizes in any one of the cells. All possible pairs of categorical variables were compared. For example, in the comparison of mode of reproduction with age at maturity, an individual species/population was classified into one of the four cells (early-oviparous, late-oviparous, early-viviparous, and late-viviparous) and the total number of species/populations in each cell is the source of the analysis.

(4) Are the above correlations and associations involving life history

DATA AND ANALYSES

traits independent of differences in body size among groups being contrasted? For example, because clutch size increases with body size in many species (Tinkle et al., 1970; Dunham and Miles, 1985), observed differences in clutch size between two groups being compared may be attributable to between-group differences in average body size. To analyze this relationship, we first report the simple regressions of clutch size on female SVL for the eight classes of categorical variables. We then compare these regressions in a one-way analysis of covariance for each variable with clutch size as the dependent variable and female SVL as the covariate. Female SVL is probably an acceptable measure of body size for comparisons within groups having similar body shapes. However, when body shapes differ (e.g., lizards versus snakes), standardization and calculation of size measures are much more complex (see Bookstein et al., 1985). Nonetheless, we were forced to base our analyses on female SVL because it is often the only reported measure.

(5) Do species cluster in discrete groups characterized by unique combinations of life history traits or are they more or less continuously distributed in character space? Such clusters suggest the existence of what Tinkle et al. (1970) referred to as "life history strategies." Clusters may also be interpreted as constraints on how life histories can evolve. We summarize the similarities among species for the five life history variables mentioned above (SVL at maturity, clutch size, age at maturity, mode of reproduction, and brood frequency) using a Prim Network Analysis (Gower and Ross, 1969). The distribution of each variable is standardized to a mean of zero and a standard deviation of one to equalize the contribution of all variables to the network. The metric used to construct the network is the coefficient of dissimilarity ($d_{i,j}$) computed as:

$$d_{i,j} = \sum^{k} |(X_{i,k} - X_{j,k})|, \qquad (1)$$

where $X_{i,k}$ is the character state of the kth character of species i. Species are then sequentially linked to the species of group with the most similar life history (smallest value of $d_{i,j}$), until all species are included in the network.

Recent theory has revealed additional factors that may influence the evolution of life history traits such as phylogenetic constraints, interactions and covariation among variables, and a wide variety of ecological factors. To assay the importance of these factors, we include the following extensions to the preceding analyses.

1. INCLUSION OF SPECIES WITH FIXED CLUTCH SIZE

We consider how fixed-clutch species fit the patterns revealed in the above analyses by including them in a second Prim network analysis. Dunham and Miles (1985) executed a much larger series of analyses with and without the fixed clutch species. Their results will be summarized with our discussion of the Prim network analyses.

2. MULTIWAY ANALYSES OF VARIANCE

Unlike Tinkle et al. (1970), we have sufficient data to compute $2 \times 2 \times 2$ factorial design analyses of variance for three life history variables. The main effects in these analyses accomplish the same end as the t-tests described above, but the added information includes the interactions between main effects. Such interactions potentially alter our interpretations of the results for the main effects. Unfortunately, these tests can include only those species/populations for which we have complete data for all dependent and independent variables. The classification variables used in these tests are mode of reproduction, brood frequency, and distribution. The dependent variables are clutch size, female SVL at first reproduction, and age at first reproduction.

3. INCLUSION OF NEW VARIABLES

Foraging mode and preferred habitat are treated as new independent variables and relative clutch mass (RCM) as a new dependent variable. First, sit-and-wait and active foragers are compared (t-tests) for differences in mean clutch size, RCM, female SVL at first reproduction, and mean female SVL. Next, the association of foraging mode with other dependent and independent variables is examined using a series of chi-square or Fisher's Exact tests. Finally, we perform an analysis of covariance with foraging mode as the independent variable, RCM as the dependent variable, and female SVL as the covariate.

4. MULTIVARIATE ANALYSES

Patterns of covariation among life history traits are examined using principal components analysis (PCA). Principal components calculates a set of new coordinates, which are rigid rotations of the original axes such that each successive component maximizes the explained variation. To summarize the phylogenetic and ecological effects on the patterns of covariation of the life history traits, we perform two sets of analyses. First, the log-transformed continuous variables (age at matu-

DATA AND ANALYSES

rity, mean adult female SVL, and clutch size) are entered into one PCA. In a subsequent analysis, data on relative clutch mass (RCM) are included. We then use the species scores from the first two principal component axes as dependent variables in an ANOVA and test the hypothesis that the species positions along the gradient of life history variation can be explained by effects due to family–level variation, mode of reproduction, frequency of breeding, or an interaction among the variables. We further analyze the positions of species in the space defined by the first two principal component axes for differences associated with foraging mode and habitat.

5. WITHIN-SPECIES COMPARISONS

Sceloporus undulatus is one of the most intensively studied North American lizards, with more than a dozen population studies in various parts of its range. Tinkle and Dunham (1986) compiled data on habitat, density, and an array of reproductive and demographic variables from 11 of the more complete studies (Table XII). *Urosaurus ornatus* has also been intensively studied, though less so than *S. undulatus*. Dunham (1982) summarized local and geographic variation in a number of life history characteristics of several populations (Table XIII). We review the studies of variation in life history traits among populations of these species.

6. SNAKES

We repeat the entire series of analyses described above for the data (Appendix) on life history variation in snakes. There are no extensive studies of geographic variation in life history for any snake species; therefore, we have not included a section on within-species comparisons for snakes.

7. EVALUATION OF THE ROLE OF TAXONOMIC REPRESENTATION

Because lizards and snakes differ with respect to patterns of variation in life history traits (Dunham and Miles, 1985), each suborder is analyzed separately. We document differences between the two groups and present an approach to quantifying the influence of phylogeny on patterns of variation in life history traits. Qualitative differences among families of squamate reptiles are illustrated by the correlations among the dependent life history variables, and then family effects for lizards as a group are more critically evaluated.

III. RESULTS

A. Life History Variation in Squamate Reptiles

Squamate reptiles are characterized by a diversity of life history habits (Table I). Our review of the literature produced life history data for ten families of lizards and five families of snakes. However, little is known about life history characteristics in the Amphisbaenia (but see Papenfuss, 1982) and the lizard families Anniellidae, Cordylidae, Helodermatidae, and Pygopodidae; and in the snake families Boidae, Leptotyphlopidae, Typhlopidae, and Uropeltidae.

Lizards tend to mature at an early age (average is 18 months) and at a small body size (62 mm). Their mean adult size (74 mm) is only slightly larger than their size at maturity. The dominant mode of reproduction in lizards is oviparity (83%); just 17% of all lizard species in our sample bear live young (see also Shine, 1985). Most species are multiple-brooded (65%), whereas a smaller fraction (35%) lay only a single clutch per year. Biennial reproduction is rarely found in lizards (but see Huey et al., 1974; Vial and Stewart, 1985). The mean clutch size is 5.3 eggs/brood, and females have a low RCM (0.24). These patterns tend to be conserved among the families we sampled. Among families, age at maturity varies from 5.5 months for chamaeleonids to more than 30 months for anguids and xantusiids. Most families are homogeneous in size at maturity and mean adult body size (this may be an artifact of the paucity of studies of large species). Mean clutch size varies from 2–3 eggs/brood in the gekkonids, gymnophthalmids, teiids, and xantusiids, to 12 eggs in the chamaeleonids. Agamids, gymnophthalmids, and teiids have the lowest values for RCM (0.16), whereas the anguids, iguanids, and lacertids have the highest values. Values for mode of reproduction and brood frequency are generally similar among families.

Snakes tend to mature at a later age (28 months) and at a larger mean body size (518 mm). In comparisons with lizards, snakes in our sample are much more likely to be viviparous (52%) and to be single-brooded (73%). Only 7% of the species produce more than one brood per season, and all of these are colubrids. A significant proportion of species (20%) is characterized by biennial reproduction. Snakes also have a higher average RCM (0.33) than lizards. Unlike the situation in lizards, considerable variation exists among families of snakes for the above variables. The viperids in our sample are primarily viviparous and are characterized by delayed maturity and usually by biennial reproduction. In contrast, colubrids and elapids mature at an earlier age and smaller body size, tend to be oviparous, and exhibit annual reproduction. Biennial reproduction is rare in these two families.

TABLE I
Summary of Data Used in Statistical Analyses

Taxon	Age	FEMAT	FSVL	CS	OFFSVL	RCM	Mode 1	Mode 2	Mode 3	BF 1	BF 2	BF 3
Sauria	**17.7** (135)	**62.0** (176)	**73.8** (152)	**5.3** (183)	**27.1** (92)	**0.24** (70)	**0.83** (158)	**0.17** (158)		**0.35**	**0.65**	**0** (158)
Agamidae	10.9 (11)	67.5 (12)	83.3 (10)	6.1 (14)	23.6 (5)	0.16 (1)	1.00 (14)	0		0.08	0.92	0 (14)
Chamaeleonidae	5.5 (2)	66.0 (2)	99.6 (2)	12.1 (2)	27.5 (2)	0.26 (2)	0.50 (2)	0.50		0	1.0	0 (2)
Anguidae	30.5 (4)	82.9 (9)	86.8 (7)	7.0 (8)	34.2 (3)	0.27 (2)	0.33 (9)	0.67		0.86	0.14	0 (9)
Gekkonidae	29.0 (4)	50.6 (18)	61.0 (12)	1.9 (18)	21.4 (12)	0.18 (6)	1.00 (18)	0		0.17	0.83	0 (18)
Gymnophthalmidae	7.0 (2)	35.0 (3)	38.7 (2)	2.0 (3)	18.1 (2)	0.16 (1)	1.00 (3)	0		0.33	0.67	0 (3)
Iguanidae	17.3 (63)	63.3 (68)	76.3 (64)	7.1 (68)	28.8 (40)	0.26 (35)	0.86 (69)	0.14		0.33	0.67	0 (69)
Lacertidae	16.1 (9)	48.7 (8)	52.9 (7)	5.0 (9)	25.6 (4)	0.32 (6)	0.89 (9)	0.11		0.33	0.67	0 (9)
Scincidae	18.3 (25)	62.5 (37)	70.7 (25)	4.8 (38)	28.2 (16)	0.22 (9)	0.73 (38)	0.27		0.63	0.37	0 (38)
Teiidae	17.0 (12)	64.5 (17)	78.8 (20)	2.9 (20)	28.1 (6)	0.15 (7)	1.00 (30)	0		0.11	0.89	0 (20)
Xantusiidae	38.0 (3)	56.5 (2)	56.1 (3)	2.4 (3)	23.0 (2)	0.22 (1)	1.00 (3)	0		1.00	0	0 (3)
Serpentes	**27.8** (57)	**518.5** (65)	**614.8** (68)	**9.1** (70)	**190.4** (50)	**0.33** (33)	**0.48** (71)	**0.52** (71)		**0.73**	**0.07**	**0.20** (69)
Acrochordidae		865.0 (2)	1007.5 (2)	10.6 (2)	310.0 (2)	0.53 (1)	0 (2)	1.00		0.50	0.50	0 (2)
Colubridae	26.5 (34)	489.5 (38)	605.8 (36)	9.8 (39)	186.4 (28)	0.31 (22)	0.60 (40)	0.40		0.79	0.13	0.08 (38)
Elapidae	24.1 (14)	421.0 (13)	471.4 (19)	7.4 (18)	145.7 (12)	0.39 (7)	0.56 (18)	0.44		0.94	0	0.06 (17)
Hydrophiidae	20.0 (1)	730.0 (1)	850.0 (1)	17.7 (1)	230.0 (1)		0 (1)	1.00		1.00	0	0 (1)
Viperidae	38.1 (9)	658.3 (12)	820.5 (11)	9.1 (11)	241.3 (8)	0.27 (3)	0 (11)	1.00		0.25	0	0.75 (12)

Age is modal age (months) of females at sexual maturity, FEMAT is average age (months) of females at maturity, FSVL is the average SVL (mm) of reproductive females, CS is the average clutch size (offspring/clutch), OFFSVL is average SVL (mm) of offspring at hatching or birth, and RCM is relative clutch mass. Mode is the proportion of species with a given mode of reproduction (1, oviparous; 2, viviparous). BF is the proportion with a given frequency of broods per year (1, annual reproduction; 2, multiple broods per year; 3, biennial reproduction).

TABLE II
Product-Moment Correlations Among Life History Traits Using All Available Data on Lizards and Snakes

Variables	Lizards	Snakes
Snout–vent length at maturity (mm) Snout–vent length of adult females (mm)	.98*** (144)	.98*** (60)
Snout–vent length at maturity (mm) Clutch size	.44*** (174)	.36** (62)
Snout–vent length at maturity (mm) Age at first reproduction (months)	.62*** (128)	.55*** (51)
Snout–vent length adult females (mm) Clutch size	.50*** (150)	.49*** (65)
Snout–vent length adult females (mm) Age at first reproduction (months)	.52*** (117)	.42*** (53)
Clutch size Age at first reproduction (mo)	.07^{ns} (134)	.14^{ns} (55)

**$P < .01$; ***$P < .001$; $^{ns}P > .05$.
Numbers in parentheses are sample sizes.

B. Life History Patterns in Lizards

1. OVERVIEW AND GENERAL TRENDS

Pairwise correlations between SVL of females at maturity, mean SVL of adult females, age of females at maturity, and clutch size are all positive (Table II), implying that lizards maturing at a later age also mature at a larger size, remain larger throughout life, and produce more eggs per clutch than do lizards maturing at an earlier age. In most cases the correlation coefficients are higher than those reported by Tinkle et al. (1970), but reflect the same trends. This increase does not necessarily reflect a simple increase in sample size, but rather it is probably due to an increase in the range of values reported for all of the dependent variables. Our results differed only for the correlation between clutch size and age at first reproduction. Tinkle et al. (1970) reported a significant positive correlation between these variables ($r = 0.31$; $n = 53$), whereas we found a nonsignificant, positive correlation ($r = 0.07$; $n = 134$). However, the partial correlation between age at maturity and clutch size, with SVL at maturity held constant, is negative ($r = -0.28$, $P < 0.01$) indicating that at a given SVL at maturity, species with delayed maturity produce smaller clutches than do early maturing species.

RESULTS

TABLE III
Summary Statistics and Results of Pairwise t-Tests on Lizard Data

Variables	Mean	Standard deviation	N	t
SVL at maturity				
oviparous	60.72 [61.64]	27.06 [18.30]	145 [59]	−1.51
viviparous	67.70 [69.92]	22.02 [21.69]	30 [12]	[−1.23]
single brood/year	75.04 [71.53]	34.30 [23.10]	53 [19]	3.49**
multiple broods/year	57.17 [58.91]	19.56 [17.47]	97 [34]	[2.07*]
tropical	64.20 [66.38]	33.47 [15.18]	70 [16]	−0.75
temperate	60.84 [62.07]	20.31 [19.98]	105 [55]	[0.92]
early maturing	51.73 [55.30]	15.15 [15.63]	72 [37]	−5.45***
late maturing	77.73 [74.26]	33.05 [20.03]	56 [23]	[−3.87**]
Mean adult female snout–vent length				
oviparous	72.65 [65.48]	33.72 [15.97]	126 [31]	−1.21
viviparous	79.21 [77.80]	22.83 [18.45]	26 [10]	[−1.89]
single brood/year	87.70 [76.29]	44.13 [22.07]	46 [7]	2.84**
multiple broods/year	67.94 [65.91]	23.11 [17.63]	93 [22]	[1.13]
tropical	81.00 [77.88]	45.41 [17.86]	52 [16]	1.61
temperate	70.25 [65.68]	21.73 [16.54]	99 [25]	[1.29]
early maturing	62.51 [62.37]	18.71 [14.18]	64 [19]	4.31***
late maturing	89.58 [80.13]	42.37 [20.75]	53 [8]	[1.29]
Clutch size				
oviparous	5.28 [5.80]	5.11 [6.11]	152 [66]	−0.68
viviparous	5.80 [7.02]	3.48 [3.94]	30 [17]	[−1.01]
single brood/year	7.41 [7.94]	6.74 [6.58]	55 [27]	2.80**
multiple broods/year	4.68 [3.99]	3.54 [3.30]	101 [40]	[2.88*]
tropical	4.22 [5.59]	5.69 [6.79]	70 [28]	−2.33*
temperate	6.06 [6.14]	4.18 [5.14]	112 [57]	[−0.38]
early maturing	5.43 [4.30]	3.52 [3.28]	75 [40]	1.72
late maturing	7.13 [7.81]	6.88 [6.52]	59 [28]	[2.63*]

*$P < .05$; **$P < .01$; ***$P < .001$.
Values in brackets are those of Tinkle et al. (1970).

We tested for differences in SVL at maturity, mean FSVL, and clutch size between levels of the categorical variables using a series of pairwise t-tests (Table III). Oviparous and viviparous lizards do not differ significantly in SVL at maturity, mean SVL of adult females, or in mean clutch size. Single-brooded species are significantly larger at maturity, remain larger, and have more offspring per clutch than do multiple-brooded species. Temperate and tropical lizards did not differ

TABLE IV
Contingency Table Analysis of Categorical Variables for Lizard Data

	Oviparous	Viviparous	p
Single brood/year	32 [16]	24 [9]	.0001 [< .001]
Multiple broods/year	100 [41]	2 [1]	
Tropical	57 [21]	13 [7]	.64 [.60]
Temperate	95 [51]	18 [9]	
Early maturing	68 [42]	8 [1]	.003 [< .001]
Late maturing	41 [18]	18 [8]	
	Tropical	Temperate	p
Single brood/year	10 [3]	46 [23]	.01 [< .001]
Multiple broods/year	36 [15]	65 [22]	
Early maturing	23 [12]	49 [31]	.0001 [.09]
Late maturing	8 [3]	44 [23]	
	Early maturing	Late maturing	p
Single brood/year	12 [2]	37 [21]	.0001 [< .001]
Multiple broods/year	60 [32]	21 [2]	

Values in brackets are those of Tinkle et al. (1970).

significantly in mean SVL at maturity or in mean FSVL. However, the mean clutch size (6.1) of temperate lizards is significantly larger than that of tropical species (4.2). Early-maturing species are significantly smaller than late-maturing species but do not differ in mean clutch size. Whereas many of these results parallel those of Tinkle et al. (1970), four exceptions occur. As mentioned above, there are significant differences in mean FSVL between single- versus multiple-brooded species and between early- versus late-maturing species. Tinkle et al. (1970) did not find the significant difference in mean clutch size between temperate and tropical species. They did report that the mean clutch size of early-maturing species was significantly smaller than that of late-maturing species, whereas we find no significant difference. These differences can be largely attributed to the increased sample size and broader taxonomic coverage in our data set.

We next examine possible associations between the categorical variables (Table IV) used in the pairwise t-tests. These comparisons indicate that (a) viviparous species are more likely to be single-brooded and

RESULTS

late-maturing than oviparous species, (b) temperate species are more frequently single-brooded than are tropical ones, and (c) early-maturing species are more frequently multiple-brooded than are late-maturing species. These relationships are similar to those found by Tinkle et al. (1970).

Part of our analysis to this point suggests that much of the observed variation in lizard life histories is correlated with variation in body size (Table II), as has been previously reported for a wide variety of organisms. Accordingly, we present the results of a series of analyses that remove the effects of body size. The question is whether the observed significant differences are simply an allometrically forced consequence of differences in body size or are independent of body size.

A series of linear regressions of clutch size on body size for lizards grouped according to whether they are oviparous or viviparous, early- or late-maturing, single- or multiple-brooded, and tropical or temperate in their distribution is presented in Table V. In most cases (the exception is viviparous species), clutch size and FSVL are positively and significantly related.

We next present results of analyses that are the equivalent of the t- tests reported in Table III, but which include female SVL as a covariate (Table VI). Our first set of analyses (under SS I) provides an estimate of the effects of the categorical variables (e.g., broods/year, mode of reproduction) on clutch size. These analyses include the effects of female body length. The second set of analyses provides an estimate of the effects of the independent variables on clutch size, but here the effects of female body size are removed, as indicated by the adjusted sum of squares (SS IV).

As in the t-tests, all comparisons are significant before taking differences in female size into account. After removing the effects of female body size, the significant differences associated with mode of reproduction and age at maturity disappear. In other words, the differences in clutch size between oviparous versus viviparous species (size-corrected values 3.9 versus 4.7, respectively, $P = 0.22$) and between early- versus late-maturing species (5.0 versus 4.2, $P = 0.44$) can be attributed to differences in body size. The analysis of frequency of reproduction reveals that single-brooded species have significantly larger clutches than multiple-brooded species even after the effects of female size are removed (5.3 versus 3.9, $P = 0.01$). Moreover, temperate species have significantly larger (size corrected) clutches than do tropical ones (5.1 versis 2.8, $P = 0.0001$).

We next computed a Prim network analysis to search for major groupings among life history patterns. The original analysis by Tinkle et

TABLE V
Results of Regression Analyses of Mean Clutch Size on Female SVL at Maturity for Several Groups of Lizards

Group	N	FSVL at MAT	Clutch size	b	a	r^2
Single brood/year	51 [19]	75.25 [71.68]	7.53 [7.07]	.088 [.090]	0.872 [.619]	.19 [.30]***
Multiple broods/year	95 [32]	57.30 [58.69]	4.74 [3.69]	.056 [.092]	1.500 [−1.440]	.09 [.23]**
Oviparous	143 [57]	60.83 [61.84]	5.31 [4.85]	.095 [.097]	−.450 [−1.148]	.24 [.27]***
Viviparous	28 [12]	67.82 [69.92]	5.94 [7.21]	.002 [.124]	5.780 [−1.460]	.00 [.35]
Early maturing	70 [35]	51.83 [55.26]	5.54 [4.27]	.081 [.114]	1.323 [−2.030]	.11 [.32]***
Late maturing	55 [22]	77.73 [72.55]	7.26 [6.48]	.094 [NR]	−.074 [NR]	.18 [.14]***
Temperate	103 [53]	60.99 [62.30]	6.20 [5.42]	.06 [.109]	2.11 [−1.371]	.10 [.36]***
Tropical	68 [16]	64.20 [66.38]	4.20 [4.74]	.09 [NR]	−1.95 [NR]	.32 [.17]***

**$P < .01$; ***$P < .001$.

Values in brackets are from Tinkle et al. (1970). NR indicates value not reported. FSVL at MAT, mean female SVL (mm) at maturity; b, estimate of slope from regression model; a, estimate of intercept from regression model. Significance levels refer to the present study only.

RESULTS

TABLE VI
Results From Analyses of Covariance for Lizards

Trait	df	SS I	F	P	SS IV	F	P
Broods/year	1	1.31	14.64	.0002	0.55	6.16	.01
FSVL at MAT	1	1.18	13.17	.004			
Mode of reproduction	1	0.29	3.09	.08	0.14	1.52	.21
FSVL at MAT	1	2.53	27.16	.0001			
Age at maturity	1	0.22	2.28	.13	0.05	0.58	.44
FSVL at MAT	1	1.51	15.94	.0001			
Distribution	1	2.60	33.41	.0001	2.93	37.64	.0001
FSVL at MAT	1	2.92	37.56	.0001			

Mean clutch size in lizards with various life history variables, FSVL at maturity introduced as a covariate. Dependent variable and covariate were log-transformed.

al. (1970) excluded species with fixed-clutch sizes. However, the general trends identified in the new Prim network did not depend on whether species with fixed-clutch size were included. Species having fixed-clutch sizes clustered among the early maturing, small bodied, multiple-clutches species. Dunham and Miles (1985) reinforced this conclusion with extensive analyses performed both with and without fixed-clutch species. In all cases, the results of the analyses, including such species, were remarkably similar to those excluding them. Of particular interest here is a series of bivariate regressions with SVL as the independent variable and clutch size, age at maturity, and brood frequency as dependent variables (Table VII). In each pair of regressions, the exclusion of species with fixed-clutch size resulted in equal or similar values for slope, intercept, and correlation between the variables. Therefore, we present only the network that includes all species.

Within the complete Prim network (Fig. 1), the primary clusters separate single- versus multiple-brooded species. The single-clutched species may be subdivided into three groups: oviparous species that exhibit delayed maturity and have large body sizes, but that either (a) have small broods (e.g., *Sauromalus obesus*, *Cyclura carinata*, *Dipsosaurus dorsalis*, and *Oedura reticulata*) or (b) have large broods (e.g., *Ctenosaura similis*, *Eumeces laticeps*, and *Phrynosoma cornutum*), or viviparous species (e.g., *Anguis fragilis*, *Typhlosaurus*, and *Barisia coerulea*). The multiple clutched species can be subdivided into two groups: (a) those that tend to be small bodied, early-maturing, and have small broods; (b) those characterized by early maturity, large body size, and large clutches. There is also a third cluster

TABLE VII

Separate Regressions of Clutch Size, Age at Maturity, and Mode and Frequency of Reproduction on Mean SVL of Adult Females in 110 Species of Lizards

Trait	Mean	r	r^2	Slope	Intercept
Clutch size	4.94	.50	.25	.40	−.11
	[5.47]	[.48]	[.23]	[.34]	[.05]
Age at maturity	15.84	.53	.28	.32	.56
	[16.30]	[.53]	[.28]	[.32]	[.56]
Mode of reproduction	1.23	.47	.22	.51	.21
	[1.27]	[.43]	[.18]	[.47]	[.31]
Broods per year	1.82	−.42	.17	−1.26	4.26
	[1.70]	[−.45]	[.20]	[−1.03]	[3.78]

Values in brackets are those resulting from exclusion from the analysis of species with fixed clutch sizes (after Dunham and Miles, 1985).

not evident in previous analyses. These species are also multiple-clutched but are late maturing, and either large bodied with large broods or small bodied with small broods. In addition, each of the main clusters were characterized by distinct patterns of covariation.

2. TRENDS WITHIN THE SINGLE-CLUTCHED SPECIES

A noteworthy subset of the oviparous group with single clutches includes species maturing at an early age and small size, but still producing large clutches. Two species in this group, *Moloch horridus* and *Phrynosoma platyrhinos*, have been noted for their convergence in ecology and morphology (Pianka and Pianka, 1970; Pianka, 1986). Both are extremely cryptic sit-and-wait predators (on ants) with broad flat bodies. They are apparently also convergent in life history pattern.

Viviparous species cluster as a specialized subset within the subset of single-clutched species. Whereas these lizards are predominantly late-maturing and produce large broods, some viviparous species, as well as some oviparous single-clutched species, are early maturing. Most of the early-maturing viviparous records are for different populations of *Sceloporus jarrovi*, but other records are for *Chamaeleo pumilis* and *Mabuya heathi*. A second trend within the viviparous species group includes species (e.g., *Xantusia vigilis*, *Barisia coerulea*, and *Typhlosaurus lineatus*) with small broods. These taxa are typically secretive or fossorial.

RESULTS

3. TRENDS WITHIN THE MULTIPLE-CLUTCHED, EARLY-MATURING SPECIES

A major source of variation within the cluster of multiple-clutched, early-maturing species involves a positive correlation between body size and clutch size. This trend absorbs what appeared to be a separate cluster (early-maturing, large-clutched, multiple-brooded species) in the analysis of Tinkle et al. (1970). In our analysis the involved species appear to form a loosely organized cluster consisting of *Chamaeleo namaquensis*, *Mabuya buettneri*, *Crotaphytus collaris*, and populations of *Sceloporus undulatus* and *Urosaurus ornatus*.

4. TRENDS WITHIN THE MULTIPLE-CLUTCHED, LATE-MATURING SPECIES

Much of the variation within the cluster of multiple-clutched, late-maturing species is associated with a positive correlation between body size and clutch size. For example, at one extreme of the cluster are species like *Gerrhonotus multicarinatus*, *Basiliscus basiliscus*, and *Sceloporus clarki*, which are relatively large and have relatively high fecundity, whereas at the other end are species like *Sceloporus graciosus*, *Mabuya quinquetaeniata*, *Podarcis taurica*, *Oedura tryoni*, and *Cnemidophorus sexlineatus*, which are small and produce relatively small clutches. Species in the former group tend to be arboreal or semiarboreal, whereas those in the latter are terrestrial or saxicolous. Thus, the life history patterns shown within this cluster may, in part, reflect selection imposed by environmental factors.

5. INTERACTIONS AMONG LIFE HISTORY VARIABLES

The previous analyses demonstrate differences in life history variation between certain categories of species without considering interactions among the independent variables. We employed a factorial ANOVA to assess the magnitude and significance of interactions among mode of reproduction, brood frequency, and distribution on variation in clutch size, female age at maturity, and female SVL at maturity (Table VIII). The results for the main effects parallel those obtained from the t tests and include significant effects in clutch size and female SVL at maturity for single-brooded versus multiple-brooded species and for tropical versus temperate species. Oviparous species are slightly larger (68 mm) at maturity than viviparous species (65 mm), but the difference is not significant ($P = 0.08$). Brood size of oviparous species does not differ significantly from that of viviparous species (4.8 versus 4.1 eggs per

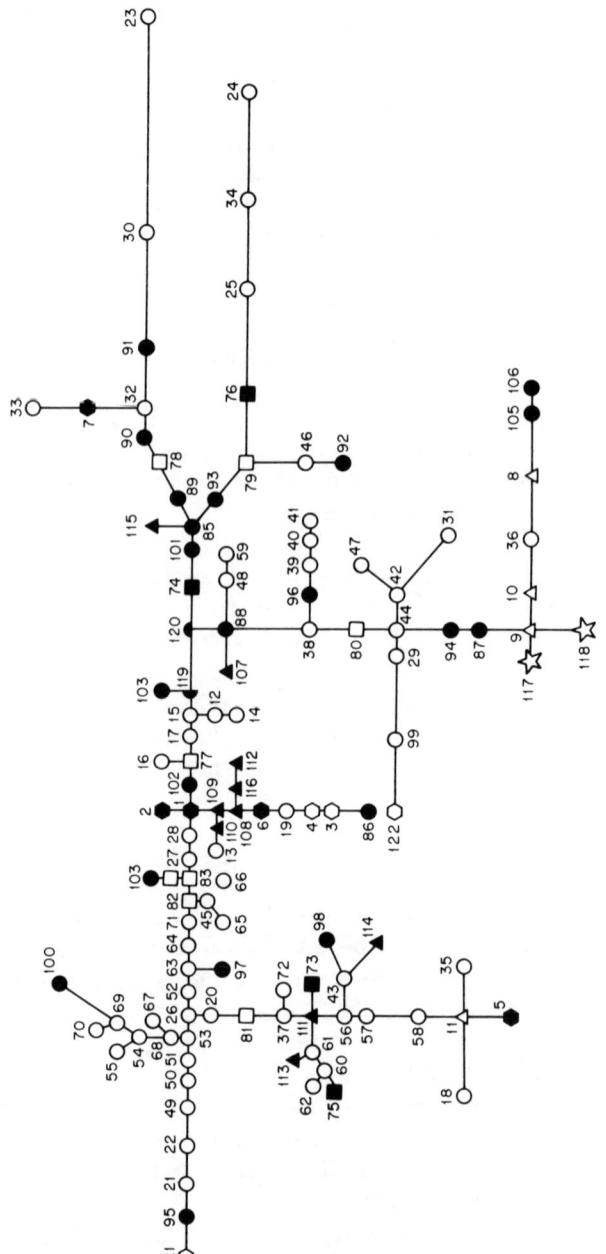

RESULTS

Fig. 1. *(facing page)* Prim network analysis of lizards, including species with invariant clutch sizes. Agamidae (solid hexagon): (1) *Amphibolurus fordi*, (2) *Amphibolurus isolepis*, (3) *Amphibolurus nuchalis*, (4) *Amphibolurus ornatus*, (5) *Calotes versicolor*, (6) *Japalura swinhonis*, (7) *Moloch horridus*. Anguidae (open triangle): (8) *Anguis fragilis*, (9) *Barisia coerulea*, (10) *Barisia coerulea*, (11) *Gerrhonotus multicarinatus*. Iguanidae (open circle): (12) *Anolis acutus*, (13) *Anolis carolinensis*, (14) *Anolis cupreus*, (15) *Anolis limifrons*, (16) *Anolis oculatus*, (17) *Anolis tropidolepis*, (18) *Basiliscus basiliscus*, (19) *Callisaurus draconoides*, (20) *Cophosaurus texanus*, (21) *Crotaphytus collaris* [KAN], (22) *Crotaphytus collaris* [TX], (23) *Ctenosaura similis*, (24) *Cyclura carinata*, (25) *Dipsosaurus dorsalis*, (26) *Holbrookia maculata* [NEB], (27) *Holbrookia maculata* [NM], (28) *Holbrookia propinqua*, (29) *Liolaemus multiformis*, (30) *Phrynosoma cornutum*, (31) *Phrynosoma douglassi*, (32) *Phrynosoma platyrhinos*, (33) *Polychrus acutirostris*, (34) *Sauromalus obesus*, (35) *Sceloporus clarki*, (36) *Sceloporus cyanogenys*, (37) *Sceloporus graciosus*, (38) *Sceloporus grammicus*, (39) *Sceloporus jarrovi* [PINALENO], (40) *Sceloporus jarrovi* [GRAHAM], (41) *Sceloporus jarrovi* [LOW], (42) *Sceloporus jarrovi* [HIGH], (43) *Sceloporus magister*, (44) *Sceloporus malachiticus*, (45) *Sceloporus merriami*, (46) *Sceloporus orcutti*, (47) *Sceloporus poinsetti*, (48) *Sceloporus scalaris*, (49) *Sceloporus undulatus* [SUN], (50) *Sceloporus undulatus* [SREL], (51) *Sceloporus undulatus* [GRANT], (52) *Sceloporus undulatus* [NEB], (53) *Sceloporus undulatus* [KAN], (54) *Sceloporus undulatus* [TX], (55) *Sceloporus undulatus* [LORD], (56) *Sceloporus undulatus* [UTAH], (57) *Sceloporus undulatus* [MESA], (58) *Sceloporus undulatus* [OHIO], (59) *Sceloporus virgatus*, (60) *Uma notata*, (61) *Uma notata*, (62) *Uma notata*, (63) *Urosaurus graciosus* [LCRV], (64) *Urosaurus graciosus* [PHX], (65) *Urosaurus ornatus* [GVH], (66) *Urosaurus ornatus* [TX], (67) *Urosaurus ornatus* [SUN], (68) *Urosaurus ornatus* [VERDE], (69) *Urosaurus ornatus* [ANIMAS], (70) *Urosaurus ornatus* [CHIRA], (71) *Uta stansburiana* [TX], (72) *Uta stansburiana* [ORE]. Gekkonidae (solid square): (73) *Gehyra variegata*, (74) *Heteronotia binoei*, (75) *Oedura tryoni*, (76) *Oedura reticulata*. Lacertidae (open square): (77) *Aporosaura anchietae*, (78) *Lacerta agilis*, (79) *Lacerta monticola*, (80) *Lacerta vivipara*, (81) *Podarcis taurica*, (82) *Takydromus tachydromoides* [1], (83) *Takydromus tachydromoides* [2], (84) *Takydromus tachydromoides* [3]. Scincidae (solid circle): (85) *Ctenotus taeniolatus*, (86) *Emoia atrocostata*, (87) *Eumeces copei*, (88) *Eumeces egregius*, (89) *Eumeces fasciatus* [1], (90) *Eumeces fasciatus* [2], (91) *Eumeces laticeps*, (92) *Eumeces obsoletus*, (93) *Eumeces skiltonianus*, (94) *Leiolopisma zelandicum*, (95) *Mabuya buettneri*, (96) *Mabuya heathi*, (97) *Mabuya maculilabris*, (98) *Mabuya quinquetaeniata*, (99) *Mabuya striata*, (100) *Menetia greyii*, (101) *Morethia boulengeri*, (102) *Panaspis nimbaensis*, (103) *Scincella lateralis*, (104) *Scincella lateralis* [FL], (105) *Typhlosaurus lineatus*, (106) *Typhlosaurus gariepensis*. Teiidae (solid triangle): (107) *Cnemidophorus exsanguis*, (108) *Cnemidophorus hyperythrus*, (109) *Cnemidophorus inornatus*, (110) *Cnemidophorus neomexicanus*, (111) *Cnemidophorus sexlineatus*, (112) *Cnemidophorus tigris*, [NM], (113) *Cnemidophorus tigris*, [PHX], (114) *Cnemidophorus tigris*, [CAL], (115) *Cnemidophorus tigris*, [ID], (116) *Cnemidophorus uniparens*. Xantusiidae (star): (117) *Klauberina riversiana*, (118) *Xantusia vigilis*. Gymnophthalmidae (solid half-circle): (119) *Gymnophthalmus speciosus*, (120) *Leposoma rugiceps*. Chamaeleonidae (open hexagon): (121) *Chamaeleo namaquensis*, (122) *Chamaeleo pumilis*. LOCALITY CODES: ANIMAS, Animas; NM; CAL, California; CHIRA, Chiricahua Mts., AZ; GRAHAM, Graham Mts., AZ; GRANT, Grant Co., NM; GVH, Grapevine Hills, TX; HIGH, High elevation, Chiricahua Mts., AZ; ID, Idaho; KAN, Kansas; LCRV, Lower Colorado River, AZ; LORD, Lordsburg, NM; LOW, Low elevation, Chiricahua Mts., AZ; MESA, Colorado; NEB, Nebraska; NM, New Mexico; OHIO, Ohio; ORE, Oregon; PINALENO, Pinaleno Mts., AZ; PHX, Phoenix, AZ; SREL, Savannah River Ecol. Lab., GA; SUN, Sunflower, AZ; TX, Texas; VERDE, Verde River, AZ.

TABLE VIII
Three-Way Factorial ANOVA Using All Available Data on Lizards: Average Fecundity, Age at Maturity, and Mean FSVL at Maturity With Mode of Reproduction, Brood Frequency, and Distribution

Dependent variable: Clutch size; $r^2 = 0.19$

Source	df	SS I	F	P	SS IV	F	P
Mode	1	0.15	1.80	.18	0.04	0.44	.50
Broods/year	1	1.25	14.23	.0002	0.01	0.06	.81
Mode × broods/year	1	0.26	2.90	.09	0.74	8.42	.004
Distribution	1	1.02	11.62	.0008	0.47	5.31	.02
Mode × distribution	1	0.02	0.28	.59	0.28	3.24	.07
Broods/year × distribution	1	0.38	4.34	.03	0.38	4.34	.03

Dependent variable: Age at maturity; $r^2 = 0.26$

Source	df	SS I	F	P	SS IV	F	P
Mode	1	0.18	3.43	.06	0.01	0.12	.73
Broods/year	1	1.75	31.79	.0001	0.54	9.74	.002
Mode × broods/year	1	0.00	0.01	.92	0.01	0.19	.66
Distribution	1	0.38	6.97	.009	0.22	4.08	.04
Mode × distribution	1	0.01	0.36	.54	0.00	0.02	.89
Broods/year × distribution	1	0.01	0.26	.60	0.01	0.26	.60

Dependent variable: FSVL at maturity; $r^2 = 0.16$

Source	df	SS I	F	P	SS IV	F	P
Mode	1	0.06	3.05	.08	0.01	0.74	.39
Broods/year	1	0.31	14.48	.0002	0.17	8.01	.005
Mode × broods/year	1	0.00	0.10	.75	0.02	0.94	.33
Distribution	1	0.12	5.72	.02	0.13	6.29	.01
Mode × distribution	1	0.00	0.01	.92	0.03	1.74	.18
Broods/year × distribution	1	0.08	3.90	.04	0.08	3.90	.04

brood, respectively). Both analyses are characterized by low r^2 values (0.19 for clutch size and 0.16 for female clutch size at maturity).

The interaction of broods/year × distribution is significant for both clutch size and female SVL at maturity. Clutches of single-brooded temperate and tropical species are significantly larger than those of temperate and tropical multiple-brooded species. Tropical, single-brooded species mature at a larger size (90 mm) than temperate, multiple-brooded species (65 mm), but temperate, multiple-brooded species have a higher SVL at maturity (58 mm) than do tropical species (57 mm). Single-brooded, oviparous species have significantly larger broods (7.1 eggs) than viviparous species (4.2); multiple-brooded, oviparous species have smaller

RESULTS

broods (3.3) than viviparous species. Clutch size is similar across all categories in the mode of reproduction × distribution comparison.

Two main effects (brood frequency and distribution) are significantly associated with variation in age at maturity (Type I SS) and match the results from the contingency table analysis. Single-brooded species mature significantly later than do multiple-brooded species (19.5 versus 10.2 months, respectively). Temperate species typically mature in their second breeding season after hatching (21.6 months), whereas tropical species mature at a significantly earlier age (12.6 months, $P < 0.01$). Oviparous species mature earlier (14.9 months) than viviparous species (17.9 months), but this difference is not significant ($P < 0.73$). Because the interaction between brood frequency and distribution is insignificant, we cannot determine the dependencies among the variables (e.g., whether single-brooded species in the temperate zone tend to be late-maturing and early-maturing, multiple-brooded species tend to be tropical). The remaining two interaction terms are not significant, thus we cannot describe the dependencies among the independent variables. The data fail to exhibit a strong distributional difference within groups of species for differing modes of reproduction or brood frequency. Furthermore, the inclusion of interaction terms in this model fails to explain much of the total variation in age at maturity. Indeed, most of the variation that is explained by the model ($r^2 = 0.25$) is attributable to the single factor, broods per year, which explains 19% of the total variation.

The small r^2 values for each of the factorial ANOVA's indicate that most of the variation in clutch size, age at maturity, and female SVL at maturity cannot be explained by differences in mode of reproduction, brood frequency, and distribution or by the interactions between them.

6. EFFECTS OF RCM, FORAGING MODE, AND PREFERRED HABITAT

Sufficient data on foraging mode, preferred habitat, and relative clutch mass (RCM) exist to merit a series of analyses similar to those reported above. T-tests of the same variables (as in Table III) reveal no significant differences among classes with different foraging mode in SVL at first reproduction or in mean SVL of adult females. However, classes of foraging behavior differ significantly in clutch size (Table IXa). Active foragers produce significantly smaller clutches (3.8 eggs) than do sit-and-wait foragers (5.9 eggs). Likewise, active foragers have significantly smaller values of RCM (0.18) than do sit-and-wait foragers (0.25). These results complement the pattern described by Vitt and Congdon (1978) and refined by Vitt and Price (1982). It should be noted that these analyses ignore the potentially confounding effects of phylogeny, which are eval-

TABLE IXa
Pairwise t-Tests of the Relationship Between Foraging Mode and Four Life History Variables for Lizards

Variables	Mean	Standard deviation	N	t
SVL at maturity (mm)				
active forager	61.72	17.77	22	.76
sit and wait forager	57.92	21.40	81	
SVL of adult females (mm)				
active forager	75.01	22.21	25	1.00
sit and wait forager	59.43	24.71	76	
Clutch size				
active foragers	3.82	2.56	26	2.96***
sit and wait foragers	5.93	4.51	82	
Relative clutch mass				
active foragers	.181	.077	13	2.56**
sit and wait foragers	.247	.082	45	

**$P < .01$; ***$P < .001$.

TABLE IXb
Results From Analyses of Covariance

Trait	df	SS I	F	P	SS IV	F	P
Foraging mode	1	0.30	3.42	.06	0.44	4.97	.02
FSVL at MAT	1	2.48	28.04	.0001			

Mean clutch size of species with differing foraging behaviors (widely foraging versus sit-and-wait foraging) with mean female SVL at maturity introduced as a covariate.

TABLE IXc
Analysis of Covariance of Relative Clutch Mass (RCM) of Widely Foraging and Sit-and-Wait Foraging Species With Mean FSVL at Maturity Entered as a Covariate

Source	df	SS I	F	P	SS IV	F	P
Foraging mode	1	.121	4.99	.02	.127	4.98	.02
FSVL at MAT	1	.00	.02	.87			

uated in Section III.D. An analysis of covariance (Tables IXb,c) demonstrates that the difference in clutch size attributable to foraging mode is independent of differences in female SVL at first reproduction. Furthermore, the difference in RCM between foraging modes remains significant after adjusting for differences in body size. Finally, based on pairwise

RESULTS

TABLE Xa
Two-Way Analysis of Variance of Ecological Variables Explaining Variation in Certain Life History Traits of Lizards

Source	Trait			
	Age at maturity	Clutch size	RCM	FSVL
Foraging mode	**	NS	***	NS
Preferred habitat	**	**	NS	NS
Interaction	NS	NS	NS	NS
r^2	.16	.15	.16	.07

$**P < .01$; $***P < .001$; NS, $P > .05$.

chi-square tests, we find no significant association between foraging mode and brood frequency, mode of reproduction, or distribution.

We now ask whether the preferred habitat of a species influences various life history traits. For example, arboreal species often have a long and narrow body shape that may constrain the number of eggs carried by a female. We compare species differing in habitat preference (e.g., saxicolous, terrestrial), for age at maturity, female SVL at maturity, clutch size, and relative clutch mass in a series of four ANOVA's. Habitat preference has significant effects on age at maturity ($F_{4,101} = 3.32$, $P < 0.01$), female SVL at maturity ($F_{4,132} = 3.48$, $P < 0.001$), and clutch size ($F_{4,140} = 2.38$, $P < 0.05$), but not on RCM. Fossorial species in our sample are characterized by delayed maturity (34 months), long body size at maturity (95 mm), and relatively low brood sizes. Saxicolous and terrestrial species mature sexually in 14.4 and 15.9 months, respectively, are at a similar body size (59 mm versus 59 mm), and produce relatively large broods (5.3 versus 4.1 eggs). Psammophilous and arboreal species are early-maturing (11.1 and 12.3 months, respectively), relatively small-bodied (56.7 and 50.8 mm), and produce small broods (3.3 and 2.9 eggs, respectively).

The significant differences in age at maturity among species with distinct habitat preferences (above) appear to be size-related (ANCOVA, $F_{4,94} = 0.83$, $P < 0.51$). However, differences in clutch size among species from different habitats remains significant after controlling for variation in female body size ($F_{4,131} = 2.83$, $P < 0.05$). The mean, size-adjusted clutch sizes of fossorial (1.8), arboreal (3.2), and psammophilous (3.4) species are significantly smaller than of terrestrial (4.1) and saxicolous (5.2) ones.

Preferred habitat is included with foraging mode in a series of two-way ANOVA's to determine whether differences among species for these ecological traits may partition the variation in life history patterns (Table X). Fossorial species are not included in the analysis because of

TABLE Xb
Analysis of Covariance of Age at Maturity, Clutch Size and RCM With Two Ecological Variables, Foraging Mode and Preferred Habitat. Female SVL at Maturity Is Introduced as the Covariate

Source	Trait		
	Age at maturity	Clutch size	RCM
Foraging mode	NS	*	**
Adjusted mean	**	NS	†
Preferred habitat	**	**	NS
Adjusted mean	*	NS	NS
Interaction	NS	NS	NS
Adjusted interaction	*	NS	NS
FSVL	***	***	NS
r^2	.27	.37	.16

†$P < .1$; *$P < .05$; **$P < .01$; ***$P < .001$; NS, $P > .05$.

incomplete information on foraging mode. All statistical tests are based on the type IV sums of squares, which correct for differences in sample size among groups and for variation due to the covariate (female body size). Sit-and-wait foragers mature significantly later (15.2 months) than widely foraging species (9.0 months), which might reflect greater rates of net energy gain in widely foraging species (Anderson and Karasov, 1981; Nagy et al., 1984). As in the previous analysis, psammophilous and arboreal species are characterized by early maturity (8.5 and 12.3 months, respectively), whereas terrestrial and saxicolous species exhibit delayed maturity (18.3 and 14.5 months, respectively). Variation in clutch size is largely explained by differences in habitat preference among species; however, as demonstrated in an earlier analysis, foraging mode alone explains variation in relative clutch mass. Variation in mean female SVL is largely unrelated to foraging mode or habitat preference. These results suggest that habitat preference and foraging behavior may exert a larger influence on life history patterns than previously thought.

The presence of two or more significant main effects suggests that interactions among the independent variables might be important for unraveling the patterns of variation. However, in all instances the ANOVA's fail to reveal any significant interaction effects (Table Xa). This may partially be due to a lack of data; because many of the cells are empty or nearly so, we cannot estimate a variance term.

Comparison of three life history variables among species that differ in foraging behavior and habitat preference after removing the effects of body size reveals several trends (Table Xb) that are not apparent from the

RESULTS

previous analyses (Table Xa). Active foraging species mature at an earlier age than sit-and-wait foraging species (adjusted means: 8.8 versus 15.5 months, respectively). Contrary to an earlier analysis, significant size-adjusted effects are now found in age at maturity for species with different habitat preferences. A significant interaction between foraging mode and habitat preferences is found and is independent of body size. For example, actively foraging, psammophilous species mature at a significantly earlier age (4.8 months) than sit-and-wait psammophilous (14.8 months) or terrestrial (18.9 months) ones. This strengthens the contention that foraging behavior and preferred habitat are significant factors that influence life history variation.

Variation in clutch size is not attributable to differences in foraging behavior or habitat preference. Thus, the differences found in the earlier analysis (Table Xa) are due to variation related to differences in body size (Table Xb). Relative clutch mass remains significantly higher in sit-and-wait foragers (0.24) than wide foragers (0.18), paralleling the result of an earlier analysis (e.g., Table IXc). Preferred habitat is not significantly associated with variation in size-corrected RCM.

These results demonstrate that foraging mode strongly influences RCM, clutch size, and age at maturity (but see Section III.D). Active foragers typically display smaller values for all three variables. Furthermore, the effects of foraging mode on these life history traits appear to be independent of female size. The influence of foraging mode is apparently independent of mode of reproduction, brood frequency, and distribution. Clutch size and age at maturity are also affected by the preferred habitat of a species. Notably, we find no significant relationship between habitat and RCM. This contrasts with Vitt's (1981) finding that morphological and behavioral adaptations associated with a particular habitat may influence the reproductive characteristics of a species, in particular RCM. These results complement and extend the conclusions of Vitt and Congdon (1978), Huey and Pianka (1981), and Vitt and Price (1982).

7. COVARIATION AMONG LIFE HISTORY TRAITS

One weakness of single factor analyses, such as performed in most life history studies, is the failure to account for covariation among traits. We have clearly demonstrated the presence of high correlations among several life history traits (Table II). Most life history theory ignores the consequences of such covariation (but see Lande, 1983) and few studies have estimated the strength of such correlations among life history variables. Following Dunham and Miles (1985), Stearns (1984), and

TABLE XIa
Principal Components Analysis of Three Life History Variables: Age at Maturity, SVL of Adult Females, and Clutch Size (N = 127) for Species From Eight Lizard Families

Trait	Eigenvector	
	I	II
Age at maturity	.591	−0.538
FSVL	.676	−0.073
Clutch size	.438	0.839
Eigenvalue	1.696	.896
Variance (%)	.565	.298

TABLE XIb
Principal Components Analysis of Four Life History Variables: Age at Maturity, SVL of Adult Females, Clutch Size, and Relative Clutch Mass for All Lizard Species (N = 56)

Trait	Eigenvector		
	I	II	III
Age at maturity	.545	.408	.514
FSVL	.504	.532	−.397
Clutch size	−.451	.579	−.473
RCM	−.494	.463	.590
Eigenvalue	1.664	1.182	.740
Variance (%)	.416	.295	.185

Trendall (1982), we use principal components analysis (PCA) calculated from correlation matrices to analyze the patterns of covariation among the life history traits in our data set. Our analysis proceeds in two steps. We first include age at maturity, female SVL at maturity, and clutch size in one PCA, and then perform a second analysis (with necessarily fewer species) in which we also include relative clutch mass (RCM).

The first principal components (PC) axis (three life history variables) explains 57% of the total variance and describes a gradient of variation consisting of small, early-maturing species with small clutches at one end, and large, late-maturing species at the opposite end (Table XIa, Fig. 2). This is very similar to the results of Dunham and Miles (1985). The second axis explains 30% of the variance and represents a strong contrast between age at maturity and clutch size. At one end of this axis are species exhibiting delayed maturity and small clutches (e.g., *Dipsosaurus dorsalis*, *Cyclura carinata*, *Typhlosaurus lineatus*, *Menetia greyii*, and *Xantusia vigilis*); at the other end are species maturing early and

RESULTS

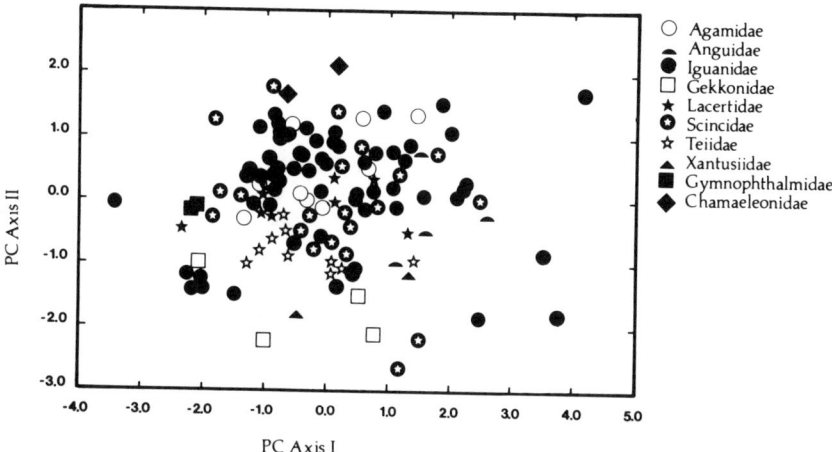

Fig. 2. Principal components analysis of lizards, including those with invariant clutch size. Analysis based on log-transformed values for age at maturity, female SVL at maturity, and mean clutch size (N = 126).

producing large clutches (e.g., *Polychrus acutirostris, Mabuya buettneri, Chamaeleo namaquensis,* and *Calotes versicolor*).

Positions of species along the first two axes defined by a PCA of three life history variables are shown in Figure 2. Species/populations in the family Iguanidae are found along and span the length of the first axis. With the exception of the Scincidae, no other family exhibits as wide a range of variation. Clustered among the Iguanidae and Scincidae are species in the families Agamidae, Lacertidae, Teiidae, and Gekkonidae. The gradient defined by PC axis II has species of *Chamaeleo* at one end and *Typhlosaurus* at the other. Interestingly, the poles of this axis are occupied by extremely arboreal species at one end and by fossorial species at the other.

Lacertids and teiids overlap along PC axis I and lie adjacent to one another along PC axis II, reflecting the tendency for lacertids to mature earlier and produce larger clutches for a given body length. Species of *Anolis,* Gekkonidae, and Gymnophthalmidae have invariant clutch sizes and cluster together in a distinct region of the space defined by these two PC axes. The gekkonids, gymnophthalmids, and *Anolis* are found on the periphery of the cluster defined by the iguanids.

The addition of RCM to the analysis produces very different results (Table XIb). The variance explained by the first PC axis decreases to 42%. The factor loadings for age at maturity and female SVL at maturity are similar to those obtained in the previous analysis; however, those for clutch size and RCM are negative and of equal magnitude, indicating an inverse relationship between these variables and age and SVL at maturity. These results describe an axis along which species increase in body size and age at maturity, but with a proportionately decreasing energetic contribution to any given clutch. The second PC axis explains 30% of the total variation and describes a gradient with a strong positive association between age at maturity, clutch size, RCM, and FSVL. At one end of this gradient are species with small clutches, and low RCM (e.g., *Heteronotia binoei*, *Gehyra variegata*, *Aporosaura anchietae*, and *Cnemidophorus tigris*), whereas the other end contains species with large clutches and high RCM (e.g., *Phrynosoma cornutum*, *Polychrus acutirostris*, *Sceloporus undulatus*, and *Lacerta vivipara*). The third PC axis explains 19% of the total variation and is similar to the second axis of the previous analysis. In this case age at maturity and RCM are negatively correlated with clutch size and FSVL. At one end of this axis are species (e.g., *Gehyra variegata*, *Takydromus tachydromoides*, *Oedura tryoni*, and *Eumeces fasciatus*) characterized by delayed maturity, small SVL at maturity, small clutches, and relative large RCM. At the other end of the axis are relatively large, early maturing species with large clutches and relatively small RCM (e.g., *Chamaeleo namaquensis*, *Moloch horridus*, *Crotaphytus collaris*, and *Sceloporus jarrovi*). The importance of these patterns of covariation among life history traits is discussed in a later section.

8. INTRASPECIFIC COMPARISONS

Broad interspecific comparisons have been the primary source of hypotheses concerning the evolution of life histories. Current theory has attempted to explain the evolution of patterns of variation and covariation in life history traits. Two major sources of selection (resource availability and demographic environment) on life history traits are involved (reviewed in Stearns, 1976). However, broad comparative studies generally lack the resolution and data on demographic and resource environments necessary to test such theory, and may include a phylogenetic bias. Comparisons of populations within a species often provide quantification of geographic variation in life history traits; and, if they include detailed ecological data, may offer tests of specific predictions from life history theory.

Tinkle and Dunham (1986) compiled data on habitat, density, and an array of reproductive and demographic variables from 11 of the more complete studies of *Sceloporus undulatus* (Table XII). They analyzed the available data on geographic variation in life history and demographic characteristics of populations of *S. undulatus* for patterns of variation and covariation in life history traits and tested two hypotheses that had been posed to explain the observed patterns. There were few strong correlations among the life history traits characterizing these populations.

RESULTS

TABLE XII
Comparison of Life History Variables Among Different
Populations of *Sceloporus undulatus*

	AZ[1]	UT[2]	CO[3]	PA[4]	LB[4]	KS[5]	NB[6]	TX[3]	OH[3]	SC[3]	GA[7]
Habitat type	C	C	C	C	G	G	G	G	W	W	W
Substrate	T	A	S	S	T	T	T	T/A	T/A	T/A	A
Clutch size	8.3	6.3	7.9	7.2	9.9	7.0	5.5	9.5	11.8	7.4	7.6
Brood frequency	3	3	2	2–3	4	1–2	2	3	2	3	2–3
Egg wet mass (gm)	.29	.36	.42	.29	.24	.26	.23	.22	.35	.33	–
RCM	.22	.21	.23	.21	.21	.28	.33	.27	.25	.23	–
Minimum SVL of mature females	60	58	58	53	54	47	45	47	66	55	52
Average SVL of adult females	65	69	70	63	68	57	55	57	75	63	62
Average age at maturity (months)	11.5	22.8	20.5	18	12	12	9.5	12	20	12	12
Survival to first reproduction	.07	.05	.11	.02	.03	.10	–	.06	.03	.11	–
Average survival of adult females	.24	.48	.37	.32	.20	.27	–	.11	.44	.49	.07

Modified from Tinkle and Dunham (1986). AZ, Sunflower, Arizona; UT, Utah; CO, Colorado; PA, Pinos Altos, New Mexico; LB, Lordsburg, New Mexico; KS, Kansas; NB, Nebraska; TX, Texas; OH, Ohio; SC, South Carolina; and GA, Georgia. Habitat classes follow Ferguson et al. (1980) and are C, canyonland; G, grassland; and W, eastern woodland. Habitat abbreviations are T, terrestrial; A, arboreal; S, saxicolous; and T/A, semiarboreal. Sources: [1]Tinkle and Dunham, 1986; [2]Tinkle, 1972; [3]Tinkle and Ballinger, 1972; [4]Vinegar, 1975a, b; [5]Ferguson et al., 1980; [6]Ballinger et al., 1981; [7]Crenshaw, 1955.

Significant rank correlations were found between age at maturity and average SVL of adult females ($r_s = 0.70$; $P < 0.05$) and between RCM and clutch frequency ($r_s = -0.64$, $P < 0.05$).

Ferguson et al., (1980) and Ballinger et al. (1981) hypothesized that similar environmental factors within a given habitat type should result in convergent life histories. To test this hypotheses, Tinkle and Dunham (1986) ranked the populations of *Sceloporus undulatus* according to nine life history traits and found no concordance between the ranks of these populations according to any life history trait and habitat type (as defined by Ferguson et al., 1980). Conspicuous exceptions occurred in every possible association.

In a second analysis, Tinkle and Dunham (1986) standardized the life history variables to a mean of 0.0 and a standard deviation of 1.0 and computed the distance metric described above (eq. 1) between all pairs of populations with the exception of the Georgia population, which was omitted due to the relatively large proportion of missing data. The populations were then clustered according to the overall similarity in their life histories as measured by values of d_{ij} into a Prim network. Inspection of the resulting network revealed significant exceptions to the clustering expected under the hypothesis of convergence in life histories (i.e., that could be attributed to similar environmental factors within common habitat types). The lack of concordance between variation in life history traits and habitat types and the clustering of populations based on overall similarity in life histories led Tinkle and Dunham (1986) to reject this hypothesis, at least for the habitat types inhabited by these populations.

Another hypothesis on patterns of similarity in life histories, such as exhibited by these populations of *Sceloporus undulatus*, is that of constraint imposed by relative recency of common ancestry (see Stearns, 1984; and Dunham and Miles, 1985). Under this hypothesis, similarity in life histories should reflect phylogenetic relatedness. Tinkle and Dunham (1986) argued that, to the degree that the extant taxonomy reflects phylogeny, the data on *S. undulatus* can be used as a crude test of this hypothesis. Examination of the Prim network revealed two cases in which populations failed to cluster with consubspecific populations on the basis of similarity in life histories. These counter-examples demonstrate that apparent relative recency of common ancestry alone cannot explain the pattern of geographic variation in life histories exhibited by these populations. However, a stronger test could be conducted if molecular data for divergence times and interpopulational relationships were available (Felsenstein, 1985).

Tinkle and Dunham (1986) suggested other hypotheses for explaining the observed pattern of life history variation among these populations of *S. undulatus*. For example, environmental factors causing lower predation rates (e.g., low density of predators or the existence of habitat refugia) should select for a different suite of life history traits (e.g., delayed maturity, lower age-specific reproductive effort, smaller clutches, and lower clutch frequency) than would be favored in environments in which predation rates are unavoidably high. However, a direct test of this hypothesis was impossible with the available data because no direct measurements of predation rates were available for any of these populations.

Dunham (1982) analyzed local and geographic variation in a number of life history characteristics of four intensively studied populations of

RESULTS

TABLE XIII
Comparison of Life History Variables Among Four Populations of *Urosaurus ornatus*

	GVH[1]	ANM[2]	CAZ[3]	SAZ[4]
Clutch size	4.7	9.0	9.0	7.1
Brood frequency	3	2 (1 year), 1 (1 year)	2 (1 year), 1 (2 years)	3
Egg wet mass (gm)	.146	.121	.143	.150
Egg dry mass (gm)	.061	.057	.073	.070
Relative clutch mass	0.31	0.40	0.50	0.36
Minimum SVL of mature females (mm)	41	39	40	45
Average SVL of adult females (mm)	48.4	48.1	49.3	50.6
Average age at maturity (months)	10.5	11.0	9.5	8.5
Mean survival to first reproduction	0.13	0.01*	0.08	0.07
Average survival of adult females	0.34	0.28*	0.33	0.23

*Data for only 1 year available.
Simplified from Dunham (1982). GVH, Grapevine Hills, Texas; ANM, Animas, New Mexico; CAZ, Chiricahua Mts., Arizona; and SAZ, Sunflower, Arizona. Sources: [1]Dunham, 1981, 1982; [2]Ballinger, 1977, 1979; Dunham, 1982; [3]Smith, 1977; Dunham, 1982; [4]Tinkle and Dunham, 1983; Dunham, 1982.

the tree lizard, *Urosaurus ornatus* (Table XIII). He examined patterns of covariation among these life history traits in terms of resource availability and predictability and the variability of the demographic environment. In addition, he provided tests of several of the explicit predictions of life history theory. He showed that neither the demographic theory nor the theory of r- and K-selection were capable of explaining the pattern of geographic variation and covariation in life history characters observed among these populations. Overall, all these data suggest that patterns of life history evolution within species are not well predicted by current theory or by between-species patterns.

C. Life History Patterns in Snakes

1. OVERVIEW AND GENERAL TRENDS

Except for the analyses of Dunham and Miles (1985) and Stearns (1984), there have been few attempts to summarize the patterns of covariation of life history traits among species of snakes. Extensive compilation of data are available on mode of reproduction, foraging mode, and relative clutch mass in snakes (Seigel and Fitch, 1984; Seigel et al., 1986); but patterns of covariation of these variables and other life history traits have not been analyzed. Seigel and Fitch (1984) described the ecological correlates of variation in RCM. They found that viviparous snakes had a significantly lower RCM than oviparous species, but could not distinguish differences between sit-and-wait versus active foragers.

Here we present the results of a series of analyses designed to complement the above lizard studies. The correlations between the life history variables (Table II) are similar to those found for lizards. All correlations are positive suggesting that large snakes mature later and produce large clutches. As in lizards, age at first reproduction and clutch size are not significantly correlated ($r = 0.14$, $n = 55$). Thus, the increase in clutch size is probably a consequence of an allometric relationship between fecundity and body size.

The t-tests reveal few significant differences in most comparisons involving life history traits and categorical variables (Table XIV). Although mean adult female SVL and female SVL at maturity are greater for viviparous species than for oviparous ones, the difference is not significant. Similarly, early-maturing species tend to be smaller at maturity and as adults than are late-maturing species, but these differences are not significant. Mean adult female SVL (745 mm) and mean SVL at maturity (617 mm) of biennial species is significantly greater than corresponding values for annual species producing a single brood per year (576 and 485 mm, respectively). Mean clutch size of oviparous species (7.1) is significantly ($P < 0.01$) lower than that of viviparous species (10.7). Species breeding every other year (biennial reproduction) do not have significantly larger clutches than do annually breeding species (9.2 young/clutch versus 9.1, respectively). Clutch size does not differ significantly between early-maturing species (7.3 eggs/brood) and late-maturing ones (9.6 eggs/brood), although the trend is similar to that found in lizards. Mean RCM does not differ significantly between actively foraging species (0.35) and sit-and-wait species (0.34), as observed previously by Seigel and Fitch (1984). However, we find no significant difference in mean RCM between oviparous (0.32) and viviparous (0.34) species, contrary to their findings (above). This discrepancy may be due to our use of a smaller data set than that of Seigel and Fitch (1984). Our data set is smaller because we included only studies for which relatively complete data (in addition to data on RCM) were available.

Our analysis of the strength of association between mode of repro-

RESULTS

TABLE XIV
Summary Statistics and Pairwise t-Tests Using All Available Life History Data on Snakes

Variables	Mean	Standard deviation	N	t
Snout–vent length at maturity (mm)				
oviparous	526.00	225.63	28	0.74
viviparous	506.80	234.59	36	
single brood/year	485.18	223.00	48	2.01*
biennial	613.53	197.71	13	
tropical	533.80	232.48	15	0.29
temperate	513.92	229.94	50	
early maturing	403.37	154.25	8	1.92†
late maturing	529.48	239.81	43	
active forager	507.44	204.37	27	1.34
sit-and-wait forager	603.13	258.45	16	
Snout–vent length of adult females (mm)				
oviparous	597.75	301.43	32	0.40
viviparous	626.70	285.11	34	
single brood/year	576.72	293.33	51	2.18*
biennial	744.76	234.12	13	
temperate	605.84	290.10	54	0.50
tropical	649.30	292.87	14	
early maturing	488.13	194.18	8	1.31
late maturing	634.26	303.55	45	
active forager	615.20	239.39	28	1.55
sit-and-wait forager	747.67	312.98	15	
Clutch size				
oviparous	7.07	3.68	32	2.99**
viviparous	10.69	6.14	36	
single brood/year	9.13	5.77	53	0.08
biennial	9.26	4.25	14	
tropical	7.83	5.02	15	1.01
temperate	9.44	5.54	55	
early maturing	7.26	4.20	8	1.30
late maturing	9.60	4.76	47	
active forager	10.18	6.06	31	0.99
sit-and-wait forager	8.53	3.62	16	
Relative clutch mass				
oviparous	.318	.115	19	0.61
viviparous	.345	.131	14	
single brood/year	.328	.130	27	0.13
biennial	.336	.085	5	
early maturing	.254	.154	7	1.55
late maturing	.348	.069	21	
active forager	.350	.108	20	0.25
sit-and-wait forager	.303	.112	5	

†$P < .10$; *$P < .05$; **$P < .01$.

TABLE XV
Results of Regression Analyses of Mean Clutch Size on Female SVL at Maturity for Snake Species Grouped According to Mode of Reproduction, Brood Frequency, Age at Maturity, Foraging Mode, and Distribution

Group	N	FSVL at MAT	Clutch size	b	a	r^2
Single brooded	45	489.54	9.46	.011	4.25	.16**
Biennial	12	613.53	9.36	−.0019	10.58	.008
Oviparous	25	523.38	7.53	.008	3.10	.22**
Viviparous	34	505.57	10.47	.008	6.22	.10*
Early maturing	7	403.38	7.26	.022	−1.55	.58**
Late maturing	40	528.00	9.81	.004	7.61	.04
Temperate	46	511.19	9.84	.006	6.58	.06
Tropical	14	533.80	7.83	.016	−0.87	.57**
Sit and wait	15	503.12	8.53	.005	5.06	.16
Active	26	507.44	10.19	.008	5.68	.08

*$P < .05$; **$P < .01$.

FSVL at MAT, mean SVL of female at maturity (mm); b, slope from regression model; a, intercept from regression. Mean values for FSVL at MAT and for clutch size differ from those in Table XIV because fewer species were available for this analysis.

duction, brood frequency, age at maturity ("early" versus "late"), distribution, and foraging mode reveals significant positive association only between mode of reproduction and brood frequency (oviparous species have more broods: $G^2 = 13.7$, $P < 0.001$), brood frequency and climate (tropical species have more broods: $G^2 = 18.4$, $P < 0.001$), age at maturity and climate (tropical species mature earlier: $G^2 = 23.7$, $P < 0.001$), and brood frequency and age at maturity (species with delayed maturity have more broods/year: $G^2 = 24.6$, $P < 0.001$).

The absence of significant differences in some comparisons may reflect the tremendous variation inherent in most life history traits as well as the low sample size for some independent variables (e.g., compare our results with those of Seigel and Fitch, 1984), which make it difficult to assess the mean and variance for a given life history trait. We encourage detailed studies, especially those of tropical and of early-maturing species.

A series of simple linear regression models examine the relationship between clutch size and body size for snakes grouped according to mode of reproduction, brood frequency, distribution, age at maturity ("early" versus "late"), and foraging mode (Table XV). Five of ten comparisons reveal significant, positive relationships of clutch size on

RESULTS

TABLE XVI
Analyses of Covariance for Differences in Clutch Size
Between Brood Frequency, Mode of Reproduction, and Distribution
for All Species of Snakes

Trait	df	SS I	F	P	SS IV	F	P
Broods/year	1	0.02	.25	.78	0.03	.28	.75
SVL at maturity	1	0.41	8.94	.004			
Mode	1	0.23	6.01	.01	0.27	6.7	.01
SVL at maturity	1	0.50	12.65	.0008			
Maturity	1	0.12	3.21	.07	0.07	1.8	.19
SVL at maturity	1	0.23	5.71	.02			
Distribution	1	0.15	3.73	.05	0.18	4.3	.04
SVL at maturity	1	0.55	13.28	.0006			

Snout–vent length at maturity entered as the covariate. Variables are log-transformed.

female SVL at maturity. Clutch size increases with body size for species that are single-brooded, oviparous or viviparous, early-maturing, and have tropical distributions.

A series of ANCOVA's examine differences in clutch size with brood frequency, mode of reproduction, age at maturity, and distribution treated as class variables and female SVL entered as a covariate (Table XVI). Biennial, single-brooded, and multiple-brooded species do not differ in mean clutch size (Table XVI, SS I). When data are adjusted for differences in SVL at maturity (Table XVI, SS IV), annual species have larger broods (8.5 offspring per clutch), than do multiple brooded (7.3), or biennial (7.8) species, but the differences are not significant. Clutch size of oviparous species is significantly smaller than that of viviparous forms (SS I), and the difference holds even when body size is controlled. Thus, egg-laying species have significantly smaller adjusted clutches (6.7 eggs/clutch) than do live-bearing ones (9.2 young/brood). This result differs from that in lizards, in which differences in clutch size between oviparous and viviparous species are attributable to allometric effects of differences in body size. Early-maturing and late-maturing species do not differ significantly in clutch size, even after adjusting for differences in SVL at maturity. However, this may reflect bias due to sample size; data for only eight early-maturing species are available. Temperate snakes have significantly larger (size-adjusted) clutch sizes (8.7) than do tropical (6.5) snakes (Type IV SS, $P < 0.05$). Thus, differences in clutch size between the distribution categories must be explained by factors other than allometric effects of differences in body size.

2. INTERACTIONS AMONG LIFE HISTORY VARIABLES

As with our analyses of lizards, we used a series of factorial ANOVA's to assay the magnitude and significance of interactions among mode of reproduction, brood frequency, and distribution in explaining the variation in age at maturity, SVL at maturity, and clutch size. We report only results based on the Type IV SS, which are the most conservative estimates and which control for differences in sample size among categories. In the analysis of FSVL at maturity, neither the main effects and nor the interaction terms are significant. In the analysis of age at maturity the only significant main effect is that due to differences in distribution (tropical species mature earlier: $F_{1,47} = 18.6$, $P < 0.001$) and only the mode of reproduction × brood frequency interaction is significant (oviparous species have more broods: $F_{2,47} = 9.8$, $P < 0.005$). The only significant effect revealed in the analysis of clutch size is the interaction between mode of reproduction and brood frequency ($F_{2,57} = 10.7$, $P < 0.001$): single-brooded, oviparous species have a much smaller clutch (5.6 eggs/brood) than do biennial, oviparous ones (13.5 eggs/brood). This result suggests that attempts to explain variation in clutch size studies require information both about frequency of reproduction and mode of reproduction.

3. COVARIATION AMONG LIFE HISTORY TRAITS

Similarities of life histories among snakes are characterized in the Prim Network (Fig. 3) based on mode of reproduction, age at maturity, SVL at maturity, clutch size, and brood frequency. The analysis reveals three major clusters. The first major cluster consists of single-brooded, oviparous species (e.g., the colubrids *Diadophis punctatus* and *Elaphe climacophora*, and elapid *Cacophis harriettae*). Within this cluster there is a gradient describing increasing body size, increasing clutch size, and the emergence of delayed maturity. This gradient has the colubrid *Sibon sanniola* at one extreme and colubrids such as *Pituophis melanoleucus* and *Coluber constrictor* at the other. A second major group consists of viviparous, annual-breeding species (e.g., an elapid *Unechis gouldii*, and the colubrids *Tropidoclonion lineatum* and *Storeria occipitomaculata*). Within this cluster, only two species (the elapids *Hemiaspis signata* and *Unechis gouldii*) exhibit early age at maturity. A trend again exists for an increase in body size and clutch size, as well as delayed maturity. The third major group consists of viviparous, biennially-reproducing species. With the exception of a population of *Thamnophis sirtalis* from Manitoba, this cluster consists entirely of species in the family Viperidae. Most of these species are large and have large clutches and delayed maturity. A

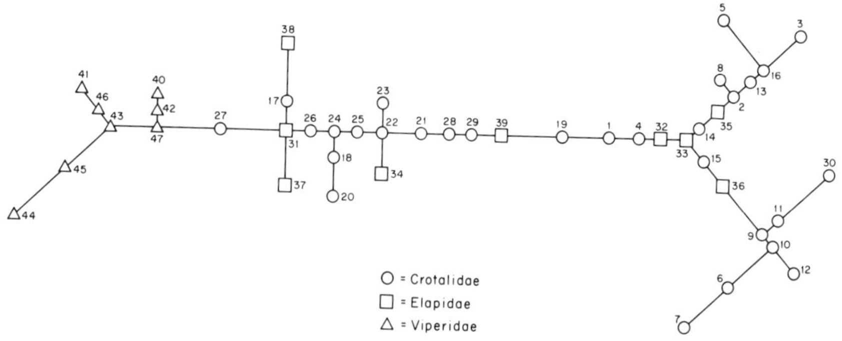

RESULTS

Fig. 3. Prim network analysis of snakes. Species names and identifying numbers follow: Colubridae: (1) *Carphophis vermis*, (2) *Coluber constrictor* [UT], (3) *Coluber constrictor* [KAN], (4) *Diadophis punctatus*, (5) *Elaphe climacophora*, (6) *Heterodon nasicus*, (7) *Heterodon platyrhinos*, (8) *Lampropeltis triangulum*, (9) *Liophis lineatus*, (9) *Liophis mossoroensis*, (11) *Liophis poecilogyrus*, (12) *Liophis viridis*, (13) *Masticophis taeniatus*, (14) *Opheodrys aestivus* [ARK], (15) *Opheodrys aestivus* [ILL], (16) *Pituophis melanoleucus*, (17) *Regina grahami*, (18) *Regina septemvittata*, (19) *Sibon sanniola*, (20) *Storeria dekayi*, (21) *Storeria occipitomaculata*, (22) *Thamnophis ordinoides*, (23) *Thamnophis proximus*, (24) *Thamnophis sauritus*, (25) *Thamnophis sirtalis* [ORE], (26) *Thamnophis sirtalis* [KAN], (27) *Thamnophis sirtalis* [MAN], (28) *Tropidoclonion lineatum*, (29) *Virginia striatula*, (30) *Waglerophis merremii*. Elapidae: (31) *Austrelaps superbus*, (32) *Cacophis harriettae*, (33) *Cacophis squamulosus*, (34) *Hemiaspis signata*, (35) *Micrurus fulvius* [FL], (36) *Micrurus fulvius* [TX], (37) *Notechis scutatus*, (38) *Pseudechis porphyriacus*, (39) *Unechis gouldii*. Viperidae: (40) *Agkistrodon contortrix*, (41) *Agkistrodon piscivorus* [FL], (42) *Agkistrodon piscivorus* [TX], (43) *Crotalus atrox*, (44) *Crotalus horridus* [PA], (45) *Crotalus horridus* [NC], (46) *Crotalus viridis* [SAS], (47) *Vipera berus*. LOCALITY CODES: ARK, Arkansas; FL, Florida; ILL, Illinois; KAN, Kansas; MAN, Manitoba; NC, North Carolina; SAS, Saskatchewan; TX, Texas.

branch off this cluster consists of relatively small-bodied species (e.g., *Vipera berus*, *Agkistrodon contortrix*, and *Agkistrodon piscivorus*) with small clutches. Another minor cluster branches off the main gradient and consists of five multiple-brooded oviparous species of the colubrid genera *Liophis* and *Waglerophis*. These early-maturing species are residents of tropical thornscrub habitat (see Vitt, 1983). Branching from this cluster are the two species of *Heterodon*, colubrids displaying biennial reproduction, delayed maturity, and relatively large broods.

Patterns of covariation in life history traits among the snake species in our sample are characterized using two PCA analyses (Table XVII). We first analyze three life history traits (age at maturity, body size at maturity, clutch size); in the subsequent analysis, we include RCM. In the first analysis, 84% of the total variation present in the data is explained by the first two PC axes (Table XVII, Fig. 4). The first axis extracts 54% of the variation and describes a gradient characterized by

TABLE XVII
Principal Components Analyses of Life History Variables: Age at Maturity, Adult Female Snout–Vent Length, and Clutch Size, and Relative Clutch Mass for Snakes

Trait	Eigenvector		Eigenvector		
	I	II	I	II	III
Age at maturity	.554	−.636	.562	.453	−.400
FSVL at maturity	.674	−.034	.611	−.375	−.385
Clutch size	.488	.770	.480	−.448	.665
RCM	—	—	.283	.672	.498
Eigenvalue	1.61	0.89	1.65	1.42	.68
Variance (%)	.54	.30	.41	.36	.17

When the first three variables are considered, N = 49 (otherwise N = 26).

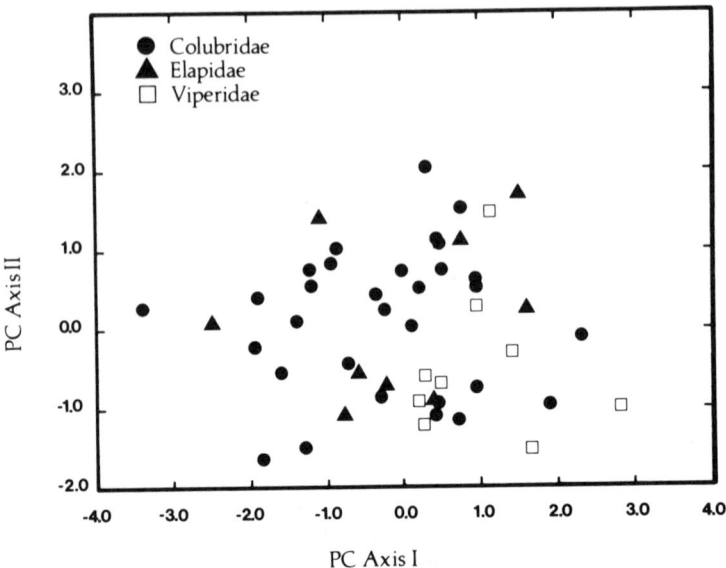

Fig. 4. Principal components analysis of snakes based on log-transformed values for age at maturity, female SVL at maturity, and mean clutch size (N = 56).

small, early-maturing species with small clutches (e.g., *Sibon sanniola*, *Unechis gouldii*, *Storeria occipitomaculata*, and *Virginia striatula*) at one end, and large, late-maturing species having large clutches (e.g., *Crotalus horridus*, *Elaphe climacophora*, and *Pseudechis porphyriacus*) at the opposite end. The second PC axis contrasts age at maturity with clutch size; late-maturing species (e.g., *Agkistrodon contortrix*, *A. piscivorus*,

RESULTS

Crotalus horridus, C. viridis, Diadophis punctatus, Lampropeltis triangulum, and *Acanthophis antarcticus*) tend to have relatively few offspring per clutch.

The position of species along the first PC axis show little clustering with respect to taxonomic affinity (Fig. 4). Viperids tend to be narrowly distributed along the axis, towards the more positive end of the gradient. Species/populations in the family Colubridae extend over the length of the axis and broadly overlap with both elapids and viperids. The elapids also exhibit a wide distribution along the first axis, but show little clustering. Species in all three families overlap extensively along PC axis II. Inspection of Figure 4 fails to reveal distinct patterns of clustering of species based on taxonomy. The only exception is the clustering of viperids along the negative values of PC axis II and for high, positive values on PC axis I.

When RCM is included in the analysis, the first two PC axes explain 77% of the total variation (Table XVII). The first PC axis has positive loadings for all variables, indicating that species (e.g., *Liophis viridis, L. mossoroensis,* and *Diadophis punctatus*) maturing at a smaller size and at an earlier age also produce smaller clutches and have relatively low RCM. Our interpretation of the second PC axis remains essentially unchanged. There is, however, a contrast between clutch size and RCM. In species producing relatively large numbers of offspring per clutch, the mass of the clutch constitutes a relatively small proportion of the female body mass.

D. Family Effects and Phylogenetic Constraints

1. OVERVIEW

The over- or underrepresentation of taxa in a comparative study, such as the one presented here, may bias the generality of the results (Clutton-Brock and Harvey, 1984). For example, are the patterns we detect generally characteristic of lizards, or are they a consequence of the predominance of data on iguanid species? We can address this bias in taxonomic representation by examining the correlations among the four life history variables for each family (Table XVIII). One criterion for evidence of a taxonomic bias in our analysis may be the deviation of family level correlations from those derived at the subordinal level. Recently, Cheverud et al. (1985) introduced a "phylogenetic correlation model" to partition variation attributable to phylogeny, allometry, and adaptation to recent environmental conditions. In an initial attempt to test for unique patterns of covariation among families, we qualitatively

TABLE XVIII
Correlations Among Four Life History Traits Calculated for Each Family: Results for Lizards and Snakes

	SVL at maturity ×			FSVL ×		Clutch ×
	FSVL	Clutch size	Age at maturity	Clutch size	Age at maturity	Age at maturity
Sauria	.97***	.49***	.62***	.50***	.52***	.07
Agamidae	.89**	−.07	.32	−.09	.48	.64*
Anguidae	.97	.86	.04	.79	−.69	−.58
Gekkonidae	.99***	.07	.57	.23	.50	.21
Iguanidae	.98***	.52***	.63***	.52***	.64***	.28*
Lacertidae	.66	.57	.79*	.79*	.82*	.89**
Scincidae	.97***	−.04	.41*	−.24	.34	.01
Teiidae	.93***	.76**	.71*	.74**	.83***	.65*
Serpentes	.98***	.36**	.55***	.50***	.42***	.14
Colubridae	.98***	.31*	.31*	.34*	.37*	.20
Elapidae	.98***	.67**	.50	.78***	.35	.06
Viperidae	.99***	.42	.15	.42	.18	−.10

*$P < .05$, **$P < .01$, ***$P < .001$.

examine correlation coefficients, as suggested by Cheverud et al. (1985), for changes in magnitude and direction.

Most lizard families do not show drastic deviations from the pooled correlations (Table XVIII). However, skinks have lower, nonsignificant correlations for all variables except for female SVL at maturity with mean adult SVL and with age at maturity: this may reflect the heterogeneous body shapes and habitats of these lizards. Agamids have low values for all correlations, but show a strong, significant association between clutch size and age at maturity. Correlations within the iguanids and the gekkonids are roughly similar to the pooled correlation matrix; but gekkonids do show lower values for all clutch size correlations, reflecting the tendency of many geckos to have a fixed clutch size (above). Anguids are characterized by low positive or strong negative correlations in all comparisons involving age at maturity. The nonsignificant relationships found for the anguids probably reflect small sample size. Interestingly, within the lacertids and the teiids, all correlations are higher than the correlations based on pooled data.

Examination of the correlation matrices for each snake family reveals that all families are generally consistent with regard to the magnitude and direction of correlations among the life history variables. Colubrids have low correlations for female SVL at maturity with age at maturity

RESULTS

and clutch size with age at maturity, but remain similar for the remaining comparisons. Within the elapids, higher correlations were found for SVL at maturity and mean adult female SVL with clutch size. Viperids were characterized by low correlations for SVL at maturity and mean adult SVL with age at maturity, but were roughly similar for the other comparisons. At this level of analysis, we do not believe that taxonomic bias has exerted a major effect on our results and conclude that the patterns we have described are representative of lizards and snakes as a whole.

2. COMPARISON OF LIZARDS AND SNAKES

To this point, we have analyzed lizards and snakes separately. We now ask whether lizards and snakes exhibit similar patterns of covariation in life history traits. Several recent studies have pointed out the importance of phylogeny in constraining the trends in variation among phenotypic traits (e.g., Lauder, 1981, 1982; Cheverud et al., 1985; Felsenstein, 1985; Huey and Bennett, 1986): Attributes describing a species may represent the influence of recent common ancestry rather than of adaptation to local environmental conditions or residual effects. Various methods and tests have been proposed in an attempt to address the importance of phylogenetic factors in the evolution of a trait (e.g., Ballinger, 1983; Cheverud et al., 1985; Dobson, 1985; Felsenstein, 1985).

Recently, Stearns (1984) asked whether the observed patterns in life history variation among squamate reptiles were size mediated or were attributable to phylogenetic influences on the correlations among life history traits. His analysis focused on removing size (mean adult female SVL) variation and examining the effect this had on patterns of covariation in four life history traits (clutch size, age at maturity, mode of reproduction, female body size) at the subordinal and family levels. His major conclusion was that the patterns of covariation within squamates were largely a consequence of variation in female body length. Differences between snakes and lizards vanished when the influence of body size was controlled.

Dunham and Miles (1985) readdressed this question and used a larger and more accurate data set than had Stearns (1984). They entered the four life history traits used by Stearns (1984) into separate nested analyses of variance with length treated as a covariate. In their analyses, lizards and snakes differed significantly in fecundity and in age at maturity even after the means were adjusted for differences in body length. Thus, contrary to Stearns (1984), life history differences between lizards and snakes are real and are only partially a consequence of difference in body size.

We present results of an expanded analysis (data from the Appendix) to determine whether the patterns of life history variation in lizards and snakes are a product of an allometric relationship between female body size or represent trends unique to each group. Four life history variables (clutch size, age at maturity, mode of reproduction, and relative clutch mass) are included in a nested ANOVA with suborder and families-within-suborder as the class variables and mean adult female body size as the covariate (but see Section II.B). Relative clutch mass was not considered in the previous analyses (above). The results here are also based on the type IV sums of squares, which is the variance term that describes size-independent variation.

Significant regressions with length are evident only for clutch size and age at maturity (Table XIX); thus variation in relative clutch mass appears to be independent of female body length. Variation in mode of reproduction is unrelated to body length, which corroborates the results presented above for both lizards and snakes. As in the Prim analysis for lizards, inclusion of species with fixed clutch sizes had no effect on the overall trends (Table XIX).

Lizards and snakes ("suborder level" in Table XIX) differ significantly in clutch size, age at maturity, mode of reproduction, and relative clutch mass. The dissimilarity between the suborders remains significant when differences in body size are standardized. Thus, at a given SVL, lizards tend to reach sexual maturity later, produce larger broods, and have broods with lower RCM. The latter result is similar to that of Seigel and Fitch (1984), who also found that snakes have a significantly higher RCM than do lizards. They attributed this difference to higher locomotion efficiencies in snakes. However, we emphasize that differences in RCM between lizards and snakes might be an artifact because of the inappropriate way in which RCM is measured and analyzed (see Dunham, et al., this volume) or to differences in body shape (see Section II.B).

We find significant family-level variation within lizards and within snakes for clutch size, age at maturity, mode of reproduction, and relative clutch mass. This suggests that the appropriate level for investigation of the importance of phylogenetic constraint on patterns of life history variation in squamate reptiles is within families (as per Table XVIII).

Stearns (1984) proposed that the life history characteristics of lizards and snakes followed a single axis of variation once the effects of adult female body length were statistically removed. Early-maturing and large-brooded species would be positioned at one end of the gradient with late-maturing, small-brooded species at the opposite end. In

RESULTS

TABLE XIX
A Test of Life History Differences Between Lizards and Snakes

Trait	Source	SS I F	SS I P	SS IV F	SS IV P	R^2
1. Clutch size (N = 214)						
	Suborder	56.18	.0001	7.54	.006	.44
		(36.11)	(.0001)	(1.60)	(.20)	(.57)
	Family (Suborder)	5.56	.0001	4.45	.0001	
		(7.83)	(.0001)	(7.73)	(.0001)	
	Length	38.30	.0001			
		(15.59)	(.0002)			
2. Age at maturity (N = 169)						
	Suborder	46.67	.0001	11.07	.001	.47
		(35.66)	(.0001)	(9.19)	(.003)	(.51)
	Family (Suborder)	4.47	.0001	4.58	.0001	
		(3.80)	(.0005)	(3.80)	(.0004)	
	Length	45.46	.0001			
		(23.98)	(.0001)			
3. Mode of reproduction (N = 217)						
	Suborder	38.75	.0001	4.35	.03	.34
		(25.84)	(.0001)	(0.0)	(.95)	(.39)
	Family (Suborder)	5.62	.001	5.42	.0001	
		(3.33)	(.001)	(3.31)	(.001)	
	Length	.11	.74			
		(1.59)	(.21)			
4. Relative clutch mass (N = 94)						
	Suborder	12.11	.0008	7.10	.0009	.32
	Family (Suborder)	2.08	.02	2.18	.02	
	Length	2.02	.15			

Nested ANOVA of clutch size, age at maturity, mode of reproduction, and relative clutch mass for suborder and families within suborder with length treated as a covariate. Values in parentheses result from excluding species with fixed clutch sizes from the analysis.

contrast, the study of Dunham and Miles (1985) showed that significant variation remains between suborders with respect to fecundity and age at maturity after eliminating variation attributable to size. The only life history traits that seem to be largely size-mediated are mode of reproduction and brood frequency. However, the use of these latter two traits (both are discrete variables) as dependent variables in an analysis of variance, which assumes that the dependent variables are linear and

TABLE XX
Analysis of Life History Differences Between Lizards and Snakes

Trait	Source	SS I			SS IV
		F	P	R^2	P
1. Oviparous, single brooded					
Clutch size	Suborder	0.88	.35	.53	.04
(N = 46)	Family (Suborder)	5.66	.0003		.0007
	Length	9.03	.004		
Age at maturity	Suborder	0.97	.33	.36	.03
(N = 39)	Family (Suborder)	0.93	.47		NS
	Length	12.39	.001		
2. Oviparous, multiple brooded					
Clutch size	Suborder	7.11	.009	.43	.04
(N = 94)	Family (Suborder)	5.49	.0001		.0001
	Length	12.90	.0006		
Age at maturity	Suborder	0.03	.85	.41	.0002
(N = 74)	Family (Suborder)	3.07	.005		.003
	Length	20.94	.0001		
3. Viviparous, single brooded					
Clutch size	Suborder	30.51	.0001	.66	NS
(N = 40)	Family (Suborder)	3.30	.009		.009
	Length	6.83	.01		
Age at maturity	Suborder	2.29	.14	.51	.02
(N = 34)	Family (Suborder)	3.67	.016		.003
	Length	7.33	.02		

Nested ANCOVA of clutch size, and age at maturity with suborder and families within suborders. Analyzed according to categories of brood frequency and mode of reproduction. Female SVL at maturity treated as a covariate.

continuously distributed, might yield misleading results. Consequently we reanalyzed the effects of phylogeny on fecundity and age at maturity according to whether species are oviparous versus viviparous, and single versus multiple-brooded (following methods outlined by Dunham and Miles, 1985). We reconsider the hypothesis (Stearns, 1984) that lizards and snakes share a common axis of life history variation.

The resulting series of three one-way nested ANCOVA's is summarized in Table XX. Analyzing variation in age at maturity and clutch size by the mode of reproduction and number of broods/year results in an increase in R^2 values. Oviparous, single-brooded snakes and lizards differ significantly for both clutch size (SS IV, $P < 0.04$; $R^2 = 0.53$) and age at maturity ($P < 0.03$; $R^2 = 0.36$). Mean adult female SVL is significantly correlated with both clutch size and age at maturity (F = 12.39, $P < 0.001$). Family-level differences are found only for clutch size ($P < 0.0007$). Among oviparous, multiple-brooded species, lizards and snakes differ significantly in clutch size ($P < 0.04$; $R^2 = 0.43$) and age at maturity ($P < 0.0002$; $R^2 = 0.41$), when the means are adjusted for size. As in the previous analyses, family-level variation within lizards and snakes is significant for clutch size ($P < 0.0001$) and age at maturity ($P < 0.003$).

The analysis of viviparous, single-brooded species yields patterns distinct from the previous two comparisons, which included the highest R^2 values for fecundity (0.66) and age at maturity (0.51). In this instance, mean clutch size does not differ significantly between lizards and snakes after adjusting for body size. Whereas the two suborders differ in the age at first reproduction, the effect ($P < 0.02$) is not nearly as strong as in previous tests. Family differences within suborders are highly significant.

Thus, the results of this analysis argue for rejection of the hypothesis (Stearns, 1984) that life history traits within the squamates follow a single axis of variation, namely body size. Both lizards and snakes differ in clutch size and age at maturity if they are analyzed within a common mode of reproduction and brood frequency. One exception to this was found for clutch size in viviparous, single-brooded species. The number of young per brood, adjusted for body size, were not significantly different for snakes (5.95 young) and lizards (7.5 young). Our analysis reinforces the suggestion that the similarities shown between lizards and snakes are not a feature of common ancestry, but are more likely to result from physiological constraints built into the mode of reproduction and the number of times these different organisms may breed during the season.

3. PHYLOGENETIC EFFECTS VERSUS ECOLOGICAL INFLUENCES

The relative importance of phylogenetic effects versus adaptation to local environmental conditions may also be approached by testing whether the positions of species in a phenotypic space, described by the axes from a principal components analysis of life history traits, may be explained at the family-level or by other ecological or life history variables. We use scores from the first two axes of variation from a PCA calculated for lizards as the dependent variables in an ANOVA with family, mode of reproduction, and frequency of reproduction as the independent variables (Table XXIa). Recall (Section II.B.6) that each PC axis represents a unique pattern of covariation among the life history

TABLE XXIa
Results From an Analysis of Variance for Residual Effects of Family, Mode of Reproduction and Brood Frequency Using the First Two Axes From the Principal Components Analysis (Based on the Analysis of Three Life History Traits) as Dependent Variables

Source	PC I	PC II
Family	*	***
Mode	NS	NS
Broods/year	***	NS
Mode × broods/year	NS	NS
r^2	.34	.30

*$P < .05$; ***$P < .001$.

TABLE XXIb
Results From an Analysis of Variance for Residual Effects of Family, Foraging Mode, and Preferred Habitat Using the First Two Axes From the Principal Components Analysis (Based on the Analysis of Three Life History Traits) as Dependent Variables

Source	PC I	PC II
Family	NS	***
Foraging mode	NS	NS
Preferred habitat	***	**
Foraging mode × preferred habit	NS	NS
r^2	.33	.53

**$P < .01$; ***$P < .001$.

traits (age at maturity, clutch size, and female body size at maturity). Briefly, the first PC axis describes an axis consisting of the emergence of delayed maturity, increasing body size at maturity, and increasing clutch size. The second PC axis, which is independent of female SVL at maturity, represents an inverse relationship between clutch size and age at maturity.

The results (Table XXIa) reveal two strong components of variance that explain the positions of species along the first PC axis. Family has an important effect: agamids, anguids, iguanids, and gymnophthalmids tend to be at the positive end of the gradient, whereas the gekkonids, lacertids, and teiids cluster toward the negative end ($F_{9,109} = 25.8$, $P < 0.02$). Frequency of reproduction also has an important effect on PC I: single-brooded species tend to have more positive scores, and multiple-brooded species have more negative ones ($F_{1,109} = 44.57$, $P < 0.0001$). However, variation in the positions of species along the second PC axis

RESULTS

are related only to differences in the positions of families ($F_{1,109} = 32.2$, $P < 0.0001$). Thus, we conclude that a strong lineage (family) effect exists for patterns of covariation in age at maturity, female SVL at maturity, and clutch size.

Scores from the first two PC axes have been used in a second analysis, which includes foraging mode and preferred habitat as independent variables (Table XXIb). Here families do not differ significantly along the first PC axis. Interestingly, preferred habitat emerges as a strong influence on this life history gradient ($F_{1,79} = 20.57$, $P < 0.002$); most of the variance explained in this model is due to habitat effects (66%). This axis separates terrestrial species, which are found mainly along the positive end of the gradient, from psammophilous and arboreal species at the other end. Saxicolous species are intermediate. Foraging mode does not contribute significantly to the variation along PC I or PC II, suggesting that correlations of foraging mode and life history traits in lizards are confounded by family-level taxonomy. Family-level differences are clearly evident, but only along the second PC axis.

We performed a similar analysis with the species scores from the PCA that included relative clutch mass. The results for the ANOVA (not shown) with family, mode of reproduction, and brood frequency paralleled the patterns found in Table XXIa. However, comparison of the positions of species along PC axis I for differences due to ecology demonstrate significant differences due only to family. The life history gradient described by the second PC axis relates significantly to differences due to foraging mode, preferred habitat, and family. Differences between this PCA and the previous one highlight the strong interdependence among foraging mode, RCM, and family-level taxonomy.

In an attempt to elucidate phylogenetic influences on the patterns of covariation among life history traits in snakes, we compare the positions of species along two PC axes based on the three above-described life history traits. There are no differences among families, between oviparous versus viviparous species, and single-brooded versus biennial species for the first PC axis. However, the distribution of the viperids along the second PC axis differs from the colubrids and elapids ($F_{2,40} = 4.7$, $P < 0.02$). The positions of the latter two families are statistically indistinguishable. Species differ strongly in the number of clutches produced per season. Biennial species have significantly lower scores on PC axis II than single-brooded species ($F_{1,40} = 12.4$, $P < 0.0006$). In the analyses which corresponded to that presented in Table XXIb, there are no significant effects due to foraging mode or preferred habitat on either the first or the second PC axis. In other words, covariation between foraging mode or preferred habitat with life history traits are confounded by their correlations with family-level taxonomy.

IV. CONCLUSIONS

A. General Patterns of Variation in Life History Traits

This chapter summarizes patterns of life history variation at different levels of resolution in a broad comparative analysis of squamate reptiles. In doing so, several distinct patterns of variation and covariation in life history variables became obvious between suborders, within suborders, and within species. The extensive data base allows refinement of the previously documented patterns of life history variation within squamate reptiles. Although certain results of Tinkle et al. (1970) are corroborated for lizards, our findings reveal complex interrelationships among the life history variables. A major contribution of this study is our demonstration that variation in life history is influenced by demography, ecology, and phylogeny.

At the most superficial level, all correlations between SVL at maturity, mean adult SVL, age at maturity, and clutch size are positive in both lizards and snakes. This suggests a similar trend in both groups, species that mature at a later age will mature at a larger size and have more eggs per clutch than those that mature early. Furthermore, those species of lizards and snakes exhibiting delayed maturity may be either oviparous or viviparous, but have only one clutch per year. The correlation analyses only begin to suggest the patterns of life history covariation. Most of the significant correlations are related to variation in body size; therefore, it cannot be determined from these analyses alone whether selection acting on clutch size, for example, has resulted in larger body sizes or whether selection acting on body size has increased clutch size.

The differences in clutch size between oviparous versus viviparous species and between early-maturing versus late-maturing species are attributable to a correlation with body size. That is, the large clutches of viviparous or late-maturing species are a consequence of increased SVL. However, the difference in clutch size between single-brooded versus multiple-brooded species is independent of body size. Interactions between the life history variables, such as brood frequency with mode of reproduction, are also important in describing variation in clutch size, and female SVL at maturity. Additional differences were found for

CONCLUSIONS

ecological variables, such as distribution, with clutch size, brood frequency, and age at maturity in lizards. At this level of resolution, both ecological (e.g., distribution) and demographic variables (especially brood frequency) appear to influence life history variation (see Wilbur et al., 1974). Nevertheless, such patterns are not evident in snakes. In this group clutch size appears to be influenced primarily by mode of reproduction rather than by brood frequency or age at maturity.

Previous studies have discussed the importance and distinctiveness of relative clutch mass (RCM), especially as this life history characteristic relates to foraging mode (e.g., Vitt and Congdon, 1978; Huey and Pianka, 1981; Seigel and Fitch, 1984) and to habitat specificity (Vitt, 1981). We found that variation in clutch size and RCM of lizards was correlated with the foraging mode. However, because of the strong lineage effects of foraging mode (Section III.D.3), the relationship between RCM and foraging mode might be a phylogenetic artifact. Even so, RCM and foraging mode are correlated in the only within-family comparison to date (Huey and Pianka, 1981). Whereas Seigel and Fitch (1984) demonstrated relationships in snakes between RCM and foraging mode and between RCM and reproductive mode, we did not. In all likelihood, these differences between our results and those of Seigel and Fitch (1984) probably reflect the larger data set used by Seigel and Fitch. Our data set was smaller because we analyzed only species/populations for which additional life history variables were known. In any case any conclusions concerning RCM must be viewed with caution because of serious methodological problems with this index (Dunham et al., this volume).

Preferred habitat also exhibits a significant association with variation in age at maturity, female SVL at maturity, and clutch size in lizards. However, only the difference in clutch size remains when female SVL is controlled. Our results partially support the hypothesis described by Vitt (1981), namely that adaptations for a particular habitat type, foraging mode, and escape behavior may involve concomitant constraints on life history traits. Again, however, phylogenetic correlations may confound these analyses (see below).

We characterized patterns of covariation of five life history variables through a Prim network analysis. This analysis provides the primary mechanism for identifying life history patterns among lizards and snakes. In each network, species are separated into clusters, primarily by number of clutches per year and mode of reproduction.

Distinct patterns of covariation are evident among the life history traits of lizards, but the picture is drastically more complex than envisaged by Tinkle et al. (1970). Lizards initially cluster on the basis of brood frequency. Three major clusters of covariation are described: single-brooded, oviparous species; single-brooded, viviparous species; and multiple-brooded, oviparous species. Within each cluster secondary trends in life history variation are defined by female SVL at maturity, age at maturity, and clutch size. Six additional groups are defined that are composed of differing combinations of the three life history traits. Collectively, ten distinct reproductive trends among lizards are distinct, suggesting the existence of consistent patterns in life history variation. For example, the trend of large body size at maturity, delayed-maturity, and large clutch size is present in multiple-brooded, oviparous species, in single-brooded, oviparous species, and in viviparous species. Three separate clusters occur within single-brooded, oviparous species, three in single-brooded, viviparous species, and four in the multiple-brooded, oviparous species. In certain instances our analyses suggest that similarities in life histories among species may be related to a common feature (e.g., foraging mode) or habitat preference (e.g., terrestrial versus arboreal). Clustering based on taxonomic affinity (relative recency of common ancestry) is not evident in this analysis. However, because foraging mode and habitat preference are often highly correlated with family-level taxonomy, analyses involving these variables may include unquantified phylogenetic effects (see Section III.D.3).

Snakes are divided into groups according to mode and frequency of reproduction. Four major groups are apparent: (a) biennial, viviparous; (b) single-brooded, viviparous; (c) single-brooded, oviparous; and (d) multiple-brooded, oviparous. Two species in our sample are biennial and oviparous. Unique patterns of covariation (based on age at maturity, SVL at maturity, and clutch size) characterize each major group. A total of five reproductive trends in snakes are described by the Prim network. Most of the differences among species are correlated with family-level taxonomy and hence, phylogeny.

Principal components analysis of three life history variables (age at maturity, female SVL at maturity, and clutch size) reveals two axes of variation, which are similar for both lizards and snakes. The first axis describes a positive relationship among all three variables, whereas the second axis represents a negative relationship between age at maturity and clutch size independent of body size. Lizards and snakes exhibit similar values for proportion of variation explained by the PCA and similar loadings on each variable. Because these axes are statistically independent, the factors responsible for major components of variation can be analyzed separately. Furthermore, the positions of species along each axis may be used to infer the existence of consistent trends in life history variation.

CONCLUSIONS

The distribution of species of lizards along the first PC axis is largely due to differences in brood frequency and preferred habitat. Family-level variation is also a significant contribution. In snakes, however, no significant trend is found for this axis.

Positions of lizards along the second PC axis are explained primarily by differences among families (Fig. 2). However, the distribution of snakes along the second axis is related both to frequency of reproduction and to family. Viperids are distinctly separated from elapids and colubrids. However, because most viperids in our sample are biennial, whereas most other snakes are not, this separation may reflect a phylogenetic effect.

B. Evaluation of the Patterns

Do our analyses suggest similar patterns of covariation in life history traits (life history strategies) for lizards and snakes? No. The nested ANOVA's clearly indicate that lizards and snakes differ in several life history traits: clutch size, age at maturity, mode of reproduction, and RCM. Because these differences persist even when size is controlled, patterns of variation in each order are distinct. Thus, the argument (Stearns, 1984) that snakes differ from lizards in life history traits only because of allometric relationships among reproductive characters cannot be supported, at least when SVL is used as the index of body size.

Life history trends are more conspicuous in the lizard analyses; known variation among snake populations (e.g., Seigel and Fitch, 1984) was not completely captured by the data available to us. This suggests further work and that a different approach is needed for analyzing life history patterns of snakes.

Explanations other than r- and K-selection or demographic influences (see Section III.B.7) for the patterns of variation in lizards have, until recently, been ignored or given minor attention. Nevertheless, local adaptation (including habitat specificity and environmental predictability), phylogenetic constraint, foraging mode, and allometric covariation may all exert important influences on the evolution of life history traits. The relative importance of such effects within any particular clade remains largely unknown.

C. Future Directions

Tests of some evolutionary hypotheses, such as the influence of frequency of reproduction on various life history traits, are now possible. However, the data required to test many specific predictions of life history theory are generally available for only a few taxa. For example, Wilbur et al. (1974) discussed several factors that may act as selective forces on life history traits. Many of the variables they considered important (resource availability, population density, size of offspring, and foraging behavior) are lacking in the data available here.

Has there been improvement in the quality of data since Tinkle et al. (1970)? Yes and no. Tinkle et al. (1970) called attention to the dearth of data of age-specific variation in reproductive traits, egg size data, and survivorship. Recent studies of life history variation among squamate reptiles have begun to include the necessary data for a comparative evolutionary study. Our review of the literature suggests a continuing need for greater detail in life history studies. For example, in our multivariate analysis of four life history traits (age at first reproduction, clutch size, SVL at maturity, and relative clutch mass), complete data are available for only 56 species of lizards and only 26 species of snakes.

Better estimates of age at first reproduction are needed. Ordinarily this age is inferred from growth rates and the minimum SVL of a female with mature ovaries (developing follicles). Similarly, very few studies provide data on age-specific survivorship, age-specific fecundity, egg size, and juvenile size. Such data, especially with respect to possible senescence in these traits, are necessary for a more complete analysis of life history patterns (e.g., Charlesworth, 1980). Our analysis reinforces the possible importance of two additional variables (RCM and foraging mode) that may have an important role in affecting the suite of life history adaptations that characterize a species. Recall, however, that the former variable has been measured inappropriately in most studies, and the latter is highly correlated with phylogeny, at least in lizards. Accordingly, additional studies will be necessary to establish the importance of these variables.

Our analyses are subject to some of the traditional weaknesses in comparative studies. Studies conducted under present conditions do not necessarily reflect conditions during the past: The magnitude and direction of selection and responses to selection are not temporally invariant (e.g., Lauder, 1981, 1982). Furthermore, it is often assumed that selection is an optimizing agent. However, a given suite of environmental conditions may favor more than one set of life history traits, thereby complicating any test.

Uncontrolled phylogenetic biases in comparative studies may result in ambiguous, unfounded, and uninterpretable conclusions. Such biases include the under- and overrepresentation of taxa in an analysis (i.e., the problem of determining the appropriate range of taxonomic representation) and the sampling constraint inherent with level of taxonomy

CONCLUSIONS

(Clutton-Brock and Harvey, 1984; Felsenstein, 1985). Finally, comparative studies involving distant taxa (e.g., families) encounter the problem that much evolution may have occurred since divergence: This makes it difficult to infer the selective bases for observed differences in life histories between current taxa (Huey and Bennett, 1986). Furthermore, tradeoffs and constraints are likely to have changed during the time that has elapsed since divergence (Cheverud et al., 1985; Dobson, 1985). As a result, the evolutionary response to a change in a given selective factor may vary among taxa.

Comparative studies of life history patterns are advantageous for reviewing a broad spectrum of variation. However, despite the accumulating base of both interspecific and intraspecific studies, our ability to test evolutionary hypotheses is limited. The patterns described in this review are interpretable in terms of a few variables (e.g., brood frequency), but we still lack crucial information for a satisfactory explanation of observed life history variation. Even the best studies contain major inadequacies that make tests of any life history theory difficult (Stearns, 1977; Dunham, 1982; Ballinger, 1983; Dunham and Miles, 1985; Tinkle and Dunham, 1986).

All these problems will remain unresolved until two problems are solved. First, the current lack of resolution of phylogenetic relationships within the squamates has forced us to use multivariate statistical approaches rather than phylogenetically-based comparative ones (e.g., Felsenstein, 1985; Cheverud et al., 1985). More stable and complete phylogenetic hypotheses are badly needed. Second, our knowledge of life history variation is scant for several important groups of squamate reptiles. More data are needed for certain diverse lizard families (Gekkonidae, Scincidae, Agamidae, and Teiidae) and also for the lesser known groups (Amphisbaenia, Pygopodidae, and Cordylidae). Information is especially limited for snakes, for which additional data are necessary for every family. Until these data become available, any attempt to characterize the life history of reptiles as a group will necessarily be inadequate simply because many of these groups are highly specialized (e.g., amphisbaenians are fossorial, most geckos are nocturnal) relative to most reptiles.

We emphasize the need for long-term studies of demographic and life history variation combined with simultaneous measurement of variation in levels of resource availability, environmentally imposed constraints (e.g., thermal ones), and intensity of predation. We also note the need for experimental demonstrations of the mechanisms by which these factors interact to affect observed densities, levels of intraspecific competition, and demographic attributes of populations (e.g., Ferguson and

Fox, 1984). Especially critical are long-term data on temporal variation in age-specific survivorship rates for a representative spectrum of local populations.

Although difficult to obtain, more precise data on egg and hatchling survivorship are required if we are to understand differing patterns of parental investment. In addition, the extent to which observed variation is due to genotypic versus environmental influences remains largely unknown. The success of "common garden" or reciprocal transplant studies has thus far been disappointing (Ballinger, 1979) but should still be encouraged. Experimental studies allowing unambiguous partitioning of observed life history variation into genetic and environmental components are critically needed. Advancement of our understanding of life history evolution first of all requires improvement of the available data. Moreover, before predictions of life history theory can be properly tested, the underlying assumptions of those theories must be validated for the organisms under investigation.

ACKNOWLEDGMENTS

We thank Carl Gans, Ray Huey, Tracy Miles, Peter Morin, Karen Overall, Richard Seigel, Doug Ruby, Laurie Vitt, and an anonymous reviewer for valuable comments on the mansucript. Richard Seigel and Laurie Vitt generously provided us with additional references. A. E. D. was supported by National Science Foundation grant DEB 81-04690. D. B. M. acknowledges support by Public Health Service grant 2T32-GM-07517-06, a Roosevelt Fund Memorial Grant, and an IBM Threshold Fellowship. Computing costs were defrayed by a grant from the Faculty of Arts and Sciences, University of Pennsylvania, and Ohio University.

REFERENCES

Alcala, A. C. and Brown, W. C. (1967). Population ecology of the tropical scincoid lizard, *Emoia atrocostata*, in the Philippines. Copeia 1967, 596–604.

Aldridge, R. D. (1979). Female reproductive cycles of the snakes *Arizona elegans* and *Crotalus viridis*. Herpetologica 35, 256–261.

Anderson, R. A. and Karasov, W. H. (1981). Contrasts in energy intake and expenditure in sit-and-wait and widely foraging lizards. Oecologia (Berl.) 49, 67–72.

Andren, C. and Nilson, G. (1983). Reproductive tactics in an island population of adders *Vipera berus* (L.) with a fluctuating food resource. Amphibia-Reptilia 4, 63–79.

Andrews, R. M. (1979). Evolution of life histories: A comparison of *Anolis* lizards from matched island and mainland habitats. Breviora 454, 1–51.

Andrews, R. M. (1984). Energetics of sit-and-wait and widely searching lizard predators. In *Vertebrate Ecology and Systematics—A Tribute to Henry S. Fitch*. R. A. Seigel, L. E.

REFERENCES

Hunt, L. Knight, L. Malaret, and N. Zuschlag (eds.). Museum of Natural History, University of Kansas, Vol. 10, pp. 137–145.

Andrews, R. M. and Rand, A. S. (1974). Reproductive effort in anoline lizards. Ecology 55, 1317–1327.

Andrews, R. M. and Rand, A. S. (1983). Limited dispersal of juvenile *Anolis limifrons*. Copeia 1983: 429–434.

Asana, J. J. (1931). The natural history of *Calotes versicolor* (Boulenger), the common blood-sucker. J. Bombay Nat. Hist. Soc. 34, 1041–1047.

Avery, R. A. (1975a). Clutch size and reproductive effort in the lizard *Lacerta vivipara* Jacquin. Oecologia (Berl.) 19, 165–170.

Avery, R. A. (1975b). Age-structure and longevity of common lizard (*Lacerta vivipara*) populations. J. Zool. (Lond.) 176, 555–558.

Baker, J. K. (1980). The rainbow skink. *Lampropholis delicata* in Hawaii. Pacific Sci. 33, 207–212.

Ballinger, R. E. (1973). Comparative demography of two viviparous iguanid lizards (*Sceloporus jarrovi* and *Sceloporus poinsetti*). Ecology 54, 269–283.

Ballinger, R. E. (1974). Reproduction of the Texas horned lizard, *Phrynosoma cornutum*. Herpetologica 30, 321–327.

Ballinger, R. E. (1976). Evolution of life history strategies: Implications of recruitment in a lizard population following density manipulations. Southwest Nat. 21, 203–208.

Ballinger, R. E. (1977). Reproductive strategies: Food availability as a source of proximal variation in a lizard. Ecology 58, 628–635.

Ballinger, R. E. (1979). Intraspecific variation in demography and life history of the lizard, *Sceloporus jarrovi*, along an altitudinal gradient in southeastern Arizona. Ecology 60, 901–909.

Ballinger, R. E. (1983). Life history variations. In *Lizard Ecology. Studies of a Model Organism*. (R. B. Huey, E. R. Pianka, and T. W. Schoener, eds.). Harvard University Press, Cambridge, MA, pp. 241–260.

Ballinger, R. E., Droge, D. L. and Jones, S. M. (1981). Reproduction in a Nebraska sandhills population of the northern prairie lizard *Sceloporus undulatus garmani*. Am. Midl. Nat. 106, 157–164.

Ballinger, R. E. and Hipp, T. G. (1985). Reproduction in the collared lizard *Crotaphytus collaris* in west central Texas. Copeia 1985, 976–980.

Ballinger, R. E., Tyler, E. D., and Tinkle, D. W. (1972). Reproductive ecology of a west Texas population of the greater earless lizard, *Cophosaurus texanus*. Am. Midl. Nat. 88, 419–428.

Barbault, R. (1976). Population dynamics and reproductive patterns of three African skinks. Copeia 1976, 483–490.

Barbault, R. (1986). Rapid-aging in males, a way to increase fitness in a short-lived tropical lizard? Oikos 46, 258–260.

Barwick, R. E. (1959). The life history of the common New Zealand skink *Leiolopisma zelandica* (Gray, 1843). Trans. Roy. Soc. New Zealand 86, 331–380.

Bauwens, D. and Thoen, C. (1981). Escape tactics and vulnerability to predation association with reproduction in the lizard *Lacerta vivipara*. J. Anim. Ecol 50, 733–743.

Bellairs, A. (1970). *The Life of Reptiles*. Vol. 2. Universe Books, New York.

Bennett, A. F., Huey, R. B. and John-Adler, H. B. (1984). Physiological correlates of natural activity and locomotor capacity in two species of lacertid lizards. J. Comp. Physiol. 154, 113–118.

Berry, K. H. (1974). The ecology and social behavior of the chuckwalla, *Sauromalus obesus obesus* Baird. Univ. Calif. Publ. Zool. 101, 1–60.

Berry, P. Y. and Lim, G. S. (1967). The breeding pattern of the puff-faced water snake, *Homalopsis buccata* Boulenger. Copeia 1967, 307–313.

Blackburn, D. G. (1982). Evolutionary origins of viviparity in the Reptilia. I. Sauria. Amphibia-Reptilia 3, 185–205.

Blackburn, D. G., Vitt, L. J. and Beuchat, C. A. (1984). Eutherian-like reproductive specializations in a viviparous reptile. Proc. Natl. Acad. Sci. U.S.A. 81, 4860–4863.

Bookstein, F. L., Chernoff, B., Elder, R. L., Humphries, J. M., Jr., Smith, G. R. and Strauss, R. E. (1985). *Morphometrics in Evolutionary Biology*. Special Publication 15. Academy of Natural Science, Philadelphia.

Bostic, D. L. (1966). A preliminary report of reproduction in the teiid lizard, *Cnemidophorus hyperythrus beldingi*. Herpetologica 22, 81–90.

Boyce, M. S. (1984). Restitution of r- and K-selection as a model of density-dependent natural selection. Ann. Rev. Ecol. Syst. 15, 427–447.

Branson, B. A. and Baker, E. C. (1974). An ecological study of the queen snake, *Regina septemvittata* (Say) in Kentucky. Tulane Stud. Zool. Bot. 18, 153–171.

Bradshaw, S. D. (1981). Ecophysiology of Australian desert lizards: Studies on the genus *Amphibolurus*. In *Ecological Biogeography of Australia*. (A. Keast, ed.). Junk, The Hague, pp. 1395–1434.

Breckenridge, W. J. (1943). The life history of the black-banded skink *Eumeces septentrionalis septentrionalis* (Baird). Am. Midl. Nat. 29, 591–606.

Brooks, G. R., Jr. (1967). Population ecology of the ground skink, *Lygosoma laterale* (Say). Ecol. Monogr. 37, 72–87.

Brown, W. S. and Parker, W. S. (1984). Growth, reproduction and demography of the racer, *Coluber constrictor mormon*, northern Utah. In *Vertebrate Ecology and Systematics: a Tribute to Henry S. Fitch*. (R. A. Seigel, L. E. Hunt, J. L. Knight, L. Malaret, and N. L. Zuschlag, eds.). Museum of Natural History, University of Kansas, Vol. 10, pp. 13–40.

Burkett, R. D. (1966). Natural history of the cottonmouth moccasin, *Agkistrodon piscivorus* (Reptilia). Univ. Kansas Mus. Nat. Hist. Publ. 17, 435–491.

Burkholder, G. L. and Walker, J. M. (1973). Habitat and reproduction of the desert whiptail lizard, *Cnemidophorus tigris* Baird and Girard, in southwestern Idaho at the northern part of its range. Herpetologica 29, 76–83.

Burrage, B. R. (1973). Comparative ecology and behaviour of *Chamaeleo pumilus pumilus* (Gmelin) and *C. namaquensis* Smith (Sauria: Chamaeleonidae). Ann. South Africa. Mus. 61, 1–158.

Bustard, H. R. (1968). The ecology of the Australian gecko, *Gehyra variegata*, in northern New South Wales. J. Zool. (Lond.) 154, 113–138.

Bustard, H. R. (1969). The ecology of the Australian gecko *Heteronotia binoei* in northern New South Wales. J. Zool. (Lond.) 156, 483–497.

Bustard, H. R. (1970). The population ecology of the Australian gekkonid lizard *Heteronotia binoei* in an exploited forest. J. Zool. (Lond.) 162, 31–42.

Bustard, H. R. (1971). A population study of the eyed gecko, *Oedura ocellata* Boulenger, in northern New South Wales, Australia. Copeia 1971, 658–669.

Charlesworth, B. (1980). *Evolution in Age-Structured Populations*. Cambridge University Press, Cambridge and London.

Cheverud, J. M., Dow, M. M. and Leuttenegger, W. (1985). The quantitative assessment of phylogenetic constraints in comparative analyses: Sexual dimorphism in body weight among primates. Evolution 39, 1335–1351.

Chondropoulos, B. P. and Lykakis, J. J. (1983). Ecology of the Balkan wall lizard, *Podarcis taurica ionica* (Sauria: Lacertidae) from Greece. Copeia 1983, 991–1001.

REFERENCES

Church, G. (1962). The reproductive cycles of the Javanese house geckos, *Cosymbotus platyurus, Hemidactylus frenatus,* and *Peropus mutilatus.* Copeia 1962, 262–269.

Clark, D. R., Jr. (1970). Ecological study of the worm snake *Carphophis vermis* (Kennicott). Univ. Kansas Publ. Mus. Nat. Hist. 19, 85–194.

Clark, D. R., Jr. (1974). The western ribbon snake *(Thamnophis proximus):* Ecology of a Texas population. Herpetologica 30, 372–379.

Clark, D. R., Jr., and Fleet, R. R. (1974). The rough earth snake *(Virginia striatula):* Ecology of a Texas population. Southwest. Nat. 20, 467–478.

Clutton-Brock, T. H. and Harvey, P. H. (1984). Comparative approaches to investigating adaptation. In *Behavorial Ecology.* (J. R. Krebs and N. B. Davies, eds.). Sinauer Associates, Sunderland, MA, pp. 7–29.

Cogger, H. G. (1978). Reproductive cycles, fat body cycles, and socio-sexual behavior in the Mallee dragon, *Amphibolurus* (Lacertilia, Agamidae). Aust. J. Zool. 26, 653–672.

Cole, L. C. (1954). The population consequences of life history phenomena. Quart. Rev. Biol. 29, 103–137.

Crenshaw, J. W., Jr. (1955). The life history of the southern spiny lizard, *Sceloporus undulatus undulatus* Latreille. Am. Midl. Nat. 54, 257–298.

Cuellar, O. (1984). Reproduction in a parthenogenetic lizard: With a discussion of optimal clutch size and a critique of the clutch weight/body weight ratio. Am. Midl. Nat. 111, 242–258.

Daniel, P. M. (1960). Growth and cyclic behavior in the West African lizard, *Agama agama africana.* Copeia 1960, 94–97.

Diller, L. V. and Wallace, R. L. (1984). Reproductive biology of the northern Pacific rattlesnake *(Crotalus viridis oreganus)* in northern Idaho. Herpetologica 40, 182–193.

Dmi'el, R. (1967). Studies on reproduction, growth, and feeding in the snake, *Spalerosophis cliffordi.* Copeia 1967, 321–346.

Dobson, F. S. (1985). The use of phylogeny in behavior and ecology. Evolution 39, 1384–1388.

Droge, D. L., Jones, S. M. and Ballinger, R. E. (1982). Reproduction of *Holbrookia maculata* in western Nebraska. Copeia 1982, 356–362.

Dunham, A. E. (1980). An experimental study of interspecific competition between the iguanid lizards *Sceloporus merriami* and *Urosaurus ornatus.* Ecol. Monogr. 50, 309–330.

Dunham, A. E. (1981). Populations in a fluctuating environment: The comparative population ecology of *Sceloporus merriami* and *Urosaurus ornatus.* Misc. Publ. Mus. Zool., Univ. Michigan 158, 1–62.

Dunham, A. E. (1982). Demographic and life history variation among populations of the iguanid lizard *Urosaurus ornatus:* Implications for the study of life-history phenomena in lizards. Herpetologica 38, 208–221.

Dunham, A. E. and Miles, D. B. (1985). Patterns of covariation in life history traits of squamate reptiles: The effects of size and phylogeny reconsidered. Am. Nat. 126, 231–257.

Elvira, B. and Vigal, C. R. (1985). Further data on the reproduction of *Lacerta monticola cyreni* (Sauria, Lacertidae) in central Spain. Amphibia-Reptilia 6, 173–179.

Felsenstein, J. (1985). Phylogenies and the comparative method. Am. Nat. 125, 1–15.

Ferguson, G. W., Bohlen, C. H. and Woolley, H. P. (1980). *Sceloporus undulatus:* Comparative life history and regulation of a Kansas population. Ecology 61, 312–322.

Ferguson, G. W. and Fox, S. F. (1984). Annual variation of survival advantage of large side-blotched lizards. *Uta stansburiana:* Its causes and evolutionary significance. Evolution 38, 342–349.

Fitch, H. S. (1935). Natural history of the alligator lizards. Trans. Acad. Sci. St. Louis 29, 1–38.

Fitch, H. S. (1954). Life history and ecology of the five-lined skink, *Eumeces fasciatus.* Univ. Kansas Publ. Mus. Nat. Hist. 8, 1–156.

Fitch, H. S. (1955). Habits and adaptations of the Great Plains Skink *(Eumeces obsoletus).* Ecol. Monogr. 25, 59–83.

Fitch, H. S. (1956). An ecological study of the collared lizard *(Crotaphytus collaris).* Univ. Kansas Publ. Mus. Nat. Hist. 8, 213–274.

Fitch, H. S. (1958). Natural history of the six-lined racerunner *(Cnemidophorus sexlineatus).* Univ. Kansas Publ. Mus. Nat. Hist. 11, 11–62.

Fitch, H. S. (1960). Autecology of the copperhead. Univ. Kansas Publ. Mus. Nat. Hist. 13, 85–288.

Fitch, H. S. (1963a). Natural history of the black rat snake *(Elaphe o. obsoleta)* in Kansas. Copeia 1963, 649–658.

Fitch, H. S. (1963b). Natural history of the racer *Coluber constrictor.* Univ. Kansas Publ. Mus. Nat. Hist. 15, 351–468.

Fitch, H. S. (1965). An ecological study of the garter snake *Thamnophis sirtalis.* Univ. Kansas Publ. Mus. Nat. Hist. 15, 493–564.

Fitch, H. S. (1972). Ecology of *Anolis tropidolepis* in Costa Rican cloud forest. Herpetologica 28, 10–21.

Fitch, H. S. (1975). A demographic study of the ringneck snake *Diadophis punctatus* in Kansas. Univ. Kansas Publ. Mus. Nat. Hist. 62, 1–53.

Fitch, H. S. and Fleet, R. R. (1970). Natural history of the milk snake *(Lampropeltis triangulum)* in northeastern Kansas. Herpetologica 26, 387–396.

Fitch, H. S. and Greene, H. W. (1965). Breeding cycle of the ground skink, *Lygosoma laterale.* Univ. Kansas Publ. Mus. Nat. Hist. 15, 565–575.

Fitch, H. S. and Henderson, R. W. (1978). Ecology and exploitation of *Ctenosaura similis.* Univ. Kansas Sci. Bull. 51, 483–500.

Flemming, T. H. and Hooker, R. S. (1975). *Anolis cupreus:* The response of a lizard to tropical seasonality. Ecology 56, 1243–1261.

Fukada, H. (1978). Growth and maturity of the Japanese rat snake, *Elaphe climacophora* (Reptilia, Serpentes, Colubridae). J. Herpetol. 12, 269–274.

Gadgil, M., and Bossert, W. (1970). Life historical consequences of natural selection. Am. Nat. 104, 1–24.

Galligan, J. H. and Dunson, W. A. (1979). Biology and status of timber rattlesnake *(Crotalus horridus)* populations in Pennsylvania. Biol. Cons. 15, 13–57.

Gannon, V. P. J. and Secoy, D. M. (1984). Growth and reproductive rates of a northern population of the prairie rattlesnake, *Crotalus v. viridis.* J. Herpetol. 18, 13–19.

Gennaro, A. L. (1974). Growth, size, and age at sexual maturity of the lesser earless lizard, *Holbrookia maculata maculata,* in eastern New Mexico. Herpetologica 30, 85–90.

Gibbons, J. W. (1972). Reproduction, growth, and sexual dimorphism in the canebreak rattlesnake. Copeia 1972, 222–226.

Gibbons, J. W., Coker, J. W. and Murphy, T. M., Jr. (1977). Selected aspects of the life history of the rainbow snake *(Farancia erythrogramma).* Herpetologica 33, 276–281.

Goldberg, S. R. (1972). Reproduction in the southern alligator lizard *Gerrhonotus multicarinatus.* Herpetologica 28, 267–273.

Goldberg, S. R. (1976). Reproduction in a mountain population of the coastal whiptail lizard, *Cnemidophorus tigris multiscutatus.* Copeia 1976, 260–266.

REFERENCES

Goldberg, S. R. and Bezy, R. L. (1974). Reproduction in the island night lizard, *Xantusia riversiana*. Herpetologica 30, 350–360.

Goldberg, S. R. and Robinson, M. D. (1979). Reproduction in two Namib Desert lacertid lizards (*Aporosaura anchietae* and *Meroles cunierostris*). Herpetologica 35, 169–175.

Gorman, G. C., Licht, P. and McCollum, F. (1981). Annual reproductive patterns in three species of marine snakes from the central Philippines. J. Herpetol. 15, 335–354.

Gower, J. C. and Ross, G. J. S. (1969). Minimum spanning trees and single linkage cluster analysis. J. Roy. Stat. Soc. Ser. C 18, 54–64.

Greene, H. W. (1969). Reproduction in a middle American skink, *Leiolopisma cherriei* (Cope). Herpetologica 25, 55–56.

Greer, A. E. (1967a). The ecology and behavior of two sympatric *Lygodactylus* geckos. Breviora 268, 1–17.

Greer, A. E. (1967b). Notes on the reproduction in anguid lizards. Herpetologica 23, 94–99.

Greer, A. E. and Parker, F. (1967). A new scincid lizard from the northern Solomon Islands. Breviora 275, 1–20.

Gregory, P. T. (1977). Life history parameters of the red-sided garter snake (*Thamnophis sirtalis parietalis*) in an extreme environment, the Interlake Region of Manitoba. Natl. Mus. Canada Publ. Zool. 13, 1–44.

Guillette, L. J. (1983). Notes concerning reproduction of the montane skink, *Eumeces copei*. J. Herpetol. 17, 144–148.

Guillette, L. J. and Casas-Andreu, G. (1980). Fall reproductive activity in the high altitude Mexican lizard, *Sceloporus grammicus microlepidotus*. J. Herpetol. 14, 143–147.

Hall, R. J. (1969). Ecological observations on Graham's watersnake (*Regina grahami* Baird and Girard). Am. Midl. Nat. 81, 156–163.

Hamlett, G. W. (1952). Notes on breeding and reproduction in the lizard *Anolis carolinensis*. Copeia 1952, 183–185.

Harris, V. A. (1964). *Life of the Rainbow Lizard*. Hutchinson and Co., London.

Hasegawa, M. (1984). Biennial reproduction in the lizard *Eumeces okadae* on Miyake-Jima, Japan. Herpetologica 40, 194–199.

Hickman, J. L. (1960). Observations on the skink lizard *Egernia whitii* (Lacépède). Proc. Roy. Soc. Tasmania 94, 111–118.

How, R. A. and Kitchener, D. J. (1983). The biology of the gecko, *Oedura reticulata* Bustard, in a small habitat isolate in the western Australian wheatbelt. Aust. Wildlife Res. 10, 543–556.

Huey, R. B. and Bennett, A. F. (1986). A comparative approach to field and laboratory studies in evolutionary biology. In *Predator–Prey Relationships. Perspectives and Approaches for the Study of Lower Vertebrates*. (M. E. Feder and G. V. Lauder eds.). Univ Chicago Press, Chicago.

Huey, R. B., Bennett, A.F., John-Alder, H. and Nagy, K. A. (1984). Locomotor capacity and foraging behaviour of lizards. Anim. Behav. 32, 41–50.

Huey, R. B. and Pianka, E. R. (1981). Ecological consequences of foraging mode. Ecology 62, 991–999.

Huey, R. B., Pianka, E. R., Egan, M. E. and Coons, L. W. (1974). Ecological shifts in sympatry: Kalahari fossorial lizards (*Typhlosaurus*). Ecology 55, 304–316.

Hulse, A. C. (1981). Ecology and reproduction of the parthenogenetic lizard *Cnemidophorus uniparens*. Ann. Carnegie Mus. 50, 353–369.

Hunsaker, D. (1959). Birth and litter sizes of the blue spiny lizard *Sceloporus cyanogenys*. Copeia 1959, 260–261.

Inger, R. F. and Greenberg, B. (1966). Annual reproductive patterns of lizards from a Bornean rain forest. Ecology 47, 1007–1021.

Iverson, J. B. (1979). Behavior and ecology of the rock iguana *Cyclura carinata*. Bull. Florida State Mus. Biol. Sci. 24, 175–358.

Jackson, D. R. and Franz, R. (1981). Ecology of the eastern coral snake *(Micrurus fulvius)* in northern peninsular Florida. Herpetologica 37, 213–228.

Judd, F. R. (1976). Demography of a barrier island population of a keeled earless lizard, *Holbrookia propinqua*. Occ. Pap. Mus. Texas Tech. Univ. 44, 1–45.

Jun-yi, L. and Kau-hung, L. (1982). Population ecology of the lizard *Japalura swinhonis formosensis* (Sauria: Agamidae) in Taiwan. Copeia 1982, 425–434.

Kofron, C. P. (1979a). Female reproductive biology of the brown snake, *Storeria dekayi*, in Louisiana. Copeia 1979, 463–466.

Kofron, C. P. (1979b). Reproduction of aquatic snakes in south-central Louisiana. Herpetologica 35, 44–50.

Kofron, C. P. (1983). Female reproductive cycle of the neotropical snail-eating snake *Sibon sanniola* in northern Yucatan, Mexico. Copeia 1983, 963–969.

Krohmer, R. W. and Aldridge, R. D. 1985. Female reproductive cycle of the lined snake. *(Tropidoclonion lineatum)*. Herpetologica 41, 39–44.

Lande, R. (1983). A quantitative genetic theory of life history evolution. Ecology 63, 607–615.

Lauder, G. V. (1981). Form and function: Structural analysis in evolutionary morphology. Paleobiology 7, 430–442.

Lauder, G. V. (1982). Historical biology and the problem of design. J. Theor. Biol. 97, 57–67.

Law, R. (1979). Optimal life histories under age-specific predation. Am. Nat. 114, 399–417.

Lewontin, R. C. (1965). Selection for colonizing ability. In *The Genetics of Colonizing Species.* (H. G. Baker and G. L. Stebbins, eds.). Academic Press, New York, pp. 77–94.

Marion, K. R. and Sexton, O. J. (1971). The reproductive cycle of the lizard *Sceloporus malachiticus* in Costa Rica. Copeia 1971, 517–526.

Martin, R. F. (1977). Variation in reproductive productivity of range margin tree lizards. *(Urosaurus ornatus)*. Copeia 1977, 83–92.

Mayhew, W. W. (1963). Reproduction in the granite spiny lizard, *Sceloporus orcutti*. Copeia 1963, 144–152.

Mayhew, W. W. (1965). Reproduction in the sand-dwelling lizard, *Uma inornata*. Herpetologica 12, 39–55.

Mayhew, W. W. (1966a). Reproduction in the arenicolous lizard, *Uma notata*. Ecology 47, 9–18.

Mayhew, W. W. (1966b). Reproduction in the psammophilous lizard, *Uma scoparia*. Copeia 1966, 114–122.

Mayhew, W. W. (1971). Reproduction in the desert lizard, *Dipsosaurus dorsalis*. Herpetologica 27, 57–77.

McCoy, C. J. (1967). Natural history note on *Crotaphytus wislizeni* (Reptilia: Iguanidae) in Colorado. Am. Midl. Nat. 77, 138–146.

Medica, P. A. (1967). Food habits, habitat preference, reproduction, and diurnal activity in four sympatric species of whiptail lizards *(Cnemidophorus)* in south central New Mexico. Bull. So. Calif. Acad. Sci. 66, 251–276.

Michod, R. E. (1979). Evolution of life histories in response to age-specific mortality factors. Am. Nat. 113, 531–550.

Miller, M. R. (1951). Some aspects of the life history of the yucca night lizard, *Xantusia vigilis*. Copeia 1951, 114–120.

Miller, M.R. (1954). Further observations on reproduction in the lizard *Xantusia vigilis*. Copeia 1954, 38–40.

REFERENCES

Morris, M. A. (1982). Activity, reproduction, and growth of *Opheodrys aestivus* in Illinois (Serpentes: Colubridae). Chicago Acad. Sci. Nat. Hist. Misc. 214, 1–11.

Mount, R. H. (1963). The natural history of the red-tailed skink, *Eumeces egregius* Baird. Am. Midl. Nat. 70, 356–385.

Nagy, K. A., Huey, R. B. and Bennett, A. F. (1984). Field energetics and foraging mode of Kalahari lacertid lizards. Ecology 65, 588–596.

Newlin, M. E. (1976). Reproduction in the bunch grass lizard, *Sceloporus scalaris*. Herpetologica 32, 171–184.

Nussbaum, R. A. and Diller, L. V. (1976). The life history of the side-blotched lizard, *Uta stansburiana* Baird and Girard, in north-central Oregon. Northwest Science 50, 243–260.

Papenfuss, T. J. (1982). The ecology and systematics of the amphisbaenian genus *Bipes*. Occ. Pap. Calif. Acad. Sci. 136, 11–42.

Parker, W. S. (1972). Ecological study of the western whiptail lizard, *Cnemidophorus tigris gracilis*, in Arizona. Herpetologica 28, 360–369.

Parker, W. S. and Brown, W. S. (1980). Comparative ecology of two colubrid snakes, *Masticophis t. taeniatus* and *Pituophis melanoleucus deserticola*, in northern Utah. Publ. Milwaukee Pub. Mus. Biol. Geol. 7, 1–104.

Pearson, O. P. (1954). Habits of the lizard *Liolaemus multiformis multiformis* at high altitudes in southern Peru. Copeia 1954, 111–116.

Pianka, E. R. (1970). On r- and K-selection. Am. Nat. 104, 592–597.

Pianka, E. R. (1971a). Comparative ecology of two lizards. Copeia 1971, 129–138.

Pianka, E. R. (1971b). Ecology of the agamid lizard *Amphibolurus isolepis* in Western Australia. Copeia 1971, 527–536.

Pianka, E. R. (1986). *Ecology and Natural History of Desert Lizards*. Princeton University Press, Princeton, NJ.

Pianka, E. R. and Parker, W. S. (1972). Ecology of the iguanid lizard *Callisaurus draconoides*. Copeia 1972, 493–508.

Pianka, E. R. and Parker, W. S. (1975a). Ecology of horned lizards with special reference to *Phrynosoma platyrhinos*. Copeia 1975, 141–162.

Pianka, E. R. and Parker, W. S. (1975b). Age-specific reproductive tactics. Am. Nat. 109, 453–464.

Pianka, E. R. and Pianka, H. D. (1970). The ecology of *Moloch horridus* (Lacertilia: Agamidae) in Western Australia. Copeia 1970, 90–103.

Platt, D. R. (1969). Natural history of the hognose snakes, *Heterodon platyrhinos* and *Heterodon nasicus*. Univ. Kansas Publ. Mus. Nat. Hist. 18, 253–420.

Pilorge, T. (1981). Structure et dynamique d'une population du lézard vivipare. Significetion adaptive de la viviparité chez les lézards. Publ. Lab. Zool. E. N. S. 18, 1–152.

Plummer, M. V. (1983). Annual variation in stored lipids and reproduction in green snakes (*Opheodrys aestivus*). Copeia 1983. 741–745.

Plummer, M. V. (1984). Female reproduction in an Arkansas population of rough green snakes (*Opheodrys aestivus*). In *Vertebrate Ecology and Systematics: A Tribute to Henry S. Fitch*. (R. A. Seigel, L. E. Hunt, J. L. Knight, L. Malaret, and N. L. Zuschlag, eds.) Museum of Natural History, University of Kansas, Vol. 10, pp. 105–113.

Prestt, I. (1971). An ecological study of the viper *Vipera berus* in southern Britain. J. Zool. (Lond.) 164, 373–418.

Quinn, H. R. (1979). Reproduction and growth of the Texas coral snake *(Micrurus fulvius tenere)*. Copeia 1979, 453–463.

Rao, M. V. S. and Rajabi, B. S. (1972). Reproduction in the ground lizard, *Sitana ponticeriana* and the garden lizard, *Calotes nemercola*. Br. J. Herpetol. 4, 245–251.

Robertson, I. A. D., Chapman, B. M. and Chapman, R. F. (1965). Notes on the biology of the lizards *Agama cyanogaster* and *Mabuya striata striata* collected in the Rukwa Valley, southwest Tanganyika. Proc. Zool. Soc. Lond. 145, 305–320.

Routman, E. J. and Hulse, A. C. (1984). Ecology and reproduction of a parthenogenteic lizard, *Cnemidophorus sonorae*. J. Herpetol. 18, 381–386.

Ruby, D. E. and Dunham, A. E. (1984). A population analysis of the ovoviviparous lizard *Sceloporus jarrovi* in the Pinaleño Mountains of southeastern Arizona. Herpetologica 40, 425–436.

Ruibal, R., Philibosian, R., and Adkins, J. L. (1972). Reproductive cycle and growth in the lizard *Anolis acutus*. Copeia 1972, 509–518.

Schaffer, W. M. (1974). Selection for optimal life histories: The effects of age structure. Ecology 55, 291–303.

Schall, J. J. (1978). Reproductive strategies in sympatric whiptail lizards *(Cnemidophorus)*: Two parthenogenetic and three bisexual species. Copeia 1978, 108–116.

Schwaner, T. D. (1980). Reproductive biology of lizards on the American Samoan Islands. Occ. Pap. Mus. Nat. Hist. Univ. Kansas No. 86, 1–53.

Seigel, R. A. and Fitch, H. S. (1984). Ecological patterns of relative clutch mass in snakes. Oecologia 61, 293–301.

Seigel, R. A., Fitch, H. S. and Ford, N. B. (1986). Variation in relative clutch mass in snakes among and within species. Herpetologica, 42, 179–185.

Semlitsch, R. D. and Moran, G. B. (1984). Ecology of the red-bellied snake *(S. occipitomaculata)* using mesic habitats in South Carolina. Am. Midl. Nat. 111, 33–40.

Sexton, O. J., Ortleb, E. P., Hathaway, L. M., Ballinger, R. E. and Licht, P. (1971). Reproductive cycles of three species of anoline lizards from the isthmus of Panama. Ecology 52, 201–215.

Sherbrooke, W. C. (1975). Reproductive cycle of a tropical teiid lizard, *Neusticurus ecpleopus* Cope in Peru. Biotropica 7, 194–207.

Shine, R. (1977). Reproduction in Australian elapid snakes. II. Female reproductive cycles. Aust. J. Zool. 25, 655–666.

Shine, R. (1978). Growth rates and sexual maturation in six species of Australian elapid snakes. Herpetologica 34, 73–79.

Shine, R. (1980a). Ecology of the Australian death adder *Acanthophis antarcticus* (Elapidae): Evidence for convergence with the Viperidae. Herpetologica 36, 281–289.

Shine, R. (1980b). Comparative ecology of three Australian snake species of the genus *Cacophis* (Serpentes: Elapidae). Copeia 1980, 831–838.

Shine, R. (1980c). Ecology of eastern Australian whipsnakes of the genus *Demansia*. J. Herpetol. 14, 381–389.

Shine, R. (1980d). "Costs" of reproduction in reptiles. Oecologia (Berl.) 46, 92–100.

Shine, R. (1983). Food habits and reproductive biology of Australian elapid snakes of the genus *Denisonia*. J. Herpetol. 17, 171–175.

Shine, R. (1984a). Reproductive biology and food habits of the Australian elapid snakes of the genus *Cryptophis*. J. Herpetol. 18, 33–39.

Shine, R. (1984b). Ecology of small fossorial Australian snakes of the genera *Neelaps* and *Simoselaps* (Serpentes, Elapidae). In *Vertebrate Ecology and Systematics: A Tribute to Henry S. Fitch*. (R. A. Seigel, L. E. Hunt, J. L. Knight, and N. L. Zuschlag, eds.). Museum of Natural History, University of Kansas, Vol. 10, 173–183.

Shine, R. (1985). The evolution of viviparity in reptiles: An ecological analysis. In *Biology of the Reptilia* Vol. 15. (C. Gans and F. Billett, eds.). Wiley, New York, pp. 607–694.

Shine, R. (1986). Ecology of a low-energy specialist: food habits and reproductive biology of the Arafura file snake (Acrochordidae). Copeia 424–437.

REFERENCES

Simbotwe, M. P. (1980). Reproductive biology of the skinks *Mabuya striata* and *Mabuya quinquetaeniata* in Zambia. Herpetologica 36, 99–104.
Smith, D. C. (1977). Interspecific competition and the demography of two lizards. Ph. D. dissertation. University of Michigan, Ann Arbor.
Smith, M. (1951). *The British Amphibians and Reptiles*. Collins, London.
Smith, R. E. (1968). Reproduction in Costa Rican *Ameiva festiva* and *Ameiva quadrilineata* (Sauria: Teiidae). Copeia 1968, 236–239.
Smyth, M. and Smith, M. J. (1974). Aspects of the natural history of three Australian skinks, *Morethia boulengeri*, *Menetia grayii*, and *Lerista bouganvillii*. J. Herpetol. 8, 329–335.
Somma, C. A. and Brooks, G. R. (1976). Reproduction in *Anolis oculatus*, *Ameiva fuscata* and *Mabuya mabouya* from Dominica. Copeia 1976, 249–256.
Stearns, S. C. (1976). Life history tactics: A review of the ideas. Quart. Rev. Biol. 51, 3–47.
Stearns, S. C. (1977). The evolution of life history traits. Ann. Rev. Ecol. Syst. 8, 145–171.
Stearns, S. C. (1980). A new view of life history evolution. Oikos 35, 266–281.
Stearns, S. C. (1983). The impact of size and phylogeny on patterns of covariation in the life-history traits of mammals. Oikos 41, 173–187.
Stearns, S. C. (1984). The effects of size and phylogeny on patterns of covariation in the life history traits of lizards and snakes. Am. Nat. 123, 56–72.
Stebbins, R. C., Lowenstein, J. M. and Cohen, N. W. (1967). A field study of the lava lizard (*Tropidurus albemarlensis*) in the Galapagos Islands. Ecology 48, 839–851.
Stewart, G. R. (1968). Some observations on the natural history of two Oregon garter snakes (Genus *Thamnophis*). J. Herpetol. 2, 71–86.
Stewart, J. R. (1985). Growth and survivorship in a California population of *Gerrhonotus coeruleus*, with comments on intraspecific variation in female size. Am. Midl. Nat. 113, 30–44.
Takenaka, S. 1980. Growth of the Japanese grass lizard *Takydromus tachydromoides* in relation to reproduction. Herpetologica 36, 305–310.
Taylor, J. A. (1985). Reproductive biology of the Australian lizard *Ctenotus taeniolatus*. Herpetologica 41, 408–418.
Telford, S. R. (1969). The ovarian cycle, reproductive potential, and structure in a population of the Japanese lizard *Takydromus tachydromoides*. Copeia 1969, 548–567.
Telford, S. R. (1971). Reproductive patterns and relative abundance of two microteiid lizard species in Panama. Copeia 1971, 670–675.
Tinkle, D. W. (1957). Ecology, maturation and reproduction of *Thamnophis sauritus proximus*. Ecology 38, 69–77.
Tinkle, D. W. (1962). Reproductive potential and cycles in female *Crotalus atrox* from northwestern Texas. Copeia 1962, 306–313.
Tinkle, D. W. (1967). The life and demography of the side-blotched lizard, *Uta stansburiana*. Misc. Publ. Mus. Zool. Univ. Michigan 132, 1–182.
Tinkle, D. W. (1969). The concept of reproductive effort and its relation to the evolution of life histories in lizards. Am. Nat. 103, 501–516.
Tinkle, D. W. (1972). The dynamics of a Utah population of *Sceloporus undalatus*. Herpetologica 28, 351–359.
Tinkle, D. W. (1973). A population analysis of the sagebrush lizard, *Sceloporus graciosus* in southern Utah. Copeia 1973, 284–296.
Tinkle, D. W. (1976). Comparative data on the population ecology of the spiny lizard, *Sceloporus magister*. Herpetologica 32, 1–6.
Tinkle, D. W. and Ballinger, R. E. (1972). *Sceloporus undulatus*: A study of the interspecific comparative demography of a lizard. Ecology 53, 570–584.

Tinkle, D. W. and Dunham, A. E. (1983). Demography of the tree lizard, *Urosaurus ornatus*, in central Arizona. Copeia 1983, 585–598.

Tinkle, D. W. and Dunham, A. E. (1986). Comparative life histories of two syntopic sceloporine lizards. Copeia 1986, 1–18.

Tinkle, D. W. and Hadley, N. F. (1973). Reproductive effort and winter activity in the viviparous montane lizard *Sceloporus jarrovi*. Copeia 1973, 272–276.

Tinkle, D. W., Wilbur, H. M. and Tilley, S. G. (1970). Evolutionary strategies in lizard reproduction. Evolution 24, 55–74.

Trendall, J. T. (1982). Covariation of life history traits in the mosquitofish, *Gambusia affinis*. Am. Nat. 119, 774–783.

Turner, F. B., Hoddenbach, G. A., Medica, P. A. and Lannom, J. R. (1970). The demography of the lizard, *Uta stansburiana* Baird and Girard, in southern Nevada. J. Anim. Ecol. 39, 505–519.

Van Devender, R. W. (1982). Comparative demography of the lizard *Basiliscus basiliscus*. Herpetologica 38, 189–208.

Van Loben Sels, R. C. and Vitt, L. J. (1984). Desert lizard reproduction: Seasonal and annual variation in *Urosaurus ornatus*. Can. J. Zool. 62, 1779–1787.

Vial, J. L. and Stewart, J. R. (1985). The reproductive cycle of *Barisa monticola*: A unique variation among viviparous lizards. Herpetologica 41, 51–57.

Vinegar, M. B. (1975a). Demography of the striped plateau lizard, *Sceloporus virgatus*. Ecology 56, 172–182.

Vinegar, M. B. (1975b). Life history phenomena in two populations of the lizard *Sceloporus undulatus* in southwestern New Mexico. Am. Midl. Nat. 93, 388–402.

Vitt, L. J. (1973). Reproductive biology of the anguid lizard, *Gerrhonotus coeruleus principis*. Herpetologica 29, 176–184.

Vitt, L. J. (1980). Ecological observations on sympatric *Philodryas* (Colubridae) in northeastern Brazil. Papeis Avulsos de Zoologia 34, 87–98.

Vitt, L. J. (1981). Lizard reproduction: Habitat specificity and constraints on relative clutch mass. Am. Nat. 117, 506–514.

Vitt, L. J. (1982a). Reproductive tactics of *Ameiva ameiva* (Lacertillia: Teiidae) in a seasonally fluctuating tropical habitat. Can. J. Zool. 60, 3113–3120.

Vitt, L. J. (1982b). Sexual dimorphism and reproduction in the microteid lizard, *Gymnophthalmus multiscutatus*. J. Herpetol. 16, 325–329.

Vitt, L. J. (1983a). Reproductive ecology of two tropical iguanid lizards: *Tropidurus torquatus* and *Platynotus semitaeniatus*. Copeia 1983, 131–141.

Vitt, L. J. (1983b). Reproduction and sexual dimorphism in the tropical teiid lizard *Cnemidophorus ocellifer*. Copeia 1983, 359–366.

Vitt, L. J. (1983c). Ecology of an anuran-eating guild of terrestrial tropical snakes. Herpetologica 39, 52–66.

Vitt, L. J. (1986). Reproductive tactics of sympatric gekkonid lizards: With a comment on the evolutionary and ecological consequences on invariant clutch size. Copeia 1986, 773–786.

Vitt, L. J. and Blackburn, D. G. (1983). Reproduction in the lizard *Mabuya heathi* (Scincidae): A comment on viviparity in New World *Mabuya*. Can. J. Zool. 61, 2798–2806.

Vitt, L. J. and Congdon, J. D. (1978). Body shape, reproductive effort and relative clutch mass in lizards: Resolution of a paradox. Am. Nat. 112, 595–608.

Vitt, L. J. and Cooper, W. E., Jr. (1985). The relationship between reproduction and lipid cycling in the skink *Eumeces laticeps* with comments on brooding ecology. Herpetologica 41, 419–432.

REFERENCES

Vitt, L. J. and Cooper, W. E., Jr. (1986). Skink reproduction and sexual dimorphism: *Eumeces fasciatus* in the southeastern United States, with notes on *Eumeces inexpectatus*. J. Herpetol. 20, 65–76.

Vitt, L. J. and Goldberg, S. R. (1983). Reproductive ecology of two tropical iguanid lizards: *Tropidurus torquatus* and *Platynotus semitaeniatus*. Copeia 1983, 131–141.

Vitt, L. J., Howland, J. M. and Dunham, A. E. (1985). The effect of formalin fixation on the weight of lizard eggs. J. Herpetol. 19, 298–299.

Vitt, L. J. and Lacher, T. E. (1981). Behavior, habitat, diet and reproduction of the iguanid lizard *Polychrus acutirostris* in the Caatinga of northeastern Brazil. Herpetologica 37, 53–63.

Vitt, L. J. and Ohmart, R. D. (1974). Reproduction and ecology of a Colorado River population of *Sceloporus magister* (Sauria: Iguanidae). Herpetologica 30, 410–417.

Vitt, L. J. and Ohmart, R. D. (1975). Ecology, reproduction and reproductive effort of the iguanid lizard *Urosaurus graciosus* on the lower Colorado River. Herpetologica 31, 56–65.

Vitt, L. J. and Price, H. J. (1982). Ecological and evolutionary determinants of relative clutch mass in lizards. Herpetologica 38, 237–255.

Vitt, L. J. and Seigel, R. A. (1985). Life history traits of lizards and snakes. Am. Nat. 125, 480–484.

Vitt, L. J., Van Loben Sels, R. C. and Ohmart, R. D. (1978). Lizard reproduction: Annual variation and environmental correlates in the iguanid lizard *Urosaurus graciosus*. Herpetologica 34, 241–253.

Voris, H. K. and Jayne, B. D. (1979). Growth, reproduction and population structure of a marine snake, *Enhydrina schistosa* (Hydrophiidae). Copeia 1979, 307–318.

Walker, J. M. (1980). Reproductive characteristics of the San Pedro Martir whiptail, *Cnemidophorus martyris*. J. Herpetol. 14, 431–432.

Walker, J. M. (1982). Reproductive characteristics of the Colima giant whiptail (*Cnemidophorus communis communis* Cope). Southwest. Nat. 27, 241–244.

Wharton, C. H. (1966). Reproduction and growth in the cottonmouths, *Agkistrodon piscivorus* Lacepede, of Cedar Keys, Florida. Copeia 1966, 149–161.

White, D. R., Mitchell, J. C. and Woolcott, W. S. (1982). Reproductive cycle and embryonic development of *Nerodia taxispilota* (Serpentes: Colubridae) at the northeastern edge of its range. Copeia 1982, 646–652.

Wilbur, H. M., Tinkle, D. W. and Collins, J. P. (1974). Environmental certainty, trophic level and resource availability in life history evolution. Am. Nat. 108, 805–817.

APPENDIX

Species	Mode	Age	FEMAT	FSVL	B	CF	CS	OFFSVL	RCM	FM	D	H	Source
Sauria													
Agamidae													
Agama agama	1	12.0	75.0	85.0	2	2.0	7.50	32.0			2	2	40
Agama agama	1	12.0		97.0	2		5.50			2	2	2	84
Amphibolurus fordi	1	8.5	48.0				2.26				1		39
Amphibolurus isolepis	1	7.5	51.0	61.0	2	2.0	3.33	24.0		2	1	2	119
Amphibolurus ornatus	1	12.0	69.0		2	2.0	3.75			2	1	1	22
Amphibolurus nuchalis	1	9.0	67.0		2	3.0	3.43			2	1	1	22
Amphibolurus nuchalis	1	12.0	86.0	88.3	2	2.0	4.10				1	3	118
Calotes nemoricola	1	8.0	64.0	98.3			13.30	25.2			2	4	128
Calotes versicolor	1	12.0	100.0		2		15.00				2		5
Draco melanopogon	1		75.0	84.0	2		1.92				2	4	91
Draco quinquefasciatus	1		85.9	97.4	2		2.71				2	4	91
Japalura swinhonis	1	11.6	53.5	76.1	2	2.0	4.27	20.0		2	1	4	95
Moloch horridus	1	12.0	86.0	93.8	1	1.0	7.23		0.157	2	1	1	122
Sitana ponticeriana	1	11.0	36.0	52.7			11.20	16.9			2	1	128
Chamaeleonidae													
Chamaeleo pumilus	2	6.0	51.0	78.8	2	4.0	11.0	22.0	0.256	2	1	4	27
Chamaeleo namaquensis	1	5.0	81.0	120.4	2	3.0	13.2	32.5	0.272	1	1	2	27
Anguidae													
Anguis fragilis	2	36.0	120.0		1	1.0	9.00				1		148
Barisia monticola	2		64.0	72.0	3	0.5	3.43			2	2		172
Barisia coerulea	2	35.9	80.0	100.0	1	1.0	6.20			2	1	1	49
Barisia coerulea	2		72.0	91.4	1	1.0	4.60	32.7		2	1	3	175
Barisia coerulea	2	32.0	75.0	87.7	1	1.0	3.80	35.9	0.250	2	1	1	154
Celestes costatus	2		75.0	84.9			5.60				2		77
Celestes crusculus	2		56.0	63.0			3.40				2		77
Gerrhonotus multicarinatus	1	18.0	92.0	108.8	2	2.0	12.00	34.0		2	1	1	70
Gerrhonotus multicarinatus	1		113.0		1	1.0	11.60				1		49

Gekkonidae										
Cosymbotus platyurus	1		50.0	54.8	2	2.00			2	35
Cyrtodactylus malayanus	1		97.9	107.7	2	1.97			2 4	91
Cyrtodactylus pubisculus	1		68.9	73.3	2	1.93			2 4	91
Gehyra mutilata	1		50.0	52.5	2	2.00			2	35
Gehyra oceanica	1		70.0			2.00			2 4	134
Gehyra variegata	1	20.0	45.0	52.5	2 2.0	1.96	29.0		2 1	30
Gymnodactylus geckoides	1		38.0	42.8	2	1.00	24.0	0.250	2 2 3	182
Hemidactylus frenatus	1		44.0	51.4	2	1.00	20.0	0.084	2 2 4	35
Hemidactylus frenatus	1		40.0			2.00			2 4	134
Heteronotia binoei	1	19.0	39.0	45.0	1 1.0	2.00	20.5		2 1 4	31,32
Lepidodactylus lugubris	1		35.0			2.00	18.0	0.099	2 2 1	134
Lygodactylus klugei	1		25.5	29.7	2 2.0	2.00	17.1		2 2 4	134
Lygodactylus picturatus	1		28.0			2.00	14.0	0.169	2 2 4	182
Lygodactylus somalicus	1		24.5		2	2.00	13.0		2 2 4	76
Nactus pelagicus	1		55.0			1.80	11.5		2 2 4	76
Oedura tryoni	1	25.0	73.0	80.0	2 2.0	2.00	35.0	0.350	2 1	134
Oedura reticulata	1	48.0	62.5	66.3	1 1.0	2.11	26.0		2 2 1 4	33
Phyllopezus pollicaris	1		65.0	75.5	2	2.00	29.0	0.114	2 2 4	87
									2 4	182
Gymnophthalmidae										
Gymnophthalmus multiscutatus	1		31.0	35.9	2 2.0	2.00		0.161	1 2 1	178
Gymnophthalmus speciosus	1	7.0	37.0	41.5	2 2.0	1.83	18.0		2 5	158
Leposoma rugiceps	1	7.0	37.0		1 1.0	2.17	18.1		2 2	158
Iguanidae										
Anolis acutus	1	11.5	36.0	42.2	2 6.0	1.00	20.0		2 2 4	132
Anolis carolinensis	1	12.0	46.5	50.0	2 6.0	1.30	23.5		2 1 4	83
Anolis cupreus	1	11.0	35.6		2	1.00			2 2 4	63
Anolis humilis	1		35.0	40.0		1.13	17.4		2 2 1	4
Anolis limifrons	1		35.0	40.0		1.10	16.0		2 2 4	4
Anolis limifrons	1	8.0	38.0	44.0	2 2.0	1.00	18.5		2 2 4	136
Anolis oculatus	1		48.0	61.0		1.00	23.8		2 2 4	4

(Continued)

APPENDIX (Continued)

Species	Mode	Age	FEMAT	FSVL	B	CF	CS	OFFSVL	RCM	FM	D	H	Source
Sauria (Continued)													
Iguanidae (Continued)													
Anolis oculatus	1	3.0	40.0	43.0	2		1.00	23.0		2	2	4	151
Anolis tropidolepis	1	8.5	42.0	50.3	2	6.0	1.00			2	2	4	58
Basiliscus basiliscus	1	20.0	135.0	168.0	2	6.0	9.49	42.0		2	2	1	170
Callisaurus draconoides	1	12.0	63.0	75.5	2	2.0	4.42	29.0	0.140	2	1	3	120
Cophosaurus texanus	1	12.0	50.0	60.0	2	3.0	6.10	22.0	0.218	2	1	3	16
Crotaphytus collaris	1	10.0	92.0	96.0	2	2.0	7.55	42.0		2	1	3	52
Crotaphytus collaris	1	9.5	70.0	85.1	2	2.0	7.47			2	1	1	14
Ctenosaura similis	1	21.0	200.0	276.0	1	1.0	43.40	57.0		2	2		62
Cyclura carinata	1	78.0	190.0	225.0	1	1.0	4.30	80.0			2		92
Dipsosaurus dorsalis	1	66.0	110.0	120.0	1	1.0	3.50			2	1	1	106
Dipsosaurus dorsalis	1				1	1.0	5.50			2	1	1	118
Gambelia wislizeni	1	22.0	96.0	105.4			7.30	44.6		2	1	1	107
Holbrookia maculata	1	12.0	45.0	54.0	2					2	1		67
Holbrookia maculata	1	12.0	42.5	49.8	2	2.0	3.50		0.184	2	1		43
Holbrookia maculata	1	12.0	45.0	54.0	2		6.10			2	1		169
Holbrookia propinqua	1	10.0	44.0	49.6	2	3.0	3.07			2	1		94
Liolaemus multiformis	2	16.0	69.0	80.6	1	1.0	5.80	28.0		2	2		117
Phrynosoma cornutum	1	24.0	70.0	87.7	1	1.0	29.00		0.310	2	1	1	10
Phrynosoma douglassi	2	24.0	66.0		1	1.0	16.00		0.254	2	1	1	121
Phrynosoma platyrhinos	1	22.0	70.0	76.5	1	1.0	8.40	27.4	0.219	2	1	1	121
Polychrus acutirostris	1	8.5	96.0	125.0	1	1.0	11.60		0.401	2	2	4	187
Sauromalus obesus	1	62.0	150.0	170.0	1	1.0	8.60	54.0		2	1	1	20
Sceloporus clarki	1	22.0	90.0	100.5	2	1.0	19.10			2	1	4	167
Sceloporus cyanogenys	2	35.9	88.0	106.0	1	1.0	13.00	29.6		2	1		90
Sceloporus graciosus	1	22.0	48.6	51.7	2	2.0	3.80	25.1	0.160	2	1	3	163
Sceloporus grammicus	2	12.0	42.0	48.5	1	1.0	5.20			2	2		81

Species											
Sceloporus jarrovi	2	15.0	65.0	77.0	1	1.0	8.40	28.5		2	1	3	9,13
Sceloporus jarrovi	2	5.0	54.0	72.4	1	1.0	7.07	28.5		2	1	3	9,13
Sceloporus jarrovi	2	5.0	54.0	72.0	1	1.0	5.60	30.7		2	1	3	131
Sceloporus jarrovi	2	6.0	55.0	75.2	1	1.0	6.75		0.150	2	1	3	168
Sceloporus magister	1	22.0	80.0	89.0	2	2.0	6.20	32.0	0.150	2	1	4	164, 188
Sceloporus malachiticus	2	18.0	65.0	79.6	1	1.0	6.00		0.190	2	2		100
Sceloporus merriami	1	12.0	43.0	50.2	2	2.0	4.51	22.0		2	1	3	44,45
Sceloporus orcutti	1	36.0	87.0	92.0	1	1.0	11.00			2	1	3	102
Sceloporus poinsetti	2	16.5	86.0	104.0	1	1.0	10.40	32.0		2	1	1	9
Sceloporus scalaris	1	8.9	47.0	51.3	1	1.0	8.38			2	1	1	113
Sceloporus undulatus	1	12.0	47.0	57.0	2	2.0	7.00		0.390	2	1	1	48
Sceloporus undulatus	1	9.5	45.0	54.5	2	2.0	5.55		0.280	2	1	2	15
Sceloporus undulatus	1	12.0	54.0	68.4	2	4.0	9.90	25.0	0.330	2	1	1	174
Sceloporus undulatus	1	24.0	58.0	69.0	2	3.0	6.30	25.0	0.211	2	1	4	162
Sceloporus undulatus	1	24.0	58.0	70.0	2	2.0	7.90	28.0	0.210	2	1	3	165
Sceloporus undulatus	1	12.0	55.0	63.0	2	3.0	7.40	23.0	0.230	2	1	1	165
Sceloporus undulatus	1	20.0	66.0	75.0	2	3.0	11.80	25.0	0.230	2	1	4	165
Sceloporus undulatus	1	12.0	47.0	57.0	2	3.0	9.50	22.0	0.250	2	1	4	165
Sceloporus undulatus	1	12.0	53.0	63.3	2	2.5	7.20		0.270	2	1	4	165
Sceloporus undulatus	1	11.0	60.0	64.7	2	3.0	8.30	27.0	0.211	2	1	3	174
Sceloporus virgatus	1	22.0	47.0	48.2	1	1.0	9.50	21.5	0.220	2	1	1	167
Tropidurus albemarlensis	1		54.0	63.0			2.27		0.291	2	2		173
Tropidurus semitaeniatus	1		58.0	70.5	2	3.5	2.00	19.0	0.150	2	2	1	152
Tropidurus torquatus	1		70.0	88.5	2	3.0	6.00	27.8	0.258	2	2	1	179,186
Uma notata	1	24.0	70.0	81.0	2	3.0	2.50			2	1	2	186
Uma notata	1	24.0	64.0	76.0	2	2.0	2.10			2	2	2	103
Uma notata	1	24.0	70.0	83.0	2	2.0	2.60			2	1	2	104
Urosaurus graciosus	1	8.0	47.0	52.2	2	1.5	5.30		0.313	2	1	2	105
Urosaurus graciosus	1	8.0	44.0	51.8	2	2.0	4.24			2	1	4	189
Urosaurus ornatus	1	11.0	39.0	48.1	2	1.5	9.00	24.5	0.400	2	1	4	190
Urosaurus ornatus	1	9.5	40.0	49.3	2	1.3	9.00	21.0	0.500	2	1	3	11,12
Urosaurus ornatus	1	10.5	41.0	48.4	2	3.0	4.70	21.0	0.310	2	1	4	45,46
Urosaurus ornatus										2	1	3	45,46

(Continued)

APPENDIX (Continued)

Species	Mode	Age	FEMAT	FSVL	B	CF	CS	OFFSVL	RCM	FM	D	H	Source
Sauria (Continued)													
Iguanidae (Continued)													
Urosaurus ornatus	1	12.0	39.0	47.8	2	3.5	5.36	21.0	0.230	2	1	4	101
Urosaurus ornatus	1	8.5	45.0	50.6	2	2.0	7.10		0.360	2	1	4	166
Urosaurus ornatus	1	8.5	45.0		2	2.0	7.40		0.210	2	1	4	171
Uta stansburiana	1	10.0	41.0	45.4	2	1.0	3.33	22.0	0.231	2	1	3	114
Uta stansburiana	1	9.0	42.0	48.9	2	3.0	3.90	22.0	0.200	2	1	2	161
Lacertidae													
Aporosaura anchietae	1	5.0	44.0	44.0	2	3.0	1.30	27.0	0.138	1	1	2	73
Lacerta agilis	1	24.0	55.0		1	1.0	9.50				1	1	148
Lacerta monticola	1	36.0	67.3		1	1.0	6.50	25.9		1	1	1	47
Lacerta vivipara	2	18.0	48.0	57.6	1	1.0	7.74		0.400	2	1	1	6,7
Meroles cuneirostris	1	7.0		49.0	2	2.0	2.90	27.5	0.137	1	1	1	73
Podarcis taurica	1	19.0	52.0	65.0	2	2.0	5.60		0.194	1	1	1	34
Takydromus tachydromoides	1	12.0	40.0	53.0	2	3.0	3.60				1	1	169
Takydromus tachydromoides	1	12.0	41.0	45.7	2	3.0	3.63	22.0	0.300		1	1	157
Takydromus tachydromoides	1	12.0	42.0	56.0	2	3.0	4.20		0.290		1	1	155
Scincidae													
Cryptoblepharus boutonii	1		40.0				1.93				2	3	134
Ctenotus taeniolatus	1	24.0	52.3	66.4	1	1.0	3.70	33.0		1	1	1	156
Egernia whitii	2		78.0	80.7	1	1.0	3.50	35.0			1	1	86
Emoia adspersa	1		70.0				1.90				2	1	134
Emoia atrocostata	1	9.0	80.0	89.9	2	3.0	2.00	35.0			2	1	1
Emoia cyanura	1		40.0				1.96	22.0	0.170		2	1	134
Emoia laxvesi	1		85.0				1.80	32.0	0.121		2	1	134
Emoia nigra	1		86.0				2.32	39.1	0.115		2	1	134
Emoia samoensis	1		84.0				5.30	31.0	0.127		2	4	134
Eumeces copei	2	24.0	60.0	67.8	1	1.0	3.53	24.7			2	2	80

Species										
Eumeces egregius	1	12.0	40.0		1	1.0	4.80	20.6		1	5	112
Eumeces fasciatus	1	24.0	65.0		1	1.0	9.16			1	1	50
Eumeces fasciatus	1	21.0	52.0	72.5	1	1.0	5.90	24.0	0.360	1	1	185
Eumeces laticeps	1	21.0	85.0	63.3	1	1.0	13.70	31.4	0.341	1	1	184
Eumeces obsoletus	1	36.0	107.0	103.8	1	1.0	11.40			1	5	51
Eumeces okadae	1		72.0		1	1.0	7.60			1		85
Eumeces septentrionalis	1	36.0		78.9	1	1.0	8.79	25.5		1	5	24
Eumeces skiltonianus	1	30.0	58.0	65.0	1	1.0	4.40			1		169
Lampropholis delicata	1			64.0	1	1.0	4.70			1		8
Lipinia noctua	2		39.0				1.75	15.5		2	1	8
Leiolopisma zelandicum	2	24.0	54.0		1	1.0	5.10			2	4	134
Lerista bougainvillei	1		52.5	59.4	1	1.0	2.83			1	1	18
Mabuya buettneri	1	6.0	84.0		2	1.5	8.40			1	5	150
Mabuya heathi	2	4.0	45.0	70.3	1	1.0	5.00	32.4	0.326	2	4	17
Mabuya mabouya	2	12.0	65.0				3.30	29.0		2		183
Mabuya maculilabris	1	6.0	58.0		2	5.5	5.50			2		151
Mabuya quinquetaeniata	1	15.0	87.0	96.6	2		4.80			2	1	17
Mabuya striata	2	15.0	61.0	78.1	2	2.0	4.20			2	3	147
Mabuya striata	2	12.0	62.0	70.0			7.00		1	2	1	147
Menetia greyii	1	12.0	28.5	34.6	2	2.0	2.00			2		129
Morethia boulengeri	1	24.0	45.0	51.6	1	1.0	3.68	17.0		1	1	150
Panaspis nimbaensis	1	6.0	45.0		2	5.0	2.50			1	1	150
Scincella lateralis	1	9.0	35.0	41.5	2	2.0	2.50			2		17
Scincella lateralis	1	12.0	38.0	47.0	2	4.0	3.80	19.0		1	1	25
Sphenomorphus cherriei	1	12.0	44.0	53.8	2	2.0	2.00			1		61
Sphenomorphus tanneri	1		41.0	45.1			2.00			2	5	75
Typhlosaurus gariepensis	2	32.0	118.0	123.0	1	1.0	1.00		0.170	2	5	78
Typhlosaurus lineatus	2	32.0	123.0	142.0	1	1.0	1.60		0.204	2	5	88
Teiidae												88
Ameiva ameiva	1		102.0	128.8	2		5.70		0.159	1	2	1	177
Ameiva festiva	1	12.0	77.0	87.3	2	3.0	2.20				2	2	149
Ameiva fuscata	1		105.0	111.0	2		4.00			1	2	1	151

(Continued)

APPENDIX (Continued)

Species	Mode	Age	FEMAT	FSVL	B	CF	CS	OFFSVL	RCM	FM	D	H	Source
Sauria (Continued)													
Teiidae (Continued)													
Ameiva quadrilineata	1	12.0	48.0	74.0	2	3.0	2.07				2		149
Cnemidophorus communis	1			96.5			6.60			1	1	1	193
Cnemidophorus exsanguis	1	11.0	60.0	75.0	1	1.0	2.72			1	1	1	108
Cnemidophorus hyperythrus	1	11.0	53.0	59.7	2	2.0	2.30	27.0		1	1	1	21
Cnemidophorus inornatus	1	12.0	48.2	58.0	2	2.0	2.15			1	1	1	108
Cnemidophorus martyris	1	11.0		68.0	2		1.29			1	1	1	192
Cnemidophorus neomexicanus	1	12.0	46.70	65.0	2	2.0	1.59			1	1	1	108
Cnemidophorus ocellifer	1		55.0	69.4	2	3.0	2.69		0.207	1	2	1	180
Cnemidophorus sexlineatus	1	24.0	55.0	72.8	2	2.0	2.10	32.0		1	1	1	53
Cnemidophorus sonorae	1		61.0	77.9	2	2.0	3.70		0.160	1	1	1	130
Cnemidophorus tesselatus	1	24.0		83.0	2	2.0	3.23		0.126	1	1	1	133
Cnemidophorus tigris	1	33.0	83.0	98.5	2	2.0	4.10	37.0	0.150	1	1	1	71
Cnemidophorus tigris	1	12.0	61.0	72.0	2	2.0	2.00			1	1	1	108
Cnemidophorus tigris	1	21.5	64.5	76.7	2	3.0	2.05	39.0	0.109	1	1	1	115
Cnemidophorus tigris	1	22.0	69.0	81.2	1	1.0	2.65			1	1	1	29
Cnemidophorus uniparens	1	10.0	58.0	65.5	2	2.0	2.77	36.0	0.144	1	1	1	89
Neusticurus ecpleopus	1		50.0	56.6	2		2.00	21.5		1	2	1	137
Xantusiidae													
Klauberina riversiana	2	42.0	75.0	88.4	1	1.0	3.76		0.268	2	1	1	72
Xantusia vigilis	2	36.0		41.0	1	1.0	1.79			2	1	1	110
Xantusia vigilis	2	36.0	38.0	39.0	1	1.0	1.78	23.0		2	1	1	109
Serpentes													
Acrochordidae													
Acrochordus arafurae	2		1130.0	1350.0	1	1.0	17.00	360.0	0.53	2	2	6	146
Acrochordus granulatus	2		600.0	665.0	1	1.0	4.13	260.0		1	2	6	74

Species											
Colubridae											
Arizona elegans		500.0	660.0	1	8.40		210.0		1	1	2
Carphophis vermis	25.5	250.0	284.4	1	2.99	1.0	114.5		1	5	36
Cerberus rhynchops		440.0	495.0	1	3.60	1.0			2	6	74
Coluber constrictor	24.0	743.0	914.0	1	11.80	1.0	214.5	0.40	1	1	56
Coluber constrictor	36.0	570.0	633.0	1	5.78	1.0	225.7	0.44	1	1	26
Diadophis punctatus	33.0	235.0	281.7	1	3.90	1.0	111.5	0.40	1	1	59
Elaphe climacophora	44.0	1080.0	1550.0	1	8.05	1.0	400.0		1	1	64
Elaphe obsoleta	48.0	900.0	1000.0	1	14.50		290.0	0.34	1		55
Farancia erytrogramma	36.0	900.0	923.0				189.0				69
Heterodon nasicus	21.0	366.0	560.0	3	9.50	0.5	153.0	0.41	1	1	123
Heterodon platyrhinos	21.0	500.0	560.0	3	19.10	0.5	234.0	0.44	1	1	123
Homalopsis buccata		400.0		1	9.26	1.0			2	6	19
Lampropeltis triangulum	36.0	530.0		1	6.70	1.0	200.0	0.44	1	1	60
Liophis lineatus	12.0	426.0	501.0	2	6.79		179.0	0.265		2	181
Liophis mossoroensis	12.0	460.0	537.0	2	6.20		230.1	0.153		2	181
Liophis poecilogyrus	12.0	490.0	605.0	2	7.38		136.0	0.123		2	181
Liophis viridis	12.0	382.0	437.0	2	3.69		160.0	0.196		2	181
Masticophis taeniatus	36.0	720.0	889.0	1	5.80	1.0	287.5	0.41	1	1	116
Nerodia cyclopion	48.0		813.3	1	18.40	1.0		0.23	1	6	97
Nerodia taxispilota		725.0	738.0	1	33.20	1.0	185.0		1	1	195
Opheodrys aestivus	24.0	347.0		1	6.10	1.0	26.0		1		111
Opheodrys aestivus	21.0	360.0	478.0	1	6.10	1.0	139.0	0.37	1	4	124,125
Philodryas nattereri		760.0	944.0	1	7.60	1.0		0.08	1	2	176
Philodryas olfersi		650.0	831.4	1	6.60	1.0	229.5	0.35	1	2	176
Pituophis melanoleucus	36.0	720.0	985.0	1	7.40	1.0	331.1	0.39	1	1	116
Regina grahami	30.0	500.0		1	15.00	1.0			1	6	82
Regina septemvittata	24.0	344.0	509.1	1	12.80	1.0	178.0	0.32	1	6	23
Sibon sanniola	8.0	201.0	228.0	1	3.40	1.0				2	98
Spalerosophis diadema	48.0		483.0	1	8.00	1.0			1	1	42
Storeria dekayi	24.0	170.0	230.0	1	14.90	1.0	37.6	0.35	2	1	96
Storeria occipitomaculata	21.0	126.0	157.3	1	9.00	1.0			1	6	135
Thamnophis ordinoides	24.0	360.0	527.2	1	9.50	1.0	61.2		1	1	153
Thamnophis proximus	24.0	515.0	571.0	1	8.40	1.0	139.0	0.28	1	1	37
Thamnophis sauritus	24.0	485.0	595.0	1	12.90	1.0			1	1	159

(Continued)

APPENDIX (Continued)

Species	Mode	Age	FEMAT	FSVL	B	CF	CS	OFFSVL	RCM	FM	D	H	Source
Serpentes (Continued)													
Colubridae (Continued)													
Thamnophis sirtalis	2	21.0	504.0	550.0	1	1.0	14.50	167.9	0.27	1	1	1	57
Thamnophis sirtalis	2	24.0	400.0	580.0	3	0.5	16.43	154.0		1	1	1	79
Thamnophis sirtalis	2	24.0	435.0	518.1	1	1.0	11.30	185.0		1	1	6	153
Tropidoclonion lineatum	2	20.0	221.0	240.0	1	1.0	7.10	89.5		1	1	5	99
Virginia striatula	2	24.0	197.0	218.0	1	1.0	5.25				1	1	38
Waglerophis merremii	1	12.0	688.0	862.0	2		16.05		0.185		2	1	181
Elapidae													
Acanthophis antarcticus	2	42.0		520.0	3	0.5	7.90	110.0		1	1	1	140
Austrelaps superbus	2	24.0	490.0	706.0	1	1.0	16.50	146.4	0.28		1	1	138,139
Cacophis harriettae	1	32.0	290.0	357.0	1	1.0	5.10			2	1		141
Cacophis krefftii	1	20.0	220.0	272.0	1						1		141
Cacophis squamulosus	1	32.0	370.0	484.0	1	1.0	6.20		0.32	2	1		141
Cryptophis nigrescens	2		285.0	357.0	1	1.0	4.10	152.0	0.60	1	1		144
Cryptophis pallidiceps	2		365.0	427.0			4.00			1	1		144
Demansia psammophis	1			529.0	1	1.0	6.03	172.0		1	1		142
Denisonia devisii	2	20.0	273.0	361.0			4.93	120.0			1	1	143
Hemiaspis signata	2	12.0	350.0	433.0	1	1.0	10.30	130.8	0.28	1	1		138,139
Micrurus fulvius	1	34.0	580.0	727.0	1	1.0	6.00	190.5		1	1	1	93
Micrurus fulvius	1	21.0	490.0	550.0	1	1.0	5.40	185.0		1	1	1	127
Neelaps bimaculatus	1			336.0	1	1.0	4.20	142.0			1	5	145
Neelaps calonotus	1			224.0	1	1.0	3.50				1	5	145
Notechis scutatus	2	24.0	650.0	808.0	1	1.0	23.60	189.4	0.42		1	1	138,139
Pseudechis porphyriacus	2	31.0	880.0	1061.0	1	1.0	12.40	237.6	0.22	1	1	1	138,139
Simoselaps bertholdi	1	20.0		208.0	1	1.0	3.50				1	5	145
Simoselaps fasciolatus	1	32.0		294.0	1	1.0	5.00				1	5	145
Unechis gouldii	2	12.0	230.0	302.0	1	1.0	4.30	138.9	0.58		1	1	138,139

Species														
Hydrophiidae														
Enhydrina schistosa	2	20.0	730.0	850.0	1	1.0	17.73		230.0			2	6	191
Viperidae														
Agkistrodon contortrix	2		36.0	520.0	625.0	3	0.5	5.46	220.0	0.29		2	1	54
Agkistrodon piscivorus	2		23.0	800.0	980.0	3	0.5	5.50	331.2			2	1	1	194
Agkistrodon piscivorus	2		36.0	450.0	545.0	3	0.5	6.50	185.0			2	1	1	28
Crotalus atrox	2		36.0	800.0	976.0	3	0.5	10.00				2	1		160
Crotalus horridus	2		72.0	1000.0	1228.0	3	0.5	12.50	380.0			2	1		68
Crotalus horridus	2		60.0	770.0	876.0	3	0.5	7.00				2	1		65
Crotalus viridis	2		24.0	800.0	976.0	3	0.5	10.20	245.0			2	1	1	66
Crotalus viridis	2			510.0	640.0	1	1.0	9.70				2	1		2
Crotalus viridis	2			550.0	659.0	1	1.0	5.50				2	1		41
Vipera berus	2		36.0	450.0		3	0.5	7.90	144.5	0.30		2	1	1	126
Vipera berus	2			520.0	671.0	3	0.5	7.50	195.0	0.24		2	1		3

Summary of data used in statistical analyses. Mode is mode of reproduction (1, oviparous; 2, viviparous). Age is modal age (months) at sexual maturity, FEMAT is average SVL (mm) of females at maturity, FSVL is the average SVL (mm) of reproductive females. B is discrete brood frequency (1, single clutch per year; 2, multiple clutches per year, 3, biennial reproduction), CF is average reported brood frequency (broods, number per year), CS is the average clutch size (offspring/clutch), OFFSVL is average SVL (mm) at hatching or birth, RCM is relative clutch mass, FM is foraging mode (1, widely foraging; 2, sit-and-wait). D is distribution (1, temperate; 2, tropical), H is preferred habitat (1, terrestrial; 2, psammophilus; 3, saxicolous; 4, arboreal; 5, fossorial; 6, aquatic), and Source is index of source of data from the following list. Foraging mode data taken from Vitt and Price (1982), or Seigel and Fitch. (1984). Sources: (1) Alcala and Brown, 1967; (2) Aldridge, 1979; (3) Andren and Nilson, 1983; (4) Andrews, 1979; (5) Asana. 1931; (6) Avery, 1975a; (7) Avery, 1975b; (8) Baker, 1980; (9) Ballinger, 1973; (10) Ballinger, 1974; (11) Ballinger, 1976; (12) Ballinger, 1977; (13) Ballinger, 1979; (14) Ballinger and Hipp, 1985; (15) Ballinger et al., 1981; (16) Ballinger et al., 1972; (17) Barbault, 1976; (18) Barwick, 1959; (19) Berry and Lim, 1967; (20) Berry, 1974; (21) Bostic, 1966; (22) Bradshaw, 1981; (23) Branson and Baker, 1974; (24) Breckenridge, 1943; (25) Brooks, 1967; (26) Brown and Parker, 1984; (27) Burrage, 1973; (28) Burkett, 1966; (29) Burkholder and Walker, 1973; (30) Bustard, 1968; (31) Bustard, 1969; (32) Bustard, 1970; (33) Bustard, 1971; (34) Chondropulos and Lykakis, 1983; (35) Church, 1962; (36) Clark, 1970; (37) Clark, 1974; (38) Clark and Fleet, 1974; (39) Cogger, 1978; (40) Daniel, 1960; (41) Diller and Wallace, 1984; (42) Dmi'el, 1967; (43) Droge et al., 1982; (44) Dunham, 1980; (45) Dunham, 1981; (46) Dunham, 1982; (47) Elvira and Vigal, 1985; (48) Ferguson et al., 1980; (49) Fitch, 1935; (50) Fitch, 1954; (51) Fitch,

(Continued)

1955; (52) Fitch, 1956; (53) Fitch, 1958; (54) Fitch, 1960; (55) Fitch, 1963a; (56) Fitch, 1963b; (57), Fitch, 1965; (58) Fitch, 1972; (59) Fitch, 1975; (60) Fitch and Fleet, 1970; (61) Fitch and Greene, 1965; (62) Fitch and Henderson, 1978; (63) Flemming and Hooker, 1975; (64) Fukada, 1978; (65) Galligan and Dunson, 1979; (66) Gannon and Secoy, 1984; (67) Gennaro, 1974; (68) Gibbons, 1972; (69) Gibbons et al., 1977; (70) Goldberg, 1972; (71) Goldberg, 1976; (72) Goldberg and Bezy, 1974; (73) Goldberg and Robinson, 1979; (74) Gorman et al., 1981; (75) Greene, 1969; (76) Greer, 1967a; (77) Greer, 1967b; (78) Greer and Parker, 1967; (79) Gregory, 1977; (80) Guillette, 1983; (81) Guillette and Caas-Andreu, 1980; (82) Hall, 1969; (83) Hamlett, 1952; (84) Harris, 1964; (85) Hasegawa, 1984; (86) Hickman, 1960; (87) How and Kitchener, 1983; (88) Huey et al. 1974; (89) Hulse, 1981; (90) Hunsaker, 1959; (91) Inger and Greenberg, 1966; (92) Iverson, 1979; (93) Jackson and Franz, 1981; (94) Judd, 1976; (95) Jun-yi and Kaua-hung, 1982; (96) Kofron, 1979a; (97) Kofron, 1979b; (98) Kofron, 1983; (99) Krohmer and Aldridge, 1985; (100) Marion and Sexton, 1971; (101) Martin, 1977; (102) Mayhew, 1963; (103) Mayhew, 1965; (104) Mayhew, 1966a; (105) Mayhew, 1966b; (106) Mayhew, 1971; (107) McCoy, 1967; (108) Medica, 1967; (109) Miller, 1951; (110) Miller, 1954; (111) Morris, 1982; (112) Mount, 1963; (113) Newlin, 1976; (114) Nussbaum and Diller, 1976; (115) Parker, 1972; (116) Parker and Brown, 1980; (117) Pearson, 1954; (118) Pianka, 1971a; (119) Pianka, 1971b; (120) Pianka and Parker, 1972; (121) Pianka and Parker, 1975a; (122) Pianka and Pianka, 1970; (123) Platt, 1969; (124) Plummer, 1983; (125) Plummer, 1984; (126) Prestt, 1971; (127) Quinn, 1979; (128) Rao and Rajabi, 1972; (129) Robertson et al., 1965; (130) Routman and Hulse, 1984; (131) Ruby and Dunham, 1984; (132) Ruibal et al., 1972; (133) Schall, 1978; (134) Schwaner, 1980; (135) Semlitsch and Moran, 1984; (136) Sexton et al., 1971; (137) Sherbrooke, 1975; (138) Shine, 1977; (139) Shine, 1978; (140) Shine, 1980a (141) Shine, 1980b; (142) Shine, 1980c; (143) Shine, 1983; (144) Shine, 1984a; (145) Shine, 1984b; (146) Shine, 1986; (147) Simbotwe, 1980; (148) Smith, 1951; (149) Smith, 1968; (150) Smyth and Smith, 1974; (151) Somma and Brooks, 1976; (152) Stebbins et al., 1967; (153) Stewart, 1968; (154) Stewart, 1985; (155) Takenaka, 1980; (156) Taylor, 1985; (157) Telford, 1969; (158) Telford, 1971; (159) Tinkle, 1957; (160) Tinkle, 1962; (161) Tinkle, 1967; (162) Tinkle, 1972; (163) Tinkle, 1973; (164) Tinkle, 1976; (165) Tinkle and Ballinger, 1972; (166) Tinkle and Dunham, 1983; (167) Tinkle and Dunham, 1986; (168) Tinkle and Hadley, 1973; (169) Tinkle et al., 1970; (170) Van Devender, 1982; (171) Van Loben Sels and Vitt, 1984; (172) Vial and Stewart, 1985; (173) Vinegar, 1975a; (174) Vinegar, 1975b; (175) Vitt, 173; (176) Vitt, 1980; (177) Vitt, 1982a; (178) Vitt, 1982b; (179) Vitt, 1983a; (180) Vitt, 1983b; (181) Vitt, 1983c; (182) Vitt, 1986; (183) Vitt and Blackburn, 1983; (184) Vitt and Cooper, 1985; (185) Vitt and Cooper, 1986; (186) Vitt and Goldberg, 1983; (187) Vitt and Lacher, 1981; (188) Vitt and Ohmart, 1974; (189) Vitt and Ohmart, 1985; (190) Vitt et al., 1978; (191) Voris and Jayne, 1979; (192) Walker, 1980; (193) Walker, 1982; (194) Wharton, 1966; (195) White et al. 1982.

CHAPTER

8

The Physiological Ecology of Reptilian Eggs and Embryos

GARY C. PACKARD AND MARY J. PACKARD
Department of Zoology, Colorado State University,
Fort Collins, Colorado

CONTENTS

I. INTRODUCTION   525

II. TYPES OF EGGS   525
    A. Testudines, 525
    B. Crocodylia, 528
    C. Lepidosauria, 529

III. TYPES OF NESTS   532
    A. Testudines, 532
    B. Crocodylia, 533
    C. Lepidosauria, 533

IV. TEMPERATURE   535
    A. Factors Affecting Temperature of Eggs, 535
    B. Temperature in Nests, 539
    C. Physiological Effects of Temperature, 544

V. WATER   554
    A. Factors Affecting Water Balance of Eggs, 554
    B. Hydration of Nests, 556
    C. Exchanges of Water by Eggs in Nature, 562
    D. Physiological Effects of Water, 563

VI. RESPIRATORY GASES   573
    A. Factors Affecting Gas Exchange, 573
    B. Gas Tensions in Nests, 575
    C. Physiological Effects of Gases, 577

VII. INTERDEPENDENCE OF ENVIRONMENTAL VARIABLES   577
    A. Effect of One Variable on Another, 577
    B. Interaction of Variables on Eggs, 578

VIII. SIGNIFICANCE OF PHYSICAL ENVIRONMENT   580
    A. Introduction, 580
    B. Size of Hatchlings, 581
    C. Length of Incubation, 583
    D. Sexual Differentiation, 583

IX. CONCLUDING REMARKS   585
    ACKNOWLEDGMENTS   586
    REFERENCES   587

I. INTRODUCTION

Oviparity is the prevalent mode of reproduction among reptiles (Shine, 1985). Females of all extant turtles and crocodilians and of most lepidosaurians lay relatively large eggs containing all of the nutrients needed to produce viable offspring. These eggs usually are deposited in subterranean nests or in other sheltered sites, and embryonic development then proceeds under physical conditions dictated largely by the location of the site, the type of nest, and prevailing weather. In this chapter, we shall summarize information on reptilian eggs and nests, on physical conditions inside these nests, and on effects of the physical environment on eggs and embryos. Our focus will be on temperature, water, and respiratory gases, because these variables are likely to be the primary determinants of metabolism, growth, and survival by embryos developing in nature. We shall also evaluate some of the methods used in recent research on reptilian eggs, and shall try to identify some of the more important topics for future study.

II. TYPES OF EGGS

A. Testudines

Many species of turtles, including all cheloniids, chelydrids, and dermochelyids and most pelomedusids and emydids, produce eggs with flexible shells (Ewert, 1979, 1985). However, morphology of flexible eggshells varies considerably among species. Eggs of sea turtles of the family Cheloniidae have a shell comprised of a relatively thick, fibrous membrane overlain by a calcareous layer formed of numerous small, often poorly defined, shell units (Fig. 1; also Baird and Solomon, 1979; G. C. and M. J. Packard, 1980; M. J. Packard et al., 1982c; Solomon and Baird, 1977). Eggshells of chelydrids and emydids are similar, except that shell units are larger and more clearly defined and the shell membrane accounts for a smaller proportion of the total thickness of the eggshell (Fig. 1; also Erben, 1970; Ewert, 1979; G. C. and M. J. Packard, 1980; M. J. Packard, 1980; M. J. Packard et al., 1982c; Solomon and Reid, 1983). Large gaps between adjacent shell units (or between groups of shell units) provide for the exchange of respiratory gases and water between embryos and the nest environment. The crystalline material in the eggshell usually is aragonite (Erben, 1970; M. J. Packard, 1980; Solomon and Reid, 1983), but traces of calcite may form at the nucleation sites for shell units (Solomon and Baird, 1976; but see Silyn-Roberts and

Fig. 1. Schematic illustrations of radial sections through shells of turtle eggs, showing the relative importance of membranous and calcareous layers and the size and configuration of shell units. All three eggshells are drawn to the same scale with the outside on top. Note the large gaps between shell units of the eggshell of *Lepidochelys kempii* (Cheloniidae) and the smaller gaps between shell units of the eggshell of *Chelydra serpentina* (Chelydridae). Occasional pores (not figured) pass between adjacent shell units of the eggshell of *Geochelone elephantopus* (Testudinidae). (Modified and redrawn from Hirsch, 1983.)

Sharp, 1985). Calcite may also comprise a portion of the calcareous layer of eggshells produced by animals reared in captivity (Baird and Solomon, 1979), which raises the possibility that characteristics of eggshells may be modified by the diet on which females are maintained.

Other species of turtles, including carettochelids, chelids, dermatemyids, kinosternids, testudinids, trionychids, and some pelomedusids and emydids, lay eggs having rigid shells (Ewert, 1979, 1985). The shell of such eggs is comprised of a relatively thin shell membrane (or two) overlain by a calcareous layer (Ewert, 1979; M. J. and G. C. Packard, 1979; Young, 1950). The calcareous layer is formed of crystals of aragonite arranged into discrete shell units that abut tightly, thereby causing the layer to be rigid and noncompliant (Fig. 1; also Erben, 1970; Erben et al., 1979; Ewert, 1985; Ewert et al., 1984; G. C. and M. J. Packard, 1980; M. J. and G. C. Packard, 1979; M. J. Packard et al., 1982c, 1984a; Thompson, 1983; Silyn-Roberts and Sharp, 1985; Woodall, 1984). The crystalline layer is interrupted occasionally by distinct pores that provide for an exchange of respiratory gases and water between the contained embryo and the nest environment. These pores are more concentrated at the equator of elliptical eggs than at the poles (Ewert et al., 1984; Thompson, 1983; Woodall, 1984); their distribution in spherical eggs has not been determined.

The ultrastructure of rigid eggshells appears at first to be very different from that of flexible eggshells (M. J. Packard et al., 1982c). However, eggs of *Kinosternon flavescens* at intermediate stages of calcification have a flexible shell that is indistinguishable from shells of

TYPES OF EGGS

oviposited eggs of chelydrids and emydids; that is, the calcareous layer has numerous small, widely spaced shell units (M. J. Packard et al., 1984b). By the time of oviposition, however, the calcareous layer is a rigid structure characterized by elongate shell units that abut tightly (M. J. Packard et al., 1984a, b). Thus, the differences in morphology of flexible and rigid eggshells may arise simply in consequence of different amounts of time that crystallization proceeds inside oviducts of females. This question deserves further attention, because control of the duration of calcification appears to be implicated in the evolution of interspecific differences in shell structure.

Turtle embryos are in the gastrula (i.e., in a presomite stage of development) at the time of oviposition, regardless of how long eggs may have been retained within the maternal oviducts prior to oviposition (e.g., Crastz, 1982; Cunningham, 1922; Decker, 1967; Domantay, 1968; Ewert, 1979, 1985; Lynn and von Brand, 1945; Mahmoud et al., 1973; Risley, 1933, 1944; Yntema, 1968). This consistency contrasts markedly with the variation in developmental stage of oviposition in squamates (Saint Girons, 1985; Shine, 1985). The cause for the apparent arrest in development at this stage has not been determined (Ewert, 1985), but hypoxia may be a factor (Risley, 1944).

Eggs of turtles have a thick layer of albumen at oviposition (Agassiz, 1857; Ewert, 1979; Mitsukuri, 1890, 1891; Morris et al., 1983; G. C. Packard et al., 1981a, 1983), and this layer holds much of the water that the female parent vests in her eggs for support of embryogenesis (Morris et al., 1983; G. C. Packard et al., 1981a, 1983). Most of the water passes from the albumen into the vitelline sac during the first 1–2 weeks of incubation, however, so the albumen layer is not prominent in eggs that have undergone much development (Agassiz, 1857; Ewert, 1979; Mitsukuri, 1890, 1891; Morris et al., 1983; G. C. Packard et al., 1981a, 1983).

Turtle eggs have a large yolk at oviposition, but the yolk becomes even larger during the first 1–2 weeks of development as water flows inward from the albumen (Morris et al., 1983; G. C. Packard et al., 1981a, 1983). Indeed, by the end of this period, the yolk occupies almost the entire interior of viable eggs. This compartment contains all of the lipid and most (or all) of the protein required to sustain metabolism and growth of embryos (Congdon et al., 1983c; Karashima, 1929; Koga et al., 1978; von Brand and Lynn, 1947). The yolk also supplies part of the calcium used by embryos for osteogenesis (Bustard et al., 1969; M. J. and G. C. Packard, 1986; M. J. Packard et al., 1984d; Simkiss, 1962, 1967) and is the proximate source of water used by embryos (Morris et al., 1983; G. C. Packard et al., 1983).

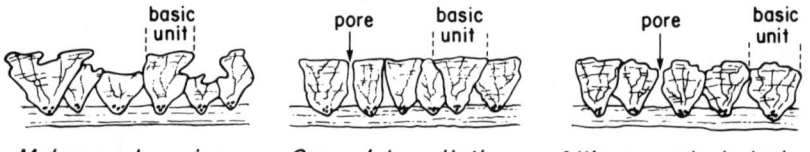

Melanosuchus niger *Crocodylus niloticus* *Alligator mississippiensis*

Fig. 2. Schematic illustrations of radial sections through shells of crocodilian eggs, showing the relative importance of membranous and calcareous layers and the size and configuration of shell units. All three eggshells are drawn to the same scale (which differs from that characterizing turtle eggshells in Fig. 1). Note the pores between shell units in eggshells of *Crocodylus niloticus* and *Alligator mississippiensis,* and the erosion craters (Ferguson, 1981a, b) on the external surface of eggshells of *Melanosuchus niger* and *Alligator mississippiensis.* (Redrawn and modified from Hirsch, 1985.)

B. Crocodylia

All crocodilians lay elliptical eggs having rigid, calcareous shells (Ferguson, 1985; Guggisberg, 1972; McIlhenny, 1935). The shell is formed of two fibrous membranes overlain by a relatively thick layer of calcium carbonate (Bigalke, 1931; Clarke, 1888, 1891; Deraniyagala, 1936, 1939; Ferguson, 1982; Reese, 1915; Voeltzkow, 1892). The calcareous layer is comprised of crystals of calcite (Erben, 1970; Ferguson, 1982; Jenkins, 1975; Schmidt and Schönwetter, 1943; Silyn-Roberts and Sharp, 1985; Solomon and Reid, 1983) organized into large, wedge-shaped shell units that abut tightly (Fig. 2), thereby conferring rigidity to the eggshell (Deraniyagala, 1936, 1939; Erben, 1970; Ferguson, 1982; Schmidt and Schönwetter, 1943). The crystalline layer occasionally is interrupted by pores that provide for an exchange of water and respiratory gases between the enclosed embryo and the nest environment. These pores tend to be more numerous around the equator of the egg than at either of the poles (Ferguson, 1982).

Embryonic crocodilians in freshly laid eggs commonly have 16–18 somites, and therefore are somewhat more advanced at oviposition than are embryonic turtles (Ferguson, 1982, 1985; Webb et al., 1983b). However, development of crocodilian embryos seems not to be arrested while eggs are retained within the maternal oviducts. Consequently, embryos may vary considerably in the stage of development they attain by the time of oviposition (Ferguson, 1985).

Crocodilian eggs contain a distinct layer of albumen at oviposition, and this albumen surrounds a large yolk (Bigalke, 1931; Clarke, 1888, 1891; Deraniyagala, 1936, 1939; Ferguson, 1982; Reese, 1915). The albumen probably contains much of the water required by the developing embryo, because the volume of albumen declines appreciably during the course of incubation (Ferguson, 1982). Additional water is contained within the yolk, which seemingly is the source also for all of the lipid and most (or all) of the protein required to sustain the embryo. Although a portion of the calcium required for skeletal ossification apparently is mobilized from the yolk, most of it comes from the calcareous layer of the eggshell (Jenkins, 1975).

C. Lepidosauria

Most oviparous lepidosaurians lay eggs with thin, flexible shells. However, both flexibility and morphology of eggshells vary considerably among and within species, so the descriptive terms that are commonly used to characterize lepidosaurian eggs (e.g., "parchment-like" and "flexible-shelled") actually encompass a wide range of morphological states.

The eggshell in some lepidosaurians is comprised of a fibrous membrane that seemingly is devoid of calcareous deposits (Fig. 3; also Andrews and Sexton, 1981; DeSalle et al., 1984; Krampitz et al., 1973; M. J. Packard et al., 1982c; Sexton et al., 1979; Trauth and Fagerberg, 1984). In other species, small amounts of calcium carbonate are found as isolated crystals among fibers of the shell membrane (Kriesten, 1975) or as larger, but widely separated, deposits on the outer surface of the membrane (M. J. Packard et al., 1982c). Finally, in still other species, a layer of calcareous material forms the outer surface of the eggshell (Fig. 3). Sometimes this calcareous layer is formed of numerous thin, flat plaques (or spheres) attached to the surface of the shell membrane (Guillette and Jones, 1985; Lillywhite and Ackerman, 1984; M. J. Packard et al., 1982a, c; Solomon and Reid, 1983), but in other instances the calcareous material is formed into columns that penetrate deeply into the membrane (M. J. Packard et al., 1982b). The calcium carbonate usually exists as crystals of calcite (M. J. Packard et al., 1982a, b), but crystals of aragonite are interspersed among the crystals of calcite in eggshells of *Python regius* (Solomon and Reid, 1983). However, variation occurs within some species both in the type of crystal forming the calcareous layer (Solomon and Reid, 1983) and in morphology of the shell itself (M. J. Packard et al., 1982a), and eggshells of a single species have occasionally been assigned to different categories by different investigators (e.g., Giersberg, 1922; Krampitz et al., 1973).

Lizards of the family Dibamidae are said to produce eggs with rigid, brittle shells (Boulenger, 1912), but the original observation has never been repeated. On the other hand, gekkonid lizards in the subfamilies Gekkoninae and Sphaerodactylinae are well known to produce eggs

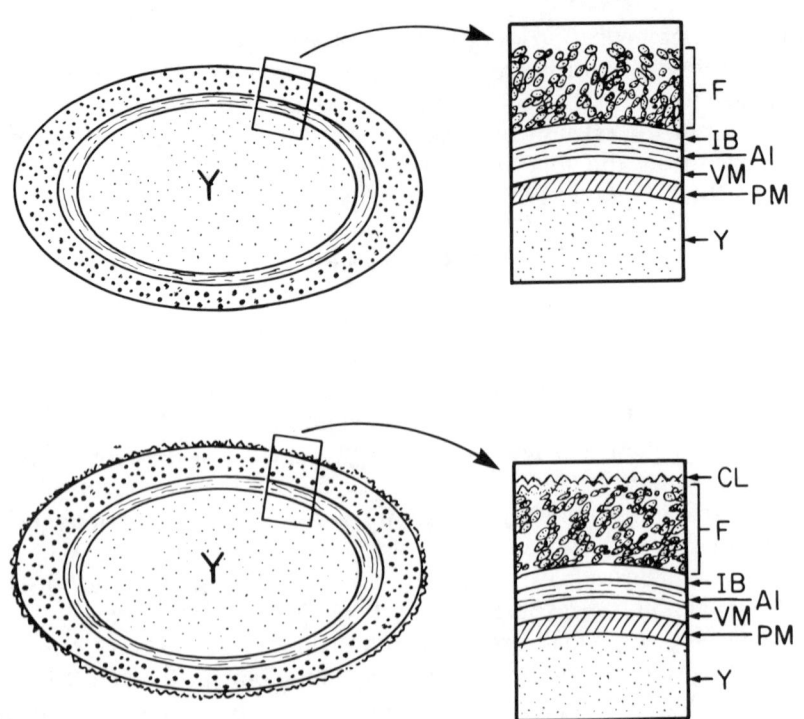

Fig. 3. Schematic illustrations of radial sections through shells of lepidosaurian eggs, showing the difference between eggs having no calcareous material in the eggshell and those having a distinct calcareous layer. Insets show enlarged sections passing from the outer surface of eggshell into the yolk. None of the layers is drawn to scale. CL, calcareous layer; F, fibers of shell membrane; IB, inner boundary of shell membrane; Al, albumen; VM, vitelline membrane; PM, plasma membrane; Y, yolk. (Redrawn and modified from M. J. Packard et al., 1982a.)

with hard, calcareous shells (Bustard, 1968; Werner, 1972). Crystals of calcite in the calcareous layer are arranged into jagged blocks that abut tightly and interlock (Erben and Newesely, 1972; Krampitz et al., 1972; M. J. Packard et al., 1982c; Schmidt, 1943), thereby rendering the layer rigid and noncompliant. The proximal portion of these calcareous blocks invests fibers at the outer surface of the shell membrane and anchors the two layers together (M. J. Packard et al., 1982c). Pores have not been observed in the calcareous layer; but all of the studies were preliminary, and pores could easily have been overlooked.

Embryos in freshly laid eggs of most lepidosaurians have attained stage 27–29 (or its equivalent) in the developmental series of Dufaure and Hubert (1961; see Shine, 1983a), and therefore have 20–30 pairs of somites (Muthukkaruppan et al., 1970). In *Opheodrys vernalis* and *Sceloporus aeneus*, however, eggs are retained for extended periods within oviducts of females, and embryonic development proceeds well beyond stage 29 (Guillette, 1981, 1982a, b; Sexton and Claypool, 1978). Oviposited eggs of these species contain embryos of substantial size, and incubation to hatching may be completed within a matter of days (Blanchard, 1933; Guillette and Lara Gongora, 1986; Sexton and Claypool, 1978). On the other hand, eggs of *Chamaeleo lateralis* contain embryos in a presomite stage of development (Blanc, 1974), and those of *Sphenodon punctatus* apparently contain embryos that are in gastrulation (Moffat, 1985). Considerable variation therefore exists in the stage of development attained by lepidosaurian embryos by the time of oviposition, but these embryos usually are more advanced than are those of turtles and crocodilians in freshly laid eggs.

Lepidosaurian eggs usually lack a distinct layer of albumen at oviposition (Badham, 1971; Clark, 1946; Dendy, 1899a, c; Fisk and Tribe, 1949; Giersberg, 1922; Harris, 1964; Jacobi, 1936; M. J. Packard et al., 1984c, 1985), but eggs of *Conolophus subcristatus* are reported to have an albumen accounting for 28% of their initial mass (Tracy and Snell, 1985). However, albumen was separated from yolk of the *Conolophus* eggs by low-speed centrifugation, so the fraction referred to as albumen may simply have been water forced out of the yolk by ultrafiltration.

The albumen of testudinian and crocodilian eggs is an important reservoir of water, so the apparent absence of an albumen layer in lepidosaurian eggs has been taken to indicate that these eggs contain insufficient water at oviposition to support embryos until hatching (G. C. and M. J. Packard, 1980; Tracy, 1982). Indeed, water represents only 63% of the initial mass in eggs of *Amphibolurus barbatus* and 59% in eggs of *Coluber constrictor* (M. J. Packard et al., 1985). However, 74% of the initial mass of eggs is water in *Pituophis melanoleucus* (Gutzke and Packard, 1987a). Comparable values for eggs of turtles fall between 68–72% (Cunningham and Hurwitz, 1936; Morris et al., 1983; G. C. and M. J. Packard, 1980; G. C. Packard et al., 1981a; Ricklefs and Burger, 1977).

Many authors have reported the presence of a large layer of albumen in squamate eggs that have undergone substantial incubation (e.g., Badham, 1971; Black et al., 1984; D. R. Clark, 1970; H. Clark, 1953b). However, the fraction they identified as albumen may actually have been material from the allantoic sac (Moffat, 1985). The allantoic sac of embryonic *Sphenodon punctatus* becomes greatly enlarged during incubation, owing to the accumulation of a clear, semigelatinous fluid resembling the albumen of an avian egg (Dendy, 1899a, c). Whenever a swollen egg ruptures, this fluid is released onto the surface of the eggshell where it could easily be mistaken for albumen.

The yolk occupies most of the interior of lepidosaurian eggs at oviposition, and presumably provides embryos with almost all of the nutrients required to support development (Body, 1985; Grodzinski, 1949; also Bellairs, 1959; Stewart and Castillo, 1984; J. Thompson, 1981). All of the water vested in eggs for support of embryogenesis is in this compartment (M. J. Packard et al., 1984c, 1985), and most (or all) of the calcium required for skeletal ossification also is stored there (Jenkins and Simkiss, 1968; M. J. Packard et al., 1984c, 1985).

III. TYPES OF NESTS

A. Testudines

Most species of turtles dig a flask-shaped hole in the ground in which eggs are deposited (e.g., Carr, 1952; Ernst and Barbour, 1972). In some instances, excavation of the nest chamber is preceded by construction of a "body pit," thereby removing surface debris and loose soil that might otherwise sift into the forming cavity (e.g., Alho and Padua, 1982; Carr, 1952; Hendrickson, 1958; Richmond, 1945). Among species producing small clutches, all of the eggs rest on the floor of the cavity and therefore have some contact with the substrate. Among species producing large clutches, however, many eggs are supported by points of contact with other eggs and consequently make no contact with the substrate (Ackerman, 1977; Hendrickson, 1958; G. C. Packard et al., 1981c). After all of the eggs have been laid, the female kicks dirt into the neck of the chamber. Some of this dirt may sift downward among the eggs, but air spaces between the eggs and at the top of the cavity usually are not obliterated completely (Ackerman, 1977; Allard, 1935; Burger, 1976; Cagle, 1937, 1950; Hendrickson, 1958; G. C. Packard et al., 1981c). These air spaces persist for the duration of incubation in nests constructed in stable soils (Breitenbach et al., 1984), but may be obliterated by infiltration of soil into nests located in less stable substrates (Hotaling et al., 1985). The infiltration of soil or sand into nests sometimes leads to increased mortality among embryos (Simon, 1975), so persistence of air spaces may be more important to successful incubation than generally is realized.

Some species of the families Chelidae and Kinosternidae depart from the pattern of nest construction characterizing most turtles. For example, *Sternotherus minor* and *Sternotherus odoratus* may simply back up to a fallen log and deposit their eggs beneath the edge; if females fail to scrape leaf litter over these "nests," the eggs remain partially exposed to the elements (Cagle, 1937; Carr, 1952). Eggs of *Phrynops gibbus* frequently are deposited on the surface of the ground or with only a thin covering of soil (Mittermeier et al., 1978). In contrast, *Kinosternon flavescens* from regions of sandy soil in the central U.S. burrow through the ground prior to oviposition, and eggs are simply deposited in the burrow system constructed by each female (J. B. Iverson, pers. comm.).

B. Crocodylia

Crocodilians construct mound nests or hole nests (Campbell, 1972; Ferguson, 1985; Greer, 1970). Mound nests, such as those characterizing *Alligator mississippiensis, Caiman crocodilus,* and *Crocodylus porosus,* are located in piles of mud and/or vegetation scraped together by gravid females (Deraniyagala, 1936, 1939; McIlhenny, 1935; Staton and Dixon, 1977; Webb et al., 1977, 1983c). A nest chamber is dug in the top of each mound, and eggs are deposited inside. Eggs at the bottom and periphery of the pile contact walls of the cavity, but those toward the center of the mass do not. The female closes the cavity after all eggs have been laid and may then crawl across the top several times, thereby compressing the loose mud and vegetation. Spaces between eggs occasionally are filled as the nest is closed (Clarke, 1888), but pockets of air usually persist within the cavity for the duration of incubation (McIlhenny, 1935).

Other crocodilians, like *Crocodylus johnsoni, Crocodylus niloticus,* and *Gavialis gangeticus,* dig a hole obliquely downward into a sand, gravel, or dirt bank (Modha, 1967; Subba Rao and Bustard, 1979; Webb et al., 1983a). The narrow tunnel leads to a spacious egg-chamber at the bottom (Whitaker and Whitaker, 1984). As eggs are laid, they simply roll to the bottom and form a pile. Eggs in the middle of the pile make no contact with the substrate, whereas those at the periphery have some contact with soil. The female subsequently closes the tunnel with sand or dirt. Some soil and debris occasionally is packed between eggs (Pooley, 1969), but air spaces usually persist inside the egg chamber (Modha, 1967; Ogden, 1978), presumably for the duration of incubation.

C. Lepidosauria

Such a diverse array of sites is used for oviposition by different species of lepidosaurians that generalization about nests of these reptiles is virtually impossible. Developing embryos of lepidosaurians encounter diverse ecological and physiological problems. This diversity represents both a challenge and an obstacle: A challenge, in that a great deal of new research is needed to describe nests in the detail required for understanding these problems; an obstacle, in that consequent variation in physiological ecology of embryos may defy simple generalization.

Because snakes lack limbs, most species apparently are unable to construct nests specifically for their eggs, and rely instead on pre-existing sites that are suitable for oviposition (see Burger and Zappalorti, 1986, for an exception). What constitutes a suitable site varies somewhat with the size of the species in question. For example, small snakes, such as the colubrid *Diadophis punctatus,* frequently deposit eggs in small crevices and ant galleries inside rotting logs and stumps (Blanchard, 1936). Eggs of larger species, like the colubrids *Coluber constrictor, Masticophis taeniatus,* and *Pituophis melanoleucus,* often are deposited in the subterranean burrows of rodents (Fitch, 1963; Parker and Brown, 1972, 1980). The largest of snakes, such as *Python sebae,* usually oviposit in large cavities beneath objects on the ground or in abandoned burrows of aardvarks and anteaters. In the absence of such sites, pythons may lay eggs on the surface of the ground in dense grass or in pockets of dead leaves (FitzSimons, 1962; Pope, 1961). Detailed descriptions are not available for nests of any snake, but the lower aspect of some (or all) eggs in a clutch probably contacts the substrate, whereas the upper surface of the eggs probably is exposed to air inside the nest cavity. The proportion of the surface contacting the substrate has important implications for temperature of eggs and for exchanges of water with the environment (see Sections IV.A, V.A), so detailed descriptions of egg chambers are badly needed.

One species or another of saurian uses almost every imaginable place to lay its eggs. Limbless lizards, such as *Ophisaurus attenuatus* and *Pygopus lepidopodus,* probably use the same kinds of sites for oviposition as are used by snakes of similar size (Vinegar, 1968; Wells and Husband, 1979). Small skinks, anoles, and other lizards lay their eggs in cavities in rotting logs or beneath surface objects (Cagle, 1940; Fitch, 1954; Magnusson and Lima, 1984; Rand, 1967; Whitaker, 1968), whereas others oviposit on the surface of the ground beneath a protective layer of leaf litter (Rand, 1967; Sexton et al., 1964). Some geckos lay their eggs beneath fallen limbs and debris (Bustard, 1969a), but others conceal their eggs beneath loose bark on standing trees or in clumps of dead leaves collecting in crotches of these trees (Sexton et al., 1964; Sexton and Turner, 1971). Many species in tropical regions, including some of the larger varanids, oviposit inside termite mounds (Cowles, 1928; Riley et al., 1985). In every case, the site selected for oviposition is a primary determinant of the physical conditions to which eggs will be exposed, but detailed descriptions of such sites are wanting for most of these saurians.

A number of species of saurians, including many agamids, chamaeleonids, iguanids, lacertids, and teiids, construct nests specifically for their eggs. A tunnel is excavated at an angle into the soil, and an enlarged chamber usually is located at the end (Bartholomew, 1966; Blair, 1960; Brown, 1956; Cooper, 1958; Hudson, 1977; Johnston, 1979; Menzies, 1958; Shaw, 1960; Subba Rao and Rajabi, 1972; Van Devender and Howard, 1973). After the female lays her eggs, the nest is closed. Females of some species apparently pack loose dirt into the nest chamber during closure, thereby obliterating air spaces among the eggs (Johnson, 1965; Rand and Dugan, 1983), whereas females of other species do not (Brown, 1956; Carpenter, 1966; Guillette and Lara Gongora, 1986; Iverson, 1979; Muth, 1977; Shaw, 1960). The presence or absence of air spaces inside nests has important implications concerning exchanges of heat, water, and gases between developing embryos and their surroundings (see Sections IV.A, V.A, VI.A). Also, obliterating these air spaces is known to increase embryonic mortality in some species (Muth, 1977). Thus, it is important to determine whether filling the cavity occurs normally in the species for which it has been reported (see Rand and Dugan, 1983) or whether the published reports are of atypical nests (see Brown, 1956).

IV. TEMPERATURE

A. Factors Affecting Temperature of Eggs

Several factors affect the temperature of reptilian eggs and embryos incubating in natural nests, as can be illustrated with a simple energy balance equation for a single egg:

$$q_S = q_M + q_{CD} + q_{CV} + q_E + q_R \qquad (1)$$

where q_S is heat storage (or loss), q_M is heat released by the embryo in intermediary metabolism, q_{CD} is heat gained (or lost) by conduction from the substrate, q_{CV} is heat gained (or lost) by convection from air inside the nest cavity, q_E is heat gained (or lost) by changes in state of water, and q_R is heat gained (or lost) by thermal radiation (see Gates, 1980; Tracy, 1982). Whenever the input of heat from various sources equals the output, storage of heat (q_S) is zero, and temperature of the egg does not change. Whenever the input of heat does not balance the output, however, heat must be stored in the egg or lost from it, and temperature of the egg therefore must increase or decrease, respectively. A fuller appreciation of the several processes affecting energy exchange and of their relative importance as determinants of egg temperature can now be gained by considering each of the terms in order.

The term for heat storage (q_S) can be expanded to read

$$q_S = m_E \times c_p \times dT_E/dt \tag{2}$$

where m_E is mass of the egg (gm), c_p is heat capacity of the egg ($J \times gm^{-1} \times °C^{-1}$), and dT_E/dt is the rate of change in temperature ($°C \times s^{-1}$). This equation confirms that storage (or loss) of heat in an egg of constant mass and heat capacity entails a change in its temperature. However, the equation also reveals that the rate of change in temperature is related inversely to mass in eggs having similar heat capacities, so the temperature of large eggs changes less with the addition (or loss) of a given amount of heat than does that of small eggs. Large eggs therefore are buffered better against changes in temperature than are small eggs.

Production of metabolic heat by an embryo (q_M, in $J \times s^{-1}$) proceeds throughout incubation, but probably is negligible just after oviposition and maximal shortly before hatching. Data for oxygen consumption of embryonic snakes and turtles support this view (Fig. 4). Interestingly, the temporal pattern of increase in oxygen consumption (and in heat production) appears to be sigmoidal in turtles and exponential in snakes (Table I). The significance (if any) of this difference has not been determined.

Energy exchange by conduction from the substrate (q_{CD}) is characterized by

$$q_{CD} = k_{CD} \times A_S \times (T_e - T_s) \tag{3}$$

whereas convective exchange (q_{CV}) is described by

$$q_{CV} = k_{CV} \times A_A \times (T_e - T_a) \tag{4}$$

where k_{CD} and k_{CV} are coefficients for conductive and convective heat transfer, respectively ($J \times s^{-1} \times cm^{-2} \times °C^{-1}$); A_S and A_A are the areas of eggshell contacting soil and air, respectively (cm^2); and T_e, T_s, and T_a are temperatures of egg, soil, and air in the nest cavity, respectively (°C). Energy exchanges by conduction and convection clearly are affected by

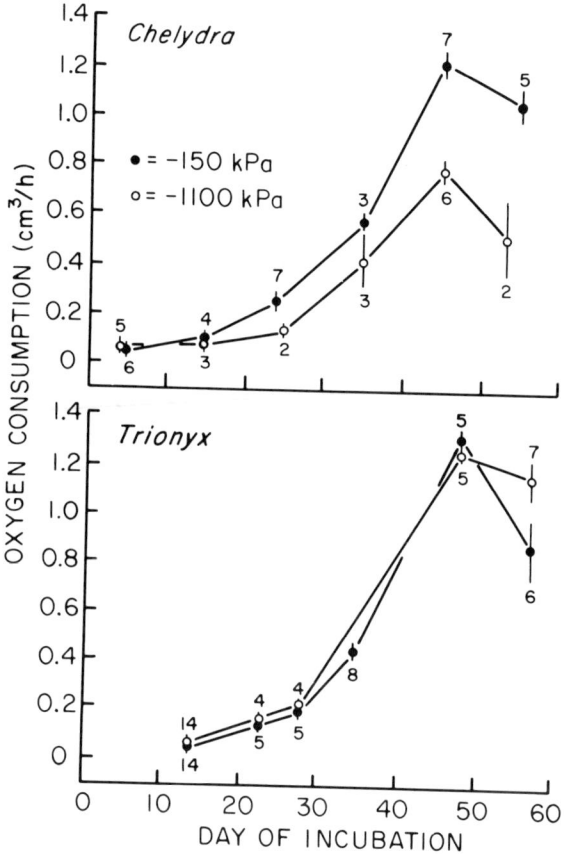

Fig. 4. Oxygen consumption of embryonic snapping turtles (*Chelydra serpentina*) and softshell turtles (*Trionyx spiniferus*) at different times in incubation. Eggs were incubated on wet (−150 kPa) and dry (−1100 kPa) substrates at an ambient temperature of 29°C. Only one measurement was taken from each egg. Plotted values are means ±1 SE for samples of the indicated size. Oxygen consumption for embryonic snapping turtles on wet substrates was significantly higher than that for embryos on dry substrates on days 45 and 53, but oxygen consumption of embryonic softshell turtles was unaffected by substrate water potential at any time in incubation. (Redrawn and modified from Gettinger et al., 1984.)

temperatures of air and soil inside reptilian nests, and numerous measurements of nest temperature have been reported (Section IV.B). However, areas of eggshell available for exchange have not been measured, and only one study has reported values for heat-transfer coefficients (Ackerman et al., 1985a).

TABLE I
Temporal Patterns in Oxygen Consumption of Embryonic Turtles and Snakes

Species	Pattern of increase	Reference
Testudines		
Caretta caretta	Logistic	Ackerman, 1981a
Chelonia mydas	Logistic	Ackerman, 1981a
Chelydra serpentina	Logistic	Gettinger et al., 1984; Lynn and von Brand, 1945
Chrysemys picta	Logistic	Lynn and von Brand, 1945
Emydura macquarrii	Logistic	Thompson, 1985
Kinosternon subrubrum	Logistic	Lynn and von Brand, 1945
Terrapene carolina	Logistic	Lynn and von Brand, 1945
Trionyx spiniferus	Logistic	Gettinger et al., 1984
Serpentes		
Cerastes cerastes	Exponential	Dmi'el, 1970
Coluber constrictor	Exponential	Clark, 1953c
Echis coloratus	Exponential	Dmi'el, 1970
Natrix tessellata	Exponential	Dmi'el, 1970
Python molurus	Exponential	Black et al., 1984
Spalerosophis diadema	Exponential	Dmi'el, 1970
Vipera xanthina	Exponential	Dmi'el, 1970

Energy exchange resulting from changes in state of water (q_E) can be described as

$$q_E = \lambda \times k_V \times A_A \times (p_E - p_A) \quad (5)$$

where λ is the latent heat of vaporization of water (J $\times$ mg^{-1}), k_V is the transfer coefficient for water vapor (mg $\times$ s^{-1} $\times$ cm^{-2} $\times$ kPa^{-1}), A_A is the area of eggshell exposed to air (including that in spaces in the soil) (cm^2), and p_E and p_A are vapor pressures of the egg and surrounding air, respectively (kPa). The vapor pressure of air in the nest clearly affects heat exchange, and some measurements for this variable have been reported (Section V.B). However, the area of eggshell available for exchange of vapor has not been assessed. Detailed studies of the transfer coefficient also are needed, because the coefficient may assume different values for portions of an egg that are exposed to air and for those that contact the substrate (Ackerman et al., 1985b).

Net exchange of energy by thermal radiation (q_R) is expressed by

$$q_R = Q_R - Q_A \quad (6)$$
$$= e \times \sigma \times A_E \times [(T_e + 273)^4 - (T_s + 273)^4] \quad (7)$$

where Q_R is thermal radiation emitted by the egg ($J \times s^{-1}$), Q_A is thermal radiation absorbed by the egg ($J \times s^{-1}$), e is emissivity (which is assumed here to be equal for egg and substrate), σ is the Stefan-Boltzmann constant ($J \times s^{-1} \times cm^{-2} \times K^{-1}$), A_E is the effective area of eggshell for absorption and emission of thermal radiation (cm^2), and the bracketed quantity is the difference in the fourth power of surface temperatures of the egg and soil (K). Thermal radiation probably is not an important mechanism for energy exchange, even in nests with air spaces that persist between eggs and at the top of the chamber (see Webb and King, 1983). However, this prediction requires verification.

B. Temperature in Nests

1. DETERMINANTS OF NEST TEMPERATURE

Numerous factors influence the heat exchange and temperature of reptilian eggs (eq. 1). Although air temperature inside the nest is only one of these factors, it is especially important because it can be measured with relative ease and because it usually yields a reasonable approximation to the temperature of the eggs themselves (see Fig.12). Thus, an understanding of the factors affecting temperature in nests is fundamental to any discussion of temperature relations of reptilian eggs.

The diurnal cycle in net radiation at the surface of bare ground is the primary determinant of temperature in the upper 50 cm of the soil profile (Marshall and Holmes, 1979; Taylor and Ashcroft, 1972). Shortwave radiation reaching the ground during daylight hours heats the surface layer and leads to a subsequent flow of heat downward (Carson and Moses, 1963). Conversely, emission of longwave radiation at night cools the surface layer and causes heat to flow upward through the soil (Carson and Moses, 1963). These cycles in heating/cooling and in heat flow are manifested as daily cycles in soil temperature (Fig. 5; also Buchan, 1982; Carson and Moses, 1963; Parton, 1984; Wierenga et al., 1969). The amplitude of the temperature cycles decreases with increasing depth, and maxima and minima occur progressively later in the day as distance from the surface increases.

Our interest in temperature cycles in the upper 50 cm of the soil centers on the fact that this is the zone in which subterranean nests of most turtles and of many crocodilians and lepidosaurians are located. With relatively few exceptions (see below), the primary determinant of temperature inside these nests is the daily cycle in heating/cooling of the surface of the soil and attendant cycles in transport of heat through upper reaches of the soil profile. This view is supported by measure-

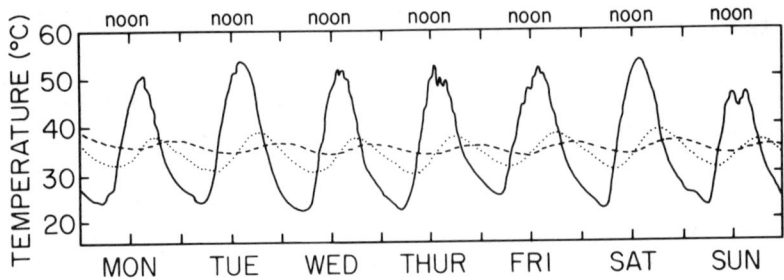

Fig. 5. Diel cycles in temperature at three depths in bare soil during a week in midsummer at Griffith, N.S.W., Australia. Solid line, 2.5 cm; dotted line, 15.0 cm; dashed line, 30.0 cm. Note that daily maxima and minima occur progressively later in the day as depth increases, and that amplitude of the cycles is reduced as depth increases. (Redrawn and modified from West, 1952.)

ments showing that temperatures at the top, middle, and bottom of hole nests located in the open exhibit the same phase-shift and damping of diel cycles with increasing depth that are expected to occur in the soil at large (Fig. 6; also Burger, 1976; G. C. Packard et al., 1985b). Indeed, the daily cycle in net radiation probably is the primary factor also influencing temperature inside the mound nests of crocodilians and inside the nests of lepidosaurians located in logs or beneath surface objects (Magnusson, 1979; Staton and Dixon, 1977; Webb et al., 1983a).

Several factors modify the impact of diel cycles in heat transport through upper layers of the soil and thereby affect temperatures at the level of nests. For example, nests located deep in the ground tend to have lower temperatures than shallower nests at the same site (Wilhoft et al., 1983), simply because of the resistance imposed by the soil itself to transport of heat from the warm surface to deeper layers in the profile. Shaded nests generally are cooler than nests located at similar depths in the open (Alho et al., 1985; Bull, 1985; G. C. Packard et al., 1985b; Webb et al., 1983a), because shading reduces insolation and heating of the surface of the soil. Moreover, temperatures are lower during periods of overcast and rainfall than during periods of fair weather (Burger, 1976; G. C. Packard et al., 1985b; Magnusson, 1979), owing to reduced insolation and to absorption of heat by infiltrating water. Finally, subtle factors like slope and aspect of the nest site influence the absorption of solar radiation (Mahrer, 1982; Mahrer and Avissar, 1985); and texture, composition, and water content of the soil influence heat transport (Marshall and Holmes, 1979; Taylor and Ashcroft, 1972).

Several notable exceptions to these generalizations occur. For example, female sea turtles (families Cheloniidae and Dermochelyidae)

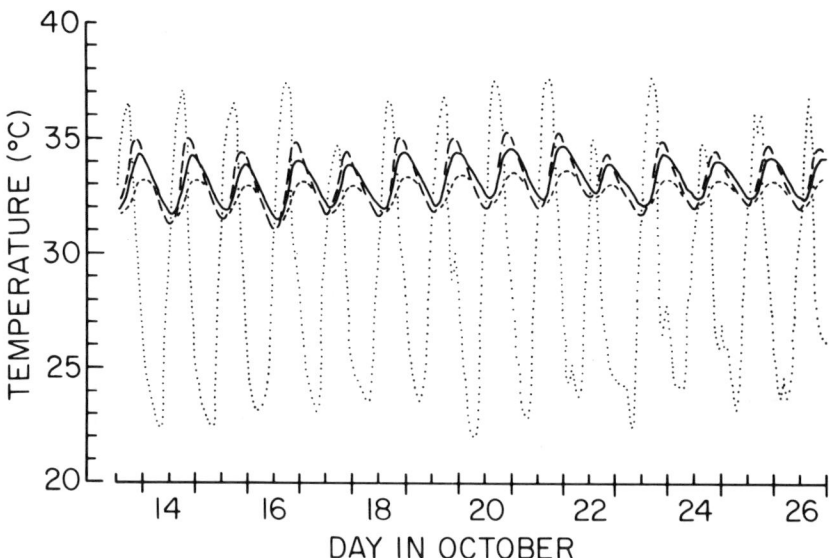

Fig. 6. Diel cycles in temperature at three levels inside a hole nest of a freshwater crocodile (*Crocodylus johnsoni*) located in the open on a sandbar. Dotted line, air above the nest; long dashed line, top of clutch; solid line, middle of clutch; short dashed line, bottom of clutch. Note that daily maxima and minima occur progressively later in the day as depth increases, and that amplitude of the cycles is reduced as well. These temperature cycles are similar to those occurring away from nests in the surrounding soil (see Fig. 5). (Redrawn and modified from Webb et al., 1983a.)

deposit large numbers of relatively large eggs in a chamber deep beneath the surface of the sand. Late in incubation, embryos in these eggs generate more heat than is transported away from the cavity, and temperature inside the chamber therefore increases by 5–7°C above that of the adjacent sand (Bustard, 1972; Carr and Hirth, 1961; Hendrickson, 1958; Raj, 1976). If nests are deep and thus unaffected by daily temperature waves, concentric gradients in temperature may be created, with eggs at the center being exposed to higher temperatures than eggs at the periphery (Bustard, 1972).

Metabolic heat generated by embryos of the turtle *Malaclemys terrapin* also causes temperature in nests to rise late in incubation by 2–7°C over temperature in adjacent soil (Burger, 1976). The magnitude of the observed increase is surprising, as the nests were shallow and each nest contained only eight eggs. Clutches this small seem to be unlikely sources for sufficient heat to elicit increases in temperature similar to those occurring in the much larger nests of sea turtles. Nevertheless, differences in temperature could not be detected between empty nests and adjacent soil, nor between nests containing freshly laid eggs and the surrounding substrate, so production of metabolic heat is a viable explanation for the findings.

Metabolic heat also may influence temperature in nests of some crocodilians, because temperature at the bottom of hole nests occasionally is higher than that at the top (Modha, 1967). However, the higher temperatures at the bottom occur at a time of day when deeper layers of the soil might be expected to be warmer than shallower layers in consequence of the difference in phase of temperature cycles occurring at these levels (see Figs. 5, 6). Thus, the question of significant metabolic heating in hole nests of crocodilians remains open.

Considerable attention has focused on the possible release of heat by fermenting vegetation forming walls of mound nests of many crocodilians (McIlhenny, 1935; Reese, 1915). Although heat of fermentation clearly affects nest temperature in some instances (Magnusson, 1979; Webb et al., 1977), it may not occur in more than a small proportion of nests (Magnusson, 1979; Webb et al., 1977) and therefore may not be a phenomenon of general importance (Magnusson et al., 1985; Staton and Dixon, 1977).

Finally, we must mention the interesting case of *Paleosuchus trigonatus*, a South American crocodilian that nests beneath a closed canopy of trees in tropical jungle in which input of heat from direct solar radiation is precluded. The mound nests of this crocodilian usually are built against, or on top of, the mounds of a termite. Metabolic heat generated by the termites helps to maintain nest temperature several degrees above ambient and within the range conducive to embryonic development (Magnusson et al., 1985). The implicit assumption is that exploitation of termite mounds as nest sites has enabled *Palaeosuchus* to occupy a habitat from which it would otherwise be excluded by ambient conditions unfavorable to reproduction.

2. MEASUREMENTS OF NEST TEMPERATURE

Temperature has been measured inside reptilian nests on numerous occasions, but most of the resulting data are of limited value in understanding the thermal environment to which reptilian eggs are exposed. In most instances, temperature was measured once in each of several nests at unspecified times during the day, and the values then were averaged. Unfortunately, values obtained in this way are not representative of temperatures to which eggs are exposed over the course of incubation, and they usually are not indicative even of an extreme. A few measurements taken with maximum/minimum thermometers provide reliable information on extremes, but again do not characterize conditions to which eggs are exposed for the greater part of incubation. Thus, the database for nest temperatures is flawed, and we have confidence in only the most general of trends and tendencies.

Average temperatures usually are 26–32°C inside nests of most testudinians (e.g., Burger, 1976; Bustard, 1972; Carr and Hirth, 1961; Goode and Russell, 1968; Hendrickson, 1958; Limpus et al., 1983a; MacFarland et al., 1974; McGehee, 1979; Pieau, 1982; Thompson, 1983; Vogt, 1980; Wilhoft et al., 1983), crocodilians (e.g., Chabreck, 1973; Deitz and Hines, 1980; Lutz and Dunbar-Cooper, 1984; Magnusson, 1979; Magnusson et al., 1985; Modha, 1967; Staton and Dixon, 1977; Webb et al., 1977, 1983a; Whitaker and Whitaker, 1984), and lepidosaurians (e.g., Bartholomew, 1966; Magnusson and Lima, 1984; Rand, 1972; Vaz-Ferreira et al., 1970). Higher values have been reported for nests of thermophilic teiids (Brown, 1956) and iguanids (Johnson, 1965), and lower temperatures have been measured in nests of relatively cryophilic skinks (Shine, 1983b) and geckos (Bustard, 1969a). Nests of montane lizards may also have relatively low temperatures (Guillette and Lara Gongora, 1986).

Superficial nests constructed in shaded areas tend to track cycles in ambient temperature relatively closely (Shine, 1983b). However, nests in the open must be located beneath a protective layer of soil or vegetation to prevent the eggs from being exposed to lethal temperatures. In such instances, cycles in temperature still occur inside nests, but they differ in mean and amplitude from cycles in ambient temperature. Eggs incubating in the large mound nests of crocodilians seldom are exposed to temperatures fluctuating by more than 2–4°C over the course of a day (Chabreck, 1973; Magnusson, 1979; Staton and Dixon, 1977; Webb et al., 1977), and a similar range characterizes the deep hole-nests of other crocodilians (Modha, 1967), some turtles (Alho and Padua, 1982; Carr and Hirth, 1961; Hendrickson, 1958; MacFarland et al., 1974; McGehee, 1979), and a few lepidosaurians (Bartholomew, 1966; Rand, 1972). However, the daily cycle in temperature in the shallow nests of a few crocodilians, many turtles, and numerous lepidosaurians commonly spans 6–10°C (Fig. 6; also Burger, 1976; Bustard, 1969a; Ewert, 1979; Guillette and Lara Gongora, 1986; Magnusson and Lima, 1984; Moll and Legler, 1971; G. C. Packard et al., 1985b; Pieau, 1982; Sexton and Claypool, 1978; Thompson, 1983; Vogt, 1980; Whitaker and Whitaker, 1984; Wilhoft et al., 1983).

Temperature in superficial nests of the snake *Opheodrys vernalis* may exceed 40°C for part of the day (Sexton and Claypool, 1978), and temperatures may briefly reach this level also in shallow nests of the turtles *Chrysemys picta* and *Pseudemys scripta* (Ewert, 1979; Moll and

Legler, 1971; Schwarzkopf and Brooks, 1985). Most surprising, however, is the report that temperatures in nests of the turtle *Podocnemis expansa* may not fall below 37°C for upwards of 9 days (Alho and Padua, 1982); prolonged exposure to temperatures this high would be lethal to embryos of most species (Section IV.C).

Eggs located at the top of nests of crocodilians and many turtles are exposed to diel cycles in temperature having higher means and greater amplitudes than are eggs at the bottom of the same nests (Fig. 6; also Ferguson and Joanen, 1982, 1983; Modha, 1967; G. C. Packard et al., 1985b; Thompson, 1983; Webb et al., 1983a; Wilhoft et al., 1983). Maxima and minima also occur somewhat earlier at the top of the egg mass than at the bottom (Fig. 6; also Burger, 1976; G. C. Packard et al., 1985b; Webb et al., 1983a; Wilhoft et al., 1983). As was indicated earlier, such cycles in temperature occur normally in the upper layers of the soil (Fig. 5), so eggs apparently are being exposed to temperature regimes appropriate for that depth in the soil profile.

C. Physiological Effects of Temperature

1. LIMITS OF TOLERANCE

Several studies have characterized the thermal tolerances of embryonic reptiles developing at constant temperatures in the laboratory. The general finding is that embryos cannot survive exposure to as great a range of temperatures as can adults of the same species. Embryonic crocodilians usually survive to hatching when incubated at temperatures of 28–34°C, but mortality increases rapidly as temperatures go above or below this range (Bustard, 1971b; Ferguson and Joanen, 1982, 1983). Young of the green turtle *Chelonia mydas* have high hatching success at 25–33°C (Bustard, 1971a; Bustard and Greenham, 1968; Miller, 1982), and a similar range of tolerances characterizes developing young of *Caretta caretta* (McGehee, 1979; Miller, 1982; Yntema and Mrosovsky, 1980) and *Chelonia depressa* (Miller, 1982). The range of thermal tolerance of embryonic *Chelydra serpentina* (Yntema, 1968, 1978), *Pseudemys scripta* (Moll and Legler, 1971), *Terrapene carolina* (Dodge et al., 1978), and *Terrapene ornata* (Legler, 1960) is similar in extent to that of sea turtles, but is displaced downward by approximately 2°C.

Data for lepidosaurians indicate that there may be a relation between limits of tolerance and local climate. Embryos of *Sceloporus undulatus*, a lizard from temperate regions of North America, have a range of thermal tolerance extending from 25°C to nearly 35°C (Sexton and Marion, 1974), whereas those of *Dipsosaurus dorsalis*, an iguanid inhabiting deserts of the American Southwest, survive exposure to 28–38°C (Muth, 1980). Furthermore, young of the tropical lizard *Iguana iguana*, which normally develop in nests that are well buffered against changes in temperature (Rand, 1972), will not complete development at temperatures departing by more than 2°C from an optimum at 30°C (Licht and Moberly, 1965). Finally, the lower limit of thermal tolerance for embryos of the snake *Python molurus* is approximately 28°C (Vinegar, 1973), suggesting adaptation of embryos to the relatively high temperatures that are likely to be encountered during incubation of this tropical species (Shine, this volume).

Causes of death in embryos developing at temperatures exceeding the limits of tolerance have not been determined. However, the high incidence of developmental anomalies among young developing at temperatures towards the extremes of the range of tolerance indicates a general disruption of highly integrated physiological systems (Bustard, 1969b; Fox, 1948; Fox et al., 1961; Gutzke and Packard, 1987a; Gutzke, 1984a; Osgood, 1978; Vinegar, 1973, 1974; Webb et al., 1983a, c; Zweifel, 1980).

Data gathered in studies performed at constant temperatures are valuable in establishing the range of conditions that embryos can withstand for extended periods, but are of limited relevance to development in nature because of the diel cycles in temperature to which eggs usually are exposed (Fig. 6). With the possible exception of those crocodilians, sea turtles, and others having nests that are buffered against changes in temperature, reptilian embryos probably are exposed periodically to temperatures exceeding the specified levels of tolerance, but they nonetheless develop normally. For example, embryos of the skinks *Eumeces fasciatus* and *Eumeces obsoletus* probably could not survive prolonged exposure to temperatures exceeding 40°C (see Muth, 1980; Sexton and Marion, 1974). Nevertheless, young can withstand temperatures of 42°C for 4 hours (Fitch and Fitch, 1967) and of 43°C for 30 min (Fitch, 1964). Thus, duration of exposure must be considered in any discussion of limits of thermal tolerance.

Embryos of numerous reptiles from temperate regions can withstand exposure for extended periods to low temperatures of 4–12°C (e.g., Cunningham, 1922; Fitch, 1954; Legler, 1960; Maderson and Bellairs, 1962), but die at temperatures below this range (Fitch, 1964; Fitch and Fitch, 1967). Older embryos may be better able to tolerate such exposure than younger ones (Holder and Bellairs, 1962). During these extended periods at low temperature, metabolism of young apparently is arrested almost completely. Development resumes when embryos are subsequently returned to favorable thermal environments, and the only apparent effect of the sojourn at low temperature is prolongation of incubation by a period equivalent to the duration of the cold exposure (Legler, 1960).

2. METABOLISM

Because reptilian embryos are ectotherms, their metabolism is expected to vary as a positive function of temperature (G. C. Packard et al., 1977). This prediction has been tested only once, however, in a study of oxygen consumption by advanced embryos of the snake *Opheodrys vernalis* (Zarrow and Pomerat, 1937). Four eggs from a single clutch found beneath a log were brought to the laboratory and studied at constant temperatures spanning the range 12–30°C. Metabolism of the embryos varied with temperature in the predicted manner, with a higher Q_{10} between 12–24°C than between 25–30°C.

A substantial body of indirect evidence also supports the concept that metabolism of embryonic reptiles is positively correlated with temperature. Embryos of the snake *Python molurus* grow more rapidly at high temperatures than they do at low temperatures (Vinegar, 1973), and developing young of numerous squamates (Clark, 1970; Dmi'el, 1967; Gutzke and Packard, 1987a; Mendelssohn, 1963, 1965; Muth, 1980; Platt, 1969; Sexton and Marion, 1974; Zweifel, 1980) and turtles (Dodge et al., 1978; Gutzke, 1984a; Legler, 1960; Miller, 1982, 1985; Miller and Limpus, 1981; Mrosovsky and Yntema, 1980; G. C. Packard et al., 1987; Yntema, 1968, 1978) complete incubation sooner in warm environments than they do in cooler ones (Fig. 7). Rapid growth and early completion of development at high temperatures presumably are reflections of higher rates of metabolism under these conditions than prevail at lower temperatures (but see Section VII.B).

Another effect of temperature is manifested as variation in size of carcasses and residual yolk of hatchlings. Painted turtles (*Chrysemys picta*) and bullsnakes (*Pituophis melanoleucus*) hatching from eggs incubated at low (22°C) and intermediate (27°C) temperatures have larger bodies, but smaller residual yolks, than young emerging from eggs held at high (32°C) temperatures (Gutzke, 1984a; Gutzke and Packard, 1987a). Similar findings have been reported for snapping turtles (*Chelydra serpentina*) incubated at 26.0°C, 28.5°C, and 31.0°C (G. C. Packard et al., 1987). Thus, embryos developing at high temperatures seemingly have higher rates of metabolism than those at low temperatures, but their metabolic efficiency—defined here as the efficiency of converting energy reserves into tissues—is reduced.

In contrast to these species, alligators (*Alligator mississippiensis*) hatch-

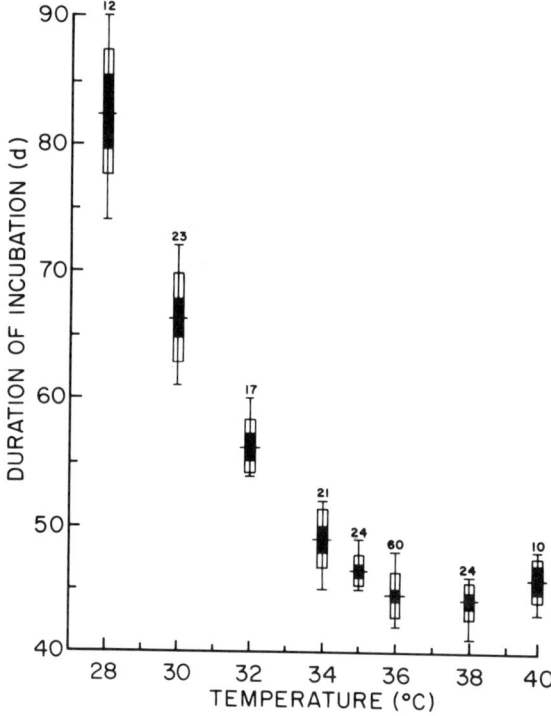

Fig. 7. Relation between length of incubation and ambient temperature for embryos of the lizard *Dipsosaurus dorsalis*. Horizontal line, mean; darkened bar, ±2 SE; open bar, ±1 SD; vertical line, range; sample size as indicated. (Redrawn and modified from Muth, 1980.)

ing from eggs incubated at high temperatures (34°C) are reported to have smaller residual yolks than animals emerging from eggs incubated at lower temperatures (30°C) (Ferguson and Joanen, 1982, 1983). The study was not based on hatchling alligators, however, but on embryos that had undergone 60 days of development irrespective of incubation temperature (Ferguson and Joanen, 1982, 1983). Embryos sampled at 34°C probably were nearer to hatching than those sampled at 30°C (Fig. 7), so findings for these two groups of embryos may not be representative of hatchlings. This study needs to be repeated to resolve the question of residual yolk size.

All of the aforementioned investigations were performed at constant temperatures. We look forward to learning whether the metabolic response of an embryo to a particular temperature is the same under transient and steady-state conditions.

3. ACID/BASE BALANCE

Acid/base physiology has been studied extensively in adult reptiles (Howell and Rahn, 1976), but not as yet in embryos. We nevertheless introduce the subject here to illustrate the pervasive effects of temperature on the physiology of reptilian embryos, and to gain perspective concerning problems of physiological control in animals exposed to sublethal fluctuations in temperature.

Consider the blood plasma of a reptilian embryo. The acid/base status of this liquid can be characterized using nine simultaneous equations for chemical equilibria (see Stewart, 1981):

(1) $K'_W = [H^+][OH^-]$

(2) $K_A [HA] = [H^+][A^-]$

(3) $[A_{TOTAL}] = [HA] + [A^-]$

(4) $[CO_2] = S_{CO_2} \times P_{CO_2}$

(5) $K'_{CO_2} [CO_2] = [H_2CO_3]$

(6) $K_{H2CO3} [H_2CO_3] = [H^+][HCO_3^-]$

(7) $K_{HCO3} [HCO_3^-] = [H^+][CO_3^{-2}]$

(8) $[CO_2] + [H_2CO_3] + [HCO_3^-] + [CO_3^{-2}] = [CO_{2TOTAL}]$

(9) $[SID] + [H^+] - [OH^-] - [A^-] - [HCO_3^-] - [CO_3^{-2}] = 0$

where K'_W is the ion product for water, $[H^+]$ is the concentration of hydrogen ions (equivalents per liter), $[OH^-]$ is the concentration of hydroxyl ions (equivalents per liter), K_A is the dissociation constant for weak acid, $[HA]$ is the concentration of weak acid in undissociated form (equivalents per liter), $[A^-]$ is the concentration of anion of the weak acid (equivalents per liter), $[A_{TOTAL}]$ is the total concentration of weak acid (equivalents per liter), $[CO_2]$ is the concentration of carbon dioxide in solution in the plasma (equivalents per liter), S_{CO_2} is the solubility coefficient for carbon dioxide in plasma (equivalents per liter per kPa), P_{CO_2} is the partial pressure of carbon dioxide (kPa), K'_{CO_2} is the equilibrium constant for hydration of carbon dioxide to form carbonic acid, $[H_2CO_3]$ is the concentration of carbonic acid (equivalents per liter), K_{H2CO3} is the dissociation constant for carbonic acid, $[HCO_3^-]$ is the concentration of bicarbonate ions (equivalents per liter), K_{HCO3} is the dissociation constant for bicarbonate, $[CO_3^{-2}]$ is the concentration of carbonate ions (equivalent per liter), $[CO_{2TOTAL}]$ is the total concentration of carbon dioxide (equivalents per liter), and [SID] is the strong ion difference (equivalents per liter). The strong ion difference is, effectively, the sum of $[Na^+]$ and $[Ca^{+2}]$ minus $[Cl^-]$.

Equation (1) is a formal statement of the dissociation of pure water into hydrogen and hydroxyl ions; equation (2) characterizes the dissociation of weak acid into its component ions; equation (3) characterizes conservation of mass for the weak acid; equation (4) quantifies the amount of dissolved carbon dioxide in the liquid; equation (5) is the equilibrium reaction for hydration of carbon dioxide to form carbonic acid; equation (6) describes the dissocation of carbonic acid into hydrogen and bicarbonate ions; equation (7) describes the dissociation of bicarbonate into hydrogen and carbonate ions; equation (8) characterizes the conservation of mass for carbon dioxide; and equation (9) satisfies the requirement for electrical neutrality of the solution (Stewart, 1981).

Three fundamentally different classes of variables appear in these several equations: independent physical variables, independent physiological variables, and dependent physiological variables (Stewart, 1981). Independent physical variables are those that are governed by laws of nature and over which developing embryos have no control; K'_W, K_A, K'_{CO2}, K_{H2CO3}, K_{HCO3}, and S_{CO2} are examples. Independent physiological variables, on the other hand, are those potentially under the direct physiological control of developing embryos, via organs such as the kidneys, intestine, or chorioallantois; we include [SID], $[A_{TOTAL}]$, and P_{CO2} in this category. Finally, dependent physiological variables are those that change passively in response to changes in both of the preceding classes of variables and that can be regulated only indirectly; $[H^+]$, $[OH^-]$, [HA], $[A^-]$, $[CO_2]$, $[H_2CO_3]$, $[HCO_3^-]$, $[CO_3^{2-}]$, and $[CO_{2TOTAL}]$ are examples.

Because all of the independent physical variables change with temperature (Albers, 1970), fluctuations in temperature of reptilian eggs presumably could elicit shifts in the several chemical equilibria characterizing blood plasma of embryos, thereby bringing about major changes in all of the dependent physiological variables. However, changes in two of the dependent physiological variables, namely [HA] and $[A^-]$, could seriously impair the capacity for embryos to exercise control over numerous metabolic functions.

A variety of proteins together comprise the weak acid found in plasma (Stewart, 1981). Some of these proteins are hormones, some function in the transport of other molecules, and some are enzymes. In almost every instance, however, the specific function of a particular protein molecule is dependent on its conformation (i.e., its tertiary and/or quaternary structure). Conformation of these proteins is affected by their net electrical charge, which is determined, in turn, by the degree of ionization of side-groups of the many amino acid residues, particularly the imidazole group of histidine (Reeves, 1977; Reeves and Rahn, 1979). To conserve conformation of all of these proteins and thereby to assure their continued role in a variety of metabolic activities, the fractional dissociation of the imidazolium must be held constant. However, the total concentration of protein, [A_{TOTAL}], probably does not vary appreciably over the course of a single day (see Stewart, 1981), so control of fractional dissociation is equivalent to holding constant the concentrations of imidazolium in ionized ([A^-]) and unionized states ([HA]).

Among adult reptiles confronted with changes in body temperature, regulation of [HA] and [A^-] is accomplished by altering the rate of ventilation relative to metabolic demand for oxygen (Howell and Rahn, 1976; Reeves, 1977). The P_{CO_2} of plasma is shifted upward at high temperatures and downward at low temperatures, thereby compensating for effects of temperature on the independent physical variables and holding [HA] and [A^-] relatively constant (Reeves, 1977; Reeves and Rahn, 1979). If a similar mechanism for compensating temperature changes is manifested by embryos, it must entail shifts in blood flow through the chorioallantois and attendant changes in resistance of the membrane to gas exchange. Of course, control of [HA] and [A^-] could be effected also by altering [SID] via the kidneys or the chorioallantois, but such mechanisms probably would be too slow to allow changes in acid/base status to keep pace with changes in temperature in the nest chamber.

This analysis could easily be extended to the intracellular compartment, where thermally-induced perturbations of acid/base status presumably would have further effects on metabolism (see Busa and Nuccitelli, 1984; Walsh and Moon, 1982; Yancey and Somero, 1978). Regardless of whether attention is focused on intracellular or extracellular compartments, however, diel cycles in temperature inside nests of many reptiles clearly have the potential to disrupt integrated metabolic systems by virtue of effects on acid/base status of embryos. The degree to which embryos regulate acid/base status in the face of continuous changes in temperature, or tolerate disruptions of metabolism attending thermally-induced shifts in acid/base status, has yet to be evaluated.

4. SEXUAL DIFFERENTIATION

All crocodilians, most turtles, and many lepidosaurians lack heteromorphic sex chromosomes (Bull, 1980). Sexual differentiation by embryos in many of these animals is affected by the temperature of incubation (Bull, 1980). For example, incubation of turtle eggs at constant temperatures above 30°C usually elicits differentiation of phenotypic females, whereas exposure of their eggs to 24–28°C usually elicits differentiation of phenotypic males. Both males and females arise from eggs exposed to 28–30°C, but proportions vary from predominantly male near 28°C to predominantly female near 30°C. This general pattern of response has been reported for numerous cheloniids, chelydrids, dermochelyids, emydids, kinosternids, pelomedusids, and testudinids (Table II). Exposure of eggs of some of these turtles to temperatures below 24°C again elicits differentiation of females, indicating that a second temperature "threshold" occasionally exists (Gutzke and Paukstis, 1984; Schwarzkopf and Brooks, 1985; Vogt et al., 1982; Yntema, 1976, 1979, 1981). However, exposure of eggs of the other species to temperatures below 24°C continues to elicit differentiation of males (Pieau, 1978).

Sexual differentiation in chelids, trionychids, and some emydids (e.g., *Clemmys insculpta*) is unaffected by temperature (Bull and Vogt, 1979; Bull et al., 1985; Thompson, 1983; Vogt and Bull, 1982b), and presumably is controlled by the genotype. Genetic control is suspected to occur also in the few emydids and kinosternids (and chelids) possessing heteromorphic sex chromosomes (Bull et al., 1974; Carr and Bickham, 1981; McBee et al., 1985; Sites et al., 1979).

Sexual differentiation by embryos of crocodilians and some lizards also is influenced by temperature. In contrast to the situation in turtles, however, the embryonic crocodilians and lizards usually differentiate as males at relatively high temperatures and as females at relatively low temperatures (Bull, 1980; Charnier, 1966; Ferguson and Joanen, 1982, 1983; Lang, 1985; Wagner, 1980). Embryos of *Gekko japonicus* and perhaps also of *Crocodylus johnsoni* are exceptional in showing patterns of sexual differentiation similar to those reported for many turtles, with females arising in eggs held at high or low temperatures and with males emerging from eggs exposed to intermediate temperatures (Tokunaga, 1985; Webb and Smith, 1984; Webb et al., 1983a).

Many lepidosaurians possess heteromorphic sex chromosomes (Bull, 1980; Gorman, 1973), and sexual differentiation in these forms presumably is under genetic control. Moreover, the process is under genetic control even in some of the species lacking distinct sex chromosomes (Muth and Bull, 1981; Raynaud and Pieau, 1972).

TABLE II
Species of Turtles in Which Environmental Control of Sexual Differentiation Has Been Reported to Occur

Species	Family	Reference
Caretta caretta	Cheloniidae	Mrosovsky et al., 1984a; Yntema and Mrosovsky, 1980, 1982
Chelonia mydas	Cheloniidae	Miller and Limpus, 1981; Morreale et al., 1982; Mrosovsky, 1982; Mrosovsky et al., 1984b
Eretmochelys imbricata	Cheloniidae	Dalrymple et al., 1985
Lepidochelys olivacea	Cheloniidae	McCoy et al., 1983; Standora and Spotila, 1985
Chelydra serpentina	Chelydridae	G. C. Packard et al., 1987; Wilhoft et al., 1983; Yntema, 1976, 1979, 1981
Dermochelys coriacea	Dermochelyidae	Dutton et al., 1985; Mrosovsky et al., 1984b; Rimblot et al., 1985
Chrysemys picta	Emydidae	Bull and Vogt, 1979, 1981; Bull et al., 1982; Gutzke and Paukstis, 1983, 1984; Paukstis et al., 1984; Schwarzkopf and Brooks, 1985
Emydoidea blandingii	Emydidae	Gutzke and Packard, 1987b
Emys orbicularis	Emydidae	Pieau, 1971, 1972, 1975, 1976, 1978, 1982; Pieau and Dorizzi, 1981; Zaborski et al., 1982
Graptemys geographica	Emydidae	Bull and Vogt, 1979; Bull et al., 1982
Graptemys ouachitensis	Emydidae	Bull and Vogt, 1979, 1981; Bull et al., 1982
Graptemys pseudogeographica	Emydidae	Bull and Vogt, 1979; Bull et al., 1982
Graptaemys pulchra	Emydidae	Bull et al., 1982
Pseudemys scripta	Emydidae	Bull et al., 1982
Terrapene ornata	Emydidae	G. C. Packard et al., 1985a
Kinosternon flavescens	Kinosternidae	Vogt et al., 1982
Sternotherus odoratus	Kinosternidae	Vogt et al., 1982
Podocnemis expansa	Pelomedusidae	Alho et al., 1985
Testudo graeca	Testudinidae	Pieau, 1971, 1972, 1975

TEMPERATURE

Patterns of sexual differentiation of embryonic turtles and crocodilians developing in natural nests generally are consistent with results of laboratory investigations, indicating that experiments performed at constant temperature are ecologically relevant. Nests of cheloniids, emydids, and pelomedusids located in warm, sunny sites give rise to a greater proportion of female hatchlings than do nests located in cool, shady settings (Alho et al., 1985; Bull, 1985; Bull and Vogt, 1979; Morreale et al., 1982; Vogt and Bull, 1984). Also, the proportion of females emerging from nests of *Emys orbicularis* is directly related to the amount of time that nest temperature is above 28.5°C (Pieau, 1982), whereas the proportion of males hatching from nests of *Chrysemys picta* seems to be related to the amount of the time eggs are exposed to temperatures between 20°C and 27.5°C (Schwarzkopf and Brooks, 1985). Hatchling *Chelydra serpentina* emerging from eggs in the warm, upper reaches of nests tend to be female, whereas those emerging from eggs in the cooler regions at the bottom of nests tend to be males (Wilhoft et al., 1983). Finally, nests of alligators (*Alligator mississippiensis*) located on levees are much warmer than nests built in open marsh, and the former yield larger proportions of males than do the latter (Ferguson and Joanen, 1982, 1983).

The middle one-third of incubation is the period in which temperature exerts its control over sexual differentiation of turtle embryos (Bull and Vogt, 1981; Pieau and Dorizzi, 1981; Yntema, 1979; Yntema and Mrosovsky, 1982), but the period of sensitivity is somewhat earlier than this in crocodilian embryos (Ferguson and Joanen, 1982, 1983). However, crocodilian embryos are slightly more advanced at oviposition than are turtle embryos (Section II.A, B), so the period of sensitivity may actually occur at equivalent stages in both groups. The period of sensitivity has not been established for any of the lizards in which environmental control of sexual differentiation occurs.

The exact way in which temperature intervenes in differentiation of the gonads is not clear (Raynaud and Pieau, 1985; Standora and Spotila, 1985; also Section VII.B). Although none of the species exhibiting environmental control of sexual differentiation possesses heteromorphic sex chromosomes (Bull, 1980), genetic males and females nonetheless can be identified, at least in turtles, by the use of H-Y antigens (Engel et al., 1981). Genetic factors are easily overridden by temperature (Zaborski et al., 1982), however, leading to differentiation of the gonads into testes or ovaries. Secretion of steroid hormones presumably induces the subsequent differentiation of secondary sexual characters appropriate to males and females (Pieau et al., 1982; Raynaud and Pieau, 1985).

V. WATER

A. Factors Affecting Water Balance of Eggs

Water presumably moves in both liquid and vapor phases down gradients in free energy in the soil–egg continuum (Corey and Klute, 1985; Taylor, 1965; Taylor and Stewart, 1960). Accordingly, any treatment of the factors affecting water transport in this continuum should be based on thermodynamic principles. Water potential is a measure of the energy required to overcome the forces of adhesion, cohesion, and ionic attraction that bind molecules of water to particles of soil (Marshall and Holmes, 1979; Taylor and Ashcroft, 1972). We therefore adopt the concept of water potential for use in the present discussion.

The water balance of a reptilian egg can be described using an equation based on the principle of conservation of mass (see Ackerman et al., 1985b; Tracy, 1982; Tracy et al., 1978):

$$m_S = m_M + m_L + m_V \tag{8}$$

where m_S is storage (or loss) of water inside the egg, m_M is water produced by the embryo in intermediary metabolism, m_L is uptake (or loss) of liquid from the environment, and m_V is uptake (or loss) of vapor from the surroundings. Whenever the uptake of water from the environment plus production of metabolic water balances water loss, there is no change in the mass of water available to support embryonic development. Whenever the uptake of water plus metabolic water does not balance water loss, however, the mass of water must change. The terms in this equation for water storage (m_S in mg $\times$ s^{-1}) and for production of metabolic water (m_M in mg $\times$ s^{-1}) are straightforward and require no special explanation, but the other two terms can be expanded to reveal more explicitly the factors affecting water transport between eggs and their environment.

Transport of liquid water can be described as

$$m_L = k_L \times A_S \times (\psi_S - \psi_E) \tag{9}$$

where k_L is a coefficient for transport of liquid water across the eggshell (mg $\times$ s^{-1} $\times$ cm^{-2} $\times$ kPa^{-1}), A_S is surface area of the eggshell contacting the substrate (cm^2), and ($\psi_S - \psi_E$) is the difference in water potential between the soil and egg (kPa). All of the independent variables in this equation are subject to change during the course of incubation, thereby making transport of liquid a very complex process.

For instance, water potential of the soil may vary appreciably over the course of incubation in concert with cycles in wetting and drying (Section V.B). The effective water potential of the egg itself changes during development as different fluid compartments (with different solute potentials) come into proximity to the inside of the eggshell (Muth, 1981; G. C. Packard et al., 1981a, 1983). Also, the surface area available for transport of liquid may change in consequence of dirt and debris infiltrating into air spaces in the nest chamber, and the transport coefficient may change in eggs with flexible shells owing to distension or contraction of fibers in the shell membrane.

The soil water potential of interest in equation (9) is that for soil contacting the surface of the eggshell. In most instances, this value will not be the same as that characterizing soil only a few centimeters away (Gutzke, 1984b; Tracy, 1982). Water generally cannot be transported through the substrate fast enough to keep pace with water exchanges at the surface of the eggshell. Consequently, the soil adjacent to the eggshell either accumulates water or is depleted of water, and therefore is at a different water potential than the soil at large. This phenomenon is familiar to plant physiologists, who have documented the major resistance to water transport imposed by soil adjacent to plant roots (e.g., Legge, 1985).

Reptilian eggs also exchange vapor with their environment, as follows:

$$m_V = k_V \times A_A \times (p_E - p_A) \qquad (10)$$

where k_V is the transport coefficient for vapor diffusing between the egg and surrounding air (including that in the soil) (mg $\times$ s^{-1} $\times$ cm^{-2} $\times$ kPa^{-1}), A_A is the area of the eggshell across which vapor is transported (cm^2), and p_E and p_A are the vapor pressures of the egg and air, respectively (kPa). All of the independent variables in this equation also are subject to change during the course of incubation, so vapor transport is another complex process. For example, vapor pressure of both the egg and surrounding air change with temperature, and therefore can be expected to change according to a daily cycle (Section IV.B) Additionally, the transport coefficient may be higher at high ambient vapor pressures than at low ambient vapor pressures (Feder et al., 1982; Lillywhite and Ackerman, 1984).

The present treatment of water balance differs in certain ways from earlier ones. A common assumption in prior research was that water produced by embryos in intermediary metabolism is not an important component of water balance (Ackerman et al., 1985b; G. C. Packard et al., 1981a; Tracy, 1982; Tracy et al., 1978). However, avian embryos produce substantial quantities of water metabolically (Ar and Rahn, 1980), so it may be premature to assume that metabolic water is unimportant to reptilian embryos. Equation (8) therefore includes a term for metabolic water.

Secondly, water exchange across reptilian eggshells has been attributed by some workers entirely to diffusion of vapor (Ackerman et al., 1985b). However, the uptake of nonvolatile dyes by incubating turtle eggs indicates that transport of liquid also occurs (Thompson, 1987). We therefore include a term in equation (8) for transport of liquid as well as one for transport of vapor. Transport of liquid may ultimately be shown to be a minor component of the water budget of an egg (Ackerman et al., 1985b), but empirical evidence must be developed in support of this view.

Finally, transport of vapor across eggshells has been assumed by some workers to be continuously in an outward direction (Tracy, 1982; Tracy et al., 1978). This assumption has recently been questioned on both theoretical (Ackerman et al., 1985b) and empirical grounds (Morris et al., 1983; G. C. Packard et al., 1979a, 1980, 1981a), and seems no longer to be tenable. We subscribe to the view that vapor passes in either direction across eggshells, with the net direction of movement being established by gradients in vapor pressure.

B. Hydration of Nests

The flexible-shelled eggs of many testudinians and lepidosaurians have long been known to respond dramatically to variation in hydration of their environment (e.g., Brimley, 1903; Coker, 1910; Cunningham and Huene, 1938; Cunningham and Hurwitz, 1936; Cunningham et al., 1939; Dendy, 1899b). However, despite the consequent awareness among herpetologists of the likely importance of water to developing young (G. C. Packard et al., 1977), relatively few workers have measured moisture in reptilian nests. The few measurements fall into three categories based on methodology.

(1) Several studies reported the mass of water per unit mass of sand or soil in the walls of subterranean nests of turtles and certain crocodilians (Bustard and Greenham, 1968; Coker, 1906; Lutz and Dunbar-Cooper, 1984; McGehee, 1979; Webb et al., 1983a), and one reported the water content of vegetation forming mound nests of another crocodilian (Chabreck, 1975). Although data such as these may reveal tendencies for walls of nests to collapse during construction (e.g., Bustard and Greenham, 1968) or for gases to diffuse through substrates into nest

WATER

cavities (e.g., Lutz and Dunbar-Cooper, 1984), they are of little value in elucidating water relations per se. This point can be illustrated most readily by drawing an analogy between the water content (and water potential) of a substrate and its heat content (and temperature).

Heat content is a familiar measure for the total kinetic energy of all the molecules comprising the substrate in question. However, information on heat content alone cannot reveal whether heat will flow between this substrate and some reference system, or whether the two media are in a thermodynamic equilibrium. The direction of heat flow is determined by the average kinetic energy of molecules in the substrate relative to that of molecules in the reference system. Thus, temperature, which is a measure of average kinetic energy, is more useful than heat content in assessing the tendency and direction for heat to move between the substrate and the reference system.

Measurements of gravimetric water-content are analogous to measurements of heat content, and measurements of water potential are analogous to measurements of temperature. Water content yields information on how much water actually is present in the substrate, but water potential yields information on the tendency for water to move isothermally between this substrate and some reference system. Thus, measurements of water potential are more useful than measurements of water content in elucidating the movements of water inside reptilian nests.

Water retention curves for three different kinds of soils illustrate this point further (Fig. 8). A sand substrate containing 4% water is at equilibrium with a clay substrate containing 21% water, because the water potential is the same in both media (i.e., −200 kPa). Thus, there is no tendency for water to flow from the clay to the sand, even though much larger quantities of water are present in the former than in the latter. Conversely, a silty substrate containing 19% water is not in equilibrium with a clay substrate at the same level of hydration, because water potential of the former is −200 kPa and that of the latter is −420 kPa. Water would flow from the silt to the clay despite the fact that water content of the two media is identical at the outset.

A surprising diversity of soil types is used for nesting by individual species of reptiles, even within a restricted geographic area (Lutz and Dunbar-Cooper, 1984; Stancyk and Ross, 1978; Thompson, 1983; Webb et al., 1983a; Whitaker and Whitaker, 1984). The different water retention characteristics for different types of soil (Fig. 8) indicate clearly that comparisons among reptilian nests in different kinds of substrates should be undertaken with measurements of water potential, but not with measurements of gravimetric water content.

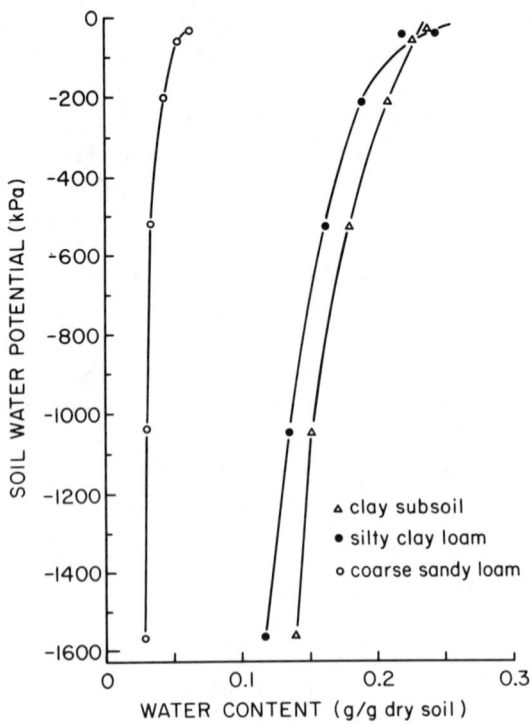

Fig. 8. Water retention curves for three substrates at a temperature of 15°C. The substrates vary in texture from a sandy loam (large particles) to a clay (fine particles). (Redrawn and modified from Taylor and Ashcroft, 1972.)

(2) Hydration inside nests of the gecko *Gehyra variegata* and of the crocodilians *Alligator mississippiensis* and *Caiman crocodilus* was assessed by measuring relative humidity (RH) of air trapped inside the egg chamber (Bustard, 1969a; Joanen, 1970; Staton and Dixon, 1977). Values of 55–80% RH were recorded in one gecko nest, and 85–98% RH in several nests of the crocodilians. Although relative humidity can be used in principle to infer water potential of substrates (Brown, 1970), the humidities in these nests would correspond to exceedingly dry conditions (Marshall and Holmes, 1979). Droplets of water nonetheless were observed in nests of one of the crocodilians (Joanen, 1970), so the nests probably were not as dry as the humidities would make it appear. We suspect that the nests were partially flushed with atmospheric air, thereby preventing vapor in air from coming into equilibrium with liquid in the substrate. This interpretation is consistent with location and construction of the nests. The gecko nest was under a loose slab of bark

lying on the surface of the ground (Bustard, 1969a), and mound nests of both crocodilians commonly have an open construction conducive to partial ventilation of the egg chamber (Chabreck, 1975; Staton and Dixon, 1977).

Partial ventilation of nests of this gecko and the two crocodilians probably is normal. Rigid-shelled eggs of geckos and crocodilians have low permeabilities to water vapor (Dunson, 1982; Dunson and Bramham, 1981; Lutz et al., 1980; G. C. Packard et al., 1979b; Tracy, 1982), so humidities such as have been reported need not lead to excessive evaporation from eggs and consequent desiccation of embryos. Furthermore, uptake of liquid water conceivably compensates for at least a portion of the vapor that may be lost (see Section V.A).

(3) Finally, two investigations reported water potentials in reptilian nests. In the first of these studies, a sample of soil was removed from the bottom of each of several iguana (*Conolophus subcristatus*) nests shortly after the young lizards had emerged from the cavity (Snell and Tracy, 1985). The samples were sealed in glass vials and later were taken to the laboratory, where water potentials apparently were measured by dewpoint hygrometry (sensu Savage et al., 1981). Values ranged from approximately -100 kPa in wet nests to less than $-11,000$ kPa in dry ones. Water potentials below $-1,500$ kPa generally lead to permanent wilting of plants (including many desert forms), so the data for iguanas indicate that their eggs may be exposed to a truly remarkable spectrum of conditions.

Collecting soil samples at the end of incubation and taking them into the laboratory for further analysis has the major advantage of being relatively simple. The important disadvantage of this method, however, is that a single measurement taken at the end of incubation affords only a rough index, at best, of the moisture conditions to which eggs were exposed throughout development. Also, the sampling-induced change in bulk density of the soil may reduce the accuracy of measurements taken in the laboratory (e.g., Box and Taylor, 1962; Campbell and Gardner, 1971; Taylor and Box, 1961).

In the second study, water potentials in nests of snapping turtles (*Chelydra serpentina*) were measured throughout incubation using indwelling thermocouple psychrometers (G. C. Packard et al., 1985b). Water potentials increased to field capacity (i.e., -100 kPa or higher) after periods of heavy rainfall, but declined below -1500 kPa during periods of fair weather (Fig. 9). During intervals of little or no rainfall, water potentials in nests exhibited diel variation, and values frequently differed between the top and bottom of nest cavities. Thus, availability

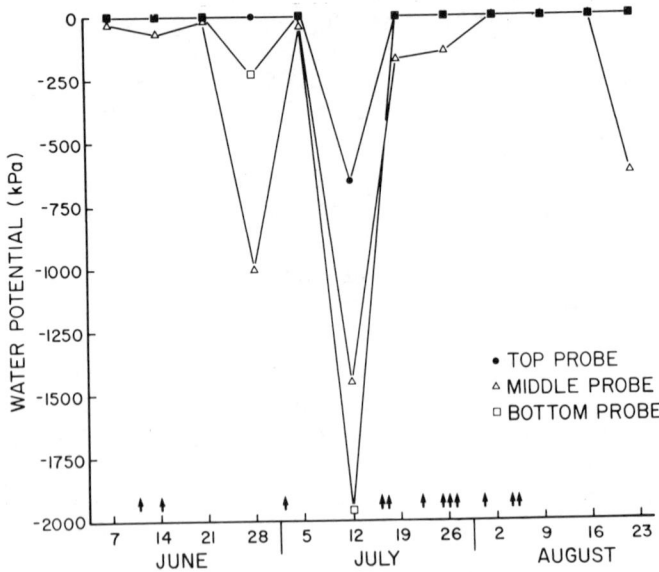

Fig. 9. Water potentials inside a nest of a snapping turtle (*Chelydra serpentina*) over the course of incubation. Measurements were made at noon on one day each week using indwelling thermocouple psychrometers. The top probe was in sand forming the plug to the nest, and was just above the egg chamber. The middle probe was in the middle of the egg mass. The bottom probe was in sand directly beneath the bottom eggs. Arrows identify days on which 1 cm or more of precipitation was recorded. (Redrawn and modified from G. C. Packard et al., 1985b.)

of water varied considerably over the course of incubation, and often at different sites within individual nests during a single day.

The use of indwelling psychrometers to monitor hydration of nests has two advantages. First, daily and seasonal variation in water potential can be assessed in the same nests, thereby providing relatively complete information on the conditions to which eggs are exposed for the duration of incubation. Second, temperatures are recorded simultaneously with readings of water potential, so thermally-induced movement of water can also be evaluated.

A knowledge of thermally-induced movements of water probably is critical to understanding water relations of eggs in natural nests. In the study of water potential in nests of snapping turtles (G. C. Packard et al., 1985b), diel cycles in temperature at the top, middle, and bottom of nests drove cycles in evaporation and condensation that led in turn to complex cycles in diffusion of water vapor through the cavities. In one nest, vapor diffused vertically upward through the chamber at 0600, and vertically downward through the cavity at 1800 (note the vapor pres-

TABLE III
Diel Cycle in Temperature, Water Potential, and Vapor Pressure Inside a Nest of a Snapping Turtle (*Chelydra serpentina*)

Time	Temperature (°C)	Water potential (kPa)	Relative humidity (%)	Saturation vapor pressure (kPa)	Nest vapor pressure (kPa)
Top of nest					
0600	22.00	0	100.0	2.643	2.643
1200	24.25	0	100.0	3.028	3.028
1800	31.00	−560	99.6	4.492	4.474
2400	26.50	0	100.0	3.461	3.461
Middle of nest					
0600	22.75	−60	100.0	2.767	2.767
1200	22.50	−40	100.0	2.725	2.725
1800	28.75	0	100.0	3.947	3.947
2400	27.00	−60	100.0	3.565	3.565
Bottom of nest					
0600	23.25	0	100.0	2.851	2.851
1200	23.00	0	100.0	2.809	2.809
1800	26.50	0	100.0	3.461	3.461
2400	26.50	0	100.0	3.461	3.461

From G. C. Packard et al., 1985b.

sures reported in Table III for the top, middle, and bottom of this nest). However, vapor diffused vertically out of the nest cavity both upward and downward at 2400, and into the egg chamber from both above and below at 1200 (Table III). Thus, eggs presumably were losing water for at least that part of the day when movement of vapor was out of the cavity, and were gaining water (by condensation onto surfaces of eggshells) for that part of the day when movement of vapor was into the nest. The differences in vapor pressure between different points in the nest may appear at first to be too small to be important in water exchange (Table III). Nevertheless, diffusion of vapor probably is more important than flow of liquid in translocating water in the upper reaches of the soil profile where reptilian nests are most likely to occur (Cary, 1966; Gurr et al., 1952; Jackson et al., 1965; Philip and de Vries, 1957; Rose, 1968a, b). The importance of these differences therefore should not be underestimated.

An important disadvantage of the psychrometric method is that it is highly labor-intensive. Even the calibration of psychrometers is extraordinarily time-consuming, because each probe should be individually calibrated against standard salt solutions before it is used in the field and again after all measurements have been completed (Brown and Bartos, 1982; Meyn and White, 1972; Savage et al., 1981, 1983). A second disadvantage concerns the extraordinary sensitivity of psychrometers to the small gradients in temperature that occur commonly in soil (Merrill and Rawlins, 1972; Wiebe and Brown, 1979; Wiebe et al., 1977). Special care must be taken in placing probes in nests and in taking readings to assure that the measurements of water potential are reliable (Brown and Bartos, 1982).

C. Exchanges of Water by Eggs in Nature

Reptilian eggs incubating in natural nests seemingly experience a net uptake of water under some conditions and a net loss of water under others. The evidence supporting this statement admittedly is fragmentary and oftentimes circumstantial, but water exchanges undoubtedly occur.

For example, flexible-shelled eggs of a lizard and a turtle have been observed to swell during incubation and to become firmly wedged into their nest chambers (Cagle, 1950; Whitaker, 1968). Additionally, flexible-shelled eggs of turtles and rigid-shelled eggs of a crocodilian have been reported to weigh more after a period of incubation than they did at oviposition (Hendrickson, 1958; M. J. Packard et al., 1982c; Staton and Dixon, 1977). Such findings are convincing evidence for net absorption of water by eggs incubating in nature.

The uptake of water by rigid-shelled eggs of turtles and crocodilians may even cause the shell to fracture under some circumstances (Goodwin and Marion, 1978; Joanen, 1970; McIlhenny, 1934, 1935; Plummer, 1976; Pooley, 1962; Webb et al., 1977, 1983c), and associated swelling may cause edges of the cracks to draw apart to expose the underlying membrane. As long as the membrane remains intact, however, the embryo usually completes development successfully (Joanen, 1970; also Ferguson, 1982). Absorption of water to the point of fracturing the calcareous layer of the eggshell probably is the exception rather than the rule (G. C. Packard et al., 1981c; Webb et al., 1977), but may happen any time that free water stands in the nest chamber for an extended period. Water may collect in nests that are subject to inundation (Plummer, 1976) or that are sufficiently "tight" as to prevent rainwater from draining away (Legler, 1954).

Conversely, flexible-shelled eggs of turtles and rigid-shelled eggs of crocodilians have also been reported on other occasions to decline in mass during incubation (Lutz and Dunbar-Cooper, 1984; Moore, 1953;

M. J. Packard et al., 1982c; Staton and Dixon, 1977), indicating that a net loss of water has occurred. The occasional formation of dents in flexible-shelled eggs of turtles (Cagle, 1937; Legler, 1954) and of air spaces inside rigid-shelled eggs of crocodilians is further evidence for loss of water from eggs incubating in natural nests (Ferguson, 1982; Webb et al., 1983c).

Thus, eggs incubating in natural nests of a particular species probably vary widely in net water-exchange with the environment and consequently in overall water balance (M. J. Packard et al., 1982c). We shall now consider the possible effects of such variation on developing embryos.

D. Physiological Effects of Water

1. METHODS OF STUDY

Most research into the importance of water to reptilian embryos has been performed in the laboratory, where the environment to which eggs are exposed is subject to a measure of control. Unfortunately, work reported before 1978 (and numerous accounts appearing more recently) suffered from inadequate characterization for hydration of the environment (Sections V.A, B), and therefore is of limited value in elucidating either the patterns of water exchange by incubating eggs or the physiological effects of such exchange on developing embryos (G. C. Packard et al., 1977). Substrates used in many of these earlier investigations seem to have been saturated with water—a condition that would have had a profound influence on patterns of water exchange by eggs and probably on physiology of developing young (G. C. Packard et al., 1980). We therefore focus on those studies appearing since 1978 in which water potentials were reported.

Recent investigations of the water relations of reptilian eggs have made use of three different methodologies. Some workers have incubated eggs over salt solutions, thereby controlling water potential of the environment more precisely than would otherwise be possible (Muth, 1980, 1981). Other investigators have incubated eggs on substrates of moistened vermiculite, primarily because of the ease and convenience in working with this material (Black et al., 1984; Gutzke, 1984a; Gutzke and Packard, 1986, 1987a; Morris et al., 1983; G. C. and M. J. Packard, 1987; G. C. Packard et al., 1979a, 1980, 1981a, b, c, 1982, 1983, 1984a, b, 1985a, 1987; M. J. and G. C. Packard, 1986; M. J. Packard et al., 1980; Tracy, 1980; Tracy et al., 1978). Still other investigators have used moistened soil or sand as a medium, thereby better simulating natural conditions for incubation (Andrews and Sexton, 1981; Thompson, 1983; Tracy and Snell, 1985).

Recent research with a mechanistic model led to the prediction that patterns of net water-exchange by reptilian eggs will be profoundly affected by the type of substrate on which they rest (Ackerman et al., 1985b). Simulations indicated that eggs resting on media of high thermal conductivity (e.g., sand) should have lower temperatures than eggs resting on media of low thermal conductivity (e.g., vermiculite), primarily because of differences in the rate at which metabolic heat released by embryos is dissipated into the environment. The differences in temperature should, in turn, affect net exchanges of water between eggs and their surroundings. Accordingly, the use of different substrates for incubating eggs may have introduced a systematic bias into earlier investigations, thereby precluding comparison among many of the studies and among the species concerned.

However, the prediction of the model was not confirmed in a recent experiment, so the model needs to be reconsidered. The flexible-shelled eggs of snapping turtles (*Chelydra serpentina*) were incubated on sand and vermiculite at different temperatures and water potentials (G. C. Packard et al., 1987). Net water-exchange by eggs was assessed, and so too were effects of the different substrates on hatching success and on characteristics of hatchlings. Although the type of substrate had a detectable influence on many (but not all) of these variables, this influence generally was minor. For instance, eggs resting on sand exhibited temporal patterns of net water-exchange that were virtually identical to those for eggs incubating on vermiculite at the same temperatures and water potentials. None of the conclusions from this investigation would have been affected by incubating eggs on just one medium or the other. Thus, valid comparisons apparently can be made even when eggs have been incubated on substrates having different physical characteristics.

Bias was much more likely to have been introduced into the earlier investigations by burying eggs in the substrate to different degrees. Some workers placed eggs on the surface so that only minimal contact was made between the eggshell and the medium (Muth, 1980, 1981). Others buried eggs partially (Andrews and Sexton, 1981; Gutzke, 1984a; Gutzke and Packard, 1986, 1987a; Morris et al., 1983; G. C. and M. J. Packard, 1987; G. C. Packard et al., 1979a, 1980, 1981a, b, c, 1982, 1983, 1984a, b, 1985a, 1987; M. J. and G. C. Packard, 1986; M. J. Packard et al., 1980; Tracy, 1980; Tracy and Snell, 1985; Tracy et al., 1978) or fully in the medium (Thompson, 1983). Both theoretical considerations (Ackerman et al., 1985b; Tracy et al., 1978) and empirical evidence (Bustard, 1966;

M. J. Packard et al., 1980; Tracy and Snell, 1985) indicate that the pattern of net water-exchange characterizing an egg will be influenced by the amount of contact between the egg and the substrate. Thus, some of the reported variation among species (see below) probably reflects on different methods for incubating eggs.

2. LIMITS OF TOLERANCE

An objective in most (but not all) studies of the water relations of reptilian eggs has been to define the hydric conditions necessary for successful completion of incubation. This goal has been elusive, however, because the water exchange between an egg and its environment is affected both by ambient temperature (and therefore egg temperature) and by water potential of the substrate (Gutzke, 1984a; Gutzke and Packard, 1987a; G. C. Packard et al., 1987). Consequently, eggs incubating on a substrate at a particular water potential may hatch at one temperature but not at another temperature within the range of thermal tolerance (G. C. Packard et al., 1987). We shall return later to this matter of interaction of temperature and water potential (Section VII.B). It suffices to say here that statements concerning effects of the hydric environment on hatching success apply only to the temperature at which the study was performed and not to other temperatures.

Flexible-shelled eggs of small lizards apparently must be deposited in settings conducive to absorption of substantial quantities of water during incubation. The mass of eggs must increase by 100–200% over their mass at oviposition; lesser increases in mass are accompanied by high mortality of embryos (Andrews and Sexton, 1981; M. J. Packard et al., 1980; Tracy, 1980). This requirement for water absorption is satisfied by substrates above -240 kPa ($T_a = 35°C$) for eggs of *Callisaurus draconoides*, by substrates above -420 kPa ($T_a = 28°C$) for eggs of *Sceloporus undulatus*, and by substrates above -1480 kPa ($T_a = 23–28°C$) for eggs of *Anolis auratus* and *Anolis limifrons*. We do not know whether eggs of *Anolis* are more tolerant of dry conditions than are eggs of *Callisaurus* and *Sceloporus*, or whether the observed survival of *Anolis* eggs at low water potentials resulted from their being incubated at lower temperatures than eggs of the other species. Embryos of *Dipsosaurus dorsalis* survive incubation on substrates at -1000 kPa ($T_a = 36°C$), but no information is available on their patterns of net water-exchange (Muth, 1980).

The flexible-shelled eggs of larger lizards and snakes will also absorb large amounts of water from suitable environments, but such uptake is not essential for the survival of embryos to hatching. Indeed, eggs of *Conolophus subcristatus*, *Coluber constrictor*, and *Pituophis melanoleucus* can sustain small (net) losses of water over the course of incubation without experiencing a reduction in hatching success (Gutzke and Packard, 1987a; G. C. and M. J. Packard, 1987; Tracy and Snell, 1985). The ability of these eggs to withstand losses of water probably is related to their relatively large size at oviposition and to the large reservoir of water that they therefore contain. In any event, eggs of *Conolophus* survive exposure to substrates at -7500 kPa ($T_a = \sim 30°C$), whereas those of *Coluber* and *Pituophis* withstand exposure to substrates at -950 kPa ($T_a = 27°C$) and -1100 kPa ($T_a = 22, 27, 32°C$), respectively.

Flexible-shelled eggs of turtles may increase in mass during incubation owing to absorption of water from the environment, but this uptake of water usually is not essential for completion of development. Eggs of many species hatch successfully even after declining appreciably in mass (Bustard, 1971a). However, species differ in the amount of water that can be lost from eggs without ill effect. Eggs of *Chelydra serpentina* frequently hatch after declining in mass by 18% over the course of incubation (Morris et al., 1983), whereas eggs of *Chrysemys picta* seldom can withstand such a loss of water (G. C. Packard et al., 1981a, 1983). The eggs of *Chelydra* are much larger than those of *Chrysemys*, and therefore contain more water at oviposition. Thus, the larger eggs of *Chelydra* may differ from the smaller eggs of *Chrysemys* by simply being better buffered against the potentially lethal effects of water loss (see Gutzke and Packard, 1985).

Flexible-shelled eggs of both *Chelydra serpentina* and *Chrysemys picta* experience increased mortality at water potentials below -500 kPa ($T_a = 26.0-31.0°C$ in *Chelydra*, $T_a = 29.0°C$ in *Chrysemys*), but this mortality is more pronounced in the latter than in the former (G. C. Packard et al., 1981a, 1983, 1987). The more rigid eggs of *Emydoidea blandingii* have high hatching success even when exposed to water potentials below -700 kPa ($T_a = 29.0°C$; G. C. Packard et al., 1982).

Rigid eggs of turtles, and presumably of crocodilians and geckos, can successfully withstand exposure to a wide range of hydric conditions (G. C. Packard et al., 1979a, 1981c; Thompson, 1983). The calcareous layer of the eggshell prevents the loss of large amounts of water to dry surroundings (Lutz et al., 1980; G. C. Packard et al., 1979a, b, 1981c; Thompson, 1983; Tracy, 1982), yet also opposes the uptake of water from wet environments (G. C. Packard et al., 1979a, 1981c; Thompson, 1983). Only the most severe of conditions are likely to elicit mortality of embryos developing in eggs such as these.

3. METABOLIC EFFECTS

Reptilian embryos in flexible-shelled eggs frequently hatch at a larger size when they are incubated in relatively wet environments than they do when they are incubated in relatively dry surroundings (Table IV). The availability of water to embryos apparently is the determining factor, because the size of hatchlings is correlated with the net exchange of water experienced by their eggs (G. C. Packard et al., 1982; M. J. Packard et al., 1982c).

Embryonic turtles take longer to develop to hatching in moist environments than they do in dry ones (Gutzke, 1984a; Morris et al., 1983; G. C. Packard et al., 1981a, 1983, 1984b, 1985a, 1987). Embryos developing in moist environments therefore have more time in which to grow before hatching than do those in dry settings. Thus, the larger size of turtles hatching in moist environments is due in part to their extended incubation. One hypothesis to account for such variation in length of incubation proposes that hatching is induced when water potential of the yolk (or some other compartment) declines to a threshold level, and that this threshold is reached sooner by embryos in dry settings than by those in wet ones (G. C. and M. J. Packard, 1984; G. C. Packard et al., 1983). Embryos of some lizards (M. J. Packard et al., 1980) and snakes (Black et al., 1984; Gutzke and Packard, 1987a) also incubate longer in wet than in dry settings, so the hypothesis may apply to these animals as well.

Embryonic turtles in flexible-shelled eggs also have higher rates of metabolism in wet environments than they do in dry ones (Fig. 4). Consequently, embryos in wet environments mobilize nutrients from the yolk more rapidly than do embryos in dry environments, and growth of embryos also is faster in wet conditions than in dry ones (Fig. 10; also Gettinger et al., 1984; M. J. and G. C. Packard, 1986). An hypothesis to account for variation in metabolism and growth of embryos proposes that intermediary metabolism is inhibited by urea accumulating inside eggs. Because less water is available inside eggs in dry conditions to serve as a diluent for the urea, concentrations of this metabolite increase more rapidly in eggs in dry environments than in eggs in wet environments. Accordingly, inhibition of embryonic metabolism and growth is greater during the last one-third of incubation in dry environments than in wet ones (G. C. and M. J. Packard, 1984; G. C. Packard et al., 1984a). Growth rates of embryos have not been studied in those lizards and snakes in which size at hatching is influenced by hydration of the environment, so we do not know whether the present hypothesis has any broader application.

TABLE IV
Effect of Hydration of the Environment on Size of Hatchling Reptiles

Species	Type of eggshell	Effect of hydration?	Measure of size[a]	Reference
Testudines				
Chelydra serpentina	Flexible	Yes	LM, DM, CL	Morris et al., 1983; G. C. Packard et al., 1980, 1981b, 1984b, 1987
Chrysemys picta	Flexible	Yes	LM, DM, CL	Gutzke, 1984a; G. C. Packard et al., 1981a, 1983; M. J. and G. C. Packard, 1986; Tracy et al., 1978
Emydoidea blandingii	Intermediate	Yes	LM, CL	G. C. Packard et al., 1982
Emydura macquarrii	Rigid	No	LM	Thompson, 1983
Terrapene ornata	Flexible	Yes	DM, CL	G. C. Packard et al., 1985a
Trionyx spiniferus	Rigid	No	LM	G. C. Packard et al., 1979a, 1981c
Sauria				
Callisaurus draconoides	Flexible	Yes	LM	M. J. Packard et al., 1980
Conolophus pallidus	Flexible	Yes	LM, SVL	Tracy and Snell, 1985
Sceloporus undulatus	Flexible	No	LM	Tracy, 1980
Serpentes				
Coluber constrictor	Flexible	No	DM	G. C. and M. J. Packard, 1987
Pituophis melanoleucus	Flexible	Yes	LM, DM, SVL	Gutzke and Packard, 1987a
Python molurus	Flexible	Yes	LM	Black et al., 1984

[a] LM, live mass of hatchling; DM, dry mass of carcass; SVL, snout-to-vent length; CL, carapace length.

Embryonic turtles developing in rigid-shelled eggs seem not to be affected by variation in hydration of the environment, because neither oxygen consumption of embryos nor size of hatchlings is related to the wetness of the substrate on which eggs are incubated (Fig. 4, Table IV). However, this does not necessarily mean that embryos in rigid-shelled eggs are more tolerant of variation in the availability of water than are embryos in flexible-shelled eggs; it may simply mean that embryos in rigid eggs are better insulated from the vagaries of the environment than

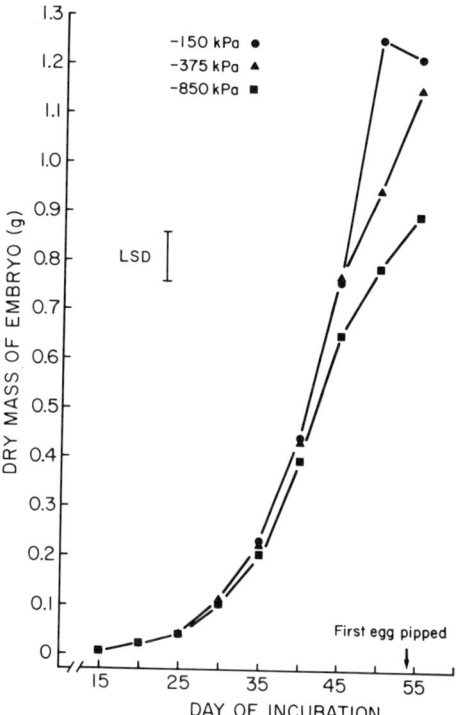

Fig. 10. Growth in dry mass of embryonic snapping turtles (*Chelydra serpentina*) incubating at 29°C on substrates of vermiculite at different water potentials. Means differing by the least significant difference (LSD) are significantly different at alpha = 0.05. (Redrawn and modified from Morris et al., 1983.)

are embryos in flexible eggs. The calcareous layer of rigid eggshells constrains movement of water between the interior and the surroundings, and rigid eggs in wet and dry environments therefore differ only slightly in net exchange of water (M. J. Packard et al., 1982c). The resultant differences in availability of water to embryos developing in wet and dry conditions presumably are too small to elicit detectable differences in physiology of the young.

No information is available as yet on the possible influence of the hydric environment on duration of incubation, metabolism, or growth of embryonic crocodilians or of those geckos developing inside rigid-shelled eggs. We anticipate that their responses will be similar to those reported for turtle embryos developing in rigid, calcareous eggs.

4. RESPONSE OF EGGS TO CHANGING HYDRATION

In most studies of the water relations of reptilian embryos, individual eggs have been exposed to one, relatively constant water potential for the duration of incubation. However, one investigation considered the effect of exposing eggs to different water potentials at different times during development. In that study, flexible-shelled eggs of painted turtles (*Chrysemys picta*) were incubated in wet (−150 kPa) and dry (−1100 kPa) environments at an ambient temperature of 28.5°C (Gutzke and Packard, 1986). Half of the eggs in each treatment were transferred to the other treatment at the end of the first trimester, and a similar shift was performed at the end of the second trimester. Thus, eight experimental groups were defined on the basis of hydric conditions to which eggs were exposed during each trimester. Some eggs were exposed to wet conditions for the first one-third of incubation and to dry conditions thereafter; other eggs were exposed to wet conditions only during the middle one-third of development; and so on.

Despite the fact that eggs on the dry substrate declined appreciably in mass during the first trimester and that eggs on the wet medium simultaneously increased in mass (Fig. 11), the condition of incubation during the first trimester had no apparent influence on survival of embryos or on size of hatchlings (Gutzke and Packard, 1986). This unexpected finding can be explained by compensatory exchanges of water occurring during the second trimester. Eggs transferred from the wet substrate to the dry substrate at the end of the first trimester lost water more rapidly during the second trimester than did eggs exposed continuously to the dry environment (Fig. 11). Consequently, the advantage held by eggs spending the first trimester in a wet environment was largely nullified by subsequent exposure to the dry setting. On the other hand, eggs transferred from the dry substrate to the wet substrate at the end of the first trimester absorbed water more rapidly during the second trimester than did eggs exposed continuously to the wet conditions (Fig. 11). Thus, the disadvantage of eggs spending the first trimester in a dry environment was largely overcome by subsequent exposure to a wet medium. Findings similar to these were reported over 30 years ago for eggs of *Coluber constrictor*, but were not widely accepted owing to uncertainty concerning the actual hydration of substrates used for incubation (Clark, 1953a). No mechanistic explanation yet exists for this phenomenon of "compensatory water exchange."

If eggs incubating in natural nests respond similarly to changing

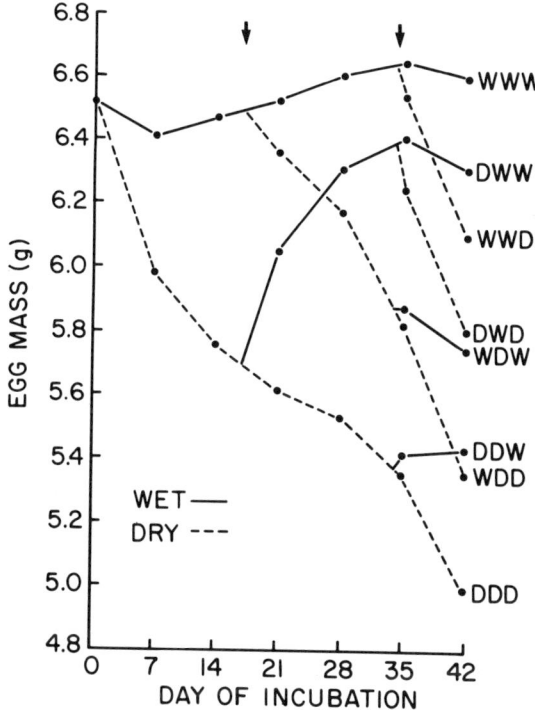

Fig. 11. Mass of eggs of painted turtles (*Chrysemys picta*) incubating on wet (−150 kPa) and dry (−1100 kPa) substrates at an ambient temperature of 28.5°C. The arrows mark the ends of the first and second trimesters of incubation, and identify times at which eggs were transferred from wet substrates to dry substrates and vice versa. The notation WWW indicates that eggs were exposed to the wet environment in all three trimesters; DWW indicates that eggs were exposed to the dry environment during the first trimester and to the wet environment during the second and third trimesters; and so on. (Redrawn from Gutzke and Packard, 1986.)

conditions of the hydric environment, these studies of *Chrysemys picta* and *Coluber constrictor* have important implications. For example, the searching behavior manifested by female turtles and lizards prior to nesting has been tentatively characterized as an attempt to select a soil-moisture regime appropriate for production of the maximal number of young of optimal size (G. C. Packard et al., 1980). However, eggs laid in a moist substrate will not necessarily produce more (or larger) young than eggs laid in a dry substrate, because conditions prevailing at oviposition need not be similar to conditions existing during the middle of development (Fig. 9). The only way that searching behavior by females could be advantageous is when conditions at oviposition correlate with conditions that will prevail later.

Another implication of this work concerns effects of intermittent rainfall during incubation (Fig. 9). Eggs presumably go into negative water balance during periods of fair weather as the walls of their nest become progressively drier. Recharging of the substrate by rainfall permits the eggs to respond to the availability of water by absorbing amounts that are largely sufficient to replace water lost during the preceding dry period. In this way, both hatching success and size of hatchlings could be maximized.

5. SEXUAL DIFFERENTIATION

One experiment has addressed the possibility that hydration of the environment influences the process of sexual differentiation in a species known already to respond to temperature. In this study, flexible-shelled eggs of the turtle *Chrysemys picta* were incubated on vermiculite at several different temperatures and water potentials (Gutzke and Paukstis, 1983). All hatchlings emerging from eggs held at higher temperatures (30.5°C, 32.0°C) were females, irrespective of the wetness of the substrate. This finding is consistent with results of earlier research on this species (Bull and Vogt, 1979, 1981). At lower temperatures (26.5°C, 27.0°C), however, the expectation that all emergent young would be males (see Bull and Vogt, 1979, 1981) was realized only for eggs exposed to higher water potentials. Significant numbers of females emerged from eggs held on drier substrates.

Eggs in dry environments at a given ambient temperature presumably had slightly higher surface temperatures than eggs in wet settings (Fig. 12), owing partly to the lower rates of dissipation of metabolic heat into dry substrates (Ackerman et al., 1985b) and partly to the smaller mass of eggs on dry media (equation 2). However, the differences in surface temperature during the period of sexual differentiation probably were only 0.1–0.2°C (Fig. 12), which is hardly sufficient to account for the formation of female turtles at ambient temperatures of both 26.5°C and 27.0°C. Because eggs in the different hydric environments experienced very different patterns of net water-exchange with their environment (see Gutzke, 1984a), the availability of water to embryos is implicated as a factor affecting sexual differentiation in this species. If this discovery is confirmed, it will add an exciting new dimension to the concept of environmental control of sexual differentiation in reptiles (see Bull, 1980).

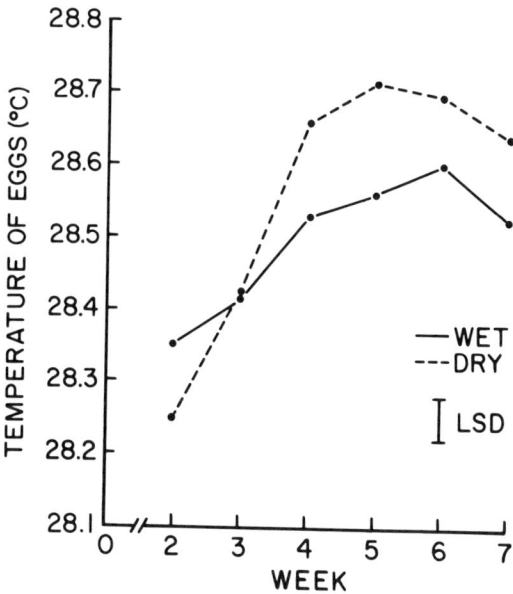

Fig. 12. Surface temperatures of eggs of painted turtles (*Chrysemys picta*) incubating on wet (−150 kPa) and dry (−1100 kPa) substrates at an ambient temperature of 28.5°C. Means differing by the least significant difference (LSD) are significantly different at alpha = 0.05. Note that surface temperatures were below ambient for the first 3 weeks and above ambient thereafter, but that the maximum difference between surface temperature and ambient temperature was only 0.2°C (on week 5). Also, the maximum difference in surface temperature between eggs on wet and dry substrates was only 0.15°C (again on week 5). Although eggs on the dry substrate had higher temperatures during the growth phase of development, metabolism (see Fig. 4) and growth (see Fig. 10) of embryos were lower in dry environments than in wet ones. (Redrawn from Gutzke, 1984a.)

VI. RESPIRATORY GASES

A. Factors Affecting Gas Exchange

Oxygen and carbon dioxide seemingly move across (or through) shells of reptilian eggs by the same process of molecular diffusion that underlies movements of these gases through pores in avian eggshells (Ackerman and Prange, 1972; Feder et al., 1982; Lutz et al., 1980). Thus, movement of both gases can be described with the Fick equation (Piiper et al., 1971) as

$$m_X = k_X \times A_A \times (p_{X,E} - p_{X,A}) \qquad (11)$$

where m_X is the mass of gass "x" crossing the eggshell (mg × s^{-1}), k_X is the transport coefficient for the gas in question (mg $\times$ s^{-1} $\times$ cm^{-2} $\times$ kPa^{-1}), A_A is the area of the eggshell across which exchange occurs (cm^2), and the term $p_{X,E} - p_{X,A}$ is the difference in partial pressure of the gas across the eggshell (kPa). The rate of diffusion clearly is proportional to the area of eggshell exposed to air in the nest cavity (including that in spaces in the soil), as well as to the difference in partial pressure between the outer surface of the eggshell and the site of exchange inside the eggshell. Diffusion is proportional also to the transport coefficient, which is profoundly affected by whether the gas is diffusing through a medium of air or water.

Gases diffusing into rigid eggs of crocodilians and many turtles pass first through discrete pores in the calcareous layer and then between fibers forming the shell membrane(s) (Erben, 1970; Ewert, 1985; Ferguson, 1982; M. J. and G. C. Packard, 1979; M. J. Packard et al., 1984a; Thompson, 1983; Woodall, 1984). The flexible-shelled eggs of lepidosaurians and many other turtles lack discrete pores in the calcareous layer (if present), so gases merely pass through the large gaps in the calcareous layer before entering spaces in the shell membrane (Lillywhite and Ackerman, 1984; M. J. Packard et al., 1982a, b, c; Solomon and Reid, 1983). The route followed by gases diffusing through the calcareous layer of the rigid-shelled eggs of geckos has not been established (M. J. Packard et al., 1982c).

The pores in testudinian and crocodilian eggshells are filled with liquid at oviposition, and therefore afford a substantial barrier to diffusion of respiratory gases (Thompson, 1985; also Feder et al., 1982). However, water is removed from these pores during the first 2 weeks of incubation by an as yet unidentified mechanism, leading thereby to a progressive increase in conductance of eggshells to both oxygen and carbon dioxide (Thompson, 1985). The drying of the shell begins at the top of the egg and then spreads downward, forming a chalky-white band that is characteristic of eggs containing viable embryos (Ewert, 1985; Ferguson, 1985). The band does not form in infertile eggs. Thus, conductance of eggs to respiratory gases changes during the course of incubation owing to intervention of the embryo itself.

Lepidosaurian eggshells do not have pores, but hydration of shells may nonetheless affect transport coefficients for gases and, therefore, gas exchange (Black et al., 1984). Eggs in wet environments have lower conductances for oxygen than do eggs in dry environments, presumably because water occludes spaces between fibers of the shell membrane (Black et al., 1984; also Feder et al., 1982). There is no indication that conductance of lepidosaurian eggs is affected by developing embryos in the manner described for testudinian and crocodilian eggs.

RESPIRATORY GASES

B. Gas Tensions in Nests

The immediate source of oxygen for reptilian embryos developing in subterranean nests is air that was trapped inside the egg chamber (or between individual particles of soil) when the nest was closed. As oxygen is withdrawn from this pocket of air, however, it is replaced by oxygen diffusing into the cavity from air-filled pores in the adjacent soil (Marshall and Holmes, 1979; Prange and Ackerman, 1974; Taylor and Ashcroft, 1972). Diffusion proceeds at a rate proportional to the difference in partial pressure between air in pores in adjacent soil and that in the nest cavity; it depends also on the volume of air in these pores, the tortuosity of the pore channels, and the presence of constrictions in the channels that prevent free movement of oxygen molecules (Flegg, 1953; Marshall, 1959; Millington, 1959; Reibel and Shair, 1982; van Bavel, 1952). Wind at the ground surface and infiltration of water following heavy rainfall may occasionally induce a mass flow of air through the upper reaches of the soil profile that partially ventilates some nests (Prange and Ackerman, 1974), but molecular diffusion is the only continuously operating mechanism for replacing oxygen (Marshall and Holmes, 1979; Taylor and Ashcroft, 1972).

Air trapped inside a nest at the outset of incubation probably has the same composition as air occupying pores in adjacent soil. Owing to aerobic respiration of soil microbes and plant roots, the partial pressure of oxygen in this air is below that of the atmosphere whereas that of carbon dioxide is higher than in atmospheric air (Marshall and Holmes, 1979; Taylor and Ashcroft, 1972). However, specific values vary among soils because of differences in oxygen demand of the soil flora and fauna and because of differences in the impedance of soils to diffusion of gases. For instance, tensions of oxygen and carbon dioxide in air held in pores of sandy loams depart only slightly from atmospheric levels, whereas those of gases in clay soils usually depart considerably from that standard (Taylor and Ashcroft, 1972).

Reptilian embryos consume relatively little oxygen during the first half of incubation (Fig. 4; also Ackerman, 1981a; Clark, 1953c; Dmi'el, 1970; Lynn and von Brand, 1945; Thompson, 1983, 1985), and oxygen in the nest cavity is replenished without undergoing an appreciable change in partial pressure (Ackerman, 1977; Lutz and Dunbar-Cooper, 1984; M. B. Thompson, 1981, 1983). Even in late stages of incubation, when oxygen requirements of individual embryos are high, the combined uptake of oxygen by embryos in a clutch usually does not cause a major decline in partial pressure of this gas in the nest cavity (*Emydura* in Fig. 13; Lutz and Dunbar-Cooper, 1984; M. B. Thompson, 1981, 1983).

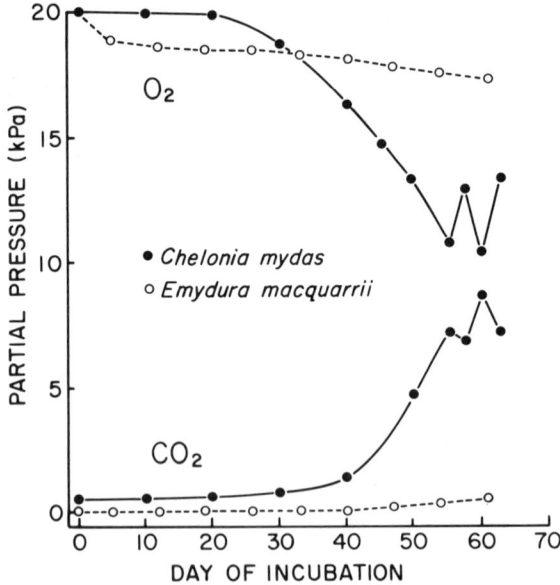

Fig. 13. Partial pressures of oxygen and carbon dioxide inside nests of two species of turtles. Note that tensions of these gases change only slightly over the course of incubation in the relatively shallow nests of *Emydura macquarrii*, but that major shifts occur in the deeper (and larger) nests of *Chelonia mydas*. (Modified and redrawn from M. B. Thompson, 1981.)

Nests of turtles of the families Cheloniidae and Dermochelyidae (and possibly the hole nests of some crocodilians; Lutz and Dunbar-Cooper, 1984) are exceptions to the preceding generalization (*Chelonia* in Fig. 13). Females of these reptiles deposit large numbers of large eggs in relatively deep nests. Late in incubation, the combined demand for oxygen by embryos causes the oxygen tension inside the nest to decline sharply (Ackerman, 1977; Ackerman and Prange, 1972; Prange and Ackerman, 1974). Although the consequent increase in the gradient in oxygen tension between adjacent soil and the nest serves to increase the rate of delivery of this gas to the nest cavity, the reduction in partial pressure of oxygen at the surface of eggshells may be sufficient to inhibit metabolism of embryos (Section VI.C).

Whenever eggs are deposited in more superficial sites (e.g., beneath rocks or logs), the tensions of oxygen and carbon dioxide adjacent to eggshells probably are at or near atmospheric levels throughout incubation. This situation reflects the generally low oxygen demand created by small clutches and the rapid replenishment of the gas by diffusion augmented by convection. This generalization presumably applies also to the mound nests of many crocodilians, because low relative humidity inside these nests indicates that they are partially ventilated (Section V.B).

C. Physiological Effects of Gases

Only one investigation has addressed the possible effects of altered tensions of oxygen and carbon dioxide on reptilian embryos. In that study, eggs of the sea turtles *Caretta caretta* and *Chelonia mydas* were incubated in sealed containers that were vented to the atmosphere through columns filled with dry sand (Ackerman, 1981b). The amount of sand in the columns was varied among containers to produce different resistances to diffusion of oxygen and carbon dioxide between the interior of containers and surrounding air. Embryos in containers with conductances to respiratory gases similar to those of nests in beach sand had higher rates of growth, shorter incubation periods, and higher hatching success than did embryos in containers with lower conductances (Ackerman, 1980, 1981b). Although data for partial pressures of gases were not reported, air in containers with low conductances probably had high tensions of carbon dioxide and low tensions of oxygen in the week or so before hatching (see Fig. 13). Thus, low tensions of oxygen and/or high tensions of carbon dioxide seemingly inhibit metabolism of reptilian embryos, probably by reducing the differences in partial pressure of these gases across eggshells. The increase in duration of incubation and decline in survival under conditions of hypoxia and hypercarbia are presumably manifestations of reduced metabolism. The relation between the metabolism of embryos and the gas tensions late in incubation needs to be quantified, however, so that the influence of varying gas tensions in natural nests can be evaluated more fully.

VII. INTERDEPENDENCE OF ENVIRONMENTAL VARIABLES

A. Effect of One Variable on Another

We have discussed each of the major components of the physical environment individually, but it was somewhat artificial to do so. The several variables are highly interdependent, and a change in one usually is accompanied by a change in one or both of the others (Taylor and Ashcroft, 1972). Indeed, this interdependence of environmental variables makes it virtually impossible to design laboratory experiments in which one factor is varied while the others are held constant. This difficulty heightens the uncertainty associated with interpretation of results (G. C. and M. J. Packard, 1984). A few examples of this interdependence of variables will illustrate our point.

Water potential of soils is influenced by temperature, even if water content remains constant. Consequently, an increase in temperature will elicit a small increase in water potential, and a decrease in temperature will cause water potential to fall slightly (Taylor, 1958; Taylor and Stewart, 1960). This phenomenon seemingly is an outcome of thermally induced changes in surface tension of water trapped in capillaries in the soil (Cary and Hanks, 1972), and is more pronounced in dry soils than in wet ones (Taylor, 1958; Taylor and Stewart, 1960). A change in temperature could therefore influence exchange of liquid water between an egg and its nest environment by altering substrate water potential.

A change in temperature also affects vapor pressure of air in the nest, primarily by altering the saturation vapor pressure of that air (Taylor and Ashcroft, 1972). Also, the rates of molecular diffusion by water vapor, oxygen, and carbon dioxide are increased at higher temperatures and decreased at lower ones. Thus, a change in ambient temperature inside nests affects diffusion of all gases; the effect on diffusion of water vapor is likely to be the most pronounced.

Similarly, an increase in water content of a substrate has effects beyond the expected one on water potential. Wet substrates have higher thermal conductivities than do dry ones (Marshall and Holmes, 1979; Taylor and Ashcroft, 1972), so transport of heat between the ground surface and lower levels in the soil profile is facilitated. Temperature of nests and eggs may thereby be affected. Furthermore, to the extent that water displaces air from pores in the soil and leads to a greater constriction at bottlenecks, diffusion of respiratory gases is impaired (Flegg, 1953; Millington, 1959; Reible and Shair, 1982). Metabolism of embryos could be inhibited if such impediments to gaseous diffusion were to cause the oxygen tension in a nest to decrease or the carbon dioxide tension to increase.

Changes in the tensions of carbon dioxide and oxygen in nests do not cause changes in temperature, and effects on the solute component of water potential probably are negligible. However, changes in gas tensions frequently signal a change in one or both of the other variables, as was indicated in prior discussion.

B. Interaction of Variables on Eggs

The effects of environmental variables on eggs and embryos may also be interactive. We illustrate this point by citing an experiment in which flexible-shelled eggs of snapping turtles (*Chelydra serpentina*) were incu-

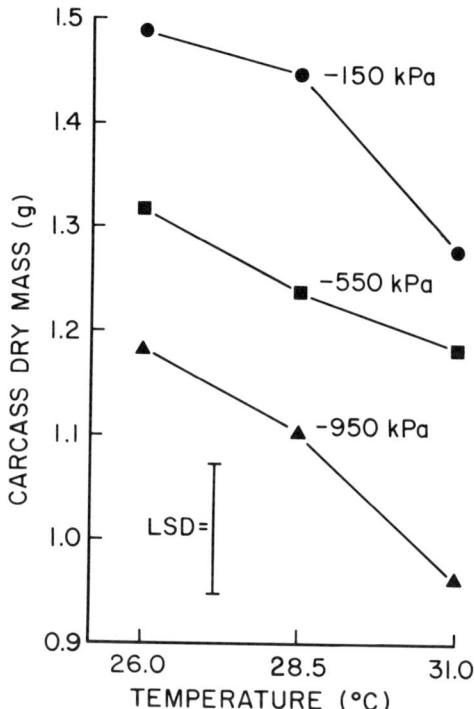

Fig. 14. Dry mass of carcasses of hatchling snapping turtles (*Chelydra serpentina*) emerging from eggs incubated on vermiculite at different temperatures and water potentials. Means differing by the least significant difference (LSD) are significantly different at alpha = 0.05. (Redrawn from G. C. Packard et al., 1987.)

bated in the laboratory at constant temperatures of 26.0°C, 28.5°C, and 31.0°C, and at water potentials of −150 kPa, −550 kPa, and −950 kPa (G. C. Packard et al., 1987). At any given water potential, turtles hatching at 31.0°C were smaller than those hatching at 28.5°C, and animals hatching at 28.5°C were smaller than those emerging at 26.0°C (Fig. 14). Because water potential of substrates was not a variable in these comparisons, a reasonable interpretation for the findings is that temperature intervened directly in physiology of developing embryos to elicit the observed variation in size of emergent young.

Unfortunately, this interpretation would be premature and possibly incorrect, because eggs incubating at different temperatures had different patterns of net water-exchange with their environment, despite the fact that they rested on media at the same water potential (Fig. 15; also Gutzke, 1984a; Gutzke and Packard, 1987a). This unexpected discovery apparently reflects on the complex effects of ambient temperature on

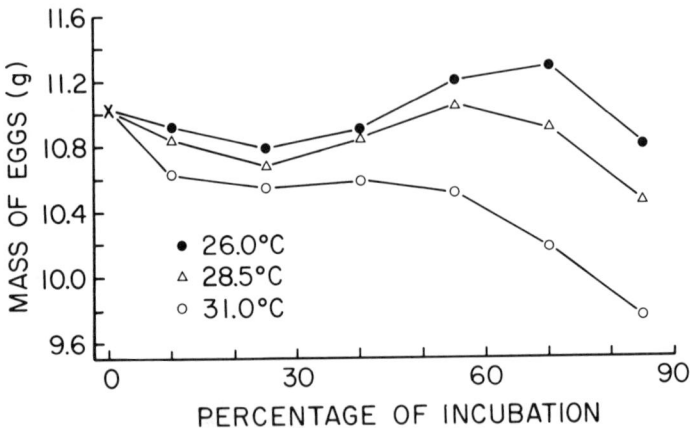

Fig. 15. Temporal changes in mass of eggs of snapping turtles (*Chelydra serpentina*) incubating on substrates of vermiculite at the same water potential (−150 kPa) but at different temperatures. Note that eggs at 31.0°C lost more mass (largely water) than did eggs at 26.0°C or 28.5°C, and that eggs at 28.5°C lost more mass than did eggs at 26.0°C. (Redrawn from G. C. Packard et al., 1987.)

temperature of eggs and on vapor pressures at the inside and outside of eggshells; it also indicates that exposing eggs to different temperatures caused them to be exposed also to different hydric environments. Consequently, the amount of water available to embryos was higher at 26.0°C than at 28.5°C, and more water was available to embryos at 28.5°C than at 31.0°C. The observed variation in size of hatchlings could have resulted from effects of water on developing embryos as easily as from effects of temperature. This possibility should be considered in the numerous studies of sexual differentiation in turtles (Section IV.C), because the implicit assumption in these investigations is that temperature was the only important variable. As is illustrated here, however, at least two important factors must have varied among experimental treatments.

VIII. SIGNIFICANCE OF PHYSICAL ENVIRONMENT

A. Introduction

Extremes of temperature, moisture, and gas tensions can lead to abnormal development and mortality of reptilian embryos, as was discussed in preceding sections. There can be little doubt concerning the significance of serious deformity or death to embryos. Within the range of tolerance to each of the aforementioned environmental variables, however, a spectrum of sublethal effects may also provide raw material for the forces of natural selection. Reptilian embryos seemingly incubate longer, consume more of their yolk during development, and hatch at a larger size when they incubate in cool conditions and/or at high water potentials than they do in warm conditions and/or at low water potentials. Large reductions in partial pressure of oxygen from atmospheric levels probably do not occur commonly in reptilian nests, but may be a normal feature of incubation of sea turtles and some crocodilians. Low tensions of oxygen (or high tensions of carbon dioxide) may prolong incubation, inhibit metabolism, and cause hatchlings to be smaller than normal. The possible importance of these sublethal effects is explored briefly in this section.

B. Size of Hatchlings

One possible product of variation in physical conditions in nests is variation in size of hatchlings, elicited by differences in rates of growth of embryos, by differences in the duration of incubation, or by a combination of these factors. Attainment of large size before hatching may be advantageous to emergent young, by conferring them with a degree of protection against predation. According to this hypothesis, larger hatchlings are more difficult for predators to capture and/or to handle and swallow than are smaller conspecifics, so the former enjoy higher rates of survival than do the latter. Survival in the wild of hatchling lizards (Ferguson and Bohlen, 1978; Ferguson and Fox, 1984; Ferguson et al., 1982; Fox, 1978; Snell, 1984) and turtles (Barrows and Schwarz, 1895; Swingland and Coe, 1979) is consistent with this proposition.

Several laboratory studies lend support to this hypothesis. The relatively large snapping turtles (*Chelydra serpentina*) hatching from eggs in wet environments are faster than the small turtles hatching from eggs in dry settings both when running on land and when swimming in water (Fig. 16). Superior performance by relatively large hatchlings could be the basis for superior survival by these animals in the wild. Also, larger hatchlings may be more aggressive than smaller hatchlings in pursuing and capturing food, and larger young may therefore sustain higher rates of growth than smaller animals in the cohort (Froese and Burghardt, 1974). High rates of growth may enable larger hatchlings to pass more rapidly through the range of body sizes in which predation is most intense, thereby contributing also to their superior survival.

On the other hand, larger offspring produced in environments

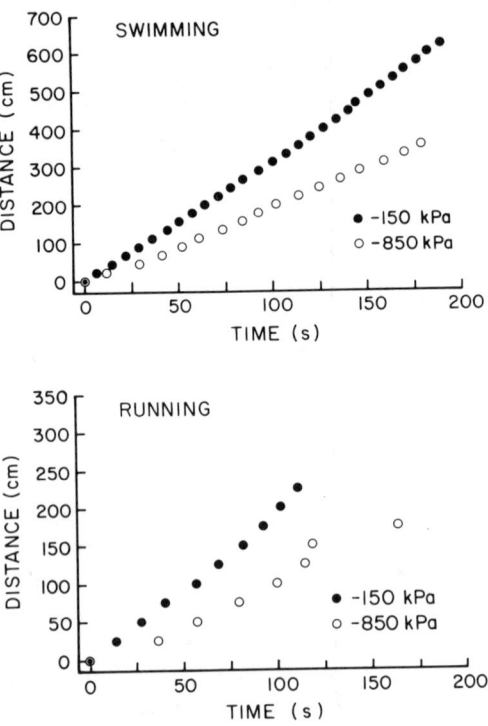

Fig. 16. Distance moved by hatchling snapping turtles (*Chelydra serpentina*) as a function of time swimming in water or running on land. Solid symbols represent turtles hatching from eggs on wet substrates (−150 kPa); open symbols represent animals emerging from eggs on dry substrates (−850 kPa). The slopes of the lines represent speeds for animals in the samples. The large turtles emerging from eggs in wet environments were able to swim and to run faster than siblings from eggs in dry environments. (Redrawn from Miller et al., 1987.)

favoring rapid growth and/or longer incubation have less residual yolk to sustain them after hatching than do smaller animals (Gutzke, 1984a; Morris et al., 1983; G. C. Packard et al., 1983, 1985a, 1987; M. J. and G. C. Packard, 1986). Because possession of a relatively large nutrient reserve may enhance survival more than large size under some circumstances, small size at hatching conceivably is beneficial. For example, young green iguanas (*Iguana iguana*) depend to a large extent on residual yolk to sustain them for the first month of life outside the nest (Troyer, 1983), so survival may be enhanced in those individuals having a large yolk, irrespective of their body size. Furthermore, hatchlings of several freshwater turtles may spend their first winter in the nest cavity without feeding (Gibbons and Nelson, 1978; Wilbur and Morin, this volume), during which time they are supported largely by lipids in the retracted yolk (Congdon and Tinkle, 1982). Again, the size of the energy reserve in the retracted yolk may be a more important determinant of survival than body size at hatching. Such possibilities need to be investigated.

C. Length of Incubation

Variation in physical conditions in nests may also influence the duration of incubation. Longer incubation is associated in some instances with conditions that allow embryos to attain large size before hatching (e.g., moist substrate), and in other instances with conditions that inhibit growth and lead to formation of small hatchlings (e.g., low partial pressure of oxygen). In all such cases, the question of significance of variation in length of incubation reduces in part to a consideration of the significance of variation in body size, as was discussed previously (Section VIII.B).

For most species, however, there is another aspect to the question. Long periods of incubation may increase the probability that nests will be destroyed by predators (Snow, 1982) or by inclement weather (Webb and Smith, 1984). Furthermore, if development is not completed before the advent of cool weather in the autumn, advanced embryos or hatchlings may be forced to pass the winter inside the nest cavity. Although embryos/hatchlings may be able to survive a mild winter (Bleakney, 1963; Cagle, 1944; Gibbons and Coker, 1977; Sexton, 1957; Toner, 1940; Trauth, 1977), mortality is likely to be high under more normal (or severe) conditions of winter weather (Breckenridge, 1960; Ewert, 1979; Hammer, 1969; Risley, 1933). Thus, rapid completion of development may be advantageous, even when conditions necessary for this outcome result in hatchlings of suboptimal size.

Duration of incubation may establish limits of distribution for oviparous reptiles in temperate or montane regions. Ground temperatures may be too low in parts of the northeastern United States to permit embryos of the terrestrial turtle *Terrapene carolina* to complete incubation during the limited growing season, thereby establishing the northern limits to distribution of this species (Allard, 1935). Similar arguments have been adduced for distribution of the lizard *Dipsosaurus dorsalis* in deserts of the American Southwest (Muth, 1980).

D. Sexual Differentiation

Environmental control of sexual differentiation in crocodilians, many turtles, and some lepidosaurians has important implications for the ecology and evolution of the species in which it occurs (Bull, 1980; Vogt and Bull, 1982a). For example, many species of turtles grow appreciably over the course of their reproductive lives. Shortly after attaining reproductive maturity, females tend to lay relatively small eggs (Congdon and Tinkle, 1982; Congdon et al., 1982, 1983a) in relatively shallow nests, where generally high temperatures may promote differentiation of females (Wilhoft et al., 1983). Later in life, the same females tend to lay relatively large eggs (Congdon and Tinkle, 1982; Congdon et al., 1982, 1983a) in relatively deep nests, where generally cool conditions may promote differentiation of males (Wilhoft et al., 1983). However, the small eggs produced early in the reproductive life of a female have a lower probability of hatching than do larger eggs produced later (Gutzke and Packard, 1985), and the small eggs give rise also to small hatchlings (Burger, 1977; Congdon et al., 1983a; Morris et al., 1983; G. C. Packard et al., 1987) that may suffer disproportionately high mortality (Barrows and Schwartz, 1895; Swingland and Coe, 1979). Consequently, first efforts at reproduction by a given female may be devoted to the relatively unsuccessful production of female offspring, whereas later efforts may be devoted to the more successful production of males. Such possibilities, if realized, would have important implications for evolution of life histories (see Congdon et al., 1983a). In particular, a high probability of producing female offspring early in reproductive life may explain why maturity is reached at relatively small body size in these species when reproduction is unlikely to be successful.

Turtles and crocodilians with protracted nesting seasons may produce offspring primarily of one sex early in the season and of the other sex later in the year, owing to seasonal changes in temperature at the level of the nest cavity (Mrosovsky et al., 1984a, b; Vogt and Bull, 1982a, 1984; Webb et al., 1983a). If catastrophic mortality from heavy rainfall (Ragotski, 1959) and run-off (Plummer, 1976) or from high tides (Fowler, 1979) were to occur in the middle of the nesting season, offspring of one sex might suffer disproportionately. Such differential mortality would have consequences for sex ratio of the hatchling cohort and possibly for a subsequent adult population as well.

Environmental control of sexual differentiation has special importance for conservation of sea turtles. For a number of years, a common practice among conservationists has been to remove eggs from nests and to incubate them in styrofoam boxes held inside a shelter near the beach (Mrosovsky, 1983). The rationale for this practice is that nests would otherwise be destroyed by predators, humans, or inclement weather. However, the conditions of artificial incubation have been relatively uniform, and relatively cool, and most turtles hatching from eggs handled in this manner probably have been males (Morreale et al., 1982; Mrosovsky, 1982). Clearly, if use of artificial hatcheries is to continue, more attention must be given to the physical environment (hydric as well as thermal; Gutzke and Paukstis, 1983) to which eggs are exposed so as to assure that young of both sexes are produced.

Finally, sea-turtle rookeries frequently are confined to very restricted stretches of beach. Because thermal conditions vary among beaches, however, offspring of one rookery may be predominantly males whereas those of another may be largely females (Limpus et al., 1983b). Although any single beach may attract large numbers of females for nesting, preservation of that beach alone may not be sufficient to assure survival of the population. Viability may depend instead on provision of enough different beaches as to assure that there is sufficient environmental heterogeneity to elicit differentiation of adequate numbers of both males and females for later recruitment into the breeding population.

IX. CONCLUDING REMARKS

In oviparous reptiles, the egg is probably the most vulnerable stage in the life cycle (e.g., Andrews, 1982; Congdon et al., 1983b; Tinkle et al., 1981; Van Devender, 1982; Webb et al., 1983a). Most of the prior research on this stage has assessed the impact of predation, but a few studies have indicated that significant mortality of embryos may also result from abiotic factors (e.g., Burger, 1977; Tinkle et al., 1981; Van Devender, 1982; Webb et al., 1983a). In addition, physiology of developing embryos may be a key factor establishing limits of geographic distribution for numerous species (Allard, 1935; Muth, 1980), and subtle effects of temperature, moisture, and respiratory gases on metabolism, growth, and sexual differentiation of developing young may induce ecologically important variation in hatchlings. Despite the apparent importance of the reptilian egg, however, knowledge of the physiological ecology of the reptilian embryo still is rudimentary.

The present state of knowledge reflects a variety of problems, some of which derive from the animals themselves and are not likely to be overcome easily. For instance, nests of many snakes and lizards have been, and are likely to continue to be, discovered opportunistically. Descriptions of the depth and dimensions of such nests, and measurements of the physical environment therein, probably never will be based on the large, representative samples that we would prefer to have.

An even greater problem, perhaps, stems from the background that we, as zoologists, bring with us to studies of reptilian eggs. Few of us are fully prepared for the change in perspective that is required when we look beneath the surface of the ground into a reptilian nest. Was any one of us not surprised just a little on first discovering that the relative humidity of air in the driest soil is likely still to be in excess of 96%, or that temperature of the soil increases with depth at certain times of day? Moreover, many of the concepts (e.g., water potential) and techniques (e.g., psychrometry) that are needed to analyze the physiological ecology of reptilian eggs are unfamiliar, and must be borrowed from the disciplines of soil physics and plant physiology. Nevertheless, these are problems that can be overcome.

More research clearly is needed on the eggs and embryos of all major groups of reptiles, but studies of the relatively large eggs laid by some squamates would probably be especially rewarding. However, future studies in both the field and laboratory should strive to characterize the physical environment as fully as possible using methods of measurement that are physically (mechanistically) meaningful. Only in this way can progress be made in distinguishing differences of biological interest from those related to experimental protocol.

We look forward especially to future research addressing the physiological effects of physical variables on developing embryos. What, for instance, are the effects of temperature and water on the ambisexual gonads of reptilian embryos? How does an increase in temperature simultaneously increase metabolism and reduce metabolic efficiency of developing embryos? And why do reptilian embryos in flexible-shelled eggs grow more slowly, yet hatch earlier, in dry environments than in wet ones?

Lastly, we look forward also to further investigation into the possible significance of variation in morphology of hatchlings induced by exposing eggs to different temperatures, water potentials, and gas tensions within the range of tolerance. We have yet to learn whether bigger really is better for hatchling reptiles, or whether there is more to this story than meets the eye.

ACKNOWLEDGMENTS

Much of the research for this article was done in the congenial surroundings of the University of New England, Armidale, New South Wales, while we were on sabbatical leave from Colorado State University. The bulk of revision was done while we enjoyed the companionship of colleagues at the University of Connecticut. We are grateful to H. Heatwole (University of New England) and T. L. Taigen (University of

Connecticut) for placing the resources of their laboratories at our disposal. We benefitted greatly from discussions of reptilian oology with M. E. Jones, C. J. Limpus, J. D. Miller, and G. J. W. Webb in Australia, and with R. D. Gettinger, W. H. N. Gutzke, K. Miller, and G. L. Paukstis in the United States. Preprints of work were graciously made available to us by R. A. Ackerman, R. D. Gettinger, L. J. Guillette, and G. J. W. Webb. Drafts of the manuscript were read and criticized by R. A. Ackerman, T. J. Boardman, J. J. Bull, R. D. Gettinger, L. J. Guillette, W. H. N. Gutzke, J. B. Iverson, J. D. Miller, K. Miller, A. Muth, and M. B. Thompson, to all of whom we owe special thanks. The illustrations were done by the expert hand of D. Carlson. Preparation of the manuscript was supported in part by the National Science Foundation (DCB 83-08555).

REFERENCES

Ackerman, R. A. (1977). The respiratory gas exchange of sea turtle nests (*Chelonia, Caretta*). Resp. Physiol. 31, 19–38.

Ackerman, R. A. (1980). Physiological and ecological aspects of gas exchange by sea turtle eggs. Am. Zool. 20, 575–583.

Ackerman, R. A. (1981a). Oxygen consumption by sea turtle (*Chelonia, Caretta*) eggs during development. Physiol. Zool. 54, 316–324.

Ackerman, R. A. (1981b). Growth and gas exchange of embryonic sea turtles (*Chelonia, Caretta*). Copeia 1981, 757–765.

Ackerman, R. A., Dmi'el, R. and Ar, A. (1985a). Energy and water vapor exchange by parchment-shelled reptile eggs. Physiol. Zool. 58, 129–137.

Ackerman, R. A. and Prange, H. D. (1972). Oxygen diffusion across a sea turtle (*Chelonia mydas*) egg shell. Comp. Biochem. Physiol. 43A, 905–909.

Ackerman, R. A., Seagrave, R. C., Dmi'el, R. and Ar, A. (1985b). Water and heat exchange between parchment-shelled reptile eggs and their surroundings. Copeia 1985, 703–711.

Agassiz, L. (1857). *Contributions to the Natural History of the United States of America. First Monograph, Volume II.* Little, Brown and Company, Boston.

Albers, C. (1970). Acid–base balance. In *Fish Physiology*. Volume IV. (W. S. Hoar and D. J. Randall, eds.). Academic Press, New York, pp. 173–208.

Alho, C. J. R., Danni, T. M. S. and Padua, L. F. M. (1985). Temperature-dependent sex determination in *Podocnemis expansa* (Testudinata: Pelomedusidae). Biotropica 17, 75–78.

Alho, C. J. R. and Padua, L. F. M. (1982). Reproductive parameters and nesting behavior of the Amazon turtle *Podocnemis expansa* (Testudinata: Pelomedusidae) in Brazil. Can. J. Zool. 60, 97–103.

Allard, H. A. (1935). The natural history of the box turtle. Scient. Mon., N.Y. 41, 325–338.

Andrews, R. M. (1982). Spatial variation in egg mortality of the lizard *Anolis limifrons*. Herpetologica 38, 165–171.

Andrews, R. M. and Sexton, O. J. (1981). Water relations of the eggs of *Anolis auratus* and *Anolis limifrons*. Ecology 62, 556–562.

Ar, A. and Rahn, H. (1980). Water in the avian egg: Overall budget of incubation. Am. Zool. 20, 373–384.

Badham, J. A. (1971). Albumen formation in eggs of the agamid *Amphibolurus barbatus barbatus*. Copeia 1971, 543–545.

Baird, T. and Solomon, S. E. (1979). Calcite and aragonite in the egg shell of *Chelonia mydas* L. J. Exp. Mar. Biol. Ecol. 36, 295–303.

Barrows, W. B. and Schwarz, E. A. (1895). The common crow of the United States. U. S. Dept. Agric. Div. Ornithol. Mammal., Bulletin no. 6.

Bartholomew, G. A. (1966). A field study of temperature relations in the Galapagos marine iguana. Copeia 1966, 241–250.

Bellairs, R. (1959). The yolk of the adder (*Vipera berus*). Br. J. Herpetol. 2, 155–158.

Bigalke, R. (1931). Note on the egg of the Nile crocodile (*Crocodylus niloticus*). Proc. Zool. Soc. Lond. 1931, 557–559.

Black, C. P., Birchard, G. F., Schuett, G. W. and Black, V. D. (1984). Influence of incubation water content on oxygen uptake in embryos of the Burmese python (*Python molurus bivittatus* [sic.]). In *Respiration and Metabolism of Embryonic Vertebrates*. (R. S. Seymour, ed.). Dr. W. Junk Publishers, Dordrecht, The Netherlands, pp. 137–145.

Blair, W. F. (1960). *The Rusty Lizard: A Population Study*. Univ. Texas Press, Austin.

Blanc, F. (1974). Table de développement de *Chamaeleo lateralis* Gray, 1831. Ann. Embryol. Morphogen. 7, 99–115.

Blanchard, F. N. (1933). Eggs and young of the smooth green snake, *Liopeltis vernalis* (Harlan). Pap. Mich. Acad. Sci. 17, 493–508.

Blanchard, F. N. (1936). Eggs and natural nests of the eastern ringneck snake, *Diadophis punctatus edwardsii*. Pap. Mich. Acad. Sci. 22, 521–532.

Bleakney, J. S. (1963). Notes on the distribution and life histories of turtles in Nova Scotia. Can. Fld. Nat. 77, 67–76.

Body, D. R. (1985). The egg-lipid composition of the "living fossil" reptile tuatara (*Sphenodon punctatus*). Experientia 41, 1055–1057.

Boulenger, G. A. (1912). *A Vertebrate Fauna of the Malay Peninsula From the Isthmus of Kra to Singapore Including the Adjacent Islands. Reptilia and Batrachia*. Taylor and Francis, London.

Box, J. E. and Taylor, S. A. (1962). Influence of soil bulk density on matric potential. Proc. Soil Sci. Soc. Am. 26, 119–122.

Breckenridge, W. J. (1960). A spiny soft-shelled turtle nest study. Herpetologica 16, 284–285.

Breitenbach, G. L., Congdon, J. D. and van Loben Sels, R. C. (1984). Winter temperatures of *Chrysemys picta* nests in Michigan: Effects on hatchling survival. Herpetologica 40, 76–81.

Brimley, C. S. (1903). Notes on the reproduction of certain reptiles. Am. Nat. 37, 261–266.

Brown, E. E. (1956). Nests and young of the six-lined racerunner *Cnemidophorus sexlineatus* Linnaeus. J. Elisha Mitchell Sci. Soc. 72, 30–40.

Brown, R. W. (1970). Measurement of water potential with thermocouple psychrometers: Construction and applications. USDA Forest Serv. Res. Pap. INT-80.

Brown, R. W. and Bartos, D. L. (1982). A calibration model for screen-caged Peltier thermocouple psychrometers. USDA Forest Serv. Res. Pap. INT-293.

Buchan, G. D. (1982). Predicting bare soil temperature. III. Extension to single-day variation. J. Soil Sci. 33, 365–373.

Bull, J. J. (1980). Sex determination in reptiles. Quart. Rev. Biol. 55, 3–21.

REFERENCES

Bull, J. J. (1985). Sex ratio and nest temperature in turtles: Comparing field and laboratory data. Ecology 66, 1115–1122.
Bull, J. J., Legler, J. M. and Vogt, R. C. (1985). Non-temperature dependent sex determination in two suborders of turtles. Copeia 1985, 784–786.
Bull, J. J., Moon, R. G. and Legler, J. M. (1974). Male heterogamety in kinosternid turtles (genus *Staurotypus*). Cytogenet. Cell Genet. 13, 419–425.
Bull, J. J. and Vogt, R. C. (1979). Temperature-dependent sex determination in turtles. Science 206, 1186–1188.
Bull, J. J. and Vogt, R. C. (1981). Temperature-sensitive periods of sex determination in emydid turtles. J. Exp. Zool. 218, 435–440.
Bull, J. J., Vogt, R. C. and McCoy, C. J. (1982). Sex determining temperatures in turtles: A geographic comparison. Evolution 36, 326–332.
Burger, J. (1976). Temperature relationships in nests of the northern diamondback terrapin, *Malaclemys terrapin terrapin*. Herpetologica 32, 412–418.
Burger, J. (1977). Determinants of hatching success in diamondback terrapin, *Malaclemys terrapin*. Am. Midl. Nat. 97, 444–464.
Burger, J. and Zappalorti, R. T. (1986). Nest site selection by pine snakes, *Pituophis melanoleucus*, in the New Jersey Pine Barrens. Copeia 1986, 116–121.
Busa, W. B. and Nuccitelli, R. (1984). Metabolic regulation via intracellular pH. Am. J. Physiol. 246, R409–R438.
Bustard, H. R. (1966). Notes on the eggs, incubation and young of the bearded dragon, *Amphibolurus barbatus barbatus* (Cuvier). Br. J. Herpetol. 3, 252–259.
Bustard, H. R. (1968). The egg-shell of gekkonid lizards: A taxonomic adjunct. Copeia 1968, 162–164.
Bustard, H. R. (1969a). The micro-environment of a natural lizard nest. Copeia 1969, 536–539.
Bustard, H. R. (1969b). Tail abnormalities in reptiles resulting from high temperature egg incubation. Br. J. Herpetol. 4, 121–123.
Bustard, H. R. (1971a). Temperature and water tolerances of incubating sea turtle eggs. Br. J. Herpetol. 4, 196–198.
Bustard, H. R. (1971b). Temperature and water tolerances of incubating crocodile eggs. Br. J. Herpetol. 4, 198–200.
Bustard, H. R. (1972). *Sea Turtles. Natural History and Conservation*. Taplinger Publ. Co., New York.
Bustard, H. R. and Greenham, P. (1968). Physical and chemical factors affecting hatching in the green sea turtle, *Chelonia mydas* (L.). Ecology 49, 269–276.
Bustard, H. R., Simkiss, K. and Jenkins, N. K. (1969). Some analyses of artificially incubated eggs and hatchlings of green and loggerhead sea turtles. J. Zool. 158, 311–315.
Cagle, F. R. (1937). Egg laying habits of the slider turtle (*Pseudemys troostii*), the painted turtle (*Chrysemys picta*), and the musk turtle (*Sternotherus odoratus*). J. Tenn. Acad. Sci. 12, 87–95.
Cagle, F. R. (1940). Eggs and natural nests of *Eumeces fasciatus*. Am. Midl. Nat. 23, 227–233.
Cagle, F. R. (1944). Activity and winter changes of hatchling *Pseudemys*. Copeia 1944, 105–109.
Cagle, F. R. (1950). The life history of the slider turtle, *Pseudemys scripta troostii* (Holbrook). Ecol. Monogr. 20, 31–54.
Campbell, G. S. and Gardner, W. H. (1971). Psychrometric measurement of soil water potential: Temperature and bulk density effects. Proc. Soil Sci. Soc. Am. 35, 8–12.

Campbell, H. W. (1972). Ecological or phylogenetic interpretations of crocodilian nesting habits. Nature 238, 404–405.
Carpenter, C. C. (1966). The marine iguana of the Galápagos Islands, its behavior and ecology. Proc. Calif. Acad. Sci. (Ser. 4) 34, 329–375.
Carr, A. (1952). *Handbook of Turtles*. Comstock Publ. Assoc., Ithaca, New York.
Carr, A. and Hirth, H. (1961). Social facilitation in green turtle siblings. Anim. Behav. 9, 68–70.
Carr, J. L. and Bickham, J. W. (1981). Sex chromosomes of the Asian black pond turtle, *Siebenrockiella crassicollis* (Testudines: Emydidae). Cytogenet. Cell Genet. 31, 178–183.
Carson, J. E. and Moses, H. (1963). The annual and diurnal heat-exchange cycles in upper layers of soil. J. Appl. Meteorol. 2, 397–406.
Cary, J. W. (1966). Soil moisture transport due to thermal gradients: Practical aspects. Proc. Soil Sci. Soc. Am. 30, 428–433.
Cary, J. W. and Hanks, R. J. (1972). The usefulness of water potential measurements in soil and related media. In *Psychrometry in Water Relations Research.* (R. W. Brown and B. P. Van Haveren, eds.). Utah Agric. Exp. Sta., Utah State Univ., Logan, pp. 137–141.
Chabreck, R. H. (1973). Temperature variation in nests of the American alligator. Herpetologica 29, 48–51.
Chabreck, R. H. (1975). Moisture variation in nests of the American alligator (*Alligator mississippiensis*). Herpetologica 31, 385–389.
Charnier, M. (1966). Action de la température sur la sex-ratio chez l'embryon d'*Agama agama* (Agamidae, Lacertilien). C. R. Seanc. Soc. Biol. 160, 620–622.
Clark, D. R., Jr. (1970). Ecological study of the worm snake *Carphophis vermis* (Kennicott). Univ. Kans. Publ. Mus. Nat. Hist. 19, 85–194.
Clark, H. (1946). Incubation and respiration of eggs of *Crotaphytus c. collaris* (Say). Herpetologica 3, 136–139.
Clark, H. (1953a). Eggs, egg-laying and incubation of the snake *Elaphe emoryi* (Baird and Girard). Copeia 1953, 90–92.
Clark, H. (1953b). Metabolism of the black snake embryo. Nitrogen excretion. J. Exp. Biol. 30, 492–501.
Clark, H. (1953c). Metabolism of the black snake embryo. II. Respiratory exchange. J. Exp. Biol. 30, 502–505.
Clarke, S. F. (1888). The nest and eggs of the alligator: *Alligator lucius* Cuv. Zool. Anz. 11, 568–570.
Clarke, S. F. (1891). The habits and embryology of the American alligator. J. Morphol. 5, 181–215.
Coker, R. E. (1906). The natural history and cultivation of the diamond-back terrapin with notes on other forms of turtles. North Carolina Geol. Surv. Bull. no. 14.
Coker, R. E. (1910). Diversity in the scutes of Chelonia. J. Morphol. 21, 1–75.
Congdon, J. D. and Tinkle, D. W. (1982). Reproductive energetics of the painted turtle (*Chrysemys picta*). Herpetologica 38, 228–237.
Congdon, J. D., Dunham, A. E. and Tinkle, D. W. (1982). Energy budgets and life histories of reptiles. In *Biology of the Reptilia.* Vol. 13. (C. Gans and F. H. Pough, eds.). Academic Press, London, pp. 233–271.
Congdon, J. D., Gibbons, J. W. and Greene, J. L. (1983a). Parental investment in the chicken turtle (*Deirochelys reticularia*). Ecology 64, 419–425.
Congdon, J. D., Tinkle, D. W., Breitenbach, G. L. and van Loben Sels, R. C. (1983b). Nesting ecology and hatching success in the turtle *Emydoidea blandingi*. Herpetologica 39, 417–429.

REFERENCES

Congdon, J. D., Tinkle, D. W. and Rosen, P. C. (1983c). Egg components and utilization during development in aquatic turtles. Copeia 1983, 264–268.

Cooper, J. S. (1958). Observations on the eggs and young of the wall lizard (*Lacerta muralis*) in captivity. Br. J. Herpetol. 2, 112–121.

Corey, A. T. and Klute, A. (1985). Application of the potential concept to soil water equilibrium and transport. J. Soil Sci. Soc. Am. 49, 3–11.

Cowles, R. B. (1928). The life history of *Varanus niloticus*. Science 67, 317–318.

Crastz, F. (1982). Embryological stages of the marine turtle *Lepidochelys olivacea* (Eschscholtz). Rev. Biol. Trop. 30, 113–120.

Cunningham, B. (1922). Some phases in the development of *Chrysemys cinerea*. J. Elisha Mitchell Sci. Soc. 38, 51–73.

Cunningham, B. and Huene, E. (1938). Further studies on water absorption by reptile eggs. Am. Nat. 72, 380–385.

Cunningham, B. and Hurwitz, A. P. (1936). Water absorption by reptile eggs during incubation. Am. Nat. 70, 590–595.

Cunningham, B., Woodward M. W. and Pridgen, J. (1939). Further studies on incubation of turtle (*Malaclemys centrata* Lat.) eggs. Am. Nat. 73, 285–288.

Dalrymple, G. H., Hampp, J. C. and Wellins, D. J. (1985). Male-biased sex ratio in a cold nest of a hawksbill sea turtle (*Eretmochelys imbricata*). J. Herpetol. 19, 158–159.

Decker, J. D. (1967). Motility of the turtle embryo, *Chelydra serpentina* (Linné). Science 157, 952–954.

Deitz, D. C. and Hines, T. C. (1980). Alligator nesting in north-central Florida. Copeia 1980, 249–258.

Dendy, A. (1899a). The life-history of the tuatara (*Sphenodon punctatum*). Trans. Proc. N.Z. Inst. 31, 249–255.

Dendy, A. (1899b). The hatching of tuatara eggs. Nature 59, 340.

Dendy, A. (1899c). Outlines of the development of the tuatara, *Sphenodon (Hatteria) punctatus*. Quar. J. Microsc. Sci. 42(NS), 1–87.

Deraniyagala, P. E. P. (1936). Reproduction of the estuarine crocodile of Ceylon. Ceylon J. Sci. (Sec. B) 19, 253–277.

Deraniyagala, P. E. P. (1939). *The Tetrapod Reptiles of Ceylon. Volume I. Testudinates and Crocodilians*. Colombo Mus. Nat. Hist. Ser., Columbo Mus., Columbo, Ceylon.

DeSalle, R., Veith, G. M. and Sexton, O. J. (1984). An enzymatic and histochemical analysis of eggshells of anoline lizards. Comp. Biochem. Physiol. 78A, 237–242.

Dmi'el, R. (1967). Studies on reproduction, growth, and feeding in the snake *Spalerosophis cliffordi* (Colubridae). Copeia 1967, 332–346.

Dmi'el, R. (1970). Growth and metabolism in snake embryos. J. Embryol. Exp. Morphol. 23, 761–772.

Dodge, C. H., Dimond, M. T. and Wunder, C. C. (1978). Effect of temperature on the incubation time of eggs of the eastern box turtle (*Terrapene carolina carolina* Linné). Fla. Mar. Res. Publ. 33, 8–11.

Domantay, J. S. (1968). Notes on the development and breeding habits of *Chelonia mydas*. Acta Manilana (Ser. A) 4, 87–109.

Dufaure, J. P. and Hubert, J. (1961). Table de développement du lézard vivipare: *Lacerta (Zootoca) vivipara* Jacquin. Arch. Anat. Microsc. Morphol. Exp. 50, 309–327.

Dunson, W. A. (1982). Low water vapor conductance of hard-shelled eggs of the gecko lizards *Hemidactylus* and *Lepidodactylus*. J. Exp. Zool. 219, 377–379.

Dunson, W. A. and Bramham, C. R. (1981). Evaporative water loss and oxygen consumption of three small lizards from the Florida keys: *Sphaerodactylus cinereus*, *S. notatus*, and *Anolis sagrei*. Physiol. Zool. 54, 253–259.

Dutton, P. H., Whitmore, C. P. and Mrosovsky, N. (1985). Masculinisation of leatherback turtle *Dermochelys coriacea* hatchlings from eggs incubated in styrofoam boxes. Biol. Conserv. 31, 249–264.
Engel, W., Klemme, B. and Schmid, M. (1981). H-Y antigen and sex-determination in turtles. Differentiation 20, 152–156.
Erben, H. K. (1970). Ultrastrukturen und Mineralisation rezenter und fossiler Eischalen bei Vögeln und Reptilien. Biomineralisation Forschungsberichte 1, 1–66.
Erben, H. K., Hoefs, J. and Wedepohl, F. H. (1979). Paleobiological and isotopic studies of eggshells from a declining dinosaur species. Paleobiology 5, 380–414.
Erben, H. K. and Newesely, H. (1972). Kristalline Bausteine und Mineralbestand von kalkigen Eischalen. Biomineralisation Forschungsberichte 6, 32–48.
Ernst, C. H. and Barbour, R. W. (1972). *Turtles of the United States*. Univ. Press Kentucky, Lexington.
Ewert, M. A. (1979). The embryo and its egg: Development and natural history. In *Turtles. Perspectives and Research*. (M. Harless and H. Morlock, eds.). Wiley, New York, pp. 333–413.
Ewert, M. A. (1985). Embryology of turtles. In *Biology of the Reptilia*. Vol. 14. (C. Gans, F. Billett and P. F. A. Maderson, eds.). Wiley, New York, pp. 75–267.
Ewert, M. A., Firth, S. J. and Nelson, C. E. (1984). Normal and multiple eggshells in batagurine turtles and their implications for dinosaurs and other reptiles. Can. J. Zool. 62, 1834–1841.
Feder, M. E., Satel, S. L. and Gibbs, A. G. (1982). Resistance of the shell membrane and mineral layer to diffusion of oxygen and water in flexible-shelled eggs of the snapping turtle (*Chelydra serpentina*). Resp. Physiol. 49, 279–291.
Ferguson, G. W. and Bohlen, C. H. (1978). Demographic analysis: A tool for the study of natural selection of behavioral traits. In *Behavior and Neurology of Lizards*. (N. Greenberg and P. D. Maclean, eds.). U.S. Dept. Health, Education, and Welfare, NIMH, Rockville, MD, pp. 227–243.
Ferguson, G. W., Brown, K. L. and DeMarco, V. G. (1982). Selective basis for the evolution of variable egg and hatchling size in some iguanid lizards. Herpetologica 38, 178–188.
Ferguson, G. W. and Fox, S. F. (1984). Annual variation of survival advantage of large juvenile side-blotched lizards, *Uta stansburiana*: Its causes and evolutionary significance. Evolution 38, 342–349.
Ferguson, M. W. J. (1981a). Increasing porosity of the incubating alligator eggshell caused by extrinsic microbial degradation. Experientia 37, 252–254.
Ferguson, M. W. J. (1981b). Extrinsic microbial degradation of the alligator eggshell. Science 214, 1135–1137.
Ferguson, M. W. J. (1982). The structure and composition of the eggshell and embryonic membranes of *Alligator mississippiensis*. Trans. Zool. Soc. Lond. 36, 99–152.
Ferguson, M. W. J. (1985). Reproductive biology and embryology of the crocodilians. In *Biology of the Reptilia*. Vol. 14. (C. Gans, F. Billett and P. F. A. Maderson, eds.). Wiley, New York, pp. 329–491.
Ferguson, M. W. J. and Joanen, T. (1982). Temperature of egg incubation determines sex in *Alligator mississippiensis*. Nature 296, 850–853.
Ferguson, M. W. J. and Joanen, T. (1983). Temperature-dependent sex determination in *Alligator mississippiensis*. J. Zool. 200, 143–177.
Fisk, A. and Tribe, M. (1949). The development of the amnion and chorion of reptiles. Proc. Zool. Soc. Lond. 119, 83–114.

REFERENCES

Fitch, A. V. (1964). Temperature tolerances of embryonic *Eumeces*. Herpetologica 20, 184–187.
Fitch, H. S. (1954). Life history and ecology of the five-lined skink, *Eumeces fasciatus*. Univ. Kans. Publ. Mus. Nat. Hist. 8, 1–156.
Fitch, H. S. (1963). Natural history of the racer *Coluber constrictor*. Univ. Kans. Publ. Mus. Nat. Hist. 15, 351–468.
Fitch, H. S. and Fitch, A. V. (1967). Preliminary experiments on physical tolerances of the eggs of lizards and snakes. Ecology 48, 160–165.
FitzSimons, V. F. M. (1962). *Snakes of Southern Africa*. Macdonald & Co., London.
Flegg, P. B. (1953). The effect of aggregation on diffusion of gases and vapours through soils. J. Sci. Fed. Agric. 4, 104–108.
Fowler, L. E. (1979). Hatching success and nest predation in the green sea turtle, *Chelonia mydas*, at Tortuguero, Costa Rica. Ecology 60, 946–955.
Fox, S. F. (1978). Natural selection on behavioral phenotypes of the lizard *Uta stansburiana*. Ecology 59, 834–847.
Fox, W. (1948). Effect of temperature on development of scutellation in the garter snake, *Thamnophis elegans atratus*. Copeia 1948, 252–262.
Fox, W., Gordon, C. and Fox, M. H. (1961). Morphological effects of low temperatures during the embryonic development of the garter snake, *Thamnophis elegans*. Zoologica 46, 57–71.
Froese, A. D. and Burghardt, G. M. (1974). Food competition in captive juvenile snapping turtles, *Chelydra serpentina*. Anim. Behav. 22, 735–740.
Gates, D. M. (1980). *Biophysical Ecology*. Springer-Verlag, New York.
Gettinger, R. D., Paukstis, G. L. and Gutzke, W. H. N. (1984). Influence of hydric environment on oxygen consumption by embryonic turtles *Chelydra serpentina* and *Trionyx spiniferus*. Physiol. Zool. 57, 468–473.
Gibbons, J. W. and Coker, J. W. (1977). Ecological and life history aspects of the cooter, *Chrysemys floridana* (Le Conte). Herpetologica 33, 29–33.
Gibbons, J. W. and Nelson, D. H. (1978). The evolutionary significance of delayed emergence from the nest by hatchling turtles. Evolution 32, 297–303.
Giersberg, H. (1922). Untersuchungen über Physiologie und Histologie des Eileiters der Reptilien und Vögel; nebst einem Beitrag zur Fasergenese. Z. wiss. Zool. 120, 1–97.
Goode, J. and Russell, J. (1968). Incubation of eggs of three species of chelid tortoises, and notes on their embryological development. Aust. J. Zool. 16, 749–761.
Goodwin, T. M. and Marion, W. R. (1978). Aspects of the nesting ecology of American alligators (*Alligator mississippiensis*) in north-central Florida. Herpetologica 34, 43–47.
Gorman, G. C. (1973). The chromosomes of the Reptilia, a cytotaxonomic interpretation. In *Cytotaxonomy and Vertebrate Evolution*. (A. B. Chiarelli and E. Capanna, eds.). Academic Press, London, pp. 349–424.
Greer, A. E. (1970). Evolutionary and systematic significance of crocodilian nesting habits. Nature 227, 523–524.
Grodzinski, M. Z. (1949). The fat in the yolk of the sand-lizard *Lacerta agilis* L. Bull. Int. Acad. Sci. Lett. Cracovie (Ser. B) 2, 367–381.
Guggisberg, C. A. W. (1972). *Crocodiles. Their Natural History, Folklore and Conservation*. Stackpole Books, Harrisburg, PA.
Guillette, L. J., Jr. (1981). On the occurrence of oviparous and viviparous forms of the Mexican lizard *Sceloporus aeneus*. Herpetologica 37, 11–15.
Guillette, L. J., Jr. (1982a). The evolution of viviparity and placentation in the high elevation, Mexican lizard *Sceloporus aeneus*. Herpetologica 38, 94–103.

Guillette, L. J., Jr. (1982b). Effects of gravidity on the metabolism of the reproductively bimodal lizard *Sceloporus aeneus.* J. Exp. Zool. 223, 33–36.
Guillette, L. J., Jr. and Jones, R. E. (1985). Ovarian, oviductal, and placental morphology of the reproductively bimodal lizard, *Sceloporus aeneus.* J. Morphol. 184, 85–98.
Guillette, L. J., Jr. and Lara Gongora, G. (1986). Notes on oviposition and nesting in the high elevation lizard, *Sceloporus aeneus.* Copeia 1986, 232–233.
Gurr, C. G., Marshall, T. J. and Hutton, J. T. (1952). Movement of water in soil due to a temperature gradient. Soil Sci. 74, 335–345.
Gutzke, W. H. N. (1984a). The Influence of Environmental Factors on Eggs and Hatchlings of Painted Turtles (*Chrysemys picta*). Ph.D. Dissertation, Colorado State University, Fort Collins.
Gutzke, W. H. N. (1984b). Modification of the hydric environment by eggs of snapping turtles (*Chelydra serpentina*). Can. J. Zool. 62, 2401–2403.
Gutzke, W. H. N. and Packard, G. C. (1985). Hatching success in relation to egg size in painted turtles (*Chrysemys picta*). Can. J. Zool. 63, 67–70.
Gutzke, W. H. N. and Packard, G. C. (1986). Sensitive periods for the influence of the hydric environment on eggs and hatchlings of painted turtles (*Chrysemys picta*). Physiol. Zool. 59, 337–343.
Gutzke, W. H. N. and Packard, G. C. (1987a). Influence of the hydric and thermal environments on eggs and hatchlings of bull snakes *Pituophis melanoleucus.* Physiol. Zool., 60, 9–17.
Gutzke, W. H. N. and Packard, G. C. (1987b). The influence of temperature on eggs and hatchlings of Blanding's turtles, *Emydoidea blandingii.* J. Herpetol., 21, 161–163.
Gutzke, W. H. N. and Paukstis, G. L. (1983). Influence of the hydric environment on sexual differentiation of turtles. J. Exp. Zool. 226, 467–469.
Gutzke, W. H. N. and Paukstis, G. L. (1984). A low threshold temperature for sexual differentiation in the painted turtle, *Chrysemys picta.* Copeia 1984, 546–547.
Hammer, D. A. (1969). Parameters of a marsh snapping turtle population Lacreek Refuge, South Dakota. J. Wildl. Mgmt. 33, 995–1005.
Harris, V. A. (1964). *The Life of the Rainbow Lizard.* Hutchinson & Co., London.
Hendrickson, J. R. (1958). The green sea turtle, *Chelonia mydas* (Linn.) in Malaya and Sarawak. Proc. Zool. Soc. Lond. 130, 455–535.
Hirsch, K. F. (1983). Contemporary and fossil chelonian eggshells. Copeia 1983, 382–397.
Hirsch, K. F. (1985). Fossil crocodilian eggs from the Eocene of Colorado. J. Paleontol. 59, 531–542.
Holder, L. A. and Bellairs, A. d'A. (1962). The use of reptiles in experimental embryology. Br. J. Herpetol. 3, 54–61.
Hotaling, E. C., Wilhoft, D. C. and McDowell, S. B. (1985). Egg position and weight of hatchling snapping turtles, *Chelydra serpentina,* in natural nests. J. Herpetol. 19, 534–536.
Howell, B. J. and Rahn, H. (1976). Regulation of acid-base balance in reptiles. In *Biology of the Reptilia.* Vol. 5. (C. Gans and W. R. Dawson, eds.). Academic Press, London, pp. 335–363.
Hudson, P. (1977). An account of egg laying by the thorny devil *Moloch horridus* (Gray). Herpetofauna 9, 23–24.
Iverson, J. B. (1979). Behavior and ecology of the rock iguana *Cyclura carinata.* Bull. Fla. St. Mus. Biol. Sci. 24, 175–358.
Jackson, R. D., Rose, D. A. and Penman, H. L. (1965). Circulation of water in soil under a temperature gradient. Nature 205, 314–316.

REFERENCES

Jacobi, L. (1936). Ovoviviparie bei einheimischen Eidechsen. Vergleichende Untersuchungen an den Eiern und am Ovidukt von *Lacerta agilis, Lacerta vivipara* und *Anguis fragilis.* Z. wiss. Zool. 148, 401–464.

Jenkins, N. K. (1975). Chemical composition of the eggs of the crocodile (*Crocodylus novaeguineae*). Comp. Biochem. Physiol. 51A, 891–895.

Jenkins, N. K. and Simkiss, K. (1968). The calcium and phosphate metabolism of reproducing reptiles with particular reference to the adder (*Vipera berus*). Comp. Biochem. Physiol. 26, 865–876.

Joanen, T. (1970). Nesting ecology of alligators in Louisiana. Proc. Twenty-third Ann. Conf. SE Assoc. Game Fish Comm., pp. 141–151.

Johnson, S. R. (1965). An ecological study of the chuckwalla, *Sauromalus obesus* Baird, in the western Mojave Desert. Am. Midl. Nat. 73, 1–29.

Johnston, G. R. (1979). The eggs, incubation and young of the bearded dragon *Amphibolurus vitticeps* Ahl. Herpetofauna 11, 5–8.

Karashima, J. (1929). Ueber das Verhalten der Fette bei der Bebrütung von Meerschildkröteneiern. J. Biochem., Tokyo 10, 375–377.

Koga, K., Fukunaga, T. and Ogura, H. (1978). The fatty acid composition of egg yolk lipids from the sea-turtle. Mem. Fac. Agric. Kagoshima Univ. 14, 117–122.

Krampitz, G., Erben, H. K. and Kriesten, K. (1972). Ueber Aminosäurenzusammensetzung und Struktur von Eischalen. Biomineralisation Forschungsberichte 4, 87–99.

Krampitz, G., Kriesten, K. and Bohme, W. (1973). Untersuchungen über Ultrastruktur und Aminosäurenzusammensetzung der Eischalen von *Natrix natrix.* Experientia 29, 416–418.

Kriesten, K. (1975). Untersuchungen über Ultrastruktur, Proteinmuster und Aminosäurenzusammensetzung der Eischalen von *Testudo elephantopus, Caiman crocodilus* und *Iguana iguana.* Zool. Jb. Anat. 94, 101–122.

Lang, J. W. (1985). Incubation temperature affects thermal selection of hatchling crocodiles. Am. Zool. 25, 18A.

Legge, N. J. (1985). Water movement from soil to root investigated through simultaneous measurement of soil and stem water potential in potted trees. J. Exp. Bot. 36, 1583–1589.

Legler, J. M. (1954). Nesting habits of the western painted turtle, *Chrysemys picta bellii* (Gray). Herpetologica 10, 137–144.

Legler, J. M. (1960). Natural history of the ornate box turtle, *Terrapene ornata ornata* Agassiz. Univ. Kans. Publ. Mus. Nat. Hist. 11, 527–669.

Licht, P. and Moberly, W. R. (1965). Thermal requirements for embryonic development in the tropical lizard *Iguana iguana.* Copeia 1965, 515–517.

Lillywhite, H. B. and Ackerman, R. A. (1984). Hydrostatic pressure, shell compliance and permeability to water vapor in flexible-shelled eggs of the colubrid snake *Elaphe obsoleta.* In *Respiration and Metabolism of Embryonic Vertebrates.* (R. S. Seymour, ed.). Dr. W. Junk Publ., Dordrecht, The Netherlands, pp. 121–135.

Limpus, C. J., Miller, J. D., Baker, V. and McLachlan, E. (1983a). The hawksbill turtle, *Eretmochelys imbricata* (L.), in north-eastern Australia: The Campbell Island rookery. Aust. Wildl. Res. 10, 185–197.

Limpus, C. J., Reed, P. and Miller, J. D. (1983b). Islands and turtles. The influence of choice of nesting beach on sex ratio. In *Proceedings: Inaugural Great Barrier Reef Conference.* (J. T. Baker, R. M. Carter, P. W. Sammarco, and K. P. Stark, eds.). James Cook Univ. Press, Townsville, Queensland, pp. 397–402.

Lutz, P. L., Bentley, T. B., Harrison, K. E. and Marszalek, D. S. (1980). Oxygen and water vapour conductance in the shell and shell membrane of the American crocodile egg. Comp. Biochem. Physiol. 66A, 335–338.

Lutz, P. L. and Dunbar-Cooper, A. (1984). The nest environment of the American crocodile (*Crocodylus acutus*). Copeia 1984, 153–161.

Lynn, W. G. and von Brand, T. (1945). Studies on the oxygen consumption and water metabolism of turtle embryos. Biol. Bull. Mar. Biol. Lab., Woods Hole 88, 112–125.

MacFarland, C. G., Villa, J. and Toro, B. (1974). The Galapagos giant tortoises (*Geochelone elephantopus*). Part II. Conservation methods. Biol. Conserv. 6, 198–212.

Maderson, P. F. A. and Bellairs, A. d'A. (1962). Culture methods as an aid to experiment on reptile embryos. Nature 195, 401–402.

Magnusson, W. E. (1979). Maintenance of temperature of crocodile nests (Reptilia, Crocodilidae). J. Herpetol. 13, 439–443.

Magnusson, W. E. and Lima, A. P. (1984). Perennial communal nesting by *Kentropyx calcaratus*. J. Herpetol. 18, 73–75.

Magnusson, W. E., Lima, A. P. and Sampaio, R. M. (1985). Sources of heat for nests of *Paleosuchus trigonatus* and a review of crocodilian nest temperatures. J. Herpetol. 19, 199–207.

Mahmoud, I. Y., Hess, G. L. and Klicka, J. (1973). Normal embryonic stages of the western painted turtle, *Chrysemys picta bellii*. J. Morphol. 141, 269–279.

Mahrer, Y. (1982). A theoretical study of the effect of soil surface shape upon the soil temperature profile. Soil Sci. 134, 381–387.

Mahrer, Y. and Avissar, R. (1985). A numerical study of the effects of soil surface shape upon the soil temperature and moisture regimes. Soil Sci. 139, 483–490.

Marshall, T. J. (1959). The diffusion of gases through porous media. J. Soil Sci. 10, 79–82.

Marshall, T. J. and Holmes, J. W. (1979). *Soil Physics*. Cambridge Univ. Press, Cambridge.

McBee, K., Bickham, J. W., Rhodin, A. G. J. and Mittermeier, R. A. (1985). Karyotypic variation in the genus *Platemys* (Testudines: Pleurodira). Copeia 1985, 445–449.

McCoy, C. J., Vogt, R. C. and Censky, E. J. (1983). Temperature-controlled sex determination in the sea turtle *Lepidochelys olivacea*. J. Herpetol. 17, 404–406.

McGehee, M. A. (1979). Factors Affecting the Hatching Success of Loggerhead Sea Turtle Eggs (*Caretta caretta caretta*). M.S. Thesis, Univ. Central Florida, Orlando.

McIlhenny, E. A. (1934). Notes on incubation and growth of alligators. Copeia 1934, 80–88.

McIlhenny, E. A. (1935). *The Alligator's Life History*. Christopher Publ. House, Boston.

Mendelssohn, H. (1963). On the biology of the venomous snakes of Israel. Part I. Israel J. Zool. 12, 143–170.

Mendelssohn, H. (1965). On the biology of the venomous snakes of Israel. II. Israel J. Zool. 14, 185–212.

Menzies, J. I. (1958). Breeding behaviour of the chamaeleon (*Chamaeleo gracilis*) in Sierra Leone. Br. J. Herpetol. 2, 130–132.

Merrill, S. D. and Rawlins, S. L. (1972). Field measurement of soil water potential with thermocouple psychrometers. Soil Sci. 113, 102–109.

Meyn, R. L. and White, R. S. (1972). Calibration of thermocouple psychrometers: A suggested procedure for development of a reliable predictive model. In *Psychrometry in Water Relations Research*. (R. W. Brown and B. P. Van Haveren, eds.). Utah Agric. Exp. Sta., Utah State Univ., Logan, pp. 56–64.

Miller, J. D. (1982). Embryology of Marine Turtles. Ph.D. Thesis, Univ. New England, Armidale, New South Wales.

Miller, J. D. (1985). Embryology of marine turtles. In *Biology of the Reptilia*. Vol. 14. (C. Gans, F. Billett and P. F. A. Maderson, eds.). Wiley, New York, pp. 269–328.

REFERENCES

Miller, J. D. and Limpus, C. J. (1981). Incubation period and sexual differentiation in the green turtle *Chelonia mydas* L. In *Proceedings of the Melbourne Herpetological Symposium*. (C. B. Banks and A. A. Martin, eds.). Zoological Board of Victoria, Parkville, Victoria, pp. 66–73.

Miller, K., Packard, G. C. and Packard, M. J. (1987). Hydric conditions during incubation influence locomotor performance of hatchling snapping turtles. J. Exp. Biol., 127, 401–412.

Millington, R. J. (1959). Gas diffusion in porous media. Science 130, 100–102.

Mitsukuri, K. (1890). On the foetal membranes of Chelonia. Anat. Anz. 5, 510–519.

Mitsukuri, K. (1891). On the foetal membranes of Chelonia. J. Coll. Sci. Imp. Univ. Tokyo 4, 1–53.

Mittermeier, R. A., Rhodin, A. G. J., Medem, F., Soini, P., Hoogmoed, M. S. and Carrillo de Espinoza, N. (1978). Distribution of the South American chelid turtle *Phrynops gibbus*, with observations on habitat and reproduction. Herpetologica 34, 94–100.

Modha, M. L. (1967). The ecology of the Nile crocodile (*Crocodylus niloticus laurenti*) on Central Island, Lake Rudolf. E. Afr. Wildl. J. 5, 74–95.

Moffat, L. A. (1985). Embryonic development and aspects of reproductive biology of the tuatara, *Sphenodon punctatus*. In *Biology of the Reptilia*. Vol. 14. (C. Gans, F. Billett and P. F. A. Maderson, eds.). Wiley, New York, pp. 493–521.

Moll, E. O. and Legler, J. M. (1971). The life history of a Neotropical slider turtle, *Pseudemys scripta* (Schoepff), in Panama. Bull. Los Angeles County Mus. Sci. no. 11.

Moore, J. C. (1953). The crocodile in the Everglades National Park. Copeia 1953, 54–59.

Morreale, S. J., Ruiz, G. J., Spotila, J. R. and Standora, E. A. (1982). Temperature-dependent sex determination: Current practices threaten conservation of sea turtles. Science 216, 1245–1247.

Morris, K. A., Packard, G. C., Boardman, T. J., Paukstis, G. L. and Packard, M. J. (1983). Effect of the hydric environment on growth of embryonic snapping turtles (*Chelydra serpentina*). Herpetologica 39, 272–285.

Mrosovsky, N. (1982). Sex ratio bias in hatchling sea turtles from artificially incubated eggs. Biol. Conserv. 23, 309–314.

Mrosovsky, N. (1983). *Conserving Sea Turtles*. The British Herpetological Society, London.

Mrosovsky, N., Dutton, P. H. and Whitmore, C. P. (1984a). Sex ratios of two species of sea turtle nesting in Suriname. Can. J. Zool. 62, 2227–2239.

Mrosovsky, N., Hopkins-Murphy, S. R. and Richardson, J. I. (1984b). Sex ratio of sea turtles: Seasonal changes. Science 225, 739–741.

Mrosovsky, N. and Yntema, C. L. (1980). Temperature dependence of sexual differentiation in sea turtles: Implications for conservation practices. Biol. Conserv. 18, 271–280.

Muth, A. (1977). Eggs and hatchlings of captive *Dipsosaurus dorsalis*. Copeia 1977, 189–190.

Muth, A. (1980). Physiological ecology of desert iguana (*Dipsosaurus dorsalis*) eggs: Temperature and water relations. Ecology 61, 1335–1343.

Muth, A. (1981). Water relations of desert iguana (*Dipsosaurus dorsalis*) eggs. Physiol Zool. 54, 441–451.

Muth, A. and Bull, J. J. (1981). Sex determination in desert iguanas: Does incubation temperature make a difference? Copeia 1981, 869–870.

Muthukkaruppan, V., Kanakambika, P., Manickavel, V. and Veeraraghavan, K. (1970). Analysis of the development of the lizard, *Calotes versicolor*. I. A series of normal stages in the embryonic development. J. Morphol. 130, 479–489.

Ogden, J. C. (1978). Status and nesting biology of the American crocodile, *Crocodylus acutus*, (Reptilia, Crocodilidae) in Florida. J. Herpetol. 12, 183–196.

Osgood, D. W. (1978). Effect of temperature on the development of meristic characters in *Natrix fasciata*. Copeia 1978, 33–37.

Packard, G. C. and Packard, M. J. (1980). Evolution of the cleidoic egg among reptilian antecedents of birds. Am. Zool. 20, 351–362.

Packard, G. C. and Packard, M. J. (1984). Coupling of physiology of embryonic turtles to the hydric environment. In *Respiration and Metabolism of Embryonic Vertebrates*. (R. S. Seymour, ed.). Dr. W. Junk Publishers, Dordrecht, The Netherlands, pp. 99–119.

Packard, G. C. and Packard, M. J. (1987). Water relations and nitrogen excretion in embryos of the oviparous snake *Coluber constrictor*. Copeia, 1987, 395–406.

Packard, G. C., Packard, M. J. and Boardman, T. J. (1981a). Patterns and possible significance of water exchange by flexible-shelled eggs of painted turtles (*Chrysemys picta*). Physiol. Zool. 54, 165–178.

Packard, G. C., Packard, M. J. and Boardman, T. J. (1982). An experimental analysis of the water relations of eggs of Blanding's turtles (*Emydoidea blandingii*). Zool. J. Linn. Soc. 75, 23–34.

Packard, G. C., Packard, M. J. and Boardman, T. J. (1984a). Influence of hydration of the environment on the pattern of nitrogen excretion by embryonic snapping turtles (*Chelydra serpentina*). J. Exp. Biol. 108, 195–204.

Packard, G. C., Packard, M. J. and Boardman, T. J. (1984b). Effects of the hydric environment on metabolism of embryonic snapping turtles do not result from altered patterns of sexual differentiation. Copeia 1984, 547–550.

Packard, G. C., Packard, M. J., Boardman, T. J. and Ashen, M. D. (1981b). Possible adaptive value of water exchanges in flexible-shelled eggs of turtles. Science 213, 471–473.

Packard, G. C., Packard, M. J., Boardman, T. J., Morris, K. A. and Shuman, R. D. (1983). Influence of water exchanges by flexible-shelled eggs of painted turtles *Chrysemys picta* on metabolism and growth of embryos. Physiol. Zool. 56, 217–230.

Packard, G. C., Packard, M. J. and Gutzke, W. H. N. (1985a). Influence of hydration of the environment on eggs and embryos of the terrestrial turtle *Terrapene ornata*. Physiol. Zool. 58, 564–575.

Packard, G. C., Packard, M. J., Miller, K. and Boardman, T. J. (1987). Influence of moisture, temperature, and substrate on snapping turtle eggs and embryos. Ecology 68, 983–993.

Packard, G. C., Paukstis, G. L., Boardman, T. J. and Gutzke, W. H. N. (1985b). Daily and seasonal variation in hydric conditions and temperature inside nests of common snapping turtles (*Chelydra serpentina*). Can. J. Zool. 63, 2422–2429.

Packard, G. C., Taigen, T. L., Boardman, T. J., Packard, M. J. and Tracy, C. R. (1979a). Changes in mass of softshell turtle (*Trionyx spiniferus*) eggs incubated on substrates differing in water potential. Herpetologica 35, 78–86.

Packard, G. C., Taigen, T. L., Packard, M. J. and Boardman, T. J. (1980). Water relations of pliable-shelled eggs of common snapping turtles (*Chelydra serpentina*). Can. J. Zool. 58, 1404–1411.

Packard, G. C., Taigen, T. L., Packard M. J. and Boardman, T. J. (1981c). Changes in mass of eggs of softshell turtles (*Trionyx spiniferus*) incubated under hydric conditions simulating those of natural nests. J. Zool. 193, 81–90.

Packard, G. C., Taigen, T. L., Packard M. J. and Shuman, R. D. (1979b). Water-vapor conductance of testudinian and crocodilian eggs (class Reptilia). Resp. Physiol. 38, 1–10.

Packard, G. C., Tracy, C. R. and Roth, J. J. (1977). The physiological ecology of reptilian

REFERENCES

eggs and embryos, and the evolution of viviparity within the class Reptilia. Biol. Rev. 52, 71–105.

Packard, M. J. (1980). Ultrastructural morphology of the shell and shell membrane of eggs of common snapping turtles (*Chelydra serpentina*). J. Morphol. 165, 187–204.

Packard, M. J., Burns, L. K., Hirsch, K. F. and Packard, G. C. (1982a). Structure of shells of eggs of *Callisaurus draconoides* (Reptilia, Squamata, Iguanidae). Zool. J. Linn. Soc. 75, 297–316.

Packard, M. J., Hirsch, K. F. and Iverson, J. B. (1984a). Structure of shells from eggs of kinosternid turtles. J. Morphol. 181, 9–20.

Packard, M. J., Hirsch, K. F. and Meyer-Rochow, V. B. (1982b). Structure of the shell from eggs of the tuatara, *Sphenodon punctatus*. J. Morphol. 174, 197–205.

Packard, M. J., Iverson, J. B. and Packard, G. C. (1984b). Morphology of shell formation in eggs of the turtle *Kinosternon flavescens*. J. Morphol. 181, 21–28.

Packard, M. J. and Packard, G. C. (1979). Structure of the shell and tertiary membranes of eggs of softshell turtles (*Trionyx spiniferus*). J. Morphol. 159, 131–143.

Packard, M. J. and Packard, G. C. (1986). Effect of water balance on growth and calcium mobilization of embryonic painted turtles (*Chrysemys picta*). Physiol. Zool. 59, 398–405.

Packard, M. J., Packard, G. C. and Boardman, T. J. (1980). Water balance of the eggs of a desert lizard (*Callisaurus draconoides*). Can. J. Zool. 58, 2051–2058.

Packard, M. J., Packard, G. C. and Boardman, T. J. (1982c). Structure of eggshells and water relations of reptilian eggs. Herpetologica 38, 136–155.

Packard, M. J., Packard, G. C. and Gutzke, W. H. N. (1984c). Calcium metabolism in embryos of the oviparous snake *Coluber constrictor*. J. Exp. Biol. 110, 99–112.

Packard, M. J., Packard, G. C., Miller, J. D., Jones, M. E. and Gutzke, W. H. N. (1985). Calcium mobilization, water balance, and growth in embryos of the agamid lizard *Amphibolurus barbatus*. J. Exp. Zool. 235, 349–357.

Packard, M. J., Short, T. M., Packard, G. C. and Gorell, T. A. (1984d). Sources of calcium for embryonic development in eggs of the snapping turtle *Chelydra serpentina*. J. Exp. Zool. 230, 81–87.

Parker, W. S. and Brown, W. S. (1972). Telemetric study of movements and oviposition of two female *Masticophis t. taeniatus*. Copeia 1972, 892–895.

Parker, W. S. and Brown, W. S. (1980). Comparative ecology of two colubrid snakes, *Masticophis t. taeniatus* and *Pituophis melanoleucus deserticola*, in northern Utah. Publ. Biol. Geol. Milwaukee Publ. Mus. no. 7.

Parton, W. J. (1984). Predicting soil temperatures in a shortgrass steppe. Soil Sci. 138, 93–101.

Paukstis, G. L., Gutzke, W. H. N. and Packard, G. C. (1984). Effects of substrate water potential and fluctuating temperatures on sex ratios of hatchling painted turtles (*Chrysemys picta*). Can. J. Zool. 62, 1491–1494.

Philip, J. R. and de Vries, D. A. (1957). Moisture movement in porous materials under temperature gradients. Trans. Am. Geophys. Un. 38, 222–232.

Pieau, C. (1971). Sur la proportion sexuelle chez les embryons de deux Chéloniens (*Testudo graeca* L. et *Emys orbicularis* L.) issus d'oeufs incubés artificiellement. C. R. Hebd. Séanc. Acad. Sci., Paris (Ser. D) 272, 3071–3074.

Pieau, C. (1972). Effets de la température sur le développement des glandes génitales chez les embryons de deux Chéloniens, *Emys orbicularis* L. et *Testudo graeca* L. C. R. Hebd. Séanc. Acad. Sci., Paris (Ser. D) 274, 719–722.

Pieau, C. (1975). Temperature and sex differentiation in embryos of two chelonians, *Emys orbicularis* L. and *Testudo graeca* L. In *Intersexuality in the Animal Kingdom*. (R. Reinboth, ed.). Springer-Verlag, New York, pp. 332–339.

Pieau, C. (1976). Données récentes sur la différenciation sexuelle en fonction de la température chez les embryons d'*Emys orbicularis* L. (Chélonien). Bull. Soc. Zool. Fr. Suppl. 4, 46–53.

Pieau, C. (1978). Effets de températures d'incubation basses et élevées, sur la différenciation sexuelle chez des embryons d'*Emys orbicularis* L. (Chélonien). C. R. Hebd. Séanc. Acad. Sci., Paris (Ser. D) 286, 121–124.

Pieau, C. (1982). Modalities of the action of temperature on sexual differentiation in field-developing embryos of the European pond turtle *Emys orbicularis* (Emydidae). J. Exp. Zool. 220, 353–360.

Pieau, C. and Dorizzi, M. (1981). Determination of temperature sensitive stages for sexual differentiation of the gonads in embryos of the turtle, *Emys orbicularis*. J. Morphol. 170, 373–382.

Pieau, C., Mignot, T., Dorizzi, M. and Guichard, A. (1982). Gonadal steroid levels in the turtle *Emys orbicularis* L.: A preliminary study in embryos, hatchlings, and young as a function of the incubation temperature of eggs. Gen. Comp. Endocrinol. 47, 392–398.

Piiper, J., Dejours, P., Haab, P. and Rahn, H. (1971). Concepts and basic quantities in gas exchange physiology. Resp. Physiol. 13, 292–304.

Platt, D. R. (1969). Natural history of the eastern and western hognose snakes *Heterodon platyrhinos* and *Heterodon nasicus*. Univ. Kans. Publ. Mus. Nat. Hist. 18, 253–420.

Plummer, M. V. (1976). Some aspects of nesting success in the turtle, *Trionyx muticus*. Herpetologica 32, 353–359.

Pooley, A. C. (1962). The Nile crocodile *Crocodilus niloticus*. Notes on the incubation period and growth rate of juveniles. Lammergeyer 2, 1–55.

Pooley, A. C. (1969). Preliminary studies on the breeding of the Nile crocodile *Crocodylus niloticus*, in Zululand. Lammergeyer 10, 22–44.

Pope, C. H. (1961). *The Giant Snakes*. Routledge & Kegan Paul, London.

Prange, H. D. and Ackerman, R. A. (1974). Oxygen consumption and mechanisms of gas exchange of green turtle (*Chelonia mydas*) eggs and hatchlings. Copeia 1974, 758–763.

Ragotzkie, R. A. (1959). Mortality of loggerhead turtle eggs from excessive rainfall. Ecology 40, 303–305.

Raj, U. (1976). Incubation and hatching success in artificially incubated eggs of the hawksbill turtle, *Eretmochelys imbricata* (L.). J. Exp. Mar. Biol. Ecol. 22, 91–99.

Rand, A. S. (1967). Communal egg laying in anoline lizards. Herpetologica 23, 227–230.

Rand, A. S. (1972). The temperatures of iguana nests and their relation to incubation optima and to nesting sites and season. Herpetologica 28, 252–253.

Rand, A. S. and Dugan, B. (1983). Structure of complex iguana nests. Copeia 1983, 705–711.

Raynaud, A. and Pieau, C. (1972). Effets de diverses températures d'incubation sur le développement somatique et sexuel des embryons de lézard vert (*Lacerta viridis* Laur.). C. R. Hebd. Séanc. Acad. Sci., Paris (Ser. D) 275, 2259–2262.

Raynaud, A. and Pieau, C. (1985). Embryonic development of the genital system. In *Biology of the Reptilia*. Vol. 15. (C. Gans and F. Billett, eds.). Wiley, New York, pp. 149–300.

Reese, A. M. (1915). *The Alligator and Its Allies*. G. P. Putnam's Sons, New York.

Reeves, R. B. (1977). The interaction of body temperature and acid-base balance in ectothermic vertebrates. Ann. Rev. Physiol. 39, 559–586.

Reeves, R. B. and Rahn, H. (1979). Patterns in vertebrate acid-base regulation. In *Evolution* of *Respiratory Processes. A Comparative Approach.* (S. C. Wood and C. Lenfant, eds.). Marcel Dekker, New York, pp. 225–252.

Reible, D. D. and Shair, F. H. (1982). A technique for the measurement of gaseous diffusion in porous media. J. Soil Sci. 33, 165–174.

Richmond, N. D. (1945). Nesting habits of the mud turtle. Copeia 1945, 217–219.

Ricklefs, R. E. and Burger, J. (1977). Composition of eggs of the diamondback terrapin. Am. Midl. Nat. 97, 232–235.

Riley, J., Stimson, A. F. and Winch, J. M. (1985). A review of Squamata ovipositing in ant and termite nests. Herpetol. Rev. 16, 38–43.

Rimblot, F., Fretey, J., Mrosovsky, N., Lescure, J. and Pieau, C. (1985). Sexual differentiation as a function of the incubation temperature of eggs in the sea-turtle *Dermochelys coriacea* (Vandelli, 1761). Amphibia-Reptilia 6, 83–92.

Risley, P. L. (1933). Observations on the natural history of the common musk turtle, *Sternotherus odoratus* (Latreille). Pap. Mich. Acad. Sci. 17, 685–711.

Risley, P. L. (1944). Arrested development of turtle embryos. Anat. Rec. 88, 454–455.

Rose, C. W. (1968a). Water transport in soil with a daily temperature wave. I. Theory and experiment. Aust. J. Soil Res. 6, 31–44.

Rose, C. W. (1968b). Water transport in soil with a daily temperature wave. II. Analysis. Aust. J. Soil Res. 6, 45–57.

Saint Girons, H. (1985). Comparative data on lepidosaurian reproduction and some time tables. In *Biology of the Reptilia.* Vol. 15. (C. Gans and F. Billett, eds.) Wiley, New York, pp. 35–58.

Savage, M. J., Cass, A. and de Jager, J. M. (1981). Calibration of thermocouple hygrometers. Irrig. Sci. 2, 113–125.

Savage, M. J., Cass, A. and de Jager, J. M. (1983). Statistical assessment of some errors in thermocouple hygrometric water potential measurement. Agric. Meteorol. 30, 83–97.

Schmidt, W. J. (1943). Ueber den Bau der kalkigen Eischale von *Lepidodactylus lugubris* D. & B. (Geckonidae). Zool. Anz. 142, 58–61.

Schmidt, W. J. and Schönwetter, M. (1943). Beiträge zur Kenntnis der Krokodileier, insbesondere ihrer Kalkschale. Z. Morphol. Ökol. Tiere 40, 17–36.

Schwarzkopf, L. and Brooks, R. J. (1985). Sex determination in northern painted turtles: Effect of incubation at constant and fluctuating temperatures. Can. J. Zool. 63, 2543–2547.

Sexton, O. J. (1957). Notes concerning turtle hatchlings. Copeia 1957, 229–230.

Sexton, O. J. and Claypool, L. (1978). Nest sites of a northern population of an oviparous snake, *Opheodrys vernalis* (Serpentes, Colubridae). J. Nat. Hist. 12, 365–370.

Sexton, O. J., Heatwole, H. and Knight, D. (1964). Correlation of microdistribution of some Panamanian reptiles and amphibians with structural organization of the habitat. Carib. J. Sci. 4, 261–295.

Sexton, O. J. and Marion, K. R. (1974). Duration of incubation of *Sceloporus undulatus* eggs at constant temperature. Physiol. Zool. 47, 91–98.

Sexton, O. J. and Turner, O. (1971). The reproductive cycle of a neotropical lizard. Ecology 52, 159–164.

Sexton, O. J., Veith, G. M. and Phillips, D. M. (1979). Ultrastructure of the eggshell of two species of anoline lizards. J. Exp. Zool. 207, 227–236.

Shaw, C. E. (1960). Notes on the eggs, incubation and young of *Chamaeleo basiliscus*. Br. J. Herpetol. 2, 182–185.

Shine, R. (1983a). Reptilian reproductive modes: The oviparity-viviparity continuum. Herpetologica 39, 1–8.

Shine, R. (1983b). Reptilian viviparity in cold climates: Testing the assumptions of an evolutionary hypothesis. Oecologia 57, 397–405.

Shine, R. (1985). The evolution of viviparity in reptiles: An ecological analysis. In *Biology of the Reptilia.* Vol. 15. (C. Gans and F. Billet, eds.). Wiley, New York, pp. 605–694.

Silyn-Roberts, H. and Sharp, R. M. (1985). Preferred orientation of calcite and aragonite in the reptilian eggshells. Proc. R. Soc. (Ser. B) 225, 445–455.

Simkiss, K. (1962). The sources of calcium for the ossification of the embryos of the giant leathery turtle. Comp. Biochem. Physiol. 7, 71–79.

Simkiss, K. (1967). *Calcium in Reproductive Physiology. A Comparative Study of Vertebrates.* Reinhold Publ. Corp., New York.

Simon, M. H. (1975). The green sea turtle (*Chelonia mydas*); collection, incubation and hatching of eggs from natural rookeries. J. Zool. 176, 39–48.

Sites, J. W., Jr., Bickham, J. W. and Haiduk, M. W. (1979). Derived X chromosome in the turtle genus *Staurotypus*. Science 206, 1410–1412.

Snell, H. L. (1984). Evolutionary Ecology of Galapagos Land Iguanas (Iguanidae: *Conolophus*). Ph.D. Dissertation, Colorado State University, Fort Collins.

Snell, H. L. and Tracy, C. R. (1985). Behavioral and morphological adaptations by Galapagos land iguanas (*Conolophus subcristatus*) to water and energy requirements of eggs and neonates. Am. Zool. 25, 1009–1018.

Snow, J. E. (1982). Predation on painted turtle nests: Nest survival as a function of nest age. Can. J. Zool. 60, 3290–3292.

Solomon, S. E. and Baird, T. (1976). Studies on the egg shell (oviducal and oviposited) of *Chelonia mydas* L. J. Exp. Mar. Biol. Ecol. 22, 145–160.

Solomon, S. E. and Baird, T. (1977). Studies on the soft shell membranes of the egg shell of *Chelonia mydas* L. J. Exp. Mar. Biol. Ecol. 27, 83–92.

Solomon, S. E. and Reid, J. (1983). The effect of the mammillary layer on eggshell formation in reptiles. Anim. Technol. 34, 1–10.

Stancyk, S. E. and Ross, J. P. (1978). An analysis of sand from green turtle nesting beaches on Ascension Island. Copeia 1978, 93–99.

Standora, E. A. and Spotila, J. R. (1985). Temperature dependent sex determination in sea turtles. Copeia 1985, 711–722.

Staton, M. A. and Dixon, J. R. (1977). Breeding biology of the spectacled caiman, *Caiman crocodilus crocodilus*, in the Venezuelan Llanos. U.S. Dept. Int. Fish Wildl. Serv. Wildl. Res. Rep. no. 5.

Stewart, J. R. and Castillo, R. E. (1984). Nutritional provision of the yolk of two species of viviparous reptiles. Physiol. Zool. 57, 377–383.

Stewart, P. A. (1981). *How to Understand Acid-Base. A Quantitative Acid-Base Primer for Biology and Medicine.* Elsevier, New York.

Subba Rao, M. V. and Bustard, H. R. (1979). Eggs and hatchlings of the gharial, *Gavialis gangeticus* Gmelin (Gavialidae, Crocodilia, Reptilia). Comp. Physiol. Ecol. 4, 114–115.

Subba Rao, M. V. and Rajabi, B. S. (1972). Reproduction in the ground lizard, *Sitana ponticeriana* and the garden lizard, *Calotes nemoricola*. Br. J. Herpetol. 4, 245–251.

Swingland, I. R. and Coe, M. J. (1979). The natural regulation of giant tortoise populations on Aldabra Atoll: Recruitment. Phil. Trans. R. Soc. (Ser. B) 286, 177–188.

Taylor, S. A. (1958). The activity of water in soils. Soil Sci. 86, 83–90.

Taylor, S. A. (1965). The influence of steady temperature gradients upon water transport in soil materials. In *Humidity and Moisture/Measurement and Control in Science and Industry.* Vol. 3. *Fundamentals and Standards.* (A. Wexler and W. A. Wildhack, eds.). Reinhold Publ. Corp., New York, pp. 343–349.

REFERENCES

Taylor, S. A. and Ashcroft, G. L. (1972). *Physical Edaphology. The Physics of Irrigated and Nonirrigated Soils.* W. H. Freeman and Co., San Francisco.

Taylor, S. A. and Box, J. E. (1961). Influence of confining pressure and bulk density on soil matric potential. Soil Sci. 91, 6–10.

Taylor, S. A. and Stewart, G. L. (1960). Some thermodynamic properties of soil water. Proc. Soil Sci. Soc. Am. 24, 243–247.

Thompson, J. (1981). A study of the sources of nutrients for embryonic development in a viviparous lizard, *Sphenomorphus quoyii*. Comp. Biochem. Physiol. 70A, 509–518.

Thompson, M. B. (1981). Gas tensions in natural nests and eggs of the tortoise *Emydura macquarii*. In *Proceedings of the Melbourne Herpetological Symposium*. (C. B. Banks and A. A. Martin, eds.). Zoological Board of Victoria, Parkville, Victoria, pp. 74–77.

Thompson, M. B. (1983). The Physiology and Ecology of the Eggs of the Pleurodiran Tortoise *Emydura macquarii* (Gray), 1831. Ph.D. Thesis, Univ. Adelaide, South Australia.

Thompson, M. B. (1985). Functional significance of the opaque white patch in eggs of *Emydura macquarii*. In *Biology of Australasian Frogs and Reptiles*. (G. Grigg, R. Shine and H. Ehmann, eds.). Royal Zoological Society of New South Wales, Sydney, pp. 387–395.

Thompson, M. B. (1987). Water exchange in reptilian eggs. Physiol. Zool., 60, 1–8.

Tinkle, D. W., Congdon, J. D. and Rosen, P. C. (1981). Nesting frequency and success: Implications for the demography of painted turtles. Ecology 62, 1426–1432.

Tokunaga, S. 1985. Temperature-dependent sex determination in *Gekko japonicus* (Gekkonidae, Reptilia). Devel. Growth Differ. 27, 117–120.

Toner, G. C. (1940). Delayed hatching in the snapping turtle. Copeia 1940, 265.

Tracy, C. R. (1980). Water relations of parchment-shelled lizard (*Sceloporus undulatus*) eggs. Copeia 1980, 478–482.

Tracy, C. R. (1982). Biophysical modeling in reptilian physiology and ecology. In *Biology of the Reptilia*. Vol. 12. (C. Gans and F. H. Pough, eds.). Academic Press, London, pp. 275–321.

Tracy, C. R., Packard, G. C. and Packard, M. J. (1978). Water relations of chelonian eggs. Physiol. Zool. 51, 378–387.

Tracy, C. R. and Snell, H. L. (1985). Interrelations among water and energy relations of reptilian eggs, embryos, and hatchlings. Am. Zool. 25, 999–1008.

Trauth, S. E. (1977). Winter collection of *Cnemidophorus sexlineatus* eggs from Arkansas. Herpetol. Rev. 8, 33.

Trauth, S. E. and Fagerberg, W. R. (1984). Ultrastructure and stereology of the eggshell in *Cnemidophorus sexlineatus* (Lacertilia: Teiidae). Copeia 1984, 826–832.

Troyer, K. (1983). Posthatching yolk energy in a lizard: Utilization pattern and interclutch variation. Oecologia 58, 340–344.

van Bavel, C. H. M. (1952). Gaseous diffusion and porosity in porous media. Soil Sci. 73, 91–104.

Van Devender, R. W. (1982). Comparative demography of the lizard *Basiliscus basiliscus*. Herpetologica 38, 189–208.

Van Devender, T. R. and Howard, C. W. (1973). Notes on natural nests and hatching success in the regal horned lizard (*Phrynosoma solare*) in southern Arizona. Herpetologica 29, 238–239.

Vaz-Ferreira, R., Covelo de Zolessi, L. and Achával, F. (1970). Oviposicion y desarrollo de ofidios y lacertilios en hormigueros de *Acromyrmex*. Physis, B. Aires 29, 431–459.

Vinegar, A. (1968). Brooding of the eastern glass lizard, *Ophisaurus ventralis*. Bull. S. Calif. Acad. Sci. 67, 65–68.

Vinegar, A. (1973). The effects of temperature on the growth and development of embryos of the Indian python, *Python molurus* (Reptilia: Serpentes: Boidae). Copeia 1973, 171–173.

Vinegar, A. (1974). Evolutionary implications of temperature induced anomalies of development in snake embryos. Herpetologica 30, 72–74.

Voeltzkow, A. (1892). On the oviposition and embryonic development of the crocodile. Ann. Mag. Nat. Hist. 9, 66–72.

Vogt, R. C. (1980). Natural history of the map turtles *Graptemys pseudogeographica* and *G. ouachitensis* in Wisconsin. Tulane Stud. Zool. Bot. 22, 17–48.

Vogt, R. C. and Bull, J. J. (1982a). Temperature controlled sex-determination in turtles: Ecological and behavioral aspects. Herpetologica 38, 156–164.

Vogt, R. C. and Bull, J. J. (1982b). Genetic sex determination in the spiny softshell *Trionyx spiniferus* (Testudines: Trionychidae)(?). Copeia 1982, 699–700.

Vogt, R. C. and Bull, J. J. (1984). Ecology of hatchling sex ratio in map turtles. Ecology 65, 582–587.

Vogt, R. C., Bull, J. J., McCoy, C. J. and Houseal, T. W. (1982). Incubation temperature influences sex determination in kinosternid turtles. Copeia 1982, 480–482.

von Brand, T. and Lynn, W. G. (1947). Chemical changes in the developing turtle embryo. Proc. Soc. Exp. Biol. Med. 64, 61–62.

Wagner, E. (1980). Gecko husbandry and reproduction. In *Reproductive Biology and Diseases of Captive Reptiles*. (J. B. Murphy and J. T. Collins, eds.). SSAR Contributions to Herpetology no. 1, pp. 115–117.

Walsh, P. J. and Moon, T. W. (1982). The influence of temperature on extracellular and intracellular pH in the American eel, *Anguilla rostrata* (le Sueur). Resp. Physiol. 50, 129–140.

Webb, D. R. and King, J. R. (1983). An analysis of the heat budgets of the eggs and nest of the white-crowned sparrow, *Zonotrichia leucophrys*, in relation to parental attentiveness. Physiol. Zool. 56, 493–505.

Webb, G. J. W., Buckworth, R. and Manolis, S. C. (1983a). *Crocodylus johnstoni* in the McKinlay River, N.T. VI. Nesting biology. Aust. Wildl. Res. 10, 607–637.

Webb, G. J. W., Buckworth, R., Sack, G. C. and Manolis, S. C. (1983b). An interim method for estimating the age of *Crocodylus porosus* embryos. Aust. Wildl. Res. 10, 563–570.

Webb, G. J. W., Messel, H. and Magnusson, W. (1977). The nesting of *Crocodylus porosus* in Arnhem Land, northern Australia. Copeia 1977, 238–249.

Webb, G. J. W., Sack, G. C., Buckworth, R. and Manolis, S. C. (1983c). An examination of *Crocodylus porosus* nests in two northern Australian freshwater swamps, with an analysis of embryo mortality. Aust. Wildl. Res. 10, 571–605.

Webb, G. J. W. and Smith, A. M. A. (1984). Sex ratio and survivorship in the Australian freshwater crocodile *Crocodylus johnstoni*. Symp. Zool. Soc. Lond. 52, 319–355.

Wells, R. and Husband, G. (1979). Comments on the reproduction of *Pygopus lepidopodus* (Lacépède). Herpetofauna 11, 22–25.

Werner, Y. L. (1972). Observations on eggs of eublepharid lizards, with comments on the evolution of the Gekkonoidea. Zool. Meded., Leiden 47, 211–224.

West, E. S. (1952). A study of the annual soil temperature wave. Aust. J. Scient. Res. (Ser. A) 5, 303–314.

Whitaker, A. H. (1968). *Leiolopisma suteri* (Boulenger), an oviparous skink in New Zealand. N.Z. J. Sci. 11, 425–432.

REFERENCES

Whitaker, R. and Whitaker, Z. (1984). Reproductive biology of the mugger (*Crocodylus palustris*). J. Bombay Nat. Hist. Soc. 81, 297–317.

Wiebe, H. H. and Brown, R. W. (1979). Temperature gradient effects on in situ hygrometer measurements of soil water potential. II. Water movement. Agron. J. 71, 397–401.

Wiebe, H. H., Brown, R. W. and Barker, J. (1977). Temperature gradient effects on in situ hygrometer measurements of water potential. Agron. J. 69, 933–939.

Wierenga, P. J., Nielsen, D. R. and Hagan, R. M. (1969). Thermal properties of a soil based upon field and laboratory measurements. Proc. Soil Sci. Soc. Am. 33, 354–360.

Wilhoft, D. C., Hotaling, E. and Franks, P. (1983). Effects of temperature on sex determination in embryos of the snapping turtle, *Chelydra serpentina*. J. Herpetol. 17, 38–42.

Woodall, P. F. (1984). The structure and some functional aspects of the eggshell of the broad-shelled river tortoise *Chelodina expansa* (Testudinata: Chelidae). Aust. J. Zool. 32, 7–14.

Yancey, P. H. and Somero, G. N. (1978). Temperature dependence of intracellular pH: Its role in the conservation of pyruvate apparent K_m values of vertebrate lactate dehydrogenases. J. Comp. Physiol. 125, 129–134.

Yntema, C. L. (1968). A series of stages in the embryonic development of *Chelydra serpentina*. J. Morphol. 125, 219–251.

Yntema, C. L. (1976). Effects of incubation temperatures on sexual differentiation in the turtle, *Chelydra serpentina*. J. Morphol. 150, 453–461.

Yntema, C. L. (1978). Incubation times for eggs of the turtle *Chelydra serpentina* (Testudines: Chelydridae) at various temperatures. Herpetologica 34, 274–277.

Yntema, C. L. (1979). Temperature levels and periods of sex determination during incubation of eggs of *Chelydra serpentina*. J. Morphol. 159, 17–27.

Yntema, C. L. (1981). Characteristics of gonads and oviducts in hatchlings and young of *Chelydra serpentina* resulting from three incubation temperatures. J. Morphol. 167, 297–304.

Yntema, C. L. and Mrosovsky, N. (1980). Sexual differentiation in hatchling loggerheads (*Caretta caretta*) incubated at different controlled temperatures. Herpetologica 36, 33–36.

Yntema, C. L. and Mrosovsky, N. (1982). Critical periods and pivotal temperatures for sexual differentiation in loggerhead sea turtles. Can. J. Zool. 60, 1012–1016.

Young, J. D. (1950). The structure and some physical properties of the testudinian eggshell. Proc. Zool. Soc. Lond. 120, 455–469.

Zaborski, P., Dorizzi, M. and Pieau, C. (1982). H-Y antigen expression in temperature sex-reversed turtles (*Emys orbicularis*). Differentiation 22, 73–78.

Zarrow, M. X. and Pomerat, C. M. (1937). Respiration of the egg and young of the smooth green snake, *Liopeltis vernalis* (Harlan). Growth 1, 103–110.

Zweifel, R. G. (1980). Aspects of the biology of a laboratory population of kingsnakes. In *Reproductive Biology and Diseases of Captive Reptiles*. (J. B. Murphy and J. T. Collins, eds.). SSAR Contributions to Herpetology no. 1, pp. 141–152.

Author Index

Abalos, J. W., 182, 217, 231
Abercromby, A. F., 285, 287, 316
Abrams, F., 425, 438
Acharjyo, L. N., 72, 137, 142, 145, 281, 285, 300, 316
Achával, F., 543, 603
Ackerman, R. A., 529, 532, 537–538, 554–556, 564, 572–577, 587, 595, 600
Adams, B. A., 7, 35, 106
Adar, O., 33, 109
Adkins, J. L., 508, 513, 522
Adolph, S. C., 70, 116
Advani, R., 11, 70, 115
Agassiz, L., 354, 369, 527, 587
Aiello, A. B., 172, 173, 217
Alberch, P., 16, 70
Albers, C., 549, 587
Alcala, A. C., 500, 516, 521
Alcock, J., 44, 54, 64–65, 70, 156–157, 160, 163, 168, 218–220
Aldridge, R. D., 357–358, 369, 378, 500, 506, 519, 522
Alho, C. J. R., 401–402, 421, 439, 532, 540, 543–544, 552–553, 587
Allard, H. A., 284, 316, 532, 583, 585, 587
Allen, E. R., 9–10, 44, 70, 113, 122, 212, 218, 292, 324, 369, 404, 421
Altland, P. D., 357–359, 369
Alvarez del Toro, M., 9–11, 13, 36, 50, 70, 113, 139, 142, 280, 283, 301, 316
Amaral, A. do A., 70, 145, 148, 175, 182, 218, 231
Amores, F., 70, 111, 113, 116, 120

Anders, G. J. R., 362, 369
Anderson, D., 364, 370
Anderson, J., 70, 146, 150–152
Anderson, J. D., 70, 121, 201, 218
Anderson, R. A., 445, 470, 500
Anderson, S. C., 21, 54, 70, 77, 91, 125, 136–138, 140–142, 152
Andren, C., 21, 49, 70, 449, 500, 521
Andrews, R. M., 55, 67, 99, 346, 349, 369, 400, 421, 445–446, 500–501, 513, 521, 529, 564–565, 585, 587
Angel, F., 70, 143, 292, 316
Anon., 300, 316
Ar, A., 537–538, 554–556, 564, 572, 587–588
Arata, A. A., 20, 96, 146, 421, 438
Arbel, A., 197, 218
Archer, W. H., 421, 439
Armitage, W. W., 41, 71, 149
Armstrong, B. L., 69, 71, 76, 152
Arndt, R. G., 338, 361, 369, 421, 437
Arnold, E. N., 23, 49, 53, 64, 66, 71, 80, 114–118, 136–141, 146, 237–238, 243, 245, 248, 250–254, 258–260, 263, 267–268, 399, 422
Arnold, S. J., 13, 15, 19, 21, 24, 55, 64–65, 67–68, 71, 123, 156, 194, 218, 224
Asana, J. J., 282, 316, 501, 512, 521
Ash, R. P., , 422, 436
Ashcroft, G. L., 539–540, 554, 558, 575, 577–578, 603
Ashen, M. D., 563–564, 568, 598
Ashton, P. S., 286, 316
Ashton, R. E., Jr., 286, 316

Asplund, K. K., 22, 71, 139, 357–358, 369
Astort, E., 199, 218
Atchley, W. R., 364, 370
Auffenberg, W., 11, 25, 71, 112, 115, 118–119, 121–122, 129, 142, 251, 268, 339–340, 342, 346, 370, 390, 396, 400–401, 403, 410, 422, 438
Austad, S. N., 209, 218
Avery, R. A., 250, 268, 501, 516, 521
Avissar, R., 540, 596

Babcock, H. L., 286, 316
Bacon, P. R., 422, 436
Badham, J. A., 531, 588
Baez, E. C., 182, 217, 231
Bagby, R. M., 45, 93, 130
Baic, D., 40, 44, 65, 67, 82, 193, 221
Bailey, N. J. T., 343, 370
Baird, T., 525–526, 588, 602
Baker, E. C., 502, 519, 521
Baker, J. K., 501, 517, 521
Baker, R. R., 211, 218
Baker, V., 543, 595
Baker, W. S., 86, 148
Bakker, R. T., 60, 71
Balasingam, E., 422, 436
Baldauf, R. J., 50, 78, 142
Baldwin, W. P., Jr., 361, 370, 403–404, 422
Balgooyen, T. G., 71, 116, 121
Ballinger, R. E., 10, 93, 116, 118, 239, 242, 248–250, 265, 268, 272, 336, 339, 341–342, 345–347, 349, 351, 354–356, 361–364, 370, 445–446, 449, 475, 477, 499–501, 503, 508–509, 513–515, 521–522
Bannikov, A. G., 182, 218, 231
Banta, B. H., 71, 340, 370
Barbault, R., 341, 345–346, 349–351, 355, 361, 370, 380, 501, 517, 521
Barber, H. S., 71, 119
Barbour, R. W., 26–27, 71, 80, 112, 134, 348, 375, 396, 426, 437, 438, 532, 592
Barbour, T., 71, 141, 144, 146–148, 151, 283, 297, 316, 422, 437
Barker, D. G., 285–286, 289, 299, 316, 324
Barker, J., 562, 605
Barnard, S. M., 285, 290, 303, 328
Barrows, W. B., 581, 584, 588
Bartholomew, G. A., 249, 268, 535, 543, 588

Barton, A. J., 360–361, 370, 422, 437
Bartos, D. L., 562, 588
Barwick, R. E., 501, 517, 521
Basu, D., 281, 317
Bates, H. W., 155, 170, 174, 180, 218
Bauer, A. M., 33, 72
Bauwens, D., 21, 72, 117, 250, 268, 445, 501
Bavay, J. E., 29, 67, 105, 137
Bayless, L. E., 337, 370
Beasom, S. L., 72, 120
Beatson, R. R., 49, 72
Beatty, R. W., 362, 365–366, 378, 430, 436
Beavers, R. A., 72, 116–117
Bechtel, H. B., 50, 72
Beebe, W., 16–18, 37, 50, 66, 72, 116, 118–123, 134, 136, 138–142, 204, 215, 218
Beer, J. R., 89, 121
Behler, J. L., 284, 292, 317, 322
Bell, B. D., 28, 101, 114
Bell, G., 406, 422
Bell, R., 341, 370
Bellairs, A. d'A., 72, 127, 237–238, 244, 265–266, 268, 448, 501, 545, 596
Bellairs, R., 532, 588, 594
Bellemin, J. M., 72
Belt, T., 72, 139
Beltz, R. E., 422, 438
Bemis, W. E., 8, 48, 72, 99, 172, 226
Benedict, F. G., 286, 317
Bennett, A. F., 5, 15, 19, 21, 24, 50, 62, 64–68, 71–72, 87, 123, 249, 268, 445–446, 470, 487, 499, 501, 505, 507
Bennett, D. H., 341, 370, 398, 428
Bennett, S. H., 401, 430
Benson, W. W., 159, 161, 218
Bentley, T. B., 559, 566, 573, 596
Berney, F. L., 288, 317
Berry, F. H., 361, 363, 372
Berry, J. F., 399, 422
Berry, K. H., 11, 72, 116, 140, 404, 434, 438, 501, 514, 521
Berry, P. Y., 502, 519, 521
Bessette, E. L., 289, 300–301, 303, 328
Beuchat, C. A., 448, 502
Bezy, R. L., 98, 121, 358, 377, 505, 518, 522
Bickham, J. W., 27, 72, 402, 422, 425, 551, 590, 596, 602
Bider, J. R., 337, 344, 354–356, 370, 380, 431, 436

Bigalke, R., 528, 588
Binder, M. H., 72, 86, 139, 144, 147, 198
Birchard, G. F., 531, 538, 563, 567–568, 574, 588
Bishop, C., 284, 317
Bissinger, B. E., 15, 49, 103, 116, 342, 383
Biswas, S., 72, 120–121, 137, 142, 145, 281, 284, 288, 300, 317
Bjorndal, K. A., 348, 370, 398, 406, 422
Black, C. P., 531, 538, 563, 567–568, 574, 588
Black, J. H., 51, 72, 141
Black, V. D., 531, 538, 563, 567–568, 574, 588
Blackburn, D. G., 448, 502, 510, 517, 522
Blackwell, K., 422, 439
Blair, W. F., 241, 268, 339, 341–342, 345–346, 349, 352, 355, 361, 363, 370–371, 405, 422, 437, 535, 588
Blanc, F., 531, 588
Blanchard, F. N., 284, 286, 317, 343, 371, 417, 422, 531, 534, 588
Bleakney, J. S., 583, 588
Blest, A. D., 173, 218
Blumer, L. S., 312, 317
Boake, B., 281, 317
Boardman, T. J., 527, 531, 556, 563, 566–569, 582, 584, 597–599
Bobisud, L. E., 156, 218
Bock, B. C., 280, 300, 319
Body, D. R., 532, 588
Bogert, C. M., 18, 24, 36, 39, 41, 43, 45, 72–73, 125, 132, 139, 150, 152, 288, 317
Bohlen, C. H., 345, 349, 375, 475, 503, 515, 521, 581, 592
Böhme, W., 29, 73, 137, 281, 317, 529, 595
Böker, H., 26, 73, 257, 268
Bokermann, W. C. A., 13, 73
Bolaños, R., 23, 73
Bookstein, F. L., 451, 502
Boos, H. E. A., 285, 289, 303–304, 306, 317
Boring, A. M., 246, 268
Bossert, W., 444, 504
Bostic, D. L., 502, 518, 521
Boswell C., 357–358, 379, 430, 437
Boulenger, G. A., 73, 115, 142, 144–150, 529, 588
Bourn, D., 340, 348, 358–361, 367, 371, 374, 398, 420, 422, 425, 438

Bourquin, O., 73, 114–115, 117–118, 287, 317
Bouskila, A., 73
Box, J. E., 559, 588, 603
Boyce, M. S., 444, 502
Boyden, T. C., 156, 157, 218
Bradshaw, S. D., 502, 512, 521
Brady, J. R., 92, 122
Brady, M., 284, 317
Brain, C. K., 73, 137, 206, 221, 252, 270
Bramble, D. M., 27, 57, 67, 73, 390, 422
Bramham, C. R., 559, 591
Branch, W. R., 8–9, 17, 73, 75, 112, 142, 148, 288, 320
Brandon, R. A., 305, 322
Branson, B. A., 502, 519, 521
Brattstrom, B. H., 50, 73, 112, 165, 176, 184, 194, 218, 261–263, 268
Breckenridge, W. J., 284, 303, 317, 340, 348, 354, 371, 422, 439, 502, 517, 521, 583, 588
Breder, R. B., 341, 371
Brehm, A. E., 280, 317
Breitenbach, G. L., 356, 365, 367, 374, 379, 395–397, 400, 404, 423, 425, 532, 585, 588, 590
Brimley, C. S., 284, 317, 556, 588
Brisban, I. L., 335, 371
Broadley, D. G., 6, 8 10, 13, 23, 55–56, 73–74, 113–115, 117–122, 143–152, 182, 218, 234, 286–288, 317
Brodie, E. D., Jr., 26, 32, 38, 78, 89, 98, 106, 131–132, 134, 138, 143 , 252, 271
Bröer, W., 74, 145
Brongersma, L. D., 39, 74
Brooks, G. R., Jr., 239, 268, 342, 345 346, 349, 371, 502, 509, 514, 517, 521–522
Brooks, R. J., 341, 380, 402, 403, 544, 551–553, 601
Brower, J. V. Z., 156, 157, 158, 164, 167, 168, 170, 180, 218, 219
Brower, L. P., 156, 157, 158, 160, 164, 167, 168, 170, 172, 180, 184, 219–221, 226
Brown, C. K., 241, 268
Brown, D. E., 60, 74
Brown, E. E., 9, 74, 112–113, 115–117, 119–120, 535, 543, 588
Brown, K. L., 362, 383, 581, 592
Brown, K. S., Jr., 184, 219

Brown, L., 6, 10, 74
Brown, R. W., 558, 562, 588, 605
Brown, W. C., 500, 516, 521
Brown, W. S., 11, 21, 74, 336, 339-340, 342-346, 348-349, 355-356, 359-360, 362-364, 366-367, 371, 380, 423, 437, 502, 507, 519, 521-522, 534, 599
Brunner, A., 74, 150
Brunson, K., 11, 73
Brunton, D. H., 57, 111
Bruton, M. N., 85, 147
Bryant, H. C., 10, 74, 116-118, 120
Bryant, S. V., 72, 127, 237-238, 244, 265-266, 268
Buchan, G. D., 539, 588
Buckworth, R., 109, 118, 119, 528, 533, 540-541, 543-545, 551, 556-557, 562-563, 585, 604
Buden, D. W., 74, 116
Buffrenil, V. de, 349, 371
Bull, J. J., 157, 222, 304, 309-311, 313, 317, 353, 371, 395, 400, 402, 423, 435, 540, 551-553, 572, 584, 588-589, 597, 604
Bulmer, M. C., 353, 371, 402, 423
Burge, B. L., 434, 438
Burger, J., 433, 43, 531-532, 534, 540-541, 543-544, 584-585, 589, 601
Burghardt, G. M., 10, 13, 15-16, 18, 20-21, 29, 31, 46, 50, 60, 65-68, 74, 84, 86, 100, 103, 109, 116, 123, 135, 129-131, 133-134, 139-140, 148, 280, 300, 319, 337, 344, 376, 581, 593
Burkett, R. D., 10, 74, 116-118, 120, 122, 502, 521
Burkholder, G. L., 74, 116, 140, 502, 518, 521
Burleson, G. L., 30, 74
Burns, L. K., 529-530, 574, 599
Burns, T. A., 423, 437
Burrage, B. R., 74, 115, 122, 137, 342, 361, 371, 502, 512, 521
Burroughs, J., 293, 317
Burt, C. E., 74, 117, 139, 284, 317
Burtt, E. H., Jr., 48, 75, 121
Bury, R. B., 9, 27, 75, 116, 135, 340, 371, 396, 398, 423
Busa, W. B., 550, 589
Busack, S. D., 37, 75

Bustard, H. R., 15, 17-18, 20, 31-33, 38, 51, 56, 68, 75, 112, 117, 122, 138, 142-143, 150, 202, 205, 219, 238, 240, 251-252, 261-262, 268, 281, 300, 303, 317-318, 339, 342, 361-362, 365, 367, 372, 396, 397, 400-401, 403-404, 409, 418, 423, 436, 502, 512-513, 521, 527, 530, 533-534, 541, 543-545, 556, 558-559, 564, 566, 589, 602
Butler, J. R., 348, 375
Butler, W. H., 75
Buxton, C. D., 8, 75, 112
Buys, P. J. C.,75, 145, 148-150
Buys, P. J., 75, 145, 148-150
Cadle, J. E., 32, 37, 39-41, 75, 78
Cagle, F. R., 284, 318, 337-338, 340-341, 347-348, 354-356, 359-361, 363, 366, 372, 403, 416-417, 423, 436-437, 532-534, 562-563, 583, 589
Cahn, A. R., 362, 372, 403, 415, 417, 424, 436, 437, 438-439
Calbert, W. H., 160, 219
Calder, W. A., III, 62, 75, 395, 424
Caldwell, D. K., 361, 363, 365, 367, 372, 424, 436
Caldwell, G. S., 43, 53, 75, 150, 168, 204, 216, 219
Caldwell, J. P., 362, 383
Calow, P., 62, 106
Calstrom, D., 343, 372
Cambefort, J. P., 168, 196, 224
Cambell, H. W., 340, 372
Camin, J. H., 49, 75
Camp, C. C., 11, 75, 116, 135, 139-140, 144, 148
Campbell, B., 75, 149
Campbell, G. S., 559, 589
Campbell, H., 283, 318
Campbell, H. W., 25, 26, 50-51, 62, 65, 75, 76, 88, 116, 133, 135, 139, 177, 178, 194, 197, 223, 533, 590
Campbell, J. A., 47, 76, 85, 124, 152, 212-214, 222, 277, 287, 297, 300, 318
Campden-Main, S. M., 76, 144, 145, 182, 220, 233
Camper, J. D., 9, 76, 118
Cansdale, G. S., 76, 143, 281, 318
Cantor, T., 249, 268

AUTHOR INDEX

Carey, H. V., 59, 111
Carey, W. M., 76, 139, 283, 318
Carl, C., 417, 424
Carl, G. C., 286, 318
Carothers, J. H., 29, 51, 57, 76, 134, 140
Carpenter, C. C., 8, 28, 33, 35, 46–47, 49, 76, 96, 110, 116, 129, 131–132, 136–137, 139–141, 151–152, 212, 213, 220, 225, 239, 249, 269, 283, 318, 338, 346, 372, 535, 590
Carpenter, G. C., 212, 213, 220
Carpenter, G. D. H., 156, 220
Carr, A. F., 12, 22–23, 26, 52, 76, 114, 120–122, 137, 140–141, 144, 146–148, 150, 152, 212, 220, 299, 308, 318, 337–339, 341, 361–363, 365–367, 372–373, 397, 401–405, 408, 412, 416, 418, 422, 424, 436–438, 532–533, 541, 543, 590
Carr, J. L., 27, 72, 422, 425, 551, 590
Carr, M. H., 365, 367, 373, 405, 408, 424, 436
Carrillo de Espinosa, N., 533, 597
Carson, J. E., 539, 590
Cary, J. W., 561, 578, 590
Casas-Andreu, G., 505, 514, 522
Case, T. J., 68, 76, 313, 318
Cass, A., 559, 562, 601
Castanet, J., 347, 349–350, 373, 380–381, 398, 425, 439
Castillo, R. E., 532, 602
Caughley, G., 334, 343–344, 373
Censky, E. J., 402, 431, 552, 596
Cerdas, L., 23, 73
Chabreck, R. H., 543, 556, 559, 590
Chadwick, W. S., 280, 318
Chaffey, W., 29, 67, 105, 137
Chaney, A. H., 337–338, 372–373
Chang, L.-F., 246, 268
Chang, W.-H., 246, 268
Channing, A., 73, 114–115, 117–118
Chapman, B. M., 508, 517, 522
Chapman, D. G., 343, 373
Chapman, F., 52, 76
Chapman, R. F., 508, 517, 522
Charles, N., 285, 289, 300–301, 303, 318
Charlesworth, B., 444, 498, 502
Charnier, M., 551, 590
Charnov, E. L., 211, 220, 402, 425

Cheke, A. S., 76, 115, 118
Chen, B-Y., 296, 323
Chenowith, W. L., 76, 124, 151
Chernoff, B., 451, 502
Cheverud, J. M., 446, 485–487, 499, 502
Cheylan, M., 347, 349, 373, 398, 425, 439
Chiszar, D., 16, 47, 64, 66, 76, 88, 99, 101, 103, 146, 152
Chondropoulos, B. P., 502, 516, 521
Choudhury, B. C., 281, 300, 303, 317–318
Christian, K. A., 50, 77, 139, 283, 318
Christiansen, J. L., 348, 355, 357–361, 365, 373, 416–417, 425, 436, 438
Church, G., 503, 513, 521
Cissé, M., 77, 114, 118
Clark, D. B., 398, 411, 425
Clark, D. L., Jr., 28, 46–47, 82, 102, 212, 214, 227
Clark, D. R., 250, 252, 255, 269, 340–342, 362, 373, 503, 519–521, 531, 546, 590
Clark, E. D., 77, 136–138, 140–142, 144–146, 151–152
Clark, H., 531, 533, 538, 570, 575, 590
Clark, R. F., 77, 120, 122, 355, 374
Clark, R. J., 77, 136–138, 140–142, 144–146, 151–152
Clarke, S. F., 280, 318, 528, 590
Clarkson, R. W., 9, 77, 113
Claypool, L., 531, 543, 601
Cloudsley-Thompson, J. L., 159, 220, 425, 438
Clutton-Brock, T. H., 446, 485, 499, 503
Coborn, J., 285, 302, 318
Cochran, D. M., 77
Cock, E. V., 73, 143, 182, 218, 234
Coe, M. J., 348, 355–356, 358–360, 365, 367, 371, 374, 383, 396, 401, 420, 425, 434, 581, 584, 602
Cogger, A. G., 425, 436, 439
Cogger, H. G., 182, 220, 233, 282–285, 290, 301, 318, 503, 512, 521
Cohen, M., 25, 56, 80, 127, 134–135
Cohen, N. W., 18, 104, 339, 383, 509, 515, 522
Cokendolpher, J., 111, 117
Coker, J. W., 427, 437, 504, 519, 522, 583, 593
Coker, R. E., 556, 590

Colbert, E. H., 29, 51, 77
Cole, L. C., 444, 503
Collins, C. T., 156, 157, 158, 170, 219
Collins, J. P., 444, 495, 498, 511
Collins, J. T., 90, 117, 283, 318
Colwell, R. K., 63, 77
Compton, A. W., 280, 318
Compton, L. V., 77, 137
Conant, R., 77, 145–148, 182, 184, 220, 230
Congdon, J. D., 11, 106, 206, 220, 239, 241, 248, 251, 253–255, 261, 266, 269, 272–273, 351, 356, 359–362, 364–365, 367, 370, 374, 376, 379, 395–398, 400–401, 404, 416–417, 423, 425, 427, 434, 437, 445, 467, 471, 495, 510, 527, 532, 583–585, 588, 590–591, 603
Conner, W. E., 25, 56, 80, 127, 135
Cook, L. M., 156–157, 219–220
Cooke, L. M., 241, 269
Coombs, W. P., Jr., 293, 318
Coons, L. W., 454, 505, 517, 522
Cooper, J. S., 535, 591
Cooper, W. E., Jr., 56, 77, 127, 239, 241, 243, 250, 252–253, 261, 263–264, 269, 273, 284, 319, 328, 355, 385, 510, 517, 522
Cope, E. D., 61, 77, 155, 164, 174, 175, 220
Coppinger, R. P., 77, 173, 220
Corben, C. J., 293, 319
Corey, A. T., 554, 591
Corkill, N. L., 77, 144, 150–151
Cormack, R. M., 343, 374
Cornelius, S. E., 8, 77
Corrington, J. D., 284, 319
Corvino, J. M., 156, 158, 167, 219
Cott, H. B., 9, 11, 77, 113, 118–122, 173, 183, 220, 239, 249, 257, 269, 277, 280–281, 299–300, 303, 319
Cott, H. G., 3, 63, 77, 124
Covelo de Zolessi, L., 543, 603
Cowles, R. B., 30, 77, 78, 123, 129, 142, 152, 292, 319, 534, 591
Cox, P. G., 260, 269
Cox, W. A., 396, 400, 425, 438
Crastz, F., 527, 591
Crawford, F. T., 99, 125
Crawshaw, P. G., Jr., 102, 118–119, 280, 319
Crenshaw, J. W., Jr., 475, 503

Creswell, R., 280, 319
Crews, D., 208, 210, 220, 224
Cristman, S. P., 340, 372
Crites, A. S., 293, 319
Crossman, E. J., 361, 385, 417, 435
Crother, B., 78, 112
Crouse, D. T., 334, 374, 406, 425
Crowder, L. B., 334, 374
Crowley, S. R., 18, 21, 29, 78
Croze, H. J., 156, 157, 219
Cruz, A., 14, 78, 116
Csanyi, V., 19, 106
Cuellar, O., 364, 374, 449, 503
Cunningham, B., 417, 425, 527, 531, 545, 556, 591
Cunningham, J. D., 78, 115–118, 120, 239, 269
Curio, E., 53–54, 57–58
Curran, E. J., 78, 138
Cutter, W. L., 78, 140
Cyrus, R. V., 359, 374

Daanje, A., 64, 68, 78
Dalrymple, G. H., 552, 591
Daniel, J. C., 283, 319
Daniel, P. M., 503, 512, 521
Daniels, C. B., 239, 248–250, 253–255, 260–261, 263, 269
Danni, T. M. S., 540, 552–553, 587
Darevsky, I. S., 54, 78, 127, 152, 182, 218, 231
Darlington, P. H., 78, 151
Darwin, C. R. 47, 78, 237, 269
David, R., 280, 319
Davies, P. M. C., 22, 69, 85
Davis, D. D., 30–31, 64, 78, 129–130, 134, 139, 145, 257, 269
Davison, E., 212, 213, 223
Dawbin, W. H., 78, 136
Dawley, E. M., 217, 220
Dawson, W. R., 249, 268
de Jager, J. M., 559, 562, 601
DeKoningh, H. L., 425, 438
DeMarco, V. G., 581, 592
DeNeira, L. E. F., 403, 425, 438
de Queiroz, K., 25, 31–32, 34–35, 38, 58, 80, 83
de Ricqles, A., 349, 373
DeSalle, R., 529, 591

AUTHOR INDEX

de Silva, A., 78, 119, 144–145
DeSola, C. R., 425, 438
de Vos, J. C., Jr., 9, 77, 113
de Vries, D. A., 561, 599
DeWitte, G. F., 78, 149
Dean, J. M., 404, 434, 436
Decker, J. D., 527, 591
Deevey, E. S., Jr., 352, 374
Deitz, D. C., 543, 591
Dejours, P., 573, 600
Demeter, A., 10, 78
Dendy, A., 531, 556, 591
Denno, R. F., 305, 327
Deoras, P. J., 211, 220
Deraniyagala, P. E. P., 280–281, 297, 301, 303, 319, 362, 374, 425, 436, 438–439, 528, 533, 591
Descourtilz, M. E., 280, 319
Dessauer, H. D., 32, 37, 39, 40, 78
Devenish, S., 280, 319
Dharmakumarsinji, K. S., 280, 300, 319
Dial, B. E., 29, 53, 78, 130, 138–139, 148, 217, 220, 239–240, 248, 250, 253–255, 257, 261, 265–266, 269, 283, 321
Dickson, N. A., 241, 248, 251, 254–255, 266, 273
Diefenbach, C. O., 245, 270
Dietz, D. C., 280–281, 300, 302, 308, 319
Diller, L. V., 78, 97, 117, 119, 503, 507, 516, 521–522
Dillon, L. S., 50, 78, 142
Dimond, M. T., 544, 546, 591
Dingle, H., 3, 78
Ditmars, R. L., 284, 286, 319
Dixon, J. R., 239, 269, 280, 327, 533, 540, 542–543, 558–559, 562–563, 602
Dmi'el, R., 503, 519, 521, 537–538, 546, 554–556, 564, 572, 575, 587, 591
Dobie, J. L., 338, 348, 355, 358–359, 361–362, 374, 426, 436
Dobson, F. S., 487, 499, 503
Dodd, C. K., 26–27, 78, 128, 131–132, 134
Dodge, C. H., 544, 546, 591
Dodge, K. R., 25, 56, 80, 127, 135
Domantay, J. S., 527, 591
Dominey, W. J., 209, 220
Donoghue, M. J., 24, 68, 92
Donoso-Barros, R., 79, 148

Dorizzi, M., 552–553, 600, 605
Douglas, A. M., 11, 79, 114–115, 117
Douglass, J. F., 111, 113
Dow, M. M., 446, 485–487, 499, 502
Dowling, H. G., 283, 285–286, 289, 291, 319, 322, 328
Downes, M. C, 335, 371
Dresner, I. G., 237, 273
Driver, P. M., 55, 88, 161, 223
Droge, D. L., 361, 363, 370, 475, 501, 503, 514–515, 521
Drummond, H., 7, 65, 79, 87, 121, 124–125, 138, 212, 220, 404, 426
Dryden, G. L., 79, 115, 117, 121
Duellman, A. S., 29, 79, 126
Duellman, W. E., 10, 29, 57, 79, 126, 175, 182, 220, 230, 231, 269, 284, 319, 426, 437
Dufaure, J. P., 530, 591
Dugan, B. A., 18, 29, 31, 50, 60, 67, 84, 116, 123–125, 130, 134, 140, 209, 221, 280, 300, 319, 535, 600
Dunbar-Cooper, A., 543, 556–557, 562, 575–576, 596
Duncan, C. J., 164, 180, 221
Dundee, H. A., 79, 146
Dunham, A. E., 336, 339, 342, 345–349, 351, 354–365, 367–368, 373–374, 382, 385, 425, 438, 445–446, 448–449, 451–453, 461–462, 471–472, 474–477, 487, 489–490, 499, 503, 508, 510–511, 514–516, 521–522, 584, 590
Dunlap, W. P., 68, 86
Dunn, E. R., 79, 118–119, 146, 150, 174, 175, 180, 221, 284, 319
Dunn, R. W., 285–286, 319
Dunson, W. A., 50, 79, 287, 320, 426, 439, 504, 521–522, 559, 591
Durham, F. E., 79, 140, 142, 147, 152
Dutton, P. H., 402, 431, 552, 584, 592, 597
Duvall, D., 16, 46, 65–66, 79, 152

Easterla, D. A., 79, 120
Echternacht, A. C., 55, 79
Edelstam, C., 343, 372
Edgren, M. K., 80
Edgren, R. A., 40, 79, 80, 426, 438
Edmunds, M., 64, 80, 159, 161, 163, 172, 173, 180, 209, 221

Egan, M. E., 454, 505, 517, 522
Eglir, A., 426, 438
Ehrengart, W., 426, 439
Ehrhart, L. M., 427, 436
Ehrlich, P. R., 49, 75
Eibl-Eibesfeldt, I., 283, 320
Einem, G. E., 366, 374, 426, 438
Eisenberg, J. F., 57, 64, 80
Eisner, T., 25, 56, 80, 127, 134–135
Eiss, I., 15, 103
Elder, R. L., 451, 502
Elvira, B., 503, 516, 521
Elzen, P. van den, 80, 135
Emerson, S. B., 64, 105
Emlen, J. M., 168, 180, 221
Emmons, L. H., 51, 80
Emsley, M. G., 183, 221
Endler, J. A., 3, 5, 22, 24, 48, 63, 80, 159, 221
Engel, W., 553, 592
Engelhardt, M., 74, 145
Engen, S., 63, 80
Erasmus, H., 288, 320
Erben, H. K., 525–526, 528, 530, 574, 592, 595
Ernst, C. H., 11, 26–27, 80, 112, 134, 337, 344, 348, 357–359, 361, 374–375, 396, 404, 417, 426, 436, 437, 438, 532, 592
Ernst, E. M., 348, 375
Eschmeyer, R. W., 343, 382
Estabrook, G. F., 156, 221
Estes, R., 25, 28, 31–32, 34–35, 38, 58, 80, 83
Evans, H. E., 284, 320
Evans, L. T., 284, 291, 320
Evans, W. E., 25, 26, 76, 133, 135, 139
Ewer, R. F., 53, 57, 64, 80
Ewert, M. A., 360, 375, 396–397, 426, 436, 525–527, 543, 574, 583, 592
Ewing, H. E., 341, 375, 426, 437
Exton, L. S., 156, 158, 161, 228

Fagerberg, W. R., 529, 603
Falconer, D. S., 389, 426
Fan, T. H., 36, 80, 125, 141, 143, 146, 147
Fawcett, J. D., 282, 327
Feaver, P. E., 336, 339, 343, 345–346, 349, 355, 362–363, 375
Feder, M. E., 67, 80, 555, 573–574, 592

Felsenstein, J., 446, 476, 487, 499, 503
Ferguson, G. W., 12, 20, 28, 33, 49, 76, 80, 89, 91, 136, 249, 269, 342, 345, 349, 355, 375, 378, 475, 499–500, 503, 515, 521, 581, 592
Ferguson, M. W. J., 335, 375, 528–529, 533, 544, 547, 551, 553, 562–563, 574, 592
Ferner, J. W., 340, 375
Ficken, R. W., 48, 80
Field, R., 285, 289, 300–301, 303, 318
Fienberg, S. E., 343–344, 346, 375
Fink, L. S., 160, 221
Fink, W. S., 68, 81
Finneran, L. C., 417, 426
Finnie, E. P., 86, 121
Finster, E. B., 343, 371
Firth, S. J., 526, 592
Fisk, A., 531, 592
Fitch, A. V., 545, 593
Fitch, H. S., 6, 10–11, 13, 15, 17, 20, 36, 41, 44, 54, 56, 81, 115–119, 121–122, 127, 131, 137, 138, 141–142, 145–146, 148, 151, 239, 250, 270, 283–284, 298, 301–303, 305, 320, 340, 342–343, 345–346, 349, 355–356, 361–362, 364, 367, 375, 382, 403–404, 426, 439, 445, 449, 478, 480, 488, 495, 497, 504, 508, 512, 514, 517–522, 534, 545, 593
Fitch, J. E., 8, 98, 121
Fitzgerald, M., 287, 320
Fitzpatrick, J. W., 81, 113
Fitzpatrick, L. C., 239–240, 248, 250, 253–255, 257, 261, 266, 269
FitzSimons, F. W., 286, 303, 306, 320
FitzSimons, V. F. M., 81, 143–152, 182, 206, 221, 234, 251–253, 270, 287, 320, 534, 593
Flaherty, S. P., 239, 253, 269
Flannery, M. A., 158, 219
Fleay, D., 81, 150, 287, 320
Fleet, R. R., 503–504, 519–522
Flegg, P. B., 575, 578, 593
Fleishman, L. J., 50, 81, 125
Flemming, T. H., 504, 513, 522
Flower, S. S., 81, 142, 144, 148, 152, 204, 221
Foekema, G. M. M., 285, 320
Fogarty, M. J., 280, 320

AUTHOR INDEX

Fogden, M., 203, 221
Fogden, P., 203, 221
Folkerts, G. W., 435, 437
Foote, R. W., 426, 439
Forbes, M., 285, 320
Ford, E. B., 156, 187, 220-221, 231
Ford, N. B., 21, 91, 449, 478, 508
Forester, D. C., 305, 320
Fowler, L. E., 404, 427, 584, 593
Fox, M. H., 545, 593
Fox, S. F., 12, 80-81, 250, 270, 499-500, 503-504, 581, 592-593
Fox, W., 545, 593
Francillion, H., 349, 375
Frank, W., 81, 143
Frankenberg, E., 32-33, 81, 109, 126, 199, 229
Franks, P., 402, 435, 540, 543-544, 552-553, 584, 605
Franson, J. C., 341, 370
Franz, R., 88, 114-115, 117-121, 506, 520, 522
Frazer, N. B., 334, 367, 375-376, 404, 406, 412, 427, 436
Frazier, J., 8, 81, 112, 348, 376, 398, 400-401, 404, 427, 436
Freiberg, M., 175, 179, 184, 221
Fretey, J., 552, 601
Frith, C. B., 287, 320
Fritts, J. H., 345, 378
Fritts, T. H., 399, 427
Froese, A. D., 337, 344, 376, 581, 593
Fuentes, E. R., 243, 270
Fukada, H., 286, 295, 306, 320, 504, 519, 522
Fukunaga, T., 527, 595
Fulbright, H. J., 100, 116, 117
Funk, R. S., 81, 115

Gadgil, M., 444, 504
Gadow, H., 175, 179, 184, 221
Gaffney, E. S., 27, 60, 81
Gallagher, M. D., 71, 115, 116, 250, 268
Gallardo, J. M., 81, 123, 148
Galligan, J. H., 504, 521-522
Gallwey, E., 286, 300, 306, 320
Gammon, B. R., 335, 371
Gannon, V. P. J., 342, 362, 371, 376, 504, 521-522

Gans, C., 4, 9-10, 21, 26, 28, 32, 34, 37, 39-40, 44, 48, 50, 55, 60-63, 65-67, 74, 81-82, 88, 114, 125-126, 128-129, 134-136, 143-145, 152, 165, 167, 168, 191, 192, 193, 194, 196, 197, 199, 206, 216, 221, 245, 252, 265, 270, 280, 307, 325
Gardner, W. H., 559, 589
Garland, T., Jr., 17, 35, 82, 134
Garman, S., 46, 83
Garner, J. A., 400, 404, 430, 437
Garrick, L. D., 83
Garrido, O. H., 103, 144
Gaskins, C. T., 364, 370
Gates, D. M., 535, 593
Gates, G. O., 83, 116-117, 120, 139-140, 145-146, 148
Gatten, R. E., Jr., 89, 137
Gauthier, J. A., 25, 31-32, 34-38, 64, 80, 83, 99, 139
Gaymer, R., 83, 135, 341, 354, 376, 427, 438
Gehlbach, F. R., 5, 15, 21-22, 38, 53, 62, 67-68, 83, 93, 109, 145-146, 148, 151-152, 167, 176, 177, 179, 187, 188, 216, 221, 222, 284, 320
Gemmell, D. J., 417, 427, 436
Gennaro, A. L., 504, 514, 522
Gentry, A. H., 51, 80
Gergits, W. F., 217, 223
Gettinger, R. D., 537-538, 567, 593
Gharpurey, K. G., 83, 144, 148, 204, 222
Gibbons, J. R. H., 49, 83, 283, 300, 320
Gibbons, J. W., 283-284, 301, 304, 311-312, 319, 328, 337-341, 345, 347-349, 353-356, 358, 360-363, 366-368, 370, 374, 376-377, 389, 394-398, 400, 405-406, 411, 415, 417, 419, 425, 427-428, 436-438, 504, 519, 521 522, 583-584, 590, 593
Gibbs, A. G., 555, 573-574, 592
Gibson, C. W. D., 348, 377
Gibson, D. O., 158, 219
Giersberg, H., 529, 531, 593
Gifford, C. E., 345, 348, 385
Gillespie, J. H., 404, 412, 428
Gillingham, J. C., 28, 46, 76, 82, 131, 151-152, 212, 225
Gingerich, P. D., 162, 222

Giovannoli, L., 341, 365, 372
Gittleman, J. L., 157, 222
Glass, B. P., 83, 148
Gloyd, H. K., 17, 83
Goddard, P., 83, 115, 117
Godley, J. S., 8, 83, 120, 148
Goeldi, E., 306, 320
Goff, C. C., 427, 437, 439
Goff, D. S., 427, 437, 439
Goldberg, S. R., 358, 361–362, 377, 385, 504–505, 511–512, 516, 518, 522
Golder, F., 83, 123, 144–145, 147–148
Goldschmidt, R. B., 157, 222
Goldsmith, S. K., 50, 83
Goldsmith, W. M., 403, 428
Goldstein, R. C., 286, 321
Gonzales, D., 83, 146
Goodale, M. A., 164, 180, 222
Goode, G. B., 155, 164, 222
Goode, J., 427, 438–439, 543, 593
Goodhart, C. G., 162, 222
Goodman, D., 367, 373, 418, 424, 436
Goodman, J. D., 176, 215, 222
Goodman, J. M., 176, 215, 222
Goodman, L. A., 334, 377
Goodwin, G. C., 11, 83, 116
Goodwin, T. M., 280, 321, 562, 593
Gordon, C., 545, 593
Gordon, E. R., 212, 220
Gordon, K. L., 84, 119
Gordon, R. E., 282, 321
Gorell, T. A., 527, 599
Gorman, G. C., 12, 83, 101, 140, 368, 379, 505, 518–519, 522, 551, 593
Gorzula, S. J., 10, 16, 18, 28, 83, 113, 135, 280, 321
Gosner, K. J., 8, 83, 132, 148
Goss, R. G., 199, 226
Gould, S. J., 16, 70, 237, 270
Goulding, M., 8, 83
Gove, D., 83, 84, 129, 148
Gow, G. F., 285, 321
Gower, J. C., 451, 505
Gracie, A. E., 84, 117
Graf, W., 84, 119
Graham, T. E., 9, 84, 112, 348, 377, 405, 411, 428, 437
Grant, C., 84, 121, 149, 367, 377

Gravelle, K., 15, 103
Greegor, D. H., Jr., 37, 84
Green, E. E., 287, 297, 321
Green, R. J., 93, 151
Greenberg, B., 505, 512–513, 522
Greenberg, N., 21, 84
Greene, H. W., 4, 5, 7, 9–15, 18, 23–35, 37–41, 43, 47, 50, 53–54, 59–60, 62–67, 74, 84–85, 88, 99, 114–122, 123, 125, 127–130, 132–134, 136, 139–140, 143–152, 162, 167, 179, 183, 184, 185, 186, 187, 188, 190, 199, 204, 208, 212, 213, 214, 216, 222, 224, 239, 243, 252, 263, 270, 283, 321, 504, 517, 522
Greene, J. L., 354, 355, 360, 367–368, 376, 395–396, 398, 400, 406, 419, 425, 427, 428, 437, 584, 590
Greenhall, A. M., 11, 83, 116
Greenham, P., 409, 423, 436, 544, 556, 589
Greenwood, P. J., 55, 63, 86, 157, 210, 222
Greer, A. E., 35, 52, 85, 127, 138, 141, 282, 283, 321, 505, 512–513, 517, 522, 533, 593
Gregory, L. A., 50, 85
Gregory, P. T., 50, 85, 339, 345–346, 355–356, 362, 364, 377, 505
Griffiths, D., 4, 85
Grigg, G. C., 285, 289–291, 301–303, 321
Grinnell, H., 85, 143
Grinnell, J., 85, 143, 145
Grobman, A. B., 174, 176, 184, 215, 222
Grodzinski, M. Z., 532, 593
Gross, M. R., 277, 312–314, 321, 329
Groves, F., 7, 85, 119
Groves, J. D., 194, 226, 277, 292, 301, 321
Grubb, P., 341, 347, 377, 398, 428, 438
Gudger, E. W., 85, 116, 121
Gudynas, E., 85, 142
Guerrero, S., 346, 369
Guese, R. K., 20, 106, 120, 123, 146
Guggisberg, C. A. W., 528, 593
Guichard, A., 553, 600
Guidry, E. V., 85, 112, 120
Guilford, T., 63, 85
Guillette, L. J., Jr., 282, 322, 505, 514, 516, 522, 529, 531, 535, 543, 593–594
Gunning, G. E., 338, 377
Guo, Y-W., 206, 323

AUTHOR INDEX

Gurr, C. G., 561, 594
Guthrie, J. E., 10, 85
Guthrie, R. D., 208, 222
Guttman, S. I., 49, 101
Gutzke, W. H. N., 402, 428, 531–532, 537–538, 540, 543–546, 551–552, 555, 559–561, 563–568, 570–573, 579, 582, 584–585
Gutzwiller, K. J., 16, 46, 65–66, 79, 152

Haab, P., 573, 600
Haacke, W. D., 25, 39, 54, 85, 98, 134, 136, 138, 140–152, 254, 270
Haber, W. A., 173, 222
Hadley, D., 280, 321
Hadley, N. F., 85, 115, 364, 384, 510, 515, 522
Hagan, P. D., 345, 378
Hagan, R. M., 539, 605
Hahn, D. E., 9, 85, 121, 145, 148, 151
Hahn, W. L., 286, 321
Haiduk, M. W., 551, 602
Hailey, A., 22, 69, 85, 340, 383
Hailman, J. P., 63, 85, 163, 173, 222
Hairston, N. G., 85, 137
Haldane, J. B. S., 239, 270
Hall, R. J., 284, 321, 505, 519, 522
Hall, T. S., 205, 222
Halpern, M., 210, 224
Halstead, B. W., 166, 222
Hamilton, J., 348, 377
Hamilton, W. D., 412, 428
Hamilton, W. J., Jr., 85, 86, 112–113, 115–120, 427, 436, 439
Hamlett, G. W., 505, 512, 522
Hamman, K. C. D., 8, 105, 122
Hammer, D. A., 338, 341, 347, 377, 403–404, 428, 436, 583, 594
Hampp, J. C., 552, 591
Hanks, R. J., 578, 590
Hanley, G. H., 86, 148
Harding, J. H., 427, 437
Hardy, R., 341, 386, 435, 438
Harless, M., 396, 428
Harlow, P., 285, 289–291, 301–303, 321
Harris, D. M., 23, 32, 35, 86, 138, 339, 377
Harris, V. A., 241, 251, 270, 355, 377, 505, 512, 522, 531, 594
Harrison, K. E., 559, 566, 573, 596

Harrisson, J. 340, 365, 367, 377, 404, 429
Hartwig, G., 281, 321
Harvey, P. H., 55, 63, 86, 157, 210, 222–223, 446, 485, 499, 503
Hasegawa, M., 284, 303, 304, 321, 505, 517, 522
Hathaway, L. M., 508, 513, 522
Hausmann, P., 429, 437, 439
Haverschmidt, F., 6, 10, 86
Hay, O. P., 46, 86, 123
Hayden, P., 434, 438
Hayes, F. E., 86, 146, 148
Hayne D. W., 343, 377
Heath, J. E., 30, 86, 133
Heatwole, H., 8, 10–11, 21, 86, 103, 116, 118, 121, 105, 144–146, 212, 213, 223, 534, 601
Hecht, M. K., 40, 86, 133, 151, 165, 174, 175, 176, 179, 181, 183, 185, 214, 223
Heckel, D. G., 344, 346, 377
Hediger, H., 286, 289, 321
Hedrick, L. E., 160, 219
Hellier, T. R., 424, 436
Henderson, R. W., 10, 17, 23, 55, 72, 86, 101, 116–118, 144, 147–149, 189, 190, 204, 214, 223, 259, 270, 429, 437, 504, 514, 522
Hendricks, F. S., 105, 149
Hendrickson, J. D., 429, 438
Hendrickson, J. R., 365–366, 377, 389, 401, 403–404, 409, 412, 418, 429, 436, 532, 541, 542, 562, 594
Hennig, C. W., 68, 86, 250, 254–255, 270
Heringhi, H. L., 55, 96
Hertz, P. E., 21, 29, 86, 132, 136–137
Herzog, H. A., 15, 65–66, 68, 86–87, 125, 138, 280, 321
Hess, G. L., 527, 596
Heulin, B., 339, 342, 345, 350, 378
Heusser, H., 21, 111
Heyer, W. R., 39, 57, 87, 138
Hibbard, C. W., 288, 321
Hickman, J. L., 505
Hicks, K., 25, 56, 80, 127, 135
Hikida, T., 283–284, 321
Hildebrand, H. H., 367, 378
Hildebrand, S. F., 354, 378
Hill, S. E., 341, 385

Hillestad, H. O., 400, 433
Hillis, D. M., 87, 148
Hilzheimer, M., 282, 321
Hine, R. L., 340, 385
Hines, T. C., 280–281, 319, 543, 591
Hipp, T. G., 361, 370, 501, 514, 521
Hirsch, K. F., 526–530, 574, 594, 599
Hirth, H. G., 342, 362, 365–367, 373, 378, 401, 406, 416, 424, 429, 436, 541, 543, 590
Hoddenbach, G. A., 336, 339, 342, 345–347, 349, 351, 356, 362, 364, 367–368, 384, 448, 510
Hodgson, J. R., 8, 90, 120–121
Hodsdon, L. A., 278, 301, 321
Hoefs, J., 526, 592
Hoek, W., 337, 344, 370
Hoffman, W., 345, 378
Hoffstetter, R., 60, 87
Hoger, C., 160, 227
Hogue, C. L., 173, 223
Hohmann, C. J., 341, 385
Holder, L. A., 545, 594
Holland, P., 280, 321
Holling, C. S., 156, 160, 168, 180, 223
Holm, E., 92, 140
Holman, J. A., 429, 436
Holmes, A., 285, 290, 318
Holmes, J. W., 539–540, 554, 558, 575, 578, 596
Holmstrom, W. F., Jr., 292, 322
Honegger, R. E., 286, 289, 322, 404, 429, 438
Hoogmoed, M. S., 9, 87, 119, 533, 597
Hooker, R. S., 504, 513, 522
Hopkins-Murphy, S. R, 402, 431, 552, 584, 597
Horn, H. G., 87, 102, 142
Horner, J. R., 293, 322
Hornocker, M. G., 10, 94, 116–118, 120
Horwich, R., 48, 80
Hotaling, E. C., 402, 435, 532, 540, 543–544, 552–553, 584, 594, 605
Hotz, H., 87, 138
Hounsome, M. V., 211, 218
Houseal, T. W., 551–552, 604
How, R. A., 505, 513, 522
Howard, C. W., 535, 603

Howard, R. D., 209, 218
Howe, P. A. W., 56, 87
Howell, B. J., 548, 550, 594
Hower, A. S., 156, 157, 219
Howland, J. M., 356. 364, 385, 449, 511
Hoyer, R. F., 54, 97
Hoyle, W. L., 75, 117, 139
Hu, Q., 36, 87
Hubert, J., 530, 591
Hudnall, J. A., 342, 378
Hudson, P., 535, 594
Huene, E., 556, 591
Huey, R. B., 5, 7, 17, 21, 27, 29, 35, 39, 59, 61, 64, 67, 83, 86, 87, 93, 106, 126, 132, 134, 136–137, 140, 206, 207, 208, 223, 242, 253, 339, 381, 445–446, 449, 454, 470–471, 487, 495, 499, 501, 505, 507, 517, 522
Hughes, R. D., 240, 268
Huheey, J. E., 156, 158, 159, 161, 168, 223, 305, 322
Hulme, J. H., 87, 150
Hulse, A. C., 11, 43, 88, 106, 118, 121, 241, 273, 348, 378, 505, 508, 518, 522
Humphries, D. A., 55, 88, 161, 223
Humphries, J. M., Jr., 451, 502
Hunsaker, D., 505, 514, 522
Hunt, R. H., 280, 282, 302, 322
Hurter, J., 284, 322
Hurwitz, A. P., 531, 556, 591
Husband, G., 534, 604
Hutchinson, J. H., 27, 57, 67, 73
Hutchinson, V. H., 285–286, 289, 291, 322, 328, 405, 428
Hutton, J. T., 561, 594
Huxley, J. S., 239, 270

Inger, R. F., 102, 150, 249, 251, 272, 505, 512–513, 522
Inglehart, F., 66, 88, 152
Ingram, G. J., 293, 319
Ingram, W. F., III, 50, 62, 65, 88, 177, 178, 194, 197, 223
Ionides, C. J. P., 88, 149, 151–152
Ireland, L. C., 26, 88, 126, 135
Iverson, J. B., 12, 25, 29, 57, 67, 71, 88, 116, 135, 139, 283, 322, 363, 367, 378, 396,

399–401, 410, 415, 422, 429, 436–439, 506, 514, 522, 531–532, 535, 594, 599
Jackson, C. G., Jr., 429, 438
Jackson, D. R., 88, 114–115, 117–121, 300, 302, 308, 319, 506, 520, 522
Jackson, J. F., 10, 50, 53, 62, 65, 67, 88, 119, 125, 140, 177, 178, 194, 197, 205, 223
Jackson, P. B. N., 56, 88
Jackson, R. D., 561, 594
Jacobi, L., 531, 595
Jacobs, G. H., 179, 184, 223
Jacobson, N. H. G., 25, 39, 54, 98, 134, 136, 138, 140–152
Jacques, J., 429, 439
Jaeger, R. G., 217, 223
Jaksić, F. M., 7, 11, 13, 60, 88, 120, 140, 208, 224, 243, 270
Janzen, D. H., 3, 5–6, 34, 60, 64–65, 88, 172, 173, 202, 224
Järvi, T., 63, 80, 156, 157, 224, 229
Jayaker, S. D., 429, 438
Jayne, B. C., 511, 521–522
Jeffords, M. R., 157, 224, 227
Jelden, D. C., 281, 322
Jenkins, N. K., 527–529, 532, 589, 595
Jennings, M. R., 89, 117
Jennison, G., 297, 300, 322
Jennrich, R. I., 242, 272
Jenssen, T. A., 33, 95, 139
Jespersen, D. C., 156, 221
Jewett, S. G., Jr., 84, 119
Jiang, Y., 36, 87
Joanen, T., 280, 322, 544, 547, 551, 553, 558, 562, 592, 595
John-Alder, H. B., 445, 501
Johnson, C. R., 18, 21, 89, 143, 145, 147, 149–150
Johnson, J. A., 32, 38, 89, 98, 138, 143
Johnson, S. R., 535, 595
Johnson, T. B., 36, 69, 92
Johnston, G. R., 535, 595
Jolly, G. M., 343, 378
Jones, M. E., 531–532, 599
Jones, R. E., 282, 290, 322, 327–328, 529, 594
Jones, S. M., 49, 89, 342, 361, 363, 370, 378, 475, 501, 506, 514–515, 521–522
Jones, T. H., 25, 56, 80, 127, 134–135

Jordon, R., 22, 89, 148
Jorgensen, C., 21, 89
Joshi, P. N., 290, 322
Jouventin, P., 168, 196, 224
Judd, F. R., 506, 514, 522
Jun-yi, L, 506, 512, 522

Kalmbach, E. R., 89, 116, 118, 120–121
Kalmus, H., 89, 123, 145
Kamel, S., 89, 137
Kanakambika, P., 531, 597
Kaplan, H. M., 341, 378
Kapoor, M., 100, 127, 138
Kar, S. K., 281, 300, 318
Kar, S., 284, 288, 317
Karashima, J., 527, 595
Karasov, W. H., 445, 470, 500
Kardong, K. V., 44, 46, 50, 89, 130, 147, 151, 197, 199, 224
Kästle, W., 89, 137
Kau-hung, L., 506, 512, 522
Kaufman, J. H., 53, 89
Kaufmann, A., 53, 89
Kaufmann, J. H., 188, 224
Kaufmann, R., 429, 436
Kearney, E. P., 156, 158, 161, 228
Keefer, T. E., 32, 51, 57, 93, 138
Keenlyne, K. D., 89, 121
Keeper, T. E., 249, 270
Keeton, G. H., 398, 428
Keiser, E. D., Jr., 215, 224
Kennedy, J. P., 89, 116–117, 119–120, 122–123, 139, 141–142, 147
Kenneweg, F. H., 89, 136
Kessell, S. R., 156, 158, 168, 226
Keyfitz, N., 334, 378
Khalaf, K. T., 182, 224, 231
Khan, M. K. B. M., 429, 436
Khan, M. S., 11, 16, 89, 90, 149
Kiester, A. R., 339, 341, 347, 378, 382, 433, 437
Kilicka, J., 527, 596
King, F. W., 284, 317
King, J. R., 539, 604
King, M. B., 16, 46, 65–66, 79, 152
King, R. B., 49, 90
King, W. W., 206, 220, 239, 254, 261, 269
Kinghorn, J. R., 285, 322
Kirk, V. M., 90, 132, 149

Kirsche, W., 429, 439
Kiss, B., 19, 106
Kitchener, D. J., 505, 513, 522
Klages, H. G., 90, 137
Klauber, L. M., 10, 13, 16, 18, 45, 47–48, 50, 53, 61, 90, 115–116, 122, 127, 129–131, 140, 145–149, 151, 292, 322
Klemme, B., 553, 592
Klicka, J., 358–360, 374, 379
Klimstra, W. D., 90, 112, 120–122
Klots, A. B., 284, 322
Kluge, A. G., 23, 31–33, 69, 86, 90, 138
Klute, A., 554, 591
Knapik, P. G., 8, 90, 120–121
Knight, D., 534, 601
Knight, J. L., 90, 117
Kochva, E., 165, 167, 224
Kofron, C. P., 90, 120–121, 506, 519, 522
Koga, K., 527, 595
Kool, K., 17, 18, 56, 90, 127, 134
Kopstein, F., 287, 322
Kraemer, J. E., 401, 430
Krampitz, G., 529–530, 595
Kratzer, H., 44, 90, 128, 132, 149, 151–152, 285, 322
Kraus, F., 46–47, 102, 212, 214, 227
Krebs, J. R., 211, 220
Kreig, H., 284, 300, 322
Kreulen, D. A., 6, 90
Kreyenberg, M., 90, 148
Kriesten, K., 529, 530, 595
Krogh, J. E., 9, 105, 116, 139
Krohmer, R. W., 357–358, 378, 506, 520, 522
Kroll, J. C., 20, 38, 40, 90, 109, 151
Kroon, C., 196, 197, 224
Kropach, C., 43, 46, 53, 101, 127, 150, 183, 203, 224, 226
Krupa, J. J., 248, 268
Kruuk, H., 10, 14, 90, 115, 118, 120
Kubie, J. L., 210, 224
Kuntz, R. E., 182, 224, 232
Kushlan, J. A., 280, 282, 292, 322
Kushlan, M. S., 280, 322
Kwiecinski, G., 48, 99, 172, 226

La Panouse, R. de, 286, 289, 291, 303, 323
LaBarbera, M., 51, 91
LaVal, R. K., 11, 106, 116
Labanick, G. M., 239, 270

Lacher, T. E., Jr., 106, 140, 249, 273, 362, 385, 511, 514, 522
Laerm, J., 51, 57, 91, 139
Lagler, K. F., 338, 378, 404, 430
Lamar, W. W., 91, 112
Lamaral, B. H., 91, 115
Lamarre-Picquot, P., 285, 322–323
Lamb, T., 9, 91, 117
Lambert, M. R. K., 430, 439
Lambert, S., 20, 91
Lamborn, W. A., 91
Lamoreaux, W. E., 96, 137, 286, 289, 324
Land, D. S., 10, 91
Lande, R., 443, 471, 506
Landers, J. L., 400, 404, 430, 437
Landwehr, J. M., 344–345, 386
Lang, J. W., 83, 551, 595
Langerwerf, B., 283, 299–300, 323
Lannom, J. R., 336, 339, 342, 345–347, 349, 351, 356, 362, 364, 367–368, 448, 510
Laposha, N. A., 47, 104
Lara Gongora, G., 531, 535, 543, 594
Lardie, R. L., 91, 133, 148, 430, 438–439
Larman, R., 285, 289, 300, 326
Latifi, M., 82, 144, 152, 196, 197, 221
Lauder, G. V., 62, 68, 91, 487, 498, 506
Laughlin, H., 91, 112
Laurent, R. F., 82, 137, 143, 145, 252, 270
Law, R., 444, 506
Lawrence, E. S., 59, 91
Lawrence, R. F., 91, 115
Lawson, R., 32, 37, 39–40, 78
Layne, J. R., Jr., 21, 91
Le Roux, S. F., 287, 323
LeBuff, C. R., Jr., 345, 362, 365–367, 378, 430, 436
Leakey, J. H. E., 287–288, 297, 303, 323
Lederer, G., 286, 323
Lee, H. T., 91, 121
Legge, N. J., 555, 595
Legler, J. M., 9, 11, 17, 21, 26–27, 57, 73, 91, 95, 112, 135, 337–339, 341, 344, 347–348, 354, 356–362, 365–367, 375, 378, 380, 394, 403–404, 414, 417, 430, 431, 437–438, 543–546, 551, 562–563, 589, 595, 597
Legler, W. K., 341, 379
Lehmann, H. D., 38, 54, 91, 134, 143, 151

AUTHOR INDEX

Leigh, C., 288, 323
Lema, T. de, 91, 142
Lemaku, P. J., 341, 379
Leroy, Y., 199, 224
Lescure, J., 552, 601
Lessells, C. M., 340, 383, 419, 434
Leuttenegger, W., 446, 485-487, 499, 502
Levins, R., 62, 91
Leviton, A. E., 54, 77, 91, 125, 138, 140-142, 144
Lewinsohn, T. M., 163, 228
Lewis, W. M., 338, 377
Lewke, R. E., 342, 379
Lewontin, R. C., 62, 91, 444, 506
Licht, P., 356, 368, 379, 505, 508, 513, 518-519, 522, 545, 595
Liem, K. F., 4, 91
Lillywhite, H. B., 49, 83, 529, 555, 574, 595
Lim, B. L., 52, 91, 137, 142, 144
Lim, G. S., 502, 519, 521
Lima, A. P., 281, 323, 534, 542-543, 596
Lima, S. L., 59, 91
Limpus, C. J., 365, 367, 379, 418, 423, 430, 436, 543, 546, 552, 585, 595, 597
Lindberg, K., 92, 149
Lindner, D. A., 425, 436
Liner, E. A., 92, 148
Lofton, J. P., Jr., 361, 370, 403-404, 422
Lofts, B., 357-358, 379, 430, 437, 439
Logan, T., 285, 289, 323
Longman, H. A., 92, 127, 137-138, 143-145, 149-150
Longstaff, G. G., 92, 137
Lönnberg, E., 92, 164, 197, 224
Lorenz, R., 10, 53, 92
Louw, G. N., 92, 140
Loveridge, A., 71, 92, 114-115, 119-122, 140, 143-144, 146-149, 152, 281, 323, 339, 379, 404, 430, 437-439
Lowe, C. H. 36, 69, 92, 241, 273, 352, 357-358, 364, 369, 377, 386
Lowenstein, J. M., 18, 104, 330, 383, 509, 515, 522
Luckenbach, R. A., 340, 371
Luke, C., 29, 51, 92
Lutz, P. L., 543, 556-557, 559, 562, 566, 573, 575-576, 596
Lykakis, J. J., 502, 516, 521

Lynch, J. D., 298, 323
Lynch, W., 92, 144
Lynn, W. G., 527, 538, 575, 596
Lyons, C. L., 341, 366, 384, 434, 438

MacCulloch, R. D., 416-417, 430, 436
MacFarland, C. B., 543, 596
Macartney, J. M., 50, 85
Mackay, R. D., 285, 323
Maddison, D. R., 24, 68, 92
Maddison, W. P., 24, 68, 92
Maderson, P. F. A., 26, 32, 82, 128, 545, 596
Maehr, D. S., 92, 122
Magnusson, W. E., 281, 301, 323, 329, 533-534, 540, 542-543, 562, 596, 604
Maharana, S., 281, 300, 303, 318
Mahendra, B. C., 92, 143
Mahmoud, I. Y., 338, 344-345, 358-360, 374, 379, 417, 430, 437-438, 527, 596
Mahrer, Y., 540, 596
Maiorana, V. C., 5, 92, 251, 270
Major, P. D., 345, 379
Maldonado, H., 161, 224
Malkmus, R., 37, 51, 92, 135, 140
Malnate, E. V., 93, 118, 137, 146, 295, 323
Mandaville, J., 93, 146
Manickavel, V., 531, 597
Manly, B. J. F., 343, 379
Manolis, S. C., 109, 118, 119, 528, 533, 540-541, 543-545, 551, 556-557, 562-563, 585, 604
Mao, S-H., 296, 323
Marcellini, D. L., 32, 33, 51, 57, 93, 138, 249, 270
March, D. H., 93, 152
Marchand, L. J., 337, 373
Marchisin, A., 93, 152
Marien, D., 165, 174, 175, 176, 179, 181, 183, 184, 185, 223
Marion, K. R., 396, 400, 415, 425, 431, 438, 506, 515, 522, 544-546, 601
Marion, W. R., 280, 321, 562, 593
Marquez, M. R., 354, 365, 367, 381, 403-404, 432, 436
Marr, J. C., 93, 116, 139
Marshall, T. J., 539-540, 554, 558, 561, 575, 578, 594, 596
Marszalek, D. S., 559, 566, 573, 596
Marten, G. G., 343-344, 379

Martin del Campo, R., 18, 36, 73, 139
Martin, D. J., 194, 224
Martin, J. H., 45, 93, 130
Martin, P. S., 60, 88, 93, 137
Martin, R. F., 449, 506, 516, 522
Martin, W. F., 39, 67, 93, 126, 134
Martof, B., 284, 323
Marx, H., 11, 44, 51, 93, 100, 113, 135–136, 139, 146, 150, 194, 224
Maslin, T. P., 47–48, 93, 99, 117, 144–145, 147–149, 151–152
Mason, E. R., 277, 282–283, 299, 300–302, 306, 324
Mason, R. T., 210, 224
Mast, S. O., 366, 379
Matthews, L. H., 237, 270
Matthiae, P. E., 48, 80
Mattox, N. T., 347, 379
Matuschka, F. R., 29, 93, 137
Maury, M. E., 349–350, 380
Mayer, G. C., 28, 101
Mayhew, W. W., 357–358, 361, 379, 506, 514–515, 522
Maynard Smith, J., 211, 224, 312–313, 323
Mays, C. E., 96, 116
Maza, B. G., 242, 272
McAllister, C. T., 51, 93, 138
McAuliffe, J. R., 398, 428
McBee, K., 551, 596
McCauley, R. H., Jr., 284, 301, 323
McCollum, F., 505, 518–519, 522
McCormick, S., 7, 93, 118, 121
McCoy, C. J., 93, 139, 148, 257, 270, 402, 423, 431, 506, 514, 522, 551–552, 589, 596, 604
McCrystal, H. K., 93, 151
McDiarmid, R. W., 5, 39, 43, 53, 85, 121, 133, 179, 183, 184, 185, 186, 187, 188, 216, 222
McDonald, H. S., 54–55, 62, 93
McDowell, S. B., 40–41, 43, 93, 202, 225, 532, 594
McEvoy, P. B., 158, 219
McGehee, M. A., 543–544, 556, 596
McGowan, N., 93, 137
McIlhenny, E. A., 93, 113, 135, 280, 300, 323, 528, 533, 543, 562, 596
McKinney, C. O., 10, 93, 116, 118, 239, 271

McLachlan, E., 543, 595
McNease, L., 280, 322
McPherson, R. J., 415, 431
McRae, W. A., 400, 404, 430, 437
Mead, G. P., 93, 94, 145, 151, 152
Meade, G. P., 286, 323
Mebs, D., 31, 32, 94, 95, 128, 138–139, 141, 144, 145, 148, 165, 225, 252, 271
Mech, H. R., 156, 158, 168, 219, 226
Medem, F., 9, 91, 94, 112, 280–281, 323, 431, 437–438, 533, 597
Medica, P. A., 239, 242, 269, 272, 336, 339, 341–342, 345–347, 349, 351, 355–356, 361–362, 364, 367–368, 379–380, 384, 434, 438, 448, 506, 510, 518, 522
Medsger, O. P., 286, 298, 301–302, 323
Meek, G., 293, 323
Meinwald, J., 25, 56, 80, 127, 134–135
Meinzer, W. P., 10, 94, 116
Melgarejo, A. R., 292, 323
Mell, R., 283–284, 286–288, 300, 304, 306, 324
Mendelssohn, H., 21, 39, 44, 82, 94, 152, 546, 596
Mengden, G. A., 287, 320
Menzies, J. I., 535, 596
Meritt, D. A., 31, 94, 140
Merrill, S. D., 562, 596
Merrotsy, B., 29, 67, 105, 137
Mertens, R., 3, 17, 26, 31, 39, 51, 65, 94, 134, 136–138, 143–150, 152, 165, 174, 180, 183, 193, 204, 225, 252, 271
Mertz, D. B., 334, 380
Messel, H., 281, 301, 329, 533, 542–543, 562, 604
Messick, J. P., 10, 94, 116–118, 120
Metzen, W. D., 280, 299–300, 305, 324
Meunier, F. J., 349, 373
Meyer-Rochow, V. B., 574, 599
Meylan, A. B., 424, 436
Meyn, R. L, 562, 596
Michod, R. E., 444, 506
Mienis, H. K., 94, 113, 120–121
Mignot, T., 553, 600
Miles, D. B., 356, 358, 368, 374, 445–446, 449, 451–453, 461–462, 471–472, 476–477, 487, 489–490, 499, 503
Milinski, M., 59, 95

AUTHOR INDEX

Miller, A. H., 95, 116
Miller, C. M., 266, 271
Miller, J. D., 531–532, 543–544, 546, 552, 563–568, 579–580, 582, 584–585, 595–597, 599
Miller, K., 582, 597–598
Miller, L., 341, 348, 380, 431, 438
Miller, M. R., 292, 324, 506, 518, 522
Millington, R. J., 575, 578, 597
Mills, M. G. L., 10, 14, 90, 115, 118, 120
Milstead, W. W., 95, 117, 142, 239, 271, 339, 359, 363, 367, 380, 431, 437
Milton, T. H., 33, 95, 139
Minckley, W. L., 57, 95, 113
Minton de Cervantes, B., 95, 119, 133
Minton, J. E., 9, 95, 140, 142, 144–145, 151
Minton, M. R., 286, 324
Minton, S. A., Jr., 17, 48, 50, 52, 54, 56, 95, 114, 115, 119, 133, 135–152, 182, 203, 225, 232, 284, 286, 324, 404, 431, 437, 439
Mishra, C. G., 281, 300, 316
Misra, R., 285, 316
Mitchell, J. C., 22, 95, 118, 146, 398–399, 415, 417, 431, 436, 511, 519, 522
Mitsukuri, K., 431, 439, 527, 597
Mittermeier, R. A., 341, 354, 380, 382, 432, 439, 533, 551, 596–597
Moberly, W. R., 31, 95, 134, 545, 595
Modha, M. L., 280–281, 300, 324, 533, 542–544, 597
Moffat, L. A., 353, 380, 531, 597
Moffitt, C. M., 158, 219
Mole, R. R., 95, 143, 144–146, 147, 287–288, 324
Moll, E. O., 8, 17, 95, 112, 135, 337–338, 341, 344, 347–348, 354–362, 365–367, 373, 380, 398, 403–404, 414, 416–417, 425, 431, 436–438, 543–544, 597
Mondolfi, E., 431, 439
Montanucci, R. R., 55, 95, 116–118, 120, 139, 141, 355, 380
Moody, S. M., 246, 271
Moon, R. G., 551, 589
Moon, T. W., 550, 604
Moore, J. C., 562, 597
Moore, P., 59, 111
Moran, G. B., 362, 383, 508, 519, 522

Morgan, C. L., 157, 225
Morgan, D., 106, 115
Morin, P. J., 242, 271
Morlock, H. , 396, 428
Morreale, S. J., 353, 380, 402–403, 431, 552–553, 585, 597
Morrell, R., 172, 225
Morris, K. A., 527, 531, 555–556, 563–564, 566–569, 582, 584, 597–598
Morris, M. A., 507, 519, 522
Mosauer, W. W., 23, 95–96, 139–142, 146, 148, 152
Moses, H., 539, 590
Mosimann, J. E., 354–356, 380, 431, 436
Mosse, A. H. E., 96, 115
Mostrom, A. M., 176, 215, 227
Mount, R. H., 239, 271, 283, 300, 324, 507, 517, 522
Moynihan, M., 5, 96
Mrosovsky, N., 402, 406, 431, 435, 544, 546, 552–553, 584–585, 592, 597, 601, 605
Müller, F., 155, 225
Muller, J. F., 431, 439
Müller, P., 96, 146, 149, 286, 324
Munger, J. C., 341, 380
Muñoz, G., 23, 73
Muntz, W. R. A., 179, 184, 225
Murphy, G. G., 338, 355, 357–361, 435, 436
Murphy, J. B., 35, 69, 71, 76, 96, 129, 132, 137, 141, 152, 212, 213, 220, 225, 286, 289, 324
Murphy, R. W., 84, 117
Murphy, T. M., Jr., 504, 519, 522
Mustill, F. J., 287, 324
Muth, A., 282, 324, 535, 545–547, 551, 555, 564–565, 583, 585, 597
Muthukkaruppan, V., 531, 597
Myers, C. W., 7, 8, 20, 23, 38, 59, 65, 96, 118–119, 129, 139, 144–146, 148–149, 205, 225
Myers, N., 61, 96

Nader, R., 182, 217, 231
Nagy, K. A., 445, 470, 507
Nakamura, K., 182, 225, 232
Nakar, O., 167, 224
Neill, W. T., 9, 27, 50, 55, 96, 113, 118, 120, 122, 130, 134–135, 145, 199, 212, 214, 218, 225, 280–281, 287, 292, 303, 324

Nelson, C. E., 526, 592
Nelson, D. H., 397, 427, 428, 583, 593
Netting, M. G., 96, 148
Nettman, H. K., 282, 324
Neve, L. C., 8, 96, 116–117
Nevo, E., 21, 29, 86, 132, 136–137
Newesely, H., 530, 592
Newlin, M. E., 507, 515, 522
Newman, D. G., 28, 101, 114
Nichols, J. T., 20, 96, 341, 380, 431, 438
Nichols, U. G., 431, 438
Nicholson, A. J., 157, 225
Nickerson, M. A., 55, 96, 116
Niekisch, M., 292, 324
Nielsen, D. R., 539, 605
Nietfeldt, J. W., 248, 268
Nikolskii, A. M., 31, 96, 130, 137
Nilson, G., 49, 70, 449, 500, 521
Noble, G. K., 68, 97, 131, 277, 282–283, 285, 289, 292, 299, 300–302, 305–306, 312, 324
Norris, K. S., 26, 48–49, 97, 124
Noske, R., 29, 67, 105, 137
Noske, S., 29, 67, 105, 137
Nouria, S., 349–350, 380
Nuccitelli, R., 550, 589
Nussbaum, R. A., 54, 97, 117, 252, 271, 311–312, 324, 507, 516, 522

O'Donald, P., 156, 168, 225, 226
Obbard, M. E., 341, 380
Obst, F. J., 29, 97, 125, 130, 137
Ogden, J. C., 280, 324–325, 533, 597
Ogren, L. H., 361–363, 365, 367, 372–373, 397, 401, 424, 436
Ogura, H., 527, 595
Ohmart, R. D., 249, 273, 362, 385, 511, 515, 522
Oliver, G. V., Jr., 85, 152
Oliver, J. A., 51, 64, 97, 124, 139, 146, 150, 278, 286–287, 297, 299, 301, 325
Orejas-Miranda, B., 97, 146
Ortenburger, A. I., 292, 325
Ortleb, E. P., 100, 148, 160, 199, 226, 227, 508, 513, 522
Orton, A. M., 21, 89
Osgood, D. W., 545, 598
Oster, G. F., 16, 62, 70, 97
Otte, D., 163, 209, 225

Ovadia, M., 167, 224
Owen, C. E., 97, 117
Owen, D., 63, 97, 117, 147, 173, 225
Owens, D. W., 406, 432
Owings, D. H., 199, 226
Ozment, J. E., 433, 438

Packard, G. C, 525–527, 529–532, 540, 543–546, 552, 554–556, 559–571, 574, 578–580, 582, 584, 594, 597–599
Packard, M. J., 525–527, 529–532, 546, 552, 554–556, 559, 562–569, 571, 574, 578–580, 582, 584, 597–599
Padua, L. F. M., 401–402, 421, 439, 532, 540, 543–544, 552–553, 587
Paine, R. T., 68, 97
Pallas, D. C., 432, 437
Panchen, A. L., 158, 219
Pandit, H., 82, 137, 143, 145
Papageorgis, C., 170, 225
Papenfuss, T. J., 10, 37, 97, 114, 253, 271, 454, 507
Parker, F., 85, 97, 141, 287, 325, 505, 517, 522
Parker, G. A., 211, 218
Parker, H. W., 47, 97, 115, 117
Parker, W. S., 9, 20, 24, 30, 50, 97, 115–118, 134, 138, 140, 206, 225, 239, 242, 252, 271, 336, 339–340, 343, 345–346, 349, 355–356, 362–364, 371, 389, 399, 432, 437, 441, 502, 507, 514, 518–519, 521–522, 534, 599
Parkes, A. S., 341, 363, 365, 383, 418, 433, 436
Parmenter, R. R., 398, 411, 432
Parmerlee, J. S., 47, 104
Parton, W. J., 539, 599
Pasteur, G., 158, 159, 160, 161, 162, 163, 164, 168, 173, 196, 224–225
Patchell, F. C., 9, 34, 97
Pattee, O. H., 72, 120
Patterson, K. K. 395, 400, 427, 428
Paukstis, G. L., 402, 428, 527, 531, 537–538, 551–552, 556, 563, 566–569, 572, 582, 584–585, 593–594, 597–598
Paulson, D. R., 97, 121
Paxton, R. J., 63, 86, 157, 222, 223
Peabody, F. E., 347, 381
Peabody, R. B., 38, 98, 143

AUTHOR INDEX

Pearse, A. S., 341, 381
Pearson, D. L., 163, 225
Pearson, J. F. W., 278, 301, 321
Pearson, O. P., 507, 514, 522
Pellier, C., 286, 289, 291, 303, 323
Pemberton, M., 157, 222
Pendlebury, G. B., 342, 381
Penman, H. L., 561, 594
Perez-Rivera, R. A., 98, 116
Pernetta, J. C., 203, 225
Perrone, M., Jr., 312–313, 325
Peters, R. H., 395, 432
Peterson, J. A., 51, 110
Petocz, R. G., 208, 222
Petters, G., 87, 142
Petzold, H. G., 98, 149–151, 287, 325, 432, 437
Phelps, T. E., 340, 345, 347, 349, 356, 383
Philibosian, R., 339, 342, 382, 508, 513, 522
Philip, J. R., 561, 599
Phillips, D. M., 529, 601
Phillips, E. J., 403–404, 432
Pianka, E. R., 9, 17, 22–24, 30, 50, 55, 59, 64, 66, 71, 87, 97–98, 114, 116–118, 134, 137–138, 140, 142, 206, 207, 208, 223, 225, 239–242, 251–253, 270–272, 339, 352, 381, 444–445, 449, 454, 462, 471, 495, 505, 507, 512, 514, 517, 522
Pianka, H. D., 30, 98, 114, 137, 239, 271, 462, 507, 512, 522
Pickwell, G. V., 8, 98, 121, 145
Pieau, C., 353, 381–382, 402, 432, 437, 543, 551–553, 599–601, 605
Pienaar, U. de V., 6, 9–11, 25, 39, 54, 98, 134, 136, 139–152
Pietruszka, R. D., 18, 21, 29, 78
Piiper, J., 573, 600
Pilecki, C., 156, 168, 225–226
Pilorge, T., 349–350, 381, 449, 507
Pitman, C. R. S., 88, 148, 151–152, 182, 233, 226, 280, 285–286, 289, 303, 325
Platt, A. P., 184, 226
Platt, D. R., 18, 30, 40, 54, 98, 112, 116–119, 121, 129, 146, 507, 519, 522, 546, 600
Platz, J. E., 11, 106, 241, 273
Plummer, M. V., 336, 340, 343, 345–346, 349, 355–356, 361–362, 364, 367, 375, 381, 403–404, 426, 432, 439, 507, 519, 522, 562, 584, 600

Polis, G. A., 7, 93, 98, 118, 121
Pollack, J. A., 86, 112–113, 115–120
Polynova, G. V., 31, 98
Pomerat, C. M., 546, 605
Pond, C. M. 34, 88, 248, 271
Pongsapipatana, S., 39, 57, 87, 138
Pooley, A. C., 280, 282, 301, 303, 325, 533, 562, 600
Pope, C. H., 98, 145, 149, 285–288, 325, 534, 600
Pope, R. D., 38, 100
Potratz, C. J., 156, 218
Potter, W. A., 338, 369
Pough, F. H., 5, 17, 21, 29, 48, 50, 57, 62–65, 67, 98, 99, 105, 147, 156, 158, 163, 164, 168, 172, 177, 178, 194, 219, 226, 305, 327, 340, 342, 381, 411, 432
Poulton, E. B., 92, 137, 161, 173, 226, 237, 271
Pounds, J. A., 50, 88, 205, 223
Powell, C. B., 359, 361, 381, 417, 432, 436, 437
Powell, R., 47, 104
Power, M., 68, 99
Prakash, I., 99, 115
Prange, H. D., 573, 575–576, 587, 600
Pregill, G. K., 36–38, 64, 67, 99, 139
Presch, W., 245, 271
Prestrude, A. M., 99, 125
Prestt, I., 99, 115, 117, 122, 340, 342–343, 345–346, 349, 356, 381, 383, 507, 521–522
Price, H. J., 445, 449, 467, 471, 511, 521
Price, J. W., Jr., 360–361, 370, 422, 437
Pridgen, J., 556, 591
Prieto, A. A., 15, 99, 116, 131, 140
Pritchard, P. C. H., 9, 11, 25, 26, 27, 68, 99, 112–113, 134, 135, 345, 354, 362, 365, 367, 381, 389–390, 396, 400, 402–406, 418, 432, 436
Procter, J. B., 26, 99
Proud, K. R. S., 37, 99, 129, 142
Pulford, E., 340, 383
Punnet, R. C., 157, 226
Punzo, F., 248, 263, 271
Pyburn, W. F., 15, 85, 150, 190, 222

Quattrini, D., 244, 261, 271

Quinn, H. R., 76, 124, 277, 287, 297, 300, 318, 507, 520, 522

Rabb, G. B., 44, 93, 194, 224
Radcliffe, C. W., 47–48, 99
Rage, J. C., 60, 87
Ragotzkie, R. A., 361, 403, 424, 432, 436, 584, 600
Rahn, H., 548, 556, 573, 588, 594, 600
Raj, U., 541, 600
Rajabi, B. S., 507, 512, 522, 535, 602
Rajendran, M. V., 99, 151
Ramm, G., 40, 86, 133, 151, 214, 223
Ramos-Costa, A. M. M., 106, 140, 148, 149
Ramsden, C. T., 71, 144, 148, 151, 283, 297, 316
Ramsey, L. W., 111, 149
Rand, A. S., 7–8, 12, 18, 21, 29, 31, 50–51, 55, 60, 63, 67, 74, 84, 96, 99–100, 116, 123–124, 130, 134, 139–140, 148, 199, 208, 210, 226, 239, 271, 280, 283, 300, 308, 319, 325, 346, 349–350, 352, 369, 381, 386, 446, 501, 534–535, 543, 545, 600
Rand, P. J., 50, 100, 140
Rand, W. M., 12, 63, 100
Rankin, P. R., 205, 226
Rao, M. V. S., 507, 512, 522
Rathor, M. S., 266, 272
Raun, G. G., 100, 123
Raven, H. C., 404, 432
Rawlins, S. L., 562, 596
Raynaud, A., 353, 382, 402, 432, 551–553, 600
Ream, C., 337–338, 382
Ream, R., 337–338, 382
Rebel, T. P., 348, 382
Rebouças-Spieker, R., 292, 325
Redford, K., 12, 100
Reed, C. A., 11, 100, 113, 135–136, 139, 146, 150
Reed, P., 585, 595
Reese, A. M., 280, 325, 528, 542, 600
Reeves, R. B., 550, 600
Regal, P. J., 100
Reible, D. D., 575, 578, 601
Reid, J., 525, 529, 574, 602
Reid, W. H., 34, 35, 100, 116, 117
Remington, C. L., 155, 156, 226

Rettenmeyer, C. W., 226
Rewcastle, S. C., 257, 272
Reynolds, H. C., 100, 119
Rhodin, A. G. J., 354, 382, 432, 439, 533, 551, 596–597
Richardson, J. I., 334, 341, 370, 382–383, 400, 402, 405–406, 412, 427, 431–433, 436, 552, 584, 597
Richmond, N. D., 39, 44, 55, 67, 82, 129, 134, 145, 192, 193, 199, 221, 366, 382, 433, 438, 532, 601
Ricklefs, R. E., 433, 437, 531, 601
Ridley, H. N., 100, 146, 152
Ridley, M., 293–295, 312, 325
Riemer, W. J., 286, 325
Rieppel, O., 100, 123, 292, 325
Riley, J., 38, 100, 306, 325, 534, 601
Rimblot, F., 552, 601
Risley, P. L., 347, 354–355, 357–359, 382, 415, 433, 438, 527, 583, 601
Rivero, J. A., 110, 139
Rivers, G. M., 293, 326
Roberson, J. B., 434, 438
Robertson, I. A. D., 508, 517, 522
Robinson, D. C., 249, 272
Robinson, M. D., 361, 377, 505, 516, 522
Robinson, M. H., 64, 66, 100, 159, 226
Robinson, St. J., 281, 326
Robison, W. G., Jr., 105, 145
Roche, E., 349, 373
Rodda, G. H., 10, 100, 116
Roe, J. H., 403, 425, 438
Roecker, R. M., 284, 320
Rogotzkie, R. A., 361, 363, 372
Rohlf, F. J., 364, 383
Rokosky, E. J., 433, 438
Romer, A. S., 293, 325
Rose, C. W., 561, 601
Rose, D. A., 561, 594
Rose, W., 35, 54, 100, 127, 138, 292, 326
Rosen, P. C., 352, 365, 367, 384, 397, 400, 404, 416–417, 425, 434, 527, 585, 591, 603
Rosenberg, H. I., 25, 32, 56, 80, 100, 127, 135, 138, 251, 272
Rosler, H., 101, 138
Ross, C. A., 335, 371
Ross, F. D., 28, 101

AUTHOR INDEX

Sneddon, I., 164, 180, 222
Snedigar, R., 433, 438
Snell, H. L., 531, 559, 564–566, 568, 581, 602–603
Snow, J. E., 383, 433, 436, 583, 602
Snyder, R. C., 248, 272
Soderberg, P. S., 104, 144, 149–150
Soini, P., 533, 597
Sokal, R. R., 364, 383
Solomon, S. E., 525–526, 528, 529, 574, 588, 602
Somero, G. N., 550, 605
Somma, C. A., 509, 514, 517, 522
Sorenson, M. W., 15, 99, 116, 131, 140
Spawls, S., 104, 145
Speck, F. G., 292, 327
Spellerberg, I. F., 340, 342–343, 345, 347, 349, 356, 383
Spoczynska, J. O. I., 433, 437
Spoecker, P. D., 339, 383
Spotila, J. R., 353, 380, 402–403, 431, 433, 552–553, 585, 597, 602
Spurway, H., 429, 438
Stamps, J. A., 34–35, 58, 68, 104, 209, 227
Stancyk, S. E., 8, 10–11, 104, 404, 434, 436, 557, 602
Standora, E. A., 353, 380, 402–403, 431, 433, 552–553, 585, 597, 602
Stanley, C., 293, 327
Stanton, M. A., 280, 327, 335, 371, 533, 540, 542–543, 558–559, 562–563, 602
Steadman, D. W., 67, 104
Stearns, S. C., 443, 446, 471, 474, 476–477, 487–488, 490–491, 497, 499, 509
Stebbins, R. C., 18, 95, 104, 116, 133, 182, 227, 230, 339, 383, 509, 515, 522
Stemmler-Gyger, O., 37, 104, 124, 143, 152
Stemmler-Morath, C., 285, 327
Sternburg, J. G., 157, 224, 227, 228
Sternfeld, R., 192, 203, 228
Stevens, R. A., 74, 145
Steward, J. W., 182, 228, 231
Stewart, G. L., 554, 578, 603
Stewart, G. R., 72, 509, 519–520, 522
Stewart, J. R., 454, 509, 512, 522, 532, 602
Stewart, M. M., 305, 327
Stewart, P. A., 548–550, 602
Stickel, L. F., 341, 383, 405, 433

Stiles, F. G., 156, 157, 219
Stille, W. T., 104, 142
Stimson, A. F., 38, 100, 306, 325, 534, 601
Stoneburner, D. L., 341, 383
Storer, T. I., 60, 85, 104, 145, 434, 437
Storm, R. M., 252, 271
Stradling, D. J., 173, 174, 228
Strasser, F. D., 104, 139
Strathmann, M. F., 307, 327
Strathmann, R. R., 307, 327
Strauss, R. E., 451, 502
Strecker, J. K., 284, 327
Stromsten, F. A., 417, 434
Stroud, R. K., 342, 379
Stuart, G. R., 434, 434, 438
Stuart, L. C., 105, 146
Stubbs, D., 340, 383, 404, 434, 439
Stull, O. G., 105, 151
Stumpel, A. H. P., 105, 149
Subba Rao, M. V., 533, 535, 602
Sutherland, S. K., 307, 327
Sutton, G. M., 13, 105
Sweeney, R. C. H., 10, 20, 39, 51, 105, 120–121, 132, 144–152, 287–288, 327
Sweet, S. S., 18, 23, 46, 48, 68, 105, 124, 194, 197, 199, 228
Swindell, D., 10, 44, 70, 113, 122
Swingland, I. R., 340, 355–356, 358–360, 365, 367, 374, 383, 396, 400–401, 404, 419–420, 434, 439, 581, 584, 602
Switak, K. H., 18, 105, 124, 285, 327

Taigen, T. L., 64, 105, 305, 327, 532, 556, 559, 562–564, 566, 568, 598
Takenaka, S., 509, 516, 522
Talbert, O. R., Jr., 404, 434, 436
Tallamy, D. W., 305, 327
Tanaka, R., 343, 346, 384
Tanner, W. W., 9, 21, 74, 89, 105, 116, 139–140, 145, 284, 327
Tardent, P., 434, 438
Tasnim, R., 11, 16, 89–90, 149
Taylor, E. H., 105, 137, 144–148, 152, 182, 228, 232, 233, 283–284, 286–287, 297, 303, 327, 361, 384
Taylor, J. A., 509, 516, 522
Taylor, S. A., 539–540, 554, 558–559, 575, 577–578, 588, 602–603
Taylor, W. P., 51, 105, 115–122

Telford, S. R., Jr., 105, 119, 144, 147, 284, 328, 509, 513, 516, 522
Terhune, E. C., 163, 170, 228
Test, F. H., 105, 144–146
Tevis, L. P., Jr., 22, 60, 104–105, 139–140, 142, 148
Thacker, J. L., 417, 434
Thoen, C., 21, 72, 117, 445, 501
Thomas, R., 32, 52, 105, 110, 139, 144, 149, 151
Thompson, J., 532, 603
Thompson, M. B., 526, 538, 543–544, 551, 556–557, 564, 566, 568, 574–576, 603
Thompson, N. B., 404–406, 434
Thomsen, L., 199, 228
Thorne, S. C., 8, 105, 122
Thornhill, G. M., 419, 434
Thornhill, R., 160, 228
Threlkeld, S. T., 47, 110
Throckmorton, G. S., 29, 67, 105, 137
Tilley, S. G., 305, 328, 443–447, 450–451, 456–461, 463, 494–495, 498, 510, 514, 516–517, 522
Timken, R. L., 338, 355–356, 384, 434, 437
Tinbergen, N., 4, 105
Tinkle, D. W., 21, 95, 106, 116–117, 239, 250, 265, 268, 272, 283, 301, 304, 308–312, 328, 333, 336, 339, 341–342, 344–352, 354–356, 359–370, 374, 377, 380, 384, 395–398, 400–401, 404, 415–417, 419, 425, 431, 434, 436–438, 443–447, 449–453, 456–461, 463, 474–477, 494–495, 498–499, 501, 509–511, 514–517, 519, 521–522, 527, 583–585, 590–591, 603
Tognetti, K. P., 403, 418, 423, 436
Tokarz, R. R., 282, 328
Tokunaga, S., 551, 603
Tollestrup, K., 30, 52, 106, 128, 140
Toner, G. C., 583, 603
Tonge, S., 106, 115
Toro, B., 543, 596
Townsend, C. R., 62, 106
Toyama, M., 284, 328
Tracy, C. R., 50, 77, 139, 283, 318, 531, 535, 546, 554–556, 559, 563–566, 568, 598, 602–603
Trauth, S. E., 529, 583, 603
Trebbau, P., 9, 11, 25, 27, 99, 112–113, 134–135, 396, 406, 432
Trendall, J. T., 472, 510
Tribe, M., 531, 592
Trillmich, K., 283, 328
Trivers, R. L., 210, 228, 277, 312, 328
Trotter, J. G., 429, 438
Trotter, M. W., 429, 438
Trotter, T. H., 429, 438
Trowbridge, A. H., 106, 120, 141, 151
Troyer, K., 582, 603
Trueb, L., 57, 79
Tryon, B. W., 20, 106, 119, 123–124, 146, 150, 277, 281, 287, 299, 328
Tschambers, B., 106, 123
Tsui, H. W., 357–358, 379, 430, 439
Turner, F. B., 242, 272, 335–336, 339, 341–342, 345–347, 349, 351, 355–356, 361–362, 364, 366–368, 379–380, 384, 405, 434, 438, 448, 510
Turner, J. R. G., 156–159, 161, 170, 184, 219, 227–228
Turner, O., 534, 601
Tuttle, M. D., 11, 106, 116
Tweedie, M. W. F., 106, 146, 167, 182, 202, 203, 228, 233, 249, 272, 287–288, 297, 328
Tyler, E. D., 361, 363, 370, 501, 514, 521
Tyler, M. J., 293, 319
Tyler, W., 340, 383

Uéno, S.-I., 182, 225, 232
Ulrich, G. F., 433, 436
Ulrich, J. F., 341, 385
Underwood, G., 38, 106, 143, 295–296, 328
Urich, F. W., 95, 145–146, 148
Uzzell, T. M., Jr., 106, 142

Vadasz, C., 19, 106
Vagvolgyi, A., 210, 224
Valdez, R., 11, 106, 116
Valenciennes, A., 285, 328
Valverde, J. A., 7, 11, 106, 114, 117
van Bavel, C. H. M., 575, 603
van Berkum, F., 7, 35, 106
Van Denburgh, F., 106, 116, 128
Van Devender, R. W., 336, 339, 342, 345, 347, 349, 351, 356, 362, 364, 384, 510, 514, 522, 585, 603
Van Devender, T. R., 50, 106, 140, 148, 284, 328, 535, 603

AUTHOR INDEX

Van Devender, W., 284, 328
Van Loben Sels, R. C., 362, 365, 367, 374, 385, 395–397, 400, 404, 423, 425, 510–511, 515–516, 522, 532, 585, 588, 590
Van Mater, J., 106, 122, 137
Van Mierop, L. H. S., 285, 289–290, 300–301, 303, 328
Vane-Wright, R. I., 159, 160, 163, 228
Vanerhaege, M., 106, 123
Vangilder, L. D., 284, 319
Vansleb, F., 280, 328
Vanzolini, P. E., 39, 106, 140, 148, 149, 292, 325, 434, 439
Vasconcellos-Neto, J., 163, 228
Vasconcellos, J. M. C., 60, 102
Vaughn, T. A., 11, 106, 115
Vaz-Ferreira, R., 543, 603
Veeraraghavan, K., 531, 597
Veith, G. M., 529, 591, 601
Venning, F. E. W., 106, 115, 149
Vermeij, G. J., 5, 11, 106
Vestjens, W. J. M., 434, 439
Vetter, R. S., 106, 138
Vial, J. L., 175, 185, 227, 230, 454, 512, 522
Vigal, C. R., 503, 516, 521
Villa, J., 106, 145, 543, 596
Villiers, A., 182, 228, 233
Vinegar, A., 283, 285–286, 289–291, 301–302, 322, 328, 534, 545–546, 604
Vinegar, M. B., 242, 272, 342, 345, 347, 349, 356, 362, 364, 385, 475, 510, 515, 522
Vinson, J. M., 34, 106, 138, 143, 152
Visser, J., 39, 106, 151, 287, 328
Vitt, L. J., 43, 50, 56, 64, 77, 106, 121, 127, 140, 148, 149, 206, 220, 239, 241, 243, 248–255, 257, 261, 263–264, 266, 269, 272–273, 284, 319, 328, 355, 356, 361–362, 364, 385, 445–449, 467, 471, 483, 495, 502, 510, 512–515, 517–522
Voeltzkow, A., 528, 604
Vogt, R. C., 340, 353, 371, 385, 395, 402, 423, 431, 434, 437, 543, 551–553, 572, 584, 589, 596, 604
Volsøe, H., 35, 102, 140, 249, 272
von Brand, T., 527, 538, 575, 596
Voous, K., 6, 10, 106, 118, 120–121
Voris, H. K., 511, 521–522
Vrba, E. S., 61, 106

Wade, E. S., 345, 348, 385
Wagner, E. P., 285, 328–329, 551, 604
Wahlquist, H., 435, 437
Waitkuwait, W. E., 280, 329
Wake, D. B., 4, 16, 70, 91, 237, 273
Wake, M. H., 8, 72
Waldbauer, G. P., 157, 224, 227–228
Walker, J. M., 502, 511, 518, 521–522
Wall, F., 7–8, 10, 15, 18, 106–109, 114–115, 118–124, 127, 136–137, 143–152, 229, 285–287, 297, 329
Wallace, A. R., 155, 164, 174, 175, 180, 184, 229
Wallace, R. L., 78, 117, 119, 503, 521
Walls, G. L., 179, 204, 229
Walsh, P. J., 550, 604
Walsh, T., 285, 329
Walters, V., 40, 86, 133, 151, 214, 223
Wang, B., 283, 329
Ward, F. P., 341, 385
Warren, E., 109, 115
Watkins, I. F., 283, 300, 320
Watkins, J. F., II, 38, 109, 151
Waytialingham, S., 280, 329
Weale, J. P. M., 155, 164, 191, 193, 229
Weary, G. G., 342, 385
Weaver, W. G., 370, 403, 422
Webb, D. R., 539, 604
Webb, G. J. W., 109, 118, 119, 281, 301, 329, 528, 533, 540–545, 551, 556–557, 562–563, 583–585, 604
Webb, R. G., 19, 146, 354, 356, 359–361, 378, 385, 435, 437, 439
Webster, T. P., 109, 139, 339, 385
Wedepohl, F. H., 526, 592
Wehekind, L., 10, 111, 113
Weingarner, C. E., 111, 113
Weinstein, S. A., 48, 95
Weldon, P. J., 15, 46, 109, 131
Wellins, D. J., 552, 591
Wellman, J., 109, 118
Wells, R., 534, 604
Wemmer, C., 57, 109
Werler, J. E., 109, 123, 142, 144, 283, 329
Werner, D. I., 283, 329
Werner, F., 193, 204, 229

Werner, Y. L., 33, 52, 109, 129, 145, 146, 147, 148, 194, 199, 204, 229, 241, 243, 261, 273, 530, 604
Werren, J. H., 312, 329
Werth, R. J., 109, 139
West, E. S., 540, 604
Wetmore, A., 111, 121
Wever, E. G., 16, 110
Wharton, C. H., 511, 521–522
Whillans, T. H., 361, 385
Whitaker, A. H., 50, 51, 55–66, 110, 138, 141, 534, 562, 604
Whitaker, R., 280–281, 301, 329, 533, 543, 557, 605
Whitaker, Z., 280–281, 301, 329, 533, 543, 557, 605
White, J. B., 338, 355, 357–361, 386, 435, 436
White, D. R., 511, 519, 522
White, R. S., 562, 596
White, S. R., 110, 137
Whitehead, J., 106, 150
Whitham, R., 8, 110, 112
Whiting, A. M., 38, 110
Whitmore, C. P., 402, 431, 552, 584, 592, 597
Wickler, W., 63, 65, 110, 159, 160, 161, 163, 173, 183, 229
Wiebe, H. H., 562, 605
Wiens, D., 161, 229
Wierenga, P. J., 539, 605
Wiewandt, T. A., 283, 289, 306, 308, 329
Wiklund, C., 63, 80
Wilbur, H. M., 334, 336–337, 340, 344–345, 347–348, 351–354, 356, 359, 361, 366, 386, 389, 397–399, 403–405, 411, 416–417, 435, 436, 443–447, 450–451, 456–461, 463, 494–495, 498, 510–511, 514, 516–517, 522
Wilcox, L. R., 417, 435
Wiley, E. O., 24, 110
Wilhoft, D. C., 402, 435, 532, 540, 543–544, 552–553, 584, 594, 605
Will, J. M., 404, 434, 436
Williams, E. C., 344, 386
Williams, E. E., 51, 83, 110, 139–140, 339, 379, 404, 430, 437–439
Williams, G. C., 46, 110, 308–309, 329
Williams, K. L., 39, 101, 129, 134, 148, 184, 185, 229, 423, 437
Williams, S. C., 85, 115
Williams, T. H., 417, 435
Williamson, G. K., 341, 383
Williamson, K. L., 158, 219
Williamson, M. A., 110, 123
Willis, L., 47, 110
Wilson, D. E., 57, 109
Wilson, E. O., 60, 62, 97, 110
Wilson, L. D., 110, 144
Wilson, V. J., 110, 147
Winch, J. M., 38, 100, 306, 325, 534, 601
Windecker, W., 157, 229
Wirklund, C., 156–157, 224, 229
Wolda, H., 110, 116
Wolfe, G. W., 7, 79, 121
Woodall, P. F., 526, 574, 605
Woodbury, A. M., 341–342, 386, 435, 438
Woodin, W. H., 43, 110, 145, 150
Woodland, W. N. F., 244, 246, 273
Woodward, M. W., 556, 591
Woolcott, W. S., 511, 519, 522
Woolfenden, G. E., 81, 113
Woolley, H. P., 345, 349, 375, 475, 503, 515, 521
Worrell, E., 280, 329
Wray, G. O., 286, 329
Wright, A. A., 110, 131, 143–149, 152
Wright, P., 7, 110
Wright, S. J., 357–358, 379
Wunder, C. C., 544, 546, 591
Wunderle, J. M., 110, 116
Wynn, A. H., 347–348, 386

Yadav, R. N., 285, 329
Yancey, P. H., 550, 605
Yin, F-Y., 296, 323
Yntema, C. L., 353, 362, 386, 402, 435, 436, 527, 544, 546, 551–553, 597, 605
Young, J. D., 526, 605

Zaborski, P., 552–553, 605
Zappalorti, R. T., 534, 589
Zaret, T. M., 312–313, 325

AUTHOR INDEX

Zarrow, M. X., 546, 605
Zhao, E., 36, 87
Zietz, F. R., 251, 273
Zingg, A., 110, 145
Zinner, H., 21, 29, 110, 134, 137

Zovickian, W. H., 435, 438
Zug, G. R., 110, 136, 347–350, 353, 382, 386
Zweifel, R. G., 26, 55, 97, 110, 184, 185, 229, 241, 273, 352, 364, 386, 545–546, 605

Subject Index

Ablepharus, 117, 141
Abronia, 115, 137
Acanthodactylus, 21, 117, 140, 213
Acanthophis, 149, 202, 213, 485, 520
Acid/base balance
    equations, 548
    factors affecting, 548–550
    imidazolium, 550
    ions, 548–550
    metabolic effects, 550
    physical/physiological variables, 549
    physiological controls, 549–550
    proteins, 549–550
    thermal dependence, 549–550
Acontias, 117, 141, 266
Acrochordidae, 119, 142, 455, 518
Acrochordus, 119, 142, 518
Adaptation, 24
Aeluroscalabotes, 249, 260
Aerial surveys, 345
Africa, 5–6
Afroedura, 115
Agama, 6, 21, 29, 114, 132, 134, 136–137, 241, 243, 251–252, 258, 512
Agamidae, 28–31, 52, 59, 114, 127, 130, 136–137, 245–246, 257–259, 282, 294, 454–455, 465, 473, 486, 492, 512
Agamodon, 37, 127, 135
Agamura, 138
Age; *see also main entries* Life history traits; Life history methods
    age-specific reproduction and survival, 240, 334, 353–356, 444, 454–455, 476–477, 498, 500
    body size/length, 334, 348
    bone rings, 347–350, 398
    distribution, 334–336, 344–353, 405
    estimating, 347–350
    fecundity, 353–368, 498
    first reproduction. *See main entry* Life history traits, reproductive maturity
    growth, 347–350
    life tables. *See main entry* Life history traits
    longevity, 333, 335, 405
    mark-recapture, 349–350
    maturity. *See main entry* Life history traits
    mortality, 333–336, 345–353, 404–405
    reproductive senescence, 353, 356, 498
    shell annuli, 347–349
    skeletochronology, 347–350, 398
    survivorship, 333–336, 345–353, 404–405, 477
    tetracycline, 348
Aggression, 352
Agkistrodon, 10, 17, 44, 47, 50, 122, 124, 127, 131, 151, 155, 214, 483–484, 521
Ahaetulla, 50, 123, 125, 144
Ailuronyx, 115
Aipysurus, 43
Albumen. *See main entries* Eggs and egg shells; Water

SUBJECT INDEX

Allantoic sac, 531
Alligator, 9, 113, 135, 280, 299–300, 302–303, 305, 335, 528, 533, 546, 553, 558
Alligatoridae, 113, 135
Alsophis, 144
Alsophylax, 138
Alternative mating strategies, 209–210
Amblyodipsas, 119, 144
Amblyrhynchus, 8, 116, 139, 249, 256, 283, 300
[*Ambystoma*], 9
Ameiva, 8, 50, 118, 141, 403, 517–518
Amphibians, 8–9, 39, 293, 304–305, 311–315
Amphibolurus, 29, 49, 67, 114, 137, 258, 464–465, 512, 531
Amphiesma, 144, 286
Amphisbaena, 37, 56, 114, 130, 136, 245, 252
Amphisbaenia, 6, 10–13, 37, 53, 56, 58, 114, 136, 265–266, 454
Amphisbaenidae, 114, 130, 136
Amplorhinus, 144
Analysis of covariance. *See main entry* Statistical analyses
Ancylocranium, 114
Anelytropsis, 35, 138
Anguidae, 35–36, 52, 115, 128, 137, 283, 296, 454–455, 465, 486, 492, 512
[*Anguilla*], 8
Anguis, 115, 137, 201, 266–267, 461, 464–465, 512
Aniliidae, 38–40, 143, 181–182
Anilius, 40, 143, 190, 230, 231
Anisolepis, 256
Anniella, 266
Anniellidae, 454
Annuli. *See main entry* Turtles, shell
Anolis, 8, 9, 12, 21, 33, 49, 51, 55, 68, 116, 126, 139, 174, 208, 210, 212, 239, 242, 249–250, 254–257, 260–261, 346, 450, 464–465, 473, 513–514, 565
[*Antechinus*], 239, 253
[*Anthia*], 206–207
Antillophis, 17, 144

Antipredator mechanisms; *see also main entries* Caudal autotomy; Mimicry; Parental care
age effects. *See* ontogeny
aggression, 16, 23, 35, 38, 40, 56, 64, 131
alarm calls, 8, 28, 212
anachronisms, 60–61, 65
aposematic coloration, 25, 36–37, 39–40, 42–43, 48, 63–64, 133, 175–178
appendage grasping, 54, 127
aspect diversity, 55
autohemorrhage. *See* blood squirting
ball forming, 22, 38, 51, 128
basic concepts and theories, 3–5, 7, 11–12, 14, 16–17, 24, 52–53, 60–63
biting, 20, 26, 28–31, 34–36, 40–41, 43, 45, 132
blood squirting, 20, 30, 40, 133
bluffs and threats, 52–53, 58, 132, 161, 173
body elevation, 31, 127, 131
body size, 307, 309, 315
body temperature, 15, 20–21
burrowing, 37, 207
camouflage. *See* crypsis
caudal autotomy. *See main entry* Caudal autotomy
cloacal discharge/defecation, 34, 36, 38–42, 45, 56, 127
coiling, 40–42, 44–45, 51, 131, 191–193, 196–197, 199, 206
concealing coloration. *See* crypsis
context, 15–16, 20, 22, 28, 45, 63
constriction, 132
convergence, 59–60
correlation with coloration, 49, 65
correlation with metabolism, 30, 50
countershading, 176
crypsis, 28, 31, 34, 40, 42, 45, 48–50, 57–58, 62–64, 124, 159, 162, 191, 205
cue removal, 54–55
death feigning, 16, 20–22, 25, 28, 35–36, 38, 40–41, 54–55, 62, 125, 161, 173
deimatic displays. *See* bluffs and threats
differences from birds and mammals, 62

Brackets indicate non-reptilian genera.

SUBJECT INDEX

disgorge meal, 43, 54, 133
diversion of attack. *See* tail display/lashing
evenomation. See under main entry Venom
evolution, 26–27, 33–34, 46–48, 55, 57, 58–61, 64, 67–69
eye marks, 172–173
fatigue, 21
faceoff/frontal displays, 128
flash colors, 206, 252
flight distance, 21
fragile skin. *See* skin tearing
future research, 65–69
gaping, 25–26, 28, 34, 44, 132
generalizations, 63–65
genetics, 16–19
geographic variation, 20, 22–24, 30, 45, 48–49, 55, 68
gliding/leaping/parachuting, 29, 32, 35, 39, 51, 57
gravidity, 21
habits and habitat, 38
habitat shift, 29–30, 36, 50, 68
habituation, 18, 20
head hiding, 42, 128, 196
head triangulation, 186, 193–194, 198–200
hemipenal eversion, 133
hierarchy, 63
hissing. *See* sound production
"hooding." *See* neck expansion
immobility, 26, 28–30, 42, 45, 124–125
inaccessibility, 35–36, 50, 126
inflation, 28, 30, 35–36, 52, 129, 131, 191, 193, 196, 208, 215
inoffensive, 125,
intraspecific variation, 14–24, 41, 68
learning, 17–18
lip flair, 132
locomotor escape, 26, 28, 31, 35–36, 41–42, 50–52, 57–58, 125–126, 177, 210–212
metabolic correlates, 30, 50, 62, 64, 134
methods, 65–67
mimicry. *See main entry* Mimicry
miscarriage, 54
misinterpretation, 68

morphological adjuncts, 24, 29–30, 56, 133–134
musk secretions, 17, 25–26, 28
neck expansion, 17, 38–39, 41–42, 128–129, 204–205, 208
neonate reptiles, 19, 40, 122–124
novel and erratic behavior, 55, 58
noxious flesh, 43, 56, 127
offensive defense, 56
ontogeny, 16–19, 28, 40, 66, 123, 177, 206–208, 212, 256, 259, 260–261
optimality, 62–63
phylogenetic patterns, 24, 48, 58–60, 68
primitive patterns, 57
problems, 65
protean behavior, 161
rattling. *See main entry* Rattlesnakes
retreat sites, 14, 50, 126
rigid postures, 38, 54
running on water, 51, 59
saltation, 33
scratching, 129
sexual differences, 20, 22, 68
shell withdrawal, 21, 25–27, 128
skin tearing, 32, 51–52, 127
social factors, 16, 18
social responses, 29, 60, 134
sound production, 15, 17–18, 26, 28, 32–34, 36, 39, 40, 42, 44, 57, 58, 69, 126, 191–193, 198–201, 252
"spitting" of venom, 39, 41, 132
startle effects, 55
systematic variation, 24–48
tail autotomy. *See main entry* Caudal autotomy
tail display/lashing. *See main entry* Tails
tail secretions, 20, 32–33, 56, 251
tameness, 12, 18, 23
taxonomic variation, 24–48
thanatosis. *See* death feigning
theory. *See* basic concepts and theories
thermal dependence. *See main entry* Temperature, body
tongue extension, 34, 129
vocalization, see sound production
versus injury frequency, 23
venom. *See main entry* Venom
wariness, 22

weapon automimicry, 208–209
"wheel," 51
wind movements, 124
writhing, 34–36, 40, 42, 130–131, 203
Aparallactus, 119, 144, 234
[*Apiformis*], 155
Aplopeltura, 144
Aporosaura, 140, 464–465, 474, 516
Apostolepis, 190, 231
Aprasia, 117
Aptycholaemus, 256–257
Aragonite, 525–526, 529
Argyrogena, 144
Aristelliger, 32, 51, 127, 138
Arizona, 119, 519
Arrhyton, 144
Arthropods. *See main entry* Invertebrates
Aspidelaps, 41, 121, 149, 234
Aspidites, 143, 285, 289, 303
[*Athene*], 199
Atheris, 44, 151
Atractaspidae, 38, 41, 119, 143
Atractaspis, 6, 41, 119, 143
Atractus, 119, 144, 186, 230–231
Atretic follicles, 360
Austrelaps, 149, 483, 520
Autarchoglossan lizards, 34–37
Autotomy. *See main entry* Caudal autotomy
Azemiops, 44, 151, 232

Bachia, 141
Bailey's triple-catch, 343–345
Baiting. *See main entry* Capture methods
Barisia, 461–462, 464–465, 512
Basiliscus, 51, 59, 116, 139, 248–249, 257, 261, 463–465, 514
Batagur, 391, 394, 409, 436
Batesian mimicry. *See main entry* Mimicry
Beak marks. *See main entry* Injuries
Bedriagaia, 140
Behavior. *See main entry* Antipredator mechanisms
Bipedidae, 114
Bipes, 114, 253
Birds, 6, 10, 13, 18, 25, 31, 34, 37, 39, 52–53, 62, 112, 156–157, 163, 165–167, 171, 173, 176, 179–181, 183–184, 188–190, 196, 199, 204, 211, 214–215, 239, 283, 312, 403, 556

Bitia, 233
Bitis, 6, 8–9, 12, 21, 122, 151–152, 191–192
Blanus, 37, 114, 131, 136
Blood, 549
Blythia, 144
Boa, 17, 40, 119, 143
Body size; *see also main entries* Antipredator mechanisms; Life history traits
  mimicry, 166–167, 206, 209–210
  parental care, 307, 309, 315
Boidae, 38, 40, 119, 123, 143, 181–182, 206, 285–286, 294, 307, 309, 315
Boiga, 119, 143, 196–197, 203, 232–233
Bolyeriidae, 143
[*Bombyx*], 172
Bone rings. *See main entry* Age
Booids, 40
Bothrops, 44, 47, 50, 56, 122, 128, 132, 152, 173, 186, 199, 201, 212, 292
Bouin's fixative, 357
Boulengerina, 41, 149
Boyleria, 143
Brachylophus, 283, 300
Bradypodion, 115
Branding. *See main entry* Marking methods
Brookesia, 29, 137
[*Bufo*], 9
Bungarus, 16, 39, 121, 149, 181, 203, 232–233, 287, 297, 299–300
Bunopus, 138
[*Buteo*], 6
[*Butorides*], 204
Butterflies. *See main entry* Invertebrates

Cacophis, 149, 482–483, 520
Caecilians, 8, 112
Caenophidia, 40–44, 143–152
Caiman, 16, 18, 28, 113, 135, 280, 533, 558
Calabaria, 37, 128, 143
Calamaria, 119, 144, 232–233
Calcite, 528–530
Calcium, 527, 529
Calcium carbonate, 528–529
Calconite, 525–526
[*Caligo*], 173
Callagur, 354, 391, 436
Calliophis, 149, 181, 203, 232–233, 287
Callisaurus, 11, 22, 53, 116, 139, 211, 212, 464–465, 514, 565, 568

SUBJECT INDEX

Callopistes, 7, 9, 13, 35, 56, 141
Calloselasma, 214, 288
Calotes, 52, 114, 137, 464–465, 473, 512
Camouflage. *See main entries* Antipredator mechanisms, crypsis; Mimicry
Candoia, 143, 202
[*Canis*], 57, 403
Cantoria, 232–233
Capture methods, 336–337, 344, 365
　capture bias, 336–338
　lizards and snakes, 339–340
　turtles, 337–339, 365
Carbon dioxide. *See main entries* Acid/base balance; Respiratory gases and embryos
Carbonic acid. *See main entry* Acid/base balance
Cardenolides, 158
Caretta, 112, 341, 362–363, 365–367, 391, 398, 400, 403–405, 436, 538, 544, 552, 577
Carphodactylus, 259
Casarea, 143
[*Casmerodius*], 204
Caterpillars. *See main entry* Invertebrates
Caudal autotomy, 31, 34, 37, 58; *see also main entry* Tails
　age, 240–242
　ancestral state. *See* evolutionary trends
　autotomy in nature, 239–243, 267
　body size, 256, 260–261
　brightly colored tails, 238, 252–254, 263–265, 267
　constraints, 247
　correlations, 242–243, 255–260, 262–263
　costs and benefits, 237, 243, 246–253, 255–259, 261–262
　ease of autotomy, 244–247, 253–255, 259–260
　"economy of autotomy," 260, 263
　effects on behavior, 255
　evidence of effectiveness, 238–239, 242, 248, 267
　evolutionary trends, 237, 244–246, 258–259
　experimental studies, 239, 242, 248, 254–255, 267
　frequency, 239–242
　future research, 267
　growth, 250, 265
　hibernation survival, 250
　histology and anatomy, 237–238, 244
　interspecific variation, 241–242, 262–263
　intravertebral and intervertebral, 244–246, 253, 255–259
　locomotor effects, 248–249, 255–259, 266–267
　loss of ability, 244–246, 255–258
　mechanisms, 244
　neurological factors, 245, 261–263
　nonpredatory, 241, 251
　ontogenetic loss, 256, 259, 260–261
　phylogenetic patterns, 31, 34, 37, 58–59, 237, 244, 259
　postautotomy behavioral changes, 255
　postautotomy tail movements, 254–255
　predation intensity, 206, 239–243
　predator inefficiency, 241–243
　re-evolution, 258–259
　reproductive capacity, 250, 264–266
　restriction to caudal base, 259–260
　short-term changes, 261–262
　snakes, 189, 259, 265–266
　social status, 250
　strategy, 238
　survivorship, 242, 267
　tail size, 253
　taxonomic distribution. *See* phylogenetic patterns
　temperature effects, 261
　theory, 237–238
　threshold, 261–263, 267
　unpalatable tails, 256
Caudal luring, 47–48, 212 214
Caudal regeneration, 244, 248, 250, 256, 265–267
Causus, 44, 46, 122, 152, 155, 191–192, 288
Celestes, 512
Cemophora, 9, 119, 144, 230, 286, 295, 305
Cerastes, 44, 48, 152, 191, 193, 213, 538
Cerberus, 144, 519
Cercaspis, 144, 232
Chalcides, 117, 141, 350
Chamaeleo, 6, 115, 122, 137, 462–465, 473–474, 512, 531
Chamaeleolis, 249, 257

Chamaeleonidae, 28–31, 115, 122, 137, 245, 257–258, 294, 454–455, 465, 512, 535
Chamaelinorops, 257
Charina, 38, 54, 128, 143, 252
Chelidae, 112, 134, 393, 399, 412, 439, 532
Chelodina, 17, 18, 127, 134, 354, 393, 439
Chelonia, 112, 362–363, 365–367, 391, 397–398, 400–401, 404–405, 408, 416, 418–419, 436, 538, 544, 552, 576–577
Cheloniidae, 112, 361, 391, 399, 412, 436, 525–526, 540–541, 551–553, 576
Chelus, 25, 27, 134, 393, 439
Chelydra, 26, 56, 112, 122, 131–132, 134, 337, 341, 347, 354, 362, 367, 391, 402–404, 436, 526, 537, 538, 544, 546, 552–553, 559–561, 564, 566, 568–569, 578–582
Chelydridae, 112, 122, 133–134, 391, 399, 412, 436, 525–526, 551–552
Chersina, 400
Chile, 7, 60
Chilomeniscus, 144, 230
Chilorhinophis, 144
Chinemys, 135
Chionactis, 22, 144, 230
Chirindia, 114
Chironius, 144
Chitra, 135
Chlamydosaurus, 137
Chondrodactylus, 115, 205, 252, 254, 260
Carphophis, 119, 483, 519
Chondropython, 143, 285, 289
Chorioallantois, 550
Chromosomes, 402
Chrysemys, 112, 337, 345, 351, 356, 358, 360, 363, 365–366, 368, 391, 397, 399–400, 403–405, 416–417, 419, 436, 538, 543, 546, 552–553, 566, 568, 570–573
Chrysopelia, 39, 51, 52, 57, 119, 123, 144, 232
[*Circaetus*], 6
Claudius, 25, 27, 128, 131–132, 134, 392, 402, 437
Clelia, 144, 231
Clemmys, 135, 337, 391, 404, 412, 437, 551

Clutch size and number. *See main entries* Life history methods; Life history traits
Cnemidophorus, 9, 14, 16–18, 22–23, 50, 55, 66, 118, 134, 141–142, 242, 248, 339, 342, 463–465, 474, 518
Coleonyx, 115, 138, 205–206, 239, 250–252, 254–255, 261, 265–266
Colopus, 115, 260
Color vision. *See main entry* Senses
Coloration; *see also main entries* Antipredator mechanisms; Caudal autotomy; Coral-snake mimicry; Mimicry; Senses; Tails; Thermal balance
Coluber, 11, 23, 41, 53, 56, 119, 123, 144, 197–198, 200, 231–232, 482–483, 519, 531, 534, 538, 566, 568, 570, 571
Colubridae, 40–41, 119–121, 123, 128, 144–149, 164–165, 167, 181–182, 286–287, 295–296, 307, 343, 454–455, 483, 485–486, 493, 519–520
Combat, 399
Common garden studies, 500
Comparative methods, 24, 50, 66–69, 294–295, 389–390, 393, 443, 446, 450, 485–487, 498–500
Competition, 416, 499
Conduction. *See main entry* Thermal balance
Coniophanes, 144, 205
Conolophus, 139, 256, 283, 300, 531, 559, 566, 568
Conophis, 123, 144
Conopsis, 119, 133
Conservation, 584–585
Constraints. *See main entry* Life history traits
Convection. *See main entry* Thermal balance
Cophosaurus, 29, 53, 116, 130, 139, 211–212, 248, 253, 350, 464–465, 514
Cophotis, 137
Copulation, 209
Corallus, 143
Coral snakes, 5, 15, 35, 42–43, 53–54
Coral-snake mimicry, 155, 174–191, 202
  aposematic coloration, 133, 183–187, 203
  concordant geographic patterns, 174, 183–187, 191–192
  crypsis versus aposematism, 175–178

SUBJECT INDEX

dual mimics, 185–186
fossoriality, 179
frequency models and mimics, 180–183
geographic patterns, 169, 181–184, 230–234
innate avoidance, 176, 179, 187–191
Mertensian mimicry, 183
Müllerian mimicry, 183
nocturnality versus diurnality, 179
paradox of deadly model, 183
predators, 178–180
senses of predators, 178–180, 184, 189–190
unpalatability, 183
Cordylidae, 35, 113, 115, 136, 138, 294, 454
Cordylus, 35, 54, 58, 138
[*Corogyps*], 403
Coronella, 202
Corpora lutea, 359–361, 365–366
Corucia, 141, 257
[*Corvus*], 13, 403
Corytophanes, 30, 64, 129, 139, 257
Costa Rica, 7
Cosymbotus, 513
Crisantophis, 144
Crocodilians
  antipredator mechanisms, 9, 25, 16, 18, 27–28, 56, 58, 66, 129–130, 135–136, 244
  eggs and embryos, 525, 528–529, 531, 544–545, 562–563, 566–569, 574
  life history, 335
  nests, 533, 541–544, 554, 576, 558–559
  parental care, 278–283, 296, 301, 307–308, 310, 313, 315
  predation on, 10–12, 27, 60, 113
  sex determination, 353, 551–553, 583–585
Crocodilurus, 249
Crocodylus, 6, 9, 11, 18, 27, 56, 113, 127, 134, 136, 280–281, 300–301, 303, 528, 533, 541, 551
[*Crocuta*], 6
Crossobamon, 260
Crotalinae. *See main entry* Viperidae
Crotalus, 7, 13, 16, 18, 23, 39, 45–48, 61, 64, 66, 69, 122, 127, 130–131, 152, 197, 199, 350, 483–485, 521

Crotaphopeltis, 119, 145, 233
Crotaphytus, 17, 50, 116, 139, 463–465, 474, 514
Crypsis. *See main entries* Antipredator mechanisms; Coral-snake mimicry; Mimicry
Cryptoblepharus, 516
Cryptophis, 149, 520
Ctenosaura, 29, 126, 134, 139, 251, 256, 260, 461, 464–465, 514
Ctenotus, 52, 117, 141, 464–465, 516
Cyclanorbis, 393, 439
Cycloderma, 393, 439
Cyclura, 12, 29, 139, 256, 260, 283, 300, 461, 464–465, 472, 514
Cylindrophis, 10, 38, 40, 143, 202, 203, 232–233
Cyrtodactylus, 139, 513

Dalophia, 114
[*Danaus*], 158
Dasypeltis, 39, 44, 48, 119, 123, 129, 134, 145, 155, 161, 167, 191–196
[*Dasypus*], 12, 403
Defensive mechanisms. *See main entries* Antipredator mechanisms; Caudal autotomy; Parental care; morphology
Deimatic behavior. *See main entry* Antipredator mechanisms
Deirochelys, 356, 391, 400, 437
Delma, 117, 205
Demansia, 149, 287, 520
Dendrelaphis, 119, 145
Dendroaspis, 6, 8, 41, 56, 121, 149
Dendrophidion, 145
Denisonia, 520
Dermatemyidae, 391, 412, 436, 526
Dermatemys, 391, 436
Dermochelyidae, 361, 391, 412, 436, 525, 540–541, 551–552, 576
Dermochelys, 354, 362, 365, 391, 396, 398, 436, 552
[*Dermophis*], 8
Development. *See main entries* Antipredator mechanisms; ontogeny; Embryos; Ontogeny
Diadophis, 11, 20, 23, 39, 119, 127, 130, 133, 145, 482–483, 485, 519, 534

Dibamidae, 35, 38, 138, 294, 529
Dicrodon, 118
Diet. *See main entries* Life history traits, diet; Predators of reptiles; Turtles
Dinodon, 145, 232
Diplodactylinae. *See main entry* Gekkonidae
Diplodactylus, 20, 32, 33, 56, 127, 138, 251–252, 259
Diploglossus, 137, 283, 297
Diporiphora, 258–259
Dipsadoboa, 145
Dipsas, 190, 230, 231
Dipsosaurus, 139, 248, 258, 461, 464–465, 472, 514, 544, 547, 565, 583
Dispholidus, 23, 119, 123, 145
Distress calls. *See main entries* Antipredator mechanisms, alarm calls; Parental care, alarm calls
Dracaena, 118, 123, 142, 249
Draco, 29, 49, 50, 51, 137, 512
Drepanoides, 231
Drift fences. *See main entry* Capture methods
Dromophis, 233
Drymarchon, 10, 145
Drymobius, 145
Drymoluber, 231
Dryocalamus, 232
Duberria, 119, 145
[Dynastor], 172, 173

Echinosaura, 54, 125, 142
Echiopsis, 149
Echis, 44–45, 48, 56, 58, 121, 123, 125, 151, 191–193, 196–198, 200, 252, 538
Egernia, 256, 516
Egg-eating snakes, 44, 155, 161, 191–196
Egg-guarding, egg-brooding. *See main entry* Parental care
Eggs and egg shells, 525; *see also main entries* Crocodilians; Lizards; Nests; Snakes; Parental care; Turtles
    air spaces, 563
    albumen, 527–532
    clutch size. *See main entries* Life history methods; Life history traits
    contact with air, 536, 638
    contact with substrate, 532–535, 538–539, 564–565

    effects of temperature. *See main entry* Nest temperature
    energy, 397
    flexible versus rigid shells, 526–527, 529–530, 556, 559, 562–563, 565–569, 574
    heat balance. *See main entry* Thermal balance
    infertile, 362
    laying, 390
    lipids, 250, 253, 264, 397
    mimics, 163
    mortality. *See* survivorship
    oviductal, 354–355, 360–362
    ovulation, 359
    pores, 525–526, 528, 530, 574
    retention, 359–360, 528, 531
    shell membranes, 525–526, 528–530, 562, 574
    size. *See main entries* Life history traits
    survivorship, 282, 298–300, 362, 403–404, 416, 418, 500
    temperature. *See main entries* Thermal balance; Nest temperature
    types and morphology, 525–532
    vapor pressure, 538, 554–556
    variation, 529
    water uptake. *See main entry* Embryos
    yolk, 527–532, 546–547, 582
[Egretta], 204
Eirenis, 145
Elaphe, 119, 123, 145, 231–232, 286, 295, 297–298, 301, 307, 482–484, 519
Elapidae, 38, 41–42, 121, 124, 149–150, 164–165, 167, 181, 202–203, 212, 287, 296, 307, 454–455, 483, 485–487, 493, 520
Elapomorphus, 145, 190, 231
Elaps, 234
Elapsoidea, 149, 233–234
Elgaria, 15, 36, 53–54, 58, 115, 127, 130, 137, 266, 279, 283, 300, 304
Elseya, 393, 439
Embryos, 525; *see also main entry* Nest temperatures
    acid/base balance. *See main entry* Acid/base balance
    allantoic sac, 531
    calcium sources, 527, 529, 532

SUBJECT INDEX

chorioallantois, 550
constant temperature studies, 545, 547
deformity, 580
development (growth) rates, 546–547, 567–569
distributional limits, 583
incubation, 531, 546–547, 567–569, 577, 580–585
limits of tolerance, 544–546, 565–566, 583
lipid sources, 527
kidneys, 550
metabolism. *See main entry* Metabolism
mortality. *See* survivorship
nutrient reserves, 582–583
nutrient sources, 527, 529, 532
parental care. *See main entry* Parental care
protein sources, 527
sexual differentiation, 551–553, 572–573, 583–585
size of hatchlings, 546–547, 567–569, 577, 579–581, 581–583
stage at oviposition, 310–311, 527–528, 530–531
survivorship, 282, 288, 298, 525, 532, 535, 544–546, 565–566, 570, 577, 580, 583, 584–585
temperature. *See main entry* Thermal balance
temperature effects. *See main entry* Temperature effects
water, 527–528, 531–532, 562–563, 565–573; *see also* Water balance of eggs and embryos
Emissivity. *See main entry* Thermal balance
Emoia, 117, 283, 464–465, 516
Empathic learning. *See main entry* Learning
Emydidae, 112, 135, 296, 354, 391–392, 399, 402, 409–410, 412–414, 436–437, 525–526, 551–553
Emydoidea, 356, 391, 397, 400, 403–404, 437, 552, 566, 568
Emydura, 393, 439, 538, 568, 576
Emys, 391, 437, 552, 553
Energy balance equation. *See main entry* Thermal balance
Enhydris, 145, 232

Environmental sex determination. *See* Sex, determination/differentiation
Enyalioides, 257, 261
Enyalius, 257
Enydrina, 149, 521
Epicrates, 17, 143
Epididymides, 355, 357
Eremias, 17, 23, 117, 140
Eretmochelys, 8, 112, 198, 367, 391, 436, 552
Eristocophis, 152
[*Eryphanis*], 173
Erythrolamprus, 129, 145, 185–186, 230–231
Eryx, 54, 123, 143
Eublepharinae. *See main entry* Gekkonidae
Eublepharis, 138, 260
Eumeces, 9, 11, 51, 56, 117, 127, 141, 250–252, 254–255, 261, 265, 283–284, 291, 294, 300–301, 303–304, 310, 315, 461, 464–465, 474, 516–517, 545
[*Eumomota*], 188
Eunectes, 10, 119
Evolution. *See main entries* Antipredator mechanisms; Caudal autotomy; Life history traits; Mimicry; Parental care
Exiliboa, 151
Extinct reptiles, 60, 67

Farancia, 119, 120, 134, 145, 286, 295, 307, 519
Fatigue, 21
Fecundity. *See main entries* Life history methods, Life history traits
Feeding mimicry. *See main entry* Mimicry
[*Felis*], 6, 69
Females
  follicles, 359–361, 365–366
  maturity criteria, 354–356
  mimicry. *See main entry* Mimicry, sexual
  reproductive cycles, 358–360, 399–400, 418–419
Fertilization, 312, 313, 315
Feylinia, 141
Ficimia, 119
Fick equation, 573
Fishes, 8, 51, 112, 163, 173, 183, 203–204, 212, 293, 308, 312–315
Fitch's method, 345
Fitness, 333
Flicker fusion. *See main entry* Senses

SUBJECT INDEX

Follicles. *See main entry* Reproduction
Food intake, 302–305, 309, 312
Foraging behavior; *see also* Life history traits, foraging mode
    antipredator mechanisms, 27, 38, 47–48, 59, 61, 64, 180–181, 206–208, 212–214, 264, 495
    parental care, 302–305
Frogs, 9, 112, 173, 242, 293, 305
Fungal infections, 292, 299, 301
Future research, 65–69, 267, 305, 368–369, 389–390, 497–500, 586

[*Galictis*], 10
Gambelia, 9, 18, 21, 29, 33, 52–53, 55, 116, 126, 139, 242, 257, 514
Gas exchange. *See main entry* Respiratory gases and embryos
Gastric brooding, 293
Gavialidae, 296
Gavialis, 281, 300, 533
Geckolepis, 138
Geckonia, 260
Gehyra, 51, 115, 138, 238, 261–262, 464–465, 474, 513, 558
Gekko, 115, 138, 551
Gekkonidae, 10, 31–34, 69, 115–116, 123, 128, 138–139, 259–260, 282, 294, 450, 454–455, 465, 473, 486, 492, 513, 543, 566
Gekkoninae. *See main entry* Gekkonidae
Gekkotan lizards. *See main entries* Gekkonidae, Pygopodidae
Genetics
    antipredator mechanisms, 16–19, 66, 68
    gene flow, 416, 419
    life history. *See main entry* Life history traits
    mimicry, 157
    quantitative, 389–390
Geochelone, 6, 113, 135, 341, 347, 354, 390, 392, 396–401, 403, 405, 419–420, 438, 526
Geoclemys, 17
[*Geococcyx*], 10, 212
Geographic variation. *See main entry* Interpopulational variation
[*Geranospiza*], 13

Gerrhonotus, 115, 128, 137, 283, 301, 304, 463–465, 512
Gerrhosaurus, 35, 115, 138
[*Ginglymostoma*], 183
Gliding, 29
Gomesophis, 145
Gonadal cycles. *See main entry* Reproduction
Gonatodes, 123, 138
Gonocephalus, 137, 258
Gonyophis, 143
Gopher snakes, 197, 199
Gopherus, 113, 134, 341, 367, 392, 400, 403–405, 437, 552
Graptemys, 112, 337, 344, 356, 362, 391, 398, 402, 404, 437, 552
Gravidity. *See main entries* Life history methods; Life history traits
Grayia, 233
[*Grison*], 53
Growth curves, 348–349, 398
Growth. *See main entries* Age; Life history traits; Parental care; Water effects on embryos
Gyalopion, 123, 145
Gymnodactylus, 259, 513
Gymnophthalmidae, 454–455, 465, 473, 492, 513
Gymnophthalmus, 118, 464–465, 513

Habitat. *See main entry* Life history traits
[*Hapalochlaena*], 307
Haplocercus, 119, 145
[*Haplochromis*], 163
Hardella, 135
Hatchlings. *See main entry* Life history traits
Heat balance equation. *See main entry* Thermal balance
Heat production. *See main entries* Parental care, shivering thermogenesis; Thermal balance
Heat storage. *See main entry* Thermal balance
Heidenhain's iron hematoxylin stain, 355
[*Heliconius*], 183
Helicops, 145–146
Heliobolus, 206–208, 242
Heloderma, 18, 36, 58, 64, 116, 139, 250

SUBJECT INDEX 645

Helodermatidae, 36, 116, 132, 139, 245, 257, 294
Hemachatus, 24, 39, 41, 55, 131, 148
Hemiaspis, 150, 482–483, 520
Hemidactylus, 115, 138, 254, 513
Hemiergis, 250
Hemipenes, 355
Hemirhagerrhis, 145
Hemitheconyx, 260
Henophidia, 38, 40, 143, 151
Heritability. *See main entry* Genetics
[*Herpetotheres*], 6, 167
Heterodon, 18, 20, 38, 40, 54–55, 119, 123, 125, 128–129, 131–132, 146, 286, 483, 519
Heteronotia, 464–465, 474, 513
Heteropholis, 249, 259
Hibernation, 210, 250, 339, 345, 357–358, 397, 582–583
Histological stains, 355, 357
Holaspis, 35, 140, 249
Holbrookia, 49, 116, 139, 211, 258, 464–465, 514
Homalopsis, 232, 519
Homopholis, 115, 138
Homopus, 392, 400, 438
Homoroselaps, 146
Homotypy. *See main entry* Mimicry
Hoplocephalus, 233
Hoplocercus, 256
Hoplodactylus, 50, 55, 138
[*Hyaena*], 6, 162
H-Y antigens, 553
Hydration. *See main entry* Water balance of eggs and embryos
Hydrodynastes, 146, 231
Hydrophiidae, 164–165, 203–204, 455, 521
Hydrophis, 150
Hydrops, 231
Hydrosaurus, 29, 51, 59, 137
[*Hylobittacus*], 160
Hypnale, 152
Hypoxia, 527
Hypsiglena, 119, 146, 206, 239

[*Ichneumoniformis*], 155
Ichnotropis, 117, 140
Iguana, 11, 18, 29–30, 50, 52, 60, 116, 123, 125, 130, 134, 139, 209, 251, 256, 260, 283, 301, 350, 545, 582

Iguanian lizards. *See main entries* Agamidae; Chamaeleonidae; Iguanidae
Iguanidae, 28–31, 59, 116–117, 123, 130, 134, 139–140, 209–210, 256–257, 282–283, 296, 299, 306, 309, 315, 355, 368, 450, 454–455, 465, 473, 486, 492, 513–516, 535, 543
Imantodes, 204, 231
Imidazolium. *See main entry* Acid/base balance
Incubation; *see also main entries* Embryos; Nests; Parental care, shivering thermogenesis
Individual variation, 19, 20–22, 41
Infrared, 163
Injuries, 11–12, 32, 37, 47, 55, 67, 156, 208, 227, 239–243, 272, 345–347, 349, 351–352, 382, 418; *see also main entry* Caudal autotomy
Insular gigantism, 399
Interpopulational variation, 20–22, 30, 400, 414–420, 441, 453, 474–477, 499
Intraspecific mimicry (deception). *See main entry* Mimicry
Invertebrates, 7–9, 17, 155–158, 160, 163–164, 166–174, 183–184, 205–208, 216, 404
Ions. *See main entry* Acid/base balance
Iteroparity. *See main entry* Life history traits

Japalura, 114, 464–465, 512
Jolly-Seber technique, 343, 345–346

Kachuga, 135, 391, 437
Kaokogecko, 260
Kentropyx, 142
Kidney, 550
Kinixys, 6, 26, 113, 135, 392, 438–439
Kinosternidae, 56, 112–113, 122, 135, 392, 399, 401, 412–414, 437–438, 526, 532, 551–552
Kinosternon, 22, 27, 112, 135, 339, 360, 366, 392, 394, 400, 403, 405, 415, 438, 526, 533, 538, 552
Klauberina, 464–465, 518

Lacerta, 21, 35, 51, 54, 56, 117, 127, 140, 243, 249–250, 254, 261–262, 265, 350

SUBJECT INDEX

Lacertidae, 35, 140–141, 206–208, 257, 282, 294, 454–455, 465, 473, 486, 492, 516, 535
Lachesis, 18, 23, 47, 64, 122, 124, 130, 152, 288
Lactate, 255
Laemanctus, 257
Lamarckian inheritance, 237
Lampropeltis, 20, 45, 55, 119–120, 123, 132, 146, 184–185, 190, 215, 230–231, 239–240, 254, 295
Lamprophis, 120, 146
Lampropholis, 517
Lanthanotidae. *See main entry* Varanidae
Lanthanotus, 37, 129, 142
[*Larus*], 397
Latastia, 117
[*Laternaria*], 173
Laticauda, 43, 287, 299–300
Latitude. *See main entries* Life history traits, distribution (tropical, temperate), latitude; Parental care
Learning, 168, 190, 194, 196, 291, 302
Leiocephalus, 115
Leiolepis, 137, 258
Leiolopisma, 21, 51, 141, 465, 517
Leiosaurus, 140, 256
Lepidochelys, 354, 365, 367, 391, 402, 404, 436, 526
Lepidodactylus, 513
Lepidophyma, 142
Leposoma, 142, 464–465, 513
[*Leptodactylus*], 9
Leptodeira, 230
Leptomicrurus, 150
Leptophis, 146
Leptotyphlopidae, 39, 121, 151, 288, 296, 454
Leptotyphlops, 7–8, 39, 120, 150, 288
Lerista, 52, 118, 141, 517
Lialis, 9, 33, 117
Liasis, 143, 285, 289, 291, 300, 303
Lichanura, 15, 38, 51, 143
Life expectancy. *See main entries* Life history methods; Life history traits
Life history methods; *see also main entries* Comparative methods; Life history traits; Statistical analyses

age estimates, 347–350
age of reproduction, 353–356, 447–448
age structure, 347–353
capture methods. *See main entry* Capture methods
clutch size and frequency, 358–368
common garden studies, 500
fecundity, 353–368, 358, 448
gonadal cycles, 356–360
gravidity, 355
growth models, 347–350
histological stains, 355
injury rates, 352; *see also main entry* Caudal autotomy
life expectancy, 351
life tables, 335–336, 351, 367
long-term studies, 333, 369, 499
marking methods. *See main entry* Marking methods
mortality rates, 350–353
multiple clutches. *See* clutch size and frequency
newborns, 346–347, 351
ovarian cycles, 358–360
population size, 343–347
predation intensity, 352
relative clutch mass, 364–365, 449, 488, 495
reproductive maturity, 345–356, 358
reproductive periodicity, 358
skeletochronology, 347–350
survivorship, 242, 267, 350–353; *see also main entry* Embryos
testicular cycles, 357–358
transplant studies, 500
X-radiography, 355, 360–361, 368
Life history traits; *see also main entries* Life history methods; Parental care
age structure. *See main entry* Age
age first reproduction. *See* reproductive maturity
analyses. *See main entry* Statistical analyses
birth rate, 333
body size, 362–365, 391–395, 398–400, 406–421, 443–444, 446, 450–451, 456–463, 466–497, 512–521
brood frequency, 333, 359, 365, 391–393, 395, 400–401, 407–409, 412, 415–

SUBJECT INDEX

421, 443–448, 450, 454–455, 457–463, 466–467, 469, 471, 475–483, 489–497, 512–521
clutch number. *See* brood frequency
clutch size, 333, 359, 391–394, 400–401, 406–421, 446–448, 450–451, 456–463, 466–498, 512–521
constraints, 398, 400–401, 412–414, 420–421, 443, 445–446, 451, 467–468, 474, 476, 485–487, 491–500
correlations among traits, 443–447, 450–453, 456–497
death rate, 333
diet, 391–394, 397–398, 406–407, 410–413, 419
distribution (tropical, temperate), 443, 449–450, 457–461, 466–467, 469, 479–480, 482, 495, 512–521
egg size, 311, 391–399, 406–414, 416, 420–421, 444, 475, 477, 498, 566, 584
emigration, 333
environmental effects, 333, 335, 400–401, 419–420, 444–445, 474, 476, 491–494, 498
evolution, 398
fecundity, 333–334, 443; *see also* brood frequency; clutch size
foraging mode, 445–446, 449, 452, 467–471, 478, 492–498, 512–521
genetics, 389, 403, 416, 419–420, 443, 445, 500
geographic variation, 400, 414–420, 441, 453, 474–477, 499
growth, 396–399
habitat, 391–394, 398, 406–413, 415, 420–421, 449, 462–463, 467–471, 475, 493–497, 512–521; *see also* distribution (tropical, temperate)
hatchling size, 396, 498, 546–547, 567–569, 577, 579–581, 581–583
immigration, 333
inaccuracies of data, 449–450, 478, 480, 495, 498
interactions among traits, 463–467, 469–470, 482
intraspecific comparisons. *See* geographic variation

intrinsic rate of increase, 406
iteroparity, 304, 389, 401, 405
latitude, 359, 368, 391–394, 397, 406–407, 414–415
life expectancy, 405, 419
life tables, 333–336, 351, 368
longevity, 333–336, 405
mode of reproduction, 292–293, 307, 313, 315, 389, 401, 405, 443–444, 446–448, 450, 454–455, 457–463, 466–467, 478–483, 488, 490–497, 512–521
morphological correlates, 445
mortality. *See* survivorship
multiple clutches. *See* brood frequency
nesting. *See main entry* Nests
nutrition, 398
parental care. *See main entry* Parental care
paternity, 209
phenotypic plasticity, 445
population size, 333–334, 343–347, 498–499
predation, 397
r-and-*K* selection, 497
relative clutch mass, 364–365, 444–445, 448–449, 452–455, 467–475, 478, 483, 485, 488–489, 493, 495, 497–498, 512–521
reproductive maturity, 209, 333–336, 389, 394, 397–399, 405, 416, 419–421, 443–444, 447, 459, 454–467, 469–498, 512–521
scaling. *See* body size
senescence, 353, 356, 498
sex determination. *See main entry* Sex, determination/differentiation
sex ratio, 353, 363, 402, 415, 418
sexual dimorphism, 399
size at maturity, 447, 454–461, 463, 466–498, 512–521
size hatchlings. *See main entry* Embryos
snakes versus lizards, 478, 481, 485–491, 494–497
social facilitation, 401
"strategies," 443–447, 451, 461–462, 471–474, 476, 482–485, 488–489, 495–497

survivorship, 333–336, 396–397, 405, 418, 444, 476–477, 498
taxonomic biases, 444, 452–453
temperature, 398, 402–403, 419
theory, 398, 399–401, 403, 405, 411–412, 443–445, 471–474, 477, 498, 500
variation, 333, 443, 449
Life tables. *See main entry* Life history traits
Limblessness, 307
[*Limenitis*], 184
Lincoln-Peterson index, 343–346
Lioheterodon, 146
Liolaemus, 29, 33, 126, 140, 242, 464–465, 514
Liophis, 120, 146, 176, 177, 190, 204, 231, 483, 485, 519
Lipids, 250, 253, 264, 397, 527
Lipinia, 517
Lissemys, 135, 393, 439
Lizards
  antipredator mechanisms, 15, 17–18, 20–21, 28–37, 39, 41, 58, 122, 136–142
  capture methods, 339–340
  caudal autotomy. *See main entry* Caudal autotomy
  eggs and embryos, 529–532, 544–546, 562, 565–568, 574
  life history, 336, 344–345, 349–350, 352, 355–356, 358, 363–365, 367–368, 403–404, 443–447, 454–477, 487–500, 512–518
  marking methods, 341–342
  mimicry, 173–174, 206–208, 242, 252
  nests, 533–535, 543, 558–559
  parental care. *See main entry* Parental care
  phylogenetic relationships, 25, 28, 31–32, 34–35, 38, 50, 69
  predation, 6–12, 114–118, 403–404; *see also main entry* Caudal autotomy
  sex determination, 353, 551–553, 583–585
Locomotion
  caudal autotomy, 243, 248–249, 255–259, 266–267
  cost, 488
  developmental effects, 581–582
  escape, 26, 28, 31, 35–36, 41–42, 50–52, 205, 210–212

foraging mode, 445–446
mimicry, 206–208
Longevity. *See main entries* Age; Life history traits
Lophognathus, 114, 258
Lopohosaurus, 249
Loxocemidae, 39
Lycodon, 120, 123, 146, 232–233, 286, 295, 305
Lycodonomorphus, 120, 146
Lycophidion, 6, 120, 146
Lygodactylus, 115, 249, 513
Lygosoma, 118, 141
[*Lynx*], 61
Lystrophis, 146, 186, 199, 231
Lytorhynchus, 146, 232

Mabuya, 118, 141, 266, 462–465, 473, 517
Macroclemys, 9, 25, 27, 212–213, 348, 358, 362, 391, 398, 436
Macropisthodon, 120, 127, 146, 233
Malaclemys, 112, 391, 394, 403, 409, 437, 541
Malacochersus, 26, 126, 135, 392, 400, 439
Males
  maturity criteria, 354–356
  reproductive cycles, 357–358
Malpolon, 120, 146
Mammals, 6–7, 10–11, 13, 15–16, 27, 31, 33, 37, 39, 41, 51–53, 57, 60–62, 64, 112, 239, 403–404, 416
[*Mandrillus*], 194
Marking methods, 49, 340–343
Mark-recapture estimates. *See main entries* Capture methods; Life history methods; Marking methods
Marsupials, 239, 253
Masticophis, 14, 18, 21–23, 53, 120, 131, 146, 483, 519, 534
Mastigodryas, 146–147
Maticora, 150, 202–203, 233
Mating balls, 210
Maturity. *See main entry* Life history traits, reproductive maturity
Mauremys, 112, 391, 437
Mehelya, 39, 120, 146
Meizodon, 120, 233
Melanochelys, 135
Melanosuchus, 281, 528

SUBJECT INDEX

[*Mellivora*], 6, 10, 14
Menetia, 118, 464–465, 472, 517
[*Mephitis*], 403
Meroles, 117, 516
Mertensian mimicry. *See main entries* Mimicry; Coral-snake mimicry
Mesalina, 140–141
Metabolism; *see also main entries* Parental care, shivering thermogenesis; Respiratory gases and embryos; Thermal balance
    aerobic versus anaerobic, 30, 50, 62, 64–65
    embryos, 536–538, 541–542, 567–569, 572
    metabolic water, 554–556
    temporal patterns of embryos, 537–538, 546, 575–576
    thermal dependence, 546–547, 550, 586
    urea effects, 567
    water dependence, 567–569
Micruroides, 42, 43, 54, 64, 126, 130, 150, 175–191, 230
Micrurus, 10, 14, 38, 53, 54, 121, 129, 133, 150, 155, 175–191, 230, 231, 253, 287, 483, 520
Migration, 401, 408, 416, 419
Mimicry
    abstract mimicry (homotypy), 157, 160, 164, 169–174, 180, 190, 193, 215
    aposematic/cryptic coloration, 157, 160, 175–178, 183–187, 196–198, 206, 210
    arthropods, 17, 155–158, 160, 163, 217
    automimicry, 208–209
    Batesian, 48, 63, 155, 157, 160–162, 190, 206
    beetles, 206–208
    behavior, 158–162, 187–196
    body size, 166–167, 206, 209–210
    by *Boiga*, 196–197
    camouflage. *See* crypsis
    centipedes, 206
    "charming" birds, 214–215
    classifications, 158–160, 163, 209
    concordant geographic patterns, 174, 183–187, 191–192, 194, 197–198, 215
    concrete mimicry (homotypy), 160, 209
    controversies, 156–159, 161–162, 168, 174–205, 215
    coral snakes. *See main entry* Coral-snake mimicry
    crypsis, 48, 159, 162, 191, 205
    definition. *See* classifications
    difficulties of studying, 160, 162–163, 172–173, 180–181, 194, 197, 199, 205
    dual mimics, 169–170, 185–186
    egg-eating snakes. *See main entry* Egg-eating snakes
    empathic learning, 168, 190, 194, 196
    evolution, 157, 190–191, 194, 197, 199, 205
    experiments, 156–157, 163, 175, 180, 187–191, 196, 202–204, 206, 210, 212, 215–216
    feeding, 212–215
    female. *See* sexual
    frequency models versus mimics, 156, 180–183
    generalization versus precision. *See* abstract mimicry
    genetics, 157, 168, 172
    geography, 172, 181–182, 184
    historical development, 155–158, 174–175
    homotypy, 159–164
    human biases, 162–163, 202, 217
    innate avoidance of models, 168, 176, 179, 187–191, 215
    by insects, 170–174, 216
    intraspecific (deception), 208–210, 215
    lethality of model, 164–169, 180, 183, 190–191, 194
    learning, 168, 190, 194, 196
    lizards, 173–174, 200–201, 205–208, 242, 252
    lures, 212–215
    Mertensian mimicry, 183
    model, mimics, and dupes, 159–162
    Mullerian, 155, 158, 160–161, 183, 194, 197
    noxiousness. *See* lethality of model; palatability spectrum
    objections. *See* controversies
    other defenses, 158, 161

SUBJECT INDEX

palatability spectrum, 158, 167
paradox of deadly model, 168, 183
pheromones, 210
phylogenetic aspects, 161–162, 181
predictions of theory, 168–205
properties of model, 164
ratio models to mimics, 156, 168–169
scorpions, 205–206
sea snakes, 183
selective agents, 156, 170–171, 194, 206
senses, 162–163, 176–180, 199–200, 202, 217
sexual, 160, 209–210, 215
taxonomic distribution, 162–164
theory, 63, 156–157, 164–170, 180
tripartite nature, 159
uncertainty of venom delivery, 166–167
unprofitable prey, 210–212
venomous snakes (mimicry of), 155, 164–205
venomous snakes (unusual features), 164–170, 216
vertebrates, 164
vocal mimicry, 199–200
weapon automimicry, 208–209
Mode of reproduction; *see also main entries* Life history traits; Parental care
Moloch, 30, 59, 61, 137, 462, 464–465, 474, 512
Monopeltis, 114
Morelia, 285, 289, 300–303
Morethia, 118, 250, 464–465, 517
Morphology
 antipredator mechanisms, 24, 28–29, 38–39, 56–57, 67, 133–134, 208–209
 anterior rib elongation, 39
 fangs, for spitting, 39
 gliding/parachuting, 51, 57
 horns/spines, 30, 52, 59, 130
 noxious flesh, 43, 56, 127
 rattlesnake rattle. *See main entry* Rattlesnakes
 scales/osteoderms, 34, 36, 59, 192–193
 skin tearing, 32, 51–52
 sound production. *See main entry* Antipredator mechanisms
 toe fringes, 29, 51, 57–58

tail autotomy. *See main entries* Caudal autotomy; Tails
Mortality; *see also under main entries* Caudal autotomy; Embryos; Life history traits, survivorship; Nests
 density dependence, 419
 rates, 342, 404–405
Multivariate analyses. *See main entry* Statistical analyses
Multiway contingency analyses. *See main entry* Statistical analyses
[*Murichthys*], 204
[*Murophis*], 204
Musculature, 130, 289–291
Müllerian mimicry. *See main entries* Coral-snake mimicry; Mimicry

Nactus, 513
Naja, 6, 12, 18, 23, 38–39, 41, 121, 124, 132, 150, 232–234, 287, 298, 299–300
[*Nasua*], 5, 52, 53, 187–188
Natriciteres, 120, 147
Natrix, 21–22, 52, 69, 120, 123, 147, 286, 300, 538
Naultinus, 249, 259
Neelaps, 520
Neoseps, 118, 284
Nephrurus, 15, 31, 138, 256, 259
Nerodia, 15, 21, 49, 66, 120, 147, 155, 177–178, 519
Nests, 401–402; *see also main entries* Crocodilians; Lizards; Snakes; Turtles; Water balance of eggs and embryos
 air spaces in, 532–535
 body pits, 532
 "arribada," 402
 delayed emergence, 397
 environmental effects 402, 416
 gas tensions, 575–577
 guarding, 282, 302, 306–308, 355
 hydration, 556–562
 incubation, 531, 546–547
 interference, 418
 migration, 401
 mortality, 403–404, 416, 418, 462; *see also main entry* Embryos
 number, 361, 365–368, 391–393
 opening of, 278–282, 288, 301, 314
 physical interactions, 577–578

SUBJECT INDEX

predation on, 403–404, 416, 418, 585
sex ratios, 553, 584–585
site selection, 416, 571–572
soils, 557–558, 564
success, 403–404
temperature. *See main entry* Nest temperature
terrestrial, 420
types, 532–535, 540–542, 558–559
ventilation, 558–559
water balance. *See main entry* Water balance of eggs and embryos
water exchange in nature, 562–563, 570–572
Nest temperature; *see also main entry* Thermal balance
determinants of, 538–544, 584
daily cycles, 539–541, 543–545, 550
measurements of, 542–544
parental care, 301–302
shivering thermogenesis, 278, 288–291, 302, 310–311
soil thermal profiles, 539–542
spatial variation within nests, 541–542, 544
Netting. *See main entry* Capture methods
Neusticurus, 142, 518
New research. *See main entry* Future research
Ninia, 17- 23, 123, 147, 204, 230
Notechis, 150, 483, 520
Nucras, 6, 117

[*Ocypoda*], 397, 403
Oedura, 115, 259, 461, 463–465, 474, 513
Oligodon, 15, 147, 232–233
Ommateremias, 140
Ontogeny. *See main entries* Age; Antipredator mechanisms; Caudal autotomy
Oophagy. *See main entry* Eggs and egg shells
Opheodrys, 50, 120, 147, 286, 295, 483, 519, 531, 543, 546
Ophiodes, 266
Ophiomorus, 141, 266
Ophiophagus, 10, 41, 42, 56, 64, 121, 124, 129, 131, 150, 278, 287, 297, 299, 301, 303

Ophisaurus, 35, 115, 137, 257, 266, 279, 283, 294, 301, 303, 307, 534
Ophisops, 141
Ophisthotropis, 147, 286, 301
Optical illusions. *See main entry* Senses
Optimality, 62–63; *see also main entries* Caudal autotomy, costs and benefits; Parental care, cost-benefit models; Reproduction
Osteogenesis, 527
Osteolaemus, 281
Otocryptis, 29, 137, 258–259
Ovarian cycles. *See main entry* Reproduction
Oviparity. *See main entry* Life history traits, mode of reproduction
Ovulation, 359
Oxybelis, 50, 123, 125, 147, 173, 215
Oxygen consumption. *See main entry* Metabolism
Oxygen. *See main entry* Respiratory gases and embryos
Oxyrhopus, 185, 230–231
Oxyuranus, 150

Pachydactylus, 51, 115, 138, 260
Paint marks. *See main entry* Marking methods
Palaeosuchus, 281, 542
Palatability spectrum. *See main entry* Mimicry
Palmatogecko, 115, 254, 260
[*Panacra*], 172
Panaspis, 6, 118, 464–465, 517
[*Panthera*], 6, 11, 27, 52, 60
[*Papio*], 194
Parachalcides, 266
[*Paracynictis*], 6
Pareas, 143, 233
Parental care
aggressiveness, 297, 299
alarm calls, 282
attending nest,
benefits, 277, 298–302, 306–308, 315
brief incubation, 310–311, 313
body size, 291, 307, 309
costs, 277, 298, 302–312, 315
cost-benefit models, 277, 298–299

SUBJECT INDEX

crocodilians, 18, 278–283, 296, 301, 307–308, 310, 313, 315
  defending young, 279–281, 288
  development, 290, 301, 310–311
  eggs and nests, 277, 279
  egg-attendance, 277, 279–282, 288, 291, 295, 297, 301, 305–306, 310–311, 314
  egg-brooding, 277–278, 288–291, 301, 314
  egg-guarding, 277, 279–281, 288–289, 299–300, 311, 314–315
  egg-manipulation, 282, 301
  egg-predation, 282, 288, 298
  environmental factors, 310–311, 315
  evolution, 294–295, 305–313, 315
  factors influencing, 306–313
  fecundity, 303, 309–310
  food intake, 302–304, 309, 312
  future studies, 305
  growth, 305
  helping birth, 292
  increasing benefits, 306–308
  independent origins, 294–295, 305–306, 315
  intermediate stages, 305–306, 313
  investment, 277
  latitude, 309–310
  lizards, 282–284, 288, 291, 296–297, 307–309, 314, 444
  learning, 291, 302
  male, female, biparental. *See* sex showing
  maturity, 308–309
  mode of fertilization, 312–313, 315
  mode of reproduction, 292–293, 307, 313, 315
  mouth brooding and transport, 292–314
  myths (apparent), 291
  nest opening, 278–282, 288, 301, 314
  non-reptiles, 293, 307, 311, 313
  oophagy. *See* egg-predation
  oviparity versus viviparity, 292–293, 307, 314–315
  rarity in reptiles, 313–314
  removing dead eggs/young, 292, 301
  sex showing, 297–298, 312–313, 315
  shivering thermogenesis, 278, 288–291, 301–302, 315

  snakes, 285–297, 307
  survivorship. *See* benefits
  swallowing young, 292–293
  taxa showing, 278–293, 289
  taxonomic biases, 293–294, 314–315
  terminology, 277
  thermal benefits. *See* shivering thermogenesis
  turtles, 278, 293, 296, 310, 314, 401, 415
  venomous species, 307, 315
  young, 277
Paroedura, 260
Parthenogenesis, 363
Partial pressure gases, 548
Pedioplanes, 208
Pelamis, 8, 43, 56, 121, 127, 150, 183, 203–204
Pelochelys, 135
Pelomedusa, 25, 113, 393, 439
Pelomedusidae, 56, 113, 135, 393, 439, 525–526, 551–553
Peltocephalus, 135
Pelusios, 6, 113, 393, 439
Pelvic canal 398
Petrosaurus, 140
Phelsuma, 51, 115
Phenacosaurus, 249, 257
Pheromones, 210
Philodryas, 7, 120, 519
Philothamnus, 51, 120, 147
[*Phocochoerus*], 194
Phrynocephalus, 23, 29, 31, 49, 53, 59, 114, 125, 128, 130, 132, 134, 137, 252, 258, 263
Phrynops, 11, 112, 114, 533
Phrynosoma, 20, 24, 30, 52–53, 59, 61, 67, 116, 125, 128, 133–134, 140, 256, 461–462, 464–465, 474, 514
Phyllodactylus, 138, 239, 248, 250, 253–255, 260, 261
Phyllopezus, 513
Phyllorhynchus, 147
Phyllurus, 138, 252, 259, 282
Phylogenetic constraints. *See* main entries Caudal autotomy; Life history traits, constraints
Phylogeny, 25; *see also* main entries Lizards; Parental care; Snakes; Turtles

SUBJECT INDEX

Physignathus, 249, 258
Physiology. *See main entries* Acid/base balance; Metabolism; Respiratory gases and embryos; Reproduction; Senses; Water balance of eggs and embryos
[*Pitangus*], 188
Pitfall traps. *See main entry* Capture methods
Pituophis, 11, 18, 23, 39, 48–49, 52, 68, 120, 123–124, 126, 130, 134, 147, 197, 286, 295, 305, 482–483, 519, 531, 534, 546, 566, 568
Plagiopholis, 147
Platemys, 134
[*Platypsaris*], 13
Platysaurus, 138
Platysternidae, 392, 412, 438
Platysternon, 25–26, 133–134, 392, 438
Plecturus, 151, 232
Pliocercus, 147, 165, 185, 187, 190, 230, 259
Podarcis, 117, 141, 243, 248–249, 261, 463–465, 516
Podocnemis, 112, 135, 393, 401, 403–404, 439, 552
Polychroides, 257
Polychrus, 116, 140, 249, 257, 464–465, 473–474, 514
Population size. *See main entry* Life history methods
Predation, 4–14, 16–17, 60, 397, 476, 499; *see also main entries* Caudal autotomy; Crocodilians; Eggs and embryos; Injuries; Lizards; Mimicry; Nests; Parental care; Snakes; Turtles
  context, 15–16
  definition, 4
  evidence of, 11–12, 239–242; *see also main entries* Caudal autotomy; Injuries
  risks to predators, 53–54, 164–170, 216, 291, 307, 309, 315, 352
  sexual differences, 21
  unsuccessful, 52; *see also main entry* Caudal autotomy
Predators of reptiles
  amphibians, 8–9, 25, 39
  arthropods, 7–8, 39
  assemblages of, 7, 60

birds, 6–7, 10, 13–14, 25, 31, 37, 39, 41, 53
  characteristics of, 13, 15
  detection by prey, 15–16, 18
  experiments, 12, 15–16, 49, 67
  fishes, 8, 25, 51
  generalizations, 12–14
  humans, 60–61, 418–419
  mammals, 6–7, 10–11, 13–15, 25, 27, 30–31, 33, 37, 39, 41, 51–53, 57, 60
  reptiles, 6–7, 9–10, 13–14, 25, 31, 33–34, 37, 39, 41–42
  regional patterns, 5–7, 12
  stimuli, 13, 15
Prim network analysis. *See main entry* Statistical analyses
Principal components analysis. *See main entry* Statistical analyses
Principle of conservation of mass, 554
[*Priodonophis*], 204
Pristurus 245, 250, 260
[*Procyon*], 403–404
Prosymna, 120, 131, 147, 234
Protean defense. *See main entry* Antipredator mechanisms
Proteins, 527
[*Proteles*], 162
Psammobates, 113, 392, 439
Psammodromus, 249
Psammodynastes, 123, 147
Psammophilus, 258–259
Psammophis, 120, 147
Psammophylax, 120, 147, 287, 307
Pseudaspis, 17, 149, 197, 287, 483–484, 520
Pseudemys, 17, 57, 68, 112, 135, 278, 301, 337, 341, 354, 356, 362, 365–367, 391, 393, 398, 400, 403–404, 411, 416, 419, 543–544, 552
Pseudoboa, 231
Pseudocerastes, 152, 198
Pseudocordylus, 115
Pseudohaje, 150
Pseudonaja, 150, 181, 205, 233, 287
[*Pseudosphinx*], 173
Pseudotrapelus, 258
Pseudoxenodon, 148
Pseustes, 129, 134, 148
Psychrometers, 559–562, 586

SUBJECT INDEX

Ptenopus, 6, 16, 59, 115, 260
Ptyas, 120, 123, 148, 287, 295, 305, 307
Ptychozoon, 32, 51, 57, 138, 249
Ptyodactylus, 116
Pygopodidae, 31–34, 69, 117, 205, 294, 454
Pygopus, 205, 534
Python, 6, 54, 119, 143, 285–286, 289–291, 294, 300–301, 303, 529, 534, 538, 545–546, 568
Pythoninae. *See main entry* Boidae
[*Pyxicephalus*], 9

Q_{10}. *See main entry* Metabolism, thermal dependence

r-and-*K* selection. *See main entry* Life history traits
Radiation. *See main entry* Thermal balance
Radiographs, 245
[*Rana*], 9, 214
Rates, birth and death. *See main entry* Life history traits
Rattlesnakes
    antipredator mechanisms, 45–48, 69, 130, 214
    evolution of rattle, 46–48, 59, 214
    mimicry of, 197, 199
    uses of rattle, 46–48
Regeneration. *See main entry* Caudal regeneration
Regina, 8, 21, 120, 148, 483, 519
Relative clutch mass. *See main entries* Life history methods; Life history traits
Relative humidity, 558–559, 586
Reproduction; *see also main entries* Eggs, embryos; Life history methods; Life history traits; Nests; Parental care
    ages, 353–356, 443
    atretic follicles, 360,
    caudal autotomy, 250, 264–266
    corpora lutea, 359–361, 365–366
    costs and benefits, 398, 419
    effects on defensive mechanisms, 21
    environmental effects 400, 402–403, 419
    fertilization, 312, 313, 315
    gonadal cycles, 356–360, 395, 399–400, 418–419
    maturity criteria, 354–356
    migration, 401
    mode. *See main entry* Life history traits, mode of reproduction
    ovulation, 359
    parental care, 303–305, 309–310
    paternity, 312
    periodicity, 367–368
    secondary sex characters, 354–356
    senescence, 353, 356, 498
    synchrony, 412
Respiratory gases and embryos
    factors influencing exchange, 532–535, 558–559, 573–575
    Fick equation, 573
    interactions, 578
    mechanistic models, 573
    metabolism, 575–576, 581
    nests. *See main entry* Nests
    physiological effects, 527, 577, 586
    pores, 528
    soils, 575
    thermal dependence, 577
Rhabderemias, 141
Rhabdophis, 52, 148, 231, 287, 304–305, 307
Rhabdops, 148
Rhadinaea, 148, 205, 259
Rhamphiophis, 120, 148, 197
Rhamphotyphlops, 121, 151, 288
Rhineura, 114, 136
Rhineuridae, 114, 136
Rhinocheilus, 14, 120, 122, 148, 230
Rhinoclemmys, 112, 135, 202, 341, 391, 409, 412, 437
Rhinophis, 122, 151
Rhinotyphlops, 39, 151, 288
Rhoptrophus, 116
Rhynchocalamus, 231
Rhynchocephalia. *See main entry* Tuatara

[*Sagittarius*], 6, 10, 167
Salamanders, 8–9, 112
Salvadora, 120, 148
Sauromalus, 11, 23, 68, 116, 131, 140, 260–261, 461, 464–465, 514
[*Saurothera*], 13
Scales. *See main entry* Morphology
Scaling. *See main entry* Body size
Scaphiodontophis, 148, 189–190, 230, 259
[*Scaphiopus*], 242

SUBJECT INDEX

Sceloporus, 8–9, 15, 17, 21, 23, 49–50, 116–117, 125, 140, 241–242, 248, 339, 342, 363, 446, 453, 463–465, 474–476, 514–515, 531, 544, 565, 568
Scelotes, 118, 266
Schnabel technique, 345
Schumacher-Eschmeyer technique, 343, 346
Scincella, 118, 141, 239–240, 248, 250, 254–255, 261, 464–465, 517
Scincidae, 34–35, 51, 59, 117–118, 123, 141, 257, 282–284, 296, 315, 455, 465, 473, 486, 516–517, 543
Scincus, 118, 141
Scolecophidia, 37–39, 151
Scolecophis, 179
Scute clipping. *See main entry* Marking methods
Secondary sexual characters, 209–210, 354–356
Selection, 49
Selfish herd, 412
Seminatrix, 120
Senescence, 353, 356, 498
Senses, 15–16, 18, 28, 62, 162–163, 177–180, 184, 189–190, 217
Sergeev's method, 348
Serpentes. *See main entry* Snakes
Sertoli cells, 357–358
Sex
    chromosomes, 402, 551
    determination/differentiation, 353, 402–403, 551–553, 572–573, 580, 583–586
    dimorphism. *See main entry* Life history traits
    hormones, 553
    H-Y antigens, 553
    mimicry, 160, 209–210, 215
    parental care, 297–298, 312–313, 315
    ratio, 353, 363, 402, 415, 418
    selection, 399
Sexual maturity, 354–356
Shaker muscle. *See main entry* Rattlesnakes
Shell. *See main entry* Turtles
Shells (egg). *See main entry* Eggs and egg shells
Shinisaurus, 36, 126, 142, 249

Shivering thermogenesis. *See main entry* Parental care
Sibon, 120, 148, 230, 482–484, 519
Sibynophis, 148, 259
Siebenrockiella, 402
Simophis, 231
Simoselaps, 150, 181, 233, 520
Sinonatrix, 148
[*Siren*], 8
Sistrurus, 16, 39, 45–48, 54, 122, 130, 152, 214
Sitana, 49, 258–259, 512
Size. *See main entries* Body size; Life history traits, body size
Skeletochronology. *See main entries* Age; Life history methods
Skin tearing, 32, 51–52
Snakebite, 164–168
Snakes
    antipredator mechanisms, 6–15, 17–19, 21, 31, 33–34, 36–48, 123–124, 142–152
    capture methods, 339–340
    caudal autotomy and regeneration, 189, 259, 265–266
    eggs and embryos, 529–532, 538, 545, 565–568, 574
    life history, 336, 345–347, 349–350, 355–357, 361–364, 367–368, 443–447, 454–456, 477–500, 518–521
    marking methods, 342–343
    mimicry. *See main entry* Mimicry
    nests, 534–538, 543
    parental care. *See main entry* Parental care
    phylogenetic relationships, 25, 37–38, 40–41
    predation on, 6–15, 37–48, 119–122
Sociality, 16, 18, 28–30, 49, 60, 134, 168, 209–210, 249–250, 401, 403, 412, 418
Sonora, 55, 120, 148, 230
Sound production. *See main entry* Antipredator mechanisms
Spain, 7, 60
Spalerosophis, 148, 198, 200, 519, 538
Sperm, 355, 357–358
[*Spermophilus*], 199
Sphaerodactylinae. *See main entry* Gekkonidae

Sphaerodactylus, 23, 32, 52, 137
Sphenodon, 9, 28, 58, 66, 114, 136, 244–245, 353, 531
Sphenodontidae. *See main entry* Tuatara
Sphenomorphus, 118, 141, 249, 255, 292, 517
Sphenops, 266
Spiders. *See main entry* Invertebrates
Spilotes, 39, 129, 134, 148
Squamates. *See main entries* Amphisbaenia; Lizards; Snakes
Stable age distribution, 351
Statistical analyses, 346, 363–365, 393–396, 406–407, 443, 445, 447, 450–453, 459, 461, 463–464, 467, 469–470, 472, 475–476, 482, 487–488, 490, 491–492
Staurotypus, 122, 135, 402
Stefan-Boltzmann constant. *See main entry* Thermal balance
Stegonotus, 233
Stellio, 258
Stenodactylus, 116, 138, 254, 260–261
Sternotherus, 8, 11, 25, 113, 122, 127, 135, 337, 354, 362, 365–367, 392, 298, 400, 403, 415, 437–438, 532, 552
Stilosoma, 120, 148, 230
Stimulus control, 15–16
Storeria, 8, 22, 120, 132, 148, 482–484, 519
Surinam, 6, 400
Survivorship. *See main entries* Embryos; Life history methods; Life history traits; Parental care
[*Sus*], 11, 404
Suta, 150
[*Synbranchus*], 204

Tachydromus, 117, 249, 464–465, 474, 516
Tachymenis, 148
Tagging. *See main entry* Marking methods
Tail autotomy. *See main entry* Caudal autotomy
Tail break frequency. *See main entry* Caudal autotomy, frequency
Tails; *see also main entry* Rattlesnakes,
   adhesive pads, 249
   autotomy. *See main entry* Caudal autotomy
   caudal luring, 47–48, 212–214, 259
   caudal plugs, 40
   coloration, 207–208, 210, 212, 252–254, 263–264, 267
   defensive uses, 247, 251–253, 256
   displays, 20, 23, 29, 31–32, 35–39, 41–48, 52–54, 130, 186, 188–189, 197, 200, 202, 205–206, 210–212, 249–250, 252–254
   diversion, 54, 253–254, 263
   fat deposits, 250, 260, 262
   gliding, 249
   harvested by predators, 251
   injuries, 37, 47, 55, 67, 208, 239–243
   lashing, 28–29, 31, 35–36, 256
   lipid, 250, 253
   locomotor/balance functions, 248–249, 255–260
   regeneration, 11–12, 22, 28, 208
   reinforcement, 54, 60
   secretions, 20, 32–33, 56, 251
   size, 192, 253
   spines, 39, 129, 247, 251
   social importance, 249–250
   unpalatable, 256
   vertebral fusion, 244–245
   waving, 252–254
Tameness, 12
Tantilla, 120–121, 148
Tarentola, 350
Tattooing. *See main entry* Marking methods
[*Taxidea*], 14
Taxonomic constraints. *See main entries* Caudal autotomy; Life history traits, constraints
Taxonomic patterns. *See main entry* Phylogeny
[*Tayassu*], 5, 187
Teiidae, 35, 118, 123, 141–142, 257, 284, 296, 454–455, 465, 473, 486, 492, 517–518, 535, 543
Telescopus, 21, 121, 129, 148, 197–198, 233–234
Temperate zone. *See main entries* Life history traits, distribution (tropical, temperate), latitude; Parental care, latitude
Temperature, body, 15, 20–21, 29, 261–262, 499

SUBJECT INDEX

Temperature. *See main entries* Nest temperature; Parental care, shivering thermogenesis
Temperature effects
  acid/base. *See main entry* Acid/base balance
  antipredator behaviors, 21, 29
  caudal autotomy, 261
  constant temperature studies, 545, 547
  life history, 398, 402–403, 419
  limits of tolerance, 544–547
  metabolism, 546–547, 550
  sex determination. *See main entry* Sex, determination/differentiation
  size of hatchlings, 567–569, 578–580
Teratolepis, 138, 200, 260
Teratoscincus, 31–32, 52, 58, 126, 128, 131, 139, 241, 252
Termite mounds, 542
Terrapene, 9, 11, 20, 21, 26, 27, 57, 112, 135, 339, 341, 345, 348, 356, 359, 362–363, 365–367, 391–394, 405, 409–410, 412, 437, 538, 544, 552, 568, 583
Testes, 355–358
Testudinidae, 113, 135, 390, 392, 397, 399, 409–410, 438–439, 526, 551–552
Testudo, 11, 113, 135, 298, 347, 392, 404–405, 430, 552
Tetracycline, 348
Thamnophis, 8, 15, 19, 21, 47, 49, 64, 68, 121, 123, 129, 148, 210, 482–483, 519–520
Thanatosis. *See main entry* Antipredator mechanisms, death feigning
Thecadactylus, 116, 139
Thelgosematic coloration, 215
Thelotornis, 20, 121, 147, 214, 215
Theory, 62–63, 237–238
Thermal balance; *see also main entries* Nest temperature; Temperature, body
  air temperature, 539
  air vapor pressure, 538
  body size (mass, area), 536, 538–539
  coloration, 49
  conduction, 535–536
  convection, 535–536
  emissivity, 538–539
  factors affecting nest temperature, 535–542

  heat balance equations, 535–539
  heat capacity, 536
  heat storage, 535–536
  metabolism, 535–537, 541–542, 546–547; *see also main entry* Parental care, shivering thermogenesis
  radiation, 535, 538–540, 542
  sexual differentiation
  soil temperatures, 537, 539–541
  Stefan-Boltzmann constant, 539
  temporal cycles, 539–541
  thermoregulation, 499
  water interactions, 565, 572–573, 577–587
Thermogenesis. *See main entry* Parental care, shivering thermogenesis
Tiliqua, 35, 123, 129, 132, 141, 205, 252, 256, 261
Toe clipping. *See main entry* Marking methods
Tolerance. *See main entries* Embryos; Temperature effects; Water effects on embryos
Toluca, 147
Toluidine Blue O stain, 355
Tomodon, 123, 147, 199
Tongue lures, 212, 215
Trachischium, 148
Trachyboa, 38, 54, 151
Trachydosaurus, 252, 256, 261
Transplant studies, 389
Trapping. *See main entry* Capture methods
Tretanorhinus, 121, 148
Tribolonotus, 141
Trimeresurus, 122, 127, 152, 172, 288
Trimorphodon, 14, 123, 149
Trionychidae, 113, 135, 393, 399, 413–414, 439, 526, 551
Trionyx, 57, 113, 135, 340, 348, 354, 361–362, 393, 396, 403–404, 439, 537, 538, 568
Tripanurgos, 231
Trodophiidae, 38, 40
Trogonophidae, 136
Trogonophis, 37, 56, 136
Tropics. *See main entries* Life history traits, distribution (tropical, temperate), latitude; Parental care, latitude
Tropidechis, 150

Tropidoclonion, 121, 149, 482–483, 520
Tropidodipsas, 230
Tropidophis, 38, 40, 133, 151
Tropidophorus, 141
Tropidurus, 7, 18, 21–22, 50, 140, 515
Tuatara, 9, 28, 58, 66, 114, 136, 308, 531–532
Tupinambis, 122, 141, 256, 261, 284, 300, 304, 306–307
Turtles
  antipredator mechanisms, 9, 17, 20–21, 25–27, 58, 66–67, 122, 134–135, 244
  capture methods, 337–339
  diet, 397–398
  eggs and embryos, 525–528, 531, 538, 544, 562–563, 565–569, 574
  feeding lures, 212–213
  life history, 335–336, 344–345, 347–349, 352–363, 365–368, 389–421, 436–439
  marking methods, 340–341
  nests, 532–533, 540–544, 553, 581
  parental care. *See main entry* Parental care
  phylogenetic relationships, 25, 390, 410, 415
  predation on, 6, 8–11, 25–27, 57, 60, 112–113, 397, 403–404, 411, 412
  sex determination, 353, 551–553, 572, 583–585
  shell, 25–27, 56–57, 347–349, 352–353, 389, 397, 400–401, 420
  size, 398–399
Tympanocryptis, 258
Typhlacontias, 118
Typhlopidae, 39, 121, 151, 288, 296, 454
Typhlops, 121, 151
Typhlosaurus, 118, 461–462, 464–465, 472–473, 517

Ultraviolet, 163
Uma, 29, 117, 140, 212, 248, 464–465, 515
Umbrivaga, 149
Unechis, 205, 282, 482–484, 520
Uracentron, 29, 130, 140, 256
Uranoscodon, 139
Urea, 567
Urination, 390
Uromacer, 149

Uromastyx, 50, 114, 137, 251–252
Uropeltidae, 38–39, 54, 121, 151, 206, 454
Uropeltis, 40, 151, 232
Uroplatus, 124, 252, 260
Urosaurus, 23, 50, 117, 140, 249, 363, 445–446, 453, 463–465, 477, 515–516
Urostrophus, 257
[*Ursus*], 11, 60
Uta, 12, 21, 49, 117, 124, 140, 242, 250, 261–262, 265, 464–465, 516

Vane-Wright Classification. *See main entry* Mimicry, classifications
Vapor pressure of air. *See main entries* Thermal balance; Eggs and egg shells
Varanidae, 36–37, 118, 123, 129, 142, 245, 257, 282, 284, 288, 296
Varanus, 6, 17, 37, 50, 52, 54, 56, 68, 118, 123, 127, 129–131, 142, 249, 251, 157, 263, 282, 284, 288, 301, 339, 342, 404, 418
Vas deferens, 355
Venom
  effects of bite, 165–166
  immunity to, 167
  mimicry, 155, 161, 164–205
  parental care, 307, 315
  phylogenetic distribution, 36, 41–42, 58, 69, 132, 164–165
  spitting, 39, 41, 132
  uncertainty of delivery, 166–167
Vermicella, 127, 150, 181, 233
Vermiculite, 563–564, 569, 579
Vipera, 18, 21, 49, 122, 152, 197–198, 201, 214, 483, 521, 538
Viperidae, 38, 44–48, 121, 123, 130–131, 151, 164–165, 167, 191–202, 212–215, 288, 296, 315, 343, 455, 482–483, 485–487, 493, 521
Virginia, 121, 132, 149, 483–484, 520
Vitelline sac, 527
Viviparity. *See main entries* Life history traits, mode of reproduction; Parental care
Voucher specimens, 336
[*Vulpes*], 10, 11

Waglerophis, 149, 199, 231, 483, 520
Walterinnesia, 150
Water

SUBJECT INDEX

albumen, 527–529
yolk, 527–528, 531–532
Water balance of eggs and embryos; *see also main entries* Water effects on embryos; Nests
   compensatory, 570–571
   exchange in nature, 562–563
   factors affecting, 527–528, 531–532, 535, 554–556
   fluctuating, 570–573
   liquid diffusion, 554–556, 559
   measuring hydration, 556–562
   mechanistic models, 554–556, 564–565
   metabolic water, 554–556
   parental care, 301
   plants, 555, 559
   principle of conservation of mass, 554
   psychrometers, 559–562, 586
   soil contact, 532–535, 538–539, 564–565
   soil types, 557–558, 563–564
   soil water potential, 554–562
   temporal variation, 554–555, 559–561
   thermal dependence, 560–561, 565, 580
   thermal interactions, 565, 572–573, 577–580, 586
   uptake, 554, 562–563
   vapor diffusion, 554–556, 559–561
   water content (gravimetric) versus water potential, 557
   water potential, 554–563, 565, 586
Water effects on embryos
   changing hydration, 570–573
   growth rates, 567–569
   limits of tolerance, 565–566
   metabolism, 567–569
   methodology, 563–564
   physiology, 527–528, 531–532, 535
   sexual differentiation, 572–573, 586
   size of hatchlings, 567–569, 579–80
Water potential. *See main entry* Water balance
Water
   albumen, 527–529
   yolk, 527–528, 531–532
Weapon automimicry, 208–209
Wheel, 51
Winter kill, 397
Wright's stain, 355

X-radiography, 355, 360–361, 368
Xantusia, 142, 241, 336, 462, 464–465, 472, 518
Xantusiidae, 34, 142, 454–455, 465, 518
Xenagama, 252
Xenocalamus, 121
Xenochrophis, 11, 121, 123, 149, 287, 305
Xenodon, 149, 199, 201
Xenopeltidae, 151
Xenopeltis, 152
Xenopholis, 231
Xenosauridae, 36, 142
Xenosaurus, 36
Xylophis, 121

Yolk. *See main entries* Eggs and egg shells; Water

Zaocys, 149
Zygaspis, 114